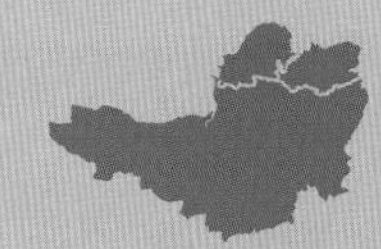

LOCAL EXPLORER

SOMERSET

www.philips-maps.co.uk

Published by Philip's a division of Octopus Publishing Group Ltd
www.octopusbooks.co.uk
Carmelite House
50 Victoria Embankment
London EC4Y 0DZ
An Hachette UK Company
www.hachette.co.uk

First edition 2022
SOMEA

ISBN 978-1-84907-603-6

Photographic acknowledgements:
Dreamstime.com: /Alexey Fedorenko II top left; /Wirestock II top right; /David Lamb III top; /Robert Baumann III bottom.
Shutterstock: Dick Kenny front cover.

Printed in China

CONTENTS

II **Best places to visit**

IV **Key to map pages**

VI **Route planning**

X **Key to map symbols**

1 **Street maps** at 3½ inches to 1 mile

122 **Street maps** at 1¾ inches to 1 mile

200 **Street maps** at 3½ inches to 1 mile

226 **Street maps of Bristol and Bath city centres** at 7 inches to 1 mile

229 **Index** of towns, villages, streets, hospitals, industrial estates, railway stations, schools, shopping centres, universities and places of interest

Best places to visit

▲ *Cheddar Gorge*

◀ *Wells Cathedral*

Outdoors

Brean Down Limestone promontory, with fine views out across the Bristol Channel. The archaeological remains of a Roman temple, as well as evidence of an Iron Age hillfort, can be seen on a circular walk on the summit. Part of the ruined Palmerston Fort, built to repel Napoleonic forces, and used again in World War II, can be explored. *Weston-super-Mare* www.nationaltrust.org **47 E2**

Cadbury Camp Remains of an Iron Age hillfort with fine views across Somerset and towards the Bristol Channel. It was constructed in the 6th century BC and remained occupied until the 1st century; it is also believed to have been used in Roman times. Wildflowers and butterflies flourish on the limestone grassland, and there are walking trails. *Tickenham* www.nationaltrust.org **8 A5**

Cheddar Gorge Limestone gorge in the Mendip Hills, a dramatic landscape of crags and pinnacles. At 400 feet deep and three miles long, it is Britain's biggest gorge. The remarkable caves, with their impressive stalactites, and the large underground river system are of geological significance. Visitors can see the feral goats that graze the steep sides of the gorge; the site is also home to rare bats and plants. www.cheddargorge.co.uk **71 E1**

Chew Valley Lake Reservoir that supplies much of Bristol's drinking water. It is popular with birdwatchers for the large variety of wildfowl, some rare, that visit the lake. There is an accessible walking route around the lake, picnic areas, playground and refreshments. Fishing and sailing can be arranged. *Chew Stoke* www.bristolwater.co.uk/chewvalleylake **57 A7**

Dunkery Beacon Highest point in Exmoor National Park and in Somerset. From the summit of the hill, walkers are rewarded with views over the surrounding rugged moorland towards Wales and Dartmoor. Heather, bracken, mosses and lichens flourish on its slopes, and deer and Exmoor ponies can be spotted. Known for its dark skies, Dunkery Beacon is a popular spot for stargazing. *Wheddon Cross* www.nationaltrust.org.uk **129 B4**

East Lambrook Manor Gardens Fine example of an English cottage garden, designed in the 1940s to 1960s by Margery Fish, an influential plant and garden expert and gardening writer. Paths wind through the colourful and abundant borders, where traditional and contemporary plants grow side by side. The gardens surround the small 15th-century East Lambrook manor house. There is a plant nursery and café on site. www.eastlambrook.com **220 C8**

Fyne Court Wild garden and nature haven in the Quantock Hills, originally the gardens of Fyne Court manor house, which was destroyed by fire in 1894. Some remnants of the house remain, but the gardens are the attraction. Visitors can spot wildlife on the waymarked trails and see the walled garden and old boathouse. Children's activities include natural play areas, pond-dipping and den-building. *Broomfield* www.nationaltrust.org.uk **152 E3**

Horner Wood Ancient oak woodland on Exmoor, a National Nature Reserve and part of the Holnicote Estate. It is unusual in being open to the surrounding heathland, with deer frequently seen grazing at the edges. There are ancient oak pollards and one tree that is over 500 years old. The woods are home to a wide variety of wildlife, fungi and lichens. *Doverhay* www.nationaltrust.org.uk **129 B7**

Prior Park Landscape Garden Georgian landscaped gardens on a steep slope descending from Prior Park house, designed in the 18th century with input from 'Capability' Brown and the poet Alexander Pope. A beautiful Palladian bridge crosses one of the many lakes, which were created by a series of dams. There are paths and children's nature activities, and it offers easy access to the longer circular walking route above Bath known as the Bath Skyline. www.nationaltrust.org.uk **45 C3**

Tintinhull Garden Small Arts and Crafts-style garden in the village of Tintinhull, divided into distinct sections or 'rooms' by neat hedges and walls. Highlights are the pool garden, fountain garden and the colourful borders with interesting planting. There is a kitchen garden and orchard. www.nationaltrust.org.uk **186 C6**

Westhay Moor National Nature Reserve Nature reserve in the Avalon Marshes of the Somerset Levels. The landscape is one of wet woodlands, reedbeds, channels and islands, with an area of rare lowland acid bog. Wildlife thrives in the reserve, with large resident populations of waders and wildfowl and vast numbers of visiting birds in winter. Sundews, sphagnum mosses and other unusual plants grow in the acid bog. There are hides and walking trails. www.somersetwildlife.org **138 D7**

Wimbleball Lake Reservoir lake within the Exmoor National Park, a popular spot for outdoor activities, including kayaking, stand-up paddleboarding, fishing, archery and many more. There are walking trails and cycle paths, providing opportunities to spot hedgehogs, weasels and deer. There is an Activity Centre, café and bird hide. Wimbleball lies within an International Dark Sky Reserve and is an excellent place to stargaze. *Brompton Regis* www.swlakestrust.org.uk/wimbleball-lake **148 C1**

Towns & villages

Bath Beautiful city, renowned for its elegant Georgian architecture and its Roman history. The well-preserved **Roman Baths** contain the remains of the temple built to honour Sulis Minerva. **Bath Abbey** church was built in the early 16th century and was substantially restored in the 19th century by Sir George Gilbert Scott. Visitors can climb the **Abbey Tower** giving impressive views over the city. The Georgian **Assembly Rooms** were the most elegant public rooms of fashionable society life in 18th-century Bath. They house the **Fashion Museum** with its world-class collection of historic and contemporary dress. The **Jane Austen Centre** gives a flavour of Austen's life in Regency Bath. The **Herschel Museum of Astronomy** relates the discovery of the planet Uranus in 1781. **No. 1 Royal Crescent** museum occupies part of one of the UK's finest examples of Georgian architecture. The **Victoria Art Gallery**, near Pulteney Bridge, houses an interesting collection of paintings, sculpture and decorative arts. www.visitbath.co.uk **228**

Frome Characterful and historic market town on the edge of the Mendip Hills. It is full of buildings and streets of architectural interest, including Catherine Hill and the medieval Cheap Street, where a spring still flows down a leat in the cobbled pavement. Active in the cloth trade and an important market town for the surrounding agricultural area, Frome still hosts regular markets of all kinds and is known for its wide variety of arts venues and galleries, one of which is housed in a well-preserved silk mill. www.discoverfrome.co.uk **119**

Glastonbury Ancient market town, long associated with the legends of King Arthur and the Holy Grail, and with an intriguing history of pagan and Christian worship. Towering over the town is **Glastonbury Tor**, which is crowned by a church tower, all that remains of the 15th-century church of St Michael; there are far-reaching views over the surrounding countryside. In the town itself, **Glastonbury Abbey**, whose foundation is linked to Joseph of Arimathea, is famed as the possible burial place of King Arthur. The substantial ruins lie within large grounds. Glastonbury is world famous for the Glastonbury Festival of performing arts. www.glastonburyabbey.com **206**

Shepton Mallet Historic market town on the edge of the Mendip Hills, originally a Roman settlement. Important in the medieval wool trade, it later became a centre for brewing and is still well known for its cider production. **Shepton Mallet Prison**, which opened in 1625, was not finally decommissioned until 2013 and has been left largely unchanged. Visitors can see the Victorian prison wings, hard labour areas and execution room, and participate in immersive activities, such as escape rooms. www.sheptonmalletprison.com **205**

Taunton County town of Somerset, in a beautiful location near the Quantock Hills and Blackdown Hills. At the centre of the town is Taunton Castle, which dates from the 12th century and now houses the **Museum of Somerset**. Its galleries explore the history of the county, its landscape and people, and its role in the Civil War and Monmouth Rebellion. There are changing exhibitions and hands-on activities. The separate **Somerset Military Museum** tells the stories of the local regiments. Other historic buildings in Taunton include St Margaret's Almshouses and Chapel, originally a 13th-century leper hospital. www.swheritage.org.uk/museum-of-somerset www.stmargaretschapel.org.uk **212-213**

Wells Historic city, the seat of the Bishop of Bath and Wells since the 13th century. The medieval centre is dominated by the magnificent Gothic-style **Wells Cathedral**, built between 1175 and 1490. It is particularly admired for the medieval stone carvings on its West Front, the Wells clock and the Chapter House. The adjoining Vicars' Close, a characterful medieval cobbled street, has been home to the adult members of the cathedral choir since the 14th century. Nearby, the early 13th-century moated **Bishop's Palace** is set within 14 acres of beautiful gardens. Visitors can see much of the original palace, the ruins of the medieval Great Hall, and the defensive guardhouse, portcullis and drawbridge. The **Wells and Mendip Museum** houses interesting local artefacts. www.wellscathedral.org.uk www.bishopspalace.org.uk www.wellsmuseum.org.uk **203**

Buildings

Barrington Court Tudor manor house, left deliberately empty of furniture and paintings, allowing visitors to experience an 'Echoes of History' atmosphere. Dating from 1538, it was acquired by the National Trust in 1907 in a state of dilapidation and was extensively restored in the 1920s. It has Arts and Crafts-style formal gardens, with orchards and kitchen gardens. Old farm buildings are now workshops for traditional crafts. www.nationaltrust.org **184 D5**

Clevedon Court Medieval manor house, dating from the 14th century, with an 18th-century terraced garden. The house has been altered over the years, but it retains a medieval core, notably the Great Hall and chapel. The Elton family, who acquired Clevedon Court in 1709, created the terraced garden, which rises up steeply behind the house. The family's collections of glass and Eltonware pottery are on display. www.nationaltrust.org **7 A4**

Coleridge Cottage Georgian cottage, furnished as it was when the poet Samuel Taylor Coleridge and his family lived here from 1797 to 1800. Visitors can learn about the significance of this period in Coleridge's life, a time when he wrote some of his most famous poems. Walkers can retrace their steps through the countryside that inspired them on the **Coleridge Way**. The cottage garden contains an orchard, bower and wildflowers. *Nether Stowey* www.nationaltrust.org **134 B2**

Dunster Castle Medieval castle, dramatically located on a hill with far-reaching views over the surrounding countryside. The castle has been transformed over the centuries into a comfortable family home; only a gatehouse and ruined tower survive from medieval times. Within the house are rare 17th-century leather wall hangings and a carved central staircase from 1680. Mediterranean plants flourish in the terraced gardens. There is an historic watermill in the grounds, which still grinds flour, and the 18th-century folly Conygar Tower. **Dunster village** itself is a well-preserved medieval village with many buildings of architectural interest, including the church, the medieval Gallox Bridge and Yarn Market. www.nationaltrust.org **201 E1**

Farleigh Hungerford Castle Remains of a 14th-century castle, home for 300 years to the Hungerford family. Little remains of the oldest part of the castle, apart from two partially ruined towers, but there is a well-preserved chapel with 14th-century wall paintings and unusual human-shaped lead coffins in the crypt. The old Priest's House contains an exhibition on the castle's history and the drama-filled lives of the Hungerford family. www.english-heritage.org.uk **82 E8**

Lytes Cary Manor Medieval manor house with Arts and Crafts-style garden. The earliest parts of the house date from the 14th century, with many additions made in the centuries that followed; highlights include the Great Hall and the patterned plasterwork ceiling of the Great Parlour. The gardens, which date from a major restoration in the early 20th century, are laid out in a series of 'rooms', with hidden paths and impressive topiary. *Somerton* www.nationaltrust.org **173 F5**

Montacute House Beautiful Elizabethan Renaissance mansion, built from local honey-coloured stone in the last decade of the 16th century. It has a symmetrical design with large windows and is surrounded by formal gardens and parkland. Inside is England's longest Long Gallery, which displays a collection of Tudor and Renaissance portraits on loan from the National Portrait Gallery. The garden has a compartmentalized design, with a great variety of plants. www.nationaltrust.org **186 B4**

Muchelney Abbey Partly ruined abbey, once one of the most important religious establishments in Somerset, with intact 16th-century abbot's house and thatched monks' lavatory. Most of the principal buildings were destroyed in 1538 during the dissolution of the monasteries, but the abbey's foundations are clearly visible, giving an idea of its impressive size. Visitors can explore inside the house, with its imposing fireplaces and stone carvings. *Langport* www.english-heritage.org.uk **172 A3**

Tyntesfield Victorian Gothic Revival house, standing in formal gardens and parkland. Originally a smaller Georgian home, it was remodelled in the 1860s, with the addition of elaborate turrets, gables and carvings. Visitors can see the lavishly decorated interior, complete with Gothic-style chapel, and some original carpets, wallpaper, furniture and paintings. The formal gardens include a rose garden and kitchen garden. There are walking trails within the large estate and woodland, children's activities and play areas. *Wraxall* www.nationaltrust.org **9 F4**

Museums & galleries

American Museum and Gardens Museum dedicated to American decorative arts and culture, housed in a Georgian manor house. Founded by two antiques collectors – one British and one American – the museum has important collections of quilts and textiles, folk art and maps. The Period Rooms were created using original materials from demolished historic American houses. The gardens reflect traditional English and American landscape design. Highlights include a replica of George Washington's garden at Mount Vernon and an arboretum with American trees. There are changing exhibitions and frequent events. *Claverton* www.americanmuseum.org **46 A5**

Coates Willows and Wetlands Centre Centre for the growing, processing and weaving of willow. Visitors can learn about all the stages involved in basket-making, from planting a willow sett and processing the willow to making the basket itself. There are walking trails through the fields where the willow is grown, and a small museum. *Stoke St Gregory* www.coatesenglishwillow.co.uk **170 D5**

Fleet Air Arm Museum Museum of naval aviation, with vast exhibition halls showcasing its large collection of Royal Naval aircraft from the earliest days of aviation to the present day, and displays on the history, technology and theory of flight. There are immersive exhibits, including the Aircraft Carrier Experience, as well as the opportunity to walk through Concorde 002. *Yeovilton* www.nmrn.org.uk/our-museum/faam **174 B3**

Haynes Motor Museum Large museum devoted to all kinds of motor vehicles from around the world. It traces the history of motoring, from the earliest motorcycles and vintage cars through to Formula 1 and luxury cars, with a vast number of vehicles on display and frequent special events when cars are driven. There are hands-on family activities and children's play areas. *Sparkford* www.haynesmuseum.org **175 A6**

The Helicopter Museum Museum with a large display of both civilian and military helicopters, with information on their history and technological developments. Highlights include a veteran Huey, used in the Vietnam War, a Russian Hind Gun Ship and the British G-LYNX, one of the world's fastest helicopters. There are frequent special events, and helicopter trips can be arranged. *Weston-super-Mare* www.helicoptermuseum.co.uk **49 E5**

The Holbourne Museum Museum and art gallery named after Sir William Holbourne, whose extensive collection of fine and decorative arts was bequeathed to the city in 1882 and forms the core of the present-day collection. Decorative arts on display include porcelain, silver, maiolica and bronze sculptures; the fine art collection includes portrait miniatures and works by Gainsborough, Stubbs and Turner. The museum is housed in what was the Sydney Hotel, and backs on to the Sydney Pleasure Gardens. *Bath* www.holburne.org **45 B7**

Somerset Rural Life Museum Museum exploring rural life in Somerset from the 1800s, on the site of the former Abbey Farm. Galleries cover the history of farming and food production in Somerset, and the way of life of those working here, with a recreation of a Victorian farmhouse kitchen, the story of village schools and education, local celebrations and religious beliefs. The museum centres on the well-preserved 14th-century Abbey Barn. Some rare cider apples are grown in the orchard. *Glastonbury.* www.swheritage.org.uk/somerset-rural-life-museum **206 E4**

Family activities

East Somerset Railway Heritage steam railway, offering five-mile round trips through the Mendip countryside. Visitors can learn about the railway in the small museum, engine shed and workshop. There is a café, miniature railway and a combined train and walking trail. *Cranmore* www.eastsomersetrailway.com **142 A5**

Grand Pier Pleasure pier in the traditional seaside resort of Weston-super-Mare. The large pavilion at the end of the pier houses an indoor theme park, with rides including a roller coaster, dodgems and go-karts, as well as traditional arcade machines and the Museum of Memories, which takes a nostalgic look at childhood. There are a variety of places to eat and frequent concerts and other events. www.grandpier.co.uk **48 D7**

▲ *Montacute House*

Noah's Ark Zoo Farm Farm park and zoo, with both traditional and exotic animal species, many of them endangered. The animals on site range from rabbits to rhinos, via African elephants, spectacled bears, giraffes and snakes, as well as cows, chickens, and many more. There are frequent keeper talks and birds of prey flying displays. Children's activities include a wildlife maze, indoor and outdoor play areas. *Wraxall* www.noahsarkzoofarm.co.uk **9 B7**

West Somerset Railway Heritage railway, an old branch line of the Great Western Railway. Restored steam and diesel locomotives run on the 20-mile line through beautiful countryside from Bishops Lydeard in the Quantock Hills and along the coast to Minehead. Visitors can get on or off at any of the 10 stations on the route, many of which have interesting sites nearby. There is a small museum, with model railway, at Bishops Lydeard station. There are walking and running routes linked to the railway. *Bishops Lydeard* www.west-somerset-railway.co.uk **167 E7**

Wookey Hole Caves Large show caves system, with vast caverns, dramatic 'waterfalls' of stalactites and an underground lake. The caves were occupied by humans at least 50,000 years ago, and explorers have found the bones of Ice Age animals, including mammoths and lions. Some of the most interesting finds are on display in the cave museum and the cave diving museum. There are a large number of other attractions on site, including Dinosaur Valley, a Victorian papermill, adventure golf, and large indoor and outdoor play areas. www.wookey.co.uk **111 E5**

► *Glastonbury Tor*

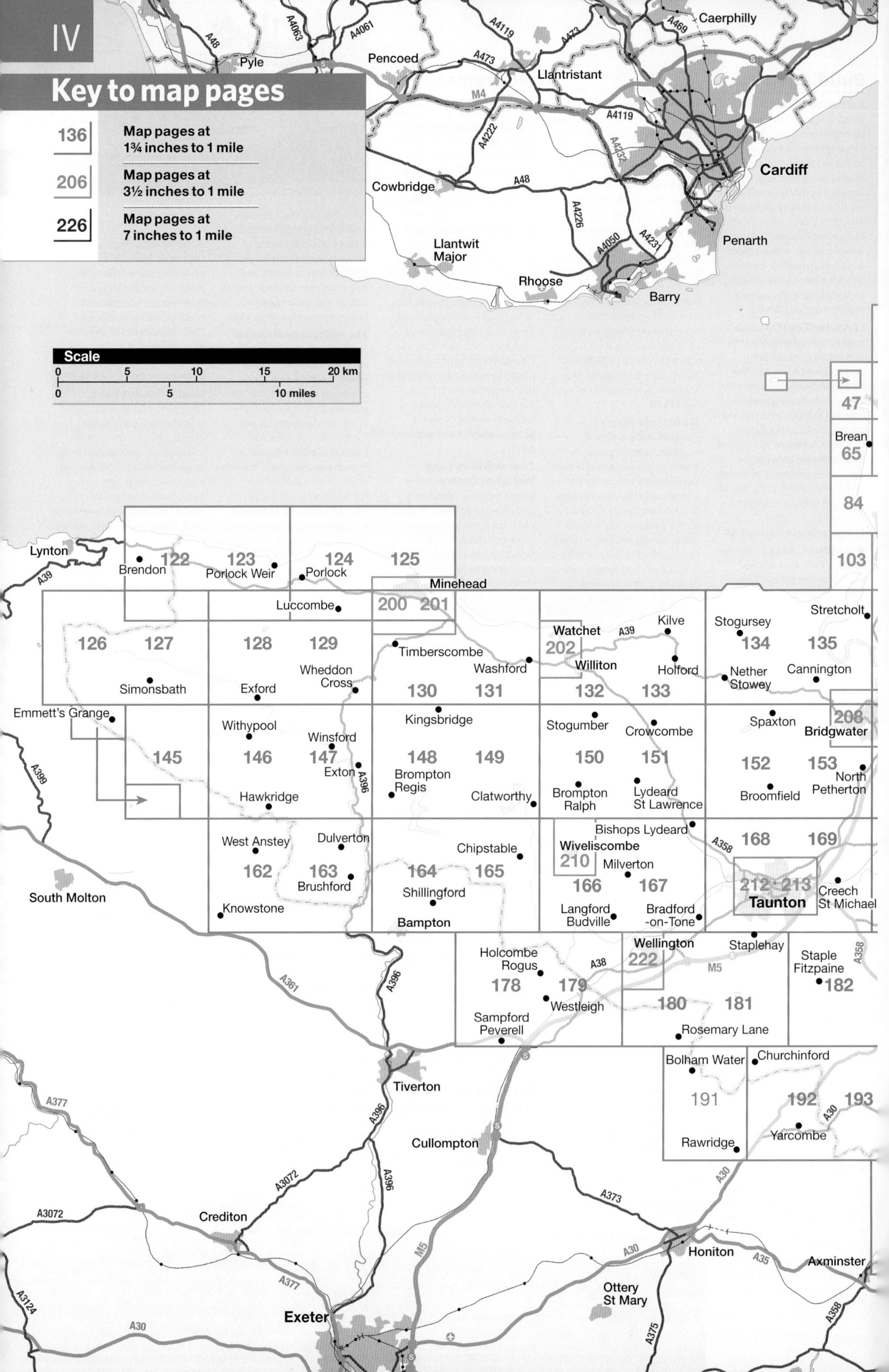
IV
Key to map pages
136 Map pages at 1¾ inches to 1 mile
206 Map pages at 3½ inches to 1 mile
226 Map pages at 7 inches to 1 mile
Scale
0 5 10 15 20 km
0 5 10 miles
Pyle
Pencoed
Caerphilly
Llantristant
Cardiff
Cowbridge
Llantwit Major
Rhoose
Barry
Penarth
A48
A4063
A4061
A4119
A473
A469
M4
A4222
A4232
A4226
A4050
A4231
47
Brean 65
84
103
Lynton
A39
Brendon
122
123
Porlock Weir
124
Porlock
125
Minehead
Luccombe
200
201
126
127
Simonsbath
128
129
Exford
Wheddon Cross
Timberscombe
Washford
130
131
Watchet
202
Williton
Kilve
Holford
132
133
Stogursey
134
135
Stretcholt
Nether Stowey
Cannington
Emmett's Grange
145
Withypool
146
Winsford
147
Exton
A396
Hawkridge
Kingsbridge
148
149
Brompton Regis
Clatworthy
Stogumber
Crowcombe
150
151
Brompton Ralph
Lydeard St Lawrence
Spaxton
152
153
208
Bridgwater
Broomfield
North Petherton
A399
West Anstey
Dulverton
162
163
Brushford
Knowstone
South Molton
Chipstable
164
165
Shillingford
Bampton
Bishops Lydeard
Wiveliscombe
210
Milverton
166
167
Langford Budville
Bradford -on-Tone
A358
168
169
212 213
Taunton
Creech St Michael
A361
Holcombe Rogus
178
179
A38
Westleigh
Sampford Peverell
Wellington
222
Staplehay
M5
180
181
Rosemary Lane
Staple Fitzpaine
182
Bolham Water
Churchinford
191
192
193
Rawridge
Yarcombe
A30
Tiverton
Cullompton
A377
A3072
Crediton
A373
Honiton
A35
Axminster
A3124
Exeter
Ottery St Mary
A375

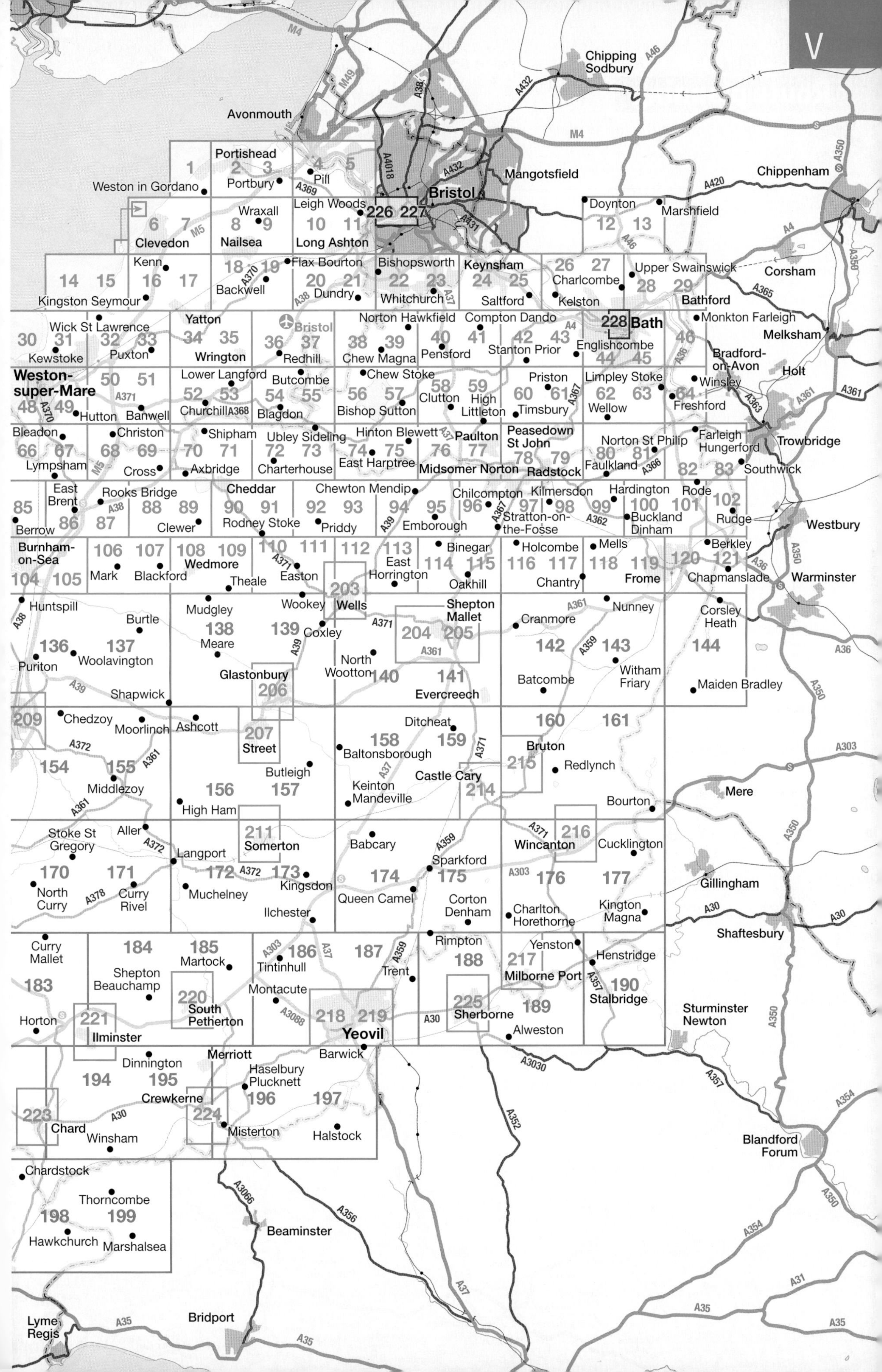

V
M4
Chipping Sodbury
A46
M49
A38
A432
Avonmouth
M4
A350
1
Portishead
2 3
4 5
Pill
A4018
A432
Mangotsfield
Chippenham
Weston in Gordano
Portbury
A369
Bristol
A420
Doynton
Marshfield
Leigh Woods
226 227
6 7
Wraxall
8 9
10 11
A431
12 13
M5
Clevedon
Nailsea
Long Ashton
A46
A4
Kenn
18 19
Flax Bourton
Bishopsworth
Keynsham
26 27
Upper Swainswick
Corsham
14 15
16 17
A370
Backwell
20 21
22 23
24 25
Charlcombe
28 29
A365
A38
Dundry
Whitchurch
A37
Saltford
Kelston
Bathford
Kingston Seymour
Wick St Lawrence
Yatton
Bristol
Norton Hawkfield
Compton Dando
228 Bath
Monkton Farleigh
30 31
32 33
34 35
36 37
38 39
40 41
42 43
A4
46
Melksham
Kewstoke
Puxton
Wrington
Redhill
Chew Magna
Pensford
Stanton Prior
Englishcombe
44 45
A36
Bradford-on-Avon
Holt
Weston-super-Mare
50 51
Lower Langford
Butcombe
Chew Stoke
58 59
Priston
Limpley Stoke
Winsley
A371
52 53
54 55
56 57
Clutton
High Littleton
60 61
A367
62 63
64
A361
A361
48 49
A370
Hutton
Banwell
Churchill
A368
Blagdon
Bishop Sutton
Timsbury
Wellow
Freshford
A363
Bleadon
Christon
Shipham
Ubley Sideling
Hinton Blewett
Paulton
Peasedown St John
Norton St Philip
Farleigh Hungerford
Trowbridge
66 67
68 69
70 71
72 73
74 75
A37
76 77
78 79
80 81
Lympsham
M5
Cross
Axbridge
Charterhouse
East Harptree
Midsomer Norton
Radstock
Faulkland
A366
82 83
Southwick
East Brent
Rooks Bridge
Cheddar
Chewton Mendip
Chilcompton
Kilmersdon
Hardington
Rode
102
85
A38
88 89
90 91
92 93
94 95
96
97 98
99
100 101
Westbury
86 87
A39
A367
Berrow
Clewer
Rodney Stoke
Priddy
Emborough
Stratton-on-the-Fosse
A362
Buckland Dinham
Rudge
Burnham-on-Sea
106 107
108 109
110 111
112 113
Binegar
Holcombe
Mells
Berkley
A350
A371
East Horrington
114 115
116 117
118 119
120 121
A36
104 105
Mark
Blackford
Wedmore
Theale
Easton
203
Oakhill
Chantry
Frome
Chapmanslade
Warminster
Huntspill
Mudgley
Wookey
Wells
Shepton Mallet
A361
Nunney
Corsley Heath
A38
Burtle
138
Meare
139
Coxley
A371
204 205
Cranmore
A359
A361
136
137
Woolavington
A39
North Wootton
140
141
142
143
Witham Friary
144
A36
Puriton
Glastonbury
Evercreech
Batcombe
Maiden Bradley
A350
A39
Shapwick
206
209
Chedzoy
Moorlinch
Ashcott
207
Street
Ditcheat
158
159
160
161
A372
Baltonsborough
A371
Bruton
A303
154
155
A361
Butleigh
215
Redlynch
Middlezoy
A37
Keinton Mandeville
Castle Cary
214
Mere
A361
156
157
High Ham
Bourton
Stoke St Gregory
Aller
211
Somerton
Babcary
A359
A371
Wincanton
216
Cucklington
A350
A372
Langport
Sparkford
A303
170
171
172
A372
173
Kingsdon
174
175
176
177
Gillingham
North Curry
A378
Curry Rivel
Muchelney
Queen Camel
Corton Denham
Charlton Horethorne
Kington Magna
A30
A30
Ilchester
Shaftesbury
Curry Mallet
184
185
A303
186
A37
187
A359
Rimpton
Yenston
Martock
Tintinhull
188
217
Henstridge
183
Shepton Beauchamp
Trent
Milborne Port
A357
190
Stalbridge
220
South Petherton
Montacute
225
189
Sturminster Newton
A350
Horton
221
A3088
218 219
A30
Sherborne
Ilminster
Yeovil
Alweston
Merriott
Barwick
A3030
Dinnington
Haselbury Plucknett
A357
194
195
196
197
Crewkerne
A352
A354
223
A30
224
Chard
Winsham
Misterton
Halstock
Blandford Forum
Chardstock
A3066
Thorncombe
A356
A350
198
199
Beaminster
A354
Hawkchurch
Marshalsea
A37
A31
Lyme Regis
A35
Bridport
A35
A35
A35

Route planning

CARDIFF
PENARTH
ABER HAFREN
MOUTH OF THE SEVERN
Avonmouth
Portishead
Redcliff Bay
Clevedon
North Somerset
Nailsea
Long Ashton
Yatton
Wrington
Weston-super-Mare
Weston Bay
Sand Bay
Kewstoke
Worle
Banwell
Churchill
Blagdon
Chew Valley Lake
Cheddar
Axbridge
Cheddar Res.
BERROW FLATS
STERT FLATS
Burnham-on-Sea
Highbridge
Brean
Wedmore
Wells
Glastonbury
Street
Bridgwater
Taunton
Somerton
Langport
South Petherton
Ilminster
Yeovil
Quantock Hills
Stogursey
Nether Stowey
Cannington
North Petherton
Westonzoyland
Curry Rivel
Ilchester
Priddy
Shepton Beauchamp
Martock
Crewkerne
Chard

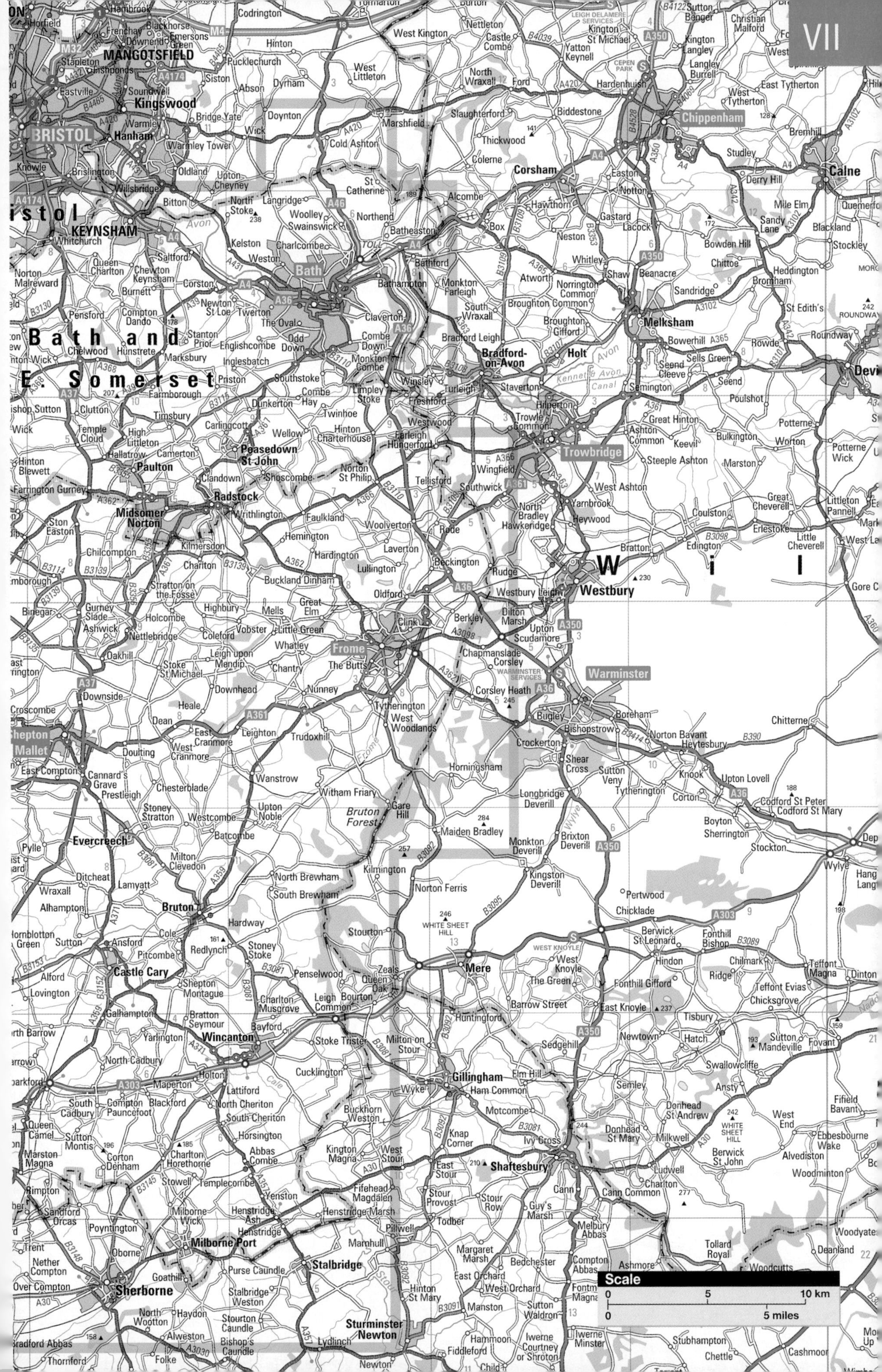
Hambrook
Codrington
Tormarton
Burton
Sutton Benger
Christian Malford
Horfield
Frenchay
Blackhorse
Emersons Green
Downend
M32
M4
Stapleton
MANGOTSFIELD
Fishponds
Pucklechurch
Hinton
West Kington
Nettleton
Castle Combe
LEIGH DELAMERE SERVICES
Kington St Michael
Yatton Keynell
Kington Langley
Langley Burrell
CEPEN PARK
Eastville
Siston
Soundwell
Kingswood
Abson
Dyrham
West Littleton
North Wraxall
Ford
Hardenhuish
East Tytherton
West Tytherton
Bridge Yate
Warmley
Doynton
Marshfield
Slaughterford
Biddestone
Chippenham
BRISTOL
Hanham
Wick
Warmley Tower
Cold Ashton
Thickwood
Bremhill
Colerne
Corsham
Studley
Calne
Knowle
Brislington
Oldland
Upton Cheyney
St Catherine
Easton
Notton
Derry Hill
Willsbridge
Bitton
North Stoke
Langridge
Northend
Alcombe
Hawthorn
Mile Elm
Quemerford
Bristol
KEYNSHAM
Whitchurch
Woolley
Swainswick
Batheaston
Box
Gastard
Lacock
Sandy Lane
Blackland
Saltford
Kelston
Charlcombe
Neston
Bowden Hill
Stockley
Queen Charlton
Chewton Keynsham
Weston
Bath
Bathford
Whitley
Shaw
Beanacre
Chittoe
Heddington
Norton Malreward
Burnett
Corston
Bathampton
Monkton Farleigh
Atworth
Norrington Common
Sandridge
Bromham
Pensford
Compton Dando
Newton St Loe
Twerton
The Oval
Claverton
South Wraxall
Broughton Common
Broughton Gifford
Melksham
St Edith's
ROUNDWAY
Stanton Prior
Englishcombe
Odd Down
Combe Down
Bradford Leigh
Bradford-on-Avon
Holt
Bowerhill
Sells Green
Rowde
Roundway
Bath and
N.E. Somerset
Chelwood
Hunstrete
Marksbury
Inglesbatch
Monkton Combe
Seend Cleeve
Seend
Devizes
Priston
Southstoke
Winsley
Turleigh
Staverton
Kennet & Avon Canal
Semington
Farmborough
Combe Hay
Limpley Stoke
Freshford
Hilperton
Poulshot
Clutton
Timsbury
Dunkerton
Twinhoe
Trowle Common
Great Hinton
Potterne
Temple Cloud
High Littleton
Carlingcott
Wellow
Hinton Charterhouse
Westwood
Farleigh Hungerford
Ashton Common
Keevil
Bulkington
Worton
Potterne Wick
Hallatrow
Camerton
Peasedown St John
Trowbridge
Steeple Ashton
Marston
Hinton Blewett
Paulton
Clandown
Shoscombe
Norton St Philip
Tellisford
Wingfield
West Ashton
Farrington Gurney
Radstock
Southwick
Midsomer Norton
Writhlington
Faulkland
Woolverton
Rode
North Bradley
Hawkeridge
Yarnbrook
Heywood
Coulston
Great Cheverell
Littleton Pannell
Erlestoke
Ston Easton
Hemington
Kilmersdon
Hardington
Laverton
Beckington
Bratton
Edington
Little Cheverell
Chilcompton
Charlton
Lullington
Rudge
Westbury
Westbury Leigh
Stratton on the Fosse
Buckland Dinham
Oldford
Gore Cross
Binegar
Gurney Slade
Highbury
Great Elm
Mells
Berkley
Dilton Marsh
Ashwick
Holcombe
Nettlebridge
Coleford
Vobster
Little Green
Clink
Upton Scudamore
Oakhill
Leigh upon Mendip
Whatley
Frome
Chapmanslade
Corsley
Stoke St Michael
Chantry
The Butts
WARMINSTER SERVICES
Warminster
Downhead
Nunney
Tytherington
Corsley Heath
Downside
Heale
West Woodlands
Bugley
Boreham
Chitterne
Croscombe
Dean
East Cranmore
Leighton
Trudoxhill
Bishopstrow
Norton Bavant
Heytesbury
Shepton Mallet
Doulting
West Cranmore
Crockerton
Shear Cross
Sutton Veny
East Compton
Cannard's Grave
Prestleigh
Wanstrow
Horningsham
Knook
Upton Lovell
Chesterblade
Witham Friary
Longbridge Deverill
Tytherington
Corton
Codford St Peter
Codford St Mary
Stoney Stratton
Upton Noble
Westcombe
Batcombe
Bruton Forest
Gare Hill
Maiden Bradley
Boyton
Sherrington
Evercreech
Monkton Deverill
Brixton Deverill
Stockton
Pylle
Wylye
Milton Clevedon
Kilmington
Kingston Deverill
Ditcheat
Lamyatt
North Brewham
Norton Ferris
Wraxall
South Brewham
Pertwood
Alhampton
Bruton
WHITE SHEET HILL
Chicklade
Hardway
Berwick St Leonard
Fonthill Bishop
Hornblotton Green
Sutton
Ansford
Cole
Redlynch
Stoney Stoke
Stourton
WEST KNOYLE
West Knoyle
Hindon
Chilmark
Teffont Magna
Dinton
Pitcombe
Alford
Castle Cary
Penselwood
Zeals
Queen Oak
Mere
The Green
Fonthill Gifford
Ridge
Teffont Evias
Chicksgrove
Lovington
Shepton Montague
Charlton Musgrove
Leigh Common
Bourton
Barrow Street
East Knoyle
Galhampton
Bratton Seymour
Bayford
Huntingford
Tisbury
North Barrow
Yarlington
Wincanton
Stoke Trister
Milton on Stour
Newtown
Hatch
Sutton Mandeville
Fovant
Sedgehill
North Cadbury
Holton
Cucklington
Gillingham
Elm Hill
Swallowcliffe
Sparkford
Maperton
Lattiford
Wyke
Ham Common
Semley
Ansty
South Cadbury
Compton Pauncefoot
Blackford
North Cheriton
Motcombe
Donhead St Andrew
Fifield Bavant
Queen Camel
South Cheriton
Buckhorn Weston
West End
Sutton Montis
Horsington
Knap Corner
Ivy Cross
Donhead St Mary
Milkwell
WHITE SHEET HILL
Ebbesbourne Wake
Marston Magna
Corton Denham
Charlton Horethorne
Abbas Combe
Kington Magna
West Stour
East Stour
Shaftesbury
Berwick St John
Alvediston
Stowell
Templecombe
Fifehead Magdalen
Ludwell
Woodminton
Rimpton
Yenston
Stour Provost
Stour Row
Cann
Charlton
Cann Common
Sandford Orcas
Milborne Wick
Henstridge Ash
Henstridge Marsh
Guy's Marsh
Poyntington
Henstridge
Pillwell
Todber
Melbury Abbas
Woodyates
Trent
Milborne Port
Marnhull
Margaret Marsh
Tollard Royal
Deanland
Oborne
Nether Compton
Purse Caundle
Stalbridge
Bedchester
Compton Abbas
Ashmore
Woodcutts
Goathill
East Orchard
Over Compton
Sherborne
Stalbridge Weston
Hinton St Mary
West Orchard
Fontmell Magna
Haydon
Manston
Sutton Waldron
North Wootton
Stourton Caundle
Sturminster Newton
Alweston
Bishop's Caundle
Lydlinch
Hammoon
Iwerne Minster
Iwerne Courtney or Shroton
Stubhampton
Bradford Abbas
Thornford
Folke
Newton
Fiddleford
Child Okeford
Chettle
Cashmoor
A4
A36
A37
A39
A303
A350
A361
A362
A365
A366
A367
A371
A420
A431
A4174
B3081
B3092
B3098
B3109
Avon
Wylye
Frome
Stour
Cale
Scale
0
5
10 km
0
5 miles

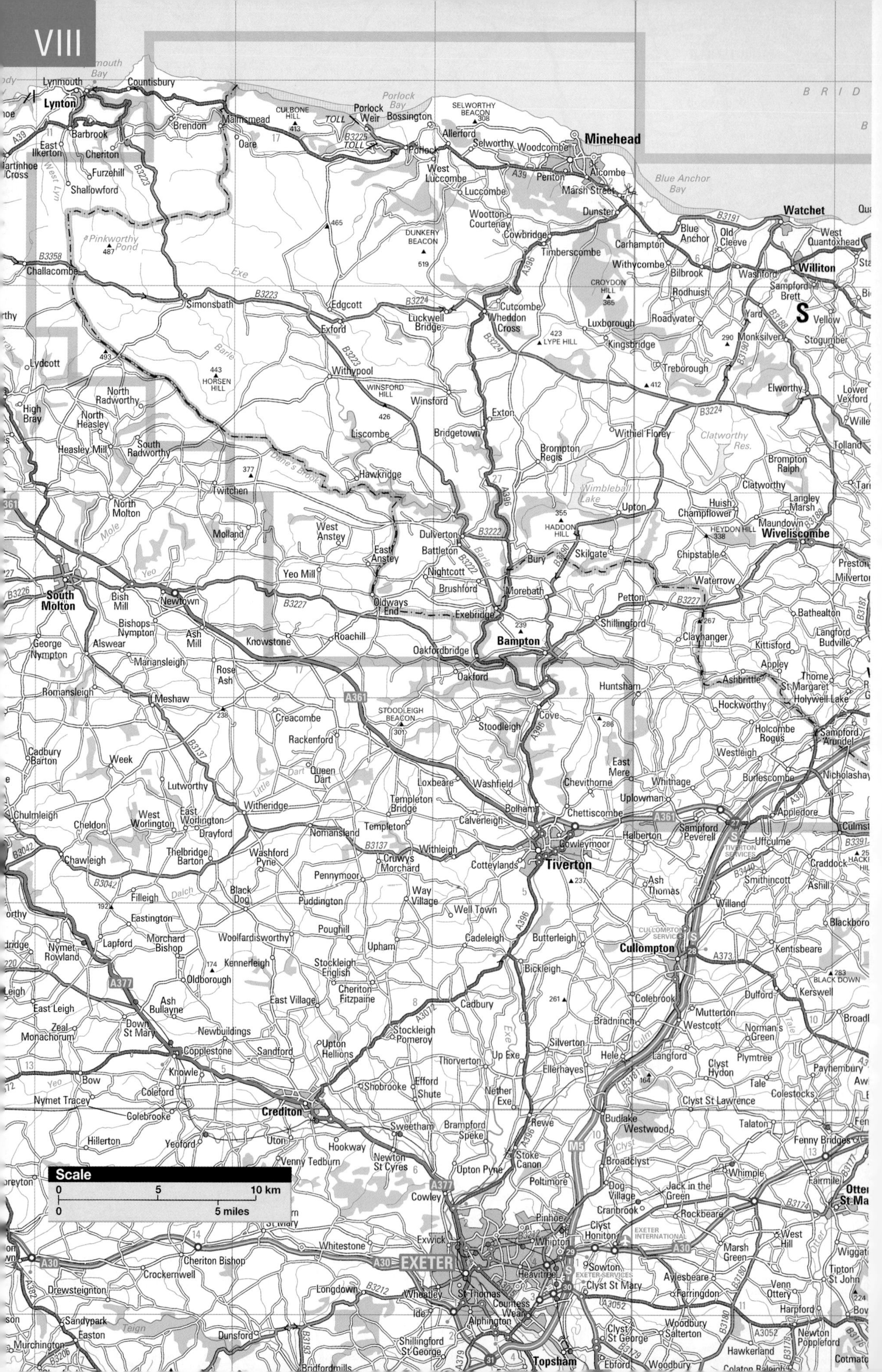
Lynmouth Bay
Lynmouth
Countisbury
Lynton
Porlock Bay
Porlock
Porlock Weir
Bossington
SELWORTHY BEACON 308
CULBONE HILL 413
TOLL
B3225
Brendon
Malmsmead
Oare
Allerford
Selworthy
Woodcombe
Minehead
Barbrook
East Ilkerton
Cheriton
Furzehill
Shallowford
West Lyn
B3223
A39
Martinhoe Cross
West Luccombe
Luccombe
Alcombe
Periton
Marsh Street
Blue Anchor Bay
Dunster
Watchet
Wootton Courtenay
Cowbridge
Timberscombe
Carhampton
Blue Anchor
Old Cleeve
West Quantoxhead
B3191
Williton
Washford
Withycombe
Bilbrook
465
DUNKERY BEACON 519
Pinkworthy Pond 487
B3358
Challacombe
Exe
Simonsbath
B3223
Edgcott
B3224
Luckwell Bridge
Cutcombe
Wheddon Cross
CROYDON HILL 365
Rodhuish
Roadwater
Sampford Brett
Yard
Vellow
Exford
Barle
443 HORSEN HILL
493
Lydcott
Withypool
WINSFORD HILL
Winsford
423 LYPE HILL
Luxborough
Kingsbridge
Treborough
290
Monksilver
Stogumber
B3190
B3188
412
Elworthy
Lower Vexford
North Radworthy
High Bray
North Heasley
Heasley Mill
South Radworthy
Liscombe
426
Exton
Bridgetown
Withiel Florey
B3224
Clatworthy Res.
Brompton Regis
Brompton Ralph
Tolland
377
Dane's Brook
Hawkridge
Twitchen
Wimbleball Lake
Clatworthy
North Molton
Mole
Molland
West Anstey
East Anstey
Dulverton
Battleton
B3222
355 HADDON HILL
Upton
Huish Champflower
Langley Marsh
Maundown
HEYDON HILL 338
Wiveliscombe
Bury
Skilgate
Chipstable
Yeo
Yeo Mill
Nightcott
Brushford
Morebath
Waterrow
Milverton
South Molton
B3226
Bish Mill
Newtown
B3227
Oldways End
Exebridge
Petton
Shillingford
Bathealton
Bishops Nympton
Ash Mill
Knowstone
Roachill
239
Bampton
267
Clayhanger
Langford Budville
George Nympton
Alswear
Oakfordbridge
Kittisford
Mariansleigh
Rose Ash
Oakford
Appley
Thorne St Margaret
Romansleigh
A361
Huntsham
Ashbrittle
Holywell Lake
Meshaw
238
Creacombe
STOODLEIGH BEACON 301
Cove
Stoodleigh
286
Hockworthy
Holcombe Rogus
Sampford Arundel
Rackenford
B3137
Westleigh
Cadbury Barton
Week
Queen Dart
Little Dart
East Mere
Burlescombe
Nicholashayne
Lutworthy
Loxbeare
Washfield
Chevithorne
Whitnage
Uplowman
Templeton Bridge
A38
Chulmleigh
West Worlington
East Worlington
Witheridge
Bolham
Chettiscombe
A361
Appledore
Cheldon
Drayford
Nomansland
Templeton
Calverleigh
Halberton
Sampford Peverell
Culmstock
Thelbridge Barton
Washford Pyne
B3137
Withleigh
Cowleymoor
TIVERTON SERVICES
Uffculme
B3391
B3042
Chawleigh
Cruwys Morchard
Cotteylands
Tiverton
237
Craddock
Pennymoor
B3440
Smithincott
Ashill
Ash Thomas
Filleigh
Dalch
Black Dog
Puddington
Way Village
192
Eastington
Well Town
Willand
Blackborough
A396
CULLOMPTON SERVICES
Poughill
Butterleigh
Nymet Rowland
Lapford
Morchard Bishop
Woolfardisworthy
Upham
Cadeleigh
Cullompton
Kentisbeare
A373
174
Kennerleigh
Stockleigh English
Bickleigh
Oldborough
283 BLACK DOWN
A377
Cheriton Fitzpaine
Dulford
Kerswell
261
Ash Bullayne
East Village
Cadbury
Colebrook
East Leigh
A3072
Bradninch
Mutterton
Zeal Monachorum
Down St Mary
Westcott
Broadhembury
Newbuildings
Stockleigh Pomeroy
Norman's Green
Culm
Copplestone
Sandford
Upton Hellions
Silverton
Langford
Plymtree
Knowle
Thorverton
Up Exe
Hele
Clyst Hydon
Payhembury
Bow
Yeo
Ellerhayes
Coleford
Shobrooke
Efford
Shute
Nether Exe
164
Tale
Colestocks
Nymet Tracey
B3181
Clyst St Lawrence
Crediton
Golebrooke
Rewe
Budlake
Talaton
Sweetham
Brampford Speke
Westwood
Hillerton
Yeoford
Uton
Hookway
Stoke Canon
M5
Fenny Bridges
Clyst
Venny Tedburn
Newton St Cyres
Upton Pyne
Broadclyst
Whimple
Scale
0
5
10 km
5 miles
A377
Poltimore
Fairmile
Cowley
Dog Village
Jack in the Green
B3174
Ottery St Mary
Cranbrook
Rockbeare
Pinhoe
St Mary
Whitestone
Exwick
B3212
Whipton
Clyst Honiton
EXETER INTERNATIONAL
West Hill
A30
Cheriton Bishop
A30
EXETER
Heavitree
Sowton
EXETER SERVICES
Marsh Green
Wiggaton
Crockernwell
Tipton St John
Drewsteignton
Longdown
B3212
Wheatley
St Thomas
Clyst St Mary
Aylesbeare
Venn Ottery
Farringdon
B3180
Ide
Countess Wear
A3052
Harpford
Sandypark
Alphington
Teign
Easton
Dunsford
Clyst St George
Woodbury Salterton
Newton Poppleford
Murchington
Shillingford St George
A379
Topsham
B3179
Hawkerland
A3052
B3193
B3206
Bridfordmills
Ebford
Woodbury
Colaton Raleigh
Cotmaton

IX
BRIDGWATER BAY
STERT FLATS
Somerset
LYME BAY
Lympsham
Biddisham
Weare
Axbridge
Cheddar Res.
Cheddar
Rooks Bridge
Badgworth
Clewer
East Brent
Berrow
Brent Knoll
Stone Allerton
Chapel Allerton
Draycott
Rodney Stoke
Burnham-on-Sea
Edithmead
West Stoughton
Cocklake
Westbury-sub-Mendip
Mark Causeway
Mark
Blackford
Wedmore
Highbridge
Latcham
Easton
Wookey Hole
Watchfield
Westham
Theale
Wells
Stolford
Steart
Huntspill
Bason Bridge
Heath House
Wookey
Henton
Mudgley
Lilstock
Kilton
Shurton
Stockland Bristol
Stretcholt
East Huntspill
East Quantoxhead
Burton
Stogursey
Otterhampton
Burtle
Coxley
Polsham
Kilve
Stringston
Combwich
Pawlett
Westhay
Godney
Southway
Puriton
Woolavington
Meare
Holford
Nether Stowey
Fiddington
Dunball
Cossington
Chilton Polden
Edington
Rodway
Cannington
Bawdrip
Catcott
Glastonbury
Over Stowey
Chilton Trinity
Stawell
Shapwick
Northover
Edgarley
Charlynch
Wembdon
Moorlinch
Ashcott
Crowcombe
Spaxton
Four Forks
Durleigh
Chedzoy
Sutton Mallet
Greinton
Pedwell
Street
West Bradley
Flaxpool
Bridgwater
Walton
Overleigh
Lower Aisholt
Enmore
Westonzoyland
Butleigh Wootton
Baltonsborough
West Bagborough
Goathurst
Bridgwater Services
Huntworth
North Petherton
Courtway
Butleigh
Lydeard St Lawrence
Compton Dundon
Dundon
Barton St David
East Combe
Cothelstone
Broomfield
Northmoor Green or Moorland
Middlezoy
Henley
Combe Florey
Cushuish
North Newton
Othery
Pathe
High Ham
Littleton
Kingweston
Keinton Mandeville
Ash Priors
Thurloxton
Burrowbridge
Aller
Low Ham
Charlton Adam
Fitzhead
Bishops Lydeard
Fulford
Kingston St Mary
Pickney
Lyng
Hedging
Athelney
Stathe
Pitney
Somerton
Halse
Nailsbourne
West Monkton
Durston
West Lyng
Charlton Mackerell
Cheddon Fitzpaine
Monkton Heathfield
Creech Heathfield
Stoke St Gregory
Langport
Bowyer
Heathfield
Staplegrove
Bathpool
North End
Meare Green
Huish Episcopi
Long Sutton
Kingsdon
Hillcommon
Norton Fitzwarren
Creech St Michael
Knapp
Curry Rivel
Oake
Bishop's Hull
Ruishton
North Curry
Muchelney
Drayton
Podimore
Hillfarance
Nynehead
East Nynehead
Bradford-on-Tone
Taunton
Thornfalcon
Henlade
Fivehead
Northover
Runnington
Trull
Stoke St Mary
Wrantage
Curry Mallet
Long Load
Ilchester
Wellington
Rockwell Green
Staplehay
West Buckland
Taunton Deane Services
Orchard Portman
Thurlbear
West Hatch
Hatch Beauchamp
Isle Abbotts
Isle Brewers
Hambridge
Kingsbury Episcopi
Stapleton
Ash
Tintinhull
Beercrocombe
Coat
Martock
Pitminster
Corfe
Hatch Green
Westport
West Lambrook
East Lambrook
Hurst
Chilthorne Domer
Angersleigh
Blagdon Hill
Staple Fitzpaine
Puckington
Barrington
Bower Hinton
Stoke sub Hamdon
Wrangway
Ford Street
Bickenhall
Ilton
South Petherton
Ashill
Stocklinch
Shepton Beauchamp
Montacute
Preston Plucknett
Staple Hill
Curland
Windmill Hill
Ilminster Services
Ashwell
Norton sub Hamdon
Odcombe
Clayhidon
Broadway
Seavington St Michael
Over Stratton
Brympton
Rosemary Lane
Churchstanton
Horton
Ilminster
Seavington St Mary
Chiselborough
Fyfett
Buckland St Mary
Donyatt
Lopen
West Chinnock
West Coker
Hemyock
Stapley
Churchinford
Crock Street
Kingstone
Dinnington
North Coker
East Coker
Bishopswood
Dowlish Wake
Hinton St George
Merriott
East Chinnock
Bolham Water
Combe St Nicholas
Cricket Malherbie
Chillington
Hardington Mandeville
Abbey
Smeatharpe
Marsh
Whitestaunton
Haselbury Plucknett
Cudworth
Closworth
Wadeford
Chaffcombe
North Perrott
Pendomer
Newcott
Howley
Cricket St Thomas
Crewkerne
Hardington Marsh
Yarcombe
Wambrook
Chard
Hewish
Sheldon
Dunkeswell
Misterton
Halstock
Upottery
Whatley
Forton
Wayford
Winsham
South Perrott
Luppitt
Rawridge
Tatworth
Clapton
Seaborough
West Chelborough
Beacon
South Chard
Mosterton
Chedington
Corscombe
Drimpton
Stockland
Furley
Chardstock
Wick
Millhayes
Membury
Tytherleigh
Thorncombe
Burstock
Monkton
Broadwindsor
Rampisham
Alston
Combe Raleigh
Heathstock
Holditch
Beaminster
Cotleigh
Churchill
Ham
Birdsmoorgate
Dalwood
Smallridge
Hawkchurch
Stoke Abbott
Wilmington
Marshalsea
Bettiscombe
Netherbury
Honiton
Offwell
Weycroft
Marshwood
Pilsdon
Mapperton
Hooke
Axminster
Gittisham
Shute
Kilmington
Melplash
Wootton Fitzpaine
Broad Oak
Salwayash
North Poorton
Church Green
Northleigh
Whitchurch Canonicorum
West Milton
Powerstock
Farway
Whitford
Ryall
Dottery
Nettlecombe
Musbury
Bradpole
Southleigh
Colyton
Morcombelake
Loders
Charmouth
Symondsbury
Bridport
Uploders
Uplyme
Colyford
Combpyne
Lyme Regis
Chideock
Walditch
Askerswell
Sidbury
Bothenhampton
Rousdon
Seatown
Eype
Shipton Gorge
Chilcombe
Harcombe
Axmouth
Sidford
West Bay
Litton Cheney
Weston
Vicarage
Seaton
Charlton Bay
Sid
Salcombe Regis
Beer
Branscombe
Seaton Bay
Burton Bradstock
Swyre
Puncknowle
Parrett
Brue
Huntspill
Whitelake
Tone
Isle
Yeo
Yarty
Axe
Char
Brit
M5
A39
A38
A358
A361
A372
A378
A303
A3088
A30
A356
A37
A35
A375
A3052
A3066
B3140
B3139
B3141
B3151
B3153
B3165
B3168
B3170
B3162
B3167
B3164
B3163
B3224
B3227
B3259
B3261
B3172
B3174
Sedgemoor Services

Key to map symbols

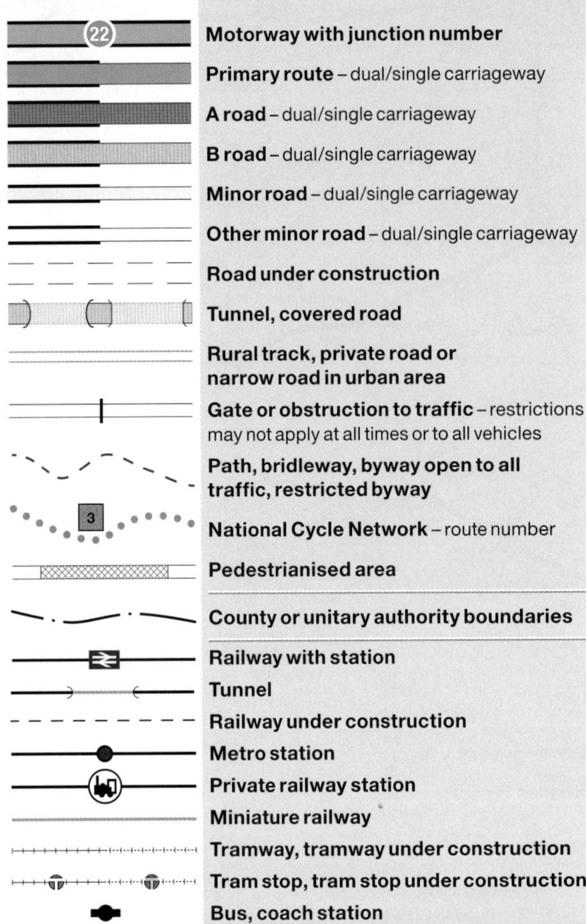

Motorway with junction number

Primary route – dual/single carriageway

A road – dual/single carriageway

B road – dual/single carriageway

Minor road – dual/single carriageway

Other minor road – dual/single carriageway

Road under construction

Tunnel, covered road

Rural track, private road or narrow road in urban area

Gate or obstruction to traffic – restrictions may not apply at all times or to all vehicles

Path, bridleway, byway open to all traffic, restricted byway

National Cycle Network – route number

Pedestrianised area

County or unitary authority boundaries

Railway with station

Tunnel

Railway under construction

Metro station

Private railway station

Miniature railway

Tramway, tramway under construction

Tram stop, tram stop under construction

Bus, coach station

Ambulance station

Coastguard station

Fire station

Police station

Accident and Emergency entrance to hospital

Hospital

Place of worship

Information centre

Shopping centre, parking

Park and Ride, Post Office

Camping site, caravan site

Golf course, picnic site

Church ROMAN FORT **Non-Roman antiquity, Roman antiquity**

Univ **Important buildings, schools, colleges, universities and hospitals**

Woods, built-up area

River Medway **Water name**

River, weir

Stream

Canal, lock, tunnel

Water

Tidal water

58 87 246 **Adjoining page indicators and overlap bands** – the colour of the arrow and band indicates the scale of the adjoining or overlapping page (see scales below)

The dark grey border on the inside edge of some pages indicates that the mapping does not continue onto the adjacent page

The small numbers around the edges of the maps identify the 1-kilometre National Grid lines

Abbreviations

Acad	**Academy**	Meml	**Memorial**
Allot Gdns	**Allotments**	Mon	**Monument**
Cemy	**Cemetery**	Mus	**Museum**
C Ctr	**Civic centre**	Obsy	**Observatory**
CH	**Club house**	Pal	**Royal palace**
Coll	**College**	PH	**Public house**
Crem	**Crematorium**	Recn Gd	**Recreation ground**
Ent	**Enterprise**	Resr	**Reservoir**
Ex H	**Exhibition hall**	Ret Pk	**Retail park**
Ind Est	**Industrial Estate**	Sch	**School**
IRB Sta	**Inshore rescue boat station**	Sh Ctr	**Shopping centre**
Inst	**Institute**	TH	**Town hall / house**
Ct	**Law court**	Trad Est	**Trading estate**
L Ctr	**Leisure centre**	Univ	**University**
LC	**Level crossing**	W Twr	**Water tower**
Liby	**Library**	Wks	**Works**
Mkt	**Market**	YH	**Youth hostel**

Enlarged maps only

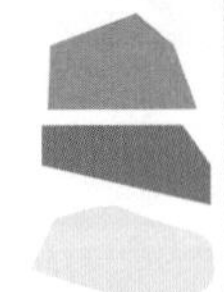

Railway or bus station building

Place of interest

Parkland

The map scale on the pages numbered in green is 1¾ inches to 1 mile
2.76 cm to 1 km • 1:36206

The map scale on the pages numbered in blue is 3½ inches to 1 mile
5.52 cm to 1 km • 1:18103

The map scale on the pages numbered in red is 7 inches to 1 mile
11.04 cm to 1 km • 1:9051

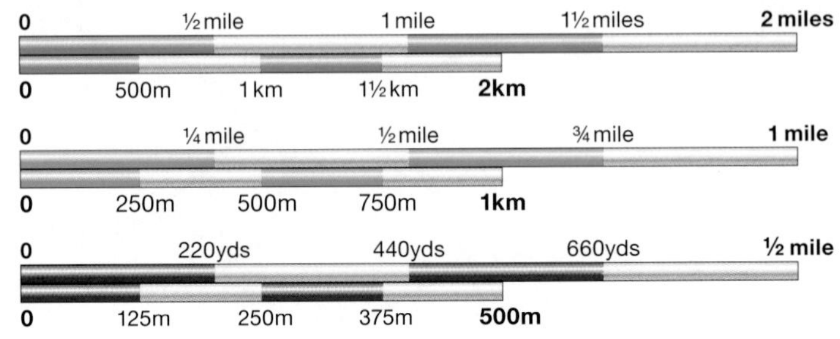

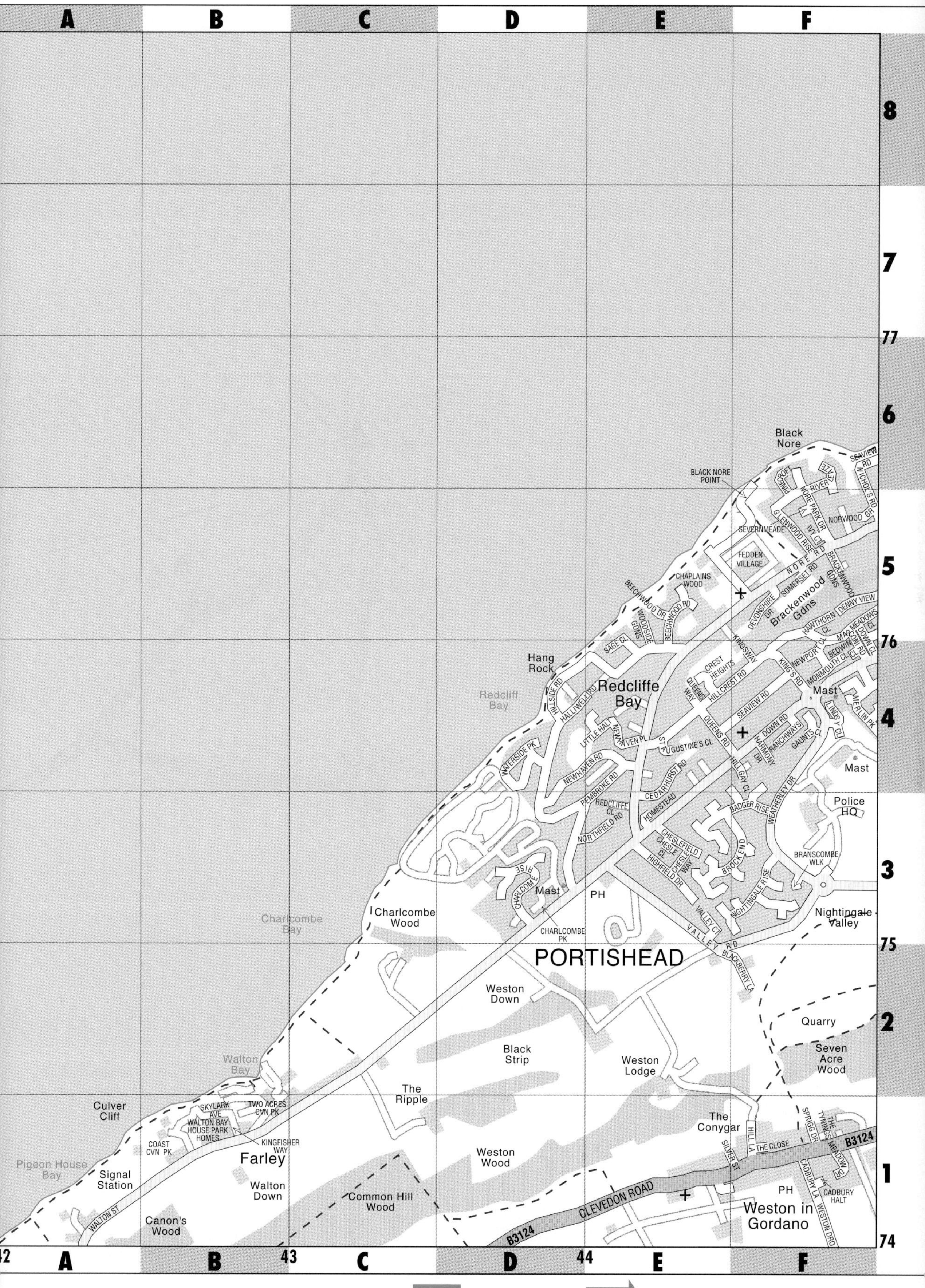
A
B
C
D
E
F
8
7
77
6
5
76
4
3
75
2
1
74
42
43
44
Black Nore
BLACK NORE POINT
SEVERNMEADE
FEDDEN VILLAGE
CHAPLAINS WOOD
BEECHWOOD DR
WOODSIDE GDNS
BEECHWOOD RD
Brackenwood Gdns
DEVONSHIRE DR
SOMERSET RD
NORE RD
GLENWOOD RISE
NORE PARK DR
IVY CL
RIVER LEAZE
NORWOOD GR
NICHOLS RD
SEAVIEW RD
BRACKENWOOD GDNS
DENNY VIEW
HAWTHORN CL
MEADOWS CL
BEDWIN CL
MONMOUTH CL
NEWPORT CL
KING'S RD
KINGSWAY
CREST HEIGHTS
HILLCREST RD
QUEENS WAY
SEAVIEW RD
Hang Rock
SAGE CL
HILLSIDE RD
HALLIWELL RD
Redcliffe Bay
Redcliff Bay
Mast
MERLIN PK
LINDSEY CL
LITTLE HALT
NEWHAVEN PL
ST AUGUSTINE'S CL
QUEENS RD
DOWN RD
RANCHWAYS
HARMONY DR
GAUNTS CL
Mast
WATERSIDE PK
NEWHAVEN RD
PEMBROKE RD
CEDARHURST RD
HILLGAY CL
REDCLIFFE CL
HOMESTEAD
NORTHFIELD RD
BADGER RISE
WEATHERLEY DR
Police HQ
CHESLEFIELD
CHESLE CL
CHESLE WAY
HIGHFIELD DR
BROCK END
BRANSCOMBE WLK
CHARLCOMBE RISE
Mast
PH
NIGHTINGALE RISE
VALLEY CL
Charlcombe Wood
Charlcombe Bay
CHARLCOMBE PK
VALLEY RD
BLACKBERRY LA
Nightingale Valley
PORTISHEAD
Weston Down
Quarry
Black Strip
Seven Acre Wood
Walton Bay
Weston Lodge
The Ripple
Culver Cliff
SKYLARK AVE
TWO ACRES CVN PK
WALTON BAY HOUSE PARK HOMES
KINGFISHER WAY
COAST CVN PK
The Conygar
HILL LA
THE CLOSE
SILVER ST
SPRIGG DR
THE TYNINGS
MEADOW RD
B3124
Farley
Weston Wood
Pigeon House Bay
Signal Station
Walton Down
Common Hill Wood
CLEVEDON ROAD
PH
CADBURY LA
CADBURY HALT
WESTON DRO
Weston in Gordano
WALTON ST
Canon's Wood
B3124

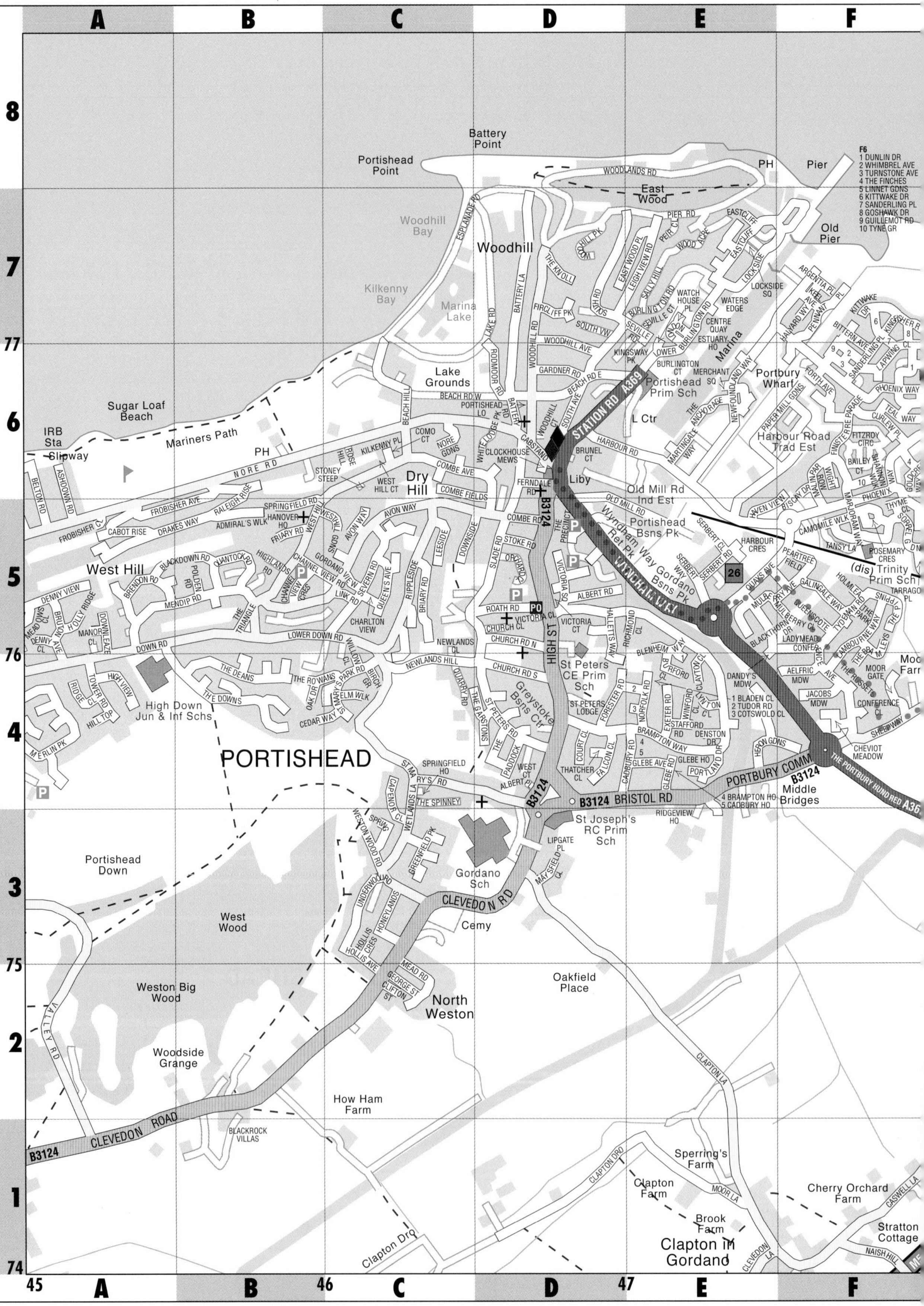

A B C D E F

F6
1 DUNLIN DR
2 WHIMBREL AVE
3 TURNSTONE AVE
4 THE FINCHES
5 LINNET GDNS
6 KITTWAKE DR
7 SANDERLING PL
8 GOSHAWK DR
9 GUILLEMOT RD
10 TYNE GR

Battery Point
Portishead Point
Woodhill Bay
Kilkenny Bay
East Wood
Woodhill
Marina Lake
Lake Grounds
Sugar Loaf Beach
IRB Sta
Slipway
Mariners Path
Dry Hill
West Hill
Portbury Wharf
Harbour Road Trad Est
Old Pier
Pier
Marina
Portishead Prim Sch
L Ctr
Liby
Old Mill Rd Ind Est
Portishead Bsns Pk
Wyndham Way Ret Pk
Gordano Bsns Pk
(dis) Trinity Prim Sch
St Peters CE Prim Sch
Greystoke Bsns Ctr
High Down Jun & Inf Schs
PORTISHEAD
Middle Bridges
St Joseph's RC Prim Sch
Gordano Sch
Cemy
Portishead Down
West Wood
Weston Big Wood
Woodside Grange
North Weston
Oakfield Place
How Ham Farm
Sperring's Farm
Clapton Farm
Brook Farm
Clapton in Gordano
Cherry Orchard Farm
Stratton Cottage

STATION RD A369
HIGH ST B3124
BRISTOL RD B3124
CLEVEDON RD
CLEVEDON ROAD B3124
PORTBURY COMM
THE PORTBURY HUNDRED A369

A B C D E F

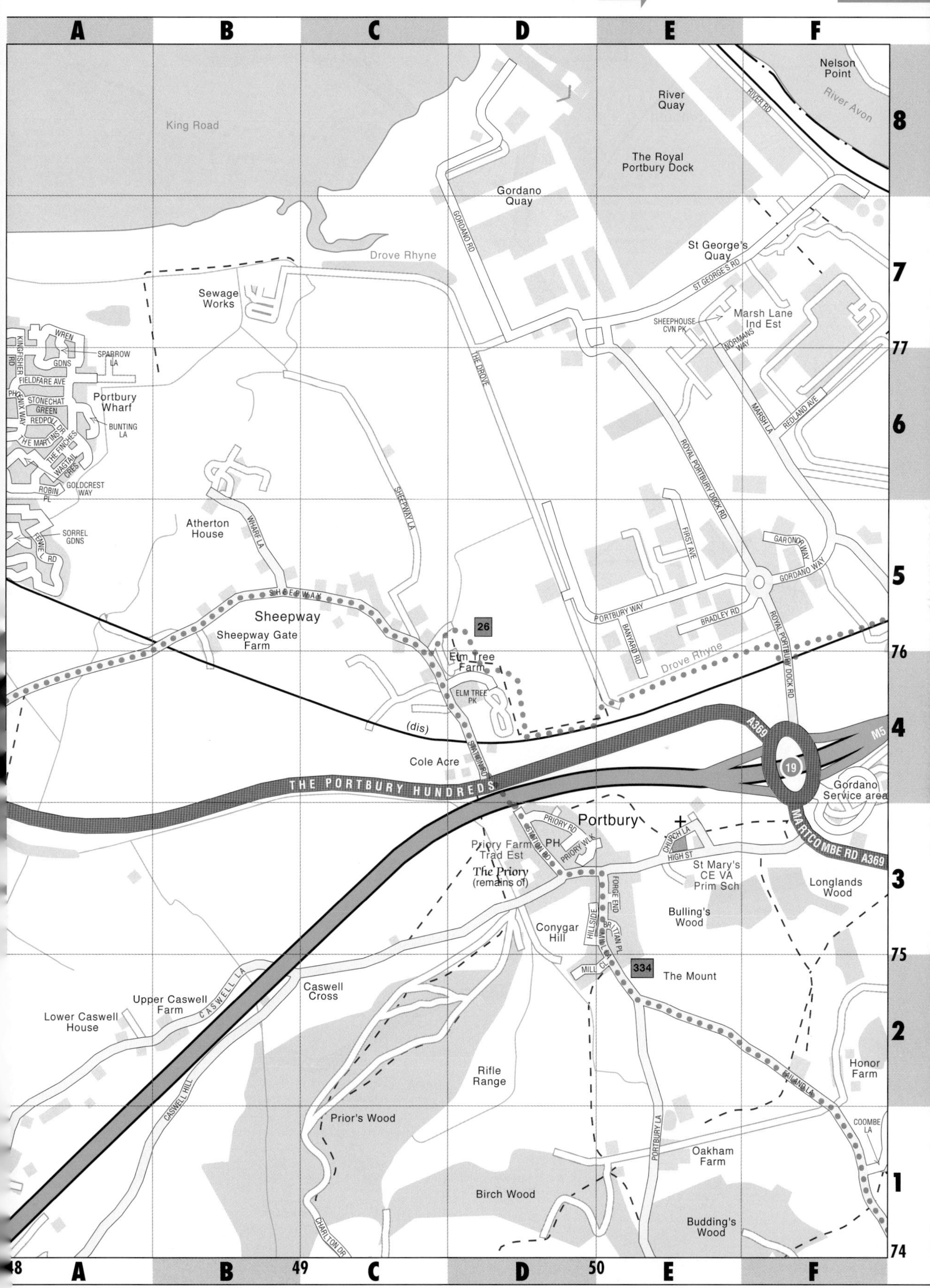
A
B
C
D
E
F
King Road
River Quay
Nelson Point
River Avon
RIVER RD
The Royal Portbury Dock
Gordano Quay
GORDANO RD
Drove Rhyne
St George's Quay
ST GEORGE'S RD
Sewage Works
SHEEPHOUSE CVN PK
Marsh Lane Ind Est
NORMANS WAY
WREN
KINGFISHER RD
SPARROW LA
GDNS
FIELDFARE AVE
STONECHAT GREEN
REDPOLL DR
THE MARTINS
THE FINCHES
WAGTAIL CRES
ROBIN PL
GOLDCREST WAY
BUNTING LA
Portbury Wharf
THE DROVE
MARSH LA
REDLAND AVE
ROYAL PORTBURY DOCK RD
SHEEPWAY LA
FIRST AVE
GARONOR WAY
GORDANO WAY
Atherton House
SORREL GDNS
FENNEL RD
WHARF LA
SHEEPWAY
Sheepway
Sheepway Gate Farm
26
Elm Tree Farm
ELM TREE PK
PORTBURY WAY
BANWARD RD
BRADLEY RD
Drove Rhyne
(dis)
A369
M5
19
Cole Acre
THE PORTBURY HUNDREDS
Gordano Service area
Portbury
PRIORY RD
STATION RD
PRIORY WLK
PH
Priory Farm Trad Est
The Priory (remains of)
CHURCH LA
HIGH ST
St Mary's CE VA Prim Sch
MARTCOMBE RD A369
Longlands Wood
FORGE END
HILLSIDE
BRITTAN PL
Conygar Hill
Bulling's Wood
MILL CL
334
The Mount
Caswell Cross
Upper Caswell Farm
CASWELL LA
Lower Caswell House
Rifle Range
Honor Farm
FAILAND LA
COOMBE LA
CASWELL HILL
Prior's Wood
PORTBURY LA
Oakham Farm
Birch Wood
Budding's Wood
CHARLTON DR
8
7
77
6
5
76
4
3
75
2
1
74
48
49
50

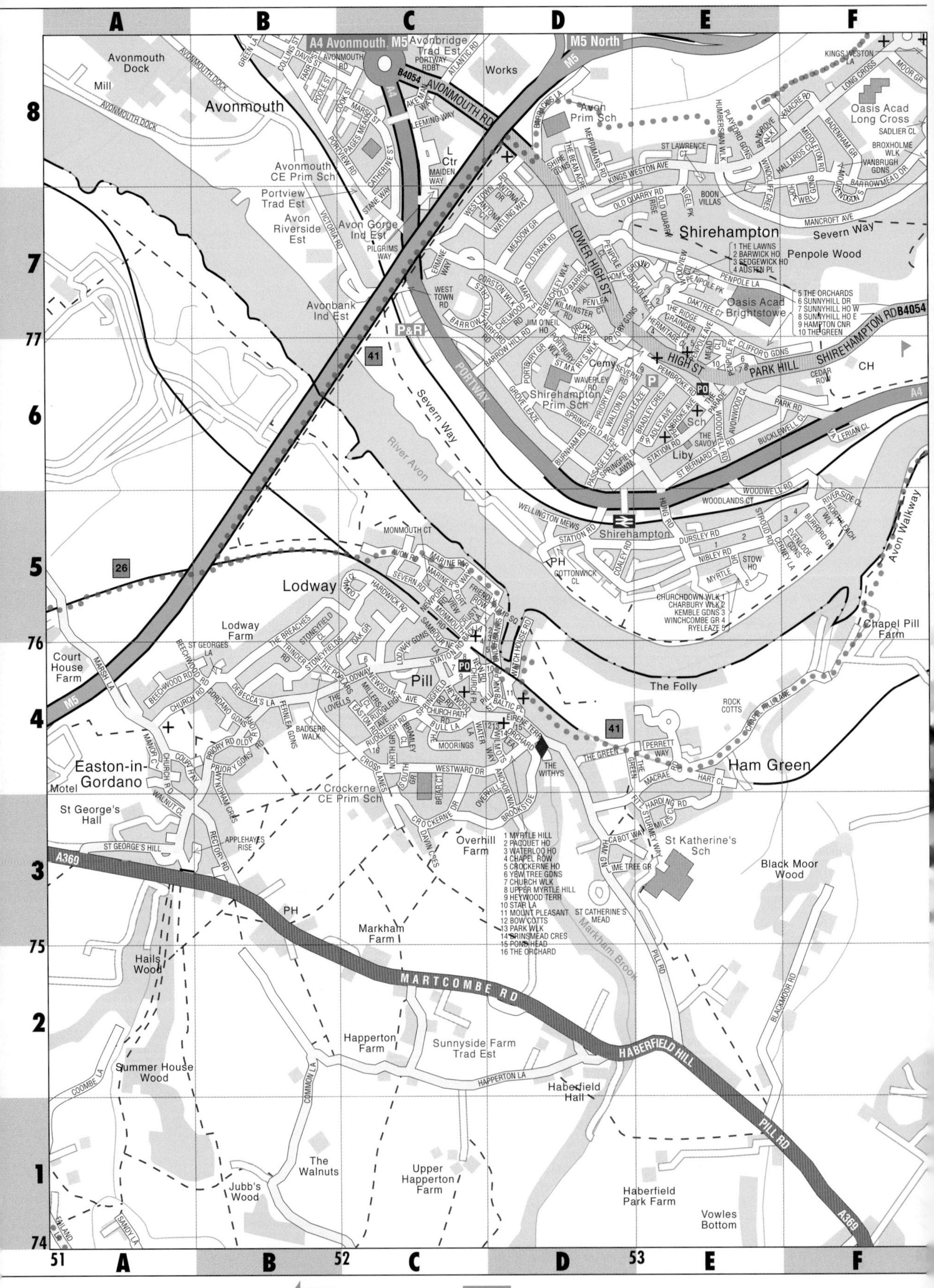
A
B
C
D
E
F
8
7
77
6
5
76
4
3
75
2
1
74
51
52
53
A4 Avonmouth
M5
M5 North
Avonbridge Trad Est
Avonmouth Dock
Mill
Avonmouth
Works
Avon Prim Sch
Oasis Acad Long Cross
L Ctr
Avonmouth CE Prim Sch
Portview Trad Est
Avon Riverside Est
Avon Gorge Ind Est
Avonbank Ind Est
Shirehampton
Severn Way
Penpole Wood
1 THE LAWNS
2 BARWICK HO
3 SEDGEWICK HO
4 AUSTEN PL
Oasis Acad Brightstowe
5 THE ORCHARDS
6 SUNNYHILL DR
7 SUNNYHILL HO W
8 SUNNYHILL HO E
9 HAMPTON CNR
10 THE GREEN
SHIREHAMPTON RD B4054
PARK HILL
HIGH ST
LOWER HIGH ST
PORTWAY
CH
A4
Cemy
Shirehampton Prim Sch
Sch
Liby
P&R
41
River Avon
Shirehampton
PH
CHURCHDOWN WLK 1
CHARBURY WLK 2
KEMBLE GDNS 3
WINCHCOMBE GR 4
RYELEAZE 5
Avon Walkway
26
Lodway
Lodway Farm
Chapel Pill Farm
Court House Farm
Pill
The Folly
ROCK COTTS
Easton-in-Gordano
Motel
Ham Green
St George's Hall
Crockerne CE Prim Sch
THE WITHYS
Overhill Farm
1 MYRTLE HILL
2 PACQUET HO
3 WATERLOO HO
4 CHAPEL ROW
5 CROCKERNE HO
6 YEW TREE GDNS
7 CHURCH WLK
8 UPPER MYRTLE HILL
9 HEYWOOD TERR
10 STAR LA
11 MOUNT PLEASANT
12 BOW COTTS
13 PARK WLK
14 BRINSMEAD CRES
15 POND HEAD
16 THE ORCHARD
St Katherine's Sch
ST CATHERINE'S MEAD
Black Moor Wood
A360
PH
Markham Farm
Markham Brook
Hails Wood
MARTCOMBE RD
HABERFIELD HILL
Happerton Farm
Sunnyside Farm Trad Est
Summer House Wood
Haberfield Hall
PILL RD
The Walnuts
Upper Happerton Farm
Jubb's Wood
Haberfield Park Farm
Vowles Bottom
A369

3
10

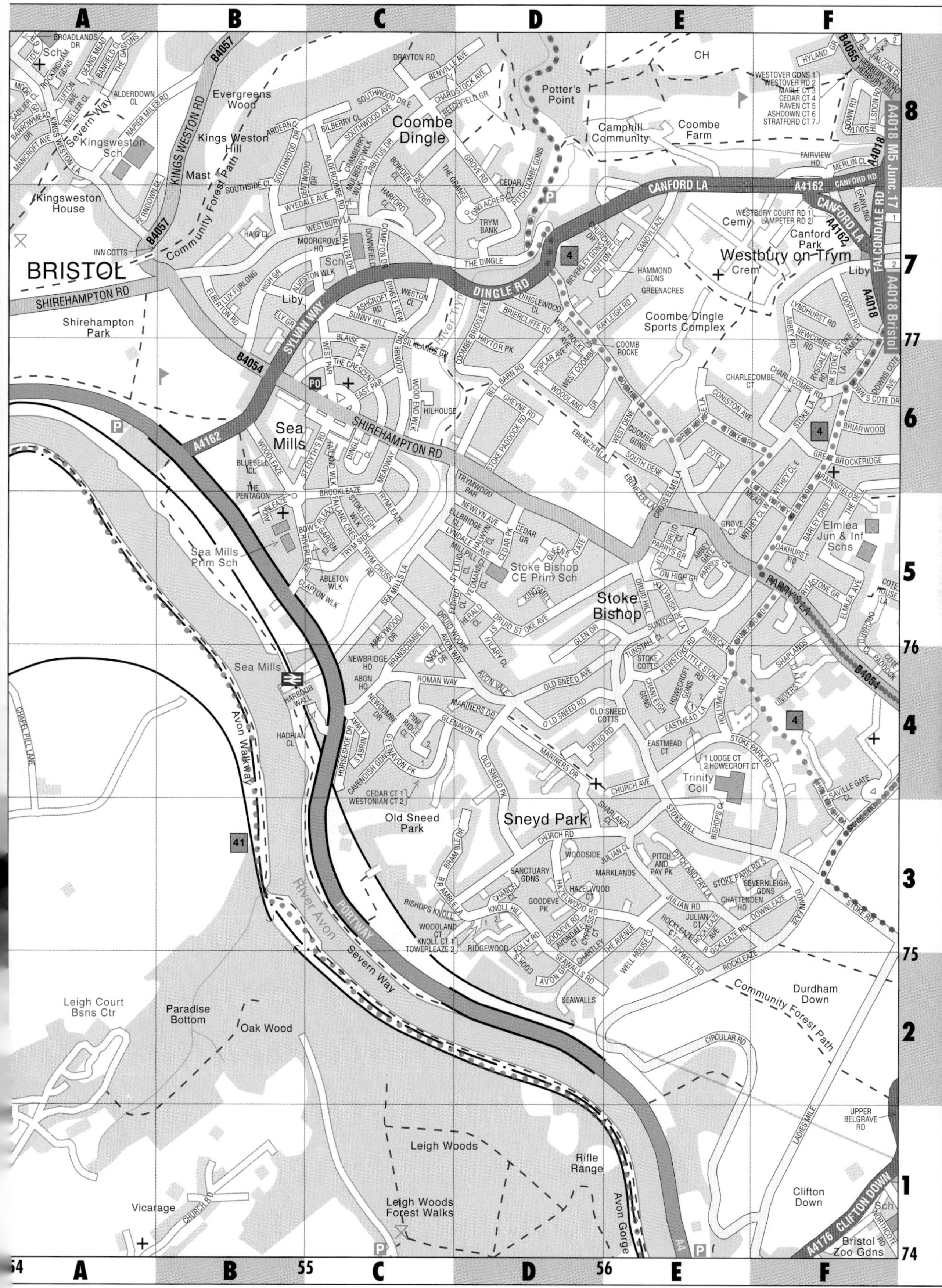
A
B
C
D
E
F
8
7
77
6
5
76
4
3
75
2
1
74
54
55
56
BRISTOL
Evergreens Wood
Kings Weston Hill
Mast
Kingsweston Sch
Kingsweston House
Severn Way
Community Forest Path
KINGS WESTON RD
B4057
SHIREHAMPTON RD
Shirehampton Park
INN COTTS
Coombe Dingle
Potter's Point
Camphill Community
Coombe Farm
CH
CANFORD LA
A4162
Westbury on Trym
Cemy
Crem
Canford Park
Liby
A4018
A4018 M5 Junc. 17
A4018 Bristol
FALCONDALE RD
B4055
WESTOVER GDNS 1
WESTOVER RD 2
MAPLE CT 3
CEDAR CT 4
RAVEN CT 5
ASHDOWN CT 6
STRATFORD CT 7
DINGLE RD
SYLVAN WAY
B4054
Sch
Liby
Coombe Dingle Sports Complex
Sea Mills
SHIREHAMPTON RD
Sea Mills Prim Sch
Stoke Bishop CE Prim Sch
Stoke Bishop
Elmlea Jun & Inf Schs
PARRY'S LA
Sea Mills
Avon Walkway
HARBOUR WALL
Old Sneed Park
Sneyd Park
Trinity Coll
1 LODGE CT
2 HOWECROFT CT
CEDAR CT 1
WESTONIAN CT 2
River Avon
PORTWAY
Severn Way
Community Forest Path
Durdham Down
Leigh Court Bsns Ctr
Paradise Bottom
Oak Wood
Leigh Woods
Rifle Range
Leigh Woods Forest Walks
Vicarage
CHURCH RD
Avon Gorge
A4
CIRCULAR RD
LADIES MILE
UPPER BELGRAVE RD
Clifton Down
A4176 CLIFTON DOWN
Bristol Zoo Gdns
Sch
41
4

11

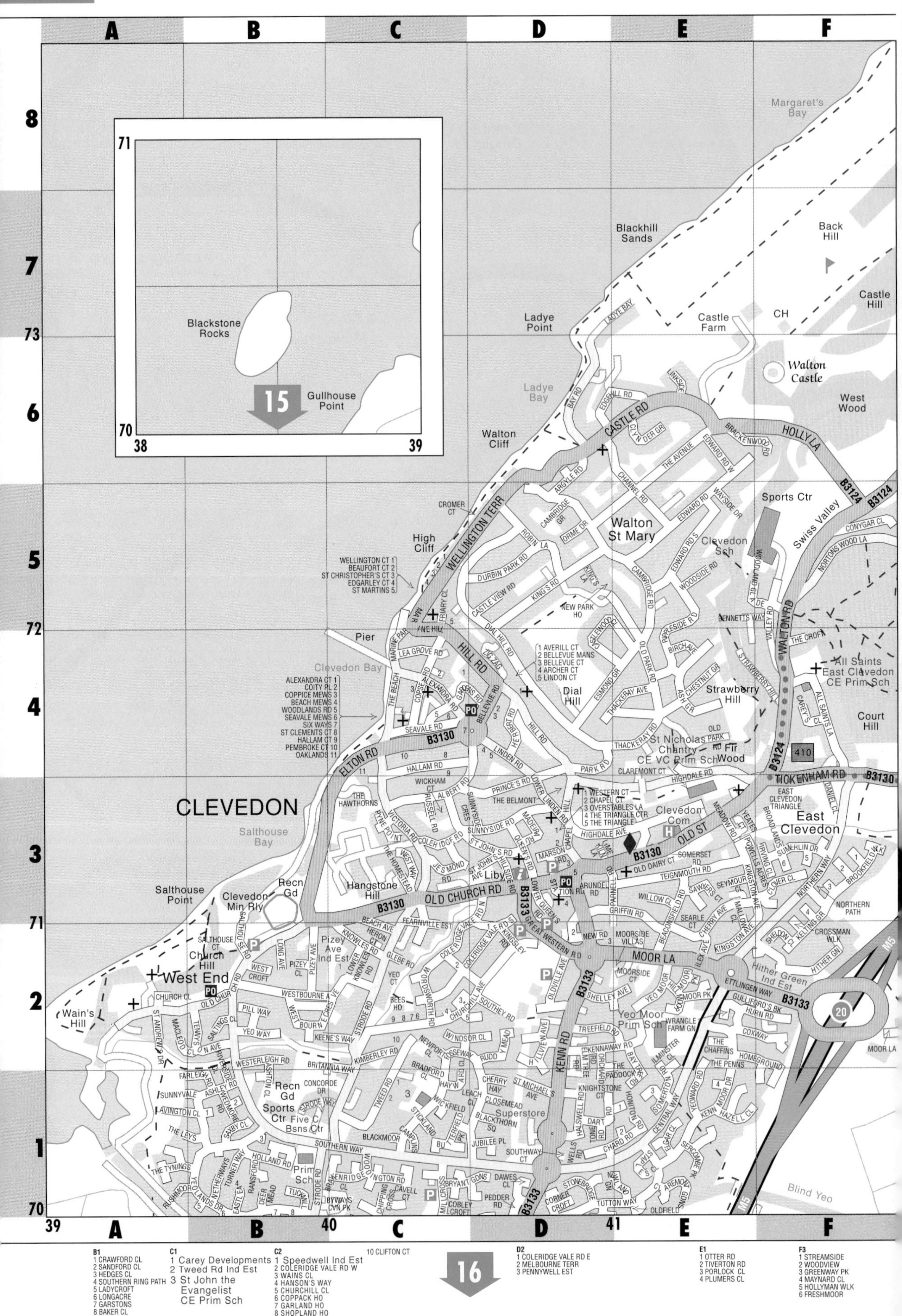

B1
1 CRAWFORD CL
2 SANDFORD CL
3 HEDGES CL
4 SOUTHERN RING PATH
5 LADYCROFT
6 LONGACRE
7 GARSTONS
8 BAKER CL

C1
1 Carey Developments
2 Tweed Rd Ind Est
3 St John the Evangelist CE Prim Sch

C2
1 Speedwell Ind Est
2 COLERIDGE VALE RD W
3 WAINS CL
4 HANSON'S WAY
5 CHURCHILL CL
6 COPPACK HO
7 GARLAND HO
8 SHOPLAND HO
9 BRIDGE HO
10 CLIFTON CT

16

D2
1 COLERIDGE VALE RD E
2 MELBOURNE TERR
3 PENNYWELL EST

E1
1 OTTER RD
2 TIVERTON RD
3 PORLOCK CL
4 PLUMERS CL

F3
1 STREAMSIDE
2 WOODVIEW
3 GREENWAY PK
4 MAYNARD CL
5 HOLLYMAN WLK
6 FRESHMOOR

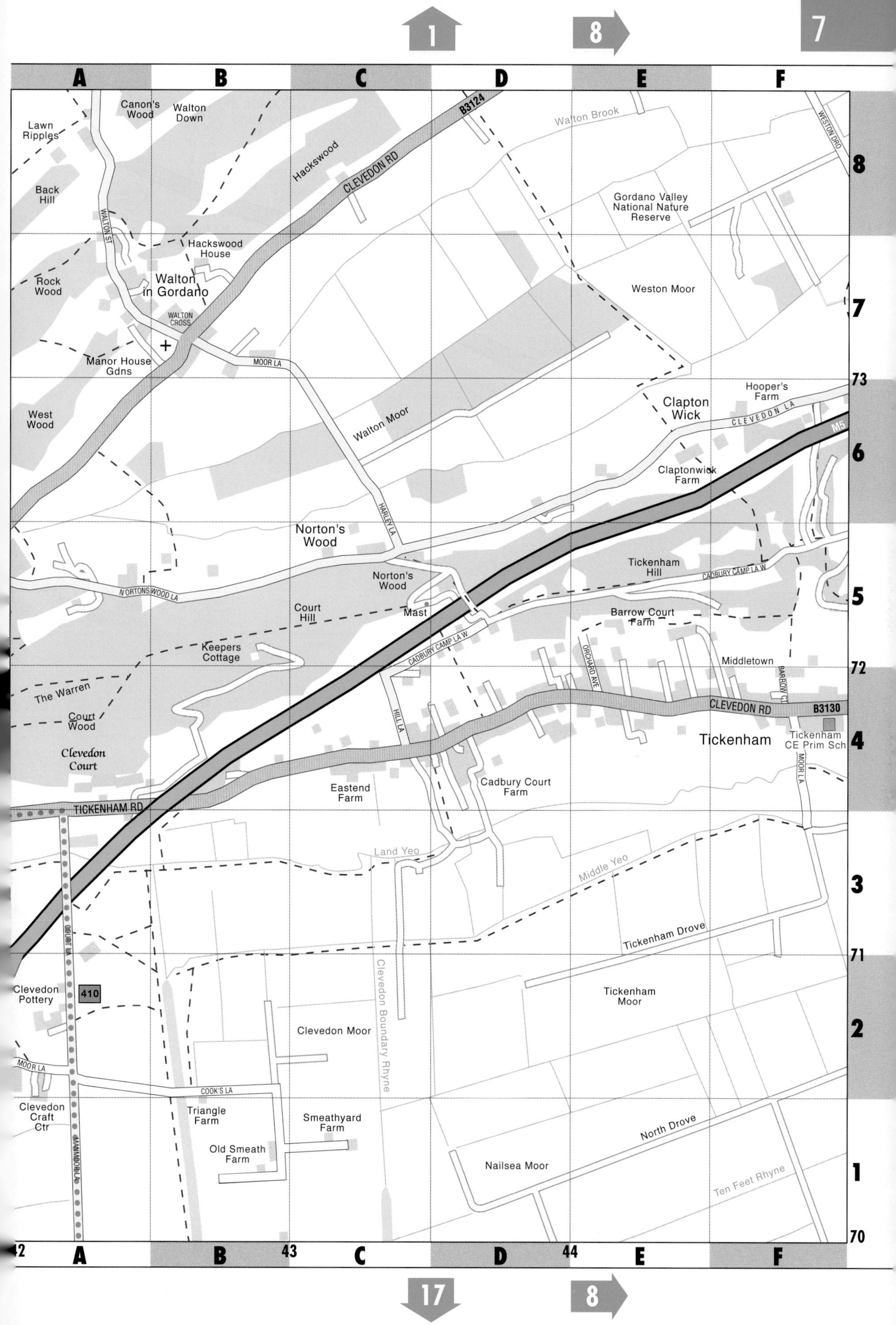

8

A B C D E F

Lawn Ripples
Canon's Wood
Walton Down
B3124
Walton Brook
WESTON DRO
8
Back Hill
Hackswood
CLEVEDON RD
WALTON ST
Gordano Valley National Nature Reserve
Hackswood House
Rock Wood
Walton in Gordano
Weston Moor
7
WALTON CROSS
Manor House Gdns
MOOR LA
73
Hooper's Farm
Clapton Wick
CLEVEDON LA
West Wood
Walton Moor
M5
6
Claptonwick Farm
HARLEY LA
Norton's Wood
Tickenham Hill
CADBURY CAMP LA W
NORTONS WOOD LA
Norton's Wood
5
Court Hill
Mast
Barrow Court Farm
Keepers Cottage
CADBURY CAMP LA W
ORCHARD AVE
Middletown
72
The Warren
BARROW CT
CLEVEDON RD
B3130
Court Wood
HILL LA
Tickenham
Tickenham CE Prim Sch
4
Clevedon Court
MOOR LA
Eastend Farm
Cadbury Court Farm
TICKENHAM RD
Land Yeo
Middle Yeo
3
COURT LA
Tickenham Drove
71
Clevedon Pottery
410
Clevedon Boundary Rhyne
Tickenham Moor
2
Clevedon Moor
MOOR LA
COOK'S LA
Clevedon Craft Ctr
Triangle Farm
Smeathyard Farm
North Drove
Old Smeath Farm
Nailsea Moor
1
MARMOOR LA
Ten Feet Rhyne
70

42 A B 43 C D 44 E F

17

8

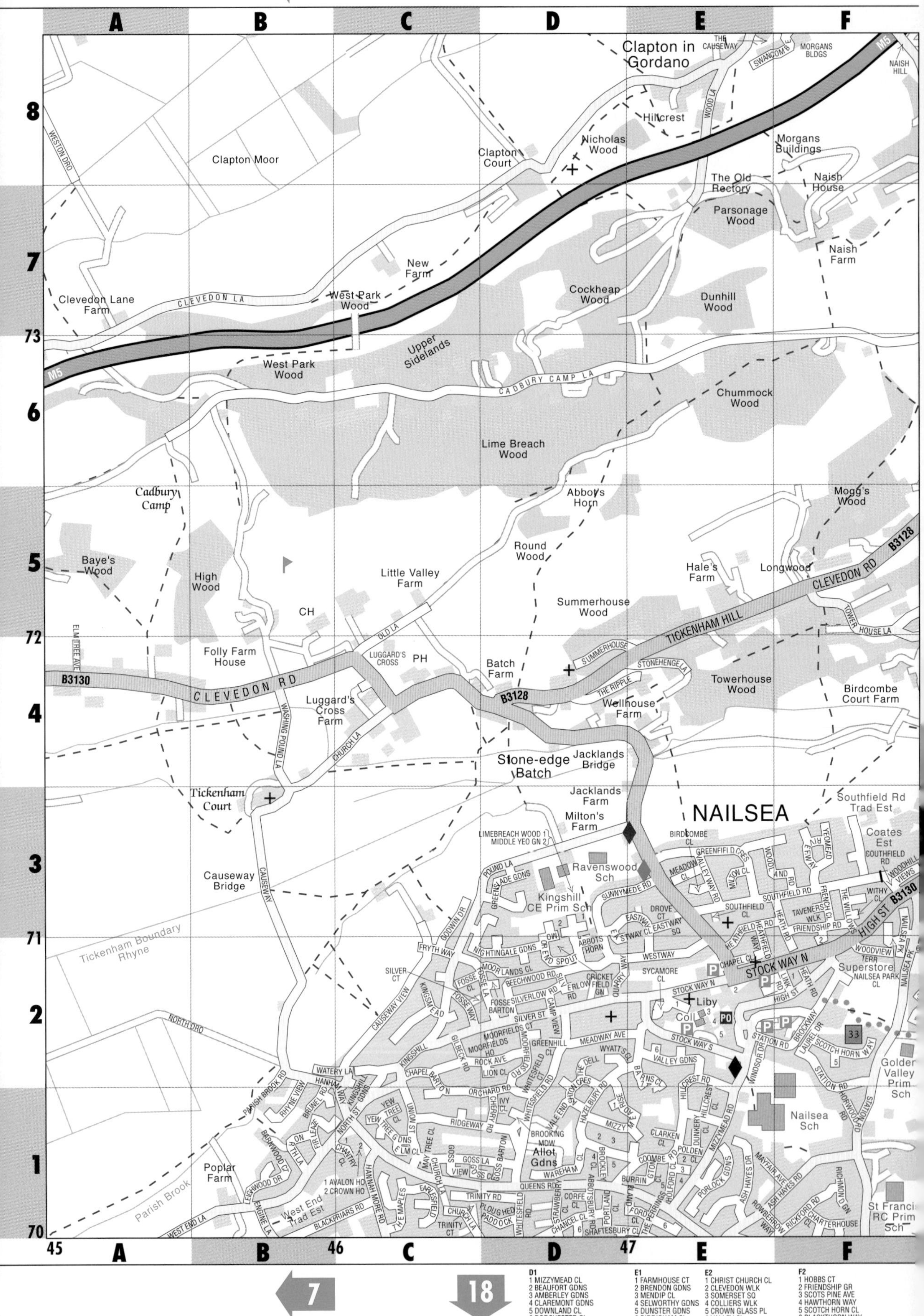
7
2
A
B
C
D
E
F
8
7
73
6
5
72
4
3
71
2
1
70
45
46
47
Clapton in Gordano
THE CAUSEWAY
SWANCOMBE
MORGANS BLDGS
NAISH HILL
M5
WOOD LA
Hillcrest
Nicholas Wood
Clapton Moor
WESTON DRO
Clapton Court
Morgans Buildings
The Old Rectory
Naish House
Parsonage Wood
Naish Farm
New Farm
Clevedon Lane Farm
CLEVEDON LA
West Park Wood
Cockheap Wood
Dunhill Wood
Upper Sidelands
CADBURY CAMP LA
Chummock Wood
Lime Breach Wood
Cadbury Camp
Abbot's Horn
Mogg's Wood
Baye's Wood
High Wood
Round Wood
Little Valley Farm
Hale's Farm
Longwood
CLEVEDON RD
B3128
Summerhouse Wood
CH
TICKENHAM HILL
TOWER HOUSE LA
ELM TREE AVE
Folly Farm House
OLD LA
LUGGARD'S CROSS
PH
Batch Farm
SUMMERHOUSE
STONEHENGE LA
B3130
CLEVEDON RD
THE RIPPLE
Towerhouse Wood
Birdcombe Court Farm
Luggard's Cross Farm
WASHING POUND LA
Wellhouse Farm
CHURCH LA
Stone-edge Batch
Jacklands Bridge
Tickenham Court
Jacklands Farm
Southfield Rd Trad Est
NAILSEA
Milton's Farm
Coates Est
Causeway Bridge
CAUSEWAY
Ravenswood Sch
Kingshill CE Prim Sch
Tickenham Boundary Rhyne
Superstore
STOCK WAY N
HIGH ST
Liby
Coll
PO
NORTH DRO
Golden Valley Prim Sch
Nailsea Sch
Allot Gdns
Poplar Farm
Parish Brook
West End Trad Est
WEST END LA
St Francis RC Prim Sch
7
18
D1
1 MIZZYMEAD CL
2 BEAUFORT GDNS
3 AMBERLEY GDNS
4 CLAREMONT GDNS
5 DOWNLAND CL
6 DORCHESTER CL
E1
1 FARMHOUSE CT
2 BRENDON GDNS
3 MENDIP CL
4 SELWORTHY GDNS
5 DUNSTER GDNS
6 BIDDISHAM CL
E2
1 CHRIST CHURCH CL
2 CLEVEDON WLK
3 SOMERSET SQ
4 COLLIERS WLK
5 CROWN GLASS PL
6 VALLEY CL
7 FARMHOUSE CL
F2
1 HOBBS CT
2 FRIENDSHIP GR
3 SCOTS PINE AVE
4 HAWTHORN WAY
5 SCOTCH HORN CL
6 BLACKTHORN WAY

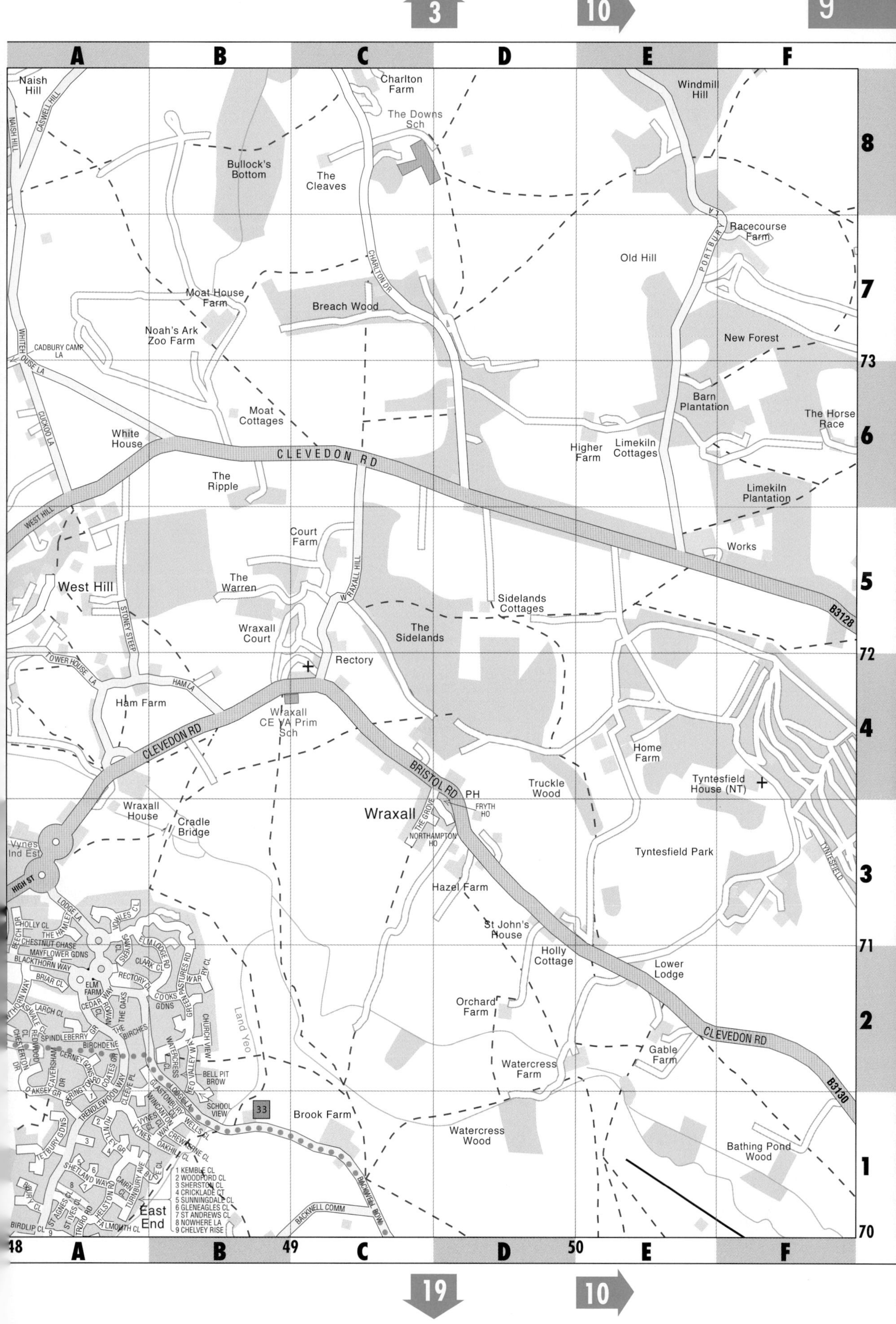

Lower Failand
Jubbs Court
Lower Failand Farm
Leigh Wood
Old Park
Old Park Wood
Poundbatch Farm
PILL RD A369
Home Farm
Failand Court
Mulberry Farm
Markham Brook
334
Three Cornered Wood
Old Park House
Glen Farm
Fish Pond Wood
West Tanpit Wood
East Tanpit Wood
Scutche's Plantation
Yew Tree Plantation
Failand Hill House
Durbans Batch
Orchard Lodge
Round Hill Clump
Failand Hill Farm
Ox House Bottom
Ferney Row
Failand Farm
Manor Farm
Failand Lodge Farm
Fifty Acre Wood
B3128
CH
B3129
PH
Works
CLEVEDON RD
BEGGAR BUSH LA
North Longwood
Redwood Lodge Hotel & Country Club
Wraxall Piece
Long Wood
Durnford Quarry
Round Plantation
Failand Lawn
Monarch's Way
Tyntesfield Plantation
Belmont Combe
WESTON RD
CLARKEN COOMBE
Clifton Lodge
Failand
Iron Plantation
Ashton Hill Plantation
The Brake
Belmont House
Mon
George's Hill Plantation
Fenn's Wood
Kingcot Farm
BELMONT HILL
Cook's Wood
Shipley Brake
Belmont Farm
Belmont Lodge
Rudge Farm
Land Yeo
Liby
B3130
51
52
53
70
71
72
73

F5
1 BRISTOL GATE
2 FARADAY RD
3 DOWRY PL
4 LITTLE CAROLINE PL
5 GRANVILLE CHAPEL
6 HUMPHRY DAVY WAY

F5
7 GRENVILLE PL
8 ASHMEAD WAY
9 CUMBERLAND RD
10 BRUNSWICK PL

F6
1 HABERFIELD HO
2 DAWES CT
3 CLEVE CT
4 BROWNE CT
5 ADAMS CT
6 CUMBERLAND PL
7 CARRICK HO
8 SOUTH GREEN ST
9 ALBERMARLE ROW
10 HOPECHAPEL HILL
11 NORTH GREEN ST
12 HINTON LA
13 WINDSOR CT

F6
14 VICTORIA TERR
15 THE POLYGON
16 GLENDALE
17 PRINCE'S BLDGS
18 WELLINGTON TERR
19 OXFORD PL

F7
1 CLIFTON CL
2 HARLEY MEWS
3 HARLEY CT
4 HARLEY PL
5 CLIFTON DOWN RD
6 GLOUCESTER ROW
7 BEAUFORT BLDGS
8 GLOUCESTER ST
9 WATERLOO ST
10 BEAUFORT MEWS

5

226

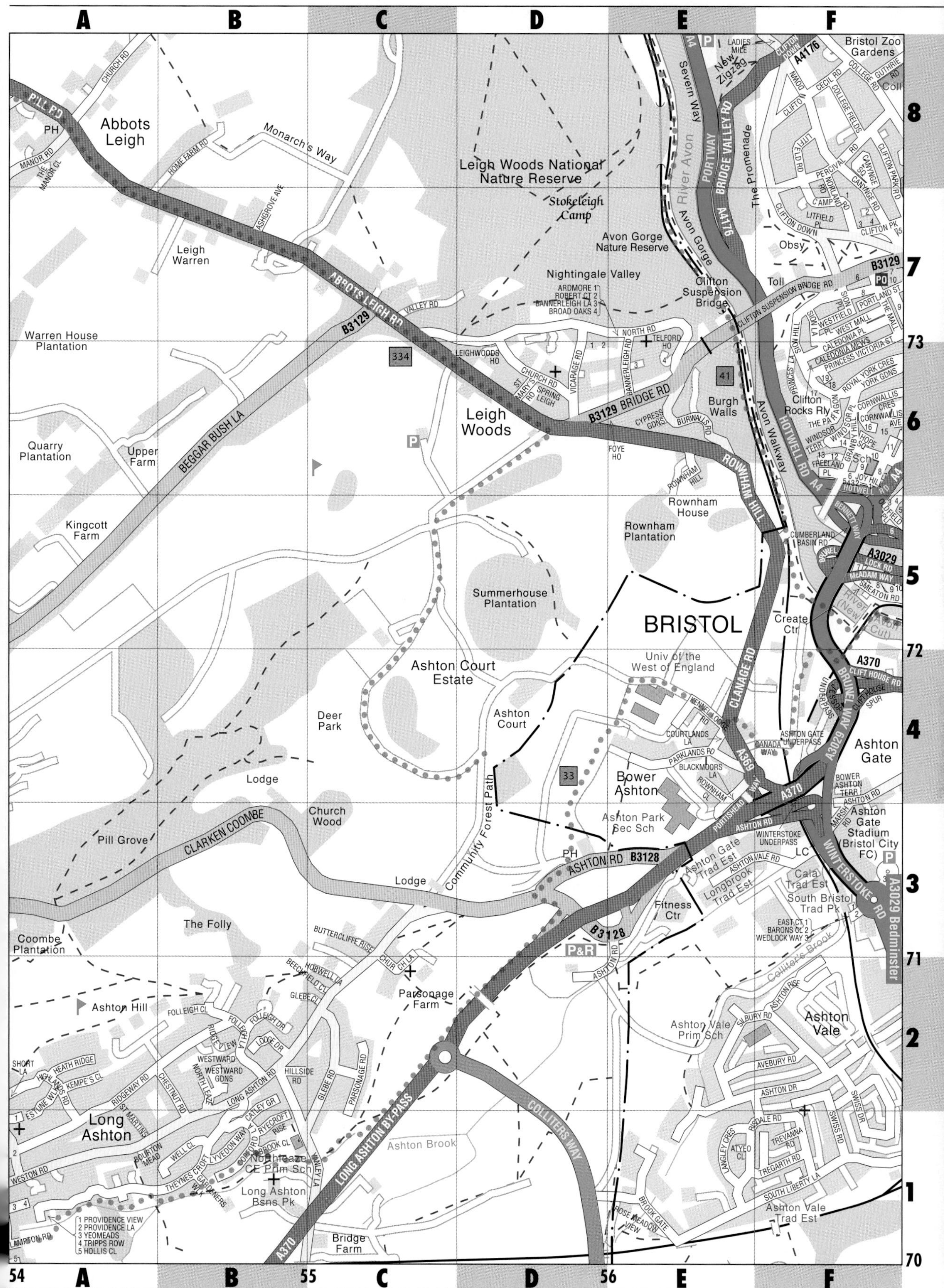

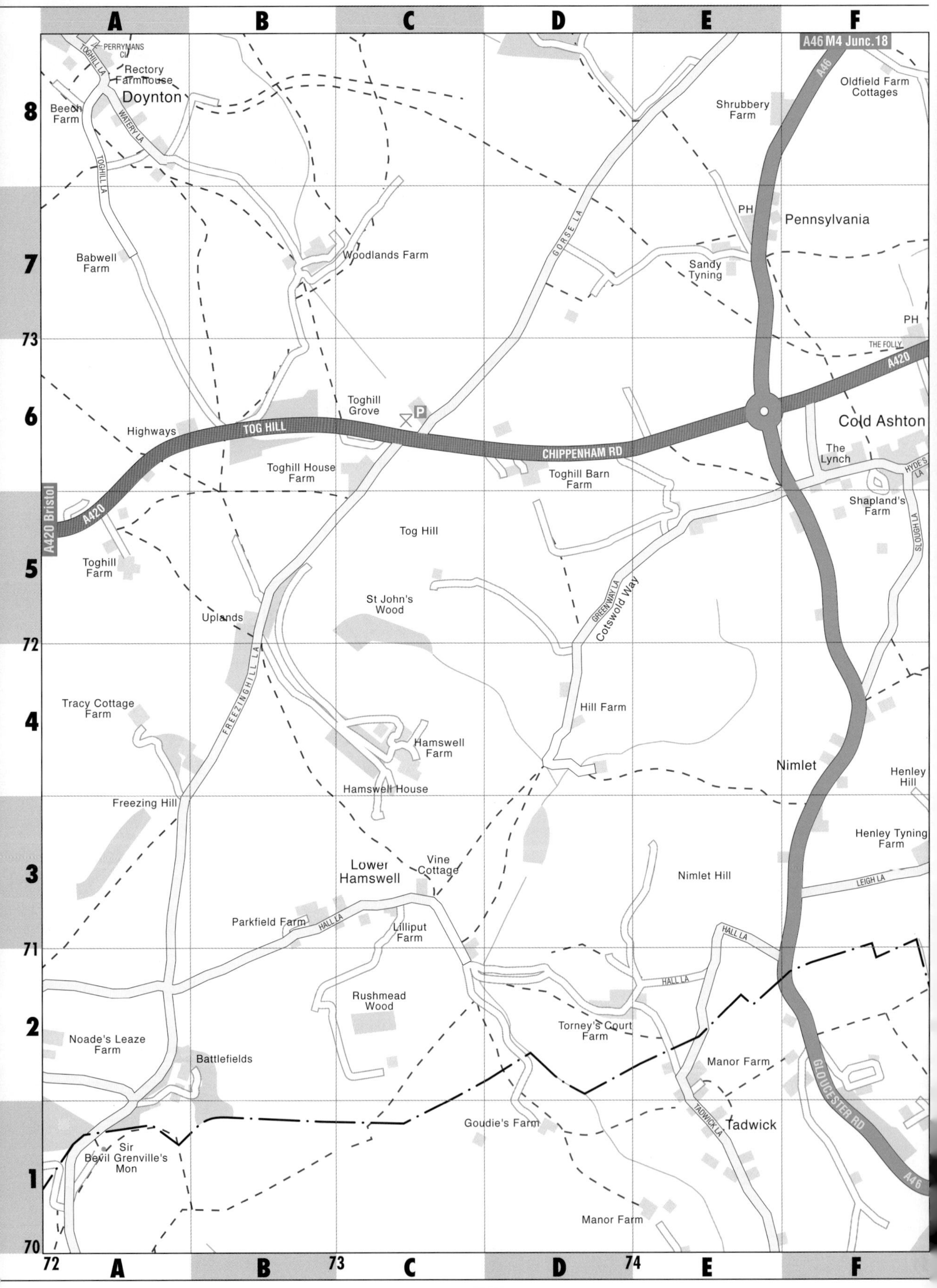
A
B
C
D
E
F
A46 M4 Junc.18
PERRYMANS CL
TOGHILL LA
Rectory Farmhouse
Doynton
Beech Farm
WATERY LA
Oldfield Farm Cottages
Shrubbery Farm
A46
8
TOGHILL LA
GORSE LA
PH
Pennsylvania
Babwell Farm
Woodlands Farm
7
Sandy Tyning
PH
THE FOLLY
73
A420
Toghill Grove
P
6
Highways
TOG HILL
Cold Ashton
CHIPPENHAM RD
The Lynch
Toghill House Farm
Toghill Barn Farm
HYDE'S LA
A420 Bristol
A420
Shapland's Farm
Tog Hill
SLOUGH LA
Toghill Farm
5
St John's Wood
GREEN WAY LA
Cotswold Way
Uplands
72
FREEZINGHILL LA
Tracy Cottage Farm
Hill Farm
4
Hamswell Farm
Nimlet
Henley Hill
Hamswell House
Freezing Hill
Henley Tyning Farm
Vine Cottage
Lower Hamswell
3
Nimlet Hill
LEIGH LA
Parkfield Farm
HALL LA
Lilliput Farm
HALL LA
71
HALL LA
Rushmead Wood
2
Torney's Court Farm
Noade's Leaze Farm
Battlefields
Manor Farm
GLOUCESTER RD
Goudie's Farm
TADWICK LA
Tadwick
Sir Bevil Grenville's Mon
1
A46
Manor Farm
70
72
73
74

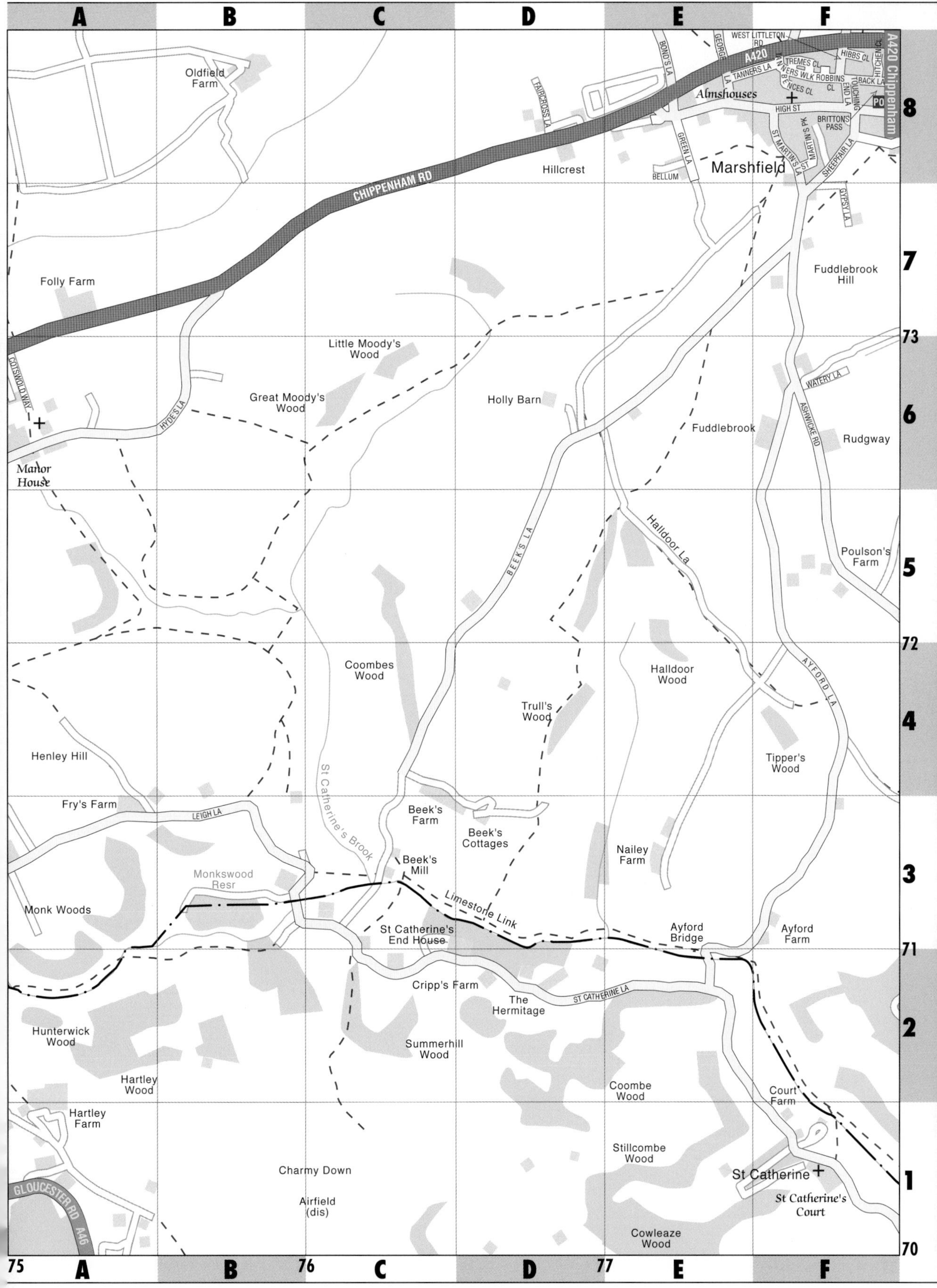
A
B
C
D
E
F
8
7
73
6
5
72
4
3
71
2
1
70
75
76
77
A420 Chippenham
CHIPPENHAM RD
A420
WEST LITTLETON RD
TANNERS LA
TREMES CL
HIBBS CL
ROBBINS CL
BACK LA
HITCHEN CL
HIGH ST
Almshouses
PO
BRITTONS PASS
ST MARTIN'S LA
ST MARTIN'S PK
SHEEPFAIR LA
GYPSY LA
BOND'S LA
FAIRCROSS LA
GREEN LA
BELLUM
Marshfield
Hillcrest
Oldfield Farm
Folly Farm
Fuddlebrook Hill
Little Moody's Wood
Great Moody's Wood
Holly Barn
HYDE'S LA
COTSWOLD WAY
Manor House
Fuddlebrook
WATERY LA
ASHWICKE RD
Rudgway
Halldoor La
BEEK'S LA
Poulson's Farm
Coombes Wood
Halldoor Wood
AYFORD LA
Trull's Wood
Henley Hill
Tipper's Wood
St Catherine's Brook
Fry's Farm
LEIGH LA
Beek's Farm
Beek's Cottages
Nailey Farm
Monkswood Resr
Beek's Mill
Monk Woods
Limestone Link
St Catherine's End House
Ayford Bridge
Ayford Farm
Cripp's Farm
The Hermitage
ST CATHERINE LA
Hunterwick Wood
Summerhill Wood
Hartley Wood
Coombe Wood
Court Farm
Hartley Farm
Stillcombe Wood
Charmy Down
St Catherine
St Catherine's Court
Airfield (dis)
GLOUCESTER RD
A46
Cowleaze Wood

28

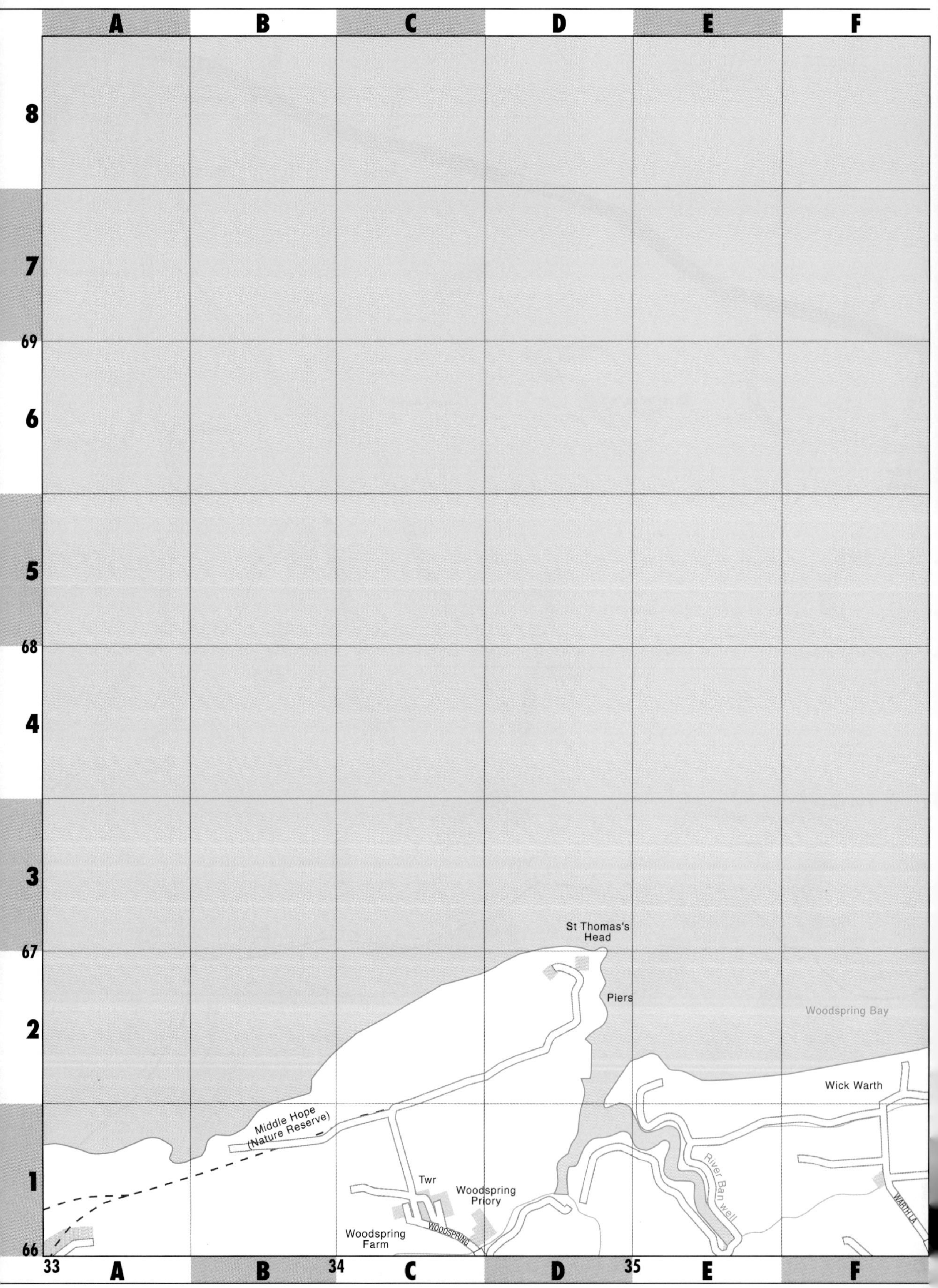

A
B
C
D
E
F
8
7
69
6
5
68
4
3
67
2
1
66
33
34
35
St Thomas's Head
Piers
Woodspring Bay
Wick Warth
Middle Hope (Nature Reserve)
River Banwell
Twr
Woodspring Priory
Woodspring Farm
WOODSPRING
WARTH LA

31

16

A
B
C
D
E
F
8
7
69
6
5
68
4
3
67
2
1
66
36
37
38
Dowlais Ditch
Kingston Pill
Hook's Ear
Seawall Farm
Treble House Farm
BACK LA
Sewage Works
Channel View Farm
MIDDLE LA
MIDDLE LA
Broadstone Rhyne
Broadstone Farm
BROADSTONE LA
Wharf Farm
HAM LA
Ham Farm
New House Farm
Pool Farm
Ham Rhyne
Sewage Works
MUDDY LA
Yeo Bank Farm
Mendip View Farm
YEO BANK LA
Mill Leaze Rhyne

32

16

6

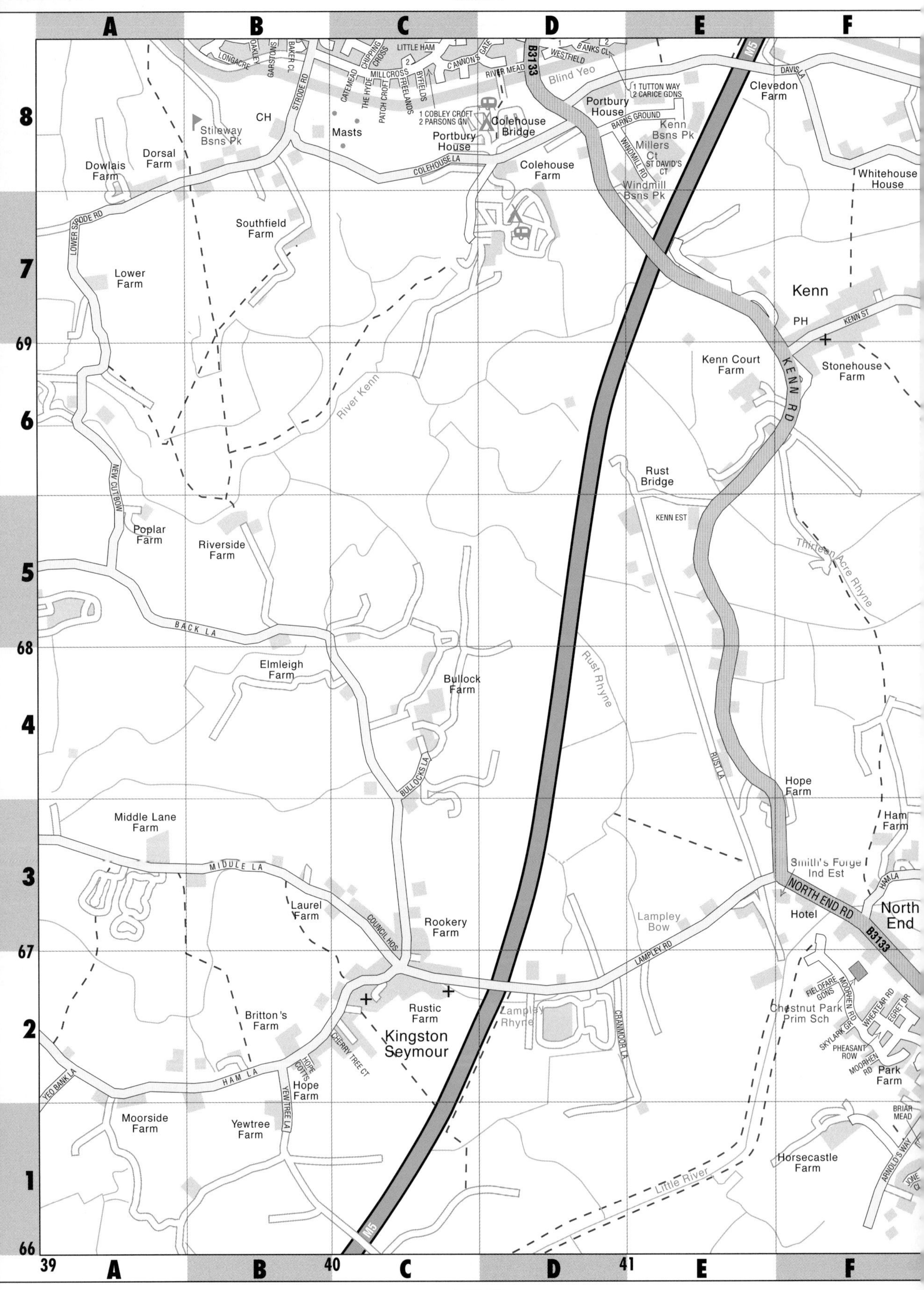
A
B
C
D
E
F
8
7
69
6
5
68
4
3
67
2
1
66
39
40
41
LONGACRE
OAKLEY
GARSTONS
BAKER CL
STRODE RD
CATEMEAD
CHIPPING CROSS
THE HYDE
PATCH CROFT
MILLCROSS
LITTLE HAM
FREELANDS
BYFIELDS
CANNONS GATE
RIVER MEAD
1 COBLEY CROFT
2 PARSONS GN
B3133
WESTFIELD
BANKS CL
Blind Yeo
1 TUTTON WAY
2 CARICE GDNS
BARNS GROUND
WINDMILL RD
ST DAVID'S CT
M5
DAVIS LA
Clevedon Farm
Stileway Bsns Pk
CH
Masts
Portbury House
Colehouse Bridge
Portbury House
Kenn Bsns Pk
Millers Ct
Windmill Bsns Pk
Dowlais Farm
Dorsal Farm
COLEHOUSE LA
Colehouse Farm
Whitehouse House
LOWER STRODE RD
Southfield Farm
Lower Farm
Kenn
PH
KENN ST
Kenn Court Farm
KENN RD
Stonehouse Farm
River Kenn
NEW CUTBOW
Rust Bridge
KENN EST
Poplar Farm
Riverside Farm
Thirteen Acre Rhyne
BACK LA
Elmleigh Farm
Bullock Farm
Rust Rhyne
RUST LA
BULLOCKS LA
Hope Farm
Middle Lane Farm
Ham Farm
MIDDLE LA
Smith's Forge Ind Est
HAM LA
Laurel Farm
COUNCIL HDS
Rookery Farm
Lampley Bow
NORTH END RD
Hotel
North End
B3133
LAMPLEY RD
FIELDFARE GDNS
MOORHEN RD
WHEATEAR RD
EGRET DR
Rustic Farm
Lampley Rhyne
Britton's Farm
Kingston Seymour
CHERRY TREE CT
CRANMOOR LA
Chestnut Park Prim Sch
SKYLARK GR
PHEASANT ROW
MOORHEN RD
Park Farm
HOPE COTTS
HAM LA
Hope Farm
YEO BANK LA
YEW TREE LA
Moorside Farm
Yewtree Farm
BRIAR MEAD
ARNOLD'S WAY
Horsecastle Farm
Little River
JONES CL
M5

33

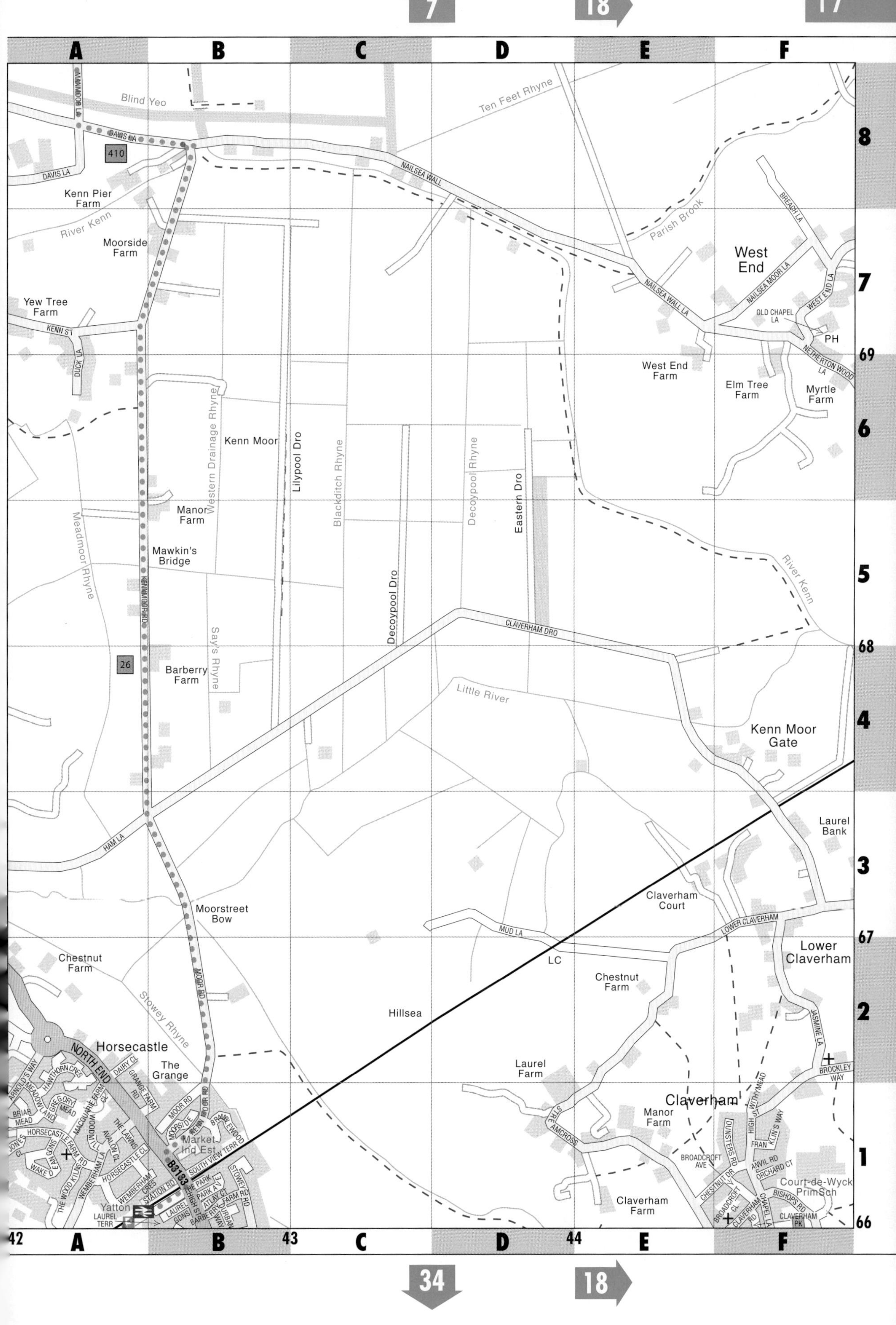
7
18
A
B
C
D
E
F
Blind Yeo
Ten Feet Rhyne
DAVIS LA
410
NAILSEA WALL
Kenn Pier
Farm
River Kenn
Moorside
Farm
Parish Brook
BREACH LA
West
End
NAILSEA MOOR LA
NAILSEA WALL LA
WEST END LA
OLD CHAPEL LA
PH
NETHERTON WOOD LA
Yew Tree
Farm
KENN ST
DUCK LA
West End
Farm
Elm Tree
Farm
Myrtle
Farm
Western Drainage Rhyne
Kenn Moor
Lilypool Dro
Blackditch Rhyne
Decoypool Rhyne
Eastern Dro
Manor
Farm
Meadmoor Rhyne
Mawkin's
Bridge
KENN MOOR RD
River Kenn
Decoypool Dro
CLAVERHAM DRO
26
Say's Rhyne
Barberry
Farm
Little River
Kenn Moor
Gate
Laurel
Bank
HAM LA
Claverham
Court
Moorstreet
Bow
LOWER CLAVERHAM
MUD LA
Lower
Claverham
LC
Chestnut
Farm
Chestnut
Farm
MOOR RD
Stowey Rhyne
Hillsea
JASMINE LA
Horsecastle
NORTH END
The
Grange
Laurel
Farm
BROCKLEY WAY
Claverham
Manor
Farm
Market
Ind Est
B3133
Yatton
Claverham
Farm
Court-de-Wyck
Prim Sch
8
7
69
6
5
68
4
3
67
2
1
66
42
43
44
34
18

17
8

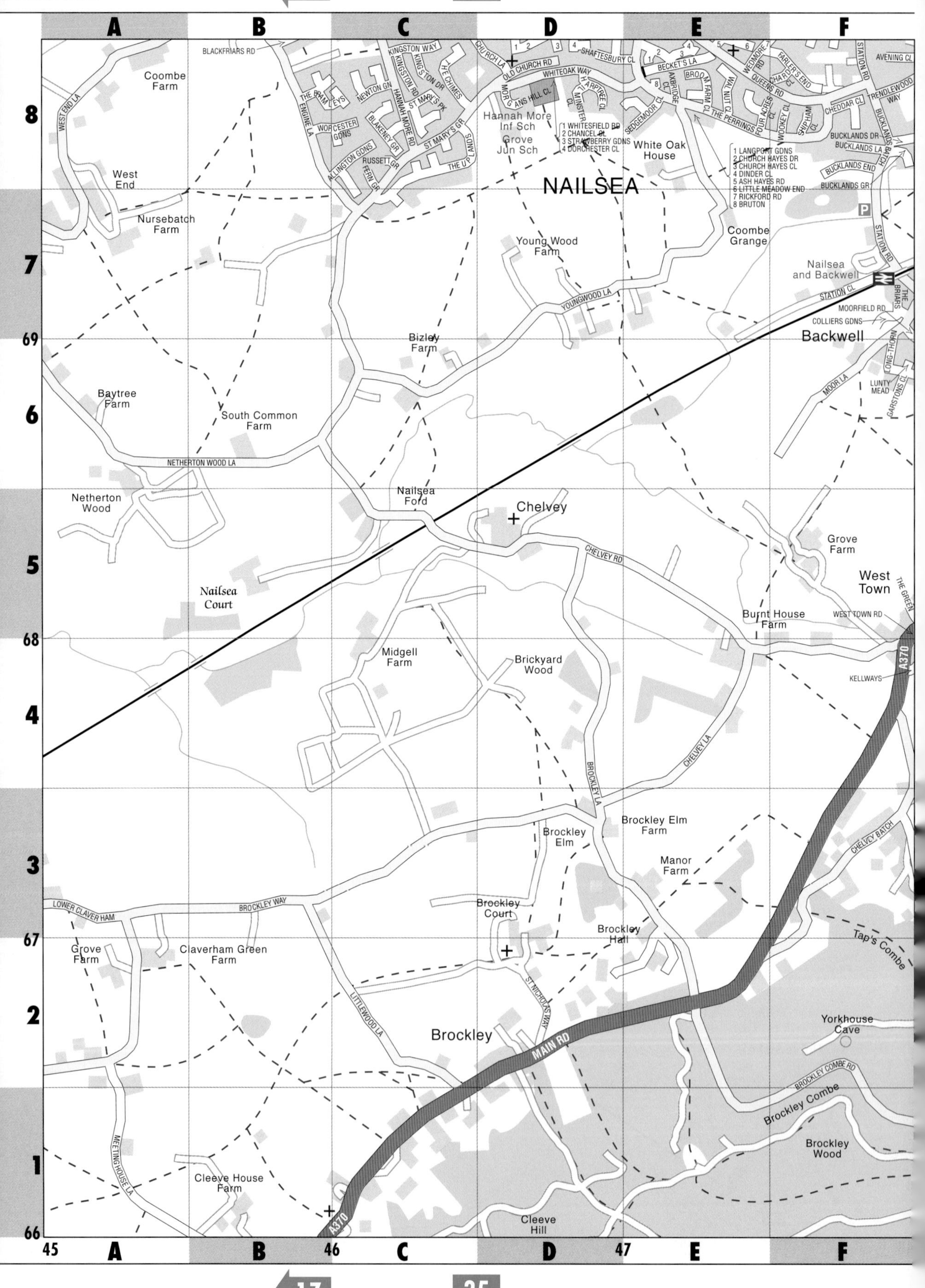
A B C D E F
8
7
69
6
5
68
4
3
67
2
1
66
45 46 47
NAILSEA
Backwell
Brockley
Chelvey
West Town
West End
Coombe Farm
Nursebatch Farm
Baytree Farm
South Common Farm
Netherton Wood
Nailsea Court
Bizley Farm
Nailsea Ford
Young Wood Farm
White Oak House
Coombe Grange
Nailsea and Backwell
Hannah More Inf Sch
Grove Jun Sch
Midgell Farm
Brickyard Wood
Grove Farm
Burnt House Farm
Brockley Elm Farm
Brockley Elm
Manor Farm
Brockley Court
Brockley Hall
Claverham Green Farm
Cleeve House Farm
Cleeve Hill
Yorkhouse Cave
Brockley Combe
Brockley Wood
Tap's Combe
NETHERTON WOOD LA
YOUNGWOOD LA
CHELVEY RD
CHELVEY LA
BROCKLEY LA
BROCKLEY WAY
LOWER CLAVER HAM
LITTLEWOOD LA
MEETING HOUSE LA
ST NICHOLAS WAY
MAIN RD
A370
BROCKLEY COMBE RD
CHELVEY BATCH
KELLWAYS
WEST TOWN RD
THE GREEN
MOOR LA
LUNTY MEAD
GARSTONS CL
LONG THORN
MOORFIELD RD
COLLIERS GDNS
STATION CL
THE BRIARS
STATION RD
BUCKLANDS GR
BUCKLANDS END
BUCKLANDS LA
BUCKLANDS DR
BUCKLANDS BATCH
TRENDLEWOOD WAY
CHEDDAR CL
SHIPHAM CL
WOOKEY CL
FOUR ACRES CL
AVENING CL
STATION RD
FARLER'S END
CHARD CL
QUEENS RD
WEDMORE RD
WALNUT CL
BROOM FARM CL
AXBRIDGE CL
BECKET'S LA
THE PERRINGS
SEDGEMOOR CL
SHAFTESBURY CL
OLD CHURCH RD
CHURCH LA
WHITEOAK WAY
MORGANS HILL CL
ILMINSTER CL
HARPTREE CL
KINGSTON WAY
KINGSTON RD
KINGSTON DR
THE CHIMES
NEWTON GN
HANNAH MORE RD
ST MARY'S PK
ST MARY'S GR
THE UPLANDS
BLAKENEY GR
RUSSETT GR
FERN GR
ALLINGTON GDNS
WORCESTER GDNS
THE BRAMBLEYS
ENGINE LA
BLACKFRIARS RD
WEST END LA
1 WHITESFIELD RD
2 CHANCEL CL
3 STRAWBERRY GDNS
4 DORCHESTER CL
1 LANGPORT GDNS
2 CHURCH HAYES DR
3 CHURCH HAYES CL
4 DINDER CL
5 ASH HAYES RD
6 LITTLE MEADOW END
7 RICKFORD RD
8 BRUTON

17
35

9
20

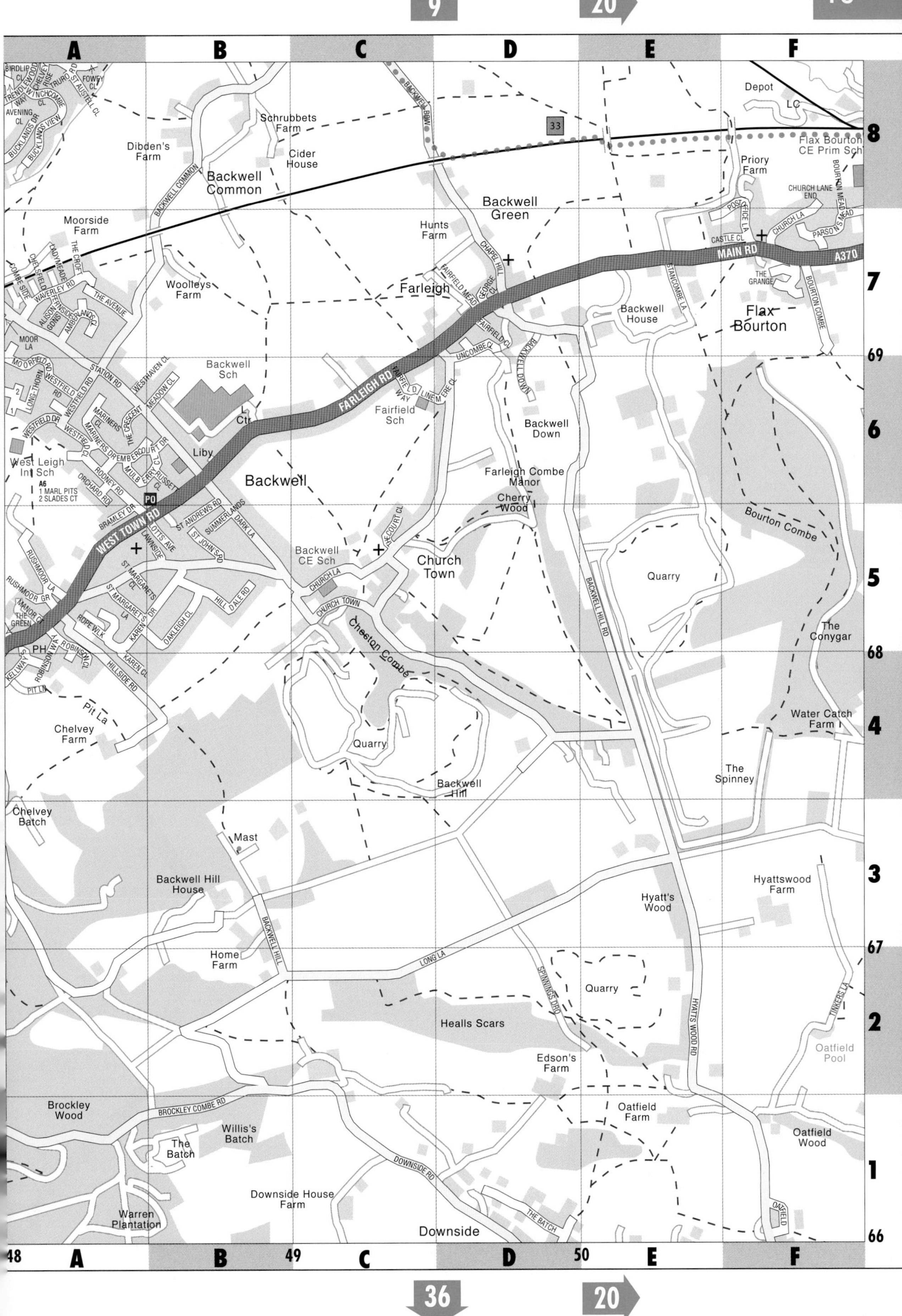
Backwell Common
Backwell Green
Farleigh
Backwell
Church Town
Flax Bourton
Backwell Down
Bourton Combe
Cheston Combe
Backwell Hill
Healls Scars
Downside
Brockley Wood
Warren Plantation
Oatfield Wood
Hyatt's Wood
Quarry
FARLEIGH RD
WEST TOWN RD
MAIN RD
A370
BACKWELL HILL RD
HYATTS WOOD RD
LONG LA
BROCKLEY COMBE RD
DOWNSIDE RD
SPINNINGS DRO
Backwell Sch
Fairfield Sch
Backwell CE Sch
West Leigh Inf Sch
Flax Bourton CE Prim Sch
Farleigh Combe Manor
Chelvey Farm
Chelvey Batch
Mast

36
20

19
10

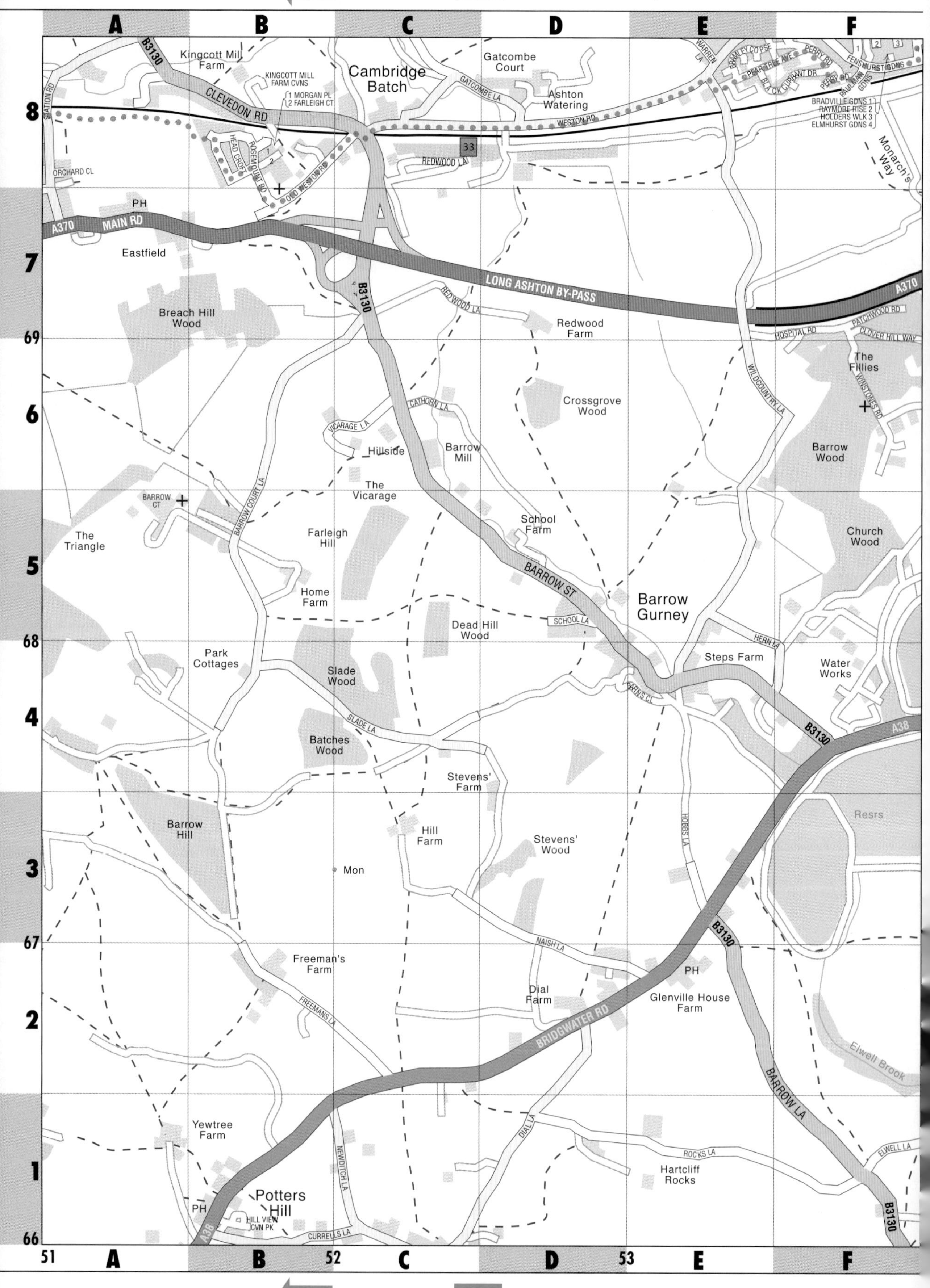
A
B
C
D
E
F
8
7
69
6
5
68
4
3
67
2
1
66
51
52
53
Kingcott Mill Farm
KINGCOTT MILL FARM CVNS
1 MORGAN PL
2 FARLEIGH CT
Cambridge Batch
Gatcombe Court
GATCOMBE LA
Ashton Watering
WESTON RD
WARREN LA
BRAMLEY COPSE
PEAR TREE AVE
BLACKCURRANT DR
PERRY RD
FENSHURST GDNS
PAULMAN GDNS
BRADVILLE GDNS 1
RAYMORE RISE 2
HOLDERS WLK 3
ELMHURST GDNS 4
Monarch's Way
B3130
CLEVEDON RD
STATION RD
HEAD CROFT
ROSEMOUNT RD
OLD WESTON RD
ORCHARD CL
33
REDWOOD LA
PH
A370
MAIN RD
Eastfield
LONG ASHTON BY-PASS
Breach Hill Wood
Redwood Farm
HOSPITAL RD
PATCHWOOD RD
CLOVER HILL WAY
The Fillies
WINSTONES RD
Crossgrove Wood
CATHORN LA
VICARAGE LA
Hillside
Barrow Mill
WILDCOUNTRY LA
Barrow Wood
The Vicarage
BARROW CT
BARROW COURT LA
The Triangle
Farleigh Hill
School Farm
Church Wood
BARROW ST
Home Farm
Barrow Gurney
Dead Hill Wood
SCHOOL LA
HERN LA
Park Cottages
Slade Wood
Steps Farm
Water Works
BARNS CL
SLADE LA
Batches Wood
Stevens' Farm
A38
Resrs
Barrow Hill
Hill Farm
Stevens' Wood
HOBBS LA
Mon
NAISH LA
Freeman's Farm
PH
Dial Farm
Glenville House Farm
FREEMANS LA
BRIDGWATER RD
Elwell Brook
BARROW LA
DIAL LA
Yewtree Farm
ROCKS LA
Hartcliff Rocks
ELWELL LA
NEWDITCH LA
Potters Hill
PH
HILL VIEW CVN PK
CURRELLS LA

19
37

11
22

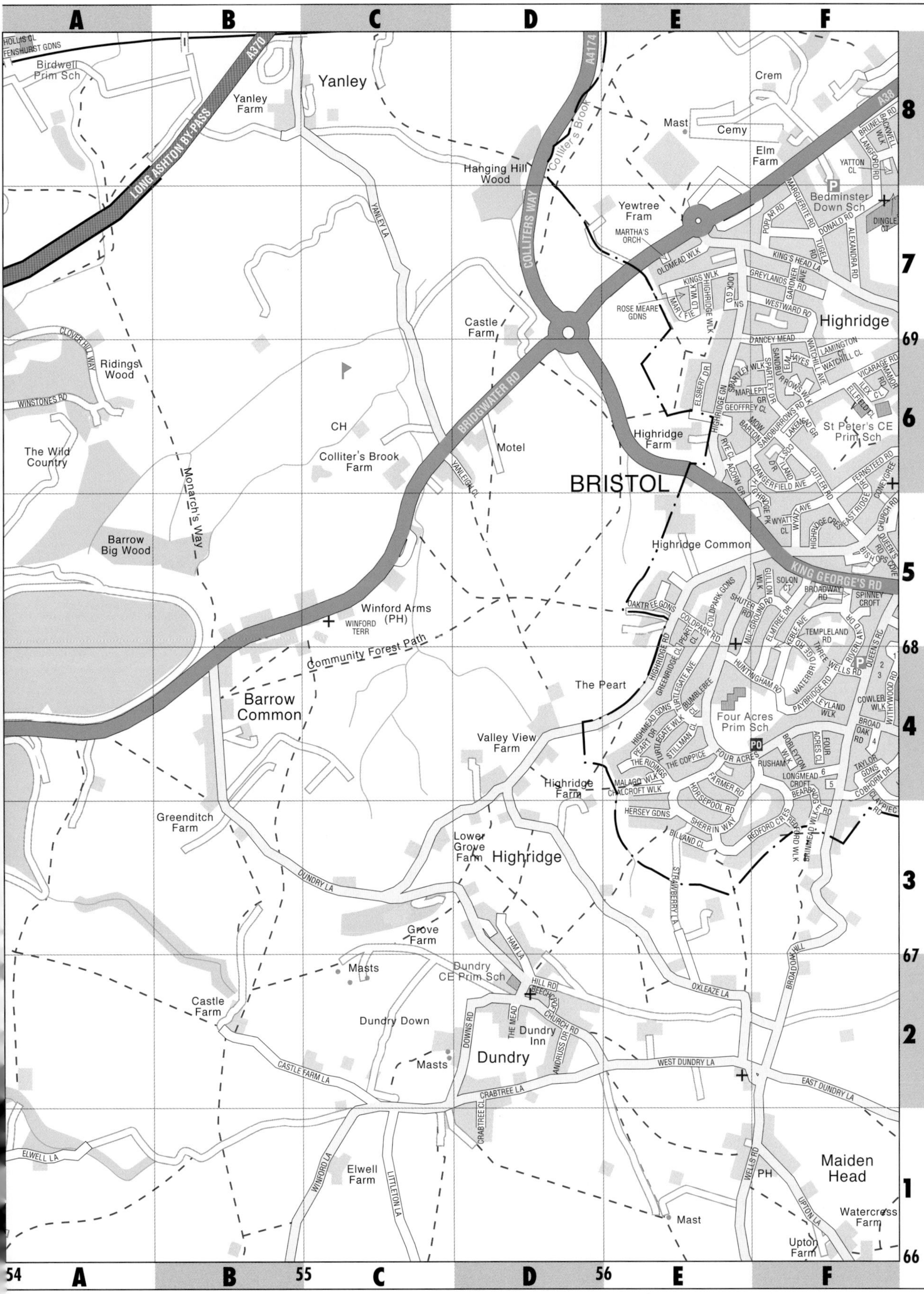

A B C D E F

8 7 69 6 5 68 4 3 67 2 1 66

Hollis Cl
Fenshurst Gdns
Birdwell Prim Sch
Yanley
Yanley Farm
A370
Long Ashton By-Pass
A4174
Colliters Way
Colliter's Brook
Crem
Mast
Cemy
Elm Farm
A38
Hanging Hill Wood
Yewtree Fram
Martha's Orch
Bedminster Down Sch
Dingle Ct
Yatton Cl
Highridge
Yanley La
Castle Farm
Clover Hill Way
Ridings Wood
Winstones Rd
CH
Colliter's Brook Farm
Bridgwater Rd
Motel
Highridge Farm
BRISTOL
St Peter's CE Prim Sch
The Wild Country
Monarch's Way
Barrow Big Wood
Yanleigh Cl
Highridge Common
King George's Rd
Winford Arms (PH)
Winford Terr
Community Forest Path
Barrow Common
The Peart
Four Acres Prim Sch
PO
Valley View Farm
Highridge Farm
Greenditch Farm
Lower Grove Farm
Highridge
Dundry La
Grove Farm
Strawberry La
Masts
Dundry CE Prim Sch
Castle Farm
Ham La
Hill Rd
Oxleaze La
Broadoak Hill
Dundry Down
Downs Rd
The Mead
Dundry Inn
Church Rd
Andruss Dr
Dundry
Masts
Castle Farm La
West Dundry La
East Dundry La
Crabtree La
Crabtree Cl
Elwell La
Winford La
Elwell Farm
Littleton La
Wells Rd
PH
Maiden Head
Mast
Upton La
Watercress Farm
Upton Farm

54 A B 55 C D 56 E F

38
22

F4
1 WITHYWOOD GDNS
2 KINGS CT
3 LAKEMEAD GDNS
4 MARGARET RD
5 ROSSITER GRANGE
6 GRANGE LANE

A8
1 Cheddar Gr Prim Sch

A5
1 GATEHOUSE CL
2 GATEHOUSE WAY
3 CORNLEAZE
4 ACRESBUSH CL
5 QUEENS RD

21

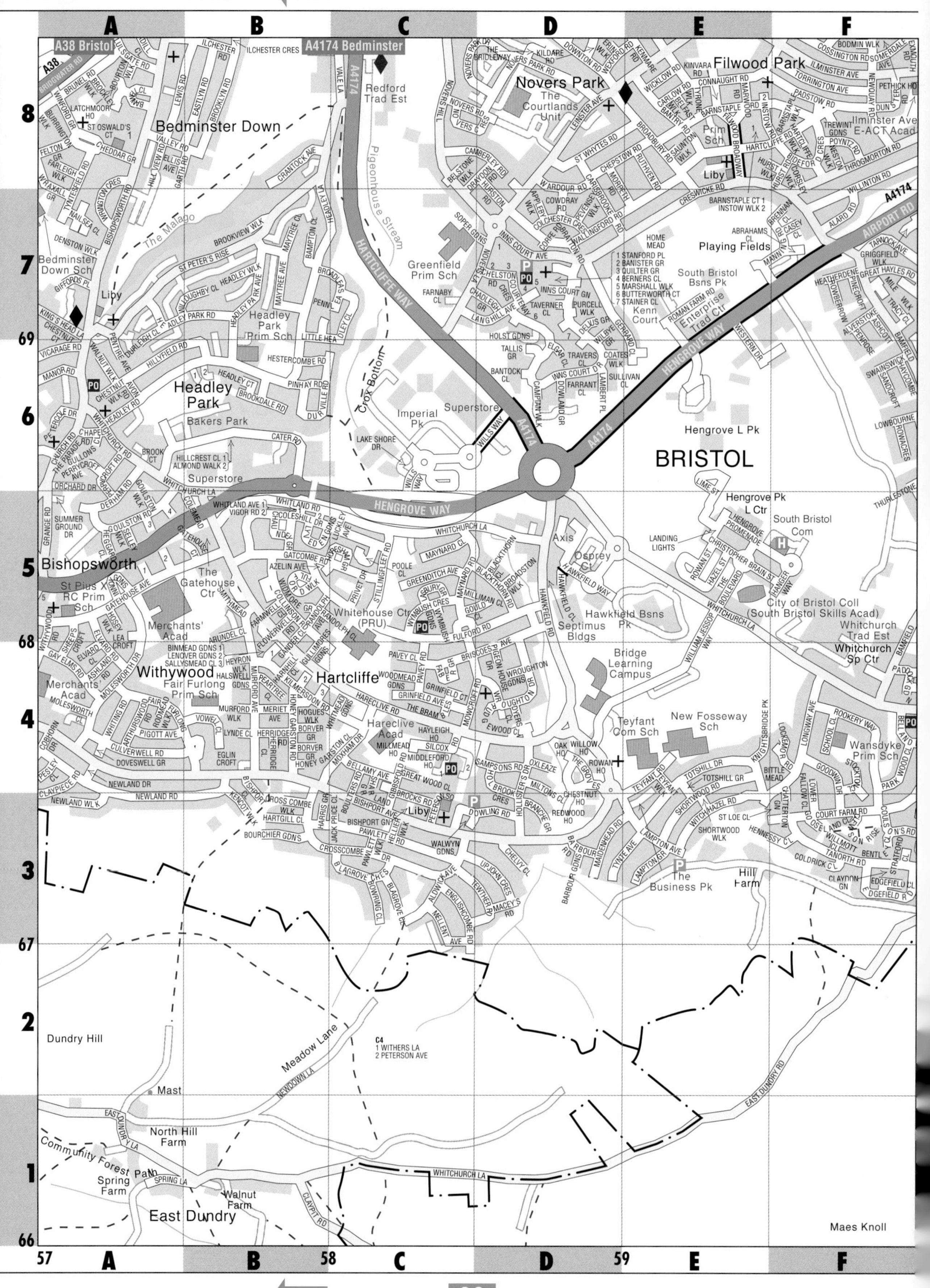

24

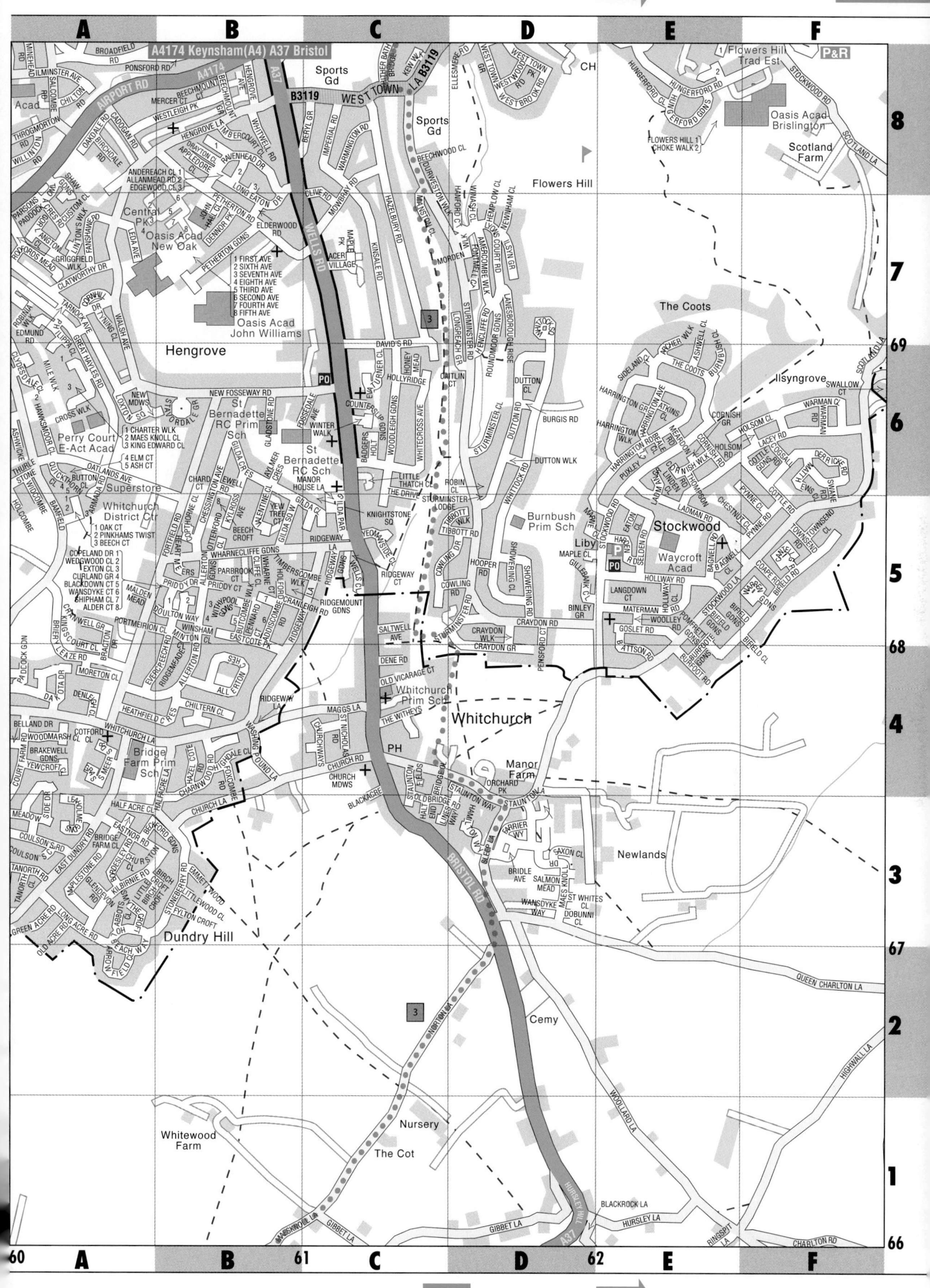

A4174 Keynsham(A4) A37 Bristol
B3119
WEST TOWN LA
AIRPORT RD
WELLS RD
BRISTOL RD
Sports Gd
Flowers Hill
Flowers Hill Trad Est
Oasis Acad Brislington
Scotland Farm
SCOTLAND LA
Central Pk
Oasis Acad New Oak
Oasis Acad John Williams
Hengrove
The Coots
Ilsyngrove
St Bernadette RC Prim Sch
St Bernadette RC Sch
Perry Court E-Act Acad
Superstore
Whitchurch District Ctr
Burnbush Prim Sch
Stockwood
Waycroft Acad
Liby
Whitchurch Prim Sch
Whitchurch
Manor Farm
Bridge Farm Prim Sch
Newlands
Dundry Hill
QUEEN CHARLTON LA
Cemy
Nursery
The Cot
Whitewood Farm
WOOLLARD LA
HIGHWALL LA
HURSLEY LA
GIBBET LA
CHARLTON RD
A
B
C
D
E
F
8
7
69
6
5
68
4
3
67
2
1
66
60
61
62

40

24

23

A
B
C
D
E
F
A4 Bristol
A4174 Bristol Northern Ring Road
Hicks Gate
BATH RD
IRONMOULD LA
16
A4174
A4
A4175
DURLEY HILL
Scotland Bottom
Avon Walkway
River Avon
Keysham Hams
Factory
Somerdale
Durleypark
DURLEY LA
Oaklease Farm
SCOTLAND LA
Cemy
KEYNSHAM BY-PASS
Recn Gd
Community Forest Path
STOCKWOOD HILL
Stockwood Vale
CH
Wood Covert
Broadlands Sch
Sports Ctr
BRISTOL RD
STATION RD
KEYNSHAM RD
Keynsham
HIGH ST
B3116
Charlton Bottom
Broadlands House
BATH HILL
Liby
L Ctr
St Keyna Prim Sch
St John's CE Prim Sch
Lays Bsns Ctr
Lays Farm
Castle Prim Sch
KEYNSHAM
Parkhouse La
Queen Charlton
Parkhouse Farm
Manor Farm
Wellfield House
Chewton Place
Manor Farm
Chewton Keynsham
WELL SWAY
REDLYNCH LA
Poplars Cottage
UPLANDS LA
OLD PENSFORD LA
Charlton Field
Harvey's Ditch
Warners Farm
DAPWELL LA
ALLOTMENT LA
PARKHOUSE LA
QUEEN CHARLTON LA
HIGHWALL LA
8
7
69
6
5
68
4
3
67
2
1
66
63
64
65

23
41

26

A
B
C
D
E
F
A4175 Willsbridge
A431 Bristol
Londonderry Farm
Nursery
Field Grove Farm
The Meadows Prim Sch
Barrow Hill
Works
Mill
Nursery
Bitton
Nursery
Mickle Mead
Broad Mead
Works
Holm Mead
Avon Walkway
River Avon
Avon Valley Rly
Monarch's Way
Community Forest Path
KEYNSHAM RD
BATH RD
HIGH ST
River Boyd
Sewage Works
Wansdyke Workshops
Mill
Avon Riverside
Avon Farm
Avon Valley Adventure & Wildlife Park
Bristol & Bath Rly Path
Superstore
Unity Ct
Ashmead Road Ind Est
TA Ctr
KEYNSHAM BY-PASS
BATH RD
B3116
IKB Acad
Pixash Bsns Ctr
1 NASH CL
2 RUBENS CL
3 CHELSEA CL
4 HILLS CL
5 REYNOLDS CL
6 TURNER CL
Wellsway Sch
Chandag Jun & Inf Sch
WORLDS END LA
Nurseries
Glenavon Farm
THE DRUMWAY
HARPSICHORD WAY
Playing Field
Keynsham Manor
Eastover Farm
MANOR RD
Liby
Saltford CE Prim Sch
Saltford
Weir
PH
CH
Uplands
Burnett Bsns Pk
Folly Wood
WELLSWAY
B3116
A4
8
7
69
6
5
68
4
3
67
2
1
66
66
67
68

42

26

25

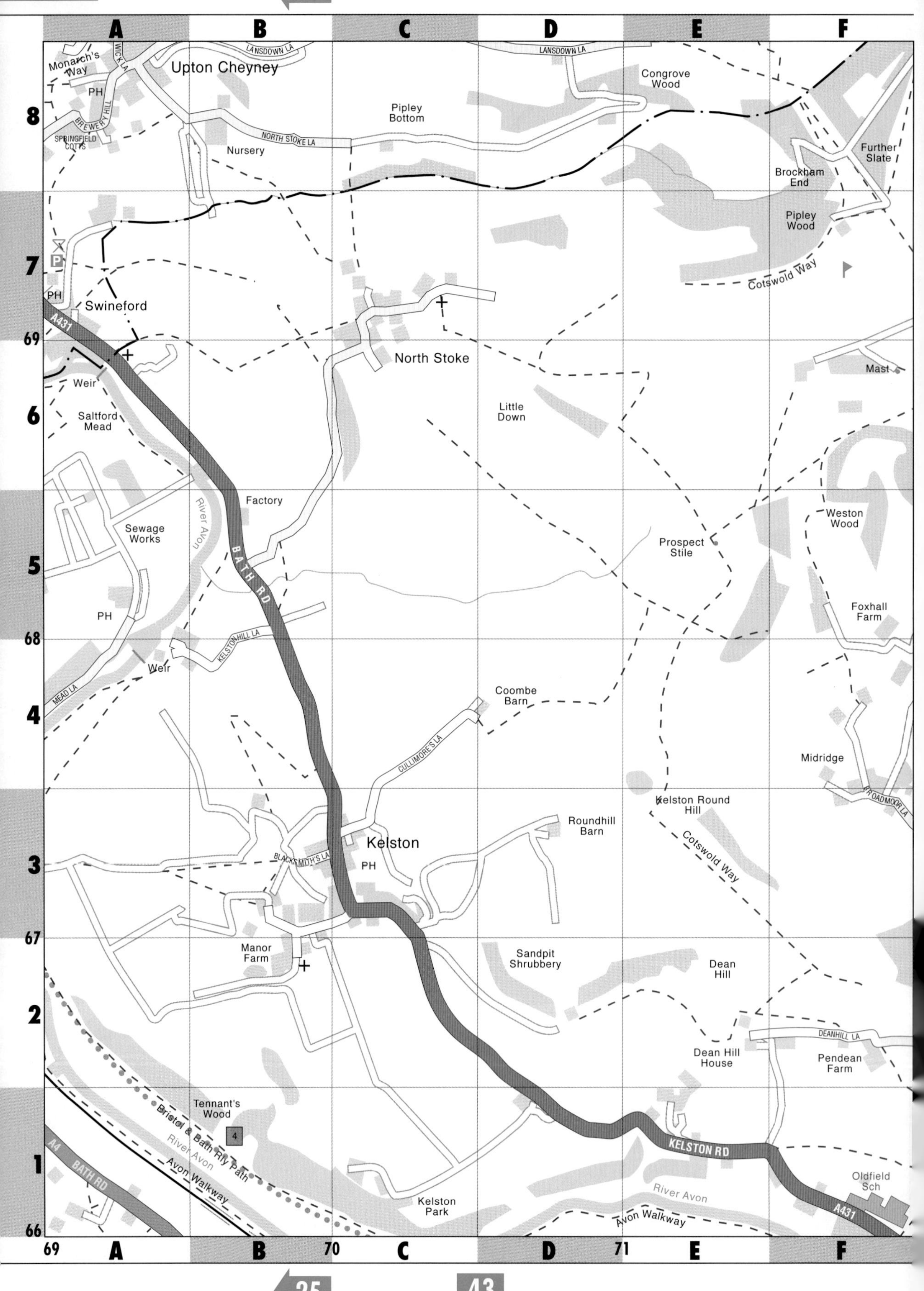
A
B
C
D
E
F
8
7
69
6
5
68
4
3
67
2
1
66
Monarch's Way
PH
Upton Cheyney
LANSDOWN LA
WICK LA
BREWERY HILL
SPRINGFIELD COTTS
Nursery
NORTH STOKE LA
Pipley Bottom
Congrove Wood
Further Slate
Brockham End
Pipley Wood
Cotswold Way
Swineford
A431
North Stoke
Mast
Weir
Saltford Mead
Little Down
Factory
Sewage Works
River Avon
BATH RD
Weston Wood
Prospect Stile
Foxhall Farm
KELSTON HILL LA
MEAD LA
Coombe Barn
CULLIMORE'S LA
Midridge
Kelston Round Hill
BROADMOOR LA
Roundhill Barn
Kelston
BLACKSMITH'S LA
Manor Farm
Sandpit Shrubbery
Dean Hill
DEANHILL LA
Dean Hill House
Pendean Farm
Tennant's Wood
Bristol & Bath Rly Path
Avon Walkway
A4
KELSTON RD
Oldfield Sch
Kelston Park
69
70
71

25
43

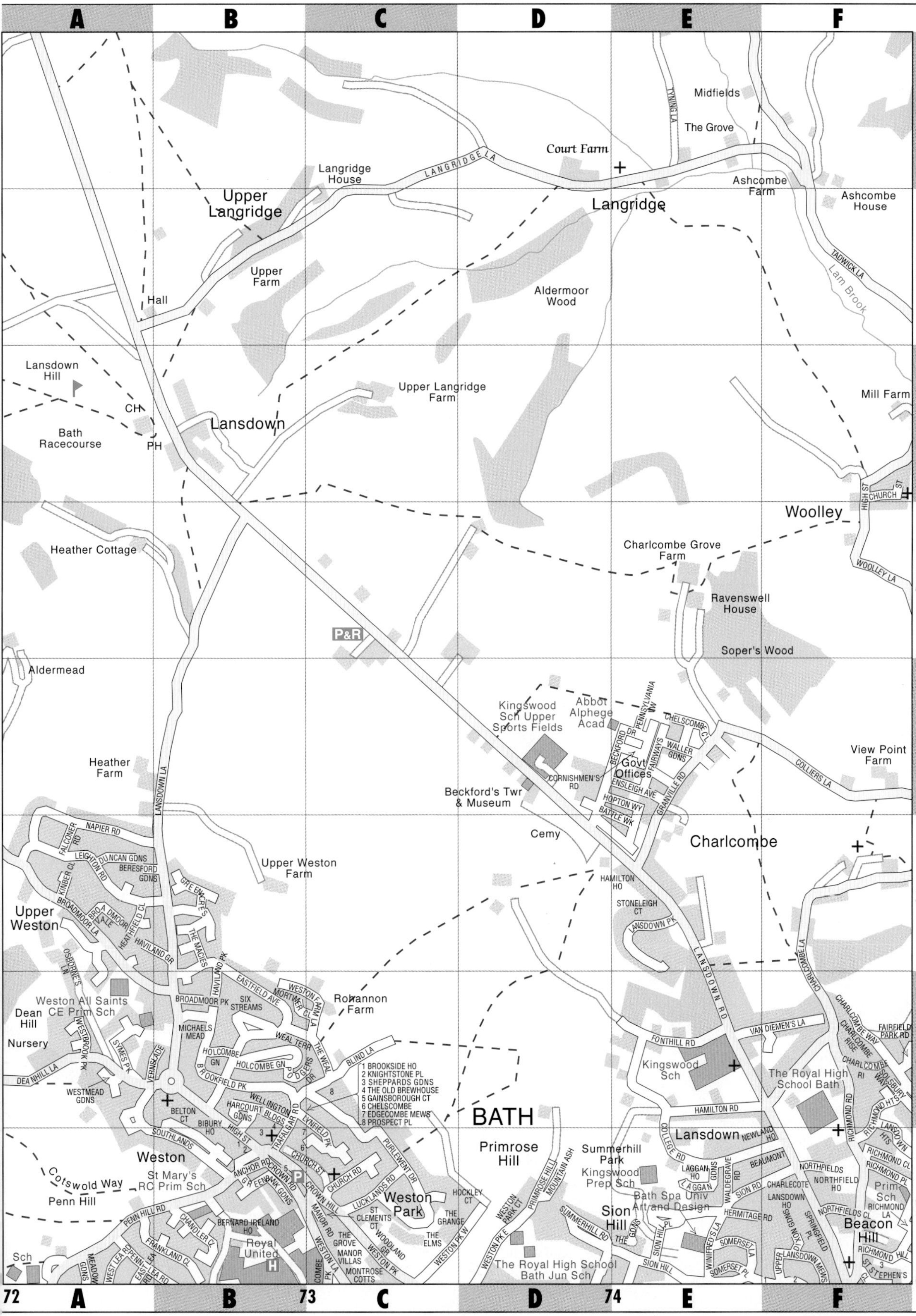

A B C D E F

8
7
69
6
5
68
4
3
67
2
1
66

Midfields
The Grove
Court Farm
LANGRIDGE LA
Langridge House
Upper Langridge
Langridge
Ashcombe Farm
Ashcombe House
TYNING LA
TADWICK LA
Lam Brook
Upper Farm
Hall
Aldermoor Wood
Lansdown Hill
CH
PH
Bath Racecourse
Lansdown
Upper Langridge Farm
Mill Farm
HIGH ST
CHURCH ST
Woolley
WOOLLEY LA
Heather Cottage
Charlcombe Grove Farm
Ravenswell House
Soper's Wood
P&R
Aldermead
Kingswood Sch Upper Sports Fields
Abbot Alphege Acad
PENNSYLVANIA VW
CHELSCOMBE CL
BECKFORD DR
FAIRWAYS
WALLER GDNS
Govt Offices
CORNISHMEN'S RD
ENSLEIGH AVE
GRANVILLE RD
HOPTON WY
BATTLE WK
COLLIERS LA
View Point Farm
Heather Farm
LANSDOWN LA
Beckford's Twr & Museum
Cemy
Charlcombe
NAPIER RD
FALCONER RD
LEIGHTON RD
DUNCAN GDNS
BERESFORD GDNS
KINBER CL
GREENACRES
Upper Weston Farm
HAMILTON HO
STONELEIGH CT
LANSDOWN PK
Upper Weston
BROADMOOR LA
BROADMOOR VALE
HEATHFIELD CL
HAVILAND GR
THE MACIES
HAVILAND PK
OSBORNE'S LN
LANSDOWN RD
CHARLCOMBE LA
Weston All Saints CE Prim Sch
Dean Hill
Nursery
BROADMOOR PK
SIX STREAMS
EASTFIELD AVE
MORTIMER CL
WESTON FARM LA
Rohannon Farm
CHARLCOMBE WAY
CHARLCOMBE RISE
FAIRFIELD PARK RD
WESTBROOK PK
SYMES PK
MICHAELS MEAD
WEAL TERR
THE WEAL
VAN DIEMEN'S LA
FONTHILL RD
HOLCOMBE GN
HOLCOMBE GR
PODGERS DR
BLIND LA
Kingswood Sch
CHARLCOMBE RI
SOLSBURY WAY
The Royal High School Bath
DEANHILL LA
VERNSLADE
BROOKFIELD PK
WESTMEAD GDNS
WELLINGTON BLDGS
HARCOURT GDNS
TRAFALGAR RD
LYNFIELD PK
BELTON CT
BIBURY HO
1 BROOKSIDE HO
2 KNIGHTSTONE PL
3 SHEPPARDS GDNS
4 THE OLD BREWHOUSE
5 GAINSBOROUGH CT
6 CHELSCOMBE
7 EDGECOMBE MEWS
8 PROSPECT PL
BATH
HAMILTON RD
RICHMOND RD
RICHMOND HTS
LANSDOWN GR
SOUTHLANDS
HIGH ST
CHURCH ST
Weston
Primrose Hill
Summerhill Park
Lansdown
NEWLAND HO
COLLEGE RD
Cotswold Way
St Mary's RC Prim Sch
ANCHOR RD
CROWN RD
GREEN BANK GDNS
CHURCH RD
PURLEWENT DR
LUCKLANDS RD
Weston Park
HOCKLEY CT
MOUNTAIN ASH
PRIMROSE HILL
WESTON PARK CT
Kingswood Prep Sch
LAGGAN HO
LAGGAN GDNS
LAGGAN
WALDEGRAVE RD
BEAUMONT
NORTHFIELDS
NORTHFIELD HO
RICHMOND CL
RICHMOND PL
Prim Sch
Penn Hill
PENN HILL RD
CHANDLER CL
BERNARD IRELAND HO
CROWN HILL
MANOR RD
ST CLEMENTS CT
THE GROVE
THE GRANGE
THE ELMS
WESTON PK W
WESTON PK E
SUMMERHILL RD
Sion Hill
Bath Spa Univ Art and Design
SION RD
CHARLECOTE
LANSDOWN HO
HERMITAGE RD
SPRINGFIELD PL
NORTHFIELDS CL
RICHMOND LA
Beacon Hill
Sch
FRANKLAND CL
Royal United
H
P
THE MANOR VILLAS
WOODLAND GR
WESTON PK
WESTON LA
COMBE PK
MONTROSE COTTS
The Royal High School Bath Jun Sch
THE GDNS
SION HILL PL
SION HILL
WINIFRED'S LA
SOMERSET LA
SOMERSET PL
UPPER LANSDOWN MEWS
DIXON GDNS
LANSDOWN MEWS
RICHMOND HILL
ST STEPHEN'S
MEADOW GDNS
WEST LEA RD
PENN LEA RD
EAST LEA RD

72 A B 73 C D 74 E F

F1
1 LANSDOWN PL W
2 LANSDOWN CRES
3 MOUNT BEACON PL

44
28

27
13

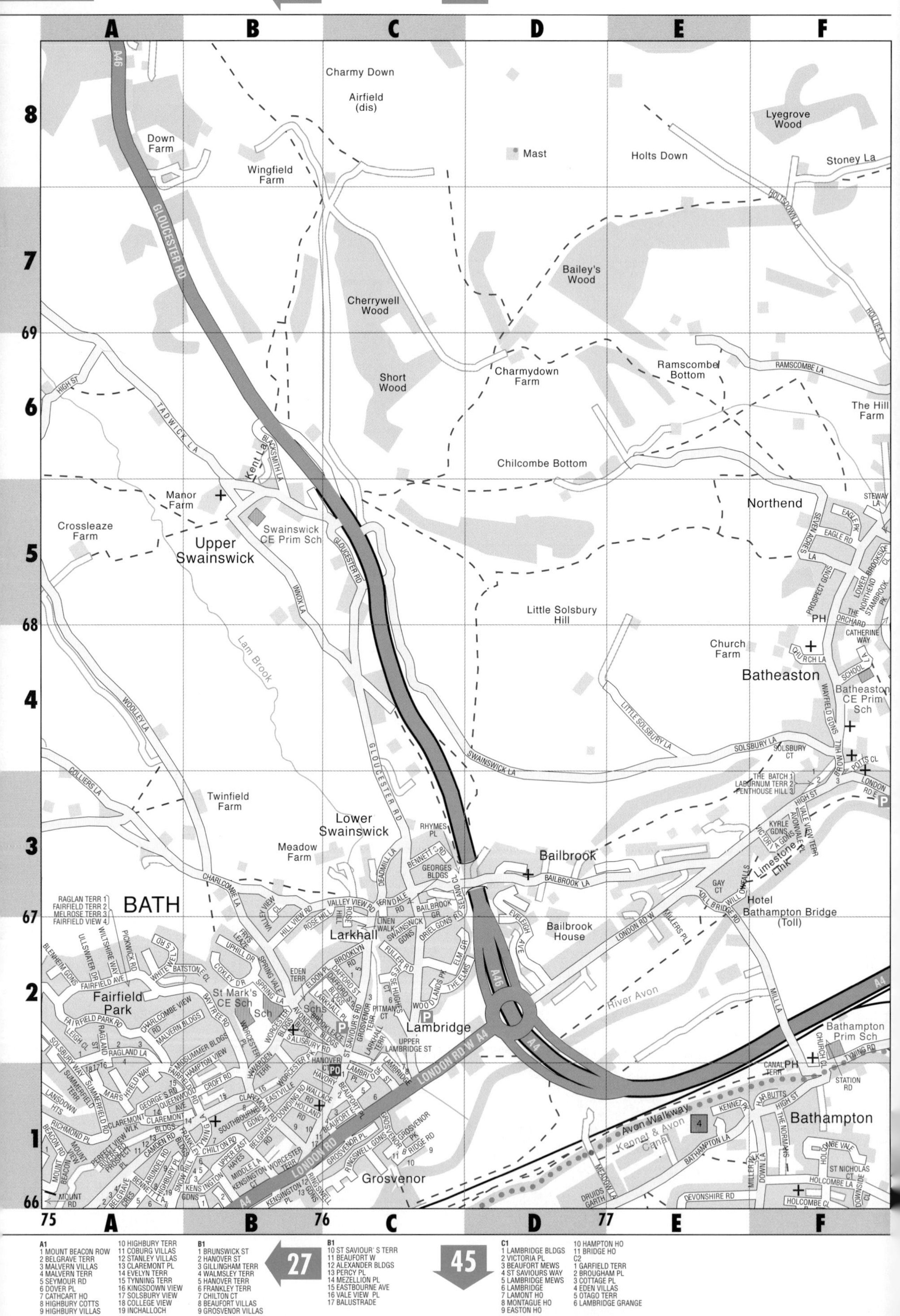

A1
1 MOUNT BEACON ROW
2 BELGRAVE TERR
3 MALVERN VILLAS
4 MALVERN TERR
5 SEYMOUR RD
6 DOVER PL
7 CATHCART HO
8 HIGHBURY COTTS
9 HIGHBURY VILLAS
10 HIGHBURY TERR
11 COBURG VILLAS
12 STANLEY VILLAS
13 CLAREMONT PL
14 EVELYN TERR
15 TYNNING TERR
16 KINGSDOWN VIEW
17 SOLSBURY VIEW
18 COLLEGE VIEW
19 INCHALLOCH

B1
1 BRUNSWICK ST
2 HANOVER ST
3 GILLINGHAM TERR
4 WALMSLEY TERR
5 HANOVER TERR
6 FRANKLEY TERR
7 CHILTON CT
8 BEAUFORT VILLAS
9 GROSVENOR VILLAS

27

B1
10 ST SAVIOUR' S TERR
11 BEAUFORT W
12 ALEXANDER BLDGS
13 PERCY PL
14 MEZELLION PL
15 EASTBOURNE AVE
16 VALE VIEW PL
17 BALUSTRADE

45

C1
1 LAMBRIDGE BLDGS
2 VICTORIA PL
3 BEAUFORT MEWS
4 ST SAVIOURS WAY
5 LAMBRIDGE MEWS
6 LAMBRIDGE
7 LAMONT HO
8 MONTAGUE HO
9 EASTON HO
10 HAMPTON HO
11 BRIDGE HO

C2
1 GARFIELD TERR
2 BROUGHAM PL
3 COTTAGE PL
4 EDEN VILLAS
5 OTAGO TERR
6 LAMBRIDGE GRANGE

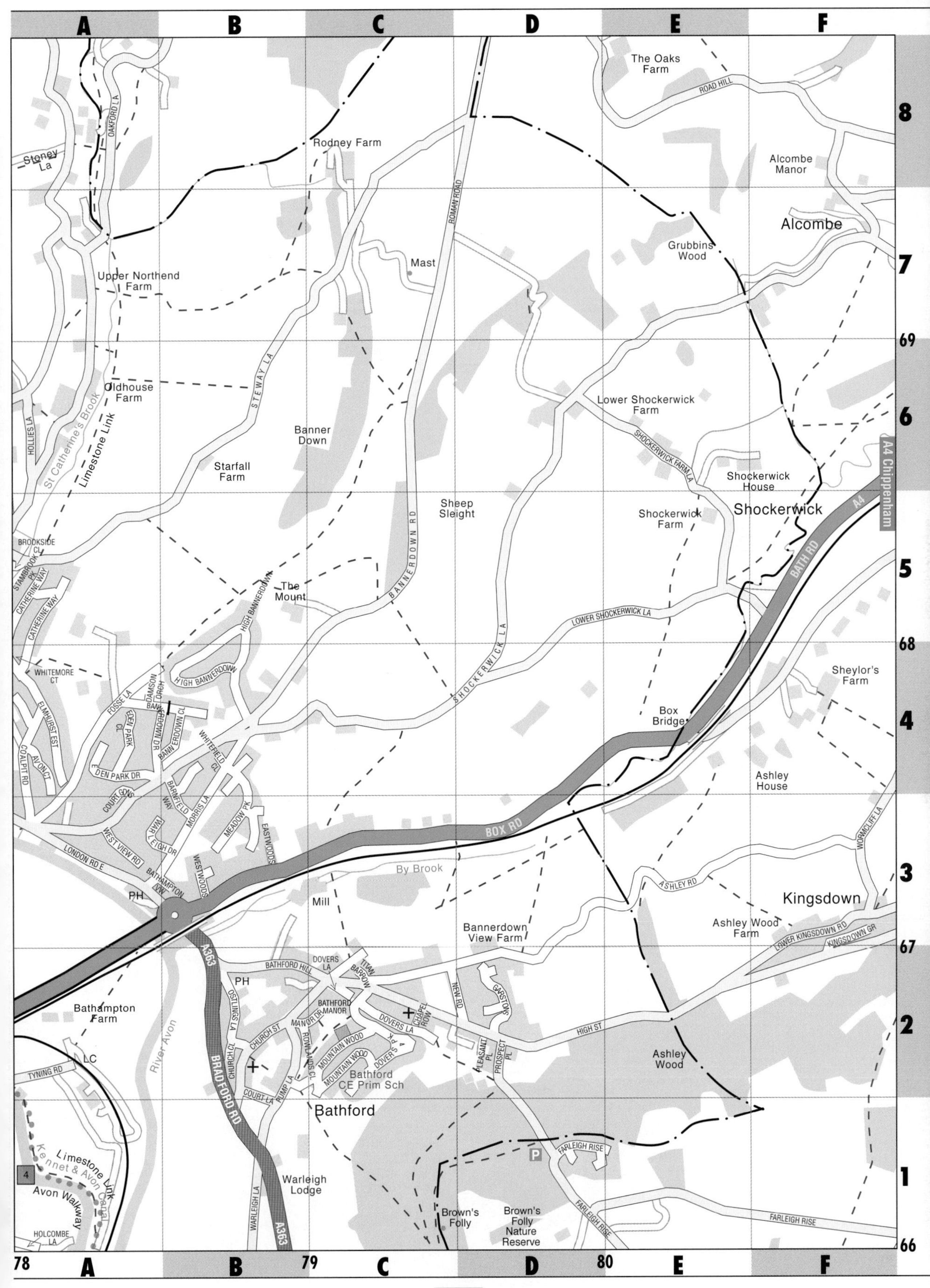

A B C D E F
8
7
69
6
5
68
4
3
67
2
1
66
78
79
80
The Oaks Farm
ROAD HILL
Alcombe Manor
Alcombe
Rodney Farm
Stoney La
OAKFORD LA
ROMAN ROAD
Mast
Grubbins Wood
Upper Northend Farm
Lower Shockerwick Farm
Oldhouse Farm
STEWAY LA
Banner Down
St Catherine's Brook
Limestone Link
HOLLIES LA
Starfall Farm
SHOCKERWICK FARM LA
Shockerwick House
A4 Chippenham
Sheep Sleight
Shockerwick Farm
Shockerwick
A4
BANNERDOWN RD
BROOKSIDE CL
STAMBROOK PK
CATHERINE WAY
The Mount
BATH RD
LOWER SHOCKERWICK LA
HIGH BANNERDOWN
SHOCKERWICK LA
Sheylor's Farm
WHITEMORE CT
FOSSE LA
DAMSON ORCH
BANNERDOWN DR
BANNERDOWN CL
WHITEFIELD CL
EDEN PARK CL
ELMHURST EST
Box Bridge
AVON CT
COALPIT RD
EDEN PARK DR
BARNFIELD WAY
MORRIS LA
Ashley House
COURT GDNS
WARLEIGH DR
MEADOW PK
EASTWOODS
WORMCLIFF LA
BOX RD
WEST VIEW RD
LONDON RD E
BATHAMPTON LA
WESTWOODS
By Brook
ASHLEY RD
PH
Mill
Kingsdown
Bannerdown View Farm
Ashley Wood Farm
LOWER KINGSDOWN RD
KINGSDOWN GR
A363
BATHFORD HILL
DOVERS LA
TITAN BARROW
PH
OSTLINGS LA
BATHFORD MANOR
CHAPEL ROW
NEW RD
GARSTONS
Bathampton Farm
CHURCH ST
MANOR DR
DOVERS LA
HIGH ST
ROWLANDS CL
MOUNTAIN WOOD
DOVER'S PK
PLEASANT PL
PROSPECT PL
Ashley Wood
LC
TYNING RD
CHURCH CL
River Avon
BRADFORD RD
Bathford CE Prim Sch
COURT LA
PUMP LA
Bathford
FARLEIGH RISE
P
Limestone Link
Kennet & Avon Canal
4
Warleigh Lodge
Avon Walkway
WARLEIGH LA
Brown's Folly
Brown's Folly Nature Reserve
FARLEIGH RISE
FARLEIGH RISE
HOLCOMBE LA

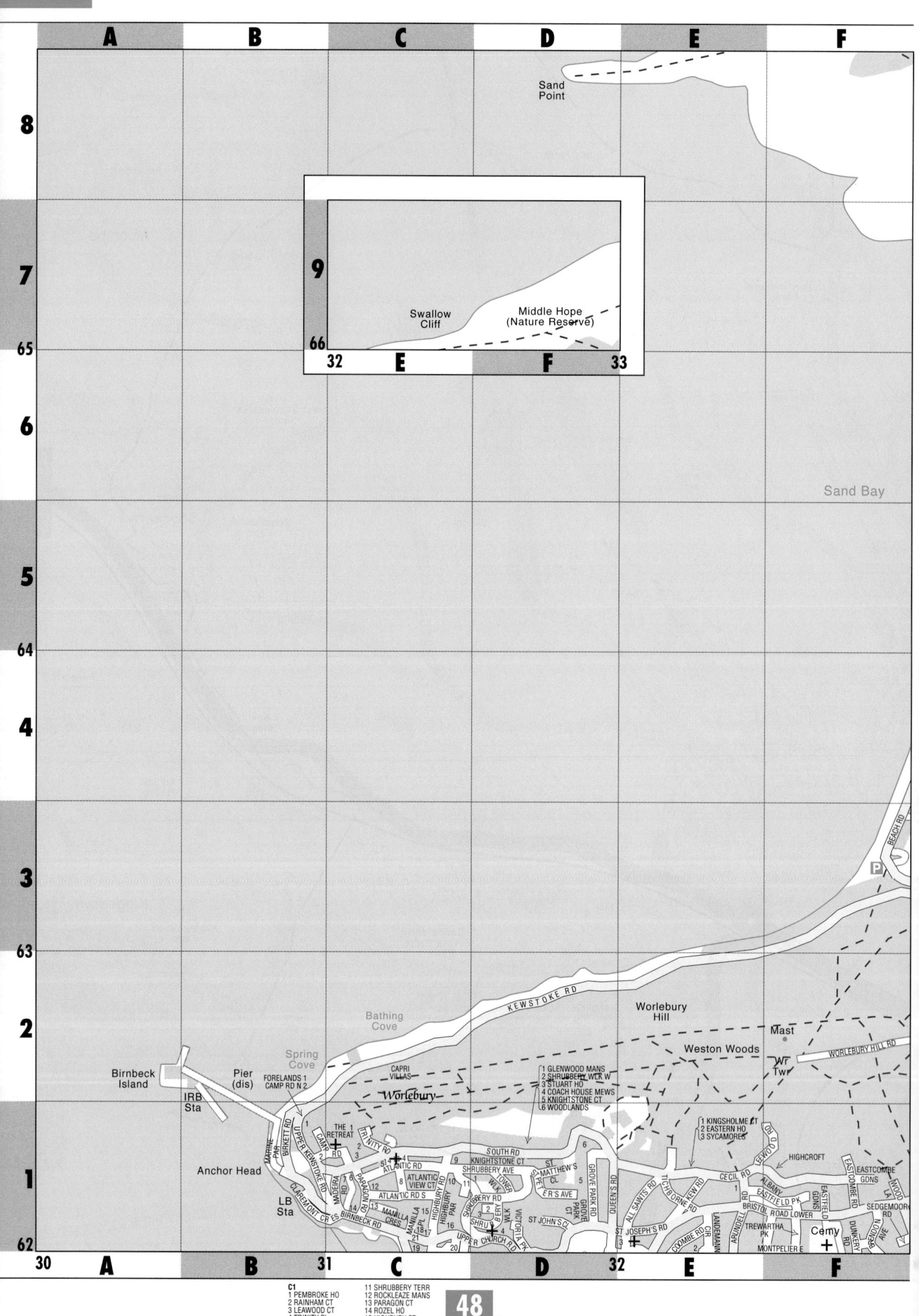

C1
1 PEMBROKE HO
2 RAINHAM CT
3 LEAWOOD CT
4 TRINITY PL
5 MORETON MANS
6 GOSFORD MANS
7 FRANKFORD MANS
8 HAMILTON RD
9 MAPLE CT
10 ROCKHALL HO
11 SHRUBBERY TERR
12 ROCKLEAZE MANS
13 PARAGON CT
14 ROZEL HO
15 HIGHBURY CT
16 VILLA ROSA
17 BADMINTON CT
18 CAIRO CT
19 GLENTWORTH CT
20 RAGLAN PL
21 MANILLA CRES

48

14
32

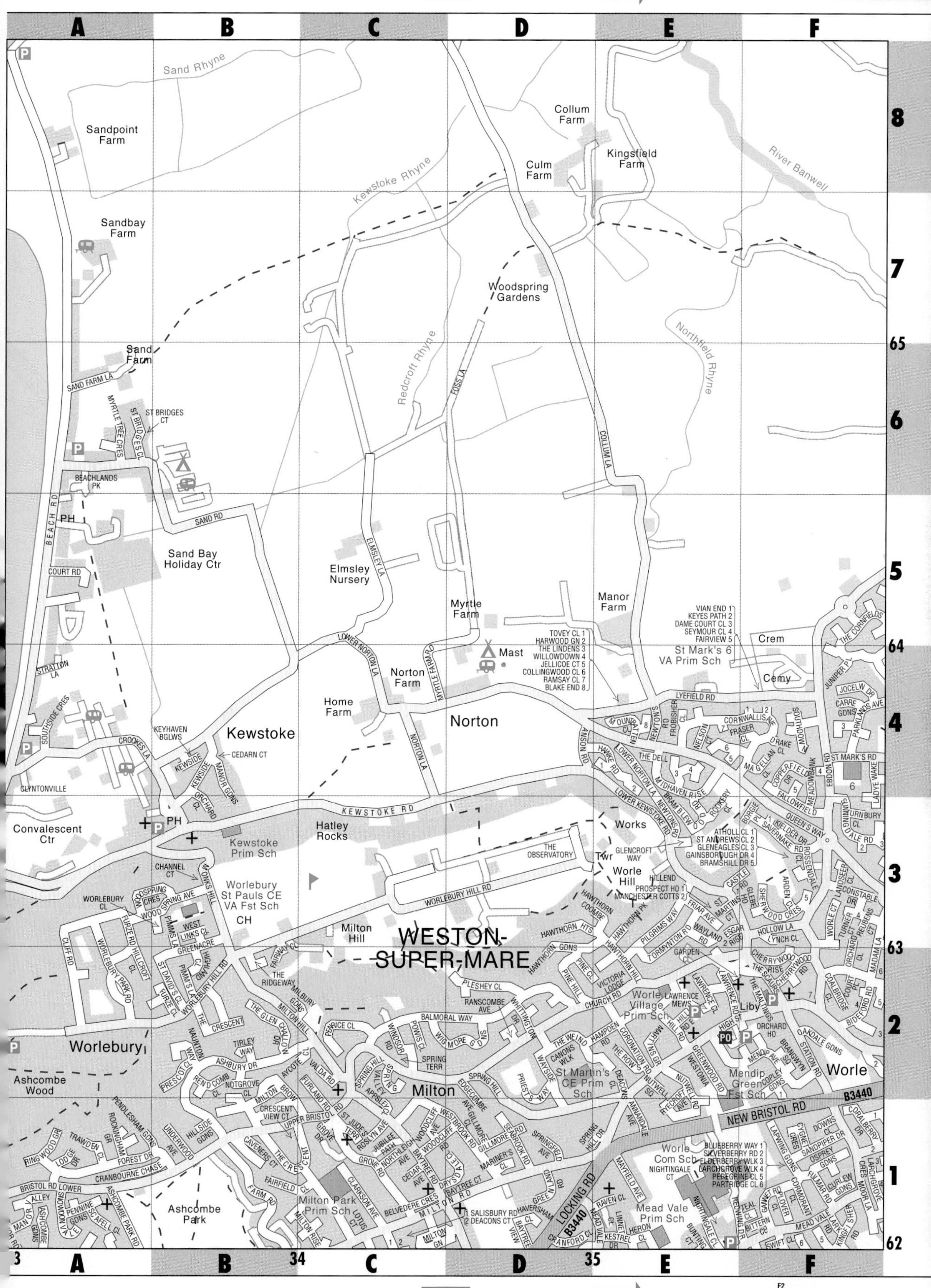

49
32

F2
1 COTMAN WLK
2 WESTWOOD CL
3 BLACKMOOR
4 APPLEDORE
5 BAMPTON
6 KENNFORD
7 KNIGHTSTONE PL

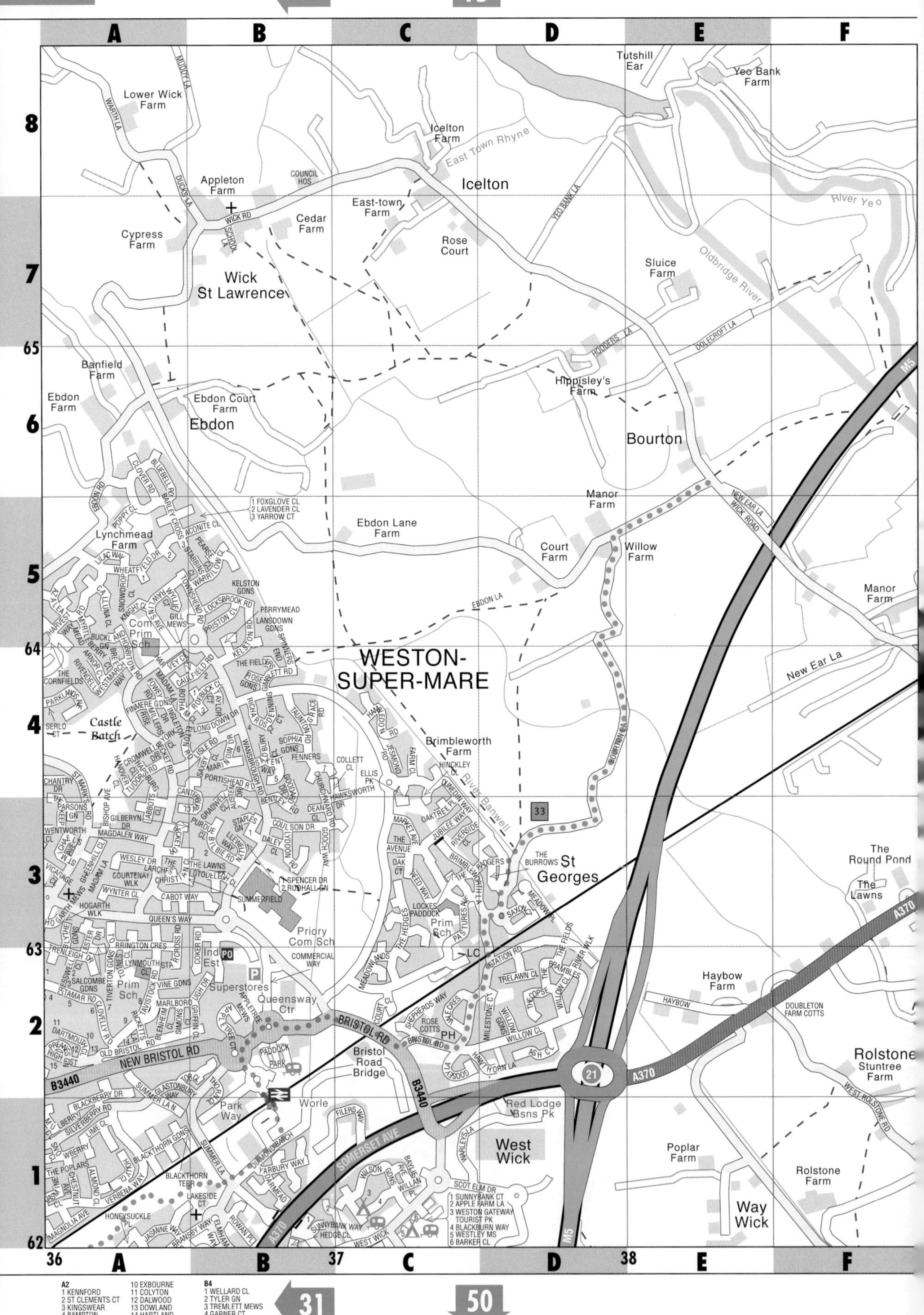

A2
1 KENNFORD
2 ST CLEMENTS CT
3 KINGSWEAR
4 BAMPTON
5 CREDITON
6 FENITON
7 INSTOW
8 IVYBRIDGE
9 HONITON
10 EXBOURNE
11 COLYTON
12 DALWOOD
13 DOWLAND
14 HARTLAND
15 EBDEN LO

B4
1 WELLARD CL
2 TYLER GN
3 TREMLETT MEWS
4 GARNER CT
5 WAINWRIGHT CL
6 EMLYN CL
7 THE SAFFRONS

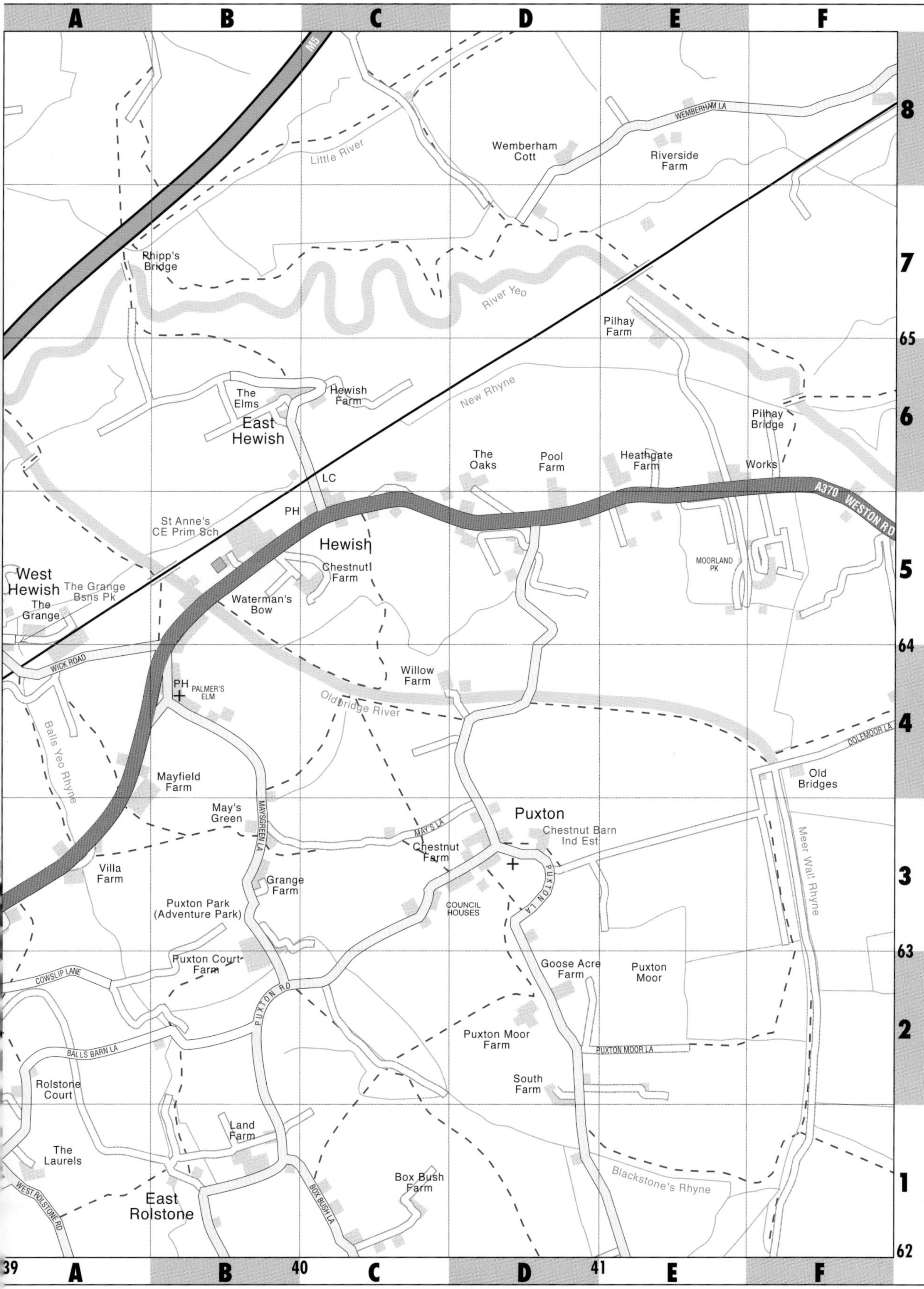

A B C D E F

M5
WEMBERHAM LA
Wemberham Cott
Riverside Farm
Little River
8
Rhipp's Bridge
7
River Yeo
Pilhay Farm
65
The Elms
Hewish Farm
East Hewish
New Rhyne
6
Pilhay Bridge
The Oaks
Pool Farm
Heathgate Farm
Works
LC
PH
A370 WESTON RD
St Anne's CE Prim Sch
Hewish
West Hewish
The Grange Bsns Pk
The Grange
Chestnut Farm
Waterman's Bow
MOORLAND PK
5
64
WICK ROAD
PH
PALMER'S ELM
Willow Farm
Oldbridge River
Balls Yeo Rhyne
4
DOLEMOOR LA
Old Bridges
Mayfield Farm
May's Green
MAYSGREEN LA
MAY'S LA
Puxton
Chestnut Barn Ind Est
Chestnut Farm
Meer Wall Rhyne
Villa Farm
Grange Farm
PUXTON LA
COUNCIL HOUSES
3
Puxton Park (Adventure Park)
63
Puxton Court Farm
COWSLIP LANE
PUXTON RD
Goose Acre Farm
Puxton Moor
BALLS BARN LA
Puxton Moor Farm
PUXTON MOOR LA
2
Rolstone Court
South Farm
Land Farm
The Laurels
Box Bush Farm
Blackstone's Rhyne
1
WEST ROLSTONE RD
East Rolstone
BOX BUSH LA
62

39 A B 40 C D 41 E F

51
34

33
17

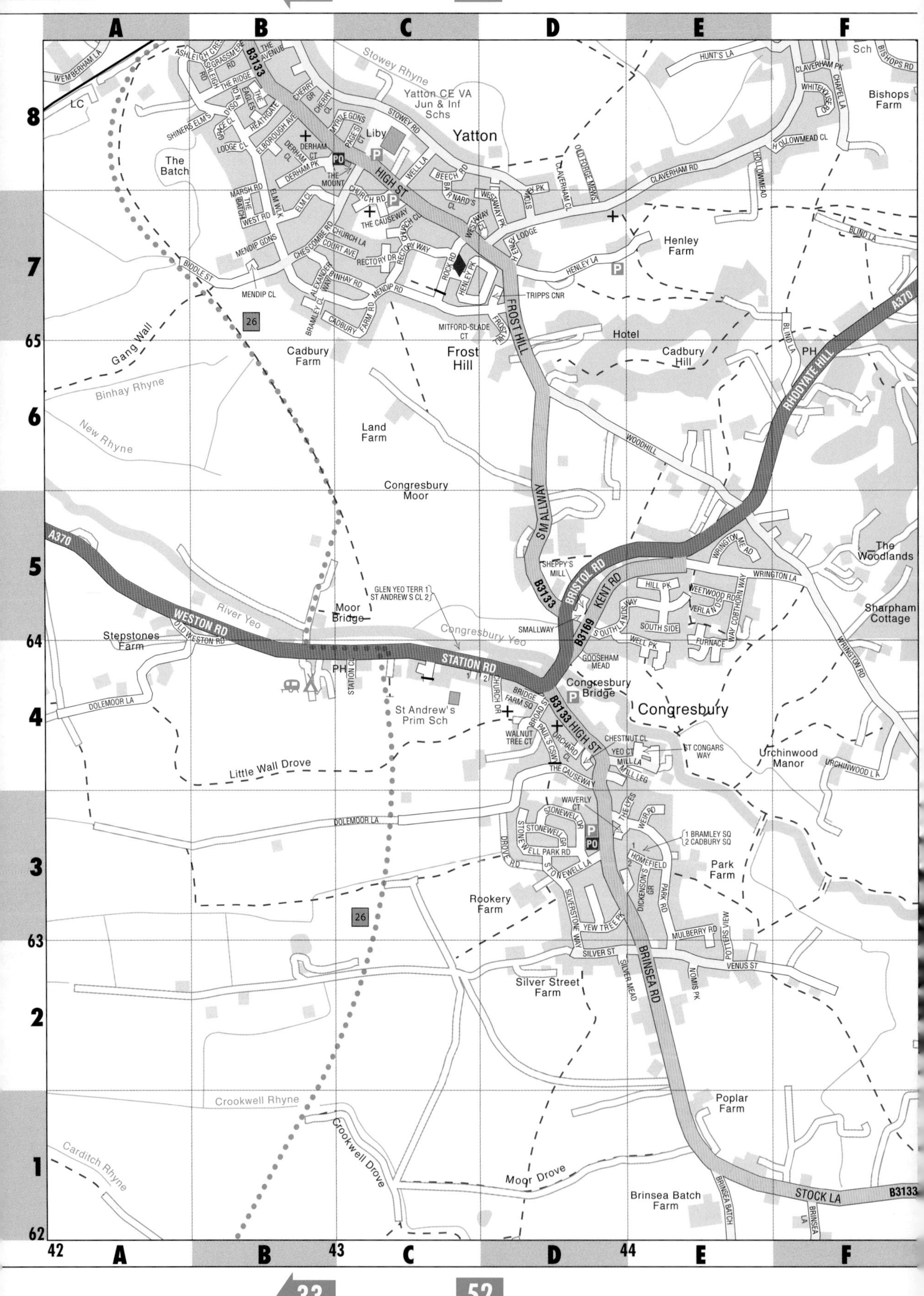
A
B
C
D
E
F
8
7
65
6
5
64
4
3
63
2
1
62
42
43
44
Yatton
Yatton CE VA
Jun & Inf
Schs
Liby
The
Batch
LC
WEMBERHAM LA
ASHLEIGH CRES
GRASSMERE RD
THE AVENUE
THE RIDGE
B3133
HIGH ST
STOWEY RD
Stowey Rhyne
CHERRY GR
CHERRY CL
MYRTLE GDNS
PAGE'S CT
SHINERS ELMS
HEATHGATE
ELBOROUGH AVE
DERHAM CT
DERHAM CL
DERHAM PK
LODGE CL
THE MOUNT
CHURCH RD
THE CAUSEWAY
CHURCH CL
WELL LA
BEECH RD
BARNARD'S CL
WESTAWAY PK
WESTAWAY CL
STOWEY PK
CLAVERHAM CL
OLD FORGE MEWS
CLAVERHAM RD
HOLLOWMEAD
HOLLOWMEAD CL
HUNT'S LA
CLAVERHAM PK
WHITEHOUSE RD
CHAPELL LA
BISHOPS RD
Sch
Bishops
Farm
MARSH RD
THE BATCH
WEST RD
ELM WLK
ELM CL
MENDIP GDNS
CHESCOMBE RD
CHURCH LA
COURT AVE
RECTORY DR
RECTORY WAY
ROCK RD
HENLEY PK
HENLEY LODGE
HENLEY LA
Henley
Farm
BLIND LA
BIDDLE ST
MENDIP CL
ALEXANDER WAY
BINHAY RD
MENDIP RD
BRAMLEY CL
CADBURY FARM RD
TRIPPS CNR
MITFORD-SLADE CT
FROST HILL
26
Gang Wall
Cadbury
Farm
Frost
Hill
Hotel
Cadbury
Hill
PH
A370
RHODYATE HILL
Binhay Rhyne
New Rhyne
Land
Farm
WOODHILL
Congresbury
Moor
SMALLWAY
The
Woodlands
WRINGTON MEAD
WRINGTON LA
Sharpham
Cottage
SHEPPY'S MILL
BRISTOL RD
B3169
KENT RD
HILL PK
WEETWOOD RD
VERLANDS
COBTHORN WAY
SOUTHLANDS WAY
SOUTH SIDE
WELL PK
FURNACE
GOOSEHAM MEAD
WRINGTON RD
WESTON RD
OLD WESTON RD
River Yeo
Stepstones
Farm
GLEN YEO TERR 1
ST ANDREW S CL 2
Moor
Bridge
Congresbury Yeo
SMALLWAY
STATION RD
PH
STATION CL
CHURCH DR
BRIDGE FARM SQ
Congresbury
Bridge
Congresbury
B3133 HIGH ST
DOLEMOOR LA
St Andrew's
Prim Sch
WALNUT TREE CT
BROAD ST
PAUL'S CSWY
ORCHARD CL
CHESTNUT CL
YEO CT
ST CONGARS WAY
MILL LA
MILL LEG
Urchinwood
Manor
URCHINWOOD LA
Little Wall Drove
THE CAUSEWAY
WAVERLY CT
STONEWELL DR
THE LYES
WEIR RD
DOLEMOOR LA
STONEWELL GR
STONEWELL PARK RD
DROVE RD
STONEWELL LA
1 BRAMLEY SQ
2 CADBURY SQ
HOMEFIELD
Park
Farm
DICKENSON'S GR
PARK RD
Rookery
Farm
SILVERSTONE WAY
YEW TREE PK
MULBERRY RD
POTTERS VIEW
SILVER ST
SILVER MEAD
BRINSEA RD
VENUS ST
NOMIS PK
Silver Street
Farm
Crookwell Rhyne
Crookwell Drove
Poplar
Farm
Carditch Rhyne
Moor Drove
Brinsea Batch
Farm
BRINSEA BATCH
STOCK LA
B3133
BRINSEA LA

33
52

18
36

A
B
C
D
E
F
8
7
65
6
5
64
4
3
63
2
1
62
45
46
47
BISHOPS RD
BISHOPS MEAD
GRAITNEY CL
CLEEVE DR
WOODVIEW DR
MILLIER RD
A370
Cleeve Combe
Cleeve Court
Cleeve
PH
Walnut Tree Farm
Cleeve Toot
Saw Mill
Wrington Warren
Warren House
WARNER CL
CHANNEL VIEW
FARM LA
CHAPEL LA
PLUNDER ST
RHODYATE LA
RHODYATE HILL
CLEEVE HILL RD
Goblin Combe
Bickley
King's Wood
Wrington Hill
Woolmers
Wrington Hill Farm
Corporation Woods
Urchin Wood
Ball Wood
Oatlands
The Island
Bracken Hill
Montreux Farm
The Grove
WRINGTON HILL
Bullhouse Lane
Udley
Uplands
Simshill Wood
WRINGTON RD
Yeowood
PH
Iwood
Gatcombe Farm Ind Est
Littler Plantation
Prestow Wood
Barley Farm
West Hay
Piercehay
Maines Batch
Iwood Farm
WEST HAY RD
CHAPEL HILL
YEOMANS ORCH
ROPER'S LA
Barley Wood Walled Garden
Iwood Manor
IWOOD LA
ALBURYS
HOME CL
ORCHARD CL
OLD HILL
BRANCHES CROSS
LONG LA
HIGH ST
BELL WLK
SCHOOL RD
Wrington CE Prim Sch
PH
LADYWELL
BROAD ST
CAMBRIDGE CT
SOUTH MDWS
LAWRENCE RD
MEMORIAL RD
HANNAH MORE CL
Court Farm
THE TRIANGLE
STATION RD
CHURCH WLK
BAKER'S BLDGS
RICKYARD RD
SILVER ST
Congresbury Yeo
Sewage Works
WILTONS
BROOKLYN
THE COTTAGES
THE GLEBE
GARSTONS CL
WESTWARD CL
OLD STATION CL
KINGS RD
BUTTS ORCH
GARSTONS
GARSTONS ORCH
Wrington
Butt's Batch
BUTT'S BATCH
COX'S GN
Stoney Croft House
Burnett Ind Est
COX'S GN
Cox's Green
STOCK LA
B3133
Beam Bridge
HALF YD
Havyat Road Trad Est
HAVYAT RD
Oakdene Farm
MILL LA
NATES LA

53
36

35
19

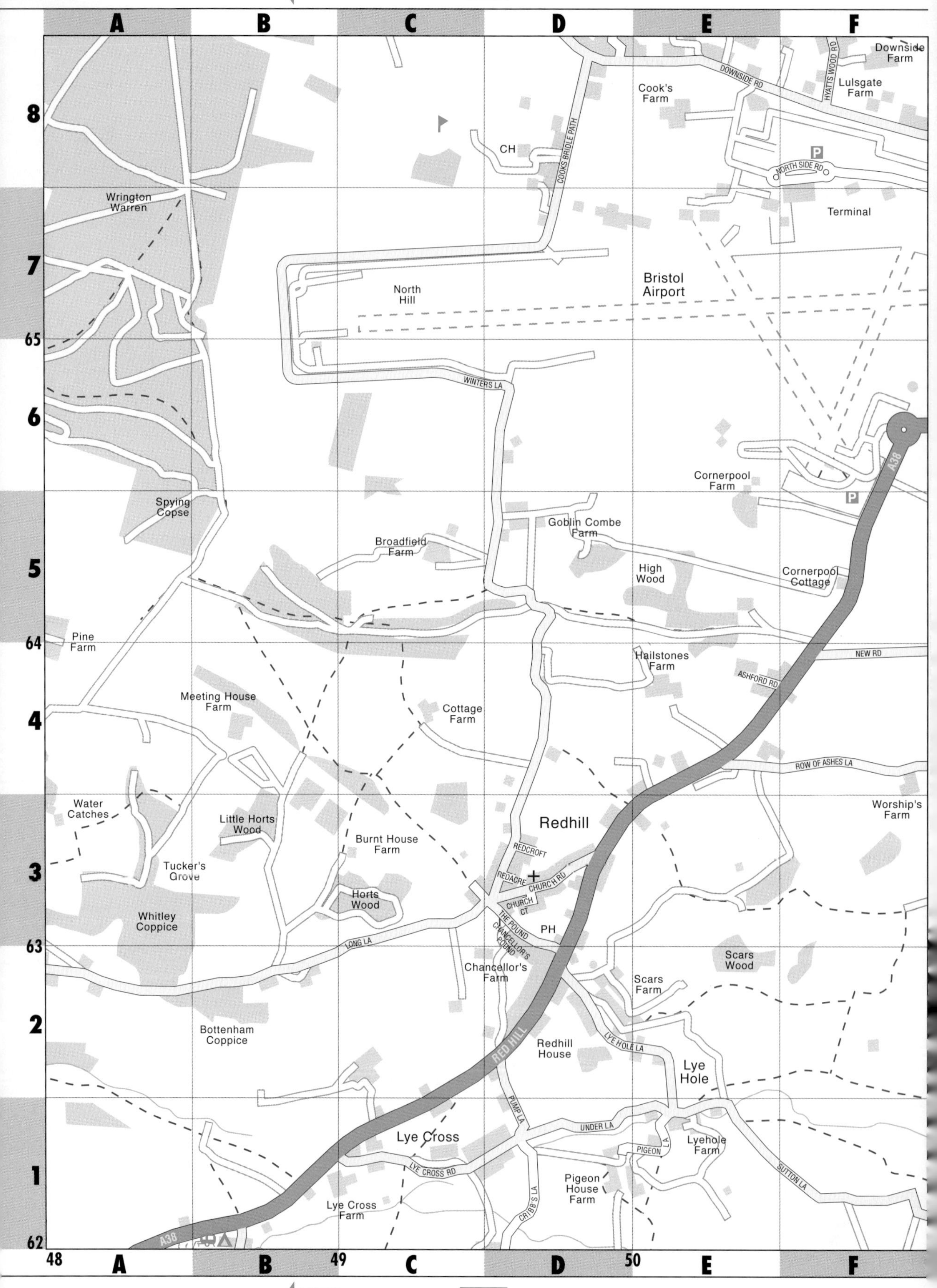
A
B
C
D
E
F
8
7
65
6
5
64
4
3
63
2
1
62
48
49
50
Downside Farm
Cook's Farm
DOWNSIDE RD
HYATTS WOOD RD
Lulsgate Farm
CH
COOKS BRIDLE PATH
P
NORTH SIDE RD
Terminal
Wrington Warren
Bristol Airport
North Hill
WINTERS LA
A38
Cornerpool Farm
Spying Copse
Goblin Combe Farm
Broadfield Farm
High Wood
Cornerpool Cottage
Pine Farm
NEW RD
Hailstones Farm
ASHFORD RD
Meeting House Farm
Cottage Farm
ROW OF ASHES LA
Water Catches
Little Horts Wood
Redhill
Worship's Farm
Burnt House Farm
REDCROFT
Tucker's Grove
REDACRE
CHURCH RD
Horts Wood
CHURCH CT
Whitley Coppice
THE POUND
PH
CHANCELLOR'S POUND
LONG LA
Chancellor's Farm
Scars Wood
Scars Farm
Bottenham Coppice
LYE HOLE LA
Redhill House
RED HILL
Lye Hole
PUMP LA
UNDER LA
Lye Cross
Lyehole Farm
PIGEON LA
LYE CROSS RD
Pigeon House Farm
SUTTON LA
CRIBB'S LA
Lye Cross Farm

35
54

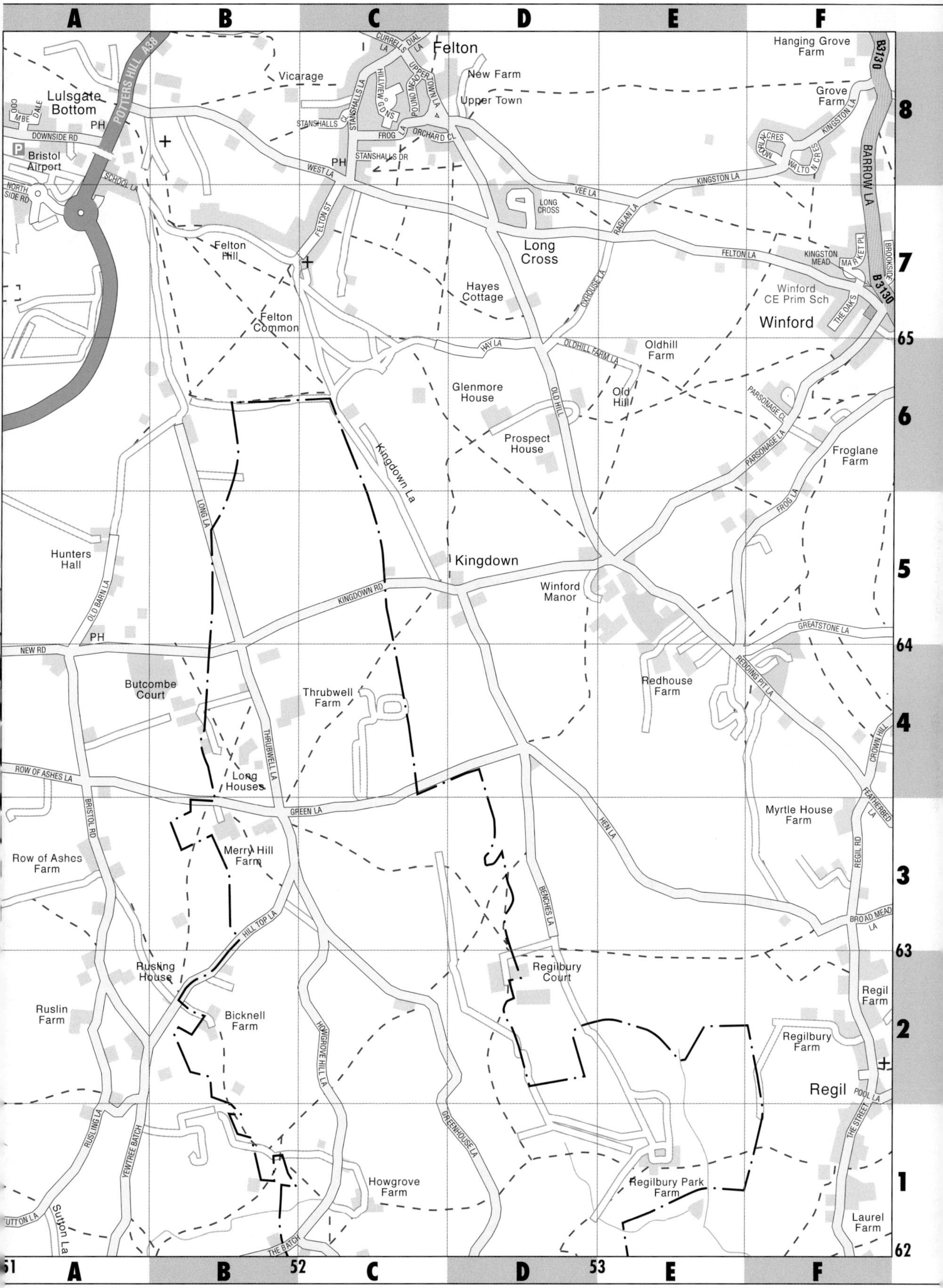

Felton
Currells La
Dial La
Hillview Gdns
Pound Mead
Upper Town La
Stanshalls La
Stanshalls Cl
Frog La
Orchard Cl
Stanshalls Dr
New Farm
Upper Town
Vicarage
Lulsgate Bottom
Coombe Dale
Downside Rd
Potters Hill A38
PH
Bristol Airport
North Side Rd
School La
West La
PH
Felton St
Vee La
Kingston La
Long Cross
Long Cross
Raglan La
Felton Hill
Felton Common
Hayes Cottage
Oxhouse La
Hay La
Oldhill Farm La
Oldhill Farm
Hanging Grove Farm
Grove Farm
Moorland Cres
Walton Cres
Kingston La
Barrow La
B3130
Felton La
Kingston Mead
Market Pl
Brookside
B3130
Winford CE Prim Sch
The Oaks
Winford
Glenmore House
Old Hill
Old Hill
Prospect House
Kingdown La
Parsonage Cl
Parsonage La
Froglane Farm
Frog La
Hunters Hall
Long La
Kingdown
Kingdown Rd
Winford Manor
Old Barn La
PH
New Rd
Greatstone La
Butcombe Court
Thrubwell Farm
Redhouse Farm
Redding Pit La
Crown Hill
Row of Ashes La
Long Houses
Thrubwell La
Green La
Featherbed La
Myrtle House Farm
Bristol Rd
Row of Ashes Farm
Merry Hill Farm
Hen La
Regil Rd
Benches La
Broad Mead La
Hill Top La
Rusling House
Regilbury Court
Ruslin Farm
Bicknell Farm
Regil Farm
Regilbury Farm
Howgrove Hill La
Regil
Pool La
The Street
Rusling La
Yewtree Batch
Greenhouse La
Howgrove Farm
Regilbury Park Farm
Sutton La
Sutton La
The Batch
Laurel Farm

A B C D E F
8 7 65 6 5 64 4 3 63 2 1 62
51 52 53

55
38

37
21

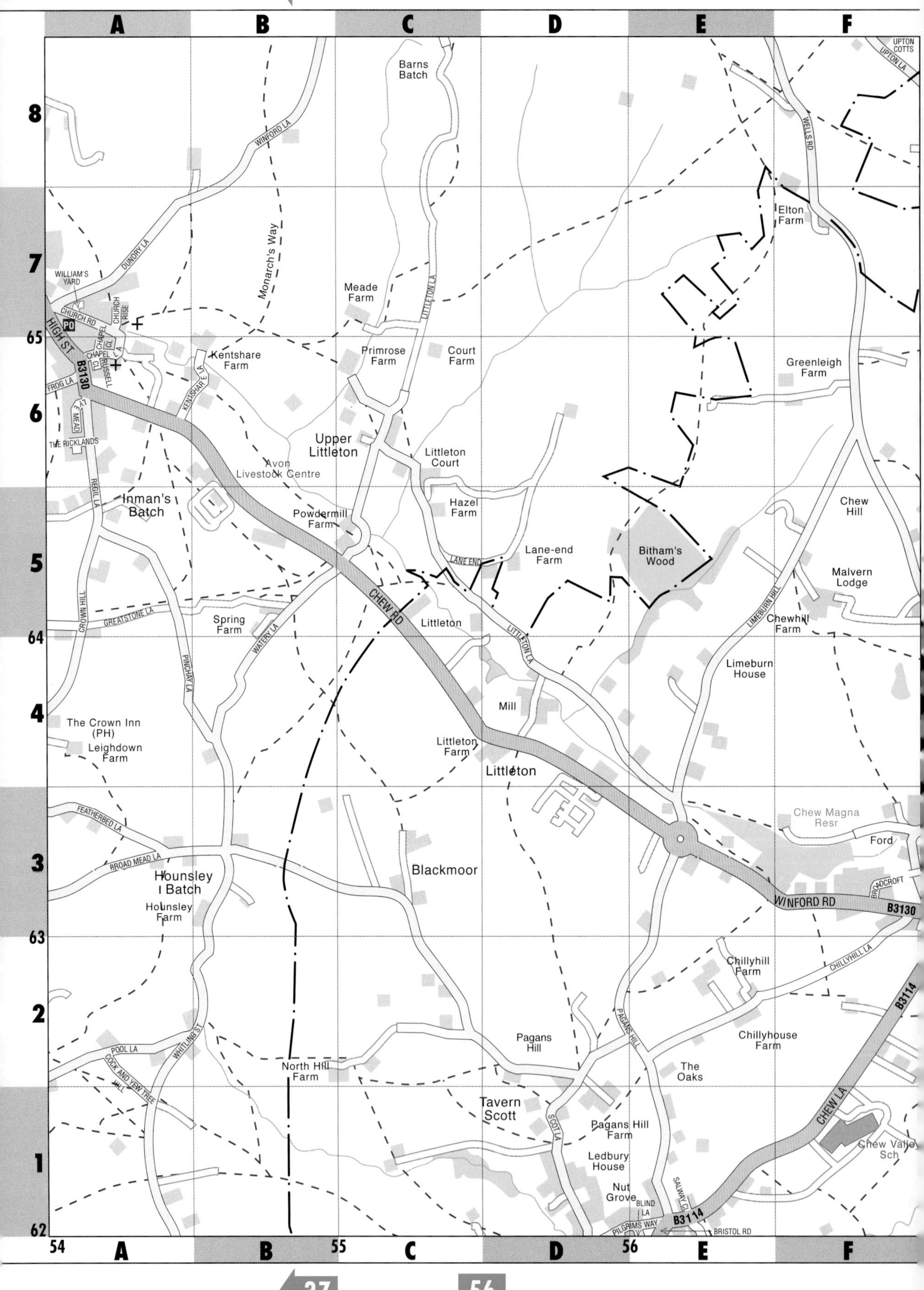
A
B
C
D
E
F
8
7
65
6
5
64
4
3
63
2
1
62
54
55
56
UPTON COTTS
UPTON LA
Barns Batch
WINFORD LA
WELLS RD
Monarch's Way
DUNDRY LA
WILLIAM'S YARD
CHURCH RD
CHURCH RISE
PO
HIGH ST
CHAPEL CL
CHAPEL LA
RUSSELL
B3130
FROG LA
LYE MEAD
THE RICKLANDS
Meade Farm
LITTLETON LA
Elton Farm
Kentshare Farm
KENTSHARE LA
Primrose Farm
Court Farm
Greenleigh Farm
Upper Littleton
Littleton Court
Avon Livestock Centre
Inman's Batch
REGIL LA
Powdermill Farm
Hazel Farm
Chew Hill
LANE END
Lane-end Farm
Bitham's Wood
Malvern Lodge
CHEW RD
CROWN HILL
GREATSTONE LA
Spring Farm
WATERY LA
Littleton
LIMEBURN HILL
Chewhill Farm
LITTLETON LA
Limeburn House
PINCHAY LA
The Crown Inn (PH)
Leighdown Farm
Mill
Littleton Farm
Littleton
FEATHERBED LA
Chew Magna Resr
Ford
BROAD MEAD LA
Hounsley Batch
Hounsley Farm
Blackmoor
BROADCROFT
WINFORD RD
B3130
Chillyhill Farm
CHILLYHILL LA
B3114
PAGANS HILL
POOL LA
WHITLING ST
COCK AND YEW TREE HILL
Pagans Hill
Chillyhouse Farm
North Hill Farm
The Oaks
Tavern Scott
SCOT LA
Pagans Hill Farm
CHEW LA
Chew Valley Sch
Ledbury House
Nut Grove
BLIND LA
SALWAY CL
PILGRIMS WAY
B3114
BRISTOL RD

37
56

22
40

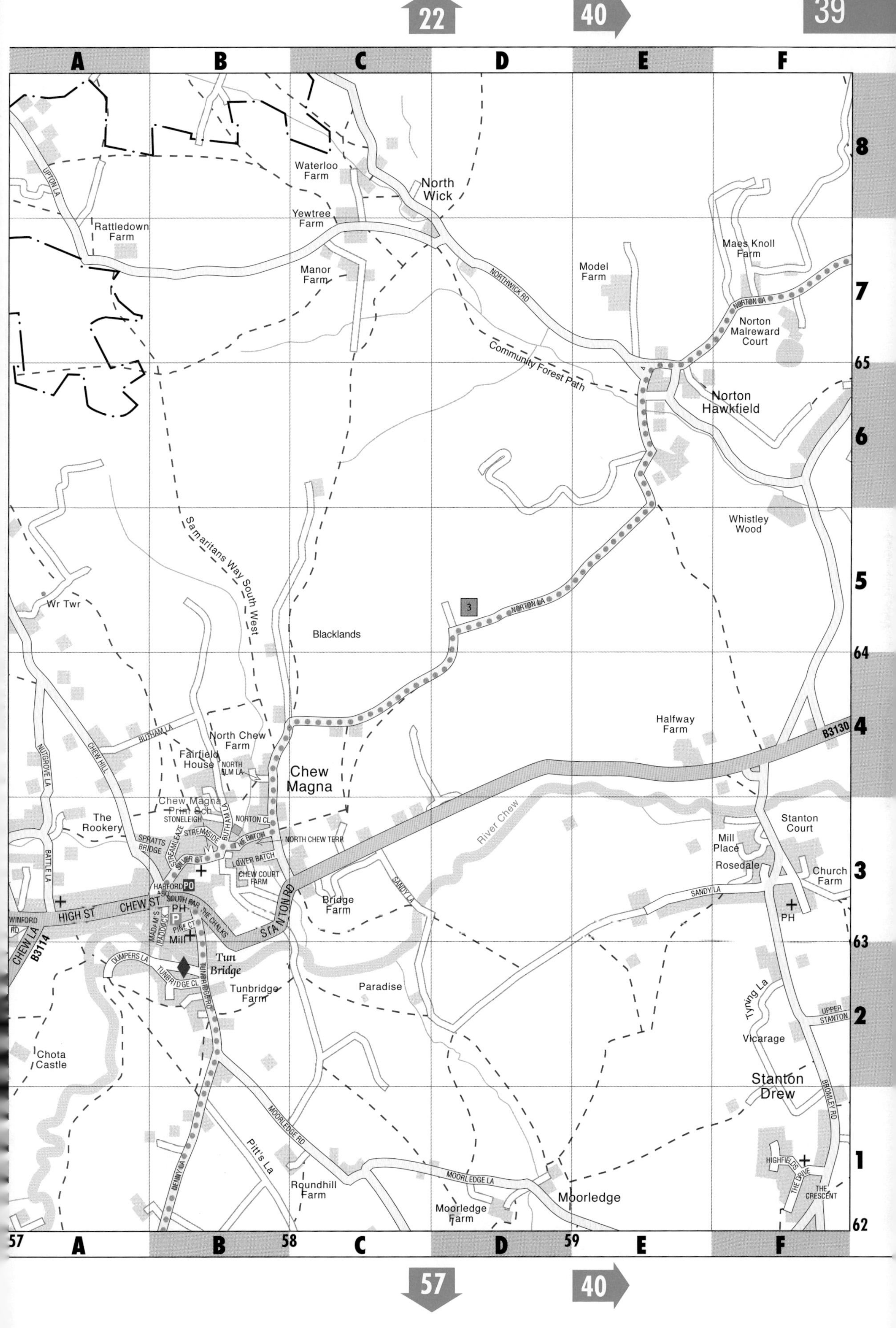
A
B
C
D
E
F
8
7
65
6
5
64
4
3
63
2
1
62
57
58
59
Waterloo Farm
North Wick
Yewtree Farm
Rattledown Farm
Manor Farm
Model Farm
Maes Knoll Farm
Norton Malreward Court
NORTHWICK RD
NORTON LA
Community Forest Path
Norton Hawkfield
UPTON LA
Whistley Wood
Samaritans Way South West
Wr Twr
Blacklands
Halfway Farm
B3130
BUTHAM LA
North Chew Farm
Fairfield House
NORTH ELM LA
Chew Magna
CHEW HILL
NUTGROVE LA
Chew Magna Prim Sch
The Rookery
STONELEIGH
STREAMSIDE
BUTHAM LA
NORTON CL
THE BATCH
NORTH CHEW TERR
SPRATTS BRIDGE
STREAMLEAZE
SILVER ST
LOWER BATCH
CHEW COURT FARM
River Chew
Stanton Court
Mill Place
Rosedale
Church Farm
BATTLE LA
HARFORD SQ
PO
HIGH ST
CHEW ST
SOUTH PAR
PH
THE CHALKS
STANTON RD
Bridge Farm
SANDY LA
SANDY LA
PH
WINFORD RD
CHEW LA
B3114
MADAM'S PADDOCK
P
PINE CT
Mill
DUMPERS LA
Tun Bridge
TUNBRIDGE CL
TUNBRIDGE RD
Tunbridge Farm
Paradise
Tyning La
UPPER STANTON
Vicarage
Chota Castle
Stanton Drew
BROMLEY RD
MOORLEDGE RD
Pitt's La
HIGHFIELDS
THE DRIVE
THE CRESCENT
DENNY LA
Roundhill Farm
MOORLEDGE LA
Moorledge Farm
Moorledge
3

57
40

39
23

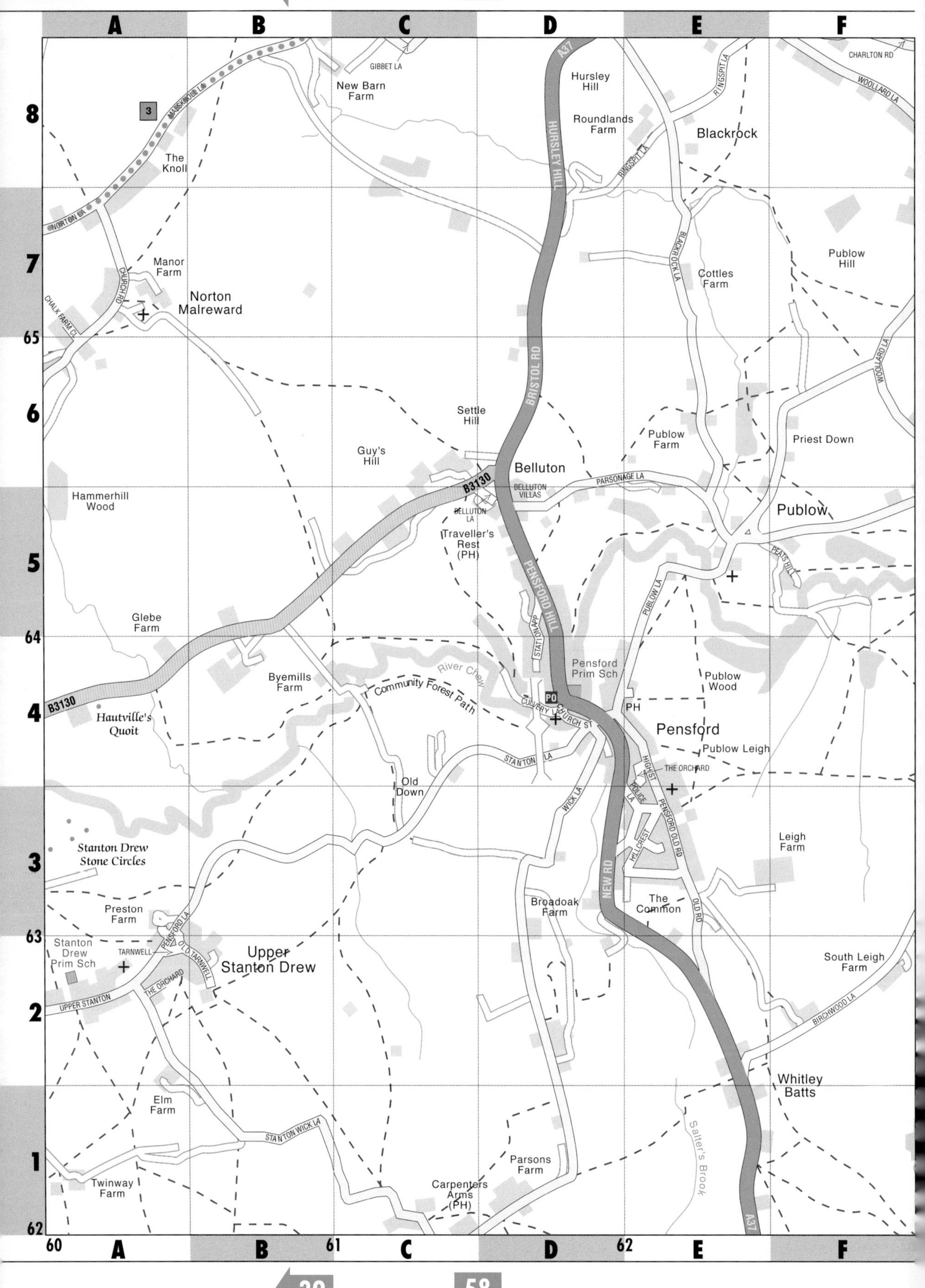
A
B
C
D
E
F
8
7
65
6
5
64
4
3
63
2
1
62
60
61
62
GIBBET LA
New Barn Farm
A37
Hursley Hill
Roundlands Farm
RINGSPIT LA
Blackrock
CHARLTON RD
WOOLLARD LA
3
The Knoll
NORTON LA
HURSLEY HILL
Manor Farm
CHURCH RD
Norton Malreward
CHALK FARM CL
BLACKROCK LA
Cottles Farm
Publow Hill
BRISTOL RD
Settle Hill
Guy's Hill
Belluton
Publow Farm
Priest Down
Hammerhill Wood
B3130
BELLUTON VILLAS
PARSONAGE LA
BELLUTON LA
Publow
Traveller's Rest (PH)
PENSFORD HILL
PEATS HILL
PUBLOW LA
Glebe Farm
STATION APP
Pensford Prim Sch
Byemills Farm
River Chew
Community Forest Path
PO
Publow Wood
B3130
CULVERY LA
CHURCH ST
PH
Pensford
Hautville's Quoit
Publow Leigh
STANTON LA
HIGH ST
THE ORCHARD
Old Down
POLICE LA
PENSFORD OLD RD
WICK LA
Stanton Drew Stone Circles
HILLCREST
Leigh Farm
NEW RD
Preston Farm
Broadoak Farm
The Common
OLD RD
Stanton Drew Prim Sch
TARNWELL
PENSFORD LA
OLD TARNWELL
Upper Stanton Drew
South Leigh Farm
UPPER STANTON
THE ORCHARD
BIRCHWOOD LA
Whitley Batts
Elm Farm
STANTON WICK LA
Salter's Brook
Parsons Farm
Twinway Farm
Carpenters Arms (PH)
A37

39
58

24
42

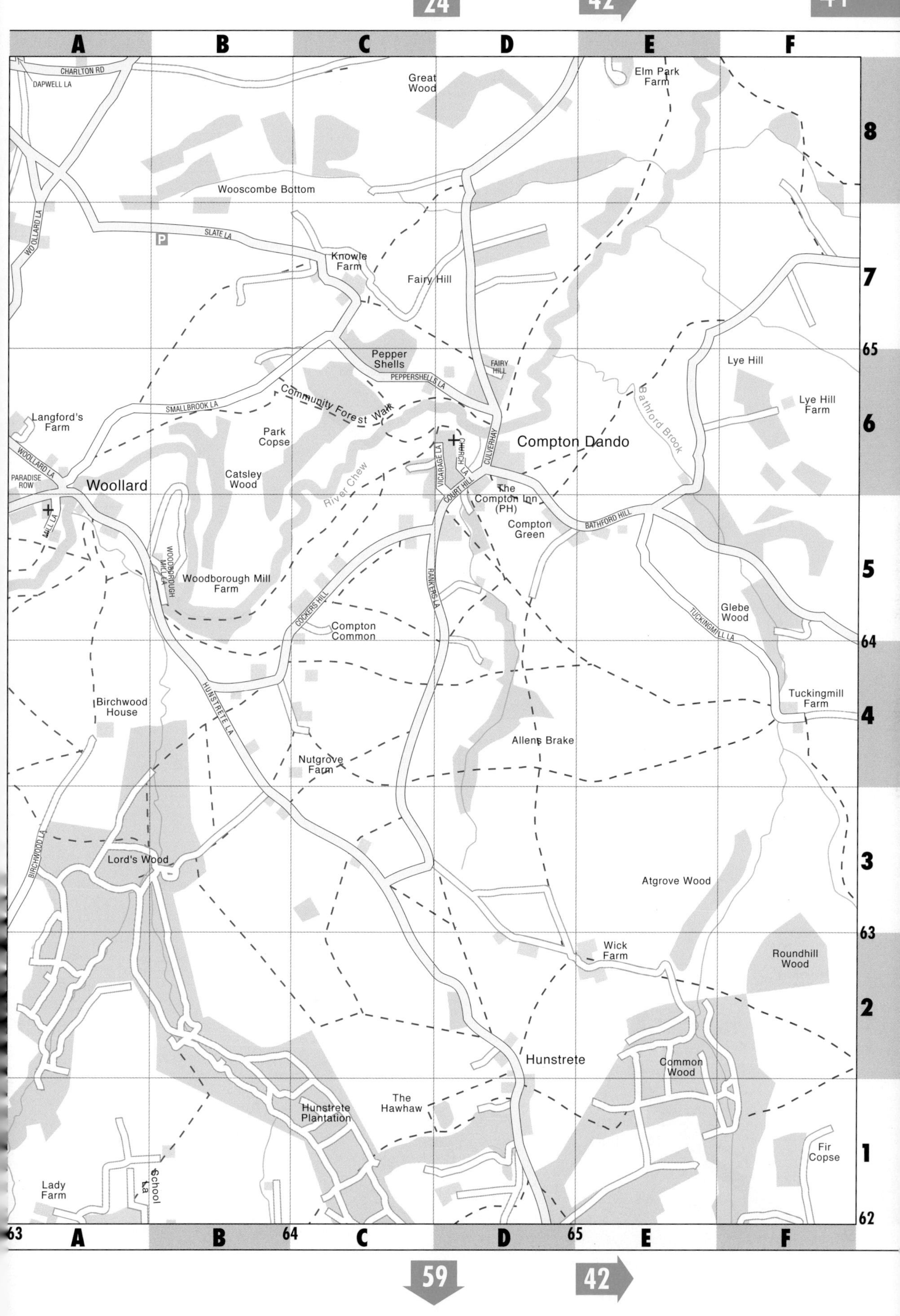
A
B
C
D
E
F
8
7
65
6
5
64
4
3
63
2
1
62
CHARLTON RD
DAPWELL LA
Great Wood
Elm Park Farm
Wooscombe Bottom
WOOLLARD LA
P
SLATE LA
Knowle Farm
Fairy Hill
Pepper Shells
FAIRY HILL
PEPPERSHELLS LA
Lye Hill
Lye Hill Farm
Community Forest Walk
SMALLBROOK LA
Langford's Farm
Park Copse
Bathford Brook
CHURCH LA
CULVERHAY
VICARAGE LA
Compton Dando
WOOLLARD LA
PARADISE ROW
Woollard
Catsley Wood
River Chew
COURT HILL
The Compton Inn (PH)
Compton Green
BATHFORD HILL
MILL LA
WOODBOROUGH MILL LA
Woodborough Mill Farm
RANKERS LA
COCKERS HILL
Compton Common
Glebe Wood
TUCKINGMILL LA
Birchwood House
HUNSTRETE LA
Tuckingmill Farm
Allens Brake
Nutgrove Farm
BIRCHWOOD LA
Lord's Wood
Atgrove Wood
Wick Farm
Roundhill Wood
Hunstrete
Common Wood
The Hawhaw
Hunstrete Plantation
Fir Copse
Lady Farm
School La
63
64
65

59
42

41
25

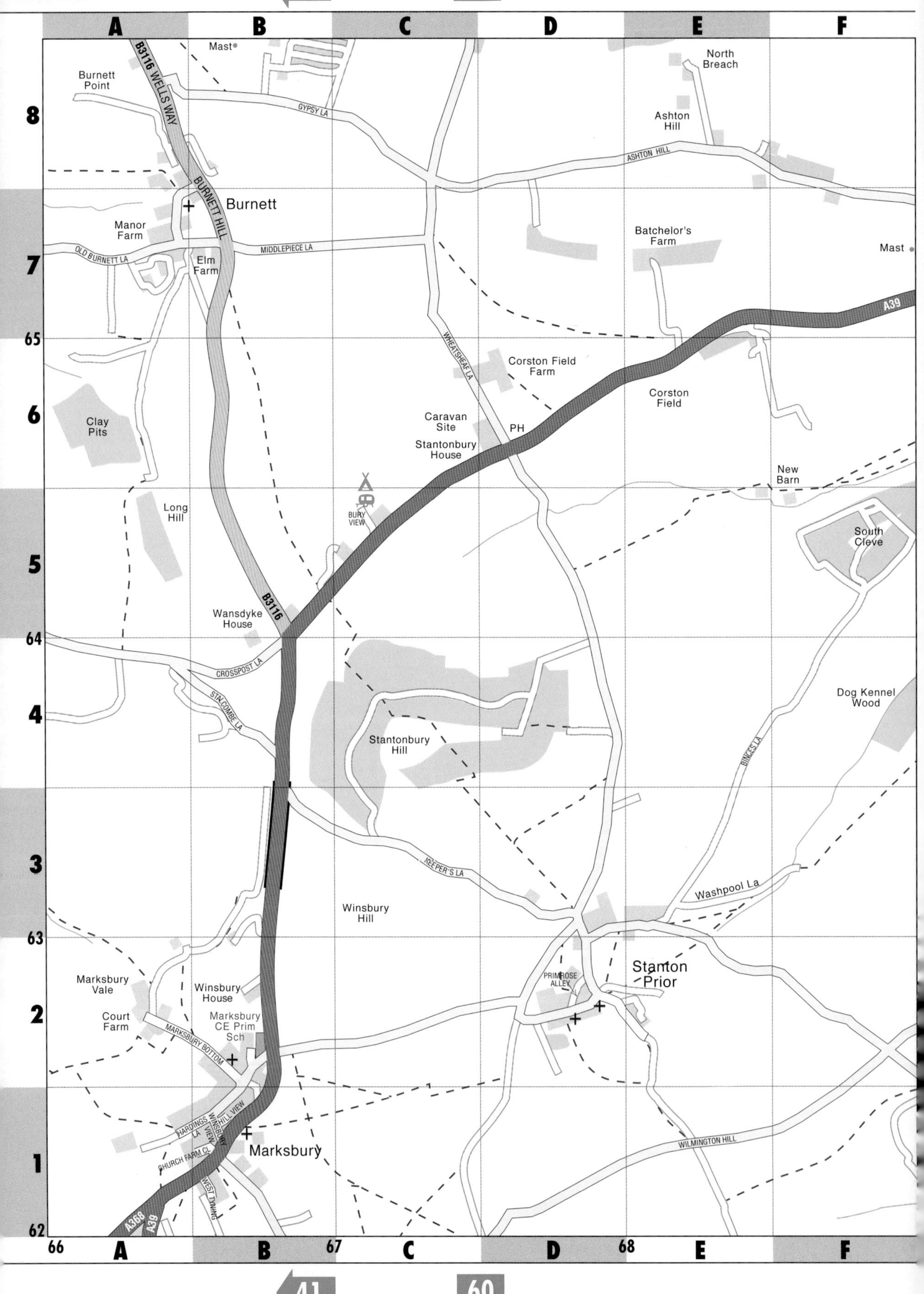
A
B
C
D
E
F
8
7
65
6
5
64
4
3
63
2
1
62
66
67
68
Mast
Burnett Point
B3116 WELLS WAY
GYPSY LA
North Breach
Ashton Hill
ASHTON HILL
BURNETT HILL
Burnett
Manor Farm
OLD BURNETT LA
Elm Farm
MIDDLEPIECE LA
Batchelor's Farm
Mast
A39
WHEATSHEAF LA
Corston Field Farm
Corston Field
Clay Pits
Caravan Site
PH
Stantonbury House
New Barn
Long Hill
BURY VIEW
South Cleve
Wansdyke House
B3116
CROSSPOST LA
STALCOMBE LA
Dog Kennel Wood
Stantonbury Hill
BINGES LA
KEEPER'S LA
Winsbury Hill
Washpool La
Marksbury Vale
Winsbury House
PRIMROSE ALLEY
Stanton Prior
Court Farm
Marksbury CE Prim Sch
MARKSBURY BOTTOM
HARDINGS LA
WINSBURY VIEW
HILL VIEW
CHURCH FARM CL
Marksbury
WILMINGTON HILL
WEST DYKING
A368
A39

41
60

26
44

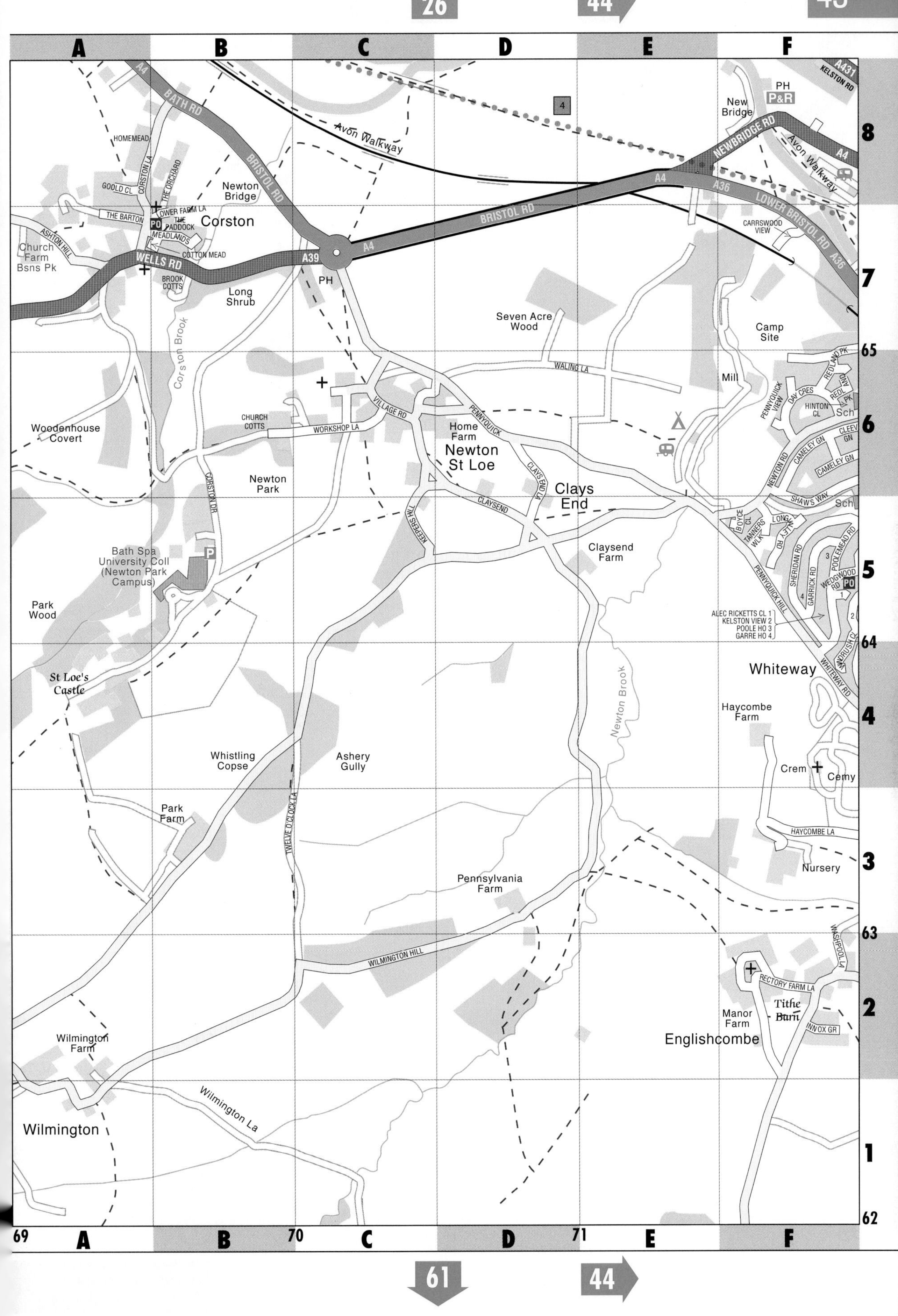
A
B
C
D
E
F
Corston
Newton Bridge
Church Farm Bsns Pk
HOMEMEAD
GOOLD CL
CORSTON LA
THE ORCHARD
THE BARTON
LOWER FARM LA
THE PADDOCK
MEADLANDS
COTTON MEAD
BROOK COTTS
ASHTON HILL
WELLS RD
BATH RD
BRISTOL RD
A4
A39
A36
A431
KELSTON RD
Avon Walkway
Long Shrub
PH
Corston Brook
Woodenhouse Covert
CHURCH COTTS
WORKSHOP LA
VILLAGE RD
Newton Park
CORSTON DR
Bath Spa University Coll (Newton Park Campus)
Park Wood
St Loe's Castle
Seven Acre Wood
WALING LA
PENNYQUICK
Home Farm
Newton St Loe
CLAYS END LA
Clays End
CLAYSEND
KEEPERS HILL
Claysend Farm
New Bridge
NEWBRIDGE RD
LOWER BRISTOL RD
CARRSWOOD VIEW
Camp Site
Mill
PENNYQUICK VIEW
DAV CRES
REDLAND PK
HINTON CL
Sch
CAMELEY GN
CLEEVE GN
NEWTON RD
SHAWS WAY
BOYCE CL
TANNERS WLK
LONGVALLEY RD
SHERIDAN RD
GARRICK RD
POOLEMEAD RD
WEDGWOOD RD
PENNYQUICK HILL
ALEC RICKETTS CL 1
KELSTON VIEW 2
POOLE HO 3
GARRE HO 4
Whiteway
WHITEWAY RD
Haycombe Farm
Crem
Cemy
HAYCOMBE LA
Nursery
Newton Brook
Whistling Copse
Ashery Gully
Park Farm
TWELVE O'CLOCK LA
Pennsylvania Farm
WILMINGTON HILL
WASHPOOL LA
RECTORY FARM LA
Tithe Barn
Manor Farm
INNOX GR
Englishcombe
Wilmington Farm
Wilmington
Wilmington La
8
7
65
6
5
64
4
3
63
2
1
62
69
70
71

61
44

B6
1 THE PARADE
2 TWERTON FARM CL
3 MILL LA
4 WATERLOO BLDGS
5 ORCHARD TERR
6 ALBANY CT
7 Locksbrook Trad Est
8 Locksbrook Ct

B7
1 ROSSLYN CL
2 HORSTMANN CL
3 WARWICK RD

43

C7
1 ASHLEY TERR
2 SHAFTESBURY AVE
3 WINDSOR VILLAS
4 WINDSOR CT
5 WINDSOR PL

27

D5
1 TRIANGLE VILLAS
2 TRIANGLE CT
3 CRANDALE RD
4 ARLINGTON RD
5 WINCHESTER RD
6 BELVOIR RD
7 SHAFTESBURY MEWS

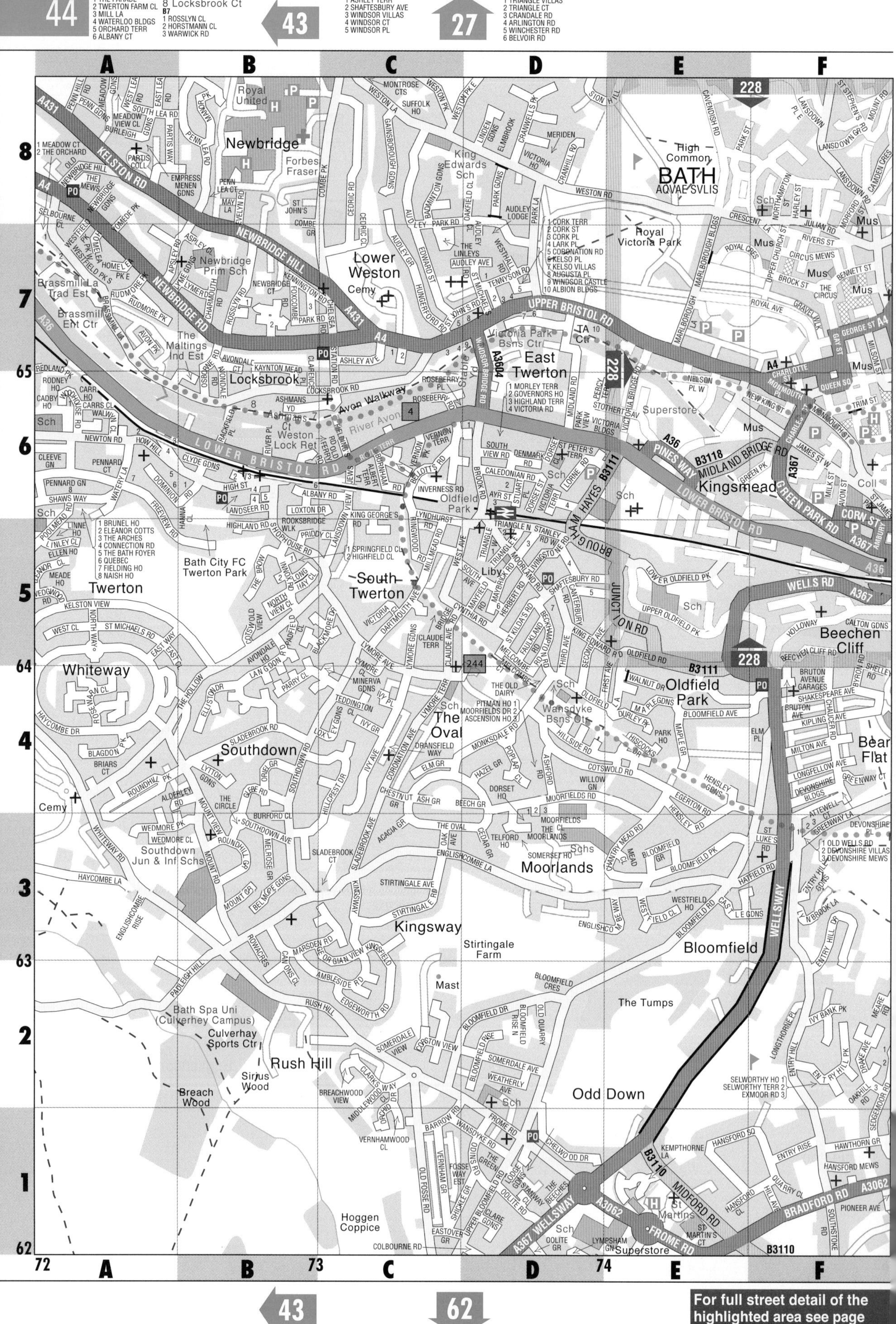

43
62

For full street detail of the highlighted area see page 228.

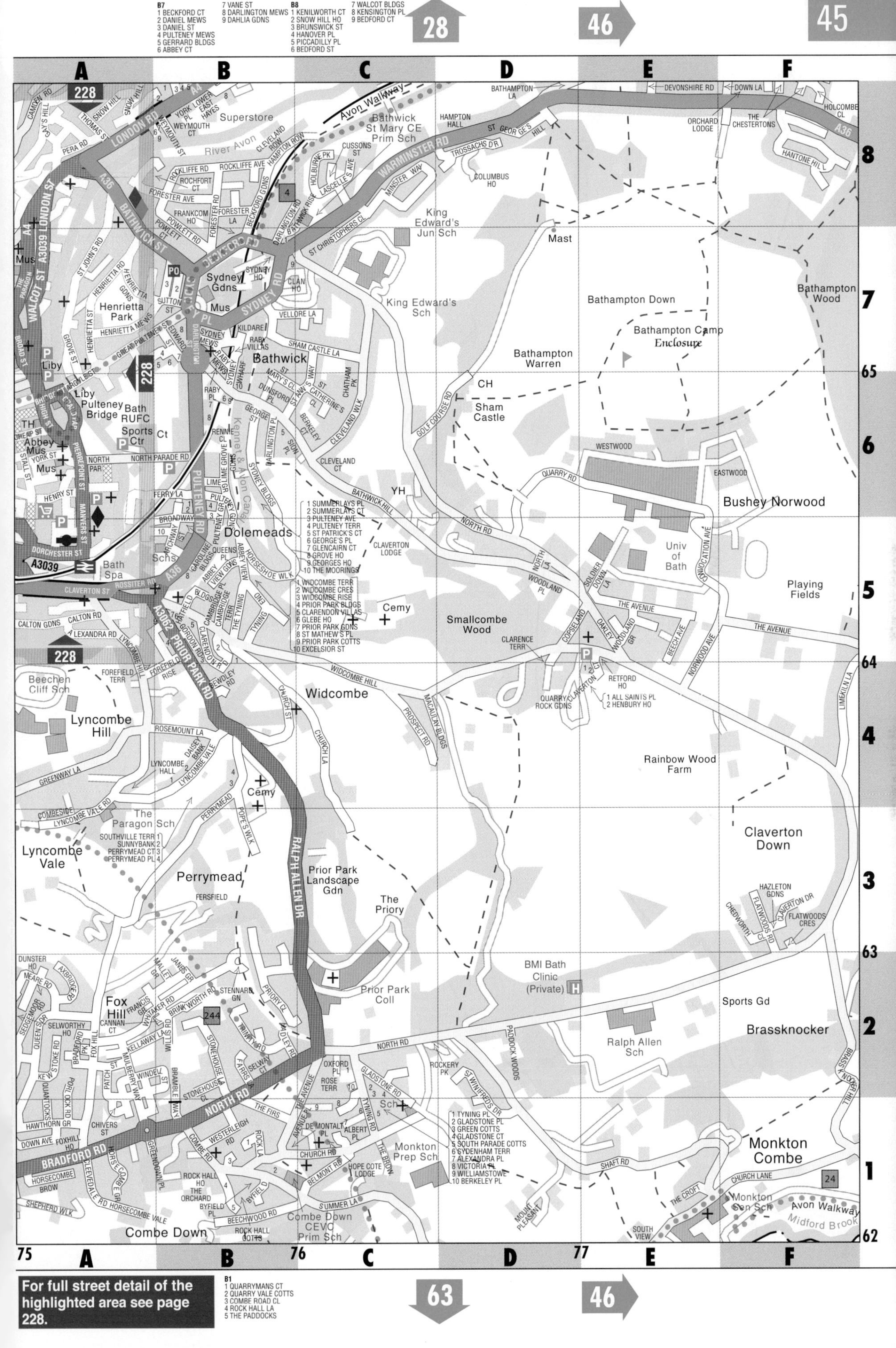

B7
1 BECKFORD CT
2 DANIEL MEWS
3 DANIEL ST
4 PULTENEY MEWS
5 GERRARD BLDGS
6 ABBEY CT
7 VANE ST
8 DARLINGTON MEWS
9 DAHLIA GDNS
B8
1 KENILWORTH CT
2 SNOW HILL HO
3 BRUNSWICK ST
4 HANOVER PL
5 PICCADILLY PL
6 BEDFORD ST
7 WALCOT BLDGS
8 KENSINGTON PL
9 BEDFORD CT
28
46
45
A
B
C
D
E
F
228
Superstore
River Avon
Avon Walkway
Bathwick St Mary CE Prim Sch
HAMPTON HALL
BATHAMPTON LA
DEVONSHIRE RD
DOWN LA
ORCHARD LODGE
THE CHESTERTONS
HOLCOMBE CL
A36
HANTONE HILL
8
WARMINSTER RD
TROSSACHS DR
COLUMBUS HO
King Edward's Jun Sch
Mast
Bathampton Down
Bathampton Wood
7
Bathampton Camp
Enclosure
King Edward's Sch
Bathampton Warren
CH
Sham Castle
65
Henrietta Park
Sydney Gdns
Mus
Bathwick
Liby
Pulteney Bridge
Bath RUFC
Sports Ctr
Ct
TH
Abbey
Mus
6
WESTWOOD
EASTWOOD
QUARRY RD
Bushey Norwood
YH
Dolemeads
CLAVERTON LODGE
Univ of Bath
Playing Fields
Bath Spa
5
1 SUMMERLAYS PL
2 SUMMERLAYS CT
3 PULTENEY AVE
4 PULTENEY TERR
5 ST PATRICK'S CT
6 GEORGE'S PL
7 GLENCAIRN CT
8 GROVE HO
9 GEORGES HO
10 THE MOORINGS
1 WIDCOMBE TERR
2 WIDCOMBE CRES
3 WIDCOMBE RISE
4 PRIOR PARK BLDGS
5 CLARENDON VILLAS
6 GLEBE HO
7 PRIOR PARK GDNS
8 ST MATHEW'S PL
9 PRIOR PARK COTTS
10 EXCELSIOR ST
Cemy
Smallcombe Wood
CLARENCE TERR
THE AVENUE
64
Beechen Cliff Sch
Widcombe
RETFORD HO
QUARRY ROCK GDNS
1 ALL SAINTS PL
2 HENBURY HO
Lyncombe Hill
4
Rainbow Wood Farm
Cemy
The Paragon Sch
SOUTHVILLE TERR 1
SUNNYBANK 2
PERRYMEAD CT 3
PERRYMEAD PL 4
Lyncombe Vale
Claverton Down
Perrymead
Prior Park Landscape Gdn
The Priory
3
HAZLETON GDNS
FLATWOODS CRES
63
Fox Hill
Prior Park Coll
BMI Bath Clinic (Private)
Sports Gd
2
Brassknocker
Ralph Allen Sch
NORTH RD
1 TYNING PL
2 GLADSTONE PL
3 GREEN COTTS
4 GLADSTONE CT
5 SOUTH PARADE COTTS
6 SYDENHAM TERR
7 ALEXANDRA PL
8 VICTORIA PL
9 WILLIAMSTOWE
10 BERKELEY PL
Monkton Prep Sch
Monkton Combe
1
BRADFORD RD
Combe Down
Combe Down CEVC Prim Sch
Monkton Sen Sch
Avon Walkway
Midford Brook
62
75
76
77
For full street detail of the highlighted area see page 228.
B1
1 QUARRYMANS CT
2 QUARRY VALE COTTS
3 COMBE ROAD CL
4 ROCK HALL LA
5 THE PADDOCKS
63
46

45
29

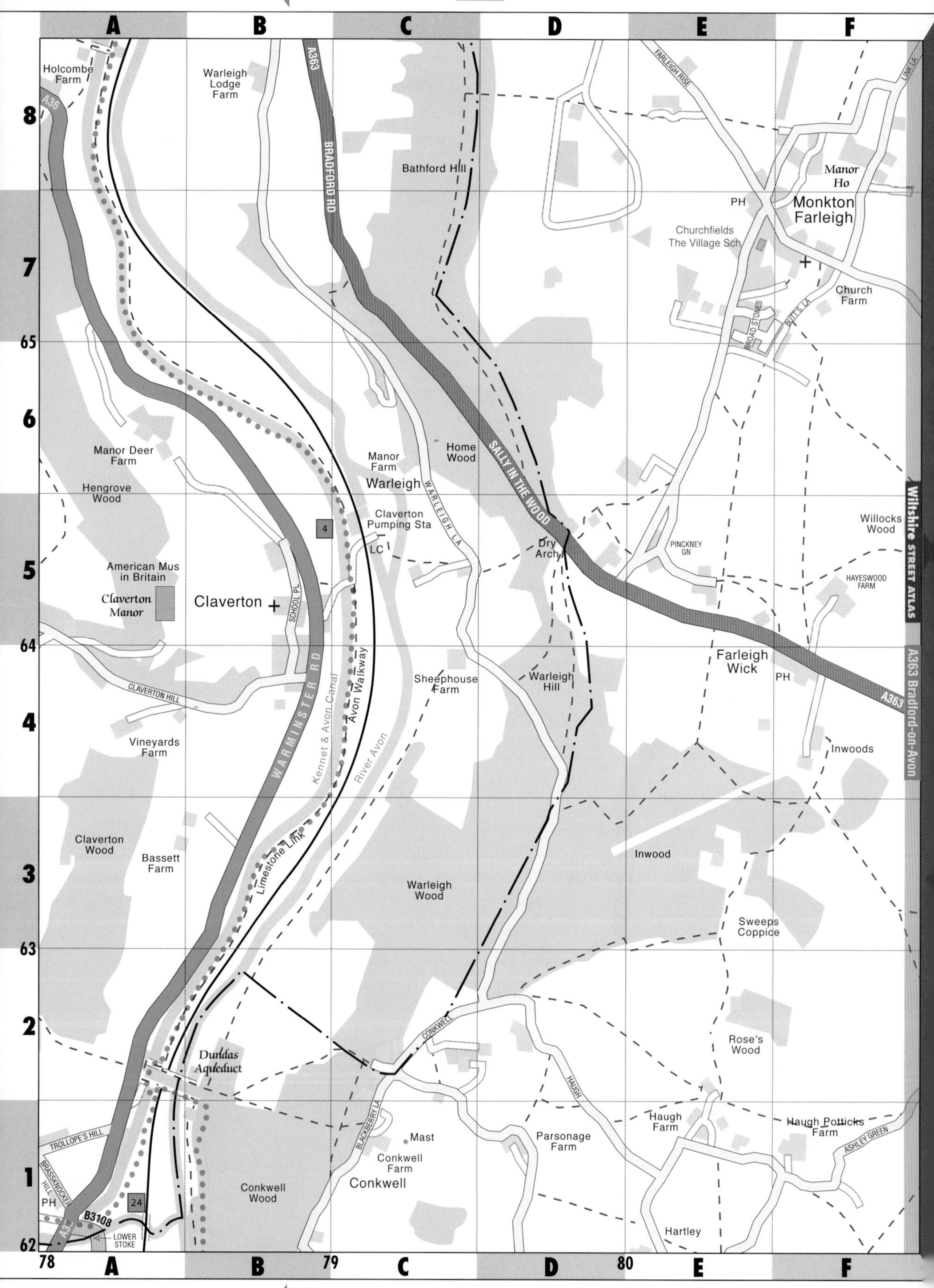
A B C D E F
8 7 65 6 5 64 4 3 63 2 1 62
78 79 80
Holcombe Farm
A36
Warleigh Lodge Farm
A363
BRADFORD RD
Bathford Hill
FARLEIGH RISE
LINK LA
Manor Ho
PH
Monkton Farleigh
Churchfields The Village Sch
Church Farm
BROAD STONES
BUTTS LA
Manor Deer Farm
Hengrove Wood
Manor Farm
Warleigh
Home Wood
SALLY IN THE WOOD
WARLEIGH LA
Claverton Pumping Sta
LC
4
Dry Arch
PINCKNEY GN
Willocks Wood
HAYESWOOD FARM
American Mus in Britain
Claverton Manor
Claverton
SCHOOL PL
CLAVERTON HILL
WARMINSTER RD
Kennet & Avon Canal
Avon Walkway
River Avon
Sheephouse Farm
Warleigh Hill
Farleigh Wick
PH
A363
Inwoods
Vineyards Farm
Claverton Wood
Bassett Farm
Limestone Link
Warleigh Wood
Inwood
Sweeps Coppice
Dundas Aqueduct
CONKWELL
HAUGH
Rose's Wood
TROLLOPE'S HILL
BRASSKNOCKER HILL
PH
A36
B3108
24
LOWER STOKE
Conkwell Wood
BLACKBERRY LA
Mast
Conkwell Farm
Conkwell
Parsonage Farm
Haugh Farm
Haugh Potticks Farm
ASHLEY GREEN
Hartley
Wiltshire STREET ATLAS
A363 Bradford-on-Avon

45
64

48

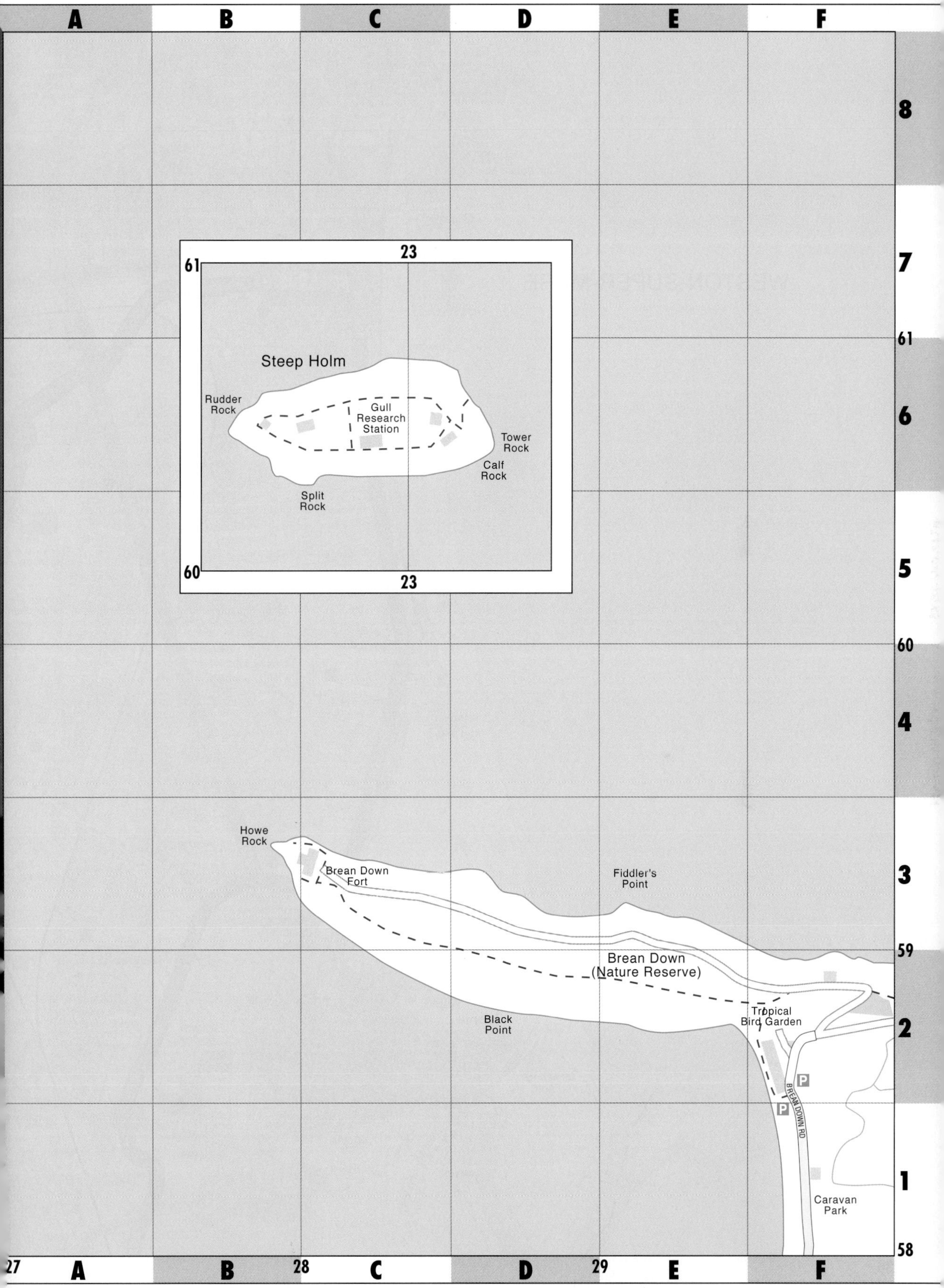

A
B
C
D
E
F
8
7
61
6
5
60
4
3
59
2
1
58
23
61
60
23
Steep Holm
Rudder Rock
Gull Research Station
Tower Rock
Calf Rock
Split Rock
Howe Rock
Brean Down Fort
Fiddler's Point
Brean Down (Nature Reserve)
Black Point
Tropical Bird Garden
P
BREAN DOWN RD
Caravan Park
27
28
29

65
48

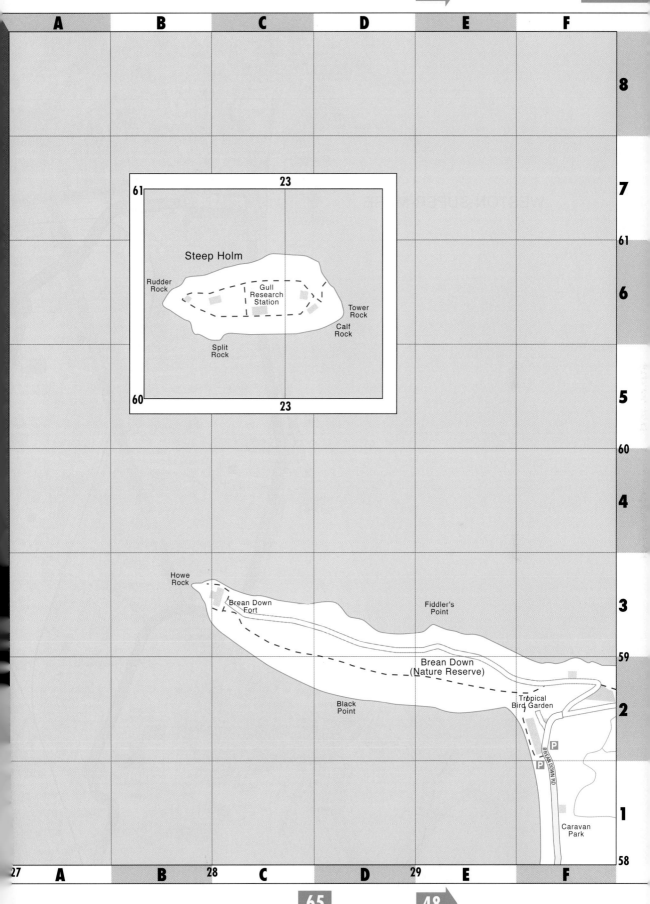

47

30

E7
1 ORCHARD PL
2 NORTH LA
3 CROSS ST
4 ALFRED CT
5 ALEXANDER MEWS
6 THE MART
7 FRANCIS FOX RD
8 STATION LODGE
9 HILDESHIEM CT
10 THE CENTRE
11 WALLISCOTE GROVE RD
12 TRAFALGAR CT
13 SWISS CT

E8
1 EDINBURGH PL
2 LANDEMANN CIRCUS
3 LONGTON GROVE RD
4 WORTHY PL
5 WORTHY LA
6 KING'S LA
7 PALMER ROW
8 JASMINE CT
9 PROSPECT PL
10 SAFFRON HO
11 HENRY BUTT HO
12 CHRIST CHURCH PATH S
13 HANS PRICE HO
14 MEADOW VILLAS
15 BURLINGTON ST
16 POPLAR PL
17 PAYNES HO
18 HANS PRICE CL

A B C D E F

8 7 61 6 5 60 4 3 59 2 1 58

WESTON-SUPER-MARE

Marine Lake

Knightstone

1 MADEIRA CT
2 UPPER CHURCH RD
3 GREENFIELD PL

PARK VILLAS 1
LOVERS' WLK 2
OLD POST OFFICE LA 3
CONNAUGHT PL 4
WESTON LODGE 5
KNIGHTSTONE HO 6
ST MARGARET'S TERR 7
Jill Dando Meml Gdn 8

Sovereign Sh Ctr

Grand Pier

SALISBURY TERR 1
WELLINGTON PL 2
RICHMOND ST 3
GLOUCESTER ST 4
UNION PL 5
OXFORD PL 6
UNION ST 7
DOLPHIN SQ 8
BIRKBECK CT 9
EDDINGTON CT 10

FERN LODGE 1
BEACH CT 2
CHANDOS CT 3

SeaQuarium

ETONHURST 4
CLIFFORD HO 5
ROYSTON LODGE 6

Model Yacht Pond

Weston Bay

Weston Miniature Rly

Clarence Park

CH

HEATHGATES 1
ROYAL CT 2
ROYAL SANDS 3

Coll

Mus

Liby

Sch

Superstore

Weston-Super-Mare

Corpus Christi RC Prim Sch

Recn Gd

1 ELLENBOROUGH CT
2 KNIGHTSTONE GN
3 ELLENBOROUGH CRES
4 PITMAN RD

OXFORD ST

LOCKING RD

MARINE PAR

BEACH RD

UPHILL RD N

DEVONSHIRE RD

DROVE RD

BRIDGWATER RD

1 RAYNESWOOD
2 LANSDOWN CT
3 BYRON CT
4 CHELWOOD

Cemy

Lancaster House Sch

5 JUBILEE CT
6 WESLEY CT

Longton Ind Est

SOMERSET MEWS

Hans Price Academy

Bournville Prim Sch

Prim Sch

Broadoak Mathematics & Computing Coll

Uphill Manor

Westhaven Sch

Uphill

Prim Sch

Weston General

Weston Coll Uni Campus

BURRINGTON CL 1
BROCKLEY CL 2

Brean Down Farm

Black Rock

Slimeridge Farm

Ferry (P)

River Axe

Marina

West Mendip Way

Windmill

HILLGROVE TERR

MANOR PK

UPHILL FARM CVN PK

30 A B 31 C D 32 E F

47

66

E5
1 SILVERCOMBE
2 WOODFORD CT
3 RALEIGH CT
4 KNIGHTSTONE PK
5 PARK CT
6 WINGARD CT
7 BERROW LODGE

F4
1 ST ANDREW'S PAR
2 BAILDON CT
3 MARLOWE HO
4 KEATS HO
5 ALEXANDER HO
6 TAVERNERS CL

F5
1 SANDRINGHAM RD
2 SANDRINGHAM CT
3 DOUGLAS CT

F7
1 ASHCOMBE CT
2 STANLEY RD
3 SIMONS MEWS
4 ASHCOMBE PL
5 WYVERN MEWS

D7
1 TEMPLARS CT
2 CLOVER CT
3 CHARLOCK CL
4 CAMPION CL

E8
1 MERLIN CL
2 KITE WLK
3 HARRIER PATH
4 THRUSH CL
5 LOMBARDY CL
6 GREENGAGE CL
7 MALLARD WLK

F8
1 SWEETGRASS RD
2 CASTLE VIEW
3 TRELISSICK GDNS
4 MONTACUTE CIR
5 THE INCLOSURES

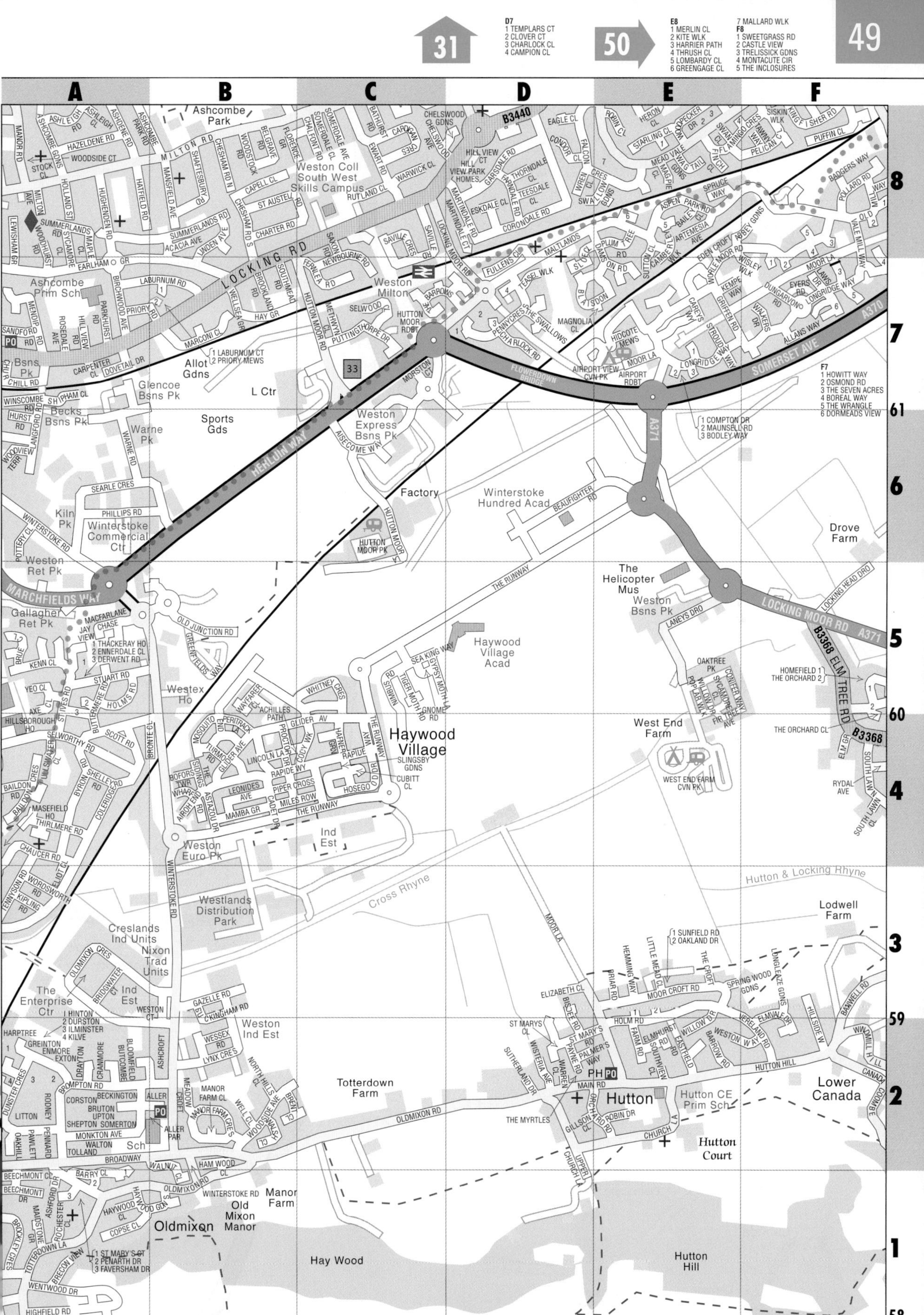

49
32

A
B
C
D
E
F
8
7
61
6
5
60
4
3
59
2
1
58
36
37
38
Liby
Superstore
Baytree Sch
Herons Moor
Acad
A370
SOMERSET AVE
WEST WICK
RDBT
MORGAN CL 1
HARVEST LA 2
SUMMER LA 3
CHURCHLAND WAY
YEW TREE DR
HAYWARD AVE
HIGHLANDS LA
CHICHESTER WAY
MERTON DR
OLD MILL WAY
BRANSBY WAY
SEFTON SQ
SHREWSBURY BOW
IVY LA
AUTUMN MEWS
MOOR LA
LONGRIDGE WAY
33
1 LANTHONY CL
2 WALTHAM END
3 HONEYSUCKLE PL
4 HIGHGROVE WLK
5 LYPSTONE CL
6 CARBERRY VIEW
7 POLESTAR WAY
8 SWEETGRASS RD
9 BOUNDARY RD
10 CHESTER CL
Westacres
Farm
WOLVERSHILL RD
KENT AVE
IRONS WAY
KENT AVE
BIRKBECK CHASE
BUCKLE PATH
DE SALIS PK
LAW GR
KENT AVE
TURNOCK GDNS
SCOT ELM DRIVE
GARDENER CL
Ivy
Cottage
Old Yeo Rhyne
Waywick
Farm
Waterloo
Farm
Cannaway's
Farm
ETON LA
Ivy House
Farm
IVY
HOUSE
COTTS
SUMMER LA
M5
BULLER RD
DEREK MEAD WAY
HARDING DR
BLEW CL
TANNER RD
Wolvershill
Manor
Wolvershill
Ind Units
Grumble Pill Rhyne
Locking Head
Cottages
LOCKING HEAD DRO
Locking Head
Farm
VARSITY WAY
WOOLVERS WAY
MERRYFIELD RD
OXFORD SQ
LARKHILL RD
CANBERRA CRES
ANSON RD
Parklands
Educate Together
Prim Sch
RUSSELL RD
LEEDHAM RD
PARKES RD
NICHOLSON RD
LOWER PARADE GROUND RD
MANSER RD
MOTTERSHEAD AVE
LEEDHAM RD
SCARF DR
ORMROD GR
CRANWELL RD
Locking
Parklands
CRUIKSHANK GR
McCRAE RD
POST OFFICE RD
CRANWELL RD
GARLAND AVE
CHAMBERLAIN RD
RUSSELL AVE
CHESHIRE AVE
HANNAH DR
BOWEN RD
FARNBOROUGH RD
MANNOCK GDNS
PARKES AVE
HECTOR CL 1
SPINNEY RD 2
PINETREE RD
TOWER HILL
BROADWAY
ADASTRAL RD
MENDIP RD
ORCHARD RD
TRENCHARD RD
PORTAL RD
FLOWERDOWN RD
WOLVERSHILL RD
Woolvers
Hill
Pool
Farm
Woolvers Hill
Batch
West Moor Rhyne
SILVER MOOR LA
Laurel
Farm
Court Farm
Country
Park
Park
Farm
SUMMER LA
Cave
View
SUMMER LANE
PARK HOMES
GROVE RD
NEW RD
IVY WLK
CENTRE DR
ASH RD
ELM CL
PARK END
SUMMER LANE
CVN PK
HILLMER RISE
Locking Farm
Ind Est
A371
LOCKING MOOR RD
HOMEFIELD CL
Homefield
Ind Est
THE ORCHARD
BEECHWOOD AVE
PLUMLEY CRES
PH
BARTLETTS WAY
LEAFY WAY
B3368
ELM TREE RD
MANOR CT
MEADOW DR
RYDAL AVE
BYRON RD
GRENVILLE AVE
SOUTH LAWN RD
LYCHGATE PK
OLD BANWELL RD
FAIRACRE CL
MENDIP RISE
LIME CL
BIRCH CL
B3368
Locking
Prim Sch
Locking
THE GREEN
Church
Farm
THE BURY
Perries
KNIGHTCOTT RD
A371
KNIGHTCOTT
KNIGHTCOTT GDNS
CHESTERFIELD CL
WILLIAM DAW CL
WATTS CL
Knightcott
Ind Est
Knightcott
WELL LA
HIGH ST
BANWELL RD
Elborough
ELBOROUGH GDNS
BEAFORT CL
MEADOW WLK
CEDERN AVE
BLUE WATER DR
Wingfield
House
Hillend
Mast
Manor
Farm
BANWELL CAVES
Mon
Banwell
Hill
Windmill
Farm
WINDMILL HILL
Benthills
Wood
Whitley
Head
Elborough
Hill
BRIDEWELL LA
Upper
Canada
CANADA COOMBE
CANADA COOMBE
Christon
Hill
Christon
Plantation
Yarberry
BANWELL RD

49
68

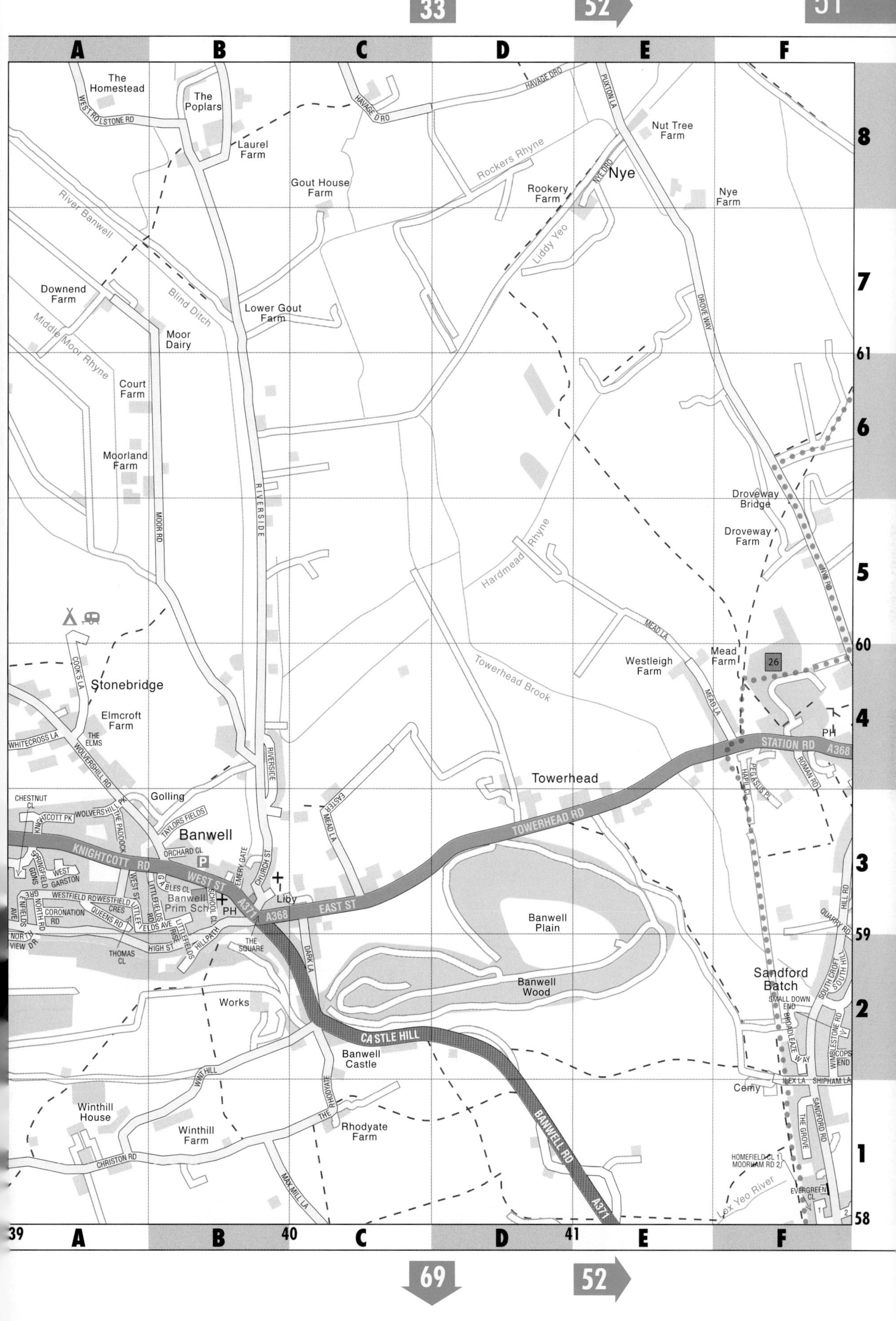
33
52
A
B
C
D
E
F
8
7
61
6
5
60
4
3
59
2
1
58
39
40
41
The Homestead
WEST RD
LSTONE RD
The Poplars
Laurel Farm
HAVAGE DRO
HAVAGE DRO
PUXTON LA
Nut Tree Farm
Rockers Rhyne
NYE DRO
Nye
Rookery Farm
Nye Farm
Gout House Farm
River Banwell
Liddy Yeo
Downend Farm
Blind Ditch
Lower Gout Farm
DROVE WAY
Middle Moor Rhyne
Moor Dairy
Court Farm
Moorland Farm
RIVERSIDE
MOOR RD
Droveway Bridge
Droveway Farm
Hardmead Rhyne
NYE RD
MEAD LA
COOK'S LA
Stonebridge
Towerhead Brook
Westleigh Farm
Mead Farm
26
Elmcroft Farm
WHITECROSS LA
THE ELMS
WOLVERSHILL RD
RIVERSIDE
MEAD LA
STATION RD
A368
PH
Towerhead
HAPIL CL
PEGASUS PL
ROMAN RD
CHESTNUT CL
KNIGHTCOTT PK
WOLVERS HILL PK
THE PADDOCK
Golling
TAYLORS FIELDS
EASTER MEAD LA
TOWERHEAD RD
Banwell
ORCHARD CL
KNIGHTCOTT RD
WEST ST
SPRINGFIELD GDNS
WEST GARSTON
EMERY GATE
CHURCH ST
WEST ST
GABLES CL
Banwell Prim Sch
SCHOOL CL
PH
A371
Liby
WESTFIELD RD
WESTFIELD CRES
QUEENS RD
CORONATION RD
NORTH RD
A368
EAST ST
HILL RD
QUARRY RD
Banwell Plain
LITTLEFIELDS
FIELDS AVE
LITTLEFIELDS RISE
HILLPATH
THE SQUARE
THOMAS CL
HIGH ST
NORTH VIEW DR
DARK LA
Banwell Wood
Sandford Batch
SMALL DOWN END
SOUTHCROFT
SOUTH HILL
Works
WIMBLESTONE RD
BROADLEAZE WAY
COPS END
CASTLE HILL
Banwell Castle
ILEX LA
SHIPHAM LA
Cemy
WINT HILL
THE RHODYATE
Winthill House
Winthill Farm
Rhodyate Farm
BANWELL RD
SANDFORD RD
THE GROVE
CHRISTON RD
HOMEFIELD CL
MOORHAM RD
MAX MILL LA
A371
Lox Yeo River
EVERGREEN CL
69
52

51 34

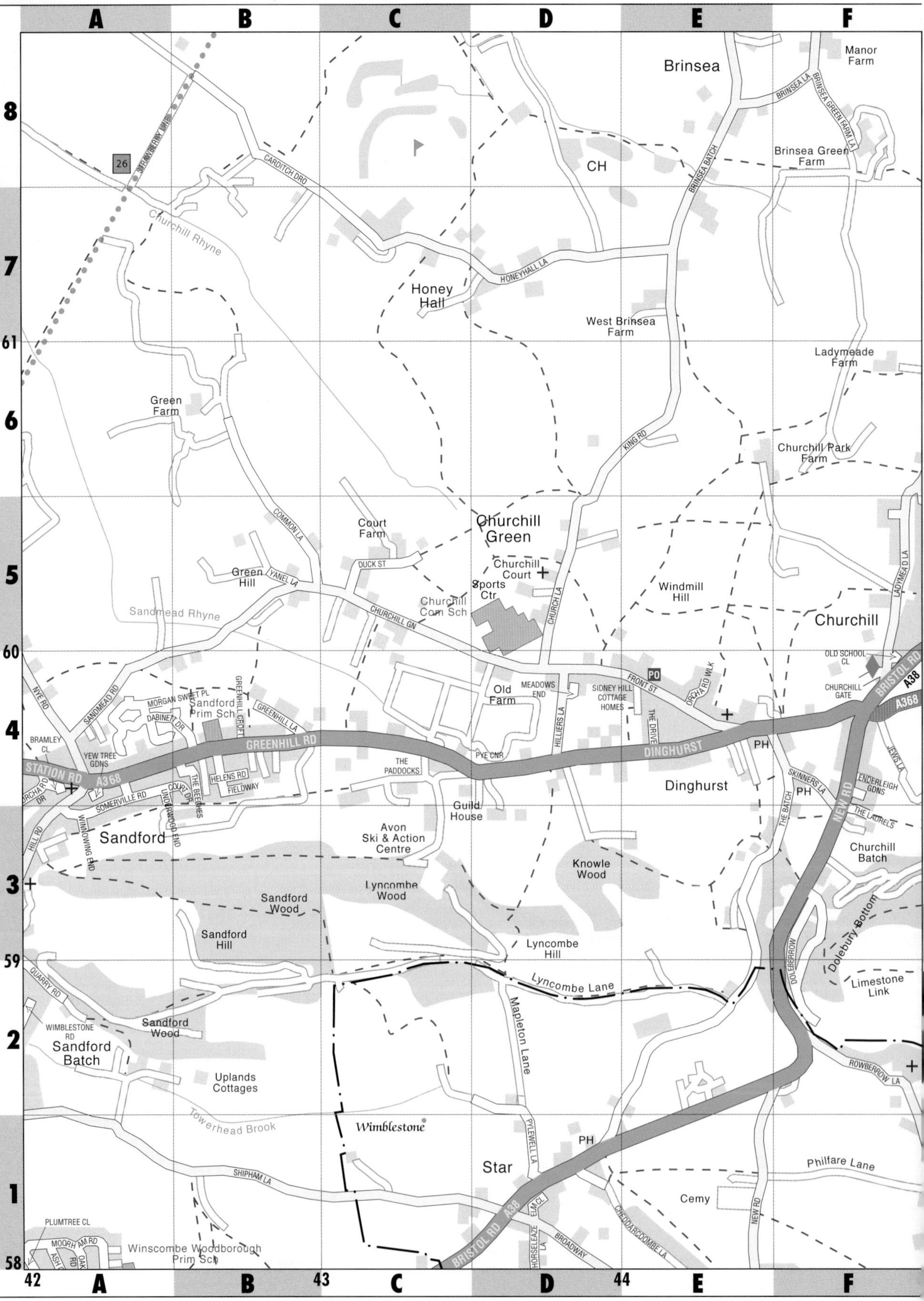

A B C D E F

8 7 61 6 5 60 4 3 59 2 58

Brinsea
Manor Farm
BRINSEA LA
BRINSEA GREEN FARM LA
Brinsea Green Farm
BRINSEA BATCH
CH
26
STRAWBERRY LINE
CARDITCH DRO
Churchill Rhyne
HONEYHALL LA
Honey Hall
West Brinsea Farm
Ladymeade Farm
Green Farm
KING RD
Churchill Park Farm
COMMON LA
Court Farm
Churchill Green
DUCK ST
Churchill Court
Green Hill
YANEL LA
Sports Ctr
Windmill Hill
Churchill Com Sch
CHURCH LA
Churchill
LADYMEAD LA
Sandmead Rhyne
CHURCHILL GN
OLD SCHOOL CL
CHURCHILL GATE
BRISTOL RD
A38
A368
PO
NYE RD
SANDMEAD RD
MORGAN SWEET PL
Sandford Prim Sch
GREENHILL CROFT
GREENHILL LA
DABINETT DR
Old Farm
MEADOWS END
SIDNEY HILL COTTAGE HOMES
FRONT ST
ORCHARD WLK
THE DRIVE
HILLIERS LA
BRAMLEY CL
YEW TREE GDNS
GREENHILL RD
DINGHURST
PH
JEWS LA
STATION RD
A368
ORCHARD DR
SOMERVILLE RD
COURT DR
THE BEECHES
HELENS RD
FIELDWAY
UNDERWOOD END
THE PADDOCKS
PYE CNR
Dinghurst
SKINNERS LA
PH
ENDERLEIGH GDNS
NEW RD
THE BATCH
THE LAURELS
HILL RD
WINNOWING END
Sandford
Guild House
Avon Ski & Action Centre
Churchill Batch
Knowle Wood
Lyncombe Wood
Sandford Wood
Sandford Hill
Dolebury Bottom
Lyncombe Hill
QUARRY RD
Lyncombe Lane
Mapleton Lane
DOLEBERROW
Limestone Link
WIMBLESTONE RD
Sandford Batch
Sandford Wood
ROWBERROW LA
Uplands Cottages
Towerhead Brook
Wimblestone
PYLEWELL LA
PH
Star
Philfare Lane
SHIPHAM LA
Cemy
NEW RD
PLUMTREE CL
MOORHAM RD
ASH
OAK
RD
Winscombe Woodborough Prim Sch
BRISTOL RD A38
ELM CL
HORSELEAZE LA
BROADWAY
CHEDDARCOOMBE LA

42 A B 43 C D 44 E F

51 70

35
54

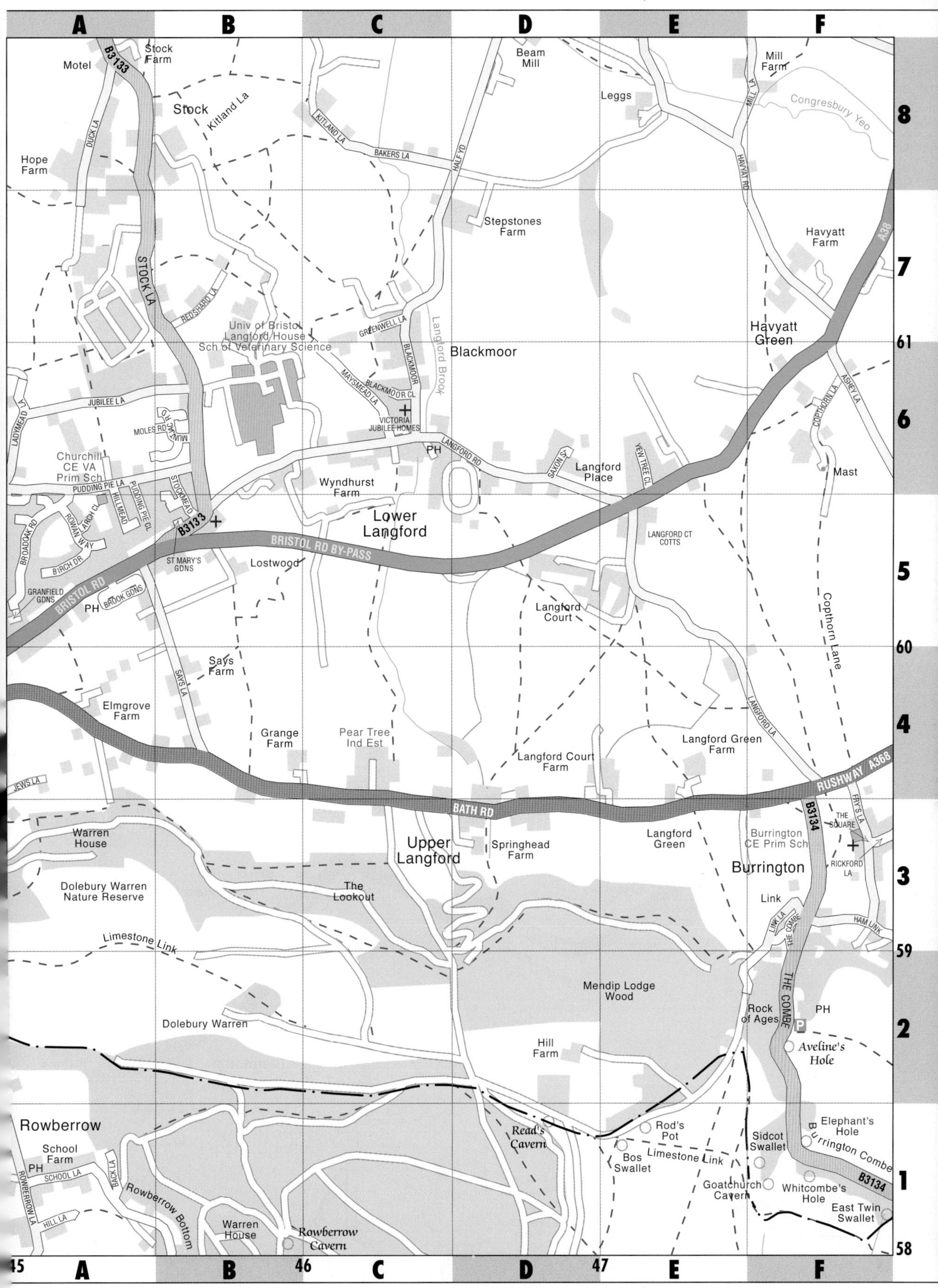
A
B
C
D
E
F
Motel
Stock Farm
B3133
Stock
Kitland La
Beam Mill
Leggs
Mill Farm
Congresbury Yeo
Hope Farm
DUCK LA
KITLAND LA
BAKERS LA
HALF YD
MILL LA
HAVYATT RD
Stepstones Farm
Havyatt Farm
A38
STOCK LA
REDSHARD LA
Univ of Bristol Langford House Sch of Veterinary Science
GREENWELL LA
Langford Brook
Blackmoor
Havyatt Green
BLACKMOOR
MAYSMEAD LA
BLACKMOOR CL
VICTORIA JUBILEE HOMES
JUBILEE LA
LADYMEAD LA
MOLES RD
PH
LANGFORD RD
ASHEY LA
COPTHORN LA
Churchill CE VA Prim Sch
PUDDING PIE LA
SAXON ST
Langford Place
YEW TREE CL
Mast
Wyndhurst Farm
STOCKMEAD
HILLMEAD
PUDDING PIE CL
Lower Langford
BROADOAK RD
ROWAN WAY
LARCH CL
BIRCH DR
ST MARY'S GDNS
BRISTOL RD BY-PASS
LANGFORD CT COTTS
Lostwood
GRANFIELD GDNS
BRISTOL RD
BROOK GDNS
Langford Court
Copthorn Lane
Says Farm
SAYS LA
Elmgrove Farm
LANGFORD LA
Grange Farm
Pear Tree Ind Est
Langford Green Farm
Langford Court Farm
JEWS LA
RUSHWAY A368
BATH RD
B3134
THE SQUARE
FRYS LA
Warren House
Upper Langford
Springhead Farm
Langford Green
Burrington CE Prim Sch
Burrington
RICKFORD LA
Dolebury Warren Nature Reserve
The Lookout
Link
LINK LA
THE COMBE
HAM LINK
Limestone Link
Mendip Lodge Wood
Rock of Ages
Dolebury Warren
Aveline's Hole
Hill Farm
Rowberrow
Read's Cavern
Rod's Pot
Elephant's Hole
Sidcot Swallet
Burrington Combe
School Farm
Bos Swallet
Limestone Link
Goatchurch Cavern
Whitcombe's Hole
ROWBERROW LA
SCHOOL LA
BACK LA
Rowberrow Bottom
HILL LA
East Twin Swallet
Warren House
Rowberrow Cavern
8
7
61
6
5
60
4
3
59
2
1
58
45
46
47

71
54

53
36

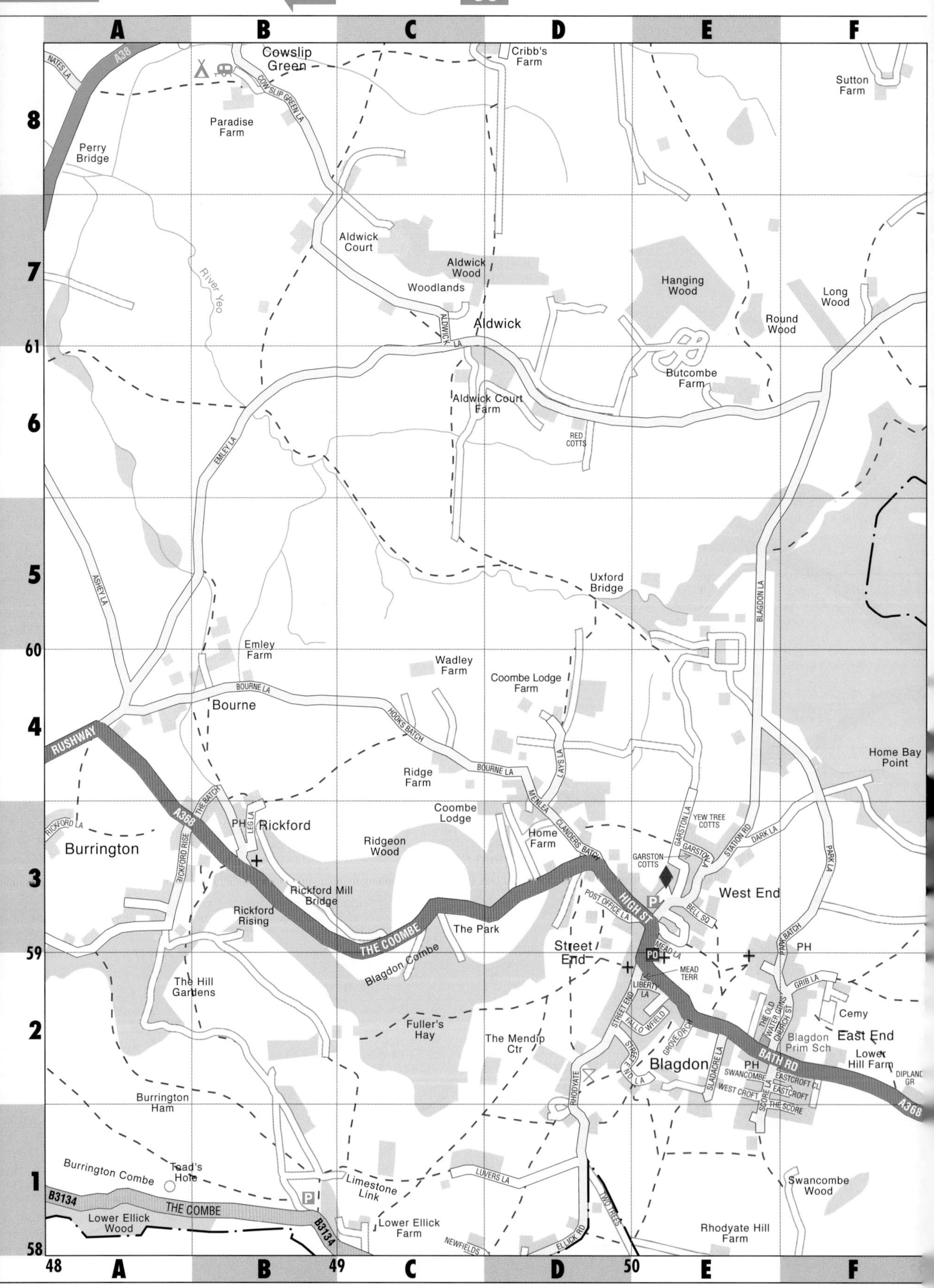
A
B
C
D
E
F
Cowslip Green
Cribb's Farm
Sutton Farm
Paradise Farm
Perry Bridge
Aldwick Court
Aldwick Wood
Woodlands
Aldwick
Hanging Wood
Long Wood
Round Wood
Butcombe Farm
Aldwick Court Farm
RED COTTS
River Yeo
Uxford Bridge
Emley Farm
Wadley Farm
Coombe Lodge Farm
Bourne
RUSHWAY
Ridge Farm
Coombe Lodge
Home Farm
Home Bay Point
Rickford
Burrington
Ridgeon Wood
Rickford Mill Bridge
Rickford Rising
GARSTON COTTS
YEW TREE COTTS
West End
The Park
THE COOMBE
Street End
Blagdon Combe
The Hill Gardens
Fuller's Hay
The Mendip Ctr
Blagdon
Blagdon Prim Sch
East End
Lower Hill Farm
Cemy
Burrington Ham
Burrington Combe
Toad's Hole
Limestone Link
Lower Ellick Wood
Lower Ellick Farm
Swancombe Wood
Rhodyate Hill Farm
A38
A368
B3134
HIGH ST
BATH RD
BOURNE LA
HOOKS BATCH
MEMLEA
CLANDERS BATCH
LAYS LA
GARSTON LA
STATION RD
DARK LA
PARK LA
BLAGDON LA
EMLEY LA
ASHEY LA
ALDWICK LA
COWSLIP GREEN LA
NATES LA
LEG LA
THE BATCH
RICKFORD RISE
RICKFORD LA
POST OFFICE LA
BELL SQ
MEAD LA
MEAD TERR
LIBERTY LA
STREET END
FALLOWFIELD
GROVE ORCH
SLADACRE LA
SWANCOMBE
WEST CROFT
EASTCROFT
EASTCROFT CL
THE SCORE
SCORE LA
CHURCH ST
THE OLD WATER GDNS
GRIB LA
PARK BATCH
RHODYATE
LUVERS LA
NEWFIELDS
ELLICK RD
TWO TREES
DIPLAND GR
PH
PO
P
8
7
61
6
5
60
4
3
59
2
1
58
48
49
50

53
72

37
56

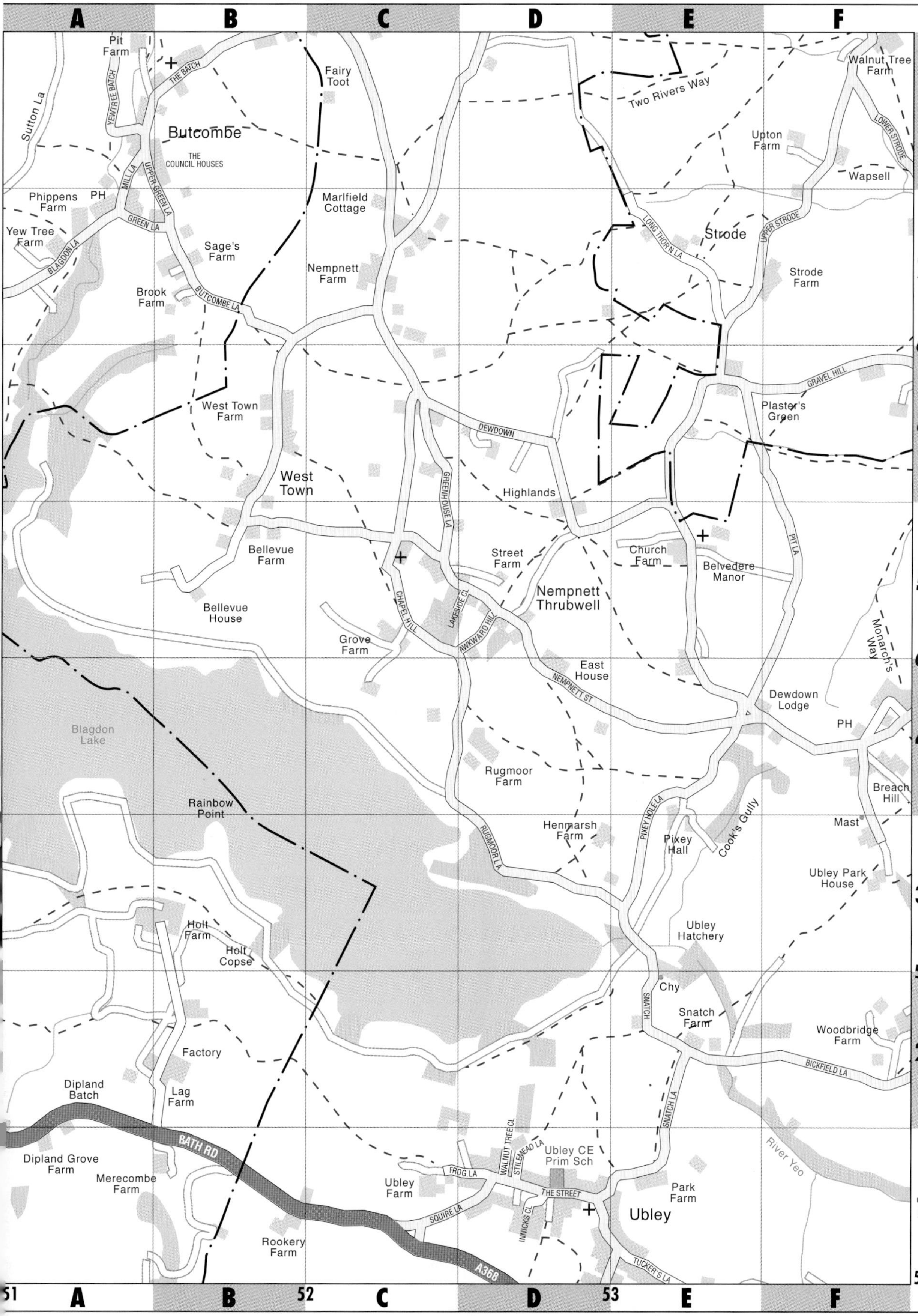

A B C D E F
8 7 61 6 5 60 4 3 59 2 1 58
51 52 53
Pit Farm
The Batch
Fairy Toot
Walnut Tree Farm
Two Rivers Way
Sutton La
Yewtree Batch
Butcombe
The Council Houses
Upton Farm
Lower Strode
Wapsell
Phippens Farm
PH
Mill La
Upper Green La
Marlfield Cottage
Green La
Yew Tree Farm
Blagdon La
Sage's Farm
Long Thorn La
Strode
Upper Strode
Nempnett Farm
Strode Farm
Brook Farm
Butcombe La
Gravel Hill
West Town Farm
Plaster's Green
Dewdown
West Town
Greenhouse La
Highlands
Bellevue Farm
Street Farm
Church Farm
Belvedere Manor
Pit La
Nempnett Thrubwell
Bellevue House
Chapel Hill
Lakeside Cl
Awkward Hill
Grove Farm
Monarch's Way
East House
Nempnett St
Dewdown Lodge
Blagdon Lake
PH
Rugmoor Farm
Breach Hill
Rainbow Point
Henmarsh Farm
Pixey Hole La
Pixey Hall
Cook's Gully
Mast
Rugmoor La
Ubley Park House
Holt Farm
Ubley Hatchery
Holt Copse
Chy
Snatch
Snatch Farm
Woodbridge Farm
Factory
Bickfield La
Dipland Batch
Lag Farm
Snatch La
Bath Rd
Walnut Tree Cl
Stilemead La
Ubley CE Prim Sch
River Yeo
Dipland Grove Farm
Merecombe Farm
Frog La
Ubley Farm
The Street
Park Farm
Squire La
Innicks Cl
Ubley
Rookery Farm
A368
Tucker's La

55
38

A
B
C
D
E
F
8
7
61
6
5
60
4
3
59
2
1
58
54
55
56
Church Farm
The Knoll
Works
Lower Strode
Chew Stoke CE Prim Sch
Chew Stoke
Lower Strode Farm
Manor Farm
Wallis Farm
Stoke Hill House
Fairseat Workshops
Woodford Hill
Perry House Farm
Rose Cottage
Woodford Lodge
Stoke Villice
Monarch's Way
Obelisk
Rookery Farm
Manor Farm
Breach Hill Common
Breach Hill
Nunnery Copse
Herons Green Farm
Herons Green
Herons Green Bay
Chew Valley Lake
Moreton Point
Moat Farm
Bickfield Farm
Villice La
Summerlea Farm
Oldbarn La
River Yeo
Scornfield La
B3114
BRISTOL RD
STOKE HILL
SCHOOL LA
SHOREDITCH
GRAVEL HILL
LOWER STRODE
WHITLING ST
BREACH HILL LA
BREACH HILL COMM
CAPLE LA
KINGSHILL LA
HERON'S GREEN LA
MORETON LA
STRATFORD LA
BICKFIELD LA
WALLY COURT RD
WALLEY LA
CHURCH LA
MILL LA
THE STREET
WEBBS MEAD
QUARRY HAY
PILGRIMS WAY
THE CEDARS
SCOT LA
PH
BILBIE RD
BILBIE CL
BUSHY THORN RD
CHAPEL
HOME ORCH
NEWCLOSE LA
A368

55
74

39
58

A
B
C
D
E
F
8
7
61
6
5
60
4
3
59
2
1
58
57
58
59
River Chew
Woodbarn Farm
DENNY LA
Pitt's La
Pitt's Farm
Moorledge Farm
MOORLEDGE LA
BROMLEY RD
Curls Farm
Curls Wood
3
Twr
Visitor Ctr
P
Chew Valley Lake Nature Trails
Knowle Hill
PH
New Town
MOORLEDGE LA
WALLEY LA
KNOWLE HILL
Knowle Hill Farm
Works
P
Double House Farm
Gold's Cross
A368
Knighton Sutton Farm
Hollow Brook
HOLLOWBROOK LA
HENGASSON LA
Sutton Court
Denny Island
Mill
BONHILL LA
Stowey Bottom
Bonhill House
BONHILL RD
STOWEY BOTTOM
HAM LA
STOWEY CROSS RDS
Stowey Mead
PO
THE STREET
STITCHINGS SHORD LA
YEATMAN CL
LOVELLS MILL
SUMMER LEAZE
Manor Farm
THE STREET
Stowey
Bishop Sutton Prim Sch
CAPPARDS RD
PH
SUTTON HILL RD
Sutton Farm
NORTHWICK GDNS
SUTTON PK
YEW TREE CL
RUSHGROVE GDNS
WICK RD
PARKFIELD
HIGH MEAD GDNS
CHURCH LA
Vine House
Stowey House Farm
ORCHARD CL
HILLSIDE GDNS
SUNNYMEAD LA
PH
Wick Farm
Bishop Sutton
Castle Wood
WOODCROFT
Wick Green Copse
Broad Wood
Hillside Farm
Sutton Wick
Burledge Hill
Barelegs Brake
Stowey Quarry
Weeks Green Farm
New Manor Farm
Burledge Common
Hill View House
Hart's Farm Cottage
BURLEDGE COMM
BURLEDGE LA
White Cross
North Widcombe
HINTON BLEWETT RD
Sparrow Grove
Curtis' Barn
P
Herriott's Bridge

75
58

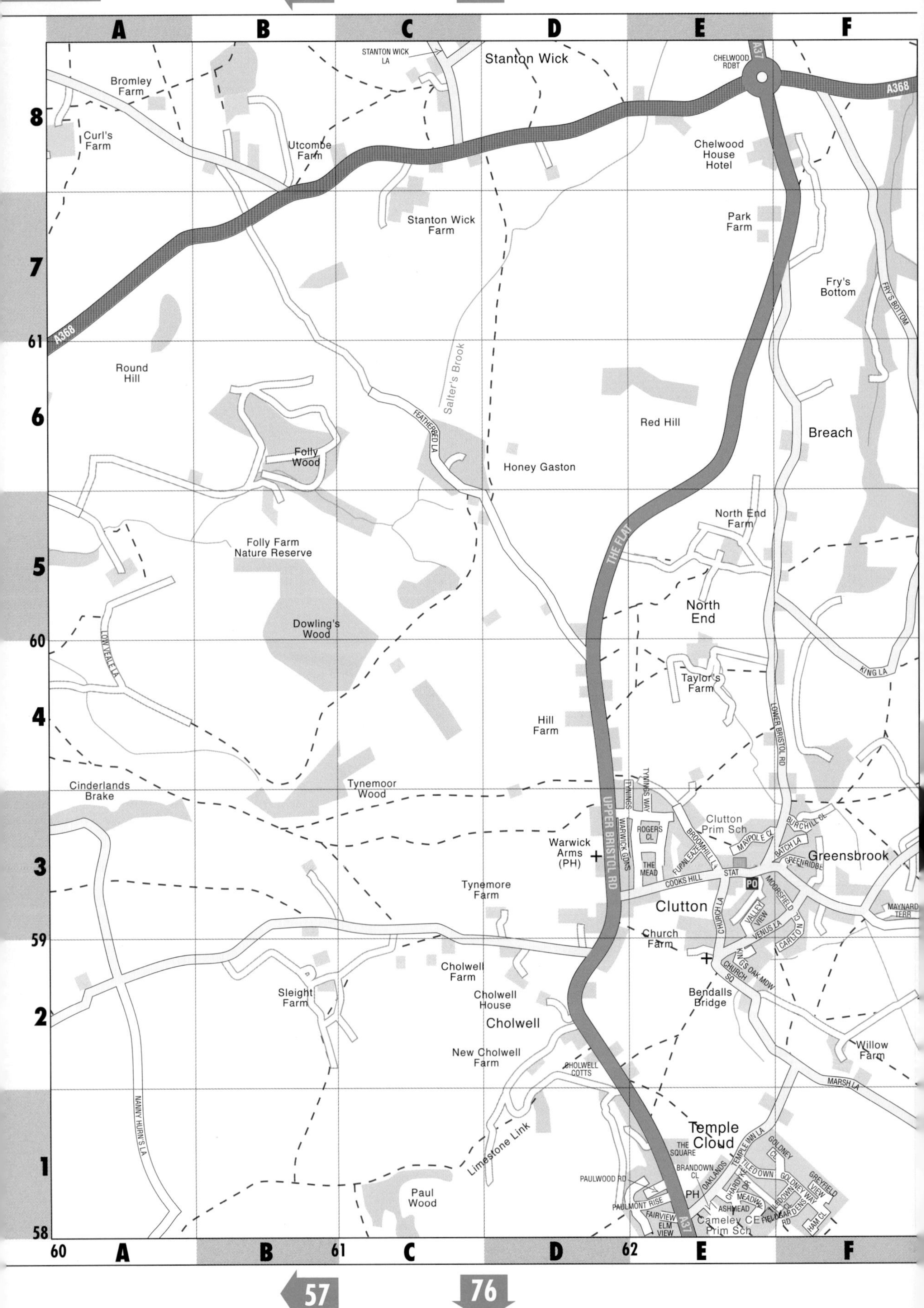
57
40
Stanton Wick
Bromley Farm
Curl's Farm
Utcombe Farm
Stanton Wick Farm
Chelwood House Hotel
Park Farm
Fry's Bottom
A368
A37
Round Hill
Salter's Brook
Red Hill
Breach
Folly Wood
Honey Gaston
North End Farm
Folly Farm Nature Reserve
North End
Dowling's Wood
Taylor's Farm
Hill Farm
Cinderlands Brake
Tynemoor Wood
Clutton Prim Sch
Greensbrook
Warwick Arms (PH)
Tynemore Farm
Clutton
Church Farm
Cholwell Farm
Sleight Farm
Cholwell House
Bendalls Bridge
Cholwell
New Cholwell Farm
Willow Farm
Temple Cloud
Limestone Link
Paul Wood
Cameley CE Prim Sch
THE FLAT
UPPER BRISTOL RD
LOWER BRISTOL RD
FEATHERBED LA
LOW VEALE LA
NANNY HURN'S LA
KING LA
MARSH LA
COOKS HILL
CHURCH LA
76

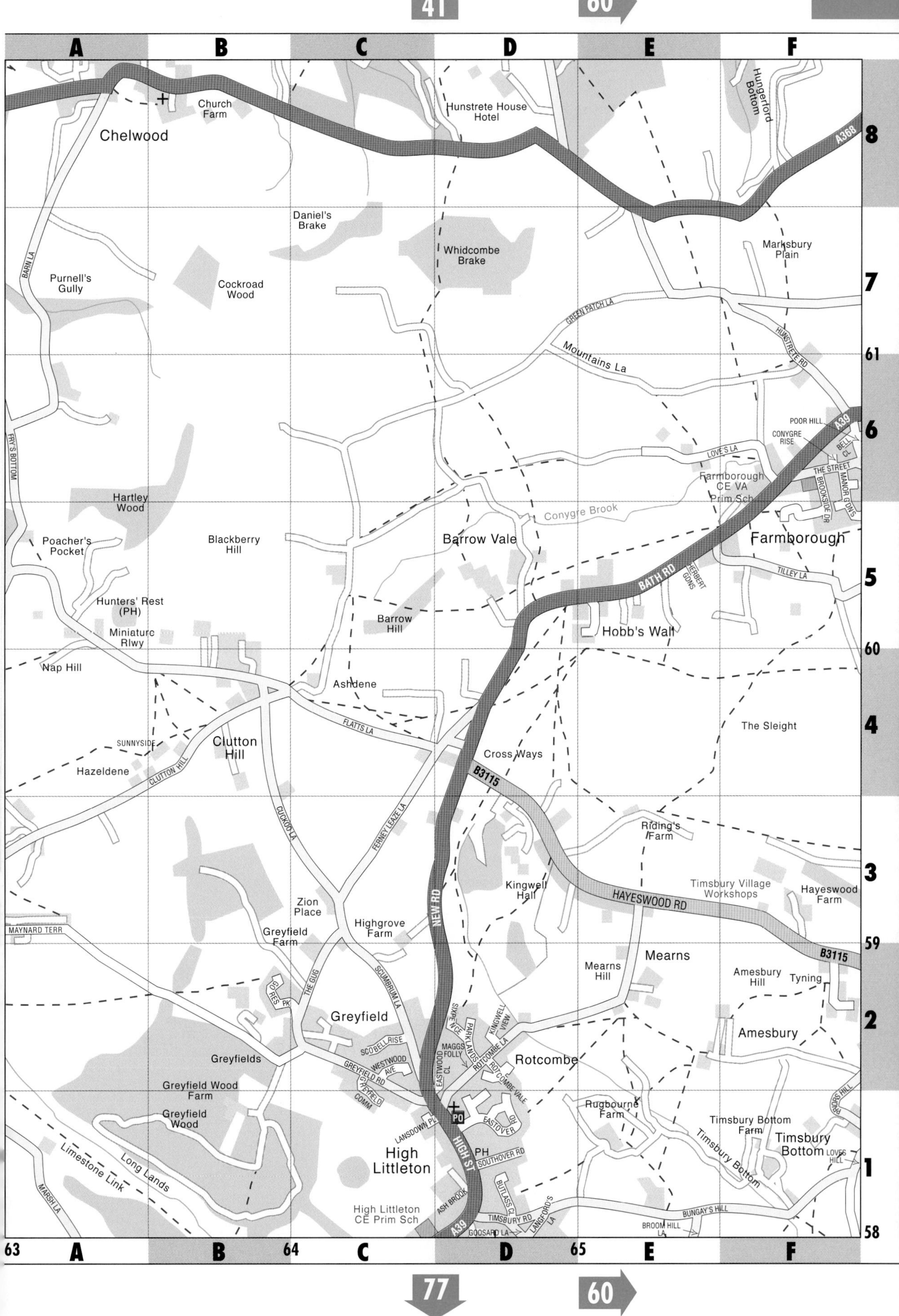
41
60
Church Farm
Chelwood
Hunstrete House Hotel
Hungerford Bottom
A368
Daniel's Brake
Whidcombe Brake
Marksbury Plain
BARN LA
Purnell's Gully
Cockroad Wood
GREEN PATCH LA
Mountains La
HUNSTRETE RD
FRY'S BOTTOM
POOR HILL
CONYGRE RISE
BELL CL
A39
LOVE'S LA
THE STREET
Farmborough CE VA Prim Sch
BROOKSIDE DR
MANOR GDNS
Hartley Wood
Conygre Brook
Poacher's Pocket
Blackberry Hill
Barrow Vale
Farmborough
BATH RD
HERBERT GDNS
TILLEY LA
Hunters' Rest (PH)
Barrow Hill
Miniature Rlwy
Hobb's Wall
Nap Hill
Ashdene
The Sleight
FLATTS LA
SUNNYSIDE
Clutton Hill
Cross Ways
Hazeldene
CLUTTON HILL
B3115
CUCKOO LA
FERNEY LEAZE LA
Riding's Farm
Kingwell Hall
Timsbury Village Workshops
Hayeswood Farm
HAYESWOOD RD
Zion Place
NEW RD
MAYNARD TERR
Greyfield Farm
Highgrove Farm
B3115
Mearns Hill
Mearns
Amesbury Hill
Tyning
GORES PK
THE GUG
SCUMBRUM LA
SIXPENCE
PARKLANDS
KINGWELL VIEW
Greyfield
Amesbury
SCOBELL RISE
MAGGS FOLLY
ROTCOMBE LA
Greyfields
WESTWOOD AVE
Rotcombe
GREYFIELD RD
EASTWOOD CL
ROTCOMBE VALE
GREYFIELD COMM
Greyfield Wood Farm
Rugbourne Farm
Timsbury Bottom Farm
PROPS HILL
Greyfield Wood
PO
EASTOVER RD
LANSDOWN PL
Timsbury Bottom
Timsbury Bottom
Limestone Link
Long Lands
High Littleton
HIGH ST
PH
SOUTHOVER RD
LOVES HILL
MARSH LA
ASH BROOK
BUTLASS CL
LANGFORD'S LA
BUNGAY'S HILL
High Littleton CE Prim Sch
TIMSBURY RD
BROOM HILL LA
GOOSARD LA
A B C D E F
1 2 3 4 5 6 7 8
58 59 60 61
63 64 65
77
60

59 42

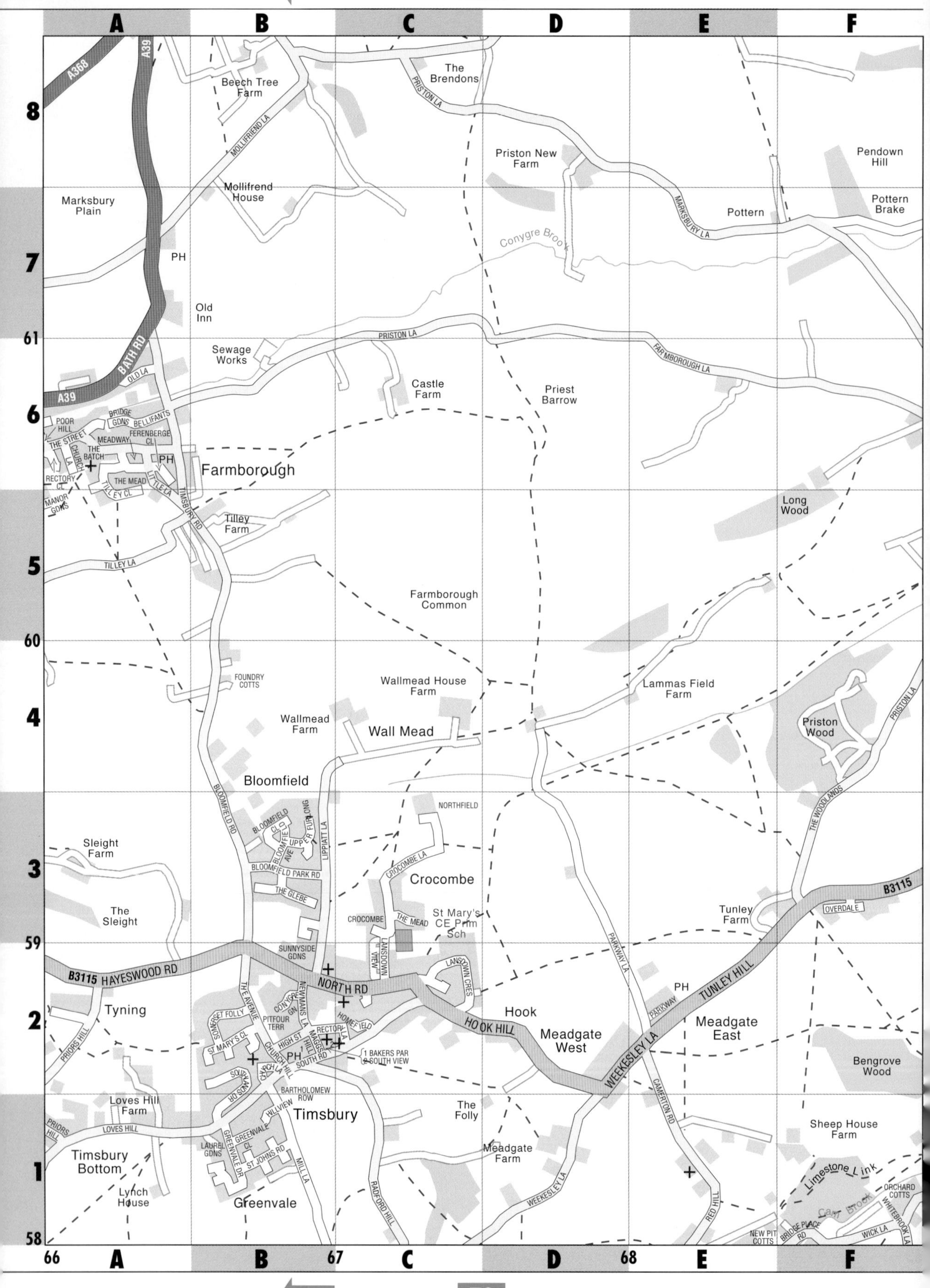
A B C D E F
8
7
61
6
5
60
4
3
59
2
1
58
66 67 68
A368
A39
Beech Tree Farm
The Brendons
PRISTON LA
MOLLIFRIEND LA
Priston New Farm
Pendown Hill
Marksbury Plain
Mollifrend House
MARKSBURY LA
Pottern
Pottern Brake
Conygre Brook
PH
Old Inn
Sewage Works
PRISTON LA
FARMBOROUGH LA
BATH RD
OLD LA
A39
Castle Farm
Priest Barrow
POOR HILL
BRIDGE GDNS
BELLIFANTS
THE STREET
MEADWAY
FERENBERGE CL
CHURCH LA
THE BATCH
PH
Farmborough
RECTORY CL
THE MEAD
LITTLE LA
TILLEY CL
MANOR GDNS
TIMSBURY RD
Tilley Farm
Long Wood
TILLEY LA
Farmborough Common
FOUNDRY COTTS
Wallmead House Farm
Lammas Field Farm
Wallmead Farm
Wall Mead
Priston Wood
PRISTON LA
Bloomfield
NORTHFIELD
THE WOODLANDS
BLOOMFIELD RD
BLOOMFIELD CL
BLOOMFIELD AVE
UPPER FURLONG
LIPPIATT LA
Sleight Farm
CROCOMBE LA
Crocombe
BLOOMFIELD PARK RD
THE GLEBE
B3115
The Sleight
CROCOMBE
THE MEAD
St Mary's CE Prim Sch
Tunley Farm
OVERDALE
SUNNYSIDE GDNS
LANSDOWN VIEW
LANSDOWN CRES
PARKWAY LA
B3115 HAYESWOOD RD
NORTH RD
PH
TUNLEY HILL
Tyning
THE AVENUE
SOMERSET FOLLY
CONYGRE GN
NEWMANS LA
HOMEFIELD
Hook
PARKWAY
PRIORS HILL
PITFOUR TERR
HOOK HILL
Meadgate West
Meadgate East
ST MARY'S CL
HIGH ST
MAGGS HILL
RECTORY LA
WEEKESLEY LA
CHURCH HILL
CHURCH LA
PH
SOUTH RD
1 BAKERS PAR
2 SOUTH VIEW
Bengrove Wood
SOUTH RD
BARTHOLOMEW ROW
Loves Hill Farm
HILLVIEW
Timsbury
The Folly
CAMERTON RD
PRIORS HILL
LOVES HILL
GREENVALE CL
GREENVALE DR
Sheep House Farm
LAUREL GDNS
ST JOHNS RD
MILL LA
Meadgate Farm
Timsbury Bottom
Limestone Link
Lynch House
RADFORD HILL
WEEKESLEY LA
RED HILL
ORCHARD COTTS
Cam Brook
Greenvale
NEW PIT COTTS
BRIDGE PLACE RD
WICK LA
WHITEBROOK LA

59 78

43
62

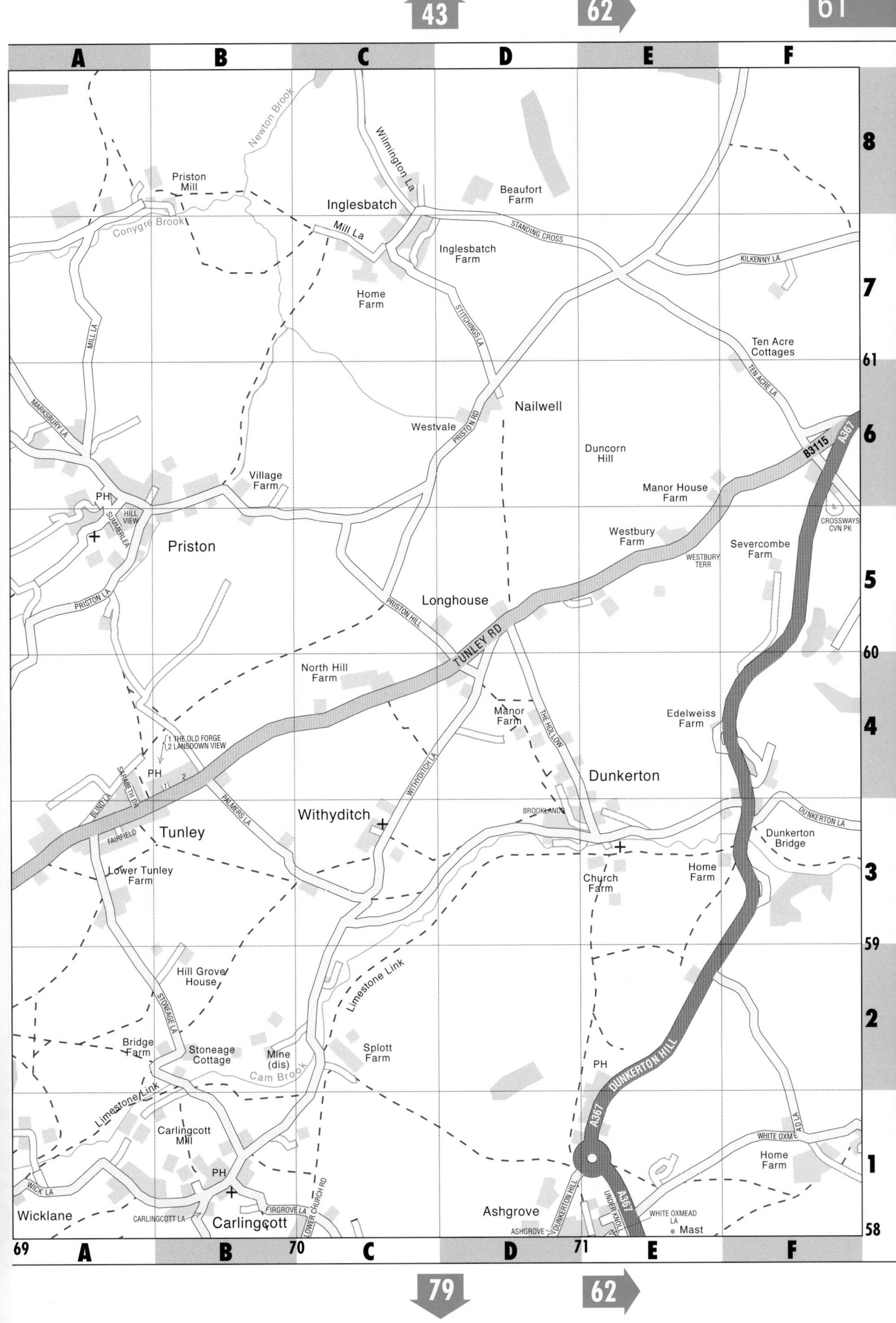
A B C D E F
8 7 61 6 5 60 4 3 59 2 1 58
69 70 71
Newton Brook
Priston Mill
Conygre Brook
Wilmington La
Inglesbatch
Mill La
Beaufort Farm
Standing Cross
Inglesbatch Farm
Kilkenny La
Home Farm
Stitchings La
Mill La
Ten Acre Cottages
Ten Acre La
Marksbury La
Nailwell
Westvale
Priston Rd
Duncorn Hill
B3115
A367
Village Farm
PH
Hill View
Summerlea
Manor House Farm
Crossways Cvn Pk
Priston
Westbury Farm
Westbury Terr
Severcombe Farm
Priston La
Longhouse
Priston Hill
Tunley Rd
North Hill Farm
Manor Farm
The Hollow
Edelweiss Farm
1 The Old Forge
2 Lansdown View
PH
Sarabeth Dr
Blind La
Withyditch La
Dunkerton
Withyditch
Brooklands
Dunkerton La
Fairfield
Tunley
Palmers La
Dunkerton Bridge
Lower Tunley Farm
Church Farm
Home Farm
Limestone Link
Hill Grove House
Stoneage La
Bridge Farm
Stoneage Cottage
Mine (dis)
Splott Farm
Cam Brook
PH
Dunkerton Hill
Limestone Link
Carlingcott Mill
White Oxmead La
Home Farm
PH
Wick La
Lower Church Rd
Dunkerton Hill
Under Knoll
Wicklane
Carlingcott La
Firgrove La
Carlingcott
Ashgrove
Ashgrove
White Oxmead La
Mast

79
62

61
44

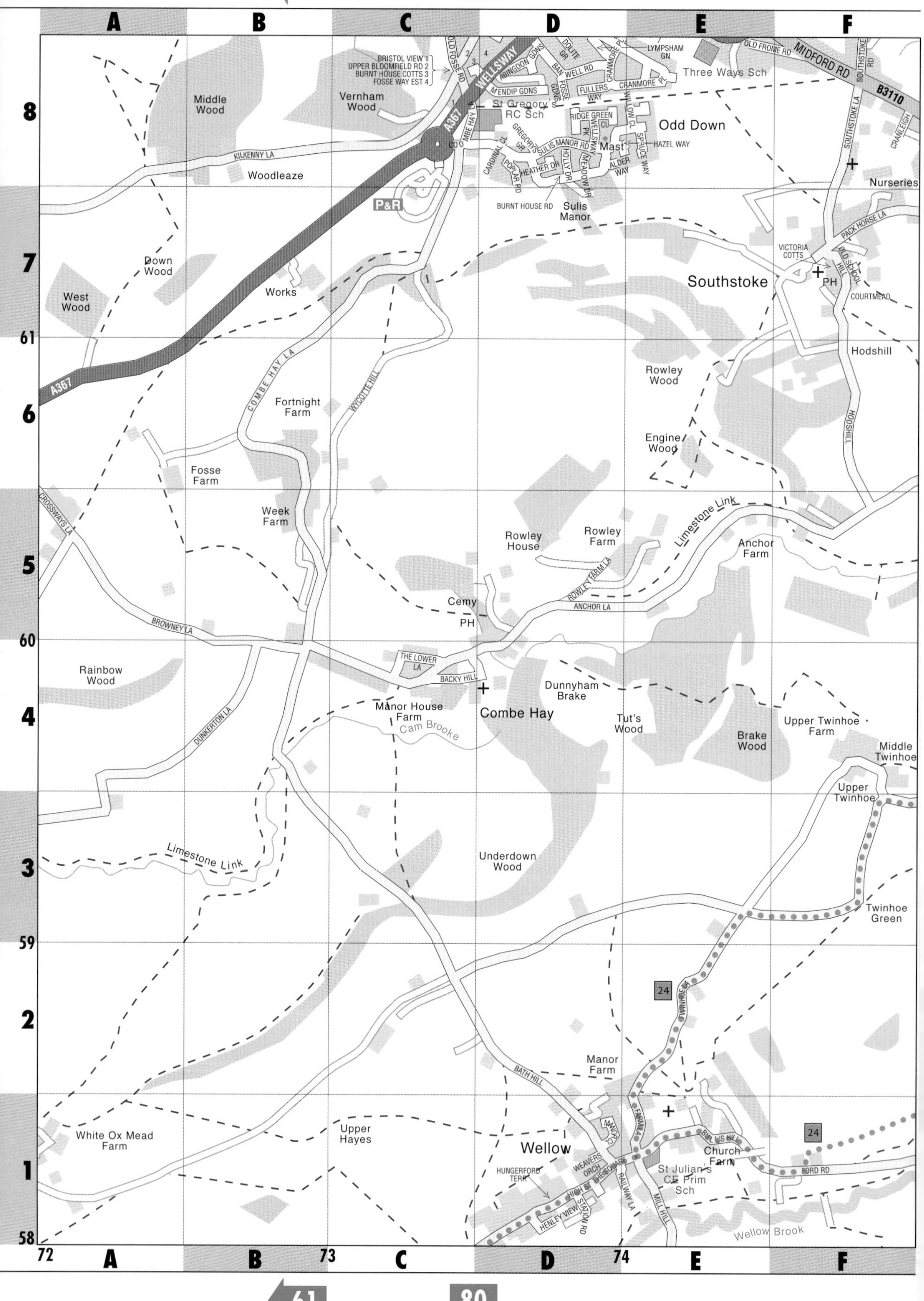
A
B
C
D
E
F
8
7
61
6
5
60
4
3
59
2
1
58
72
73
74
Middle Wood
Vernham Wood
BRISTOL VIEW 1
UPPER BLOOMFIELD RD 2
BURNT HOUSE COTTS 3
FOSSE WAY EST 4
OLD FOSSE RD
WELLSWAY
A367
ABINGDON GDNS
MENDIP GDNS
LYMPSHAM GN
Three Ways Sch
OLD FROME RD
MIDFORD RD
B3110
SOUTHSTOKE RD
St Gregory RC Sch
Odd Down
RIDGE GREEN CL
FULLERS WAY
CRANMORE PL
SULIS MANOR RD
Mast
HAZEL WAY
SPRUCE WAY
ALDER WAY
HEATHER DR
POPLAR RD
CARDINAL CL
HOLLY DR
MEADOW DR
BURNT HOUSE RD
Sulis Manor
KILKENNY LA
Woodleaze
P&R
SOUTHSTOKE LA
CRANLEIGH
Nurseries
PACK HORSE LA
VICTORIA COTTS
OLD SCHOOL HILL
Southstoke
PH
COURTMEAD
Down Wood
West Wood
Works
Hodshill
HODSHILL
Rowley Wood
COMBE HAY LA
Fortnight Farm
WYCOTTE HILL
Engine Wood
Fosse Farm
Week Farm
CROSSWAYS LA
Rowley House
Rowley Farm
Limestone Link
Anchor Farm
ROWLEY FARM LA
ANCHOR LA
Cemy
PH
BROWNEY LA
Rainbow Wood
THE LOWER LA
BACKY HILL
Dunnyham Brake
Manor House Farm
Combe Hay
Cam Brooke
Tut's Wood
Brake Wood
Upper Twinhoe Farm
Middle Twinhoe
DUNKERTON LA
Upper Twinhoe
Limestone Link
Underdown Wood
Twinhoe Green
24
TWINHOE LA
Manor Farm
BATH HILL
FARM LA
White Ox Mead Farm
Upper Hayes
Wellow
24
Church Farm
BULLS HILL
FORD RD
HUNGERFORD TERR
WEAVERS ORCH
THE SQUARE
HIGH ST
RAILWAY LA
St Julian's CE Prim Sch
MILL HILL
HENLEY VIEW
STATION RD
Wellow Brook

61
80

45
64

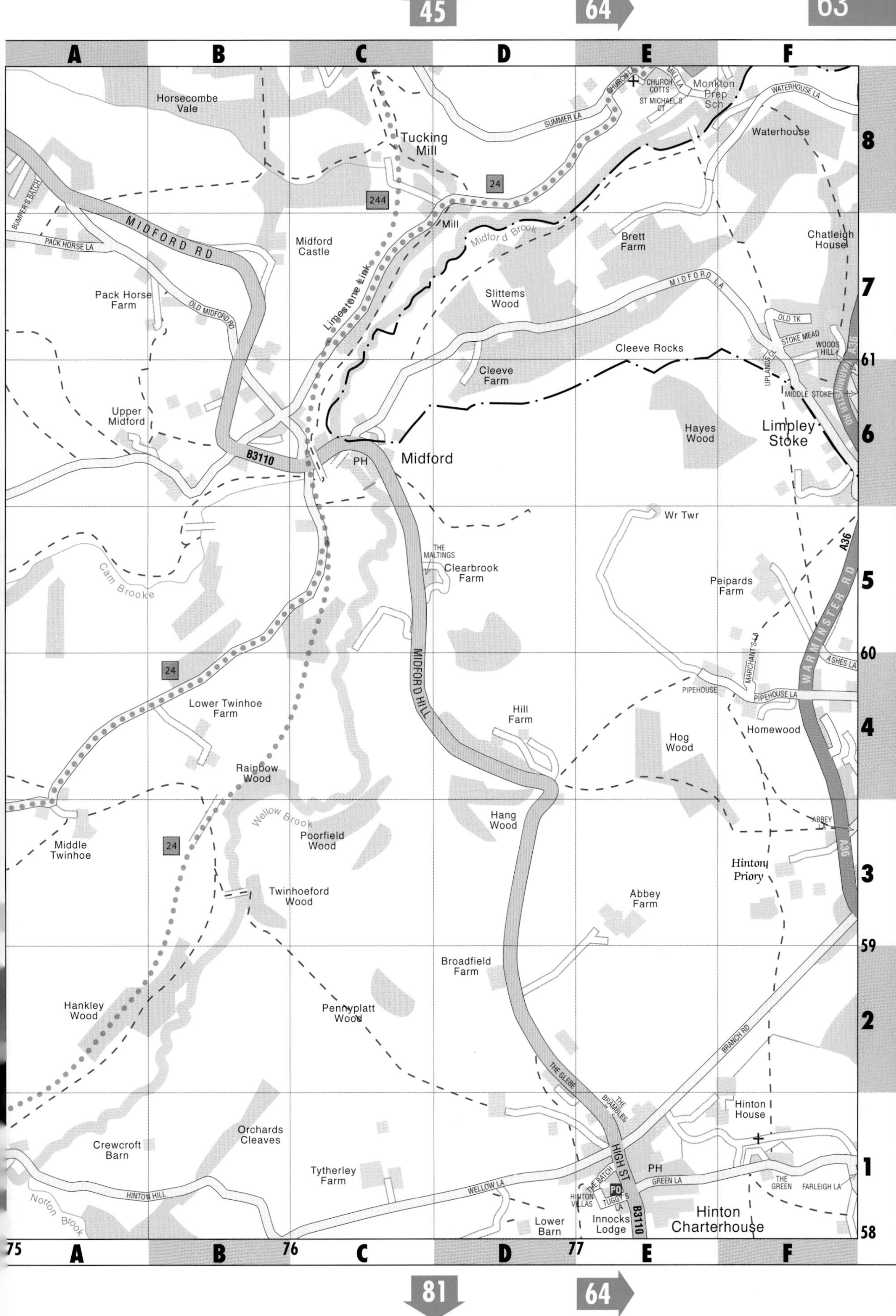
A
B
C
D
E
F
Horsecombe Vale
Tucking Mill
Monkton Prep Sch
CHURCH COTTS
ST MICHAEL'S CT
CHURCH LA
MILL LA
WATERHOUSE LA
Waterhouse
SUMMER LA
244
24
Mill
MIDFORD RD
BUMPER'S BATCH
PACK HORSE LA
Midford Castle
Midford Brook
Brett Farm
Chatleigh House
Pack Horse Farm
OLD MIDFORD RD
Limestone Link
Slittems Wood
MIDFORD LA
OLD TK
STOKE MEAD
WOODS HILL
Cleeve Rocks
UPLANDS CL
Cleeve Farm
MIDDLE STOKE
WARMINSTER RD
A36
Upper Midford
Hayes Wood
Limpley Stoke
B3110
PH
Midford
Wr Twr
THE MALTINGS
Clearbrook Farm
Cam Brooke
Peipards Farm
MIDFORD HILL
MARCHANT'S LA
ASHES LA
PIPEHOUSE
PIPEHOUSE LA
Lower Twinhoe Farm
Hill Farm
Hog Wood
Homewood
Rainbow Wood
Wellow Brook
Hang Wood
ABBEY LA
Middle Twinhoe
Poorfield Wood
Hinton Priory
Twinhoeford Wood
Abbey Farm
Broadfield Farm
Hankley Wood
Pennyplatt Wood
BRANCH RD
THE GLEBE
THE BRAMBLES
Hinton House
Orchards Cleaves
Crewcroft Barn
HIGH ST
PH
GREEN LA
THE GREEN
FARLEIGH LA
Tytherley Farm
THE BATCH
HINTON HILL
WELLOW LA
HINTON VILLAS
PO
TUGGY'S LA
Norton Brook
Lower Barn
Innocks Lodge
Hinton Charterhouse
8
7
61
6
5
60
4
3
59
2
1
58
75
76
77

81
64

63
46

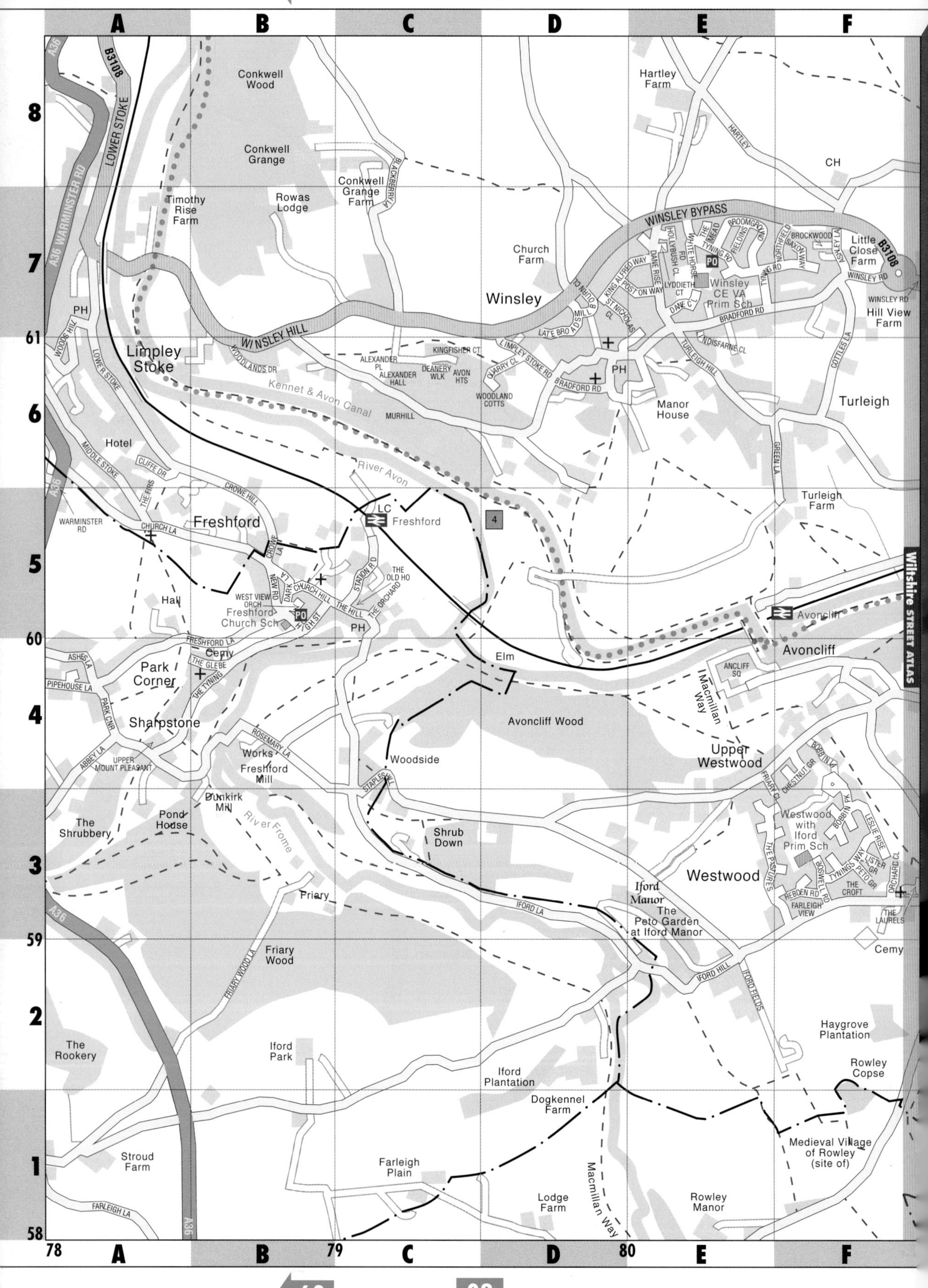
Conkwell Wood
Conkwell Grange
Timothy Rise Farm
Rowas Lodge
Conkwell Grange Farm
Hartley Farm
CH
Church Farm
Winsley
WINSLEY BYPASS
WINSLEY HILL
Little Close Farm
Winsley CE VA Prim Sch
Hill View Farm
Limpley Stoke
PH
Kennet & Avon Canal
Manor House
Turleigh
Hotel
River Avon
Freshford
Turleigh Farm
Hall
Freshford Church Sch
Avoncliff
Park Corner
Cemy
Elm
Sharpstone
Avoncliff Wood
Macmillan Way
Upper Westwood
Works
Freshford Mill
Woodside
Dunkirk Mill
The Shrubbery
Pond House
River Frome
Shrub Down
Westwood with Iford Prim Sch
Westwood
Friary
Iford Manor
The Peto Garden at Iford Manor
Friary Wood
Haygrove Plantation
The Rookery
Iford Park
Iford Plantation
Rowley Copse
Dogkennel Farm
Stroud Farm
Farleigh Plain
Medieval Village of Rowley (site of)
Lodge Farm
Rowley Manor
Wiltshire STREET ATLAS

63
82

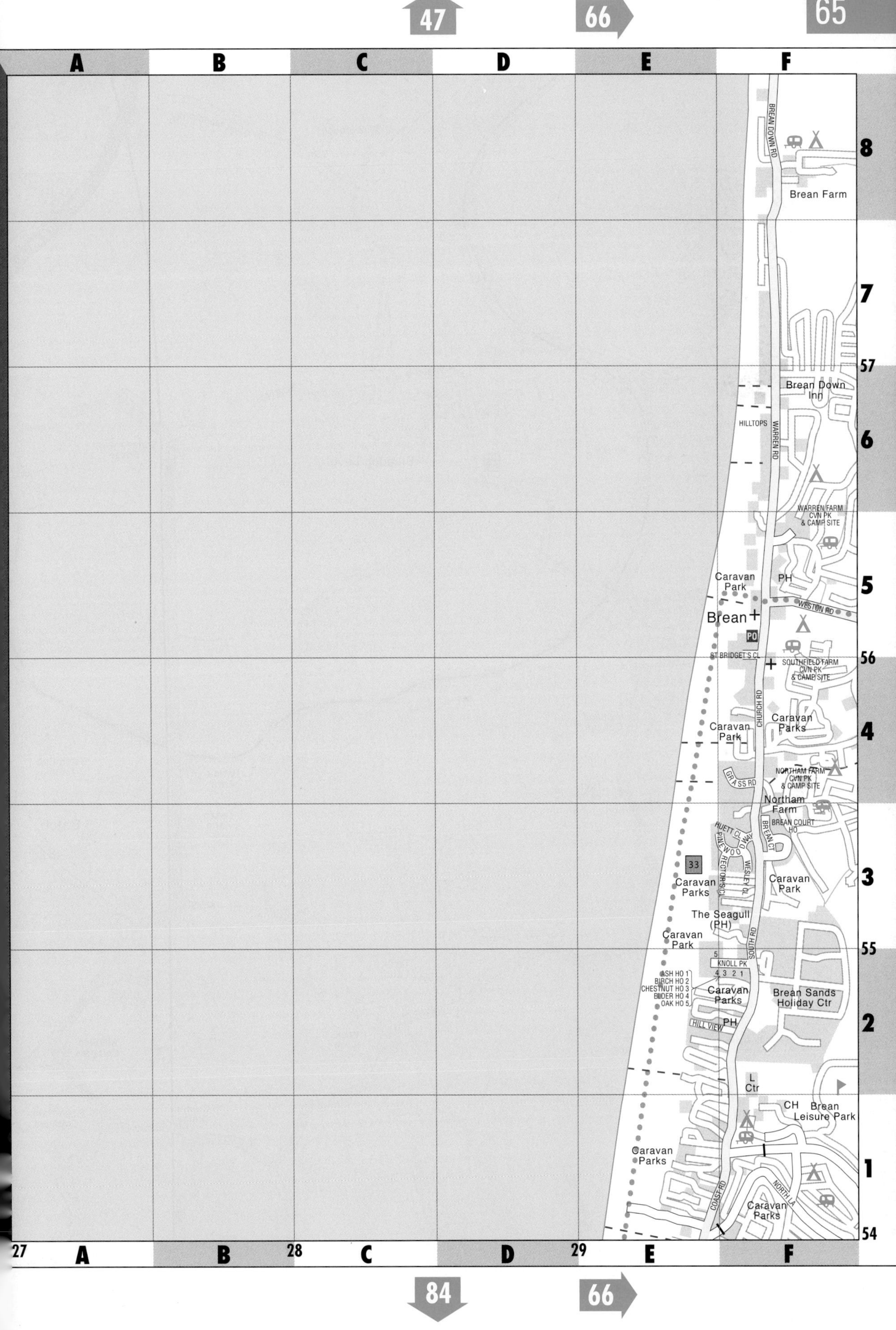
47
66
A
B
C
D
E
F
8
7
57
6
5
56
4
3
55
2
1
54
27
28
29
BREAN DOWN RD
Brean Farm
Brean Down Inn
HILLTOPS
WARREN RD
WARREN FARM CVN PK & CAMP SITE
Caravan Park
PH
WESTON RD
Brean
PO
ST BRIDGET'S CL
SOUTHFIELD FARM CVN PK & CAMP SITE
CHURCH RD
Caravan Parks
Caravan Park
NORTHAM FARM CVN PK & CAMP SITE
GRASS RD
Northam Farm
BREAN COURT HO
HUETT CL
PINEWOOD WAY
BREAN CT
RECTOR'S CL
WESLEY CL
33
Caravan Parks
Caravan Park
The Seagull (PH)
SOUTH RD
Caravan Park
KNOLL PK
ASH HO 1
BIRCH HO 2
CHESTNUT HO 3
ELDER HO 4
OAK HO 5
Caravan Parks
Brean Sands Holiday Ctr
HILL VIEW
PH
L Ctr
CH
Brean Leisure Park
Caravan Parks
COAST RD
NORTH LA
Caravan Parks
84
66

65
48

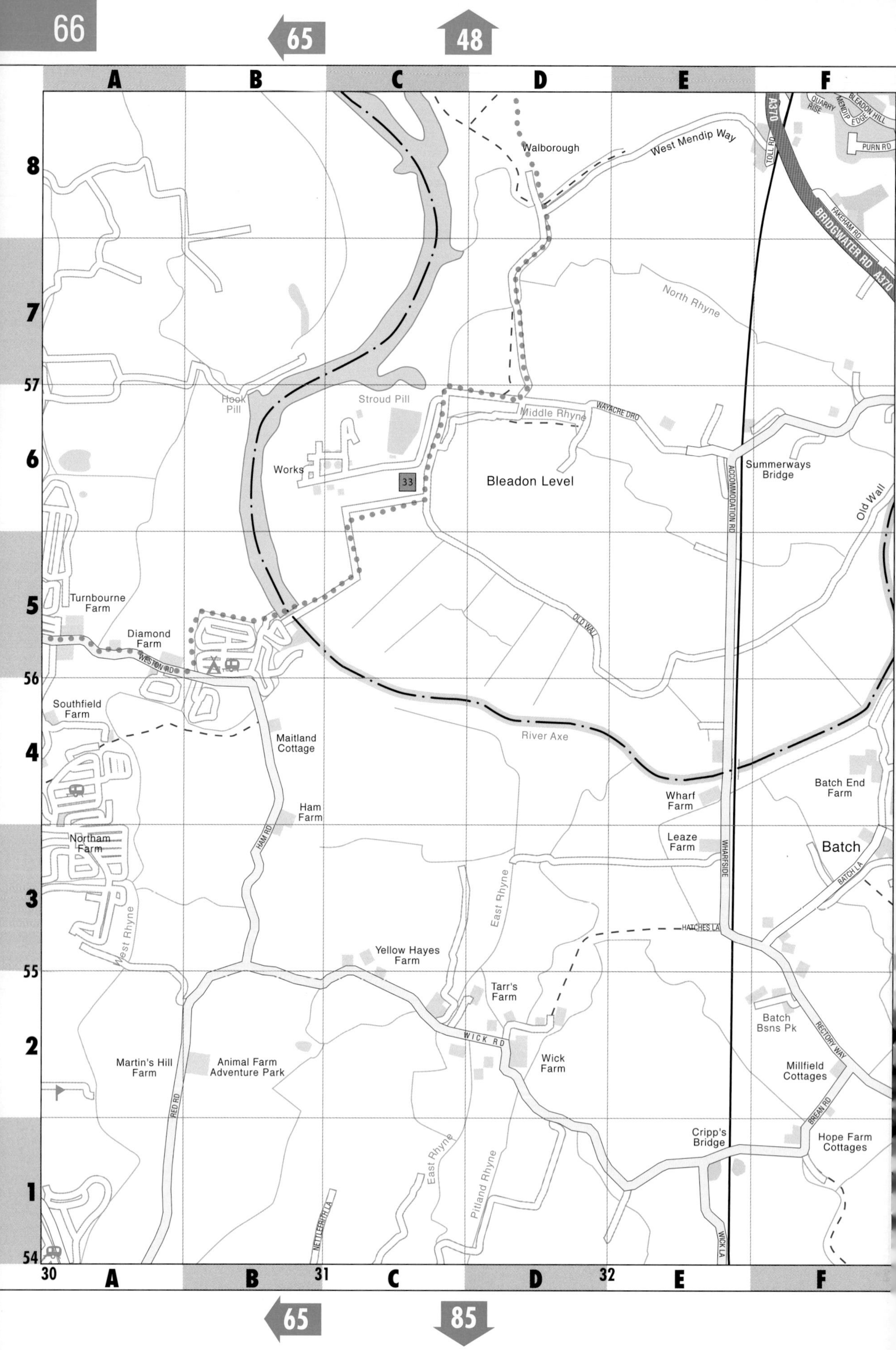
A
B
C
D
E
F
8
7
57
6
5
56
4
3
55
2
1
54
30
31
32
Walborough
West Mendip Way
A370
TOLL RD
QUARRY RISE
MENDIP EDGE
BLEADON HILL
PURN RD
FAKEHAM RD
BRIDGWATER RD
North Rhyne
Hook Pill
Stroud Pill
Middle Rhyne
WAYACRE DRO
Works
33
Bleadon Level
Summerways Bridge
ACCOMMODATION RD
Old Wall
Turnbourne Farm
Diamond Farm
WESTON RD
OLD WALL
Southfield Farm
Maitland Cottage
River Axe
Ham Farm
HAM RD
Wharf Farm
Batch End Farm
Northam Farm
Leaze Farm
WHARFSIDE
Batch
BATCH LA
East Rhyne
West Rhyne
HATCHES LA
Yellow Hayes Farm
Tarr's Farm
Batch Bsns Pk
RECTORY WAY
WICK RD
Martin's Hill Farm
Animal Farm Adventure Park
Wick Farm
Millfield Cottages
RED RD
BREAN RD
Cripp's Bridge
Hope Farm Cottages
East Rhyne
Pitland Rhyne
NETTLEBRIDGE LA
WICK LA

65
85

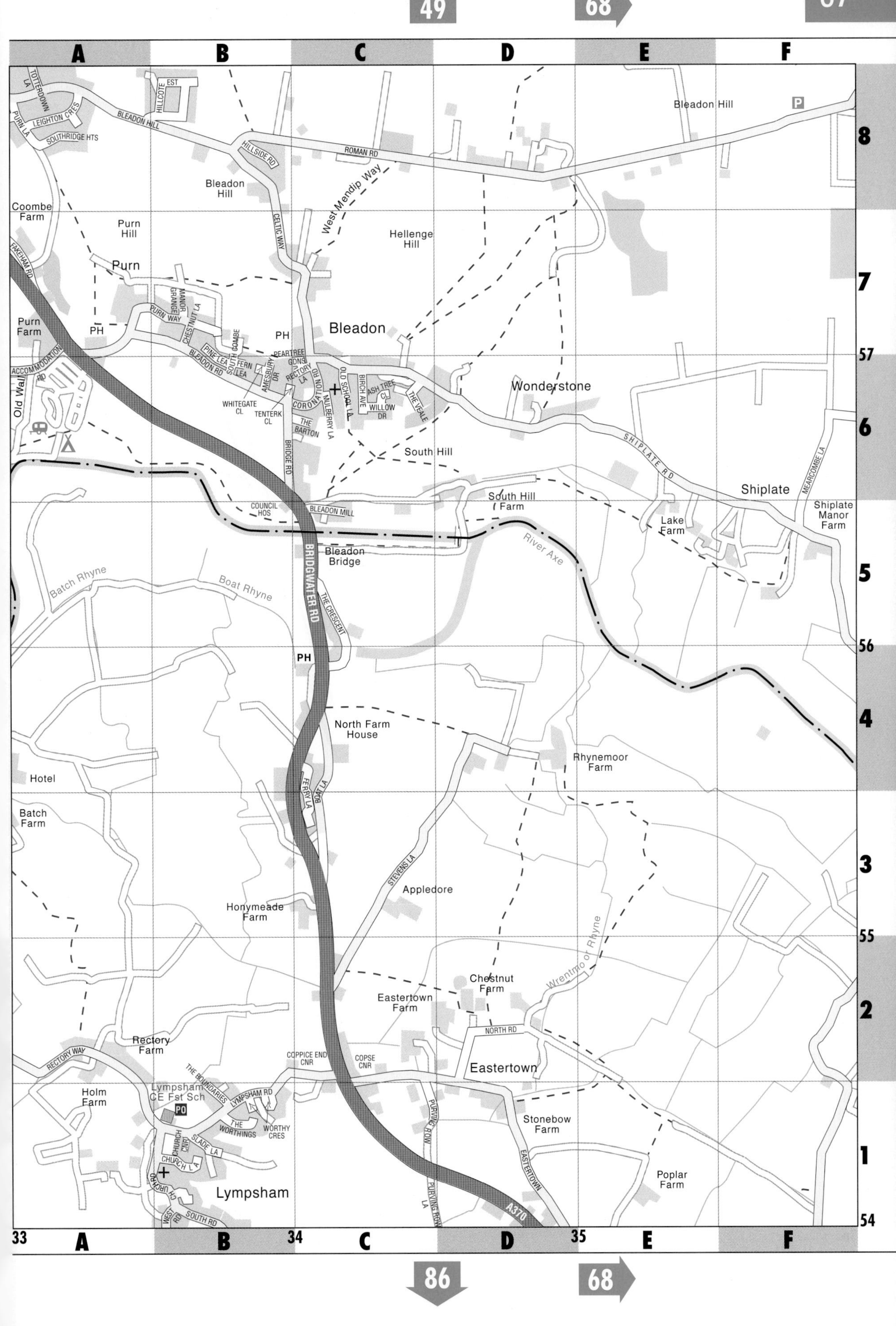
49
68
A
B
C
D
E
F
8
7
57
6
5
56
4
3
55
2
1
54
33
34
35
TOTTERDOWN LA
HILLCOTE
EST
LEIGHTON CRES
PURN LA
SOUTHRIDGE HTS
BLEADON HILL
HILLSIDE RD
ROMAN RD
Bleadon Hill
Bleadon Hill
Coombe Farm
Purn Hill
West Mendip Way
CELTIC WAY
Hellenge Hill
FAKEHAM RD
Purn
MANOR GRANGE
CHESTNUT LA
PURN WAY
Purn Farm
PH
PH
Bleadon
SOUTH COMBE
PINE LEA
FERN LEA
BLEADON RD
PEARTREE GDNS
AMESBURY DR
RECTORY LA
CORONATION RD
OLD SCHOOL LA
BIRCH AVE
ASH TREE CL
WILLOW DR
THE VEALE
MULBERRY LA
Wonderstone
ACCOMMODATION RD
Old Wall
WHITEGATE CL
TENTERK CL
THE BARTON
BRIDGE RD
South Hill
SHIPLATE RD
Shiplate
MEARCOMBE LA
COUNCIL HOS
BLEADON MILL
South Hill Farm
Lake Farm
Shiplate Manor Farm
Bleadon Bridge
River Axe
BRIDGWATER RD
THE CRESCENT
Batch Rhyne
Boat Rhyne
PH
North Farm House
Rhynemoor Farm
Hotel
FERRY LA
BOX LA
Batch Farm
STEVENS LA
Appledore
Honymeade Farm
Wrentmoor Rhyne
Chestnut Farm
Eastertown Farm
NORTH RD
Rectory Farm
RECTORY WAY
COPPICE END CNR
COPSE CNR
Eastertown
THE BOUNDARIES
Holm Farm
Lympsham CE Fst Sch
LYMPSHAM RD
PO
THE WORTHINGS
WORTHY CRES
PURVING ROW
Stonebow Farm
CHURCH CNR
SLADE LA
CHURCH LA
ORCHARD
EASTERTOWN
Poplar Farm
Lympsham
A370
WEST RD
SOUTH RD
PURVING ROW LA
86
68

67
50

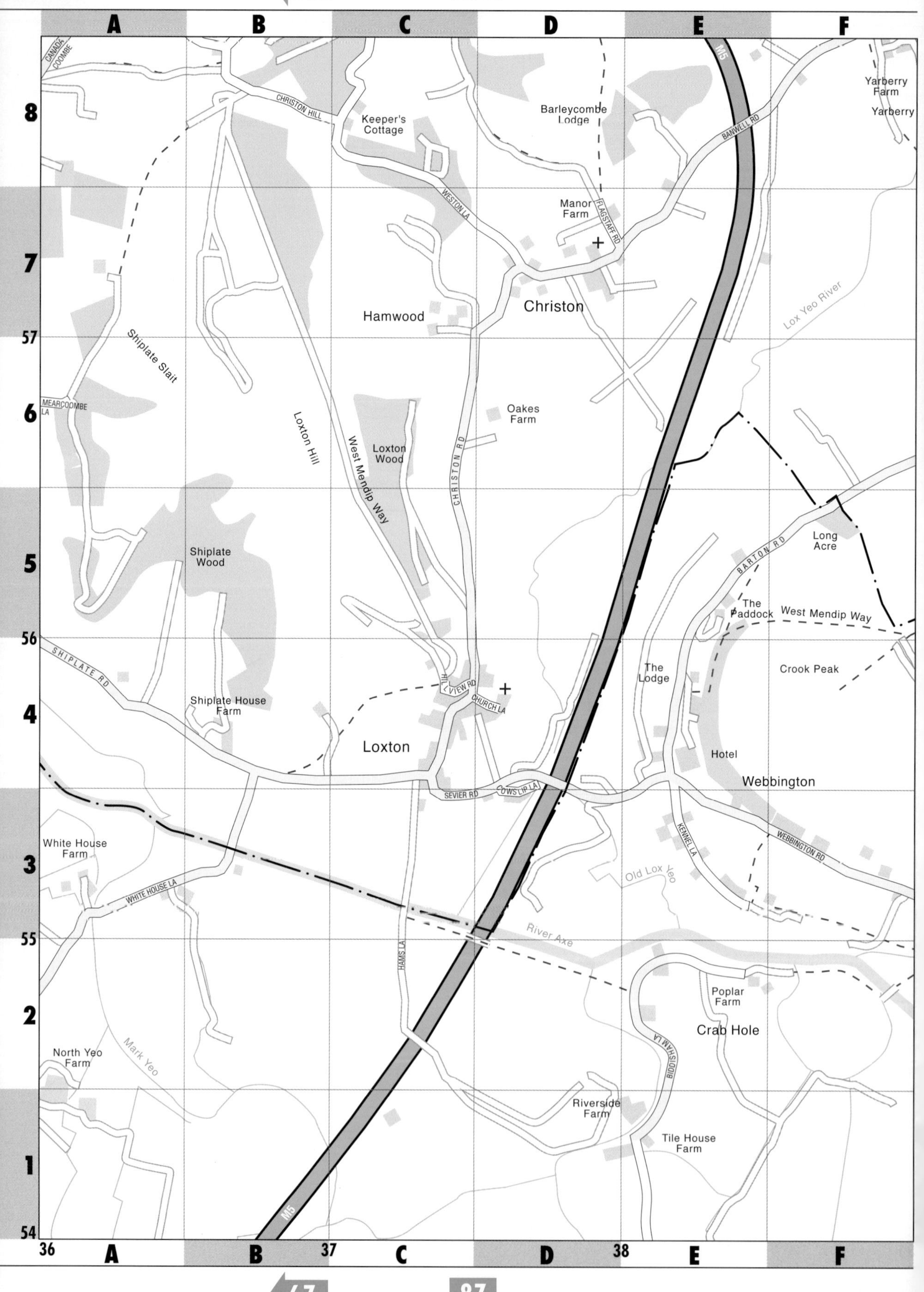
A
B
C
D
E
F
8
7
57
6
5
56
4
3
55
2
1
54
36
37
38
CANADA COOMBE
CHRISTON HILL
Keeper's Cottage
Barleycombe Lodge
M5
Yarberry Farm
Yarberry
BANWELL RD
WESTON LA
Manor Farm
FLAGSTAFF RD
Christon
Hamwood
Lox Yeo River
Shiplate Slait
MEARCOOMBE LA
Loxton Hill
West Mendip Way
Oakes Farm
Loxton Wood
CHRISTON RD
Long Acre
BARTON RD
Shiplate Wood
The Paddock
West Mendip Way
SHIPLATE RD
The Lodge
Crook Peak
HILLVIEW RD
CHURCH LA
Shiplate House Farm
Loxton
Hotel
Webbington
SEVIER RD
COWSLIP LA
White House Farm
KENNEL LA
WEBBINGTON RD
Old Lox Yeo
WHITE HOUSE LA
River Axe
HAMS LA
Poplar Farm
Crab Hole
BIDDISHAM LA
North Yeo Farm
Mark Yeo
Riverside Farm
Tile House Farm
A
B
C
D
E
F

67
87

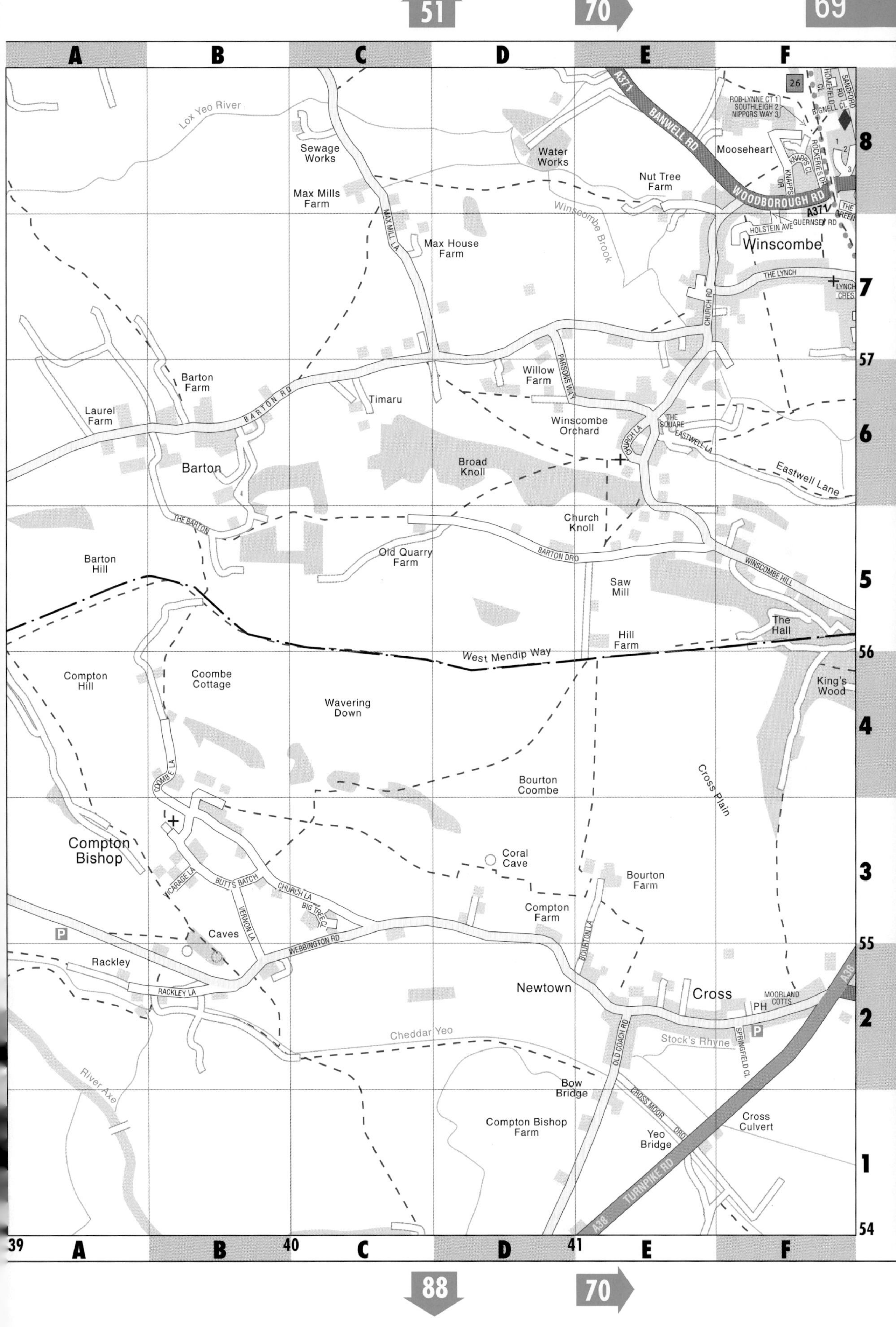
51
70
A
B
C
D
E
F
Lox Yeo River
Sewage Works
Max Mills Farm
Water Works
Nut Tree Farm
Mooseheart
BANWELL RD
A371
WOODBOROUGH RD
ROB-LYNNE CT 1
SOUTHLEIGH 2
NIPPORS WAY 3
HOMEFIELD CL
SANDFORD RD
BIGNELL CL
ROCKERIES DR
KNAPPS CL
KNAPPS DR
HOLSTEIN AVE
GUERNSEY RD
THE GREEN
Winscombe
Winscombe Brook
MAX MILL LA
Max House Farm
THE LYNCH
LYNCH CRES
CHURCH RD
Barton Farm
BARTON RD
Timaru
Willow Farm
PARSONS WAY
Laurel Farm
Winscombe Orchard
THE SQUARE
EASTWELL LA
CHURCH LA
Eastwell Lane
Barton
Broad Knoll
THE BARTON
Church Knoll
Old Quarry Farm
BARTON DRO
WINSCOMBE HILL
Barton Hill
Saw Mill
The Hall
Hill Farm
West Mendip Way
Compton Hill
Coombe Cottage
King's Wood
Wavering Down
Cross Plain
COOMBE LA
Bourton Coombe
Compton Bishop
Coral Cave
VICARAGE LA
BUTTS BATCH
CHURCH LA
BIG TREE CL
VERNON LA
Bourton Farm
Compton Farm
Caves
WEBBINGTON RD
BOURTON LA
P
Rackley
RACKLEY LA
Newtown
Cross
MOORLAND COTTS
PH
A38
Cheddar Yeo
OLD COACH RD
Stock's Rhyne
SPRINGFIELD CL
River Axe
Bow Bridge
CROSS MOOR DRO
Compton Bishop Farm
Yeo Bridge
Cross Culvert
TURNPIKE RD
8
7
57
6
5
56
4
3
55
2
1
54
39
40
41
88
70

69
52

A
B
C
D
E
F
Winscombe Woodborough Prim Sch
Queensmead Court
Paddington House
Woodborough
Winterhead
Winterhead Farm
Sidcot Sch
Sidcot
Shipham CE Fst Sch
Shipham
Hotel
Playing Field
Oakridge Farm
Sidcot Hill Farm
Winterhead Hill Farm
Winterhead Hill
Cuck Hill
Gatcombe
Hotel
Hale Coombe
West Mendip Way
Lillypool Cheese & Cider Farm
Callow Hill
Hale Coppice
Shute Shelve Farm
Callow Drove
Works
Callow Rock Quarry
Mast
Fry's Hill
Rose Wood
Shute Shelve Hill
Axbridge Hill
Cheddar Wood
Manor Farm
St Michael's Cheshire Home
Cemy
Hillside
Townsend Farm
Axbridge
Axbridge CE Fst Sch
Bloomfield Farm
Boat Yard
Yacht Club
Allot Gdns
Cheddar Resr
Sewage Works
Middle Rhyne
Ellenge Stream
A38
A371
BRISTOL RD
SIDCOT LA
BRIDGWATER RD
AXBRIDGE BYPASS
CROSS LA
CHEDDAR RD
AXBRIDGE RD
SHIPHAM HILL
SHIPHAM RD
WINSCOMBE DRO
WINSCOMBE HILL
WINSCOMBE DR
Pastwell La
LONGBOTTOM
1 MENDIP LODGE
2 WOODBOROUGH CT
3 APPLE TREE DR
4 DUNSTER CT
1 ALLENS LA
2 COURT LA
3 NORTH DOWN CL
1 MEADOW ST
2 THE SQUARE
3 CHURCH LA
4 THE BUNGALOWS
8
7
57
6
5
56
4
3
55
2
1
54
42
43
44
26

69
89

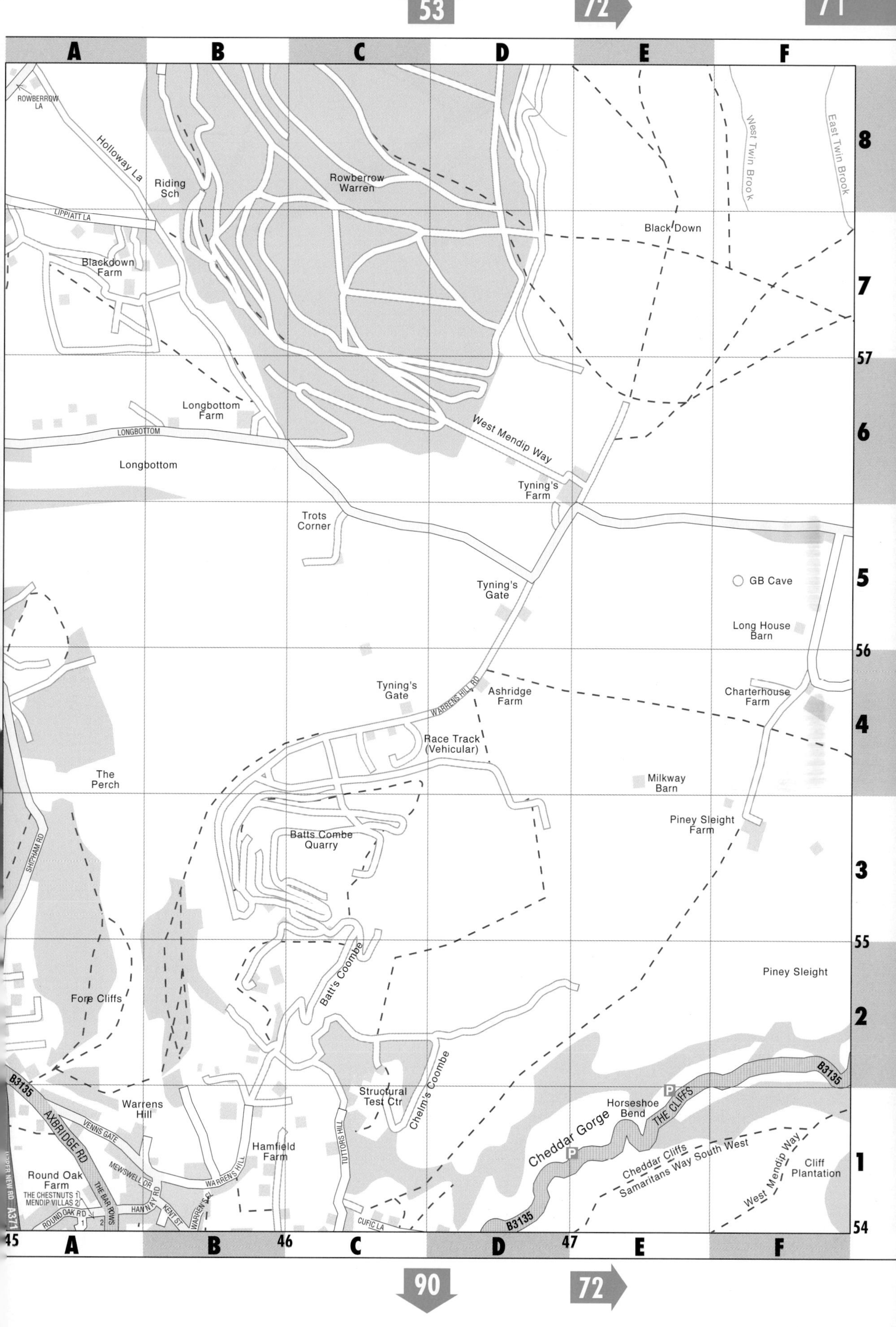
53
72
A
B
C
D
E
F
8
7
57
6
5
56
4
3
55
2
1
54
ROWBERROW LA
Holloway La
Riding Sch
Rowberrow Warren
West Twin Brook
East Twin Brook
LIPPIATT LA
Black Down
Blackdown Farm
Longbottom Farm
LONGBOTTOM
Longbottom
West Mendip Way
Tyning's Farm
Trots Corner
Tyning's Gate
GB Cave
Long House Barn
Tyning's Gate
WARRENS HILL RD
Ashridge Farm
Charterhouse Farm
Race Track (Vehicular)
The Perch
Milkway Barn
Piney Sleight Farm
Batts Combe Quarry
SHIPHAM RD
Piney Sleight
Batt's Coombe
Fore Cliffs
Chelm's Coombe
B3135
B3135
Structural Test Ctr
Horseshoe Bend
THE CLIFFS
Warrens Hill
AXBRIDGE RD
VENNS GATE
Cheddar Gorge
Hamfield Farm
TUTTORS HILL
Cheddar Cliffs
Samaritans Way South West
West Mendip Way
Cliff Plantation
MEWSWELL DR
Round Oak Farm
THE CHESTNUTS
MENDIP VILLAS
THE BAR ROWS
HANNAY RD
KENT ST
WARRENS HILL
WARREN'S CL
ROUND OAK RD
CUFIC LA
B3135
A371
45
46
47
90
72

71
54

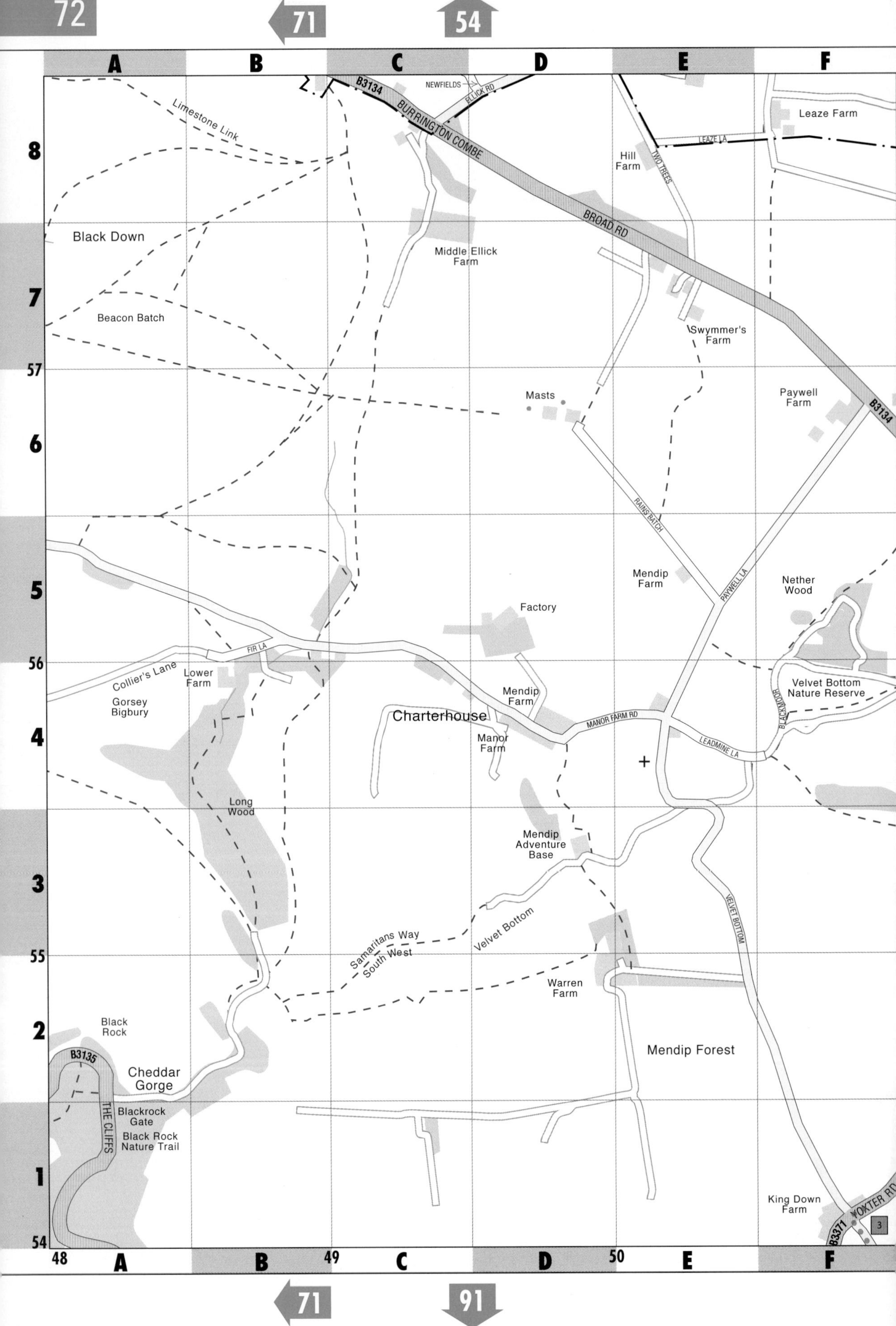
A
B
C
D
E
F
8
7
57
6
5
56
4
3
55
2
1
54
48
49
50
Limestone Link
Black Down
Beacon Batch
B3134
NEWFIELDS
ELLICK RD
BURRINGTON COMBE
BROAD RD
Middle Ellick
Farm
Hill
Farm
TWO TREES
LEAZE LA
Leaze Farm
Swymmer's
Farm
Paywell
Farm
B3134
Masts
RAINS BATCH
Mendip
Farm
PAYWELL LA
Nether
Wood
Factory
FIR LA
Collier's Lane
Lower
Farm
Gorsey
Bigbury
Mendip
Farm
Charterhouse
Manor
Farm
MANOR FARM RD
LEADMINE LA
BLACKMOOR
Velvet Bottom
Nature Reserve
Long
Wood
Mendip
Adventure
Base
Velvet Bottom
Samaritans Way
South West
VELVET BOTTOM
Warren
Farm
Black
Rock
B3135
Cheddar
Gorge
Mendip Forest
THE CLIFFS
Blackrock
Gate
Black Rock
Nature Trail
King Down
Farm
B3371
YOXTER RD
3

71
91

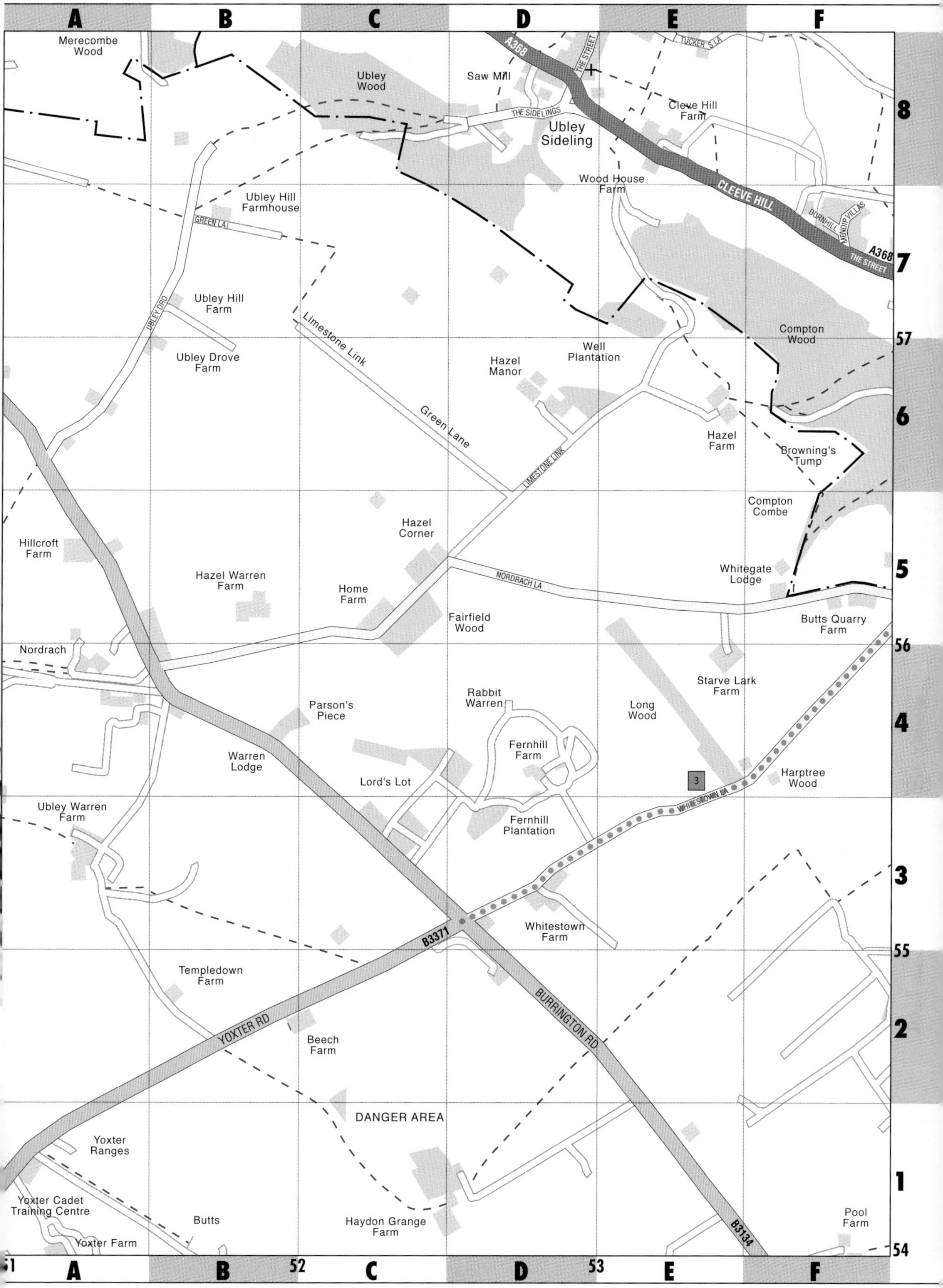

A B C D E F

Merecombe Wood
Ubley Wood
Saw Mill
THE STREET
TUCKER'S LA
A368
THE SIDELINGS
Ubley Sideling
Cleve Hill Farm
8
Wood House Farm
CLEEVE HILL
Ubley Hill Farmhouse
GREEN LA
DORNHILL
MENDIP VILLAS
A368
THE STREET
7
Ubley Hill Farm
UBLEY DRO
Limestone Link
Compton Wood
57
Ubley Drove Farm
Well Plantation
Hazel Manor
Green Lane
6
Hazel Farm
Browning's Tump
LIMESTONE LINK
Compton Combe
Hazel Corner
Hillcroft Farm
Hazel Warren Farm
5
Whitegate Lodge
NORDRACH LA
Home Farm
Fairfield Wood
Butts Quarry Farm
Nordrach
56
Starve Lark Farm
Rabbit Warren
Parson's Piece
Long Wood
4
Fernhill Farm
Warren Lodge
Lord's Lot
3
Harptree Wood
Ubley Warren Farm
WHITESTOWN LA
Fernhill Plantation
3
Whitestown Farm
B3371
55
Templedown Farm
BURRINGTON RD
YOXTER RD
Beech Farm
2
DANGER AREA
Yoxter Ranges
1
Yoxter Cadet Training Centre
Butts
Haydon Grange Farm
Pool Farm
B3134
Yoxter Farm
54

51 A B 52 C D 53 E F

92
74

73
56

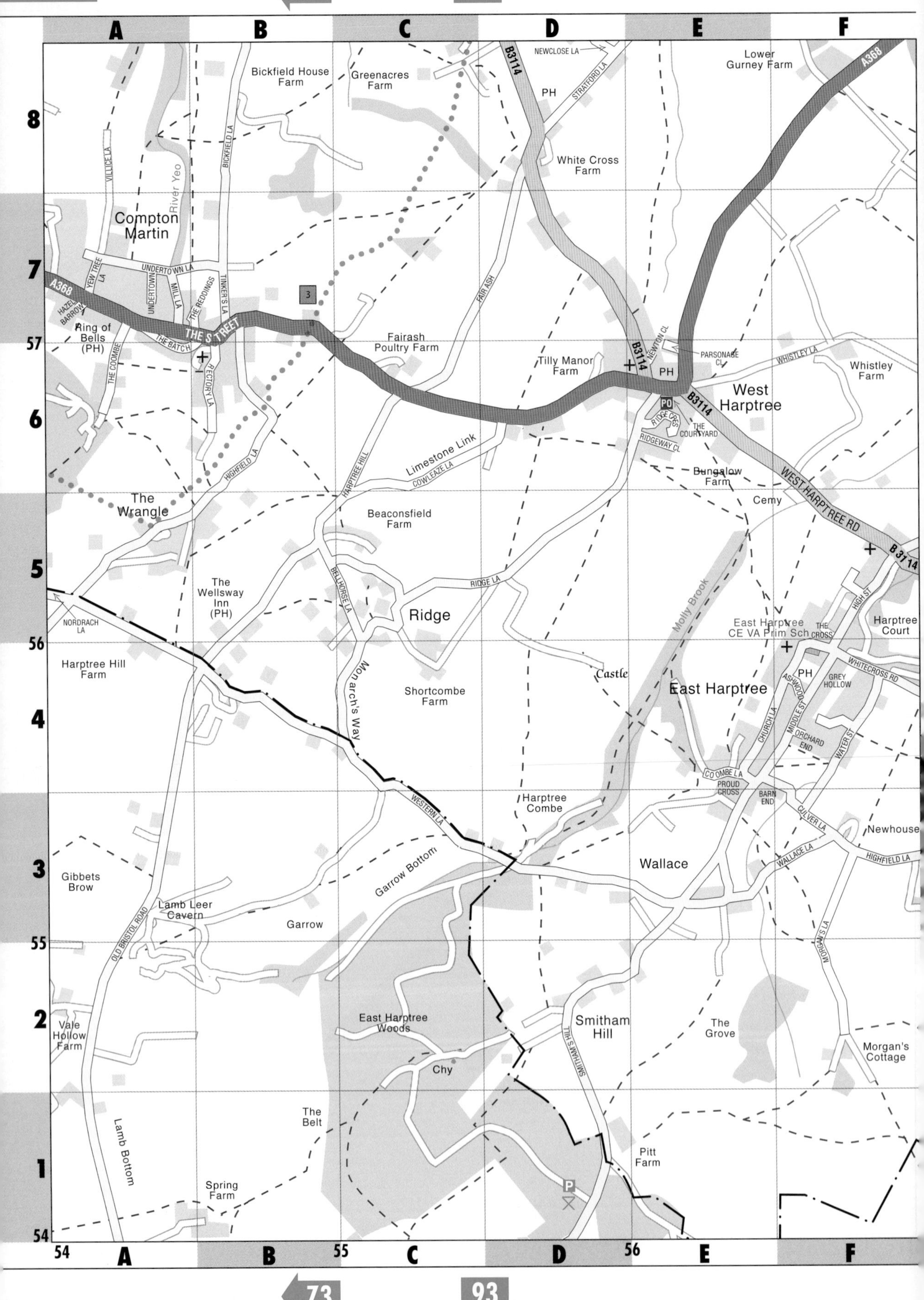
Compton Martin
Bickfield House Farm
Greenacres Farm
Lower Gurney Farm
White Cross Farm
River Yeo
Ring of Bells (PH)
Fairash Poultry Farm
Tilly Manor Farm
West Harptree
Whistley Farm
Limestone Link
Bungalow Farm
Cemy
The Wrangle
Beaconsfield Farm
West Harptree Rd
The Wellsway Inn (PH)
Ridge
East Harptree CE VA Prim Sch
Harptree Court
Harptree Hill Farm
Castle
Shortcombe Farm
East Harptree
Monarch's Way
Molly Brook
Harptree Combe
Newhouse
Gibbets Brow
Garrow Bottom
Wallace
Lamb Leer Cavern
Garrow
Vale Hollow Farm
East Harptree Woods
Smitham Hill
The Grove
Morgan's Cottage
Chy
The Belt
Lamb Bottom
Pitt Farm
Spring Farm

73
93

57
76

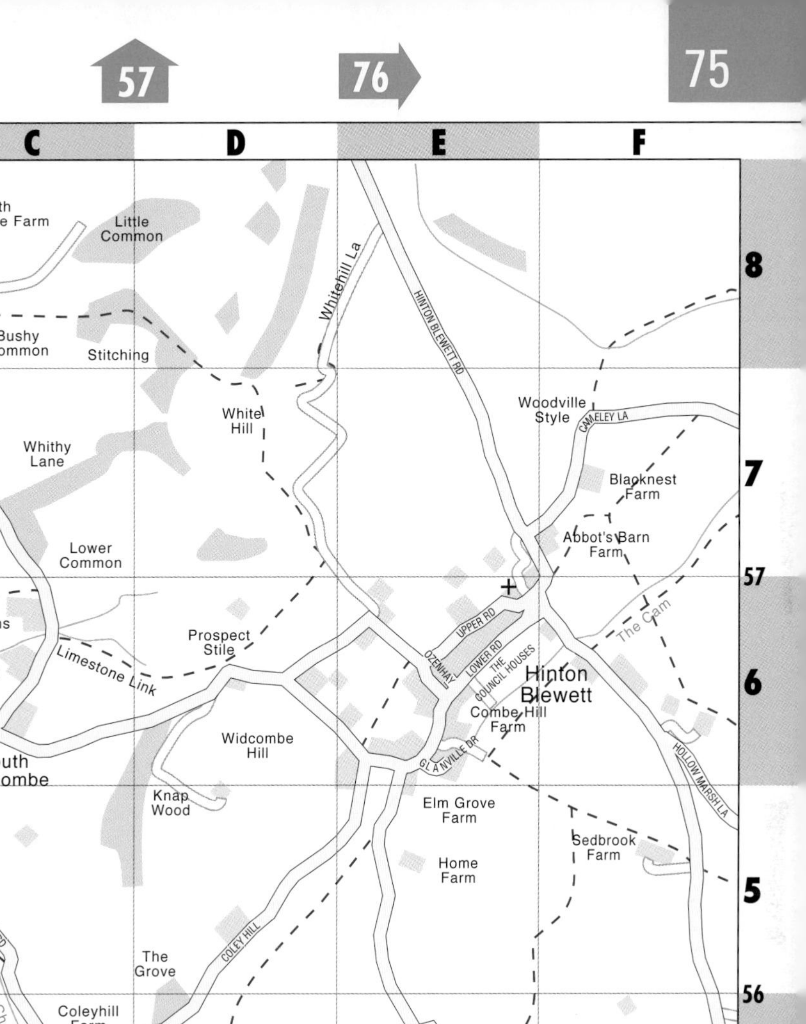
Herriotts Mill Pond
Widcombe Common
North Widcombe Farm
Little Common
Molly Brook
Bushy Common
Stitching
Whitehill La
HINTON BLEWETT RD
White Hill
Whithy Lane
Woodville Style
CAMELEY LA
Blacknest Farm
Abbot's Barn Farm
Lower Common
Shrowl Bridge
Haydons Farm
Prospect Stile
UPPER RD
LOWER RD
OZENHAY
THE COUNCIL HOUSES
The Cam
Hinton Blewett
Limestone Link
Edgehill Farm
SHROWLE
Combe Hill Farm
Widcombe Hill
South Widcombe
GLANVILLE DR
HOLLOW MARSH LA
Knap Wood
Tudor Farm
Elm Grove Farm
Sedbrook Farm
Home Farm
TOWNSEND
PERRY MEAD RD
COLEY HILL
River Chew
The Grove
The Park
Coleyhill Farm
COLEY RD
WHITECROSS RD
Coley Hill
HOOK LA
Hinton Field Farm
Peak's Girt Wood
Coley Manor Farm
Coley
Lower Resr
Shortwood House
Higher Shortwood Farm
Eastwood Manor
Shortwood Common
HIGHFIELD LA
COLEY NARROW
Upper Resr
Elm Tree Farm
Sherborne
HOLLOW MARSH LA
Eastwood Manor Farm
WHITEHOUSE LA
Arm Cover
BENLEAZE RD
EASTWOOD
The Dell
SHORTWOOD LA
BACK LA
Benleaze
Litton
PH
STONEYARD LA
LITT HILL
Lady Wood
Wickham's Gully
SHORT LA
Buckley Wood
STRAIGHTMEAD
HARPTREE LA
Wooten Hall
Litton Wood
BACK LA
Hook's Hill
ASHEL'S BATCH
FORD LA
B3114
A
B
C
D
E
F
8
7
57
6
5
56
4
3
55
2
1
54
57
58
59

94
76

75
58

A B C D E F

8
7
57
6
5
56
4
3
55
2
1
54

Camway Cottage
NANNY HURN'S LA
Lower Farm
Church Farm
Cameley
CAMELEY RD
The Cam
Cameley House
Limestone Link
Jame's Brake
Mill Farm
Brook House
PETERSIDE
Temple Cloud
A37
MOLLY CL
PERRIN CL
CAMELEY CL
EASTCOURT RD
CAMBROOK HO
East Court
Temple Bridge Farm
Temple Bridge
Temple Bridge Bsns Pk
WHITE CROSS
White Cross
WELLS RD
A39
WHITE CROSS GATE
Brick House Farm
Red House Farm
GREEN LA
The Croft
Field Farm
Hollow Marsh
Long Dale Wood
HOLLOW MARSH LA
BRISTOL RD
Farrington Inn (PH)
HAM LA
PITWAY LA
CHAPEL CL
CHURCH LA
MAIN ST
PITWAY CL
GOURNAY CT
A362
Chewton Wood
Easton Wood
Hengrove Wood
RUSH HILL
MARSH LA
A39
Hollowmarsh Cottage
North Lawn
Ston Easton
The Retreat
EASTON CT
A37 HIGH ST
Ston Easton Park
Terrace Wood
Hotel
FIELD LA
LINTON RD
A39

60 A B 61 C D 62 E F

75
95

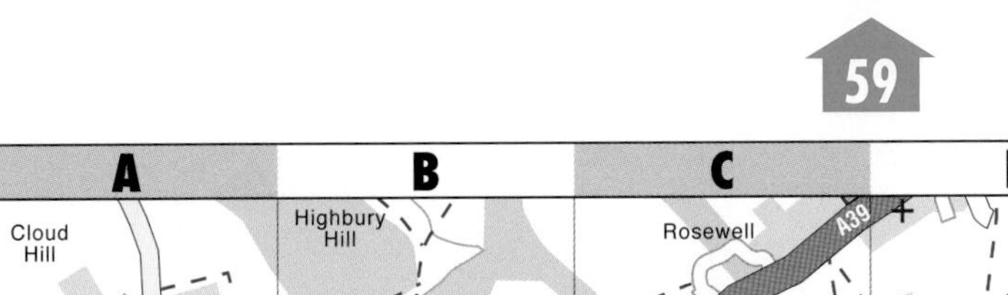

59
78

A
B
C
D
E
F
Cloud Hill
Highbury Hill
Rosewell
Withy Mills Farm
Cloud Hill Ind Est
Stephen's Hill
Goosard Bridge
Factory
EASTCOURT RD
MARSH LA
Cloud Hill Farm
Highbury Farm Bsns Pk
LANGFORDS LA
GOOSARD LA
BROOM HILL
Sewage Wks
Southside House
HIGHBURY RD
Cam Brook
HARTS LA
The Court
Hanham House
Limestone Link
Hallatrow Bridge
HANHAM LA
BRISTOL RD
Hallatrow
THE GROVE
B3355
PAULTON RD
CLAREMONT GDNS
Allard's Farm
WELLS RD
A39
Tenniscourt Farm
COMBE LA
PH
HALLATROW RD
Butt's Lane
OLD PRINT WORKS RD
VICTORIA SOUTH TERR
BATH RD
BRITTENS
WALLENGE CL
Brittens
Plummer's Hill
Cemy
SPRINGHILL CL
ROMAN WAY
TWELVE ACRES CL
SHOE LA
PAPER LA
MANOR FARM CL
THE TRIANGLE
PO
P
CHURCH ST
HIGH ST
HILLSIDE CL
THE FOLLY
PAULTON HILL
White Cross Farm
BRISTOL RD
A37
CAMVIEW
HIGH PK
New Town
WOODVIEW
DOWNSWAY
WESTVIEW
VICTORIA PL
PARK CL
CARTER RD
LAUREL DR
ASHMANS GATE
Liby
CHESTNUT CL
SOMERSET WAY
BROOKSIDE CL
SIMON'S CL
Paulton
FARRINGTON RD
ABBOTTS FARM CL
PARK RD
THE MEAD
LUDWELLS
Paulton Jun & Inf Sch
Ham
SPECKLEMEAD
TENNIS COURT AVE
TENNIS COURT RD
GREENVALE RD
BADMAN CL
ELM RD
SPRING GROUND RD
RUDGEWAY RD
WINTERFIELD RD
HIGH ACRE
Towns End
HAYBORO WAY
WINTERFIELD PK
NENDIP CL
OAKLANDS
CLOVER CL
ALPINE CL
CLANDOWN RD
Salisbury Farm
ST JULIEN'S CL 1
HOLWELL CL 2
FIR TREE AVE
Meml
MEADOW RD
Farrington Gurney CE Prim Sch
PAULTON RD
PHILLIS HILL
SALISBURY RD
Paulton Memorial
CHURCH LA
FRANKLYN TERR
SCHOOL LA
Manor House
MANOR GDNS
RUETT LA
MONGER COTTS
GOURNAY CT
FARRINGTON WAY
MEADOW CL
MAIN ST
Farrington Fields Trad Est
FARRINGTON FIELDS
OLD MILLS LA
MONGER LA
SOMER RIDGE
FARRINGTON GURNEY BY-PASS
THE CRESCENT
BRIDGE BLDGS
HILL VIEW
SUNNYSIDE
Farrington Gurney
MARSH LA
PADDOCK
Thicket Mead
BUSHY COMBE 1
BLUEBELL RISE 2
BLACKBERRY WAY
BOXBURY HILL
B3355
Old Mills
Superstore
WEST RD
A362
SPRINGFIELD BLDGS
Superstore
Old Mills Ind Est
SUNNYMEAD
Thicketmead Bridge
CH
Langley Down Lane
NORTHMEAD AVE
HAYES PARK RD
SOMER AVE
SOMER RD
UNDERHILL AVE
NORTHMEAD RD
ST LUKE'S RD
Hillier's Down Wood
MIDSOMER NORTON
UNDERHILL LA
HAYES RD
Hillier's Down
LANGLEYS LA
Underhill Wood
HIGH MDWS
THE DYMBORO
Underhill Farm
NORTH RD
ORCHARD AVE
Bull's Wood
PINEWOOD AVE
PINEWOOD RD
DYMBORO AVE
PAULTON RD
Wellow Brook
White Bridge
CLAPTON RD
GREENACRES
Longvernal Prim Sch
LONGVERNAL
MANDY MDWS
Providence Place
8
7
57
6
5
56
4
3
55
2
1
54
63
64
65

96
78

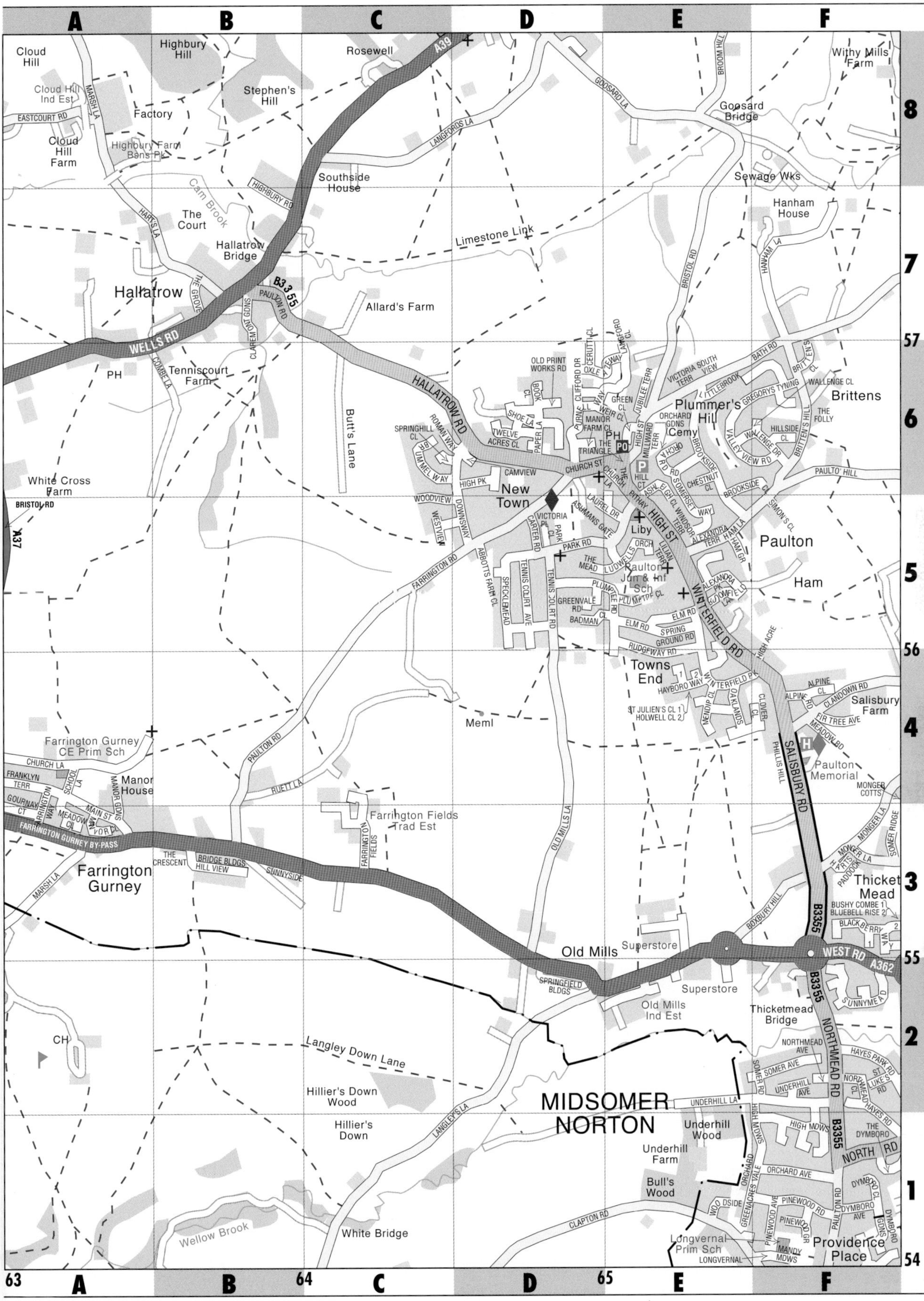

77
60

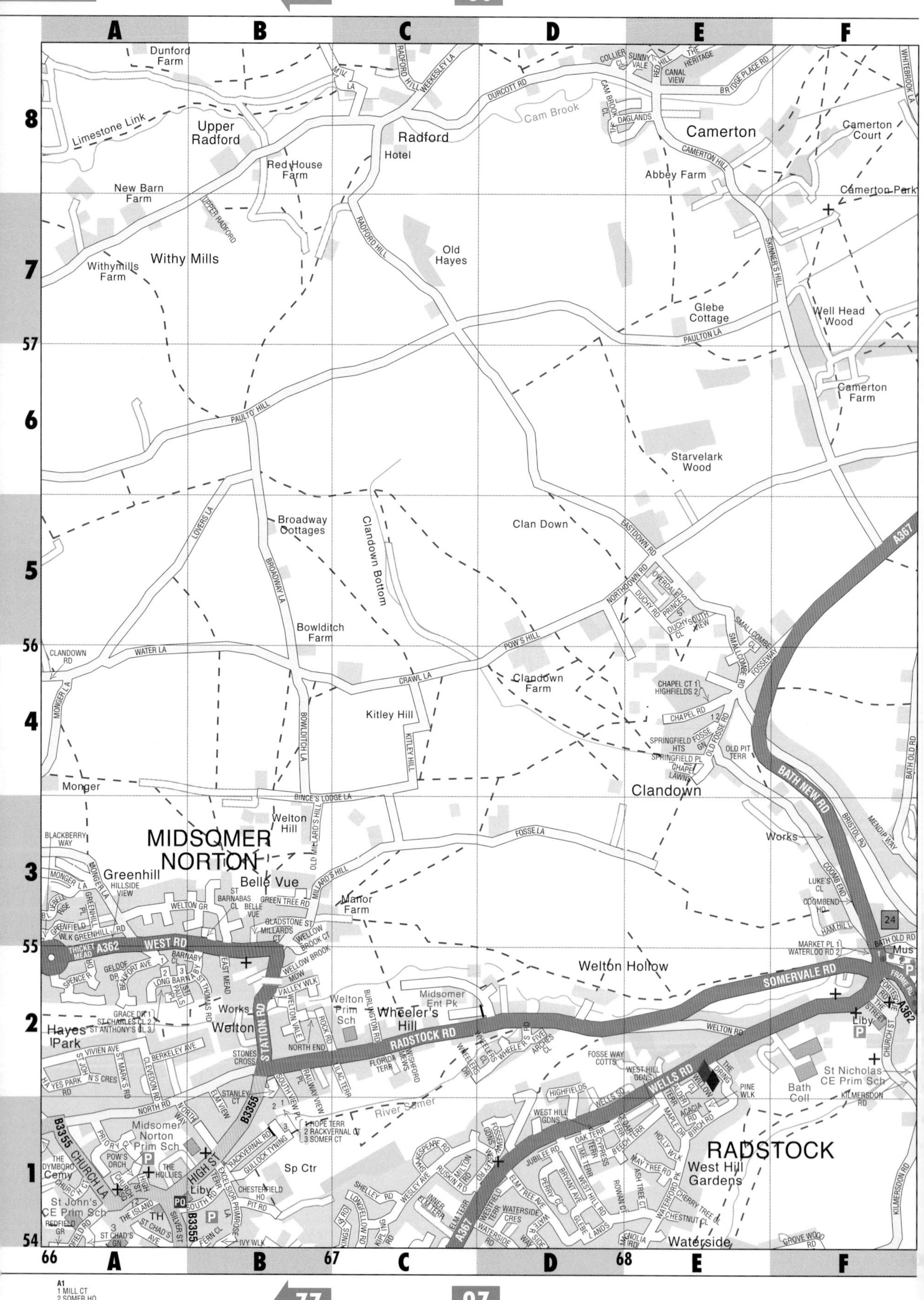
A
B
C
D
E
F
8
7
57
6
5
56
4
3
55
2
1
54
66
67
68
Dunford Farm
Limestone Link
Upper Radford
Radford
Hotel
Red House Farm
New Barn Farm
Withy Mills
Withymills Farm
Old Hayes
Camerton
Camerton Court
Abbey Farm
Camerton Park
Cam Brook
Glebe Cottage
Well Head Wood
Camerton Farm
Starvelark Wood
Clan Down
Broadway Cottages
Clandown Bottom
Bowlditch Farm
Clandown Farm
Kitley Hill
Monger
Clandown
Welton Hill
MIDSOMER NORTON
Greenhill
Belle Vue
Manor Farm
Works
Welton Hollow
Hayes Park
Welton
Welton Prim Sch
Wheeler's Hill
Midsomer Ent Pk
Midsomer Norton Prim Sch
Cemy
St John's CE Prim Sch
Liby
Sp Ctr
River Somer
RADSTOCK
West Hill Gardens
Waterside
Bath Coll
St Nicholas CE Prim Sch
Mus
PAULTON HILL
PAULTON LA
WATER LA
CRAWL LA
POW'S HILL
BINCE'S LODGE LA
FOSSE LA
WEST RD
RADSTOCK RD
SOMERVALE RD
WELLS RD
STATION RD
BATH NEW RD
A367
A362
B3355
HIGH ST
CHURCH LA
BROADWAY LA
LOVERS LA
BOWLDITCH LA
KITLEY HILL
RADFORD HILL
EASTDOWN RD
NORTHDOWN RD
FOSSEWAY
WELTON RD

77
97

A1
1 MILL CT
2 SOMER HO
3 Somervale Sch

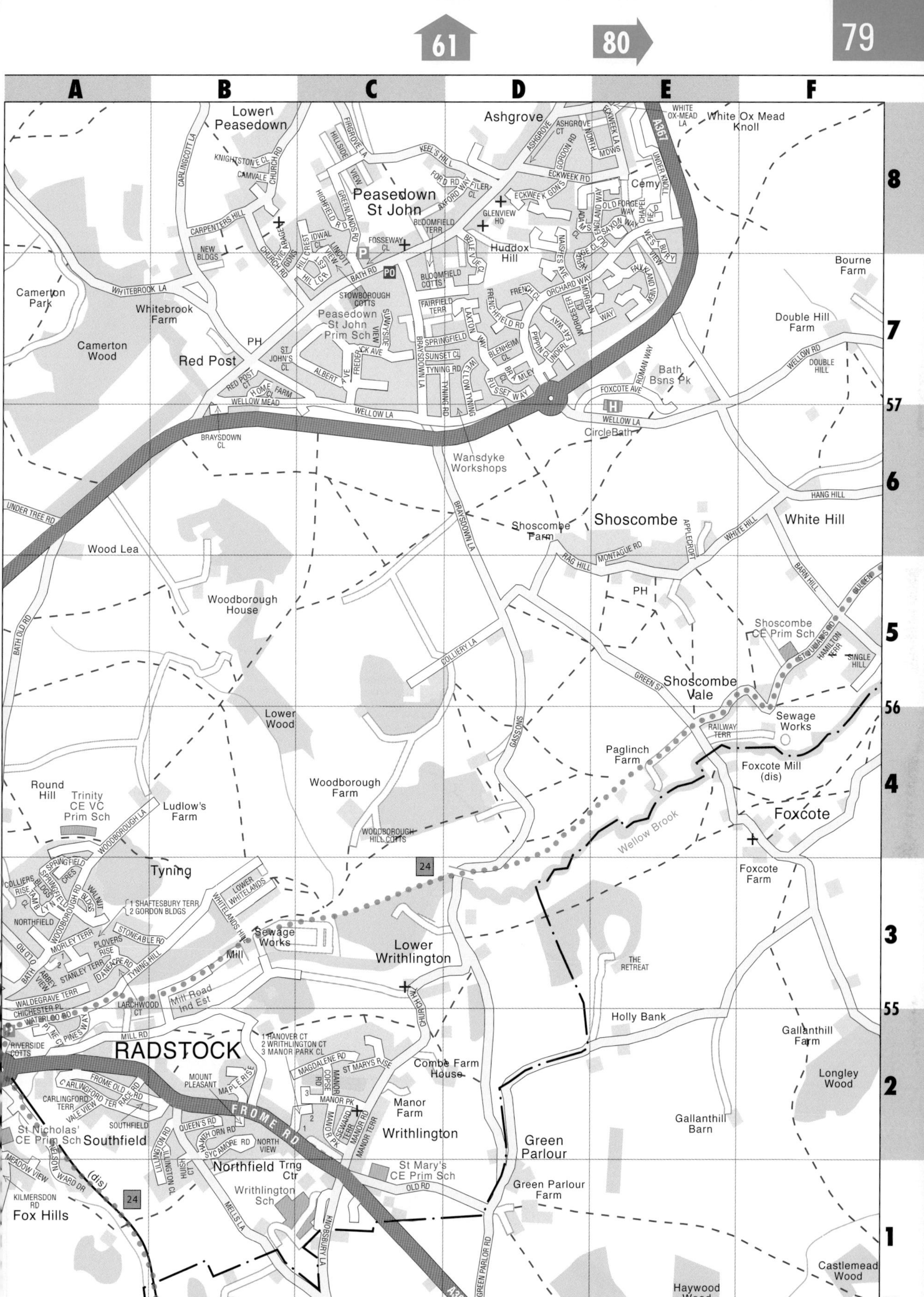

61
80
Lower Peasedown
Ashgrove
White Ox Mead Knoll
Peasedown St John
Huddox Hill
Cemy
Bourne Farm
Camerton Park
Whitebrook Farm
Camerton Wood
Red Post
Peasedown St John Prim Sch
Double Hill Farm
Bath Bsns Pk
CircleBath
Wansdyke Workshops
Shoscombe Farm
Shoscombe
White Hill
Wood Lea
Woodborough House
Shoscombe CE Prim Sch
Shoscombe Vale
Lower Wood
Sewage Works
Paglinch Farm
Foxcote Mill (dis)
Woodborough Farm
Round Hill
Trinity CE VC Prim Sch
Ludlow's Farm
Foxcote
Wellow Brook
Tyning
Foxcote Farm
Lower Writhlington
The Retreat
Mill Road Ind Est
Holly Bank
RADSTOCK
Gallanthill Farm
Combe Farm House
Longley Wood
Manor Farm
Writhlington
Gallanthill Barn
St Nicholas' CE Prim Sch
Southfield
Green Parlour
Northfield
Trng Ctr
St Mary's CE Prim Sch
Green Parlour Farm
Writhlington Sch
Fox Hills
Castlemead Wood
Haywood Wood
98
80

79
62

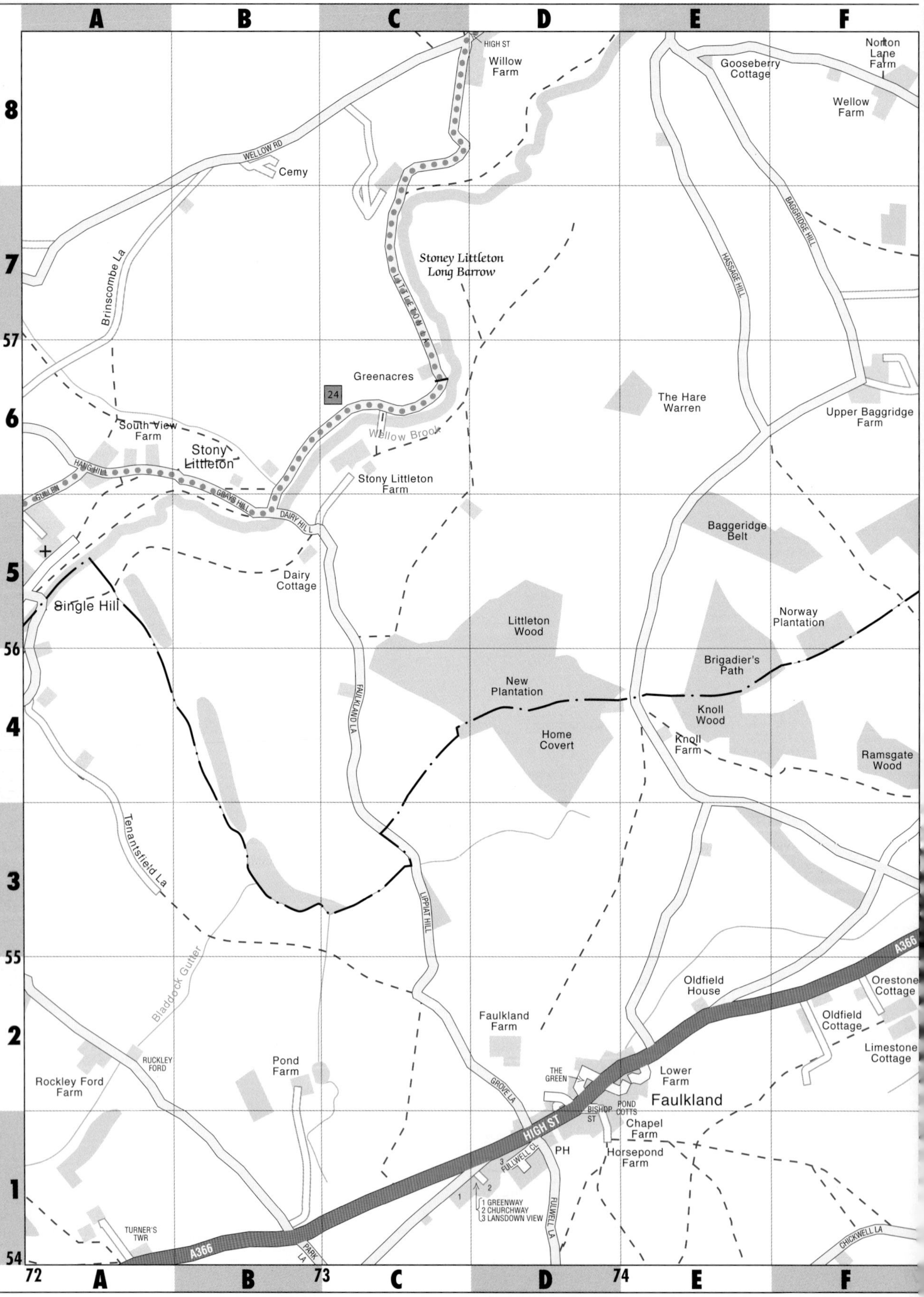

A B C D E F

8
7
57
6
5
56
4
3
55
2
1
54

HIGH ST
Willow Farm
Norton Lane Farm
Gooseberry Cottage
Wellow Farm
WELLOW RD
Cemy
BAGGRIDGE HILL
HASSAGE HILL
Brinscombe La
Stoney Littleton Long Barrow
LITTLETON LA
Greenacres
24
The Hare Warren
Upper Baggridge Farm
South View Farm
Stony Littleton
Wellow Brook
HANG HILL
GULLBIN
GRAYS HILL
DAIRY HILL
Stony Littleton Farm
Baggeridge Belt
Dairy Cottage
Single Hill
Littleton Wood
Norway Plantation
Brigadier's Path
New Plantation
FAULKLAND LA
Knoll Wood
Home Covert
Knoll Farm
Ramsgate Wood
Tenantsfield La
LIPPIAT HILL
Bladdock Gutter
A366
Oldfield House
Orestone Cottage
Oldfield Cottage
Faulkland Farm
Limestone Cottage
RUCKLEY FORD
Pond Farm
Rockley Ford Farm
THE GREEN
Lower Farm
GROVE LA
Faulkland
BISHOP ST
POND COTTS
HIGH ST
Chapel Farm
PH
FULLWELL CL
Horsepond Farm
1 GREENWAY
2 CHURCHWAY
3 LANSDOWN VIEW
FULLWELL LA
TURNER'S TWR
PARK LA
CHICKWELL LA

72 A B 73 C D 74 E F

79
99

63
82

A
B
C
D
E
F
New Town
8
Norton Barn
B3110
Prestick Wood
Cleaves Wood
Tait Wood
Norwood Wood
Tuckson Wood
NORTON LA
7
Norwood Farm
Lower Baggridge Farm
57
Hinton Field
Breach Brake
Kingsfield Brake
Ring Wood
6
Norton Brook
New Plantation
Broadlands
BATH RD
Mast
Hassage Wood
Rainbow Brake
5
WELLOW LA
A366
Hassage Cottage
Sewage Works
Norton Ho
FARLEIGH RD
NORTON GRANGE
CHEVER'S LA
SOHO
LYDE GN
NORTH ST
SOUTH PADDOCK
56
THE BARTON
BELL HILL
LONGMEAD CL
UPPER FARM CL
TOWN BARTON
SPRINGFIELD
RINGWELL LA
FAIR CL
THE PLAIN
PH
HIGH ST
CHAPEL ROW
Norton St Philip
RINGWELL
CHURCH ST
4
Hassage
Norton St Philip CE Fst Sch
VICARAGE LA
FORTESCUE ST
Vicarage
Mount Pleasant Farm
TOWN END
SOUTHFIELD
TELLISFORD LA
HASSAGE FARM
FROME RD
CHATLEY FURLONG
Tucker's Grave Bottom
Tucker's Grave Inn (PH)
WELLS RD
Watery La
Southfield Farm
3
B3110
Bingwell Farm
MACKLEY LA
55
CHILKWELL LA
2
Chickwell New Farm
Peart Farm
CHICKWELL LA
Marrow Pole La
1
Chickwell Farm
ROW LA
HAMMER LA
54
75
76
77

100
82

81
64

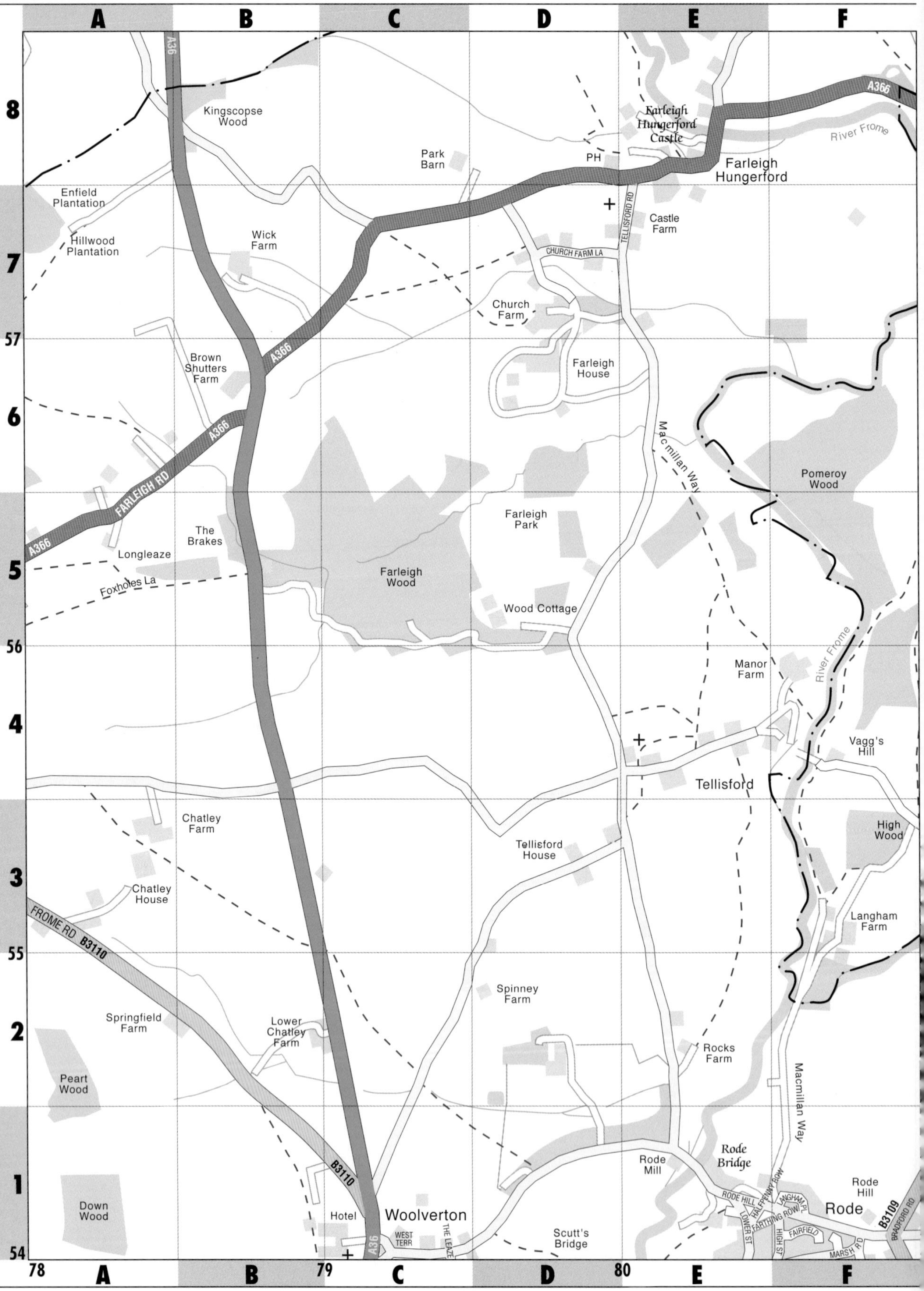

A B C D E F

8
7
57
6
5
56
4
3
55
2
1
54

Kingscopse Wood
Enfield Plantation
Hillwood Plantation
Park Barn
PH
Farleigh Hungerford Castle
Farleigh Hungerford
River Frome
A366
A36
Wick Farm
Castle Farm
TELLISFORD RD
CHURCH FARM LA
Church Farm
Brown Shutters Farm
Farleigh House
Macmillan Way
Pomeroy Wood
FARLEIGH RD
The Brakes
Farleigh Park
Longleaze
Foxholes La
Farleigh Wood
Wood Cottage
Manor Farm
Vagg's Hill
Tellisford
Chatley Farm
Tellisford House
High Wood
Chatley House
FROME RD
B3110
Langham Farm
Spinney Farm
Springfield Farm
Lower Chatley Farm
Rocks Farm
Peart Wood
Rode Bridge
Rode Mill
Rode Hill
Down Wood
Hotel
Woolverton
RODE HILL
HALFPENNY ROW
LANGHAM PL
LOWER ST
FARTHING ROW
HIGH ST
FAIRFIELD
MARSH RD
Rode
B3109
BRADFORD RD
WEST TERR
THE LEAZE
Scutt's Bridge

78 79 80
A B C D E F

81
101

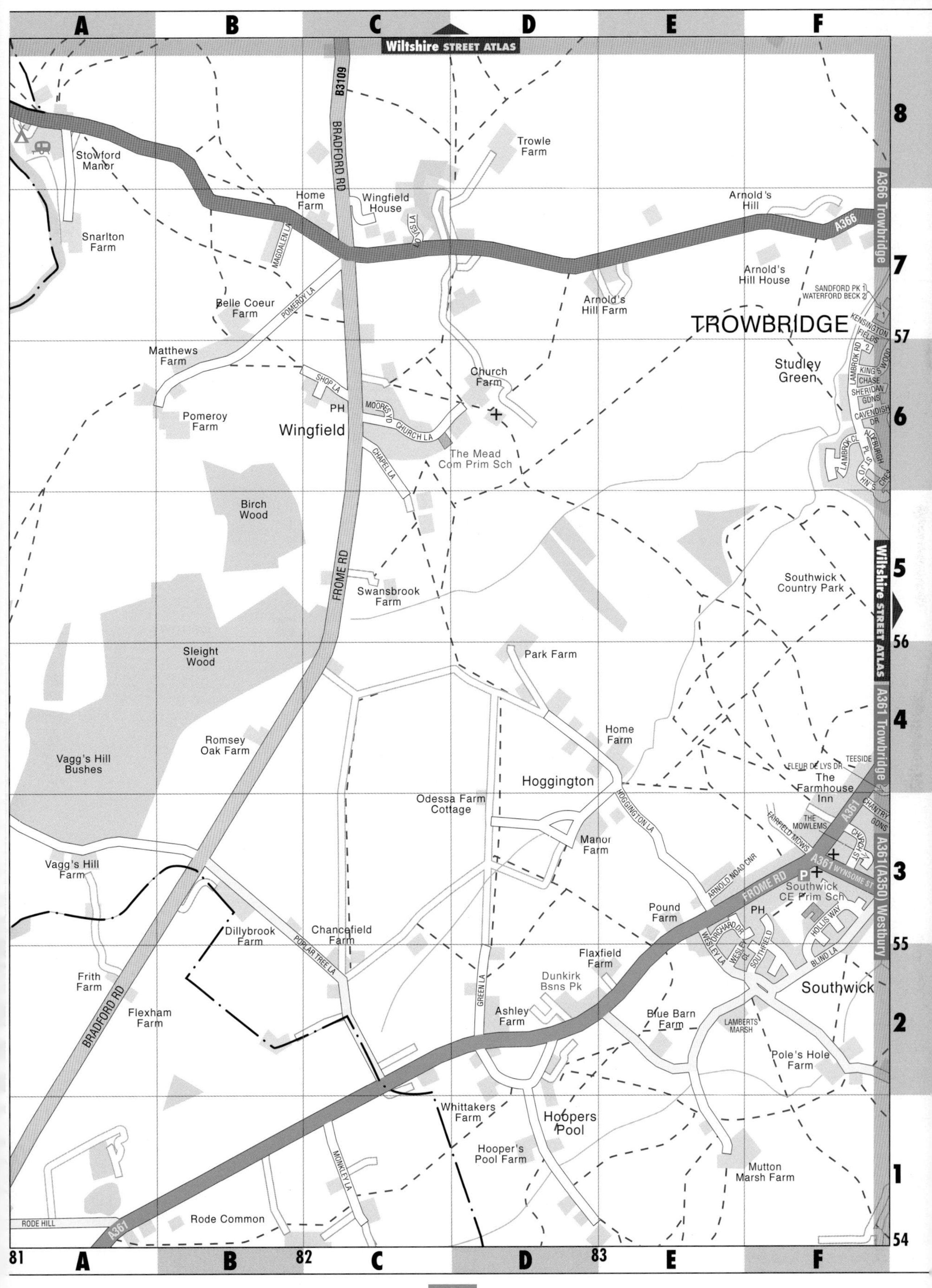
Wiltshire STREET ATLAS
A
B
C
D
E
F
8
7
57
6
5
56
4
3
55
2
1
54
81
82
83
B3109
BRADFORD RD
Stowford Manor
Snarlton Farm
Home Farm
Wingfield House
MAGDALEN LA
LOVES LA
Trowle Farm
Arnold's Hill
A366
A366 Trowbridge
Arnold's Hill House
Arnold's Hill Farm
TROWBRIDGE
Studley Green
Belle Coeur Farm
POMEROY LA
Matthews Farm
Pomeroy Farm
SHOP LA
PH
Wingfield
MOORES YD
CHURCH LA
CHAPEL LA
Church Farm
The Mead Com Prim Sch
Birch Wood
FROME RD
Swansbrook Farm
Southwick Country Park
Sleight Wood
Park Farm
Romsey Oak Farm
Home Farm
Hoggington
Vagg's Hill Bushes
Odessa Farm Cottage
HOGGINGTON LA
Manor Farm
Vagg's Hill Farm
The Farmhouse Inn
A361 Trowbridge
A361(A350) Westbury
ARNOLD NOAD CNR
Southwick CE Prim Sch
Pound Farm
Dillybrook Farm
Chancefield Farm
POPLAR TREE LA
Flaxfield Farm
Dunkirk Bsns Pk
GREEN LA
Ashley Farm
Blue Barn Farm
Southwick
LAMBERTS MARSH
Pole's Hole Farm
Frith Farm
Flexham Farm
BRADFORD RD
Whittakers Farm
Hoopers Pool
Hooper's Pool Farm
Mutton Marsh Farm
MONKLEY LA
Rode Common
RODE HILL
A361

65

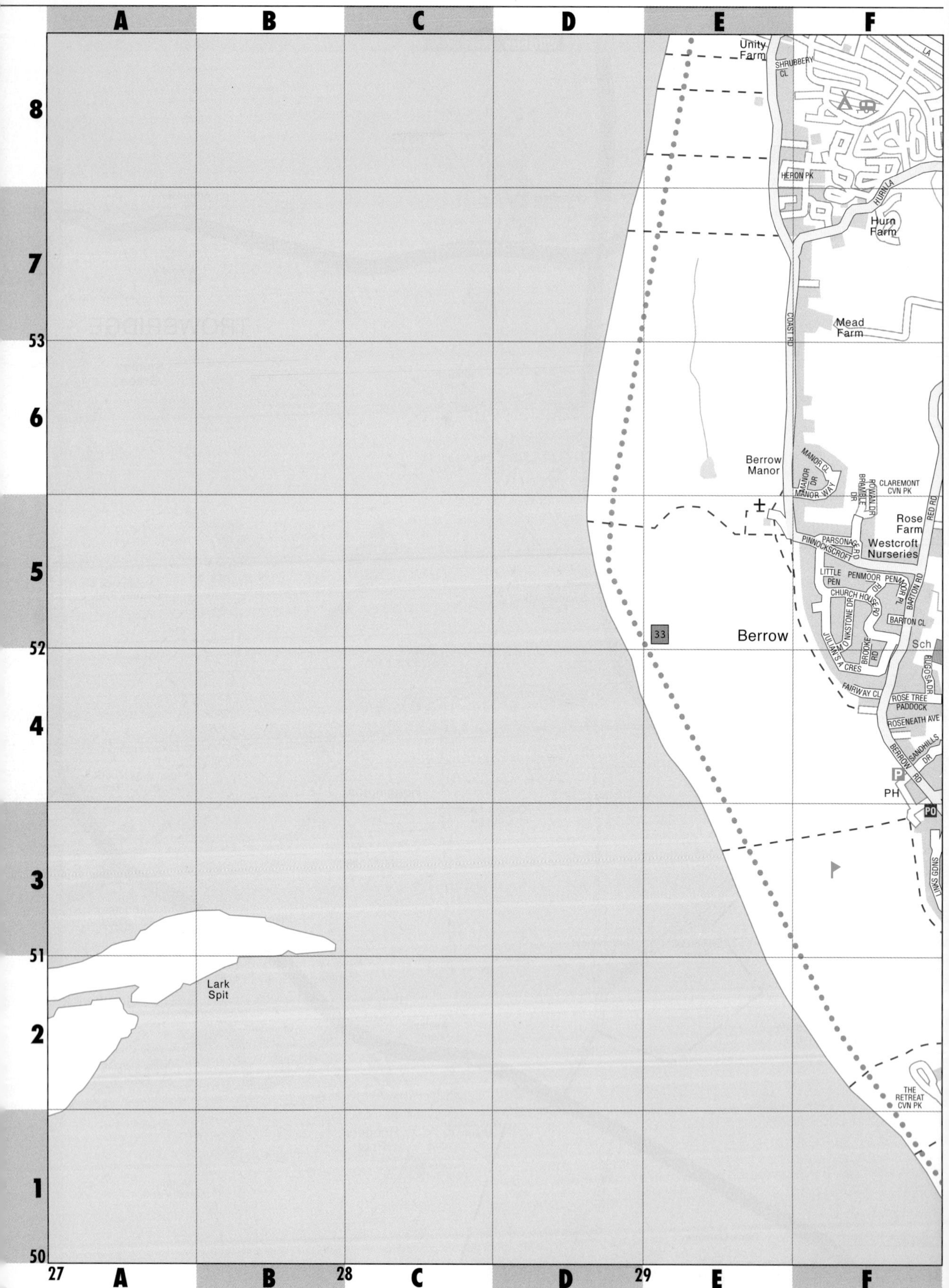

A
B
C
D
E
F
8
7
53
6
5
52
4
3
51
2
1
50
27
28
29
Unity Farm
SHRUBBERY CL
HERON PK
HURN LA
Hurn Farm
COAST RD
Mead Farm
Berrow Manor
MANOR CL
MANOR DR
MANOR WAY
BRAMBLE DR
ROWAN DR
CLAREMONT CVN PK
RED RD
Rose Farm
PARSONAGE RD
PINNOCKSCROFT
Westcroft Nurseries
LITTLE PEN
PENMOOR RD
PENMOOR PL
CHURCH HOUSE RD
MONKSTONE DR
BARTON RD
BARTON CL
33
Berrow
JULIAN'S A CRES
BROOKE RD
Sch
FAIRWAY CL
ROSE TREE PADDOCK
ROSENEATH AVE
BERROW RD
SANDHILLS DR
PH
PO
Lark Spit
THE RETREAT CVN PK

103

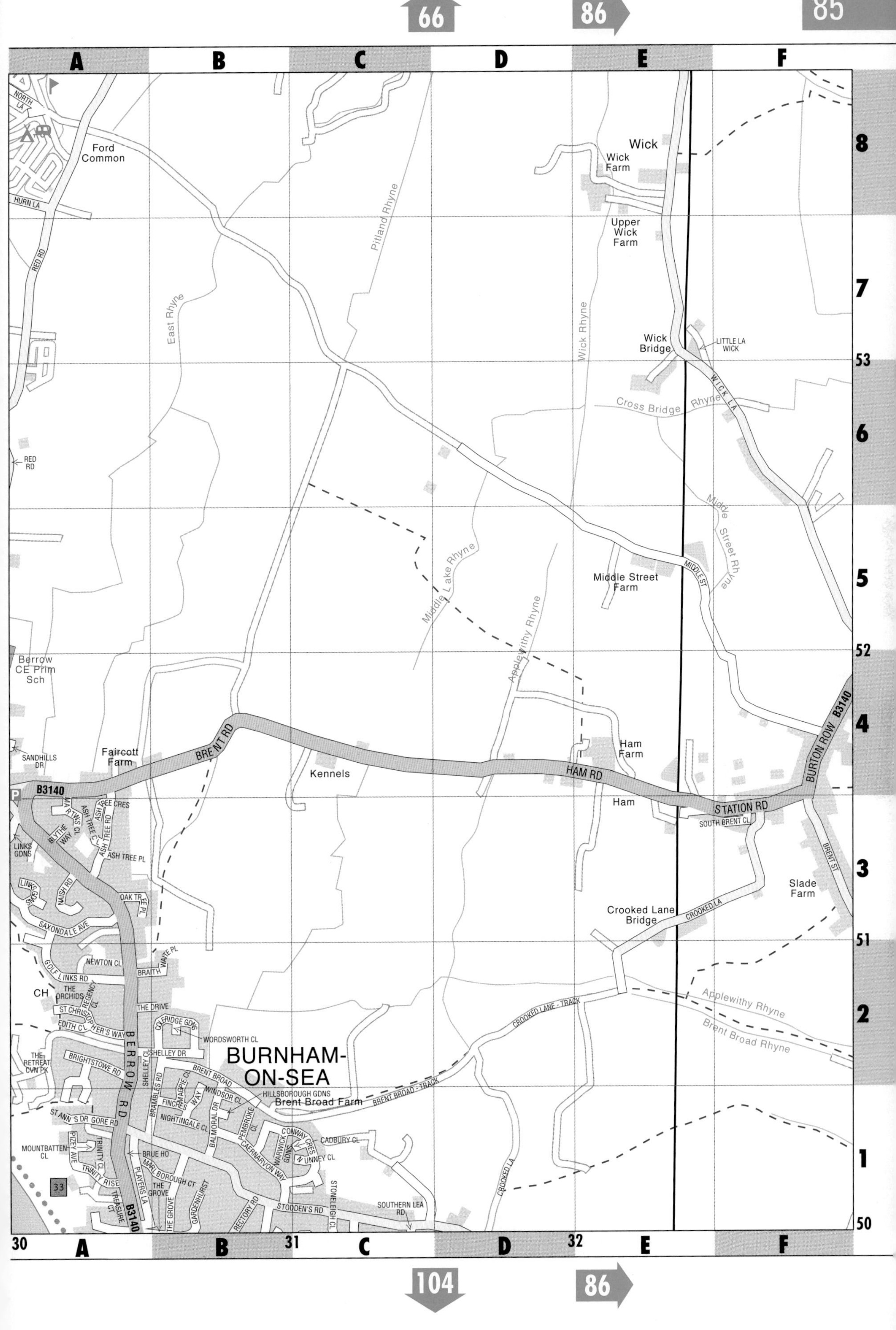
66
86
104
86
A
B
C
D
E
F
8
7
53
6
5
52
4
3
51
2
1
50
30
31
32
Wick
Wick Farm
Upper Wick Farm
Ford Common
NORTH LA
HURN LA
RED RD
Pitland Rhyne
East Rhyne
Wick Rhyne
Wick Bridge
LITTLE LA WICK
WICK LA
Cross Bridge Rhyne
Middle Street Rhyne
MIDDLE ST
Middle Street Farm
Middle Lake Rhyne
Applewithy Rhyne
Berrow CE Prim Sch
SANDHILLS DR
Faircott Farm
BRENT RD
Kennels
HAM RD
Ham Farm
Ham
STATION RD
SOUTH BRENT CL
BURTON ROW
B3140
BRENT ST
Slade Farm
Crooked Lane Bridge
CROOKED LA
CROOKED LANE - TRACK
Applewithy Rhyne
Brent Broad Rhyne
BRENT BROAD - TRACK
Brent Broad Farm
HILLSBOROUGH GDNS
BURNHAM-ON-SEA
BLYTHE WAY
MARTINS CL
ASH TREE CL
ASH TREE RD
ASH TREE CRES
ASH TREE PL
LINKS GDNS
NAISH RD
OAK TREE PL
SAXONDALE AVE
NEWTON CL
GOLF LINKS RD
BRAITHWAITE PL
CH
THE ORCHIDS
REGENCY CL
ST CHRISTOPHER'S WAY
EDITH CL
THE DRIVE
COLERIDGE GDNS
WORDSWORTH CL
SHELLEY DR
SHELLEY CL
THE RETREAT CVN PK
BRIGHTSTOWE RD
BERROW RD
BRENT BROAD
WINDSOR CL
BRAMBLES RD
FINCHES
MAGPIE CL
NIGHTINGALE CL
BALMORAL DR
PEMBROKE CL
CAERNARVON WAY
CONWAY CRES
WARWICK GDNS
UNNEY CL
CADBURY CL
ST ANN'S DR
GORE RD
MOUNTBATTEN CL
PIZEY AVE
TRINITY CL
TRINITY RISE
BRUE HO
MARLBOROUGH CT
PLAYERS LA
THE GROVE
GARDENHURST
TREASURE CT
RECTORY RD
STODDEN'S RD
STONELEIGH CL
SOUTHERN LEA RD
33

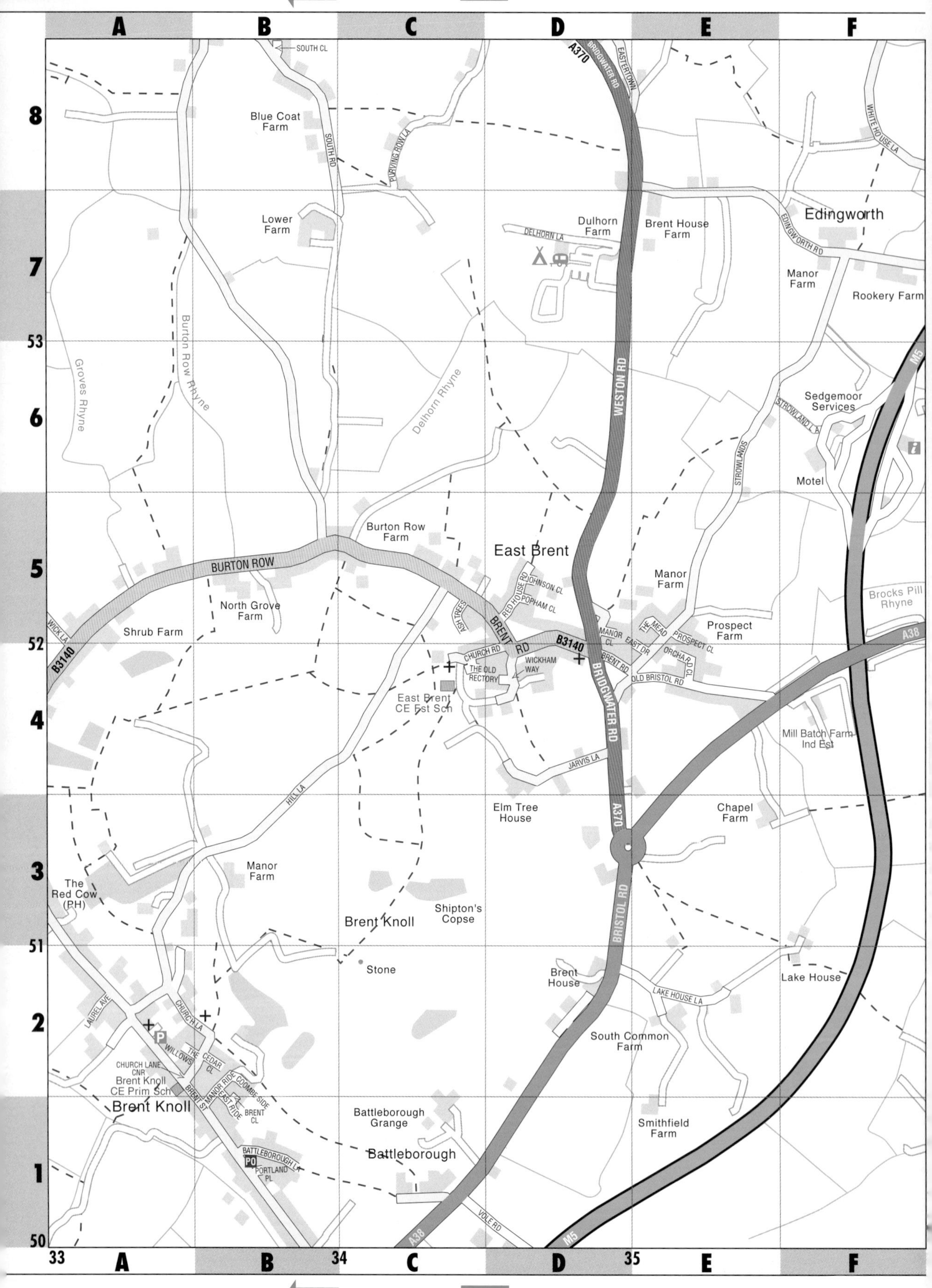
85
67
A
B
C
D
E
F
8
7
53
6
5
52
4
3
51
2
1
50
33
34
35
Blue Coat Farm
Lower Farm
Dulhorn Farm
Brent House Farm
Edingworth
Manor Farm
Rookery Farm
Sedgemoor Services
Motel
Groves Rhyne
Burton Row Rhyne
Delhorn Rhyne
Burton Row Farm
East Brent
Manor Farm
North Grove Farm
Shrub Farm
BURTON ROW
B3140
Prospect Farm
Brocks Pill Rhyne
East Brent CE Fst Sch
Mill Batch Farm Ind Est
Elm Tree House
Chapel Farm
Manor Farm
The Red Cow (PH)
Brent Knoll
Shipton's Copse
Stone
Brent House
Lake House
South Common Farm
Smithfield Farm
Battleborough Grange
Battleborough
Brent Knoll CE Prim Sch
Brent Knoll
WESTON RD
BRIDGWATER RD
BRISTOL RD
A370
A38
M5
HILL LA
JARVIS LA
LAKE HOUSE LA
VOLE RD
STROWLANDS
EDINGWORTH RD
DELHORN LA
SOUTH RD
SOUTH CL
PURVING ROW LA
EASTERTOWN
WHITE HOUSE LA
CHURCH LA
WILLOWS
THE CEDAR CL
BATTLEBOROUGH LA
PORTLAND PL
LAUREL AVE
WICK LA
85
105

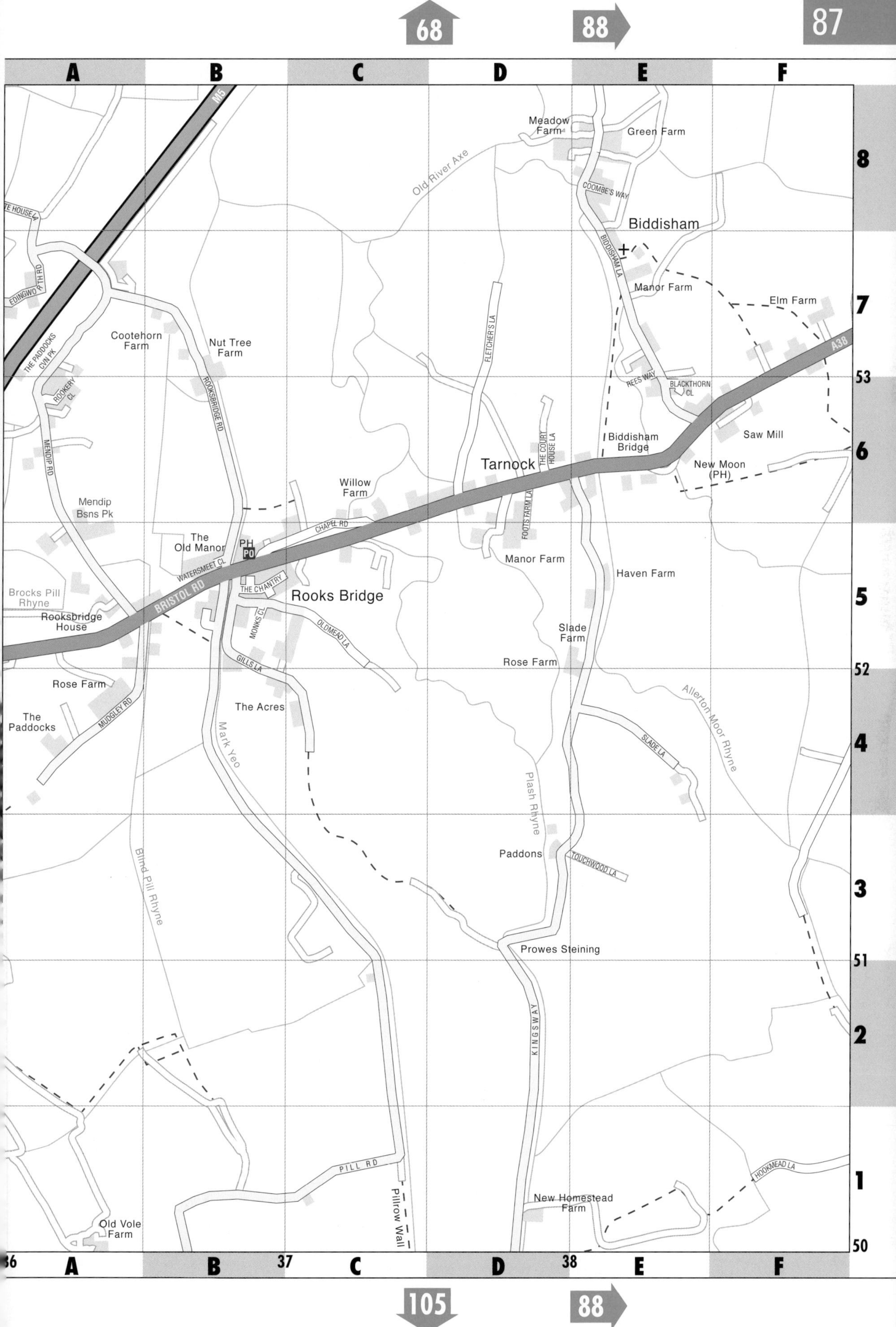
68
88
A
B
C
D
E
F
8
7
53
6
5
52
4
3
51
2
1
50
36
37
38
M5
Meadow Farm
Green Farm
Old River Axe
COOMBE'S WAY
Biddisham
BIDDISHAM LA
Manor Farm
Elm Farm
A38
Cootehorn Farm
Nut Tree Farm
FLETCHER'S LA
THE PADDOCKS CVN PK
ROOKERY CL
ROOKSBRIDGE RD
REES WAY
BLACKTHORN CL
Saw Mill
MENDIP RD
Biddisham Bridge
THE COURT HOUSE LA
Tarnock
New Moon (PH)
Willow Farm
Mendip Bsns Pk
CHAPEL RD
FOOTS FARM LA
The Old Manor
PH
PO
Manor Farm
WATERSMEET CL
Haven Farm
Brocks Pill Rhyne
BRISTOL RD
THE CHANTRY
Rooks Bridge
Rooksbridge House
MONKS CL
OLDMEAD LA
Slade Farm
Rose Farm
GILLS LA
Rose Farm
Allerton Moor Rhyne
The Paddocks
MUDGLEY RD
The Acres
Mark Yeo
SLADE LA
Plash Rhyne
Paddons
TOUCHWOOD LA
Blind Pill Rhyne
Prowes Steining
KINGSWAY
PILL RD
HOOKMEAD LA
New Homestead Farm
Pillrow Wall
Old Vole Farm
105
88

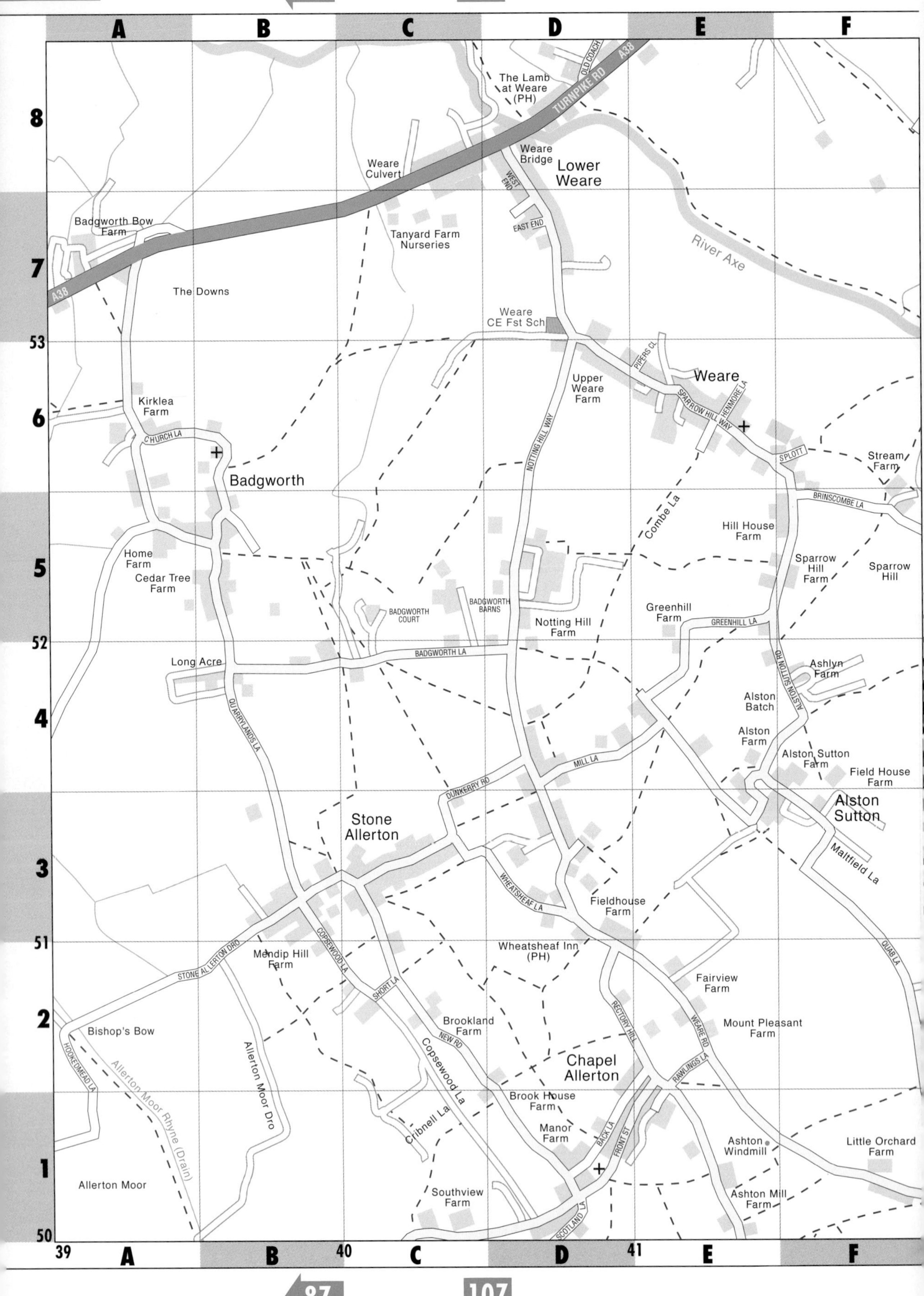
87
69
A
B
C
D
E
F
8
7
53
6
5
52
4
3
51
2
1
50
39
40
41
107
The Lamb at Weare (PH)
OLD COACH
TURNPIKE RD
A38
Weare Culvert
Weare Bridge
Lower Weare
WEST END
EAST END
Badgworth Bow Farm
Tanyard Farm Nurseries
River Axe
The Downs
Weare CE Fst Sch
PIPERS CL
Weare
Upper Weare Farm
HENMORE LA
SPARROW HILL WAY
Kirklea Farm
CHURCH LA
NOTTING HILL WAY
SPLOTT
Stream Farm
Badgworth
BRINSCOMBE LA
Combe La
Hill House Farm
Home Farm
Sparrow Hill Farm
Sparrow Hill
Cedar Tree Farm
BADGWORTH BARNS
BADGWORTH COURT
Greenhill Farm
Notting Hill Farm
GREENHILL LA
Long Acre
BADGWORTH LA
Ashlyn Farm
ALSTON SUTTON RD
Alston Batch
QUARRYLANDS LA
Alston Farm
Alston Sutton Farm
MILL LA
Field House Farm
DUNKERRY RD
Alston Sutton
Stone Allerton
Maltfield La
WHEATSHEAF LA
Fieldhouse Farm
STONE ALLERTON DRO
COPSEWOOD LA
Mendip Hill Farm
Wheatsheaf Inn (PH)
QUAB LA
Fairview Farm
SHORT LA
Bishop's Bow
Brookland Farm
Mount Pleasant Farm
NEW RD
RECTORY HILL
WEARE RD
HOOKEDMEAD LA
Allerton Moor Rhyne (Drain)
Allerton Moor Dro
Copsewood La
Chapel Allerton
RAWLINGS LA
Brook House Farm
Cribnell La
Manor Farm
BACK LA
FRONT ST
Ashton Windmill
Little Orchard Farm
Allerton Moor
Southview Farm
Ashton Mill Farm
SCOTLAND LA

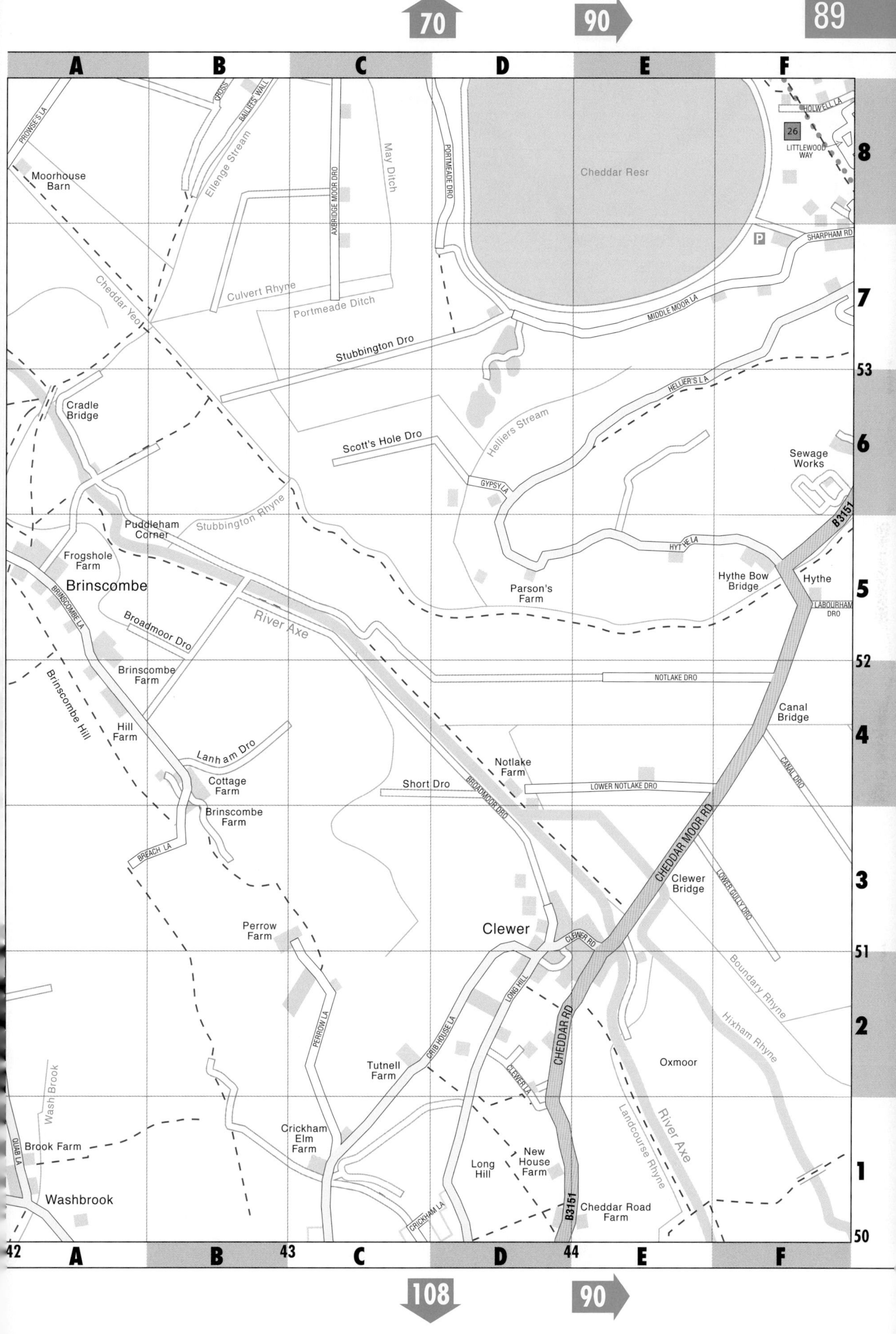

70
90
A
B
C
D
E
F
8
7
53
6
5
52
4
3
51
2
1
50
42
43
44
108
90
PROWSE'S LA
CROSS
BAILIFFS WALL
Moorhouse Barn
Ellenge Stream
AXBRIDGE MOOR DRO
May Ditch
PORTMEADE DRO
Cheddar Resr
HOLWELL LA
26
LITTLEWOOD WAY
SHARPHAM RD
Culvert Rhyne
Portmeade Ditch
Cheddar Yeo
Stubbington Dro
MIDDLE MOOR LA
Cradle Bridge
HELLIER'S LA
Helliers Stream
Scott's Hole Dro
Sewage Works
GYPSY LA
Puddleham Corner
Stubbington Rhyne
B3151
Frogshole Farm
HYTHE LA
Brinscombe
BRINSCOMBE LA
Parson's Farm
Hythe Bow Bridge
Hythe
LABOURHAM DRO
Broadmoor Dro
River Axe
Brinscombe Farm
NOTLAKE DRO
Brinscombe Hill
Canal Bridge
Hill Farm
Lanham Dro
Notlake Farm
CANAL DRO
Cottage Farm
Short Dro
BROADMOOR DRO
LOWER NOTLAKE DRO
Brinscombe Farm
BREACH LA
CHEDDAR MOOR RD
Clewer Bridge
LOWER GULLY DRO
Perrow Farm
Clewer
CLEWER RD
Boundary Rhyne
LONG HILL
CRIB HOUSE LA
CHEDDAR RD
Hixham Rhyne
PERROW LA
Tutnell Farm
Oxmoor
CLEWER LA
Wash Brook
Landcourse Rhyne
River Axe
Brook Farm
Crickham Elm Farm
New House Farm
QUAB LA
Long Hill
Washbrook
CRICKHAM LA
B3151
Cheddar Road Farm

89
71

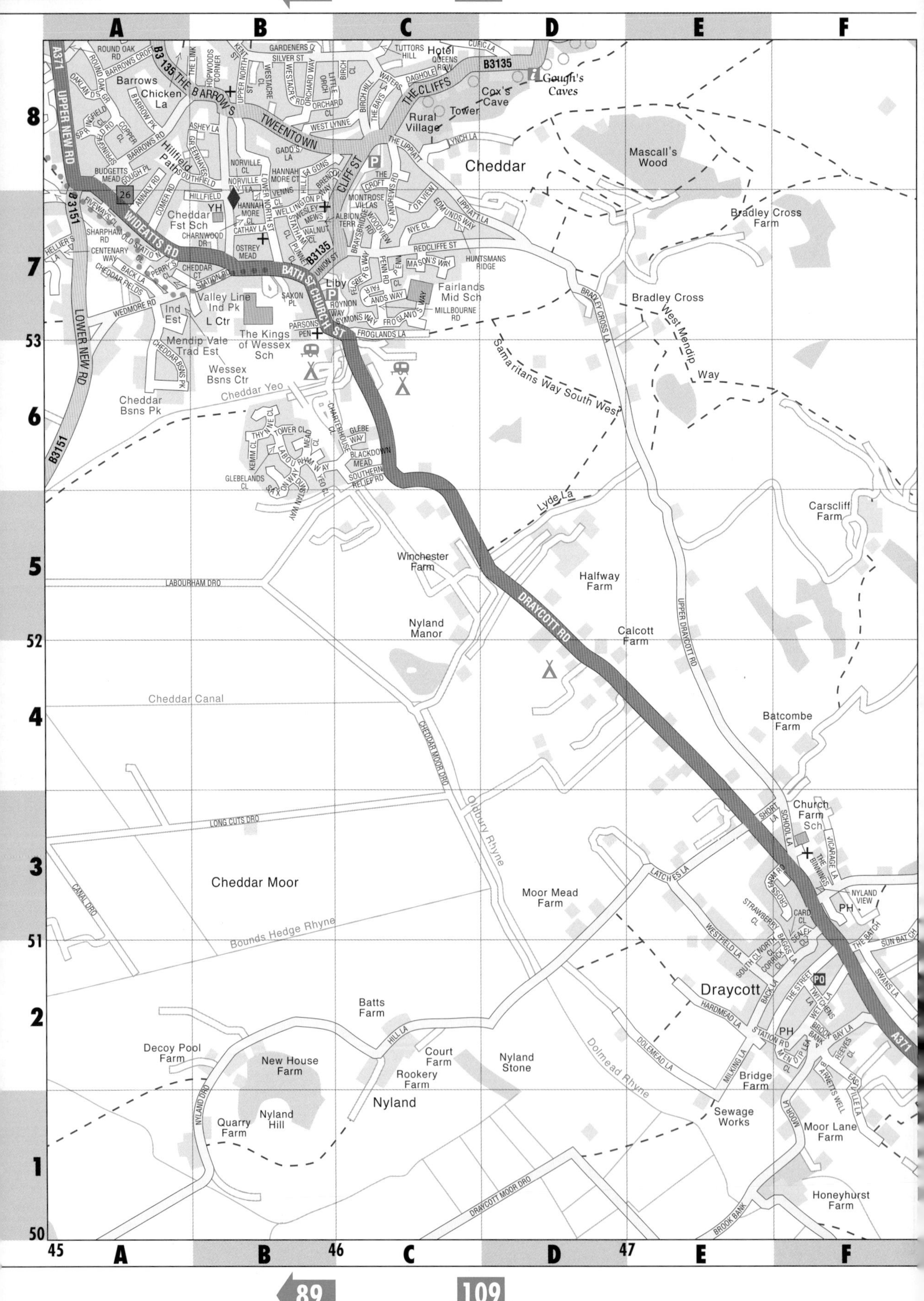
A
B
C
D
E
F
8
7
53
6
5
52
4
3
51
2
1
50
45
46
47
A371
UPPER NEW RD
ROUND OAK RD
BARROWS CROFT
B3 135 THE BARROWS
THE LINK
HOPWOODS CORNER
KENT ST
UPPER NORTH ST
GARDENERS CL
SILVER ST
WESTACRE
WESTACRE RD
ORCHARD WAY
LITTLE ORCH
BIRCH CL
BIRCH HILL
TUTTORS HILL
Hotel
QUEENS ROW
CURIC LA
B3135
Gough's Caves
THE CLIFFS
DAGHOLE
WATERS LA
THE BAYS
ORCHARD CL
WEST LYNNE
TWEENTOWN
Cox's Cave
Tower
Rural Village
LYNCH LA
Barrows
Chicken La
OAKLANDS
ROUND OAK GR
SPRINGFIELD
SPRINGFIELD RD
COPPER CL
BARROW PK
BARROWS RD
ASHEY LA
Hillfield Paths
GREENHAYES
SOUTHFIELD
NORVILLE CL
GADD'S LA
HANNAH MORE CT
JENNS
HILL LA GDNS
BREWERY
CLIFF ST
THE LIPPIATT
Cheddar
Mascall's Wood
BUDGETTS MEAD
GOUGH PL
ANNALY RD
COMER RD
HILLFIELD
NORVILLE LA
LOWER NORTH ST
WELLINGTON PL
WESLEY MEWS
THE CROFT
MONTROSE VILLAS
ST ANDREWS RD
TOR VIEW
EDMUNDS WAY
LIPPIATT LA
Bradley Cross Farm
26
B3151
WIDEATTS RD
YH
Cheddar Fst Sch
HANNAH MORE CL
CATHAY LA
STATHAM CL
WALNUT CL
ALBION TERR
BRAYSBRIDGE RD
WOODVIEW
NYE CL
REDCLIFFE ST
HUNTSMANS RIDGE
SHARPHAM RD
CENTENARY WAY
CHARNWOOD DR
OSTREY MEAD
PUNNETT CL
B3135
UNION ST
MASON'S WAY
BACK LA
PERRY'S CL
CHEDDAR CT
STATION RD
BATH ST
CHURCH ST
Liby
FUSSELL'S WAY
PENN RD
Fairlands Mid Sch
MILLBOURNE RD
BRADLEY CROSS LA
Bradley Cross
West Mendip Way
CHEDDAR FIELDS
WEDMORE RD
Valley Line Ind Pk
L Ctr
SAXON PL
ROYNON WAY
SYMONS WAY
FROGLANDS WAY
Ind Est
PARSONS PEN
FROGLANDS LA
Samaritans Way South West
LOWER NEW RD
Mendip Vale Trad Est
CHEDDAR BSNS PK
The Kings of Wessex Sch
Wessex Bsns Ctr
Cheddar Yeo
Cheddar Bsns Pk
THYNNE CL
TOWER CL
CHARTERHOUSE CL
GLEBE WAY
KEMM CL
LABOURHAM WAY
MEAD CL
BLACKDOWN MEAD
SOUTHERN RELIEF RD
GLEBELANDS CL
SAXON WAY
DUNSTAN WAY
YEO CL
Lyde La
Carscliff Farm
Winchester Farm
LABOURHAM DRO
Halfway Farm
DRAYCOTT RD
Nyland Manor
Calcott Farm
UPPER DRAYCOTT RD
Cheddar Canal
CHEDDAR MOOR DRO
Batcombe Farm
Oldbury Rhyne
LONG CUTS DRO
Church Farm
Sch
SHORT LA
SCHOOL LA
VICARAGE LA
THE BINNINGS
Cheddar Moor
CANAL DRO
Moor Mead Farm
LATCHES LA
CROSS FARM RD
STRAWBERRY CL
CARD CL
NYLAND VIEW
PH
Bounds Hedge Rhyne
WESTFIELD LA
SOUTH CL
NORTH CL
CORRICK CL
BRIGGS LA
SEALEY CL
THE BATCH
SUN BATCH
SWANS LA
Draycott
PO
BACK LA
THE STREET
TWITCHENS LA
WELLS RD
A371
Batts Farm
HARDMEAD LA
STATION RD
PH
BROOK BANK
BAY LA
REEVES CL
Decoy Pool Farm
HILL LA
New House Farm
Court Farm
Nyland Stone
Dolmead Rhyne
DOLEMEAD LA
MILKING LA
MENDIP LEA CL
Bridge Farm
BARNETTS WELL
EASTVILLE LA
Rookery Farm
Nyland
NYLAND DRO
Quarry Farm
Nyland Hill
Sewage Works
MOOR LA
Moor Lane Farm
DRAYCOTT MOOR DRO
BROOK BANK
Honeyhurst Farm
45
A
B
46
C
D
47
E
F

89
109

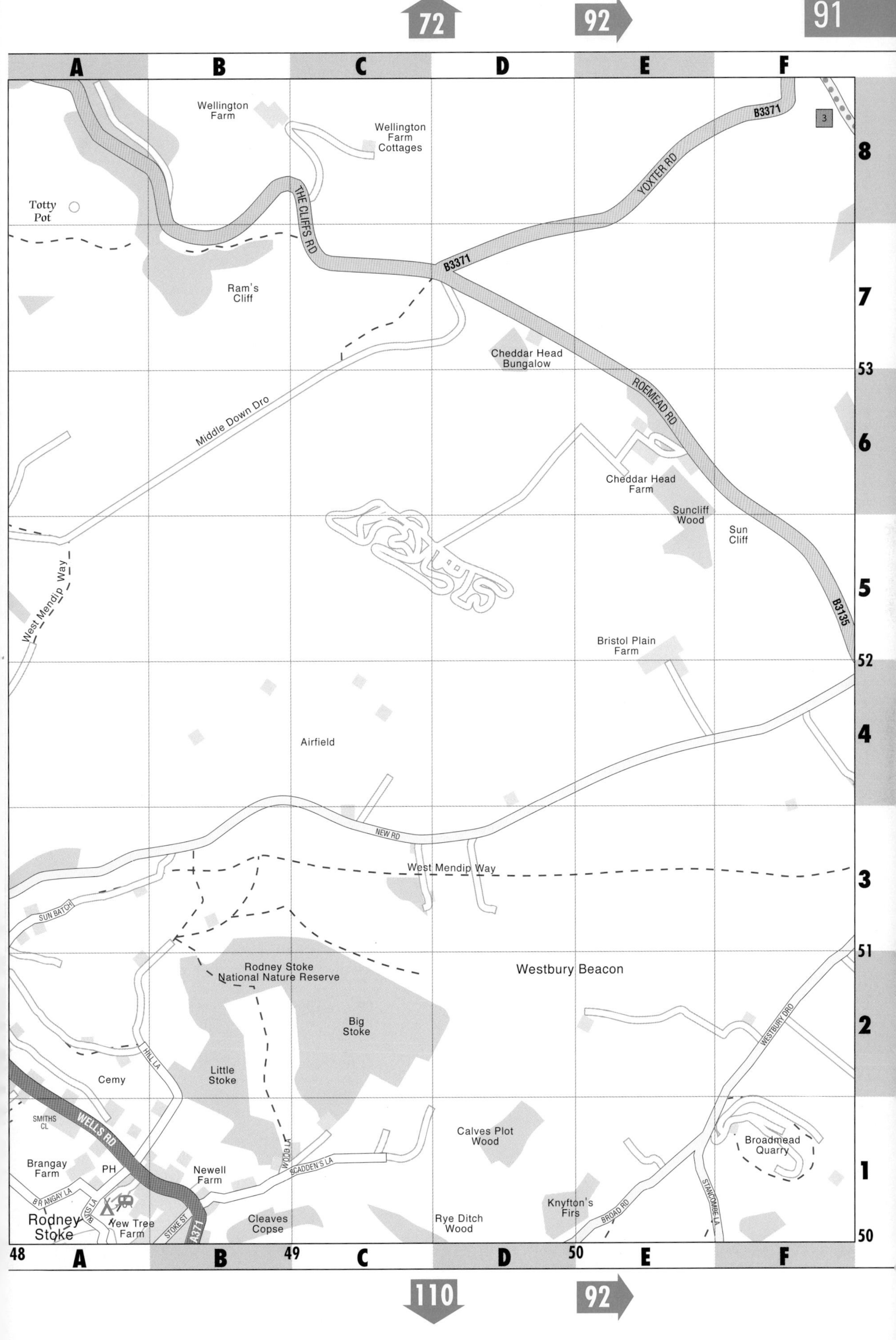
72
92
A
B
C
D
E
F
Wellington
Farm
Wellington
Farm
Cottages
Totty
Pot
THE CLIFFS RD
YOXTER RD
B3371
Ram's
Cliff
Cheddar Head
Bungalow
ROEMEAD RD
Middle Down Dro
Cheddar Head
Farm
Suncliff
Wood
Sun
Cliff
West Mendip Way
B3135
Bristol Plain
Farm
Airfield
NEW RD
West Mendip Way
SUN BATCH
Westbury Beacon
Rodney Stoke
National Nature Reserve
Big
Stoke
WESTBURY DRO
Little
Stoke
Cemy
HILL LA
SMITHS
CL
WELLS RD
Calves Plot
Wood
Broadmead
Quarry
Brangay
Farm
PH
Newell
Farm
WOOD LA
SCADDEN'S LA
BRANGAY LA
Rodney
Stoke
Yew Tree
Farm
STOKE ST
A371
Cleaves
Copse
Rye Ditch
Wood
Knyfton's
Firs
BROAD RD
STANCOMBE LA
8
7
53
6
5
52
4
3
51
2
1
50
48
49
50
110
92

91
73

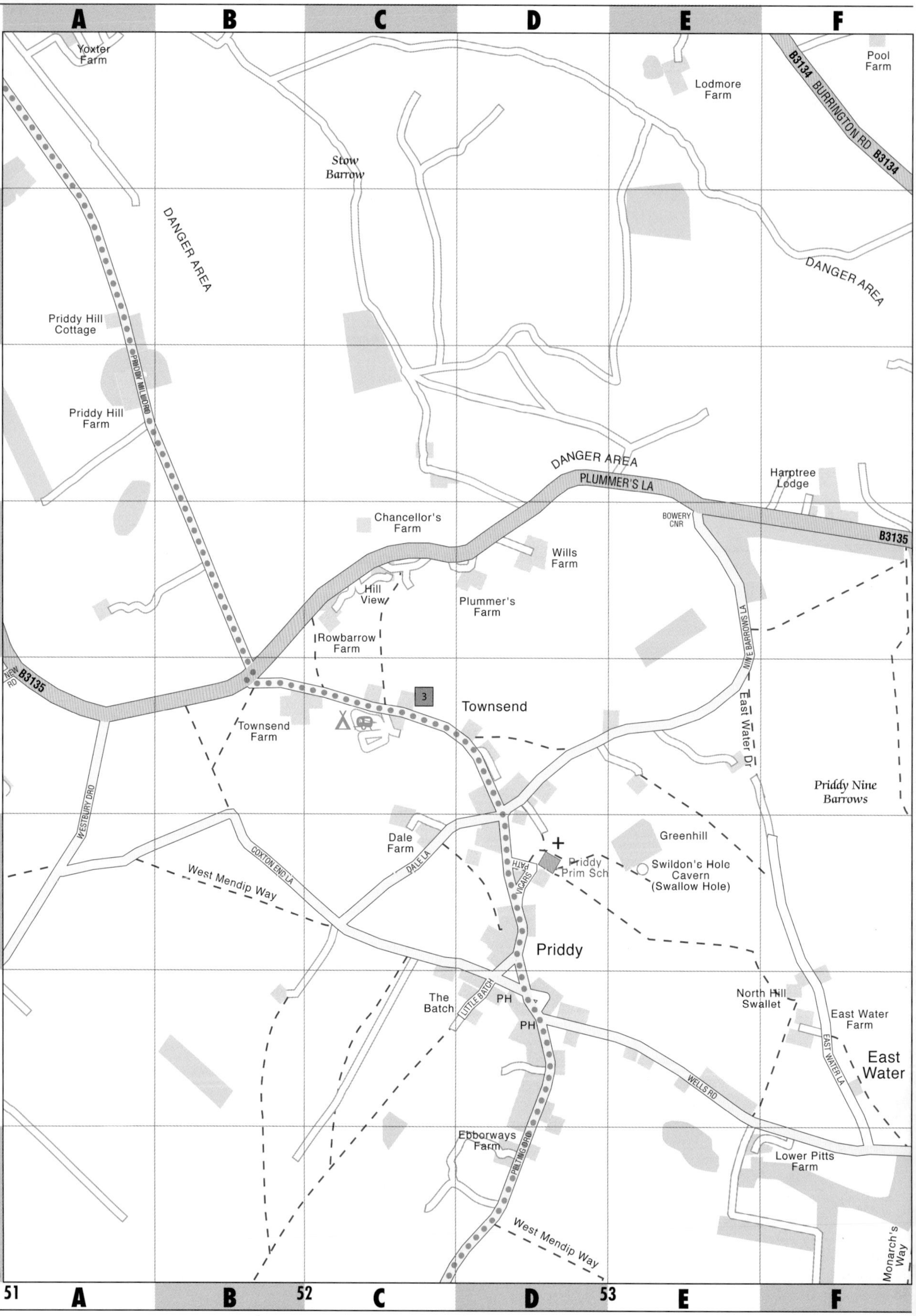

A B C D E F

8 7 53 6 5 52 4 3 51 2 1 50

Yoxter Farm
Pool Farm
Lodmore Farm
B3134 BURRINGTON RD B3134
Stow Barrow
DANGER AREA
DANGER AREA
Priddy Hill Cottage
PRIDDY HILL DRO
Priddy Hill Farm
DANGER AREA
PLUMMER'S LA
Harptree Lodge
BOWERY CNR
B3135
Chancellor's Farm
Wills Farm
Hill View
Plummer's Farm
Rowbarrow Farm
NINE BARROWS LA
NEW RD
B3135
3
Townsend
Townsend Farm
East Water Dr
Priddy Nine Barrows
WESTBURY DRO
Dale Farm
Greenhill
COXTON END LA
DALE LA
VICARS PATH
Priddy Prim Sch
Swildon's Hole Cavern (Swallow Hole)
West Mendip Way
Priddy
North Hill Swallet
The Batch
LITTLE BATCH
PH
PH
East Water Farm
EAST WATER LA
East Water
WELLS RD
Ebborways Farm
PELTING DRO
Lower Pitts Farm
West Mendip Way
Monarch's Way

51 A B 52 C D 53 E F

91
111

74
94
A
B
C
D
E
F
Devil's Punch Bowl
OLD BRISTOL RD
Swallet Farm
Mast
SMITHAMS HILL
Wurt Pit (dis)
Roadside Clump
Big Clump
Nett Wood Farm
Greendown Batch
8
Hill Grange
B3134 BURRINGTON RD
Hill Farm
Niver Hill
7
Castle of Comfort (PH)
53
Castle Farm
Priddy Circles
OLD BRISTOL RD
The Belt
Monarch's Way
Bendall's Grove
Eaker Hill Farm
EAKER HILL LA
West End
Wigmore Farm
6
Cranmore View
Miners' Arms
B3134
Eaker Hill
5
Red Quarr Farm
52
TOR HOLE RD
4
North Hill
Monarch's Way
MINERY RD
3
Priddy Mineries
Bendalls Farm
B3135
51
Stockhill
2
Under Barrow Farm
Nursery
Cuckoo Cleeves
Tower Hill
1
Ash Plantation
Hunters Lodge Inn
HILLGROVE RD
50
54
55
56
112
94

93
75

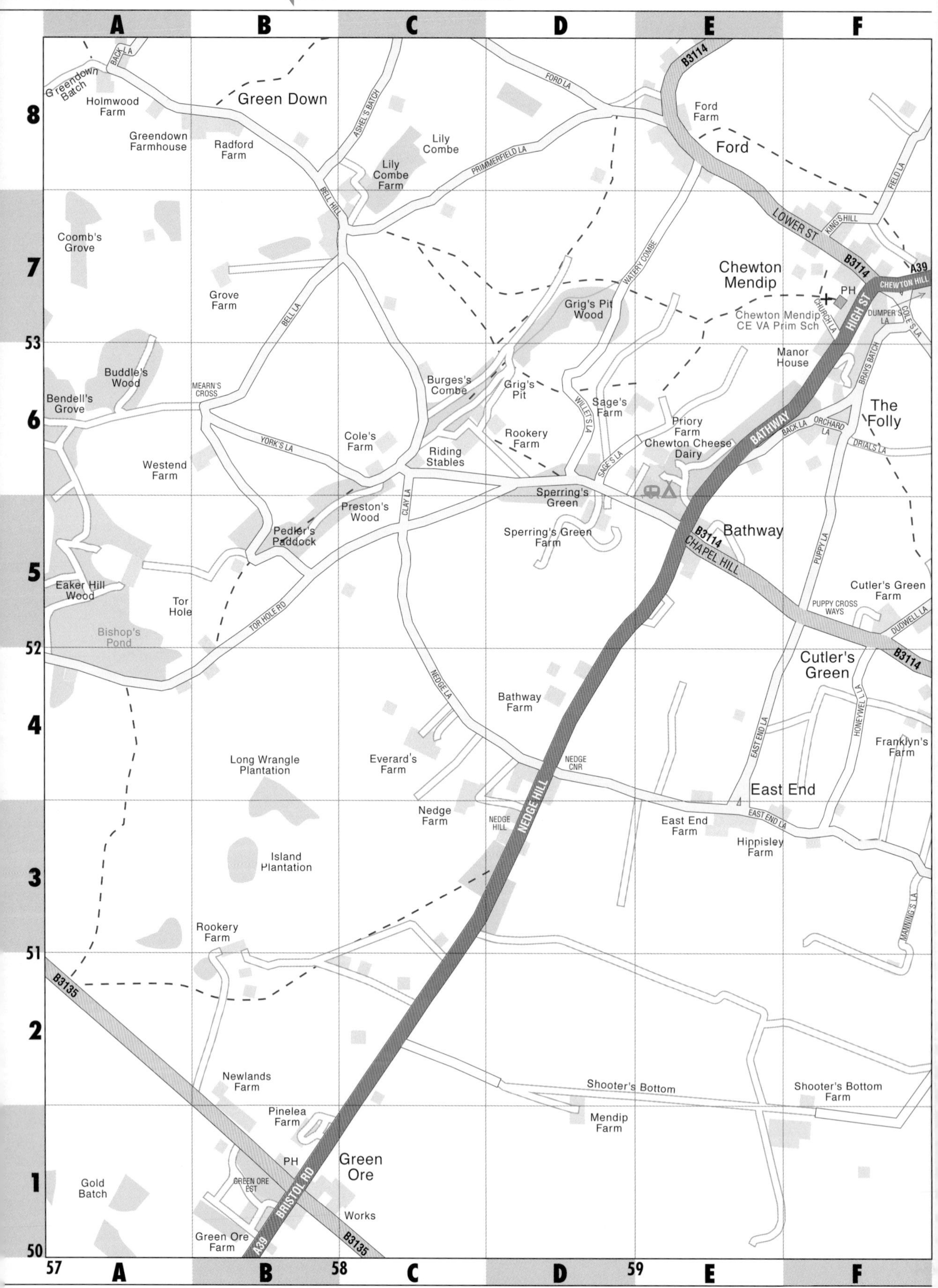
A
B
C
D
E
F
8
7
53
6
5
52
4
3
51
2
1
50
57
58
59
Greendown Batch
BACK LA
Holmwood Farm
Green Down
Greendown Farmhouse
Radford Farm
ASHEL'S BATCH
Lily Combe
Lily Combe Farm
FORD LA
B3114
Ford Farm
Ford
PRIMMERFIELD LA
BELL HILL
FIELD LA
Coomb's Grove
LOWER ST
KING'S HILL
Chewton Mendip
B3114
A39
CHEWTON HILL
WATERY COMBE
Grove Farm
BELL LA
Grig's Pit Wood
PH
Chewton Mendip CE VA Prim Sch
CHURCH LA
HIGH ST
DUMPER'S LA
COLE'S LA
Buddle's Wood
MEARN'S CROSS
Burges's Combe
Grig's Pit
Sage's Farm
WILLET'S LA
Manor House
BRAYS BATCH
Bendell's Grove
The Folly
YORK'S LA
Cole's Farm
Riding Stables
Rookery Farm
Priory Farm
Chewton Cheese Dairy
BATHWAY
BACK LA
ORCHARD LA
DRIALS LA
SAGE'S LA
Westend Farm
Sperring's Green
Preston's Wood
CLAY LA
Pedler's Paddock
Sperring's Green Farm
Bathway
B3114
CHAPEL HILL
PUPPY LA
Eaker Hill Wood
Tor Hole
TOR HOLE RD
Cutler's Green Farm
PUPPY CROSS WAYS
DUDWELL LA
Bishop's Pond
Cutler's Green
B3114
NEDGE LA
Bathway Farm
EAST END LA
HONEYWELL LA
Long Wrangle Plantation
Everard's Farm
NEDGE CNR
Franklyn's Farm
NEDGE HILL
East End
Nedge Farm
NEDGE HILL
East End Farm
EAST END LA
Hippisley Farm
Island Plantation
MANNING'S LA
Rookery Farm
B3135
Newlands Farm
Shooter's Bottom
Shooter's Bottom Farm
Mendip Farm
Pinelea Farm
PH
Green Ore
Gold Batch
GREEN ORE EST
BRISTOL RD
Works
Green Ore Farm
A39
B3135

93
113

76
96

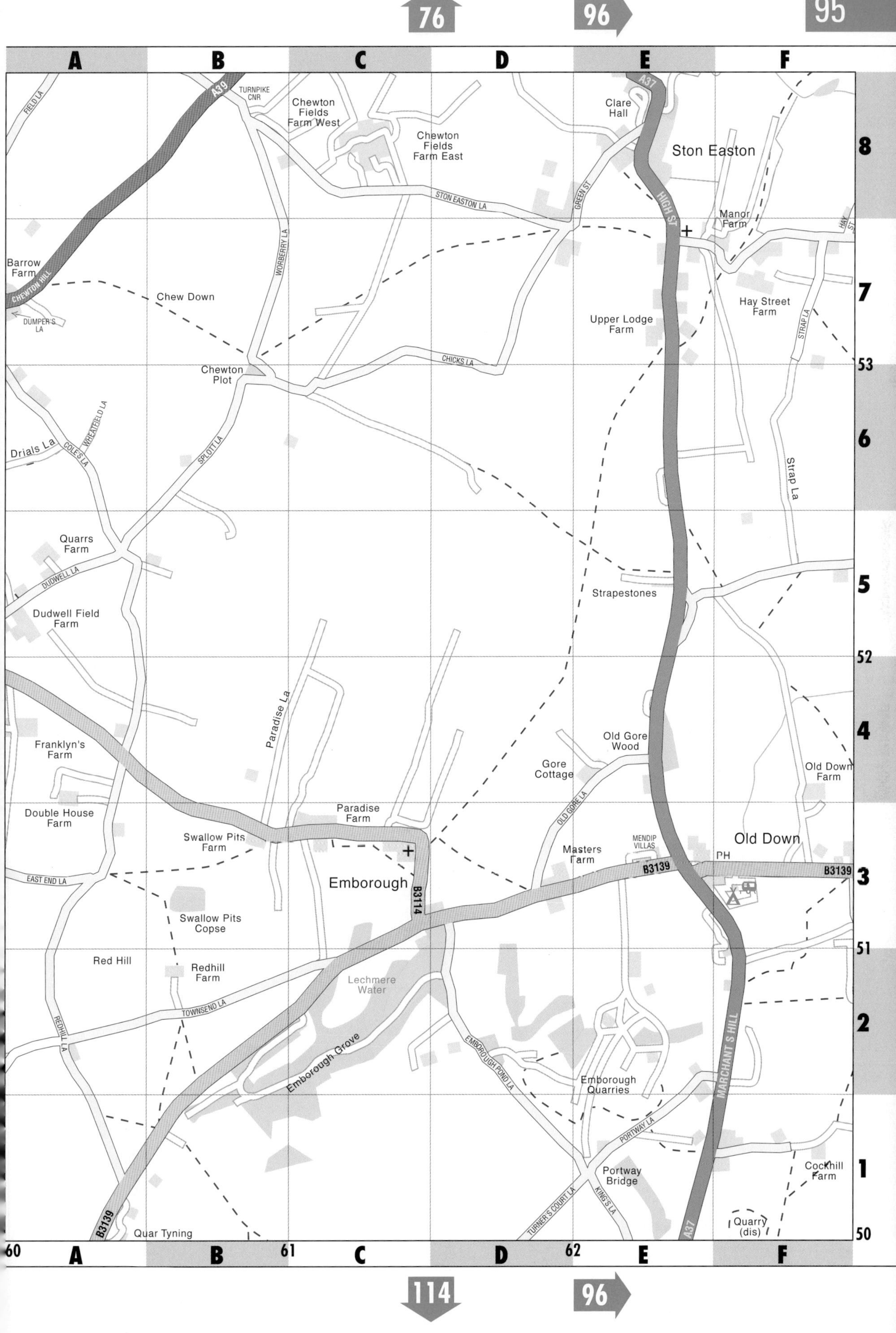
A
B
C
D
E
F
8
7
53
6
5
52
4
3
51
2
1
50
60
61
62
TURNPIKE CNR
Chewton Fields Farm West
Chewton Fields Farm East
Clare Hall
Ston Easton
STON EASTON LA
GREEN ST
HIGH ST
Manor Farm
HAY ST
Barrow Farm
CHEWTON HILL
DUMPER'S LA
Chew Down
WORBERRY LA
Hay Street Farm
Upper Lodge Farm
STRAP LA
CHICKS LA
Chewton Plot
FIELD LA
WHEATFIELD LA
Drials La
COLE'S LA
SPLOTT LA
Strap La
Quarrs Farm
DUDWELL LA
Strapestones
Dudwell Field Farm
Paradise La
Old Gore Wood
Franklyn's Farm
Gore Cottage
Old Down Farm
Double House Farm
Paradise Farm
OLD GORE LA
Swallow Pits Farm
MENDIP VILLAS
Masters Farm
Old Down
PH
B3139
EAST END LA
Emborough
B3114
Swallow Pits Copse
Red Hill
Redhill Farm
Lechmere Water
TOWNSEND LA
REDHILL LA
MARCHANT'S HILL
Emborough Grove
EMBOROUGH POND LA
Emborough Quarries
PORTWAY LA
Portway Bridge
Cockhill Farm
TURNER'S COURT LA
KING'S LA
Quarry (dis)
A37
A39
Quar Tyning

114
96

95
77

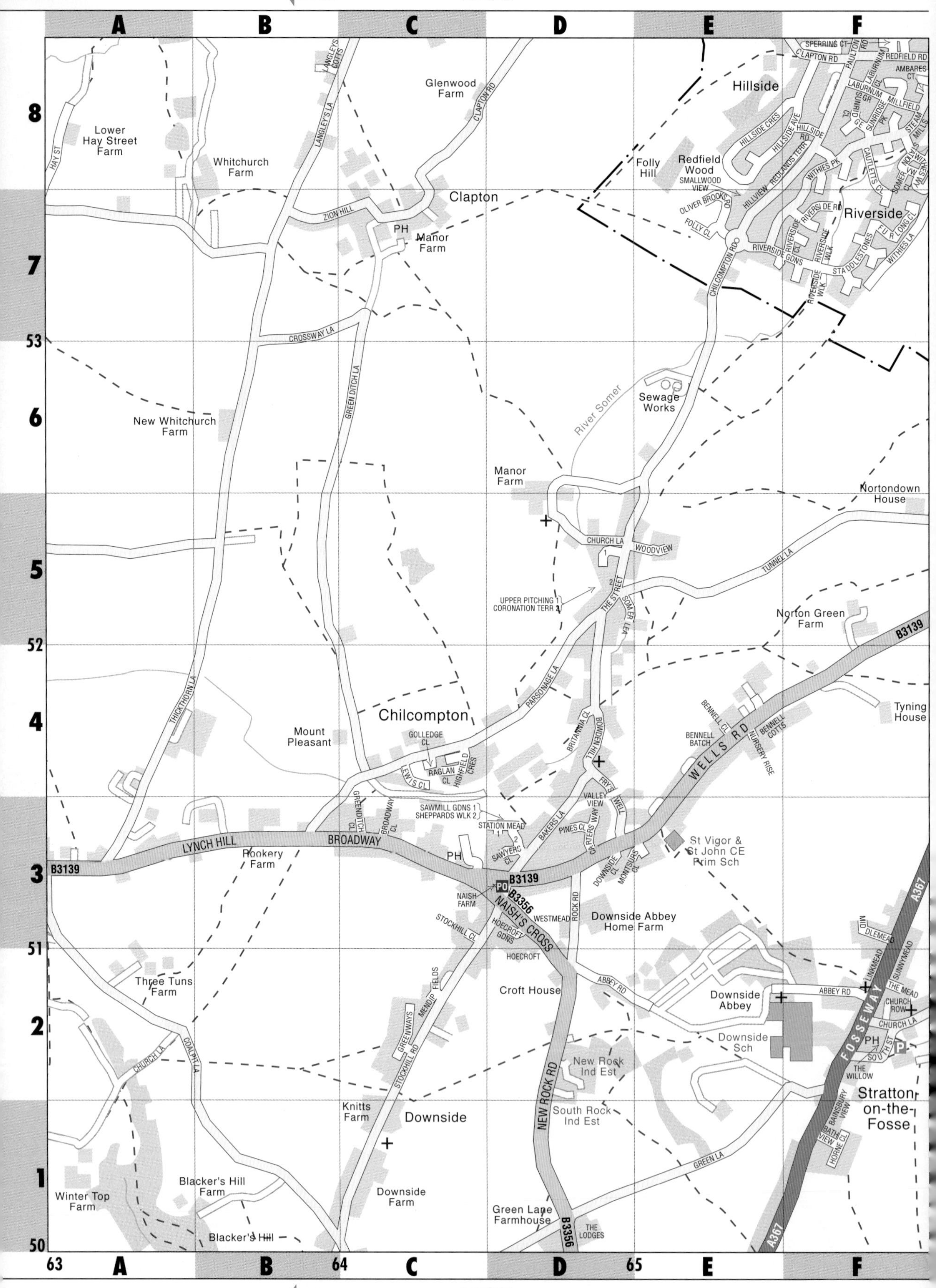
A
B
C
D
E
F
8
7
53
6
5
52
4
3
51
2
1
50
63
64
65
Lower Hay Street Farm
HAY ST
Whitchurch Farm
LANGLEYS COTTS
LANGLEY'S LA
Glenwood Farm
CLAPTON RD
Hillside
SPERRING CT
CLAPTON RD
PAULTON RD
LABURNUM
REDFIELD RD
AMBARES CT
LABURNUM GR
MILLFIELD
SUNRIDGE CL
SUNRIDGE PK
HILLSIDE CRES
HILLSIDE AVE
HILLSIDE RD
REDLANDS TERR
Folly Hill
Redfield Wood
SMALLWOOD VIEW
OLIVER BROOKS RD
FOLLY CL
HILLVIEW
WITHIES PK
CAUTLETTS CL
RIVERSIDE RD
Riverside
RIVERSIDE GDNS
RIVERSIDE CL
RIVERSIDE WLK
STADDLESTONES
WITHIES LA
CHILCOMPTON RD
ZION HILL
Clapton
PH
Manor Farm
CROSSWAY LA
GREEN DITCH LA
New Whitchurch Farm
River Somer
Sewage Works
Manor Farm
Nortondown House
CHURCH LA
WOODVIEW
TUNNEL LA
UPPER PITCHING 1
CORONATION TERR 2
THE STREET
SOMER LEA
Norton Green Farm
B3139
THICKTHORN LA
Chilcompton
Mount Pleasant
PARSONAGE LA
GOLLEDGE CL
LEWIS CL
RAGLAN CL
HIGHFIELD CRES
BRITANNIA CL
BOWDEN HILL
FRY'S WELL
BENNELL CL
BENNELL BATCH
WELLS RD
BENNELL COTTS
NURSERY RISE
Tyning House
GREENDITCH CL
BROADWAY CL
SAWMILL GDNS 1
SHEPPARDS WLK 2
STATION MEAD
BAKERS LA
VALLEY VIEW
PINES CL
CARTERS WAY
LYNCH HILL
BROADWAY
Rookery Farm
PH
SAWYERS CL
St Vigor & St John CE Prim Sch
DOWNSIDE CL
MONTSURS CL
B3139
PO
B3139
NAISH FARM
B3356
NAISH'S CROSS
WESTMEAD
ROCK RD
Downside Abbey Home Farm
STOCKHILL CL
HOECROFT GDNS
HOECROFT
A367
MIDDLEMEAD
SUNNYMEAD
LINKMEAD
THE MEAD
Three Tuns Farm
MENDIP FIELDS
Croft House
ABBEY RD
Downside Abbey
ABBEY RD
CHURCH ROW
CHURCH LA
GREENWAYS
STOCKHILL RD
CHURCH LA
COALPIT LA
New Rock Ind Est
Downside Sch
FOSSEWAY
PH
SOUTH ST
THE WILLOW
Knitts Farm
Downside
NEW ROCK RD
South Rock Ind Est
Stratton-on-the-Fosse
BAINSBURY VIEW
BATH VIEW
HORNE CL
GREEN LA
Winter Top Farm
Blacker's Hill Farm
Downside Farm
Green Lane Farmhouse
B3356
THE LODGES
Blacker's Hill
A367

95
115

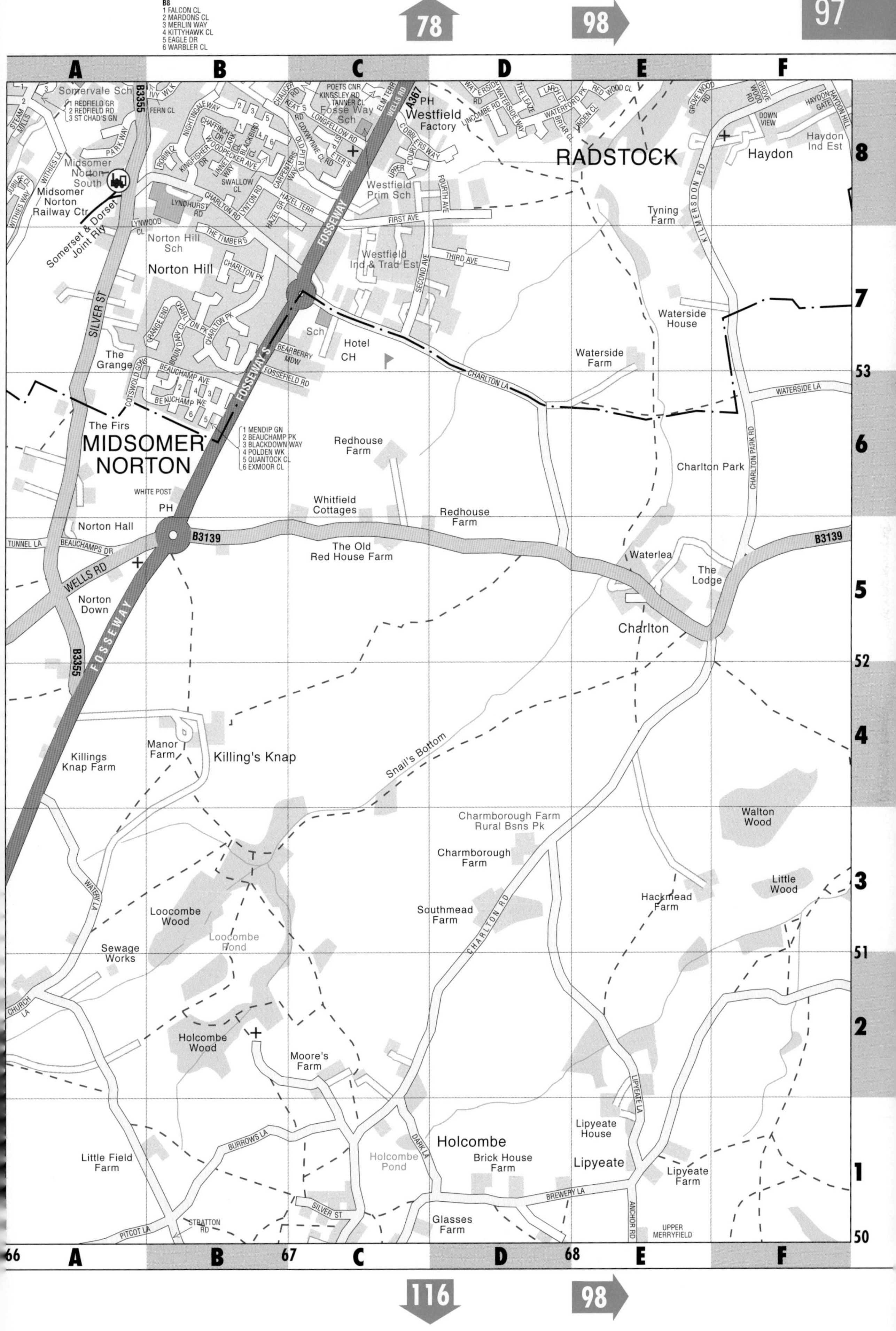
B8
1 FALCON CL
2 MARDONS CL
3 MERLIN WAY
4 KITTYHAWK CL
5 EAGLE DR
6 WARBLER CL
78
98
A
B
C
D
E
F
Somervale Sch
1 REDFIELD GR
2 REDFIELD RD
3 ST CHAD'S GN
POETS CNR
KINGSLEY RD
TANNER CL
Fosse Way Sch
PH
Westfield
Factory
RADSTOCK
Haydon
Haydon Ind Est
Midsomer Norton South
Midsomer Norton Railway Ctr
Somerset & Dorset Joint Rly
Westfield Prim Sch
Tyning Farm
Norton Hill Sch
Norton Hill
Westfield Ind & Trad Est
FIRST AVE
THIRD AVE
SECOND AVE
FOURTH AVE
FOSSEWAY
SILVER ST
B3355
A367
WELLS RD
Waterside House
Sch
Hotel
CH
The Grange
Waterside Farm
CHARLTON LA
WATERSIDE LA
The Firs
MIDSOMER NORTON
1 MENDIP GN
2 BEAUCHAMP PK
3 BLACKDOWN WAY
4 POLDEN WK
5 QUANTOCK CL
6 EXMOOR CL
Redhouse Farm
Charlton Park
CHARLTON PARK RD
WHITE POST
PH
Whitfield Cottages
Redhouse Farm
Norton Hall
B3139
The Old Red House Farm
TUNNEL LA
BEAUCHAMPS DR
Waterlea
The Lodge
Norton Down
Charlton
Manor Farm
Killing's Knap
Killings Knap Farm
Snail's Bottom
Walton Wood
Charmborough Farm Rural Bsns Pk
Charmborough Farm
Little Wood
Hackmead Farm
Loocombe Wood
Southmead Farm
CHARLTON RD
Loocombe Pond
Sewage Works
WATERY LA
CHURCH LA
Holcombe Wood
Moore's Farm
LIPYEATE LA
Lipyeate House
Holcombe
Little Field Farm
BURROWS LA
Holcombe Pond
DARK LA
Brick House Farm
Lipyeate
Lipyeate Farm
BREWERY LA
SILVER ST
Glasses Farm
PITCOT LA
STRATTON RD
ANCHOR RD
UPPER MERRYFIELD
8
7
53
6
5
52
4
3
51
2
1
50
66
67
68
116
98

97
79

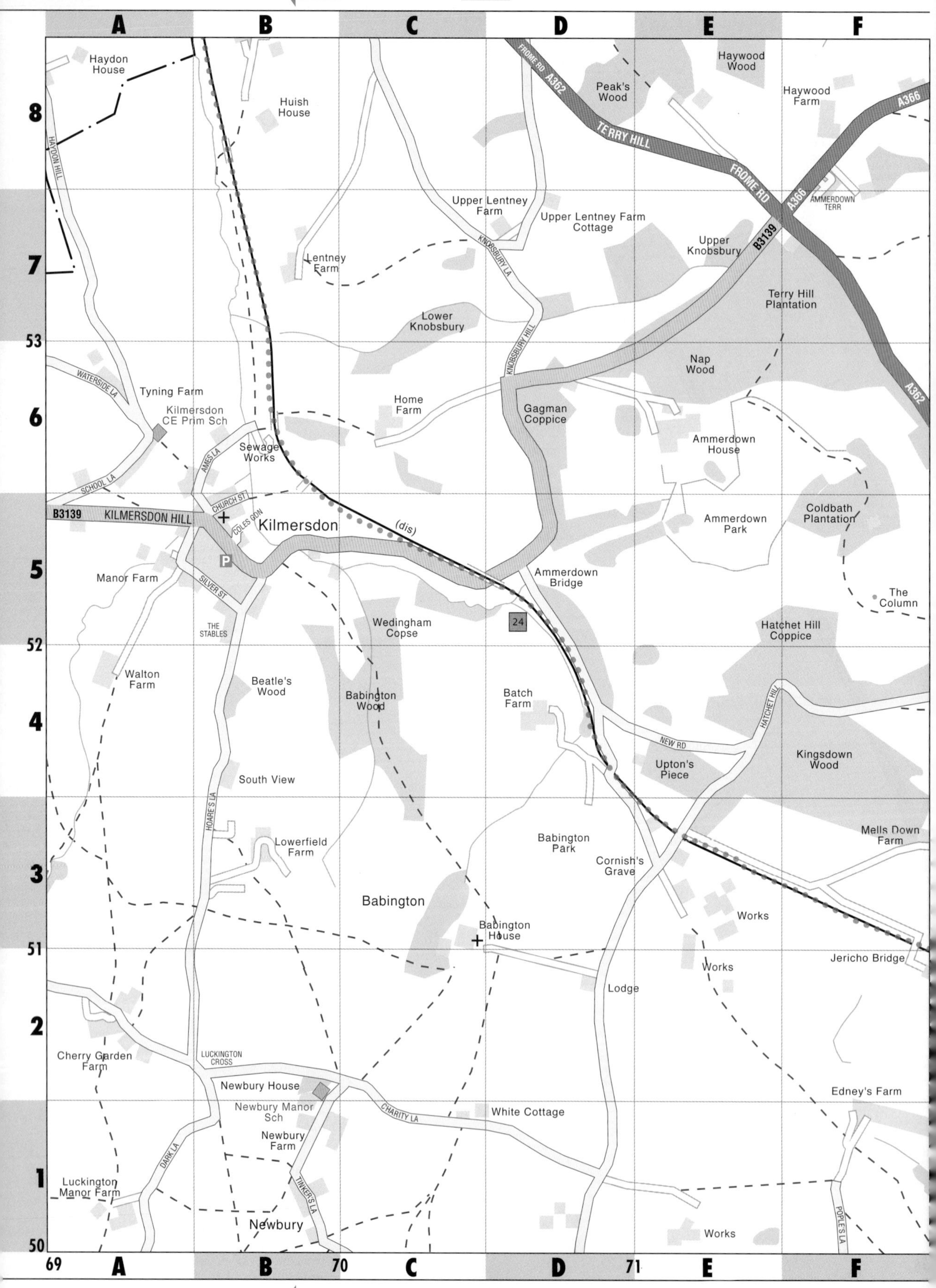
A
B
C
D
E
F
8
7
53
6
5
52
4
3
51
2
1
50
69
70
71
Haydon House
Haydon Hill
Huish House
Peak's Wood
Haywood Wood
Haywood Farm
Frome Rd
A362
Terry Hill
Frome Rd
A366
Ammerdown Terr
Upper Lentney Farm
Upper Lentney Farm Cottage
Lentney Farm
Knobsbury La
Upper Knobsbury
B3139
Terry Hill Plantation
Lower Knobsbury
Knobsbury Hill
Nap Wood
Waterside La
Tyning Farm
Kilmersdon CE Prim Sch
Home Farm
Gagman Coppice
A362
Ames La
Sewage Works
Ammerdown House
School La
Church St
Coldbath Plantation
B3139
Kilmersdon Hill
Coles Gdn
Kilmersdon
(dis)
Ammerdown Park
P
Manor Farm
Silver St
Ammerdown Bridge
The Column
The Stables
Wedingham Copse
24
Hatchet Hill Coppice
Walton Farm
Beatle's Wood
Babington Wood
Batch Farm
Hatchet Hill
New Rd
Kingsdown Wood
Upton's Piece
South View
Hoare's La
Babington Park
Mells Down Farm
Lowerfield Farm
Cornish's Grave
Babington
Works
Babington House
Works
Jericho Bridge
Lodge
Cherry Garden Farm
Luckington Cross
Newbury House
Newbury Manor Sch
Charity La
White Cottage
Edney's Farm
Newbury Farm
Dark La
Luckington Manor Farm
Tinker's La
Newbury
Works
Pople's La

97
117

80
100

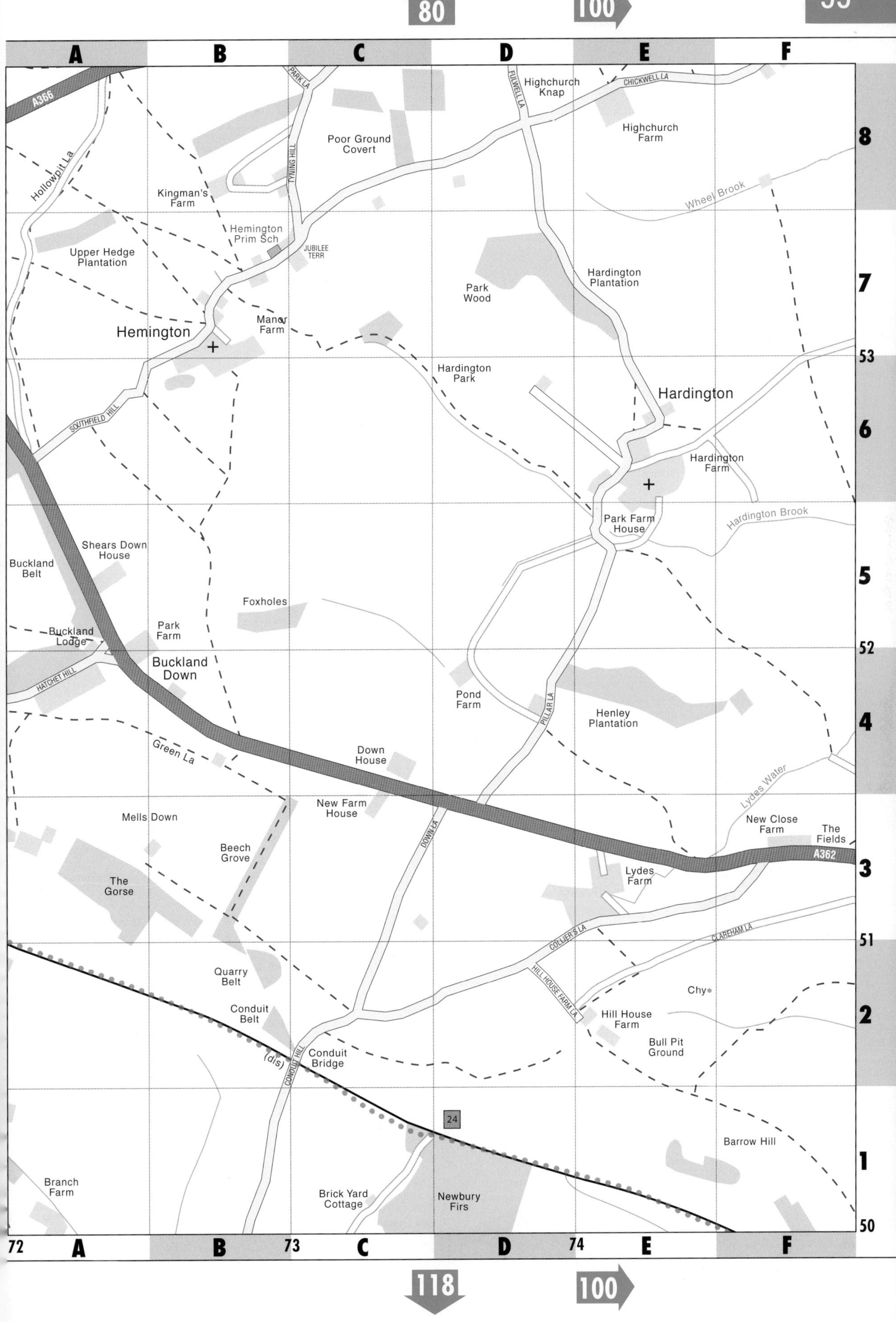
A
B
C
D
E
F
A366
Hollowpit La
Park La
Tyning Hill
Fulwell La
Highchurch Knap
Chickwell La
Highchurch Farm
Poor Ground Covert
Kingman's Farm
Wheel Brook
Hemington Prim Sch
Jubilee Terr
Upper Hedge Plantation
Hardington Plantation
Park Wood
Hemington
Manor Farm
Hardington Park
Hardington
Southfield Hill
Hardington Farm
Park Farm House
Hardington Brook
Shears Down House
Buckland Belt
Foxholes
Buckland Lodge
Park Farm
Hatchet Hill
Buckland Down
Pond Farm
Pillar La
Henley Plantation
Green La
Down House
New Farm House
Lydes Water
Mells Down
New Close Farm
The Fields
Beech Grove
Down La
A362
The Gorse
Lydes Farm
Collier's La
Clareham La
Quarry Belt
Hill House Farm La
Chy
Conduit Belt
Hill House Farm
Bull Pit Ground
(dis)
Conduit Hill
Conduit Bridge
24
Barrow Hill
Branch Farm
Brick Yard Cottage
Newbury Firs
8
7
53
6
5
52
4
3
51
2
1
50
72
73
74

118
100

99
81

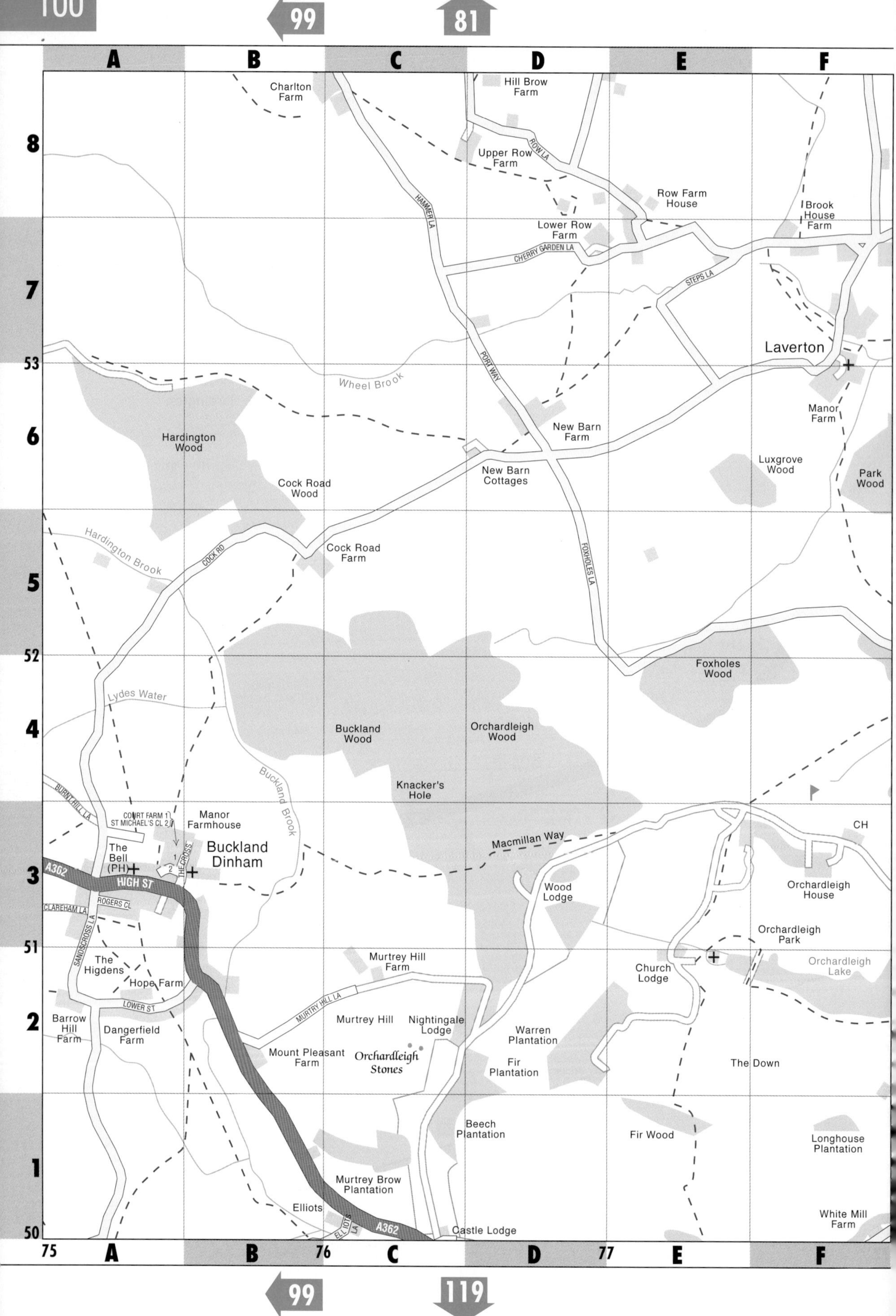
A
B
C
D
E
F
8
7
53
6
5
52
4
3
51
2
1
50
75
76
77
Charlton Farm
Hill Brow Farm
Upper Row Farm
ROW LA
Row Farm House
Brook House Farm
HAMMER LA
Lower Row Farm
CHERRY GARDEN LA
STEPS LA
Laverton
PORT WAY
Wheel Brook
Hardington Wood
New Barn Farm
Manor Farm
New Barn Cottages
Luxgrove Wood
Park Wood
Cock Road Wood
Hardington Brook
COCK RD
Cock Road Farm
FOXHOLES LA
Foxholes Wood
Lydes Water
Buckland Wood
Orchardleigh Wood
Knacker's Hole
Buckland Brook
BURNT HILL LA
COURT FARM 1
ST MICHAEL'S CL 2
Manor Farmhouse
The Bell (PH)
Buckland Dinham
THE CROSS
Macmillan Way
CH
A362
HIGH ST
ROGERS CL
CLAREHAM LA
SANDSCROSS LA
Wood Lodge
Orchardleigh House
Orchardleigh Park
The Higdens
Hope Farm
Murtrey Hill Farm
Church Lodge
Orchardleigh Lake
LOWER ST
MURTRY HILL LA
Barrow Hill Farm
Dangerfield Farm
Murtrey Hill
Nightingale Lodge
Warren Plantation
Mount Pleasant Farm
Orchardleigh Stones
Fir Plantation
The Down
Beech Plantation
Fir Wood
Longhouse Plantation
Murtrey Brow Plantation
Elliots
ELLIOTS LA
Castle Lodge
White Mill Farm

99
119

Woolverton
Manor Farm
Scutt's Bridge
Rode
Rode Methodist VA Fst Sch
Church Row
Bell Inn (PH)
Church Farm
Church Row Farm
Merfield House
Sleight Farm
Shawford
Shawford Farm
Green Park Pond
Henham Bridge
Henhambridge Brook
Macmillan Way
Clifford Farm
Recn Gd
Motel
Priors Court Farm
Beckington Mill
Park Farm
Lullington Court Farm
Tower Hill
Sewage Works
Gloucester Farm
Lullington
Gloucester Lodge
River Frome
Dairy House Farm
Beckington CE Fst Sch
Beckington
Springmead Sch
Poor Ground Plantation
Longclose Plantation
Cemy
Temple Plantation
Limerick Farm
Orchardleigh Lake
Creamery
Winkley Bottom
Pond Head Plantation
Wks
Bonnyleigh Hill
Great Bridge
Newlands Farm
Whitechapel Farm
St George's Farm
Oldford Farm
Longhouse Farm
Iron Mill
The Ship (PH)
Oldford
OLDFORD RESIDENTIAL PK
A36
A361
B3090
B3109
FROME BYPASS
FROME RD
SHAWFORD LA
PARKGATE LA
GREEN PARK LA
STRAIGHT LA
CROOKED LA
COOPER'S LA
HENHAMBRIDGE WAY
RUDGE LA
BATH RD
MILL LA
HORSE CL
GREAT DUNNS CL
GOOSE ST
WARMINSTER RD
CHURCH HILL
CHURCH ST
STUBB'S LA
CASTLE CNR
BERKLEY LA
LULLINGTON LA
LIMERICK LA
WHITECHAPEL LA
WINDSBATCH LA
WINDSBATCH HILL
OLDFORD HILL
IRON MILL LA
POT LA
ST GEORGE'S CROSS
THE LEAZE
WALNUT CL
THE MEAD
HUGHES CT
LOWER ST
HIGH ST
MARSH RD
WILTS LA
CHURCH LA
CLAY LA
CHURCHFIELDS
BRADFORD RD
THE OLD BR
GREEN PK
PO
HOMEFIELD CL
RYLANDS
SANDY LA
THE WEAVERS
SANDY VIEW
WEBBS MEAD
SHEPHERDS WAY
ST LUKES RD
THE LAYS
LAHS PL
PH
A B C D E F
8 7 6 5 4 3 2 1
53 52 51 50
78 79 80

101
83
A
B
C
D
E
F
8
7
53
6
5
52
4
3
51
2
1
50
BRADFORD RD
B3109
A361
Parsonage Farm
Rode Farm
Monkley La
The Devil's Bed & Bolster
Mount Pleasant
Duck Pool La
Castley Farm
Norris Hill Farm
Overcourt Farm
Seymour's Court
RUDGE LA
DUCK POOL LA
Duck Pool Farm
CASLEY LA
Silver Street Farm
Brokerswood Country Pk
Hazel Wood
Upper Castley Farm
Waterslade
Church Farm
FAIRWOOD RD
Honeybridge Farm
Round Wood
Lower Rudge Hill Farm
RUDGE HILL
Rudge
The Kicking Donkey (PH)
Brokerswood
SCOTLAND LA
Full Moon (PH)
White Row Farm
Lower Rudge
Carter's Bridge
DADLEY LA
Scotland Farm
Stourton Bushes
STANDERWICK
RUDGE LA
A36
Standerwick Court
Trees Farm
Palmer's Farm
Court Farm
LC
Standerwick
TENNIS CORNER DRO
Bell Inn (PH)
RUDGE RD
Fairwood Farm
Round Wood
Leigh Farm
STANDERWICK CROSS
Barber's Wood
Cuzner's Farm
B3099
Frome Market
MARSH RD
BERKLEY ST
FOX'S DRO
Five Lords Farm
CLIVEY
Westbury View
A36
Clivey
Clivey Farm
CLEARWOOD
B3099
81
82
83
Wiltshire STREET ATLAS
101
121

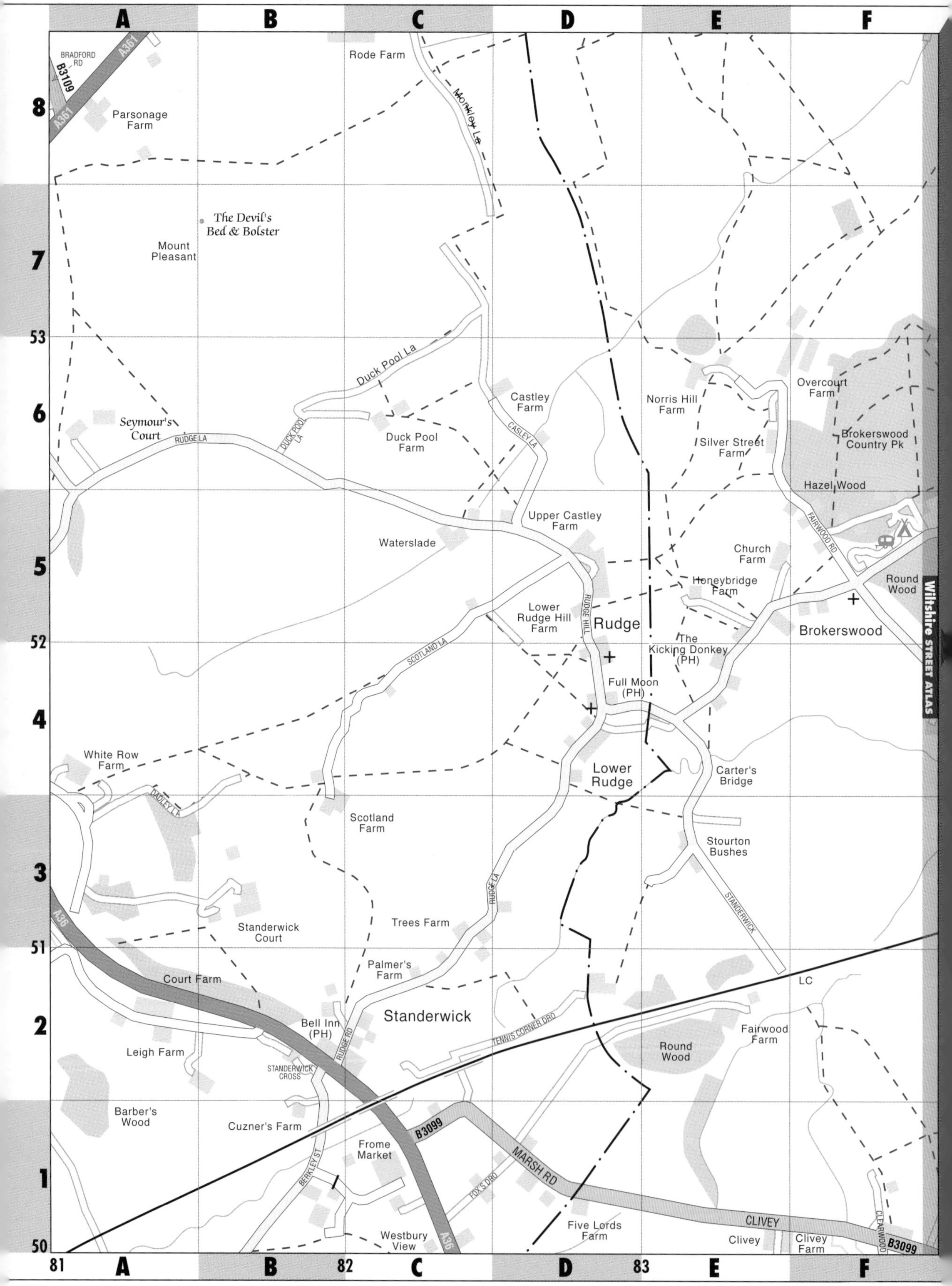

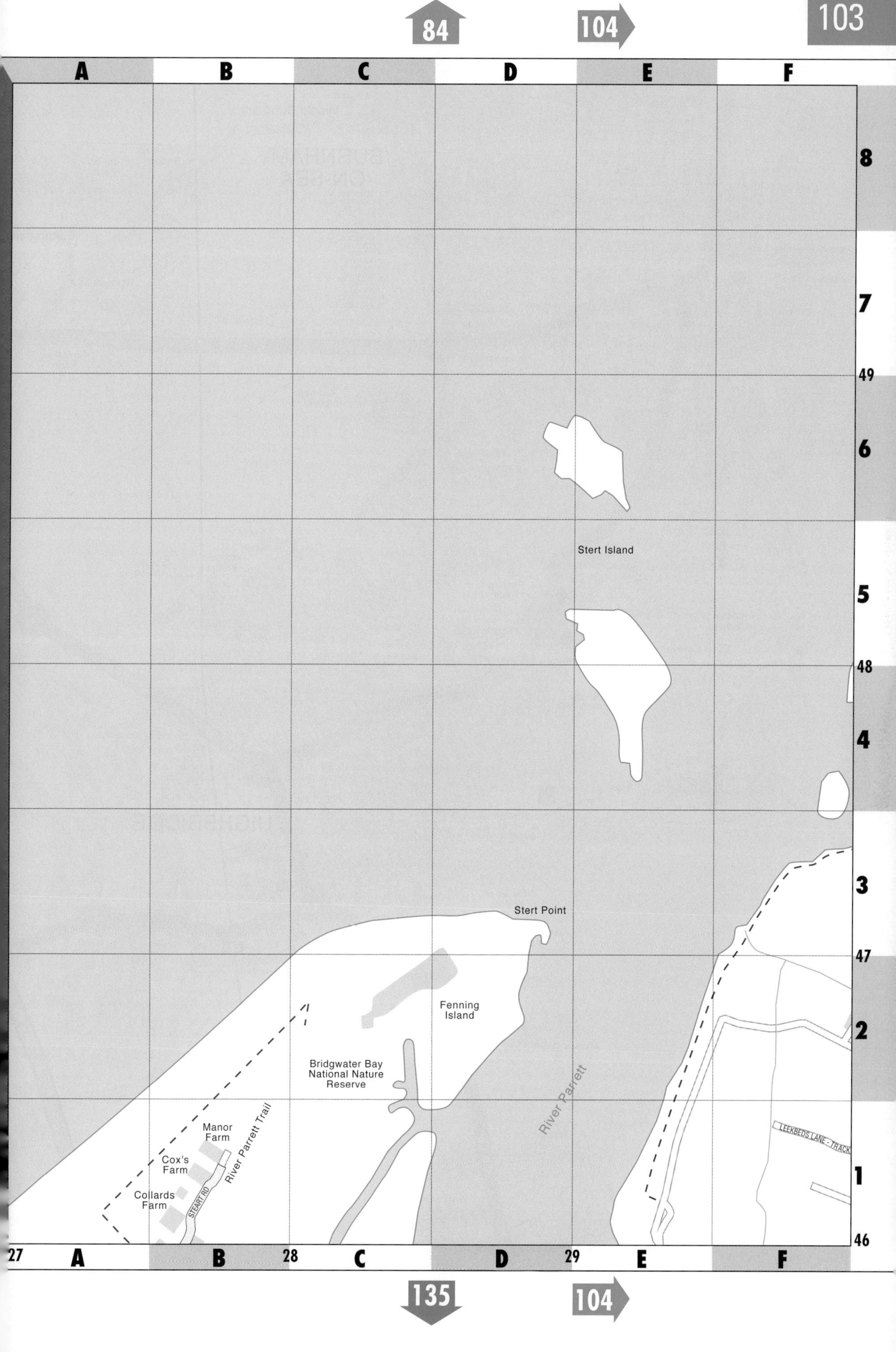
84
104
A
B
C
D
E
F
8
7
49
6
Stert Island
5
48
4
3
Stert Point
47
Fenning
Island
2
Bridgwater Bay
National Nature
Reserve
River Parrett
Manor
Farm
River Parrett Trail
Cox's
Farm
Collards
Farm
STEART RD
LEEKBEDS LANE - TRACK
1
46
27
28
29
135
104

103 85

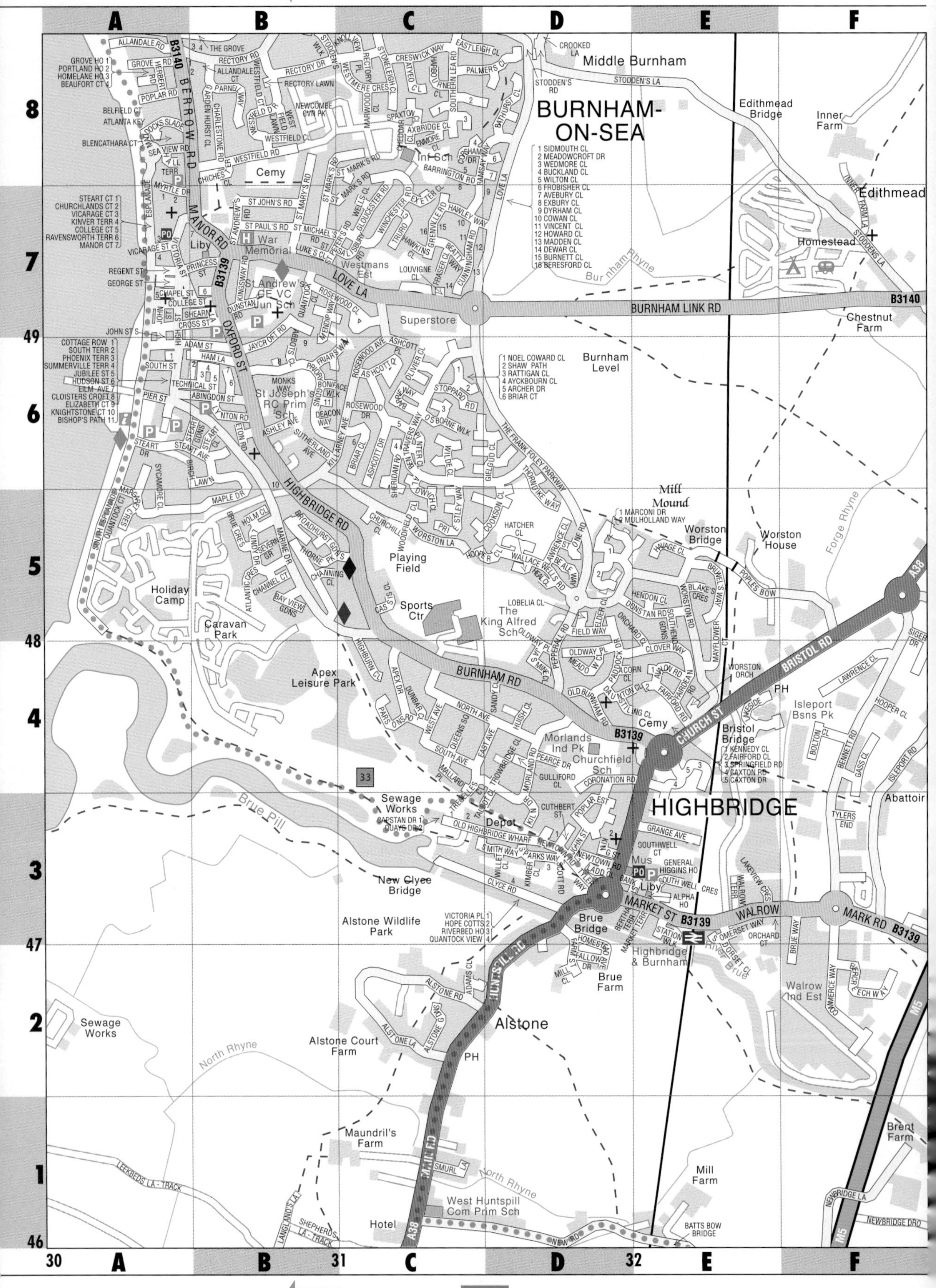
BURNHAM-ON-SEA
HIGHBRIDGE
Middle Burnham
Burnham Level
Alstone
Edithmead
B3140
B3139
A38
M5
BURNHAM LINK RD
BURNHAM RD
HIGHBRIDGE RD
CHURCH ST
BRISTOL RD
MARKET ST
MARK RD
LOVE LA
OXFORD ST
MANOR RD
BERROW RD
HUNTSPILL RD
MAIN RD
Brue Pill
North Rhyne
River Brue
Sewage Works
Holiday Camp
Caravan Park
Apex Leisure Park
Playing Field
Sports Ctr
Superstore
Highbridge & Burnham
Alstone Wildlife Park
Alstone Court Farm
Maundril's Farm
West Huntspill Com Prim Sch
Isleport Bsns Pk
Walrow Ind Est
Morlands Ind Pk
Churchfield Sch
Mill Mound
Brent Farm
Mill Farm
Brue Farm
Abattoir

103 136

86
106

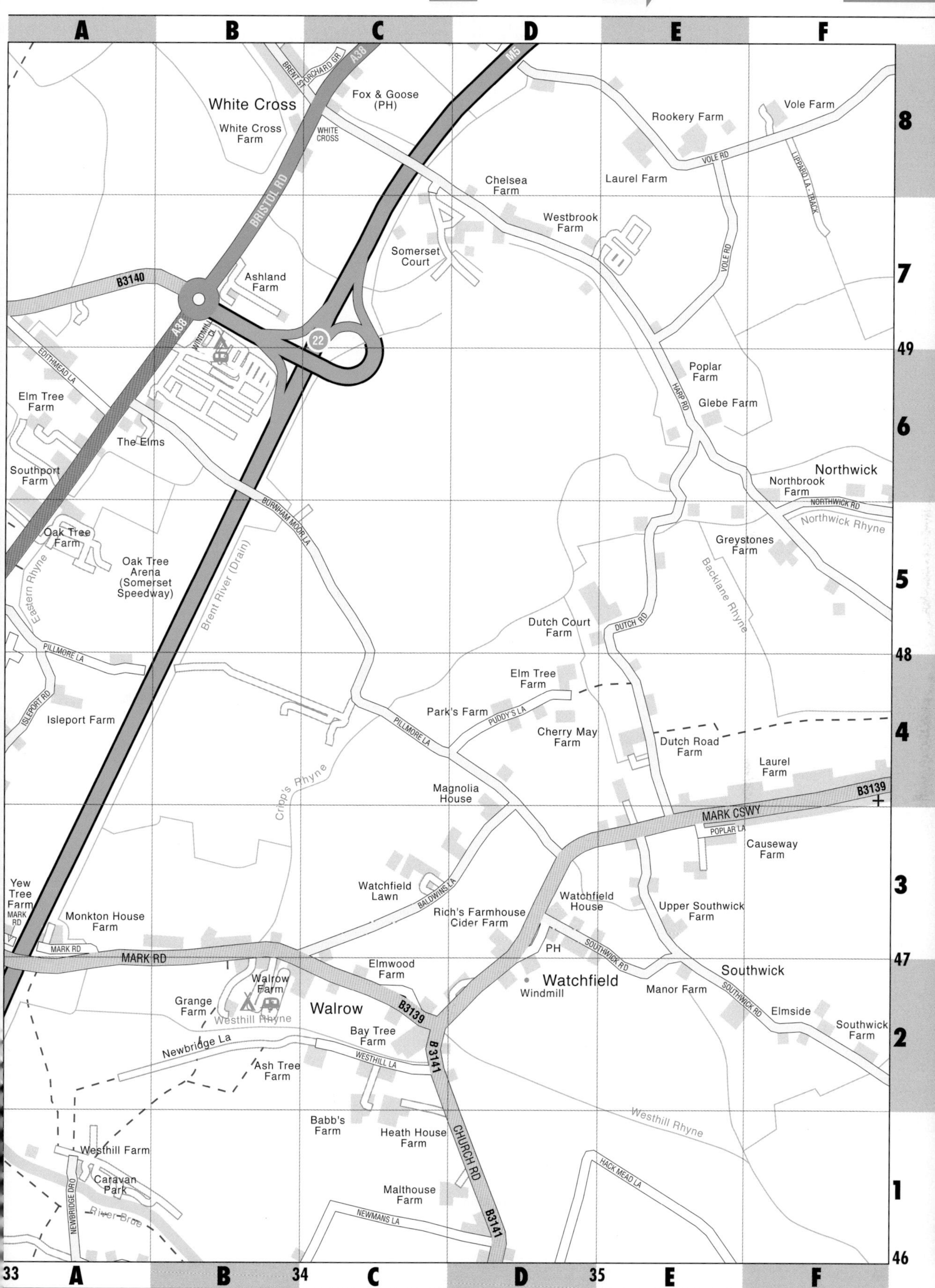
White Cross
White Cross Farm
Fox & Goose (PH)
WHITE CROSS
BRENT ST
ORCHARD GR
A38
M5
BRISTOL RD
Rookery Farm
Vole Farm
VOLE RD
LIPPARD LA - TRACK
Laurel Farm
Chelsea Farm
Westbrook Farm
Somerset Court
Ashland Farm
B3140
WINDMILL CL
22
EDITHMEAD LA
Elm Tree Farm
The Elms
Southport Farm
Poplar Farm
HARP RD
Glebe Farm
Northwick
Northbrook Farm
NORTHWICK RD
Northwick Rhyne
BURNHAM MOOR LA
Oak Tree Farm
Oak Tree Arena (Somerset Speedway)
Eastern Rhyne
Brent River (Drain)
Greystones Farm
Backlane Rhyne
Dutch Court Farm
DUTCH RD
PILLMORE LA
ISLEPORT RD
Isleport Farm
Elm Tree Farm
Park's Farm
PUDDY'S LA
Cherry May Farm
Dutch Road Farm
Laurel Farm
Cripp's Rhyne
Magnolia House
B3139
MARK CSWY
POPLAR LA
Causeway Farm
Yew Tree Farm
MARK RD
Monkton House Farm
Watchfield Lawn
BALDWINS LA
Rich's Farmhouse Cider Farm
Watchfield House
Upper Southwick Farm
PH
SOUTHWICK RD
MARK RD
Walrow Farm
Elmwood Farm
Watchfield
Windmill
Manor Farm
Southwick
Grange Farm
Westhill Rhyne
Walrow
B3139
Elmside
Southwick Farm
Bay Tree Farm
Newbridge La
WESTHILL LA
Ash Tree Farm
B3141
Babb's Farm
Heath House Farm
CHURCH RD
Westhill Rhyne
Westhill Farm
Caravan Park
NEWBRIDGE DRO
River Brue
Malthouse Farm
NEWMANS LA
HACK MEAD LA
A B C D E F
8 7 49 6 5 48 4 3 47 2 1 46
33 34 35

136
106

105
87

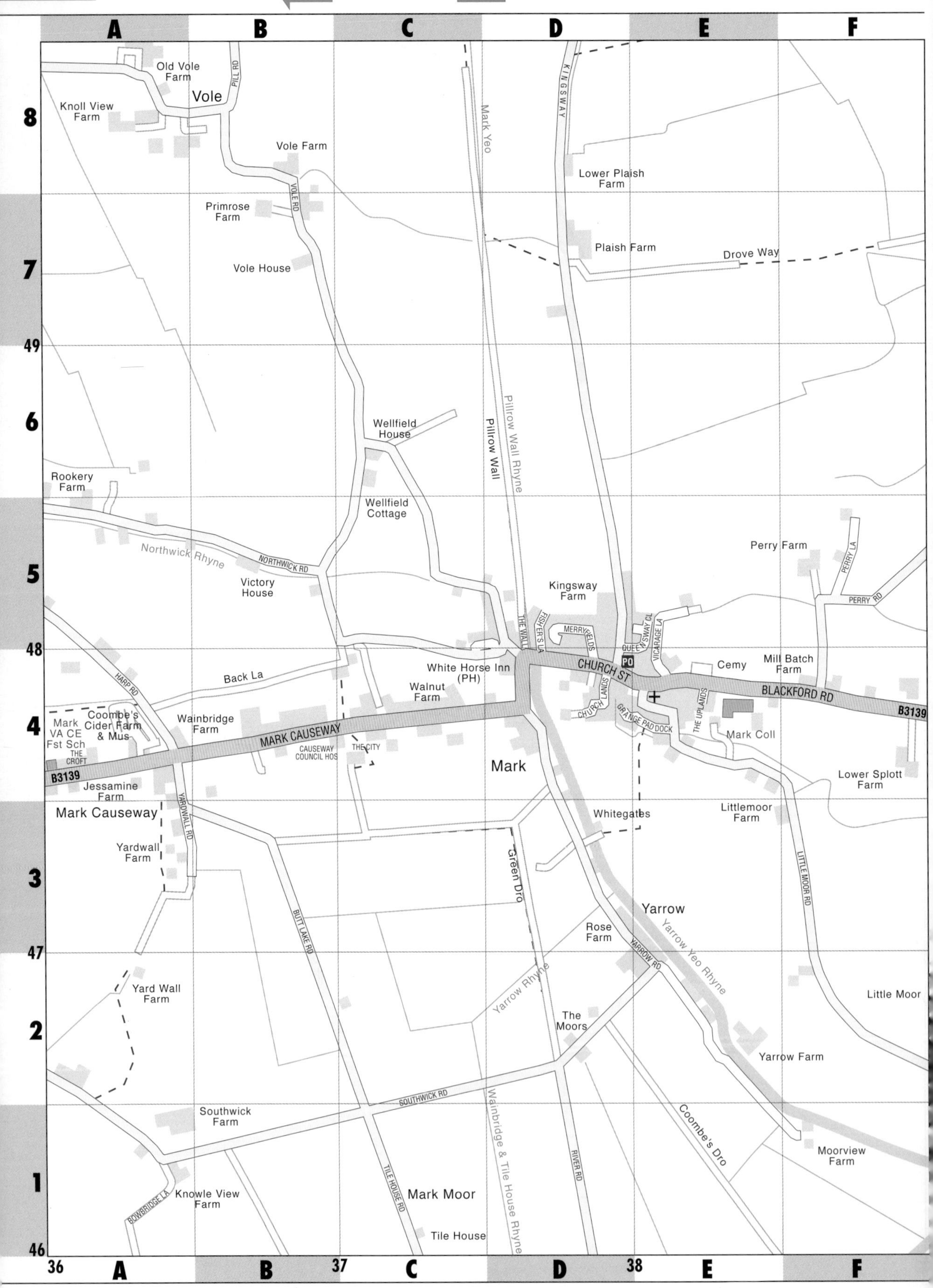
A
B
C
D
E
F
8
7
49
6
5
48
4
3
47
2
1
46
36
37
38
Old Vole Farm
Vole
PILL RD
Knoll View Farm
Vole Farm
Mark Yeo
KINGSWAY
Lower Plaish Farm
Primrose Farm
VOLE RD
Plaish Farm
Drove Way
Vole House
Wellfield House
Pillrow Wall
Pillrow Wall Rhyne
Rookery Farm
Wellfield Cottage
Perry Farm
PERRY LA
Northwick Rhyne
NORTHWICK RD
Victory House
Kingsway Farm
PERRY RD
THE WALL
FISHER'S LA
MERRYFIELDS
QUEENSWAY
KINGSWAY CL
VICARAGE LA
Back La
White Horse Inn (PH)
CHURCH ST
PO
Cemy
Mill Batch Farm
HARP RD
Walnut Farm
CHURCH LANDS
BLACKFORD RD
Mark VA CE Fst Sch
Coombe's Cider Farm & Mus
Wainbridge Farm
MARK CAUSEWAY
GRANGE PADDOCK
THE UPLANDS
B3139
Mark Coll
THE CROFT
CAUSEWAY COUNCIL HOS
THE CITY
Mark
Lower Splott Farm
B3139
Jessamine Farm
Mark Causeway
YARDWALL RD
Whitegates
Littlemoor Farm
Yardwall Farm
Green Dro
BUTT LAKE RD
LITTLE MOOR RD
Yarrow
Yarrow Yeo Rhyne
Rose Farm
YARROW RD
Yard Wall Farm
Yarrow Rhyne
Little Moor
The Moors
Yarrow Farm
Southwick Farm
SOUTHWICK RD
Wainbridge & Tile House Rhyne
Coombe's Dro
Moorview Farm
RIVER RD
TILE HOUSE RD
Knowle View Farm
BOWBRIDGE LA
Mark Moor
Tile House

105
137

88
108

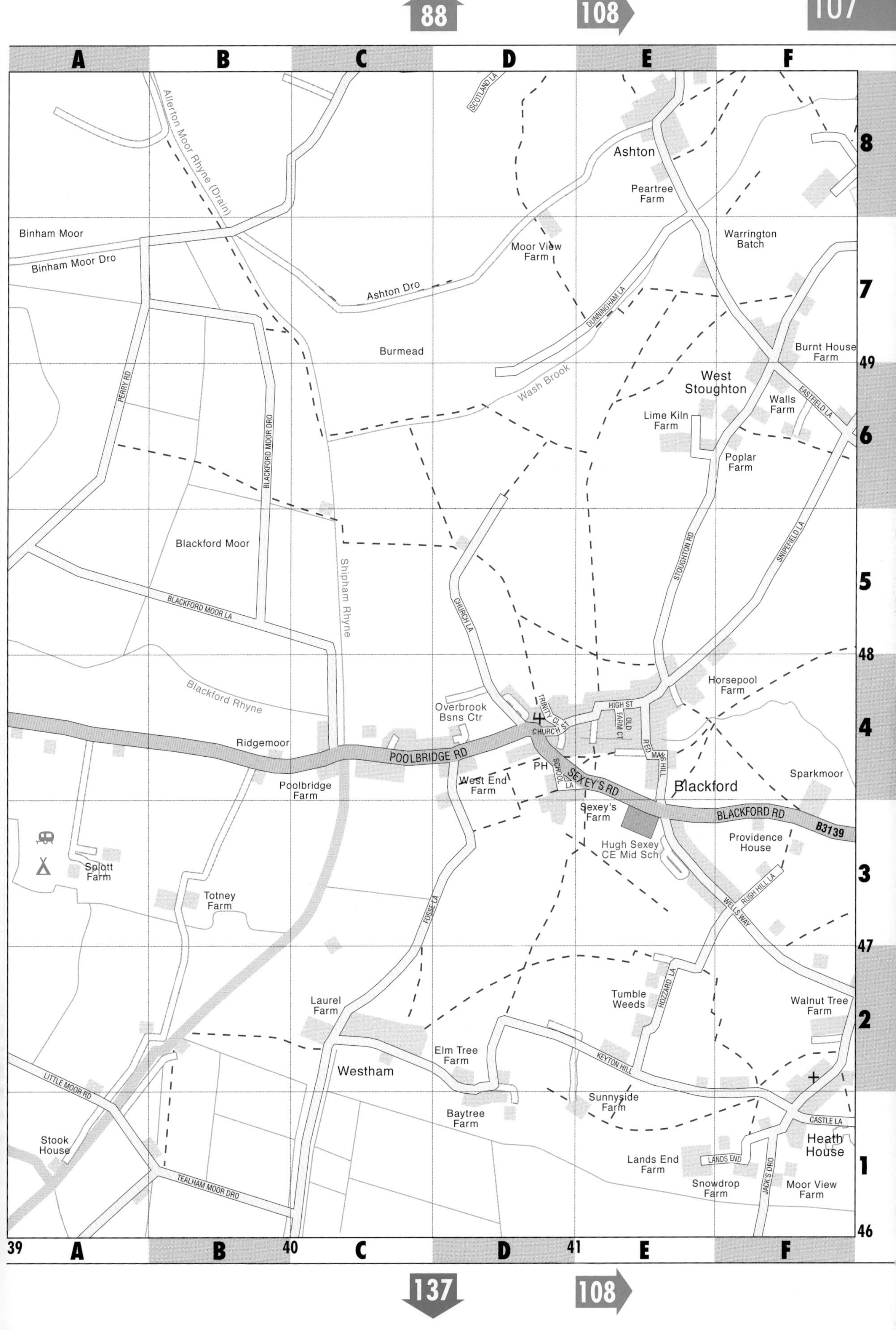
A
B
C
D
E
F
8
7
6
5
4
3
2
1
49
48
47
46
39
40
41
Ashton
Peartree Farm
Binham Moor
Binham Moor Dro
Allerton Moor Rhyne (Drain)
SCOTLAND LA
Warrington Batch
Moor View Farm
Ashton Dro
DUNNINGHAM LA
Burmead
Burnt House Farm
West Stoughton
Wash Brook
Walls Farm
EASTFIELD LA
Lime Kiln Farm
PERRY RD
BLACKFORD MOOR DRO
Poplar Farm
Blackford Moor
Shipham Rhyne
STOUGHTON RD
SNIPEFIELD LA
BLACKFORD MOOR LA
CHURCH LA
Blackford Rhyne
Horsepool Farm
Overbrook Bsns Ctr
TRINITY CL
ST
HIGH ST
OLD FARM CT
CHURCH
Ridgemoor
POOLBRIDGE RD
RED MAN'S HILL
Sparkmoor
PH
SCHOOL LA
SEXEY'S RD
Poolbridge Farm
West End Farm
Blackford
Sexey's Farm
BLACKFORD RD
B3139
Providence House
Hugh Sexey CE Mid Sch
Splott Farm
RUSH HILL LA
Totney Farm
WELLS WAY
FOSSE LA
Tumble Weeds
HOZZARD LA
Laurel Farm
Walnut Tree Farm
Elm Tree Farm
KEYTON HILL
Westham
LITTLE MOOR RD
Sunnyside Farm
Baytree Farm
CASTLE LA
Stook House
Heath House
Lands End Farm
LANDS END
Snowdrop Farm
JACK'S DRO
Moor View Farm
TEALHAM MOOR DRO

137
108

107
89

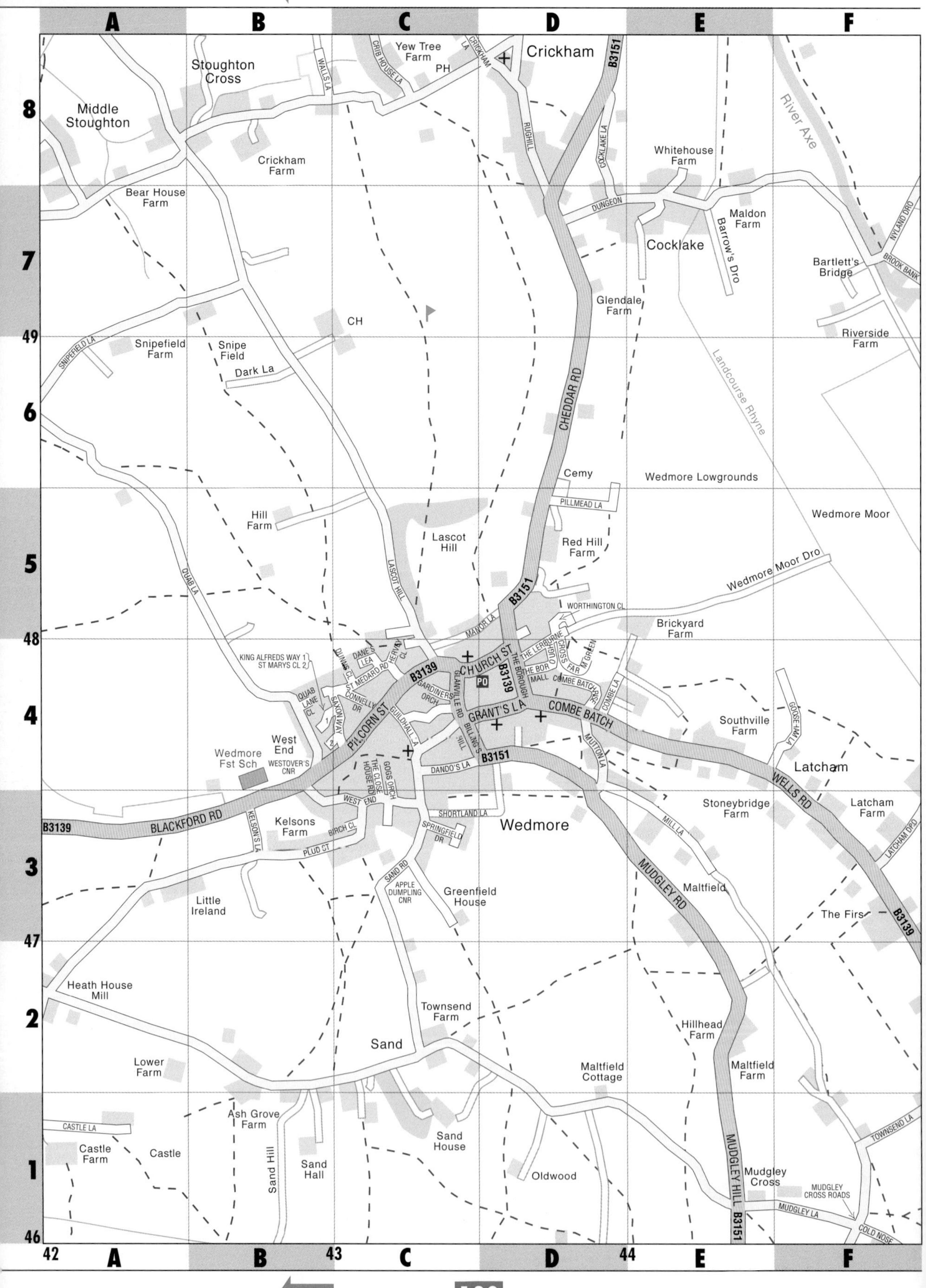
A
B
C
D
E
F
8
7
49
6
5
48
4
3
47
2
1
46
42
43
44
Stoughton Cross
Middle Stoughton
Crickham Farm
Bear House Farm
Yew Tree Farm
PH
Crickham
B3151
River Axe
Whitehouse Farm
Maldon Farm
Cocklake
Barrow's Dro
Bartlett's Bridge
Glendale Farm
Riverside Farm
CH
Snipefield Farm
Snipe Field
Dark La
Landcourse Rhyne
CHEDDAR RD
Cemy
Wedmore Lowgrounds
Wedmore Moor
Hill Farm
Lascot Hill
Red Hill Farm
Wedmore Moor Dro
Brickyard Farm
Southville Farm
Latcham
West End
Wedmore Fst Sch
Kelsons Farm
Stoneybridge Farm
Latcham Farm
Wedmore
Greenfield House
Little Ireland
Maltfield
The Firs
Heath House Mill
Townsend Farm
Sand
Hillhead Farm
Lower Farm
Maltfield Cottage
Maltfield Farm
Ash Grove Farm
Castle Farm
Castle
Sand Hill
Sand Hall
Sand House
Oldwood
Mudgley Cross
MUDGLEY CROSS ROADS
BLACKFORD RD
B3139
PILCORN ST
CHURCH ST
GRANT'S LA
COMBE BATCH
WELLS RD
MUDGLEY RD
MUDGLEY HILL
MUDGLEY LA
COLD NOSE
TOWNSEND LA
CASTLE LA
SNIPEFIELD LA
QUAB LA
LASCOT HILL
RUGHILL
COCKLAKE LA
DUNGEON
NYLAND DRO
BROOK BANK
PILLMEAD LA
WORTHINGTON CL
MANOR LA
KING ALFREDS WAY 1
ST MARYS CL 2
DANE'S LEA
ST MEDARD RD
HERVEY CL
DUNNS CL
QUAB LANE CL
SAXON WAY
CONNELLY DR
GARDINERS ORCH
GUILDHALL LA
GLANVILLE RD
BILLINGS HILL
THE BOROUGH
THE LERBURNE
THE BOR MALL
COMBE BATCH
COMBE LA
MUTTON LA
DANDO'S LA
SHORTLAND LA
SPRINGFIELD DR
WESTOVER'S CNR
WEST END
HOUSE RD
THE CLOSE
GOGS ORCH
BIRCH CL
PLUD ST
KELSON'S LA
SAND RD
APPLE DUMPLING CNR
MILL LA
GOOSE LA
LATCHAM DRO
CRIB HOUSE LA
WALLS LA
CRICKHAM LA
PO
B3151

107
138

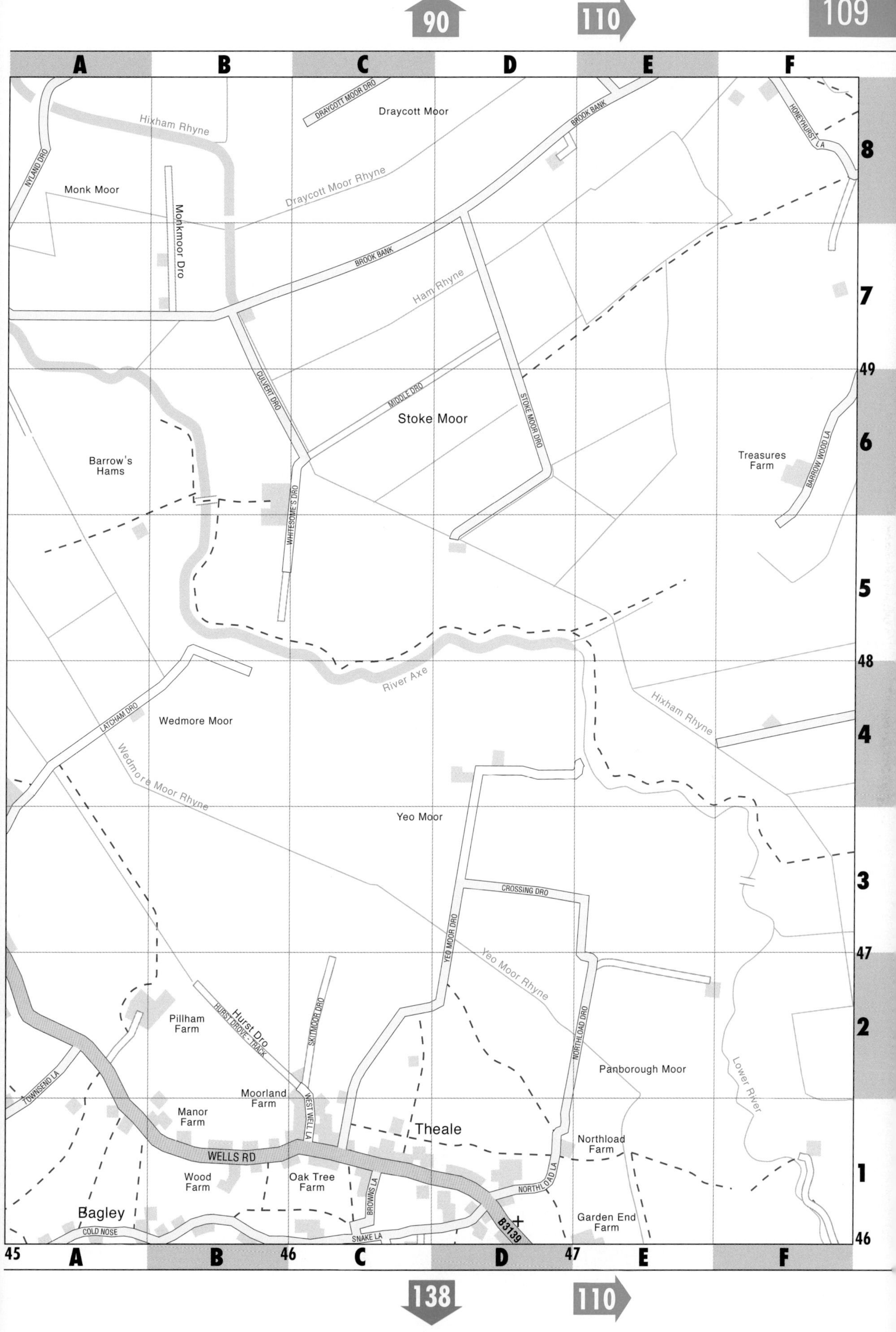

90
110
A
B
C
D
E
F
8
7
49
6
5
48
4
3
47
2
1
46
45
46
47
Hixham Rhyne
DRAYCOTT MOOR DRO
Draycott Moor
BROOK BANK
HONEYHURST LA
NYLAND DRO
Monk Moor
Monkmoor Dro
Draycott Moor Rhyne
BROOK BANK
Ham Rhyne
CULVERT DRO
MIDDLE DRO
Stoke Moor
STOKE MOOR DRO
Barrow's Hams
Treasures Farm
BARROW WOOD LA
WHITESOME'S DRO
River Axe
Hixham Rhyne
LATCHAM DRO
Wedmore Moor
Wedmore Moor Rhyne
Yeo Moor
CROSSING DRO
YEO MOOR DRO
Yeo Moor Rhyne
NORTHLOAD DRO
Pillham Farm
Hurst Dro
HURST DROVE - TRACK
SKITMOOR DRO
Panborough Moor
Lower River
TOWNSEND LA
Manor Farm
Moorland Farm
WEST WELL LA
Theale
Northload Farm
WELLS RD
Wood Farm
Oak Tree Farm
BROWNS LA
NORTHLOAD LA
Bagley
COLD NOSE
SNAKE LA
B3139
Garden End Farm
138
110

109
91

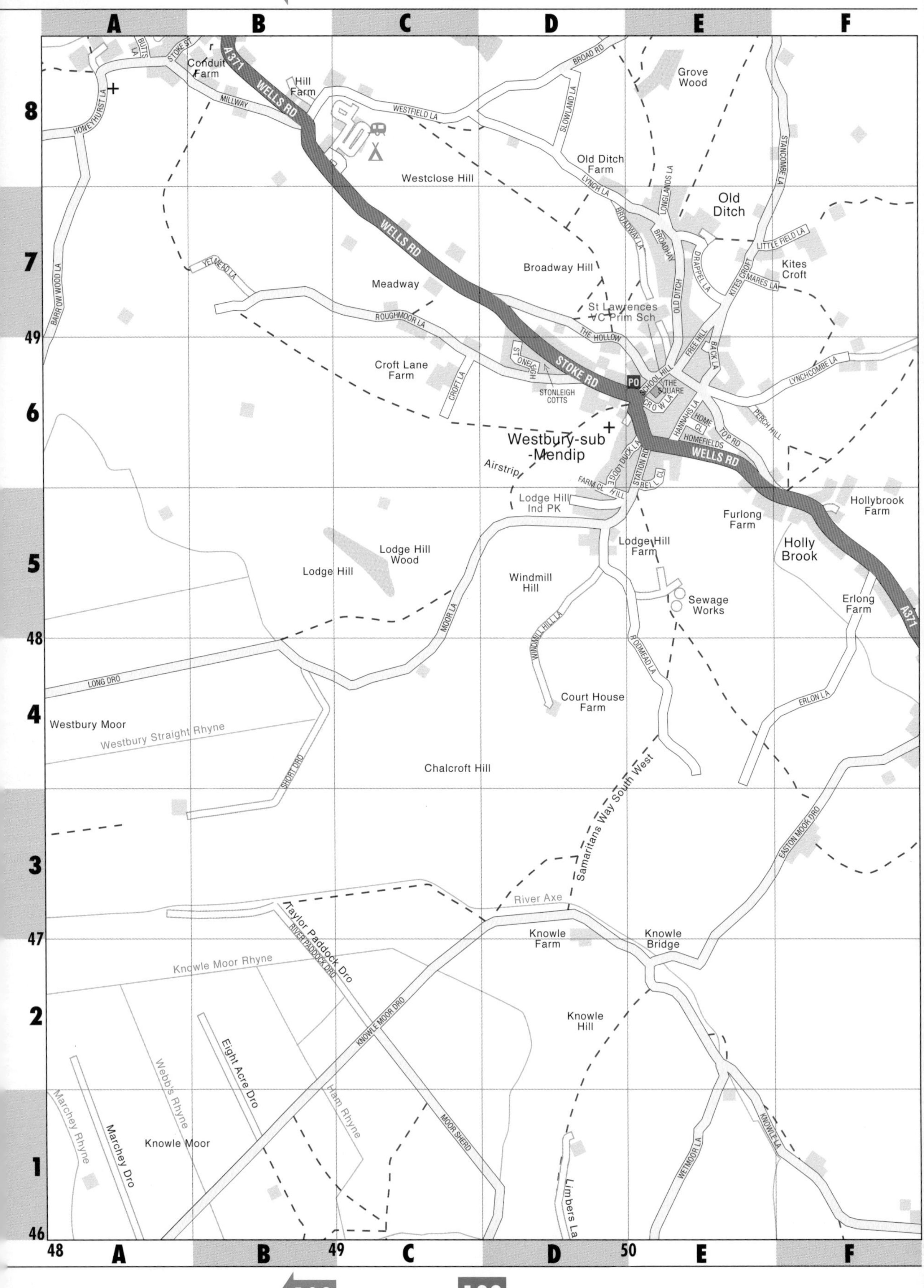
A
B
C
D
E
F
8
7
49
6
5
48
4
3
47
2
1
46
BUTTS LA
STOKE ST
Conduit Farm
A371
WELLS RD
MILLWAY
HONEYHURST LA
Hill Farm
WESTFIELD LA
BROAD RD
SLOWLAND LA
Grove Wood
STANCOMBE LA
Westclose Hill
Old Ditch Farm
LYNCH LA
LONGLANDS LA
Old Ditch
BROADWAY LA
BROADWAY
DRAPPEL LA
OLD DITCH
LITTLE FIELD LA
Kites Croft
KITES CROFT
MARES LA
YETMEAD LA
Broadway Hill
Meadway
St Lawrences VC Prim Sch
ROUGHMOOR LA
THE HOLLOW
FREE HILL
BACK LA
BARROW WOOD LA
Croft Lane Farm
CROFT LA
STONELEIGH
STONLEIGH COTTS
STOKE RD
PO
SCHOOL HILL
THE SQUARE
CROW LA
HANNAHS LA
HOME CL
TOP RD
HOMEFIELDS
LYNCHCOMBE LA
PERCH HILL
Westbury-sub -Mendip
Airstrip
GOOSE LA
STATION RD
BELL CL
FARM CL
HILL
WELLS RD
Lodge Hill Ind PK
Furlong Farm
Hollybrook Farm
Holly Brook
Lodge Hill Wood
Lodge Hill
Windmill Hill
Lodge Hill Farm
Sewage Works
Erlong Farm
A371
MOOR LA
WINDMILL HILL LA
RODMEAD LA
48
LONG DRO
Court House Farm
ERLON LA
Westbury Moor
Westbury Straight Rhyne
SHORT DRO
Chalcroft Hill
Samaritans Way South West
EASTON MOOR DRO
River Axe
Taylor Paddock Dro
RIVER PADDOCK DRO
Knowle Farm
Knowle Bridge
Knowle Moor Rhyne
KNOWLE MOOR DRO
Knowle Hill
Eight Acre Dro
Webb's Rhyne
Ham Rhyne
Marchey Rhyne
Marchey Dro
Knowle Moor
MOOR SHERD
WETMOOR LA
KNOWLE LA
Limbers La
48
A
B
49
C
D
50
E
F

109
139

92
112

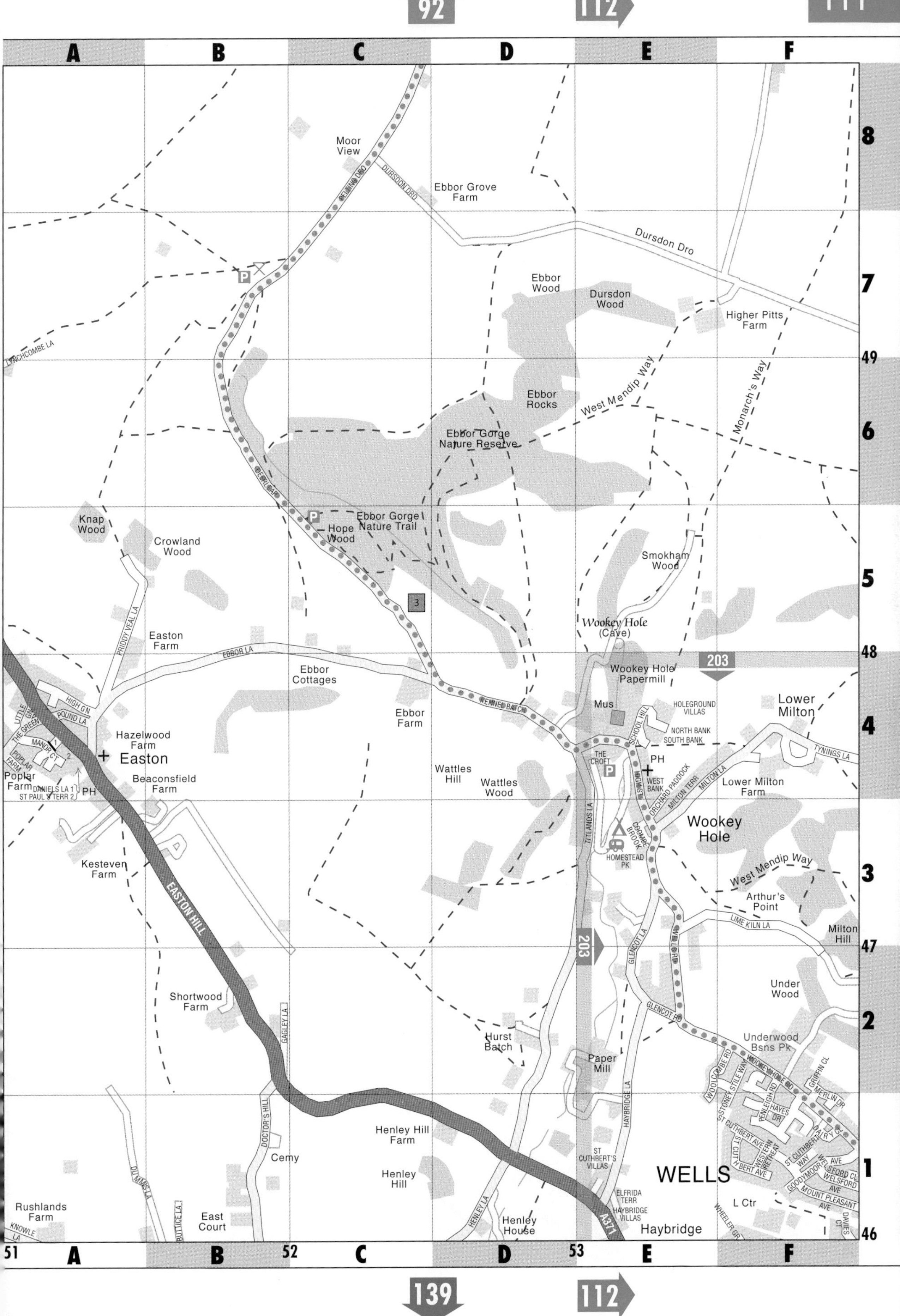
A
B
C
D
E
F
8
7
49
6
5
48
4
3
47
2
1
46
51
52
53
Moor View
Ebbor Grove Farm
Dursdon Dro
Ebbor Wood
Dursdon Wood
Higher Pitts Farm
West Mendip Way
Monarch's Way
Ebbor Rocks
Ebbor Gorge Nature Reserve
Knap Wood
Crowland Wood
Hope Wood
Ebbor Gorge Nature Trail
Smokham Wood
Wookey Hole (Cave)
Easton Farm
EBBOR LA
Ebbor Cottages
Wookey Hole Papermill
203
Mus
HOLEGROUND VILLAS
Lower Milton
NORTH BANK
SOUTH BANK
TYNINGS LA
Hazelwood Farm
Easton
Ebbor Farm
KENNEL BATCH
PH
Poplar Farm
Beaconsfield Farm
Wattles Hill
Wattles Wood
THE CROFT
WEST BANK
ORCHARD PADDOCK
MILTON TERR
MILTON LA
Lower Milton Farm
Wookey Hole
Kesteven Farm
EASTON HILL
TITLANDS LA
COOMBE BROOK
HOMESTEAD PK
West Mendip Way
Arthur's Point
LIME KILN LA
Milton Hill
GLENCOT LA
Under Wood
Shortwood Farm
GAGLEY LA
GLENCOT RD
Hurst Batch
Underwood Bsns Pk
Paper Mill
HAYBRIDGE LA
DOCTOR'S HILL
Henley Hill Farm
Cemy
Henley Hill
ST CUTHBERT'S VILLAS
WELLS
Rushlands Farm
East Court
HENLEY LA
Henley House
ELFRIDA TERR
HAYBRIDGE VILLAS
A371
Haybridge
L Ctr
WHEELER GR
DAVIES CT
KNOWLE LA
PRIDDY VEAL LA
HIGH GN
POUND LA
THE GREEN
LITTLE GN
MANOR CT
POPLAR FARM
DANIELS LA
ST PAUL'S TERR
LYNCHCOMBE LA
DURSDON DRO
SCHOOL HILL
WOOKEY HOLE RD
WOOLCOMBE RD
STONEY STILE WAY
HAYES DR
GRIFFIN CL
MERLIN DR
ST CUTHBERT AVE
WESTERN RETREAT
WELSFORD CL
WELSFORD AVE
MOUNT PLEASANT AVE
GOODYMOOR AVE
3

139
112

111
93

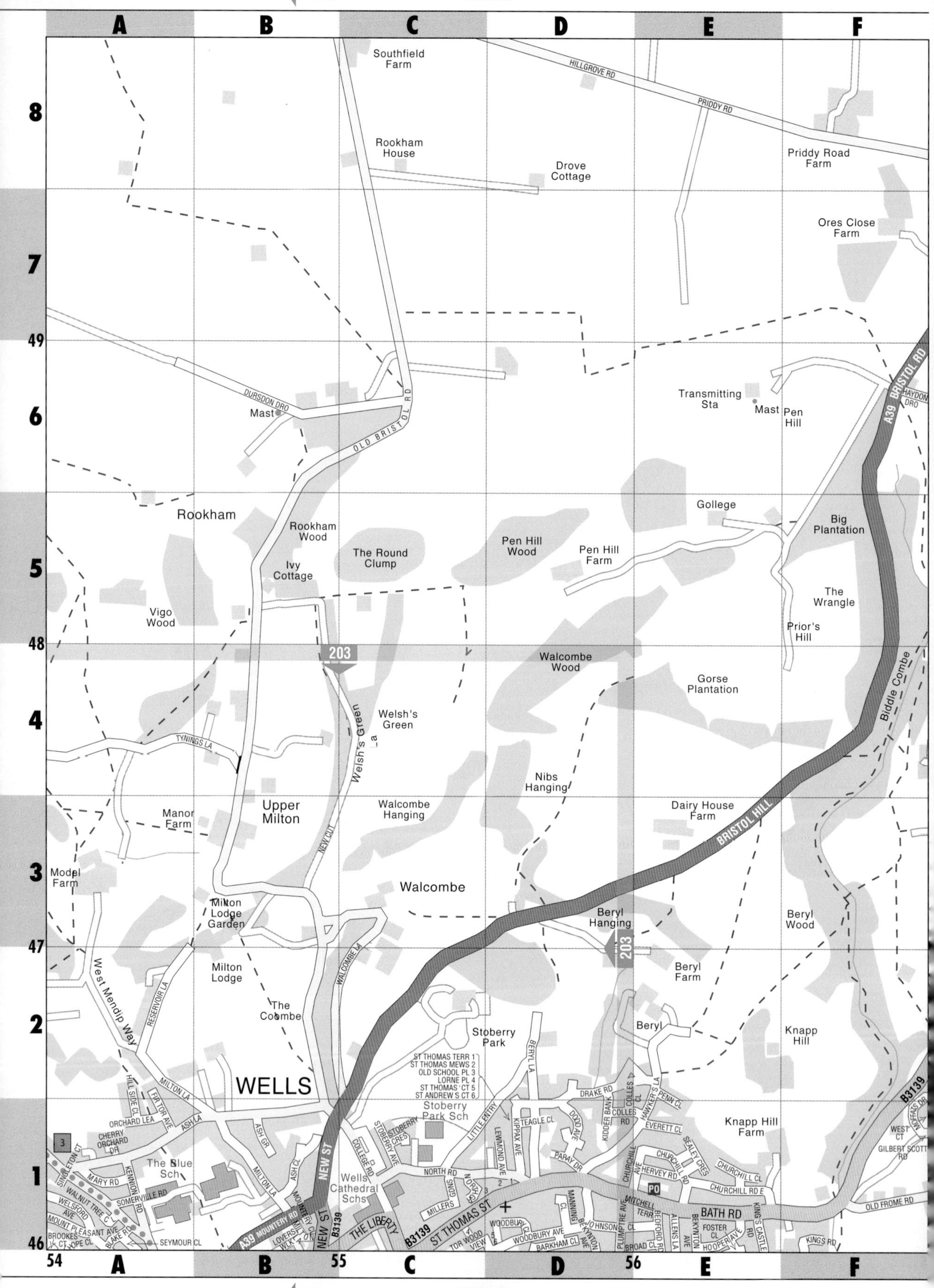
Southfield Farm
HILLGROVE RD
PRIDDY RD
Rookham House
Drove Cottage
Priddy Road Farm
Ores Close Farm
DURSDON DRO
Mast
OLD BRISTOL RD
Transmitting Sta
Mast
Pen Hill
A39 BRISTOL RD
HAYDON DRO
Rookham
Rookham Wood
The Round Clump
Pen Hill Wood
Pen Hill Farm
Gollege
Big Plantation
Ivy Cottage
Vigo Wood
The Wrangle
Prior's Hill
203
Walcombe Wood
Gorse Plantation
Welsh's Green
Welsh's Green La
TYNINGS LA
Biddle Combe
Nibs Hanging
Manor Farm
Upper Milton
Walcombe Hanging
Dairy House Farm
BRISTOL HILL
NEW CUT
Model Farm
Walcombe
Milton Lodge Garden
Beryl Hanging
Beryl Wood
Milton Lodge
West Mendip Way
RESERVOIR LA
WALCOMBE LA
Beryl Farm
The Coombe
Stoberry Park
BERYL LA
Beryl
Knapp Hill
WELLS
ST THOMAS TERR 1
ST THOMAS MEWS 2
OLD SCHOOL PL 3
LORNE PL 4
ST THOMAS' CT 5
ST ANDREW S CT 6
MILTON LA
HILL SIDE CL
FIR TOR AVE
ORCHARD LEA
ASH LA
CHERRY ORCHARD DR
ASH GR
Stoberry Park Sch
STOBERRY CRES
STOBERRY AVE
COLLEGE RD
LITTLE ENTRY
LEMMOND AVE
KIPPAX AVE
TEAGLE CL
DOOD AVE
DRAKE RD
KIDDER BANK
COLLES CL
COLLES RD
HAWKER'S LA
PENN CL
EVERETT CL
SEALEY CRES
Knapp Hill Farm
B3139
WEST CT
GILBERT SCOTT RD
The Blue Sch
SINGLETON CT
MARY RD
KENNION RD
MILTON LA
ASH CL
NEW ST
Wells Cathedral Schs
NORTH RD
PARAY DR
CHURCHILL AVE
HERVEY RD
CHURCHILL RD
CHURCHILL CL
CHURCHILL RD E
WALNUT TREE CL
SOMERVILLE RD
WELSFORD AVE
MOUNT PLEASANT AVE
BROOKES CT
BLAKE RD
SEYMOUR CL
A39 MOUNTERY RD
MOUNTERY CL
LOVERS WLK
B3139
THE LIBERTY
MILLERS GDNS
B3139
ST THOMAS ST
WOODBURY CL
WOODBURY AVE
TOR WOOD VIEW
BARKHAM CL
MANNING CL
BEKYNTON AVE
JOHNSON CL
PLUMPTRE AVE
MITCHELL TERR
BROAD CL
BEDFORD RD
ALLENS LA
BEKYNTON AVE
PO
BATH RD
FOSTER CL
HOOPER AVE
KING'S CASTLE RD
KINGS RD
OLD FROME RD
54
55
56
46
47
48
49
A B C D E F
1 2 3 4 5 6 7 8

111
140

94
114

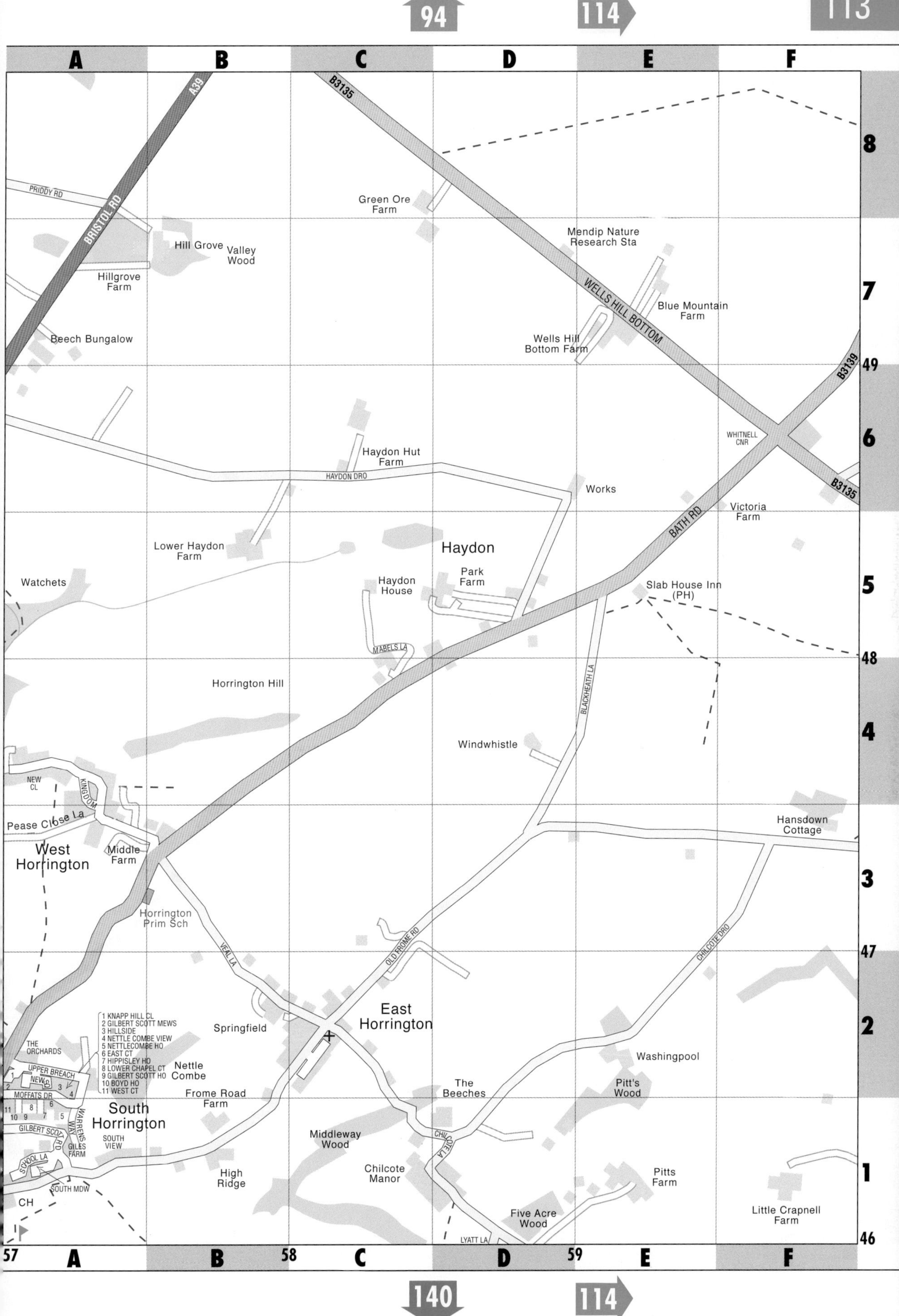
A
B
C
D
E
F
8
7
49
6
5
48
4
3
47
2
1
46
57
58
59
A39
BRISTOL RD
PRIDDY RD
B3135
Green Ore Farm
Hill Grove
Valley Wood
Hillgrove Farm
Beech Bungalow
Mendip Nature Research Sta
WELLS HILL BOTTOM
Blue Mountain Farm
Wells Hill Bottom Farm
B3139
WHITNELL CNR
B3135
Haydon Hut Farm
HAYDON DRO
Works
Victoria Farm
BATH RD
Lower Haydon Farm
Haydon
Park Farm
Haydon House
Watchets
Slab House Inn (PH)
MABELS LA
Horrington Hill
BLACKHEATH LA
Windwhistle
NEW CL
KINGDOM
Pease Close La
West Horrington
Middle Farm
Hansdown Cottage
Horrington Prim Sch
OLD FROME RD
VEAL LA
CHILCOTE DRO
East Horrington
Springfield
1 KNAPP HILL CL
2 GILBERT SCOTT MEWS
3 HILLSIDE
4 NETTLE COMBE VIEW
5 NETTLECOMBE HO
6 EAST CT
7 HIPPISLEY HO
8 LOWER CHAPEL CT
9 GILBERT SCOTT HO
10 BOYD HO
11 WEST CT
THE ORCHARDS
UPPER BREACH
NEWS
MOFFATS DR
Nettle Combe
Frome Road Farm
South Horrington
WARRENS WAY
GILBERT SCOTT RD
GILES FARM
SOUTH VIEW
SCHOOL LA
SOUTH MDW
CH
Washingpool
Pitt's Wood
The Beeches
CHILCOTE LA
Middleway Wood
Chilcote Manor
High Ridge
Pitts Farm
Five Acre Wood
LYATT LA
Little Crapnell Farm

140
114

113
95

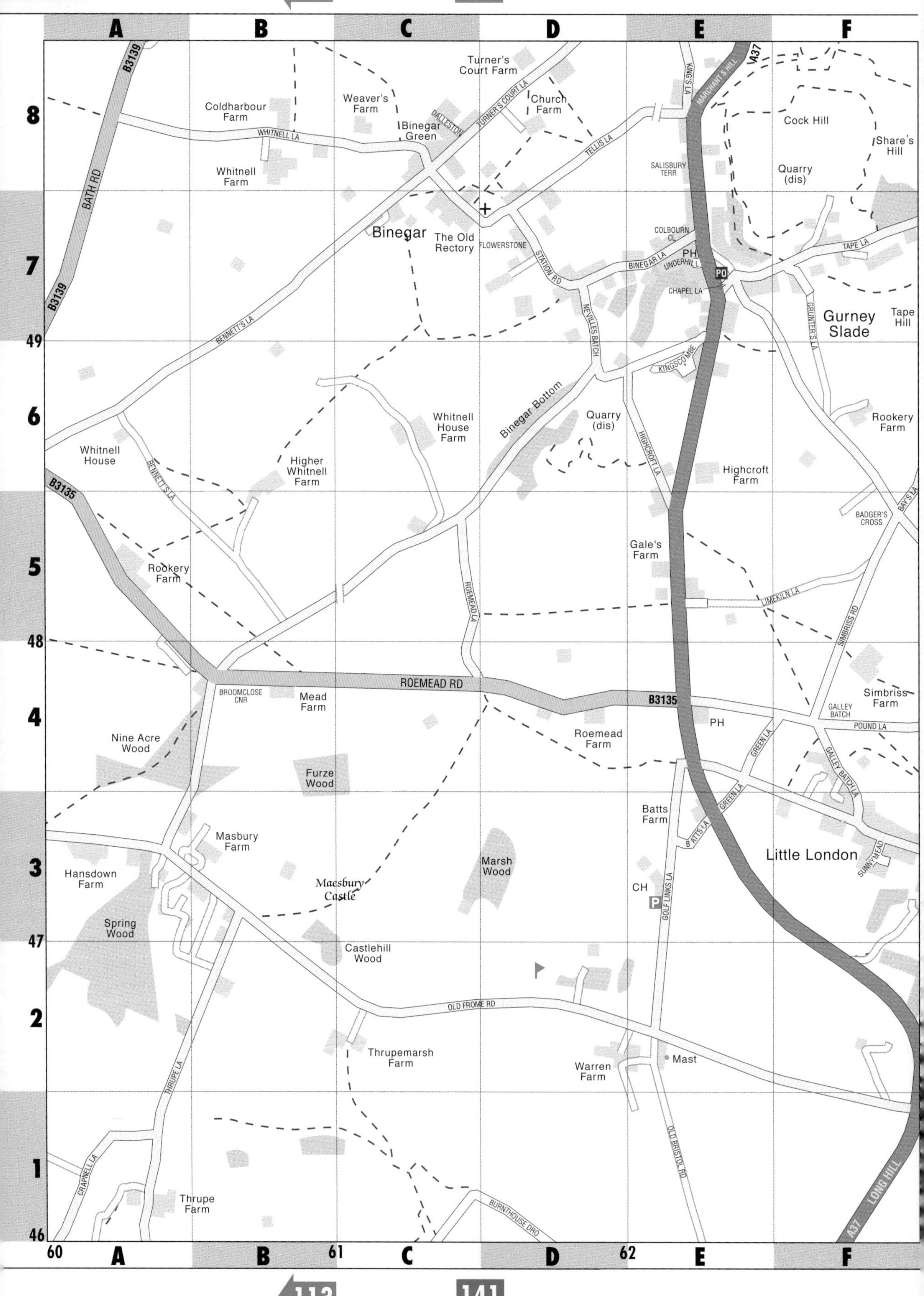
A
B
C
D
E
F
8
7
49
6
5
48
4
3
47
2
1
46
60
61
62
B3139
BATH RD
Coldharbour Farm
WHITNELL LA
Whitnell Farm
Weaver's Farm
Binegar Green
DALLESTON
TURNER'S COURT LA
Turner's Court Farm
Church Farm
TELLIS LA
KING'S LA
MARCHANT'S HILL
A37
Cock Hill
Share's Hill
Quarry (dis)
SALISBURY TERR
COLBOURN CL
Binegar
The Old Rectory
FLOWERSTONE
STATION RD
BINEGAR LA
UNDERHILL
PH
PO
CHAPEL LA
TAPE LA
GRUNTER'S LA
Gurney Slade
Tape Hill
BENNETT'S LA
NEVILLES BATCH
KINGSCOMBE
Binegar Bottom
Whitnell House Farm
Quarry (dis)
HIGHCROFT LA
Rookery Farm
Whitnell House
Higher Whitnell Farm
Highcroft Farm
B3135
BADGER'S CROSS
BAY'S LA
Gale's Farm
Rookery Farm
ROEMEAD LA
LIMEKILN LA
SIMBRISS RD
ROEMEAD RD
BROOMCLOSE CNR
Mead Farm
B3135
Simbriss Farm
GALLEY BATCH
POUND LA
PH
Nine Acre Wood
Roemead Farm
GREEN LA
GALLEY BATCH LA
Furze Wood
Batts Farm
BATTS LA
Masbury Farm
Hansdown Farm
Marsh Wood
Little London
SUNNYMEAD
Maesbury Castle
CH
P
GOLF LINKS LA
Spring Wood
Castlehill Wood
OLD FROME RD
Thrupemarsh Farm
Warren Farm
Mast
THRUPE LA
CRAPNELL LA
OLD BRISTOL RD
LONG HILL
A37
Thrupe Farm
BURNTHOUSE DRO

113
141

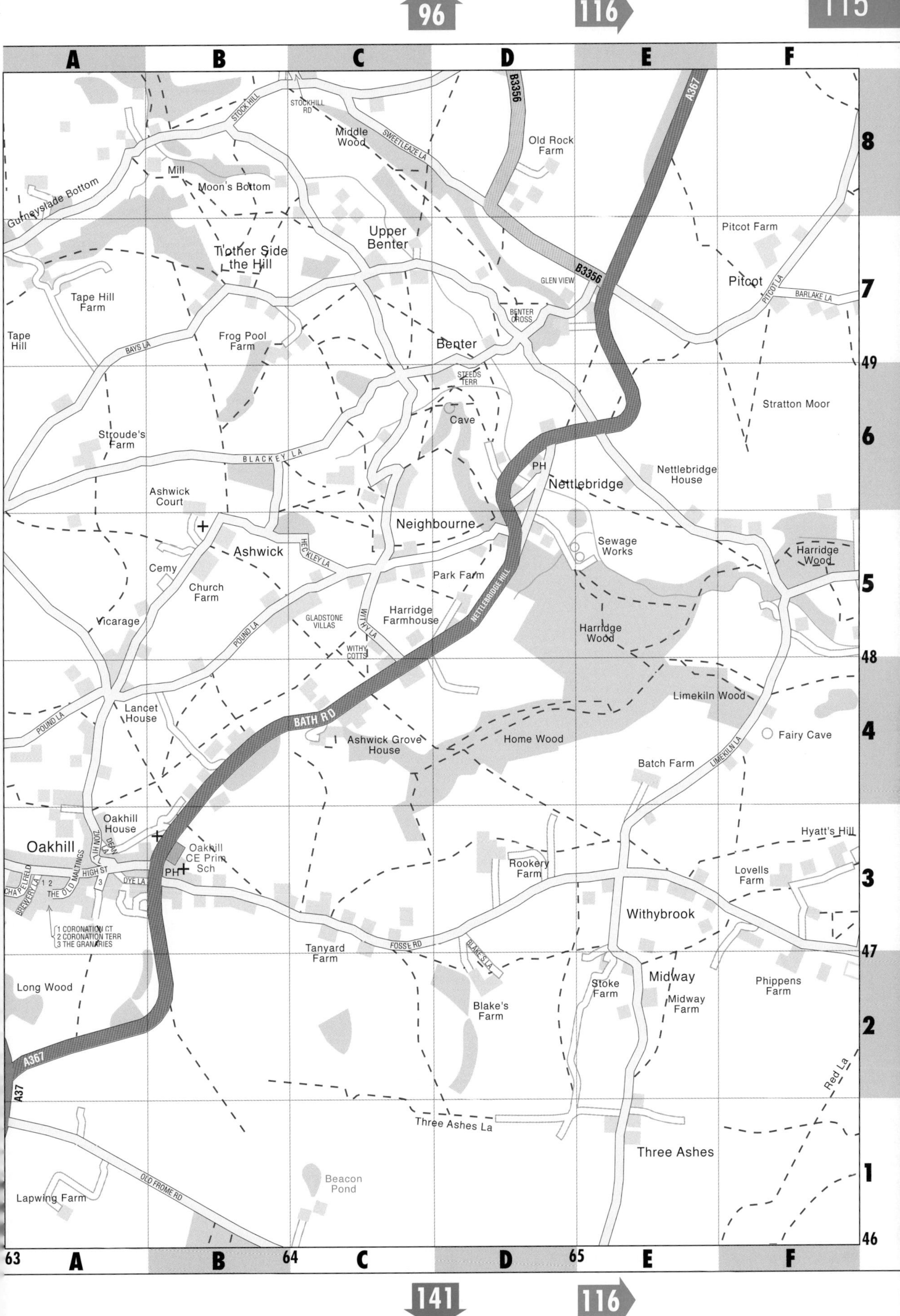
96
116
A
B
C
D
E
F
8
7
49
6
5
48
4
3
47
2
1
46
63
64
65
141
116
A367
B3356
Old Rock Farm
Middle Wood
STOCKHILL RD
STOCK HILL
SWEETLEAZE LA
Mill
Moon's Bottom
Gurneyslade Bottom
Upper Benter
T'other Side the Hill
Pitcot Farm
Pitcot
PITCOT LA
BARLAKE LA
GLEN VIEW
BENTER CROSS
Tape Hill Farm
Tape Hill
Frog Pool Farm
BAYS LA
Benter
STEEDS TERR
Cave
Stratton Moor
Stroude's Farm
BLACKEY LA
PH
Nettlebridge
Nettlebridge House
Ashwick Court
Neighbourne
Sewage Works
Harridge Wood
Ashwick
HECKLEY LA
Cemy
Church Farm
Park Farm
NETTLEBRIDGE HILL
Vicarage
POUND LA
GLADSTONE VILLAS
WITHY LA
Harridge Farmhouse
WITHY COTTS
Harridge Wood
Limekiln Wood
Lancet House
BATH RD
Ashwick Grove House
Home Wood
Fairy Cave
Batch Farm
LIMEKILN LA
Oakhill House
Oakhill
ZION HILL
DEAN LA
Oakhill CE Prim Sch
PH
Rookery Farm
Hyatt's Hill
Lovells Farm
CHAPELFIELD
BREWERY LA
THE OLD MALTINGS
HIGH ST
DYE LA
THE OLD MALTINGS
1 CORONATION CT
2 CORONATION TERR
3 THE GRANARIES
Withybrook
Tanyard Farm
FOSSE RD
BLAKE'S LA
Midway
Stoke Farm
Midway Farm
Phippens Farm
Long Wood
Blake's Farm
A367
A37
Red La
Three Ashes La
Three Ashes
Beacon Pond
Lapwing Farm
OLD FROME RD

115
97

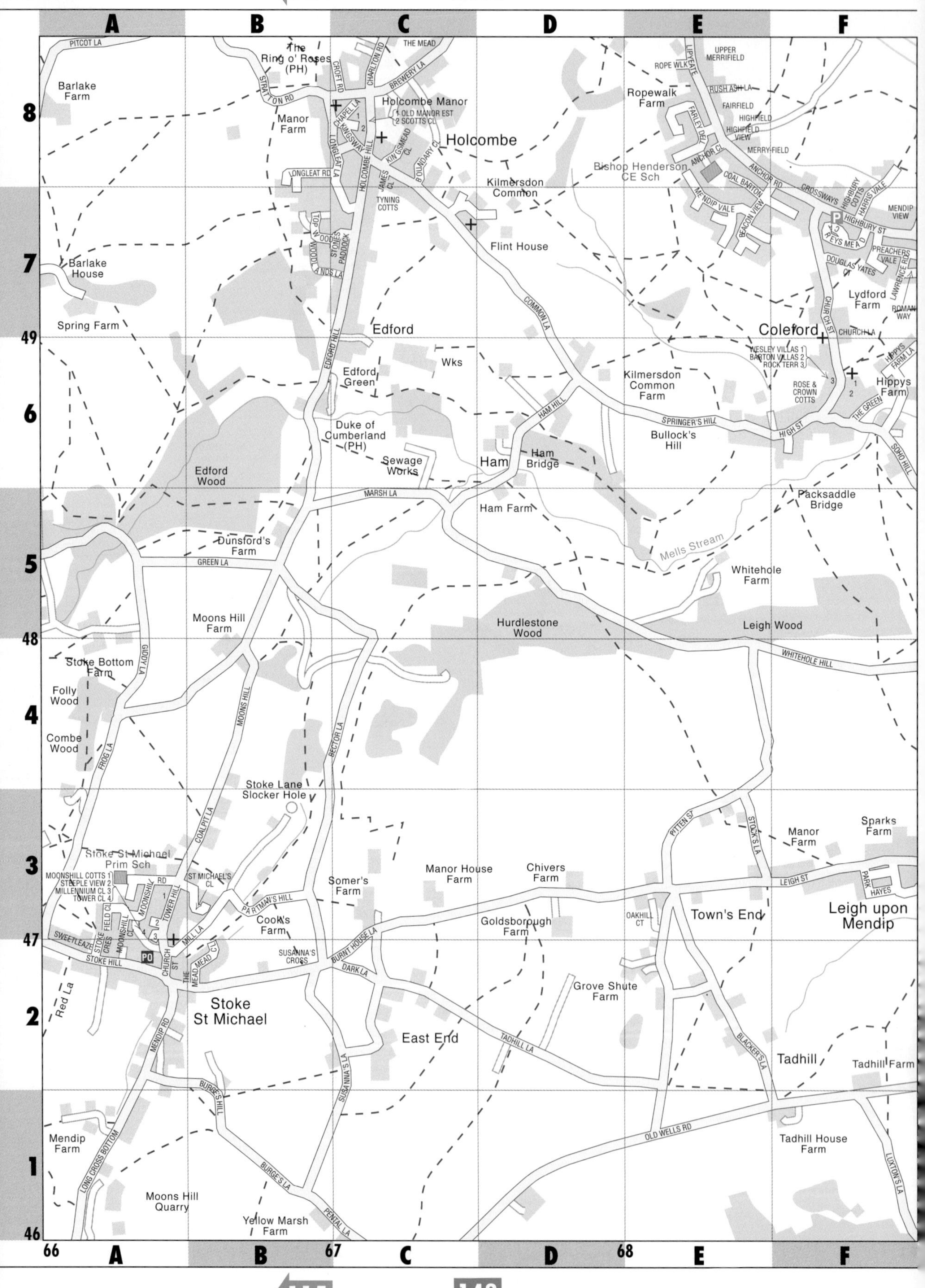
A
B
C
D
E
F
8
7
49
6
5
48
4
3
47
2
1
46
66
67
68
Barlake Farm
Barlake House
Spring Farm
The Ring o' Roses (PH)
Manor Farm
Holcombe Manor
Holcombe
Kilmersdon Common
Flint House
Edford
Edford Green
Wks
Duke of Cumberland (PH)
Sewage Works
Ham
Ham Bridge
Ham Farm
Edford Wood
Dunsford's Farm
Moons Hill Farm
Hurdlestone Wood
Stoke Bottom Farm
Folly Wood
Combe Wood
Stoke Lane Slocker Hole
Stoke St Michael Prim Sch
Ropewalk Farm
Bishop Henderson CE Sch
Coleford
Lydford Farm
Kilmersdon Common Farm
Bullock's Hill
Hippys Farm
Packsaddle Bridge
Mells Stream
Whitehole Farm
Leigh Wood
Manor Farm
Sparks Farm
Manor House Farm
Chivers Farm
Somer's Farm
Cook's Farm
Goldsborough Farm
Town's End
Leigh upon Mendip
Grove Shute Farm
Stoke St Michael
East End
Tadhill
Tadhill Farm
Tadhill House Farm
Mendip Farm
Moons Hill Quarry
Yellow Marsh Farm
Red La
PO
P
PITCOT LA
STRATTON RD
CROFT RD
CHARLTON RD
THE MEAD
BREWERY LA
CHAPEL LA
KINGSWAY
LONGLEAT LA
LONGLEAT RD
HOLCOMBE HILL
KINGSMEAD CL
BOUNDARY CL
JAMES CL
TYNING COTTS
1 OLD MANOR EST
2 SCOTTS CL
TOP WOODS
STONES PADDOCK
WOODLANDS LA
EDFORD HILL
COMMON LA
HAM HILL
MARSH LA
GREEN LA
GIDDY LA
MOONS HILL
FROG LA
COALPIT LA
BECTOR LA
ST MICHAEL'S CL
PARTMAN'S HILL
MOONSHILL COTTS 1
STEEPLE VIEW 2
MILLENNIUM CL 3
TOWER CL 4
MOONSHILL RD
TOWER HILL
FIELD CL
SWEETLEAZE
STOKE CRES
STOKE HILL
CHURCH ST
MILL LA
THE MEAD
MEAD CL
SUSANNA'S CROSS
BURNT HOUSE LA
DARK LA
MENDIP RD
BURGE'S HILL
BURGE'S LA
SUSANNA'S LA
PENTAL LA
LONG CROSS BOTTOM
TADHILL LA
OLD WELLS RD
BLACKER'S LA
LUXTON'S LA
OAKHILL CT
PITTEN ST
STOCK'S LA
LEIGH ST
PARK
HAYES
WHITEHOLE HILL
SPRINGER'S HILL
HIGH ST
THE GREEN
SOHO HILL
UPPER MERRIFIELD
LIPYEATE
ROPE WLK
RUSH ASH LA
FAIRFIELD
HIGHFIELD
HIGHFIELD VIEW
MERRYFIELD
FARLEY DELL
ANCHOR CL
ANCHOR RD
COAL BARTON
MENDIP VALE
BEACON VIEW
CROSSWAYS
HIGHBURY COTTS
HARRIS VALE
MENDIP VIEW
HIGHBURY ST
REYS MEAD
PREACHERS VALE
DOUGLAS YATES CT
LAWRENCE RD
ROMAN WAY
CHURCH ST
CHURCH LA
WESLEY VILLAS 1
BARTON VILLAS 2
ROCK TERR 3
ROSE & CROWN COTTS
HIPPYS FARM LA

115
142

98
118

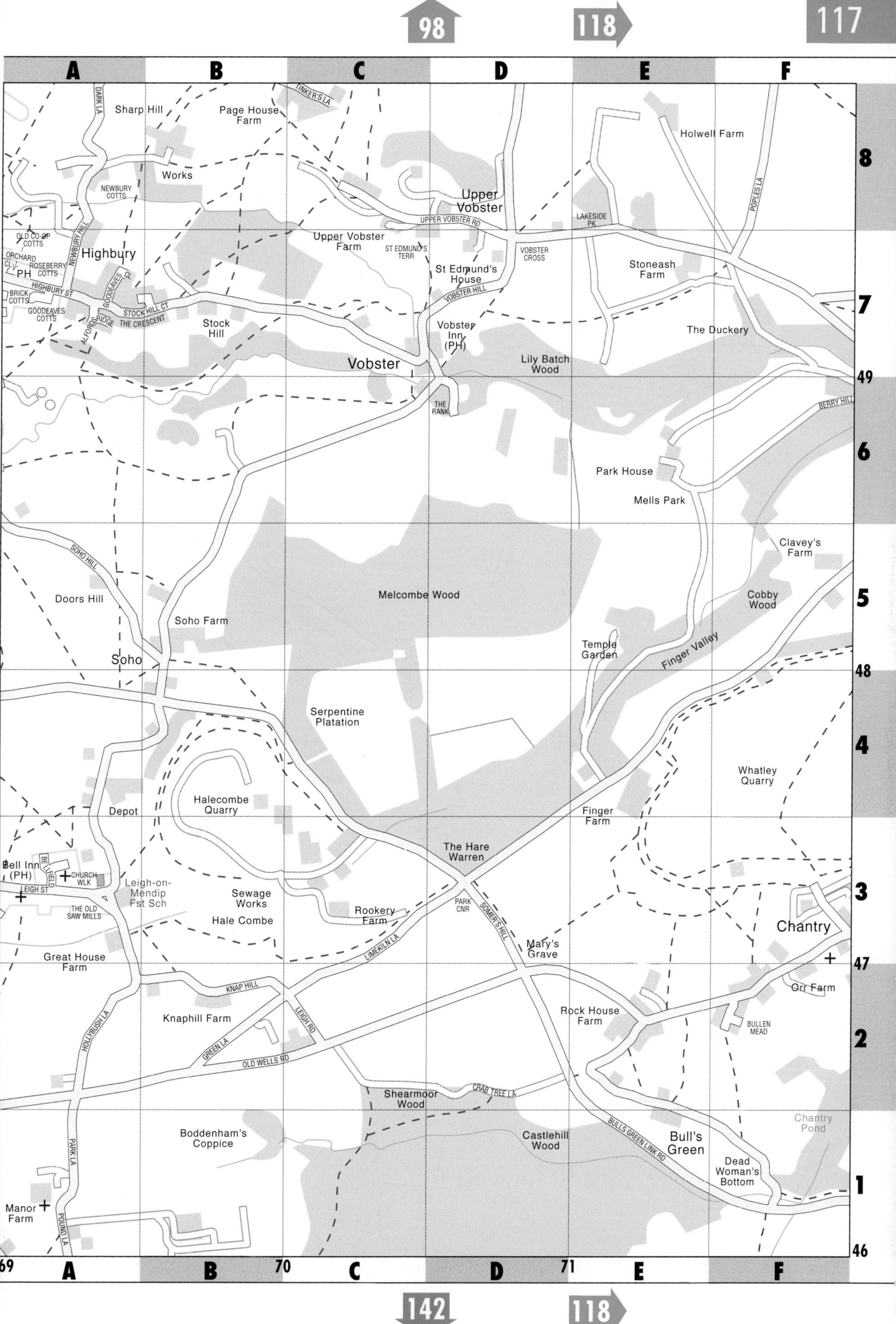
A
B
C
D
E
F
8
7
49
6
5
48
4
3
47
2
1
46
69
70
71
Sharp Hill
Page House Farm
Holwell Farm
Works
Newbury Cotts
Upper Vobster
Upper Vobster Rd
Lakeside Pk
Poples La
Highbury
Upper Vobster Farm
St Edmund's Terr
St Edmund's House
Vobster Cross
Stoneash Farm
Vobster Hill
Stock Hill
Vobster Inn (PH)
The Duckery
Vobster
Lily Batch Wood
The Rank
Berry Hill
Park House
Mells Park
Soho Hill
Clavey's Farm
Doors Hill
Melcombe Wood
Cobby Wood
Soho Farm
Temple Garden
Finger Valley
Soho
Serpentine Platation
Whatley Quarry
Halecombe Quarry
Depot
Finger Farm
The Hare Warren
Bell Inn (PH)
Church Wlk
Leigh St
Leigh-on-Mendip Fst Sch
Sewage Works
Hale Combe
Rookery Farm
Park Cnr
Somer's Hill
Chantry
The Old Saw Mills
Great House Farm
Limekiln La
Mary's Grave
Orr Farm
Knap Hill
Knaphill Farm
Rock House Farm
Bullen Mead
Hollybush La
Leigh Rd
Green La
Old Wells Rd
Shearmoor Wood
Crab Tree La
Boddenham's Coppice
Castlehill Wood
Bulls Green Link Rd
Bull's Green
Chantry Pond
Dead Woman's Bottom
Park La
Manor Farm
Pound La
Dark La
Newbury Hill
Old Co-op Cotts
Orchard Cl
Roseberry Cotts
PH
Highbury St
Goodeaves Cl
Brick Cotts
Goodeaves Cotts
Stock Hill Ct
Alfords Ridge
The Crescent
Tinker's La
Bell Field

142
118

117
99

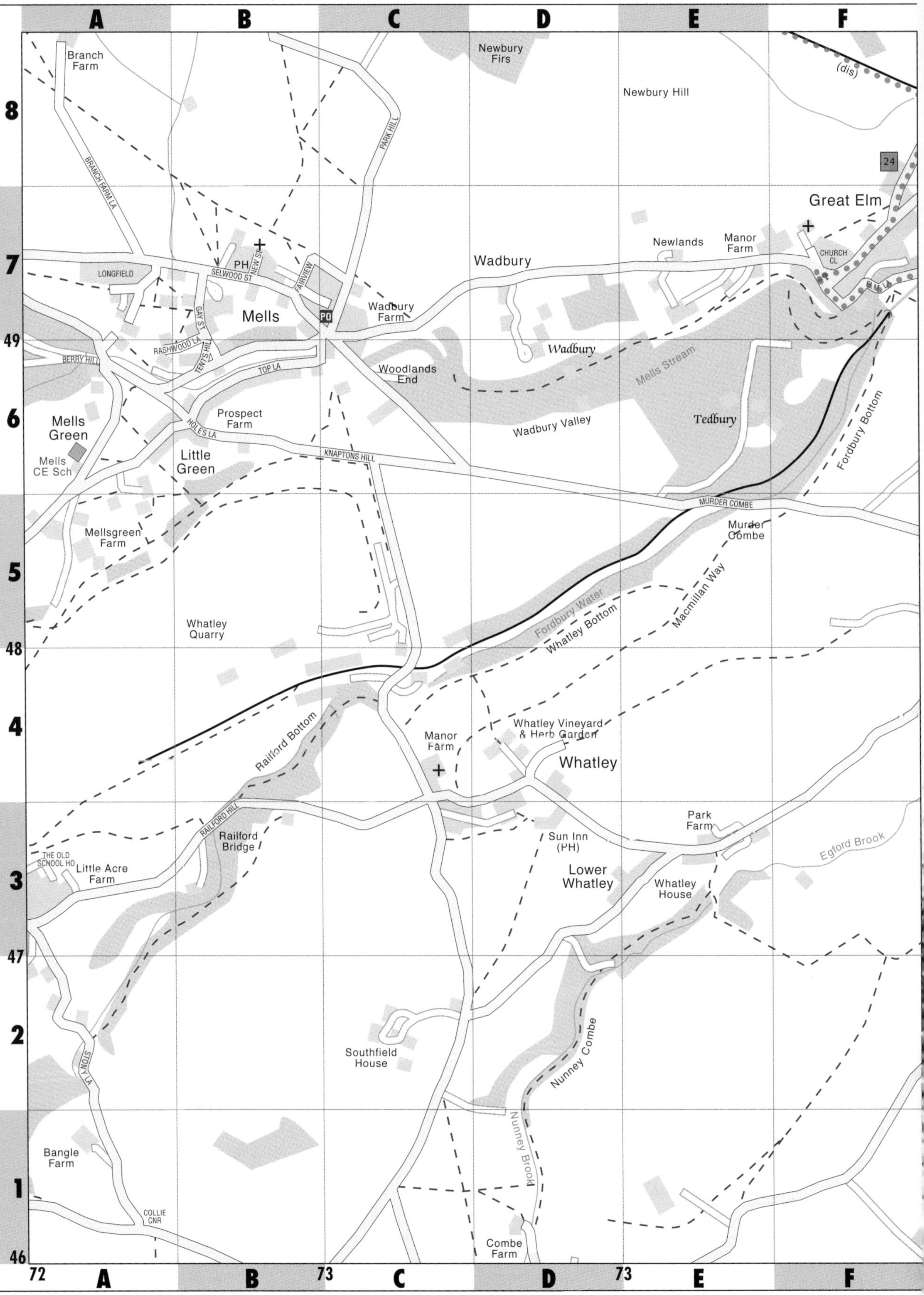

A B C D E F

8 7 49 6 5 48 4 3 47 2 1 46

Branch Farm
Newbury Firs
Newbury Hill
(dis)
24
Great Elm
BRANCH FARM LA
PARK HILL
Newlands
Manor Farm
CHURCH CL
ELM LA
PH
NEW ST
FAIRVIEW
LONGFIELD
SELWOOD ST
Wadbury
Wadbury Farm
Mells
PO
GAY ST
RASHWOOD LA
TENTS HILL
BERRY HILL
TOP LA
Woodlands End
Wadbury
Mells Stream
Tedbury
Mells Green
Mells CE Sch
Prospect Farm
HOLES LA
Little Green
KNAPTONS HILL
Wadbury Valley
Fordbury Bottom
MURDER COMBE
Murder Combe
Mellsgreen Farm
Macmillan Way
Fordbury Water
Whatley Bottom
Whatley Quarry
Railford Bottom
Manor Farm
Whatley Vineyard & Herb Garden
Whatley
RAILFORD HILL
Railford Bridge
Sun Inn (PH)
Park Farm
Egford Brook
THE OLD SCHOOL HO
Little Acre Farm
Lower Whatley
Whatley House
Nunney Combe
Southfield House
STONY LA
Bangle Farm
Nunney Brook
COLLIE CNR
Combe Farm

72 A B 73 C D 73 E F

117
143

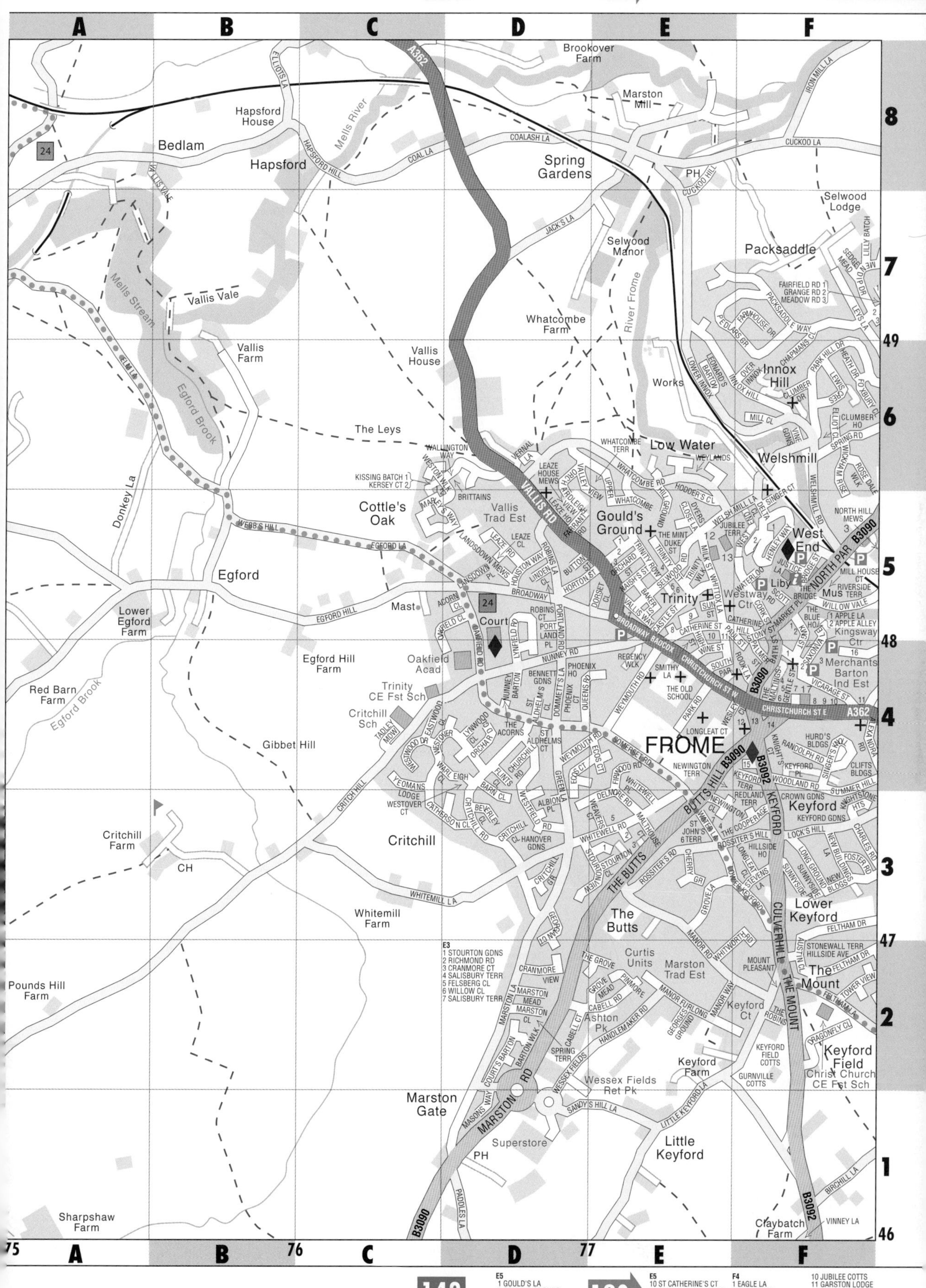
A
B
C
D
E
F
8
7
49
6
5
48
4
3
47
2
1
46
75
76
77
A362
Brookover Farm
Marston Mill
Hapsford House
Bedlam
Hapsford
Mells River
HAPSFORD HILL
COALASH LA
COAL LA
Spring Gardens
CUCKOO LA
PH
CUCKOO HILL
Selwood Lodge
JACK'S LA
Selwood Manor
Packsaddle
Mells Stream
Vallis Vale
River Frome
Whatcombe Farm
FAIRFIELD RD 1
GRANGE RD 2
MEADOW RD 3
PACKSADDLE WAY
Vallis Farm
Vallis House
Egford Brook
Works
Innox Hill
The Leys
Low Water
Welshmill
WALLINGTON WAY
KISSING BATCH 1
KERSEY CT 2
VALLIS RD
BRITTAINS
Cottle's Oak
Vallis Trad Est
Gould's Ground
Donkey La
WEBB'S HILL
EGFORD LA
West End
NORTH PAR
B3090
Egford
BROADWAY
Trinity
Westway Ctr
Liby
Mus
Lower Egford Farm
Mast
EGFORD HILL
Court
BROADWAY BADCOX
CHRISTCHURCH ST W
Egford Hill Farm
Oakfield Acad
NUNNEY RD
Kingsway Ctr
Merchants Barton Ind Est
Red Barn Farm
Trinity CE Fst Sch
Critchill Sch
CHRISTCHURCH ST E
Egford Brook
Gibbet Hill
FROME
B3092
Keyford
Critchill Farm
CH
Critchill
CRITCHILL RD
THE BUTTS
ROSSITER'S RD
Lower Keyford
WHITEMILL LA
Whitemill Farm
The Butts
CULVERHILL
Curtis Units
Marston Trad Est
E3
1 STOURTON GDNS
2 RICHMOND RD
3 CRANMORE CT
4 SALISBURY TERR
5 FELSBERG CL
6 WILLOW CL
7 SALISBURY TERR
The Mount
Pounds Hill Farm
Ashton Pk
Keyford Ct
MARSTON RD
THE MOUNT
Keyford Field
Christ Church CE Fst Sch
Keyford Farm
Wessex Fields Ret Pk
Marston Gate
SANDY'S HILL LA
LITTLE KEYFORD LA
Superstore
Little Keyford
PH
Sharpshaw Farm
Claybatch Farm
VINNEY LA
PADDLES LA

119
99

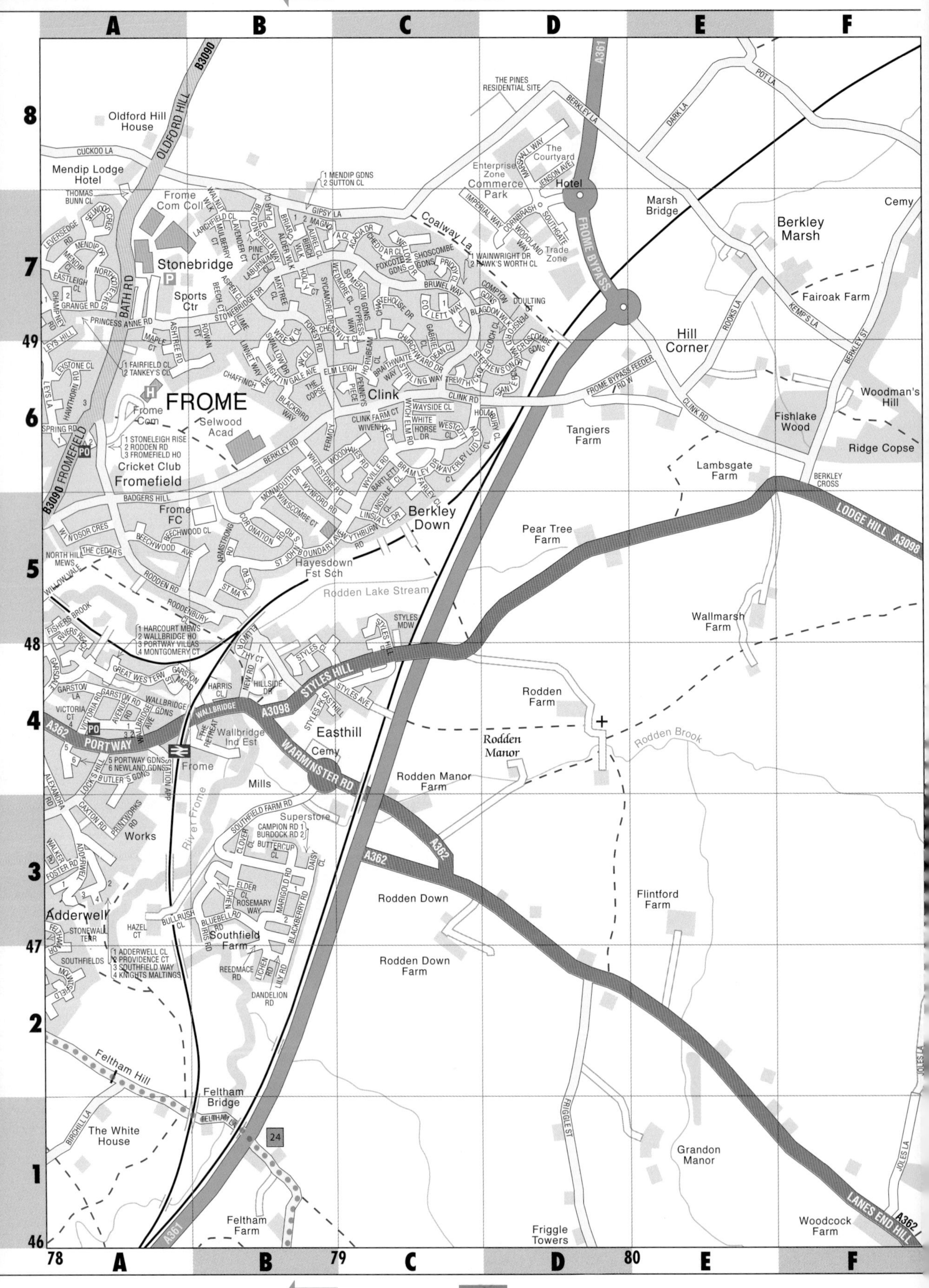
A
B
C
D
E
F
8
7
49
6
5
48
4
3
47
2
1
46
78
79
80
Oldford Hill House
OLDFORD HILL
B3090
CUCKOO LA
Mendip Lodge Hotel
THOMAS BUNN CL
Frome Com Coll
Stonebridge
Sports Ctr
BATH RD
PRINCESS ANNE RD
GRANGE RD
EASTLEIGH CL
MENDIP CL
LEVERSEDGE RD
SELWOOD CRES
NORTHCOTE CRES
CHAMPNEY RD
LEYS HILL
LEYSTONE CL
HAWTHORN RD
LEYS LA
SPRING RD
1 FAIRFIELD CL
2 TANKEY'S CL
FROME
Frome Com
Selwood Acad
1 STONELEIGH RISE
2 RODDEN RD
3 FROMEFIELD HO
Cricket Club
Fromefield
B3090 FROMEFIELD
BADGERS HILL
Frome FC
BEECHWOOD CL
BEECHWOOD AVE
WINDSOR CRES
THE CEDARS
NORTH HILL MEWS
WILLOW VALE
RODDEN RD
RODDENBURY CL
FISHERS BROOK
RIVERS REACH
1 HARCOURT MEWS
2 WALLBRIDGE HO
3 PORTWAY VILLAS
4 MONTGOMERY CT
GREAT WESTERN
GARSTON MEAD
GARSTON LA
GARSTON RD
VICTORIA CT
VICTORIA RD
WALLBRIDGE GDNS
WALLBRIDGE AVE
A362 PORTWAY
5 PORTWAY GDNS
6 NEWLAND GDNS
BUTLER'S GDNS
LOCK'S HILL
STATION APP
Frome
ALEXANDRA RD
CAXTON RD
PRINTWORKS RD
Works
WALKER RD
FOSTER RD
ADDERWELL
Adderwell
STONEWALL TERR
HAZEL CT
SOUTHFIELDS
1 ADDERWELL CL
2 PROVIDENCE CT
3 SOUTHFIELD WAY
4 KNIGHTS MALTINGS
Feltham Hill
BIRCHILL LA
The White House
Feltham Bridge
FELTHAM LA
24
A361
Feltham Farm
1 MENDIP GDNS
2 SUTTON CL
GIPSY LA
WALNUT WLK
MULBERRY CT
LARCHFIELD CL
LAVENDER CT
BEACONSFIELD WAY
PINE CT
LABURNUM WLK
STONEBRIDGE DR
ASHTREE RD
ROWAN CT
MAPLE CT
BEECH CT
ASPEN CL
LIME CL
LINNET WAY
CHAFFINCH AVE
MAYTREE CL
BRIAR CL
ALDER WLK
HOLLY CT
BIRCH CL
LAUREL CL
MAGNOLIA
SYCAMORE DR
FOREST RD
WREN CL
SWALLOW DR
NIGHTINGALE AVE
BLACKBIRD WAY
WEDMORE CL
SOMERTON GDNS
CYPRESS WAY
CHESTNUT CL
HORNBEAM
ACACIA DR
CHEDDAR CL
WELLOW DR
SHOSCOMBE GDNS
FOXCOTE GDNS
PRIDDY CL
BRUWEL WAY
COLLETT WAY
GABRIEL CL
DEAN CL
CHURCHWARD DR
BRAITHWAITE WAY
STIRLING WAY
ELM LEIGH
THE COPSE
PENNEYS PIECE
Clink
CLINK RD
CLINK FARM CT
WIVENHOE CT
WAYSIDE CL
WHITE HORSE DR
WESTCOTT CL
WYCH ELM RD
HOLMBURY CL
BERKLEY RD
FERMOY
WHITESTONE RD
WOODHAYES RD
WYNFORD RD
MONMOUTH DR
WINSCOMBE CT
CORONATION RD
ARMSTRONG RD
ST JOHNS RD
BOUNDARY AVE
NEWBURY RD
LINSVALE DR
LINSVALE CL
BARTLETT RD
BRAMLEY DR
WAVERLEY CL
FARLEY CL
Berkley Down
Hayesdown Fst Sch
Rodden Lake Stream
ST MARY'S RD
COMPTON GDNS
DOULTING CT
BLAGDON WLK
GOOCH CL
PENSFORD WAY
CROSCOMBE GDNS
STEPHENSON DR
TREVITHICK CL
STANLEY CL
Coalway La
1 WAINWRIGHT DR
2 HAWK'S WORTH CL
THE PINES RESIDENTIAL SITE
BERKLEY LA
Enterprise Zone
Commerce Park
The Courtyard
MARSHALL WAY
JENSON AVE
Hotel
IMPERIAL WAY
CORNBRASH
WOODLAND WAY
SOUTHGATE
Trade Zone
FROME BYPASS
FROME BYPASS FEEDER RD W
Marsh Bridge
DARK LA
POT LA
Berkley Marsh
Cemy
Fairoak Farm
KEMP'S LA
ROOKS LA
BERKLEY ST
Hill Corner
Woodman's Hill
Fishlake Wood
Ridge Copse
Tangiers Farm
Lambsgate Farm
BERKLEY CROSS
LODGE HILL A3098
Pear Tree Farm
Wallmarsh Farm
STYLES MDW
STYLES HILL
STYLES CL
ELLIOTT HO
THYNNE CT
NEW RD
HILLSIDE DR
HARRIS CL
THE RETREAT
WALLBRIDGE
A3098
STYLES AVE
EASTHILL
STYLES PK
Easthill
Cemy
Wallbridge Ind Est
Mills
WARMINSTER RD
Rodden Farm
Rodden Manor
Rodden Manor Farm
Rodden Brook
SOUTHFIELD FARM RD
Superstore
CAMPION RD 1
BURDOCK RD 2
BUTTERCUP CL
CLOVER CL
DAISY CL
ELDER CL
ROSEMARY WAY
LICHEN RD
MARIGOLD RD
BLACKBERRY RD
BLUEBELL RD
IRIS RD
BULLRUSH CL
Southfield Farm
REEDMACE RD
LICHEN RD
LILY RD
DANDELION RD
River Frome
A362
Rodden Down
Rodden Down Farm
Flintford Farm
FRIGGLE ST
Friggle Towers
Grandon Manor
JOLES LA
Woodcock Farm
LANES END HILL
A362

119
144

102

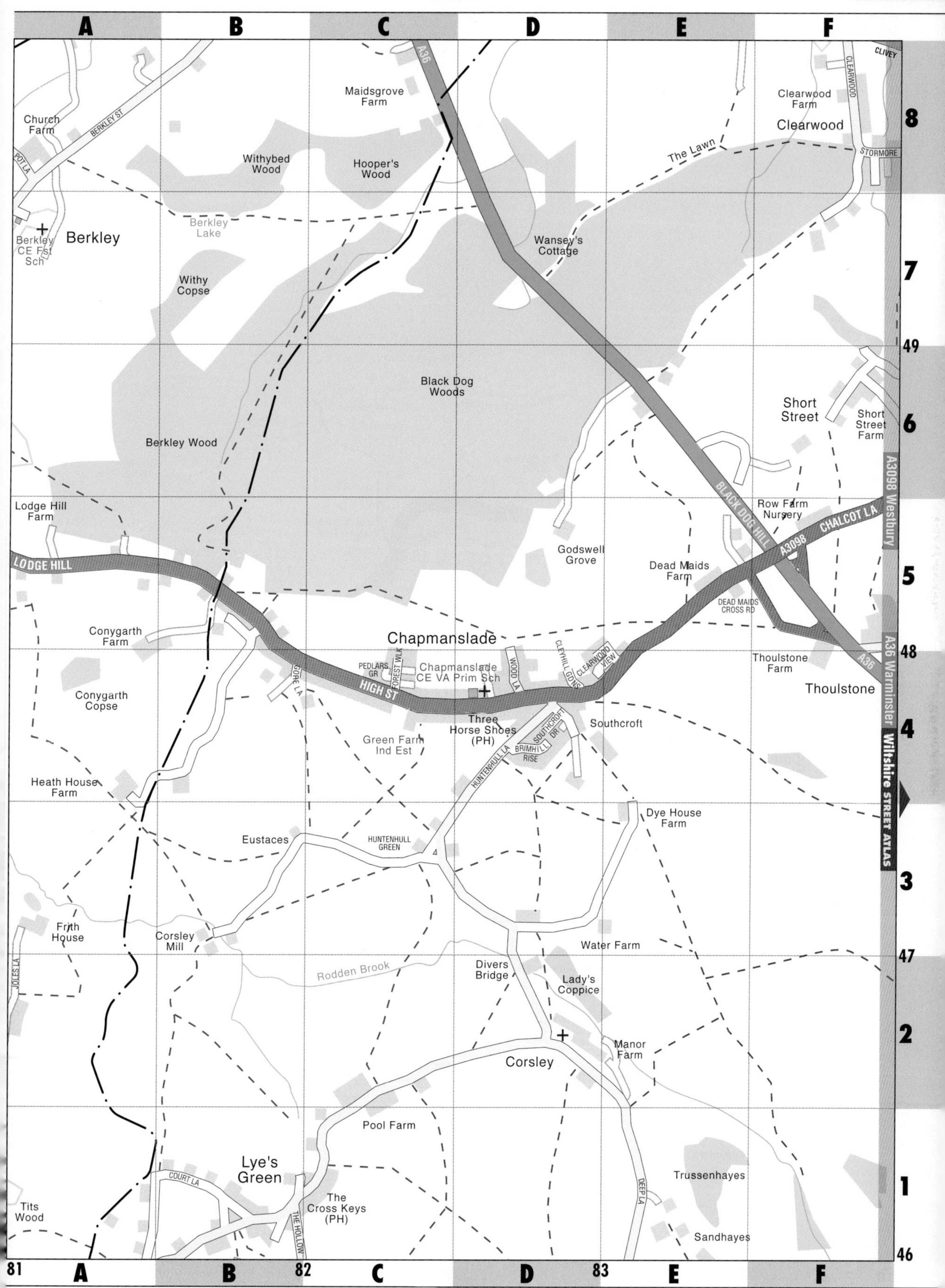
A
B
C
D
E
F
Church Farm
BERKLEY ST
POT LA
Berkley
Berkley CE Fst Sch
Maidsgrove Farm
Withybed Wood
Hooper's Wood
Berkley Lake
Withy Copse
Clearwood Farm
Clearwood
CLEARWOOD
CLIVEY
STORMORE
The Lawn
Wansey's Cottage
A36
Black Dog Woods
Berkley Wood
Short Street
Short Street Farm
Lodge Hill Farm
LODGE HILL
Row Farm Nursery
CHALCOT LA
A3098
BLACK DOG HILL
Godswell Grove
Dead Maids Farm
DEAD MAIDS CROSS RD
Conygarth Farm
Chapmanslade
PEDLARS GR
FOREST WLK
Chapmanslade CE VA Prim Sch
WOOD LA
CLEYHILL GDNS
CLEARWOOD VIEW
GORE LA
HIGH ST
Thoulstone Farm
Thoulstone
Conygarth Copse
Three Horse Shoes (PH)
Southcroft
SOUTHCROFT DR
BRIMHILL RISE
HUNTENHULL LA
Green Farm Ind Est
Heath House Farm
Dye House Farm
Eustaces
HUNTENHULL GREEN
Frith House
Corsley Mill
Water Farm
Rodden Brook
Divers Bridge
Lady's Coppice
JOLES LA
Manor Farm
Corsley
Pool Farm
Lye's Green
COURT LA
Trussenhayes
DEEP LA
Tits Wood
The Cross Keys (PH)
THE HOLLOW
Sandhayes
A3098 Westbury
A36 Warminster
Wiltshire STREET ATLAS
8
7
49
6
5
48
4
3
47
2
1
46
81
82
83

141

Scale: 1¾ inches to 1 mile

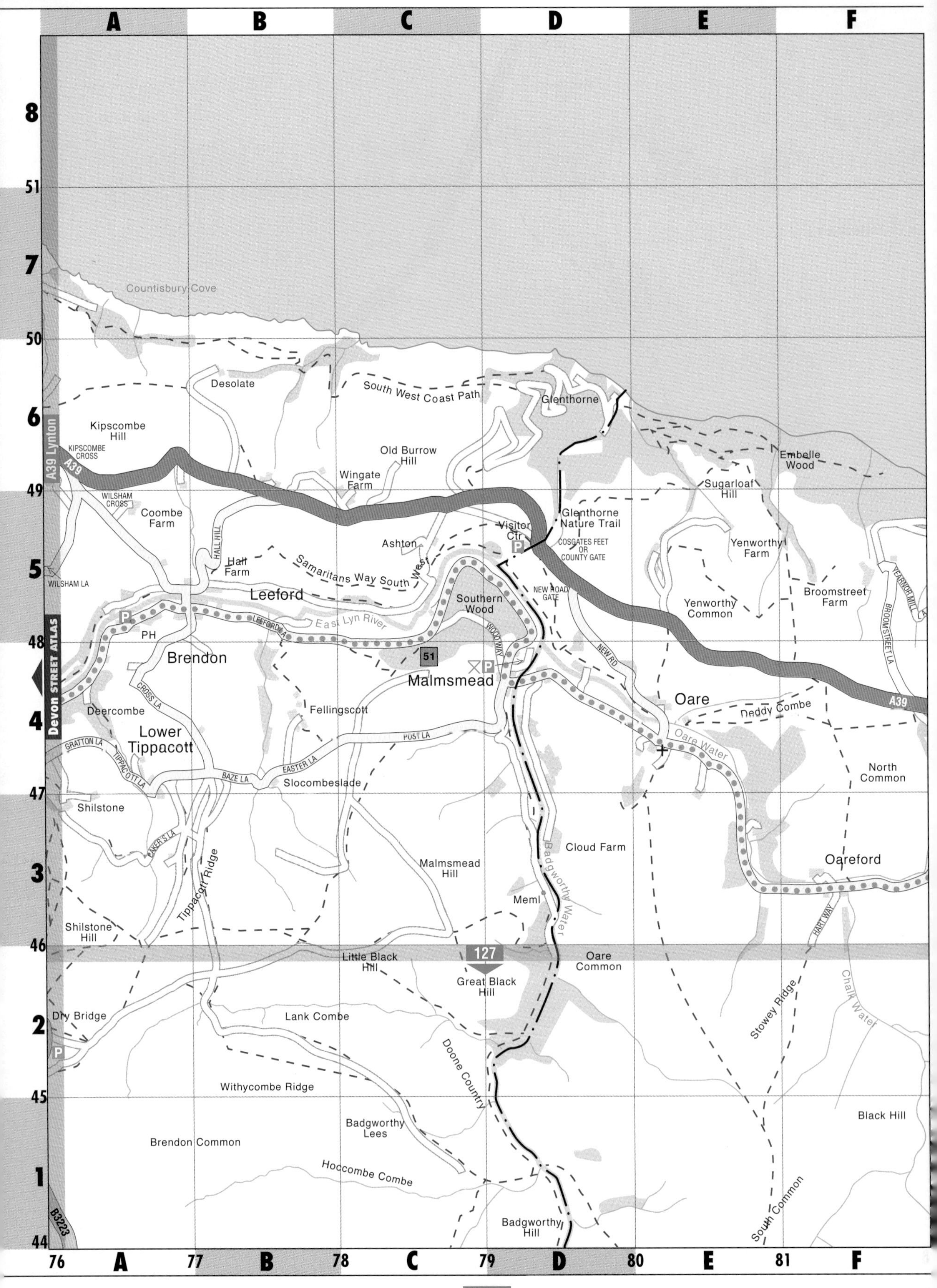

A B C D E F
8
51
7
Countisbury Cove
50
Desolate
South West Coast Path
Glenthorne
6
Kipscombe Hill
KIPSCOMBE CROSS
A39 Lynton
A39
Old Burrow Hill
Embelle Wood
Wingate Farm
49
WILSHAM CROSS
Coombe Farm
Sugarloaf Hill
Glenthorne Nature Trail
Visitor Ctr
COSGATES FEET OR COUNTY GATE
Ashton
Yenworthy Farm
HALL HILL
Hall Farm
Samaritans Way South West
5
WILSHAM LA
Leeford
Southern Wood
NEW ROAD GATE
Broomstreet Farm
Yenworthy Common
YEARNOR MILL
BROOMSTREET LA
LEEFORD LA
East Lyn River
PH
48
Devon STREET ATLAS
WOODWAY
NEW RD
Brendon
51
Malmsmead
Oare
A39
CROSS LA
Deercombe
Fellingscott
Deddy Combe
4
Lower Tippacott
GRATTON LA
TIPPACOTT LA
POST LA
Oare Water
EASTER LA
BAZE LA
North Common
Slocombeslade
47
Shilstone
BAKER'S LA
Cloud Farm
Badgworthy Water
3
Tippacott Ridge
Malmsmead Hill
Oareford
Meml
Shilstone Hill
HART WAY
46
127
Little Black Hill
Oare Common
Great Black Hill
Chalk Water
Stowey Ridge
2
Dry Bridge
Lank Combe
Doone Country
Withycombe Ridge
45
Black Hill
Badgworthy Lees
Brendon Common
1
Hoccombe Combe
B3223
Badgworthy Hill
South Common
44
76 A 77 B 78 C 79 D 80 E 81 F

127

Scale: 1¾ inches to 1 mile
0 ¼ ½ mile
0 250m 500m 750m 1 km

124

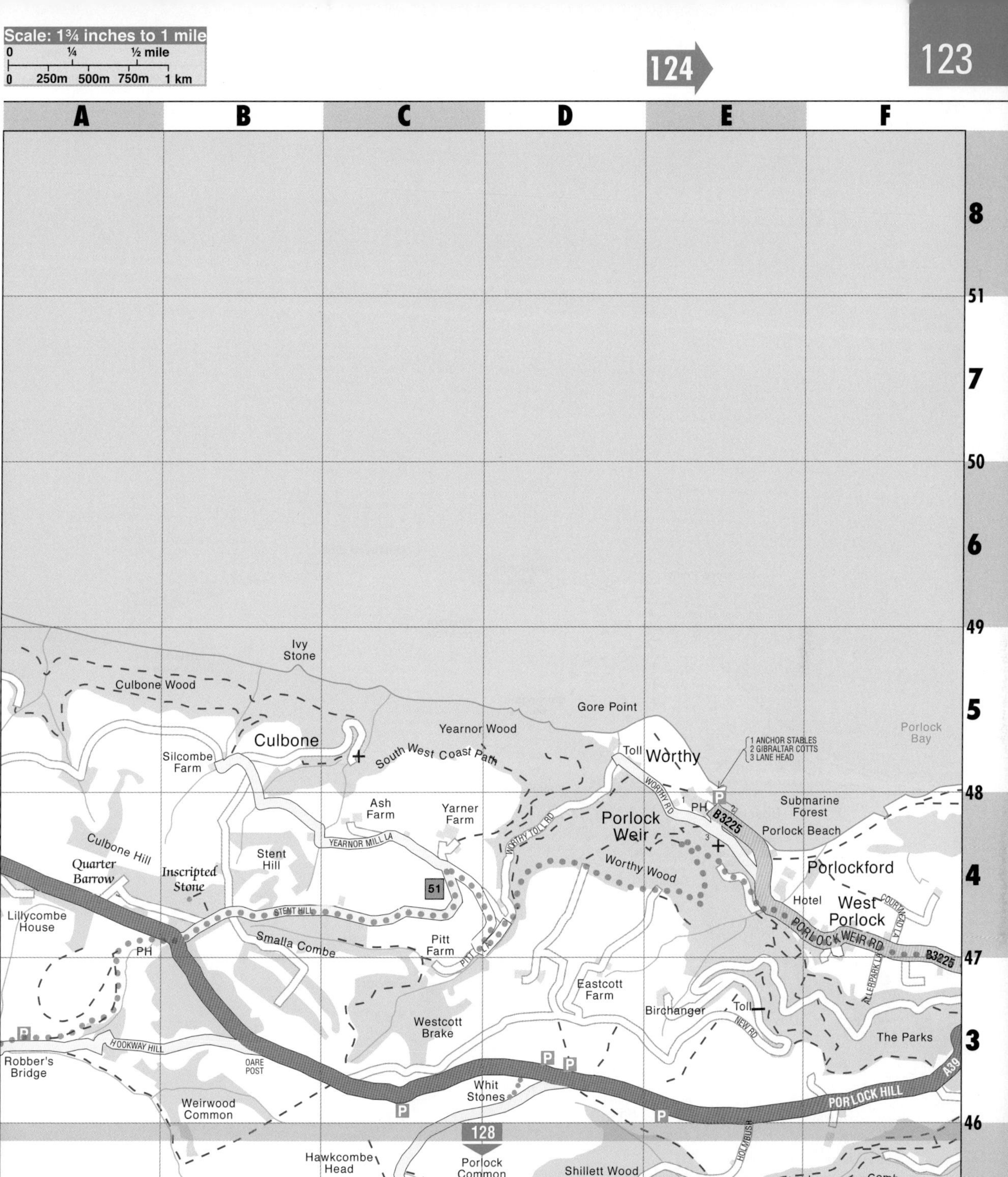

128
124

123

Scale: 1¾ inches to 1 mile
0 ¼ ½ mile
0 250m 500m 750m 1 km

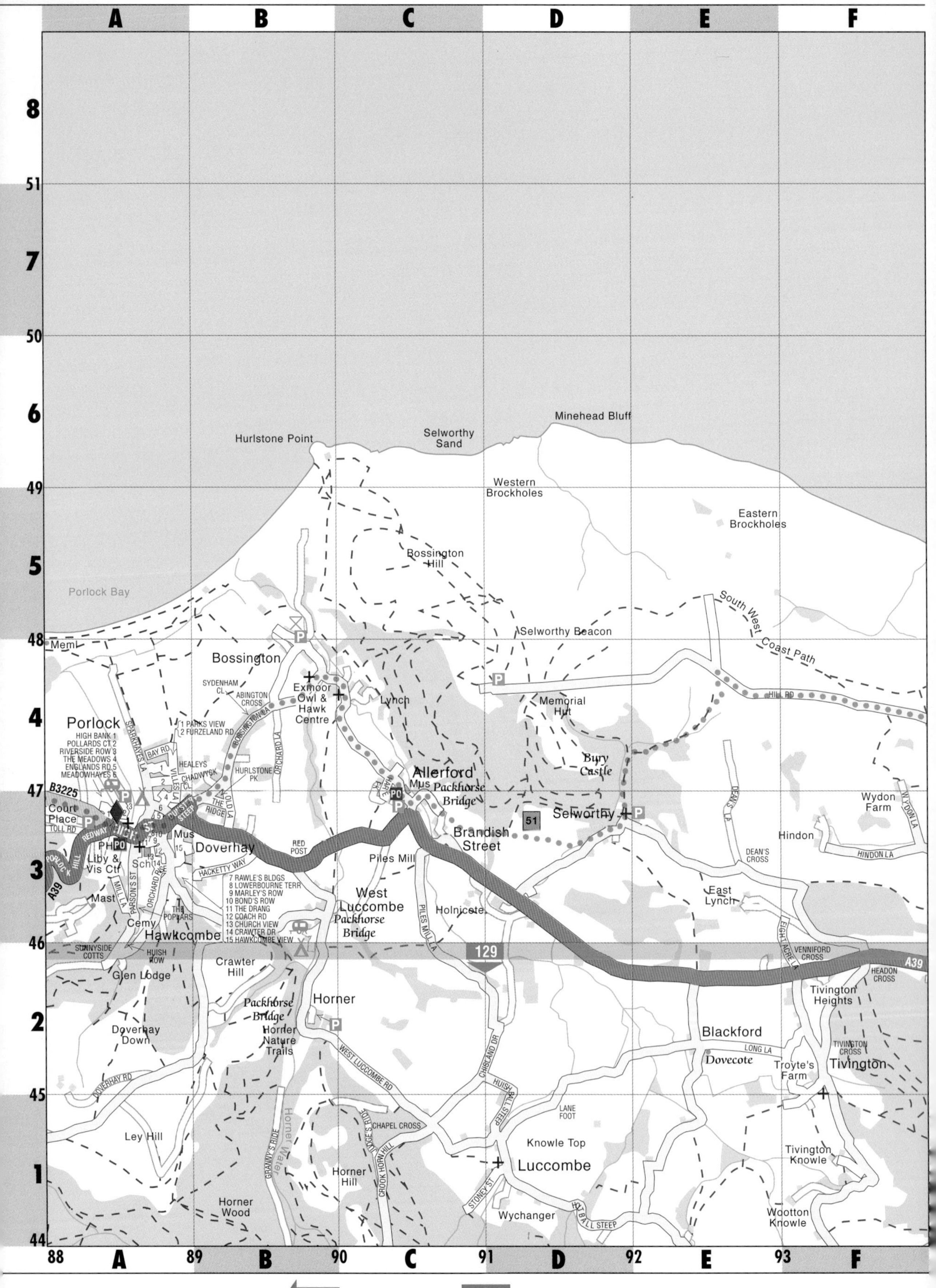

123
129

Scale: 1¾ inches to 1 mile

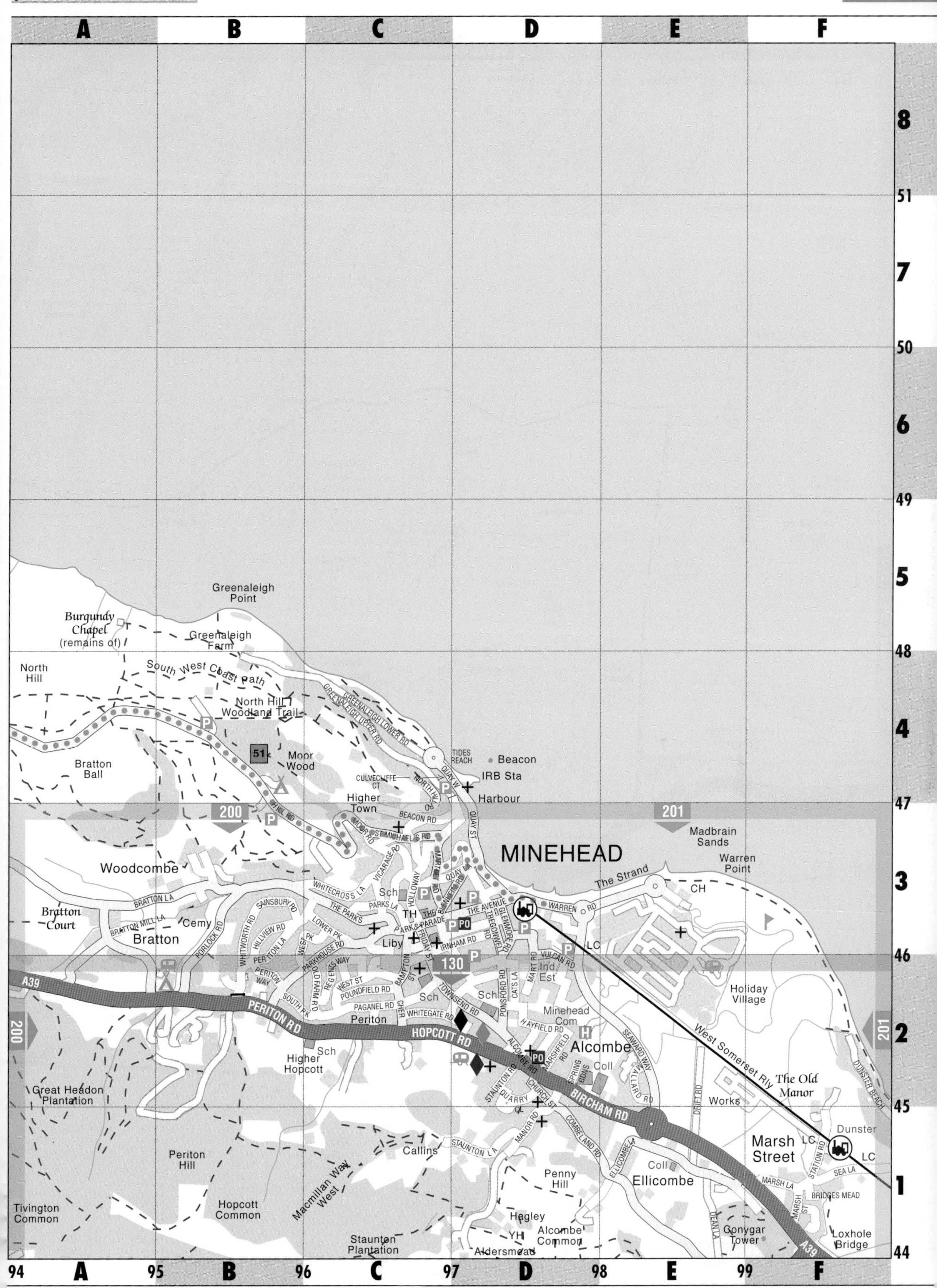

130
131
For full street detail of the highlighted areas see pages 200 and 201.

Scale: 1¾ inches to 1 mile

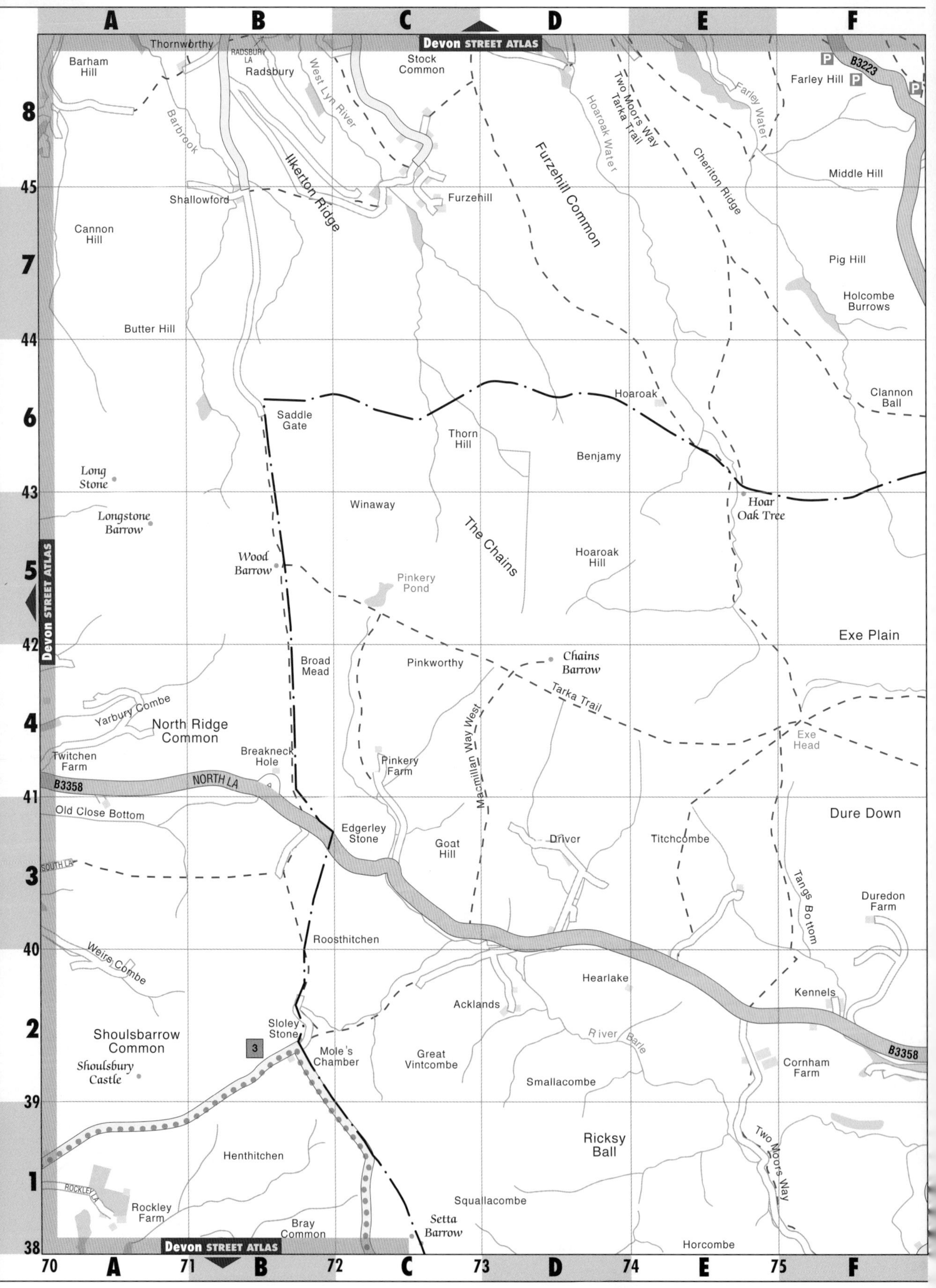

Devon STREET ATLAS
Thornworthy
Barham Hill
Radsbury
RADSBURY LA
West Lyn River
Stock Common
Two Moors Way
Tarka Trail
Hoaroak Water
Farley Water
Farley Hill
B3223
Barbrook
Ilkerton Ridge
Furzehill Common
Cheriton Ridge
Middle Hill
Shallowford
Furzehill
Cannon Hill
Pig Hill
Holcombe Burrows
Butter Hill
Hoaroak
Clannon Ball
Saddle Gate
Thorn Hill
Benjamy
Long Stone
Winaway
Hoar Oak Tree
Longstone Barrow
The Chains
Hoaroak Hill
Wood Barrow
Pinkery Pond
Exe Plain
Broad Mead
Pinkworthy
Chains Barrow
Tarka Trail
Yarbury Combe
North Ridge Common
Macmillan Way West
Exe Head
Twitchen Farm
Breakneck Hole
Pinkery Farm
B3358
NORTH LA
Old Close Bottom
Dure Down
Edgerley Stone
Goat Hill
Driver
Titchcombe
SOUTH LA
Tangs Bottom
Duredon Farm
Roosthitchen
Weirs Combe
Hearlake
Kennels
Acklands
Shoulsbarrow Common
Sloley Stone
River Barle
3
Mole's Chamber
Great Vintcombe
B3358
Cornham Farm
Shoulsbury Castle
Smallacombe
Ricksy Ball
Henthitchen
Two Moors Way
ROCKLEY LA
Rockley Farm
Bray Common
Squallacombe
Setta Barrow
Horcombe

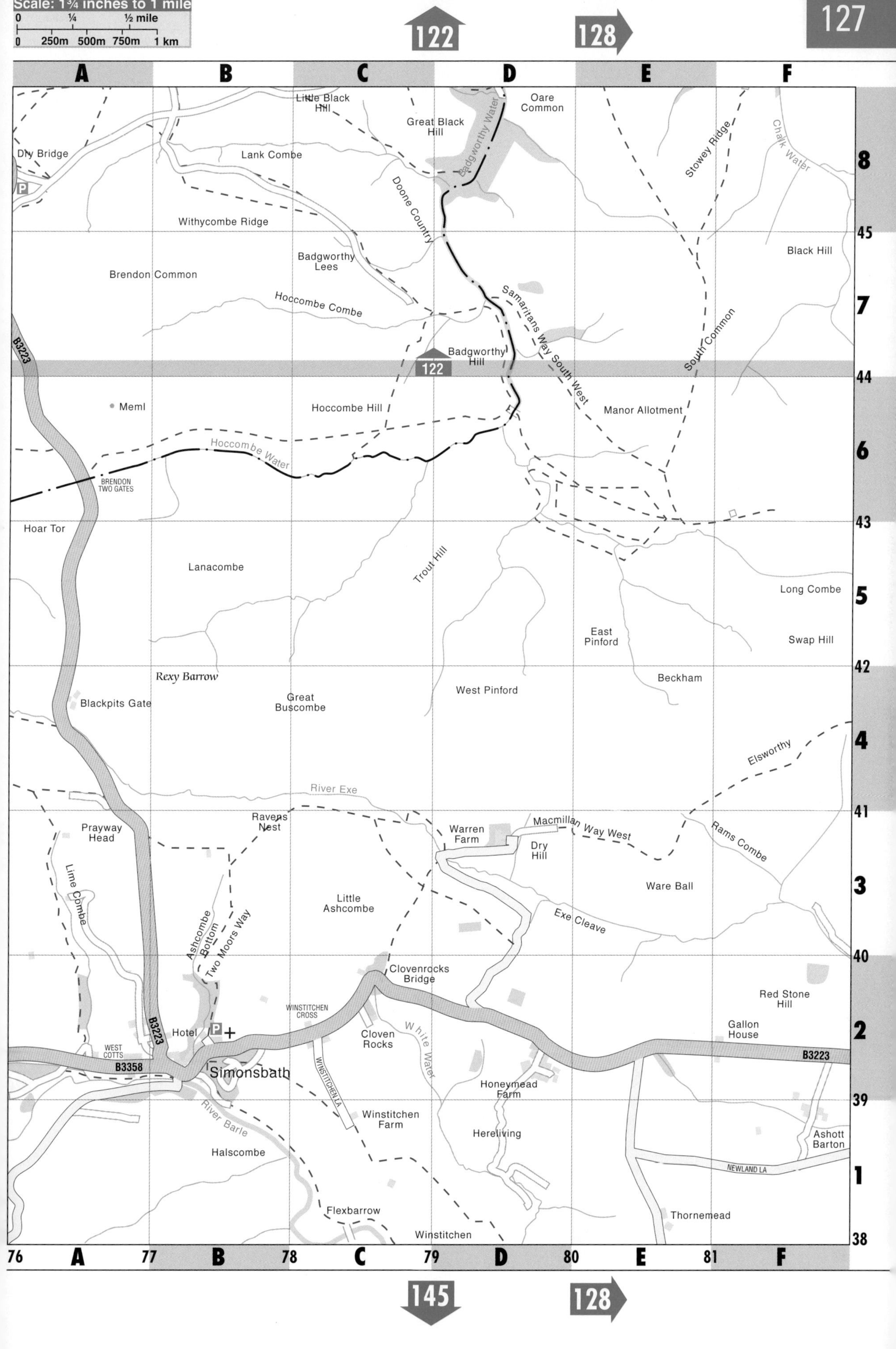

Scale: 1¾ inches to 1 mile
0 ¼ ½ mile
0 250m 500m 750m 1 km
122
128
A B C D E F
Little Black Hill
Oare Common
Great Black Hill
Badgworthy Water
Dry Bridge
Lank Combe
Stowey Ridge
Chalk Water
Doone Country
Withycombe Ridge
Black Hill
Badgworthy Lees
Brendon Common
Hoccombe Combe
Samaritans Way South West
South Common
B3223
Badgworthy Hill
122
Meml
Hoccombe Hill
Manor Allotment
Hoccombe Water
BRENDON TWO GATES
Hoar Tor
Lanacombe
Trout Hill
Long Combe
East Pinford
Swap Hill
Rexy Barrow
Beckham
Great Buscombe
West Pinford
Blackpits Gate
Elsworthy
River Exe
Ravens Nest
Prayway Head
Warren Farm
Macmillan Way West
Dry Hill
Rams Combe
Lime Combe
Ware Ball
Little Ashcombe
Ashcombe Bottom
Two Moors Way
Exe Cleave
Clovenrocks Bridge
WINSTITCHEN CROSS
Red Stone Hill
Hotel
White Water
Cloven Rocks
Gallon House
WEST COTTS
B3358
Simonsbath
B3223
Honeymead Farm
River Barle
WINSTITCHEN LA
Winstitchen Farm
Hereliving
Ashott Barton
Halscombe
NEWLAND LA
Flexbarrow
Thornemead
Winstitchen
8 45 7 44 6 43 5 42 4 41 3 40 2 39 1 38
76 77 78 79 80 81
145
128

127

Scale: 1¾ inches to 1 mile
0 ¼ ½ mile
0 250m 500m 750m 1 km

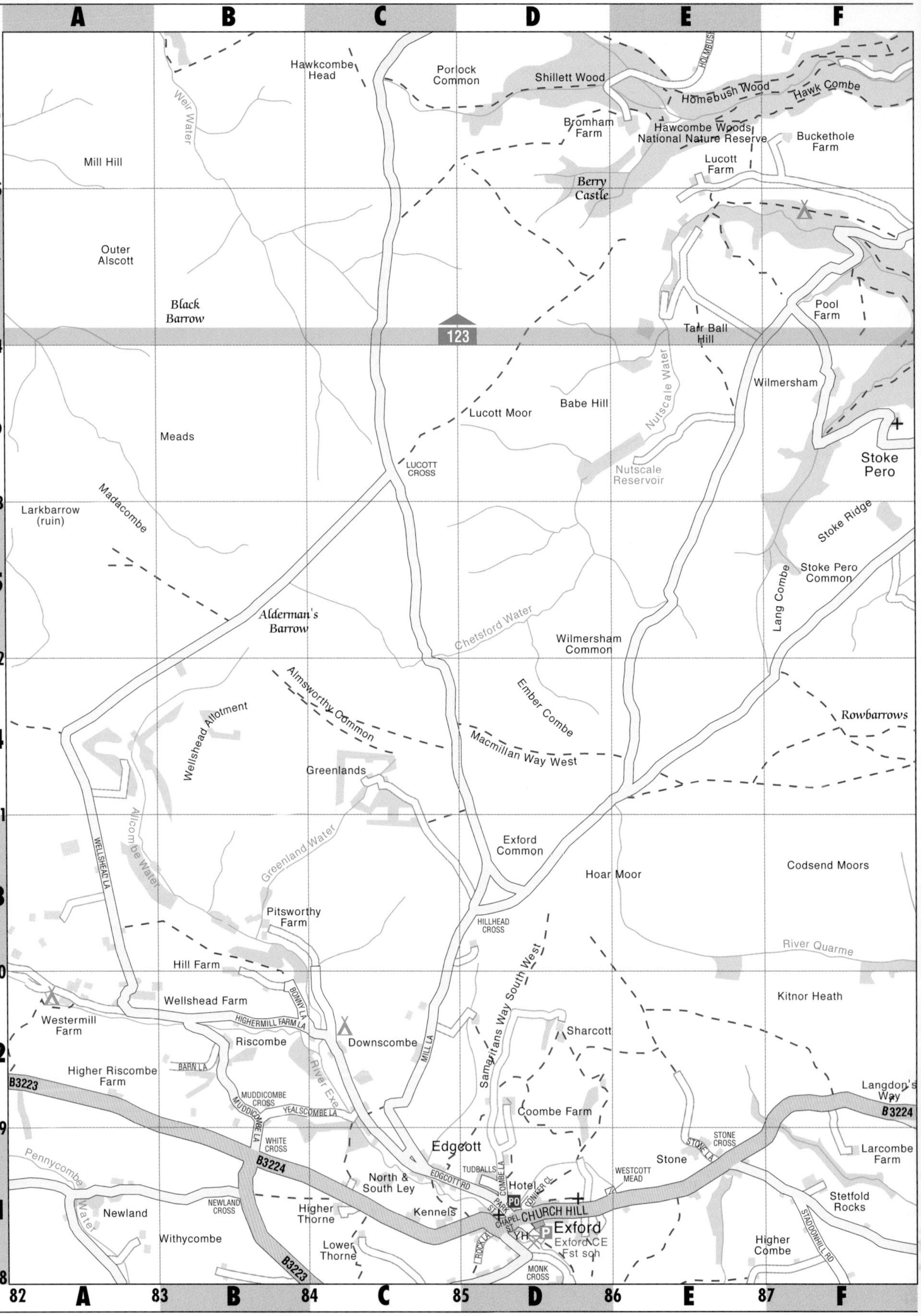

A B C D E F

Hawkcombe Head
Porlock Common
Shillett Wood
HOLMBUSH
Homebush Wood
Hawk Combe
Weir Water
Bromham Farm
Hawcombe Woods National Nature Reserve
Buckethole Farm
Mill Hill
Lucott Farm
Berry Castle
Outer Alscott
Black Barrow
Pool Farm
123
Tar Ball Hill
Wilmersham
Meads
Lucott Moor
Babe Hill
Nutscale Water
Stoke Pero
LUCOTT CROSS
Nutscale Reservoir
Larkbarrow (ruin)
Madacombe
Stoke Ridge
Stoke Pero Common
Lang Combe
Alderman's Barrow
Chetsford Water
Wilmersham Common
Almsworthy Common
Ember Combe
Rowbarrows
Wellshead Allotment
Macmillan Way West
Greenlands
WELLSHEAD LA
Allcombe Water
Greenland Water
Exford Common
Hoar Moor
Codsend Moors
Pitsworthy Farm
HILLHEAD CROSS
River Quarme
Samaritans Way South West
Hill Farm
Kitnor Heath
Wellshead Farm
BONNY LA
Westermill Farm
HIGHERMILL FARM LA
Downscombe
MILL LA
Sharcott
Riscombe
BARN LA
River Exe
Higher Riscombe Farm
Langdon's Way
B3223
MUDDICOMBE CROSS
YEALSCOMBE LA
Coombe Farm
B3224
MUDDICOMBE LA
WHITE CROSS
STONE CROSS
Edgcott
Larcombe Farm
Pennycombe
B3224
North & South Ley
TUDBALLS
COMBE LA
Stone
STONE LA
WESTCOTT MEAD
EDGCOTT RD
Hotel
PO
CONIFER CL
Stetfold Rocks
Water
Newland
NEWLAND CROSS
Higher Thorne
Kennels
PARK ST
CHAPEL ST
CHURCH HILL
Exford
Withycombe
YH
P
Exford CE Fst sch
Higher Combe
STADDONHILL RD
Lower Thorne
ROCK LA
MONK CROSS
B3223

45 44 43 42 41 40 39 38
8 7 6 5 4 3 2 1

82 83 84 85 86 87
A B C D E F

127
146

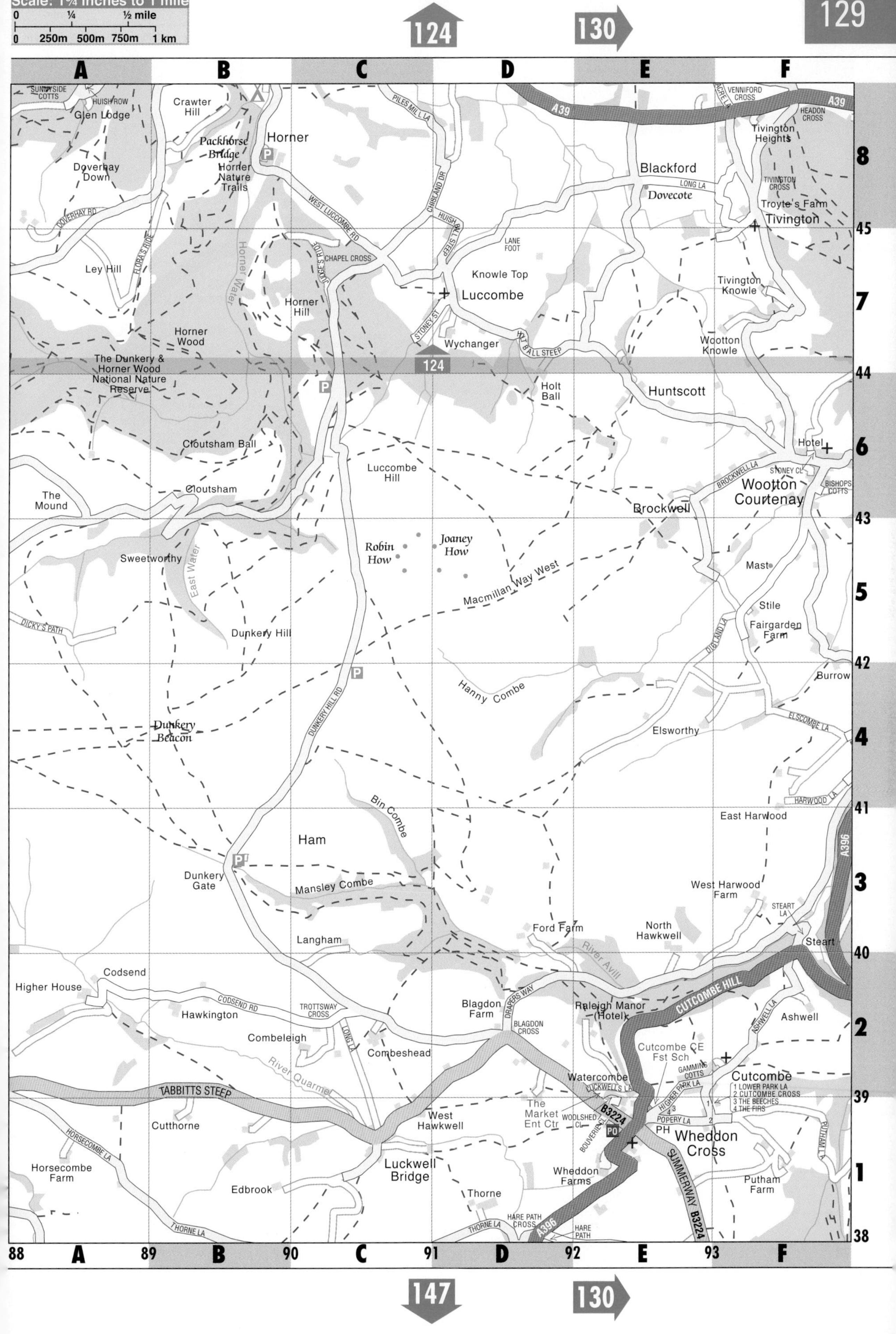
Scale: 1¾ inches to 1 mile
0 ¼ ½ mile
0 250m 500m 750m 1 km
124
130
A B C D E F
Glen Lodge
Crawter Hill
Horner
Packhorse Bridge
Horner Nature Trails
Doverhay Down
DOVERHAY RD
Ley Hill
FLORA'S RIDE
Horner Water
WEST LUCCOMBE RD
CHAPEL CROSS
JUDGE'S RIDE
Horner Hill
Horner Wood
The Dunkery & Horner Wood National Nature Reserve
PILES MILL LA
CHISLAND DR
HUISH BALL STEEP
LANE FOOT
Knowle Top
Luccombe
STONEY ST
Wychanger
HOLT BALL STEEP
A39
Blackford
LONG LA
Dovecote
VENNIFORD CROSS
HEADON CROSS
Tivington Heights
TIVINGTON CROSS
Troyte's Farm
Tivington
Tivington Knowle
Wootton Knowle
Holt Ball
Huntscott
Cloutsham Ball
Cloutsham
The Mound
Luccombe Hill
Hotel
BROCKWELL LA
STONEY CL
BISHOPS COTTS
Wootton Courtenay
Brockwell
Sweetworthy
East Water
Robin How
Joaney How
Macmillan Way West
Mast
Stile
Fairgarden Farm
DICKY'S PATH
Dunkery Hill
DIGLAND LA
Burrow
Hanny Combe
DUNKERY HILL RD
Dunkery Beacon
Elsworthy
ELSCOMBE LA
HARWOOD LA
Bin Combe
East Harwood
A396
Ham
Dunkery Gate
Mansley Combe
West Harwood Farm
STEART LA
Ford Farm
North Hawkwell
Steart
Langham
River Avill
Codsend
Higher House
CODSEND RD
Hawkington
TROTTSWAY CROSS
Combeleigh
LONG LA
Blagdon Farm
DRAPERS WAY
BLAGDON CROSS
Raleigh Manor (Hotel)
CUTCOMBE HILL
Ashwell
ASHWELL LA
Combeshead
Cutcombe CE Fst Sch
GAMMINS COTTS
River Quarme
Watercombe
LUCKWELL'S LA
HIGHER PARK LA
Cutcombe
1 LOWER PARK LA
2 CUTCOMBE CROSS
3 THE BEECHES
4 THE FIRS
TABBITTS STEEP
The Market Ent Ctr
WOOLSHED CL
B3224
POPERY LA
PH
Wheddon Cross
West Hawkwell
Cutthorne
BOUVERIE CL
PO
HORSECOMBE LA
SUMMERWAY B3224
PUTHAM LA
Luckwell Bridge
Horsecombe Farm
Wheddon Farms
Putham Farm
Edbrook
Thorne
HARE PATH CROSS
THORNE LA
HARE PATH
A396
8 45 7 44 6 43 5 42 4 41 3 40 2 39 1 38
88 89 90 91 92 93
147

129
125

Scale: 1¾ inches to 1 mile
0 ¼ ½ mile
0 250m 500m 750m 1 km

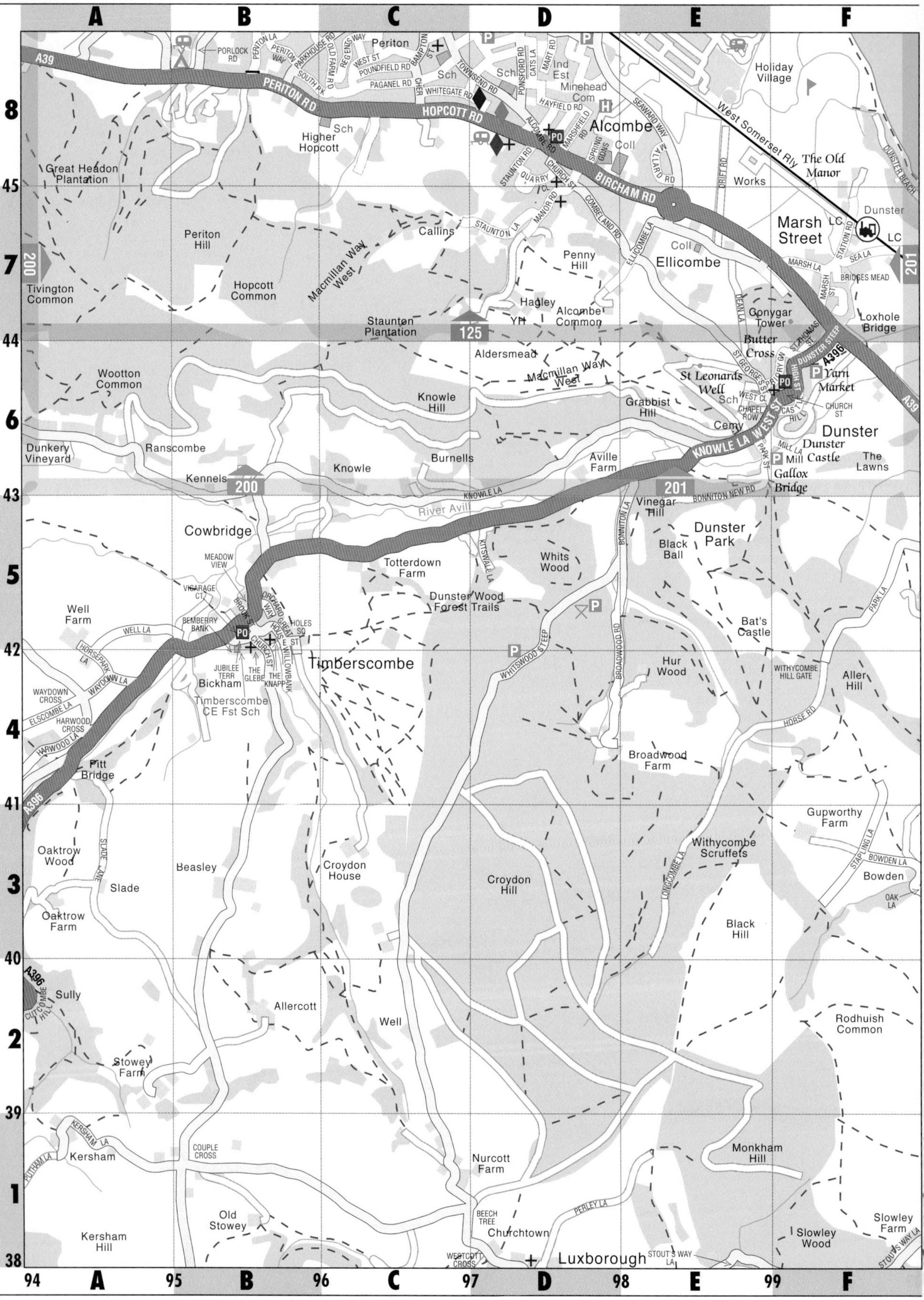
A
B
C
D
E
F
8
7
6
5
4
3
2
1
45
44
43
42
41
40
39
38
94
95
96
97
98
99
200
201
125
A39
PERITON RD
HOPCOTT RD
BIRCHAM RD
A396
KNOWLE LA WEST ST
Periton
PORLOCK RD
PERITON LA
PERITON WAY
PARKHOUSE RD
SOUTH PK
OLD FARM RD
REGENTS WAY
WEST ST
POUNDFIELD RD
BAMPTON ST
PAGANEL RD
WHITEGATE RD
TOWNSEND RD
PONSFORD RD
CATS LA
MART RD
Ind Est
Minehead Com
HAYFIELD RD
SEAWARD WAY
Alcombe
MARSHFIELD RD
SPRING GDNS
Coll
MALLARD RD
ALCOMBE RD
STAUNTON RD
QUARRY CL
CHURCH ST
MANOR RD
COMBELAND RD
Higher Hopcott
Sch
Great Headon Plantation
Periton Hill
Hopcott Common
Tivington Common
Macmillan Way West
Callins
STAUNTON LA
Staunton Plantation
Hagley
YH
Penny Hill
Alcombe Common
ELLICOMBE LA
Ellicombe
Holiday Village
West Somerset Rly
DRIFT RD
Works
The Old Manor
DUNSTER BEACH
Dunster
LC
Marsh Street
STATION RD
MARSH LA
SEA LA
BRIDGES MEAD
MARSH ST
Loxhole Bridge
Conygar Tower
DEAN LA
Butter Cross
ST THOMAS ST
DUNSTER STEEP
HIGH ST
Yarn Market
St Leonards Well
ST GEORGES ST
PRIORY GN
WEST CL
CHAPEL ROW
CASTLE HILL
CHURCH ST
Dunster
Cemy
Mill
MILL LA
Dunster Castle
PARK ST
Gallox Bridge
The Lawns
Wootton Common
Aldersmead
Knowle Hill
Grabbist Hill
Dunkery Vineyard
Ranscombe
Knowle
Burnells
Aville Farm
Kennels
KNOWLE LA
River Avill
BONNITON NEW RD
Vinegar Hill
Cowbridge
MEADOW VIEW
VICARAGE CT
Totterdown Farm
KITSWALL LA
Whits Wood
BONNITON LA
Black Ball
Dunster Park
Dunster Wood Forest Trails
Well Farm
BEMBERRY BANK
WELL LA
BROOK ST
ORCHARD WAY
GREAT HOUSE ST
HOLES SQ
CHURCH ST
WILLOWBANK
PO
JUBILEE TERR
THE GLEBE
THE KNAPP
Bickham
Timberscombe
Timberscombe CE Fst Sch
HORSEPARK LA
WAYDOWN LA
WAYDOWN CROSS
ELSCOMBE LA
HARWOOD CROSS
HARWOOD LA
WHITSWOOD STEEP
BROADWOOD RD
Hur Wood
Bat's Castle
WITHYCOMBE HILL GATE
Aller Hill
PARK LA
HORSE RD
Pitt Bridge
Broadwood Farm
Gupworthy Farm
Oaktrow Wood
SLADE LANE
Slade
Beasley
Croydon House
Croydon Hill
Withycombe Scruffets
LONGCOMBE LA
STAPLING LA
BOWDEN LA
Bowden
OAK LA
Oaktrow Farm
Black Hill
Sully
CUTCOMBE HILL
Allercott
Well
Rodhuish Common
Stowey Farm
KERSHAM LA
Kersham
PITHAM LA
COUPLE CROSS
Nurcott Farm
Monkham Hill
Old Stowey
BEECH TREE
Churchtown
PERLEY LA
Slowley Wood
Slowley Farm
Kersham Hill
WESTCOTT CROSS
Luxborough
STOUT'S WAY LA

For full street detail of the highlighted areas see pages 200 and 201.

129
148

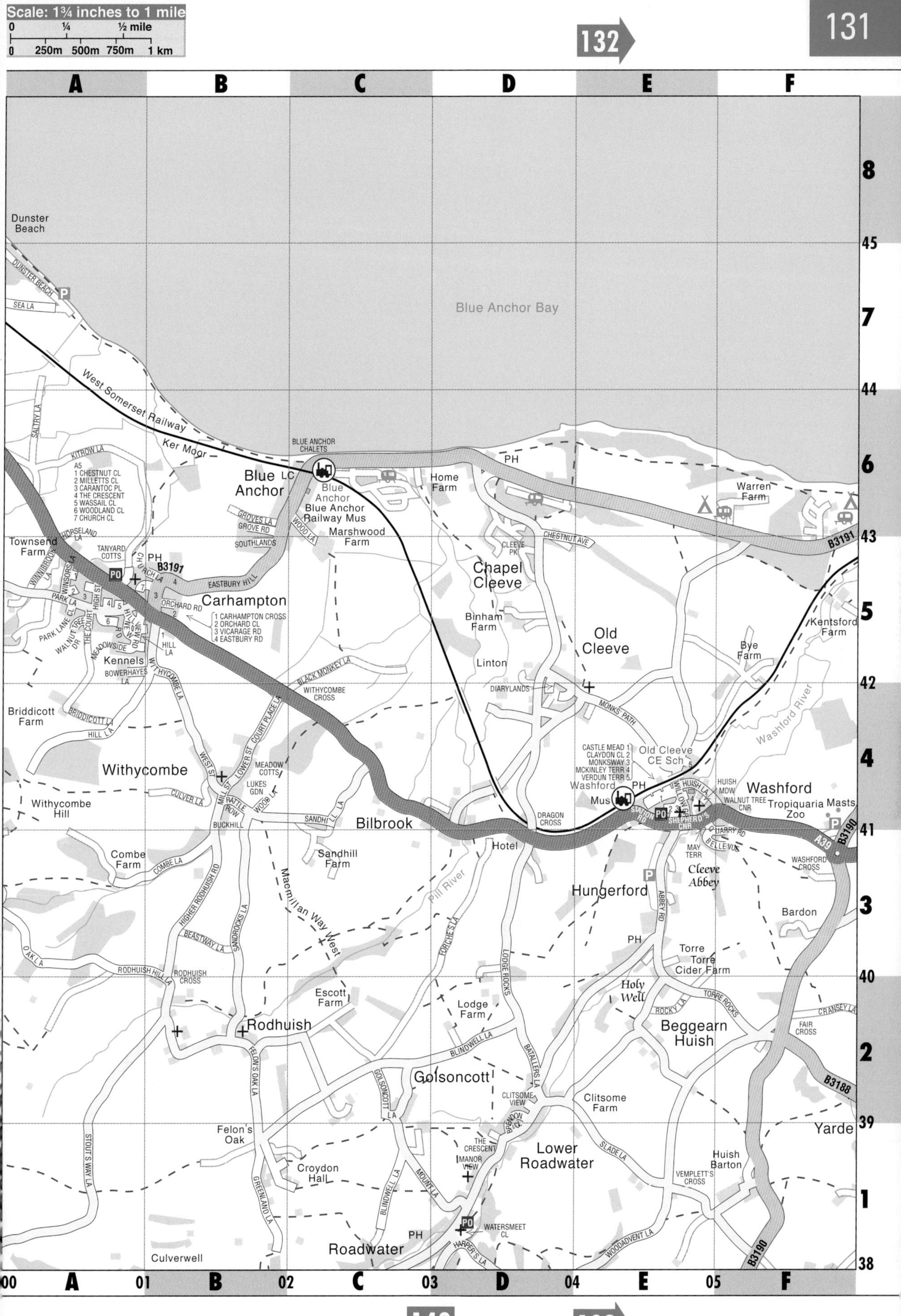
Scale: 1¾ inches to 1 mile
0 ¼ ½ mile
0 250m 500m 750m 1 km
132
A B C D E F
8 7 6 5 4 3 2 1
45 44 43 42 41 40 39 38
00 01 02 03 04 05
Dunster Beach
Blue Anchor Bay
West Somerset Railway
Ker Moor
Blue Anchor
Blue Anchor Railway Mus
Marshwood Farm
Home Farm
Chapel Cleeve
Binham Farm
Linton
Old Cleeve
Warren Farm
Kentsford Farm
Bye Farm
Washford
Washford River
Tropiquaria Zoo
Masts
Carhampton
Townsend Farm
Kennels
Briddicott Farm
Withycombe
Withycombe Hill
Combe Farm
Bilbrook
Sandhill Farm
Macmillan Way West
Pill River
Hotel
Hungerford
Cleeve Abbey
Bardon
Torre
Torre Cider Farm
Holy Well
Beggearn Huish
Escott Farm
Lodge Farm
Rodhuish
Golsoncott
Clitsome Farm
Felon's Oak
Croydon Hall
Lower Roadwater
Roadwater
Culverwell
Huish Barton
Yarde
B3191
A39
B3190
B3188
149
132

131

Scale: 1¾ inches to 1 mile

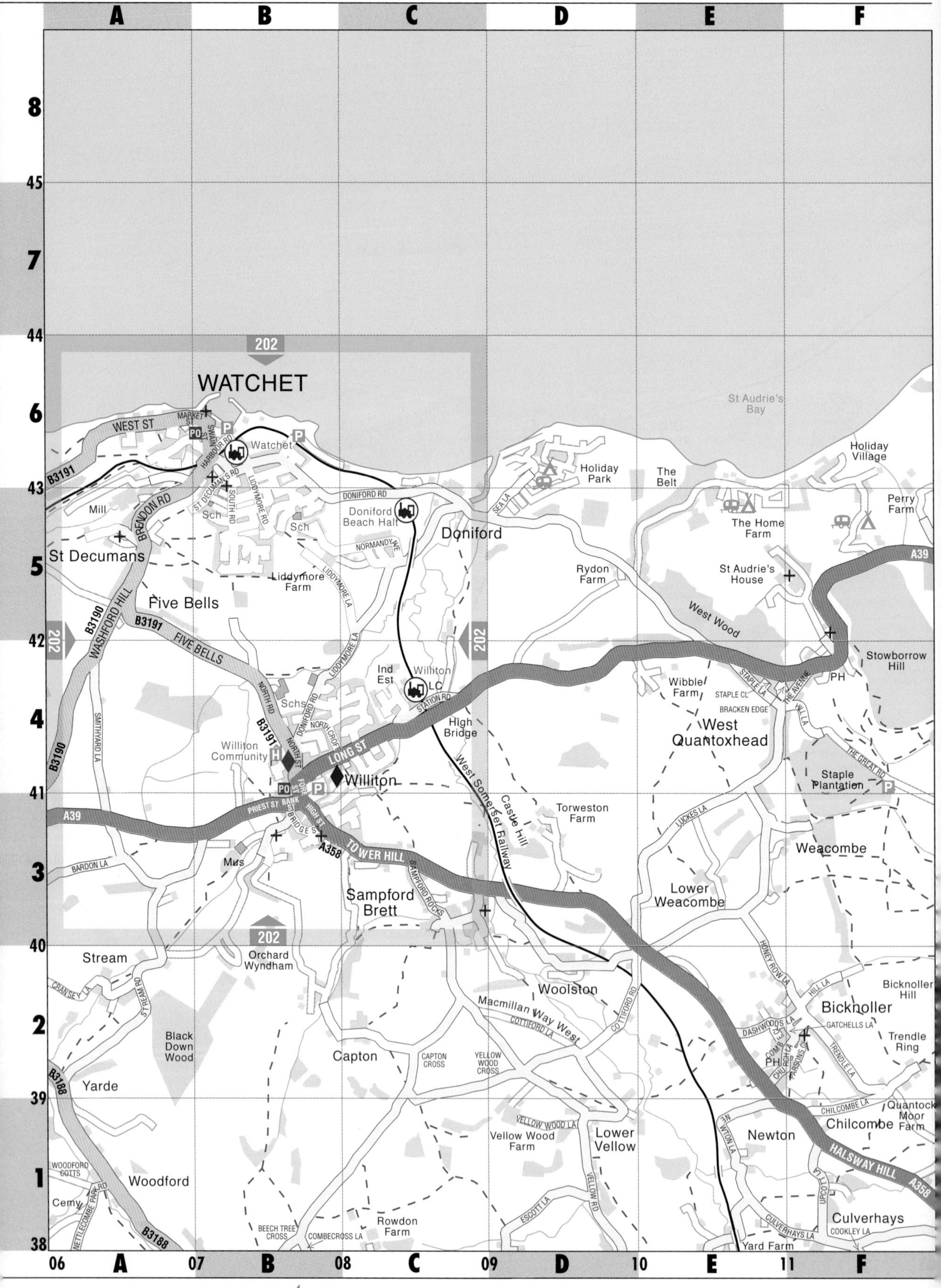

For full street detail of the highlighted area see page 202.

131

150

Scale: 1¾ inches to 1 mile
0 ¼ ½ mile
0 250m 500m 750m 1 km

134

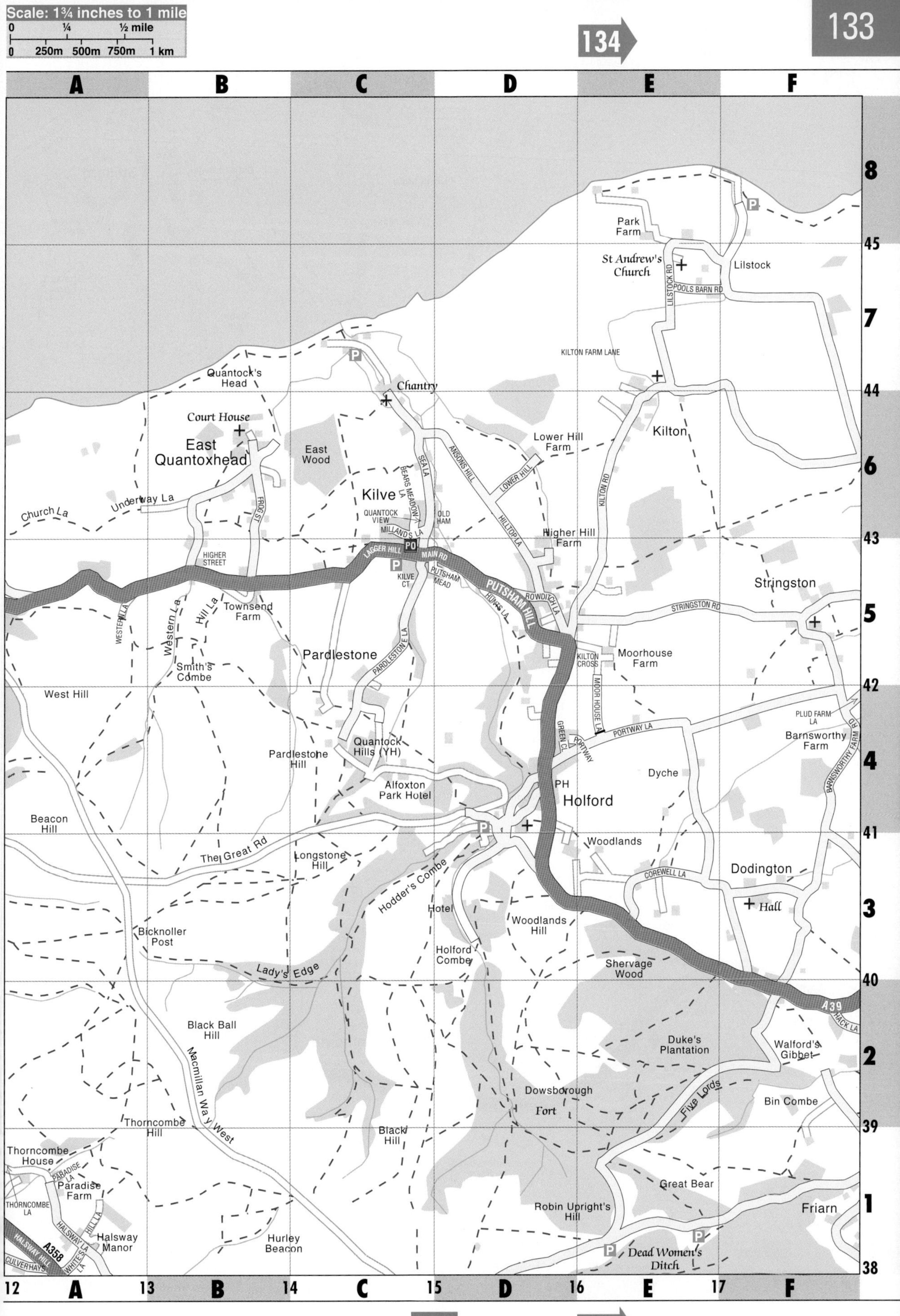

151 134

133

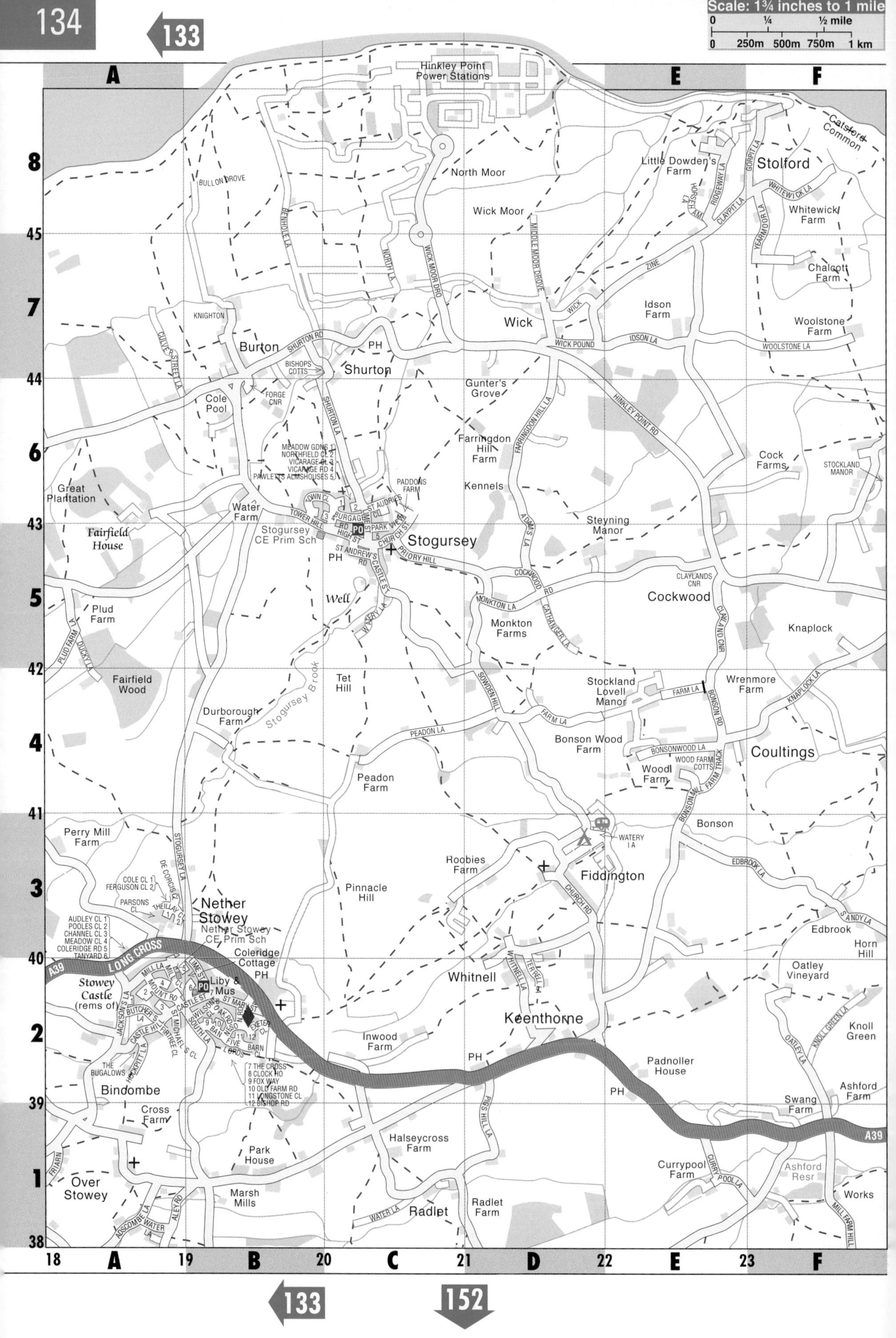
Scale: 1¾ inches to 1 mile
0 ¼ ½ mile
0 250m 500m 750m 1 km
A
E
F
8
45
7
44
6
43
5
42
4
41
3
40
2
39
1
38
18
19
20
21
22
23
B
C
D
Hinkley Point
Power Stations
North Moor
Wick Moor
Little Dowden's
Farm
Stolford
Catsford
Common
Whitewick
Farm
Chalcott
Farm
Idson
Farm
Woolstone
Farm
WOOLSTONE LA
IDSON LA
WICK POUND
Wick
Burton
Shurton
PH
Gunter's
Grove
Farringdon
Hill
Farm
Kennels
Cole
Pool
Great
Plantation
Water
Farm
Fairfield
House
Stogursey
CE Prim Sch
Stogursey
Steyning
Manor
Cock
Farms
STOCKLAND
MANOR
Cockwood
CLAYLANDS
CNR
Knaplock
Plud
Farm
Well
Monkton
Farms
Fairfield
Wood
Tet
Hill
Stockland
Lovell
Manor
Wrenmore
Farm
Durborough
Farm
Stogursey Brook
Bonson Wood
Farm
Coultings
Wood
Farm
Peadon
Farm
Perry Mill
Farm
Bonson
Roobies
Farm
Fiddington
Pinnacle
Hill
Nether
Stowey
Nether Stowey
CE Prim Sch
Coleridge
Cottage
Liby &
Mus
Edbrook
Horn
Hill
Oatley
Vineyard
Whitnell
Keenthorne
Knoll
Green
Stowey
Castle
(rems of)
Inwood
Farm
Padnoller
House
Bindombe
Cross
Farm
Halseycross
Farm
Swang
Farm
Ashford
Farm
Park
House
Currypool
Farm
Ashford
Resr
Over
Stowey
Marsh
Mills
Radlet
Radlet
Farm
Works
A39
LONG CROSS
BULL ON DROVE
BENHOLE LA
NORTH LA
WICK MOOR DRO
MIDDLE MOOR DROVE
HORSE LA
RIDGEWAY LA
GORPIT LA
CLAYPIT LA
WHITEWICK LA
YEARMOOR LA
ZINE
KNIGHTON
CULVER STREET LA
SHURTON RD
BISHOPS
COTTS
FORGE
CNR
SHURTON LA
HINKLEY POINT RD
FARRINGDON HILL LA
MEADOW GDNS 1
NORTHFIELD CL 2
VICARAGE CL 3
VICARAGE RD 4
PAWLETTS ALMSHOUSES 5
PADDONS
FARM
TOWN CL
TOWER HILL
BURGAGE RD
HIGH ST
ST AUDRIES CL
PARK VIEW
CHURCH ST
ST ANDREW'S RD
CASTLE ST
PRIORY HILL
ADAM'S LA
COCKWOOD RD
MONKTON LA
CATHANGER LA
CLAYLAND CNR
PLUD FARM LA
DUCKY LA
WATERY LA
SOWDEN HILL
FARM LA
BONSON RD
KNAPLOCK LA
PEADON LA
BONSONWOOD LA
WOOD FARM
COTTS
BONSON HILL FARM TRACK
WATERY
LA
EDBROOK LA
CHURCH RD
SANDY LA
STOGURSEY LA
DE CORCIS CL
COLE CL 1
FERGUSON CL 2
PARSONS CL
THEILLAY CL
AUDLEY CL 1
POOLES CL 2
CHANNEL CL 3
MEADOW CL 4
COLERIDGE RD 5
TANYARD 6
MILL LA
MOUNT RD
LIME ST
CASTLE ST
ST MARY ST
JACKSON'S LA
BUTCHER'S LA
CASTLE HILL
ST MICHAEL'S CL
FIRTREE CL
SOUTH LA
WILSONS
OAK RD
EXETER CL
BARN CL
LORDS
FIVE
THE
BUGALOWS
HOCKPITT LA
7 THE CROSS
8 CLOCK HO
9 FOX WAY
10 OLD FARM RD
11 LONGSTONE CL
12 BISHOP RD
WHITNELL LA
TERRETT LA
OATLEY LA
KNOLL GREEN LA
PIGS HILL LA
CURRY POOL LA
MILL FARM HILL
FRIARN
ALEY RD
ADSCOMBE LA
WATER LA

133
152

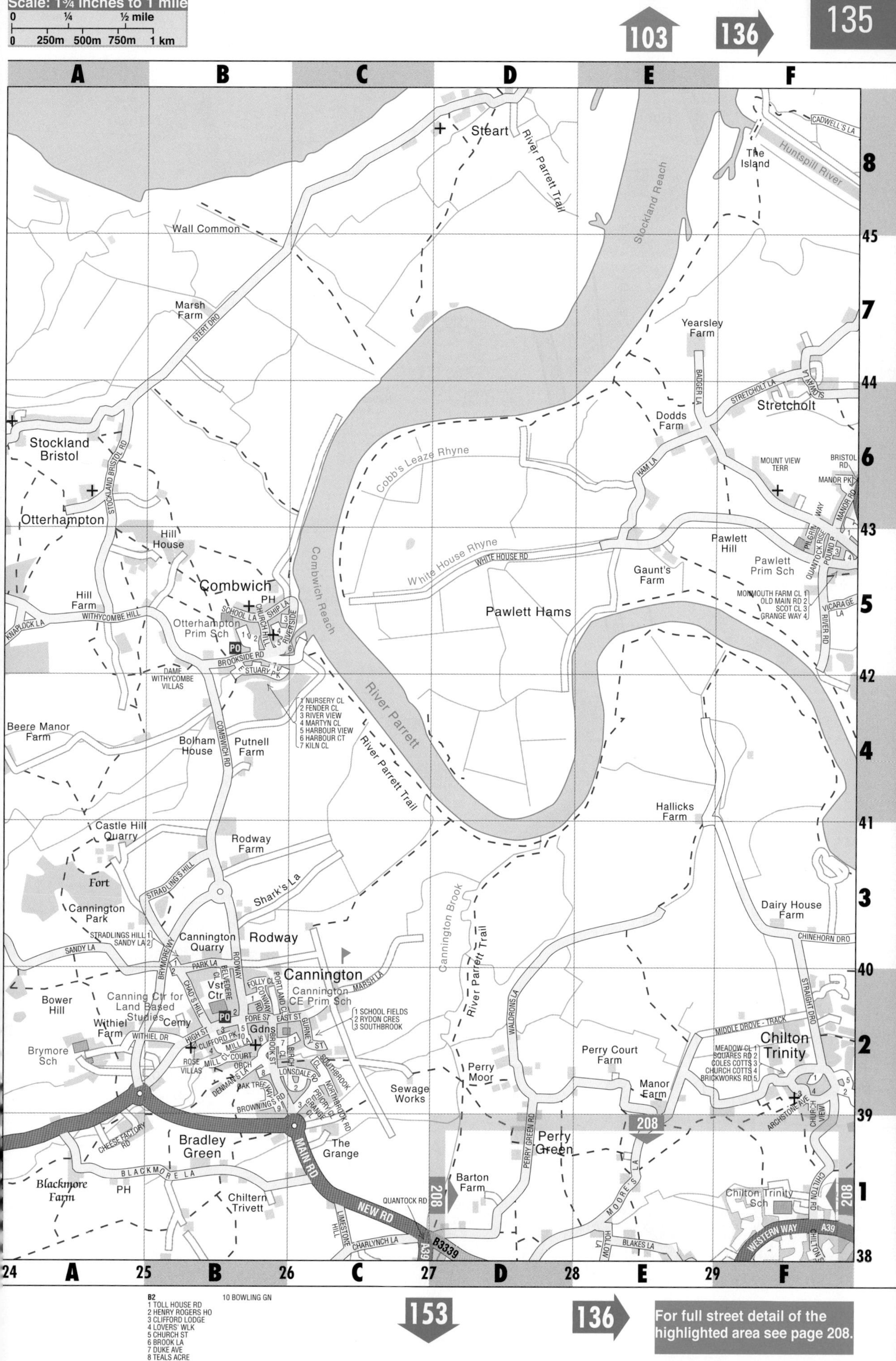
Scale: 1¾ inches to 1 mile
0 ¼ ½ mile
0 250m 500m 750m 1 km
103
136
A B C D E F
Steart
River Parrett Trail
The Island
Huntspill River
CADWELL'S LA
Stockland Reach
Wall Common
Marsh Farm
STERT DRO
Yearsley Farm
BADGER LA
STRETCHOLT LA
Stretcholt
Dodds Farm
Stockland Bristol
STOCKLAND BRISTOL RD
Cobb's Leaze Rhyne
HAM LA
MOUNT VIEW TERR
BRISTOL RD
MANOR PK
Otterhampton
Hill House
Combwich Reach
White House Rhyne
WHITE HOUSE RD
Pawlett Hill
Pawlett Prim Sch
Gaunt's Farm
Combwich
PH
Hill Farm
WITHYCOMBE HILL
KNAPLOCK LA
SCHOOL LA
CHURCH HILL
SHIP LA
RIVERSIDE
Otterhampton Prim Sch
PO
BROOKSIDE RD
ESTUARY PK
DAME WITHYCOMBE VILLAS
Pawlett Hams
MONMOUTH FARM CL 1
OLD MAIN RD 2
SCOT CL 3
GRANGE WAY 4
VICARAGE LA
RIVER RD
1 NURSERY CL
2 FENDER CL
3 RIVER VIEW
4 MARTYN CL
5 HARBOUR VIEW
6 HARBOUR CT
7 KILN CL
River Parrett
Beere Manor Farm
Bolham House
Putnell Farm
COMBWICH RD
Hallicks Farm
Castle Hill Quarry
Rodway Farm
Fort
STRADLING'S HILL
Shark's La
Cannington Brook
Cannington Park
Dairy House Farm
STRADLINGS HILL 1
SANDY LA 2
SANDY LA
Cannington Quarry
Rodway
River Parrett Trail
CHINEHORN DRO
BRYMORE WY
PARK LA
Cannington
MARSH LA
Bower Hill
Canning Ctr for Land Based Studies
Vst Ctr
Cannington CE Prim Sch
1 SCHOOL FIELDS
2 RYDON CRES
3 SOUTHBROOK
WALDRONS LA
STRAIGHT DRO
Withiel Farm
Cemy
Gdns
FORE ST
EAST ST
MIDDLE DROVE - TRACK
Chilton Trinity
Brymore Sch
WITHIEL DR
HIGH ST
CLIFFORD PK
MILL LA
Perry Court Farm
MEADOW CL 1
SQUARES RD 2
COLES COTTS 3
CHURCH COTTS 4
BRICKWORKS RD 5
ROSE VILLAS
COURT ORCH
LONSDALE RD
SOUTHBROOK
NORTHBROOK RD
Perry Moor
Sewage Works
Manor Farm
OAK TREE WAY
BROWNINGS RD
PRIORY CL
GRANGE CL
ARCHSTONE AVE
CHURCH VIEW
208
CHEESE FACTORY RD
Bradley Green
MAIN RD
The Grange
Perry Green
PERRY GREEN RD
BLACKMORE LA
Barton Farm
MOORE'S LA
Blackmore Farm
PH
Chiltern Trivett
QUANTOCK RD
NEW RD
Chilton Trinity Sch
CHILTON RD
LIMESTONE HILL
CHARLYNCH LA
A39
B3339
HOLLOW LA
BLAKES LA
WESTERN WAY
24 25 26 27 28 29
8 45 7 44 6 43 5 42 4 41 3 40 2 39 1 38
B2
1 TOLL HOUSE RD
2 HENRY ROGERS HO
3 CLIFFORD LODGE
4 LOVERS' WLK
5 CHURCH ST
6 BROOK LA
7 DUKE AVE
8 TEALS ACRE
9 HAWKERS CL
10 BOWLING GN
153
136
For full street detail of the highlighted area see page 208.

Scale: 1¾ inches to 1 mile
0 ¼ ½ mile
0 250m 500m 750m 1 km

A B C D E F

Huntspill
1 PLYMOR RD
2 CARAMIA PK
3 CHAPEL FORGE CL
4 SUNNY CL
5 GREENWOOD CL

CADWELL'S LA
CHURCH RD
GRANGE RD
MILLGREEN
GROVE
SILVER ST
SWELL CL
SEALEYS CL
ILEX CL
RINGSTONE
LABURNUM LODGES
CADWELL'S DV
MAIN RD
A38
NEWBRIDGE LA
STONE END COTTAGE LA
M5
Secret World Wildlife Rescue
NEW RD
CATHERINE ST
East Huntspill Sch
FOSTERS FARM LA
Hackness
Brue Bsns Pk
FACTORY LA
MERRY LA
HACK MEAD LA
Moor Row
B3141
ORCHARD CL
CHAPEL LA
HACKNESS RD
COMBE TERR
1 NUT TREE CL
2 CHURCH CL
CHURCH LA
CHURCH RD
HLEA PK
MILL LA
WILLOW CT
33
East Huntspill
PH
Cote
WHITE HOUSE LA
CORNMOOR CRES
Huntspill Level
SLOWAY LA
OLD PAWLETT RD
Bleak Bridge
OLD WITHY RD
WITHY ROAD FARM LA
WITHY RD
ASHTON FARM LA
WEST CORNMOOR DRO
MIDDLE CORNMOOR DRO
PAWLETT RD
West Huntspill
PURITON RD
STRAIGHT DRO
RUGG'S DRO
LC
HARDY MEAD DRO
WITHY GR
Withy Grove Farm
Huntspill River
Cornmoor Farm
CORNMOOR LA
BURTLE RD
HAGGETTS LA
COTE CNR
Withy Farm
Huntspill River National Nature Reserve
Huntspill Moor
GOLD CORNER DRO
LC
OLD BLACKDITCH RD
Landfill Site
CAUSEWAY
Pyde Dro
Pawlett
OLD MAIN RD
PO
VICARAGE LA
North Farm
PAWLETT MEAD DRO
WALPOLE DRO
Middle Moor Dro
Moormead Dro
Middlemoor Water Park

PARSONAGE CT 1
PURITON MANOR 2
COURT GR 3
POOL CL 4
ROOKERY CL 5
PUREWELL 6
CULVERHAY CL 7
WALNUT CL 8

BATCH RD
Factory
Puriton Level
Woolavington Level
PURITON RD
PEAR TREE LA
PAWLETT RD
Walpole
Motte & Baileys
WALPOLE LA
Bannock Dro
North Mead Dro
CHURCH FIELD LA
GREENACRES
BATCH CL
RYE
Puriton
WATERLOO
WATERLOO CL
WOOLAVINGTON RD
WEST APPROACH RD
EAST APPROACH RD
CAUSEWAY CL
MORTIMER CL
HECTORS STONES
LOWER RD
HIGHER RD
CHERTSEY CL
CROCKERS HILL
REEDS DR
CHILPITTS
SCHOOL LA
ELM LA
LOCKSWELL
DAWBINS DR
EDGEBURY
TAPPS LA

1 THE DRIVE
2 THE SQUARE
3 CHURCH ST
3 VICARAGE RD

Woolavington
DOWNEND TERR
DOWN END RD
DOWNEND CRES
Down End
Dunball Ind Est
DUNBALL DROVE
Factory
Dunball
23
A39
RIVERTON RD
PURITON HILL
HALL RD
ROWLANDS RISE
HILLSIDE
CYPRESS DR
PURITON PK
WEBBERS WAY
STATION RD
FREDERICKS LA
Puriton Prim Sch

9 HILLSIDE DR
10 HILLSIDE CRES
11 ROWAN CL
12 BIRCH AVE
13 MAPLE CL
14 MANSE LA
15 SPRING RISE
16 ELM LEA CL

Woolavington Village Prim Sch
HORTON WAY
MEADWAY
KIDNER CL
BAWDEN
TOR VIEW
HIGHCROFT
COMBE LA

5 CROSSMEAD
6 CLARK CL
7 BROADLAWN
8 MOUNT VIEW
9 HILLSBORO
10 ORCHARD WAY

Gardiners Bsns Pk
BRISTOL RD
PURITON HILL
King's Sedgemoor Drain
CRANCOMBE LA
SEDGEMOOR RD
GEMOOR
KNOWLE END
SOUTHFIELD CL
COSSINGTON LA
PARK CL
STATION RD
WALNUT LA
CHINEHOR DRO
River Parrett

MARTLAND CL 10
POLDEN WLK 11
WINDMILL CRES 12
BITHAM WLK 13
MILL WLK 14

MAPLE TREE CT 1
THE COPSE 2
MANOR CT 3

PARK CRES
MANOR CL
ST MARY'S CL
MILL MOOT
FAIRWAYS CVN PK
Cossington
MANOR RD
Knowle Hall
FIELD LANE TRACK
WOOLAVINGTON HILL
B3141
Woodlands Court Bsns Pk
Horsey Pill
Horsey Level
Crandon Bridge
BATH RD
PH
BAWDRIP LA
NEW RD
CHURCH WLK
Brook La
A39
Little Wall La
GREENFIELD LA
EAST SIDE LA
The Polden Bsns Ctr
KINGS RD

1 Sedgemount Ind Pk
2 The Wireworks Est
3 KINGS DR
4 CLARENCE TER
5 IMPERIAL WAY
6 WESTMINSTER WAY
7 WHITEHALL DR
8 BALRAVIA DR
9 ROYAL DR
10 LANCASTER CL

HORSEY LA
Marsh La
ST MICHAELS CT
Knowle
Kingsmoor Prim Sch
King's Farm
THISTLEDOO VINE
Express Pk
SQUARES RD
SOUTH VIEW
3
Bawdrip
Stone Dro
Bawdrip Level
Horsey
209
MANOR FARM LA
BRADNEY LA
Peasey Farm
Sewage Works
Crypton Tech Bsns Pk
Acad
BRIDGWATER
Bradney
NORTHMOOR DRO
Ind Est
209
H
SIDE LA
Slape Cross
209
WOOD LA
Pendon Hill
WYLDS RD
Works
A38
A39
BOWER LA
WHITFIELD RD
CHEDZOY LA
M5
WEST END CT

8 45 7 44 6 43 5 42 4 41 3 40 2 39 1 38
30 31 32 33 34 35

For full street detail of the highlighted area see page 209.

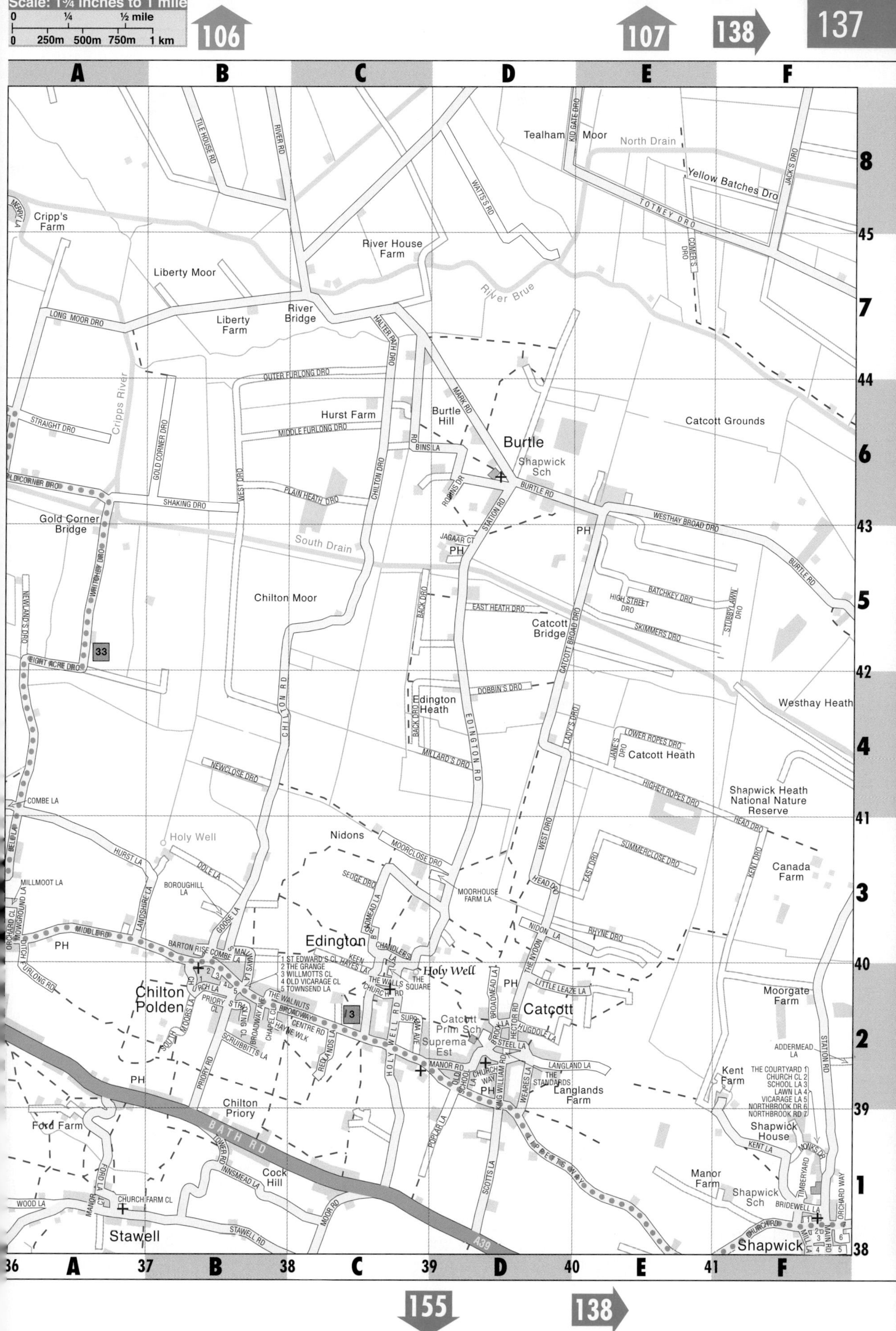
Scale: 1¾ inches to 1 mile
0 ¼ ½ mile
0 250m 500m 750m 1 km
106
107
138
A
B
C
D
E
F
8
7
6
5
4
3
2
1
45
44
43
42
41
40
39
38
36
37
38
39
40
41
155
138
Tealham Moor
KID GATE DRO
North Drain
Yellow Batches Dro
JACK'S DRO
TOTNEY DRO
COMER'S DRO
TILE HOUSE RD
RIVER RD
WATTS'S RD
Cripp's Farm
River House Farm
Liberty Moor
River Brue
Liberty Farm
River Bridge
LONG MOOR DRO
HALTER PATH DRO
OUTER FURLONG DRO
MARK RD
Cripps River
STRAIGHT DRO
Hurst Farm
MIDDLE FURLONG DRO
Burtle Hill
Catcott Grounds
GOLD CORNER DRO
BINS LA
Burtle
Shapwick Sch
CHILTON DRO
ROBINS DR
BURTLE RD
GOLD CORNER DRO
SHAKING DRO
WEST DRO
PLAIN HEATH DRO
STATION RD
WESTHAY BROAD DRO
Gold Corner Bridge
JAGAAR CT
PH
South Drain
WITCHEY DRO
NEWLAND'S DRO
Chilton Moor
BACK DRO
EAST HEATH DRO
BATCHKEY DRO
HIGH STREET DRO
SKIMMERS DRO
STUBBY LAWN DRO
BURTLE RD
Catcott Bridge
CATCOTT BROAD DRO
33
EIGHT ACRE DRO
DOBBIN'S DRO
Edington Heath
BACK DRO
Westhay Heath
CHILTON RD
EDINGTON RD
LADY'S DRO
LOWER ROPES DRO
JANE'S DRO
Catcott Heath
MILLARD'S DRO
NEWCLOSE DRO
HIGHER ROPES DRO
Shapwick Heath National Nature Reserve
COMBE LA
HEAD DRO
Holy Well
Nidons
WEST DRO
HURST LA
MOORCLOSE DRO
SUMMERCLOSE DRO
KENT RD
BELL LA
DOLE LA
MILLMOOT LA
BOROUGHILL LA
SEDGE DRO
Canada Farm
MOORHOUSE FARM LA
HEAD DRO
EAST DRO
LANDSHIRE LA
GOOSE LA
NIDON LA
RHYNE DRO
MIDDLE RD
PH
Edington
CHANDLERS
BARTON RISE
COMBE LA
MALTWAYS LA
1 ST EDWARD'S CL
2 THE GRANGE
3 WILLMOTTS CL
4 OLD VICARAGE CL
5 TOWNSEND LA
HAYES LA
KEEN
Holy Well
THE SQUARE
THE WALLS
CHURCH RD
THE NYDON
LITTLE LEAZE LA
BROADMEAD LA
Moorgate Farm
FURLONG RD
Chilton Polden
CHURCH LA
PRIORY CL
THE WALNUTS
BROADWAY
CENTRE RD
HAYNE WLK
CHAPEL CL
3
Catcott
Catcott Prim Sch
Suprema Est
HOLY WELL RD
HECTOR RD
HUGDOLE LA
STEEL LA
ADDERMEAD LA
STATION RD
SOUTH
MOORS LA
SCRUIBBITTS LA
REDLANDS LA
MANOR RD
CHURCH WAY
LANGLAND LA
THE STANDARDS
Langlands Farm
PH
PRIORY RD
OLD SCHOOL LA
KING WILLIAM RD
WEARES LA
Kent Farm
THE COURTYARD 1
CHURCH CL 2
SCHOOL LA 3
LAWN LA 4
VICARAGE LA 5
NORTHBROOK DR 6
NORTHBROOK RD 7
Chilton Priory
Ford Farm
BATH RD
POPLAR LA
Shapwick House
KENT LA
MONKS DR
TONER RD
INNSMEAD LA
Cock Hill
SCOTTS LA
LIPPETTS WAY
Manor Farm
TIMBERYARD
ORCHARD WAY
FORD LA
CHURCH FARM CL
WOOD LA
MANOR CT
MOOR RD
Shapwick Sch
BRIDEWELL LA
Stawell
STAWELL RD
A39
CHURCH RD
Shapwick
MILL LA
MAIN RD

137
108
109

Scale: 1¾ inches to 1 mile

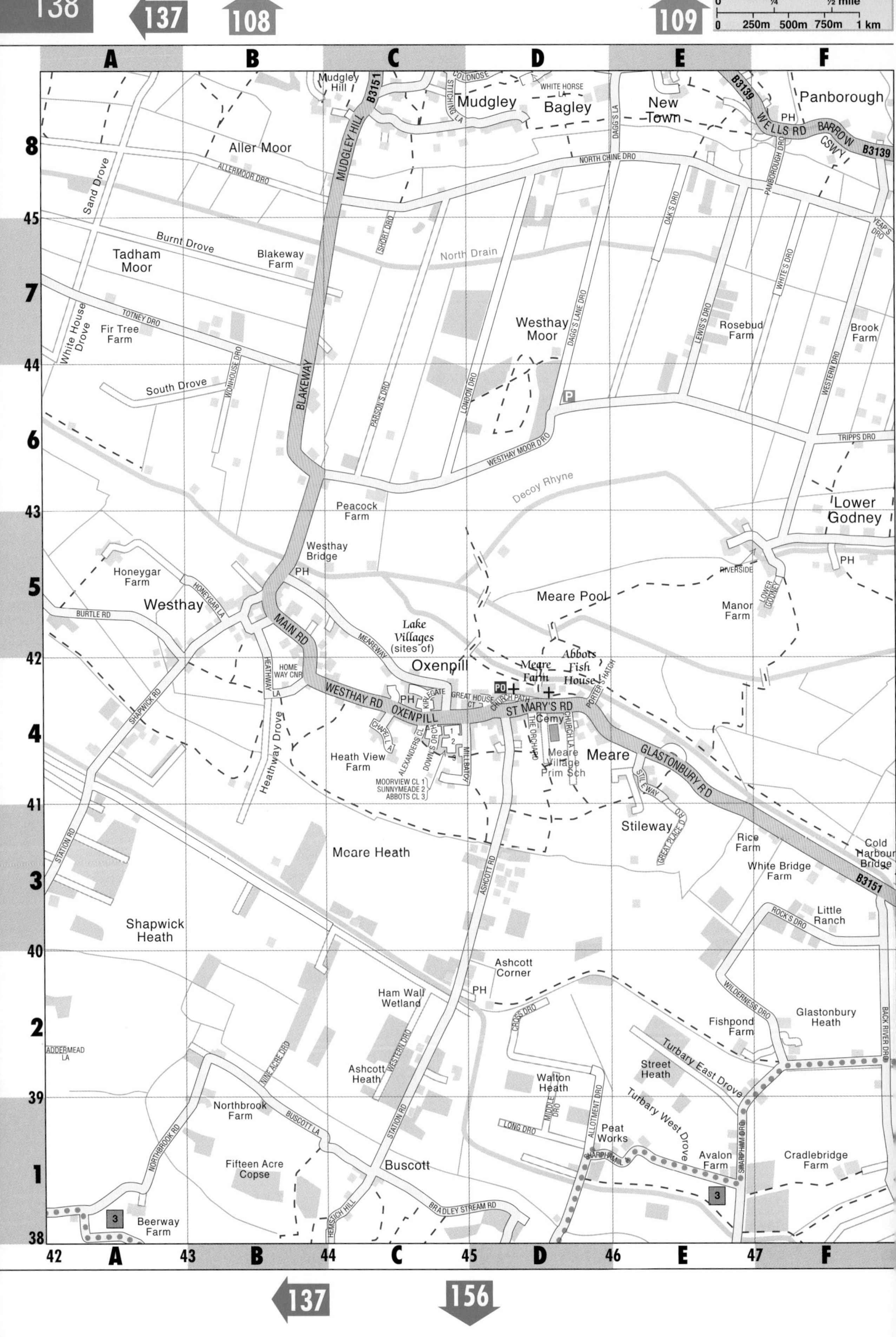
Mudgley Hill
Mudgley
Bagley
New Town
Panborough
Aller Moor
Sand Drove
Tadham Moor
Burnt Drove
Blakeway Farm
North Drain
Fir Tree Farm
White House Drove
South Drove
Westhay Moor
Rosebud Farm
Brook Farm
Peacock Farm
Decoy Rhyne
Lower Godney
Honeygar Farm
Westhay
Westhay Bridge
Meare Pool
Manor Farm
Lake Villages (sites of)
Oxenpill
Meare Farm
Abbots Fish House
Heath View Farm
Heathway Drove
Meare
Meare Village Prim Sch
Stileway
Rice Farm
White Bridge Farm
Cold Harbour Bridge
Meare Heath
Shapwick Heath
Little Ranch
Ashcott Corner
Ham Wall Wetland
Glastonbury Heath
Fishpond Farm
Turbary East Drove
Street Heath
Walton Heath
Ashcott Heath
Northbrook Farm
Turbary West Drove
Peat Works
Avalon Farm
Cradlebridge Farm
Fifteen Acre Copse
Buscott
Beerway Farm
BLAKEWAY
MUDGLEY HILL
MAIN RD
WESTHAY RD
OXENPILL
ST MARY'S RD
GLASTONBURY RD
ASHCOTT RD
STATION RD
SHAPWICK RD
BURTLE RD
WELLS RD
B3151
B3139

137
156

Scale: 1¾ inches to 1 mile

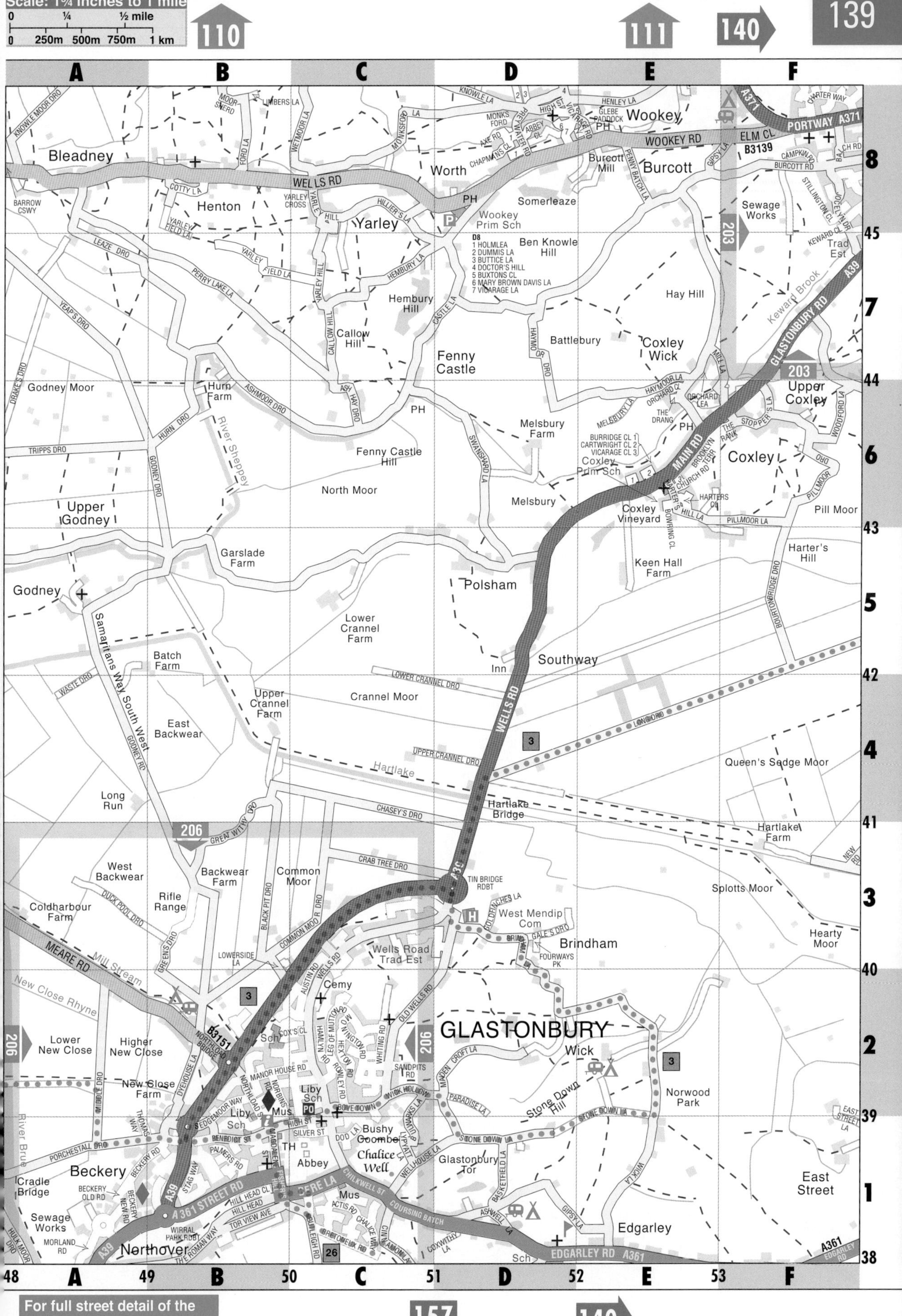

For full street detail of the highlighted areas see pages 203 and 206.

139 112 113

Scale: 1¾ inches to 1 mile
0 ¼ ½ mile
0 250m 500m 750m 1 km

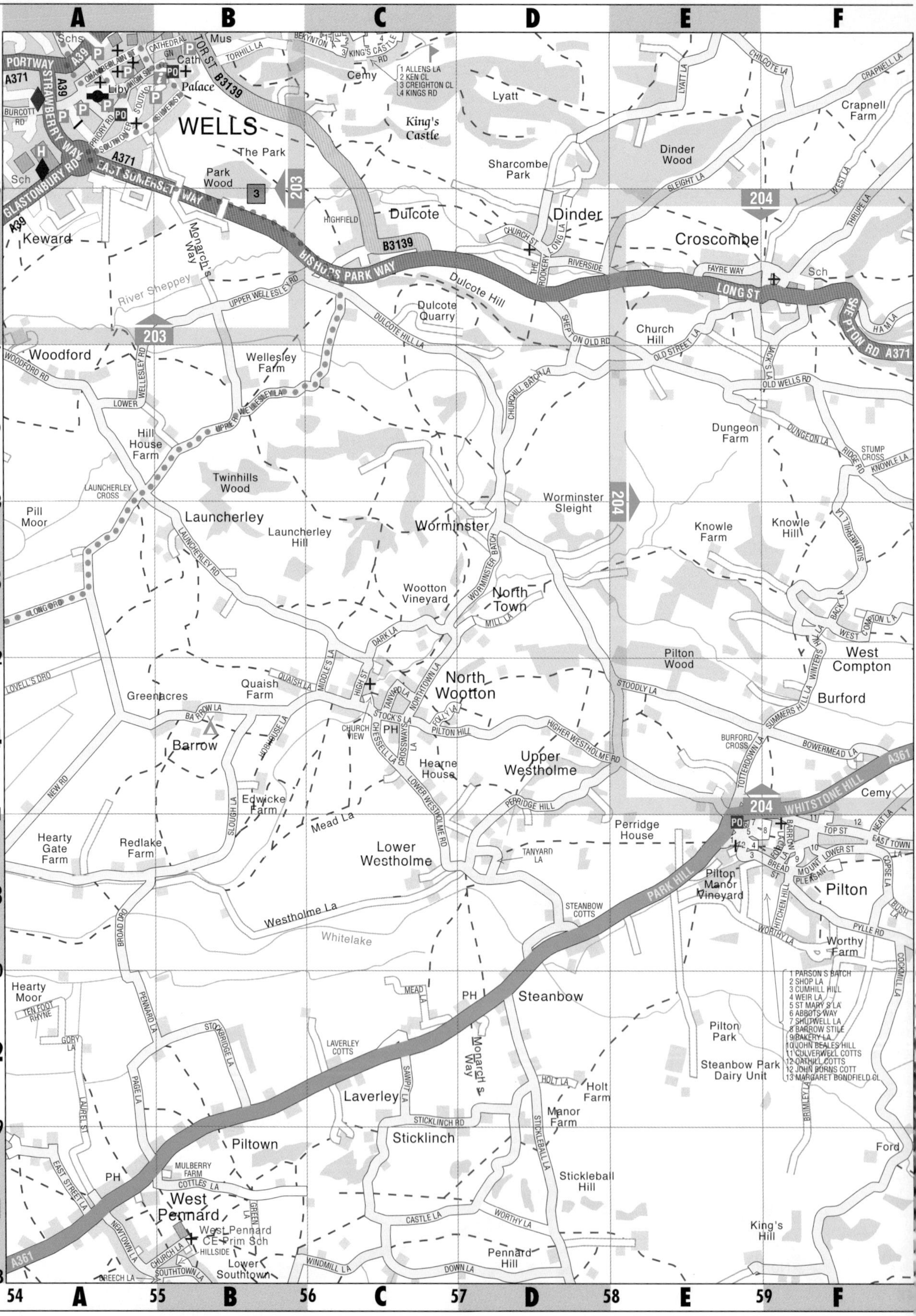

A B C D E F

8
45
7
44
6
43
5
42
4
41
3
40
2
39
1
38

WELLS
Schs
PORTWAY
A371
A39
STRAWBERRY WAY
BURCOTT RD
PRIORY RD
SOUTHOVER
SOUTH ST
SILVER ST
CHAMBERLAIN ST
CATHEDRAL GN
Liby
Cath
Mus
Palace
TOR ST
TORHILL LA
B3139
Sch
GLASTONBURY RD
EAST SOMERSET WAY
The Park
Park Wood
Keward
Monarch's Way
River Sheppey
UPPER WELLESLEY RD
BEKYNTON AV
KING'S CASTLE RD
Cemy
1 ALLENS LA
2 KEN CL
3 CREIGHTON CL
4 KINGS RD
King's Castle
Lyatt
LYATT LA
Sharcombe Park
Dinder Wood
CHILCOTE LA
CRAPNELL LA
Crapnell Farm
SLEIGHT LA
WEST LA
THRUPE LA
HIGHFIELD
Dulcote
B3139
CHURCH ST
THE ROOKERY
LONG LA
Dinder
RIVERSIDE
Croscombe
FAYRE WAY
LONG ST
Sch
SHEPTON RD A371
HAM LA
BISHOPS PARK WAY
Dulcote Hill
Dulcote Quarry
DULCOTE HILL LA
SHEPTON OLD RD
Church Hill
OLD STREET LA
JACK'S LA
OLD WELLS RD
Woodford
WOODFORD RD
WELLESLEY RD
Wellesley Farm
LOWER
UPPER WELLESLEY LA
CHURCHILL BATCH LA
Dungeon Farm
DUNGEON LA
RIDGE RD
STUMP CROSS
KNOWLE LA
Hill House Farm
Twinhills Wood
LAUNCHERLEY CROSS
Worminster Sleight
Pill Moor
Launcherley
Launcherley Hill
Worminster
Knowle Farm
Knowle Hill
SUMMERHILL LA
LAUNCHERLEY RD
WORMINSTER BATCH
Wootton Vineyard
North Town
LONG DRO
MILL LA
BACK LA
COMPTON LA
WEST COMPTON LA
DARK LA
LOVELL'S DRO
Pilton Wood
West Compton
QUAISH LA
MIDDLE'S LA
HIGH ST
Quaish Farm
North Wootton
NORTHTOWN LA
TANYARD LA
STOODLY LA
WINTERS HILL LA
Greenacres
Burford
BARROW LA
STOCK'S LA
FOLLY LA
SUMMERS HILL LA
HOPHOUSE LA
CHURCH VIEW
PH
PILTON HILL
HIGHER WESTHOLME RD
BURFORD CROSS
BOWERMEAD LA
A361
Barrow
CHESSELL LA
CROSSWAYS LA
Hearne House
Upper Westholme
TOTTERDOWN LA
NEW RD
Edwicke Farm
SLOUGH LA
LOWER WESTHOLME RD
PERRIDGE HILL
WHITSTONE HILL
Cemy
Mead La
Perridge House
PO
BARROW LA
TOP ST
NEAT LA
EAST TOWN LA
Hearty Gate Farm
Redlake Farm
Lower Westholme
TANYARD LA
LOWER ST
MOUNT PLEASANT
BREAD ST
COPSE LA
Pilton Manor Vineyard
Pilton
PARK HILL
BROAD DRO
Westholme La
STEANBOW COTTS
HITCHEN HILL
BUSH LA
Whitelake
WORTHY LA
PYLLE RD
Worthy Farm
COCKMILL LA
Hearty Moor
TEN FOOT RHYNE
PENNARD LA
MEAD LA
PH
Steanbow
1 PARSON'S BATCH
2 SHOP LA
3 CUMHILL HILL
4 WEIR LA
5 ST MARY'S LA
6 ABBOTS WAY
7 SHUTWELL LA
8 BARROW STILE
9 BAKERY LA
10 JOHN BEALES HILL
11 CULVERWELL COTTS
12 OATHILL COTTS
12 JOHN BURNS COTT
13 MARGARET BONDFIELD CL
GORY LA
STOCKBRIDGE LA
LAVERLEY COTTS
Monarch's Way
Pilton Park
PAGE LA
LAUREL ST
SAWPIT LA
HOLT LA
Holt Farm
Steanbow Park Dairy Unit
BRIMLEY LA
Laverley
Manor Farm
STICKLINCH RD
Sticklinch
STICKLEBALL LA
Piltown
Ford
EAST STREET LA
PH
MULBERRY FARM
COTTLES LA
Stickleball Hill
West Pennard
GREEN LA
CASTLE LA
WORTHY LA
King's Hill
NEWTOWN LA
West Pennard CE Prim Sch
HILLSIDE
CHURCH LA
Pennard Hill
A361
BREECH LA
SOUTHTOWN LA
Lower Southtown
WINDMILL LA
DOWN LA

54 A 55 B 56 C 57 D 58 E 59 F

203
204
For full street detail of the highlighted area see pages 203 and 204.
139 158

Scale: 1¾ inches to 1 mile
0 ¼ ½ mile
0 250m 500m 750m 1 km

114
115
142

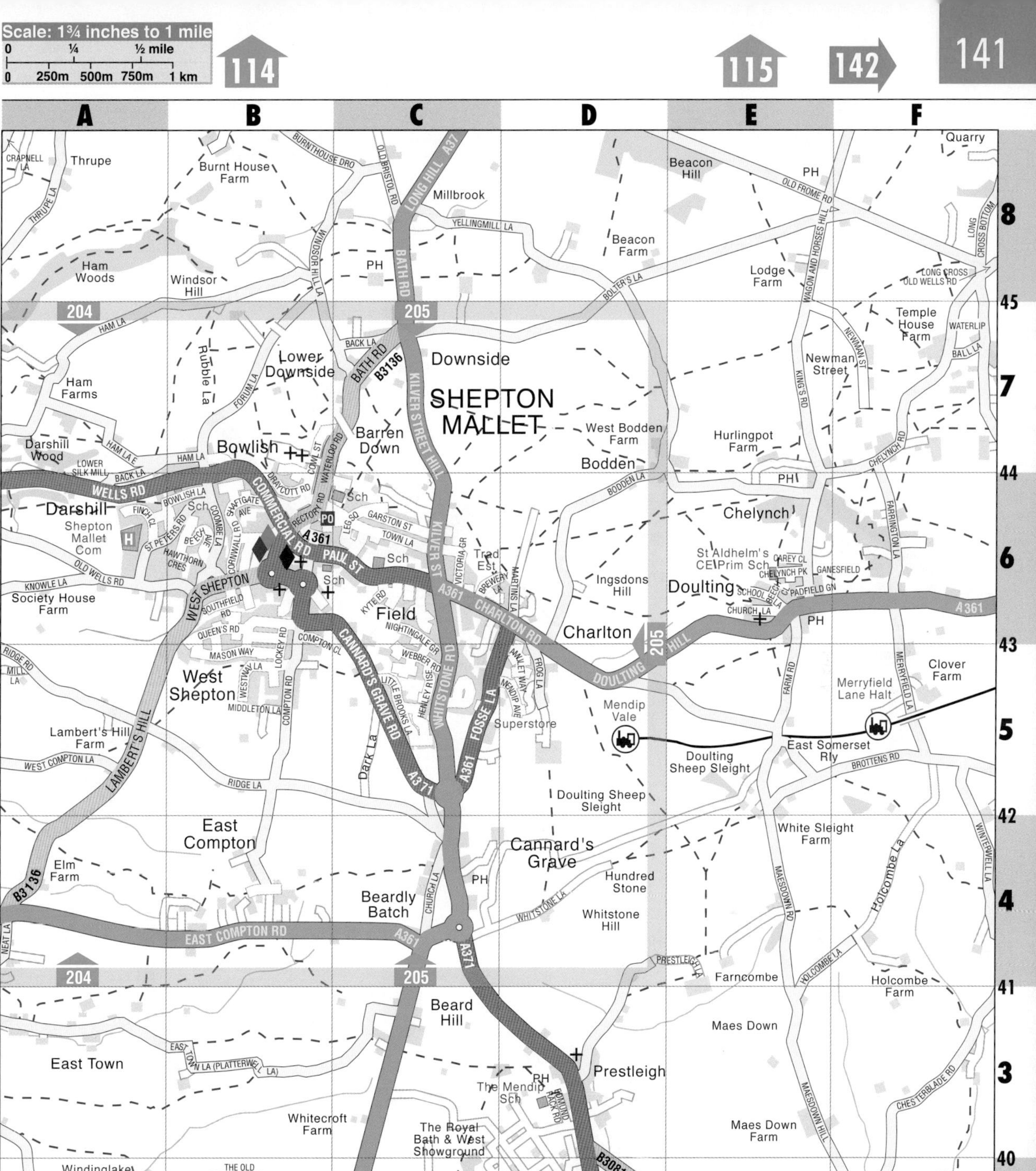

A B C D E F

159
142
For full street detail of the highlighted area see pages 204 and 205.

141 116 117

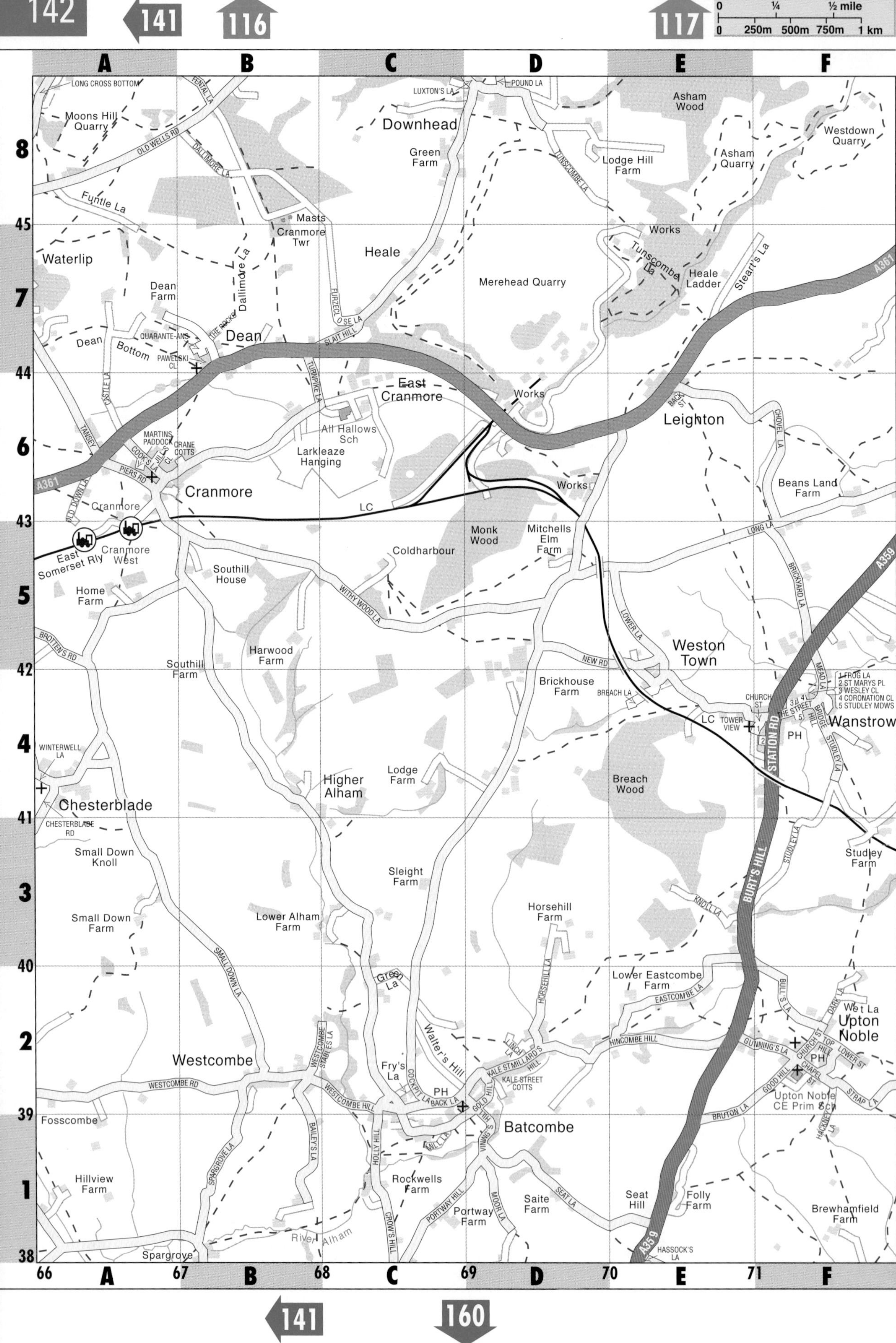
Scale: 1¾ inches to 1 mile
Downhead
Green Farm
Asham Wood
Asham Quarry
Westdown Quarry
Lodge Hill Farm
Moons Hill Quarry
Funtle La
Masts
Cranmore Twr
Heale
Works
Waterlip
Dean Farm
Dallimore La
Merehead Quarry
Tunscombe La
Heale Ladder
Steart's La
Dean
Dean Bottom
East Cranmore
Works
Leighton
All Hallows Sch
Larkleaze Hanging
Cranmore
Beans Land Farm
Works
LC
Monk Wood
Mitchells Elm Farm
Coldharbour
East Somerset Rly
Cranmore West
Southill House
Home Farm
Weston Town
Harwood Farm
Southill Farm
Brickhouse Farm
LC
Wanstrow
PH
Higher Alham
Lodge Farm
Breach Wood
Chesterblade
Small Down Knoll
Studley Farm
Sleight Farm
Horsehill Farm
Small Down Farm
Lower Alham Farm
Lower Eastcombe Farm
Green La
Walter's Hill
Wet La
Upton Noble
Westcombe
Fry's La
PH
PH
Fosscombe
Batcombe
Upton Noble CE Prim Sch
Hillview Farm
Rockwells Farm
Saite Farm
Seat Hill
Folly Farm
Portway Farm
Brewhamfield Farm
River Alham
Spargrove
A361
A359
BURT'S HILL
STATION RD
A B C D E F
66 67 68 69 70 71
38 39 40 41 42 43 44 45
1 2 3 4 5 6 7 8

141 160

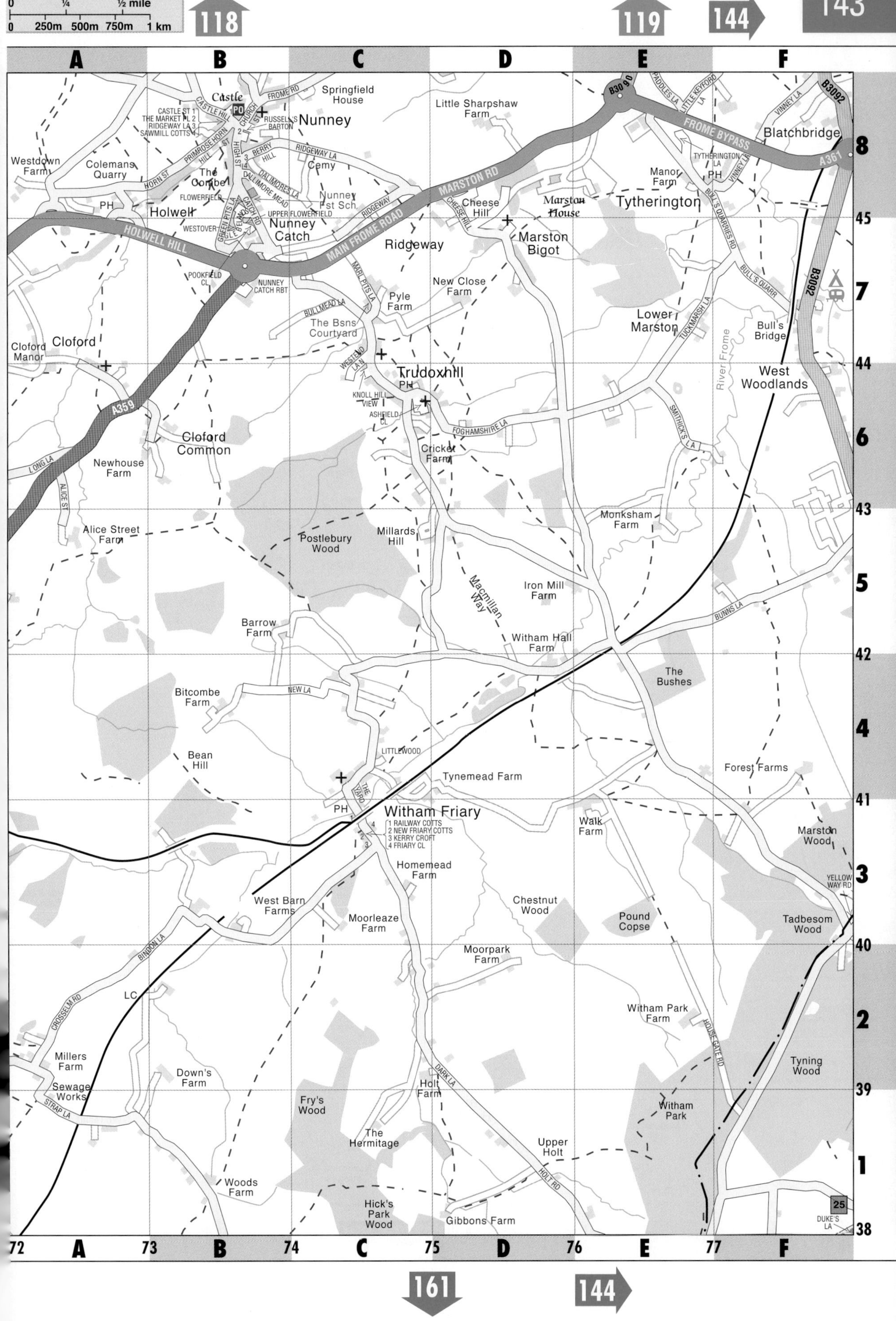
Scale: 1¾ inches to 1 mile
0 ¼ ½ mile
0 250m 500m 750m 1 km
118
119
144
A B C D E F
Castle
PO
Springfield House
Nunney
Little Sharpshaw Farm
Blatchbridge
FROME BYPASS
B3090
B3092
A361
Westdown Farm
Colemans Quarry
The Combe
Cemy
Nunney Fst Sch
Holwell
PH
HOLWELL HILL
Nunney Catch
MAIN FROME ROAD
MARSTON RD
Cheese Hill
Marston House
Tytherington
Manor Farm
Marston Bigot
Ridgeway
NUNNEY CATCH RBT
POOKFIELD CL
Pyle Farm
New Close Farm
Lower Marston
Bull's Bridge
The Bsns Courtyard
BULLMEAD LA
Cloford Manor
Cloford
Trudoxhill
West Woodlands
River Frome
A359
Cloford Common
FOGHAMSHIRE LA
Cricket Farm
Newhouse Farm
LONG LA
ALICE ST
Alice Street Farm
Postlebury Wood
Millards Hill
Monksham Farm
Macmillan Way
Iron Mill Farm
Barrow Farm
Witham Hall Farm
BUNNS LA
The Bushes
Bitcombe Farm
NEW LA
Bean Hill
LITTLEWOOD
Tynemead Farm
Forest Farms
Witham Friary
1 RAILWAY COTTS
2 NEW FRIARY COTTS
3 KERRY CROFT
4 FRIARY CL
Walk Farm
Marston Wood
Homemead Farm
YELLOW WAY RD
West Barn Farms
Moorleaze Farm
Chestnut Wood
Pound Copse
Tadbesom Wood
Moorpark Farm
BINDON LA
LC
CROSSELM RD
Witham Park Farm
HOUSE GATE RD
Millers Farm
Down's Farm
Sewage Works
STRAP LA
Holt Farm
DARK LA
Tyning Wood
Witham Park
Fry's Wood
The Hermitage
Upper Holt
HOLT RD
Woods Farm
Hick's Park Wood
Gibbons Farm
25
DUKE'S LA
8 45 7 44 6 43 5 42 4 41 3 40 2 39 1 38
72 73 74 75 76 77
161
144

Scale: 1¾ inches to 1 mile

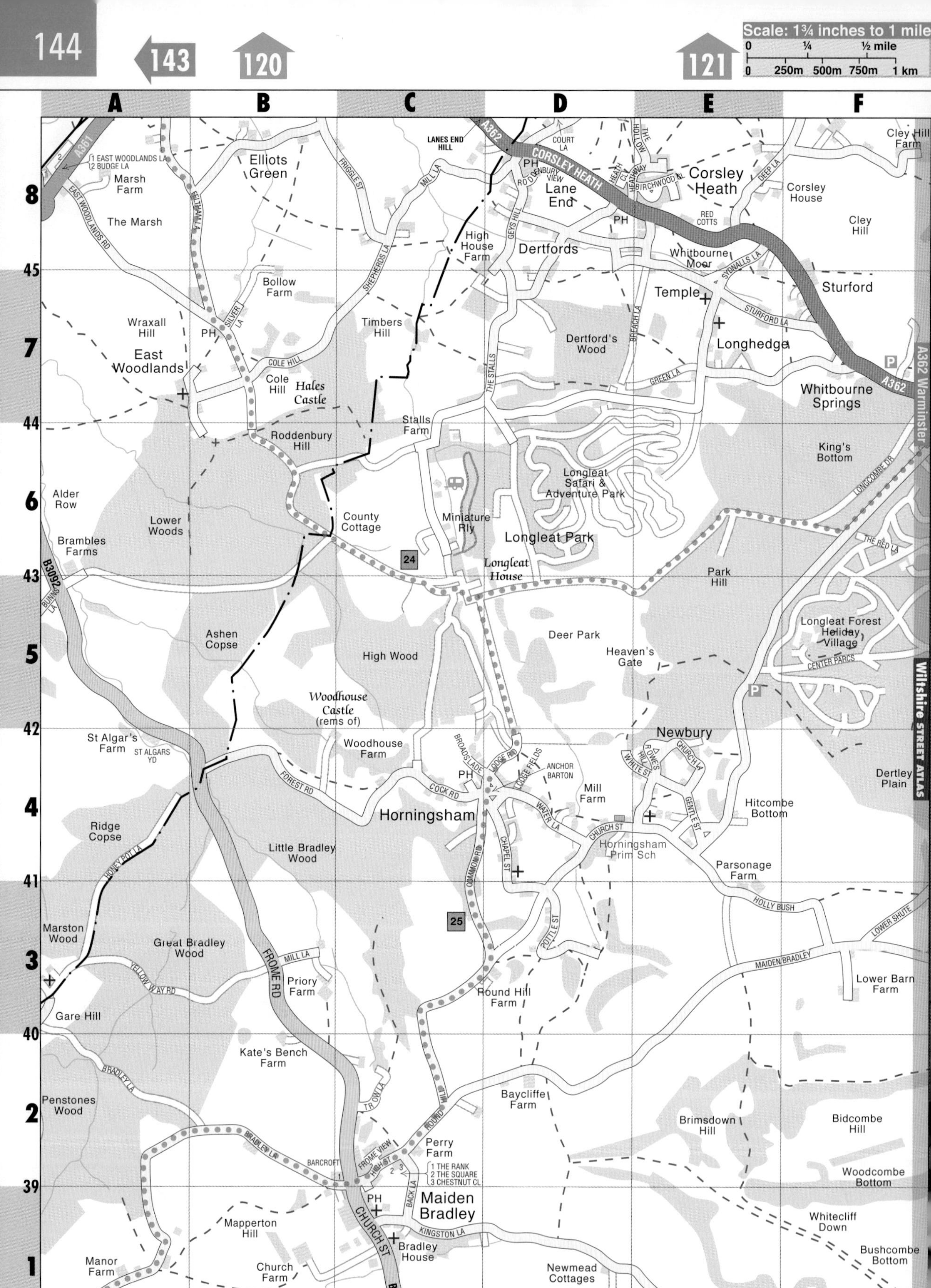
Elliots Green
Marsh Farm
The Marsh
Lanes End Hill
Corsley Heath
Lane End
Corsley House
Cley Hill Farm
Cley Hill
High House Farm
Dertfords
Whitbourne Moor
Temple
Sturford
Longhedge
Bollow Farm
Wraxall Hill
East Woodlands
Timbers Hill
Dertford's Wood
Cole Hill
Hales Castle
Whitbourne Springs
Stalls Farm
Roddenbury Hill
King's Bottom
Longleat Safari & Adventure Park
Alder Row
Lower Woods
County Cottage
Miniature Rly
Longleat Park
Brambles Farms
Longleat House
Park Hill
Ashen Copse
Deer Park
Heaven's Gate
Longleat Forest Holiday Village
High Wood
Woodhouse Castle (rems of)
St Algar's Farm
Woodhouse Farm
Newbury
Mill Farm
Dertley Plain
Horningsham
Hitcombe Bottom
Ridge Copse
Little Bradley Wood
Horningsham Prim Sch
Parsonage Farm
Marston Wood
Great Bradley Wood
Priory Farm
Round Hill Farm
Lower Barn Farm
Gare Hill
Kate's Bench Farm
Penstones Wood
Baycliffe Farm
Brimsdown Hill
Bidcombe Hill
Perry Farm
Woodcombe Bottom
Maiden Bradley
Mapperton Hill
Whitecliff Down
Bradley House
Manor Farm
Church Farm
Newmead Cottages
Bushcombe Bottom
Newmead Farm
A362 Warminster
Wiltshire STREET ATLAS

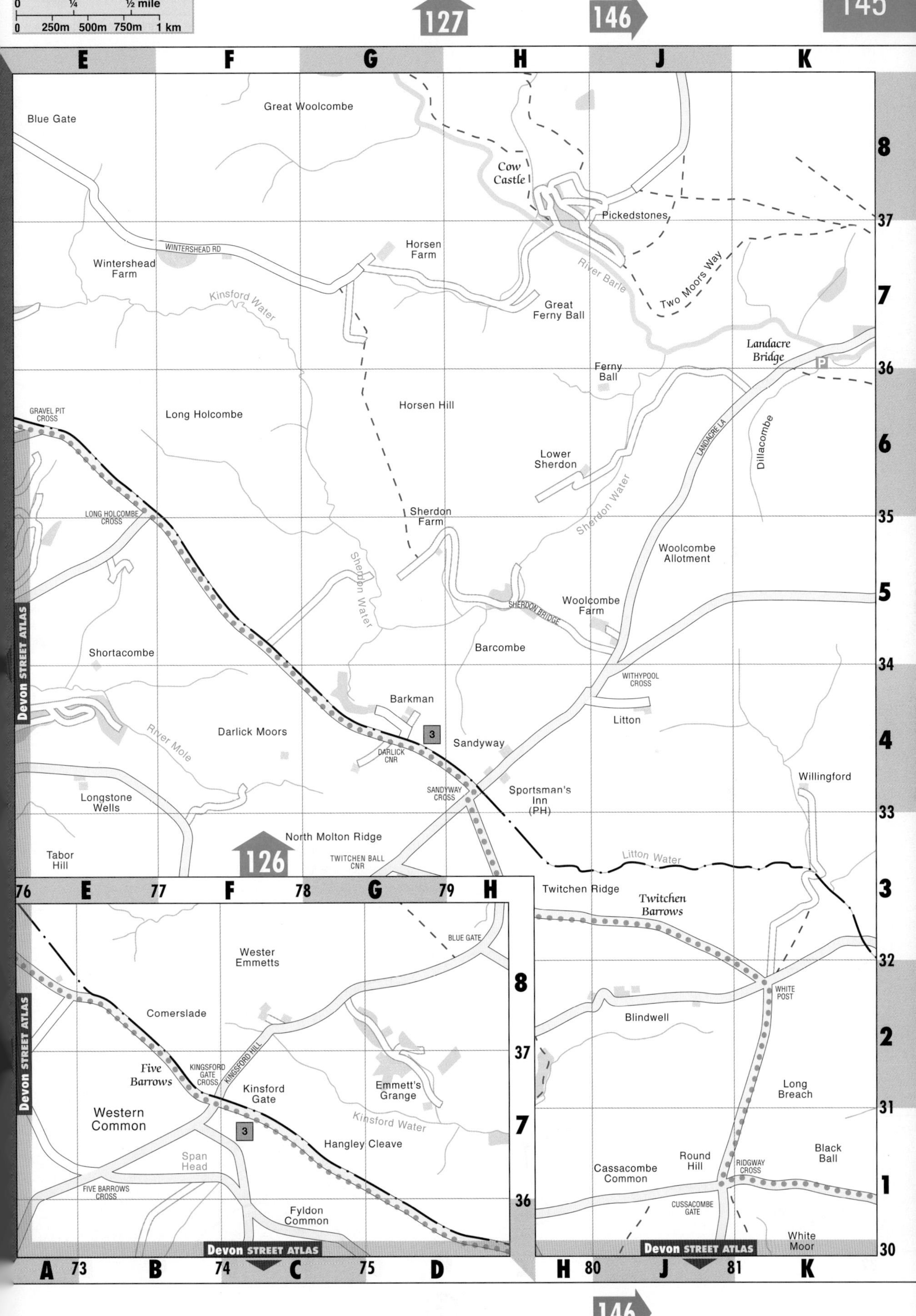
Scale: 1¾ inches to 1 mile
0 ¼ ½ mile
0 250m 500m 750m 1 km
127
146
E F G H J K
Blue Gate
Great Woolcombe
Cow Castle
Pickedstones
8
37
Wintershead Farm
WINTERSHEAD RD
Horsen Farm
River Barle
Two Moors Way
Kinsford Water
Great Ferny Ball
7
Landacre Bridge
Ferny Ball
36
GRAVEL PIT CROSS
Long Holcombe
Horsen Hill
LANDACRE LA
Dillacombe
Lower Sherdon
6
LONG HOLCOMBE CROSS
Sherdon Farm
Sherdon Water
35
Woolcombe Allotment
Sherdon Water
Woolcombe Farm
SHERDON BRIDGE
5
Shortacombe
Barcombe
34
WITHYPOOL CROSS
Devon STREET ATLAS
Barkman
Litton
River Mole
Darlick Moors
3
Sandyway
DARLICK CNR
4
SANDYWAY CROSS
Sportsman's Inn (PH)
Willingford
Longstone Wells
33
North Molton Ridge
126
Tabor Hill
TWITCHEN BALL CNR
Litton Water
Twitchen Ridge
Twitchen Barrows
3
76 E 77 F 78 G 79 H
BLUE GATE
Wester Emmetts
8
32
WHITE POST
Comerslade
Blindwell
2
37
KINGSFORD HILL
Five Barrows
KINGSFORD GATE CROSS
Kinsford Gate
Emmett's Grange
Long Breach
Devon STREET ATLAS
Western Common
3
Kinsford Water
7
31
Hangley Cleave
Black Ball
Span Head
Round Hill
Cassacombe Common
RIDGWAY CROSS
1
FIVE BARROWS CROSS
36
Fyldon Common
CUSSACOMBE GATE
White Moor
Devon STREET ATLAS
Devon STREET ATLAS
30
A 73 B 74 C 75 D
H 80 J 81 K
146

145
128

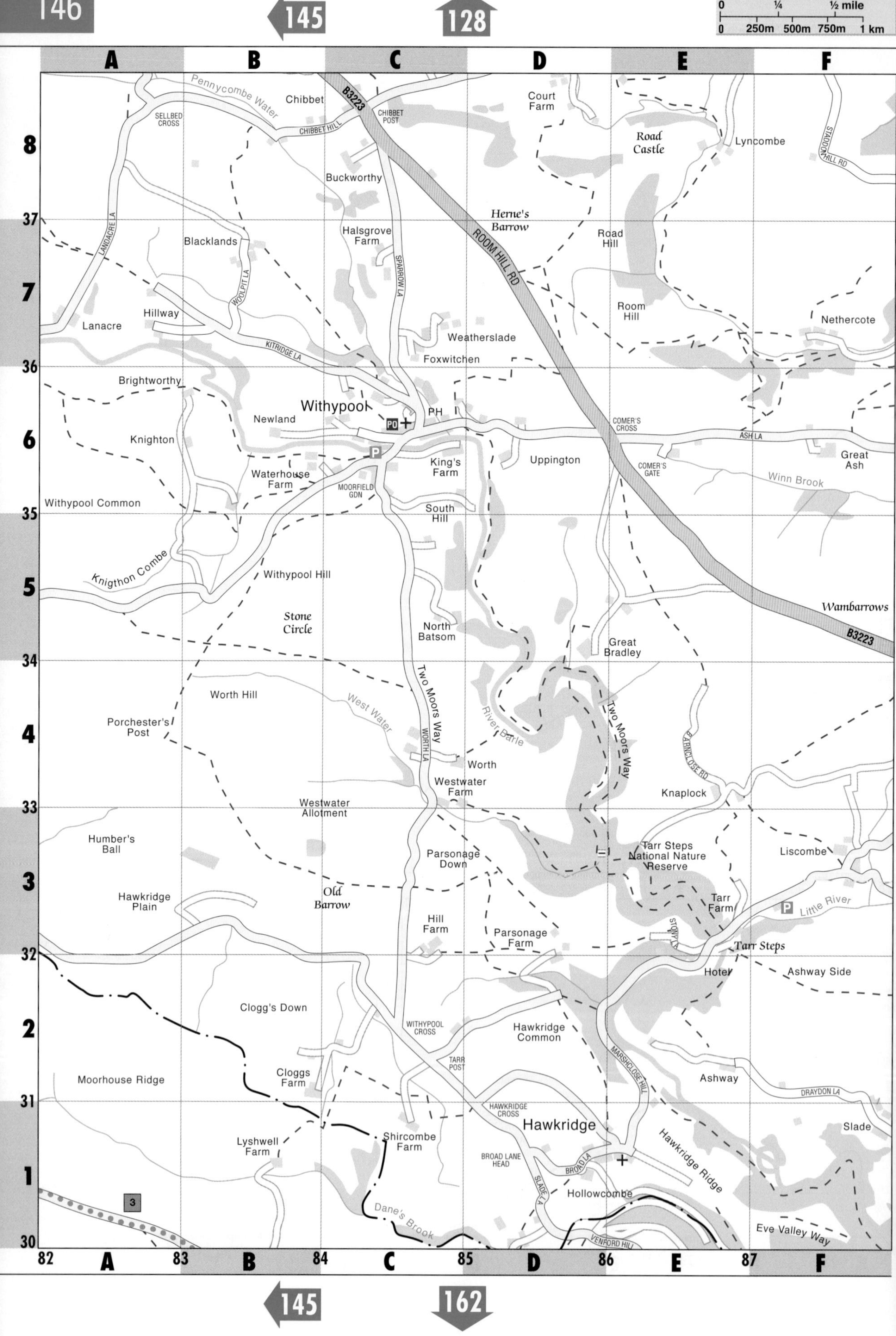
Scale: 1¾ inches to 1 mile
0 ¼ ½ mile
0 250m 500m 750m 1 km
A B C D E F
8 7 6 5 4 3 2 1
37 36 35 34 33 32 31 30
82 83 84 85 86 87
Pennycombe Water
Chibbet
B3223
CHIBBET POST
SELLBED CROSS
CHIBBET HILL
Court Farm
Road Castle
Lyncombe
STADDON HILL RD
Buckworthy
Herne's Barrow
ROOM HILL RD
Road Hill
LANDACRE LA
Blacklands
Halsgrove Farm
SPARROW LA
WOOLPIT LA
Room Hill
Nethercote
Lanacre
Hillway
Weatherslade
KITRIDGE LA
Foxwitchen
Brightworthy
Withypool
PH
Newland
PO
COMER'S CROSS
ASH LA
Knighton
Uppington
King's Farm
COMER'S GATE
Great Ash
Waterhouse Farm
Winn Brook
MOORFIELD GDN
South Hill
Withypool Common
Knigthon Combe
Withypool Hill
Stone Circle
Wambarrows
North Batsom
Great Bradley
Worth Hill
Two Moors Way
West Water
River Barle
Porchester's Post
WORTH LA
Worth
BARNCLOSE RD
Westwater Farm
Knaplock
Westwater Allotment
Humber's Ball
Tarr Steps National Nature Reserve
Liscombe
Parsonage Down
Hawkridge Plain
Old Barrow
Tarr Farm
Little River
Hill Farm
Parsonage Farm
STONY LA
Tarr Steps
Hotel
Ashway Side
Clogg's Down
WITHYPOOL CROSS
Hawkridge Common
MARSHCLOSE HILL
TARR POST
Ashway
Moorhouse Ridge
Cloggs Farm
DRAYDON LA
HAWKRIDGE CROSS
Hawkridge
Slade
Lyshwell Farm
Shircombe Farm
BROAD LANE HEAD
BROAD LA
Hawkridge Ridge
SLADE LA
Hollowcombe
3
Dane's Brook
VENFORD HILL
Eve Valley Way

145
162

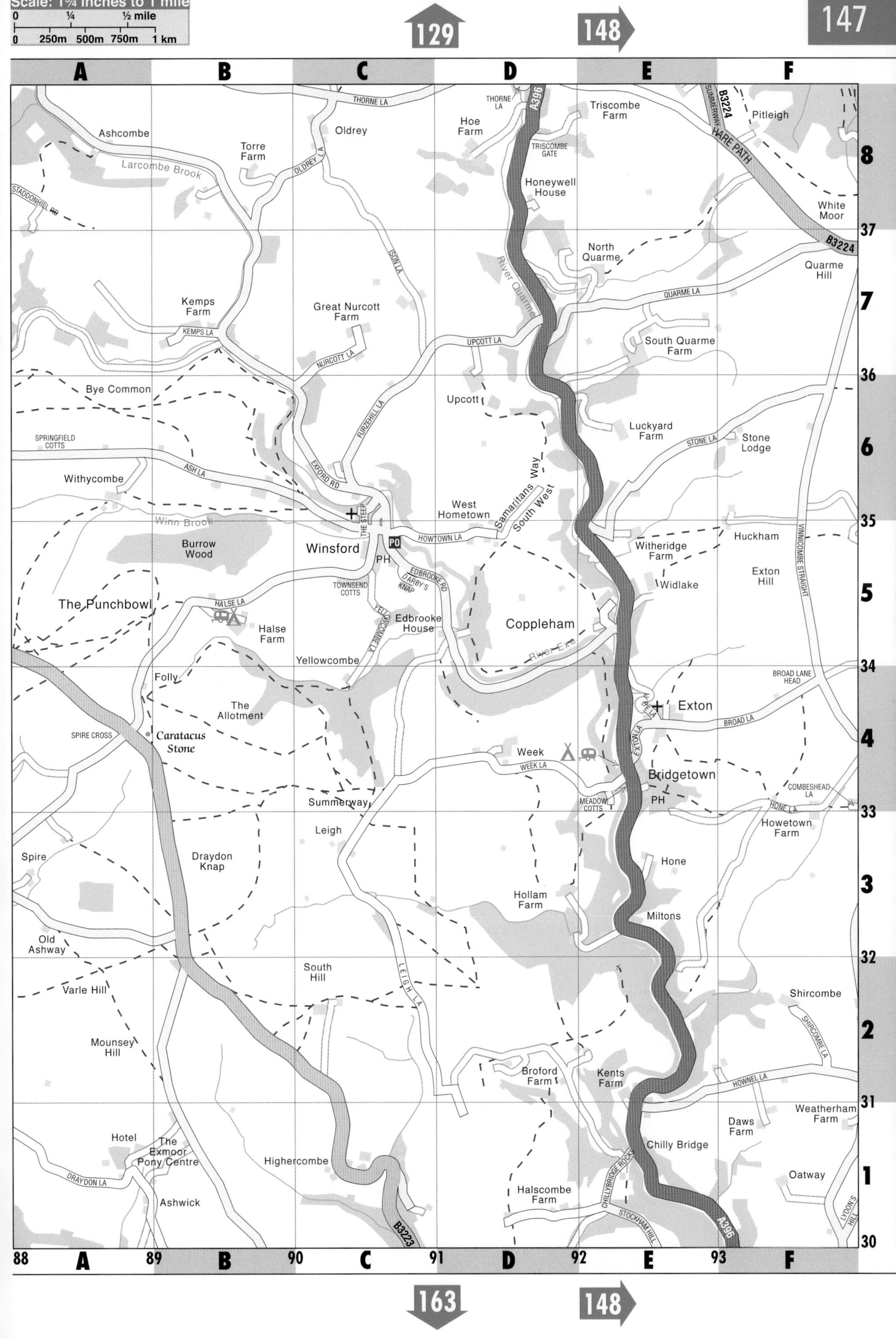
Scale: 1¾ inches to 1 mile
0 ¼ ½ mile
0 250m 500m 750m 1 km
129
148
A B C D E F
Ashcombe
Larcombe Brook
STADDONHILL RD
Torre Farm
Oldrey
OLDREY LA
THORNE LA
Hoe Farm
A396
Triscombe Farm
TRISCOMBE GATE
B3224
SUMMERWAY
HARE PATH
Pitleigh
Honeywell House
White Moor
North Quarme
River Quarme
ISON LA
Quarme Hill
QUARME LA
Kemps Farm
KEMPS LA
Great Nurcott Farm
NURCOTT LA
UPCOTT LA
South Quarme Farm
Bye Common
Upcott
Luckyard Farm
SPRINGFIELD COTTS
FURZEHILL LA
STONE LA
Stone Lodge
Withycombe
ASH LA
EXFORD RD
Samaritans Way South West
West Hometown
Winn Brook
THE STEEP
HOWTOWN LA
Witheridge Farm
Huckham
Burrow Wood
Winsford
PO
PH
EDBROOKE RD
DARBY'S KNAP
Widlake
Exton Hill
VINNICOMBE STRAIGHT
TOWNSEND COTTS
The Punchbowl
HALSE LA
Halse Farm
YELLOWCOMBE LA
Edbrooke House
Coppleham
River Exe
Yellowcombe
BROAD LANE HEAD
Folly
The Allotment
Exton
EXTON LA
BROAD LA
SPIRE CROSS
Caratacus Stone
Week
WEEK LA
Bridgetown
COMBESHEAD LA
Summerway
MEADOW COTTS
PH
HONE LA
Howetown Farm
Leigh
Spire
Draydon Knap
Hone
Holtam Farm
Miltons
Old Ashway
South Hill
LEIGH LA
Shircombe
Varle Hill
SHIRCOMBE LA
Mounsey Hill
Broford Farm
Kents Farm
HOWNEL LA
Weatherham Farm
Daws Farm
Hotel
The Exmoor Pony Centre
Highercombe
Chilly Bridge
CHILLYBRIDGE ROCKS
Oatway
DRAYDON LA
Ashwick
Halscombe Farm
STOCKHAM HILL
LYDON'S HILL
B3223
8 37 7 36 6 35 5 34 4 33 3 32 2 31 1 30
88 89 90 91 92 93
163
148

147
130
Scale: 1¾ inches to 1 mile

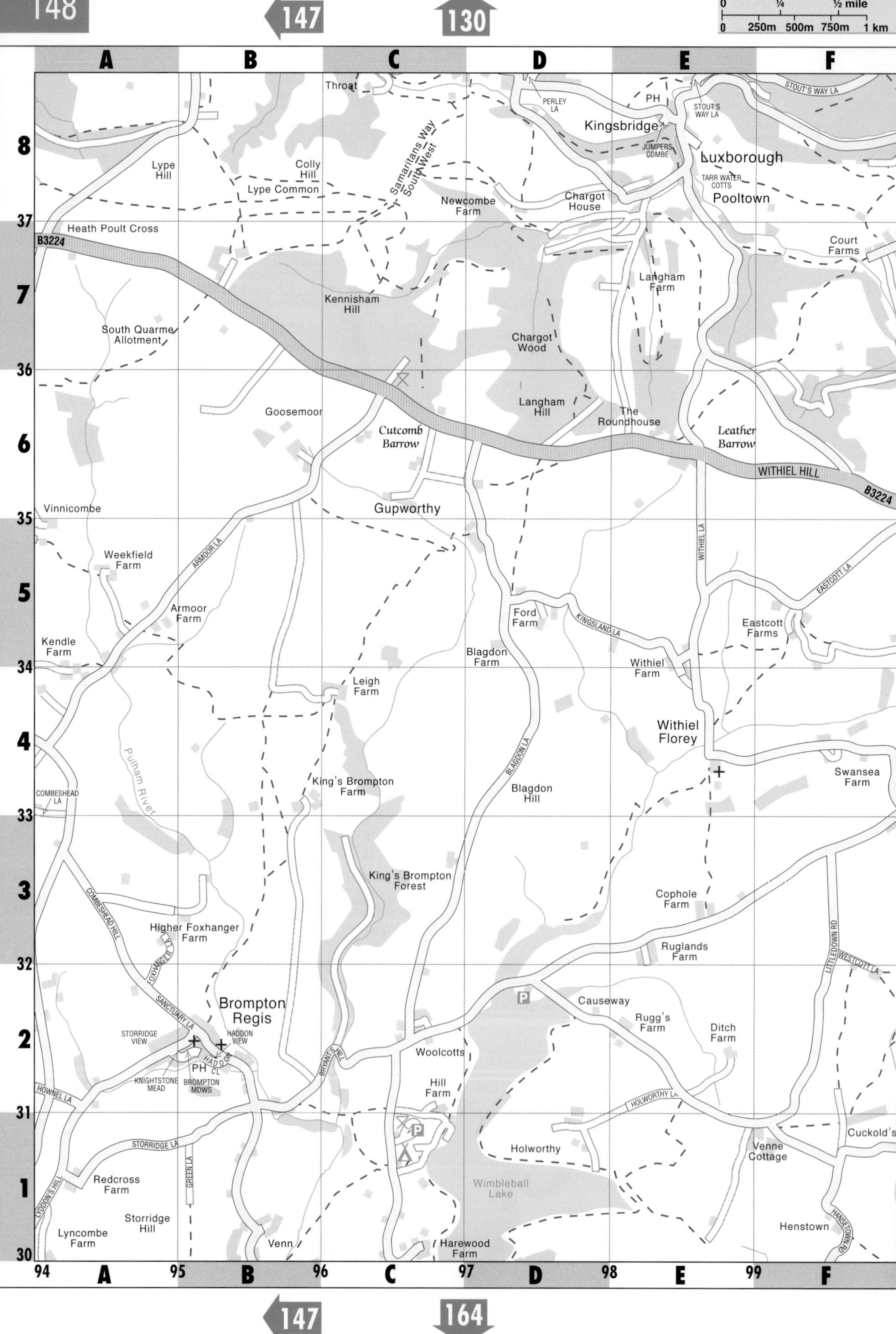
Throat
PERLEY LA
PH
STOUT'S WAY LA
Kingsbridge
JUMPERS COMBE
Luxborough
TARR WATER COTTS
Pooltown
Lype Hill
Colly Hill
Lype Common
Samaritans Way South West
Newcombe Farm
Chargot House
Heath Poult Cross
B3224
Court Farms
Langham Farm
Kennisham Hill
South Quarme Allotment
Chargot Wood
Goosemoor
Langham Hill
The Roundhouse
Cutcomb Barrow
Leather Barrow
WITHIEL HILL
Gupworthy
Vinnicombe
WITHIEL LA
Weekfield Farm
ARMOOR LA
EASTCOTT LA
Armoor Farm
Ford Farm
KINGSLAND LA
Eastcott Farms
Kendle Farm
Blagdon Farm
Withiel Farm
Leigh Farm
Withiel Florey
Pulham River
King's Brompton Farm
BLAGDON LA
Blagdon Hill
Swansea Farm
COMBESHEAD LA
King's Brompton Forest
Cophole Farm
COMBESHEAD HILL
Higher Foxhanger Farm
FOXHANGER LA
Ruglands Farm
LITTLEDOWN RD
WESTCOTT LA
Brompton Regis
SANCTUARY LA
Causeway
Rugg's Farm
STORRIDGE VIEW
HADDON VIEW
Ditch Farm
Woolcotts
BRYANT'S HILL
PH
HADDON CL
KNIGHTSTONE MEAD
BROMPTON MDWS
HOWNEL LA
Hill Farm
HOLWORTHY LA
STORRIDGE LA
Cuckold's
Holworthy
Venne Cottage
Redcross Farm
GREEN LA
Wimbleball Lake
LYDDON'S HILL
Storridge Hill
Henstown
HANSETOWN RD
Lyncombe Farm
Venn
Harewood Farm

147
164

Scale: 1¾ inches to 1 mile
0 ¼ ½ mile
0 250m 500m 750m 1 km

131
150

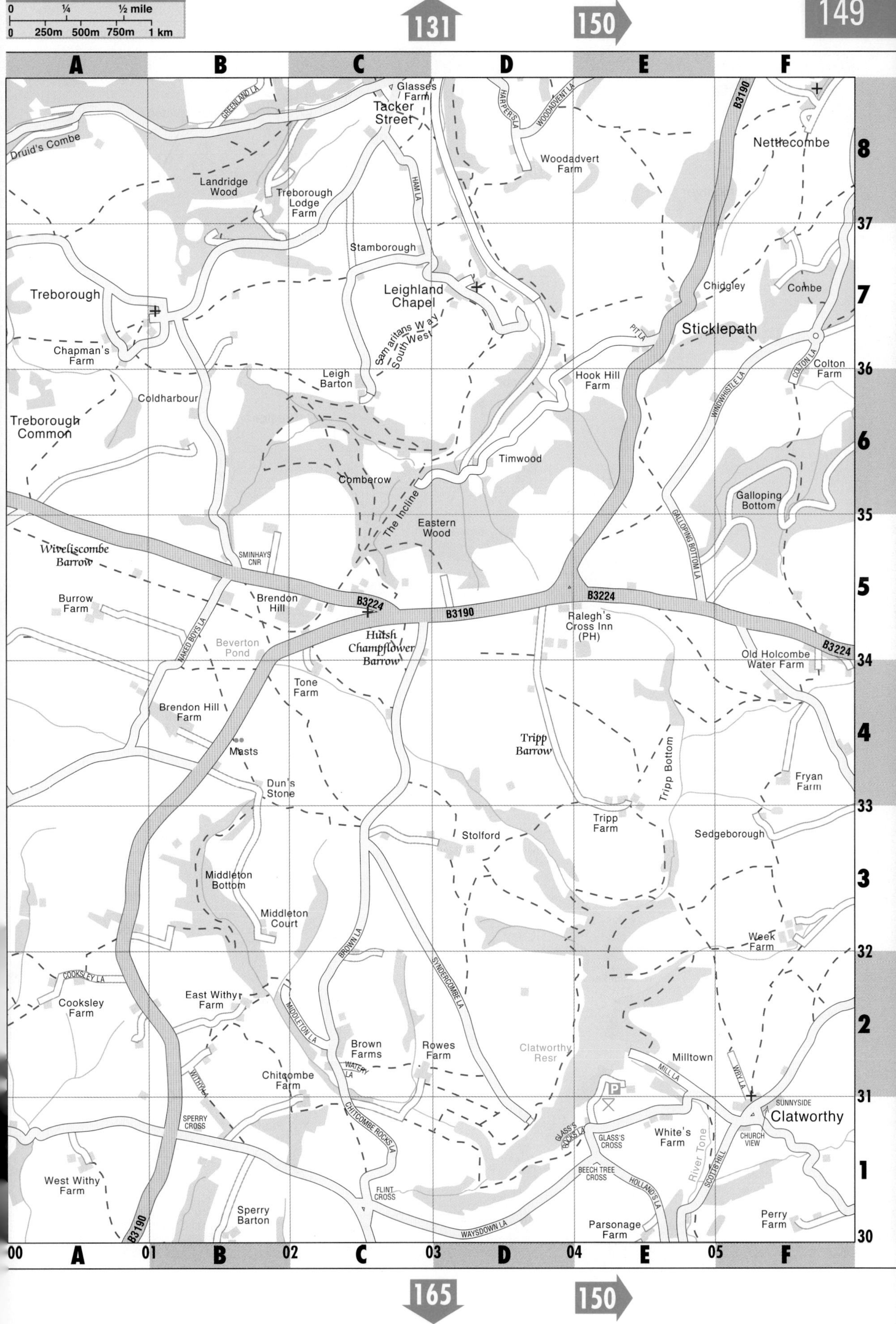

165
150

149
132

Scale: 1¾ inches to 1 mile

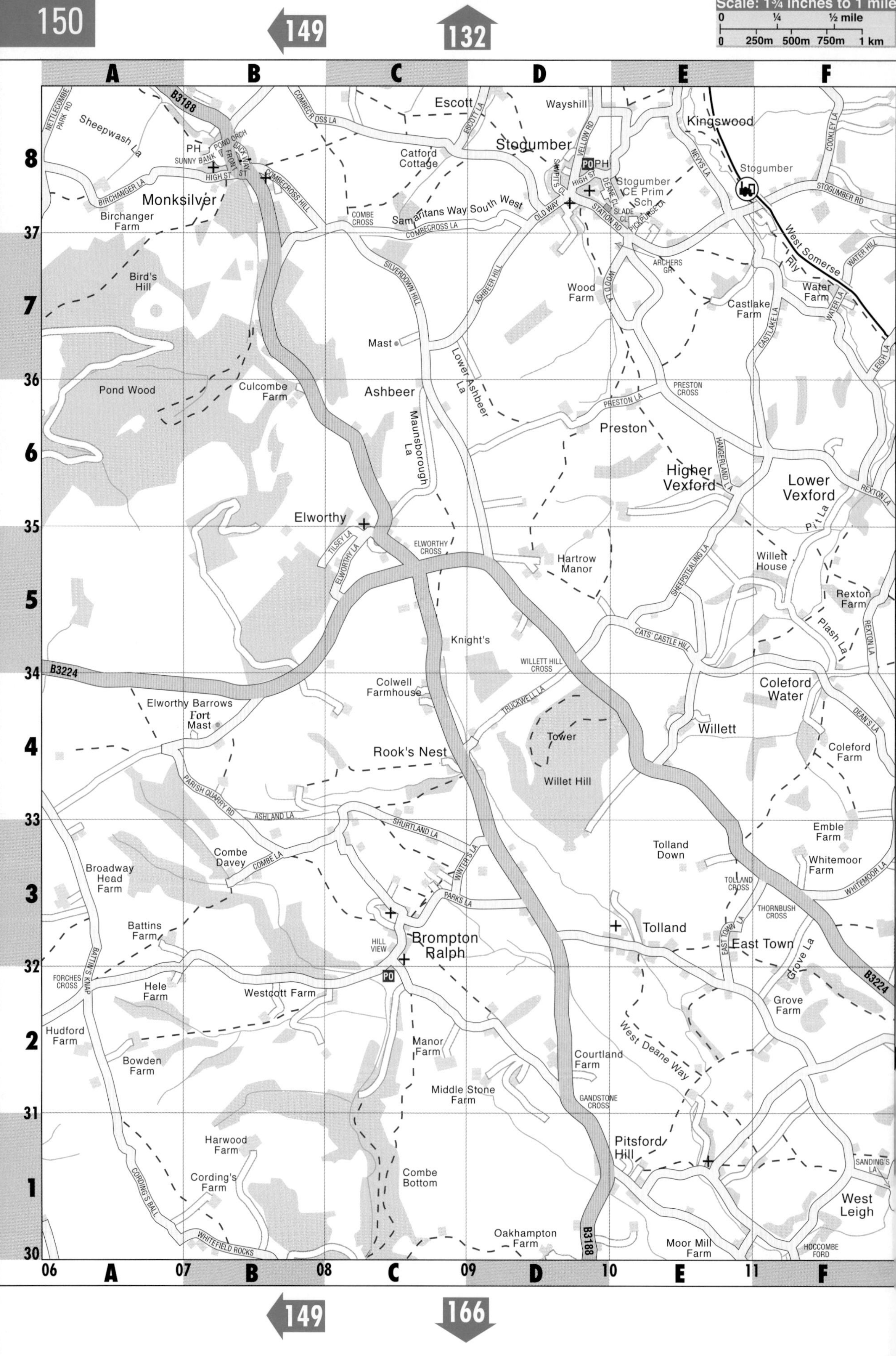
Escott
Wayshill
Kingswood
Stogumber
Sheepwash La
Monksilver
Birchanger Farm
Catford Cottage
Samaritans Way South West
Stogumber CE Prim Sch
West Somerset Rly
Bird's Hill
Wood Farm
Castlake Farm
Water Farm
Mast
Pond Wood
Culcombe Farm
Ashbeer
Lower Ashbeer La
Maunsborough La
Preston
Higher Vexford
Lower Vexford
Elworthy
Hartrow Manor
Willett House
Rexton Farm
Knight's
Colwell Farmhouse
Coleford Water
Elworthy Barrows
Fort
Willett
Tower
Rook's Nest
Coleford Farm
Willet Hill
Combe Davey
Broadway Head Farm
Tolland Down
Emble Farm
Whitemoor Farm
Battins Farm
Brompton Ralph
Tolland
East Town
Hele Farm
Westcott Farm
Grove Farm
Hudford Farm
Bowden Farm
Manor Farm
West Deane Way
Courtland Farm
Middle Stone Farm
Harwood Farm
Pitsford Hill
Cording's Farm
Combe Bottom
West Leigh
Oakhampton Farm
Moor Mill Farm
B3188
B3224

149
166

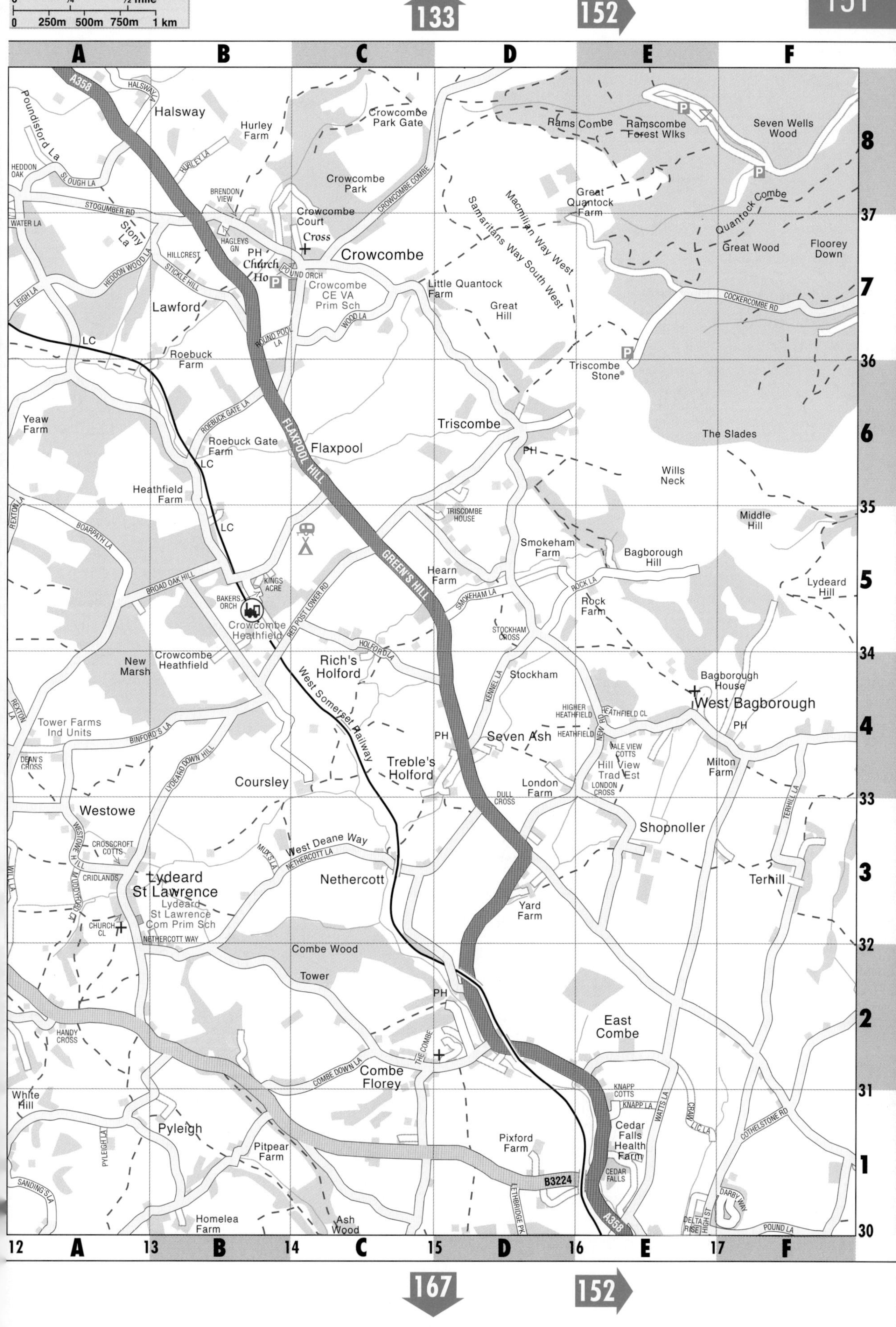
Scale: 1¾ inches to 1 mile
0 ¼ ½ mile
0 250m 500m 750m 1 km
133
152
A B C D E F
Halsway
Hurley Farm
Crowcombe Park Gate
Rams Combe
Ramscombe Forest Wlks
Seven Wells Wood
Poundisford La
Heddon Oak
Slough La
Hurley La
Brendon View
Crowcombe Park
Great Quantock Farm
Quantock Combe
Stogumber Rd
Water La
Stony La
Crowcombe Court
Cross
Crowcombe Combe
Macmillan Way West
Samaritans Way South West
Hagleys Gn
Hillcrest
PH
Church Ho
Crowcombe
Great Wood
Floorey Down
Heddon Wood La
Stickle Hill
Pound Orch
Crowcombe CE VA Prim Sch
Little Quantock Farm
Great Hill
Cockercombe Rd
Leigh La
Lawford
Wood La
Round Pool La
LC
Roebuck Farm
Triscombe Stone
Roebuck Gate La
Yeaw Farm
Flaxpool Hill
Triscombe
The Slades
Roebuck Gate Farm
Flaxpool
Wills Neck
Heathfield Farm
Triscombe House
Middle Hill
Rexton La
Boarpath La
Smokeham Farm
Bagborough Hill
Green's Hill
Hearn Farm
Lydeard Hill
Broad Oak Hill
Kings Acre
Bakers Orch
Red Post Lower Rd
Smokeham La
Rock La
Rock Farm
Crowcombe Heathfield
Stockham Cross
Holford La
New Marsh
Rich's Holford
Kennel La
Stockham
Bagborough House
West Somerset Railway
Higher Heathfield
Heathfield Cl
West Bagborough
Tower Farms Ind Units
Binford's La
PH
Seven Ash
Heathfield
New Rd
Dean's Cross
Lydeard Down Hill
Vale View Cotts
Hill View Trad Est
Milton Farm
Treble's Holford
Coursley
London Farm
Dull Cross
London Cross
Terhill La
Westowe
Shopnoller
Westowe Hill
Crosscroft Cotts
West Deane Way
Mux's La
Nethercott La
Will La
Cridlands
Lydeard St Lawrence
Nethercott
Terhill
Lydeard St Lawrence Com Prim Sch
Church Cl
Yard Farm
Nethercott Way
Combe Wood
Tower
East Combe
Handy Cross
The Combe
Combe Down La
Combe Florey
White Hill
Knapp Cotts
Knapp La
Watts La
Craw Lic La
Cothelstone Rd
Pyleigh
Pyleigh La
Pitpear Farm
Pixford Farm
Cedar Falls Health Farm
B3224
Cedar Falls
Lethbridge Pk
Sanding's La
Darby Way
Homelea Farm
Ash Wood
A358
Delta Rise
High St
Pound La
8 37 7 36 6 35 5 34 4 33 3 32 2 31 1 30
12 A 13 B 14 C 15 D 16 E 17 F
167
152

151
134

Scale: 1¾ inches to 1 mile

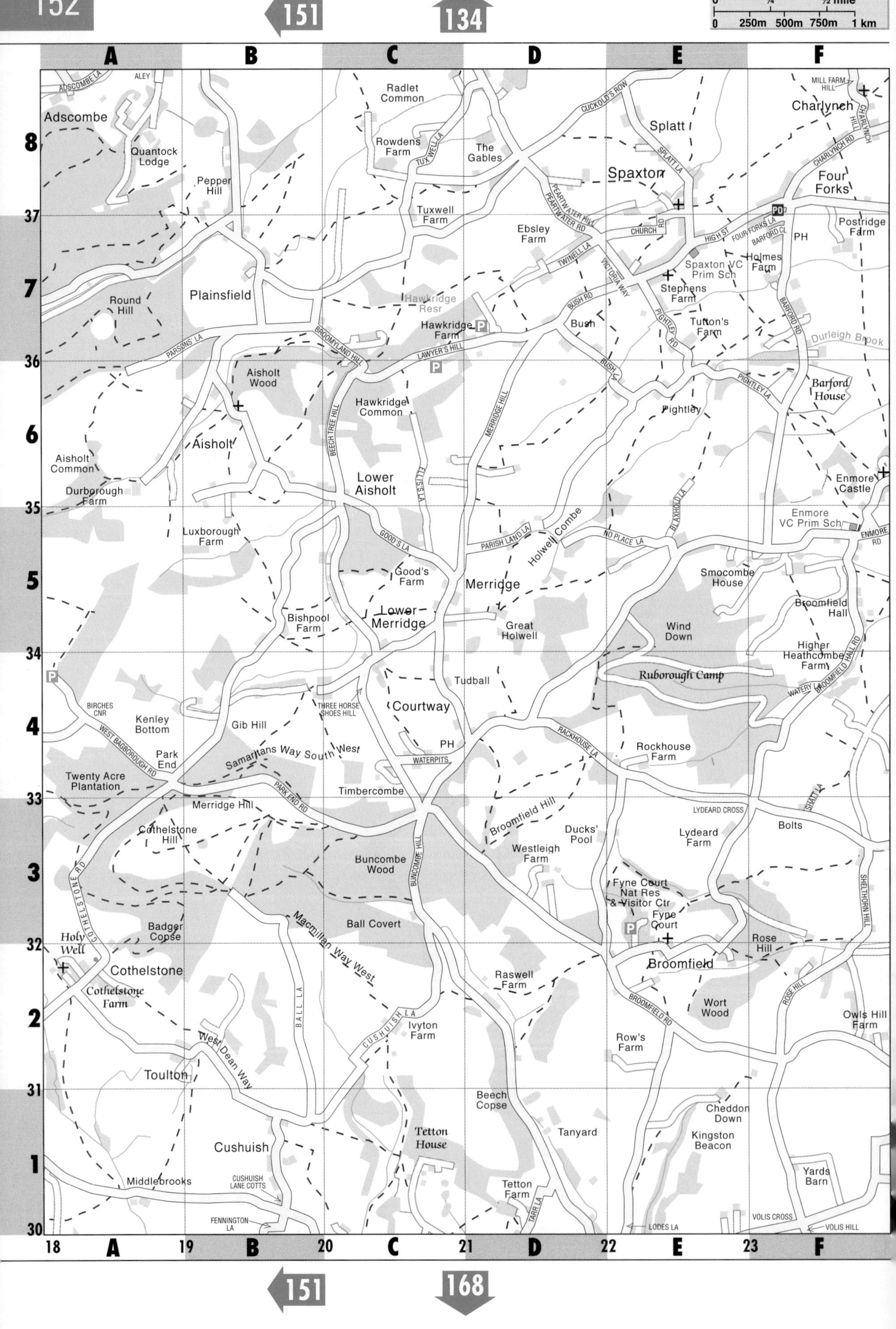
0
¼
½ mile
0
250m
500m
750m
1 km
A
B
C
D
E
F
Adscombe
Quantock Lodge
Pepper Hill
Radlet Common
Rowdens Farm
The Gables
Splatt
Spaxton
Charlynch
Four Forks
Postridge Farm
Tuxwell Farm
Ebsley Farm
Spaxton VC Prim Sch
Holmes Farm
Stephens Farm
Plainsfield
Round Hill
Hawkridge Resr
Hawkridge Farm
Bush
Tutton's Farm
Durleigh Brook
Aisholt Wood
Hawkridge Common
Pightley
Barford House
Aisholt
Aisholt Common
Durborough Farm
Lower Aisholt
Enmore Castle
Enmore VC Prim Sch
Luxborough Farm
Holwell Combe
Good's Farm
Merridge
Smocombe House
Broomfield Hall
Bishpool Farm
Lower Merridge
Great Holwell
Wind Down
Higher Heathcombe Farm
Ruborough Camp
Tudball
Courtway
Kenley Bottom
Gib Hill
Park End
Rockhouse Farm
Twenty Acre Plantation
Samaritans Way South West
Timbercombe
Merridge Hill
Cothelstone Hill
Broomfield Hill
Ducks' Pool
Lydeard Farm
Bolts
Westleigh Farm
Buncombe Wood
Fyne Court Nat Res & Visitor Ctr
Fyne Court
Ball Covert
Badger Copse
Macmillan Way West
Rose Hill
Holy Well
Cothelstone
Cothelstone Farm
Raswell Farm
Broomfield
Wort Wood
Owls Hill Farm
Ivyton Farm
Row's Farm
West Dean Way
Toulton
Beech Copse
Cheddon Down
Kingston Beacon
Tetton House
Tanyard
Cushuish
Middlebrooks
Tetton Farm
Yards Barn
ALEY
ADSCOMBE LA
MILL FARM HILL
CHARLYNCH HILL
CHARLYNCH RD
CUCKOLD'S ROW
SPLATT LA
TUXWELL LA
PEARTWATER HILL
PEARTWATER RD
CHURCH RD
HIGH ST
FOUR FORKS LA
BARFORD CL
TWINELL LA
VICTORIA WAY
BUSH RD
PIGHTLEY RD
BARFORD RD
PARSONS LA
BROOMYLAND HILL
LAWYER'S HILL
BUSH LA
PIGHTLEY LA
BEECH TREE HILL
MERRIDGE HILL
ELLIS'S LA
BLAXHOLD LA
GOOD'S LA
PARISH LAND LA
NO PLACE LA
ENMORE RD
WATERY LA
BROOMFIELD HALL RD
BIRCHES CNR
WEST BAGBOROUGH RD
THREE HORSE SHOES HILL
RACKHOUSE LA
WATERPITS
PARK END RD
LYDEARD CROSS
SHATT LA
COTHELSTONE RD
BUNCOMBE HILL
SHELTHORN HILL
BALL LA
CUSHUISH LA
BROOMFIELD RD
ROSE HILL
CUSHUISH LANE COTTS
FENNINGTON LA
TARR LA
LODES LA
VOLIS CROSS
VOLIS HILL
PH
P
PO
8
37
7
36
6
35
5
34
4
33
3
32
2
31
1
30
18
19
20
21
22
23

151
168

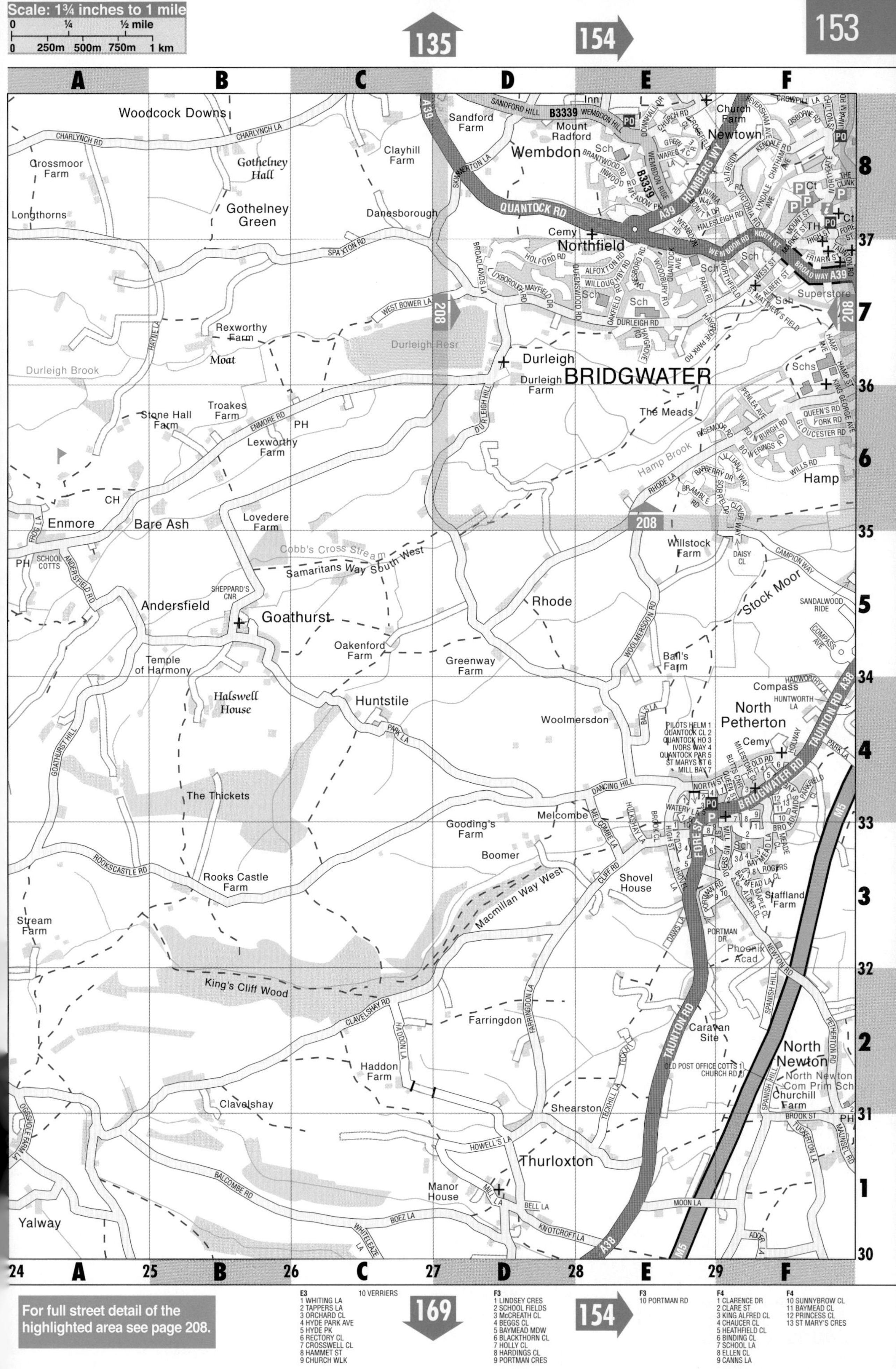
Scale: 1¾ inches to 1 mile
0 ¼ ½ mile
0 250m 500m 750m 1 km
135
154
Woodcock Downs
CHARLYNCH RD
CHARLYNCH LA
Crossmoor Farm
Longthorns
Gothelney Hall
Gothelney Green
Clayhill Farm
Danesborough
SPAXTON RD
Sandford Farm
Mount Radford
Wembdon
Newtown
Church Farm
QUANTOCK RD
Northfield
Cemy
Superstore
BROADWAY
A39
B3339
WEST BOWER LA
208
Rexworthy Farm
Moat
Durleigh Brook
Durleigh Resr
Durleigh
Durleigh Farm
BRIDGWATER
Stone Hall Farm
Troakes Farm
ENMORE RD
PH
Lexworthy Farm
The Meads
Hamp Brook
Hamp
RHODE LA
CH
Enmore
Bare Ash
Lovedere Farm
Cobb's Cross Stream
Samaritans Way South West
Willstock Farm
Stock Moor
CAMPION WAY
SCHOOL COTTS
ANDERSFIELD RD
Andersfield
SHEPPARD'S CNR
Goathurst
Rhode
WOOLMERSDON RD
Oakenford Farm
Greenway Farm
Ball's Farm
Temple of Harmony
Halswell House
Huntstile
PARK LA
Woolmersdon
Compass
North Petherton
HUNTWORTH LA
TAUNTON RD
A38
GOATHURST HILL
The Thickets
DANCING HILL
Melcombe
Gooding's Farm
Boomer
Macmillan Way West
Shovel House
Staffland Farm
ROOKSCASTLE RD
Rooks Castle Farm
Stream Farm
King's Cliff Wood
Phoenix Acad
CLAVELSHAY RD
Farringdon
FARRINGDON LA
HADDON LA
Haddon Farm
Caravan Site
North Newton
North Newton Com Prim Sch
Churchill Farm
Clavelshay
Shearston
HOWELL'S LA
Thurloxton
BALCOMBE RD
Manor House
MILL LA
BELL LA
MOON LA
Yalway
BOEZ LA
WHITELEAZE LA
KNOTCROFT LA
M5
ADDER LA
For full street detail of the highlighted area see page 208.
169
154
E3
1 WHITING LA
2 TAPPERS LA
3 ORCHARD CL
4 HYDE PARK AVE
5 HYDE PK
6 RECTORY CL
7 CROSSWELL CL
8 HAMMET ST
9 CHURCH WLK
10 VERRIERS
F3
1 LINDSEY CRES
2 SCHOOL FIELDS
3 McCREATH CL
4 BEGGS CL
5 BAYMEAD MDW
6 BLACKTHORN CL
7 HOLLY CL
8 HARDINGS CL
9 PORTMAN CRES
F3
10 PORTMAN RD
F4
1 CLARENCE DR
2 CLARE ST
3 KING ALFRED CL
4 CHAUCER CL
5 HEATHFIELD CL
6 BINDING CL
7 SCHOOL LA
8 ELLEN CL
9 CANNS LA
F4
10 SUNNYBROW CL
11 BAYMEAD CL
12 PRINCESS CL
13 ST MARY'S CRES

153
136

Scale: 1¾ inches to 1 mile
0 ¼ ½ mile
0 250m 500m 750m 1 km

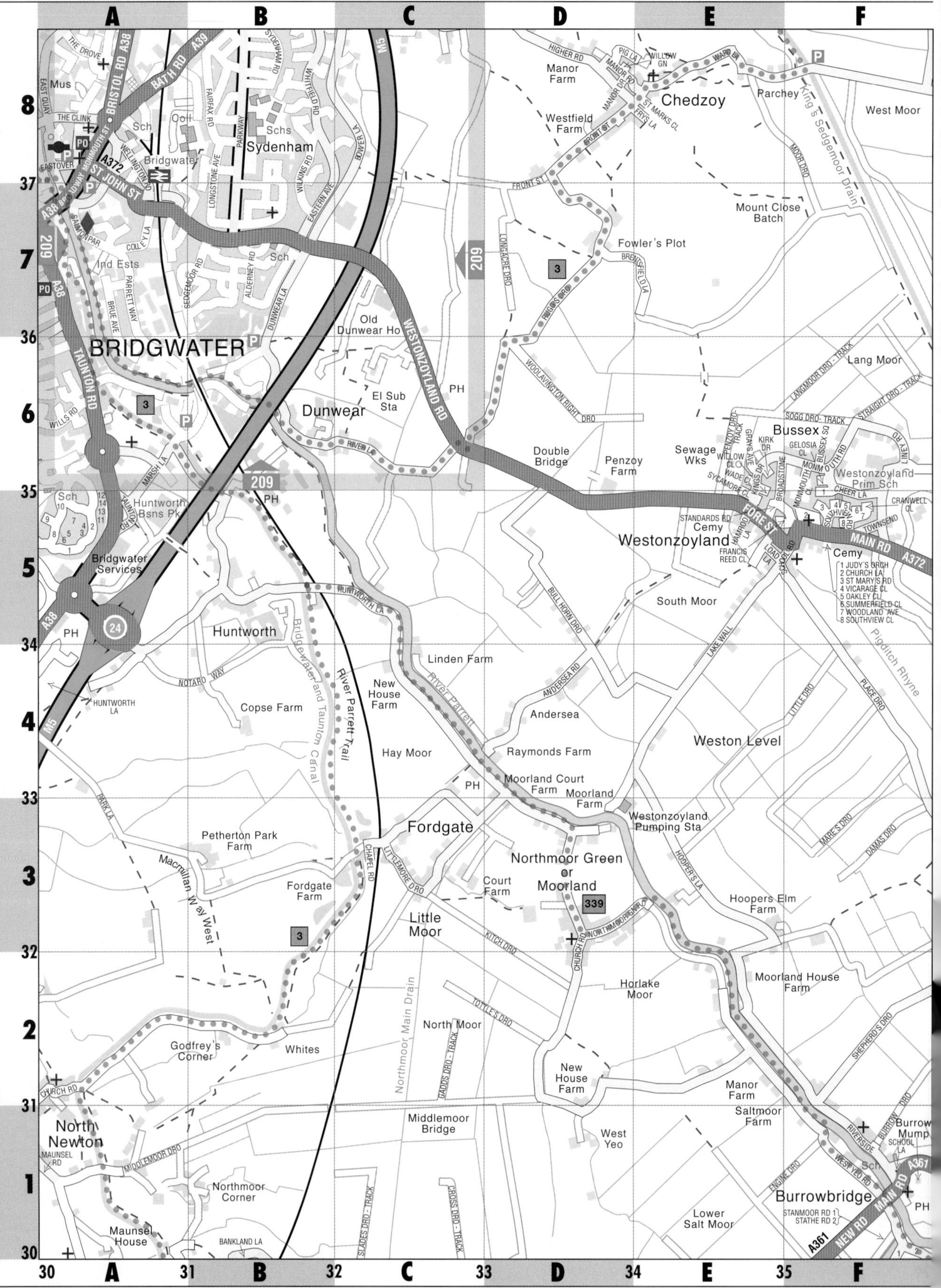

For full street detail of the highlighted area see page 209
153
170

A5
1 MUSCOVY DR
2 ROMNEY RD
3 SAVANNAH DR
4 VIENNA WAY
5 TUNDRA WALK
6 CHEVIOT ST
7 MERINO WAY
8 CHAROLAIS DR
9 TEESWATER WAY
10 STOCKMOOR DR
11 CHAMBRAY RD
12 ANGUS WAY
13 SHIRE ST
14 CHILLINGHAM DRO

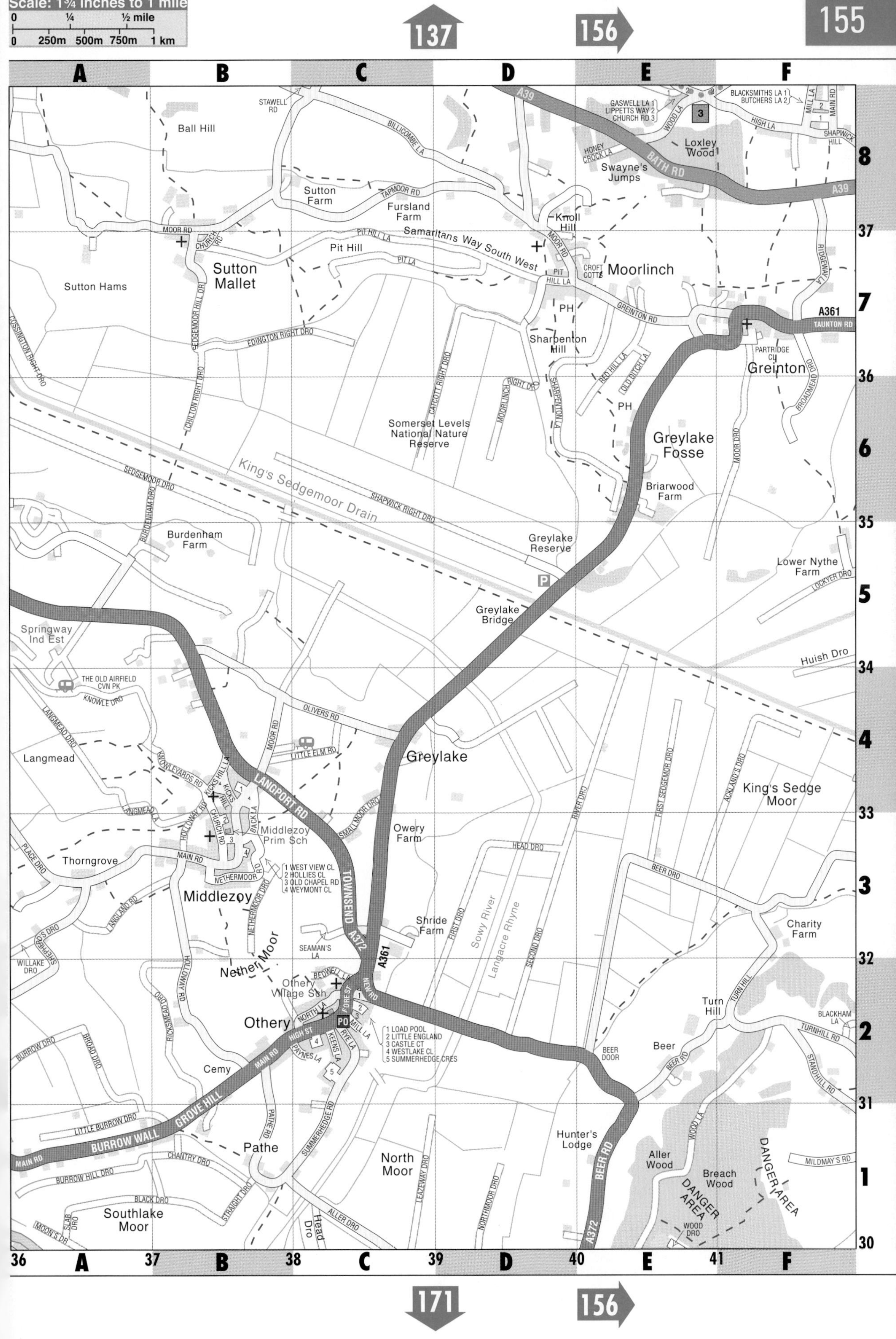

Scale: 1¾ inches to 1 mile
0 ¼ ½ mile
0 250m 500m 750m 1 km
137
156
Sutton Mallet
Moorlinch
Greinton
Greylake Fosse
Greylake
King's Sedge Moor
Middlezoy
Othery
Nether Moor
Pathe
Southlake Moor
North Moor
Thorngrove
Langmead
Sutton Hams
Ball Hill
Pit Hill
Sutton Farm
Fursland Farm
Swayne's Jumps
Loxley Wood
Knoll Hill
Sharpenton Hill
Somerset Levels National Nature Reserve
King's Sedgemoor Drain
Burdenham Farm
Greylake Reserve
Greylake Bridge
Briarwood Farm
Lower Nythe Farm
Springway Ind Est
THE OLD AIRFIELD CVN PK
Owery Farm
Shride Farm
Charity Farm
Turn Hill
Beer
Hunter's Lodge
Aller Wood
Breach Wood
DANGER AREA
Samaritans Way South West
Middlezoy Prim Sch
Othery Village Sch
Cemy
1 WEST VIEW CL
2 HOLLIES CL
3 OLD CHAPEL RD
4 WEYMONT CL
1 LOAD POOL
2 LITTLE ENGLAND
3 CASTLE CT
4 WESTLAKE CL
5 SUMMERHEDGE CRES
GASWELL LA 1
LIPPETTS WAY 2
CHURCH RD 3
BLACKSMITHS LA 1
BUTCHERS LA 2
A39
A361
A372
BATH RD
LANGPORT RD
TOWNSEND
BURROW WALL
GROVE HILL
BEER RD
171
156

155
138

Scale: 1¾ inches to 1 mile
0 ¼ ½ mile
0 250m 500m 750m 1 km

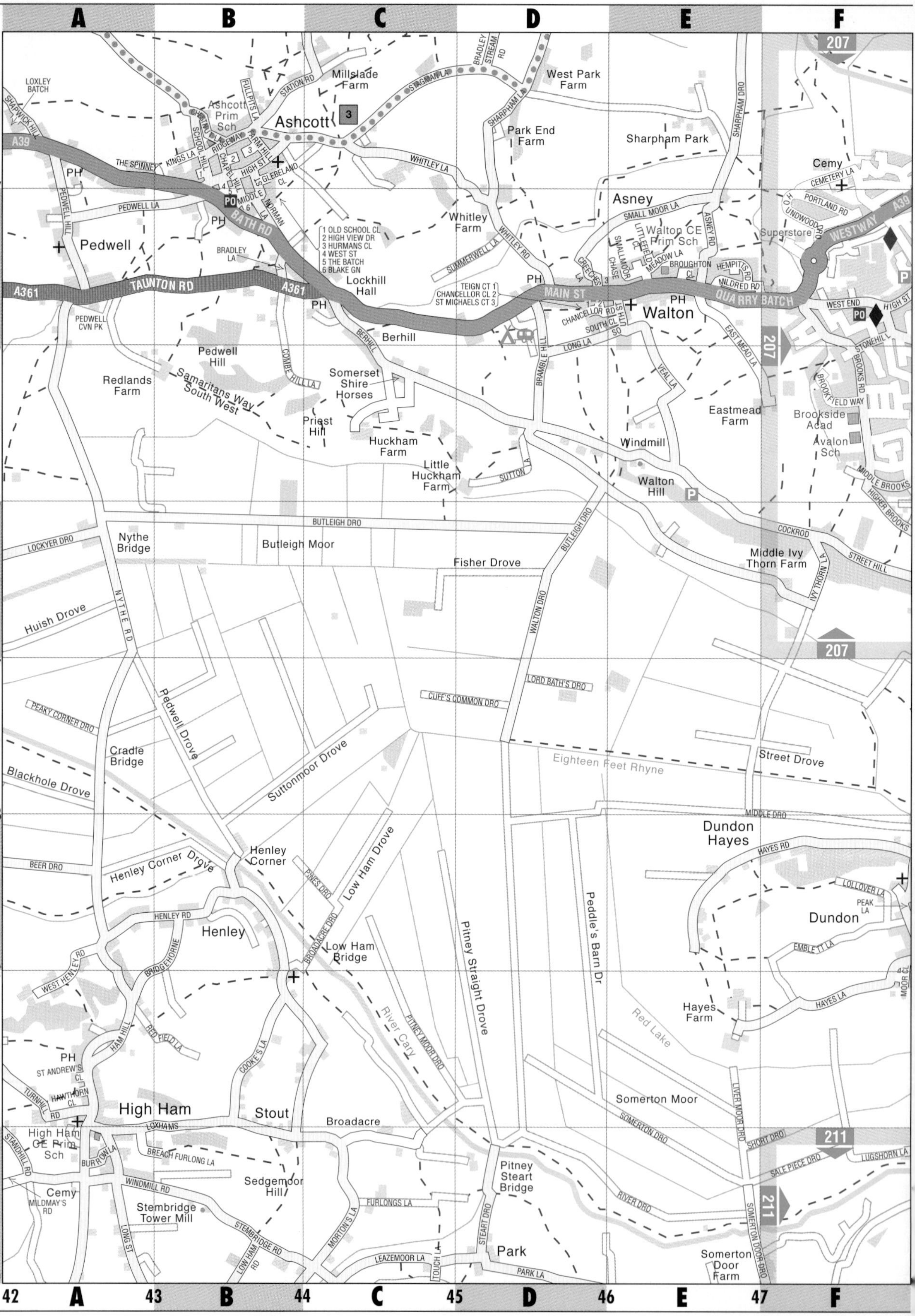
A B C D E F
8
37
7
36
6
35
5
34
4
33
3
32
2
31
1
30
42 A 43 B 44 C 45 D 46 E 47 F
207
211
LOXLEY BATCH
SHAPWICK HILL
A39
Ashcott Prim Sch
Ashcott
STATION RD
Millslade Farm
FULLPITS LA
STAGMAN LA
BRADLEY STREAM RD
West Park Farm
SHARPHAM LA
Park End Farm
Sharpham Park
SHARPHAM DRO
THE SPINNEY
KINGS LA
SCHOOL HILL
RIDGEWAY
CHAPEL HILL
HIGH ST
GLEBELAND CL
MIDDLE ST
NORMAN LA
WHITLEY LA
PH
PEDWELL HILL
PEDWELL LA
PO
BATH RD
Pedwell
BRADLEY LA
1 OLD SCHOOL CL
2 HIGH VIEW DR
3 HURMANS CL
4 WEST ST
5 THE BATCH
6 BLAKE GN
Lockhill Hall
Whitley Farm
WHITLEY RD
SUMMERWELL LA
Asney
SMALL MOOR LA
Walton CE Prim Sch
LITTLEFIELD CL
SMALLMOOR CHASE
MEADOW LA
BROUGHTON CL
ASNEY RD
HEMPITTS RD
MILDRED RD
Cemy
CEMETERY LA
PORTLAND RD
UNDWOOD DR
Superstore
WESTWAY
A361
TAUNTON RD
TEIGN CT 1
CHANCELLOR CL 2
ST MICHAELS CT 3
MAIN ST
CHANCELLOR RD
SOUTH CL
LONG LA
Walton
QUARRY BATCH
WEST END
HIGH ST
PEDWELL CVN PK
Berhill
BRAMBLE HILL
VEALLA
EAST MEAD LA
STONEHILL
BROOKS RD
BROOKFIELD WAY
Redlands Farm
Pedwell Hill
Samaritans Way South West
COMBE HILL LA
Somerset Shire Horses
Priest Hill
Huckham Farm
Little Huckham Farm
SUTTON LA
Windmill
Eastmead Farm
Brookside Acad
Avalon Sch
Walton Hill
MIDDLE BROOKS
HIGHER BROOKS
BUTLEIGH DRO
COCKROD
LOCKYER DRO
Nythe Bridge
Butleigh Moor
Fisher Drove
Middle Ivy Thorn Farm
IVY THORN LA
STREET HILL
Huish Drove
NYTHE RD
WALTON DRO
LORD BATH'S DRO
CUFF'S COMMON DRO
PEAKY CORNER DRO
Pedwell Drove
Cradle Bridge
Suttonmoor Drove
Street Drove
Eighteen Feet Rhyne
Blackhole Drove
MIDDLE DRO
Dundon Hayes
HAYES RD
Henley Corner
Low Ham Drove
BEER DRO
Henley Corner Drove
PINES DRO
LOLLOVER LA
PEAK LA
Dundon
HENLEY RD
Henley
BROADACRE DRO
Low Ham Bridge
Pitney Straight Drove
Peddle's Barn Dr
EMBLETT LA
WEST HENLEY RD
BRIDGEHORNE
River Cary
PITNEY MOOR DRO
Red Lake
Hayes Farm
HAYES LA
MOOR LA
HAM HILL
RED FIELD LA
COOKE'S LA
PH
ST ANDREW'S CL
HAWTHORN CL
TURNHILL RD
High Ham
Stout
Broadacre
Somerton Moor
SOMERTON DRO
LIVER MOOR DRO
SHORT DRO
High Ham CE Prim Sch
LOXHAMS
STANDHILL RD
BURROW LA
BREACH FURLONG LA
Pitney Steart Bridge
SALE PIECE DRO
LUGSHORN LA
Cemy
MILDMAY'S RD
WINDMILL RD
Sedgemoor Hill
FURLONGS LA
RIVER DRO
Stembridge Tower Mill
STEMBRIDGE RD
LONG ST
LOW HAM RD
MORTON'S LA
STEART DRO
LEAZEMOOR LA
TOUCH LA
Park
PARK LA
SOMERTON DOOR DRO
Somerton Door Farm

155
172

For full street detail of the highlighted area see pages 207 and 211.

Scale: 1¾ inches to 1 mile

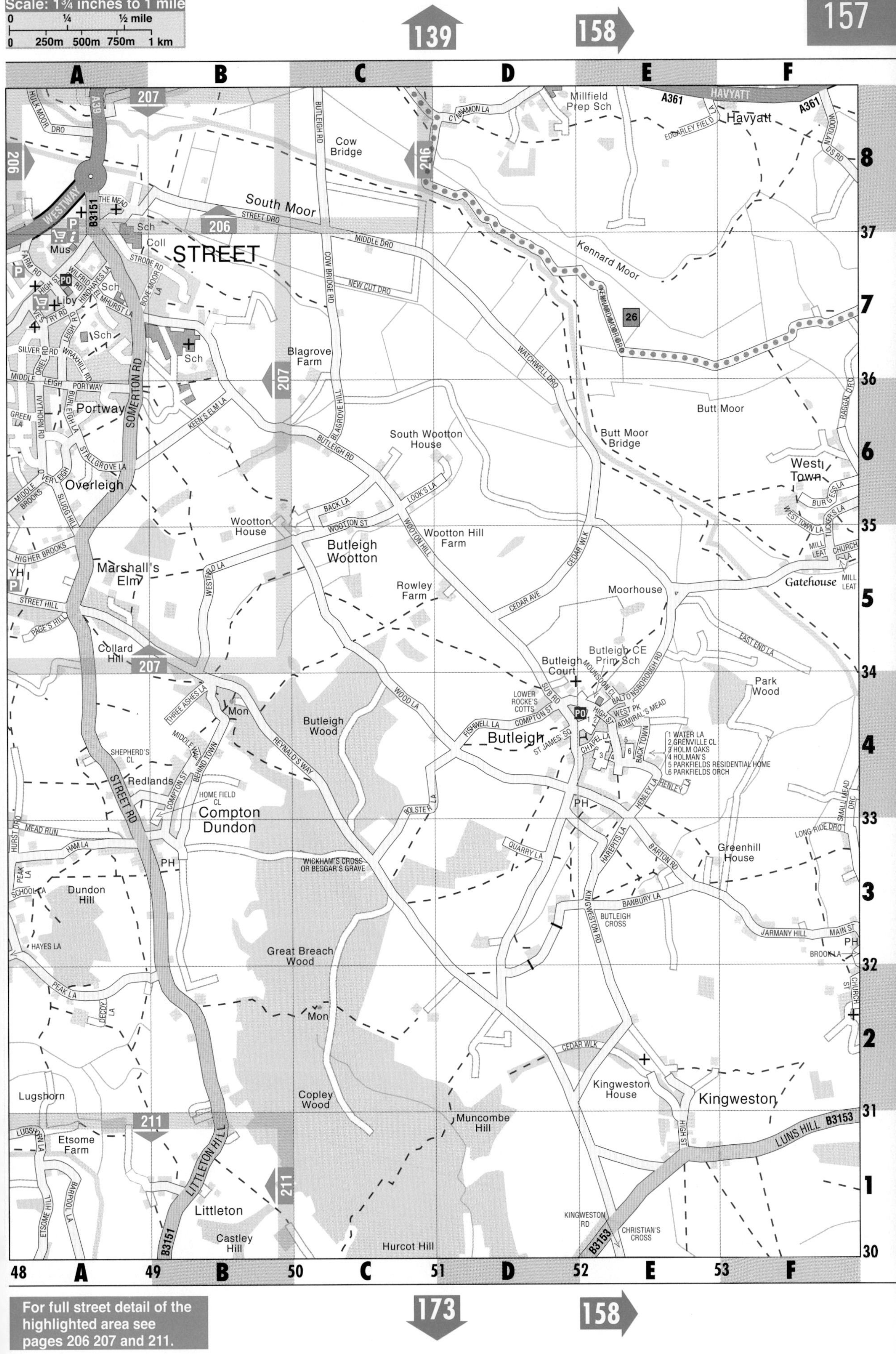

139
158
173
158
For full street detail of the highlighted area see pages 206 207 and 211.

157
140

Scale: 1¾ inches to 1 mile
0 ¼ ½ mile
0 250m 500m 750m 1 km

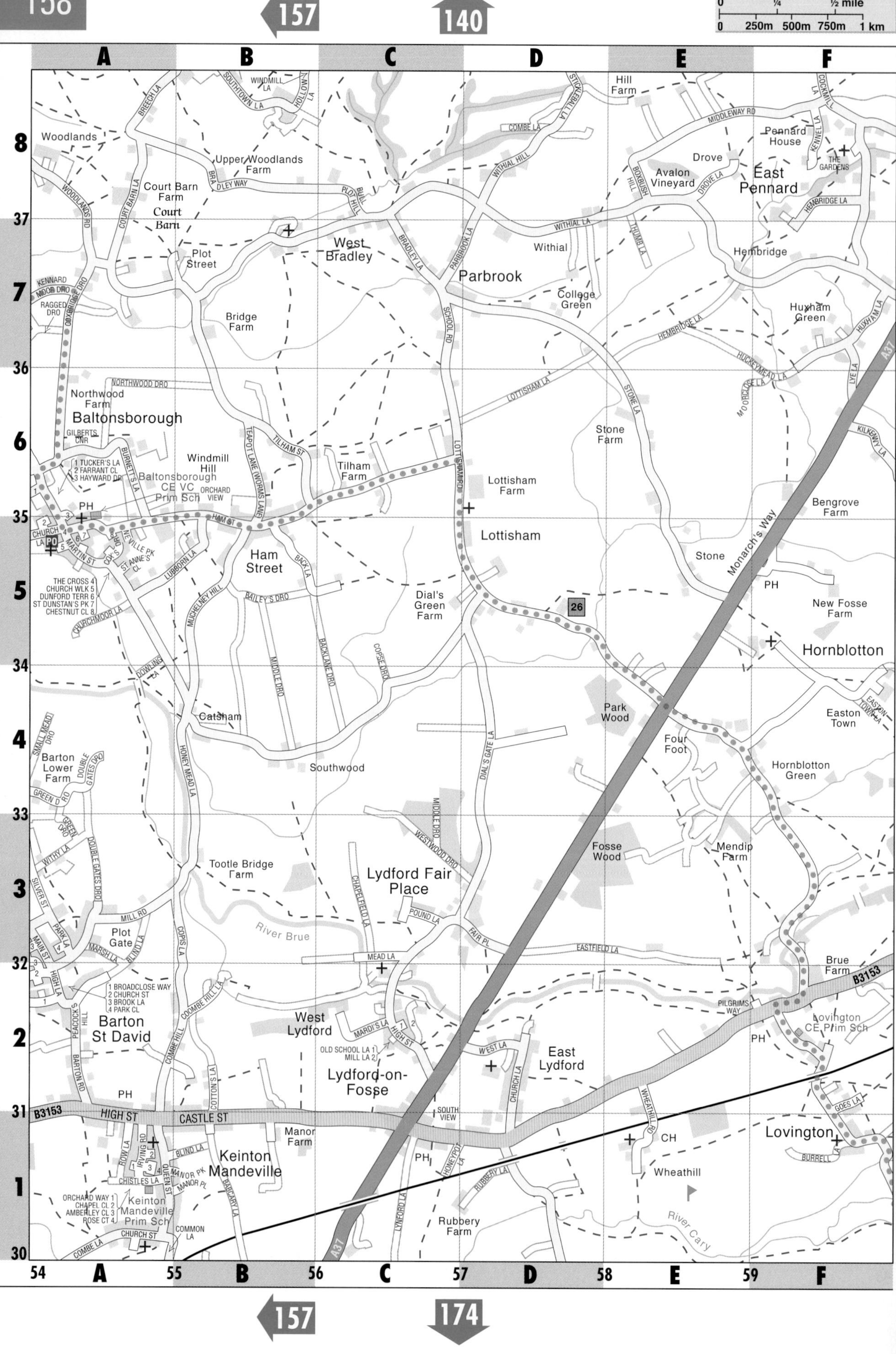

157
174

141
160

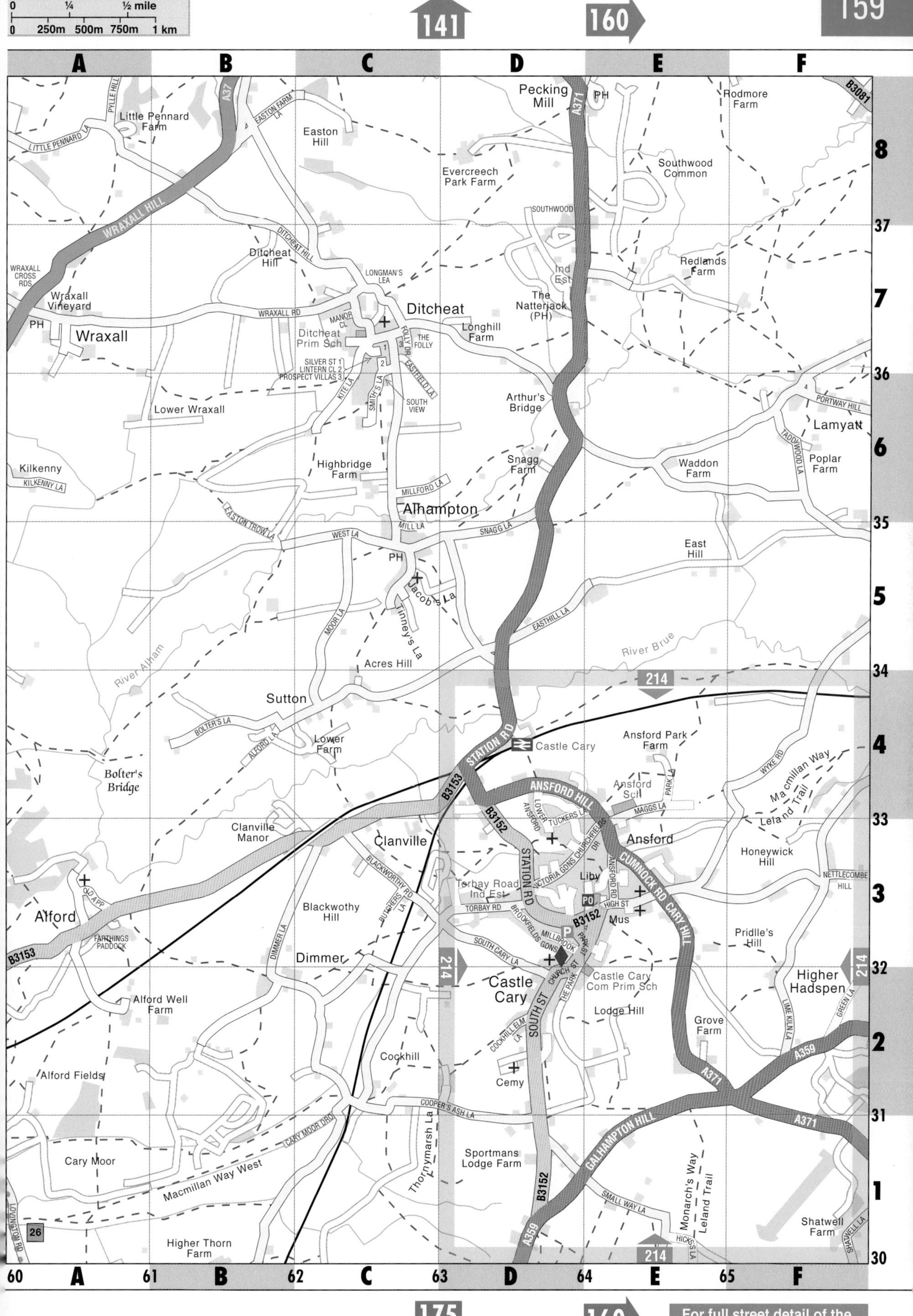

175
160
For full street detail of the highlighted area see page 214.

159
142

Scale: 1¾ inches to 1 mile
0 ¼ ½ mile
0 250m 500m 750m 1 km

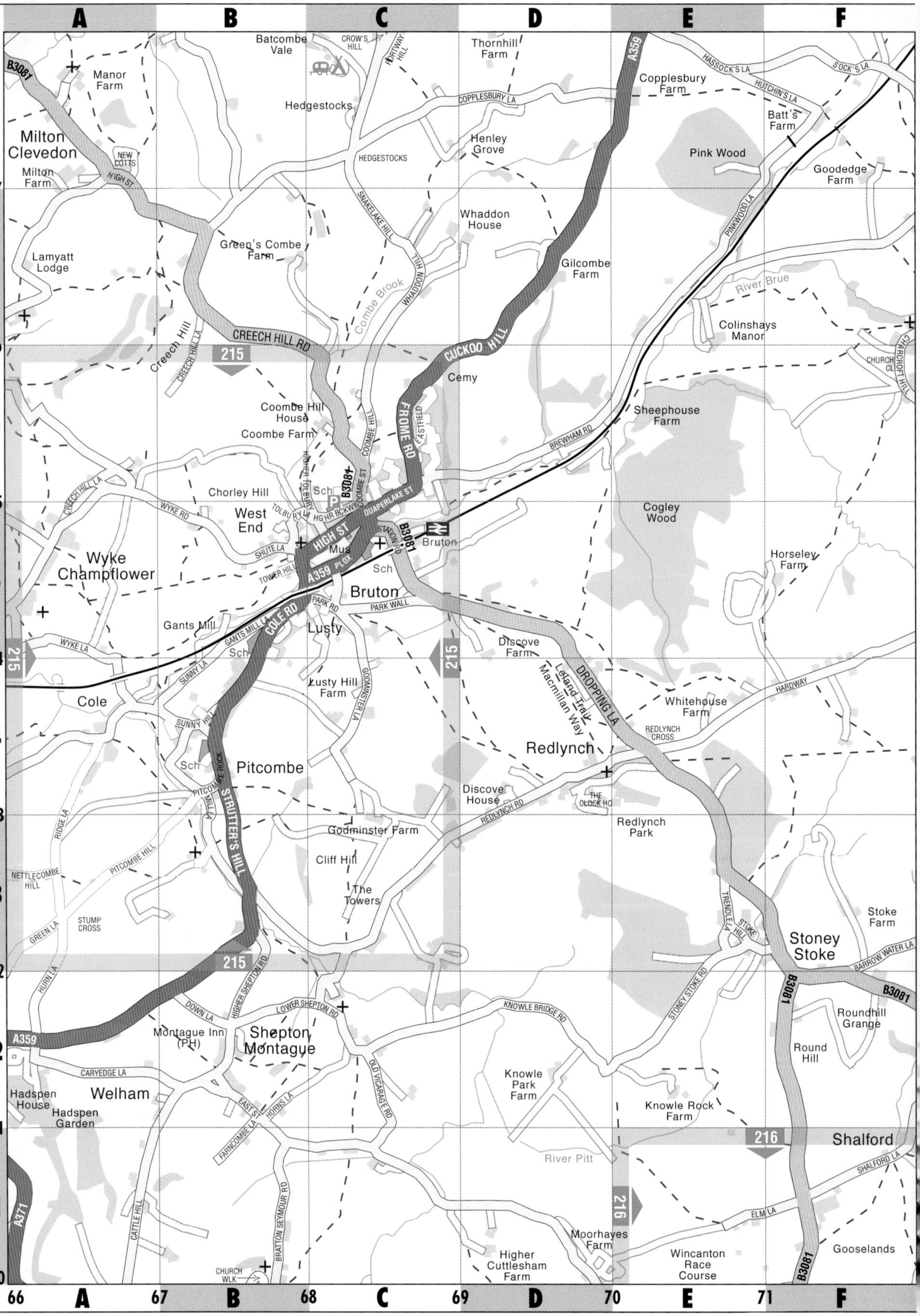

A B C D E F

Batcombe Vale
CROW'S HILL
FORTWAY HILL
Thornhill Farm
Manor Farm
B3081
A359
Copplesbury Farm
HASSOCK'S LA
SOCK'S LA
HUTCHIN'S LA
Hedgestocks
COPPLESBURY LA
Batt's Farm
Milton Clevedon
NEW COTTS
Henley Grove
Pink Wood
Milton Farm
HIGH ST
HEDGESTOCKS
Goodedge Farm
SNAKELAKE HILL
Whaddon House
PINKWOOD LA
Lamyatt Lodge
Green's Combe Farm
WHADDON HILL
Gilcombe Farm
Combe Brook
River Brue
Colinshays Manor
CREECH HILL RD
Creech Hill
CREECH HILL LA
CUCKOO HILL
CHURCH CL
CHURCROFT HILL
Cemy
Coombe Hill House
FROME RD
EASTFIELD
Sheephouse Farm
Coombe Farm
COOMBE HILL
HIGHER TOLBURY LA
BREWHAM RD
CREECH HILL LA
Chorley Hill
Sch
B3081
COOMBE ST
WYKE RD
West End
TOLBURY LA
HIGHER BCKWY
QUAPERLAKE ST
Cogley Wood
HIGH ST
STATION RD
B3081
Bruton
Wyke Champflower
SHUTE LA
Mus
PLOX
Sch
Horseley Farm
TOWER HILL
A359
Bruton
PARK RD
PARK WALL
Gants Mill
COLE RD
Lusty
GANTS MILL LA
Discove Farm
WYKE LA
Sch
DROPPING LA
SUNNY LA
Lusty Hill Farm
GODMINSTER LA
Leland Trail
Macmillan Way
Whitehouse Farm
HARDWAY
Cole
SUNNY HILL
REDLYNCH CROSS
Redlynch
Sch
Pitcombe
PITCOMBE ROCK
Discove House
THE CLOCK HO
PITCOMBE HILL
STRUTTER'S HILL
REDLYNCH RD
Redlynch Park
RIDGE LA
Godminster Farm
Cliff Hill
PITCOMBE HILL
NETTLECOMBE HILL
The Towers
TRENDLE LA
STOKE HILL
Stoke Farm
STUMP CROSS
GREEN LA
Stoney Stoke
BARROW WATER LA
HURN LA
HIGHER SHEPTON RD
STONEY STOKE RD
B3081
B3081
DOWN LA
LOWER SHEPTON RD
KNOWLE BRIDGE RD
Roundhill Grange
A359
Montague Inn (PH)
Shepton Montague
Round Hill
CARYEDGE LA
OLD VICARAGE RD
Knowle Park Farm
Hadspen House
Welham
Hadspen Garden
EAST ST
HORNS LA
Knowle Rock Farm
FARNCOMBE LA
Shalford
River Pitt
SHALFORD LA
A371
BRATTON SEYMOUR RD
ELM LA
CATTLE HILL
Moorhayes Farm
Wincanton Race Course
Gooselands
Higher Cuttlesham Farm
CHURCH WLK
B3081

Grid numbers: 8, 37, 7, 36, 6, 35, 5, 34, 4, 33, 3, 32, 2, 31, 1, 30
66 A 67 B 68 C 69 D 70 E 71 F

215
215
215
215
216
216

For full street detail of the highlighted area see pages 215 and 216.

159
176

Scale: 1¾ inches to 1 mile

143

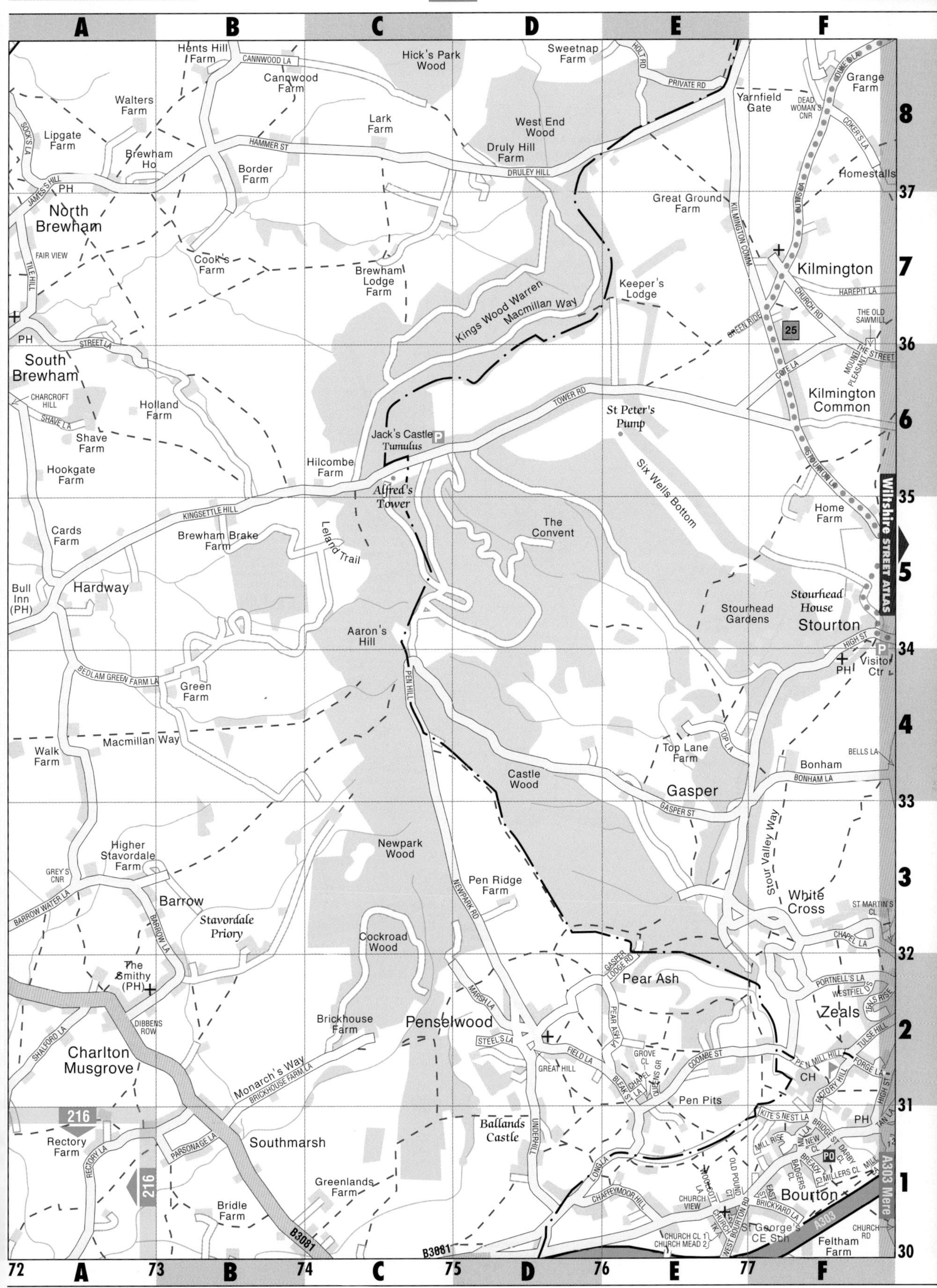

216

F1
1 SILTON RD
2 THE MEADOWS

For full street detail of the highlighted area see page 216.

177

146

Scale: 1¾ inches to 1 mile
0 ¼ ½ mile
0 250m 500m 750m 1 km

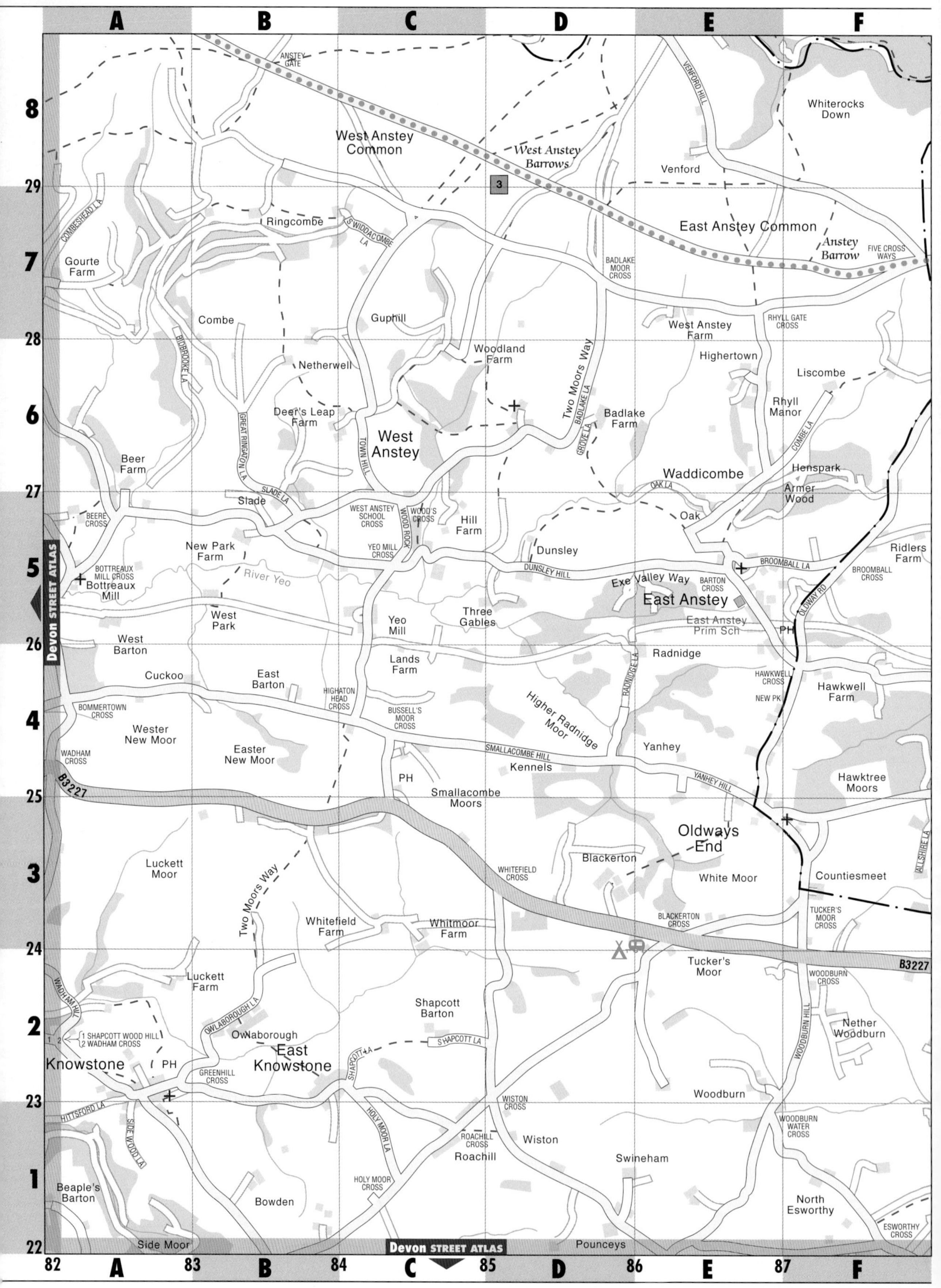

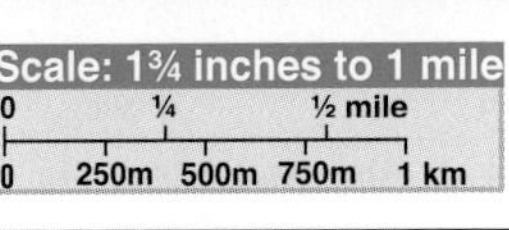

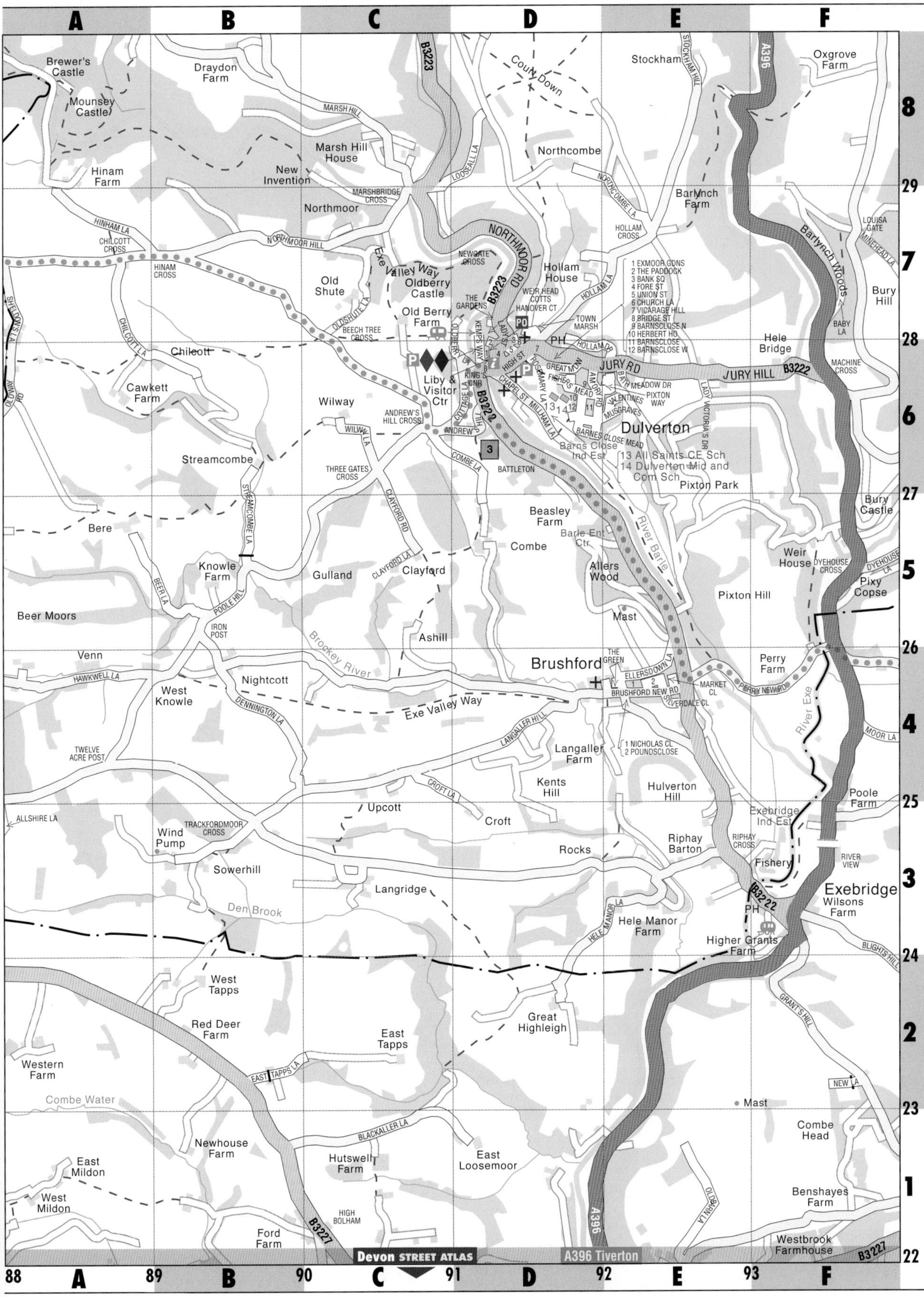

147
164

A B C D E F

8
Brewer's Castle
Draydon Farm
Stockham
STOCKHAM HILL
Oxgrove Farm
Mounsey Castle
MARSH HILL
Court Down
A396
B3223
Marsh Hill House
Northcombe
Hinam Farm
New Invention
LOOSEALL LA
29
NORTHCOMBE LA
Barlynch Farm
MARSHBRIDGE CROSS
Northmoor
HINHAM LA
NORTHMOOR RD
HOLLAM CROSS
LOUISA GATE
CHILCOTT CROSS
NORTHMOOR HILL
NEWGATE CROSS
Barlynch Woods
MINEHEAD LA
7
HINAM CROSS
Exe Valley Way
Old Shute
Oldberry Castle
Hollam House
1 EXMOOR GDNS
2 THE PADDOCK
3 BANK SQ
4 FORE ST
5 UNION ST
6 CHURCH LA
7 VICARAGE HILL
8 BRIDGE ST
9 BARNSCLOSE N
10 HERBERT HO
11 BARNSCLOSE
12 BARNSCLOSE W
Bury Hill
WEIR HEAD COTTS
THE GARDENS
HANOVER CT
HOLLAM LA
SHELDON'S LA
OLDSHUTE LA
Old Berry Farm
PO
TOWN MARSH
BABY LA
CHILCOTT LA
BEECH TREE CROSS
OLDBERRY LA
KEMPS WAY
LADY ST
PH
HOLLAM DR
Hele Bridge
28
Chilcott
HIGH ST
JURY RD
JURY HILL
B3222
MACHINE CROSS
GREAT MDW
FISHERS MEAD
BATH MEADOW DR
P
Liby & Visitor Ctr
KING GDNS
COTTAGE LA
CHAPEL ST
ROSEMARY LA
AMORY RD
LADY VICTORIA'S DR
Cawkett Farm
Wilway
VALENTINES
PIXTON WAY
MILLHAM LA
MUSGRAVES
ANDREW'S HILL CROSS
ANDREW HILL
6
WILWAY LA
BARNES CLOSE MEAD
Dulverton
Barns Close Ind Est
13 All Saints CE Sch
14 Dulverton Mid and Com Sch
Streamcombe
COMBE LA
BATTLETON
THREE GATES CROSS
Pixton Park
STREAMCOMBE LA
CLAYFORD RD
27
Bury Castle
Beasley Farm
Bere
Barle Ent Ctr
Combe
River Barle
Weir House
DYEHOUSE CROSS
DYEHOUSE LA
Knowle Farm
Gulland
CLAYFORD LA
Clayford
Allers Wood
5
Pixy Copse
Pixton Hill
BEER LA
POOLE HILL
Beer Moors
IRON POST
Mast
Ashill
Brockey River
26
Venn
THE GREEN
Perry Farm
Brushford
ELLERSDOWN LA
HAWKWELL LA
Nightcott
MARKET CL
PERRY NEW RD
West Knowle
BRUSHFORD NEW RD
SILVERDALE CL
River Exe
DENNINGTON LA
Exe Valley Way
LANGALLER HILL
4
MOOR LA
1 NICHOLAS CL
2 POUNDSCLOSE
TWELVE ACRE POST
Langaller Farm
Kents Hill
Hulverton Hill
CROFT LA
Poole Farm
25
ALLSHIRE LA
Upcott
Exebridge Ind Est
TRACKFORDMOOR CROSS
Croft
Wind Pump
Riphay Barton
RIPHAY CROSS
RIVER VIEW
Rocks
Sowerhill
Fishery
3
Exebridge
Langridge
Wilsons Farm
Den Brook
HELE MANOR LA
Hele Manor Farm
Higher Grants Farm
BLIGHTS HILL
24
West Tapps
GRANT'S HILL
Red Deer Farm
Great Highleigh
2
East Tapps
Western Farm
EAST TAPPS LA
NEW LA
Combe Water
Mast
23
Combe Head
BLACKALLER LA
Newhouse Farm
East Mildon
Hutswell Farm
East Loosemoor
1
West Mildon
OLDBARN LA
Benshayes Farm
HIGH BOLHAM
A396
B3227
Ford Farm
Westbrook Farmhouse
22

88 A 89 B 90 C 91 D 92 E 93 F

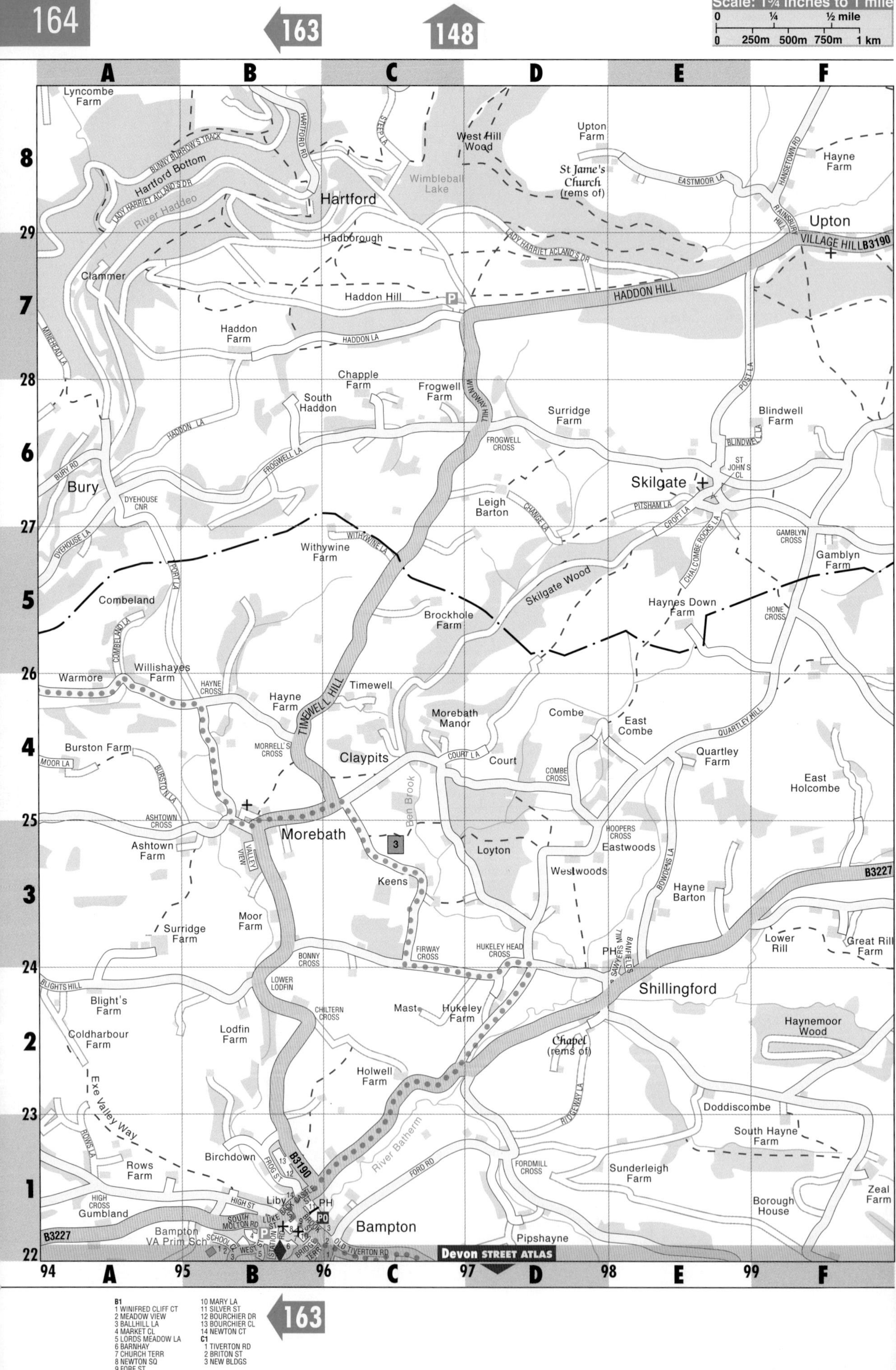
163
148
Scale: 1¾ inches to 1 mile
0
¼
½ mile
0
250m
500m
750m
1 km
A
B
C
D
E
F
8
29
7
28
6
27
5
26
4
25
3
24
2
23
1
22
94
95
96
97
98
99
Lyncombe Farm
Hartford Bottom
BUNNY BURROW'S TRACK
LADY HARRIET ACLAND'S DR
River Haddeo
HARTFORD RD
STEEP LA
Hartford
West Hill Wood
Wimbleball Lake
Upton Farm
St James's Church (rems of)
EASTMOOR LA
HANSETOWN RD
Hayne Farm
RAINSBURY HILL
Upton
VILLAGE HILL
B3190
Hadborough
LADY HARRIET ACLAND'S DR
Clammer
Haddon Hill
P
HADDON HILL
MINEHEAD LA
Haddon Farm
HADDON LA
Chapple Farm
Frogwell Farm
WINDWAY HILL
POST LA
South Haddon
HADDON LA
Surridge Farm
Blindwell Farm
BLINDWELL LA
FROGWELL CROSS
FROGWELL LA
BURY RD
Bury
ST JOHN'S CL
Skilgate
DYEHOUSE CNR
Leigh Barton
CHANGE LA
PITSHAM LA
CROFT LA
CHALCOMBE ROCKS LA
GAMBLYN CROSS
DYEHOUSE LA
WITHYWINE LA
Withywine Farm
Gamblyn Farm
PORT LA
Skilgate Wood
Combeland
Haynes Down Farm
Brockhole Farm
HONE CROSS
COMBELAND LA
26
Warmore
Willishayes Farm
Timewell
HAYNE CROSS
Hayne Farm
TIMEWELL HILL
Morebath Manor
Combe
East Combe
QUARTLEY HILL
Burston Farm
MORRELL'S CROSS
Claypits
COURT LA
Court
Quartley Farm
MOOR LA
BURSTON LA
Ben Brook
COMBE CROSS
East Holcombe
ASHTOWN CROSS
HOOPERS CROSS
Ashtown Farm
VALLEY VIEW
Morebath
3
Loyton
Eastwoods
BOWDENS LA
Westwoods
B3227
Keens
Hayne Barton
Moor Farm
Surridge Farm
SAWYERS MILL
BANFIELDS
Lower Rill
Great Rill Farm
FIRWAY CROSS
HUKELEY HEAD CROSS
PH
BONNY CROSS
BLIGHTS HILL
LOWER LODFIN
Shillingford
Blight's Farm
CHILTERN CROSS
Mast
Hukeley Farm
Haynemoor Wood
Coldharbour Farm
Lodfin Farm
Chapel (rems of)
Holwell Farm
Exe Valley Way
RIDGEWAY LA
Doddiscombe
ROWS LA
River Batherm
South Hayne Farm
Birchdown
FROG ST
B3190
FORD RD
Rows Farm
FORDMILL CROSS
Sunderleigh Farm
Zeal Farm
HIGH CROSS
HIGH ST
Liby
CASTLE ST
PH
Borough House
Gumbland
SOUTH MOLTON RD
LUKE ST
BROOK ST
PO
Bampton
B3227
Bampton VA Prim Sch
SCHOOL CL
WEST ST
STATION RD
BRIDGE TERR
OLD TIVERTON RD
Pipshayne
Devon STREET ATLAS
B1
1 WINIFRED CLIFF CT
2 MEADOW VIEW
3 BALLHILL LA
4 MARKET CL
5 LORDS MEADOW LA
6 BARNHAY
7 CHURCH TERR
8 NEWTON SQ
9 FORE ST
10 MARY LA
11 SILVER ST
12 BOURCHIER DR
13 BOURCHIER CL
14 NEWTON CT
C1
1 TIVERTON RD
2 BRITON ST
3 NEW BLDGS
163

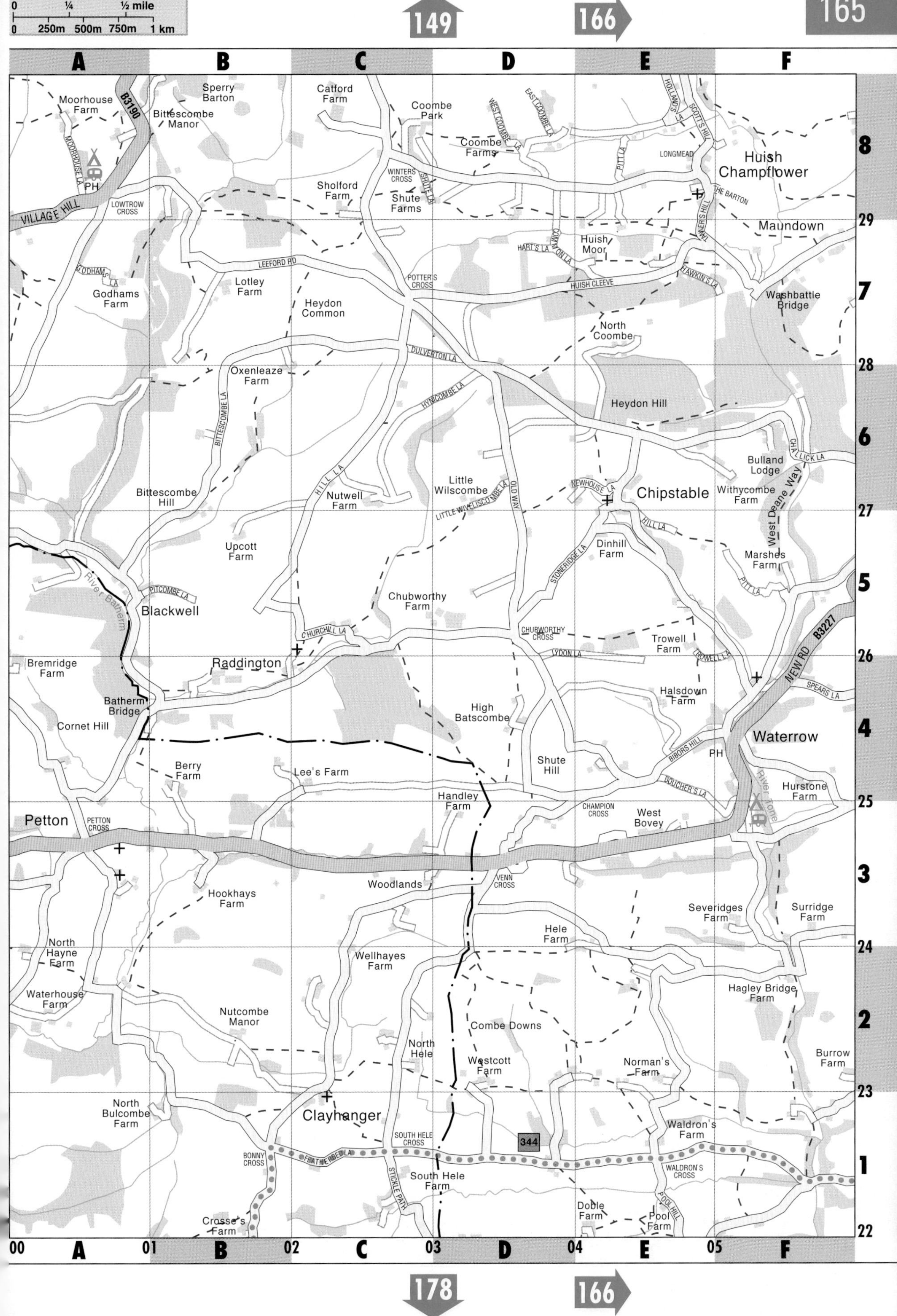
Scale: 1¾ inches to 1 mile
0 ¼ ½ mile
0 250m 500m 750m 1 km
149
166
A B C D E F
Moorhouse Farm
Sperry Barton
Bittescombe Manor
Catford Farm
Coombe Park
Coombe Farms
Huish Champflower
Maundown
Sholford Farm
Shute Farms
Winters Cross
Lowtrow Cross
Village Hill
Godhams Farm
Lotley Farm
Leeford Rd
Heydon Common
Potter's Cross
Huish Moor
Huish Cleeve
Washbattle Bridge
North Coombe
Oxenleaze Farm
Dulverton La
Hyncombe La
Heydon Hill
Bittescombe La
Bittescombe Hill
Nutwell Farm
Little Wilscombe
Old Way
Chipstable
Withycombe Farm
Bulland Lodge
Challick La
West Deane Way
Upcott Farm
Dinhill Farm
Hill La
Stoneridge La
Marshes Farm
Pitt La
Blackwell
Pitcombe La
River Batherm
Chubworthy Farm
Churchill La
Chubworthy Cross
Trowell Farm
Trowell La
Lydon La
Raddington
Bremridge Farm
Batherm Bridge
Cornet Hill
High Batscombe
Halsdown Farm
New Rd
B3227
Spears La
Waterrow
PH
Berry Farm
Lee's Farm
Shute Hill
Bibors Hill
Boucher's La
River Tone
Hurstone Farm
Petton
Petton Cross
Handley Farm
Champion Cross
West Bovey
Hookhays Farm
Woodlands
Venn Cross
Severidges Farm
Surridge Farm
Hele Farm
North Hayne Farm
Wellhayes Farm
Hagley Bridge Farm
Waterhouse Farm
Nutcombe Manor
Combe Downs
North Hele
Westcott Farm
Norman's Farm
Burrow Farm
North Bulcombe Farm
Clayhanger
South Hele Cross
Waldron's Farm
344
Bonny Cross
Featherbed La
Waldron's Cross
South Hele Farm
Stickle Path
Pool Hill
Crosse's Farm
Doble Farm
Pool Farm
Longmead
The Barton
Tanner's Hill
Scott's Hill
Holland's La
Pitt La
Common La
Hart's La
Hawkin's La
West Coombe La
East Coombe La
Shute La
Godhams La
Moorhouse La
B3190
Newhouse La
Little Wiveliscombe La
Hill La
8 29 7 28 6 27 5 26 4 25 3 24 2 23 1 22
00 01 02 03 04 05
178
166

165
150

Scale: 1¾ inches to 1 mile
0 ¼ ½ mile
0 250m 500m 750m 1 km

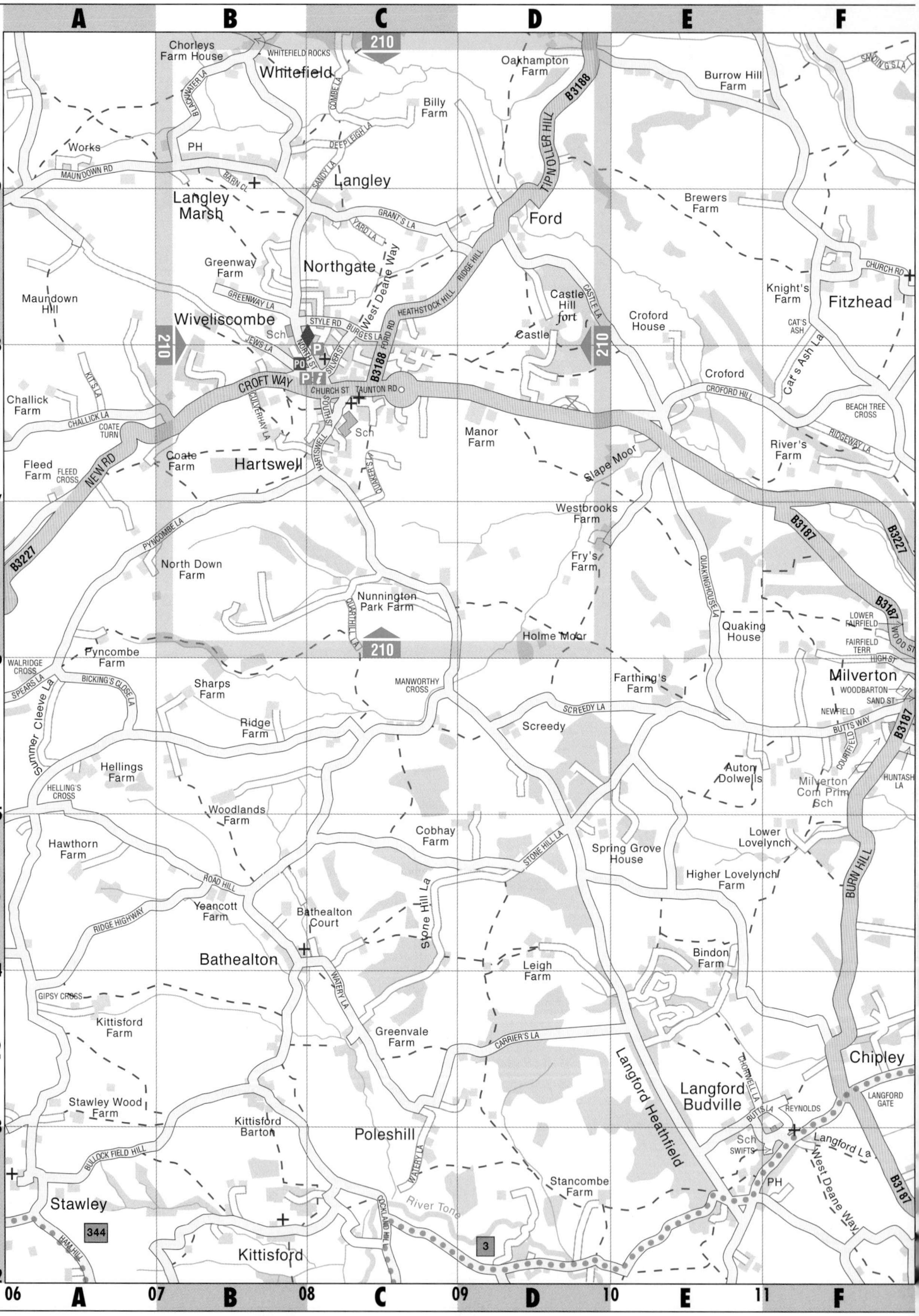

A B C D E F

Chorleys Farm House
WHITEFIELD ROCKS
Whitefield
210
Oakhampton Farm
B3188
Burrow Hill Farm
SMOKING LA
8
BLACKWATER LA
COMBE LA
Billy Farm
Works
PH
DEEPLEIGH LA
TIPNOLLER HILL
MAUNDOWN RD
BARN CL
SANDY LA
Langley
29
Langley Marsh
GRANT'S LA
Brewers Farm
YARD LA
Ford
7
Greenway Farm
Northgate
West Deane Way
RIDGE HILL
CHURCH RD
Maundown Hill
GREENWAY LA
HEATHSTOCK HILL
Castle Hill fort
CASTLE LA
Knight's Farm
Croford House
Fitzhead
Wiveliscombe
STYLE RD
BURGES LA
Sch
Castle
210
CAT'S ASH
28
210
JEWS LA
NORTH ST
SILVER ST
P
PO
FORE ST
B3188
Car's Ash La
P i
CROFT WAY
CHURCH ST
TAUNTON RD
Croford
CROFORD HILL
KITS LA
Challick Farm
BEACH TREE CROSS
6
CHALLICK LA
COATE TURN
CULVERHAY LA
SOUTH ST
Sch
Manor Farm
RIDGEWAY LA
HARTSWELL
River's Farm
Fleed Farm
FLEED CROSS
NEW RD
Coate Farm
Hartswell
Slape Moor
27
Westbrooks Farm
B3187
B3227
PYNCOMBE LA
B3227
North Down Farm
Fry's Farm
5
QUAKINGHOUSE LA
Nunnington Park Farm
B3187
LOWER FAIRFIELD
WOOD ST
QUARTHILL LA
Quaking House
210
Holme Moor
FAIRFIELD TERR
26
WALRIDGE CROSS
Pyncombe Farm
HIGH ST
SPEARS LA
BICKING'S CLOSE LA
Sharps Farm
MANWORTHY CROSS
Farthing's Farm
Milverton
WOODBARTON
SAND ST
SCREEDY LA
NEWFIELD
Summer Cleeve La
Ridge Farm
Screedy
BUTTS WAY
B3187
4
COURTFIELD
Hellings Farm
Auton Dolwells
HUNTASH LA
HELLING'S CROSS
Milverton Com Prim Sch
25
Woodlands Farm
Hawthorn Farm
Cobhay Farm
STONE HILL LA
Spring Grove House
Lower Lovelynch
ROAD HILL
3
Higher Lovelynch Farm
BURN HILL
Yeancott Farm
Bathealton Court
RIDGE HIGHWAY
Stone Hill La
Bindon Farm
Bathealton
24
Leigh Farm
WATERY LA
GIPSY CROSS
Kittisford Farm
Greenvale Farm
2
CARRIER'S LA
Langford Heathfield
Chipley
CHORWELL LA
Langford Budville
LANGFORD GATE
Stawley Wood Farm
BUTTS LA
REYNOLDS
23
Kittisford Barton
Poleshill
Sch
SWIFTS
Langford La
WATERY LA
West Deane Way
BULLOCK FIELD HILL
Stancombe Farm
PH
B3187
1
Stawley
River Tone
COCKLAND HILL
344
HAM HILL
3
Kittisford
22

06 A 07 B 08 C 09 D 10 E 11 F

For full street detail of the highlighted area see page 210.

165
179

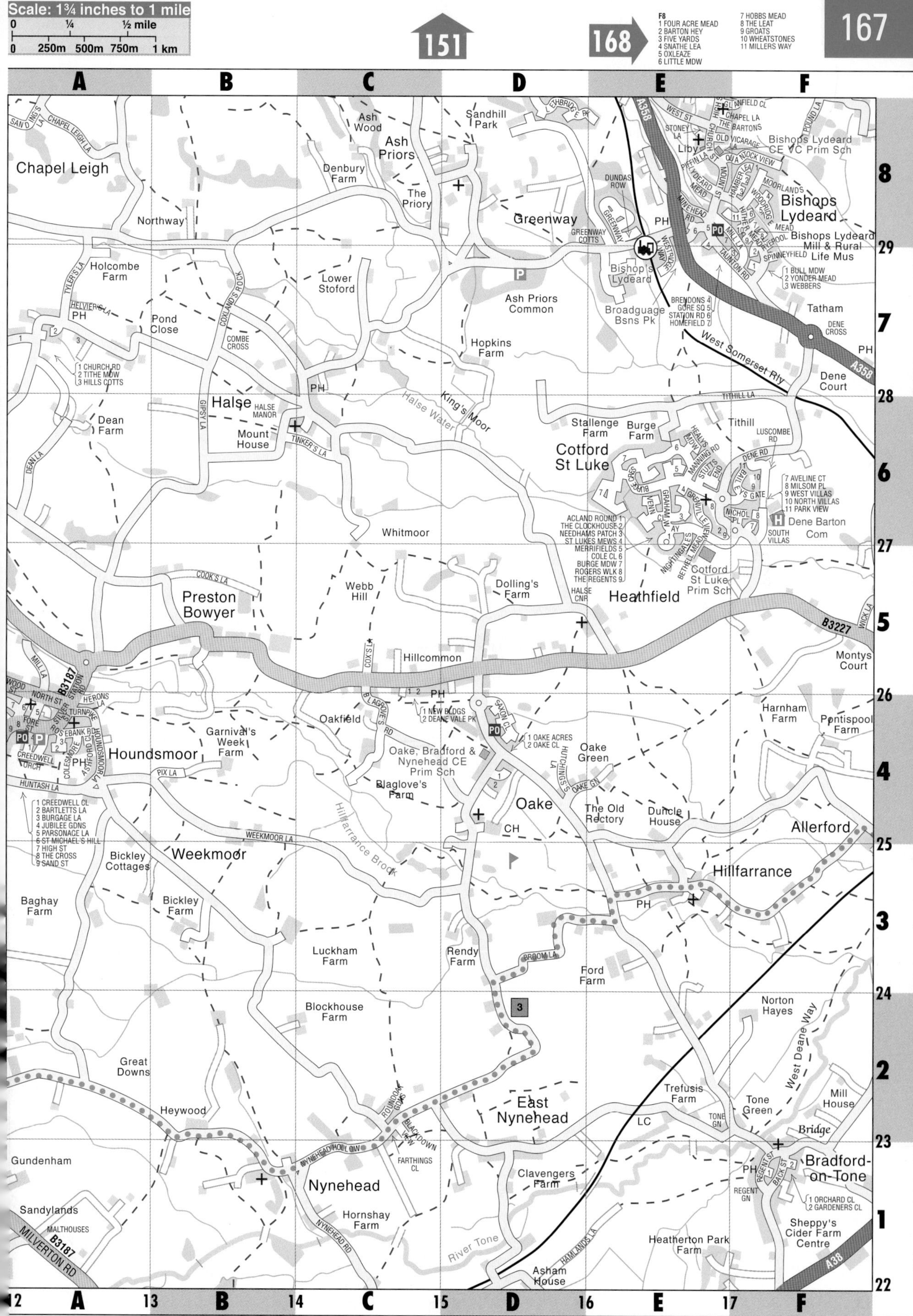

Scale: 1¾ inches to 1 mile
0 ¼ ½ mile
0 250m 500m 750m 1 km
151
168
F8
1 FOUR ACRE MEAD
2 BARTON HEY
3 FIVE YARDS
4 SNATHE LEA
5 OXLEAZE
6 LITTLE MDW
7 HOBBS MEAD
8 THE LEAT
9 GROATS
10 WHEATSTONES
11 MILLERS WAY
A
B
C
D
E
F
Chapel Leigh
CHAPEL LEIGH LA
Ash Wood
Ash Priors
Sandhill Park
Denbury Farm
The Priory
Northway
Greenway
DUNDAS ROW
GREENWAY COTTS
WEST ST
STONEY LA
CHURCH ST
HIGH ST
CHAPEL LA
THE BARTONS
OLD VICARAGE
QUANTOCK VIEW
Bishops Lydeard CE VC Prim Sch
Bishops Lydeard
Bishops Lydeard Mill & Rural Life Mus
MOORLANDS
WOODRIDGE
MEAD
PYEPOOL
SPINNEYFIELD
TAUNTON RD
MINEHEAD RD
MILL LA
MOUNT ST
LYDEARD MEAD
PIFFIN LA
HAMBER LEA
A358
Holcombe Farm
TYLER'S LA
HELVIER'S LA
PH
Lower Stoford
Ash Priors Common
Bishop's Lydeard
Broadguage Bsns Pk
BRENDONS 4
GORE SQ 5
STATION RD 6
HOMEFIELD 7
1 BULL MDW
2 YONDER MEAD
3 WEBBERS
Tatham
DENE CROSS
Pond Close
COXLAND'S ROCK
COMBE CROSS
1 CHURCH RD
2 TITHE MDW
3 HILLS COTTS
Hopkins Farm
West Somerset Rly
Dene Court
Halse
HALSE MANOR
GIPSY LA
Dean Farm
Mount House
TINKER'S LA
Halse Water
King's Moor
TITHILL LA
Stallenge Farm
Burge Farm
Tithill
LUSCOMBE RD
Cotford St Luke
DENE RD
HEALYS MDW
MANNING RD
STUTTS END
7 AVELINE CT
8 MILSOM PL
9 WEST VILLAS
10 NORTH VILLAS
11 PARK VIEW
DEAN LA
GRAHAM WY
VENN CL
GRENVILLE VIEW
MICHOL PL
Dene Barton Com
SOUTH VILLAS
Whitmoor
ACLAND ROUND 1
THE CLOCKHOUSE 2
NEEDHAMS PATCH 3
ST LUKES MEWS 4
MERRIFIELDS 5
COLE CL 6
BURGE MDW 7
ROGERS WLK 8
THE REGENTS 9
NIGHTINGALES
BETHELL MEAD
Cotford St Luke Prim Sch
COOK'S LA
Preston Bowyer
Webb Hill
Dolling's Farm
HALSE CNR
Heathfield
B3227
WICK LA
Montys Court
MILL LA
B3187
Hillcommon
COX'S LA
NORTH ST
STATION RD
HERONS LA
SILVER ST
TURNPIKE
FORE ST
ROSEBANK RD
Houndsmoor
COLESMORE
ASHFORD CL
HOUNDSMOOR LA
CREEDWELL
TORCH
HUNTASH LA
BLAGROVE'S RD
1 NEW BLDGS
2 DEANE VALE PK
Oakfield
Garnival's Week Farm
SAXON CL
1 OAKE ACRES
2 OAKE CL
HUTCHINGS LA
Oake Green
OAKE GN
Harnham Farm
Pontispool Farm
PIX LA
Oake, Bradford & Nynehead CE Prim Sch
Blaglove's Farm
Hillfarrance Brook
Oake
CH
The Old Rectory
Duncle House
Allerford
1 CREEDWELL CL
2 BARTLETTS LA
3 BURGAGE LA
4 JUBILEE GDNS
5 PARSONAGE LA
6 ST MICHAEL'S HILL
7 HIGH ST
8 THE CROSS
9 SAND ST
WEEKMOOR LA
Bickley Cottages
Weekmoor
Hillfarrance
Baghay Farm
Bickley Farm
Luckham Farm
Rendy Farm
BROOM LA
Ford Farm
Blockhouse Farm
Norton Hayes
West Deane Way
Great Downs
Heywood
ROUNDOAK GDNS
East Nynehead
Trefusis Farm
Tone Green
Mill House
TONE GN
LC
Bridge
BLACKDOWN VIEW
NYNEHEAD HOLLOW
FARTHINGS CL
Gundenham
Nynehead
Clavengers Farm
REGENT ST
BACK ST
Bradford-on-Tone
REGENT GN
1 ORCHARD CL
2 GARDENERS CL
Sandylands
MALTHOUSES
MILVERTON RD
Hornshay Farm
NYNEHEAD RD
River Tone
HAMLANDS LA
Heatherton Park Farm
Sheppy's Cider Farm Centre
A38
Asham House
8
29
7
28
6
27
5
26
4
25
3
24
2
23
1
22
12
13
14
15
16
17

167
152

Scale: 1¾ inches to 1 mile
0 ¼ ½ mile
0 250m 500m 750m 1 km

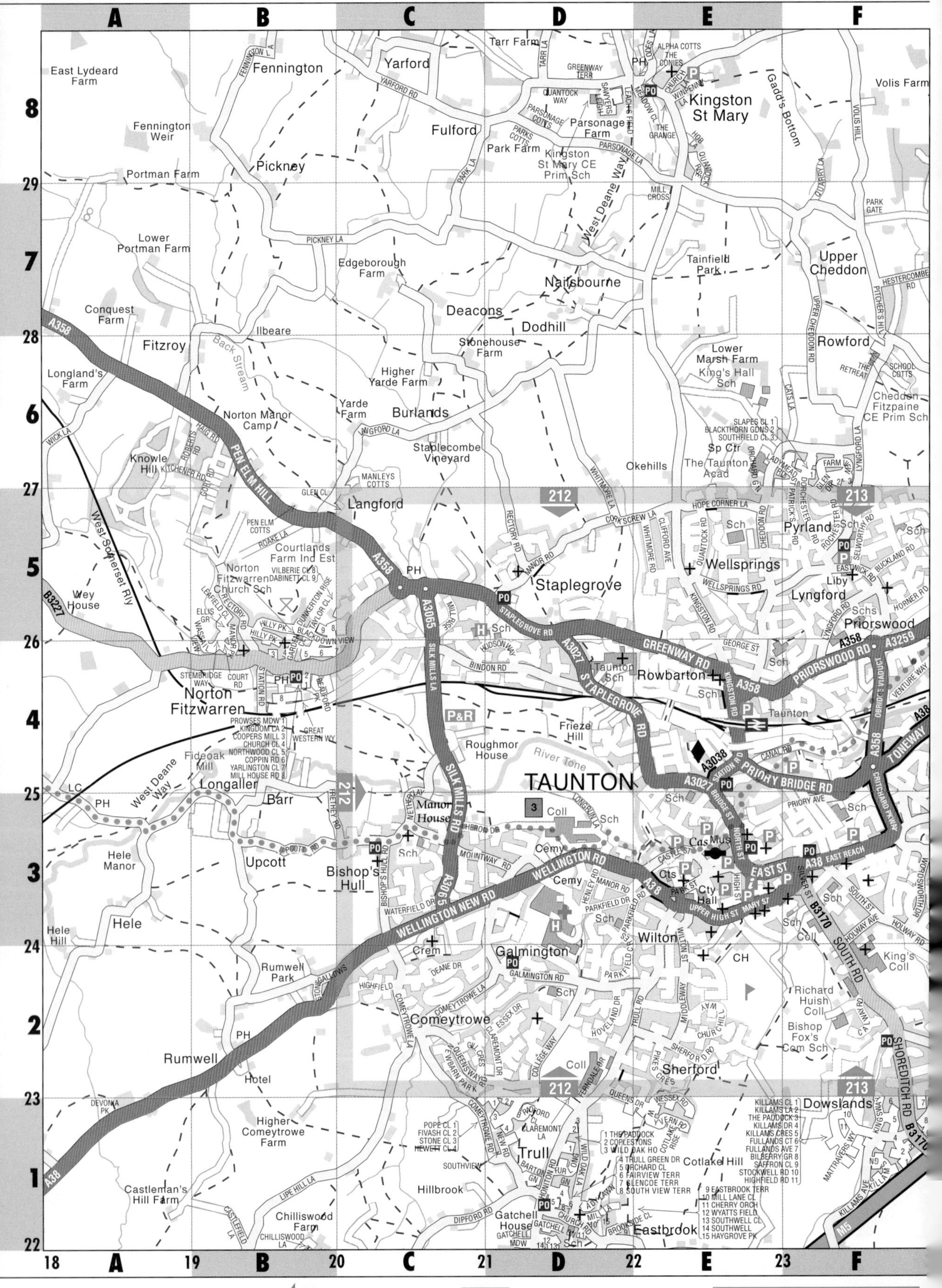

167
181

For full street detail of the highlighted area see pages 212 and 213.

For full street detail of the highlighted area see page 213.

169
154

Scale: 1¾ inches to 1 mile
0 ¼ ½ mile
0 250m 500m 750m 1 km

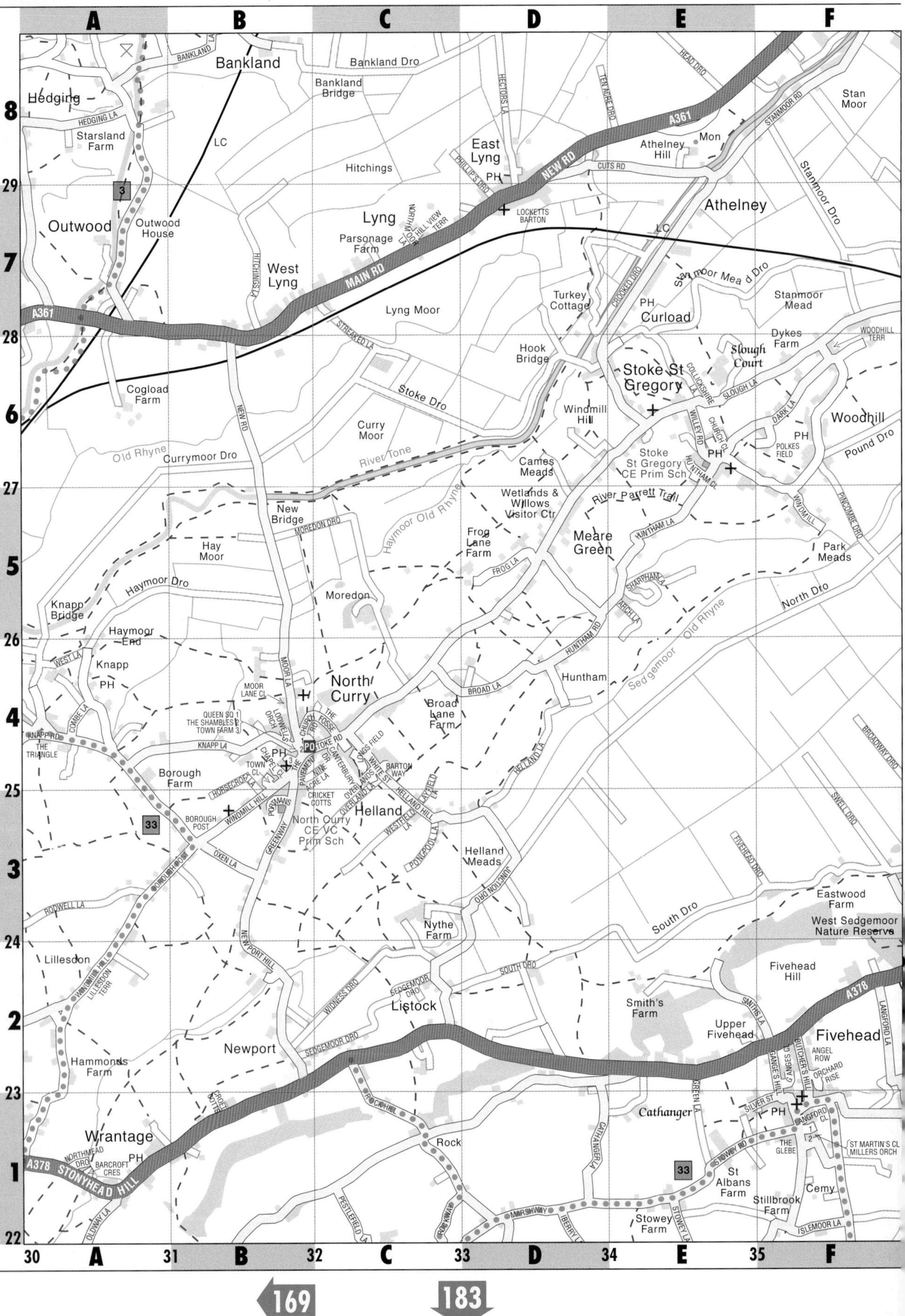

30 A 31 B 32 C 33 D 34 E 35 F

169
183

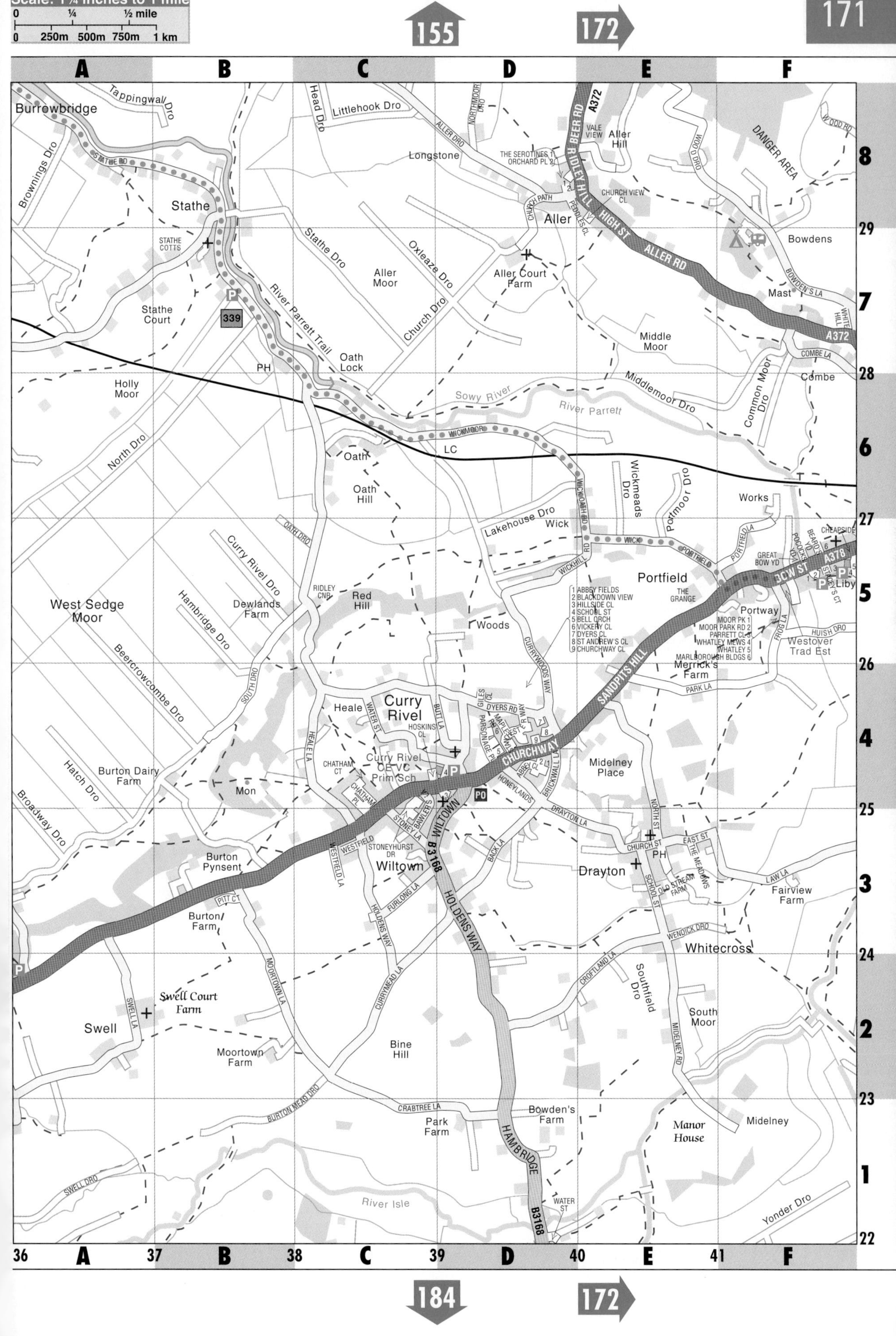
Scale: 1¾ inches to 1 mile
155
172
Burrowbridge
Stathe
Statthe Court
Aller
Aller Moor
Oath Lock
Holly Moor
Oath
Oath Hill
West Sedge Moor
Dewlands Farm
Red Hill
Curry Rivel
Heale
Portfield
Portway
Merrick's Farm
Westover Trad Est
Midelney Place
Burton Dairy Farm
Burton Pynsent
Wiltown
Drayton
Whitecross
Fairview Farm
Swell
Swell Court Farm
Moortown Farm
Bine Hill
South Moor
Park Farm
Bowden's Farm
Manor House
Midelney
River Isle
River Parrett
Sowy River
184
172

171
156

Scale: 1¾ inches to 1 mile
0 ¼ ½ mile
0 250m 500m 750m 1 km

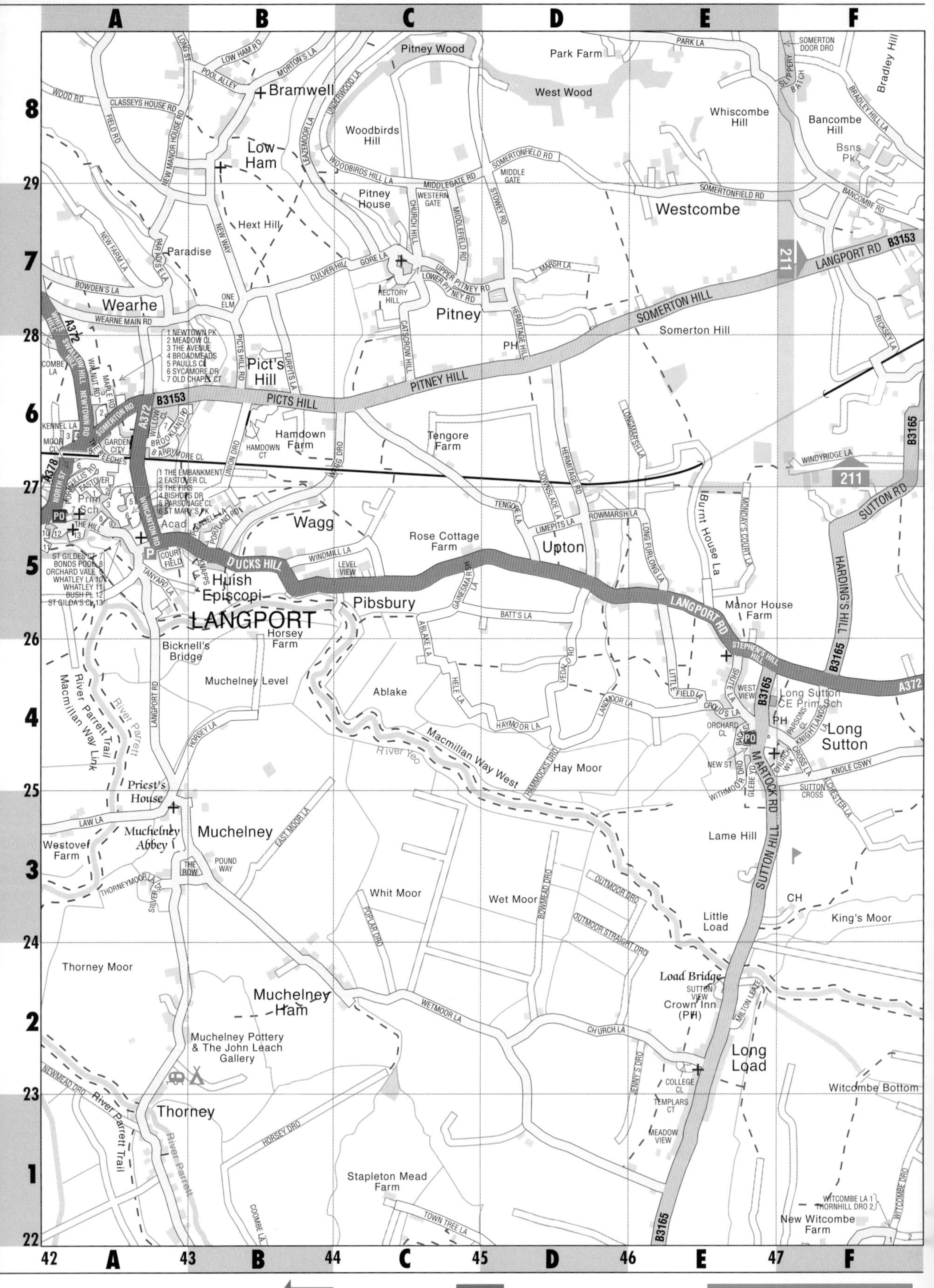

171
185

For full street detail of the highlighted area see page 211.

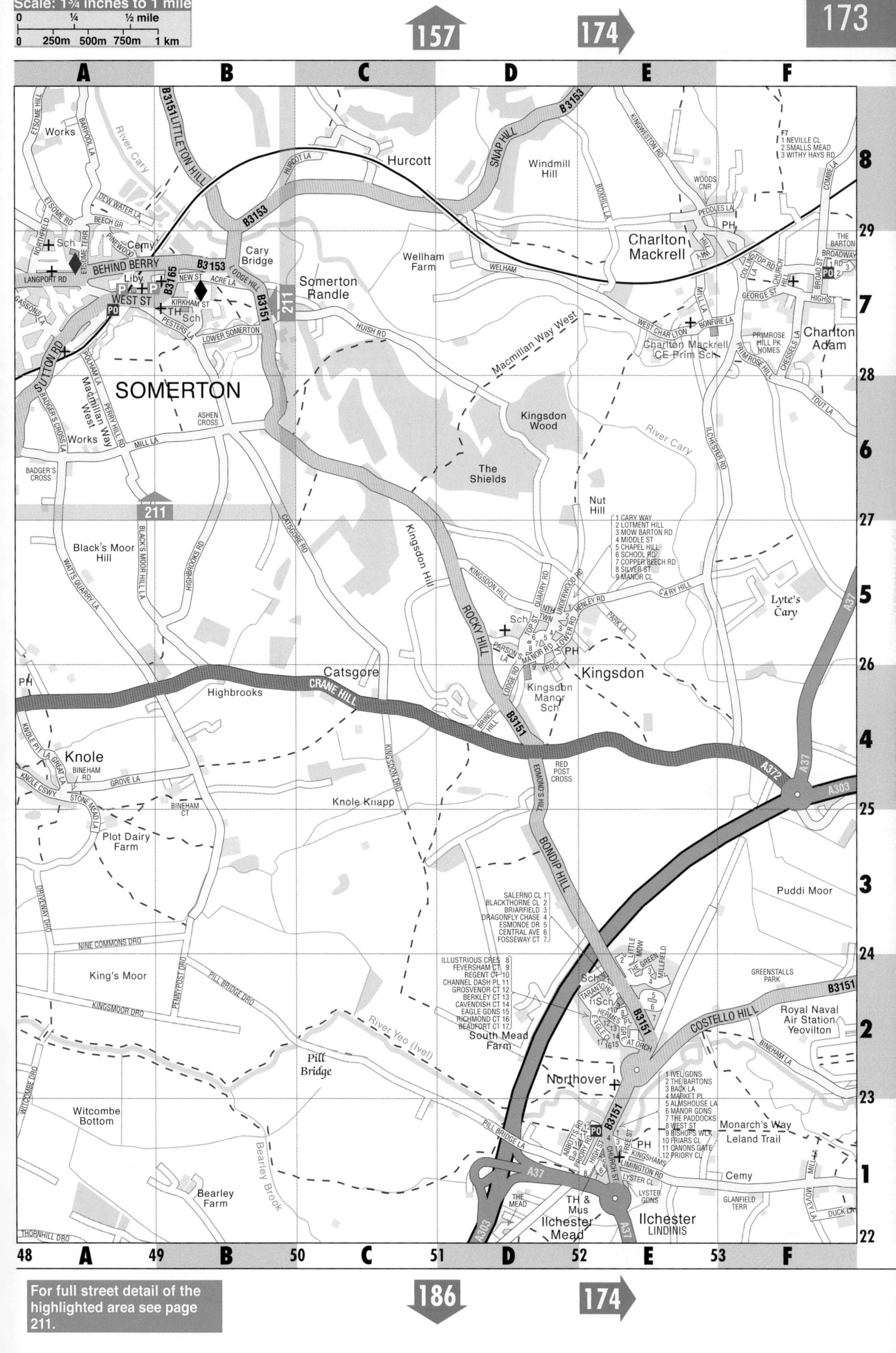

For full street detail of the highlighted area see page 211.

173
158

Scale: 1¾ inches to 1 mile
0 ¼ ½ mile
0 250m 500m 750m 1 km

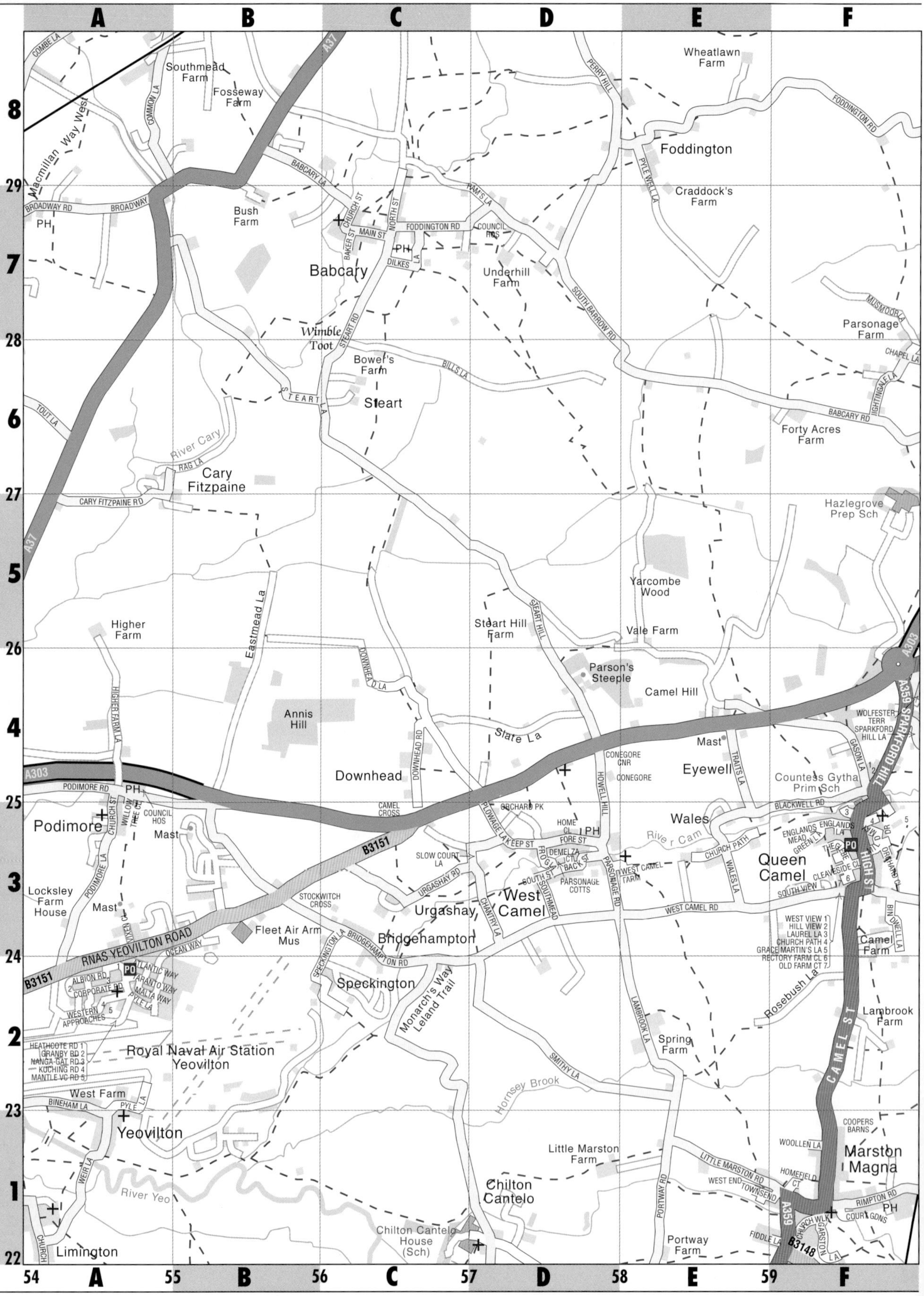

173
187

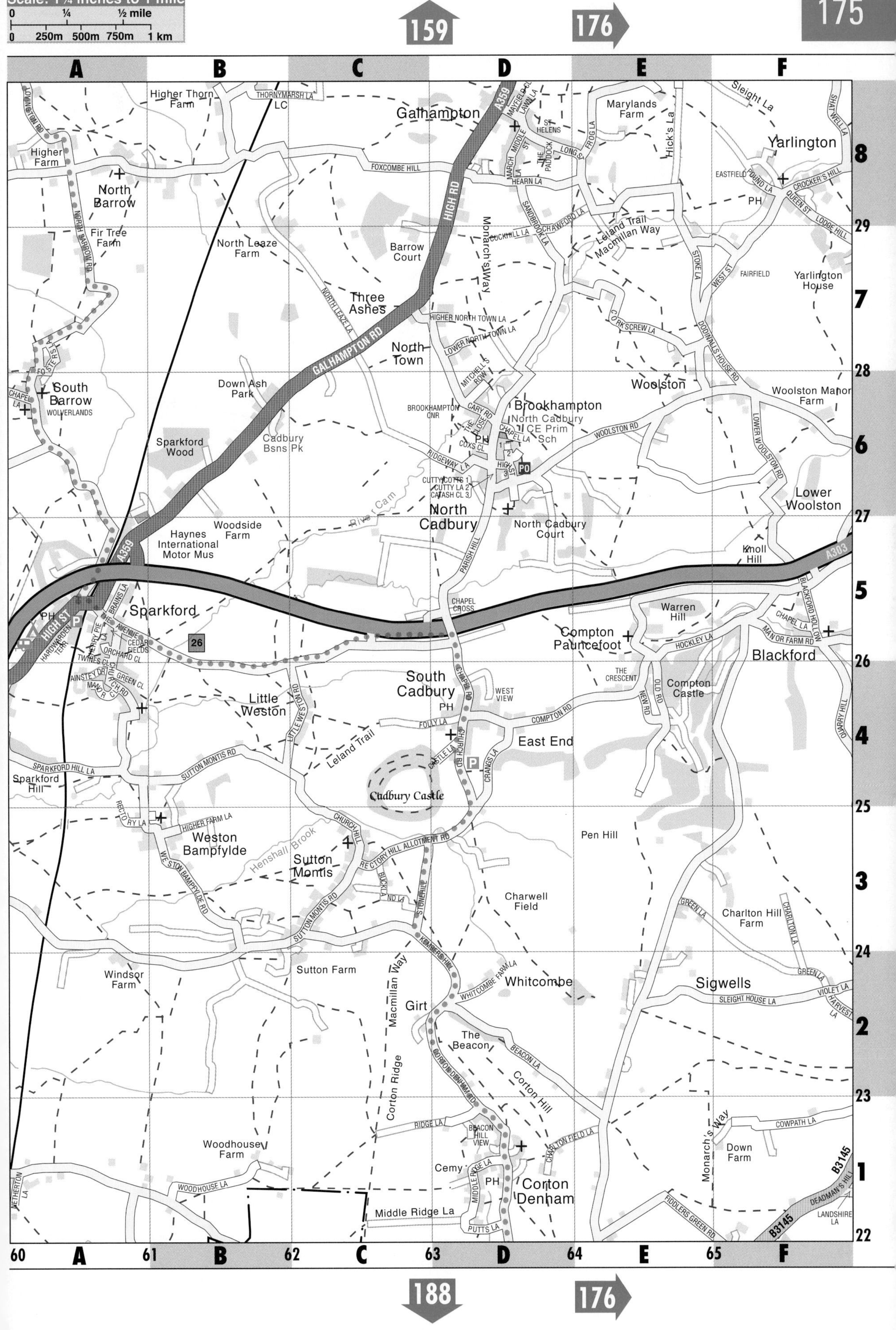
Scale: 1¾ inches to 1 mile
0 ¼ ½ mile
0 250m 500m 750m 1 km
159
176
A B C D E F
8 29 7 28 6 27 5 26 4 25 3 24 2 23 1 22
60 61 62 63 64 65
188
176
Higher Thorn Farm
THORNYMARSH LA
LC
Galhampton
A359
MAYFIELD CL
LAWN LA
ST HELENS
FROG LA
Marylands Farm
Hick's La
Sleight La
SHATWELL LA
Yarlington
Higher Farm
North Barrow
FOXCOMBE HILL
HIGH RD
MIDDLE ST
MARCH LA
THE PADDOCK
LONG ST
HEARN LA
EASTFIELD
POUND LA
CROCKER'S HILL
QUEEN ST
LODGE HILL
PH
NORTH BARROW RD
Fir Tree Farm
North Leaze Farm
Barrow Court
Monarch's Way
SANDBROOK LA
CRAWFORD LA
Leland Trail
Macmillan Way
STOKE LA
WEST ST
FAIRFIELD
Yarlington House
Three Ashes
NORTH LEAZE LA
GALHAMPTON RD
HIGHER NORTH TOWN LA
LOWER NORTH TOWN LA
CORKSCREW LA
DODINGTON HOUSE RD
North Town
MITCHELL'S ROW
South Barrow
WOLVERLANDS
CHAPEL LA
Down Ash Park
Woolston
Woolston Manor Farm
BROOKHAMPTON CNR
CARY RD
Brookhampton
North Cadbury CE Prim Sch
WOOLSTON RD
LOWER WOOLSTON RD
Sparkford Wood
Cadbury Bsns Pk
COXS CL
CHAPEL LA
RIDGEWAY LA
HIGH ST
PO
CUTTY COTTS 1
CUTTY LA 2
CATASH CL 3
River Cam
North Cadbury
North Cadbury Court
Lower Woolston
Haynes International Motor Mus
Woodside Farm
PARISH HILL
Knoll Hill
A303
Sparkford
HIGH ST
BRAINS LA
CHAPEL CROSS
Warren Hill
BLACKFORD HOLLOW
CHAPEL LA
MANOR FARM RD
26
Compton Pauncefoot
HOCKLEY LA
Blackford
HARDWARDEN TERR
HENRY PIE LA
THE AVENUE
CEDAR FIELDS
ORCHARD CL
TWINES CL
AINSTEY DR
CHURCH RD
GREEN CL
MANOR CL
THE CRESCENT
South Cadbury
CHAPEL RD
WEST VIEW
NEW RD
OLD RD
Compton Castle
Little Weston
LITTLE WESTON RD
FOLLY LA
COMPTON RD
East End
QUARRY HILL
Leland Trail
CASTLE LA
CHURCH RD
CRANGS LA
SUTTON MONTIS RD
SPARKFORD HILL LA
Sparkford Hill
Cadbury Castle
RECTORY LA
HIGHER FARM LA
Weston Bampfylde
Henshall Brook
CHURCH HILL
Sutton Montis
RECTORY HILL
ALLOTMENT RD
Pen Hill
WESTON BAMPFYLDE RD
BUCKLA
STONEHILL
Charwell Field
GREEN LA
Charlton Hill Farm
CHARLTON LA
SUTTON MONTIS RD
KEMBERS HILL
Windsor Farm
Sutton Farm
Macmillan Way
WHITCOMBE FARM LA
Whitcombe
Sigwells
GREEN LA
SLEIGHT HOUSE LA
VIOLET LA
HARVEST LA
Girt
The Beacon
BEACON LA
CORTON DENHAM RD
Corton Ridge
Corton Hill
Monarch's Way
RIDGE LA
BEACON HILL VIEW
CHARLTON FIELD LA
COWPATH LA
Woodhouse Farm
Down Farm
Cemy
MIDDLE RIDGE LA
PH
Corton Denham
B3145
DEADMAN'S HILL
WETHERTON LA
WOODHOUSE LA
Middle Ridge La
PUTTS LA
FIDDLERS GREEN RD
LANDSHIRE LA

175
160

Scale: 1¾ inches to 1 mile
0 ¼ ½ mile
0 250m 500m 750m 1 km

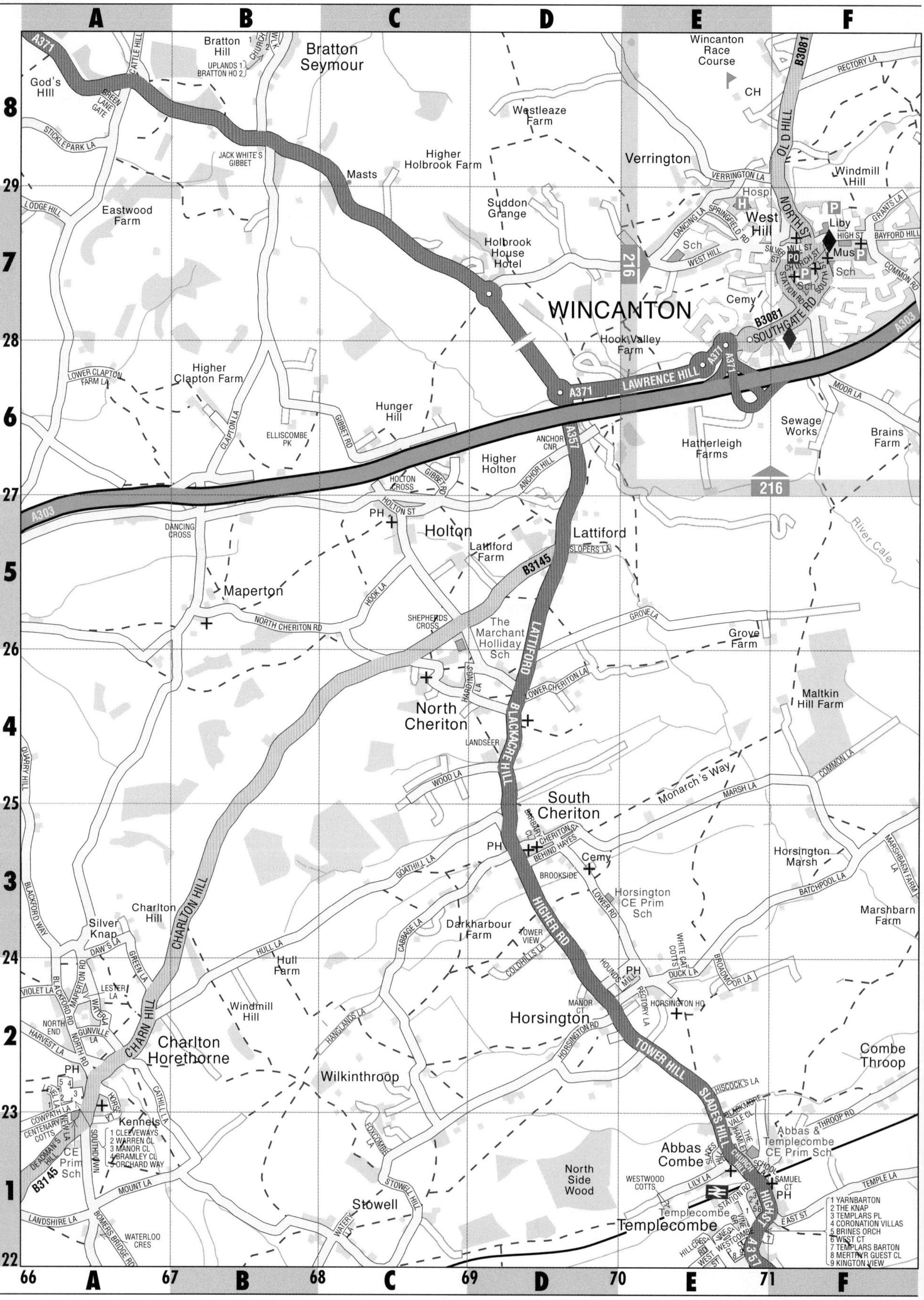

66 67 68 69 70 71

175
189

For full street detail of the highlighted area see page 216.

Scale: 1¾ inches to 1 mile

161

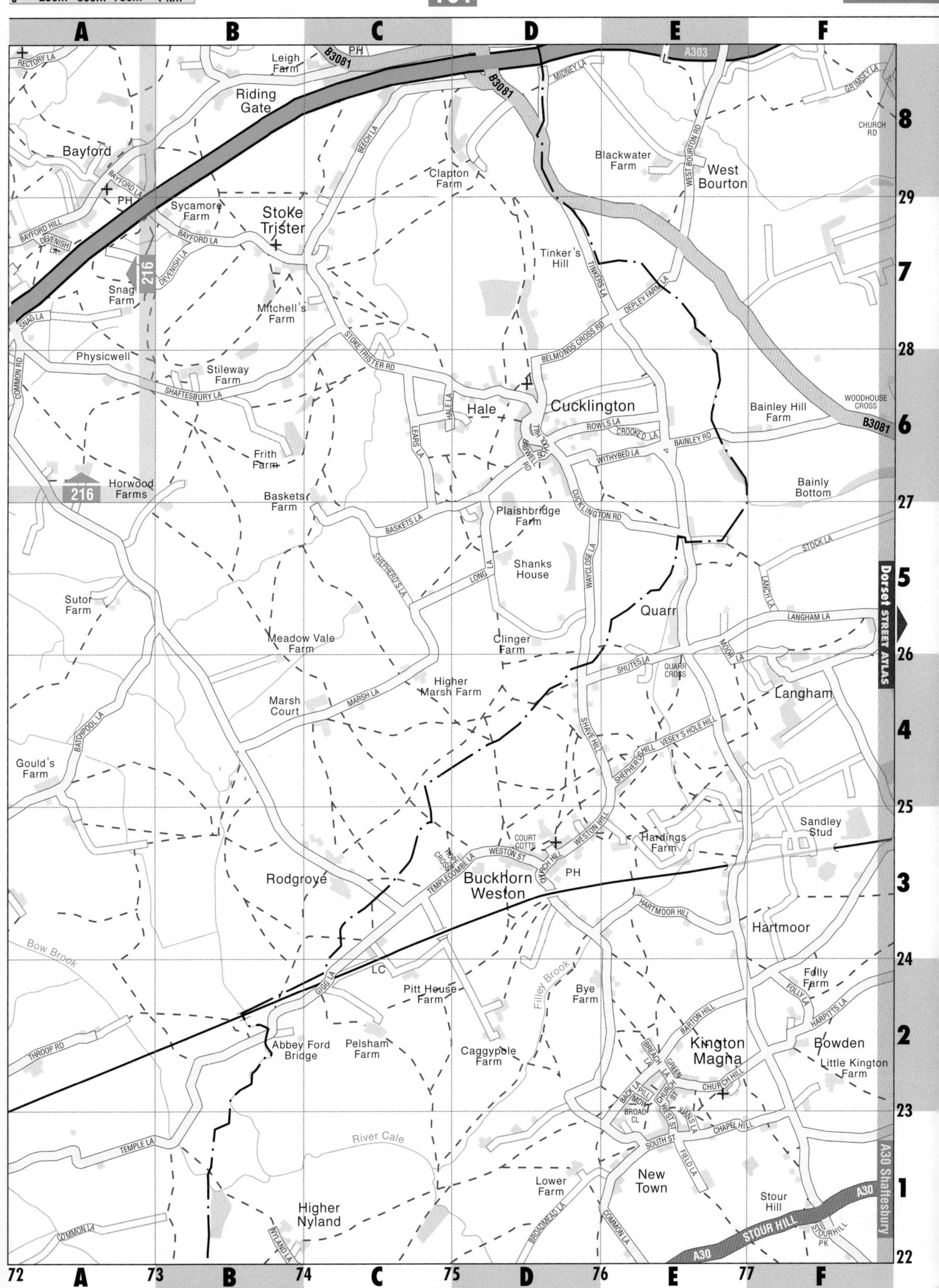

190

For full street detail of the highlighted area see page 216.

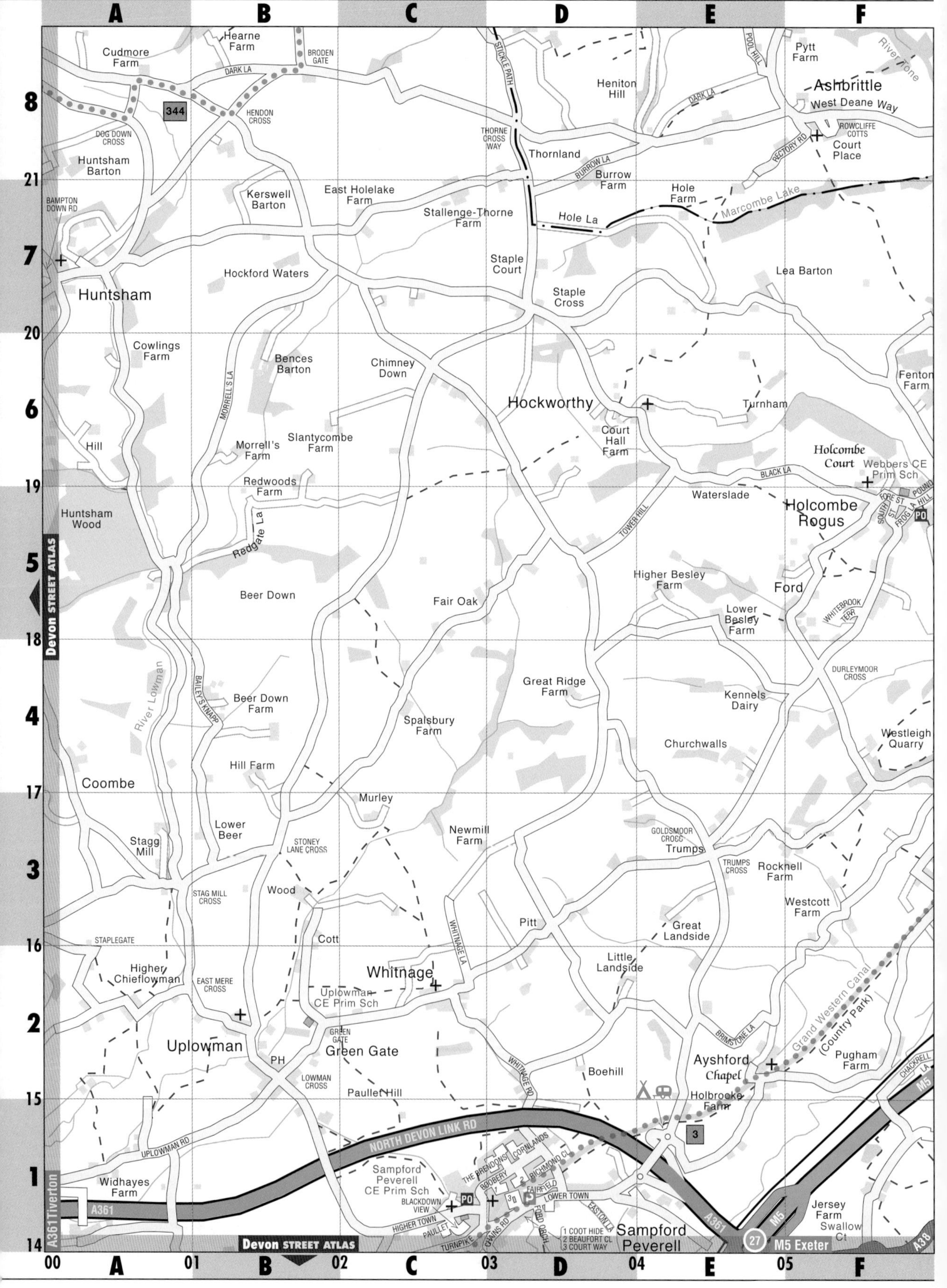

165
Scale: 1¾ inches to 1 mile
Cudmore Farm
Hearne Farm
Huntsham Barton
Kerswell Barton
East Holelake Farm
Stallenge-Thorne Farm
Thornland
Burrow Farm
Heniton Hill
Pytt Farm
Ashbrittle
West Deane Way
Court Place
Hole Farm
Hole La
Marcombe Lake
Staple Court
Staple Cross
Lea Barton
Hockford Waters
Huntsham
Cowlings Farm
Bences Barton
Chimney Down
Hockworthy
Turnham
Fenton Farm
Court Hall Farm
Holcombe Court
Webbers CE Prim Sch
Morrell's Farm
Slantycombe Farm
Redwoods Farm
Hill
Waterslade
Holcombe Rogus
Huntsham Wood
Redgate La
Beer Down
Fair Oak
Higher Besley Farm
Ford
Lower Besley Farm
Great Ridge Farm
Kennels Dairy
Beer Down Farm
Spalsbury Farm
Churchwalls
Westleigh Quarry
River Lowman
Hill Farm
Coombe
Murley
Lower Beer
Newmill Farm
Trumps
Rocknell Farm
Stagg Mill
Wood
Westcott Farm
Pitt
Great Landside
Cott
Higher Chieflowman
Whitnage
Little Landside
Uplowman CE Prim Sch
Uplowman
Green Gate
Ayshford Chapel
Pugham Farm
Boehill
Paullet Hill
Holbrooke Farm
Grand Western Canal (Country Park)
NORTH DEVON LINK RD
Widhayes Farm
Sampford Peverell CE Prim Sch
Sampford Peverell
Jersey Farm
Swallow Ct
M5 Exeter
Devon STREET ATLAS

Scale: 1¾ inches to 1 mile

166
180

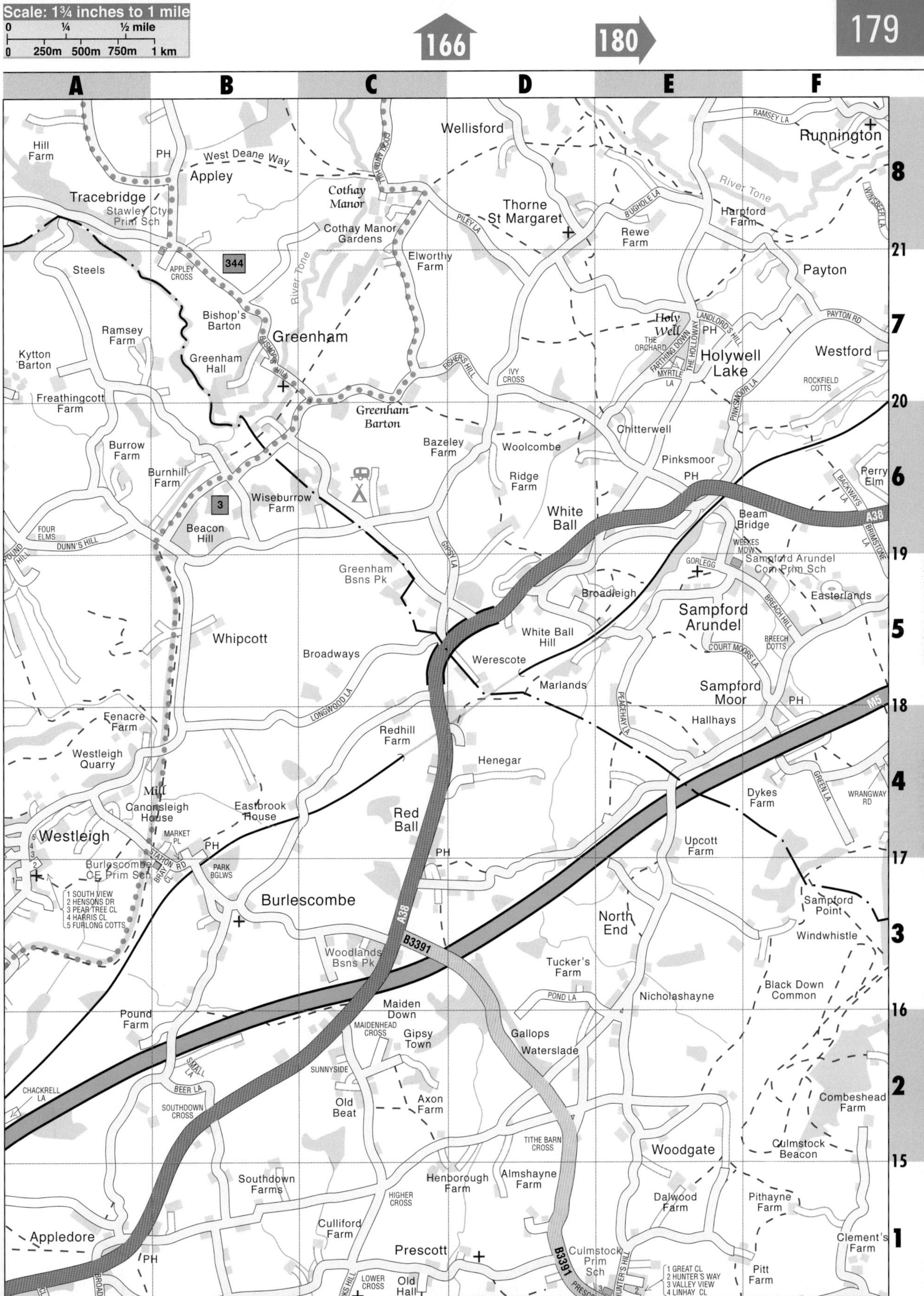
Hill Farm
Tracebridge
Stawley Cty Prim Sch
Appley
West Deane Way
Cothay Manor
Cothay Manor Gardens
Wellisford
Thorne St Margaret
Rewe Farm
Harpford Farm
River Tone
Runnington
Steels
Appley Cross
344
Bishop's Barton
Greenham
Greenham Hall
Elworthy Farm
Payton
Ramsey Farm
Kytton Barton
Holy Well
Holywell Lake
Westford
Freathingcott Farm
Greenham Barton
Ivy Cross
Rockfield Cotts
Burrow Farm
Burnhill Farm
Bazeley Farm
Woolcombe
Chitterwell
Pinksmoor
Ridge Farm
Perry Elm
Wiseburrow Farm
3
Beacon Hill
White Ball
Beam Bridge
Four Elms
Dunn's Hill
Greenham Bsns Pk
Sampford Arundel Com Prim Sch
Broadleigh
Easterlands
Sampford Arundel
Whipcott
White Ball Hill
Broadways
Werescote
Marlands
Sampford Moor
Hallhays
Fenacre Farm
Westleigh Quarry
Redhill Farm
Henegar
Dykes Farm
Mill
Canonsleigh House
Eastbrook House
Red Ball
Westleigh
Upcott Farm
Burlescombe CE Prim Sch
1 South View
2 Hensons Dr
3 Pear Tree Cl
4 Harris Cl
5 Furlong Cotts
Burlescombe
Sampford Point
North End
Windwhistle
Woodlands Bsns Pk
Tucker's Farm
Black Down Common
Nicholashayne
Pound Farm
Maiden Down
Maidenhead Cross
Gipsy Town
Gallops
Waterslade
Chackrell La
Beer La
Southdown Cross
Sunnyside
Old Beat
Axon Farm
Combeshead Farm
Tithe Barn Cross
Woodgate
Culmstock Beacon
Southdown Farms
Henborough Farm
Almshayne Farm
Higher Cross
Dalwood Farm
Pithayne Farm
Appledore
Culliford Farm
Prescott
Culmstock Prim Sch
Clement's Farm
Pitt Farm
1 Great Cl
2 Hunter's Way
3 Valley View
4 Linhay Cl
Spiceland
Lower Cross
Old Hall
Millmoor
A38
M5
B3391
Devon Street Atlas

180

179
167

Scale: 1¾ inches to 1 mile
0 ¼ ½ mile
0 250m 500m 750m 1 km

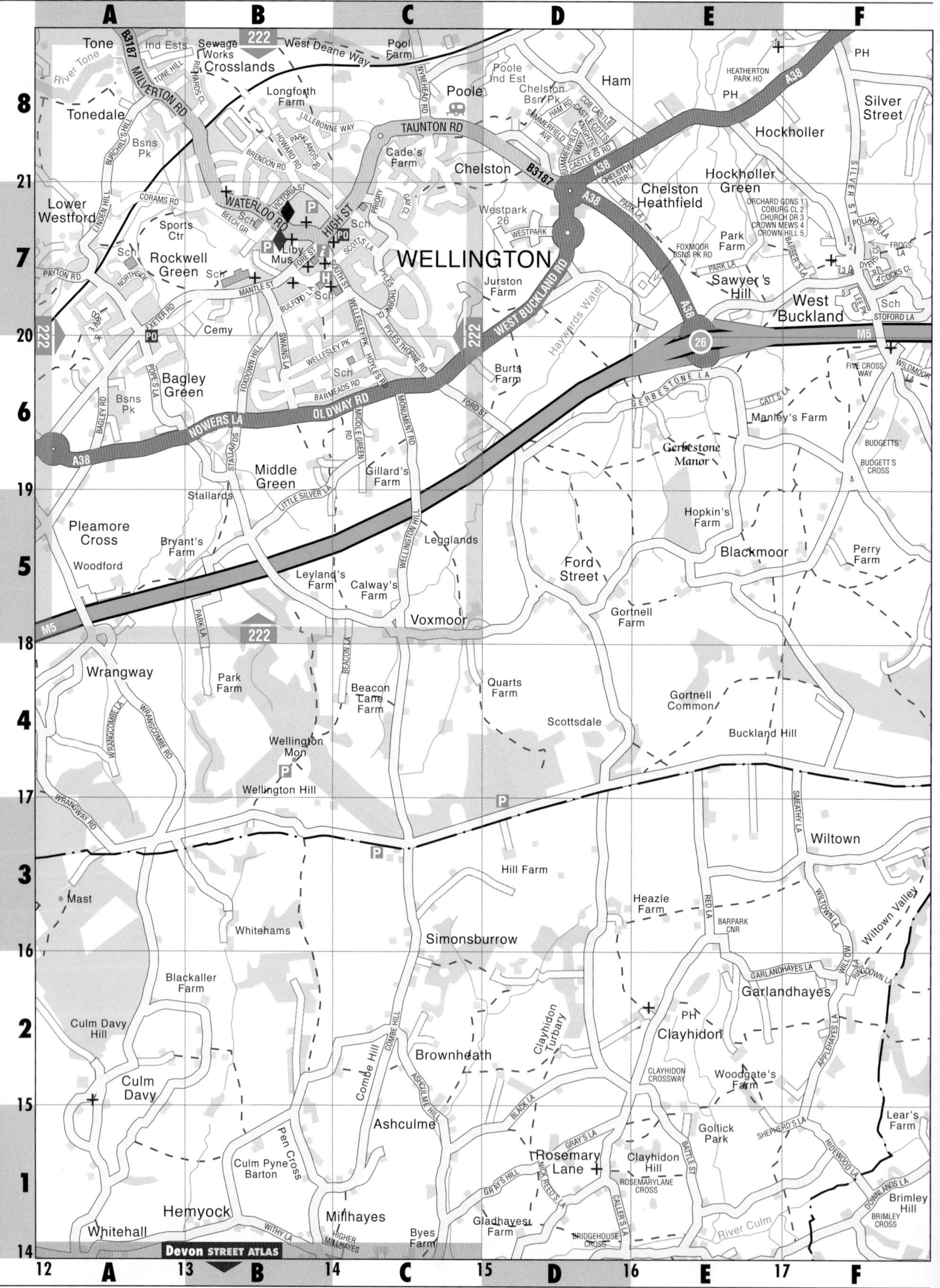

For full street detail of the highlighted area see page 222.
179
191

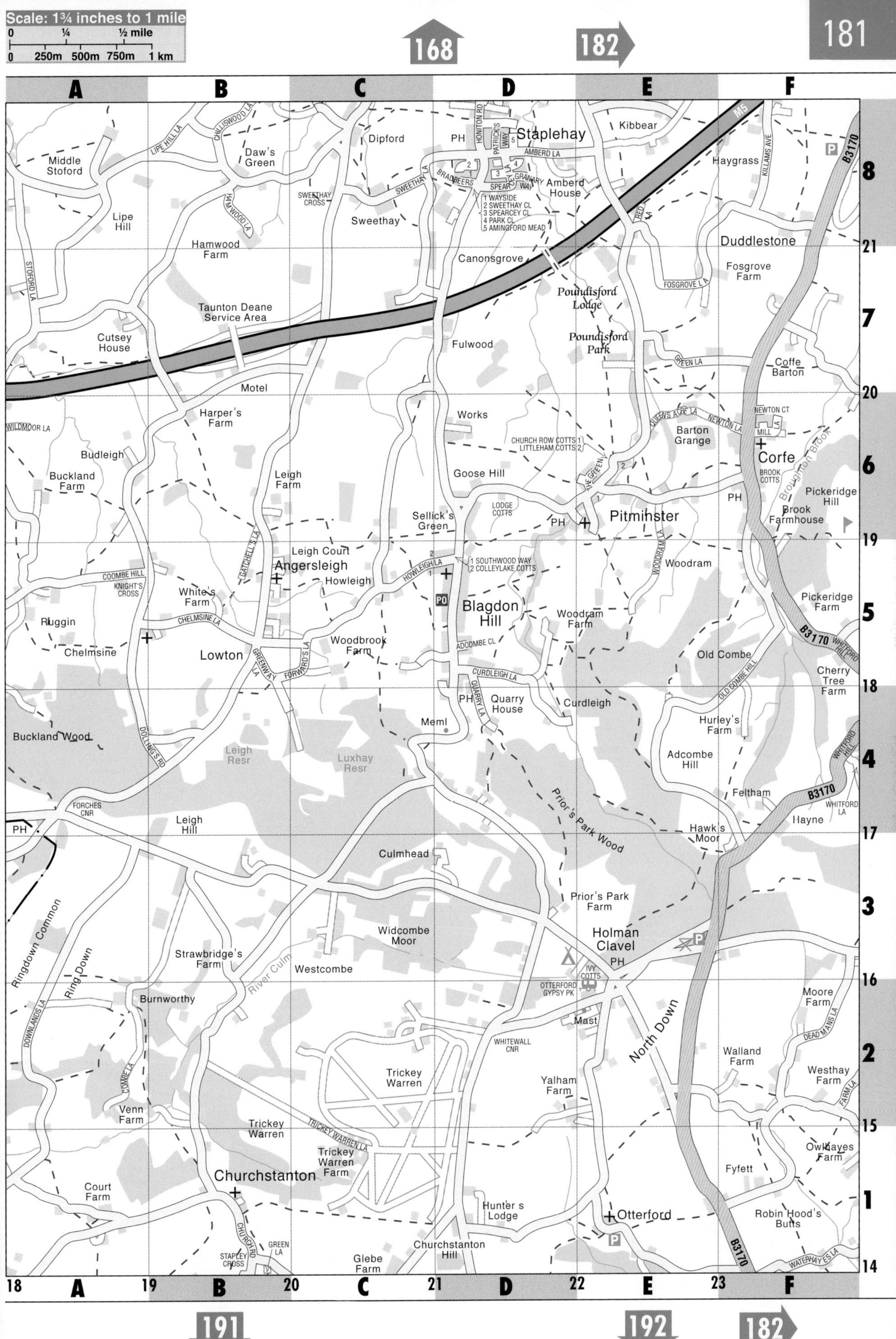
Scale: 1¾ inches to 1 mile
168
182
Staplehay
Kibbear
Dipford
Daw's Green
Middle Stoford
Lipe Hill
Hamwood Farm
Sweethay
Amberd House
Haygrass
Duddlestone
Fosgrove Farm
Canonsgrove
1 WAYSIDE
2 SWEETHAY CL
3 SPEARCEY CL
4 PARK CL
5 AMINGFORD MEAD
Poundisford Lodge
Poundisford Park
Taunton Deane Service Area
Cutsey House
Fulwood
Coffe Barton
Motel
Harper's Farm
Works
Barton Grange
Corfe
Budleigh
Buckland Farm
Leigh Farm
Goose Hill
CHURCH ROW COTTS
LITTLEHAM COTTS
Pickeridge Hill
Brook Farmhouse
Sellick's Green
Pitminster
Leigh Court
Angersleigh
Howleigh
Woodram
1 SOUTHWOOD WAY
2 COLLEYLAKE COTTS
White's Farm
Blagdon Hill
Woodram Farm
Pickeridge Farm
Ruggin
Chelmsine
Lowton
Woodbrook Farm
Old Combe
Cherry Tree Farm
Quarry House
Curdleigh
Hurley's Farm
Buckland Wood
Meml
Leigh Resr
Luxhay Resr
Adcombe Hill
Prior's Park Wood
Feltham
Hayne
Leigh Hill
Hawk's Moor
Culmhead
Prior's Park Farm
Widcombe Moor
Holman Clavel
Strawbridge's Farm
Westcombe
Ringdown Common
Ring Down
River Culm
Burnworthy
Moore Farm
Mast
North Down
Walland Farm
Westhay Farm
Trickey Warren
Yalham Farm
Venn Farm
Trickey Warren Farm
Owlkayes Farm
Fyfett
Churchstanton
Court Farm
Hunter's Lodge
Otterford
Robin Hood's Butts
Churchstanton Hill
Glebe Farm
M5
B3170
191
192
182

181
169

Scale: 1¾ inches to 1 mile
0 ¼ ½ mile
0 250m 500m 750m 1 km

A B C D E F

8 21 7 20 6 19 5 18 4 17 3 16 2 15 1 14

Orchard Portman
Greenway Farm
Stoke Court
Thurlbear
Thurlbear CE Prim Sch
Philpotts Farm
Meare Court Farm
Vincent's Farm
Netherclay
Nature Reserve
West Hatch
Winter Well
Hill Farm
Stroud's Farm
Slough Green
Boon's Farm
Hatch Park
Heale
Frost Street
Badger Street
Animal Centre (RSPCA)
Sparks Farm
Lime Ridge Wood
Witch Lodge
Street Farm House
Piddle Wood
Bickenhall Farm
Park Farm
CH
Staple Lawns Farm
Forest Lodge
Staple Farm
Staple Lawns
Staple Fitzpaine
Bickenhall
Batten's Green
Whitty
Myrtle Farm
Staple Park Farm
Manor Ho
Abbey Hill
Perry Hall
Staple Park Wood
Underhill Farm
Bulford
Bow Green
Curland
Newtown Farm
New Town
Curland Common
Barrington Hill
South Hill Farm
Quarrystone Farm
Mount Fancy Farm
Ruttersleigh Common
Venner's Farm
Staple Common
Castle Farm
Castle Neroche
Castle Plain
Castle Neroche Forest Trail
Hisbeer's Farm
Britty Common
Old Castle Farm
Hare
Staple Hill Farm
Blackwater
Buckland Farm
White's Farm
Rydiness Farm
Dommett
Beehive Farm
Blindmoor
Roses Farm
Dingford Farm
River Ding
Lower Burnt House Farm
Dommett Moor
Colley Farm
Birchwood

Race Course, B3170, Broughton Brook, Whitford Hill, Whitford La, Netherclay La, Stoke Hill, Slough Green Cvn Pk, Church La, West Hatch La, West Hatch La, Griffin Rd, Griffin La, Oldway La, Higher West Hatch La, Prey La, Myrtle Cotts, Slough Hill, PH, Bickenhall La, Village Rd, Old Barn La, Hatch Green La, A358, 33, Cold Rd, Staple Hill, Crughay La, Dairy House La, New Rd, St Peters Cl, Green Dro, Abbey Hill Dro, Curry Mallet Dr, Bickenhall Plain, Forest Dro, Underhill La, Parsonage La, Middleroom Dro, Middleroom La, Barrington Hill Rd, Green La, Long Dro, Farm La, Hare La, Broomfield La, Hare La, Dommett Rd, Castlemain, Ding Rd, Charmoor La, Rackley La, Aplins La, Hornsey La, Pound La, Folly La, Hamway La, Hamley La, Charmoor Dro, Blind La

24 A 25 B 26 C 27 D 28 E 29 F

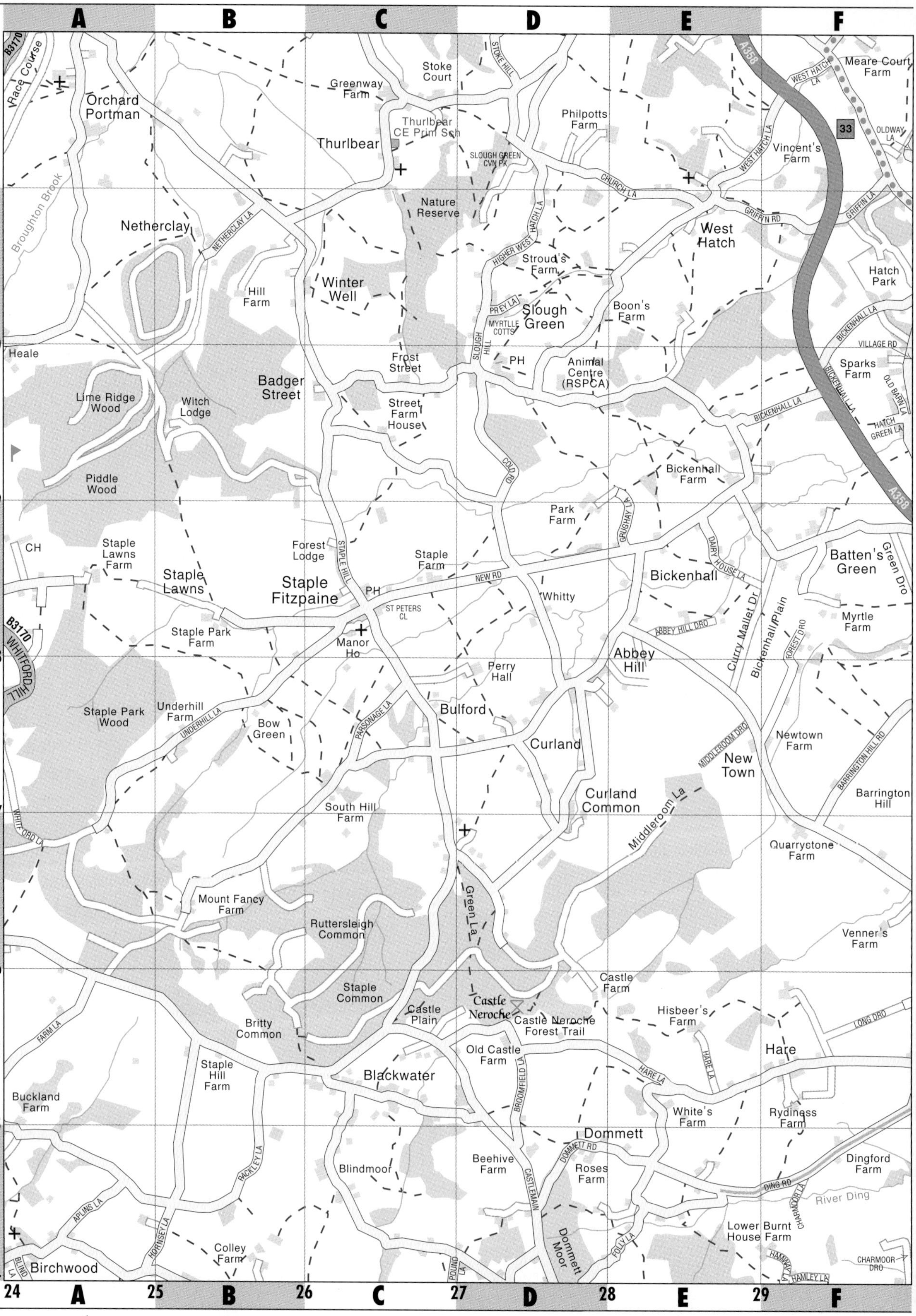

181
192
193

Scale: 1¾ inches to 1 mile
0 ¼ ½ mile
0 250m 500m 750m 1 km

170
184

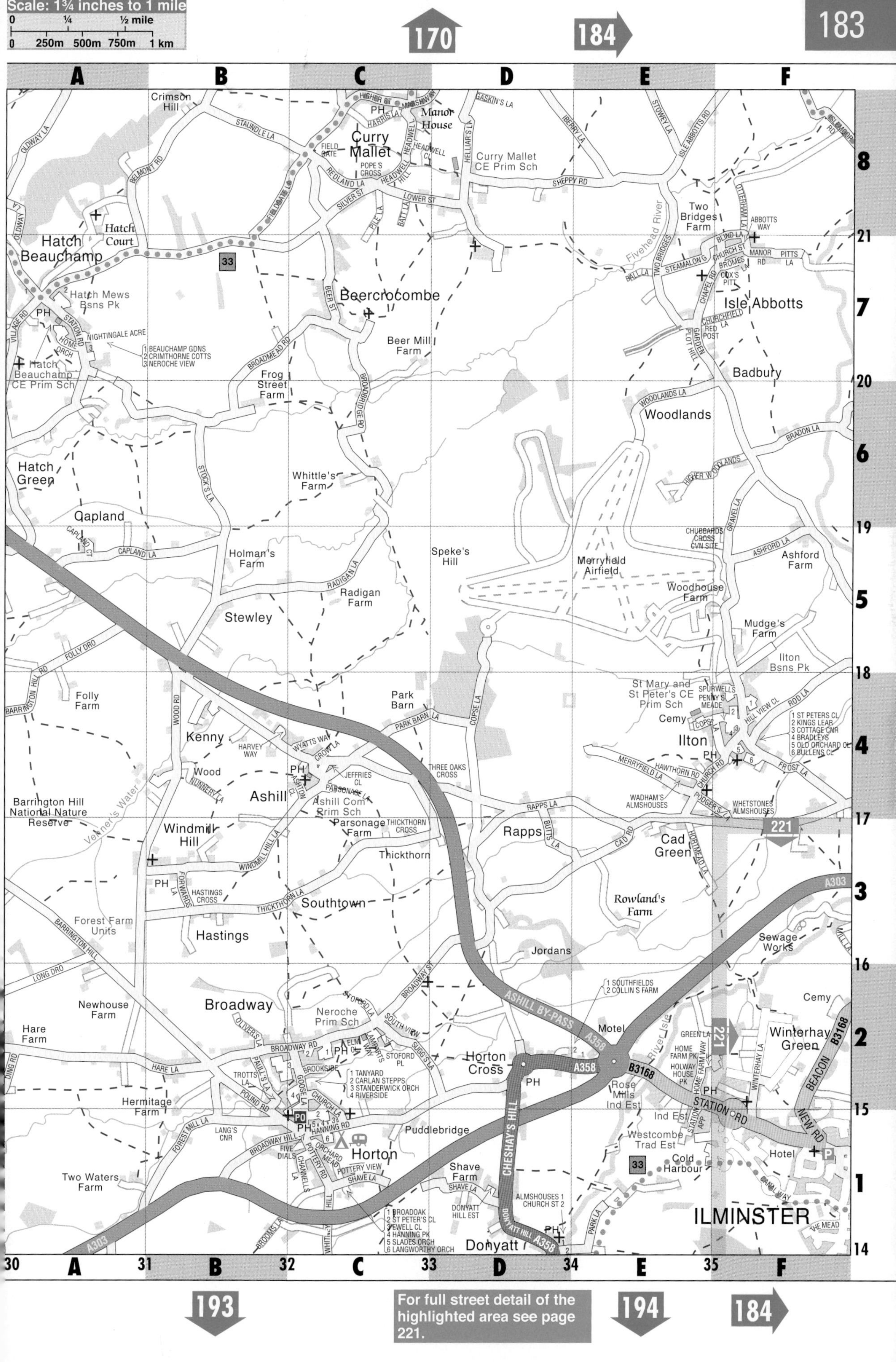

193
For full street detail of the highlighted area see page 221.
194
184

183
171

Scale: 1¾ inches to 1 mile

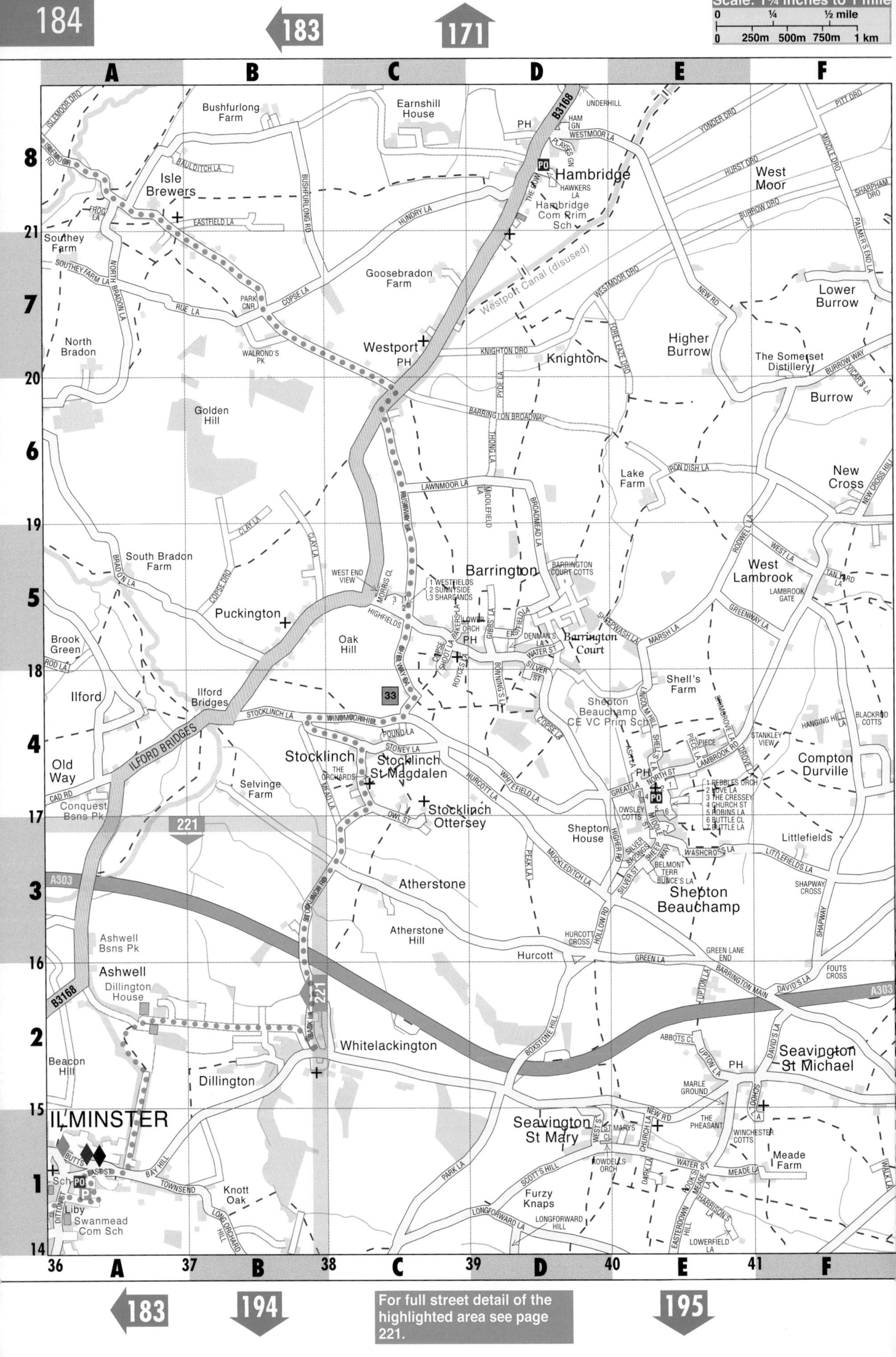

183
194
For full street detail of the highlighted area see page 221.
195

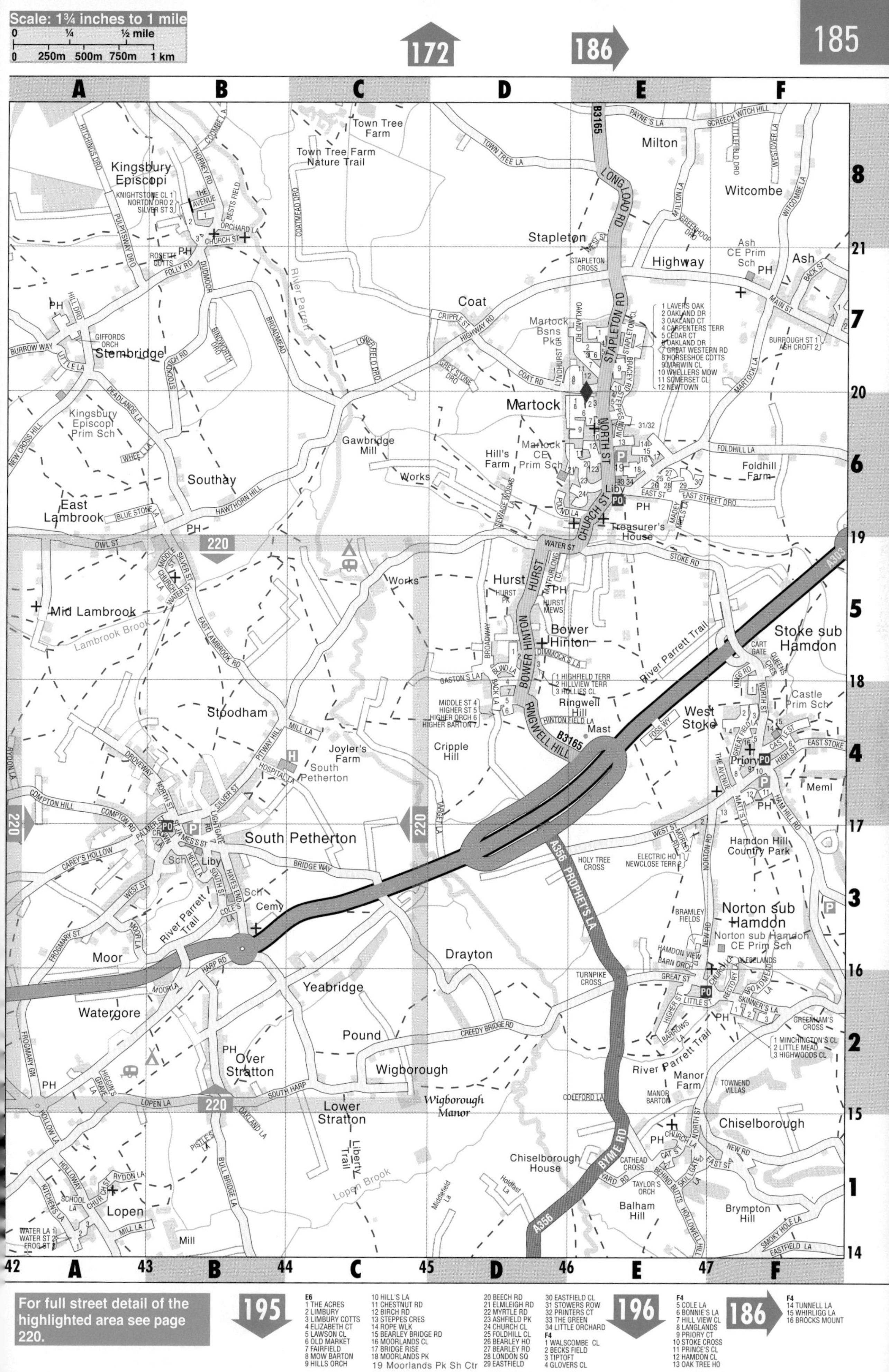
Scale: 1¾ inches to 1 mile
0 ¼ ½ mile
0 250m 500m 750m 1 km
172
186
A B C D E F
8 21 7 20 6 19 5 18 4 17 3 16 2 15 1 14
42 43 44 45 46 47
Town Tree Farm
Town Tree Farm Nature Trail
Kingsbury Episcopi
KNIGHTSTONE CL 1
NORTON DRO 2
SILVER ST 3
Milton
Witcombe
Stapleton
STAPLETON CROSS
Highway
Ash CE Prim Sch
Ash
Coat
Martock Bsns Pk
1 LAVERS OAK
2 OAKLAND DR
3 OAKLAND CT
4 CARPENTERS TERR
5 CEDAR CT
6 OAKLAND DR
7 GREAT WESTERN RD
8 HORSESHOE COTTS
9 MARWIN CL
10 WHELLERS MDW
11 SOMERSET CL
12 NEWTOWN
BURROUGH ST 1
ASH CROFT 2
GIFFORDS ORCH
Stembridge
Kingsbury Episcopi Prim Sch
Martock
Gawbridge Mill
Hill's Farm
Martock CE Prim Sch
Works
Foldhill Farm
Southay
East Lambrook
Treasurer's House
220
Hurst
HURST PK
HURST MEWS
Mid Lambrook
Lambrook Brook
Bower Hinton
Stoke sub Hamdon
CART GATE
1 HIGHFIELD TERR
2 HILLVIEW TERR
3 HOLLIES CL
Ringwell Hill
MIDDLE ST 4
HIGHER ST 5
HIGHER ORCH 6
HIGHER BARTON 7
Castle Prim Sch
West Stoke
Stoodham
Mast
Joyler's Farm
Cripple Hill
South Petherton
Priory
Meml
South Petherton
Hamdon Hill Country Park
HOLY TREE CROSS
ELECTRIC HO 1
NEWCLOSE TERR 2
Norton sub Hamdon
Norton sub Hamdon CE Prim Sch
BRAMLEY FIELDS
Moor
Drayton
TURNPIKE CROSS
Yeabridge
Watergore
Pound
1 MINCHINGTON'S CL
2 LITTLE MEAD
3 HIGHWOODS CL
Over Stratton
Wigborough
River Parrett Trail
Manor Farm
TOWNEND VILLAS
MANOR BARTON
Wigborough Manor
Lower Stratton
Chiselborough
Liberty Trail
Chiselborough House
CATHEAD CROSS
TAYLOR'S ORCH
Lopen Brook
Balham Hill
Brympton Hill
Lopen
WATER LA 1
WATER ST 2
FROG ST 3
Mill
A303
A356
B3165
For full street detail of the highlighted area see page 220.
195
E6
1 THE ACRES
2 LIMBURY
3 LIMBURY COTTS
4 ELIZABETH CT
5 LAWSON CL
6 OLD MARKET
7 FAIRFIELD
8 MOW BARTON
9 HILLS ORCH
10 HILL'S LA
11 CHESTNUT RD
12 BIRCH RD
13 STEPPES CRES
14 ROPE WLK
15 BEARLEY BRIDGE RD
16 MOORLANDS CL
17 BRIDGE RISE
18 MOORLANDS PK
19 Moorlands Pk Sh Ctr
20 BEECH RD
21 ELMLEIGH RD
22 MYRTLE RD
23 ASHFIELD PK
24 CHURCH CL
25 FOLDHILL CL
26 BEARLEY HO
27 BEARLEY RD
28 LONDON SQ
29 EASTFIELD
30 EASTFIELD CL
31 STOWERS ROW
32 PRINTERS CT
33 THE GREEN
34 LITTLE ORCHARD
F4
1 WALSCOMBE CL
2 BECKS FIELD
3 TIPTOFT
4 GLOVERS CL
196
F4
5 COLE LA
6 BONNIE'S LA
7 HILL VIEW CL
8 LANGLANDS
9 PRIORY CT
10 STOKE CROSS
11 PRINCE'S CL
12 HAMDON CL
13 OAK TREE HO
186
F4
14 TUNNELL LA
15 WHIRLIGG LA
16 BROCKS MOUNT

185
173

Scale: 1¾ inches to 1 mile
0 ¼ ½ mile
0 250m 500m 750m 1 km

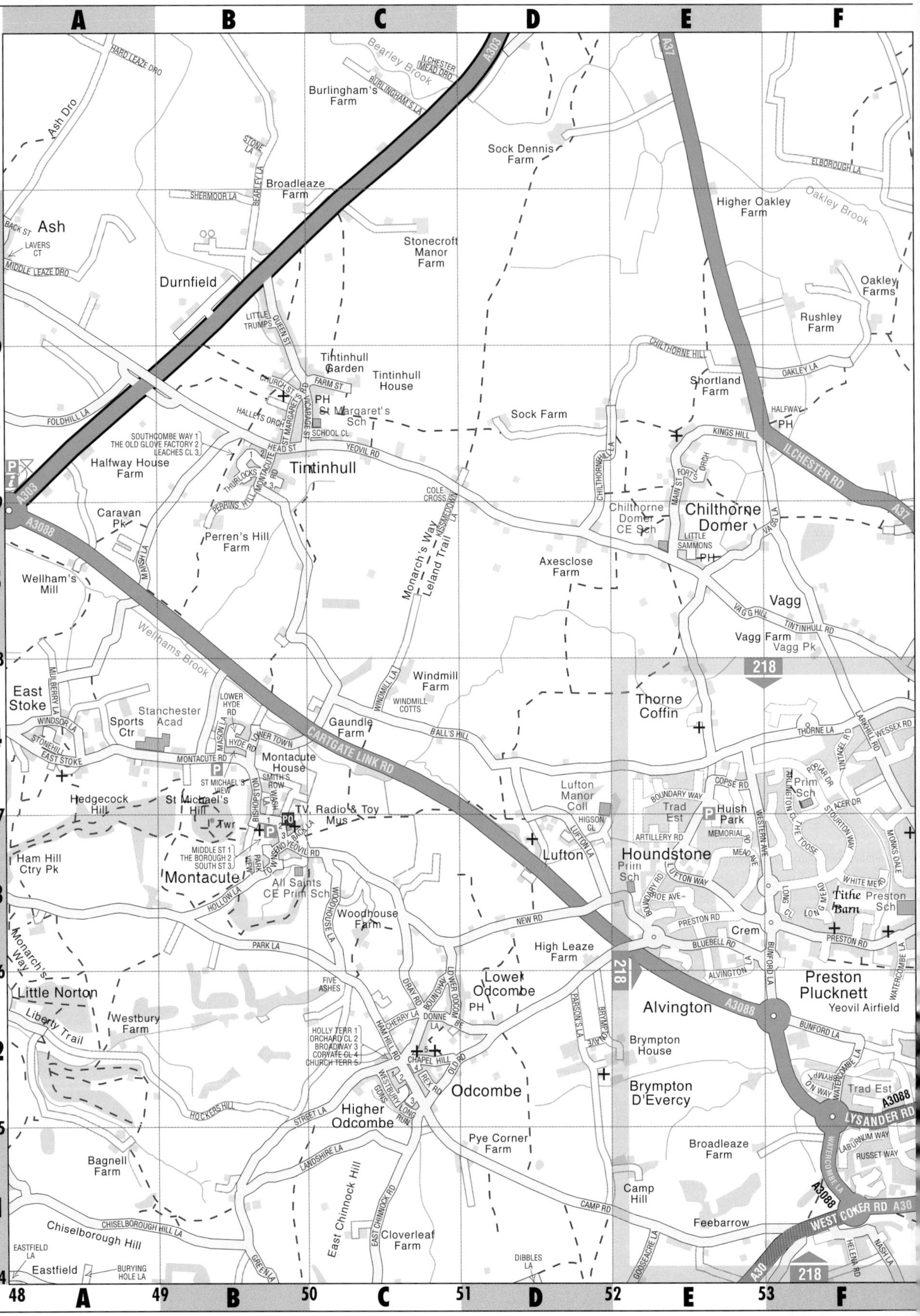

A B C D E F

8
21
7
20
6
19
5
18
4
17
3
16
2
15
1
14

48 49 50 51 52 53

Ash
Ash Dro
HARD LEAZE DRO
BACK ST
LAVERS CT
MIDDLE LEAZE DRO
Bearley Brook
ILCHESTER MEAD DRO
BURLINGHAM'S LA
Burlingham's Farm
A303
STONE LA
BEARLEY LA
SHERMOOR LA
Broadleaze Farm
Sock Dennis Farm
A37
ELBOROUGH LA
Higher Oakley Farm
Oakley Brook
Stonecroft Manor Farm
Durnfield
LITTLE TRUMPS
QUEEN ST
Oakley Farms
Rushley Farm
Tintinhull Garden
Tintinhull House
CHURCH ST
FARM ST
VICARAGE ST
ST MARGARET'S RD
PH
St Margaret's Sch
SCHOOL CL
HALLETS ORCH
FOLDHILL LA
CHILTHORNE HILL
OAKLEY LA
Shortland Farm
HALFWAY PH
Sock Farm
KINGS HILL
ILCHESTER RD
SOUTHCOMBE WAY 1
THE OLD GLOVE FACTORY 2
LEACHES CL 3
HEAD ST
YEOVIL RD
Halfway House Farm
Tintinhull
THURLOCKS
MONTACUTE RD
PERRINS HILL
COLE CROSS
KISSMEDOWN LA
CHILTHORNE LA
MAIN ST
FORTS ORCH
Caravan Pk
A3088
Chilthorne Domer CE Sch
Chilthorne Domer
VAGG LA
LITTLE SAMMONS
PH
Perren's Hill Farm
Monarch's Way
Leland Trail
Axesclose Farm
MARSH LA
Wellham's Mill
Vagg
VAGG HILL
TINTINHULL RD
Vagg Farm
Vagg Pk
Wellhams Brook
218
Windmill Farm
WINDMILL LA
WINDMILL COTTS
MULBERRY LA
East Stoke
LOWER HYDE RD
Stanchester Acad
Sports Ctr
Thorne Coffin
WINDSOR LA
STONEHILL
EAST STOKE
MASON LA
HYDE RD
LOWER TOWN
Gaundle Farm
BALL'S HILL
CARTGATE LINK RD
THORNE LA
WESSEX RD
LARKHILL RD
MONTACUTE RD
Montacute House
SMITH'S ROW
Lufton Manor Coll
COPSE RD
POLAR DR
Prim Sch
TINTAGEL RD
TARLINGTON CL
ST MICHAEL'S VIEW
BISHOPSTON
WASH LA
BOUNDARY WAY
Trad Est
Huish Park
ST ACER DR
Hedgecock Hill
St Michael's Hill
TV, Radio & Toy Mus
HIGSON CL
MEMORIAL RD
STOURTON WAY
THE TOOSE
Twr
BACK LA
PO
LUFTON LA
ARTILLERY RD
WESTERN AVE
MONKS DALE
MIDDLE ST 1
THE BOROUGH 2
SOUTH ST 3
TOWNSEND
YEOVIL RD
Lufton
Houndstone
MEAD AVE
Ham Hill Ctry Pk
PARK LA
VIEW
Montacute
All Saints CE Prim Sch
Prim Sch
LUFTON WAY
WHITE MEAD
HOLLOW LA
WOODHOUSE LA
BOUNDARY RD
ROE AVE
LONG CL
Tithe Barn
Preston Sch
Woodhouse Farm
NEW RD
PRESTON RD
Crem
PRESTON RD
PARK LA
High Leaze Farm
BLUEBELL RD
Monarch's Way
WATERCOMBE LA
Little Norton
FIVE ASHES
Lower Odcombe
ALVINGTON LA
Preston Plucknett
Yeovil Airfield
BUNFORD LA
Westbury Farm
DRAY RD
BOUNDARY
LOWER ODCOMBE
PARSON'S LA
BRYMPTON LA
Alvington
Liberty Trail
HOLLY TERR 1
ORCHARD CL 2
BROADWAY 3
CORYATE CL 4
CHURCH TERR 5
HAM HILL RD
CHERRY LA
DONNE LA
PH
Brympton House
BUNFORD LA
CHAPEL HILL
OLD RD
REX RD
WESTBURY
GONS LA
LONG RUN
Odcombe
Brympton D'Evercy
WATERCOMBE LA
ON WAY
Trad Est
A3088
HOCKERS HILL
STREET LA
Higher Odcombe
LYSANDER RD
LABURNUM WAY
Pye Corner Farm
Broadleaze Farm
RUSSET WAY
Bagnell Farm
LANDSHIRE LA
East Chinnock Hill
EAST CHINNOCK RD
Camp Hill
WATERCOMBE LA
CAMP RD
WEST COKER RD
A30
Chiselborough Hill
CHISELBOROUGH HILL LA
Cloverleaf Farm
Feebarrow
EASTFIELD LA
Eastfield
BURYING HOLE LA
GREEN LA
DIBBLES LA
GOOSEACRE LA
HELENA RD
MASH LA
218

185
196
197
For full street detail of the highlighted area see page 218.

Scale: 1¾ inches to 1 mile
0 ¼ ½ mile
0 250m 500m 750m 1 km

174
188

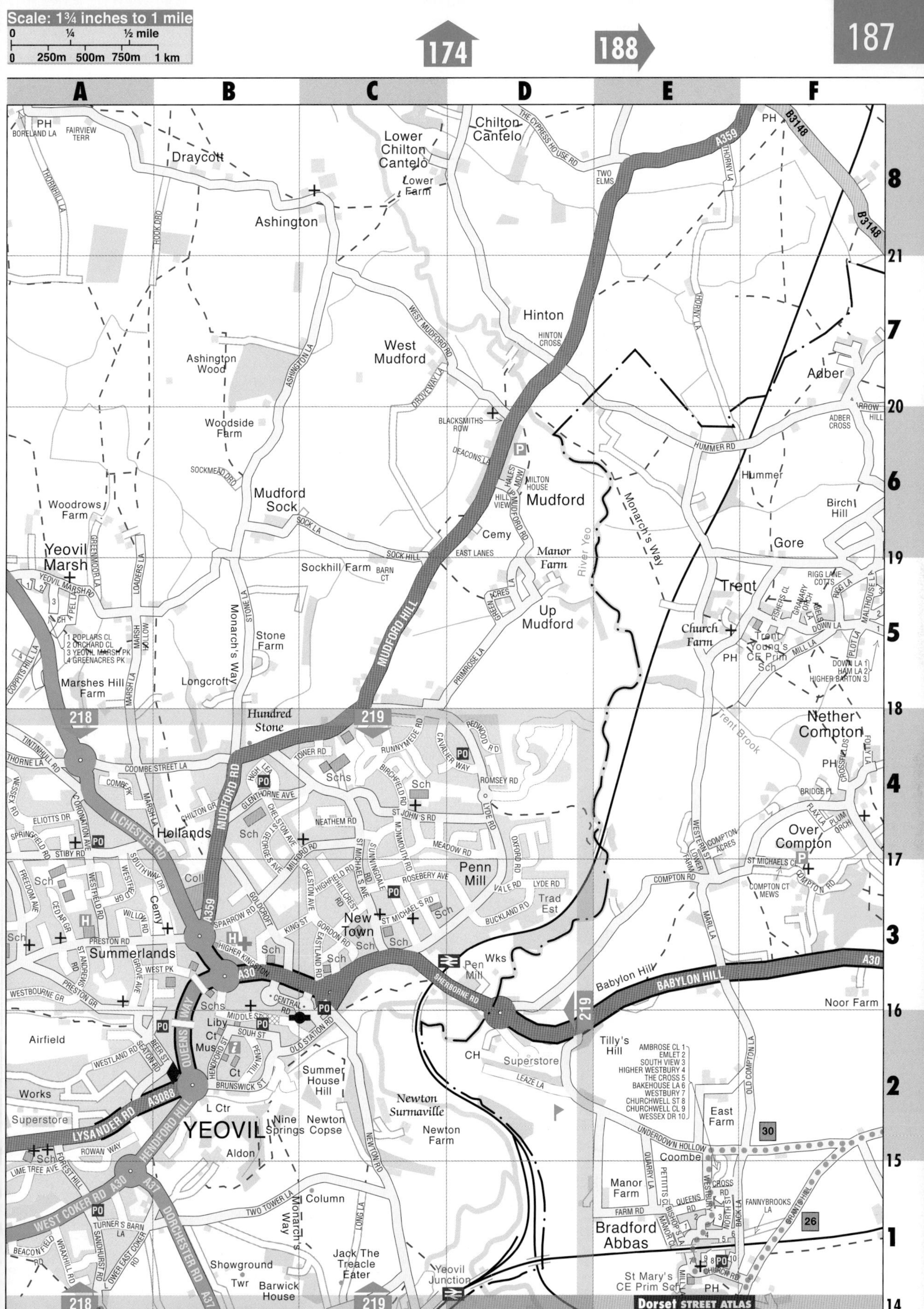

For full street detail of the highlighted area see pages 218 and 219.

197
188

187
175

Scale: 1¾ inches to 1 mile
0 ¼ ½ mile
0 250m 500m 750m 1 km

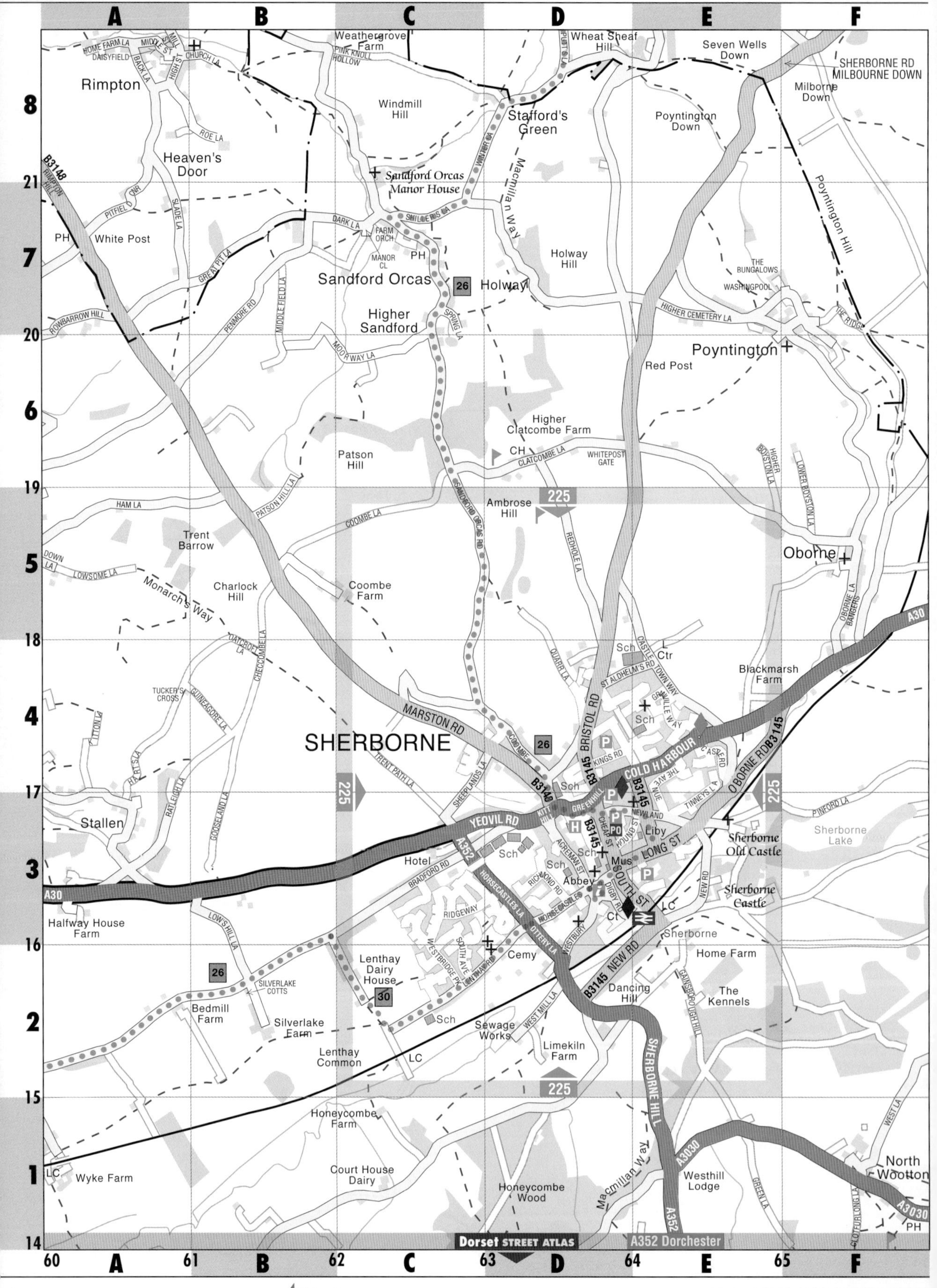

187

For full street detail of the highlighted area see page 225.

Scale: 1¾ inches to 1 mile

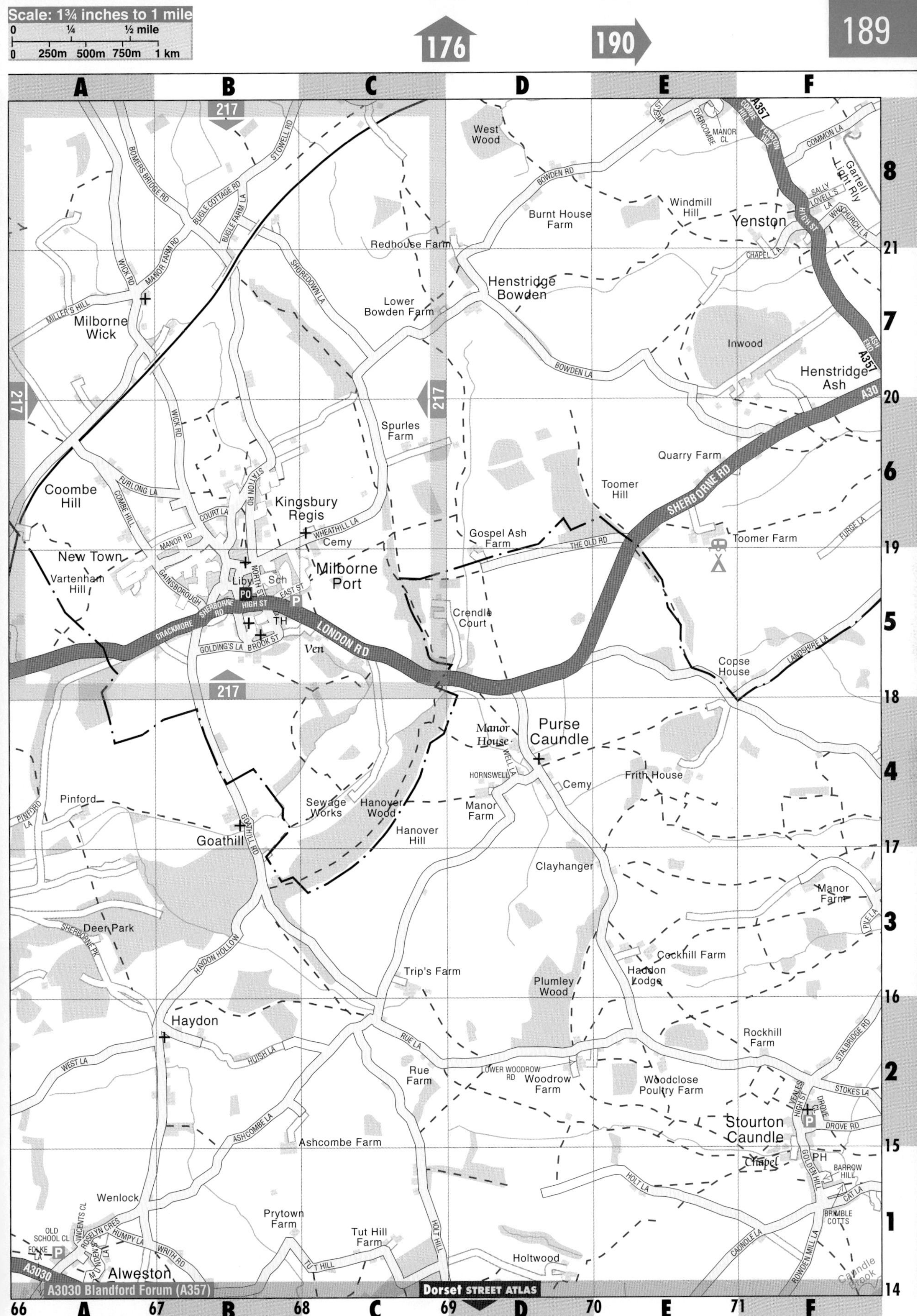

For full street detail of the highlighted area see page 217.

A6
1 VIRGINIA CL
2 PLAYFIELD CL
3 BROOKLAND WAY
4 ST NICHOLAS CL
5 POND CL
6 BLACKMOOR LA
7 BROOK LA
8 CHURCH ST
9 THE CROSS
10 TOWNSEND GN
11 BUGLE CT
12 WOODHAYES HO
13 COTTON CNR
14 VICTORIA TERR
15 VICTORIA GDNS
16 ELIZABETH GDNS
17 WINDSOR TERR
18 CHURCH FARM PL
19 WOODHAYES CT

189

177

Scale: 1¾ inches to 1 mile
0 ¼ ½ mile
0 250m 500m 750m 1 km

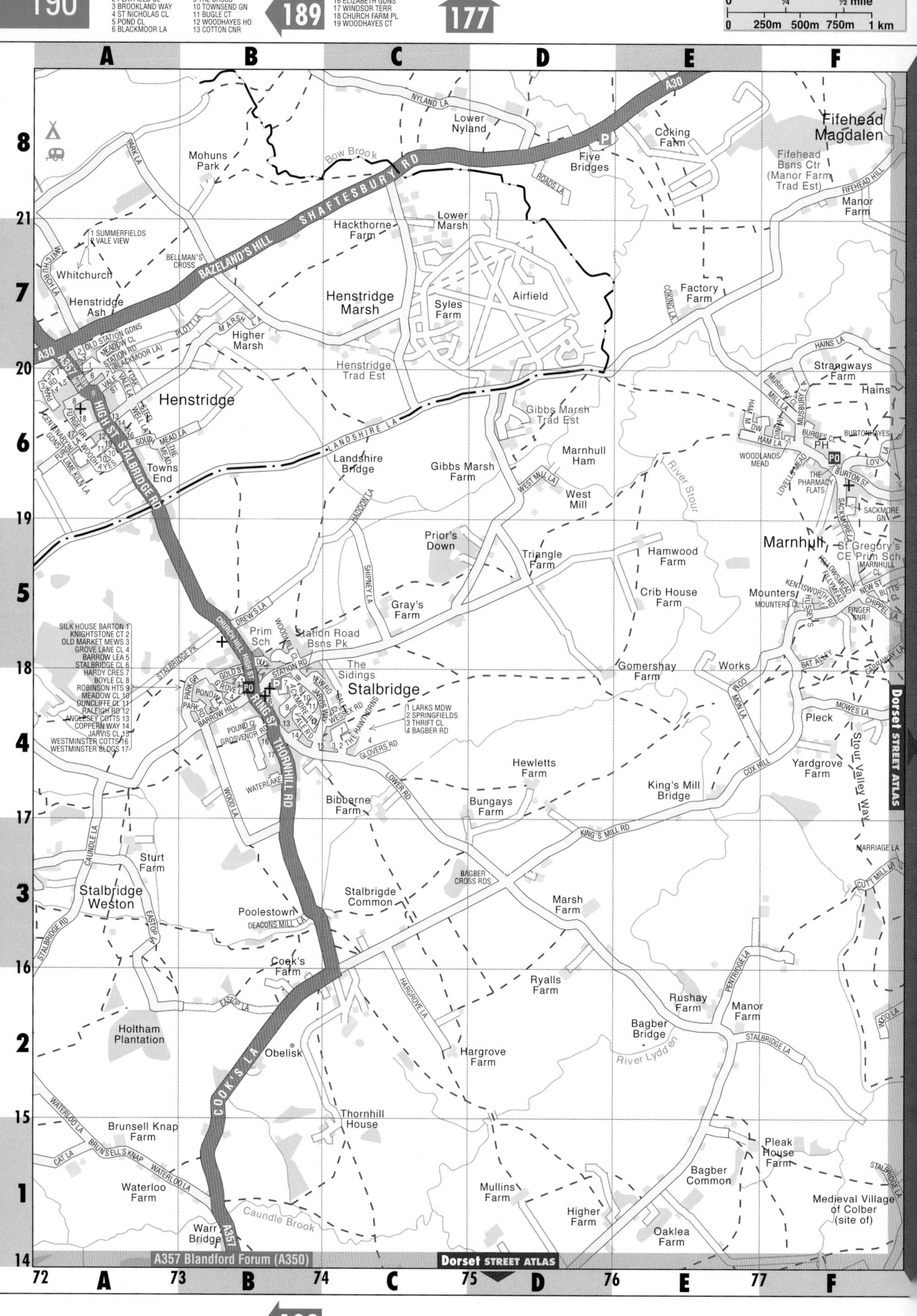

189

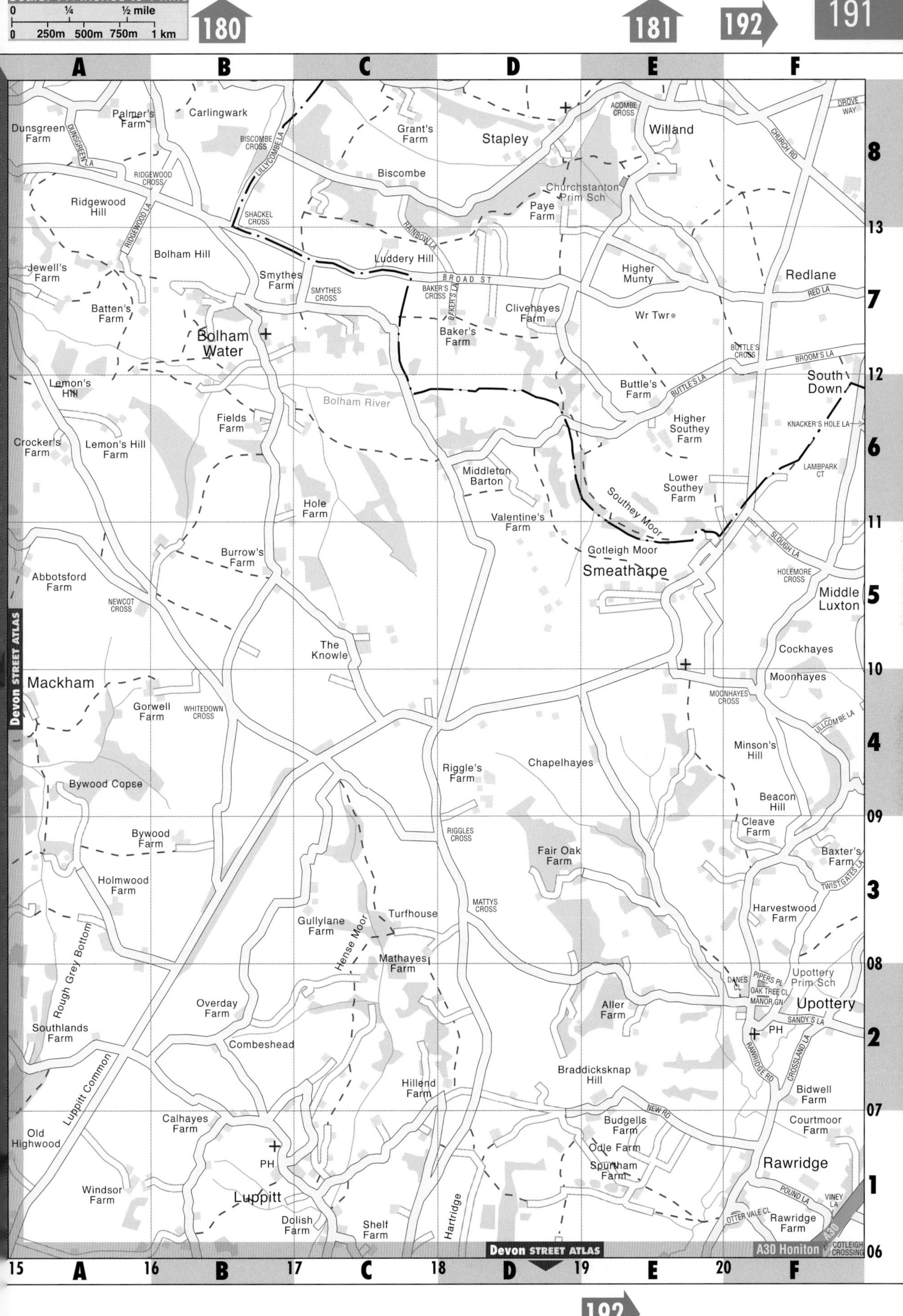

Scale: 1¾ inches to 1 mile
0 ¼ ½ mile
0 250m 500m 750m 1 km
180
181
192
A B C D E F
8
13
7
12
6
11
5
10
4
09
3
08
2
07
1
06
15 16 17 18 19 20
Dunsgreen Farm
Palmer's Farm
Carlingwark
Grant's Farm
Stapley
Willand
Ridgewood Hill
Biscombe
Churchstanton Prim Sch
Paye Farm
Bolham Hill
Luddery Hill
Jewell's Farm
Smythes Farm
Higher Munty
Redlane
Batten's Farm
Bolham Water
Clivehayes Farm
Baker's Farm
Wr Twr
Lemon's Hill
Buttle's Farm
South Down
Bolham River
Fields Farm
Higher Southey Farm
Crocker's Farm
Lemon's Hill Farm
Middleton Barton
Lower Southey Farm
Hole Farm
Southey Moor
Valentine's Farm
Burrow's Farm
Gotleigh Moor
Smeatharpe
Abbotsford Farm
Middle Luxton
The Knowle
Cockhayes
Mackham
Moonhayes
Gorwell Farm
Minson's Hill
Chapelhayes
Riggle's Farm
Bywood Copse
Beacon Hill
Cleave Farm
Bywood Farm
Fair Oak Farm
Baxter's Farm
Holmwood Farm
Harvestwood Farm
Gullylane Farm
Turfhouse
Hense Moor
Mathayes Farm
Rough Grey Bottom
Upottery Prim Sch
Overday Farm
Aller Farm
Upottery
Southlands Farm
Combeshead
PH
Braddicksknap Hill
Hillend Farm
Bidwell Farm
Luppitt Common
Calhayes Farm
Budgells Farm
Courtmoor Farm
Old Highwood
Odle Farm
Rawridge
Spurtham Farm
Windsor Farm
Luppitt
Dolish Farm
Shelf Farm
Hartridge
Rawridge Farm
DUNSGREEN LA
RIDGEWOOD CROSS
RIDGEWOOD LA
BISCOMBE CROSS
LILLYCOMBE LA
SHACKEL CROSS
RAINBOW LA
ACOMBE CROSS
CHURCH RD
DROVE WAY
BROAD ST
SMYTHES CROSS
BAKER'S CROSS
BAKER'S LA
RED LA
BUTTLE'S CROSS
BROOM'S LA
BUTTLE'S LA
KNACKER'S HOLE LA
LAMBPARK CT
SLOUGH LA
HOLEMORE CROSS
NEWCOT CROSS
WHITEDOWN CROSS
MOONHAYES CROSS
ULLCOMBE LA
RIGGLES CROSS
MATTYS CROSS
TWISTGATES LA
DANES CL
PIPERS PL
OAK TREE CL
MANOR GN
SANDY'S LA
RAWRIDGE RD
CROSSLAND LA
NEW RD
POUND LA
VINEY LA
OTTER VALE CL
A30
COTLEIGH CROSSING
A30 Honiton
Devon STREET ATLAS

191
181
182

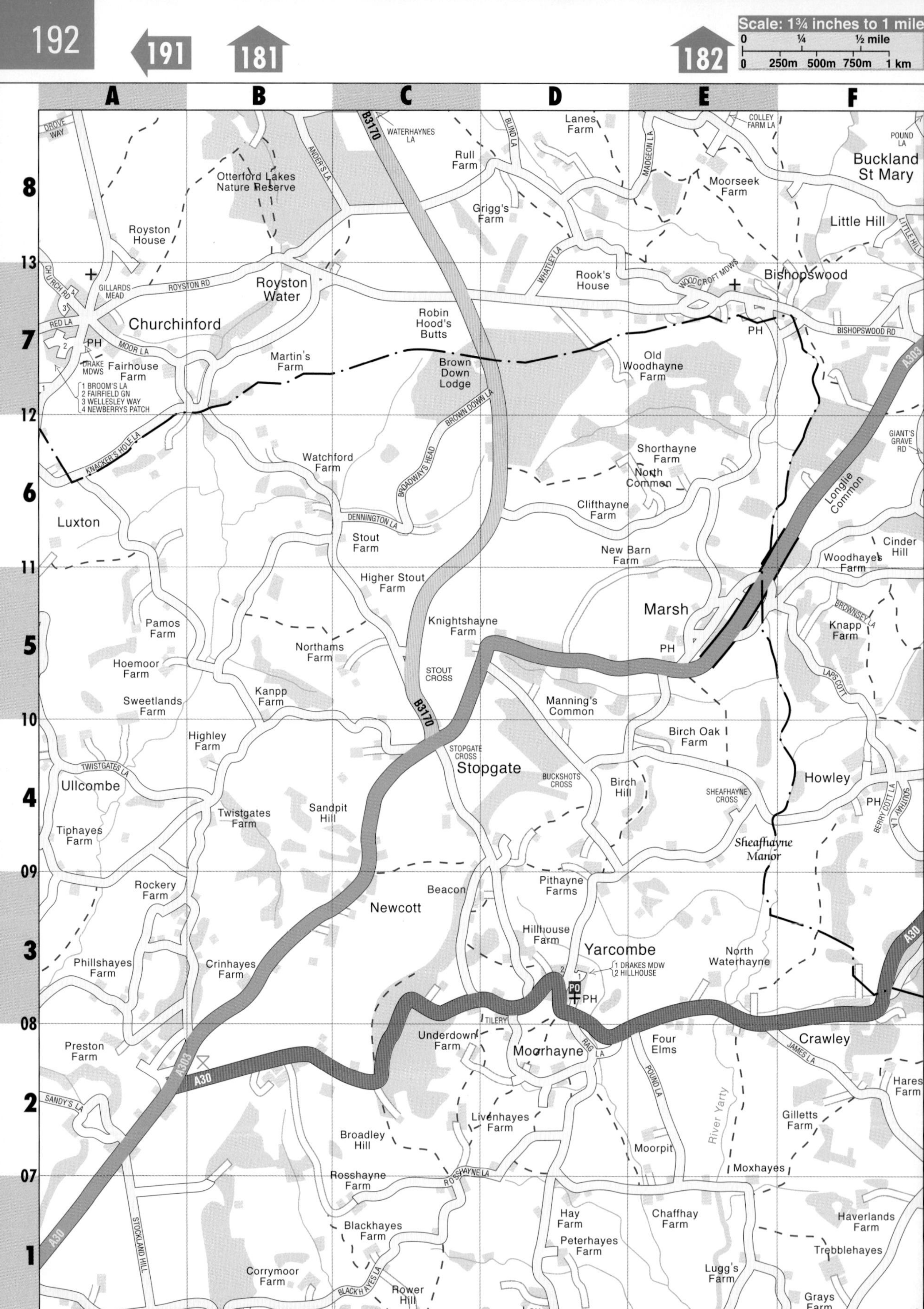
Scale: 1¾ inches to 1 mile
0 ¼ ½ mile
0 250m 500m 750m 1 km
A B C D E F
Otterford Lakes Nature Reserve
Royston House
Churchinford
Royston Water
Robin Hood's Butts
Brown Down Lodge
Martin's Farm
Fairhouse Farm
Rull Farm
Grigg's Farm
Lanes Farm
Moorseek Farm
Buckland St Mary
Little Hill
Bishopswood
Rook's House
Old Woodhayne Farm
Shorthayne Farm
North Common
Clifthayne Farm
New Barn Farm
Marsh
Longlie Common
Cinder Hill
Woodhayes Farm
Knapp Farm
Watchford Farm
Luxton
Stout Farm
Higher Stout Farm
Knightshayne Farm
Northams Farm
Pamos Farm
Hoemoor Farm
Sweetlands Farm
Kanpp Farm
Highley Farm
Manning's Common
Birch Oak Farm
Stopgate
Birch Hill
Howley
Ullcombe
Tiphayes Farm
Twistgates Farm
Sandpit Hill
Sheafhayne Manor
Rockery Farm
Newcott
Beacon
Pithayne Farms
Hillhouse Farm
Yarcombe
North Waterhayne
Phillshayes Farm
Crinhayes Farm
Preston Farm
Underdown Farm
Moorhayne
Four Elms
Crawley
Hares Farm
Gilletts Farm
Livenhayes Farm
Broadley Hill
Moorpit
River Yarty
Moxhayes
Rosshayne Farm
Blackhayes Farm
Hay Farm
Chaffhay Farm
Haverlands Farm
Peterhayes Farm
Trebblehayes
Corrymoor Farm
Rower Hill
Lugg's Farm
Grays Farm
Ley Farm
B3170
A303
A30
PH
PO
1 BROOM'S LA
2 FAIRFIELD GN
3 WELLESLEY WAY
4 NEWBERRYS PATCH
1 DRAKES MDW
2 HILLHOUSE
Devon STREET ATLAS
21 22 23 24 25 26
06 07 08 09 10 11 12 13
1 2 3 4 5 6 7 8

191

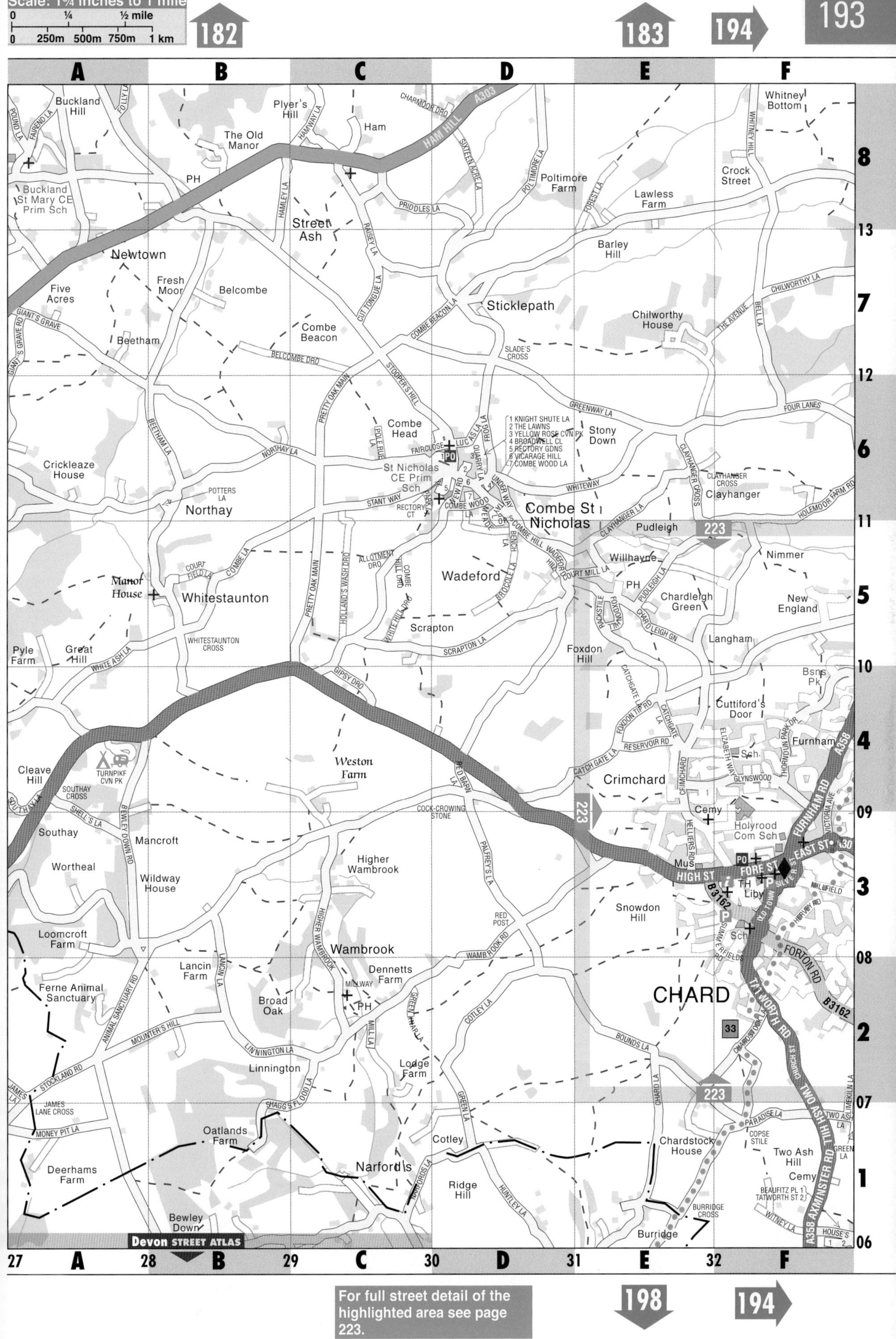

For full street detail of the highlighted area see page 223.

198
194

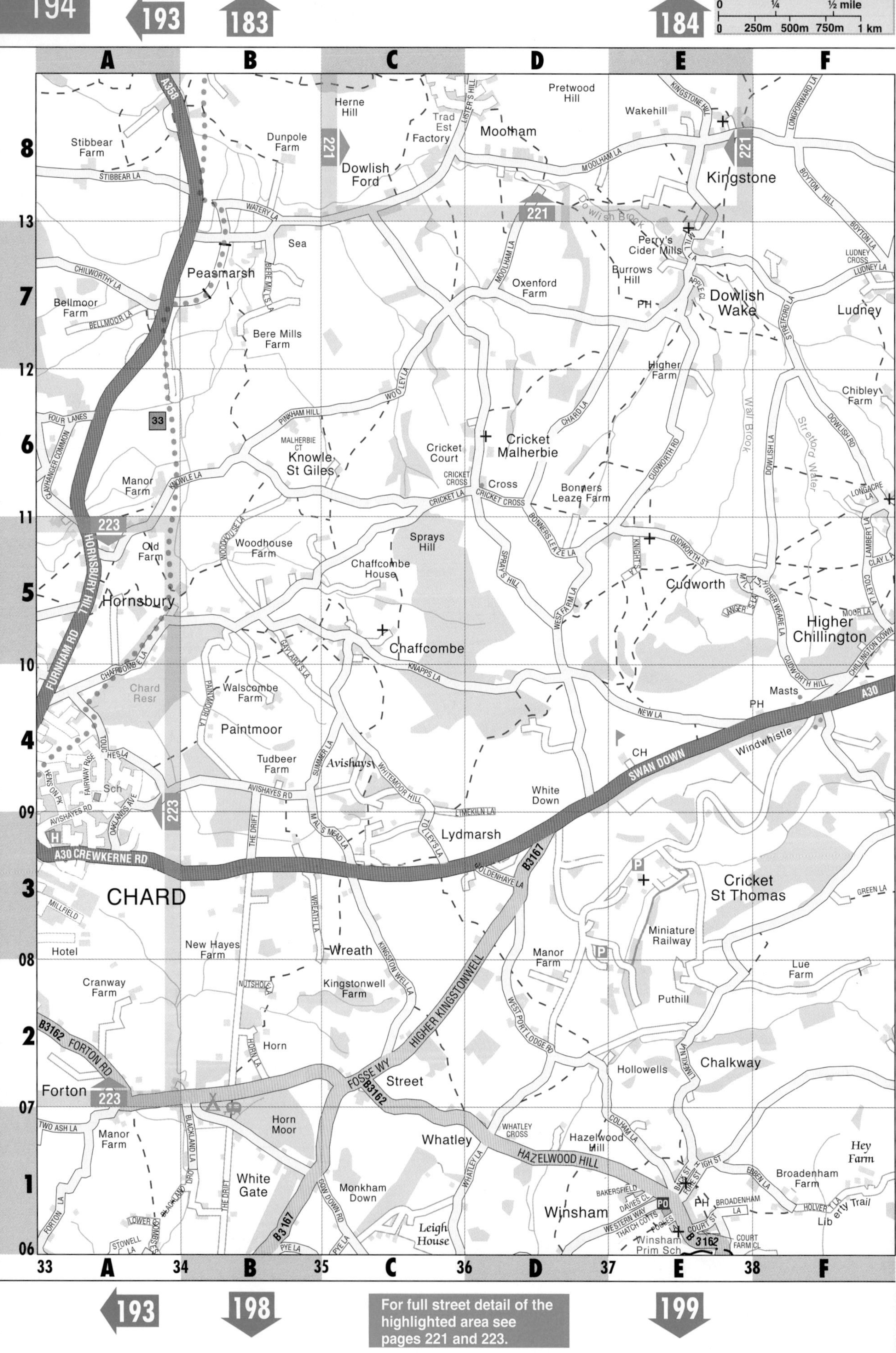
193
183
184
Scale: 1¾ inches to 1 mile
0 ¼ ½ mile
0 250m 500m 750m 1 km
A B C D E F
Stibbear Farm
Dunpole Farm
Herne Hill
Trad Est Factory
Moolham
Pretwood Hill
Wakehill
Kingstone
Dowlish Ford
Peasmarsh
Sea
Perry's Cider Mills
Burrows Hill
Oxenford Farm
Bellmoor Farm
Bere Mills Farm
Dowlish Wake
Ludney
Higher Farm
Chibley Farm
Manor Farm
Knowle St Giles
Cricket Court
Cricket Malherbie
Cross
Bonners Leaze Farm
Old Farm
Woodhouse Farm
Sprays Hill
Chaffcombe House
Cudworth
Hornsbury
Chaffcombe
Higher Chillington
Chard Resr
Walscombe Farm
Paintmoor
Tudbeer Farm
Avishays
Masts
PH
CH
Windwhistle
White Down
Lydmarsh
CHARD
Cricket St Thomas
Miniature Railway
Hotel
New Hayes Farm
Wreath
Manor Farm
Cranway Farm
Kingstonwell Farm
Lue Farm
Puthill
Horn
Forton
Street
Hollowells
Chalkway
Manor Farm
Horn Moor
Whatley
Hazelwood Hill
Hey Farm
White Gate
Monkham Down
Winsham
Broadenham Farm
Leigh House
Liberty Trail
Winsham Prim Sch
A30 CREWKERNE RD
SWAN DOWN
HIGHER KINGSTONWELL
HAZELWOOD HILL
FOSSE WY
33 34 35 36 37 38
193
198
199
For full street detail of the highlighted area see pages 221 and 223.

F7
1 BAKEHOUSE
2 THE PIECE
3 SHERLANDS GDNS
4 SHERLANDS
5 OLD HITCHEN
6 FARR'S ORCH
7 GLEBELANDS
8 SHYNERS TERR
9 THE CLOSE
10 MANOR DR
11 GOUGH CL

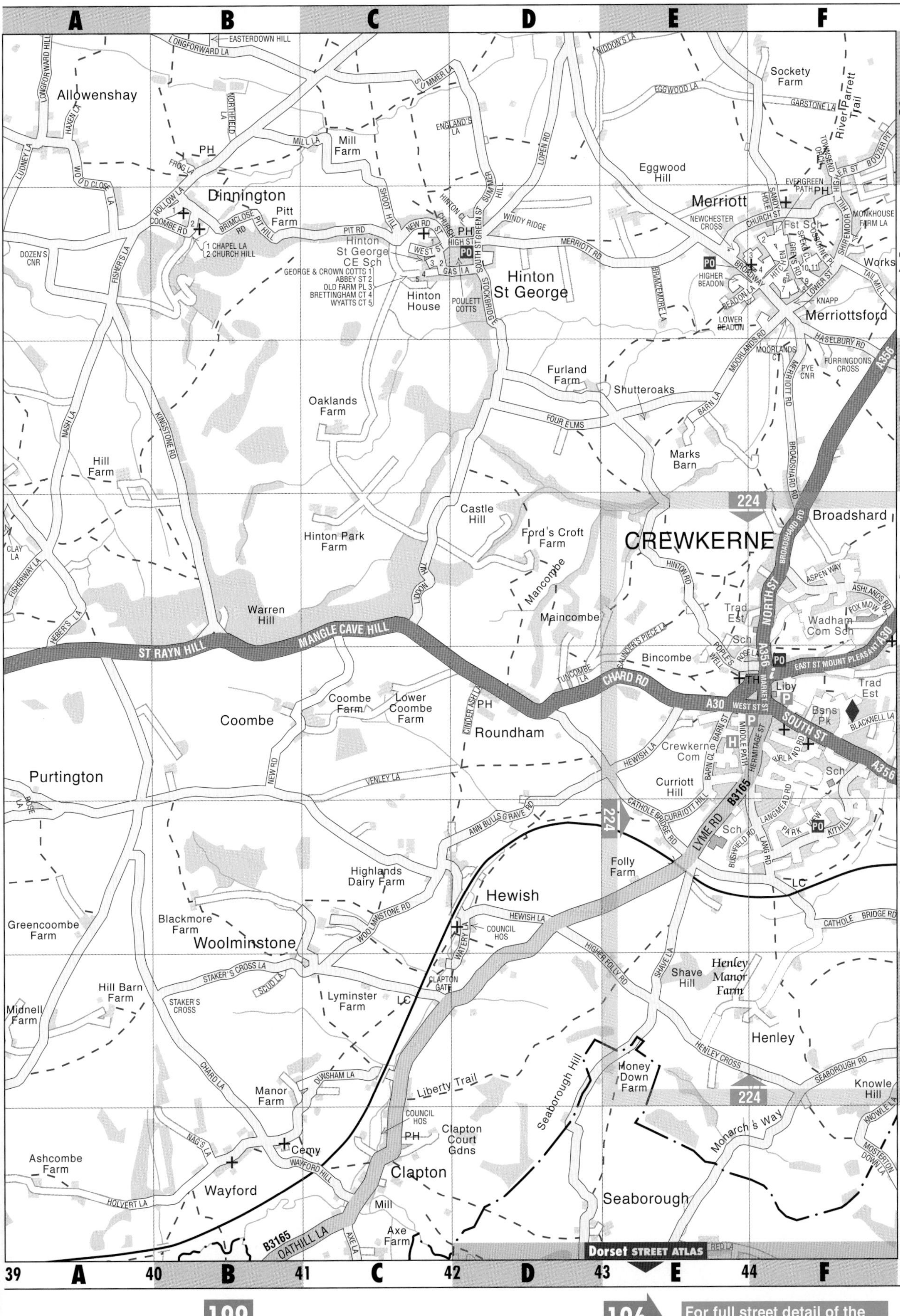

A B C D E F
8 7 6 5 4 3 2 1
13 12 11 10 09 08 07 06
39 40 41 42 43 44
Allowenshay
Dinnington
Pitt Farm
Mill Farm
Hinton St George
Hinton St George CE Sch
Hinton House
POULETT COTTS
GEORGE & CROWN COTTS 1
ABBEY ST 2
OLD FARM PL 3
BRETTINGHAM CT 4
WYATTS CT 5
1 CHAPEL LA
2 CHURCH HILL
DOZEN'S CNR
Eggwood Hill
Sockety Farm
River Parrett Trail
Merriott
NEWCHESTER CROSS
HIGHER BEADON
LOWER BEADON
Merriottsford
Works
KNAPP
MOORLANDS CT
PYE CNR
FURRINGDONS CROSS
Furland Farm
Shutteroaks
Oaklands Farm
Marks Barn
Hill Farm
Castle Hill
Ford's Croft Farm
Hinton Park Farm
Broadshard
CREWKERNE
Mancombe
Maincombe
Warren Hill
Trad Est
Wadham Com Sch
Bincombe
ST RAYN HILL
MANGLE CAVE HILL
CHARD RD
Coombe Farm
Lower Coombe Farm
Coombe
Roundham
Purtington
Crewkerne Com
Curriott Hill
Bsns Pk
Highlands Dairy Farm
Hewish
Folly Farm
Greencoombe Farm
Blackmore Farm
Woolminstone
Hill Barn Farm
STAKER'S CROSS
Lyminster Farm
CLAPTON GATE
Shave Hill
Henley Manor Farm
Midnell Farm
Henley
HENLEY CROSS
Honey Down Farm
Seaborough Hill
Knowle Hill
Manor Farm
Liberty Trail
Monarch's Way
COUNCIL HOS
Clapton Court Gdns
Ashcombe Farm
Wayford
Cemy
Clapton
Seaborough
Mill
Axe Farm
B3165
A30
A356
224
Dorset STREET ATLAS

For full street detail of the highlighted area see page 224.

195
185
186

Scale: 1¾ inches to 1 mile
0 ¼ ½ mile
0 250m 500m 750m 1 km

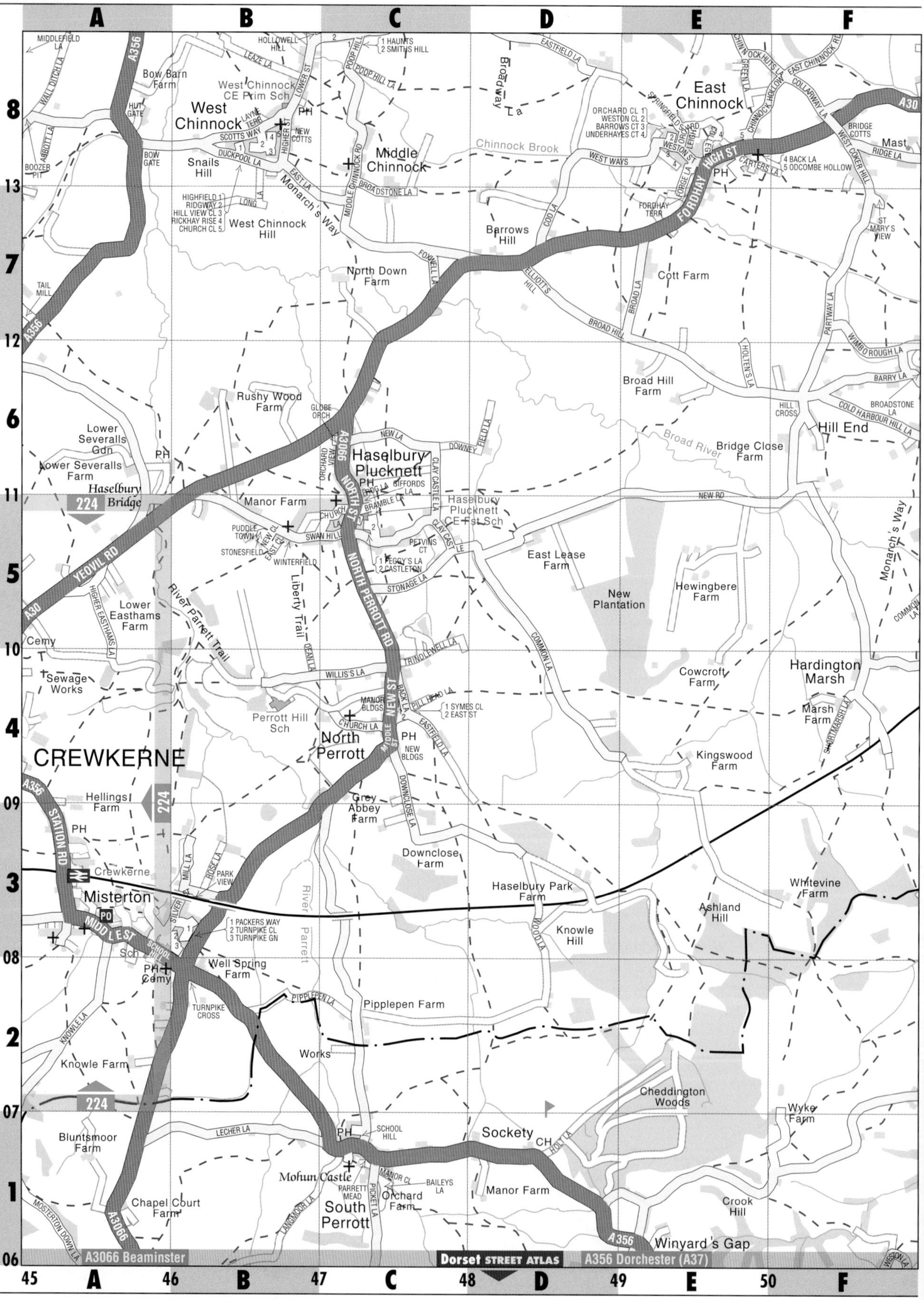

West Chinnock
West Chinnock CE Prim Sch
Middle Chinnock
East Chinnock
Snails Hill
West Chinnock Hill
Bow Barn Farm
Barrows Hill
North Down Farm
Cott Farm
Broad Hill Farm
Rushy Wood Farm
Lower Severalls Gdn
Lower Severalls Farm
Haselbury Bridge
Haselbury Plucknett
Haselbury Plucknett CE Fst Sch
Manor Farm
Bridge Close Farm
Hill End
East Lease Farm
New Plantation
Hewingbere Farm
Lower Easthams Farm
Sewage Works
Perrott Hill Sch
North Perrott
Cowcroft Farm
Hardington Marsh
Marsh Farm
Kingswood Farm
CREWKERNE
Hellings Farm
Grey Abbey Farm
Downclose Farm
Haselbury Park Farm
Crewkerne
Misterton
Knowle Hill
Ashland Hill
Whitevine Farm
Well Spring Farm
Pipplepen Farm
Works
Knowle Farm
Cheddington Woods
Bluntsmoor Farm
Sockety
Wyke Farm
Mohun Castle
South Perrott
Orchard Farm
Manor Farm
Chapel Court Farm
Crook Hill
Winyard's Gap
Chinnock Brook
Broad River
River Parrett
Monarch's Way
River Parrett Trail
Liberty Trail
A356
A30
A3066
YEDVIL RD
NORTH ST
NORTH PERROTT RD
NEW ST
MIDDLE ST
STATION RD
FORDHAY
HIGH ST
MIDDLE ST

A3066 Beaminster
Dorset STREET ATLAS
A356 Dorchester (A37)

For full street detail of the highlighted area see page 224.
195

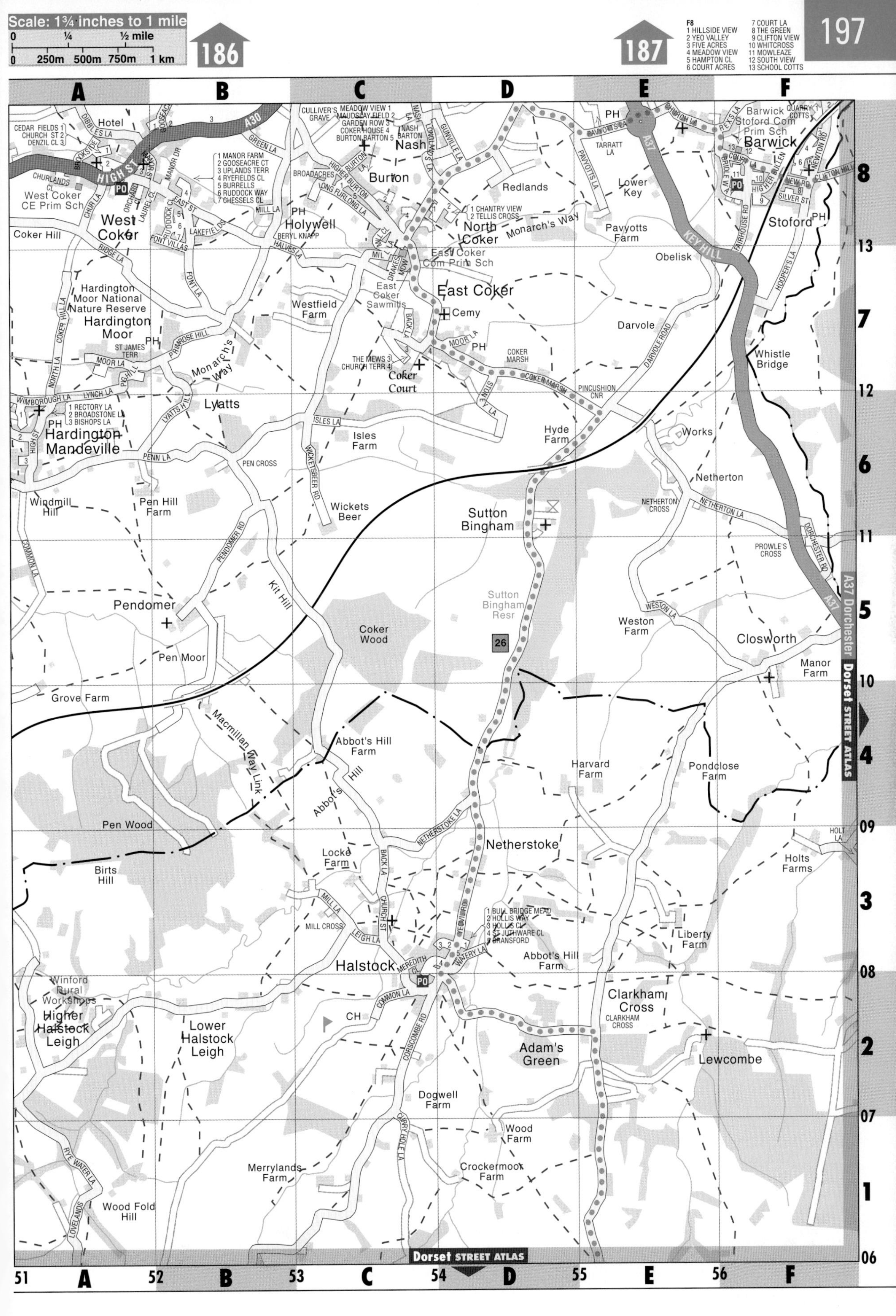
Scale: 1¾ inches to 1 mile
0 ¼ ½ mile
0 250m 500m 750m 1 km
186
187
F8
1 HILLSIDE VIEW
2 YEO VALLEY
3 FIVE ACRES
4 MEADOW VIEW
5 HAMPTON CL
6 COURT ACRES
7 COURT LA
8 THE GREEN
9 CLIFTON VIEW
10 WHITCROSS
11 MOWLEAZE
12 SOUTH VIEW
13 SCHOOL COTTS
A
B
C
D
E
F
Hotel
CEDAR FIELDS 1
CHURCH ST 2
DENZIL CL 3
A30
HIGH ST
CHURLANDS CL
West Coker CE Prim Sch
West Coker
Coker Hill
1 MANOR FARM
2 GOOSEACRE CT
3 UPLANDS TERR
4 RYEFIELDS CL
5 BURRELLS
6 RUDDOCK WAY
7 CHESSELS CL
CULLIVER'S GRAVE
MEADOW VIEW 1
MAUDSLAY FIELD 2
GARDEN ROW 3
COKER HOUSE 4
BURTON BARTON 5
NASH BARTON
Nash
Burton
BROADACRES
PH
Holywell
BERYL KNAPP
1 CHANTRY VIEW
2 TELLIS CROSS
Redlands
North Coker
Monarch's Way
East Coker Com Prim Sch
East Coker Sawmills
East Coker
Cemy
Westfield Farm
Hardington Moor National Nature Reserve
Hardington Moor
ST JAMES TERR
MOOR LA
PRIMROSE HILL
Monarch's Way
THE MEWS 3
CHURCH TERR 4
Coker Court
COKER MARSH
WIMBOROUGH LA
LYNCH LA
1 RECTORY LA
2 BROADSTONE LA
3 BISHOPS LA
Hardington Mandeville
Lyatts
ISLES LA
Isles Farm
PENN LA
PEN CROSS
WICKETSBEER RD
Hyde Farm
PINCUSHION CNR
DARVOLE ROAD
Darvole
Obelisk
KEY HILL
Pavyotts Farm
Lower Key
TARRATT LA
PH
Barwick Stoford Com Prim Sch
Barwick
Stoford
QUARRY COTTS
NEWTON RD
CLIFTON HILL
SILVER ST
HIGHER BULLEN
FAIRHOUSE RD
HOOPER'S LA
Whistle Bridge
Works
Netherton
NETHERTON CROSS
NETHERTON LA
PROWLE'S CROSS
DORCHESTER RD
Windmill Hill
Pen Hill Farm
Wickets Beer
Sutton Bingham
Sutton Bingham Resr
26
COMMON LA
PENDOMER RD
Kit Hill
Pendomer
Pen Moor
Coker Wood
Weston Farm
WESTON LA
Closworth
Manor Farm
A37 Dorchester
Dorset STREET ATLAS
Grove Farm
Macmillan Way Link
Abbot's Hill Farm
Abbot's Hill
Harvard Farm
Pondclose Farm
Pen Wood
NETHERSTOKE LA
Netherstoke
HOLT LA
Holts Farms
Birts Hill
Locke Farm
BACK LA
MILL LA
CHURCH ST
MILL CROSS
LEIGH LA
1 BULL BRIDGE MEAD
2 HOLLIS WAY
3 HOLLIS CL
4 ST JUTHWARE CL
5 BRANSFORD
YEOVIL RD
WATERY LA
Abbot's Hill Farm
Liberty Farm
Halstock
MEREDITH CL
PO
COMMON LA
Winford Rural Workshops
Higher Halstock Leigh
Lower Halstock Leigh
CH
CORSCOMBE RD
Clarkham Cross
CLARKHAM CROSS
Adam's Green
Lewcombe
Dogwell Farm
CARRY HOLE LA
Wood Farm
RYE WATER LA
Merrylands Farm
Crockermoor Farm
LOVELANDS
Wood Fold Hill
Dorset STREET ATLAS
8
13
7
12
6
11
5
10
4
09
3
08
2
07
1
06
51
52
53
54
55
56

193
194

Scale: 1¾ inches to 1 mile
0 ¼ ½ mile
0 250m 500m 750m 1 km

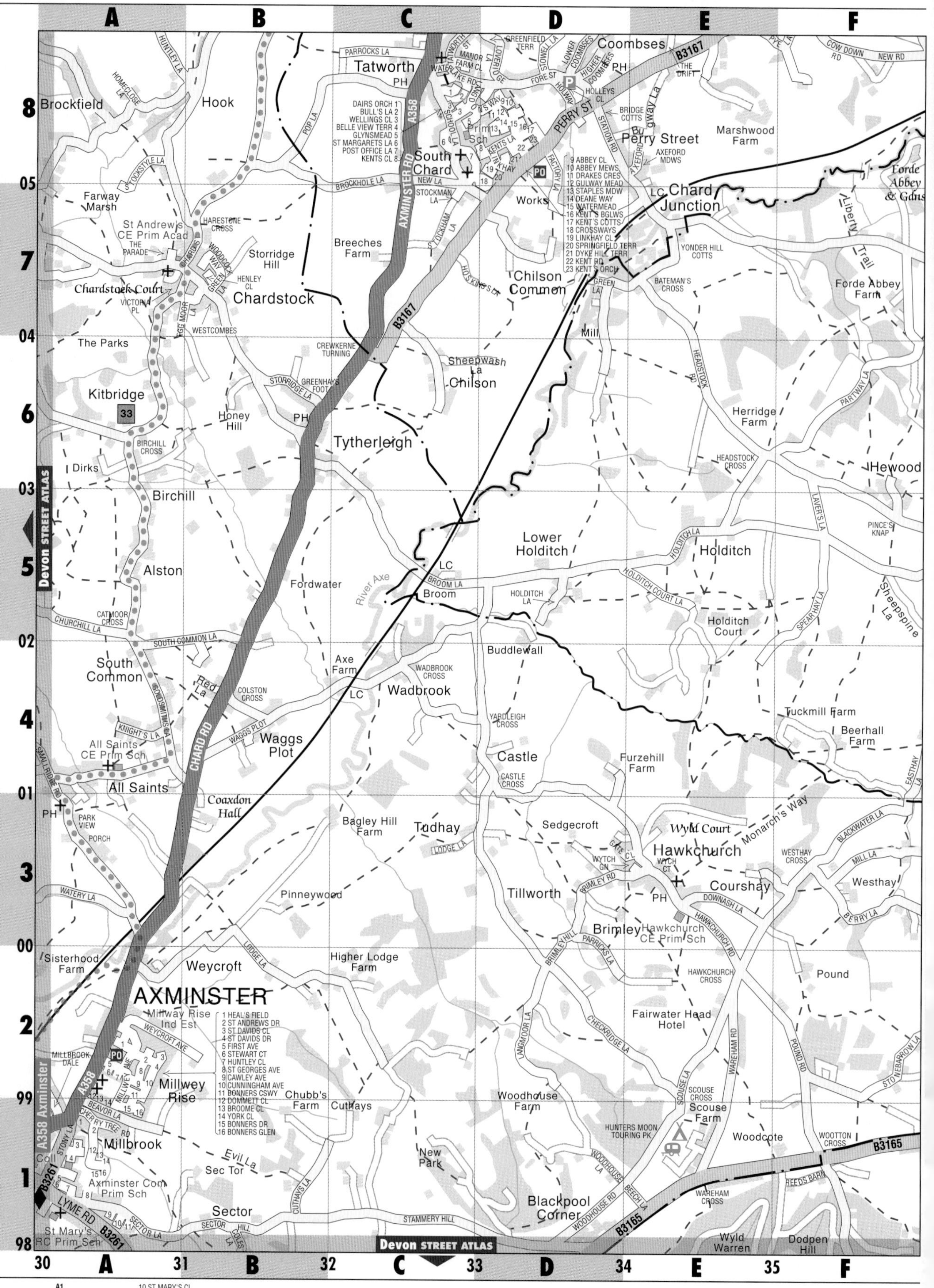

A1
1 MILLBROOK CROSS
2 CATNIP CL
3 JEFFS WAY
4 NEWBERY CL
5 LORETTO GDNS
6 MONKSTONE GDNS
7 CRIDLAKE
8 TIGERS WY
9 PRESTOR
10 ST MARY'S CL
11 SALWAY GDNS
12 FLAX MEADOW LA
13 BLEACHFIELD RI
14 LOWER MEAD
15 LINSEED DR
16 UPPER MEAD

LEIGH LA
Bridge
Ammerham
WHATLEY LA
AMMERHAM LA
Bere Farm
B3162
Bere Chapel
OATHILL LA
B3165
Oathill
AXE LA
Netherhay
8
Copse House
MAUDLIN CROSS
MAUDLIN LA
Maudlin
OAXHAYES 1
HOLLY LA 2
BRIDPORT RD 3
MARKSMEAD 4
APPLEFIELD RD 5
NETHERHAY LA
ORCHARD CL
05
SHEDRICK HILL
WHEEL HOUSE LA
Shedrick Hill
Greenham House
Drimpton
B3162 CHARD RD
SPEAR MEAD
POST OFFICE YD
Squirrel Inn
PARK LA
Forde Grange
Laymore
B3162
GREENHAM LA
GREENHAM YD
BRIDGE COTTS
DRIMPTON CROSS
BURSTOCK LA
Greenham
7
Horn Ash
Stony Knaps
THREE ASHES
GRANGE CNR
Chaffeigh Farm
CUCKOO LA
WOOD LA
04
Gribb
Vennacott Farm
Kittwhistle
Childhay
CHILDHAY LA
BLIND LA
VENN HILL
SCHOOL LA
Monarch's Way
Moor La
Temple Brook
KNOWLE CROSS
BLIND LA
Holway
Blackdown Hill
Whetham Farm
GRIBB VIEW
TANSEY HILL
HORSESHOE RD
Synderford
6
St Mary's CE Prim Sch
CHARD ST
FORE ST
CAUSEWAY LA
WHETHAM MILL LA
Yewtree Farm
Greenhill
WITHEY'S
HIGH ST
ORCHARD LA
Thorncombe
Blackdown
03
COOMBE WATER LA
THORNCOMBE THORN
River Synderford
WHETHAM MILL CROSS
Holmbush
PARK WATER LA
5
School House
SHEARING CROSS
SADBOROW POUND
HAINES LA
Cole's Cross
COLES CROSS COTTS
Lowdown Farm
Knapp Farm
Sadborow
02
WHACKER'S HOLE LA
EASTHAY LA
Racedown
Pilsdon Pen
Jubilee Trail
Elmore Farm
Grighay Farm
Home Farm
SADBOROW LA
4
Easthay
Payne's Down
COCKPIT HILL
Attisham
B3165
Wessex Ridgeway
Birdsmoorgate
ATTISHAM LA
B3164
01
PH
B3164
Templeman's Ash
Northay
GASHAY LA
Gashay Farm
Pilsdon Barn
NORTHAY LA
Blackwater River
HORSE MILL CROSS
Sliding Hill
NORTHAY CROSS
3
CULVERLAKE LA
Liberty Trail
Bettiscombe Manor
YARD LA
Colmer Farm
Marshalsea
Revelshay Farm
PILSDON LA
BERRY LA
MARSHALSEA EST
Wellfield Farm
Bettiscombe
00
STONEBARROW LA
Bottle La
PH
WELLFIELD HILL
Pilsdon Manor
HAWKMOOR HILL
Marshwood
Lower House Farm
Pilsdon
Marshwood CE Prim Sch
Manshay Barton
Marshwood Manor
2
TURNER'S LA
Bridewell
Lambert's Castle (Fort)
Sminhay Farms
BATTS LA
Purcombe Farm
MANSHAY LA
99
NASH LA
Nash Farm
Baber's Farm
Cowdea Farm
MUTTON ST
P
Lambert's Castle Hill
Oakford Farm
FISHPOND BOTTOM RD
Higher Park Farm
MARSHWOOD CROSS
2
PETER'S GORE
HOLDSCROFT LA
1
SANSOM'S CROSS
WOOTTON HILL
Fishpond Bottom
ABBOTT'S
WOOTTON LA
TAPHOUSE LA
POORHOUSE LA
CHARING CROSS
2
SHAVE CROSS
98

Dorset STREET ATLAS

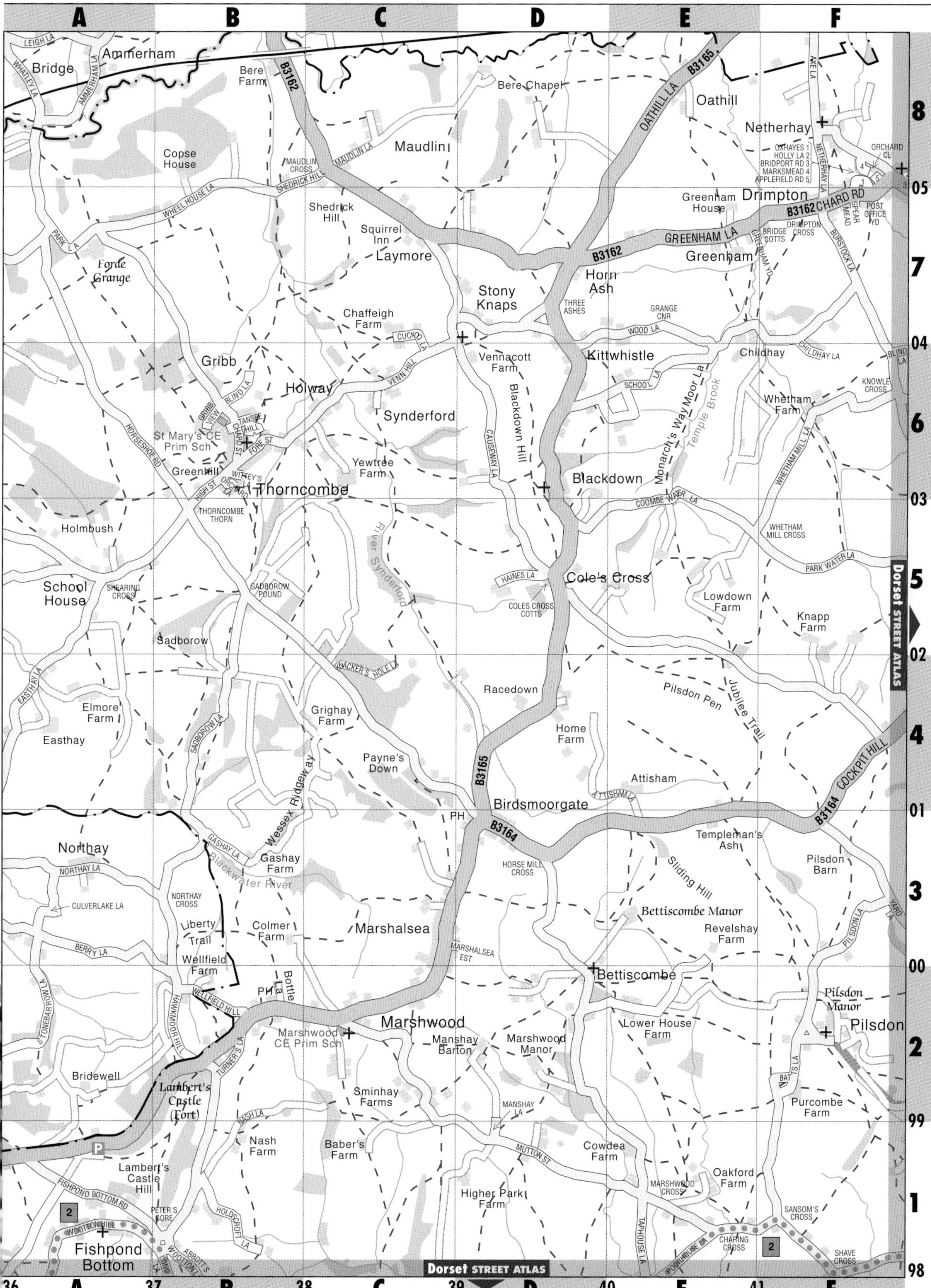

124
125

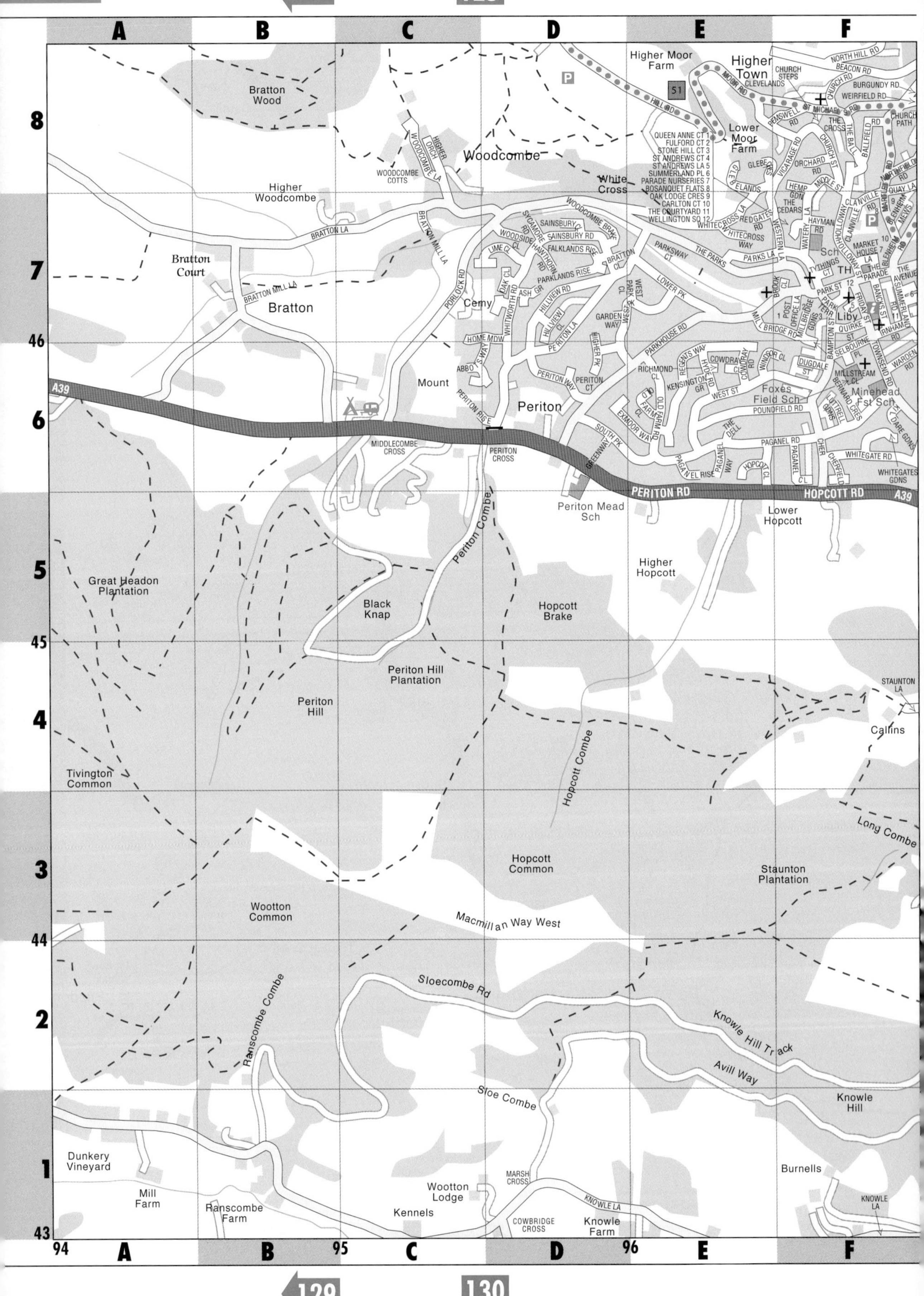
A
B
C
D
E
F
8
7
46
6
5
45
4
3
44
2
1
43
94
95
96
Bratton Wood
Higher Moor Farm
Higher Town
Lower Moor Farm
Woodcombe
WOODCOMBE COTTS
Higher Woodcombe
White Cross
BRATTON LA
Bratton Court
BRATTON MILL LA
Bratton
Cemy
Mount
Periton
PERITON RISE
MIDDLECOMBE CROSS
PERITON CROSS
A39
PERITON RD
HOPCOTT RD
Periton Mead Sch
Lower Hopcott
Higher Hopcott
Foxes Field Sch
Minehead Fst Sch
Sch
Liby
TH
Periton Combe
Great Headon Plantation
Black Knap
Hopcott Brake
Periton Hill Plantation
Periton Hill
Tivington Common
Hopcott Combe
Callins
STAUNTON LA
Long Combe
Hopcott Common
Staunton Plantation
Wootton Common
Macmillan Way West
Sloecombe Rd
Ranscombe Combe
Knowle Hill Track
Avill Way
Sloe Combe
Knowle Hill
Dunkery Vineyard
Mill Farm
Ranscombe Farm
Wootton Lodge
Kennels
MARSH CROSS
COWBRIDGE CROSS
KNOWLE LA
Knowle Farm
Burnells
QUEEN ANNE CT 1
FULFORD CT 2
STONE HILL CT 3
ST ANDREWS CT 4
ST ANDREWS LA 5
SUMMERLAND PL 6
PARADE NURSERIES 7
BOSANQUET FLATS 8
OAK LODGE CRES 9
CARLTON CT 10
THE COURTYARD 11
WELLINGTON SQ 12
NORTH HILL RD
BEACON RD
BURGUNDY RD
WEIRFIELD RD
CHURCH STEPS
CLEVELANDS
CHURCH PATH
ORCHARD RD
GLEBELANDS
VICARAGE RD
THE CEDARS
WHITECROSS LA
WHITECROSS WAY
PARKS LA
THE PARKS
PARKSWAY CT
LOWER PK
WOODCOMBE BRAKE
SAINSBURY CL
SAINSBURY RD
FALKLANDS RISE
PARKLANDS RISE
HILLVIEW RD
PORLOCK RD
WHITWORTH RD
HOME MDW
PARKHOUSE RD
RICHMOND CL
KENSINGTON GR
WEST ST
POUNDFIELD RD
SOUTH PK
EXMOOR WAY
GREENWAY
PAGANEL RD
PAGANEL RISE
HOPCOTT CL
WHITEGATE RD
WHITEGATES GDNS
DUGDALE ST
MILLSTREAM CL
SELBOURNE PL
TOWNSEND RD
BAMPTON ST
FRIDAY ST
PARK ST
MARKET HOUSE LA
THE PARADE
THE AVENUE
QUAY LA
WARDEN RD

129
130

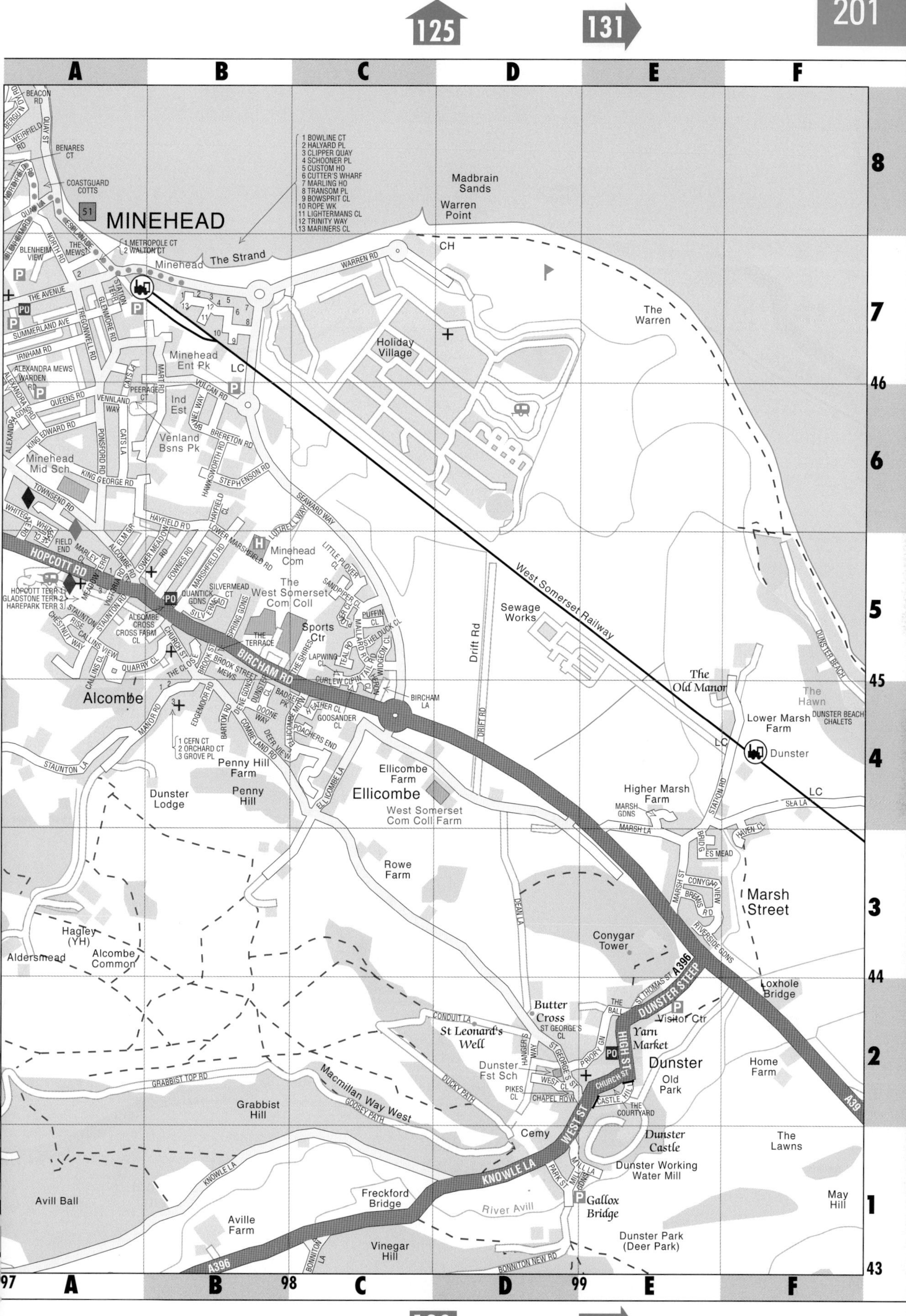
125
131
A
B
C
D
E
F
8
7
46
6
5
45
4
3
44
2
1
43
97
98
99
MINEHEAD
51
BEACON RD
QUAY ST
WEIRFIELD RD
BENARES CT
COASTGUARD COTTS
QUAY LA
ESPLANADE
NORTH RD
BLENHEIM RD
BLENHEIM VIEW
THE MEWS
1 METROPOLE CT
2 WALTON CT
Minehead
The Strand
1 BOWLINE CT
2 HALYARD PL
3 CLIPPER QUAY
4 SCHOONER PL
5 CUSTOM HO
6 CUTTER'S WHARF
7 MARLING HO
8 TRANSOM PL
9 BOWSPRIT CL
10 ROPE WK
11 LIGHTERMANS CL
12 TRINITY WAY
13 MARINERS CL
Madbrain Sands
Warren Point
CH
WARREN RD
The Warren
STATION TERR
THE AVENUE
SUMMERLAND AVE
TREGONWELL RD
GLENMORE RD
IRNHAM RD
ALEXANDRA MEWS
WARDEN RD
QUEENS RD
ALEXANDRA GDNS
KING EDWARD RD
Holiday Village
Minehead Ent Pk
LC
MART RD
CATS LA
PEERAGE CT
VENNLAND WAY
Ind Est
VULCAN RD
BRUNEL WAY
Venland Bsns Pk
BRERETON RD
HAWKSWORTH RD
STEPHENSON RD
Minehead Mid Sch
PONSFORD RD
KING GEORGE RD
TOWNSEND RD
WHITECROSS RD
HAYFIELD RD
HAYFIELD CL
LUTTRELL WAY
SEAWARD WAY
LOWER MARSHFIELD RD
FIELD END
MARLEY CL
ELM GR
ALCOMBE RD
LOWER MEADOW RD
FOWNES RD
MARSHFIELD RD
Minehead Com
LITTLE PLOVER CL
HOPCOTT RD
HOPCOTT TERR 1
GLADSTONE TERR 2
HAREPARK TERR 3
MEADOW TERR
VICTORIA RD
QUANTICK GDNS
SILVERMEAD CT
SILVERMEAD
SPRING GDNS
The West Somerset Com Coll
SANDPIPER CL
PUFFIN CL
STAUNTON RISE
STAUNTON RD
CHESTNUT WAY
CALLINS VIEW
ALCOMBE CROSS
CROSS FARM CL
CHURCH ST
THE TERRACE
Sports Ctr
MALLARD RD
SHELDUCK CL
WIDGEON CL
Sewage Works
West Somerset Railway
Drift Rd
DRIFT RD
CALLINS CL
QUARRY CL
THE CLOSE
BROOK ST
BROOK STREET MEWS
BIRCHAM RD
THE SHIRES
LAPWING CL
TEAL RD
PINTAIL RD
HERON
CURLEW CL
BIRCHAM LA
The Old Manor
The Hawn
DUNSTER BEACH
DUNSTER BEACH CHALETS
Lower Marsh Farm
Dunster
Alcombe
MANOR RD
EDGEMOOR RD
BARTON RD
DENE GDNS
DOONE WAY
COMBELAND RD
DEER VIEW
BADGER PK
ALLICOMBE MDW
HEATHER CL
GOOSANDER CL
POACHERS END
1 CEFN CT
2 ORCHARD CT
3 GROVE PL
STAUNTON LA
Penny Hill Farm
Penny Hill
Dunster Lodge
ELLICOMBE LA
Ellicombe Farm
Ellicombe
West Somerset Com Coll Farm
Higher Marsh Farm
MARSH GDNS
MARSH LA
STATION RD
SEA LA
HAVEN CL
ES MEAD
BRIDGE
Rowe Farm
MARSH ST
CONYGAR VIEW
Marsh Street
RIVERSIDE GDNS
DEAN LA
Conygar Tower
Hagley (YH)
Aldersmead
Alcombe Common
A396
ST THOMAS ST
DUNSTER STEEP
Loxhole Bridge
THE BALL
Visitor Ctr
Butter Cross
CONDUIT LA
St Leonard's Well
ST GEORGE'S CL
HANGER'S WAY
PRIORY GN
HIGH ST
Yarn Market
Dunster
Home Farm
Dunster Fst Sch
ST GEORGE'S ST
WEST CL
CHURCH ST
Old Park
PIKES CL
CHAPEL ROW
CASTLE HILL
THE COURTYARD
A39
GRABBIST TOP RD
Macmillan Way West
DUCKY PATH
GOOSEY PATH
Grabbist Hill
Cemy
WEST ST
Dunster Castle
The Lawns
Dunster Working Water Mill
KNOWLE LA
PARK ST
MILL LA
MILL GDNS
Gallox Bridge
Freckford Bridge
River Avill
May Hill
Avill Ball
Aville Farm
Vinegar Hill
Dunster Park (Deer Park)
BONNITON LA
BONNITON NEW RD
130
131

131 132

A B C D E F
8 7 6 5 4 3 2 1
43 42 41 40
06 07 08
Warren Bay
Western Pier
Eastern Pier
Watchet Harbour
Caravan Park
Watchet
Helwell Bay
Daw's Castle
West Somerset Railway
Tuck's Brake
Paper Mill
Holy Well
Snailholt Farm
St Decumans
WATCHET
Buckland Sch
Trad Est
Parsonage Farm
Knights Templar CE Meth Com Sch
Doniford Beach Halt
Court Farm
Doniford
Liddymore Farm
Five Bells
Grove Copse
Egrove Farm
Doniford Stream
Smithyard Cottage
St Peter's CE Fst Sch
Danesfield CE Com Mid Sch
Roughmoor Ind Est
Williton Ind Est
Williton
High Bridge
Outmoor Wood
Williton Com
Williton
Macmillan Way West
Mamsey Bridge
The Bakelite Mus
Porch Elm
Eastfield House
Sampford Mill Farm
Dowry Copse
Rankin's Copse
Burrow Copse
Sampford Brett
Manor Farm
1 PORTLAND TERR
2 ALMYR TERR
3 SEVERN TERR
4 LITTLE SILVER CT
5 THE CROFT
6 THE ROPE WLK
7 PEEL CT
1 LIMPET SHELL LA
2 FORESTERS CL
3 SIR GILBERT SCOTT CT
WEST ST
CLEEVE HILL
SWAIN ST
BRENDON RD
WASHFORD HILL
FIVE BELLS
NORTH RD
LONG ST
PRIEST ST
BANK ST
HIGH ST
TOWER HILL
DONIFORD RD
B3191
B3190
A39
A358

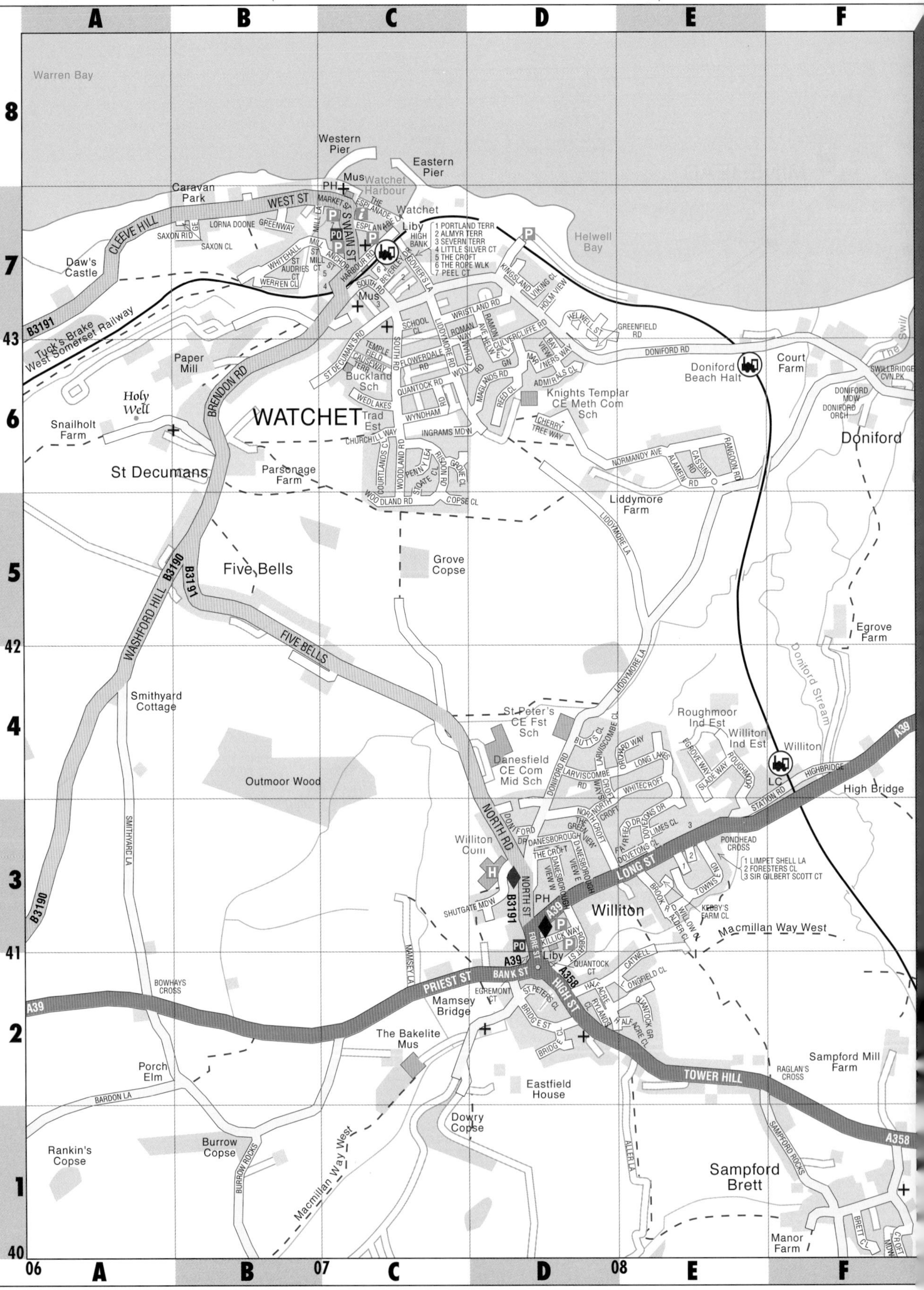

131 132 132

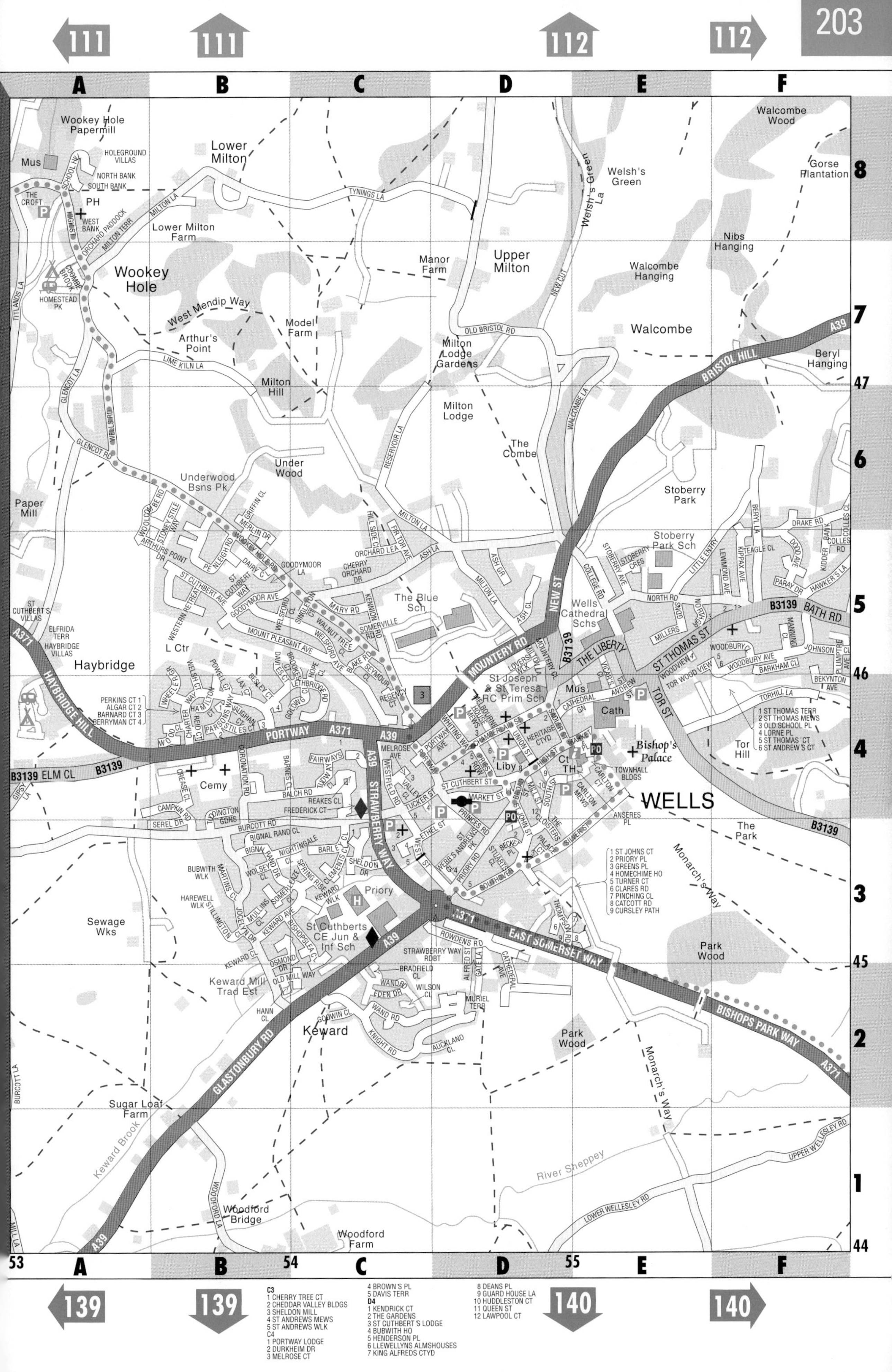
111
111
112
112
A
B
C
D
E
F
8
7
47
6
5
46
4
3
45
2
1
44
53
54
55
Wookey Hole Papermill
Mus
HOLEGROUND VILLAS
NORTH BANK
SOUTH BANK
THE CROFT
PH
WEST BANK
Lower Milton
Lower Milton Farm
TYNINGS LA
MILTON LA
MILTON TERR
ORCHARD PADDOCK
Wookey Hole
HOMESTEAD PK
TITLANDS LA
West Mendip Way
Arthur's Point
LIME KILN LA
Model Farm
Manor Farm
Upper Milton
Milton Hill
Milton Lodge Gardens
Milton Lodge
OLD BRISTOL RD
NEW CUT
Welsh's Green
Welsh's Green La
Walcombe Wood
Gorse Plantation
Nibs Hanging
Walcombe Hanging
Walcombe
Beryl Hanging
BRISTOL HILL
A39
WALCOMBE LA
The Combe
RESERVOIR LA
Under Wood
Underwood Bsns Pk
GLENCOT LA
GLENCOT RD
WELLS RD
Paper Mill
Stoberry Park
Stoberry Park Sch
MILTON LA
ORCHARD LEA
CHERRY ORCHARD DR
ASH LA
ASH GR
GOODYMOOR LA
GOODYMOOR AVE
ST CUTHBERT AVE
WESTERN RETREAT
ARTHURS POINT DR
MARY RD
SOMERVILLE RD
The Blue Sch
NEW ST
Wells Cathedral Schs
NORTH RD
BATH RD
B3139
ST CUTHBERT'S VILLAS
ELFRIDA TERR
HAYBRIDGE VILLAS
Haybridge
HAYBRIDGE HILL
A371
L Ctr
MOUNT PLEASANT AVE
MOUNTERY RD
THE LIBERTY
ST THOMAS ST
TOR ST
St Joseph & St Teresa RC Prim Sch
Mus
Cath
Bishop's Palace
Tor Hill
1 ST THOMAS TERR
2 ST THOMAS MEWS
3 OLD SCHOOL PL
4 LORNE PL
5 ST THOMAS' CT
6 ST ANDREW'S CT
PERKINS CT 1
ALGAR CT 2
BARNARD CT 3
BERRYMAN CT 4
PORTWAY
B3139 ELM CL
Cemy
Liby
Ct
TH
TOWNHALL BLDGS
WELLS
The Park
B3139
MARKET ST
ST CUTHBERT ST
STRAWBERRY WAY
BURCOTT RD
SEREL DR
CAMPKIN RD
Priory
St Cuthberts CE Jun & Inf Sch
1 ST JOHNS CT
2 PRIORY PL
3 GREENS PL
4 HOMECHIME HO
5 TURNER CT
6 CLARES RD
7 PINCHING CL
8 CATCOTT RD
9 CURSLEY PATH
Monarch's Way
Sewage Wks
EAST SOMERSET WAY
STRAWBERRY WAY RDBT
Park Wood
Keward Mill Trad Est
OLD MILL WAY
BRADFIELD CL
WILSON CL
MURIEL TERR
Keward
GLASTONBURY RD
AUCKLAND CL
KNIGHT RD
BISHOPS PARK WAY
Park Wood
BURCOTT LA
Sugar Loaf Farm
Keward Brook
River Sheppey
UPPER WELLESLEY RD
LOWER WELLESLEY RD
WOODFORD LA
Woodford Bridge
Woodford Farm
MILL LA
139
139
140
140
C3
1 CHERRY TREE CT
2 CHEDDAR VALLEY BLDGS
3 SHELDON MILL
4 ST ANDREWS MEWS
5 ST ANDREWS WLK
C4
1 PORTWAY LODGE
2 DURKHEIM DR
3 MELROSE CT
4 BROWN'S PL
5 DAVIS TERR
D4
1 KENDRICK CT
2 THE GARDENS
3 ST CUTHBERT'S LODGE
4 BUBWITH HO
5 HENDERSON PL
6 LLEWELLYNS ALMSHOUSES
7 KING ALFREDS CTYD
8 DEANS PL
9 GUARD HOUSE LA
10 HUDDLESTON CT
11 QUEEN ST
12 LAWPOOL CT

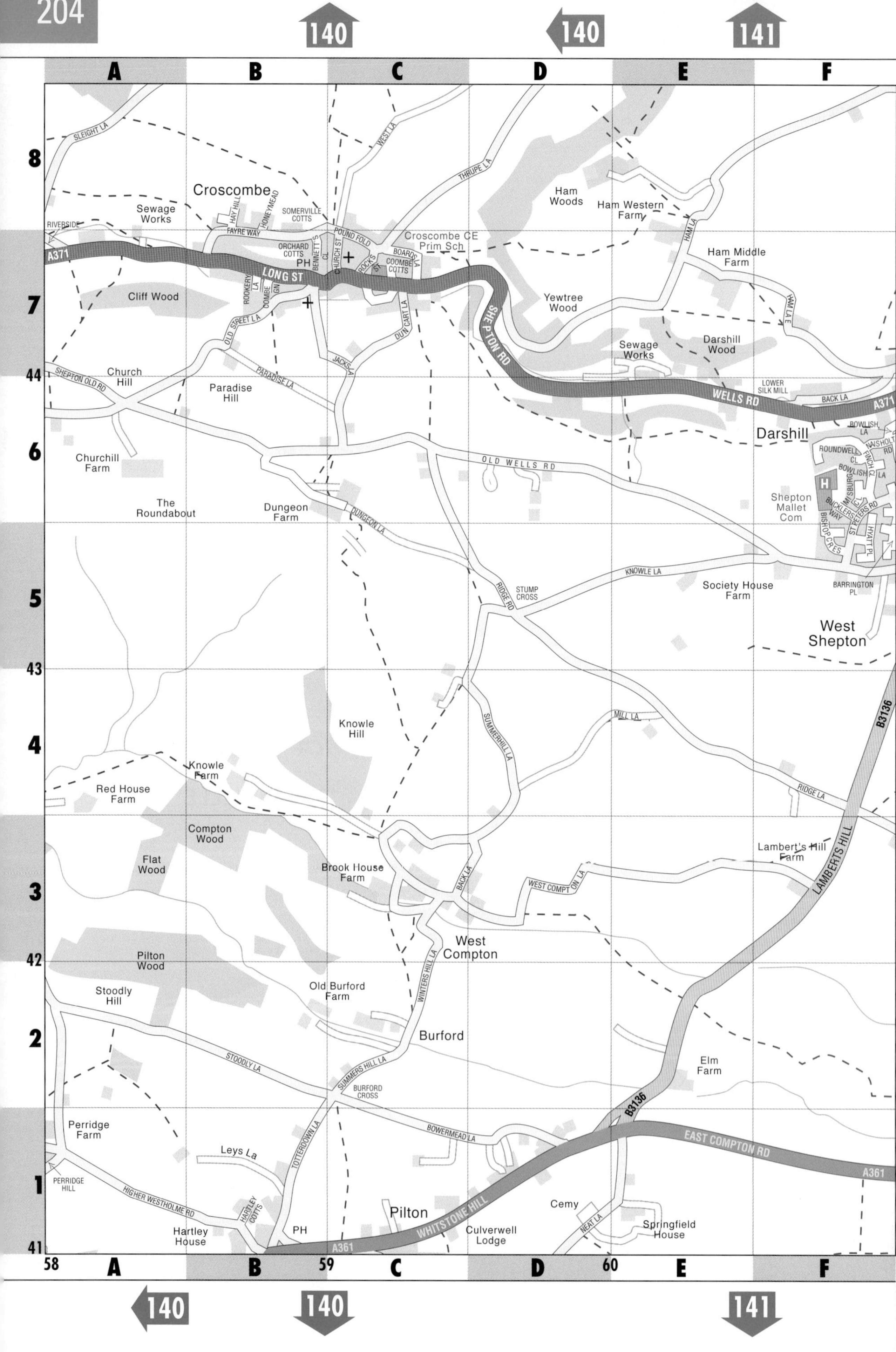
140
140
141
A
B
C
D
E
F
8
7
44
6
5
43
4
3
42
2
1
41
58
59
60
Croscombe
Sewage Works
Cliff Wood
Church Hill
Paradise Hill
Churchill Farm
The Roundabout
Dungeon Farm
Ham Woods
Ham Western Farm
Croscombe CE Prim Sch
Ham Middle Farm
Yewtree Wood
Sewage Works
Darshill Wood
Darshill
Shepton Mallet Com
Society House Farm
West Shepton
Knowle Hill
Knowle Farm
Red House Farm
Compton Wood
Flat Wood
Brook House Farm
Lambert's Hill Farm
West Compton
Pilton Wood
Stoodly Hill
Old Burford Farm
Burford
Elm Farm
Perridge Farm
Pilton
Hartley House
Culverwell Lodge
Cemy
Springfield House
A371
LONG ST
SHEPTON RD
WELLS RD
OLD WELLS RD
KNOWLE LA
RIDGE LA
SUMMERHILL LA
WEST COMPTON LA
LAMBERTS HILL
B3136
EAST COMPTON RD
A361
WHITSTONE HILL
STOODLY LA
BOWERMEAD LA
HIGHER WESTHOLME RD
TOTTERDOWN LA
SUMMERS HILL LA
WINTERS HILL LA
BURFORD CROSS
STUMP CROSS
SLEIGHT LA
WEST LA
THRUPE LA
HAM LA
DUNGEON LA
PARADISE LA
JACKS LA
DUNCART LA
OLD STREET LA
SHEPTON OLD RD
MILL LA
BACK LA
NEAT LA
PERRIDGE HILL
Leys La
PH
LOWER SILK MILL
BARRINGTON PL
RIVERSIDE
FAYRE WAY
HAY HILL
HONEYMEAD
SOMERVILLE COTTS
ORCHARD COTTS
POUND FOLD
BENNETT'S CL
CHURCH ST
ROCKS ST
BOARDS LA
COOMBE COTTS
ROOKERY LA
COMBE GN
ROUNDWELL CL
BOWLISH LA
BOWLISH CL
FINCH CL
NASHOLT RD
BUCKLERS WAY
BISHOP CRES
ST PETERS RD
HYATT PL
HARTLEY COTTS

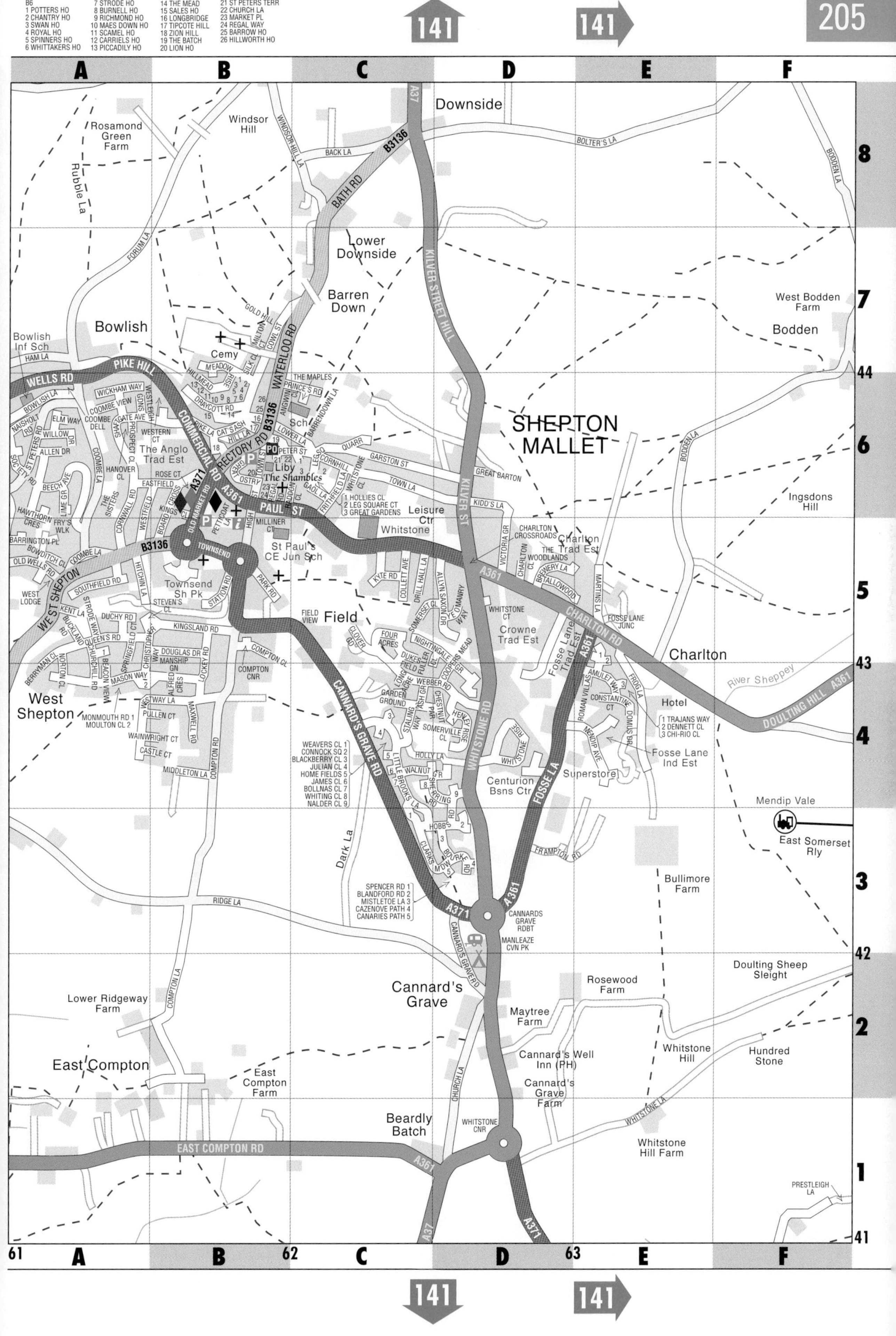

B6
1 POTTERS HO
2 CHANTRY HO
3 SWAN HO
4 ROYAL HO
5 SPINNERS HO
6 WHITTAKERS HO
7 STRODE HO
8 BURNELL HO
9 RICHMOND HO
10 MAES DOWN HO
11 SCAMEL HO
12 CARRIELS HO
13 PICCADILY HO
14 THE MEAD
15 SALES HO
16 LONGBRIDGE
17 TIPCOTE HILL
18 ZION HILL
19 THE BATCH
20 LION HO
21 ST PETERS TERR
22 CHURCH LA
23 MARKET PL
24 REGAL WAY
25 BARROW HO
26 HILLWORTH HO
141
141
205
A
B
C
D
E
F
Downside
Windsor Hill
Rosamond Green Farm
Rubble La
BACK LA
B3136
BOLTER'S LA
BODDEN LA
8
BATH RD
FORUM LA
Lower Downside
Barren Down
KILVER STREET HILL
West Bodden Farm
7
Bodden
Bowlish
Bowlish Inf Sch
HAM LA
GOLD HILL
Cemy
WATERLOO RD
WELLS RD
PIKE HILL
44
THE MAPLES
PRINCE'S RD
WICKHAM WAY
COOMBE VIEW
BOWLISH LA
ELM WAY
WILLOW DR
ALLEN DR
COMMERCIAL RD
Sch
SHEPTON MALLET
The Anglo Trad Est
RECTORY RD
QUARR
GARSTON ST
6
HANOVER CL
EASTFIELD
A371
A361
Liby
The Shambles
TOWN LA
GREAT BARTON
KILVER ST
Ingsdons Hill
1 HOLLIES CL
2 LEG SQUARE CT
3 GREAT GARDENS
Leisure Ctr
KIDD'S LA
PAUL ST
MILLINER CT
Whitstone
BARRINGTON PL
B3136
TOWNSEND
St Paul's CE Jun Sch
CHARLTON CROSSROADS
Charlton Trad Est
THE WOODLANDS
WEST SHEPTON
Townsend Sh Pk
SOUTHFIELD RD
STATION RD
KYTE RD
COLLETT AVE
DRILL HALL LA
A361
WEST LODGE
5
STEVEN'S CL
KINGSLAND RD
Field
FIELD VIEW
WHITSTONE CT
Crowne Trad Est
FOSSE LANE JUNC
CHARLTON RD
Charlton
COMPTON CL
COMPTON CNR
CANNARD'S GRAVE RD
NIGHTINGALE
43
River Sheppey
West Shepton
MONMOUTH RD 1
MOULTON CL 2
Hotel
1 TRAJANS WAY
2 DENNETT CL
3 CHI-RIO CL
DOULTING HILL
A361
WHITSTONE RD
4
WEAVERS CL 1
CONNOCK SQ 2
BLACKBERRY CL 3
JULIAN CL 4
HOME FIELDS 5
JAMES CL 6
BOLLNAS CL 7
WHITING CL 8
NALDER CL 9
MIDDLETON LA
COMPTON RD
Fosse Lane Ind Est
Superstore
Centurion Bsns Ctr
FOSSE LA
Mendip Vale
East Somerset Rly
Dark La
FRAMPTON RD
Bullimore Farm
3
SPENCER RD 1
BLANDFORD RD 2
MISTLETOE LA 3
CAZENOVE PATH 4
CANARIES PATH 5
RIDGE LA
A371
A361
CANNARDS GRAVE RDBT
MANLEAZE CVN PK
42
Doulting Sheep Sleight
Rosewood Farm
Lower Ridgeway Farm
COMPTON LA
Cannard's Grave
Maytree Farm
2
Cannard's Well Inn (PH)
Whitstone Hill
Hundred Stone
East Compton
East Compton Farm
Cannard's Grave Farm
CHURCH LA
Beardly Batch
WHITSTONE CNR
WHITSTONE LA
Whitstone Hill Farm
EAST COMPTON RD
A361
1
PRESTLEIGH LA
A37
A371
41
61
62
63
141
141

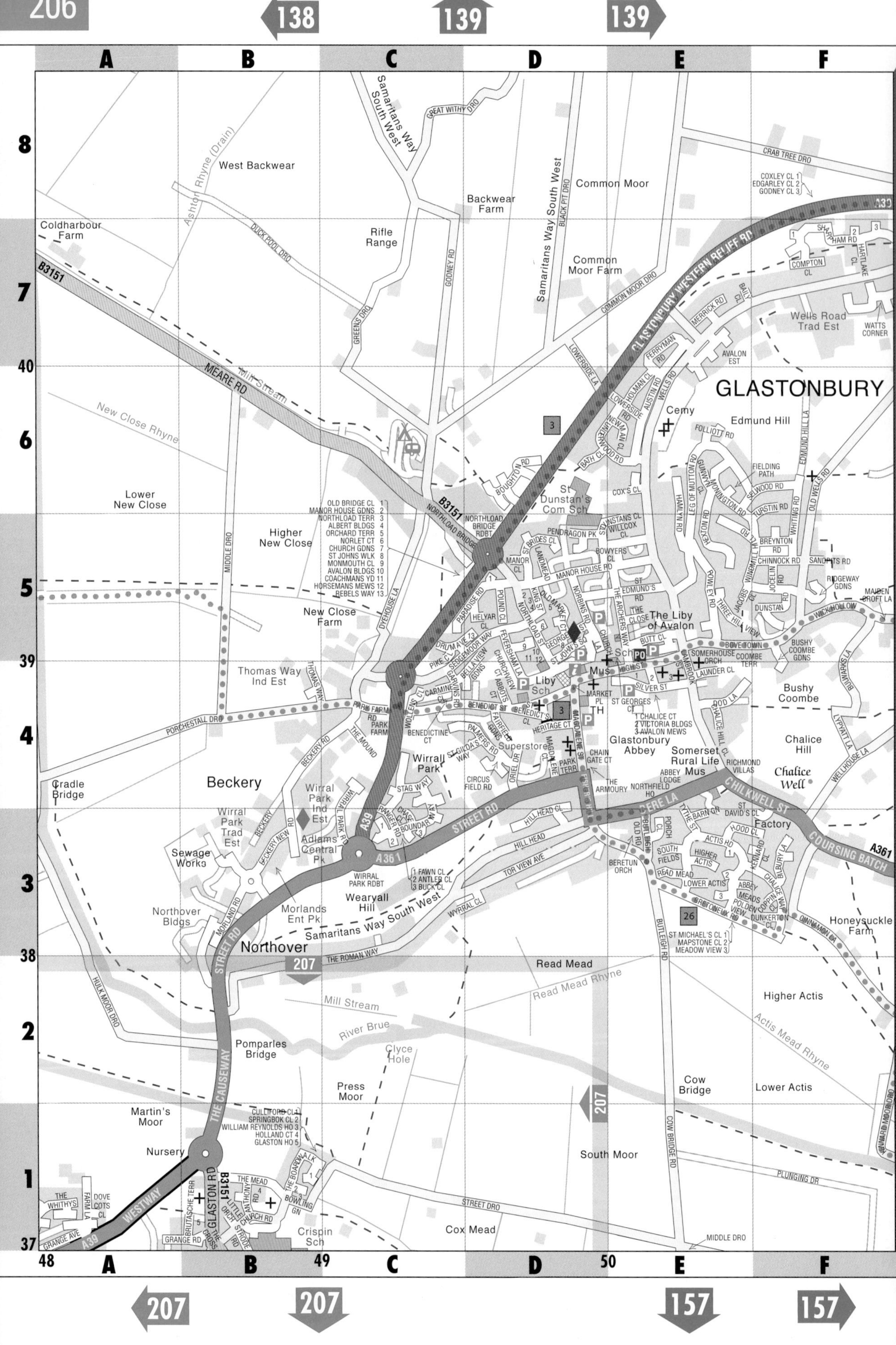
138
139
139
A
B
C
D
E
F
8
7
40
6
5
39
4
3
38
2
1
37
48
49
50
207
207
157
157
GLASTONBURY
West Backwear
Coldharbour Farm
B3151
MEARE RD
Mill Stream
New Close Rhyne
Lower New Close
Higher New Close
Ashton Rhyne (Drain)
DUCK POOL DRO
Rifle Range
Samaritans Way South West
GREAT WITHY DRO
Backwear Farm
GODNEY RD
GREENS DRO
Common Moor
Common Moor Farm
BLACK PIT DRO
COMMON MOOR DRO
LOWERSIDE LA
GLASTONBURY WESTERN RELIEF RD
CRAB TREE DRO
COXLEY CL 1
EDGARLEY CL 2
GODNEY CL 3
A39
SHARP HAM RD
HARTLAKE CL
COMPTON CL
BAILY CL
MERRICK RD
Wells Road Trad Est
WATTS CORNER
AVALON EST
FERRYMAN RD
HOLMAN CL
LOWERSIDE RD
AUSTIN RD
WELLS RD
Cemy
Edmund Hill
FOLLIOTT RD
FIELDING PATH
EDMUND HILL LA
OLD WELLS RD
SELWOOD RD
TURSTIN RD
WHITING RD
BREYNTON RD
CHINNOCK RD
SANDPITS RD
RIDGEWAY GDNS
MAIDEN CROFT LA
WICK HOLLOW
DUNSTAN RD
JOCELIN RD
JACOBS
WINDMILL HILL RD
THREE HILL VIEW
ROWLEY RD
HEXTON RD
LEG OF MUTTON RD
HAMLYN RD
GUNWYN
WINNINGTON RD
BATH CL
NEWMAN CL
ELMWOOD RD
COX'S CL
St Dunstan's Com Sch
ST DUNSTANS CL
WILLCOX CL
PENDRAGON PK
BOWYERS CL
MANOR HOUSE RD
ST EDMUND'S RD
THE CLOSE
The Liby of Avalon
BUTT CL
BOVE TOWN
BUSHY COOMBE GDNS
COOMBE TERR
SOMERHOUSE ORCH
LAUNDER CL
Bushy Coombe
BULWARKS LA
OLD BRIDGE CL 1
MANOR HOUSE GDNS 2
NORTHLOAD TERR 3
ALBERT BLDGS 4
ORCHARD TERR 5
NORLET CT 6
CHURCH GDNS 7
ST JOHNS WLK 8
MONMOUTH CL 9
AVALON BLDGS 10
COACHMANS YD 11
HORSEMANS MEWS 12
REBELS WAY 13
NORTHLOAD BRIDGE
NORTHLOAD BRIDGE RDBT
BOUGHTON RD
ST BRIDES CL
LANDMEAD
MANOR CL
PARADISE RD
POUND CL
NORTHLOAD ST
KING ST
OLD MARKET CT
NORBINS RD
THE ARCHERS WAY
CHURCH LA
HIGH ST
MAGDALENE ST
ST JOHN'S SQ
HELYAR CL
New Close Farm
DYEHOUSE LA
Thomas Way Ind Est
THOMAS WAY
PORCHESTALL DRO
MIDDLE DRO
PARK FARM RD
PARK FARM
DRUMMOND
SEDGEMOOR WAY
PIKE CL
BELLA VIEW GDNS
CHURCHILL
FEVERSHAM LA
CHURCHVIEW CT
ABBOTS CT
CARMINE
GAWAINS
WOLLENS CL
BENEDICT ST
BENEDICTINE CT
Liby
Sch
Mus
MARKET PL
TH
PO
SILVER ST
ST GEORGES CT
1 CHALICE CT
2 VICTORIA BLDGS
3 AVALON MEWS
CHALICE HILL CL
DOD LA
Glastonbury Abbey
Somerset Rural Life Mus
Chalice Hill
Chalice Well
RICHMOND VILLAS
LYPYATT LA
WELLHOUSE LA
HERITAGE CT
Superstore
PALMERS RD
FAIRFIELD GDNS
ST GILDA'S WAY
ORIEL DR
MAGDALENE LA
PARK TERR
CHAIN GATE CT
THE ARMOURY
NORTHFIELD HO
ABBEY LODGE
Wirrall Park
CIRCUS FIELD RD
THE MOUND
Beckery
BECKERY RD
Cradle Bridge
Wirral Park Trad Est
Wirral Park Ind Est
Adlams Central Pk
WIRRAL PARK RD
BECKERY NEW RD
Sewage Works
STAG WAY
RANGER RD
CHASE CL
BOUNDARY WAY
STREET RD
A361
WIRRAL PARK RDBT
1 FAWN CL
2 ANTLER CL
3 BUCK CL
HILL HEAD CL
HILL HEAD
TOR VIEW AVE
DERE LA
OLD RD
BUTLEIGH RD
PORCH CL
TYTHE ST
BARN GN
ST DAVID'S CL
CHILKWELL ST
Factory
COURSING BATCH
SOUTH FIELDS
HIGHER ACTIS
ACTIS RD
HOOD CL
KENNARD CL
BILBURY LA
CHALICE WAY
READ MEAD
LOWER ACTIS
ABBEY MEADS
POLDEN VIEW
COPPIN CL
DUNKERTON CL
BRETONEUX RD
CINNAMON LA
Honeysuckle Farm
BERETUN ORCH
ST MICHAEL'S CL 1
MAPSTONE CL 2
MEADOW VIEW 3
Wearyall Hill
Morlands Ent Pk
Northover
Northover Bldgs
MORLAND RD
STREET RD
WYRRAL CL
THE ROMAN WAY
Read Mead
Read Mead Rhyne
HULK MOOR DRO
Mill Stream
River Brue
Pomparles Bridge
Clyce Hole
Press Moor
Higher Actis
Actis Mead Rhyne
Cow Bridge
Lower Actis
COW BRIDGE RD
BUTLEIGH RD
South Moor
PLUNGING DR
MIDDLE DRO
Martin's Moor
THE CAUSEWAY
Nursery
CULLIFORD CL 1
SPRINGBOK CL 2
WILLIAM REYNOLDS HO 3
HOLLAND CT 4
GLASTON HO 5
THE BOARDWALK
BOWLING GN
THE MEAD
CHURCH RD
LITTLE ORCH
ANTHONY RD
STRODE RD
GLASTON RD
BRUTASCHE TERR
THE CROSS
GRANGE RD
Crispin Sch
STREET DRO
Cox Mead
WESTWAY
THE WHITHYS
FARM LA
DOVE COTS CL
GRANGE AVE
26

138
206
206

C5
1 VESTRY CT
2 MILLTHORN HO
3 DURSTON HO
4 The Bayliss Ctr

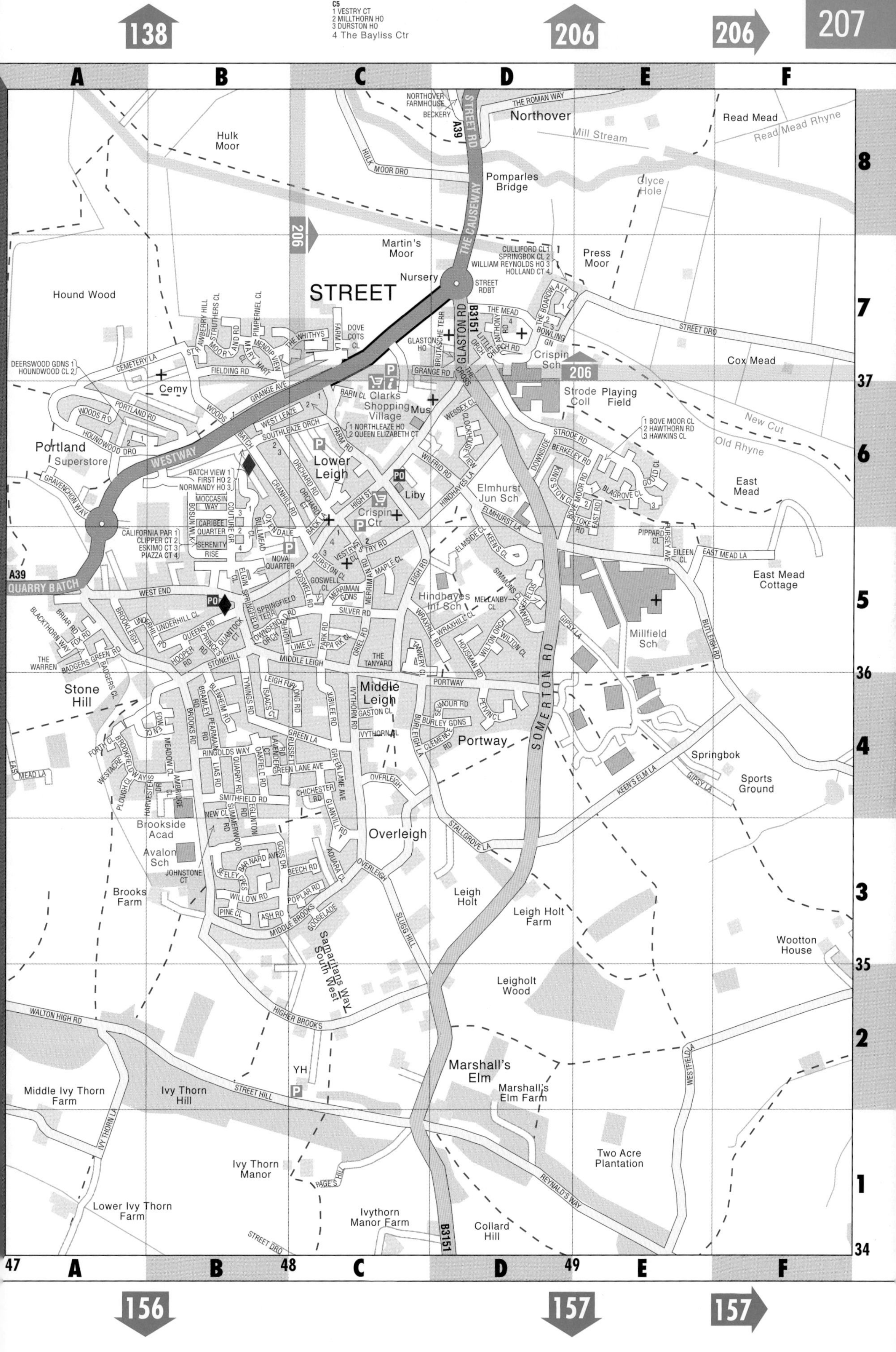

156
157
157

135
135

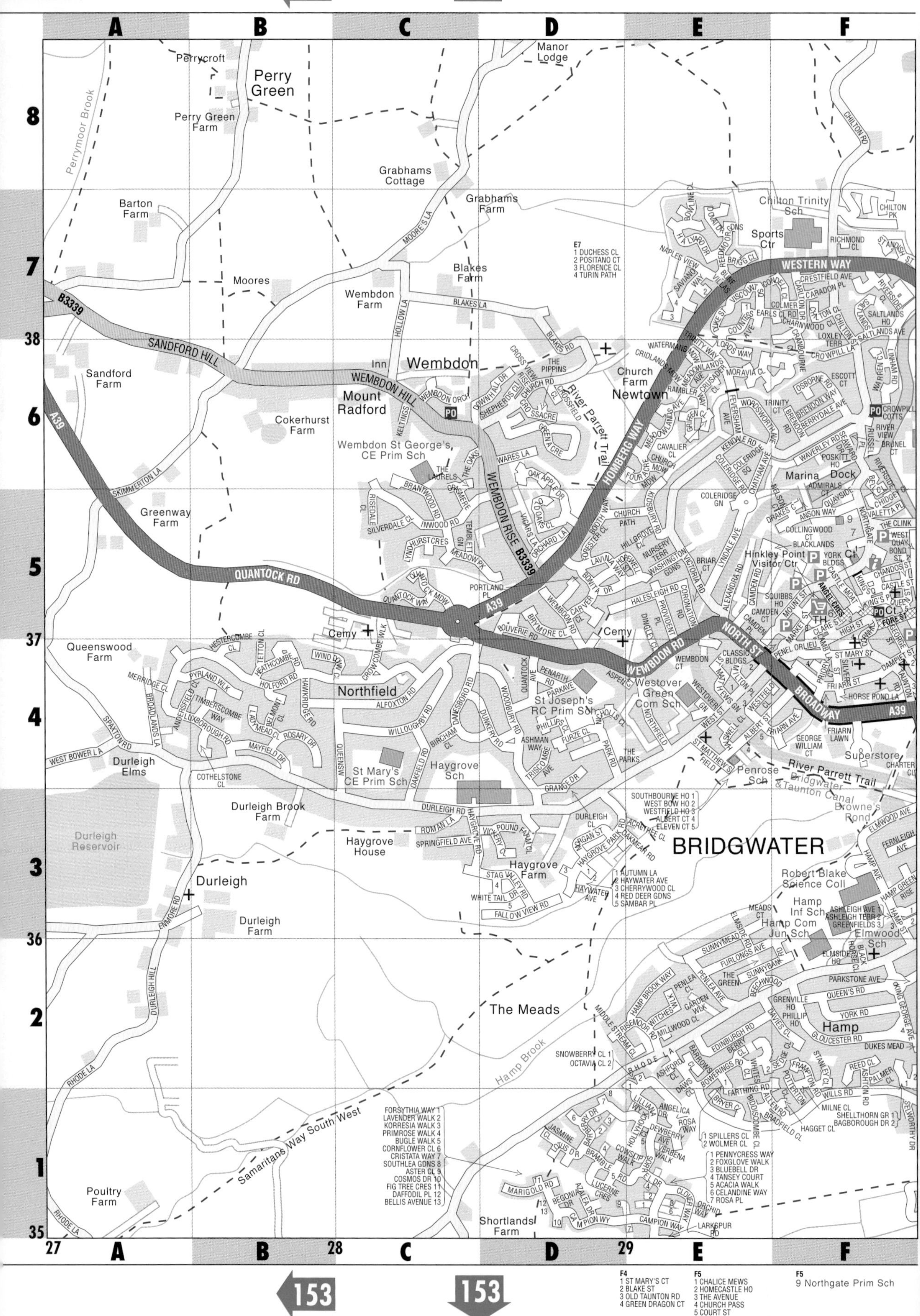

153
153

F4
1 ST MARY'S CT
2 BLAKE ST
3 OLD TAUNTON RD
4 GREEN DRAGON CT

F5
1 CHALICE MEWS
2 HOMECASTLE HO
3 THE AVENUE
4 CHURCH PASS
5 COURT ST
6 Angel Place Sh Ctr
7 Bridgwater Ent Ctr
8 MARKET CT

F5
9 Northgate Prim Sch

136
136

A1
1 BRETON CL
2 TORI GREEN
3 SAXONY PL
4 EMBDEN WALK
5 TOULOUSE RD
6 COTTON PATCH WLK
7 LONGHORN DR
8 DEXTER WALK
9 RHYNE BRIDGE

B4
1 PARKSIDE CT
2 STEAM PACKET TERR
3 PATHFINDER TERR
4 OXFORD TERR
5 THE MEWS
6 HUGHES CL
7 GRAVES CL
8 MOONRAKER CL
9 APPLEDORE DR
10 PEPLOE WY
11 MARSA WY

C4
1 NIGHTINGALE CL
2 HERON HO
3 DUNWEAR HO

154
154

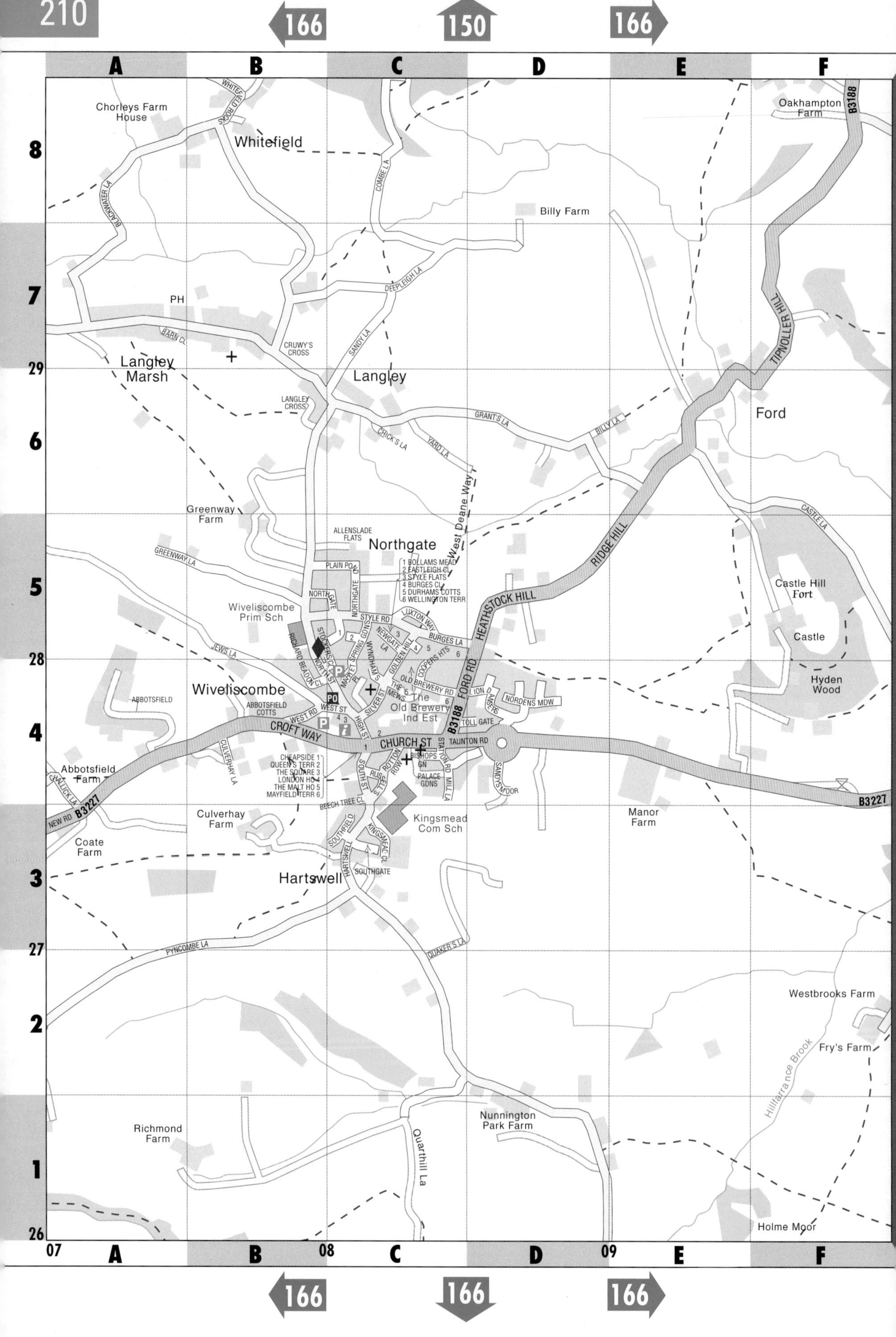
166
150
166
A
B
C
D
E
F
8
7
29
6
5
28
4
3
27
2
1
26
07
08
09
Chorleys Farm House
Whitefield
WHITEFIELD ROCKS
Oakhampton Farm
B3188
COMBE LA
BLACKWATER LA
Billy Farm
DEEPLEIGH LA
PH
BARN CL
CRUWY'S CROSS
SANDY LA
Langley Marsh
Langley
TIPNOLLER HILL
LANGLEY CROSS
GRANT'S LA
BILLY LA
Ford
CHICK'S LA
YARD LA
West Deane Way
Greenway Farm
CASTLE LA
RIDGE HILL
ALLENSLADE FLATS
Northgate
GREENWAY LA
PLAIN POND
1 BOLLAMS MEAD
2 EASTLEIGH CL
3 STYLE FLATS
4 BURGES CL
5 DURHAMS COTTS
6 WELLINGTON TERR
Castle Hill Fort
NORTH GATE
NORTHGATE
HEATHSTOCK HILL
Wiveliscombe Prim Sch
STYLE RD
LUXTON WAY
Castle
BURGES LA
JEWS LA
RICHARD BEADON CL
STOCKERS CL
NORTH ST
MARKET PL
SPRING GDNS
NEWGATE LA
WYNDHAMS
GOLDEN HILL
COOPERS HTS
FORD RD
Hyden Wood
Wiveliscombe
THE MEWS
OLD BREWERY RD
The Old Brewery Ind Est
LION D
MASERS
NORDENS MDW
ABBOTSFIELD
ABBOTSFIELD COTTS
PO
WEST ST
SILVER ST
WEST RD
B3188
TOLL GATE
CROFT WAY
HIGH ST
CHURCH ST
TAUNTON RD
CULVERHAY LA
CHEAPSIDE 1
QUEEN'S TERR 2
THE SQUARE 3
LONDON HO 4
THE MALT HO 5
MAYFIELD TERR 6
ROTTON ROW
BISHOPS GN
STATION RD
SOUTH ST
RUSSELLS
PALACE GDNS
MILL LA
SANDYS MOOR
Abbotsfield Farm
CHALICK LA
B3227
B3227
BEECH TREE CL
Manor Farm
NEW RD
Culverhay Farm
Kingsmead Com Sch
SOUTHFIELD
KINGSMEAD CL
Coate Farm
HARTSWELL
SOUTHGATE
Hartswell
PYNCOMBE LA
QUAKER'S LA
Westbrooks Farm
Fry's Farm
Hillfarrance Brook
Nunnington Park Farm
Richmond Farm
Quarthill La
Holme Moor
166
166
166

156 156 157 157

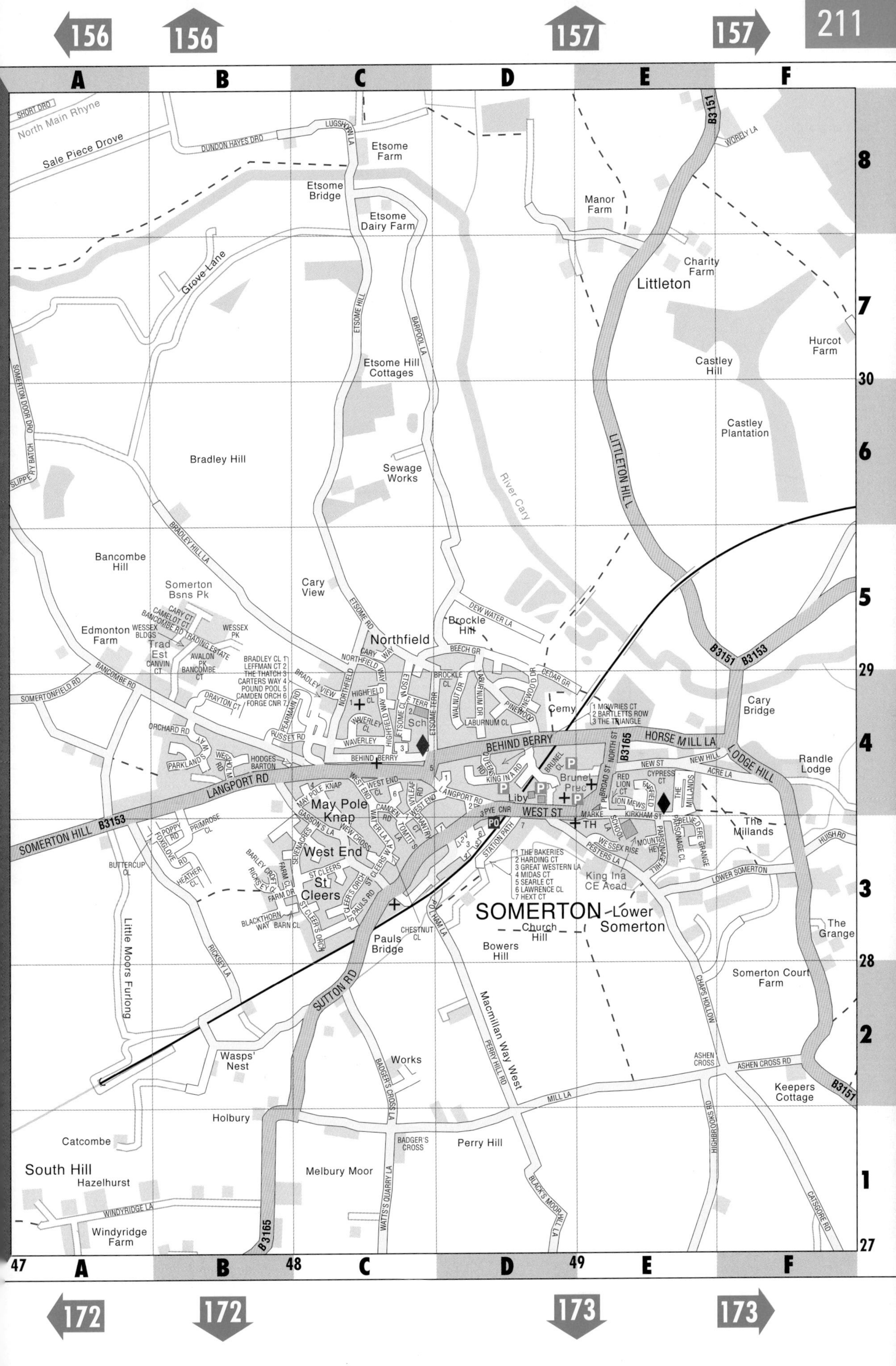
A
B
C
D
E
F
8
7
30
6
5
29
4
3
28
2
1
27
47
48
49
SHORT DRO
North Main Rhyne
Sale Piece Drove
DUNDON HAYES DRO
LUGSHORN LA
Etsome Farm
Etsome Bridge
Etsome Dairy Farm
B3151
WORELY LA
Manor Farm
Charity Farm
Littleton
Grove Lane
ETSOME HILL
BARPOOL LA
Hurcot Farm
Castley Hill
Etsome Hill Cottages
SOMERTON DOOR DRO
Castley Plantation
SLIPPERY BATCH
Bradley Hill
Sewage Works
River Cary
LITTLETON HILL
BRADLEY HILL LA
Bancombe Hill
Somerton Bsns Pk
Cary View
ETSOME RD
DEW WATER LA
Brockle Hill
Edmonton Farm
CARY CT
CAMELOT CT
BANCOMBE RD
WESSEX BLDGS
TRADING ESTATE
WESSEX PK
Trad Est
CANVIN CT
AVALON PK
BANCOMBE CT
Northfield
CARY WAY
BEECH GR
B3151
B3153
BRADLEY CL 1
LEFFMAN CT 2
THE THATCH 3
CARTERS WAY 4
POUND POOL 5
CAMDEN ORCH 6
FORGE CNR 7
NORTHFIELD WAY
BRADLEY VIEW
NORTHFIELD
HIGHFIELD CL
ETSOME TERR
BROCKLE CL
LAURNUM DR
WALNUT DR
NEWOOD DR
CEDAR GR
PINEWOOD
LABURNUM CL
Cemy
1 MOWRIES CT
2 BARTLETTS ROW
3 THE TRIANGLE
Cary Bridge
BANCOMBE RD
SOMERTONFIELD RD
DRAYTON CT
PEARMAIN RD
HIGHFIELD
WAVERLEY CL
WAVERLEY
Sch
ORCHARD RD
RUSSET RD
BEHIND BERRY
HORSE MILL LA
B3165
NORTH ST
PARKLANDS
WESTHOLM RD
HODGES BARTON
BEHIND BERRY
QUEENS RD
BRUNEL CL
NEW ST
NEW HILL
ACRE LA
LODGE HILL
Randle Lodge
KING INA RD
Brunel Prec
BROAD ST
RED LION CT
CYPRESS CT
ENFIELD
THE MILLANDS
LANGPORT RD
MAY POLE KNAP
WEST END CL
WEST END
May Pole Knap
VYLEAF CT
LANGPORT RD
Liby
LION MEWS
KIRKHAM ST
MARKET
TH
SCHOOL LA
PARSONAGE HILL
BELVEDERE GRANGE
PARSONAGE CL
The Millands
HUISH RD
SOMERTON HILL
B3153
POPPY RD
PRIMROSE CL
GASSON'S LA
CAMDEN RD
TOMTITS LA
WEST END
PYE CNR
WEST ST
PO
STATION PATH
WESSEX RISE
MOUNT HEY
PESTERS LA
FOXGLOVE RD
West End
SEVENACRES
NEW CROSS
WATER LA
ST CLEERS WAY
1 THE BAKERIES
2 HARDING CT
3 GREAT WESTERN LA
4 MIDAS CT
5 SEARLE CT
6 LAWRENCE CL
7 HEXT CT
LOWER SOMERTON
BUTTERCUP CL
HEATHER CL
BARLEY CROFT
FARM CL
St Cleers
ST CLEERS
King Ina CE Acad
RICKSEY CL
FARM DR
ST CLEER'S ORCH
ST PAULS RD
SOMERTON
Lower Somerton
The Grange
BLACKTHORN WAY
BARN CL
Church Hill
Pauls Bridge
CHESTNUT CL
POLHAM LA
Little Moors Furlong
Bowers Hill
RICKSEY LA
Somerton Court Farm
SUTTON RD
Macmillan Way West
CHAPS HOLLOW
Wasps' Nest
Works
BADGER'S CROSS LA
PERRY HILL RD
ASHEN CROSS
ASHEN CROSS RD
Keepers Cottage
B3151
MILL LA
Holbury
Catcombe
BADGER'S CROSS
Perry Hill
HIGHBROOKS RD
South Hill
Hazelhurst
Melbury Moor
BLACK'S MOOR HILL LA
CATSGORE RD
WINDYRIDGE LA
Windyridge Farm
WATTS'S QUARRY LA
B3165

172 172 173 173

168
168

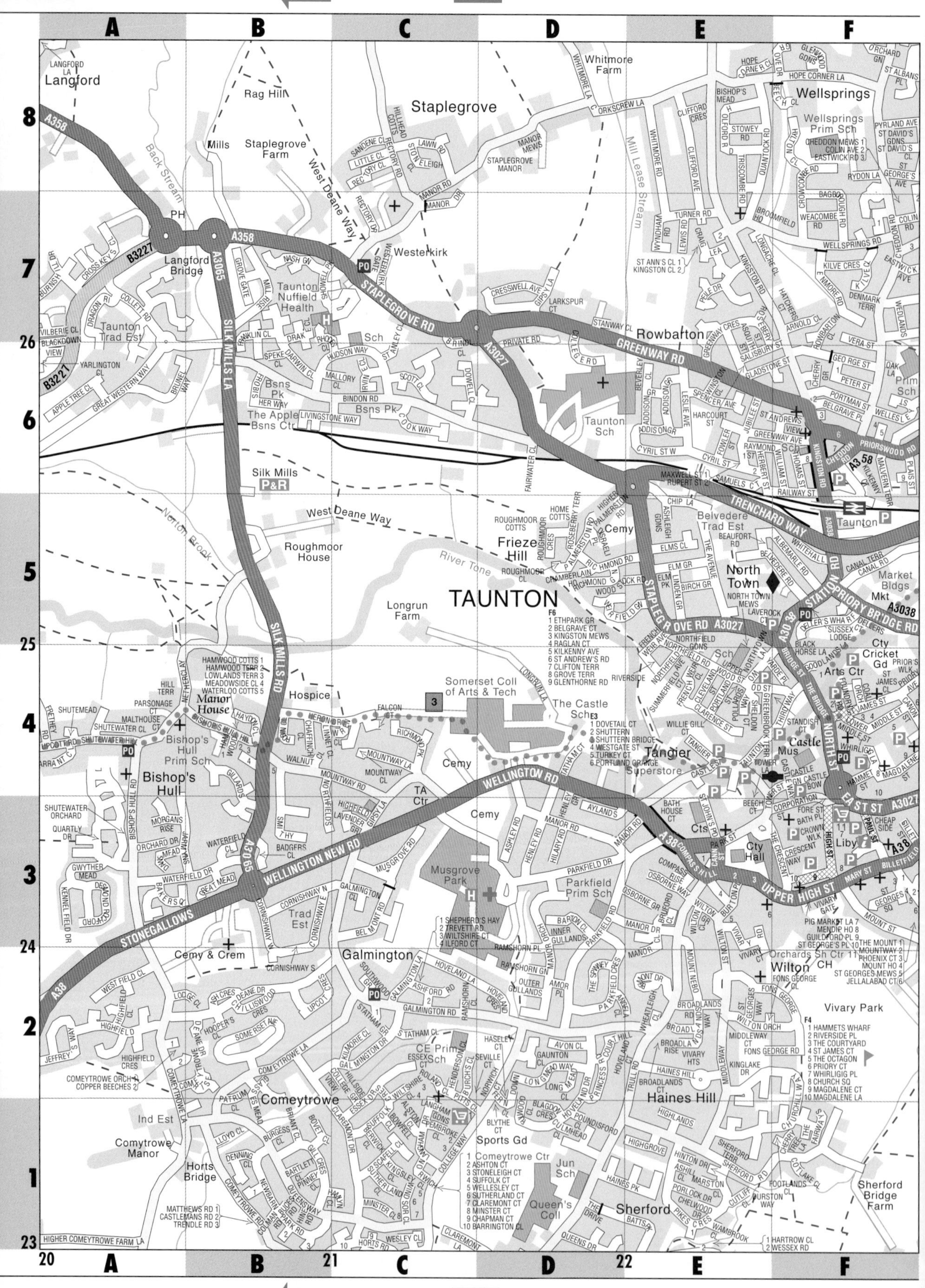
A
B
C
D
E
F
8
7
26
6
5
25
4
3
24
2
1
23
20
21
22
Langford
Rag Hill
Whitmore Farm
Staplegrove
Wellsprings
Wellsprings Prim Sch
Mills
Staplegrove Farm
West Deane Way
Back Stream
Mill Lease Stream
STAPLEGROVE MANOR
PH
Langford Bridge
Westerkirk
Taunton Nuffield Health
Taunton Trad Est
Sch
Rowbarton
STAPLEGROVE RD
GREENWAY RD
A358
B3227
A3065
A3027
A3038
A38
SILK MILLS LA
Bsns Pk
Bsns Pk
The Apple Bsns Ctr
Taunton Sch
Prim Sch
Silk Mills
P&R
Norton Brook
West Deane Way
Roughmoor House
Frieze Hill
Cemy
Belvedere Trad Est
TRENCHARD WAY
Taunton
River Tone
North Town
Market Bldgs
Mkt
TAUNTON
Longrun Farm
STAPLEGROVE RD
PRIORY BRIDGE RD
STATION RD
Cty Cricket Gd
F6
1 ETHPARK GR
2 BELGRAVE CT
3 KINGSTON MEWS
4 RAGLAN CT
5 KILKENNY AVE
6 ST ANDREW'S RD
7 CLIFTON TERR
8 GROVE TERR
9 GLENTHORNE RD
Somerset Coll of Arts & Tech
The Castle Sch
Arts Ctr
Hospice
Manor House
Bishop's Hull Prim Sch
Bishop's Hull
HAMWOOD COTTS 1
HAMWOOD TERR 2
LOWLANDS TERR 3
MEADOWSIDE CL 4
WATERLOO COTTAGES 5
E3
1 DOVETAIL CT
2 SHUTTERN
3 SHUTTERN BRIDGE
4 WESTGATE ST
5 TURKEY CT
6 PORTLAND GRANGE
Cemy
Tangier
Superstore
Mus
Castle
WELLINGTON RD
TA Ctr
Cemy
Cts
City Hall
Liby
NORTH ST
EAST ST
UPPER HIGH ST
WELLINGTON NEW RD
STONEGALLOWS
Musgrove Park
Parkfield Prim Sch
Trad Est
Cemy & Crem
Galmington
1 SHEPHERD'S HAY
2 TREVETT RD
3 WILTSHIRE CT
4 ILFORD CT
PIG MARKET LA 7
MENDIP HO 8
GUILDFORD PL 9
ST GEORGE'S PL 10
Orchards Sh Ctr 11
THE MOUNT 1
MOUNTWAY 2
PHOENIX CT 3
MOUNT HO 4
ST GEORGES MEWS 5
JELLALABAD CT 6
Wilton
CH
Vivary Park
F4
1 HAMMETS WHARF
2 RIVERSIDE PL
3 THE COURTYARD
4 ST JAMES CT
5 THE OCTAGON
6 PRIORY CT
7 WHIRLIGIG PL
8 CHURCH SQ
9 MAGDALENE CT
10 MAGDALENE LA
COMEYTROWE ORCH 1
COPPER BEECHES 2
CE Prim Sch
Comeytrowe
Haines Hill
Ind Est
Comytrowe Manor
Sports Gd
1 Comeytrowe Ctr
2 ASHTON CT
3 STONELEIGH CT
4 SUFFOLK CT
5 WELLESLEY CT
6 SUTHERLAND CT
7 CLAREMONT CT
8 MINSTER CT
9 CHAPMAN CT
10 BARRINGTON CL
Jun Sch
Queen's Coll
Sherford
Horts Bridge
MATTHEWS RD 1
CASTLEMANS RD 2
TRENDLE RD 3
HIGHER COMEYTROWE FARM LA
Sherford Bridge Farm
1 HARTROW CL
2 WESSEX RD

168
168

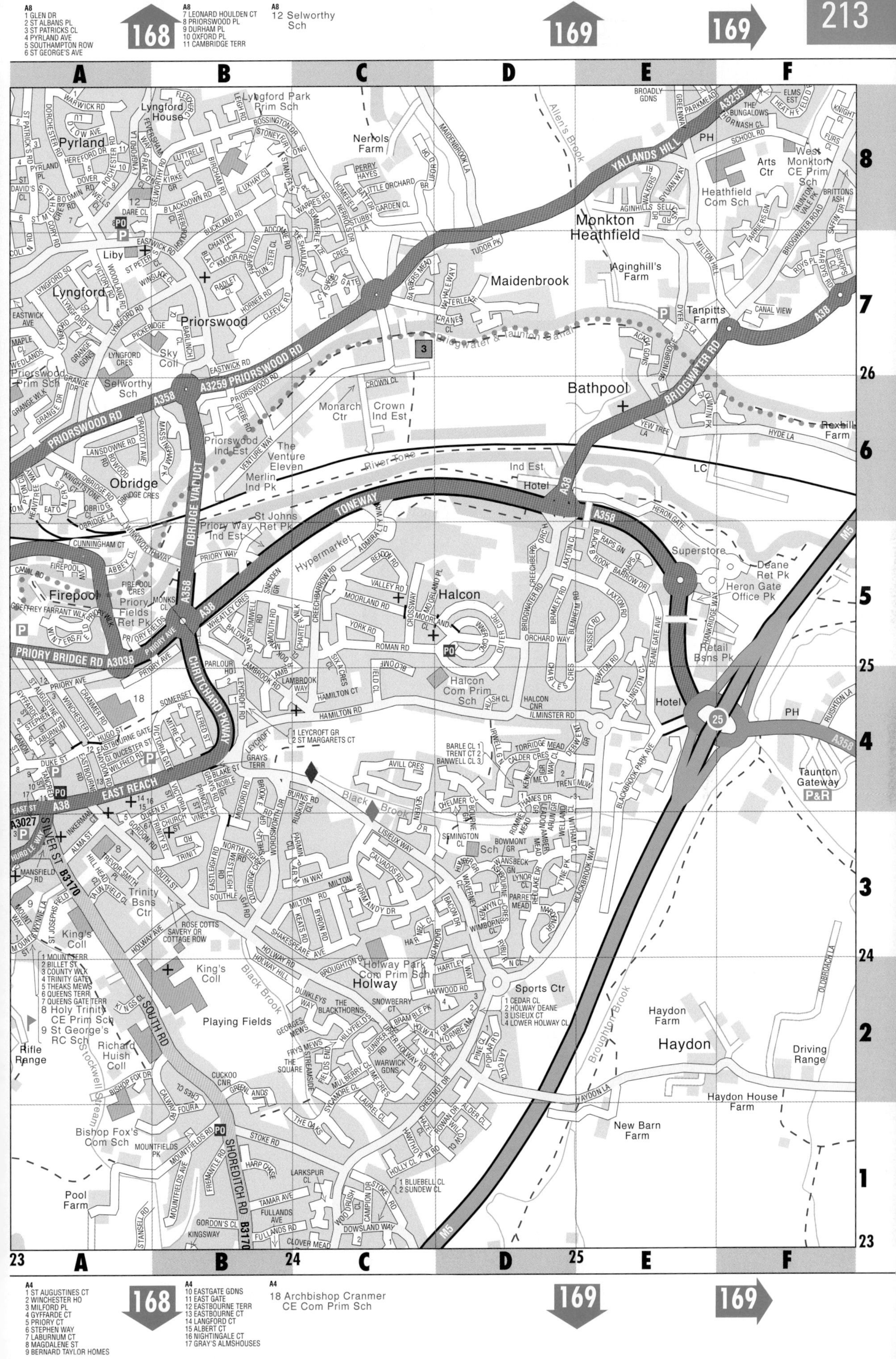

213
168
169
169
A8
1 GLEN DR
2 ST ALBANS PL
3 ST PATRICKS CL
4 PYRLAND AVE
5 SOUTHAMPTON ROW
6 ST GEORGE'S AVE
A8
7 LEONARD HOULDEN CT
8 PRIORSWOOD PL
9 DURHAM PL
10 OXFORD PL
11 CAMBRIDGE TERR
A8
12 Selworthy Sch
A
B
C
D
E
F
Pyrland
Lyngford House
Lyngford Park Prim Sch
Nerrols Farm
Allen's Brook
YALLANDS HILL
A3259
Monkton Heathfield
Heathfield Com Sch
Arts Ctr
West Monkton CE Prim Sch
Aginghill's Farm
Maidenbrook
Lyngford
Priorswood
Sky Coll
Tanpitts Farm
Bridgwater & Taunton Canal
Priorswood Prim Sch
Selworthy Sch
PRIORSWOOD RD
A3259 PRIORSWOOD RD
A358
Monarch Ctr
Crown Ind Est
Bathpool
BRIDGWATER RD
Rexhill Farm
Priorswood Ind Est
The Venture Eleven
Merlin Ind Pk
River Tone
Ind Est
Hotel
LC
Obridge
OBRIDGE VIADUCT
TONEWAY
A38
St Johns Ret Pk
Priory Way Ind Est
Hypermarket
Superstore
Deane Ret Pk
Heron Gate Office Pk
Firepool
Priory Fields Ret Pk
Halcon
Retail Bsns Pk
PRIORY BRIDGE RD A3038
CHRITCHARD PKWAY
Halcon Com Prim Sch
Hotel
PH
25
A358
1 LEYCROFT GR
2 ST MARGARETS CT
EAST REACH
Taunton Gateway
P&R
Black Brook
A3027
SILVER ST
B3170
Trinity Bsns Ctr
King's Coll
Sch
Holway Park Com Prim Sch
Holway
Sports Ctr
1 CEDAR CL
2 HOLWAY DEANE
3 LISIEUX CT
4 LOWER HOLWAY CL
1 MOUNT TERR
2 BILLET ST
3 COUNTY WLK
4 TRINITY GATE
5 THEAKS MEWS
6 QUEENS TERR
7 QUEENS GATE TERR
8 Holy Trinity CE Prim Sch
9 St George's RC Sch
King's Coll
Playing Fields
Rifle Range
Richard Huish Coll
Stockwell Stream
Broughton Brook
Haydon Farm
Haydon
Driving Range
Haydon House Farm
New Barn Farm
Bishop Fox's Com Sch
SOUTH RD
SHOREDITCH RD
B3170
M5
M5
Pool Farm
1 BLUEBELL CL
2 SUNDEW CL
8
7
26
6
5
25
4
3
24
2
1
23
23
24
25
A
B
C
D
E
F
A4
1 ST AUGUSTINES CT
2 WINCHESTER HO
3 MILFORD PL
4 GYFFARDE CT
5 PRIORY CT
6 STEPHEN WAY
7 LABURNUM CT
8 MAGDALENE ST
9 BERNARD TAYLOR HOMES
168
A4
10 EASTGATE GDNS
11 EAST GATE
12 EASTBOURNE TERR
13 EASTBOURNE CT
14 LANGFORD CT
15 ALBERT CT
16 NIGHTINGALE CT
17 GRAY'S ALMSHOUSES
A4
18 Archbishop Cranmer CE Com Prim Sch
169
169

159 159 215

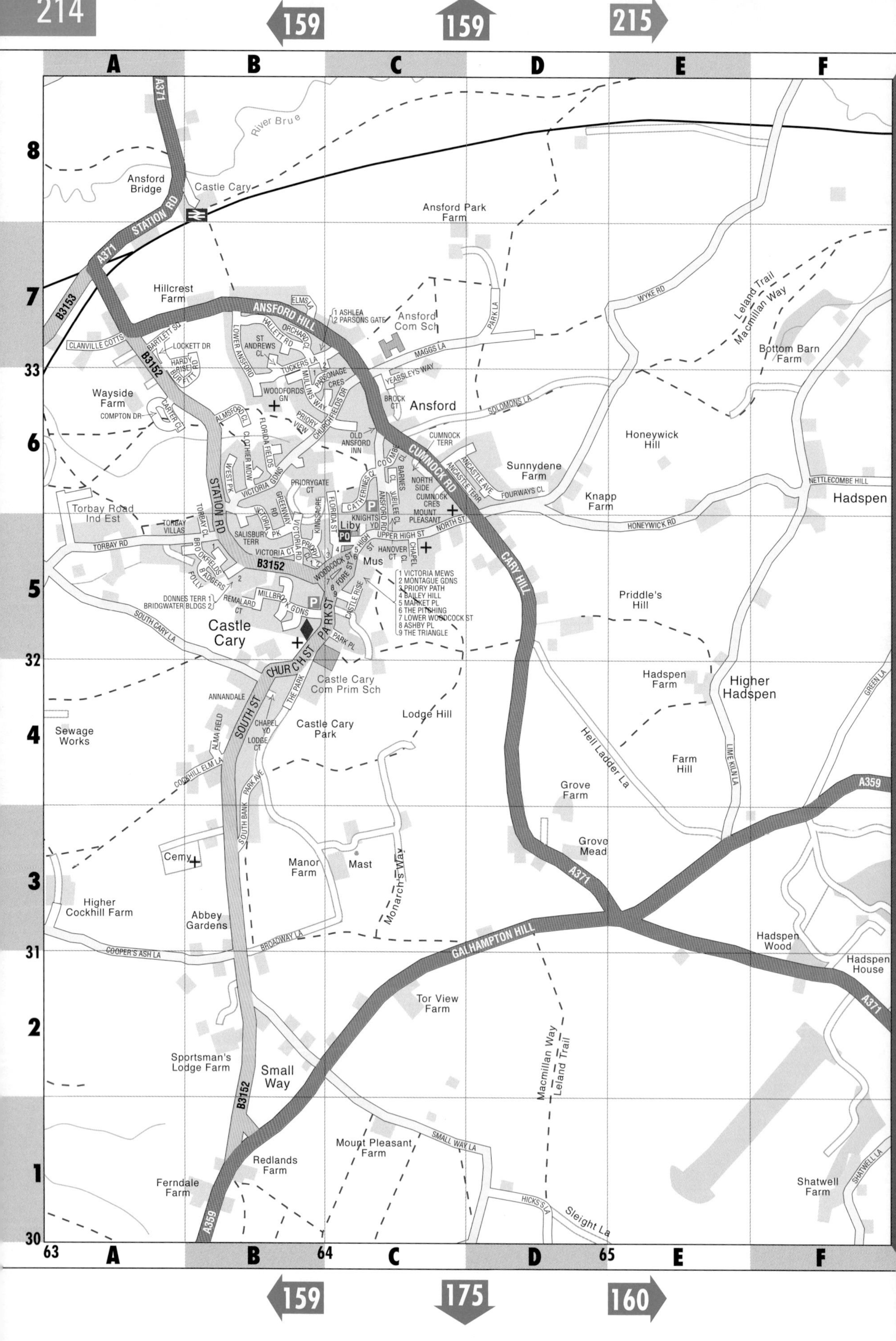
A
B
C
D
E
F
8
7
33
6
5
32
4
3
31
2
1
30
63
64
65
River Brue
Ansford Bridge
Castle Cary
Ansford Park Farm
Hillcrest Farm
ANSFORD HILL
Ansford Com Sch
Ansford
Wayside Farm
Bottom Barn Farm
Leland Trail
Macmillan Way
WYKE RD
MAGGS LA
PARK LA
SOLOMONS LA
Honeywick Hill
Sunnydene Farm
Knapp Farm
Hadspen
NETTLECOMBE HILL
HONEYWICK RD
FOURWAYS CL
CUMNOCK RD
CARY HILL
STATION RD
Torbay Road Ind Est
TORBAY RD
B3152
B3153
A371
Castle Cary
Priddle's Hill
1 VICTORIA MEWS
2 MONTAGUE GDNS
3 PRIORY PATH
4 BAILEY HILL
5 MARKET PL
6 THE PITCHING
7 LOWER WOODCOCK ST
8 ASHBY PL
9 THE TRIANGLE
SOUTH CARY LA
Castle Cary Com Prim Sch
Hadspen Farm
Higher Hadspen
Lodge Hill
Castle Cary Park
Sewage Works
Hell Ladder La
Farm Hill
Grove Farm
Grove Mead
LIME KILN LA
GREEN LA
A359
Cemy
Manor Farm
Mast
Monarch's Way
Higher Cockhill Farm
Abbey Gardens
COOPER'S ASH LA
BROADWAY LA
GALHAMPTON HILL
Hadspen Wood
Hadspen House
Tor View Farm
Sportsman's Lodge Farm
Small Way
Mount Pleasant Farm
SMALL WAY LA
Redlands Farm
Ferndale Farm
HICKS'S LA
Sleight La
Shatwell Farm
SHATWELL LA

159 175 160

160
160

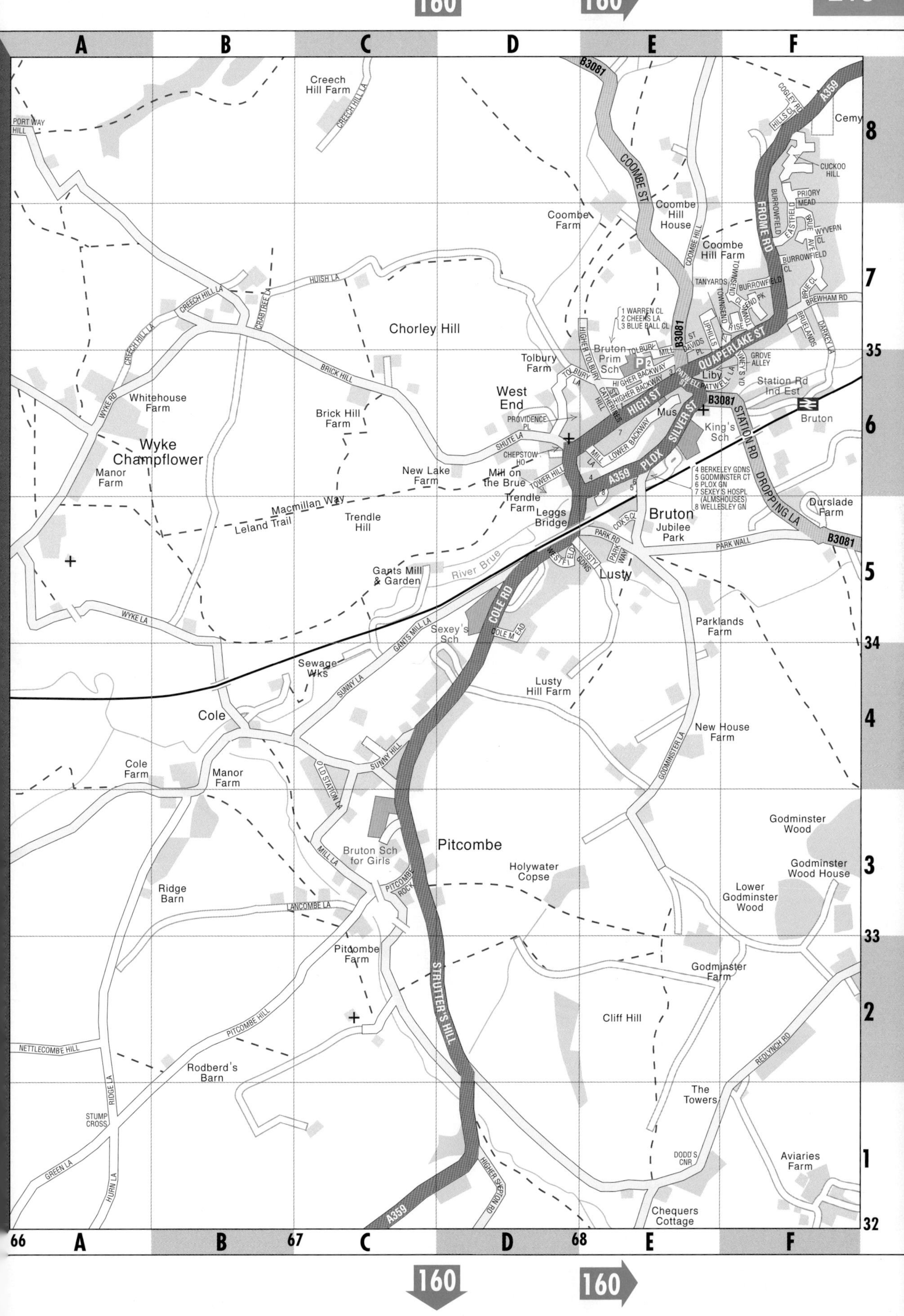
A
B
C
D
E
F
Creech Hill Farm
Cemy
Coombe Farm
Coombe Hill House
Coombe Hill Farm
Chorley Hill
Tolbury Farm
Bruton Prim Sch
Liby
West End
Whitehouse Farm
Wyke Champflower
Manor Farm
Brick Hill Farm
New Lake Farm
Mill on the Brue
Mus
King's Sch
Station Rd Ind Est
Bruton
Macmillan Way
Leland Trail
Trendle Hill
Trendle Farm
Leggs Bridge
Bruton
Jubilee Park
Durslade Farm
Gants Mill & Garden
River Brue
Lusty
Sexey's Sch
Sewage Wks
Parklands Farm
Lusty Hill Farm
Cole
New House Farm
Cole Farm
Manor Farm
Pitcombe
Bruton Sch for Girls
Holywater Copse
Godminster Wood
Godminster Wood House
Lower Godminster Wood
Ridge Barn
Pitcombe Farm
Godminster Farm
Cliff Hill
Rodberd's Barn
The Towers
Aviaries Farm
Chequers Cottage
1 WARREN CL
2 CHEEKS LA
3 BLUE BALL CL
4 BERKELEY GDNS
5 GODMINSTER CT
6 PLOX GN
7 SEXEY'S HOSPL (ALMSHOUSES)
8 WELLESLEY GN
B3081
A359
B3087
COOMBE ST
FROME RD
HIGH ST
QUAPERLAKE ST
SILVER ST
PLOX
STATION RD
DROPPING LA
PARK WALL
COLE RD
STRUTTER'S HILL
HIGHER BACKWAY
LOWER BACKWAY
BRICK HILL
HUISH LA
CREECH HILL LA
CRABTREE LA
WYKE RD
WYKE LA
GANTS MILL LA
SUNNY LA
SUNNY HILL
OLD STATION LA
MILL LA
LANCOMBE LA
PITCOMBE HILL
NETTLECOMBE HILL
RIDGE LA
STUMP CROSS
GREEN LA
HURN LA
HIGHER SHEPTON RD
GODMINSTER LA
REDLYNCH RD
DODD'S CNR
PORT WAY HILL
COGLEY RD
HILLS CL
CUCKOO HILL
PRIORY MEAD
BURROWFIELD
FASTFIELD
WYVERN CL
BURROWFIELD CL
BREWHAM RD
BRUELANDS
DARKEY LA
GROVE ALLEY
PATWELL LA
TANYARDS
TOWNSEND
SHUTE LA
CHEPSTOW HO
PROVIDENCE PL
TOWER HILL
COX'S CL
PARK RD
COLE MEAD
66
67
68
8
7
35
6
5
34
4
3
33
2
1
32

160
160

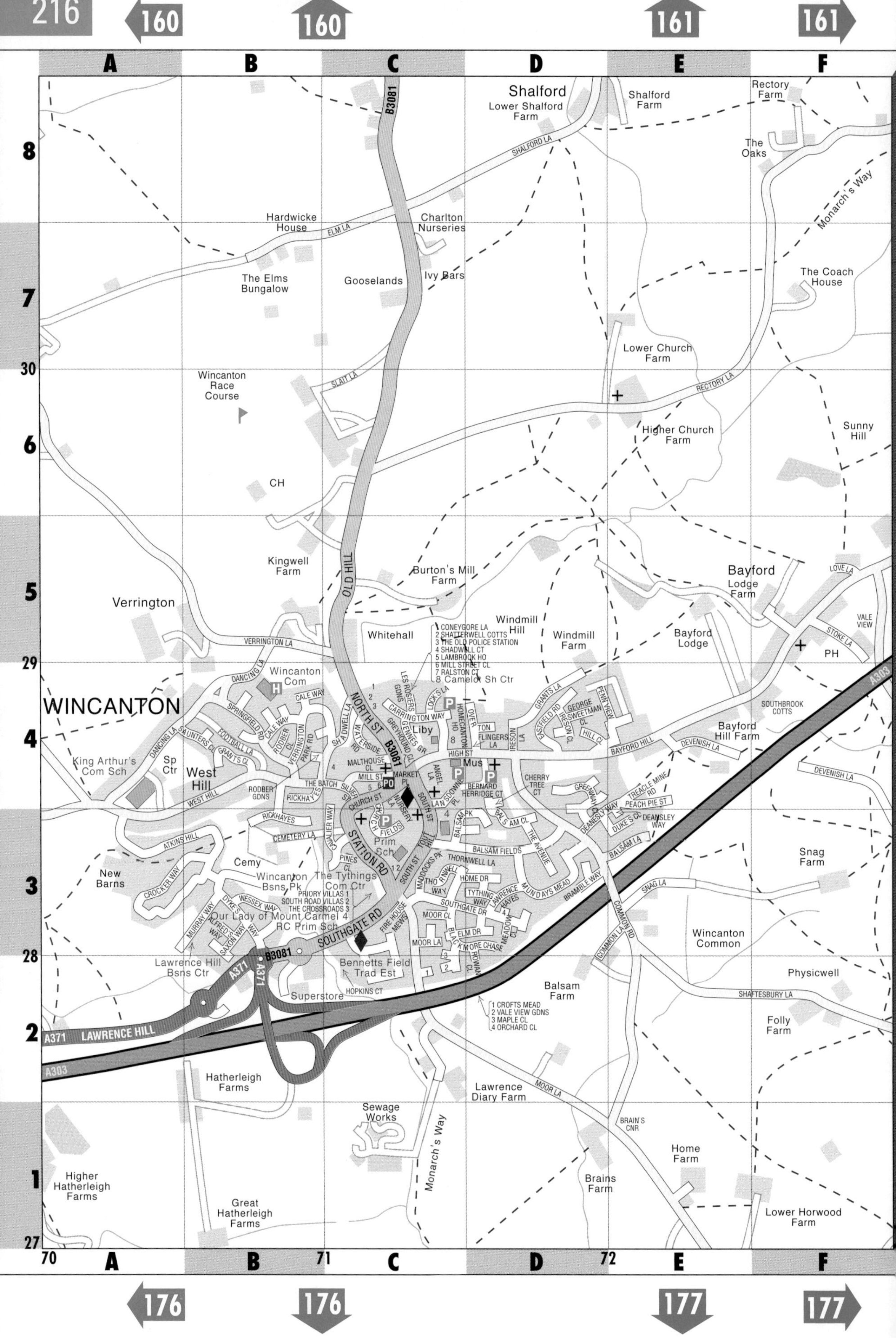
160
160
161
161
A
B
C
D
E
F
8
7
30
6
5
29
4
3
28
2
1
27
Shalford
Lower Shalford Farm
Shalford Farm
Rectory Farm
The Oaks
SHALFORD LA
Monarch's Way
B3081
Hardwicke House
ELM LA
Charlton Nurseries
The Elms Bungalow
Gooselands
Ivy Bars
The Coach House
Lower Church Farm
Wincanton Race Course
SLAIT LA
RECTORY LA
Higher Church Farm
Sunny Hill
CH
Kingwell Farm
OLD HILL
Burton's Mill Farm
Bayford
Lodge Farm
LOVE LA
Verrington
Whitehall
Windmill Hill
Windmill Farm
Bayford Lodge
VALE VIEW
STOKE LA
PH
VERRINGTON LA
1 CONEYGORE LA
2 SHATTERWELL COTTS
3 THE OLD POLICE STATION
4 SHADWELL CT
5 LAMBROOK HO
6 MILL STREET CL
7 RALSTON CT
8 Camelot Sh Ctr
A303
DANCING LA
Wincanton Com
WINCANTON
CALE WAY
SPRINGFIELD RD
NORTH ST
CARRINGTON WAY
LOCK'S LA
GRANTS LA
PENN VIEW
EASTFIELD RD
GEORGE SWEETMAN CL
IRESON CL
HILL CL
SOUTHBROOK COTTS
Liby
HOMECANTON HO
FLINGERS LA
IRESON LA
Bayford Hill Farm
BAYFORD HILL
DEVENISH LA
DEVENISH LA
SAUNTERS CL
FOOTBALL LA
GRANTS CL
RODBER CL
VERRINGTON PARK RD
SHADWELL LA
WATERSIDE RD
GREYHOUND CL
HIGH ST
King Arthur's Com Sch
Sp Ctr
West Hill
MALTHOUSE CL
MILL ST
MARKET PL
Mus
CHERRY TREE CT
TREACLE MINE RD
PEACH PIE ST
DEANESLY WAY
DUKE'S CL
BALSAM LA
THE BATCH
PO
BERNARD HERRIDGE CT
RODBER GDNS
WEST HILL
RICKHAYES
CHURCH ST
NURSERY
SOUTH ST
BALSAM PK
RICKHAYES
CEMETERY LA
CAVALIER WAY
STATION RD
Prim Sch
BALSAM FIELDS
THE AVENUE
Snag Farm
ATKINS HILL
Cemy
PINES CL
THORNWELL LA
New Barns
CROCKER WAY
Wincanton Bsns Pk
The Tythings Com Ctr
MADDOCKS PK
HOME DR
TYTHING WAY
LAWRENCE HAYES
MUNDAYS MEAD
BRAMBLE WAY
SNAG LA
PRIORY VILLAS 1
SOUTH ROAD VILLAS 2
THE CROSSROADS 3
SOUTHGATE DR
WESSEX WAY
Our Lady of Mount Carmel RC Prim Sch
SOUTHGATE RD
FIRE HOUSE MEWS
MOOR CL
ELM DR
MEADOW CL
COMMON RD
COMMON LA
Wincanton Common
MURRAY WAY
ALFRED'S WAY
SAXON WAY
MOOR LA
BLACKMORE CHASE
ROWAN CL
B3081
Lawrence Hill Bsns Ctr
A371
A371
Bennetts Field Trad Est
Superstore
HOPKINS CT
Balsam Farm
Physicwell
SHAFTESBURY LA
1 CROFTS MEAD
2 VALE VIEW GDNS
3 MAPLE CL
4 ORCHARD CL
A371
LAWRENCE HILL
Folly Farm
A303
Hatherleigh Farms
Lawrence Diary Farm
MOOR LA
Sewage Works
BRAIN'S CNR
Monarch's Way
Home Farm
Higher Hatherleigh Farms
Brains Farm
Great Hatherleigh Farms
Lower Horwood Farm
70
71
72
176
176
177
177

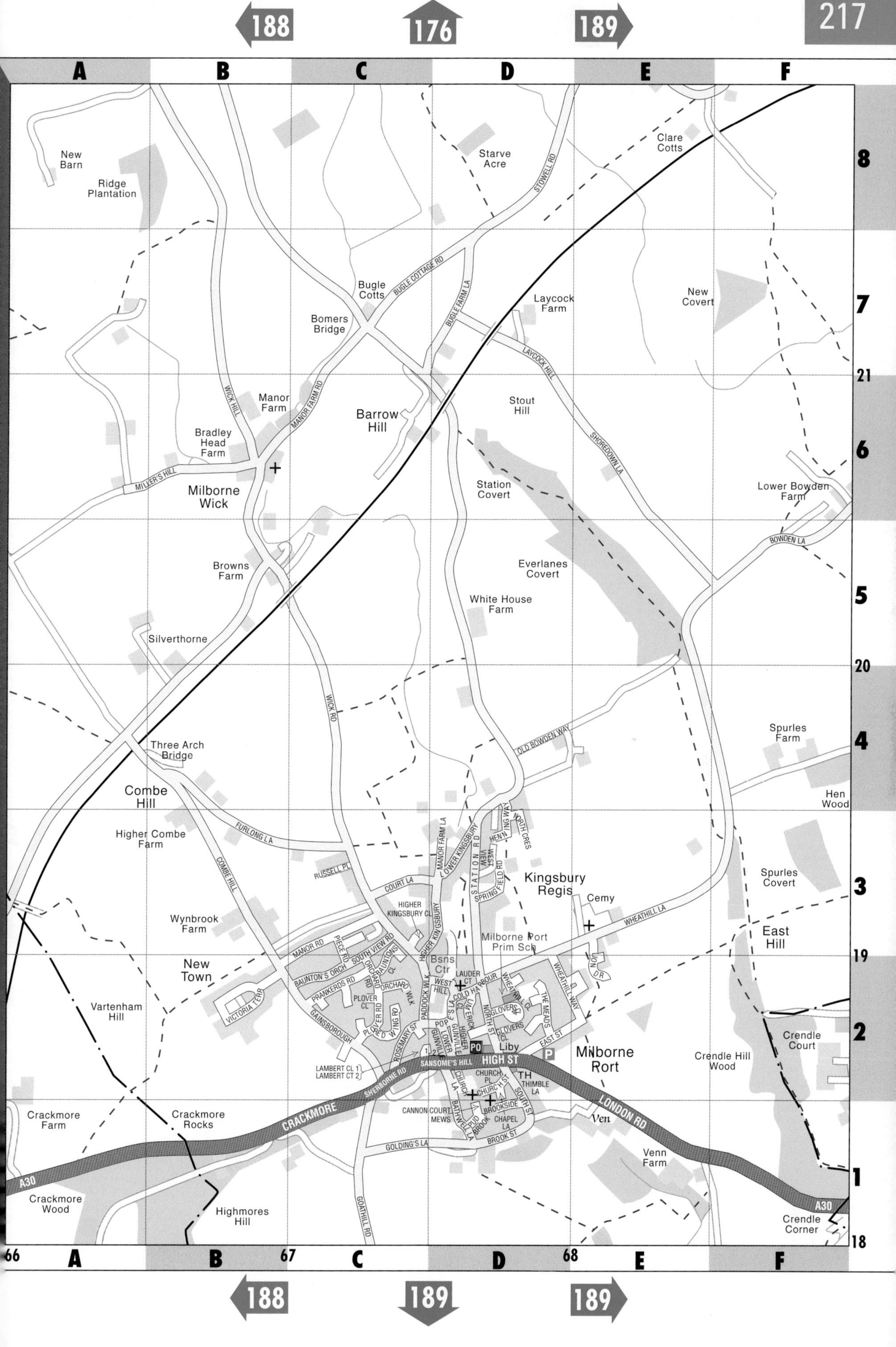
217
188
176
189
A
B
C
D
E
F
8
7
21
6
5
20
4
3
19
2
1
18
66
67
68
New Barn
Ridge Plantation
Starve Acre
Clare Cotts
STOWELL RD
Bugle Cotts
BUGLE COTTAGE RD
Bomers Bridge
BUGLE FARM LA
Laycock Farm
New Covert
LAYCOCK HILL
Manor Farm
MANOR FARM RD
WICK HILL
Barrow Hill
Stout Hill
Bradley Head Farm
SHOREDOWN LA
MILLER'S HILL
Milborne Wick
Station Covert
Lower Bowden Farm
BOWDEN LA
Browns Farm
Everlanes Covert
White House Farm
Silverthorne
WICK RD
Spurles Farm
OLD BOWDEN WAY
Three Arch Bridge
Combe Hill
Hen Wood
Higher Combe Farm
FURLONG LA
MANOR FARM LA
LOWER KINGSBURY
STATION RD
NORTH CRES
RUSSELL PL
COMBE HILL
WEST VIEW
SPRINGFIELD RD
Kingsbury Regis
Spurles Covert
COURT LA
HIGHER KINGSBURY CL
HIGHER KINGSBURY
Cemy
WHEATHILL LA
Wynbrook Farm
Milborne Port Prim Sch
East Hill
MANOR RD
PIECE RD
SOUTH VIEW RD
BAUNTONS CL
New Town
Bsns Ctr
LAUDER CT
BAUNTON'S ORCH
ORCHARD RD
ORCHARD
PRANKERDS RD
WEST HILL
COLD HARBOUR
WHEATHILL CL
THE MEADS
WHEATHILL WAY
VICTORIA TERR
PLOVER CL
PLOVER RD
PADDOCK WLK
Vartenham Hill
GAINSBOROUGH
REDWING RD
ROSEMARY ST
POP
LOWER GUNVILLE
HIGHER GUNVILLE
NORTH ST
GLOVERS CL
EAST ST
Crendle Court
PO
HIGH ST
P
Milborne Port
Liby
TH
LAMBERT CL
LAMBERT CT
SANSOME'S HILL
SHERBORNE RD
CHURCH PL
THIMBLE LA
Crendle Hill Wood
CHURCH LA
SOUTH ST
BROOKSIDE
CANNON COURT MEWS
BATHWELL LA
CHAPEL LA
BROOK ST
LONDON RD
Ven
Crackmore Farm
Crackmore Rocks
CRACKMORE
GOLDING'S LA
Venn Farm
A30
Crackmore Wood
Highmores Hill
GOATHILL RD
Crendle Corner
188
189
189

186
186
C6
1 KINGSLAND GRANGE
2 HAWKINS WAY
3 TRELLECH CT
4 THE REGENTS
5 GREAT CNR
6 MALMESBURY CT
187
F7
1 THATCHAM CT
2 THATCHAM CL
3 NEWBERRY TERR
4 LOCKWOOD CT

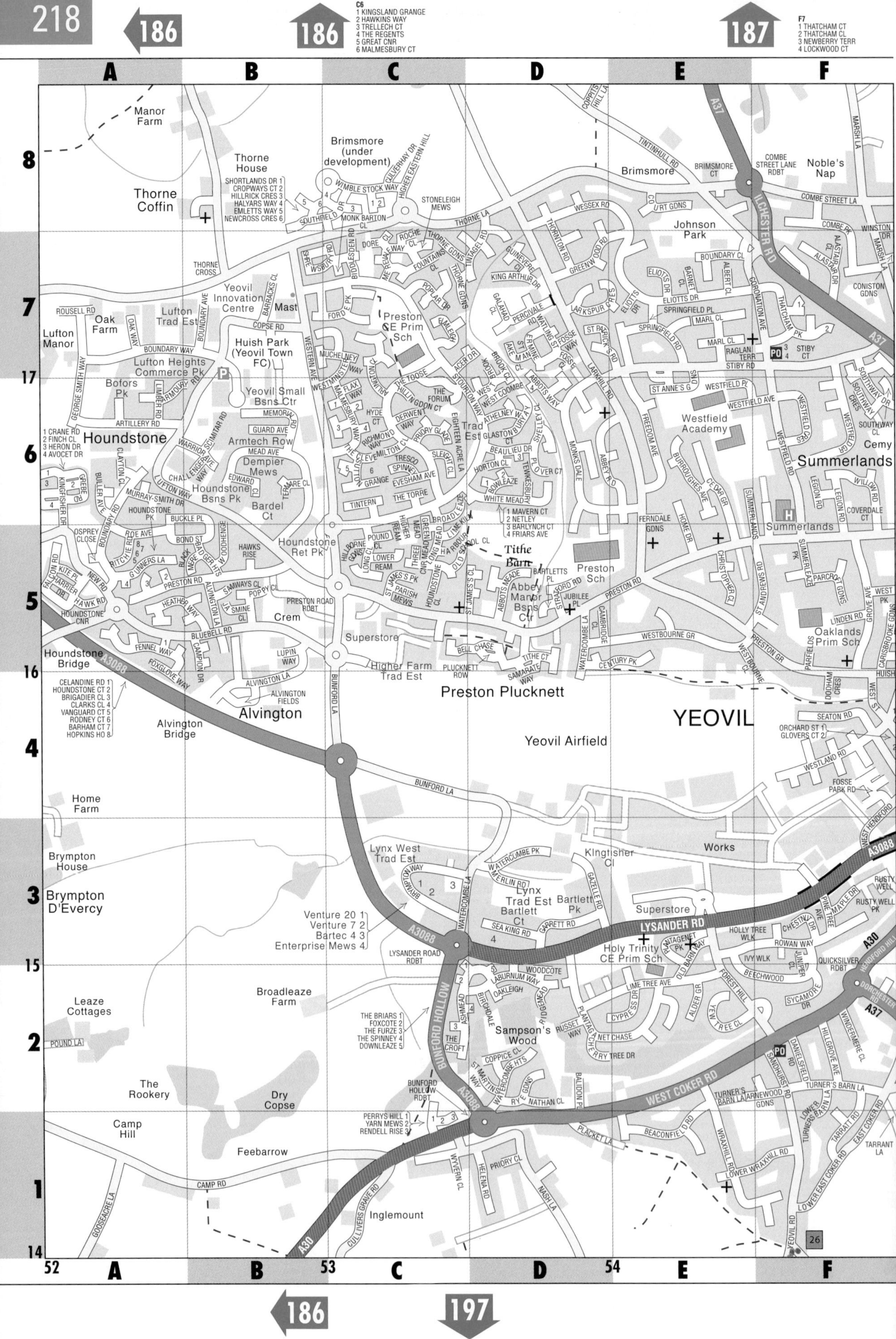

186
197

187
187

B8
1 GRENVILLE RD
2 SOMERVILLE CL
3 LIVINGSTONE DR
4 BLAKE CL
5 MOUNTBATTEN RD
6 CARTIER CL

B8
7 COLUMBUS CL
8 CAVENDISH CL

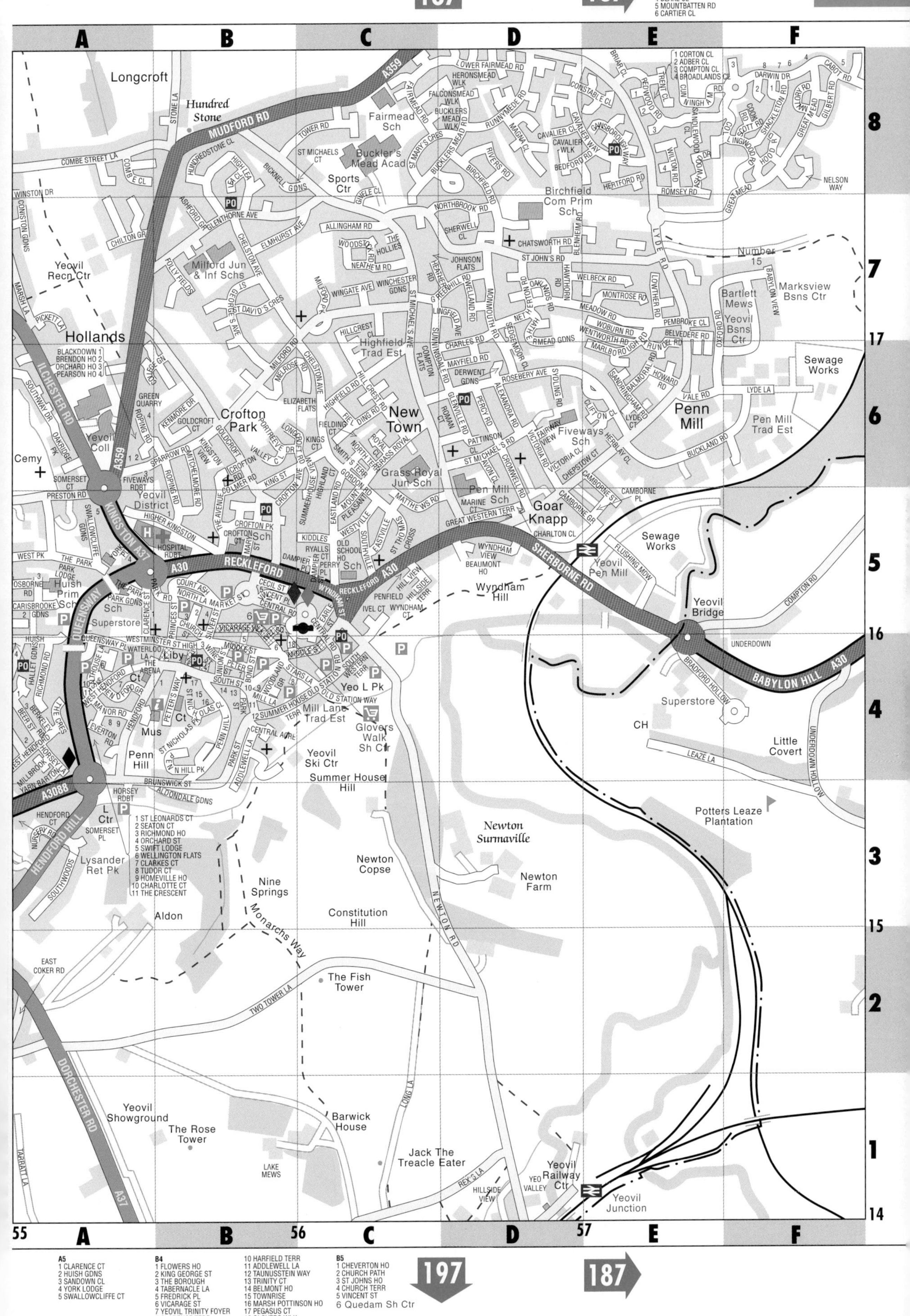

A5
1 CLARENCE CT
2 HUISH GDNS
3 SANDOWN CL
4 YORK LODGE
5 SWALLOWCLIFFE CT

B4
1 FLOWERS HO
2 KING GEORGE ST
3 THE BOROUGH
4 TABERNACLE LA
5 FREDRICK PL
6 VICARAGE ST
7 YEOVIL TRINITY FOYER
8 CLARENCE TERR
9 BROAD OAK
10 HARFIELD TERR
11 ADDLEWELL LA
12 TAUNUSSTEIN WAY
13 TRINITY CT
14 BELMONT HO
15 TOWNRISE
16 MARSH POTTINSON HO
17 PEGASUS CT
18 GLOVERS WLK

B5
1 CHEVERTON HO
2 CHURCH PATH
3 ST JOHNS HO
4 CHURCH TERR
5 VINCENT ST
6 Quedam Sh Ctr

197
187

184 185 185

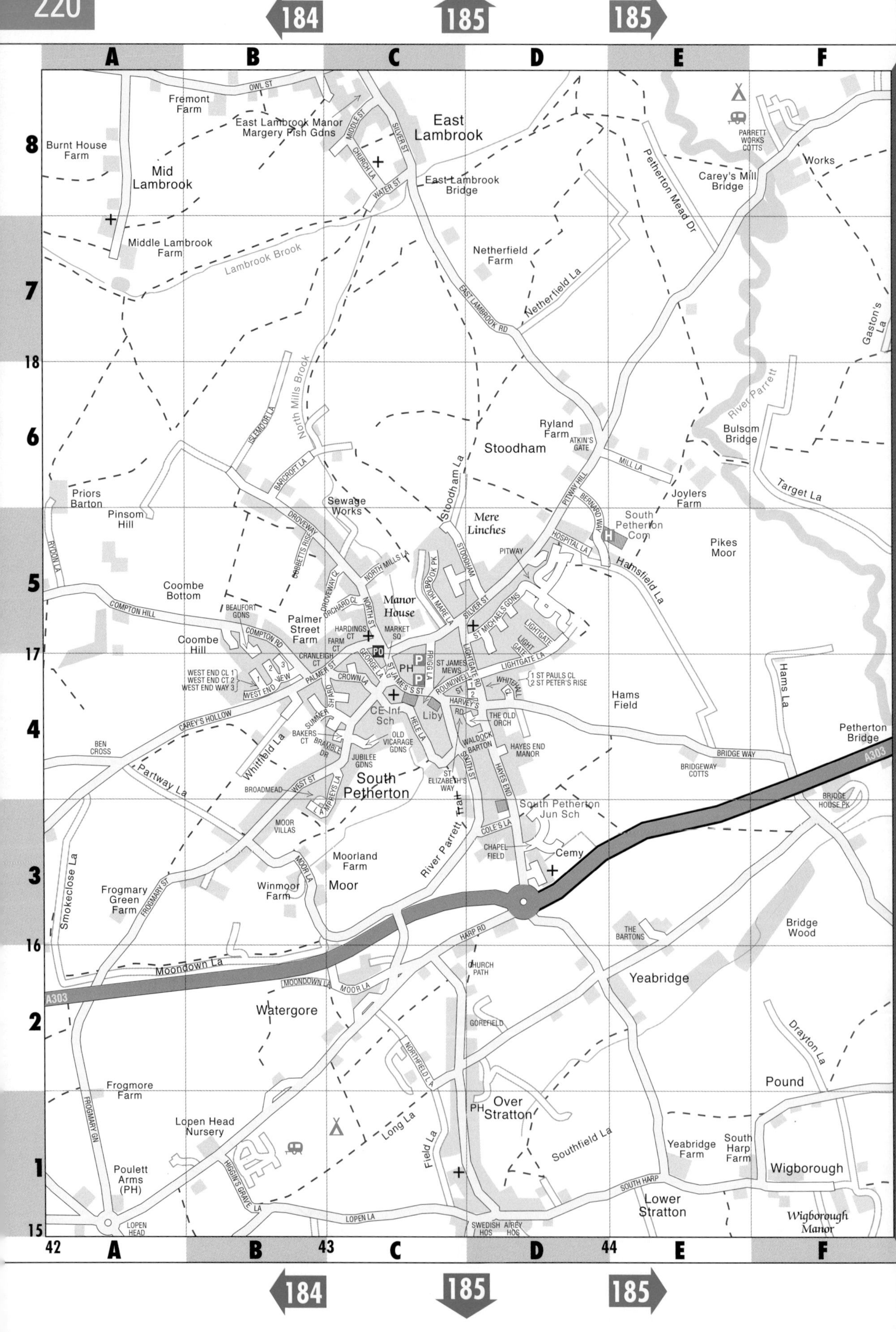
A
B
C
D
E
F
8
7
18
6
5
17
4
3
16
2
1
15
42
43
44
OWL ST
Fremont Farm
East Lambrook Manor Margery Fish Gdns
MIDDLE ST
SILVER ST
CHURCH LA
WATER ST
East Lambrook
East Lambrook Bridge
Burnt House Farm
Mid Lambrook
Middle Lambrook Farm
Lambrook Brook
Netherfield Farm
Netherfield La
EAST LAMBROOK RD
Petherton Mead Dr
PARRETT WORKS COTTS
Works
Carey's Mill Bridge
Gaston's La
River Parrett
Bulsom Bridge
North Mills Brook
ISLEMOOR LA
BARCROFT LA
Ryland Farm
ATKIN'S GATE
Stoodham
MILL LA
Target La
Joylers Farm
Priors Barton
Pinsom Hill
Sewage Works
DROVEWAY
COBBETTS RISE
Stoodham La
Mere Linches
PITWAY HILL
BERNARD WAY
South Petherton Com
HOSPITAL LA
Pikes Moor
RYDON LA
Coombe Bottom
NORTH MILLS LA
HOLBROOK PK
STOODHAM
PITWAY
Hamsfield La
COMPTON HILL
BEAUFORT GDNS
Palmer Street Farm
DROVEWAY CL
ORCHARD CL
NORTH ST
Manor House
MARE LA
SILVER ST
ST MICHAEL'S GDNS
LIGHTGATE
LIGHT GATE LA
Coombe Hill
COMPTON RD
HARDINGS CT
FARM CT
MARKET SQ
PO
PH
P
PRIGG LA
ST JAMES MEWS
LIGHTGATE RD
LIGHTGATE LA
1 ST PAULS CL
2 ST PETER'S RISE
WHITEHALL
Hams Field
Hams La
CRANLEIGH CT
GEORGE LA
ST JAMES'S ST
ROUNDWELL ST
HARVEY'S RD
WEST END CL 1
WEST END CT 2
WEST END WAY 3
YEW
WEST END
PALMER ST
CROWN LA
CE Inf Sch
Liby
HELE LA
THE OLD ORCH
CAREY'S HOLLOW
SHAPWAY
SUMMER
BAKERS CT
BRAMBLE DR
OLD VICARAGE GDNS
WALDOCK BARTON
HAYES END MANOR
BRIDGE WAY
Petherton Bridge
A303
BEN CROSS
Whitfield La
JUBILEE GDNS
SOUTH ST
BRIDGEWAY COTTS
Partway La
BROADMEAD
WEST ST
HUMPREYS LA
South Petherton
ST ELIZABETH'S WAY
HAYES END
River Parrett Trail
South Petherton Jun Sch
BRIDGE HOUSE PK
MOOR VILLAS
COLE'S LA
CHAPEL FIELD
Cemy
Smokeclose La
Moorland Farm
MOOR LA
Frogmary Green Farm
FROGMARY ST
Winmoor Farm
Moor
HARP RD
THE BARTONS
Bridge Wood
Moondown La
CHURCH PATH
Yeabridge
MOONDOWN LA
MOOR LA
Watergore
GOREFIELD
Drayton La
NORTHFIELD LA
Pound
Frogmore Farm
FROGMARY GN
Over Stratton
Lopen Head Nursery
Long La
Field La
Southfield La
Yeabridge Farm
South Harp Farm
Wigborough
Poulett Arms (PH)
HIGGIN'S GRAVE LA
SOUTH HARP
Lower Stratton
LOPEN HEAD
LOPEN LA
SWEDISH HOS
AIREY HOS
Wigborough Manor

184 185 185

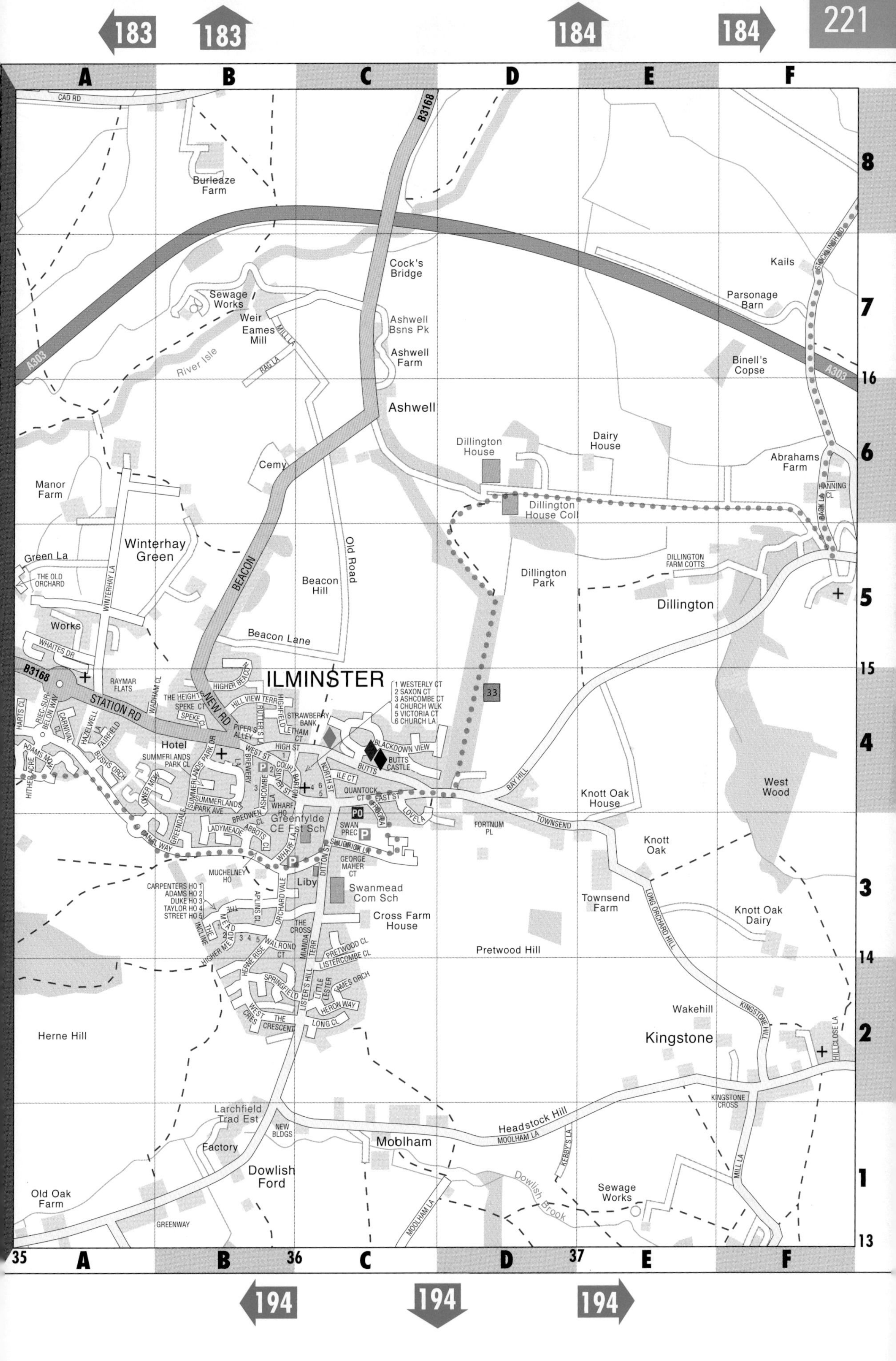
183
183
184
184
ILMINSTER
Ashwell
Winterhay Green
Dillington
Kingstone
Moolham
Dowlish Ford
Burleaze Farm
Sewage Works
Weir
Eames Mill
Cock's Bridge
Ashwell Bsns Pk
Ashwell Farm
Kails
Parsonage Barn
Binell's Copse
Dillington House
Dairy House
Abrahams Farm
Dillington House Coll
Manor Farm
Cemy
Beacon Hill
Beacon Lane
Old Road
Dillington Park
Works
Hotel
Greenfylde CE Fst Sch
Liby
Swanmead Com Sch
Cross Farm House
Knott Oak House
West Wood
Knott Oak
Townsend Farm
Knott Oak Dairy
Pretwood Hill
Wakehill
Herne Hill
Larchfield Trad Est
Factory
Old Oak Farm
Sewage Works
Headstock Hill
Dowlish Brook
River Isle
A303
B3168
STATION RD
NEW RD
BEACON
TOWNSEND
BAY HILL
LONG ORCHARD HILL
KINGSTONE HILL
MOOLHAM LA
KEBBY'S LA
MILL LA
HILLCLOSE LA
GREENWAY
CAD RD
Green La
1 WESTERLY CT
2 SAXON CT
3 ASHCOMBE CT
4 CHURCH WLK
5 VICTORIA CT
6 CHURCH LA
CARPENTERS HO 1
ADAMS HO 2
DUKE HO 3
TAYLOR HO 4
STREET HO 5
194
194
194

179 167 180

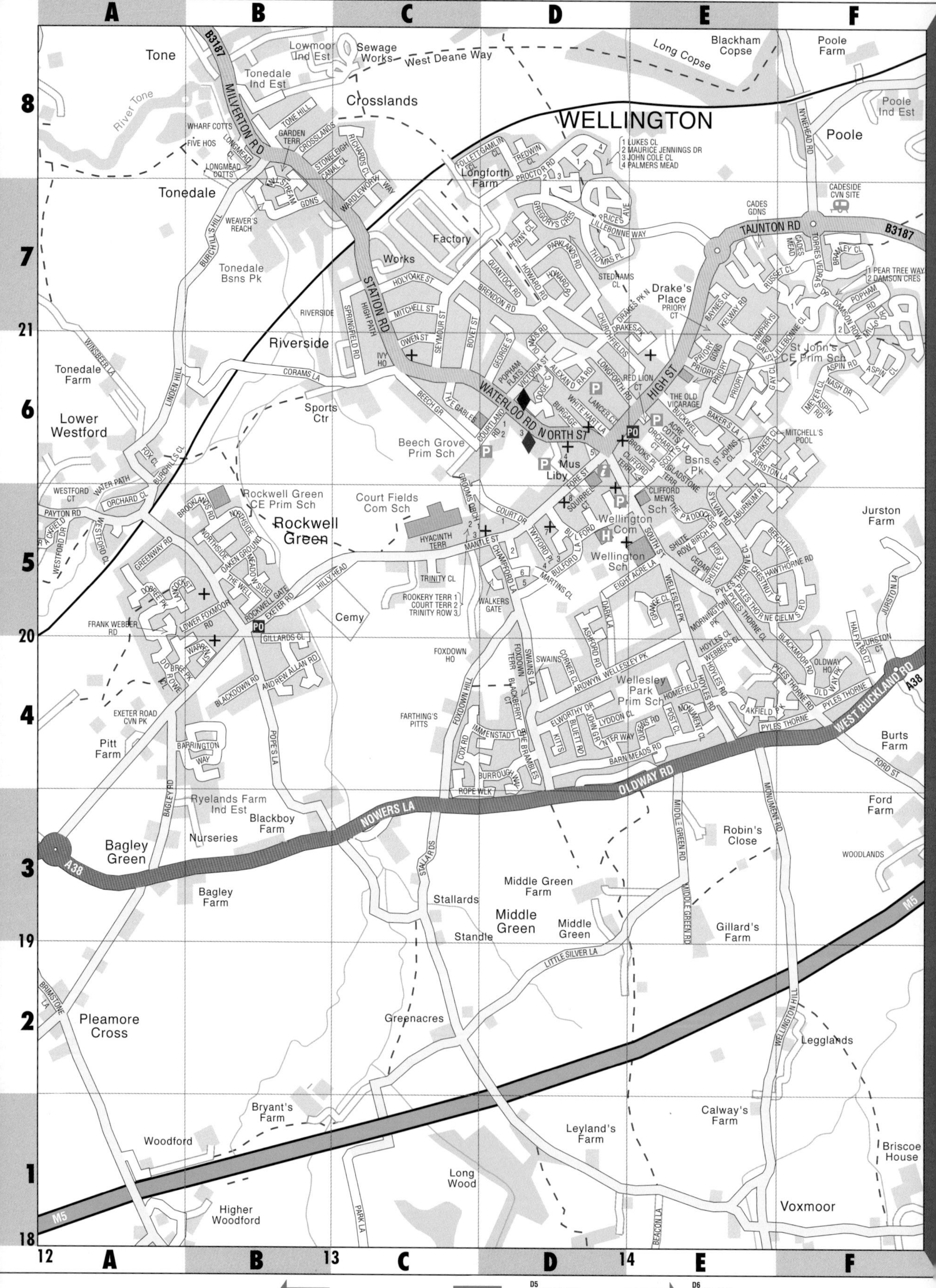

179 180 180

D5
1 THE GARDENS
2 CHAMPFORD MEWS
3 POUND TERR
4 MARTINS BLDGS
5 IMPROVEMENT PL
6 WILLCOCKS CL
7 LABURNUM COTTS
8 JUBILEE CT

D6
1 THE LAWN
2 BEECH CT
3 BELVEDERE CT
4 BISHOPS CT
5 CORNHILL

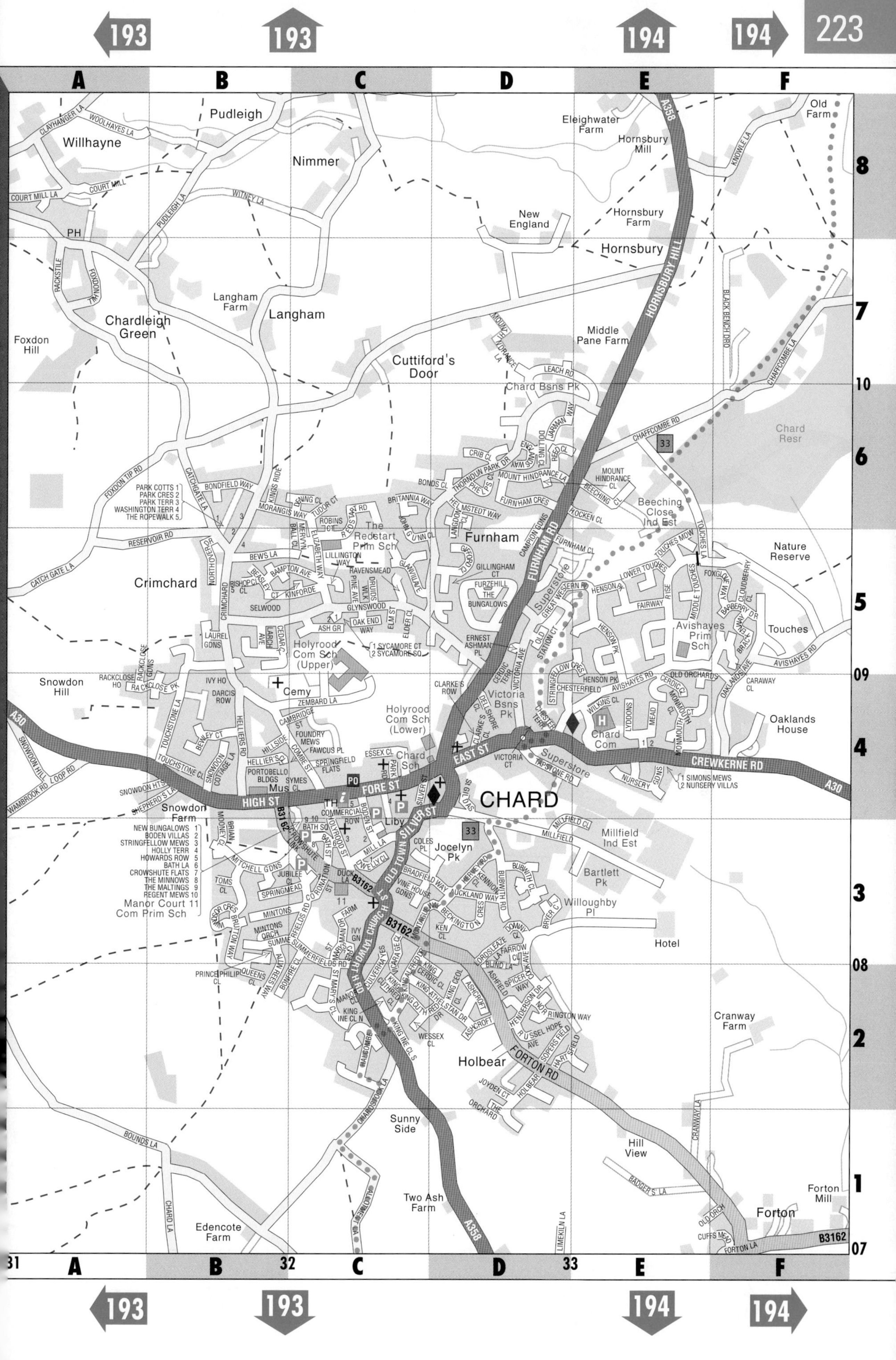
193
193
194
194
A
B
C
D
E
F
Pudleigh
Willhayne
Nimmer
Eleighwater Farm
Hornsbury Mill
Old Farm
New England
Hornsbury Farm
Hornsbury
HORNSBURY HILL
A358
Langham Farm
Langham
Chardleigh Green
Foxdon Hill
Cuttiford's Door
Middle Pane Farm
Chard Bsns Pk
Chard Resr
Beeching Close Ind Est
Furnham
FURNHAM RD
The Redstart Prim Sch
Crimchard
Nature Reserve
Touches
Avishayes Prim Sch
Holyrood Com Sch (Upper)
Snowdon Hill
Cemy
Holyrood Com Sch (Lower)
Victoria Bsns Pk
Chard Com
Oaklands House
Chard Sch
EAST ST
CREWKERNE RD
A30
HIGH ST
FORE ST
CHARD
Superstore
Mus
Liby
Snowdon Farm
Jocelyn Pk
Millfield Ind Est
Bartlett Pk
Willoughby Pl
Manor Court Com Prim Sch
Hotel
Cranway Farm
Holbear
FORTON RD
Sunny Side
Hill View
Two Ash Farm
Edencote Farm
Forton
Forton Mill
B3162
8
7
10
6
5
09
4
3
08
2
1
07
31
32
33

195 195 196 196

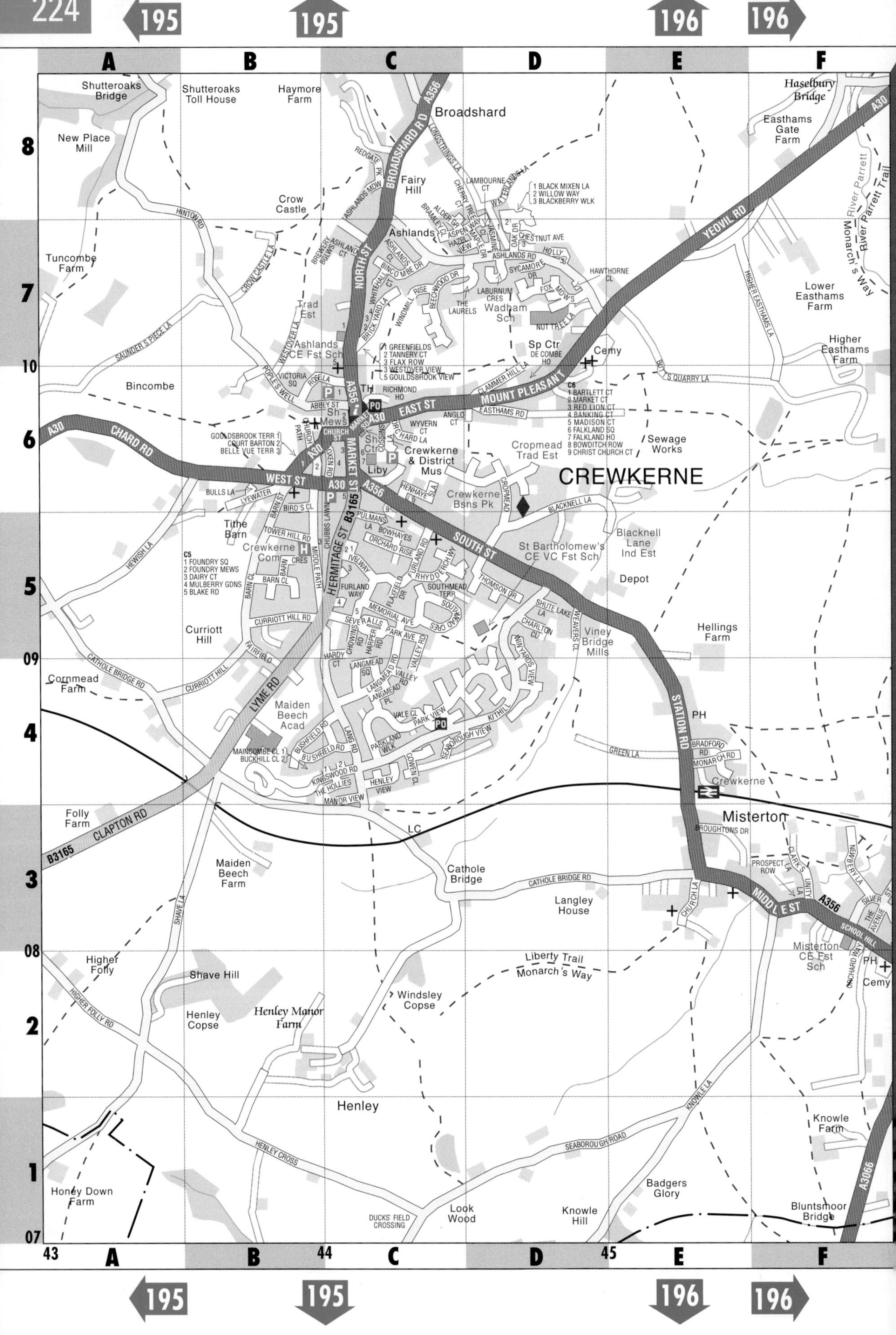
A B C D E F
8
7
10
6
5
09
4
3
08
2
1
07
43 44 45
Shutteroaks Bridge
Shutteroaks Toll House
Haymore Farm
Broadshard
Haselbury Bridge
Easthams Gate Farm
New Place Mill
Fairy Hill
Crow Castle
Ashlands
Tuncombe Farm
Trad Est
Ashlands CE Fst Sch
Wadham Sch
Sp Ctr
Cemy
Lower Easthams Farm
Higher Easthams Farm
River Parrett
River Parrett Trail
Monarch's Way
Bincombe
YEOVIL RD
MOUNT PLEASANT
EAST ST
CHARD RD
WEST ST
NORTH ST
BROADSHARD RD
MARKET ST
SOUTH ST
HERMITAGE ST
A30
A356
B3165
1 GREENFIELDS
2 TANNERY CT
3 FLAX ROW
4 WESTOVER VIEW
5 GOULDSBROOK VIEW
1 BLACK MIXEN LA
2 WILLOW WAY
3 BLACKBERRY WLK
C6
1 BARTLETT CT
2 MARKET CT
3 RED LION CT
4 BANKING CT
5 MADISON CT
6 FALKLAND SQ
7 FALKLAND HO
8 BOWDITCH ROW
9 CHRIST CHURCH CT
C5
1 FOUNDRY SQ
2 FOUNDRY MEWS
3 DAIRY CT
4 MULBERRY GDNS
5 BLAKE RD
GOULDSBROOK TERR 1
COURT BARTON 2
BELLE VUE TERR 3
Sh Mews
Sh Ctr
Liby
TH
PO
Crewkerne & District Mus
Cropmead Trad Est
Sewage Works
CREWKERNE
Crewkerne Bsns Pk
Tithe Barn
Crewkerne Com
St Bartholomew's CE VC Fst Sch
Blacknell Lane Ind Est
Depot
Curriott Hill
Viney Bridge Mills
Hellings Farm
Cornmead Farm
Maiden Beech Acad
STATION RD
LYME RD
PH
Crewkerne
Misterton
Folly Farm
CLAPTON RD
Maiden Beech Farm
LC
Cathole Bridge
Langley House
MIDDLE ST
Misterton CE Fst Sch
Higher Folly
Shave Hill
Liberty Trail
Monarch's Way
Windsley Copse
Henley Copse
Henley Manor Farm
Henley
Knowle Farm
Honey Down Farm
Badgers Glory
Look Wood
Knowle Hill
DUCKS' FIELD CROSSING
Bluntsmoor Bridge
A3066
SEABOROUGH ROAD
HENLEY CROSS
HIGHER FOLLY RD
KNOWLE LA
SHAVE LA
CATHOLE BRIDGE RD

188
188
188
A
B
C
D
E
F
8
7
18
6
5
17
4
3
16
2
1
15
62
63
64
SHERBORNE
Ambrose Hill
Coombe Farm
Oborne Wood
COOMBE LA
Macmillan Way
Lower Clatcombe House
The Gryphon Sch
L Ctr
REDHOLE LA
BRICKKILN LA
SANDFORD ORCAS RD
B3145
B3148
B3145
A30
A352
HARDING'S HOUSE LA
QUARR LANE PK
QUARR LA
QUARR DR
STONEDENE
BRISTOL RD
ST ALDHELM'S RD
CASTLE TOWN WAY
ST PAUL'S FLATS
ST PAUL'S GN
MC CREERY
Blackmarsh Farm
UNDERDOWN LA
Coldharbour Bsns Pk
DODGE CROSS
KINGS CT 1
QUEENS TERR 2
GLOVERS
Hotel
Prim Sch
GRANVILLE WAY
ALBANY CL
ADMIRALS CL
LAMBS FIELD
VERNALLS RD
SIMONS RD
KINGS CRES
THE FURLONGS
KINGS RD
HARBOUR WAY
WOOTTON GR
HARBOUR TERR
DAIRY FLATS
TERRACE VIEW
COLD HARBOUR
LANGDONS
EARLS CL
CASTLE RD
CASTLE TOWN WAY
OBORNE RD
CHANDLERS
FRANCIS WLK
HILL HOUSE CL
THE AVENUE
MILLER WAY
BEDE ST
DUNS
ALBERT ROW
LUSH PATH
SAFFRON CT
TINNEYS LA
SCHOOL DR
KNOTTS PADDOCK
WATERLOO TERR
MANOR CT
NORTH RD
ST SWITHINS RD
NEWLAND
CASTLETON RD
Sherborne Old Castle
PINFORD LA
TRENT PATH LA
HIGHMORE RD
NETHERCOOMBE LA
COOMBE
THE SHEEPLA
SHEEPLANDS LA
TWELVE ACRES
DAIRY CL
KEARVELL WAY
WARREN WAY
AMORS DROVE
STAFFORD RD
MULBERRY GDNS
BLACKBERRY LA
COOMBE TERR
PRIESTLANDS
Sherborne Sch Int Coll
JOSELIN CT
PRIESTLANDS LA
D4
1 THE GREEN
2 THE OLD GREEN
3 HIGHER CHEAP ST
NEWELL
GREENHILL
GEORGE ST
BARTON GDNS
YEOVIL RD
KITT HILL
OXLEY COTTS
CORNHILL
OLD FARM
BACK LA
HOSPITAL LA
Yeatman
HILLBROOK CT
CHEAP ST
SWAN YD
HOUND ST
Liby
THORNBANK CT
LONG ST
EAST MILL LA
Hotel
MILDENHALL RD
Sherborne Girls Sch
ACREMAN CT
ACREMAN ST
CULVERS CL
RICHMOND RD
POWY'S GN
POWY'S LA
ABBEY RD
Sch
THE CLOISTERS
THE MALTINGS
RALEIGH CT
Weir
Sherborne Castle
Boat House
CHURCH
Mus
Abbey
FINGER LA
JOHNSON'S CTYD
BRIDGEWELL CT
LUDBOURNE RD
Superstore
ST CATHERINE'S WAY
HORSECASTLES LA
HORSECASTLES
BRADFORD RD
KENELM CL
GAINSBOROUGH DR
ST MARY'S RD
ST CATHERINE'S CRES
RIDGEWAY
RICHMOND CL
RICHMOND GN
HALF ACRE
Sherborne Prep Sch
ACREMAN PL
DURRANT
COOKS LA
DIGBY RD
DIGBY CT
DALWOODS
PAGEANT DR
SOUTH ST
STATION RD
GAS HOUSE HILL
Sherborne
LC
NEW RD
Lodge
West End
MIDLEAZE
ABBOTTS WAY
WYDFORD CL
ASKWITH CL
LITTLEFIELD
WYNNES CL
WYNDHAM RD
WESTRIDGE
LENTHAY CT
THE GARDENS
HORSECASTLES
THE OLD SCHOOL PL
CRICKET VIEW 1
THE GROVE 2
WESTBURY
WILLIS WAY
South Western Bsns Pk
RALIEGH PL
OTTERY LA
WESTBRIDGE PK
WESTFIELD
SOUTH AVE
SOUTH CT
NOAKE RD
LENTHAY CL
Cemy
The Old Yarn Mills
Lenthay Dairy House
LENTHAY LA
NAPIER CT
HUNTS MEAD
LEET CT
HONEYCOOMBE RISE
LENTHAY RD
30
26
NEW RD
The Slopes
Home Farm
Home Convert
GAINSBOROUGH HILL
The Kennels
Dancing Hill
WESTBURY
B3145
Sewage Works
WEST MILL LA
Sherborne Abbey CE Prim Sch
Yetman's Copse
Limekiln Cottages
SHERBORNE HILL
LC
West Mill
Limekiln Farm
River Yeo
Lovers Grove
D3
1 ST ANTONYS SQ
2 WESTBURY TERR
3 LOWER ACREMAN ST
4 WESSEX CT
5 TILTON CT
6 HALF MOON ST
7 ABBEY CL
E4
1 CASTLETON
2 CHRYSANTHEMUM FLATS
3 CHRYSANTHEMUM CL
4 CHRYSANTHEMUM ROW
5 NEWLAND FLATS
6 SUNNYSIDE TERR
7 FAIRMONT TERR
8 NEWLAND GDN
9 THE WILDERNESS
10 FOSTERS
11 EAST MILL CT
12 EASTFIELD GDN

House numbers
1 59
HIGH ST

11

One-way Streets

Scale: 7 inches to 1 mile
0 110 yards 220 yards
0 125 m 250 m

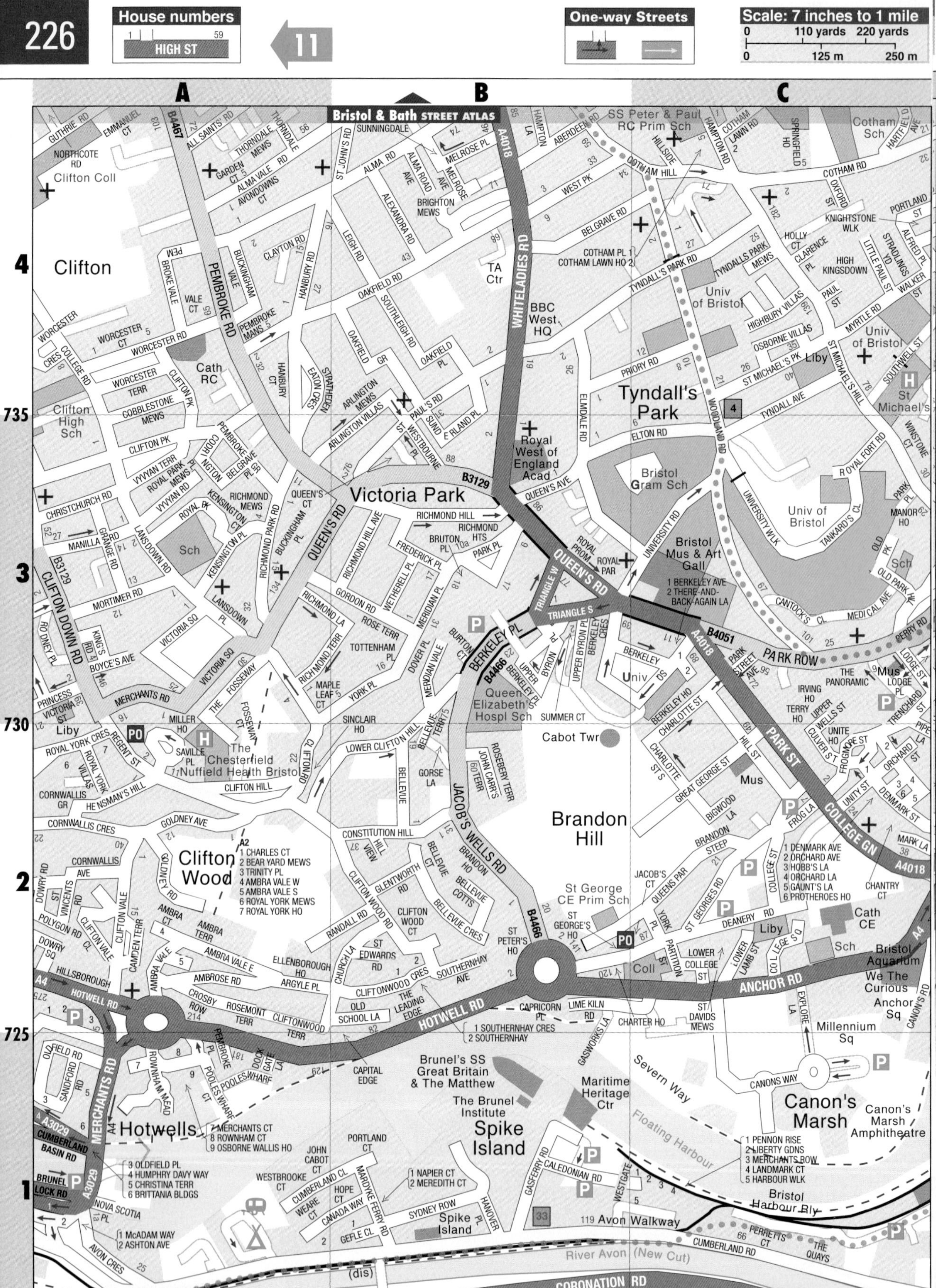

11

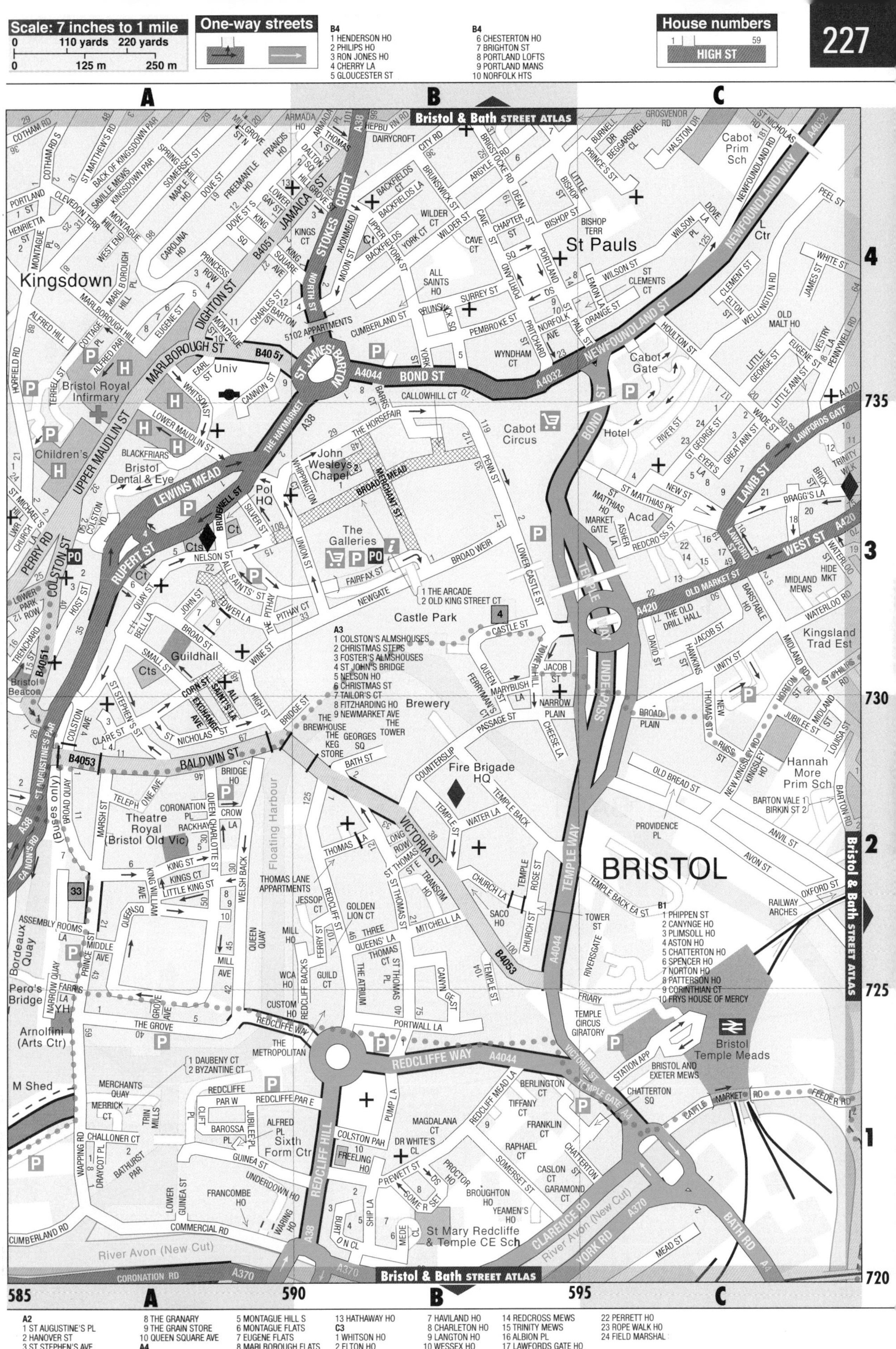

A2
1 ST AUGUSTINE'S PL
2 HANOVER ST
3 ST STEPHEN'S AVE
4 MARSH ST
5 ST NICHOLAS ALMSHOUSES
6 MERCHANTS ALMSHOUSES
7 KING GEORGE V PL
8 THE GRANARY
9 THE GRAIN STORE
10 QUEEN SQUARE AVE

A4
1 KNIGHTSTONE HO
2 COLSTON FORT
3 DIGHTON CT
4 MONTAGUE CT
5 MONTAGUE HILL S
6 MONTAGUE FLATS
7 EUGENE FLATS
8 MARLBOROUGH FLATS
9 HAYMARKET WLK
10 BLENHEIM CT
11 HAMILTON CT
12 CHERRY CT
13 HATHAWAY HO

C3
1 WHITSON HO
2 ELTON HO
3 ELBRIDGE HO
4 NEW STREET FLATS
5 TYNDALL HO
6 JOHN COZENS HO
7 HAVILAND HO
8 CHARLETON HO
9 LANGTON HO
10 WESSEX HO
11 GLOUCESTER HO
12 SOMERSET HO
13 STEEVENS HO (ALMSHOUSES)
14 REDCROSS MEWS
15 TRINITY MEWS
16 ALBION PL
17 LAWFORDS GATE HO
18 GLOUCESTER LA
19 WATERLOO PL
20 THE OLD TANNERY
21 ST JUDES HO
22 PERRETT HO
23 ROPE WALK HO
24 FIELD MARSHAL

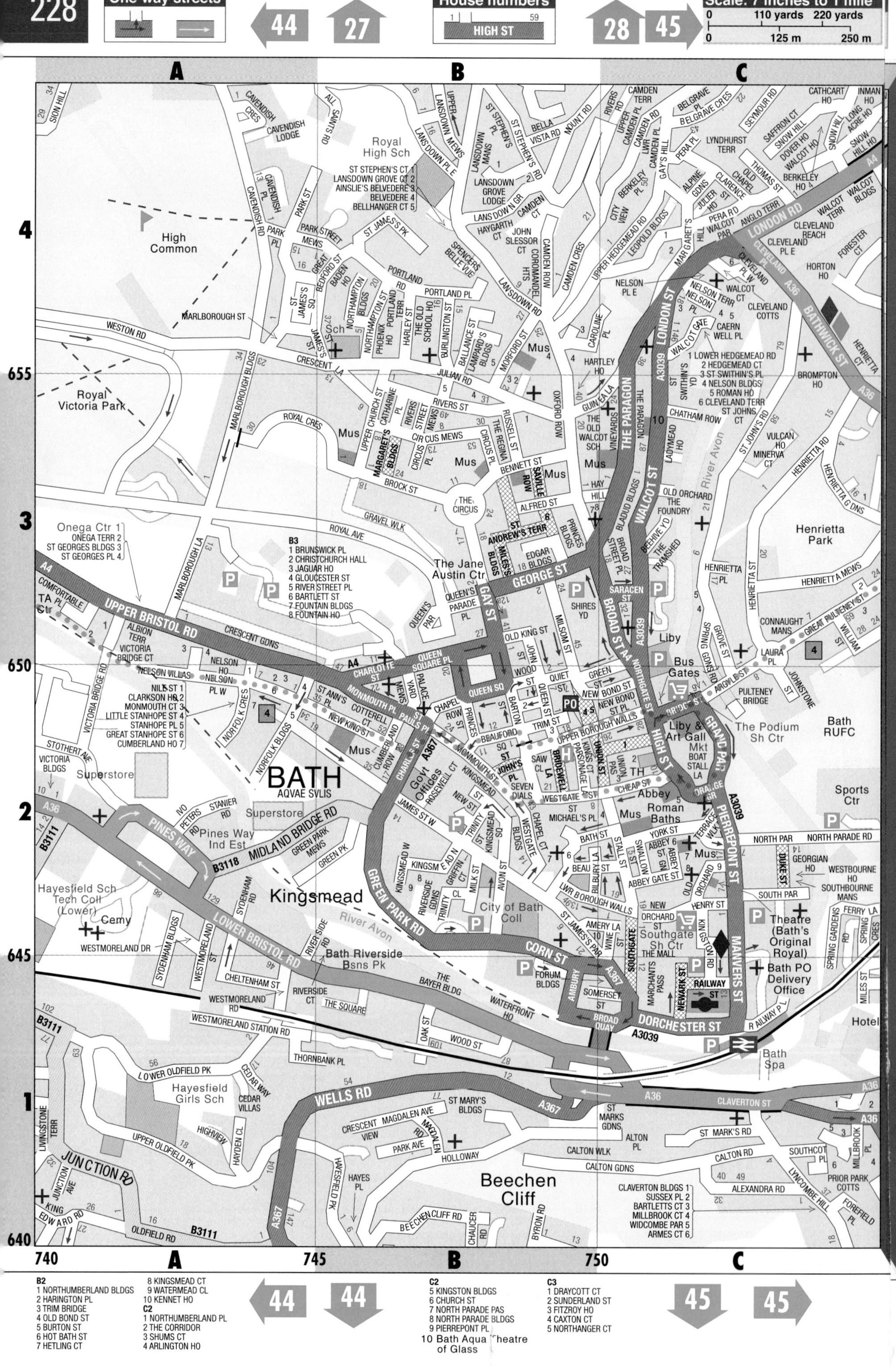
228
One-way streets
House numbers
HIGH ST
Scale: 7 inches to 1 mile
0 110 yards 220 yards
0 125 m 250 m
44
27
28
45
A
B
C
4
655
3
650
2
645
1
640
740
745
750
SION HILL
CAVENDISH CRES
CAVENDISH LODGE
CAVENDISH PL
CAVENDISH RD
ALL SAINTS RD
Royal High Sch
LANSDOWN MEWS
UPPER LANSDOWN MEWS
LANSDOWN PL E
ST STEPHEN'S CT 1
LANSDOWN GROVE CT 2
AINSLIE'S BELVEDERE 3
BELVEDERE 4
BELLHANGER CT 5
ST STEPHEN'S PL
ST STEPHEN'S RD
LANSDOWN MANS
LANSDOWN GROVE LODGE
BELLA VISTA RD
MOUNT RD
RIVERS RD
CAMDEN TERR
UPPER CAMDEN PL
CAMDEN RD
LWR CAMDEN PL
GAY'S HILL
BELGRAVE PL
BELGRAVE CRES
SEYMOUR RD
CATHCART HO
INMAN HO
PERA PL
LYNDHURST TERR
SAFFRON CT
SNOW HILL
DOVER HO
WALCOT HO
SNOW HILL
LONG ACRE HO
SNOW HILL HO
High Common
PARK ST
PARK STREET MEWS
PARK PL
ST JAMES'S PK
SPENCERS BELLEVUE
LANSDOWN GR
HAYGARTH CT
CAMDEN CT
JOHN SLESSOR CT
COROMANDEL HTS
CAMDEN ROW
CAMDEN CRES
CITY VIEW
BERKELEY PL
LEOPOLD BLDGS
UPPER HEDGEMEAD RD
ALPINE GDNS
CLARENCE ST
OLD CHAPEL
THOMAS ST
BERKELEY HO
WALCOT TERR
WALCOT BLDGS
JULIER HO
PERA RD
WALCOT PAR
ANGLO TERR
LONDON RD
CLEVELAND REACH
CLEVELAND PL E
CLEVELAND PL
FORESTER CT
HORTON HO
A4
GREAT BEDFORD ST
BADEN HO
ST JAMES'S SQ
NORTHAMPTON BLDGS
NORTHAMPTON ST
PORTLAND RD
PORTLAND TERR
PORTLAND PL
PHOENIX HO
HARLEY ST
THE OLD SCHOOL HO
BURLINGTON ST
BALLANCE ST
LAMPARD'S BLDGS
MORFORD ST
LANSDOWN RD
MARGARET'S HILL
NELSON PL E
NELSON TERR
NELSON PL W
WALCOT CT
CLEVELAND COTTS
CAERN WELL PL
BATHWICK ST
HENRIETTA CT
MARLBOROUGH ST
WESTON RD
ST JAMES'S ST
Sch
CRESCENT LA
JULIAN RD
Mus
CAROLINE PL
HARTLEY HO
LONDON ST
WALCOT GATE
1 LOWER HEDGEMEAD RD
2 HEDGEMEAD CT
3 ST SWITHIN'S PL
4 NELSON BLDGS
5 ROMAN HO
6 CLEVELAND TERR
ST JOHNS CT
BROMPTON HO
Royal Victoria Park
MARLBOROUGH BLDGS
ROYAL CRES
UPPER CHURCH ST
CATHARINE PL
RIVERS ST
RIVERS STREET MEWS
CIRCUS MEWS
CIRCUS PL
CIRCUS PL
RUSSELL ST
OXFORD ROW
GUINEA LA
THE OLD WALCOT SCH
VINEYARDS
THE PARAGON
CHATHAM ROW
ST SWITHIN'S YD
ST JOHN'S RD
VULCAN HO
MINERVA CT
HENRIETTA RD
HENRIETTA GDNS
MARGARET'S BLDGS
BROCK ST
BENNETT ST
SAVILLE ROW
LADYMEAD HO
River Avon
THE CIRCUS
ALFRED ST
HAY HILL
BLADUD BLDGS
WALCOT ST
OLD ORCHARD
THE FOUNDRY
Henrietta Park
Onega Ctr 1
ONEGA TERR 2
ST GEORGES BLDGS 3
ST GEORGES PL 4
GRAVEL WLK
ROYAL AVE
B3
1 BRUNSWICK PL
2 CHRISTCHURCH HALL
3 JAGUAR HO
4 GLOUCESTER ST
5 RIVER STREET PL
6 BARTLETT ST
7 FOUNTAIN BLDGS
8 FOUNTAIN HO
ST ANDREW'S TERR
MILES'S BLDGS
EDGAR BLDGS
PRINCES BLDGS
BROAD STREET PL
BEEHIVE YD
THE TRAMSHED
HENRIETTA PL
HENRIETTA ST
HENRIETTA MEWS
MARLBOROUGH LA
The Jane Austin Ctr
GEORGE ST
SARACEN ST
QUEEN'S PARADE PL
QUEEN'S PAR
GAY ST
SHIRES YD
BROAD ST
NORTHGATE ST
A3039
Liby
SPRING GDNS RD
GROVE ST
CONNAUGHT MANS
GREAT PULTENEY ST
WILLIAM ST
COMFORTABLE PL
TA Ctr
UPPER BRISTOL RD
ALBION TERR
VICTORIA BRIDGE CT
CRESCENT GDNS
OLD KING ST
JOHN ST
MILSOM ST
LAURA PL
JOHNSTONE ST
CHARLOTTE ST
QUEEN SQUARE PL
WOOD ST
QUIET ST
GREEN ST
NEW BOND ST
Bus Gates
ARGYLE ST
PULTENEY BRIDGE
NELSON VILLAS
NELSON HO
NELSON PL W
NILE ST 1
CLARKSON HO 2
MONMOUTH CT 3
LITTLE STANHOPE ST 4
STANHOPE PL 5
GREAT STANHOPE ST 6
CUMBERLAND HO 7
VICTORIA BRIDGE RD
NORFOLK CRES
NORFOLK BLDGS
ST ANN'S PL
MONMOUTH PL
COTTERELL CT
NEW KING ST
ST PAULS PL
MONMOUTH ST
QUEEN SQ
PALACE YARD MEWS
CHAPEL ROW
PRINCES ST
BARTON ST
QUEEN ST
PO
NEW BOND ST PL
UPPER BOROUGH WALLS
BRIDGE ST
Liby & Art Gall
GRAND PAR
The Podium Sh Ctr
Bath RUFC
STOTHERT AVE
VICTORIA BLDGS
Superstore
CUMBERLAND ROW
CHARLES ST
A367
BEAUFORD SQ
TRIM ST
KINGS CT
PARSONAGE LA
UNION ST
UNION PAS
Mkt
BOAT STALL LA
BATH
AQVAE SVLIS
Govt Offices
ROSEWELL CT
KINGSMEAD ST
SAW CL
ST JOHN'S PL
BRIDEWELL LA
TH
CHEAP ST
SEVEN DIALS
WESTGATE ST
ORANGE GR
Abbey
Roman Baths
Sports Ctr
A36
PINES WAY
IVO PETERS RD
STANIER RD
Pines Way Ind Est
MIDLAND BRIDGE RD
GREEN PARK MEWS
GREEN PK
JAMES ST W
NEW ST
TRINITY ST
KINGSMEAD SQ
WESTGATE BLDGS
CHAPEL CT
ST MICHAEL'S PL
BATH ST
STALL ST
SWALLOW ST
YORK ST
ABBEY ST
ABBEY GN
TERRACE WLK
PIERREPONT ST
NORTH PAR
NORTH PARADE RD
B3111
B3118
KINGSMEAD W
KINGSMEAD N
GRIFFIN CT
MILK ST
AVON ST
BEAU ST
BILBURY LA
ABBEY GATE ST
OLD ORCHARD ST
DUKE ST
GEORGIAN HO
WESTBOURNE HO
SOUTHBOURNE MANS
Hayesfield Sch Tech Coll (Lower)
Cemy
SYDENHAM RD
Kingsmead
RIVERSIDE GDNS
TRINITY CL
City of Bath Coll
LWR BOROUGH WALLS
AMERY LA
NEW ORCHARD ST
HENRY ST
KINGSTON RD
SOUTH PAR
Theatre (Bath's Original Royal)
FERRY LA
SPRING CRES
SPRING GARDENS RD
WESTMORELAND DR
SYDENHAM BLDGS
WESTMORELAND ST
LOWER BRISTOL RD
GREEN PARK RD
RIVER SIDE RD
Bath Riverside Bsns Pk
CORN ST
ST JAMES'S PAR
WINE ST
SOUTHGATE
Southgate Sh Ctr
THE MALL
MANVERS ST
Bath PO Delivery Office
CHELTENHAM ST
THE BAYER BLDG
FORUM BLDGS
AMBURY
MARCHANTS PASS
RAILWAY ST
NEWARK ST
MILES ST
WESTMORELAND RD
RIVERSIDE CT
THE SQUARE
WATERFRONT HO
SOMERSET ST
BROAD QUAY
DORCHESTER ST
RAILWAY PL
Hotel
WESTMORELAND STATION RD
OAK ST
WOOD ST
THORNBANK PL
Bath Spa
LOWER OLDFIELD PK
CEDAR WAY
Hayesfield Girls Sch
CEDAR VILLAS
WELLS RD
ST MARY'S BLDGS
ST MARKS GDNS
CLAVERTON ST
LIVINGSTONE TERR
HIGHVIEW
HAYDEN CL
UPPER OLDFIELD PK
CRESCENT VIEW
MAGDALEN AVE
MAGDALEN RD
PARK AVE
HOLLOWAY
ALTON PL
ST MARK'S RD
SOUTHCOT PL
MILLBROOK PL
JUNCTION RD
JUNCTION AVE
HAYESFIELD PK
HAYES PL
Beechen Cliff
CALTON WLK
CALTON GDNS
CALTON RD
PRIOR PARK COTTS
ALEXANDRA RD
LYNCOMBE HILL
FOREFIELD PL
CLAVERTON BLDGS 1
SUSSEX PL 2
BARTLETTS CT 3
MILLBROOK CT 4
WIDCOMBE PAR 5
ARMES CT 6
KING EDWARD RD
OLDFIELD RD
BEECHEN CLIFF RD
CHAUCER RD
BYRON RD
B2
1 NORTHUMBERLAND BLDGS
2 HARINGTON PL
3 TRIM BRIDGE
4 OLD BOND ST
5 BURTON ST
6 HOT BATH ST
7 HETLING CT
8 KINGSMEAD CT
9 WATERMEAD CL
10 KENNET HO
C2
1 NORTHUMBERLAND PL
2 THE CORRIDOR
3 SHUMS CT
4 ARLINGTON HO
44
44
C2
5 KINGSTON BLDGS
6 CHURCH ST
7 NORTH PARADE PAS
8 NORTH PARADE BLDGS
9 PIERREPONT PL
10 Bath Aqua Theatre of Glass
C3
1 DRAYCOTT CT
2 SUNDERLAND ST
3 FITZROY HO
4 CAXTON CT
5 NORTHANGER CT
45
45

Index

Place name May be abbreviated on the map → **Church Rd** 6 Beckenham BR2..........**53** C6

Location number Present when a number indicates the place's position in a crowded area of mapping

Locality, town or village Shown when more than one place has the same name

Postcode district District for the indexed place

Page and grid square Page number and grid reference for the standard mapping

Cities, towns and villages are listed in CAPITAL LETTERS

Public and commercial buildings are highlighted in **magenta** **Places of interest** are highlighted in blue with a star★

Abbreviations used in the index

Acad	**Academy**	Comm	**Common**	Gd	**Ground**	L	**Leisure**	Prom	**Promenade**
App	**Approach**	Cott	**Cottage**	Gdn	**Garden**	La	**Lane**	Rd	**Road**
Arc	**Arcade**	Cres	**Crescent**	Gn	**Green**	Liby	**Library**	Recn	**Recreation**
Ave	**Avenue**	Cswy	**Causeway**	Gr	**Grove**	Mdw	**Meadow**	Ret	**Retail**
Bglw	**Bungalow**	Ct	**Court**	H	**Hall**	Meml	**Memorial**	Sh	**Shopping**
Bldg	**Building**	Ctr	**Centre**	Ho	**House**	Mkt	**Market**	Sq	**Square**
Bsns, Bus	**Business**	Ctry	**Country**	Hospl	**Hospital**	Mus	**Museum**	St	**Street**
Bvd	**Boulevard**	Cty	**County**	HQ	**Headquarters**	Orch	**Orchard**	Sta	**Station**
Cath	**Cathedral**	Dr	**Drive**	Hts	**Heights**	Pal	**Palace**	Terr	**Terrace**
Cir	**Circus**	Dro	**Drove**	Ind	**Industrial**	Par	**Parade**	TH	**Town Hall**
Cl	**Close**	Ed	**Education**	Inst	**Institute**	Pas	**Passage**	Univ	**University**
Cnr	**Corner**	Emb	**Embankment**	Int	**International**	Pk	**Park**	Wk, Wlk	**Walk**
Coll	**College**	Est	**Estate**	Intc	**Interchange**	Pl	**Place**	Wr	**Water**
Com	**Community**	Ex	**Exhibition**	Junc	**Junction**	Prec	**Precinct**	Yd	**Yard**

Index of towns, villages, streets, hospitals, industrial estates, railway stations, schools, shopping centres, universities and places of interest

5102 Apartments BS1 .... **227** B4

A

ABBAS COMBE **176** E1
Abbas & Templecombe CE Prim Sch BA8 .... **176** E1
Abbey Cl
Curry Rivel TA10 .... **171** D4
Firepool TA1 .... **213** A5
Keynsham BS31 .... **24** F6
7 Sherborne DT9 .... **225** D3
Tatworth TA20 .... **198** D8
Wookey BA5 .... **139** D8
Abbey Ct 6 BA2 .... **45** B7
Abbey Fields TA10 .... **171** D4
Abbey Gate BS9 .... **5** E5
Abbey Gate St BA1 .... **228** C2
Abbey Gdns BS22 .... **49** E8
Abbey Gn BA1 .... **228** C2
ABBEY HILL **182** E5
Abbey Hill Dro TA3 .... **182** E5
Abbey La BA3 .... **64** A4
Abbey Lodge BA6 .... **206** E4
Abbey Manor Bsns Ctr BA21 .... **218** D5
Abbey Meads BA6 .... **206** E3
Abbey Mews TA20 .... **198** D8
Abbey Pk BS31 .... **24** F6
Abbey Rd
Bristol BS9 .... **5** F7
Chilcompton BA3 .... **96** D2
Sherborne DT9 .... **225** D4
Stratton-on-t F BA3 .... **96** F2
Washford TA23 .... **131** E3
Yeovil BA21 .... **218** D6
Abbey St
Bath BA1 .... **228** C2
Crewkerne TA18 .... **224** C6
Hinton St George TA17 .... **195** C7
Abbey Trad Est BA21 .... **218** D6
Abbey View
Bath BA2 .... **45** B5
Radstock BA3 .... **79** A3
Abbey View Gdns BA2 .... **45** B5
Abbeywood Dr BS9 .... **5** C5
Abbot Alphege Acad
Bath BA1 .... **27** E4
Charlcombe BA1 .... **27** D4
Abbotsbury Rd BS48 .... **8** D1
Abbots Cl
Bristol BS14 .... **23** A3
Abbots Cl *continued*
Burnham-on-S TA8 .... **104** B6
Ilminster TA19 .... **221** B3
Oxenpill BA6 .... **138** C4
Seavington St Michael TA19 .... **184** E2
Abbot's Cl BS22 .... **32** A3
Abbots Ct BA6 .... **206** D4
Abbotsfield TA4 .... **210** A4
Abbotsfield Cotts TA4 .... **210** B4
Abbots Fish House★ BA6 .... **138** D4
Abbots Horn BS48 .... **8** D2
ABBOTS LEIGH **11** A8
Abbots Leigh Rd BS8 .... **11** C7
Abbots Meade BA21 .... **218** D5
Abbots Way
Minehead TA24 .... **200** C6
Pilton BA4 .... **140** E3
Sherborne DT9 .... **225** B3
Yeovil BA21 .... **218** D6
Abbotswood Cl BS31 .... **24** D3
Abbott La TA16 .... **196** A8
Abbotts Farm Cl BS39 .... **77** D5
Abbotts Rd BA22 .... **173** D1
Abbotts Way TA3 .... **183** F7
Abbott's Wootton La DT6 .... **199** B1
Abels La DT9 .... **187** F5
Aberdeen Rd BS6 .... **226** B4
Abingdon Gdns BA2 .... **62** D8
Abingdon St TA8 .... **104** B6
Abington Cross TA24 .... **124** B4
Ablake La TA10 .... **172** C5
Ableton Wlk BS9 .... **5** C5
Abon Ho BS9 .... **5** C4
Abrahams Cl BS4 .... **22** F7
Acacia Ave BS23 .... **49** B8
Acacia Ct BS31 .... **24** C4
Acacia Dr BA11 .... **120** C7
Acacia Gdns TA2 .... **213** E7
Acacia Gr BA2 .... **44** C3
Acacia Rd BA3 .... **78** E1
Acacia Walk TA6 .... **208** E1
Accommodation Rd BS24 .... **66** E6
Acer Dr BA21 .... **218** C7
Acer Village BS14 .... **23** C7
Achilles Path BS23 .... **49** B4
Ackland's Dro TA10 .... **155** F4
Acland Round TA4 .... **167** E6
Acombe Cross TA3 .... **191** E8
Aconite Cl BS22 .... **32** B5
Acorn Cl
Frome BA11 .... **119** D5
Highbridge TA9 .... **104** D4
Acorn Gr BS13 .... **21** E6
Acre Cotts TA21 .... **222** E6
Acre La TA11 .... **211** F4
Acreman Ct DT9 .... **225** C4
Acreman Pl DT9 .... **225** D3
Acreman St DT9 .... **225** D4
Acresbush Cl BS13 .... **22** A5
Acres Ct BA22 .... **197** F8
Acres The 1 TA12 .... **185** E6
Acretree Cl TA6 .... **208** E3
Actis Rd BA6 .... **206** E3
Adams Cl
Highbridge TA9 .... **104** C2
Peasedown St John BA2 .... **79** D8
Adams Ct 5 BS8 .... **11** F6
ADAM'S GREEN **197** D2
Adams Ho TA19 .... **221** B3
Adam's La TA5 .... **134** D6
Adams Mdw TA19 .... **221** A4
Adam St TA8 .... **104** B6
Adastral Rd BS24 .... **50** D4
ADBER **187** F7
Adber Cl BA21 .... **219** E8
Adber Cross DT9 .... **187** F6
Adcombe Cl TA3 .... **181** D5
Adcombe Rd TA2 .... **213** B8
Adder La TA7 .... **169** F8
ADDERWELL **120** A3
Adderwell BA11 .... **120** A3
Adderwell Cl BA11 .... **120** A3
Addicott Rd BS23 .... **48** E6
Addiscombe Rd
Bristol BS14 .... **23** B5
Weston-super-Mare BS23 .... **48** E4
Addison Gr TA2 .... **212** E6
Addlewell La 11 BA20 .... **219** B4
Adlams Central Pk BA6 .... **206** B3
Admirals Cl
Sherborne DT9 .... **225** E5
Watchet TA23 .... **202** D6
Admirals Ct TA6 .... **208** F5
Admiral's Mead BA6 .... **157** E4
Admiral's Wlk BS20 .... **2** B5
Admiralty Way TA1 .... **213** C5
ADSBOROUGH **169** D8
Adsborough Hill TA2 .... **169** D7
Adsborough La
Adsborough TA7 .... **169** E8
West Monkton TA2 .... **169** D7
ADSCOMBE **152** A8
Adscombe Ave TA6 .... **209** C6
Adscombe La TA5 .... **134** A1
Aelfric Mdw BS20 .... **2** F4
Aesop Dr BS31 .... **24** C3
Aginhills Dr TA2 .... **213** E8
Ainslie's Belvedere BA1 .... **228** B4
Ainstey Dr BA22 .... **175** A4
Airey Hos TA13 .... **220** D1
Airoh End BS24 .... **49** B4
Airport Rd BS14 .... **23** A8
Airport Rdbt BS24 .... **49** E7
Airport View Cvn Pk BS24 .... **49** D7
Aisecome Way BS22 .... **49** C6
AISHOLT **152** B6
Akeman Cl BA21 .... **218** D7
Akeman Way BS11 .... **4** C8
Alamein Rd TA23 .... **202** E6
Alard Rd BS4 .... **22** F7
Alastair Cl BA21 .... **218** F7
Alastair Dr BA21 .... **218** F7
Albany BS23 .... **30** F1
Albany Cl DT9 .... **225** E6
Albany Ct 6 BA1 .... **44** B6
Albany Rd BA2 .... **44** C6
Albemarle Rd TA1 .... **212** F5
Albermarle Row 9 BS8 .... **11** F6
Albert Ave
Peasedown St John BA2 .... **79** C7
Weston-super-Mare BS23 .... **48** E6
Albert Bldgs BA6 .... **206** D5
Albert Cl BA21 .... **218** E7
Albert Ct
Bridgwater TA6 .... **208** E4
15 Taunton TA1 .... **213** A4
Weston-super-Mare BS23 .... **48** E6
Albert Pl
Bath BA2 .... **45** C1
Portishead BS20 .... **2** D4
Albert Quadrant BS23 .... **48** E8
Albert Rd
Clevedon BS21 .... **6** C3
Keynsham BS31 .... **24** E5
Portishead BS20 .... **2** D5
Weston-super-Mare BS23 .... **48** E6
Albert Row DT9 .... **225** E4
Albert St TA6 .... **208** E4
Albert Terr BA2 .... **44** C6
Albion Bldgs BA1 .... **44** D7
Albion Cl TA6 .... **209** B5
Albion Pl
16 Bristol BS2 .... **227** C3
Frome BA11 .... **119** D3
Albion Rd BA22 .... **174** A2
Albion Terr
Bath BA1 .... **228** A3
Cheddar BS27 .... **90** B7
Alburys BS40 .... **35** D3
Alcina Way BS31 .... **24** C2
ALCOMBE
Kingsdown **29** F7
Minehead **201** A4
Alcombe Cross TA24 .... **201** B5
Alcombe Rd TA24 .... **201** A5
Aldeburgh Pl BA14 .... **83** F6
Alder Cl
North Petherton TA6 .... **153** F3
Taunton TA1 .... **213** D1
Williton TA4 .... **202** E3
Aldercombe Rd BS9 .... **5** C8
Alder Ct BS14 .... **23** B5
Alderdown Cl BS11 .... **5** A8
Alder Gr
Crewkerne TA18 .... **224** C7
Yeovil BA20 .... **218** E2
Alderley Rd BA2 .... **44** B4
Alderney Rd TA6 .... **209** C3
Alder Terr BA3 .... **78** E2
Alder Way BA2 .... **62** D8
Alder Wlk BA11 .... **120** B7
Aldondale Gdns BA20 .... **219** B3
ALDWICK **54** D7
Aldwick Ave BS13 .... **22** C3
Aldwick La BS40 .... **54** C7
Aldwych Cl TA8 .... **104** C6
Alec Ricketts Cl BA2 .... **43** F5
Alexander Bldgs 12 BA1 .... **28** B1
Alexander Cl TA3 .... **169** D5
Alexander Hall BA3 .... **64** C6
Alexander Ho 5 BS23 .... **48** F4
Alexander Mews 5 BS23 .... **48** E7
Alexander Pl BA3 .... **64** C6
Alexander Rd BS31 .... **24** C2
Alexanders Cl BA6 .... **138** C4
Alexander Way BS49 .... **34** B7
Alexandra Ct BS21 .... **6** C4
Alexandra Gdns TA24 .... **201** A6
Alexandra Mews TA24 .... **201** A7
Alexandra Par BS23 .... **48** E7
Alexandra Pk BS39 .... **77** E5
Alexandra Pl BA2 .... **45** C1
Alexandra Rd
Bath BA2 .... **228** C1
Bridgwater TA6 .... **208** E5
Bristol BS8 .... **226** B4
Bristol, Highridge BS13 .... **21** F7
Clevedon BS21 .... **6** C4
Frome BA11 .... **119** F4

Alexandra Rd *continued*
Minehead TA24 201 A6
Wellington TA21 222 D6
Yeovil BA21 219 D6
Alexandra Terr BS39 77 E5
Alexevia Cvn Pk TA3 169 C3
Aley TA5 152 A8
Aley Rd TA5 134 A1
ALFORD 159 A3
Alford La BA4, BA7 159 B4
Alfords Ridge BA3 117 A7
Alfoxton Rd TA6 208 C4
Alfred Cres BA4 205 B4
Alfred Ct 4 BS23 48 E7
Alfred Hill BS2 227 A4
Alfred Par BS2 227 A4
Alfred Pl
BS1 227 A1
Bristol BS2 226 C4
Alfred St
Bath BA1 228 B3
Taunton TA1 213 B4
Wells BA5 203 D3
Weston-super-Mare BS23 48 E8
Alfred's Twr* BA10 161 C6
Alfred's Way BA9 216 B3
Algar Ct BA5 203 B4
ALHAMPTON 159 C6
Alice St BA11 143 A6
Alison Gdns BS48 19 A7
Allandale Ct TA8 104 B8
Allandale Rd TA8 104 A8
Allanmead Rd BS14 23 B8
Allans Way BS24 49 F7
Allen Dr BA4 205 A6
Allen Rd TA6 208 F1
Allens La
Shipham BS25 70 F8
Wells BA5 112 E1
Allenslade Flats TA4 210 C5
ALLER 171 D8
Aller BS24 49 B2
Aller Dro
Aller TA10 171 D8
Othery TA7 155 C1
ALLERFORD
Porlock 124 C4
Taunton 167 F4
Aller La TA4 202 E1
Allermoor Dro BS28 138 B8
Aller Par BS24 49 B2
Allerpark La TA24 123 F3
Aller Rd TA10 171 E7
Allerton Cres BS14 23 B4
Allerton Gdns BS14 23 B5
Allerton Rd
Bridgwater TA6 209 B7
Bristol BS14 23 B4
All Hallows Sch BA4 142 C6
Allingham Rd BA21 219 C7
Allington Cl TA1 213 E4
Allington Gdns BS48 18 C8
Allington Rd BS3 226 C1
Allotment Dro
Combe St Nicholas TA20 193 C5
Glastonbury BA16 138 D1
Allotment La
Chard TA20 223 C1
Keynsham BS31 24 B2
Keynsham BS31 24 B2
Allotment Rd BA22 175 C3
ALLOWENSHAY 195 A8
ALL SAINTS 198 A4
All Saints CE Prim Sch
Axminster EX13 198 A4
Dulverton TA22 163 D6
Montacute TA15 186 B3
All Saints East Clevedon CE Prim Sch BS21 6 F4
All Saints Ho BS2 227 B4
All Saints La BS21 6 F4
All Saints' La BS1 227 A2
All Saints Pl BA2 45 E4
All Saints Rd BA1 228 B4
All Saints' Rd
Bristol BS8 226 A4
Weston-super-Mare BS23 30 E1
All Saints' St BS1 227 A3
All Saints' Terr TA6 209 B4
Allshire La EX16 162 F3
Allyn Saxon Dr BA4 205 D5
Alma Field BA7 214 B4
Alma Rd BS8 226 B4
Alma Road Ave BS8 226 B4
Alma St
Taunton TA1 213 A3
Weston-super-Mare BS23 48 E7
Alma Vale Rd BS8 226 A4
Almond Cl BS22 32 A1
Almond Tree Cl TA6 209 D4
Almond Wlk BS13 22 B6
Almsford Cl BA7 214 B6
Almshouse La BA22 173 E1
Almshouses
Donyatt TA19 183 D1
Marshfield SN14 13 E8
Almyr Terr TA23 202 C7
Alpha Cotts TA2 168 E8
Alpha Ho TA9 104 E3
Alpine Cl BS39 77 F4
Alpine Gdns BA1 228 C4
Alpine Rd BS39 77 F4
ALSTON 198 A5
Alston Cl TA1 212 C1
Alstone Gdns TA9 104 C2
Alstone La TA9 104 C2
Alstone Rd TA9 104 C2
Alstone Wildlife Pk* TA9 104 C3
ALSTON SUTTON 88 F3
Alston Sutton Rd BS26 88 F4
Alton Pl BA2 228 C1
Alun Rees Way TA20 223 B3
Alverstoke BS14 22 F7
Alveston Wlk BS9 5 B7
ALVINGTON 218 B4
Alvington Fields BA22 218 B4
Alvington La BA22 218 B5
ALWESTON 189 A1
Alweston DT9 189 A1
Ambares Ct BA3 96 F8
Amber Cl TA7 209 C8
Amberd La TA3 181 D8
Amberey Rd BS23 48 F5
Amberlands Cl BS48 19 A7
Amberley Cl
Keinton Mandeville TA11 158 A1
Keynsham BS31 24 E4
Amberley Gdns 3 BS48 8 D1
Amber Mead TA1 213 D3
Ambleside Rd BA2 44 C2
Ambra Ct BS8 226 A2
Ambra Terr BS8 226 A2
Ambra Vale BS8 226 A2
Ambra Vale E BS8 226 A2
Ambra Vale S 5 BS8 226 A2
Ambra Vale W 4 BS8 226 A2
Ambridge Cl BA16 207 B4
Ambrose Cl DT9 187 E1
Ambrose Rd BS8 226 A2
Ambury BA1 228 B1
Amercombe Wlk BS14 23 D7
American Mus in Britain* BA2 46 A5
Amery La BA1 228 C2
AMESBURY 59 F2
Amesbury Dr BS24 67 B6
Ames La BA3 98 B6
Ammerdown Terr BA3 98 F7
AMMERHAM 199 A8
Ammerham La TA20 199 A8
Amor Pl TA1 212 D2
Amors Dro DT9 225 B4
Amory Rd TA22 163 D6
Amulet Way BA4 205 E4
Ancastle Ave BA7 214 D6
Ancastle Terr BA7 214 C6
Anchorage The BS20 2 E6
Anchor Barton BA12 144 D3
Anchor Cl BA3 116 E8
Anchor Cnr BA9 176 D6
Anchor Hill BA9 176 D6
Anchor La BA2 62 D5
Anchor Rd
Bath BA1 27 B1
Bristol BS1 226 C2
Coleford BA3 116 E8
Anchor Sq BS1 226 C2
Anchor St TA23 202 C7
Anchor Stables TA24 123 E4
Anchor Way BS20 4 D4
Ancliff Sq BA15 64 E4
Andalusia Acad BS2 227 C3
Andereach Cl BS14 23 B8
Andersea Rd TA7 154 D4
ANDERSFIELD 153 B5
Andersfield Cl TA6 208 A4
Andersfield Rd TA5 153 A5
Ander's La TA3 192 B8
Andrew Allan Rd TA21 222 B4
Andrew's Hill TA22 163 D6
Andrew's Hill Cross TA22 163 C6
Andruss Dr BS41 21 D2
Angela Cl TA1 212 D2
Angel Cres TA6 208 F5
Angelica Dr TA6 208 E1
Angel La BA9 216 C4
Angel Place Sh Ctr 6 TA6 208 F5
Angel Row TA3 170 F2
ANGERSLEIGH 181 C5
Anglesey Cotts DT10 190 B4
Anglo Ct TA18 224 C6
Anglo Terr BA1 228 C4
Anglo Trad Est The BA4 205 B6
Angoni Pl TA6 209 B6
Angus Way 12 TA6 154 A5
Angwin Cl BA4 205 B6
Animal Farm Adventure Park* TA8 66 B2
Animal Sanctuary Rd EX14 193 A2
Annaly Rd BS27 90 A7
Annandale BA7 214 B4
Annandale Ave BS22 31 E1
Ann Bulls Grave Rd TA18 195 D3
Anseres Pl BA5 203 E4
ANSFORD 214 C6
Ansford Hill BA7 214 B7
Ansford Rd BA7 214 C6
Ansford Sch BA7 214 C7
Anson Cl BS31 25 D2
Anson Rd
Locking BS24 50 B6
Weston-super-Mare BS22 31 D4
Anson Way TA6 208 F5
Anstey Gate TA22 162 B8
Anthony Rd BA16 207 D7
Antler Cl BA6 206 C3
Antona Ct BS11 4 D7
Antona Dr BS11 4 D7
Anvil Rd BS49 17 F1
Anvil St BS2 227 C2
Apex Dr TA9 104 C4
Aplins Cl TA19 221 B3
Aplins La TA20 182 A1
Apple Alley BA11 119 F5
Apple Bsns Ctr The TA2 212 B6
Appleby Wlk BS4 22 D7
Apple Cl TA19 194 E7
Applecroft BA2 79 E6
APPLEDORE 179 A1
Appledore 4 BS22 31 F2
Appledore Cl BS14 23 B8
Appledore Dr 9 TA6 209 B4
Apple Dumpling Cnr BS28 108 C3
Apple Farm La BS24 32 B1
Applefield Rd DT8 199 F8
Applehayes La EX15 180 F2
Applehayes Rise BS20 4 B3
Apple La BA11 119 F5
Apple Tree Cl TA6 209 D4
Appletree Ct BS22 32 B2
Apple Tree Dr BS25 70 A8
Appletree Mews BS22 32 B2
APPLEY 179 B8
Appley Cross TA21 179 B7
Appsley Cl BS22 31 C1
Apricot Tree Cl TA6 209 D5
Apsley Rd BA1 44 A7
Aquara Cl BA16 207 C3
Arbutus Dr BS9 5 C8
Arcade The BS1 227 B3
Arcadius Way BS31 24 F8
Archbishop Cranmer CE Com Prim Sch
18 Holway TA1 213 A4
Taunton TA1 213 A4
Arch Cl BS41 10 F1
Archer Ct BS21 6 D4
Archer Dr TA8 104 C6
Archers Grove TA4 150 E7
Archers Way The BA6 206 E5
Archer Wlk BS14 23 E6
Arches The BA2 44 A6
Archgrove BS41 10 F1
Arch La TA3 170 E4
Archstone Ave TA5 135 F2
Archway St BA2 45 B5
Arden Cl BS22 31 F3
Ardern Cl BS9 5 B8
Ardmore BS8 11 D7
Ardwyn TA21 222 D4
Arena The BA20 219 A4
Argentia Pl BS20 2 F7
Argyle Ave BS23 48 F4
Argyle Pl BS8 226 A2
Argyle Rd
Bristol BS2 227 B4
Clevedon BS21 6 D6
Argyle St BA2 228 C2
Argyle Terr BA2 44 C6
Arlington Cl
Bridgwater TA6 209 A2
Yeovil BA21 218 C7
Arlington Ho 4 BA1 228 C2
Arlington Mans BS8 226 B4
Arlington Rd 4 BA2 44 D5
Arlington Villas BS8 226 B3
Armada Ho BS2 227 A4
Armada Pl BS1 227 B4
Armada Rd BS14 23 A6
Armes Ct BA2 228 C1
Armoor Lane TA22 148 A4
Armoury Rd BA22 218 A6
Armoury The BA6 206 D4
Armstrong Rd BA11 120 B5
Armtech Row BA22 218 B6
Arnewood Gdns BA20 218 F2
Arnold Cl TA2 212 F7
Arnold Noad Cnr BA14 83 E3
Arnold's Way BS49 17 A2
Arnolfini (Arts Ctr)* BS1 227 A1
Arnor Cl BS22 32 A4
Arrowfield Cl BS14 23 A2
Artemesia Ave BS22 49 E8
Arthurs Point Dr BA5 203 A5
Arthurswood Rd BS13 22 A4
Artillery Rd BA22 218 A6
Arundel Cl BS13 22 B5
Arundell Ct BS23 48 E8
Arundell Rd BS23 30 E1
Arundells Way TA3 169 D4
Arundel Rd
Bath BA1 28 A1
Clevedon BS21 6 D3
Yeovil BA21 219 E6
Arundel Wlk BS31 24 D5
Arun Gr TA1 213 D4
Ascension Ho BA2 44 D4
ASH
Martock 185 F7
Taunton 169 E1
ASHBEER 150 C6
Ashbeer Hill TA4 150 D7
Ashbourne Cres TA1 213 D3
ASHBRITTLE 178 F8
Ash Brook BS39 59 D1
Ashbrooke House Sch BS23 48 D6
Ashbury Dr BS22 31 B2
Ashby Pl BA7 214 C5
Ash CE Prim Sch TA12 185 F7
Ash Cl
Bridgwater TA6 209 D4
Wells BA5 203 D5
Weston-super-Mare BS22 32 D2
Winscombe BS25 52 A1
Ashcombe Ct
Ilminster TA19 221 B4
1 Weston-super-Mare BS23 48 F7
Ashcombe Gdns BS23 49 A8
Ashcombe La
Alweston DT9 189 B2
Ilminster TA19 221 B4
Ashcombe Park Rd BS23 31 A1
Ashcombe Pl 4 BS23 48 F7
Ashcombe Prim Sch BS23 49 A7
Ashcombe Rd BS23 48 F7
ASHCOTT 156 B8
Ashcott BS14 22 F7
Ashcott Cl TA8 104 C6
Ashcott Dr TA8 104 C6
Ashcott Pl TA8 104 C6
Ashcott Prim Sch TA7 156 B8
Ashcott Rd BA6 138 D3
Ash Cres TA1 212 B2
Ashcroft
Chard TA20 223 D2
Weston-super-Mare BS24 49 B2
Ash Croft TA12 185 F7
Ashcroft Ave BS31 24 D5
Ashcroft Rd BS9 5 C7
Ash Cross TA3 169 E2
Ash Ct BS14 23 A6
ASHCULME 180 C2
Ashculme Hill EX15 180 C2
Ashdene Rd BS23 49 A8
Ashdown Ct BS9 5 F8
Ashdown Rd BS20 2 A6
Ashel's Batch BA3 94 C8
Ashen Cross TA11 211 E2
Ashen Cross Rd TA11 211 F2
Ash End BA8 189 F7
Asher La BS2 227 C3
Ashes La BA3 64 A4
Ashey La
Burrington BS40 54 A5
Cheddar BS27 90 B8
Ashfield TA20 223 D2
Ashfield Cl BA11 143 C6
Ashfield Pk 23 TA12 185 E6
Ashford Cl
Bridgwater TA6 208 E2
Milverton TA4 167 A4
Ashford Dr BS24 49 A1
Ashford Gr BA21 219 B7
Ashford La TA19 183 F5
Ashford Rd
Bath BA2 44 D4
Redhill BS40 36 E4
Taunton TA1 212 C2
Wellington TA21 222 D4
Ash Gr
Bath BA2 44 C4
Chard TA20 223 C5
Clevedon BS21 6 E4
Minehead TA24 200 D7
Shepton Mallet BA4 205 C4
Wells BA5 203 D5
Weston-super-Mare BS23 48 E2
ASHGROVE 79 D8
Ashgrove BA2 79 D8
Ashgrove Ave BS8 11 B7
Ashgrove Ct BA2 79 D8
Ash Grove Way TA6 209 D7
Ash Hay Dro BA5 139 C6
Ash Hayes Dr BS48 8 E1
Ash Hayes Rd BS48 8 F1
Ash Ho TA8 65 F2
ASHILL 183 B4
Ashill Cl TA1 212 E1
Ashill Com Prim Sch TA19 183 C4
ASHINGTON 187 B8
Ashington La BA21 187 B7
Ash La
Shepton Beauchamp TA19 184 E4
Wells BA5 203 C5
Winsford TA24 147 B6
Ashland Ct TA18 224 C7
Ashland La TA4 150 B4
Ashland Rd BS13 22 A4
Ashlands CE Fst Sch TA18 224 C7
Ashlands Cl TA18 224 C7
Ashlands Mdw TA18 224 C8
Ashlands Rd TA18 224 D7
Ashlea BA7 214 B6
Ashlea Pk TA9 136 E8
Ashleigh Ave TA6 209 A3
Ashleigh Cl
Paulton BS39 77 E6
Weston-super-Mare BS23 49 A8
Ashleigh Cres BS49 34 B8
Ashleigh Gdns TA1 212 E5
Ashleigh Rd
Weston-super-Mare BS23 49 A8
Yatton BS49 34 B8
Ashleigh Terr TA6 209 A3
Ashley Ave
Bath BA1 44 C7
Burnham-on-S TA8 104 B6
Ashley Cl BS25 70 A7
Ashley Green BA15 46 F1
Ashley La BA15 64 F7
Ashley Rd
Bathford BA1 29 E3
Clevedon BS21 6 B1
Taunton TA1 212 D3
Ashley Terr 1 BA1 44 C7
Ashmans Ct BA1 44 B6
Ashmans Gate BS39 77 E5
Ashmans Yd BA1 44 B6
Ashman Way TA6 208 D4
Ashmead
Temple Cloud BS39 58 E1
Yeovil BA20 218 C2
Ashmead Rd BS31 25 B5
Ashmead Road Ind Est BS31 25 B5
Ashmead Way 8 BS1 11 F5
Ashmoor Dro BA5 139 C6
ASH PRIORS 167 C8
Ash Rd
Banwell BS29 50 E4
Street BA16 207 B3
ASHTON 107 E8
Ashton Ave BS1 226 A1
Ashton Cl
Ashill TA19 183 C4
Clevedon BS21 6 B1
Ashton Court Estate* BS41 11 C4
Ashton Cres BS48 8 D1
Ashton Ct TA1 212 C1
Ashton Dr BS3 11 F2
Ashton Farm La TA9 136 D7
ASHTON GATE 11 F4
Ashton Gate Stadium (Bristol City FC)* BS3 11 F3
Ashton Gate Trad Est BS3 11 E3
Ashton Gate Underpass BS3 11 F3
Ashton Hill
Burnett BA2 42 E8
Corston BA2 43 A7
Ashton Park Sec Sch BS3 11 E3
Ashton Pk BA11 119 E2
Ashton Rd
Bridgwater TA6 208 F2
Bristol BS3 11 D2
Bristol, Ashton Gate BS3 11 F4
Bristol, Bower Ashton BS3 11 D3
Ashton Rise BS3 11 F2
ASHTON VALE 11 F2
Ashton Vale Prim Sch BS3 11 F2
Ashton Vale Rd BS3 11 E3
Ashton Vale Trad Est BS3 11 F1
Ashton Way BS31 24 E6
Ashton Windmill* BS28 88 E1
Ashtown Cross EX16 164 A3
Ash Tree Cl
Bleadon BS24 67 C6
Burnham-on-S TA8 85 A3
Ash Tree Cres TA8 85 A3
Ash Tree Ct BA3 78 E1
Ash Tree Pl TA8 85 A3
Ashtree Rd BA11 120 A6
Ash Tree Rd TA8 85 A3
Ash Trees TA9 86 C5
Ashvale Cl BS48 9 A2
ASHWELL 221 C6
Ashwell Bsns Pk TA19 221 C7
Ashwell Cl BS14 23 E6
Ashwell La
Glastonbury BA6 139 D1
Wheddon Cross TA24 129 F2
ASHWICK 115 B5
Ashwicke BS14 23 A6
Ash Wlk BA8 190 A6
Ashwood BS40 74 F4
Ashwood Dr BA21 219 E8
Askwith Cl DT9 225 B3
ASNEY 156 E7
Asney Rd BA16 156 E7
Aspen Cl BA11 120 B7
Aspen Ct TA6 208 E4
Aspen Park Rd BS22 49 E8
Aspen Way TA18 224 D7
Aspin Cl TA21 222 F6
Aspin Rd
Wellington TA21 222 F6
Wellington TA21 222 F6
Aspley Cl BA1 44 B7
Asquith St TA2 212 E6
Assembly Rooms La BS1 227 A2
Astazou Dr BS24 49 B4
Aster Cl TA6 208 D1
Aston Ho 4 BS1 227 B1
Athelney Way BA21 218 D6
ATHERSTONE 184 C3
Athlone Rd TA6 209 A2
Atholl Cl BS22 31 F3
Atkins Cl BS14 23 E6
Atkin's Gate TA13 220 D6
Atkins Hill BA9 216 A3
Atlanta Key TA8 104 A8
Atlantic Cres TA8 104 B5
Atlantic Rd
Bristol BS11 4 C8
Weston-super-Mare BS23 30 C1
Atlantic Rd S BS23 30 C1
Atlantic View Ct BS23 30 C1
Atlantic Way BA22 174 A2
Atlay Ct BS49 17 B1
Atrium The BS1 227 B2
Attewell Ct BA2 44 F4
Attisham La DT6 199 D4
Atyeo Cl
Bristol BS3 11 E1
Burnham-on-S TA8 104 C8
Aubrey Meads BS30 25 E8
Auckland Cl
Wells BA5 203 C2
Weston-super-Mare BS23 48 F3
Auckland Way TA20 223 D3
Audley Ave BA1 44 D7
Audley Cl
Bath BA1 44 D7
Nether Stowey TA5 134 A2
Audley Gr BA1 44 C7
Audley Lodge BA1 44 D7
Audley Park Rd BA1 44 C7
Augusta Pl BA1 44 D7
Augustine's Cl BS20 1 E4
Augustus Ave BS31 24 F7

Aurelius Cl BS31 24 F8
Austen Dr BS22 32 B4
Austen Pl BS11 4 E7
Austin Cl BA11 119 F2
Austin Rd BA6 206 E6
Autumn La TA6 208 D3
Autumn Mews BS24 50 A8
Avalon Bldgs BA6 206 D5
Avalon Cl BS49 17 A1
Avalon Est BA6 206 E7
Avalon Ho BS48 8 C1
Avalon Mews BA6 206 E4
Avalon Pk TA11 211 B5
Avalon Rd
Bridgwater TA6 209 D5
Highbridge TA9 104 E4
Avalon Sch BA16 207 B3
Avalon Vineyard BA4 158 E8
Avebury Cl TA8 104 D8
Avebury Dr TA6 209 D5
Avebury Rd BS3 11 F2
Aveline Ct TA4 167 F6
Avening Cl BS48 19 A8
Avenue Pl BA2 45 B1
Avenue Rd BA11 120 A4
Avenue The
Backwell BS48 19 A7
Bath, Bushey Norwood BA2 45 E5
Bath, Combe Down BA2 45 C1
Bicknoller TA4 132 F4
3 Bridgwater TA6 208 F5
Bristol, Sneyd Park BS9 5 E3
Chard TA20 193 F7
Clevedon BS21 6 E6
Keynsham BS31 24 E6
Kingsbury Episcopi TA12 185 B8
Langport TA10 172 A6
Minehead TA24 201 A7
Misterton TA18 224 F3
Sherborne DT9 225 E5
Sparkford BA22 175 A5
Stoke sub Hamdon TA14 185 F4
Taunton TA1 212 E5
Timsbury BA2 60 B2
Weston-super-Mare BS22 32 C3
Wincanton BA9 216 D3
Winscombe BS25 70 C8
Yatton BS49 34 B8
Yeovil BA21 219 B5
Averill Ct BS21 6 D4
Avill Cres TA1 213 C4
Avishayes Prim Sch TA20 223 E5
Avishayes Rd TA20 223 D4
Avocet Dr BA22 218 A6
Avonbank Ind Est BS11 4 B7
Avonbridge Trad Est BS11 4 C8
Avon Cl
Keynsham BS31 24 F6
Taunton TA1 212 D2
Weston-super-Mare BS23 48 F2
Yeovil BA21 219 D6
AVONCLIFF 64 F4
Avoncliff Halt BA15 64 F5
Avon Cres BS1 226 A1
Avon Ct BA1 29 A4
Avondale Bldgs BA1 28 B2
Avondale Ct
Bath BA1 44 B7
Bristol, Sneyd Park BS9 5 D3
Avondale Ho
Bath BA2 44 B5
Bridgwater TA6 209 A2
Avondale Rd BA1 44 B6
Avondowns Ct BS8 226 A4
Avon Gorge Ind Est BS11 4 C7
Avon Gorge Nature Reserve★ BS8 11 E7
Avon Gr BS9 5 D2
Avon Hts BA3 64 C6
Avon La BS31 25 F5
Avonleaze BS9 5 B5
Avon Livestock Ctr BS40 38 B6
Avonmead BS2 227 B4
Avon Mill La BS31 24 F6
AVONMOUTH 4 B8
Avonmouth CE Prim Sch BS11 4 C8
Avonmouth Dock BS11 4 A8
Avonmouth Rd BS11 4 C8
Avon Pk BA1 44 A7
Avon Prim Sch BS11 4 D8
Avon Rd
Bristol BS13 22 A6
Keynsham BS31 24 F5
Pill BS20 4 C5
Avon Riverside Est BS11 4 B7
Avon Riverside Sta★ BS30 25 E6
Avon Ski & Action Centre★ BS25 52 C3
Avon & Somerset Pol HQ BS20 1 F3
Avon St
Bath BA1 228 B2
Bristol BS2 227 C2
Avon Vale BS9 5 D4
Avonvale Pl BA1 28 F3
Avon Valley Adventure & Wildlife Pk★ BS31 25 D6
Avon Valley Rly★ BS30 25 D7
Avon Way
Bristol, Sneyd Park BS9 5 C4
Portishead BS20 2 C5
Avonwood Cl BS11 4 E6
Awkward Hill BS40 55 D5
AXBRIDGE 70 B1
Axbridge Bypass BS26 70 A3
Axbridge CE Fst Sch BS26 70 C1
Axbridge Cl
Burnham-on-S TA8 104 C8
Nailsea BS48 18 E8
Axbridge & District Mus★ BS26 70 C2
Axbridge Moor Dro BS26 70 C1
Axbridge Rd
Bath BA2 45 A2
Cheddar BS27 70 F2
Axe Cl BS23 49 A5
Axeford TA20 198 E8
Axeford Mdws TA20 198 E8
Axe La
Clapton DT8 195 C1
Drimpton DT8 199 F8
Axe Rd
Bridgwater TA6 209 B3
Wookey BA5 139 D8
Axe Valley Com Coll The EX13 198 A1
Axford Way BA2 79 D8
Axis BS14 22 D5
AXMINSTER 198 B2
Axminster Com Prim Sch EX13 198 A1
Axminster Rd TA20 198 C7
Ayckbourn Cl TA8 104 C6
Aycote Cl BS22 31 C2
Ayford La SN14 13 F4
Aylands Rd TA1 212 D3
Aylmer Cres BS14 23 B6
Ayr St BA2 44 D6
AYSHFORD 178 E2
Azalea Dr TA6 208 D1
Azalea Rd BS22 32 A5
Azelin Ave BS13 22 B5

B

BABCARY 174 C7
Babcary La BA22 174 B8
Babcary Rd TA11 174 F6
Babwell Rd BA9 177 D6
Baby La TA22 163 F7
Babylon Hill
Sherborne DT9 188 A3
Yeovil BA21 219 F4
Babylon View BA21 219 F7
Backfields BS2 227 B4
Backfields Ct BS2 227 B4
Backfields La BS2 227 B4
Back La
Axbridge BS26 70 C2
Baltonsborough BA6 158 B5
Batcombe BA4 142 C2
Bradford Abbas DT9 187 F1
Chapel Allerton BS26 88 D1
Cheddar BS27 90 A7
Chewton Mendip BA3 75 B1
Curry Rivel TA10 171 D3
Draycott BS27 90 F2
East Chinnock BA22 196 E8
East Coker BA22 197 C7
Halstock BA22 197 C3
Ilchester BA22 173 E1
Keynsham BS31 24 E6
Kingston Seymour BS21 16 A5
Kington Magna SP8 177 E2
Litton BA3 75 E2
Maiden Bradley BA12 144 C2
Marshfield SN14 13 F8
Martock TA12 185 D4
Middlezoy TA7 155 B3
Montacute TA15 186 B3
North Perrott TA18 196 C4
Pill BS20 4 C5
Pilton BA4 204 D3
Rimpton BA22 188 A8
Rowberrow BS25 53 A1
Shepton Mallet, Darshill BA4 204 F6
Shepton Mallet, Downside BA4 205 C8
Sherborne DT9 225 D4
Stoney Stratton BA4 141 F2
Street BA16 207 C6
Street, Butleigh Wootton BA6 157 C6
Westbury-sub-Mendip BA5 110 E6
Whitelackington TA19 221 F6
Backlane Dro BA6 158 C5
Back Of Kingsdown Par BS6 227 A4
Back River Dro BA16 138 F2
Back St
Ash TA12 186 A7
Bampton EX16 164 B1
Bradford On Tone TA4 167 F1
Leighton BA11 142 E6
Long Sutton TA10 172 E4
Martock TA12 185 F7
West Camel BA22 174 D3
Weston-super-Mare BS23 48 E7
Winsham TA20 194 E1
Back Stoke La BS9 5 F6
Back Town BA6 157 E4
Back Way TA4 150 B8
Backways La TA21 179 F6
BACKWELL 19 B6
Backwell Bow BS48 9 C1
Backwell CE Jun Sch BS48 19 C5
Backwell Comm BS48 19 B8
BACKWELL COMMON 19 B8
BACKWELL GREEN 19 D8
Backwell Hill BS48 19 B3
Backwell Hill Rd BS48 19 E5
Backwell Sch BS48 19 B6
Backwell Wlk BS13 21 F8
Backy Hill BA2 62 C4
Bacon Dr TA1 213 D3
BADBURY 183 F7
Badcox BA11 119 E4
Badenham Gr BS11 4 F8
Baden Ho BA1 228 B4
Badger Hts BA22 218 B5
Badger Pk TA24 201 C4
Badger Rise BS20 1 F3
Badgers Cl
Bourton SP8 161 F1
Street BA16 207 A5
Taunton TA1 212 B3
Badger's Cross
Oakhill BA3 114 F5
Somerton TA11 211 C1
Badger's Cross La TA11 211 C2
Badgers Folly BA7 214 B5
Badgers Green Rd BA16 207 A5
Badgers Hill BA11 120 A5
Badgers Holt BS14 23 C6
Badgers' La TA20 223 E1
Badgers The BS22 32 D3
BADGER STREET 182 B6
Badgers Way BS24 49 F8
Badgers Wlk BS20 4 B4
BADGWORTH 88 B6
Badgworth Barns BS26 88 D5
Badgworth Ct BS26 88 C5
Badgworth La BS26 88 C4
Badlake La EX36 162 D6
Badlake Moor Cross TA22 162 D7
Badman Cl BS39 77 D5
Badminton Ct 17 BS23 30 C1
Badminton Gdns BA1 44 C8
Bagber Cross Rds DT10 190 D3
Bagber Rd BA8 190 C4
Bagborough Dr TA6 208 F2
Bagborough La BA4 141 C2
Bagborough Rd TA2 212 F7
Baggridge Hill BA2 80 F7
Baggs La BS27 90 F2
BAGLEY 109 A1
BAGLEY GREEN 222 A3
Bagley Rd TA21 222 A3
Bagnell Cl BS14 23 E5
Bagnell Rd BS14 23 E5
BAILBROOK 28 D3
Bailbrook Gr BA1 28 C3
Bailbrook La BA1 28 D3
Baildon Cres BS23 49 A4
Baildon Ct 2 BS23 48 F4
Baildon Rd BS23 49 A4
Bailey Cl BS22 49 E8
Bailey Ct BS20 2 F6
Bailey Hill BA7 214 C5
Bailey's Dro BA6 158 B5
Baileys Gate TA4 167 F6
Bailey's Knapp EX16 178 B4
Baileys La DT8 196 C1
Bailey's La BA4 142 B1
Baileys St TA6 209 B5
Bailiffs Cl BS26 70 C1
Bailiffs' Wall BS26 70 B1
Baily Cl BA6 206 E7
Bainley Rd BA9 177 E6
Bainsbury View BA3 96 F1
Bakehouse 1 TA16 195 F7
Bakehouse La DT9 187 E1
Bakelite Mus The★ TA4 202 C2
Baker Cl 8 BS21 6 B1
Bakeries The TA11 211 D3
Baker's Bldgs BS40 35 D2
Bakers Cl TA1 212 A3
Baker's Cross TA3 191 D7
Bakers Ct TA13 220 C4
Bakersfield TA20 194 E1
Bakers La
Barrington TA19 184 C5
Chilcompton BA3 96 D3
Lower Langford BS40 53 C8
Baker's La
Churchinford TA3 191 D7
Shilstone EX35 122 A3
Wellington TA21 222 E6
Bakers Orch TA4 151 B5
Bakers Par BA2 60 B2
Bakers Pk BS13 22 B6
Baker St
Babcary TA11 174 C7
Frome BA11 119 E5
Weston-super-Mare BS23 48 E8
Bakery La BA4 140 F3
Balch Rd BA5 203 C4
Balcombe Rd TA6 153 B1
Baldwin Rd TA1 213 B5
Baldwins La TA9 105 C3
Baldwin St BS1 227 A2
Balidon Pl BA20 218 D2
Ballance St BA1 228 B4
Ballfield Rd TA24 200 F8
Ballhill La EX16 164 B1
Ball La
Doulting BA4 141 F7
Isle Abbotts TA3 183 E7
Spaxton TA2 & TA5 152 B2
Balls Barn La BS24 33 A2
Ball's Hill BA22, TA15 186 C4
Ball's La TA5 153 E4
Ball The
Dunster TA24 201 E2
Minehead TA24 200 F8
Balmoral Dr TA8 85 B1
Balmoral Ho TA6 209 C4
Balmoral Rd
Keynsham BS31 24 E4
Yeovil BA21 219 E6
Balmoral Way BS22 31 D2
Balsam Cl BA9 216 D3
Balsam Fields BA9 216 D3
Balsam La BA9 216 E3
Balsam Pk BA9 216 C3
Baltic Pl BS20 4 D4
BALTONSBOROUGH 158 A6
Baltonsborough CE Prim Sch BA6 158 A6
Baltonsborough CE VC Prim Sch BA6 158 A6
Baltonsborough Rd BA6 157 E4
Balustrade 17 BA1 28 B1
Bamfield BS14 23 A6
BAMPTON 164 C1
Bampton 5 BS22 31 F2
Bampton Ave TA20 223 B5
Bampton Cl BS13 22 B7
Bampton Down Rd EX16 178 A7
Bampton Prim Sch EX16 164 B1
Bampton St TA24 200 F6
Banbury La BA6 157 E3
Bancks St TA24 200 F7
Bancombe Ct TA11 211 B5
Bancombe Rd TA11 211 A4
Bancombe Rd Trading Estate TA11 211 B5
Banfield Cl BS11 5 A8
Bangers DT9 188 F5
Bangrove Wlk BS11 4 E8
Banister Gr BS4 22 D7
Banking Ct 4 TA18 224 C6
Bankland La TA7 154 B1
Bank Pl BS20 4 D4
Banks Cl BS21 16 D8
Bank Sq TA22 163 D6
Bank St
Highbridge TA9 104 D3
Williton TA4 202 D2
Bannerdown Cl BA1 29 B4
Bannerdown Dr BA1 29 A4
Bannerdown Rd BA1 29 C5
Bannerleigh La BS8 11 E6
Bannerleigh Rd BS8 11 E6
Banneson Rd TA5 134 B2
Bantock Cl BS4 22 D6
Bantry Rd BS4 22 E8
BANWELL 51 B3
Banwell Caves BS26 50 E2
Banwell Cl
Bristol BS13 22 A8
Keynsham BS31 25 A2
Taunton TA1 213 D4
Banwell Prim Sch BS29 51 B3
Banwell Rd
Banwell BS26, BS29 68 E8
Bath BA2 62 D8
Locking BS24 50 B3
Winscombe BS25, BS29 69 E8
Banyard Rd BS20 3 E5
Barbary Cl BA8 176 D3
Barberry Dr
Bridgwater TA6 208 D1
Chard TA20 223 F5
Barberry Farm Rd BS49 17 B1
Barber's La TA21 180 F7
Barbers Mead TA2 213 C7
Barbour Gdns BS13 22 D3
Barbour Rd BS13 22 D3
Barclay St TA6 209 A5
Barcroft BA12 144 B2
Barcroft Cres TA3 170 A1
Barcroft La TA13 220 B6
Bardel Ct BA22 218 B6
Bardon La
Williton TA4 132 A3
Williton TA4 202 A2
BARE ASH 153 B6
Barford Cl TA5 152 F7
Barford Rd TA5 152 F7
Barham Ct BA22 218 A5
Barhams Cl TA6 209 A7
Barker Cl BS24 32 C1
Barkham Cl BA5 203 F5
Barlake La BA3 115 F7
Barle Cl TA1 213 D4
Barle Ent Ctr TA22 163 D5
Barley Cl BA5 203 C3
Barley Croft
Bristol BS9 5 F5
Somerton TA11 211 B3
Barley Cross BS22 32 A5
Barley Wood Walled Garden★ BS40 35 F3
Barlinch Cl TA2 213 B7
Barlynch Ct BA21 218 D6
Barnabas Cl BS26 70 D2
Barnaby Cl BA3 78 B2
Barnard Ave BA16 207 B3
Barnard Ct BA5 203 B4
Barnard's Cl BS49 34 C7
Barnard Wlk BS31 24 D4
Barn Cl
Crewkerne TA18 224 B5
Frome BA11 119 D3
Nether Stowey TA5 134 B2
Somerton TA11 211 B3
Street BA16 207 C6
Wiveliscombe TA4 210 A7
Barnclose Rd TA22 146 E4
Barn Cres TA18 224 B5
Barn Ct BA21 187 C5
Barn End BS40 74 E3
Barnes Cl
Castle Cary BA7 214 C6
Wells BA5 203 B4
Barnes Close Mead TA22 163 D6
Barnet Cl BA21 218 E7
Barnetts Well BS27 90 F2
Barnfield Way BA1 29 B3
Barn Gn BA6 206 E3
Barnhay 6 EX16 164 B1
Barn Hill BA2 79 F5
Barn La
Clutton BS39 59 A7
Crewkerne TA18 195 E6
Riscombe TA24 128 B2
Barn Meads Rd TA21 222 E4
Barn Orchard TA14 185 E3
Barn Pool BS25 70 F8
Barns Cl
Barrow Gurney BS48 20 E4
Nailsea BS48 8 E2
Barnsclose TA22 163 D6
Barns Close Ind Est TA22 163 D6
Barnsclose N TA22 163 D6
Barnsclose W TA22 163 D6
Barns Gd BS21 16 E8
Barn St TA18 224 B6
Barnstaple Ct BS4 22 E8
Barnstaple Rd BS4 22 E8
Barnstaple Wlk BS4 22 F8
Barnsworthy Farm Rd TA5 133 F4
Barnwood Ct BS48 8 B1
Baron Cl BS30 25 E8
Barons Cl BS3 11 F3
Barossa Pl BS1 227 A1
Barpark Cnr EX15 180 E3
Barpool La TA11 211 D6
BARR 168 B3
Barracks Cl BA22 218 B7
Barrack's La BS11 4 D8
BARREN DOWN 205 C7
Barrendown La BA4 205 C6
Barrie Way TA8 104 C6
BARRINGTON 184 D5
Barrington Broadway TA10 184 D6
Barrington Cl TA1 212 C1
Barrington Court★ TA19 184 D5
Barrington Court Cotts TA19 184 D5
Barrington Hill TA19 183 A3
Barrington Hill National Nature Reserve★ TA19 183 A4
Barrington Hill Rd TA19 182 F4
Barrington Main TA19 184 E2
Barrington Pl BA4 204 F5
Barrington Rd TA8 104 C8
Barrington Wy TA21 222 B4
BARROW
Wells 140 B4
Wincanton 161 B3
BARROW COMMON 21 B4
Barrow Court La BS19 20 B5
Barrow Cswy BA5 138 F8
Barrow Ct
Barrow Gurney BS48 20 A5
Tickenham BS21 7 F4
Barrow Dr TA1 213 E5
BARROW GURNEY 20 E5
Barrow Hill
Stalbridge DT10 190 B4
Stourton Caundle DT10 189 F1
Barrow Hill Cres BS11 4 C7
Barrow Hill Rd BS11 4 D6
Barrow Ho 25 BA4 205 B6
Barrow La
Charlton Musgrove BA9 161 B3
North Wootton BA4 140 B4
Pilton BA4 140 F3
Winford BS40 20 F1
Barrow Lea DT10 190 B4
Barrowmead Dr BS11 4 F7
Barrow Pk BS27 90 A8
Barrow Rd
Bath BA2 44 C1
Hutton BS24 49 E2
Barrows Cl TA6 208 E2
Barrows Croft BS27 90 A8
Barrows Ct BA22 196 E8
Barrows La TA14 185 E2
Barrows Rd BS27 90 A8
Barrow St BS48 20 D5
Barrows The
Cheddar BS27 90 A8
Weston-super-Mare BS22 49 C7
Barrow Stile BA4 140 F3
BARROW VALE 59 D5
Barrow Water La BA9 161 A3
Barrow Wood La BS27 110 A7
Barrs Ct BS1 227 B3
Barry Cl BS24 49 A1
Barry La BA22 196 F6
Barrymore Cl TA10 172 A6
Barstable Ho BS2 227 C3
Bartec 4 BA20 218 C3
Bartholomew Row BA2 60 B2
Bartlett Cl
Frome BA11 120 C6
Taunton TA1 212 B1
Bartlett Ct 1 TA18 224 C6
Bartlett Ct BA20 218 D3
Bartlett Mews BA21 219 F7
Bartlett Pk
Chard TA20 223 E3
Yeovil BA20 218 D3
Bartletts Ct BA2 228 C1
Bartletts La TA4 167 A4
Bartletts Pl BA21 218 D5
Bartlett Sq BA7 214 A7
Bartletts Row TA11 211 D4

Bartlett St 6 BA1 228 B3
Bartletts Way BS24 50 A4
BARTON 69 B6
Barton Cl
Berrow TA8 84 F5
Taunton TA1 212 D3
Barton Cross EX16 162 E5
Barton Dro BS25 69 D5
Barton Gdns DT9 225 B4
Barton Gn TA3 168 D1
Barton Hey 2 TA4 167 F8
Barton Hill SP8 177 E2
Barton La TA3 169 C4
Barton Rd
Barton St David TA11 158 A2
Berrow TA8 84 F4
Bristol BS2 227 C2
Butleigh BA6 157 E3
Minehead TA24 201 B4
Winscombe BS26 69 C6
Barton Rise TA7 137 B3
BARTON ST DAVID 158 A2
Barton St
Bath BA1 228 B2
Bristol BS1 227 A4
Bartons The
Bishops Lydeard TA4 167 E8
Ilchester BA22 173 E1
South Petherton TA13 220 E3
Barton The
Bleadon BS24 67 C6
Charlton Adam TA11 173 F7
Corston BA2 43 A7
Huish Champflower TA4 165 E8
Norton St Philip BA2 81 E4
Barton Vale BS2 227 C2
Barton Villas BA3 116 F6
Barton Way TA3 170 C4
Barton Wlk BA11 119 D2
BARWICK 197 F8
Barwick Ho BS11 4 E7
Barwick Stoford Com Prim Sch BA22 197 F8
Barwick & Stoford Com Prim Sch BA22 197 F8
Basketfield La BA6 139 D1
Baskets La BA9 177 C5
Batallers La TA23 131 D2
Bat Alley DT10 190 F5
BATCH 66 F3
Batch Bsns Pk BS24 66 F2
Batch Cl TA7 136 C4
Batch La
Clutton BS39 58 F3
Lympsham BS24 66 F3
Batchpool La BA8 176 F3
Batch Rd TA7 136 B5
Batch The
Ashcott TA7 156 B7
Backwell BS48 19 D1
Batheaston BA1 28 F3
Burrington BS40 54 B3
Butcombe BS40 55 B8
Chew Magna BS40 39 B3
Churchill BS25 52 F4
Draycott BS27 90 F2
Farmborough BA2 60 A6
Hinton Charterhouse BA2 63 E1
Saltford BS31 25 F3
19 Shepton Mallet BA4 205 B6
Wincanton BA9 216 B4
Yatton BS49 34 B7
Batch View BA16 207 B6
BATCOMBE 142 D1
Bateman's Cross TA20 198 E7
BATH 228 A2
Bath Abbey★ BA1 228 C2
BATHAMPTON 28 F1
Bathampton La BA2 28 E1
Bathampton Prim Sch BA2 28 F2
Bathampton View BA1 29 B3
Bath Aqua Theatre of Glass★ 10 BA1 228 C3
Bath Bridge Bsns Pk TA6 209 B6
Bath Bsns Pk BA2 79 E7
Bath City FC Twerton Park BA2 44 B5
Bath Cl BA6 206 D6
Bath Coll BA3 78 F2
BATHEALTON 166 B3
BATHEASTON 28 F4
Batheaston CE Prim Sch BA1 28 F4
BATHFORD 29 C1
Bathford CE Prim Sch BA1 29 C2
Bathford Hill
Bathford BA1 29 B2
Compton Dando BS39 41 E5
Bathford Manor BA1 29 C2
Bath Foyer The BA2 44 A6
Bath Hill
Keynsham BS31 24 F5
Wellow BA2 62 D2
Bath House Ct TA1 212 E3
Bath La TA20 223 C3
Bath Meadow Dr TA22 163 E6
Bath New Rd BA3 78 F4
Bath Old Rd BA3 78 F4
Bath Pl TA1 212 F3
BATHPOOL 213 E6
Bath Postal Mus★ BA1 228 C3
Bath Racecourse★ BA1 27 A6
Bath Rd
Ashcott TA7 156 B7
Bawdrip TA7 136 D2
Bath Rd *continued*
Beckington BA11 101 D5
Bitton BS30 25 D8
Blagdon BS40 55 B1
Bridgwater TA6 209 C7
Bristol BS2 227 C1
Farmborough BA2 59 E5
Frome BA11 120 A7
Horrington BA3, BA5 113 D5
Kelston BA1, BS30 26 B6
Kingsdown SN13 29 F5
Moorlinch TA7 155 E8
Norton St Philip BA2 81 E5
Oakhill BA3 115 B3
Paulton BS39 77 F6
Peasedown St John BA2 79 C7
Saltford BS31 25 D3
Shepton Mallet BA4 141 C8
Stawell TA7 137 B1
Upper Langford BS40 53 D3
Wells BA5 112 E1
Bath Riverside Bsns Pk BA2 228 B1
Bath's Original Theatre Royal & Masonic Mus★ BA1 228 C2
Bath Spa Sta BA1 228 C1
Bath Spa Univ Art and Design
Bath BA1 27 E1
Bath BA1 27 E1
Bath Spa Univ Coll BA1 27 E1
Bath Spa University Coll (Newton Pk Campus) BA2 43 B5
Bath Spa University (Culverhey Campus) BA2 44 B2
Bath Sq TA20 223 C3
Bath St
Bath BA1 228 C2
Bristol BS1 227 B2
Chard TA20 223 C3
Cheddar BS27 90 B7
Frome BA11 119 F4
Bathurst Cl TA8 104 D8
Bathurst Par BS1 227 A1
Bathurst Rd BS22 49 C8
Bath View BA3 96 F1
BATHWAY 94 E5
Bathwell La DT9 217 D1
BATHWICK 45 B7
Bathwick Hill BA2 45 C6
Bathwick Rise BA2 45 B7
Bathwick St Mary CE Prim Sch
Bathwick BA2 45 C8
Bathwick BA2 45 C8
Bathwick St BA1, BA2 228 C4
Batstone Cl BA1 28 B2
Batt Dr TA2 213 C8
BATTEN'S GREEN 182 F5
Battery La BS20 2 D7
Battery Rd BS20 2 D6
Battin's Knap TA4 150 A3
Batt La TA3 183 C8
BATTLEBOROUGH 86 C1
Battleborough La TA9 86 B1
Battle La BS40 39 A3
Battle St EX15 180 E1
Battleton TA22 163 D6
Battle Wk BA1 27 E4
Batts Bow Bridge TA9 104 E1
Batts La
Oakhill BA3 114 E3
Pilsdon DT6 199 F2
Batt's La TA10 172 D5
Battson Rd BS14 23 E4
Batts Pk TA1 212 E1
Bauldltch La TA3 184 B8
Baunton's Cl DT9 217 C2
Baunton's Orch DT9 217 C2
Bawden Cl TA7 136 E4
BAWDRIP 136 E2
Bawdrip La TA7 136 E2
Bawler Rd TA2 169 B2
Bawler's La TA10 171 C3
Bayer Bldg The BA2 228 B1
BAYFORD 216 F5
Bayford Hill BA9 216 E4
Bayford La BA9 177 B7
Bayford Rd TA6 209 C6
Bay Hill TA19 221 D4
Bay La BS27 90 F2
Baylie Ave BS24 32 C1
Bayliss Ctr The 4 BA16 207 C5
Baymead Cl 11 TA6 153 F4
Baymead La TA6 153 F3
Baymead Mdw 5 TA6 153 F3
Baynes Cl TA21 222 E7
Bay Rd
Clevedon BS21 6 D6
Porlock TA24 124 A4
Bay's La BA3 115 A7
Bays The BS27 90 C8
Baytree Ct BS22 31 D1
Baytree Rd BS22 31 C1
Bay Tree Rd
Bath BA1 28 B2
Clevedon BS21 6 E1
Baytree Sch BS24 50 A8
Baytree View BS22 31 D1
Bay Tree View BS22 31 D1
Bay View TA23 202 D6
Bay View Gdns TA8 104 B5
Baze La EX35 122 B4
Bazelands Hill BA8 190 B7
Beach Ave BS21 6 C2
Beach Ct BS23 48 D6
Beach End Rd BS23 48 C2
Beach Hill BS20 2 C6
Beachlands Pk BS22 31 A6
Beachley Wlk BS11 4 D7
Beach Mews BS21 6 C4
Beach Rd
Weston-super-Mare BS23 48 D6
Weston-super-Mare, Kewstoke BS22 31 A5
Beach Rd E BS20 2 D6
Beach Rd W BS20 2 C6
Beach The BS21 6 C4
Beach Tree Cross TA4 166 F6
Beacon TA19 221 B5
Beacon Cl 7 TA2 169 C5
Beaconfield Ho TA6 209 A2
Beaconfield Rd BA20 218 E1
BEACON HILL 27 F1
Beacon Hill View DT9 175 D1
Beacon La
Corton Denham DT9 175 D2
Wellington TA21 180 C4
Beacon Rd
Bath BA1 28 A1
Minehead TA24 200 F8
Beaconsfield Rd
Clevedon BS21 6 E3
Weston-super-Mare BS23 48 E7
Beaconsfield Way BA11 120 B7
Beacon View
Coleford BA3 116 E7
Shepton Mallet BA4 205 A4
Beadon La TA16 195 F7
Beadon Rd TA1 213 C5
Beafort Cl BS24 50 C3
Beale Cl BS14 23 E6
Beale Way TA8 104 D5
Bean Acre The BS11 4 D8
Bearbridge Rd BS13 21 F4
BEARD HILL 141 C3
BEARDLY BATCH 205 C1
Beard's Yd TA10 171 F5
BEAR FLAT 44 F4
Bearley Bridge Rd 15 TA12 185 E6
Bearley Ho 26 TA12 185 E6
Bearley La BA22 186 B7
Bearley Rd 27 TA12 185 E6
Bears Meadow La TA5 133 C6
Bear Yard Mews 2 BS8 226 A2
Beasley Ct TA20 223 B5
Beastway La TA24 131 B3
Beatty Way TA8 104 C7
Beauchamp Ave BA3 97 B6
Beauchamp Gdns TA3 183 A7
Beauchamp Pk BA3 97 B6
Beauchamps Dr BA3 97 A5
Beaufighter Rd BS24 49 D6
Beaufitz Pl TA20 193 F1
Beauford Pk TA2 168 B4
Beauford Sq BA1 228 B2
Beaufort Ave BA3 78 A2
Beaufort Bldgs 7 BS8 11 F7
Beaufort Cl EX16 178 D1
Beaufort Ct
Clevedon BS21 6 C5
Ilchester BA22 173 E2
Beaufort E BA1 28 C1
Beaufort Gdns
2 Nailsea BS48 8 D1
South Petherton TA13 220 B5
Beaufort Mews
3 Bath BA1 28 C1
10 Bristol BS8 11 F7
Beaufort Pl BA1 28 C1
Beaufort Rd
Taunton TA1 212 E5
Weston-super-Mare BS23 48 F7
Beaufort Villas 8 BA1 28 B1
Beaufort W 11 BA1 28 B1
Beauley Rd BS3 226 B1
Beaulieu Dr BA21 218 D6
Beaumont BA1 27 F1
Beaumont Cl BS23 48 F4
Beaumont Ho BA21 219 D5
Beau St BA1 228 B2
Beavor La EX13 198 A1
BECKERY 206 B4
Beckery BA6 206 B3
Beckery New Rd BA6 206 B3
Beckery Rd BA6 206 B4
Becket Dr BS22 32 A3
Becket Pl BA5 203 D3
Becket Prim Sch BS22 32 A2
Becket Rd BS22 32 A4
Becket's La BS48 18 E8
Beckford Ct 1 BA2 45 B7
Beckford Dr BA1 27 E4
Beckford Gdns
Bath BA2 45 B8
Bristol BS14 23 A3
Beckford Rd BA2 45 B7
Beckford's Twr & Mus★ BA1 27 D4
Beckhampton Rd BA2 44 D5
BECKINGTON 101 E4
Beckington BS24 49 A2
Beckington CE Fst Sch BA11 101 E4
Beckington Cres TA20 223 D3
Becks Bsns Pk BS23 49 A7
Becks Field 2 TA14 185 F4
Beckworth Cl TA6 209 C3
Bector La BA3 116 C4
Bede St DT9 225 E5
Bedford Cl TA6 209 C3
Bedford Ct BA1 45 B8
Bedford Rd
Wells BA5 112 E1
Weston-super-Mare BS23 48 E4
Yeovil BA21 219 D8
Bedford St BA1 45 B8
BEDLAM 119 B8
Bedlam Green Farm La BA10 161 A4
BEDMINSTER DOWN 22 B8
Bedminster Down Sch
Bedminster Down BS13 22 A7
Bristol BS13 21 F7
Bedwell La TA7 155 C2
Bedwin Cl BS20 1 F4
Beech Ave
Bath BA2 45 E5
Shepton Mallet BA4 205 A6
Beech Bsns Pk TA6 209 A7
Beech Cl
Doulting BA4 141 E6
Shipham BS25 70 F8
Taunton TA2 212 F8
Beechcroft BS41 21 D2
Beech Croft BS14 23 B5
Beech Ct
Bristol BS14 23 A5
Frome BA11 120 B7
Taunton TA1 212 E3
2 Wellington TA21 222 D6
Beech Dr
Bridgwater TA6 209 D5
Nailsea BS48 9 A3
Shipham BS25 70 E8
BEECHEN CLIFF 228 B1
Beechen Cliff Rd BA2 228 B1
Beechen Cliff Sch BA2 45 A4
Beeches The
Bath BA2 44 D1
Langport TA10 172 A6
Sandford BS25 52 B4
Wheddon Cross TA24 129 E1
Beechfield Cl BS41 11 C2
Beechfield Gr BS9 5 C8
Beech Gr
Bath BA2 44 D4
Somerton TA11 211 D5
Wellington TA21 222 C6
Beech Grove Prim Sch TA21 222 C6
Beech Hill TA21 222 F5
Beeching Cl TA20 223 E6
Beeching Close Ind Est TA20 223 E6
Beech La
Axminster EX13 198 E1
Stoke Trister BA9 177 C8
Beechmont Dr BS24 49 A1
Beechmount Cl BS24 48 F1
Beechmount Ct BS14 23 B8
Beechmount Gr BS14 23 B8
Beech Rd
Bridgwater TA6 209 D5
20 Martock TA12 185 E6
Saltford BS31 25 E3
Shipham BS25 70 F8
Street BA16 207 C3
Yatton BS49 34 C8
Beech Terr BA3 78 E1
Beech Tree TA23 130 D1
Beech Tree Cl TA4 210 C4
Beech Tree Cross
Clatworthy TA4 149 E1
Dulverton TA22 163 C7
Monksilver TA4 132 B1
Beech Tree Hill TA5 152 C6
Beech Way BA4 141 E1
Beechwood
Bridgwater TA6 208 E2
Yeovil BA20 218 F2
Beechwood Ave
Frome BA11 120 A5
Locking BS24 50 A5
Beechwood Cl
Bristol BS14 23 C8
Frome BA11 120 A5
Beechwood Dr
Crewkerne TA18 224 C7
Portishead BS20 1 E5
Beechwood Rd
Bath BA2 45 B1
Easton-in-G BS20 4 A4
Nailsea BS48 8 D2
Portishead BS20 1 E5
Beehive Yd BA1 228 C3
Beek's La SN14, BA1 13 D5
Beer Door TA10 155 E2
Beer Dro TA10 155 E3
Beere Cross EX36 162 A5
Beer La
Burlescombe EX16 179 B2
Dulverton TA22 163 B5
Beer Rd TA10 155 E1
Beer St
Curry Mallet TA3 183 C7
Yeovil BA20 219 A4
Bees Ho BS21 6 C2
Beetham La TA20 193 B6
Beggar Bush La BS8 11 B6
Beggarswell Cl BS2 227 C4
BEGGEARN HUISH 131 E2
Beggs Cl 4 TA6 153 F3
Begonia Dr TA6 208 D1
Behind Berry TA11 211 D4
Behind Butts TA14 185 E1
Behind Hayes BA8 176 D3
Behind Town TA11 157 B4
Bekynton Ave BA5 203 F4
Belcombe Dro TA20 193 B7
Belfast Wlk BS4 22 E8
Belfield Ct TA8 104 A8
Belgrave Cres BA1 228 C4
Belgrave Ct 2 TA2 212 F6
Belgrave Pl
Bath BA1 228 C4
Bristol BS8 226 A3
Taunton TA2 212 F6
Belgrave Rd
Bath BA1 28 B1
Bristol BS8 226 B4
Weston-super-Mare BS22 49 B8
Belgrave Terr 2 BA1 28 A1
Belgravia Rd TA6 136 B2
Bellamy Ave BS13 22 C4
Belland Dr BS14 22 F4
Bella View Gdns BA6 206 D4
Bella Vista Rd BA1 228 B4
Bell Barn Rd BS9 5 D6
Bell Chase BA20 218 D5
Bell Cl
Bridgwater TA6 208 F6
Farmborough BA2 59 F6
Westbury-sub-Mendip BA5 110 E6
Belle View Terr TA20 198 C8
Bellevue BS8 226 B2
BELLE VUE 78 B3
Belle Vue
Midsomer Norton BA3 78 B3
Washford TA23 131 E3
Belle Vue Cl BA2 79 D7
Bellevue Cotts BS8 226 B2
Bellevue Cres BS8 226 B2
Bellevue Ct
Bristol BS8 226 B2
Clevedon BS21 6 D4
Bellevue Mans BS21 6 D4
Bellevue Rd BS21 6 D4
Bellevue Terr BS8 226 B2
Belle Vue Terr TA18 224 B6
Bellfield BA3 117 A3
Bellhanger Ct BA1 228 B4
Bell Hill
Chewton Mendip BA3 94 B7
Norton St Philip BA2 81 E4
Bellhorse La BS40 74 C5
Bellifants BA2 60 A6
Bellis Avenue TA5 208 D1
Bell La
Bristol BS1 227 A3
Chard TA19, TA20 193 F7
Chewton Mendip BA3 94 B7
Cossington TA7 137 A3
Thurloxton TA2 153 D1
Bell Language Sch The BA1 44 C8
Bellman's Cross BA8 190 B7
Bellmoor La TA19 194 A7
Bell Orch TA10 171 D4
Bellotts Rd BA2 44 C6
Bell Pit Brow BS48 9 B2
Bell Sq BS40 54 E3
Bellum SN14 13 E8
BELLUTON 40 D6
Belluton La BS39 40 D5
Belluton Villas BS39 40 D5
Bell Wlk BS40 35 E2
Belmonds Cross Rd BA9 177 D7
Belmont Cl TA6 208 B4
Belmont Dr
Failand BS8 10 B3
Taunton TA1 212 E2
Belmont Hill BS48 10 B1
Belmont Ho 14 BA20 219 B4
Belmont Rd
Bath BA2 45 C1
Hatch Beauchamp TA3 183 A8
Taunton TA1 212 C3
Winscombe BS25 70 A8
Belmont Terr TA19 184 E3
Belmont The BS21 6 D3
Belmore Gdns BA2 44 B3
Belstone Wlk BS4 22 C8
Belton Ct BA1 27 B2
Belton Rd BS20 2 A6
Belvedere BA1 228 B4
Belvedere Cl TA5 135 B2
Belvedere Cres BS22 31 C1
Belvedere Ct 3 TA21 222 D6
Belvedere Grange TA11 211 E3
Belvedere Rd
Taunton TA1 212 F5
Yeovil BA21 219 E7
Belvedere Trad Est TA1 212 E5
Belvoir Rd 6 BA2 44 D5
Bemberry Bank TA24 130 B5
Benares Ct TA24 201 A8
Bences Cl SN14 13 F8
Benches La BS40 37 D3
Bench La TA20 193 D5
Ben Cross TA13 220 A4
Benedictine Ct BA6 206 C4
Benedict St BA6 206 D4
Benhole La TA5 134 B8
Benleaze Rd BS40 75 C2
Bennell Batch BA3 96 E4
Bennell Cl BA3 96 E4
Bennell Cotts BA3 96 E4
Bennett Gdns BA11 119 D4
Bennett La BA1 28 A1
Bennett Rd TA9 104 F4
Bennetts Cl BA5 204 B7
Bennetts Field Trad Est BA9 216 C2
Bennett's La BA3, BA5 114 B7
Bennett's Rd BA1 28 C3
Bennett St BA1 228 B3
Bennetts Way BS21 6 E5
Bennett Way BS1, BS8 11 F5
BENTER 115 D7
Benter Cross BA3 115 D7
Bentley Cl BS14 22 F3

Bentley Rd BS22 32 B3
Ben Travers Way TA8 104 C6
Benville Ave BS9 5 C8
Bere La BA6 206 E4
Bere Mills La TA19 194 B7
Beresford Cl
Burnham-on-S TA8 104 C7
Saltford BS31 25 E2
Beresford Gdns BA1 27 A3
Beretun Orch BA6 206 E3
Berhill TA7 156 C7
Berkeley Ave
Bristol BS8 226 C3
Midsomer Norton BA3 78 A2
Berkeley Cres
Bristol BS8 226 B3
Weston-super-Mare BS23 48 C2
Berkeley Ct BA2 45 C6
Berkeley Gdns
Bruton BA10 215 E6
Keynsham BS31 24 E4
Berkeley Ho
Bath BA1 228 C4
Bristol BS1 226 C3
Berkeley Pl
Bath BA1 228 C4
Bristol BS8 226 B3
Berkeley Rd
Street BA16 207 E6
Yeovil BA20 219 A4
Berkeley Sq BS8 226 B3
BERKLEY 121 A7
Berkley Ave BS8 226 B3
Berkley CE Fst Sch BA11 121 A7
Berkley Cross BA11 120 F6
Berkley Ct BA22 173 E2
BERKLEY DOWN 120 C5
Berkley La
Beckington BA11 101 D3
Frome BA11 120 D8
BERKLEY MARSH 120 F7
Berkley Rd BA11 120 B6
Berkley St BA11 121 A8
Berlington Ct BS1 227 B1
Bernard Cres TA24 200 F6
Bernard Herridge Ct BA9 216 D4
Bernard Ireland Ho BA1 27 B1
Bernard Taylor Homes 9 TA1 213 A4
Bernard Way TA13 220 D6
Berners Cl BS4 22 D7
BERROW 84 E5
Berrow CE Prim Sch TA8 84 F4
Berrow Lodge 7 BS23 48 E5
Berrow Rd TA8 85 A2
Berry Cl TA6 208 E2
Berry Cott La TA20 192 F4
Berrydale Ave TA6 208 F6
Berry Hill
Mells BA11 118 A6
Nunney BA11 143 B8
Berry La EX13 198 F3
Berryman Cl BA4 205 A5
Berryman Ct BA5 203 B4
Bertha Terr TA9 104 D3
Berwick Cl TA1 212 C1
Beryl Gr BS14 23 C8
Beryl Knapp BA22 197 B8
Beryl La BA5 203 F6
Besley Ct BA5 203 B4
Bests Field TA12 185 B8
Bethell Mead TA4 167 E6
BETTISCOMBE 199 E2
Bevan Rd BS30 25 E8
Beverley Cl
Frome BA11 119 D3
Taunton TA2 212 E6
Beverley Dr TA23 202 C7
Beverley Gdns BS9 5 D7
Bewdley Rd BA2 45 B4
Bewley Ct TA20 223 B4
Bewley Down Rd TA20 193 A3
Bews La TA20 223 B5
Bibors Hill TA4 165 E4
Bibury Cl BS48 9 A1
Bibury Ho BA1 27 B2
BICKENHALL 182 E5
Bickenhall La TA3 182 F6
Bickfield La
Compton Martin BS40 74 B8
Ubley BS40 55 F2
Bicking's Close La TA4 166 A4
Bicknell Gdns BA21 219 B8
BICKNOLLER 132 F2
Bidbrooke La EX36 162 A6
Biddiscombe Cl TA6 208 E1
BIDDISHAM 87 E8
Biddisham Cl 6 BS48 8 E1
Biddisham La BS26 87 E7
Biddlesden Rd BA21 218 C7
Biddle St BS49 34 B7
Bideford Cres BS4 22 F8
Bideford Rd BS22 31 F2
Bifield Cl BS14 23 F5
Bifield Gdns BS14 23 E5
Bifield Rd BS14 23 F5
Bignal Rand Cl BA5 203 B3
Bignal Rand Dr BA5 203 B3
Bignell Cl BS25 69 F8
Big Tree Cl BS26 69 C3
Bigwood La BS1 226 C2
Bilberry Cl BS9 5 C8
Bilberry Gr TA1 168 F1
Bilbie Cl BS40 56 E8
Bilbie Rd
Chew Stoke BS40 56 E8
Weston-super-Mare BS22 32 B3
BILBROOK 131 C4
Bilbury La
Bath BA1 228 B2
Glastonbury BA6 206 F3
Billand Cl BS13 21 E3
Billetfield TA1 212 F3
Billet St TA1 212 F3
Billicombe La TA7 155 C8
Billing's Hill BS28 108 C4
Bills La TA11 174 C6
Binces La BA2 42 E3
Bince's Lodge La BA3 78 B3
BINCOMBE 134 A2
Bincombe Dr TA18 224 C7
Bincombe Rd TA6 209 C4
Binding Cl 6 TA6 153 F4
Bindon La BA11 143 B2
Bindon Rd TA2 212 C6
Bindwell La BA22 174 F3
Bindworth Dro TA12 185 A7
BINEGAR 114 C7
Binegar La BA3 114 E7
Bineham Ct TA10 173 B4
Bineham La
Ilchester BA22 173 F2
Yeovilton BA22 174 A2
Bineham Rd TA10 173 A4
Binford Pl TA6 209 A5
Binford's La TA4 151 A4
Binhay Rd BS49 34 C7
Binley Gr BS14 23 D5
Binmead Gdns BS13 22 B4
Binnings The BS27 90 F3
Birbeck Chase BS24 50 C8
Birbeck Rd BS9 5 E5
Bircham Cl TA6 208 C4
Bircham La TA24 201 C4
Bircham Rd
Minehead TA24 201 B5
Taunton TA2 213 B8
Birchanger La TA4 150 A8
Birch Ave
Bleadon BS24 67 C6
Clevedon BS21 6 E4
Puriton TA7 136 C4
Birch Cl
Bridgwater TA6 209 D5
Cannington TA5 135 B2
Cheddar BS27 90 C8
Locking BS24 50 B4
Wedmore BS28 108 C3
Birch Croft BS14 23 A3
Birch Ct BS31 24 C4
Birchdale BA20 218 D2
Birchdale Rd BS14 23 A8
Birchdene BS48 9 A2
Birch Dr BS40 53 A5
Birches Cnr TA4 152 A4
Birches The BS48 9 A2
Birchfield Com Prim Sch BA21 219 D7
Birchfield Rd BA21 219 D8
Birch Gr
Portishead BS20 2 C4
Taunton TA1 212 E5
Birch Hill BS27 90 C8
Birch Ho TA8 65 F2
BIRCHILL 198 A5
Birchill Cross EX13 198 A6
Birchill La BA11 120 A1
Birch Lawn TA8 104 B6
Birch Rd
12 Martock TA12 185 E6
Radstock BA3 78 E1
Wellington TA21 222 E5
Birch Wlk BA11 120 B7
BIRCHWOOD 182 A1
Birchwood Ave BS23 49 A7
Birchwood Cl BA12 144 E8
Birchwood Dr BS8 10 B3
Birchwood La BS39 40 F2
Birdcombe Cl BS48 8 E3
Birdlip Cl BS48 9 A1
Bird's Cl TA18 224 B6
BIRDSMOORGATE 199 D4
Birdwell La BS41 10 F1
Birdwell Prim Sch BS41 21 A8
Birdwell Rd BS41 10 F1
Birkbeck Ct BS23 48 D7
Birkett Rd BS23 30 B1
Birkin St BS2 227 C2
Birnbeck Rd BS23 30 C1
Biscay Dr BS20 2 F6
Biscombe Cross TA3 191 B8
Bisdee Rd BS24 49 D2
Bishop Ave BS22 32 A3
Bishop Cl TA20 223 B5
Bishop Cres BA4 204 F5
Bishop Fox Dr TA1 213 A2
Bishop Fox's Com Sch TA1 213 A1
Bishop Henderson CE Prim Sch
Taunton TA1 212 C2
Taunton TA2 212 C2
Bishop Henderson CE Sch BA3 116 E8
Bishop Rd TA5 134 B2
Bishops Cl
Bristol BS9 5 E3
Taunton TA2 213 F7
Bishops Cotts
Stogursey TA5 134 B7
Wootton Courtenay TA24 129 F6
Bishops Cove BS13 21 F5
Bishops Ct 4 TA21 222 D6
Bishops Dr TA10 172 A5
Bishops Gn TA4 210 C4
Bishop's Hill TA21 179 B7
BISHOP'S HULL 212 A4
Bishop's Hull Hill TA1 212 B4
Bishop's Hull Prim Sch TA1 212 B4
Bishop's Hull Rd TA1 212 A3
Bishops Knoll BS9 5 C3
Bishops La BA22 197 A6
Bishop's La DT9 187 E1
Bishopslea Cl BA5 203 C3
BISHOPS LYDEARD 167 F8
Bishops Lydeard CE Prim Sch TA4 167 E8
Bishops Lydeard Mill & Rural Life Mus★ TA4 167 F8
Bishops Lydeard Mill & Rural Life Mus TA4 167 F8
Bishop's Lydeard Sta TA4 167 E7
Bishops Mead BS49 35 A8
Bishop's Mead TA2 212 E8
Bishop's Palace★ BA5 203 E4
Bishops Park Way BA5 203 F2
Bishop's Path TA8 104 B6
Bishops Rd BS49 35 A8
Bishop St
Bristol BS2 227 B4
Faulkland BA3 80 D2
Bishopston TA15 186 B4
BISHOP SUTTON 57 D3
Bishop Sutton Prim Sch BS39 57 D4
Bishops Wlk BA22 173 D1
BISHOPSWOOD 192 E7
Bishopswood Rd TA20 192 F7
BISHOPSWORTH 22 A5
Bishopsworth Rd BS13 22 A7
Bishop Terr BS2 227 C4
Bishport Ave BS13 22 C3
Bishport Cl BS13 22 B4
Bishport Gn BS13 22 C3
Bitham Wlk TA7 136 E3
Bittern Ave BS20 2 F7
Bittern Cl BS22 31 F1
Bittescombe La TA4 165 B6
Bittlemead BS13 22 F4
BITTON 25 E7
Blackacre BS14 23 C4
Blackacre Hill BA8 176 D4
Blackaller La EX16 163 C1
Black Bench Dro TA20 223 F7
Blackberry Cl BA4 205 C4
Blackberry Ct TA21 222 D4
Blackberry Dr BS22 32 A2
Blackberry La
Portishead BS20 1 F2
Sherborne DT9 225 D5
Winsley BA3, BA15 64 C8
Blackberry Rd BA11 120 B3
Blackberry Way BA3 77 F3
Blackberry Wlk TA18 224 D7
Blackberry Wy BS31 24 E3
Blackbird Cl BA3 97 B8
Blackbird Way BA11 120 B6
Blackbrook Park Ave TA1 213 E4
Blackbrook Prim Sch TA1 213 D3
Blackbrook Rd TA1 213 E5
Blackbrook Way TA1 213 E3
Blackburn Wy BS24 32 C1
Blackcurrant Dr BS41 20 E8
Black Dog Hill BA13 121 E6
BLACKDOWN 199 D6
Blackdown BA21 219 A6
Blackdown Bsns Pk TA21 222 E6
Blackdown Ct BS14 23 B5
Blackdown Mead BS27 90 C6
Blackdown Rd
Bridgwater TA6 209 D4
Portishead BS20 2 B5
Rockwell Green TA21 222 B4
Taunton TA2 213 B8
Blackdown View
Curry Rivel TA10 171 D4
Ilminster TA19 221 C4
Norton Fitzwarren TA2 168 B5
Nynehead TA21 167 C2
Sampford Peverell EX16 178 C1
Blackdown Way BA3 97 B6
Black Dro TA7 155 A1
Blacker's La BA3 116 E2
Blackerton Cross EX16 162 E3
Blackey La BA3 115 B6
BLACKFORD
Minehead 129 E8
Wedmore 107 E4
Wincanton 175 F5
Blackford Hollow BA22 175 F5
Blackford Moor Dro BS26, BS28 107 B6
Blackford Moor La TA9, BS28 107 B5
Blackford Rd
Charlton Horethorne DT9 176 A2
Mark TA9 106 F4
Wedmore BS28 108 A3
Blackford Way DT9 176 A3
Blackfriars BS1 227 A3
Blackfriars Rd BS48 8 B1
Blackham La TA10 155 F2
Blackhayes La EX14 192 C1
Blackheath La BA5 113 E4
Black Horse Cl TA6 208 F2
Black Horse La TA1 212 F5
Black La
Axbridge BS26 70 E2
Hemyock EX15 180 D2
Holcombe Rogus TA21 178 E6
Blackland Dro TA20 194 A1
Blackland La TA20 194 B1
Blacklands TA6 208 F5
Black Mere BA22 218 B5
Black Mixen La TA18 224 C7
Black Monkey La TA24 131 C5
BLACKMOOR
Chew Stoke 38 C3
Churchill 53 D6
Wellington 180 E5
Blackmoor
Charterhouse BS40 72 F4
Clevedon BS21 6 C1
Lower Langford BS40 53 C6
3 Weston-super-Mare BS22 31 F2
Blackmoor Cl BS40 53 C6
Blackmoor La 6 BA8 190 A6
Blackmoor Rd
Abbots Leigh BS8 4 E2
Taunton TA2 213 B7
Wellington TA21 222 F4
Blackmoors La BS3 11 E4
Blackmore Chase BA9 216 D3
Blackmore Dr BA2 44 C5
Blackmore La TA5 135 B1
Blackmore Rd DT10 190 B4
Blackmore Vale Cl BA8 176 E1
Blacknell La TA18 224 D6
Blacknell Lane Ind Est TA18 224 E5
Black Nore Point BS20 1 F5
Black Pit Dro BA6 206 D8
BLACKPOOL CORNER 198 D1
BLACKROCK 40 E8
Blackrock La BS39 40 E7
Black Rock Nature Trail★ BA5 72 A1
Blackrock Villas BS20 2 B1
Blackrod Cotts TA13 184 F4
Blacksmith La BA1 28 B6
Blacksmiths La TA7 155 F8
Blacksmith's La BA1 26 B3
Blacksmiths Row BA21 187 D6
Black's Moor Hill La TA11 173 A5
Blackthorn Cl
Biddisham BS26 87 E6
Bristol BS13 22 D5
6 North Petherton TA6 153 F3
Blackthorn Dr BS20 2 E5
Blackthorne Cl BA22 173 E2
Blackthorn Gdns
Taunton TA2 168 F6
Weston-super-Mare BS22 32 A1
Blackthorn Rd BS13 22 D5
Blackthorn Sq BS21 6 D1
Blackthorns The TA1 213 C2
Blackthorn Terr BS22 32 A1
Blackthorn Way
Nailsea BS48 9 A2
Somerton TA11 211 B3
Street BA16 207 A5
BLACKWATER 182 C2
Blackwater La
Axminster EX13 198 F3
Wiveliscombe TA4 210 A8
BLACKWELL 165 B5
Blackwell Rd BA22 174 F3
Blackworthy Rd BA7 159 C3
Bladen Cl BS20 2 E4
Bladud Bldgs BA1 228 C3
BLAGDON 54 E2
Blagdon Cl BS24 48 F1
Blagdon Cres TA1 212 D1
Blagdon Cross TA24 129 D2
BLAGDON HILL 181 D5
Blagdon La
Blagdon BS40 54 F6
Brompton Regis TA22, TA24 148 D4
Blagdon Pk BA2 44 A4
Blagdon Prim Sch BS40 54 F2
Blagdon Wlk BA11 120 D7
Blagrove Cl
Bristol BS13 22 C3
Street BA16 207 E6
Blagrove Cres BS13 22 C3
Blagrove Hill BA6 157 C6
Blagrove's Rd TA4 167 C4
Blaisdon BS22 49 D7
Blaise Wlk BS9 5 C6
Blake Cl 4 BA21 219 F8
Blake End BS22 31 E4
Blake Gn TA7 156 B7
Blake Ind Est TA6 209 A3
Blake Mus The★ TA6 209 A4
Blakeney Gr BS48 18 C8
Blake Pl TA6 209 A5
Blake Rd
5 Crewkerne TA18 224 C5
Wells BA5 203 C5
Blake's Cres TA9 104 E5
Blakes La TA5, TA6 208 C7
Blake's La BA3 115 D2
Blakes Rd TA6 208 D6
Blake St
2 Bridgwater TA6 208 F4
Taunton TA1 213 B4
Blakeway BS28 138 B6
Blandford Cl BS48 8 E1
Blandford Rd BA4 205 D3
BLATCHBRIDGE 143 F8
Blaxhold La TA5 152 E5
Bleachfield Rise 13 EX13 198 A1
BLEADNEY 139 A8
BLEADON 67 C7
Bleadon Hill BS23, BS24 67 A8
Bleadon Mill BS24 67 C5
Bleadon Rd BS24 67 B7
Bleak St BA9 161 E2
Blencathara Ct TA8 104 A8
Blenheim Cl
Peasedown St John BA2 79 D7
Blenheim Cl *continued*
Weston-super-Mare BS22 32 A2
Blenheim Ct 10 BS1 227 A4
Blenheim Gdns BA1 28 A2
Blenheim Mews TA24 200 F7
Blenheim Rd
Bridgwater TA6 209 D7
Minehead TA24 201 A7
Street BA16 207 B4
Taunton TA1 213 D5
Yeovil BA21 219 D7
Blenheim View TA24 201 A7
Blenheim Way BS20 2 E5
Blew Cl BS29 50 C7
Blights Hill EX16, TA22 163 F3
Blindhouse La 7 BA11 119 F4
Blind La
Barton St David TA11 158 A2
Bath BA1 27 C2
Buckland St Mary TA20 182 A1
Chard TA20 223 D2
Chew Stoke BS40 56 E8
Congresbury BS49 34 F6
Drimpton DT8 199 F6
Isle Abbotts TA3 183 F8
Keinton Mandeville TA11 158 B1
Martock TA12 185 D5
Southwick BA14 83 F2
Thorncombe TA20 199 B6
Tunley BA2 61 A4
Yatton BS49 34 F7
Blindwell La
Golsoncott TA23, TA24 131 C1
Skilgate TA4 164 E6
BLOOMFIELD
Bath 44 E3
Timsbury 60 B4
Bloomfield BS24 49 A2
Bloomfield Ave
Bath BA2 44 E4
Timsbury BA2 60 B3
Bloomfield Cl
Taunton TA1 213 C5
Timsbury BA2 60 B3
Bloomfield Cotts BA2 79 C7
Bloomfield Cres BA2 44 D2
Bloomfield Dr BA2 44 D2
Bloomfield Gr BA2 44 E3
Bloomfield La BS39 77 E5
Bloomfield Park Rd BA2 60 B3
Bloomfield Pk BA2 44 E3
Bloomfield Rd
Bath BA2 44 E3
Timsbury BA2 60 B3
Bloomfield Rise BA2 44 D2
Bloomfield Rise N BA2 44 D2
Bloomfield Terr BA2 79 C7
Bloom Row TA6 209 D5
Blossom Cl TA6 209 C5
BLUE ANCHOR 131 B6
Blue Anchor Chalets TA24 131 C6
Blue Anchor Railway Mus★ TA24 131 C6
Blue Anchor Sta TA24 131 C6
Blue Ball Cl BA10 215 E6
Bluebell Cl
Bristol BS9 5 B6
Taunton TA1 213 C1
Bluebell Dr
Bridgwater TA6 208 E1
Keynsham BS31 24 D3
Bluebell Rd
Frome BA11 120 B3
Weston-super-Mare BS22 32 A6
Yeovil BA22 218 B5
Bluebell Rise BA3 77 F3
Blueberry Way BS22 31 F1
Blue Gate TA24 145 D8
Blue Ho The BA11 119 F5
Blue Reef Aquarium★ BS1 226 C2
Blue Sch The BA5 203 C5
Blue Stone La TA13 185 B6
Bluett Rd TA21 222 D4
Blue Water Dr BS24 50 D3
Blundells La TA2 169 C7
Blythe Ct TA1 212 D1
Blythe Gdns BS22 32 A3
Blythe Way TA8 85 A3
BMI Bath Clinic Private Hospl BA2 45 D2
Board Cross BA4 205 B6
Boards La BA5 204 C7
Boards Rd TA6 209 A6
Boardwalk The BA16 207 D7
Boarpath La TA4 151 A5
Boat La BS24 67 C3
Boat Stall La BA2 228 C2
Bobbin La BA15 64 F4
Bobbin Pk BA15 64 F3
BODDEN 205 F7
Bodden La BA4 205 E6
Boden St TA20 223 C3
Boden Villas TA20 223 C3
Bodley Way BS24 49 E7
Bodmin Rd TA2 213 A8
Bodmin Wlk BS4 22 F8
Boez La TA2 153 D1
Bofors Pk BA22 218 A6
Bofors Twr BS23 49 B4
BOLHAM WATER 191 B7
Bollams Mead TA4 210 C5
Bollnas Cl BA4 205 C4
Bolster La BA6 157 C4

Bolter's La
  Alhampton BA4, BA7 159 B4
  Shepton Mallet BA4 141 D8
Bolton Cl TA9 104 F4
Bomers Bridge Rd
  Charlton Horethorne DT9 176 A1
  Milborne Wick DT9 189 A8
Bommertown Cross EX36 162 A4
Bondfield Way TA20 223 B6
Bondip Hill BA22, TA11 173 D3
Bonds Cl TA20 223 D6
Bond's La SN14 13 E8
Bonds Pool TA10 172 A5
Bond's Row TA24 124 A3
Bond St
  Bridgwater TA6 208 F5
  Bristol BS1 227 B3
  Yeovil BA20 219 B4
  Yeovil, Houndstone BA22 218 B5
Bonfire Cl TA20 223 C2
Bonfire La TA11 173 E7
Bonham La BA12 161 F4
Bonhill La BS39 57 D5
Bonhill Rd BS39 57 D5
Boniface Wlk TA8 104 B6
Bonita Dr TA6 208 D5
Bonners Cswy EX13 198 A2
Bonners Dr EX13 198 A1
Bonners Glen EX13 198 A1
Bonners Leaze La TA20 194 D5
Bonnie's La 6 TA14 185 F4
Bonning's La TA19 184 D4
Bonniton La TA24 130 E5
Bonniton New Rd TA24 201 D1
Bonny Cross
  Clayhanger EX16 165 B1
  Morebath EX16 164 B3
Bonny La TA24 128 B2
Bonson Hill TA5 134 E3
Bonson Mill Farm Track
  TA5 134 E4
Bonson Rd TA5 134 E4
Bonsonwood La TA5 134 E4
Boobery EX16 178 D1
Book Cl BS39 77 D6
Boome La TA2 169 C7
Boons Orch TA3 169 C3
Boon Villas BS11 4 E7
Booth Way TA6 208 D5
Boozer Pit TA16 195 F8
Borden Gate EX16 178 B8
Bordesley Rd BS14 23 A3
Boreal Way 4 BS24 49 F7
Boreland La BA22 187 A8
Borgie Pl BS22 31 F3
Borleyton Wlk BS13 21 F4
Borough Mall The BS28 108 D4
Borough Post
  Helland TA3 170 A3
  North Curry TA3 170 B3
Borough The
  Montacute TA15 186 B3
  Wedmore BS28 108 D4
  3 Yeovil BA20 219 B4
Borver Gr BS13 22 B4
Bosanquet Flats TA24 200 F7
BOSSINGTON 124 B4
Bossington Dr TA2 213 B8
Bossington La TA24 124 B4
Bosun Wlk BA16 207 B6
Boswell Rd BA15 64 F3
Botham Cl BS22 32 A4
Bottreaux Mill Cross
  EX36 162 A5
Boucher's La TA4 165 E4
Boughton Rd BA6 206 D6
Boulevard BS23 48 E8
Boulevard The BS14 22 E5
Boulters Rd BS13 22 C4
Boundaries The BS24 67 B1
Boundary Ave
  Frome BA11 120 B5
  Yeovil BA22 218 B7
Boundary Cl
  Holcombe BA3 116 C8
  Midsomer Norton BA3 97 B7
  Weston-super-Mare BS23 48 E3
  Yeovil BA21 218 E7
Boundary Rd
  Weston-super-Mare BS24 50 A7
  Yeovil BA22 218 A5
Boundary Way
  Glastonbury BA6 206 C3
  Yeovil BA22 218 A7
Boundhay BA22 186 C2
Bounds La TA20 223 A1
Bourchier Cl 13 EX16 164 B1
Bourchier Dr 12 EX16 164 B1
Bourchier Gdns BS13 22 B3
Bourke Rd BA4 205 D3
BOURNE 54 B4
Bourne Gr TA1 213 D4
Bourne La
  Blagdon BS40 54 C4
  Burrington BS40 54 B4
Bournville Prim Sch BS23 48 F5
Bournville Rd BS23 48 F4
BOURTON
  Gillingham 161 F1
  Weston-super-Mare 32 E6
Bourtonbridge Dro BA5 139 F5
Bourton Combe BS48 19 F7
Bourton La
  Cross BS26 69 E3
  Weston-super-Mare BS22 32 D4
Bourton Mead
  Flax Bourton BS48 19 F8
  Long Ashton BS41 11 A1
Bourton Wlk BS13 22 A8
Bouverie Cl TA24 129 E1
Bouverie Rd TA6 208 D5
Bove Moor Cl BA16 207 E6
Bove Moor Rd BA16 207 E6
Bovet Cl TA1 212 B1
Bove Town BA6 206 E5
Bovet St TA21 222 C6
Bowbridge La TA9 106 A1
Bow Cotts BS20 4 C4
BOWDEN 177 F2
Bowden Cl BS9 5 C8
Bowden Hill BA3 96 D4
Bowden La
  Milborne Port BA8 217 F5
  Rodhuish TA24 130 F3
  Yenston BA8 189 D7
Bowden Rd BA8 189 D8
Bowdens La EX16 164 E3
Bowden's La TA10 171 F7
Bowden Way BS8 10 B3
Bowditch Cl BA4 205 A5
Bowditch Row 8 TA18 224 C6
Bowen Rd BS24 50 C5
BOWER ASHTON 11 E4
Bower Ashton Terr BS3 11 F4
Bower Ave TA6 209 C6
Bower Fields TA6 209 D6
Bowerhayes La TA24 131 A5
BOWER HINTON 185 D5
Bower Hinton TA12 185 D5
Bowerings Rd TA6 208 E2
Bower La TA6 209 E6
Bowerleaze BS9 5 C5
Bower Manor Sh Ctr TA6 209 D6
Bowermead La BA4 204 C1
Bowery Cnr BA5 92 E5
Bowfell Cl TA1 212 C1
Bow Gate TA18 196 A8
Bowhayes TA18 224 C5
Bowhays Cross TA4 202 A2
Bowlditch La BA3 78 B4
Bowleaze BA21 218 D6
Bowline Cl TA6 208 E7
Bowline Ct TA24 201 B7
Bowling Gn
  10 Cannington TA5 135 B2
  Street BA16 207 D7
BOWLISH 205 A7
Bowlish Inf Sch
  Shepton Mallet BA4 205 A6
  Shepton Mallet BA4 205 A6
Bowlish La BA4 205 A6
Bowmead Dro TA10 172 D3
Bowmont Gr TA1 213 D3
Bowns Cl BA4 141 E1
Bowood Rd TA2 213 A6
Bowring Cl
  Bristol BS13 22 C3
  Coxley BA5 139 E6
Bowsprit Cl TA24 201 B7
Bow St TA10 171 F5
Bowyers Cl BA6 206 E5
Boxbury Hill BS39 77 F3
Boxbush Hill BA4 158 E8
Box Bush La BS24 33 C1
Boxhill La TA11 173 E8
Box Rd BA1 29 C3
Boxstone Hill TA19 184 D2
Box Wlk BS31 24 C4
Boyce Cl BA2 43 F5
Boyce's Ave BS8 226 A3
Boyd Ho BA5 113 A1
Boyd Rd BS31 25 D3
Boyle Cl DT10 190 B4
Boyton Hill TA19 194 F8
Boyton La TA19 194 F7
Bracey Rd TA12 185 E7
Bracken Edge TA4 132 E4
Bracken Way TA20 223 F5
Brackenwood Gdns* BS20 1 F5
Brackenwood Rd BS21 6 E6
Bracton Dr BS14 23 A5
Bradbeers TA3 181 D8
Bradfield Cl
  Bridgwater TA6 208 E1
  Wells BA5 203 C2
Bradfield Way TA20 223 C3
BRADFORD ABBAS 187 E1
Bradford Cl
  Clevedon BS21 6 C1
  Taunton TA1 168 D1
Bradford Hollow BA21 219 E4
BRADFORD ON TONE 167 F1
Bradford Pk BA2 45 A2
Bradford Rd
  Bath BA2 45 A1
  Bathford BA1 29 B2
  Misterton TA18 224 E4
  Rode BA11, BA14 83 A2
  Sherborne DT9 225 B3
  Wingfield BA14, BA15 83 C8
  Winsley BA15 64 D6
  Winsley BA15 64 E7
Bradley Ave BS11 4 E6
Bradley Cl TA11 211 C4
Bradley Cres BS11 4 E6
Bradley Cross La BS27 90 D7
BRADLEY GREEN 135 B1
Bradley Hill La TA11 211 B5
Bradley La
  Ashcott TA7 156 B7
  Maiden Bradley BA11, BA12 144 B2
  Parbrook BA6 158 C7
Bradley Rd BS20 3 E5
Bradleys TA19 183 F4
Bradley Stream Rd BA16,
  TA7 138 C1
Bradley View TA11 211 C4
Bradley Way BA6 158 B8
BRADNEY 136 D1
Bradney La TA7 136 D1
Bradon La
  Isle Abbotts TA3 183 F6
  Stocklinch TA19 184 A5
Bradville Gdns BS41 20 F8
Brae Rd BS25 70 B8
Brae Rise BS25 70 A8
Bragg's La BS2 227 C3
Braikenridge Cl BS21 6 C1
Brain's Cnr BA9 216 E1
Brainsfield BS9 5 F6
Brains La BA22 175 A5
Braithwaite Pl TA8 85 A2
Braithwaite Way BA11 120 C6
Brakewell Gdns BS14 23 A4
Bramble Dr
  Berrow TA8 84 F5
  Bristol BS9 5 D3
  South Petherton TA13 220 C4
Bramble Hill BA16 156 D6
Bramble La
  Bristol BS9 5 C3
  Haselbury Plucknett TA18 196 C5
Bramble Pk TA1 213 C2
Bramble Rd TA6 208 D1
Brambles Rd TA8 85 B1
Brambles The
  Bristol BS13 22 C4
  Hinton Charterhouse BA2 63 E1
  Keynsham BS31 24 D3
  Wellington TA21 222 D4
  Weston-super-Mare BS22 32 D2
Bramble Way BA2 45 B1
Bramblewood BS49 17 B1
Bramblewood Rd BS22 31 E3
Bramley Cl
  Charlton Horethorne DT9 176 A2
  Crewkerne TA18 224 C7
  Locking BS24 50 A5
  Peasedown St John BA2 79 D7
  Pill BS20 4 C4
  Sandford BS25 52 A4
  Wellington TA21 222 F7
  Yatton BS49 34 B7
Bramley Copse BS41 20 E8
Bramley Dr
  Backwell BS48 19 A5
  Frome BA11 120 C6
Bramley Fields TA14 185 E3
Bramley Rd
  Street BA16 207 B4
  Taunton TA1 213 D5
Bramley Sq BS49 34 E3
Bramleys The
  Nailsea BS48 18 B8
  Portishead BS20 2 F5
Brampton Ho BS20 2 E4
Brampton Way BS20 2 E4
Bramshill Dr BS22 31 F3
BRAMWELL 172 B8
Branche Gr BS13 22 D3
Branches Cross BS40 35 E3
Branch Farm La BA11 118 A7
Branch Rd BA2 63 F2
BRANDISH STREET 124 C3
BRANDON HILL 226 B2
Brandon Ho BS8 226 B2
Brandon St BS1 226 C2
Brandon Steep BS1 226 C2
Brandown Cl BS39 58 E1
Brangay La BS27 91 A1
Brangwyn Sq BS22 31 F2
Branksome Ave TA6 209 B5
Bransby Way BS24 50 A8
Branscombe Rd BS9 5 C4
Branscombe Wlk BS20 1 F3
Bransford BA22 197 D3
Brantwood Rd TA6 208 C5
BRASSKNOCKER 45 F2
Brassknocker Hill BA2 45 F2
Brassmill Ent Ctr BA1 44 A7
Brassmill La BA1 44 A7
Brassmill Lane Trad Est
  BA1 44 A7
BRATTON 200 B7
Bratton Cl TA24 200 D7
Bratton Ho BA9 176 B8
Bratton La TA24 200 B7
Bratton Mill La
  Minehead, Bratton TA24 200 B7
  Minehead, Woodcombe
  TA24 200 C7
Bratton Rd BS4 22 D7
BRATTON SEYMOUR 176 C8
Bratton Seymour Rd BA9 160 B1
Bray Cl EX16 179 B3
Brays Batch BA3 94 F6
Braysbridge BS27 90 C7
Braysdown Cl BA2 79 B6
Braysdown La BA2 79 C7
BREACH 58 F6
Breach Cl SP8 161 F1
Breaches The BS20 4 B5
Breach Furlong La TA10 156 A1
Breach Hill TA21 179 F5
Breach Hill Comm BS40 56 A5
Breach Hill La BS40 56 C6
Breach La
  Brinscombe BS26 89 B3
  Corsley Heath BA12 144 E7
  Kington Magna SP8 177 E2
  Nailsea BS48 17 F7
Breach La *continued*
  Weston Town BA4 142 E4
Breachwood View BA2 44 C2
Bread And Cheese La
  Seavington St Mary TA19 184 C1
  Seavington St Mary TA19 184 C1
Bread St BA4 140 F3
BREAN 65 F5
Brean Court Ho TA8 65 F3
Brean Ct TA8 65 F3
Brean Down Ave BS23 48 E4
Brean Down Rd TA8 47 F1
Brean Leisure Pk* TA8 65 F1
Brean Rd BS24 66 F1
Brecon View BS24 49 A1
Breech Cotts TA21 179 F5
Breech La BA6 158 A8
Bree Cl BS22 32 A4
Bremis Rd TA24 201 E3
BRENDON 122 A4
Brendon Ave BS23 48 F8
Brendon Cl TA23 131 D2
Brendon Gdns 2 BS48 8 E1
Brendon Ho BA21 219 A6
Brendon Rd
  Bridgwater TA6 208 F6
  Portishead BS20 2 A5
  Watchet TA23 202 B6
  Wellington TA21 222 D7
Brendons TA4 167 E8
Brendons The EX16 178 D1
Brendon Two Gates TA24 127 A6
Brendon View TA4 151 B7
Brendon Way
  Bridgwater TA6 208 F6
  Cheddar BS27 90 C8
Brennan Cl BS4 22 F7
Brent Broad
  Burnham-on-S TA8 85 B2
  Burnham-on-Sea TA8 85 C1
Brent Cl
  Brent Knoll TA9 86 B1
  Weston-super-Mare BS24 49 B2
BRENT KNOLL 86 A1
Brent Knoll CE Prim Sch
  TA9 86 A2
Brent Rd
  Burnham-on-S TA8, TA9 85 B4
  Cossington TA7 136 F3
  East Brent TA9 86 C5
Brentsfield La TA7 154 E7
Brent St TA9 86 A2
Breowen Cl TA19 221 B3
Brereton Rd TA24 201 B6
Breton Cl 1 TA6 209 A1
Bretoneux Rd BA6 206 E3
Brett Cl TA4 202 F1
Brettingham Ct TA17 195 C7
Brewery Bglws TA18 224 C7
Brewery Hill BS30 25 F7
Brewery La
  Holcombe BA3 97 D1
  Ilminster TA19 221 B4
  Oakhill BA3 115 A3
  Shepton Mallet BA4 205 D5
Brewham Rd BA10 160 D6
Brewhouse The BS1 227 B2
Brewhouse Theatre & Arts
  Ctr* TA1 212 F4
Breynton Rd BA6 206 F5
Brian Mooney Cl TA20 223 B3
Briant Cl TA1 212 B1
Briar Cl
  Burnham-on-S TA8 104 C6
  Frome BA11 120 B7
  Nailsea BS48 9 A2
  Radstock BA3 97 D8
  Yeovil BA21 219 E8
Briar Ct
  Bridgwater TA6 208 E5
  Burnham-on-S TA8 104 C6
  Pill BS20 4 C4
Briarfield BA22 173 E2
Briar Mead BS49 17 A1
Briar Rd
  Hutton BS24 49 E3
  Street BA16 207 A5
Briars Ct BA2 44 A4
Briars The
  Backwell BS48 18 F7
  Yeovil BA20 218 C2
Briarwood BS9 5 F6
Briary Rd BS20 2 C5
Brick Cotts BA3 117 A7
Brick Hill BA10 215 C6
Brickhouse Farm La BA9 161 B2
Brickkiln La DT9 225 E7
Brick St BS2 227 C3
Brickwall La TA10 171 D3
Brickworks Rd TA5 135 A2
Brickyard La
  Bourton SP8 161 F1
  Wanstrow BA4 142 F5
Brick Yard La TA18 224 C7
Briddicott La TA24 131 A4
Bridewell La
  Bath BA1 228 B2
  Hutton BS24, BS26, BS29 50 D1
  Shapwick TA7 137 F1
Bridewell St BS1 227 A3
BRIDGE 199 A8
Bridge Bldgs BS39 77 B3
Bridge Cl
  Evercreech BA4 141 E2
  Whitchurch BS14 23 C4
  Williton TA4 202 D2
Bridge Cotts
  Chard Junction TA20 198 D8
Bridge Cotts *continued*
  Drimpton DT8 199 F7
  East Chinnock BA22 196 F8
Bridge Farm Cl BS14 23 A3
Bridge Farm Inf Sch BS14 23 A4
Bridge Farm Jun Sch BS14 23 A4
Bridge Farm Prim Sch
  Whitchurch BS14 23 A4
  Whitchurch BS4 23 A4
Bridge Farm Sq BS49 34 D4
Bridge Gdns BA2 60 A6
BRIDGEHAMPTON 174 C3
Bridgehampton Rd BA22 174 C3
Bridge Hill BA4 142 F4
Bridge Ho
  11 Bath BA1 28 C1
  Bristol BS1 227 A2
  9 Clevedon BS21 6 C2
  Weston-super-Mare BS23 48 F6
Bridgehorne TA10 156 B3
Bridgehouse Cross EX15 180 D1
Bridge House Pk TA13 220 F4
Bridge Learning Campus
  BS13 22 D4
Bridge Pl DT9 187 F4
Bridge Place Rd BA2 78 E8
Bridge Rd
  Bath BA2 44 C5
  Bleadon BS24 67 B6
  Leigh Woods BS8 11 E6
  Weston-super-Mare BS23 48 F6
Bridge Rise 17 TA12 185 E6
Bridges Mead TA24 201 E3
Bridge St
  Bath BA2 228 C2
  Bourton SP8 161 F1
  Bristol BS1 227 A2
  Dulverton TA22 163 D6
  Frome BA11 119 F5
  Taunton TA1 212 F4
  Williton TA4 202 D2
Bridge Terr EX16 164 B1
Bridge The
  Frome BA11 119 F5
  Taunton TA1 212 F4
BRIDGETOWN 147 E4
Bridge Valley Rd BS8 11 E8
Bridge Way TA13 220 E4
Bridgeway Cotts TA13 220 E4
Bridgewell Ct DT9 225 E3
BRIDGWATER 208 E3
Bridgwater TA6 208 F4
Bridgwater Bay National
  Nature Reserve* TA5 103 C2
Bridgwater Bldgs BA7 214 B5
Bridgwater Coll TA6 209 B5
Bridgwater Com Hospl
  TA6 209 D7
Bridgwater Ct BS24 49 A3
Bridgwater Ent Ctr 7
  TA6 208 F5
Bridgwater Rd
  Dundry BS41, BS13, BS48 21 D6
  East Brent TA9 86 D4
  Lympsham BS24 67 C5
  North Petherton TA6 153 F4
  Taunton TA1 213 D5
  Taunton, Bathpool TA2 213 F7
  Weston-super-Mare BS23,
  BS24 48 F2
  Winscombe BS25 70 A5
Bridgwater Ret Pk TA6 209 A5
Bridgwater Sta TA6 209 B4
Bridle Ave BS14 23 D3
Bridle Way BA22 197 F8
Bridleway The BS4 22 D8
Bridport Rd DT8 199 F8
Briercliffe Rd BS9 5 D7
Briery Leaze Rd BS14 23 A4
Brigadier Cl BA22 218 A5
Brigg Cl TA6 208 E7
Brighton Mews BS8 226 B4
Brighton Rd BS23 48 E6
Brighton St 7 BS2 227 B4
Brightstowe Rd TA8 85 A2
Brigstocke Rd BS2 227 B4
Brimble Cotts DT10 189 F1
Brimbleworth La BS22 32 C3
Brimclose Rd TA17 195 B7
Brimgrove La TA19 184 E4
Brimhill Rise BA13 121 D4
BRIMLEY 198 D3
Brimley Cross TA3 180 F1
Brimley Hill EX13 198 D2
Brimley La BA4 140 F2
Brimley Rd EX13 198 D3
Brimridge Rd BS25 70 A8
Brimsmore Ct BA21 218 E8
Brimstone La
  Rockwell Green TA21 222 A2
  Sampford Arundel TA21 179 F6
  Sampford Peverell EX16 178 E2
Brimzemore La TA16 195 E6
Brincil Hill TA11 173 D4
BRINDHAM 139 D3
Brindham La BA6 139 D3
Brindle Cl TA2 212 C7
Brines Orch BA8 176 E1
Brinkworth Rd BA2 45 B2
Brinmead Wlk BS13 21 F3
BRINSCOMBE 89 A5
Brinscombe La BS26 89 A5
BRINSEA 52 E8
Brinsea Batch BS49 52 E8
Brinsea Green Farm La
  BS49 52 F8
Brinsea La BS49 52 F8
Brinsea Rd BS49 34 E2

Brinsmead Cres BS20 4 D4
Briscoes Ave BS13 22 D4
BRISTOL 227 B3
Bristol Airport BS48 36 E7
Bristol and Exeter Mews
BS1 227 C1
Bristol Cathedral Sch
BS1 226 C2
Bristol Dental Hospl BS1 227 A3
Bristol Eye Hospl BS1 227 A3
Bristol Gate 1 BS8 11 F5
Bristol Gram Sch BS8 226 C3
Bristol Harbour Rly* BS1 226 C1
Bristol Hill BA5 112 E3
Bristol Mus & Art Gall*
BS8 226 C3
Bristol Rd
Bridgwater TA6 209 B7
Chew Stoke BS40 56 E8
Chewton Mendip BA5 113 A8
Churchill BS25 53 A5
Congresbury BS49 34 D5
Farrington Gurney BS39 76 F5
Highbridge TA9 104 F4
Horrington BA5 112 F6
Keynsham BS31 24 E6
Newton St Loe BA2 43 D7
Paulton BS39 77 E7
Pensford BS39 40 D6
Portishead BS20 2 E4
Radstock BA3 78 F3
Redhill BS40 37 A3
Rooks Bridge BS26, TA9 87 B5
Sherborne DT9 225 D5
Walpole TA6 136 B3
Weston-super-Mare BS22 32 C2
Whitchurch BS14 23 D3
Winscombe BS25 70 C8
Wraxall BS48 9 D4
Bristol Rd By-pass BS40 53 C5
Bristol Rd Lower BS23 30 F1
Bristol Road Lower BS23 30 E1
Bristol Royal Hospl for
Children BS2 227 A3
Bristol Royal Infirmary
BS2 227 A4
Bristol Temple Meads Sta
BS1 227 C1
Bristol View BA2 62 C8
Bristol Zoo Gdns* BS8 5 F1
Britannia Cl BA3 96 D4
Britannia Way
Chard TA20 223 C6
Clevedon BS21 6 C1
Briton St 2 EX16 164 C1
Brittains BA11 119 D6
Brittania Bldgs BS8 226 A1
Brittan Pl BS20 3 E3
BRITTENS 77 F6
Britten's Cl BS39 77 F6
Britten's Hill BS39 77 F6
Brittons Ash TA2 213 F8
Brittons Pass SN14 13 F8
Broadacre Dro TA10 156 C3
Broadacres BA22 197 C8
Broadbridge Rd TA3 183 C6
Broadbury Rd BS4 22 E8
Broad Cl
Kington Magna SP8 177 E1
Wells BA5 112 E1
Broadclose Way TA11 158 A2
Broadcroft BS40 38 F3
Broadcroft Ave BS49 17 F1
Broadcroft Cl BS49 17 F1
Broad Dro
Burrowbridge TA7 155 A2
North Wootton BA4 140 A3
Broadenham La TA20 194 E1
Broadfield Rd BS4 23 A8
Broadguage Bsns Pk TA4 167 E7
Broadhay BA5 110 E7
Broad Hill BA22 196 D7
Broadhurst Gdns TA8 104 B5
Broad La
East Chinnock BA22 196 E7
Hawkridge TA22 146 D1
North Curry TA3 170 D4
Winsford TA22 147 F4
Broadlands BS21 6 F3
Broadlands Ave
Keynsham BS31 24 D6
North Petherton TA6 153 F4
Broadlands Cl BA21 219 E8
Broadlands Ct TA1 212 E2
Broadlands Dr BS11 5 A8
Broadlands La TA5 208 A4
Broadlands Rd TA1 212 E2
Broadlands Rise TA1 212 E2
Broadlands Sch BS31 24 D6
Broadlands Way TA1 212 E2
Broad Lane Head
Hawkridge TA22 146 D1
Winsford TA22 147 F4
Broadlawn TA7 136 E4
Broadleas BS13 22 C7
Broadleaze
Bristol BS11 4 E7
Yeovil BA21 218 C6
Broadleaze Way BS25 51 F2
Broadly Gdns TA2 213 E8
Broadmead
Bristol BS1 227 B3
Keynsham BS31 25 B5
Kingsbury Episcopi TA12 185 B7
South Petherton TA13 220 B4
Broadmead Dro TA7 155 F6
Broadmead La
Barrington TA19 184 D6
Broadmead La *continued*
Catcott TA7 137 D2
Edington TA7 137 C3
Keynsham BS31 25 A6
Kington Magna SP8 177 D1
Norton Sub Hamdon TA14 185 F2
Broad Mead La BS40 38 A3
Broadmead Rd TA3 183 B7
Broadmeads TA10 172 A6
Broadmoor Dro BS28 89 D3
Broadmoor La
Bath BA1 27 A3
Horsington BA8 176 E2
Broadmoor Pk BA1 27 B2
Broadmoor Vale BA1 27 A3
Broadoak TA19 183 C1
Broad Oak 9 BA20 219 B4
Broadoak Hill BS41 21 F2
Broad Oak Hill TA4 151 B5
Broadoak Mathematics &
Computing Coll BS23 48 E3
Broadoak Rd
Bridgwater TA6 209 D5
Churchill BS40 53 A5
Weston-super-Mare BS23 48 D3
Broad Oak Rd BS13 21 F4
Broad Oaks BS8 11 E6
Broad Path EX15 179 A1
Broad Plain BS2 227 C2
Broad Quay
Bath BA1 228 C1
Bristol BS1 227 A2
Broad Rd
Blagdon BS40 72 D8
Rodney Stoke BA5 91 E1
Broadshard Rd TA18 224 C8
Broadslade BA12 144 C3
Broad St
Bath BA1 228 C3
Bristol BS1 227 A3
Charlton Adam TA11 173 F7
Churchinford TA3 191 D7
Congresbury BS49 34 D4
Somerton TA11 211 E4
Stoney Stratton BA4 141 F2
Wells BA5 203 D4
Wrington BS40 35 D2
Broadstone TA7 154 E6
Broadstone La
Hardington Mandeville
BA22 197 A6
Kingston Seymour BS21 15 F3
West Chinnock TA18 196 C7
Broad Stones BA15 46 E7
Broadstone Wlk BS13 22 D5
Broad Street Pl BA1 228 C3
BROADWAY 183 B2
Broadway
Bath BA2 45 B6
Bridgwater TA6 208 F4
Charlton Adam TA11 174 A7
Chilcompton BA3 96 C3
Chilton Polden TA7 137 B2
Frome BA11 119 D5
Locking BS24 50 D4
Merriott TA16 195 F7
Odcombe BA22 186 C2
Saltford BS31 25 D3
Shipham BS25 70 E8
Weston-super-Mare BS24 49 A2
Broad Way TA12 185 D5
Broadway Acres BS27 70 F1
Broadway Ave TA7 137 B2
Broadway Cl BA3 96 C3
Broadway Dro TA3 170 F4
Broadway Hill TA19 183 B1
Broadway La
Castle Cary BA22 214 B3
Midsomer Norton BA3 78 B5
Westbury-sub-Mendip BA5 110 D7
Broadway Rd
Bristol, Bishopsworth BS13 21 F5
Charlton Adam TA11 173 F7
Horton TA19 183 C2
Broadways Head EX14,
TA20 192 C6
Broadway St TA19 183 C2
Broad Weir BS1 227 B3
Broadwell Cl TA20 193 D6
Broadwood Rd TA24 130 D4
Brock Ct BA7 214 C6
Brock End BS20 1 F3
BROCKFIELD 198 A8
Brockhole La EX13, TA20 198 B7
Brockle Cl TA11 211 D4
BROCKLEY 18 C2
Brockley Cl
Nailsea BS48 8 D1
Weston-super-Mare BS24 48 F1
Brockley Combe Rd BS48 19 B1
Brockley Cres BS24 48 F1
Brockley La BS48 18 D4
Brockley Rd BS31 25 D3
Brockley Way BS49 18 B3
Brockley Wlk BS13 22 A8
Brocks La BS41 10 F1
Brocks Mount 16 TA14 185 F4
Brocks Rd BS13 22 C3
Brock St BA1 228 B3
Brockway BS48 8 F2
BROCKWELL 129 E6
Brockwell La TA24 129 F6
Brockwood BA15 64 F7
Brocole La TA20 193 D5
Broderip TA7 136 F3
BROKERSWOOD 102 F5
Brokerswood Country Pk*
BA13 102 F6
Bromes La TA3 183 F7
Bromley Rd BS39 39 F1
Brompton Ho BA2 228 C4
Brompton Mdws TA22 148 B2
BROMPTON RALPH 150 C3
Brompton Rd BS24 49 A2
BROMPTON REGIS 148 B2
Bronte Cl BS23 49 B4
Brook Bank
Draycott BS27 90 F2
Rodney Stoke BS27 109 C7
Brook Cl
Long Ashton BS41 11 B1
Minehead TA24 200 F7
North Petherton TA6 153 E3
Yeovil BA21 218 D7
Brook Cotts
Corfe TA3 181 F6
Corston BA2 43 B7
Brook Ct BS13 22 A6
Brookdale Rd BS13 22 B6
Brooke Rd
Berrow TA8 84 F4
Taunton TA1 213 B4
Brookes Ct BA5 203 C5
Brookfield Pk BA1 27 B2
Brookfields BA7 214 B5
Brookfield Way BA16 207 A4
Brookfield Wlk BS21 6 F3
Brook Gate BS3 11 E1
Brook Gdns BS40 53 A5
BROOKHAMPTON 175 D6
Brookhampton Cnr BA22 175 D6
Brooking Mdw BS48 8 D1
Brook La
Barton St David BA6 157 F3
6 Cannington TA5 135 B2
Catcott TA7 137 D2
7 Henstridge BA8 190 A6
Brookland Rd
Langport TA10 172 A6
Weston-super-Mare BS22 49 B7
Brooklands
Bridgwater TA6 209 C5
Dunkerton BA2 61 D3
Brooklands Rd TA21 222 B5
Brookland Way 3 BA8 190 A6
Brookleaze
Bristol BS9 5 C5
Keynsham BS31 24 D6
Brookleaze Bldgs BA1 28 B2
Brookleigh BA16 207 A5
Brooklyn BS40 35 D2
Brooklyn Rd
Bath BA1 28 C2
Bristol BS13 22 B8
Brooklyn Terr BA5 139 E6
Brook Rd
Bath BA2 44 D6
Williton TA4 202 E3
Brook's Hill EX15 179 C1
Brookside
Broadway TA19 183 C2
Milborne Port DT9 217 D1
Paulton BS39 77 E6
Pill BS20 4 D3
South Cheriton BA8 176 D3
West Coker BA22 197 A8
Brookside Acad BA16 207 B4
Brookside Cl
Batheaston BA1 28 F5
Paulton BS39 77 E6
Taunton TA3 168 D1
Brookside Dr BA2 59 F6
Brookside Ho BA1 27 B1
Brookside Rd TA5 135 B5
Brooks Pl TA21 222 E6
Brooks Rd BA16 207 B4
Brook St
Bampton EX16 164 B1
Cannington TA5 135 B2
Milborne Port DT9 217 D1
Minehead TA24 201 B5
North Newton TA7 153 F1
Timberscombe TA24 130 B5
Brook Street Mews TA24 201 B5
Brookview Wlk BS13 22 B7
Broomball Cross TA22 162 F5
Broomball La EX16 162 E5
Broomclose Cnr BA3 114 B4
Broome Cl EX13 198 A1
Broom Farm Cl BS48 18 E8
BROOMFIELD 152 E2
Broomfield Hall Rd TA5 152 F4
Broomfield Ho TA2 212 E7
Broomfield La TA20 182 D2
Broomfield Rd TA5 152 E2
Broomground BA15 64 E7
Broomhill La BS39 58 E3
Broom Hill La BS39 77 E8
Broom La
Chardstock EX13 198 C5
Oake TA4 167 D3
Brooms La TA19 183 B1
Broom's La TA3 191 F7
Broomstreet La TA24 122 F5
Broomyland Hill TA5 152 C7
Brottens Rd
Cranmore BA4 142 A5
Doulting BA4 141 F5
Brougham Hayes BA2 44 D6
Brougham Pl 2 BA1 28 C2
Broughton Cl
Taunton TA1 213 C2
Walton BA16 156 E7
Broughton Ho BS1 227 B1
Broughton La TA3 169 B1
Broughton Pk TA3 169 A1
Broughtons Dr TA18 224 E3
Brow Hill BA2 28 F4
Brown Down La TA20 192 C7
Browne Ct 4 BS8 11 F6
Browney La BA2 62 A5
BROWNHEATH 180 C2
Brownings Rd TA5 135 B2
Brown La TA4, TA23 149 C3
Brownlow Rd BS23 48 E4
Browns Ct BS23 48 E6
Brownsey La TA20 192 F5
Brown's Folly Nature
Reserve* BA15 29 D1
Browns La BS28 109 C1
Brown's Pl 4 BA5 203 C4
Brow The
Bath BA2 44 B5
Bath, Combe Down BA2 45 C1
Broxholme Wlk BS11 4 F8
Brue Ave
Bridgwater TA6 209 B3
Bruton BA10 215 F7
Brue Bsns Pk TA9 136 E8
Brue Cl
Bruton BA10 215 F7
Weston-super-Mare BS23 49 A5
Brue Cres TA8 104 B5
Brue Ho TA8 85 A1
Bruelands BA10 215 F7
Brue Way TA9 104 F3
Bruford Cl TA1 212 E3
Bruford Dr TA2 213 C8
Brummel Way BS39 77 C6
Brunel Cl
Somerton TA11 211 D4
Weston-super-Mare BS24 48 F1
Brunel Ct
Bridgwater TA6 208 F6
Portishead BS20 2 D6
Brunel Ho BA2 44 A6
Brunel Institute The*
BS3 226 B1
Brunel Lock Rd BS1 11 F5
Brunel Prec TA11 211 D4
Brunel Rd
Bristol BS13 22 A8
Nailsea BS48 8 B1
Brunel's SS Great Britain &
The Matthew* BS1 226 B1
Brunel's Way TA9 104 E5
Brunel Way
Bristol BS1, BS3 11 F4
Frome BA11 120 C7
Minehead TA24 201 B6
Taunton TA2 212 A6
Brunsell's Knap DT10 190 A1
Brunswick Pl
1 Bath BA1 228 B3
10 Bristol BS1 11 F5
Brunswick Sq BS2 227 B4
Brunswick St
1 Bath BA1 28 B1
Bristol BS2 227 B4
Yeovil BA20 219 A4
BRUSHFORD 163 D4
Brushford New Rd TA22 163 E4
Brutasche Terr BA16 207 D7
BRUTON 215 E5
Bruton BS24 49 A2
Bruton Ave
Bath BA2 44 F4
Portishead BS20 2 A5
Bruton Avenue Garages
BA2 44 F4
Bruton Cl BS48 18 E8
Bruton La BA4 142 F2
Bruton Mus* BA10 215 E6
Bruton Pl BS8 226 B3
Bruton Prim Sch BA10 215 E6
Bruton Rd BA4 141 F1
Bruton Sch for Girls BA10 215 C3
Bruton Sta BA10 215 F6
Brutton Way TA20 223 B3
Bryant Ave BA3 78 D1
Bryant Gdns BS21 6 C1
Bryant's Hill TA22 148 C2
Bryer Cl
Bridgwater TA6 208 E1
Chard TA20 223 D3
Brymore Cl TA6 208 D5
Brymore Sch TA5 135 A2
Brympton Ave BA22 186 D2
BRYMPTON D'EVERCY 218 A3
Brympton Way BA20 218 C3
Bsns Courtyard The BA11 143 C7
Bubwith Cl TA20 223 D3
Bubwith Ho 4 BA5 203 D4
Bubwith Rd TA20 223 D3
Bubwith Wlk BA5 203 B3
Buces Rd TA1 212 B1
Buck Cl BA6 206 C3
Buckhill TA24 131 B4
Buckhill Cl TA18 224 C4
BUCKHORN WESTON 177 D3
Buckingham Cl TA6 209 A2
Buckingham Pl BS8 226 A3
Buckingham Rd BS24 49 B2
Buckingham Vale BS8 226 A4
Buckland Cl TA8 104 C8
BUCKLAND DINHAM 100 A3
BUCKLAND DOWN 99 B4
Buckland Gn BS22 32 A5
Buckland La BA22 175 C3
Buckland Rd
Shepton Mallet BA4 205 A5
Taunton TA2 213 B8
Yeovil BA21 219 E6
BUCKLAND ST MARY 192 F8
Buckland St Mary CE Prim
Sch TA20 193 A8
Bucklands Batch BS48 18 F8
Buckland Sch TA23 202 C6
Bucklands Dr BS48 19 A8
Bucklands End BS48 18 F8
Bucklands Gr BS48 18 F8
Bucklands La BS48 18 F8
Bucklands View BS48 19 A8
Buckle Path BS24 50 C8
Buckle Pl BA22 218 B6
Buckler's Mead Acad
BA21 219 C8
Bucklers Mead Rd BA21 219 D8
Bucklers Mead Wlk BA21 219 D8
Bucklers Way BA4 204 F6
Bucklewell Cl BS11 4 F6
Buckshots Cross EX14 192 D4
Buckwell TA21 222 E6
Bude Cl BS48 9 B1
Budge La BA11 144 A8
Budgetts TA21 180 F6
Budgett's Cross TA21 180 F6
Bughole La TA21 179 E8
Bugle Cottage Rd
Barrow Hill DT9 217 C7
Milborne Wick DT9 189 B8
Bugle Ct 11 BA8 190 A6
Bugle Farm La
Barrow Hill DT9 217 D7
Milborne Wick DT9 189 B8
Bugle Wlk TA6 208 D1
Building of Bath Mus*
BA1 228 C3
BULFORD 182 C4
Bulford TA21 222 D5
Bulford La TA21 222 D5
Bull Bridge La TA13 185 B1
Bull Bridge Mead BA22 197 D3
Bullen Mead BA11 117 F2
Bullens Cl TA19 183 F4
Buller Ave BA22 218 A6
Buller Rd BS29 50 C7
Bull Horn Dro TA7 154 D5
Bull La BS20 4 C4
Bull Mdw TA4 167 F7
Bullmead Cl BA16 207 B5
Bullmead La BA11 143 C7
Bullock Field Hill TA21 166 B2
Bullocks La BS21 16 C4
Bullon Drove TA5 134 B7
Bull Plot Hill BA6 158 C8
Bullrush Cl BA11 120 A3
BULL'S GREEN 117 E1
Bulls Green Link Rd BA11 117 E1
Bull's Hill BA2 62 E1
Bulls La TA18 224 B6
Bull's La
Tatworth TA20 198 C8
Upton Noble BA4 142 F2
Bull's Quarr BA11 143 E8
Bull's Quarries Rd BA11 143 F7
Bull St TA3 169 D4
Bulwarks La BA6 206 F4
Bumblebee Cl BS13 21 E4
Bumper's Batch BA2 63 A8
Bunce's La TA19 184 E3
Buncombe Hill TA5 152 C3
Bune Villas TA6 208 E7
Bunford Hollow
Yeovil BA20 218 C2
Yeovil, Preston Plucknett
BA20 218 D5
Bunford Hollow Rdbt
BA20 218 D1
Bunford La BA20, BA21 218 C4
Bungalows The
Axbridge BS26 70 C2
Chard TA20 223 D5
Monkton Heathfield TA2 213 F8
Nether Stowey TA5 134 A2
Poyntington DT9 188 E7
Bungay's Hill BA2, BS39 59 E1
Bunker Military Mus The*
TA9 104 D3
Bunns La
Horningsham BA11 144 A5
Witham Friary BA11 143 F5
Bunny Burrow's Track
TA22 164 A8
Bunting Ct BS22 31 E1
Bunting La BS20 3 A6
Burchill Cl BS39 58 F3
Burchills Cl TA21 222 A6
Burchill's Hill TA21 222 B7
Burch's Cl TA1 212 C2
BURCOTT 139 E8
Burcott La
Coxley BA5 139 E7
Wells BA5 203 A3
Burcott Mill* BA5 139 E8
Burcott Rd BA5 203 B3
Burdenham Dro TA7 155 A6
Burdock Rd BA11 120 B3
Burfitt Rd BA7 214 A6
Burfoote Gdns BS14 23 E4
Burfoot Rd BS14 23 E4
BURFORD 204 C2
Burford Cl
Bath BA2 44 B3
Portishead BS20 2 E4
Burford Cross BA4 204 C2
Burford Gr BS11 4 F5
Burgage TA21 222 D6
Burgage La TA4 167 A4

Burgage Rd TA5 134 C6
Burge Cres TA4 167 E6
Burge Mdw TA4 167 E6
Burges Cl
 Marnhull DT10 190 F6
 Wiveliscombe TA4 210 C5
Burge's Hill BA3 116 B1
Burges La TA4 210 C5
Burge's La BA3 116 B1
Burgess Cl TA1 212 B1
Burgess La BA6 157 F6
Burgis Rd BS14 23 D6
Burgundy Rd TA24 201 A8
BURLANDS 168 C6
Burledge Comm BS39 57 B1
Burledge La BS39 57 D1
Burleigh Gdns BA1 44 A8
Burleigh La BA16 207 C4
BURLESCOMBE 179 B3
Burlescombe CE Prim Sch
 EX16 179 B3
Burley Gdns BA16 207 D4
Burlingham's La BA22 186 C8
Burlington Ct BS20 2 E6
Burlington Rd
 Midsomer Norton BA3 78 C2
 Portishead BS20 2 E7
Burlington St
 Bath BA1 228 B4
 15 Weston-super-Mare BS23 48 E8
Burnbush Cl BS14 23 E6
Burnbush Prim Sch BS14 23 D5
Burnell Dr BS2 227 C4
Burnell Ho 8 BA4 205 B6
BURNETT 42 B7
Burnett Bsns Pk BS31 25 B1
Burnett Cl TA8 104 C7
Burnett Hill BS31 42 B8
Burnett Ind Est BS40 35 E1
Burnett's La BA6 158 A6
Burnham Cl BS24 48 F1
Burnham Dr BS24 48 F1
Burnham Link Rd TA8 104 E7
Burnham Moor La TA9 105 B5
BURNHAM-ON-SEA 104 D8
Burnham-on-Sea Inf Sch
 TA8 104 C8
Burnham Rd
 Bath BA2 44 C6
 Bristol BS11 4 D6
 Highbridge TA9 104 D4
Burn Hill TA4, TA21 166 F3
Burnshill Dr TA2 212 A7
Burns Rd TA1 213 C4
Burnt Hill La BA11 100 A3
Burnt House Cotts BA2 62 C8
Burnthouse Dro BA5 141 B8
Burnt House La BA3 116 C2
Burnt House Rd BA2 62 D8
Burrell La BA7 158 F1
Burrells BA22 197 B8
Burridge Cl BA5 139 E6
Burridge Cross TA20 193 E1
BURRINGTON 53 F3
Burrington Ave BS24 48 F1
Burrington CE Prim Sch
 BS40 53 F3
Burrington Cl
 Nailsea BS48 8 E1
 Weston-super-Mare BS24 48 F1
Burrington Combe BS40 72 C8
Burrington Coombe*
 BS40 54 A1
Burrington La
 Burrington BS40 54 A3
 Burrington BS40 54 A3
Burrington Rd
 Townsend BS40 92 F8
 Ubley Sideling BS40 73 D2
 West End BS40 93 A7
Burrington Wlk BS13 22 A8
Burroughes Ave BA21 218 E6
Burrough St TA12 185 F7
Burrough Way TA21 222 D4
BURROW 184 F6
BURROWBRIDGE 154 F1
Burrowbridge CE Sch
 TA7 154 F1
Burrow Dro
 Burrowbridge TA7 154 F1
 Hambridge TA12 184 F8
Burrowfield BA10 215 F7
Burrowfield Cl BA10 215 F7
Burrow Hill Dro TA7 155 A1
Burrow La
 Ashbrittle TA21 178 D8
 High Ham TA10 156 A1
Burrow Mump* TA7 154 F1
Burrow Rocks TA4 202 B1
Burrows La BA3 97 B1
Burrows The BS22 32 D3
Burrow Wall TA7 155 A1
Burrow Way
 Hambridge TA12 184 F7
 Kingsbury Episcopi TA12 185 A7
Burstock La DT8 199 F7
Burston La EX16 164 A4
BURTLE 137 D6
Burtle Rd
 Burtle TA7 137 D6
 East Huntspill TA9 136 E7
 Westhay BA6 138 A5
BURTON
 Stogursey 134 B7
 Yeovil 197 C8
Burton Barton BA22 197 C8
Burton Cl BS1 227 B1
Burton Ct BS8 226 B3
Burtonhayes DT10 190 F6
Burton La BA22 197 C8
Burton Mead Dro TA10 171 B1
Burton Pl TA1 212 E3
Burton Row TA9 86 A5
Burton St
 5 Bath BA1 228 B2
 Marnhull DT10 190 F6
Burt's Hill BA4 142 F3
Burwalls Rd BS8 11 E6
BURY 164 A6
Burying Hole La BA22 186 A1
Bury Rd TA22 164 A6
Bury The BS24 50 A3
Bury View BA2 42 C5
BUSCOTT 138 C1
Buscott La TA7 138 B1
BUSHEY NORWOOD 45 F6
Bushfield Rd TA18 224 B4
Bushfurlong Rd TA3 184 B8
Bush La
 Pilton BA4 140 F3
 Spaxton TA5 152 E6
Bush Pl TA10 172 A5
Bush Rd TA5 152 D7
Bushs Orch TA19 221 A4
Bushy Combe BA3 77 F3
Bushy Coombe Gdns BA6 206 F5
Bushy Cross La TA3 169 C3
Bushy Thorn Rd BS40 56 E8
Business Pk The BS13 22 E3
Bussell's Moor Cross
 EX36 162 C4
BUSSEX 154 F6
Bussex Sq TA7 154 F6
Butcher's Hill TA3 170 F2
Butchers La
 Castle Cary BA7 159 C3
 Shapwick TA7 155 F8
Butcher's La TA5 134 A2
BUTCOMBE 55 B8
Butcombe BS24 49 A2
Butcombe La BS40 55 B7
Butcombe Wlk BS14 23 B5
Butham La
 Chew Magna BS40 39 A4
 Chew Magna BS40 39 B3
Butlass Cl BS39 59 D1
BUTLEIGH 157 D4
Butleigh CE Prim Sch
 Butleigh BA6 157 E4
 Butleigh BA6 157 E4
Butleigh Cl TA6 209 D4
Butleigh Cross BA6 157 E3
Butleigh Dro
 Ashcott TA7, BA16 156 C5
 Walton BA16 156 D6
Butleigh Old Rd BA6 206 E3
Butleigh Rd
 Glastonbury BA6 206 E3
 Street BA16 207 E5
BUTLEIGH WOTTON 157 C5
Butler's Gdns BA11 120 A4
Butt Cl BA6 206 E5
Buttercliffe Rise BS41 11 C3
Buttercup Cl
 Frome BA11 120 B3
 Somerton TA11 211 B3
Buttercup La
 Street BA16 207 D6
 Street BA16 207 D6
Butterfield Pk BS21 6 C1
Buttermere Rd BS23 49 A5
Butterworth Ct BS4 22 D7
Buttice La BA5 111 B1
Butt La TA10 171 D4
Butt Lake Rd TA9 106 B3
Buttle Cl TA19 184 E4
Buttle La TA19 184 E3
Buttle's Cross TA3 191 F7
Buttle's La TA3 191 E6
Button Cl BS14 23 A6
Button St BA11 119 D5
Butts TA19 221 C4
Butts Batch BS26 69 B3
BUTT'S BATCH 35 D1
Butt's Batch BS40 35 D1
Butts Castle TA19 221 C4
Butts Cl
 Marnhull DT10 190 F5
 Williton TA4 202 D4
Butts Cnr TA6 153 F4
Butts Hill BA11 119 E3
Butts La
 Ilton TA19 183 D3
 Kilmington BA12 161 F7
 Langford Budville TA21 166 F2
 Rodney Stoke BS27 91 A1
Butts Orch BS40 35 D1
Butts Quarry La TA18 224 E6
BUTTS THE 119 E3
Butts The BA11 119 E3
Butts Way TA4 166 F4
Buxtons Cl 5 BA5 139 D8
Byfield BA2 45 B1
Byfield Pl BA2 45 B1
Byfields BS21 16 C8
Byme Rd TA14 185 E1
Byron Cl BS24 50 A4
Byron Ct BS23 48 F8
Byron Pl BS8 226 B3
Byron Rd
 Bath BA2 44 F4
 Locking BS24 50 A4
 Taunton TA1 213 C3
Byron Rd *continued*
 Weston-super-Mare BS23 49 A4
Byways Cvn Pk BS21 6 C1
Byzantine Ct BS1 227 A1

C

Cabbage La BA8 176 C3
Cabell Ct BA11 119 D2
Cabell Rd BA11 119 E2
Cabot Circus Sh Ctr BS1 227 B3
Cabot Cl BS31 25 D2
Cabot Gate BS2 227 C4
Cabot Prim Sch BS2 227 C4
Cabot Rd BA21 219 F8
Cabot Rise BS20 2 A5
Cabot Twr* BS8 226 B2
Cabot Way
 Bristol BS8 11 F5
 Pill BS20 4 D3
 Weston-super-Mare BS22 32 A3
Cabstand BS20 2 D6
Cadbury Bsns Pk BA22 175 B6
Cadbury Camp La BS20 8 D6
Cadbury Camp La W BS21 7 C5
Cadbury Castle* BA22 175 C4
Cadbury Cl TA8 85 C1
Cadbury Farm Rd BS49 34 C7
Cadbury Halt BS20 1 F1
Cadbury Ho BS20 2 E4
Cadbury La BS20 1 F1
Cadbury Rd
 Keynsham BS31 25 A2
 Portishead BS20 2 E4
Cadbury Sq BS49 34 E3
Cadby Ho BA2 44 A6
Cades Gdns TA21 222 E7
Cadeside Cvn Site TA21 222 F7
Cades Mead TA21 222 F7
Cadet Dr BS24 49 B4
CAD GREEN 183 E3
Cadogan Rd BS14 23 A8
Cad Rd
 Ilminster TA19 221 A8
 Ilton TA19 183 E3
Cadwell's Dv TA9 136 A8
Cadwell's La TA9 136 A8
Caernarvon Cl BS31 24 C5
Caernarvon Rd BS31 24 C4
Caernarvon Way TA8 85 B1
Caern Well Pl BA1 228 C4
Cairn Cl BS48 9 A1
Cairo Ct 18 BS23 30 C1
Caitlin Ct BS14 23 D6
Cala Trad Est BS3 11 F3
Calder Cl BS31 25 A4
Calder Cres TA1 213 D4
Cale Cl DT10 190 C4
Caledonia Mews BS8 11 F6
Caledonian Rd
 Bath BA2 44 D6
 Bristol BS1 226 B1
Caledonia Pl BS8 11 F7
Cale Way BA9 216 B4
California Par BA16 207 B6
Caller's La EX15 180 D1
Callins Cl TA24 201 A5
Callins View TA24 201 A5
Callow Hill BA5 139 C7
Callowhill Ct BS1 227 B3
Calluna Cl BS22 32 A5
Calton Gdns BA2 228 C1
Calton Rd BA2 228 C1
Calton Wlk BA2 228 B1
Calvados Rd TA1 213 C3
Calway Rd TA1 213 B2
Camberley Rd BS4 22 D8
Camberley Wlk BS22 49 E8
Camborne Gr BA21 219 E5
Camborne Pl BA21 219 E5
Camborne St BA21 219 E5
CAMBRIDGE BATCH 20 C8
Cambridge Cl BA20 218 D5
Cambridge Ct BS40 35 D2
Cambridge Gr BS21 6 D5
Cambridge Pl
 Bath BA2 45 B5
 Weston-super-Mare BS23 48 D8
Cambridge Rd BS21 6 D5
Cambridge St TA20 223 C4
Cambridge Terr
 Bath BA2 45 B5
 11 Taunton TA2 213 A8
Cam Brook Cl BA2 78 D8
Cambrook Ho BS39 76 F8
Camden Cres BA1 228 B4
Camden Ct
 Bath BA1 228 B4
 Bridgwater TA6 208 E5
Camden Orch TA11 211 C4
Camden Pl TA6 208 E5
Camden Rd
 Bath BA1 28 A1
 Bridgwater TA6 208 E5
 Bristol BS3 226 B1
 Somerton TA11 211 C4
Camden Row BA1 228 B4
Camden Terr
 Bath BA1 228 C4
 Bristol BS8 226 A2
 Weston-super-Mare BS23 48 E7
Camel Cross BA22 174 C3
CAMELEY 76 C8
Cameley CE Prim Sch BS39 58 E1
Cameley Cl BS39 76 E8
Cameley Gn BA2 43 F6
Cameley La BS39 75 F7
Cameley Rd BS39 76 C8
Camelot Ct TA11 211 B5
Camelot Sh Ctr BA9 216 C4
Camel St BA22 174 F2
Cameroons Cl BS31 24 E4
CAMERTON 78 E8
Camerton Cl BS31 25 E3
Camerton Hill BA2 78 E8
Camerton Rd BA2 60 E1
Camomile Wlk BS20 2 F5
Campian Wlk BS4 22 D6
Campion Cl 4 BS22 49 D7
Campion Dr
 Taunton TA1 213 C1
 Yeovil BA22 218 B5
Campion Gdns TA20 223 D5
Campion Rd BA11 120 B3
Campion Way TA6 208 E1
Campkin Rd BA5 203 B4
Camplins BS21 6 C1
Camp Rd
 Bristol BS8 11 F7
 Weston-super-Mare BS23 30 C1
 Yeovil BA22 186 D1
Camp Rd N BS23 30 B1
Camp View BS48 8 D2
Camvale BA2 79 B8
Camview BS39 77 D6
Canada Coombe BS24 50 A1
Canada Way BS1 226 B1
Canada Wy BS3 11 F4
Canal Cl TA21 222 B8
Canal Dro BS27, BS28 90 A3
Canal Rd TA1 212 F5
Canal Terr
 Bathampton BA2 28 F1
 Taunton TA1 212 F5
Canal View
 Bridgwater TA6 209 A4
 Taunton TA2 213 F7
Canal Way TA19 221 A3
Canaries Path BA4 205 D3
Canberra Cres BS24 50 B6
Canberra Rd BS23 48 F3
Canford La BS9 5 E8
Canford Rd BS9 5 F8
Cannan Ct BA2 45 A2
CANNARD'S GRAVE 205 D2
Cannard's Grave Rd BA4 205 C4
Cannards Grave Rdbt
 BA4 205 D3
Canning Ctr for Land Based
 Studies TA5 135 B2
CANNINGTON 135 C2
Cannington CE Prim Sch
 TA5 135 C2
Cannington College Gdns*
 TA5 135 B2
Cannington Countryside Vst
 Ctr* TA5 135 B2
Cannon Cl TA6 209 B5
Cannon Court Mews
 DT9 217 D1
Cannons Gate BS21 16 C8
CANNON'S MARSH 226 C1
Cannon St BS1 227 A4
Canns La
 9 North Petherton TA6 153 F4
 Puriton TA7 136 C4
Cann St TA1 212 E3
Cannwood La BA10 161 B8
Canons Cl BA2 44 B2
Canons Gate BA22 173 E1
Canon's Marsh
 Amphitheatre*
 BS1 226 C1
Canons Rd BS1 226 C2
Canon's Rd BS1 226 C2
Canon St TA1 213 A4
Canons Way BS1 226 C1
Canons Wlk BS22 31 D2
Cantell Gr BS14 23 F5
Canterbury Cl BS22 32 B3
Canterbury Dr TA3 170 C4
Canterbury Rd BA2 44 D5
Cantock's Cl BS8 226 C3
Canvin Ct TA11 211 B5
Canworth Way TA6 209 C3
Canynge Ho 2 BS1 227 B1
Canynge Rd BS8 11 F8
Canynge Sq BS8 11 F8
Canynge St BS1 227 B2
Capell Cl BS22 49 B8
Capenor Cl BS20 2 C4
Capes Cl TA6 209 A5
Capital Edge BS8 226 B1
CAPLAND 183 A6
Capland Ct TA3 183 A5
Capland La TA3 183 A5
Caple La BS40 56 B5
Cappards Rd BS39 57 D4
Capricorn Pl BS8 226 B2
Capri Villas BS23 30 C2
CAPTON 132 C2
Capton TA4 132 C2
Capton Cross TA4 132 C2
Caradon Pl TA6 208 F7
Caramia Pk TA9 136 A8
Carantoc Pl 3 TA24 131 A5
Caraway Cl TA20 223 F5
Caray Gr TA3 169 D4
Carberry View BS24 50 A8
Card Cl BS27 90 F3
Cardigan Cres BS22 49 C8
Cardill Cl BS13 22 A8
Cardinal Cl BA2 62 D8
Carditch Dro BS49 52 B8
Carey Cl BA4 141 E6
Carey Developments 1
 BS21 6 C1
Carey's Cl BS21 6 F4
Carey's Hollow TA13 220 B4
Careys Mead BA3 116 F7
Careys Way BS24 49 E7
CARHAMPTON 131 B5
Carhampton Cross TA24 131 B5
Caribee Quarter BA16 207 B5
Carice Gdns BS21 16 D8
Carisbrooke Gdns BA20 218 F5
Carisbrooke Rd BS4 22 D7
Carlan Stepps TA19 183 C2
CARLINGCOTT 61 B1
Carlingcott La
 Carlingcott BA2 61 B1
 Peasedown St John BA2 79 B8
Carlingford Terr BA3 79 A2
Carlingford Terrace Rd
 BA3 79 A2
Carlow Rd BS4 22 E8
Carlton Cl BS39 58 F3
Carlton Ct
 Minehead TA24 200 F7
 Wells BA5 203 E4
Carlton Dr TA6 208 F7
Carlton Mans BS23 48 D7
Carlton Mews BA5 203 E4
Carlton St BS23 48 D7
Carmine Cl BA6 206 C4
Carnival Cl TA19 221 A4
Carolina Ho BS2 227 A4
Caroline Bldgs BA2 45 B5
Caroline Cl BS31 24 C4
Caroline Pl BA1 228 B4
Carpenter Cl BS23 49 A7
Carpenters Cl TA3 169 C3
Carpenters Hill BA2 79 B8
Carpenters Ho TA19 221 B3
Carpenters La BS31 24 E5
Carpenters Terr TA12 185 E7
Carpenters Way BA3 97 B8
Carraway La DT10 190 F5
Carre Gdns BS22 31 F4
Carr Ho BA2 44 A6
Carrick Ho 7 BS8 11 F6
Carriels Ho 12 BA4 205 B6
Carrier's La TA21 166 C2
Carrington Way BA9 216 C4
Carrs Cl BA2 44 A6
Carrswood Vw BA2 43 F7
Carstons Cl BS48 18 F6
Carter Cl BA7 214 A6
Carter Rd BS39 77 D5
Carters La BA22 196 E8
Carters Way
 Chilcompton BA3 96 D3
 Somerton TA11 211 C4
Cart Gate TA14 185 F5
Cartgate Link Rd TA15 186 C4
Cartier Cl 6 BA21 219 F8
Cartwright Cl BA5 139 E6
Carver Cl TA6 208 D5
Carvers Rd TA6 209 A5
Cary Ct TA11 211 B5
Caryedge La BA7 160 A2
CARY FITZPAINE 174 B6
Cary Fitzpaine Rd BA22 174 A5
Cary Hill
 Castle Cary BA7 214 D5
 Kingsdon TA11 173 E5
Cary Moor Dro BA7 159 C1
Cary Rd BA22 175 D6
Cary Way
 Kingsdon TA11 173 D5
 Somerton TA11 211 C5
Casey Cl BS4 22 F7
Cashford Gate TA2 213 C7
Casion Ct BS1 227 B1
Casley La BA11 102 D6
Cassino Rd TA23 202 E6
Cassis Cl TA8 104 C5
Castlake La TA4 150 F7
CASTLE 198 D4
Castle Batch Prim Sch
 BS22 32 A5
Castle Bow TA1 212 F4
CASTLE CARY 214 B5
Castle Cary Com Prim Sch
 BA7 214 C4
Castle Cary Mus* BA7 214 C5
Castle Cary Sta BA7 214 B8
Castle Cl BS48 19 F7
Castle Cnr BA11 101 D3
Castle Cotts TA21 180 D8
Castle Cross EX13 198 D4
Castle Ct
 Othery TA7 155 C2
 Shepton Mallet BA4 205 A4
Castle Farm La BS41 21 B2
Castle Field Ind Est TA6 209 A6
Castlefield La TA4 168 B1
Castle Gdns BA2 44 E3
Castle Gn TA1 212 F4
Castle Hill
 Banwell BS29 51 C2
 Dunster TA24 201 E2
 Nether Stowey TA5 134 A2
 Nunney BA11 143 B8
Castle La
 Cranmore BA4 142 A6
 South Cadbury BA22 175 D4
 Wedmore BS28 108 A1
 West Pennard BA6 140 C1
 Wiveliscombe TA4 210 F6
 Yarley BA5 139 D7
Castlemain TA20 182 D2
Castlemans Rd TA1 212 B1

Castle Mead TA23 131 E4
Castle Moat TA6 208 F5
Castle Neroche Forest Trail* TA20 182 D2
Castle Prim Sch BS31 24 D4
Castle Rd
Clevedon BS21 6 E6
Sherborne DT9 225 F5
Wellington TA21 180 D8
Weston-super-Mare BS22 31 E3
Castle Rise BA7 214 C5
Castle Sch The TA1 212 D4
Castle St
Bampton EX16 164 B1
Bridgwater TA6 208 F5
Bristol BS1 227 B3
Frome BA11 119 E5
Keinton Mandeville TA11 158 B1
Nether Stowey TA5 134 B2
Nunney BA11 143 B8
Stogursey TA5 134 C5
Stoke sub Hamdon TA14 185 F4
Taunton TA1 212 E4
Castleton
Haselbury Plucknett TA18 196 C5
1 Sherborne DT9 225 E4
Castleton Rd DT9 225 F4
Castle Town Way DT9 225 E6
Castle View 2 BS24 49 F8
Castle View Rd BS21 6 D5
Castle Way TA1 212 F4
Castlewood Cl BS21 6 D4
Caswell Hill BS20 3 B1
Caswell La BS20 3 B2
Catash Cl BA22 175 D6
Catchgate La
Chard TA20 193 E4
Crimchard TA20 223 B6
Catch Gate La TA20 223 A5
Catch Rd BA11 143 B7
CATCOTT 137 D2
Catcott Broad Dro TA7 137 D5
Catcott Prim Sch TA7 137 D2
Catcott Rd BA5 203 E3
Catcott Right Dro TA7 155 D6
Catemead BS21 16 C8
Cater Rd BS13 22 B6
Cathanger La
Fivehead TA3 170 D1
Stogursey TA5 134 D5
Catharine Pl BA1 228 B3
Cathay La BS27 90 B7
Cathcart Ho 7 BA1 28 A1
Cathead Cross TA14 185 E1
Cathederal Ave BA5 203 D2
Cathedral Church of The Holy & Undivided Trinity* BS1 226 C2
Cathedral Gn BA5 203 E4
Catherine Hill BA11 119 F5
Catherines Cl BA7 214 C6
Catherine St
Avonmouth BS11 4 C8
East Huntspill TA9 136 D8
Frome BA11 119 E5
Catherson Cl BA11 119 D3
Cathill La DT9 176 A2
Cathole Bridge Rd TA18 224 A4
Cathorn La BS48 20 C6
Cat La
Stalbridge DT10 190 A1
Stourton Caundle DT10 189 F1
Catley Gr BS41 11 B2
Catmoor Cross EX13 198 A5
Catnip Cl 2 EX13 198 A1
Cat's Ash
Fitzhead TA4 166 F7
Shepton Mallet BA4 205 B6
Cats' Castle Hill TA4 150 E5
Catscrow Hill TA10 172 C6
CATSGORE 173 C4
Catsgore Rd TA11 173 C5
Cats La
Minehead TA24 201 A6
Taunton TA2 168 F6
Cat St TA14 185 E1
Cattle Hill
Bratton Seymour BA9 176 A8
Welham BA7 160 A1
Cattle Market Rd BS1 227 C1
Catt's La TA21 180 E6
Catwell TA4 202 E2
Caulfield Rd BS22 32 B4
Caundle La
Stalbridge Weston DT10 190 A3
Stourton Caundle DT10 189 F1
Causeway
Nailsea BS48 8 B3
Woolavington TA7, TA9 136 E6
Causeway Cl TA7 136 E4
Causeway Council Hos TA9 106 B4
Causeway La DT8 199 D6
Causeway Terr TA23 202 C6
Causeway The
Congresbury BS49 34 D4
Nailsea BS20 8 F8
Street BA16 207 D8
Yatton BS49 34 C7
Causeway View BS48 8 C2
Cautletts Cl BA3 96 F8
Cavalier Cl
Wembdon TA6 208 E6
Yeovil BA21 219 D8
Cavalier Way
Wincanton BA9 216 C3
Yeovil BA21 219 E8
Cavalier Wlk BA21 219 D8
Cave Ct BS2 227 B4
Cavell Ct BS21 6 C1
Cavendish Cl
8 Longcroft BA21 219 F8
Saltford BS31 25 D2
Cavendish Cres BA1 228 A4
Cavendish Ct BA22 173 E2
Cavendish Dr BA14 83 F6
Cavendish Gdns BS9 5 C4
Cavendish Lodge BA1 228 A4
Cavendish Pl BA1 228 A4
Cavendish Rd BA1 228 A4
Caveners Ct BS22 31 B1
Caversham Dr BS48 9 A2
Cave St BS2 227 B4
Cawley Ave EX13 198 A2
Caxton Ct 4 BA2 228 C3
Caxton Dr 5 TA9 104 E4
Caxton Rd
Frome BA11 120 A3
4 Highbridge TA9 104 E4
Cazenove Path BA4 205 D3
Cecil Rd
Bristol, Clifton BS8 11 F8
Weston-super-Mare BS23 30 E1
Cecil St BA20 219 B5
Cecil Terr TA6 209 B4
Cedar Ave
Butleigh BA6 157 D5
Weston-super-Mare BS22 31 C1
Cedar Cl
Brent Knoll TA9 86 B2
Bridgwater TA6 209 C3
Chard TA20 223 B5
Long Ashton BS41 10 F1
Taunton TA1 213 D2
Cedar Ct
Bristol, Combe Dingle BS9 5 D7
Bristol, Sneyd Park BS9 5 C4
Bristol, Westbury on T BS9 5 F8
Martock TA12 185 E7
Wellington TA21 222 E5
Cedar Dr BS31 24 D4
Cedar Falls TA4 151 E1
Cedar Fields
Sparkford BA22 175 A5
West Coker BA22 197 A8
Cedar Gr
Bath BA2 44 D3
Bristol BS9 5 D5
Somerton TA11 211 D4
Yeovil BA21 218 E6
Cedarhurst Rd BS20 1 E4
Cedarn Ct BS22 31 B4
Cedar Pk BS9 5 D5
Cedar Row BS11 4 F6
Cedars The
Chew Stoke BS40 56 D8
Evercreech BA4 141 E1
Minehead TA24 200 F7
Cedar Terr BA3 78 D1
Cedar Villas BA2 228 A1
Cedar Way
Bath BA2 228 A1
Nailsea BS48 9 A2
Portishead BS20 2 C4
Cedar Wlk
Butleigh BA6 157 E5
Kingweston TA11 157 E2
Cedern Ave BS24 50 C3
Cedric Cl BA1 44 C7
Cedric Rd BA1 44 C8
Cefn Ct TA24 201 B4
CE Inf Sch TA13 220 C4
Celandine Mead TA1 169 A1
Celandine Rd BA22 218 A5
Celandine Way TA6 208 E1
Cello Cl BS31 25 B4
Celtic Way BS24 67 B7
Cemetery La
Street BA16 207 A7
Wincanton BA9 216 B3
Centenary Cotts DT9 176 A1
Centenary Gdns BA8 190 A6
Centenary Way BS27 90 A7
Center Parcs BA12 144 F5
Central Acre BA20 219 B4
Central Ave BA22 173 E2
Central Pk BS14 23 B7
Central Rd BA20 219 B5
Central Way BS21 6 E1
Centre Dr BS29 50 E4
Centre Quay BS20 2 E7
Centre Rd TA7 137 C2
Centre The
Keynsham BS31 24 F5
10 Weston-super-Mare BS23 48 E7
Centurion Bsns Ctr BA4 205 D4
Century Pk BA20 218 E5
CE Prim Sch DT9 176 A1
Cerdic Cl TA20 223 E4
Cerdic Terr TA20 223 D4
Cerney Gdns BS48 9 A2
Cerney La BS11 4 E5
Cerutti Cl BS39 77 D6
CE VA Prim Sch TA6 209 D4
Chackrell La EX16 178 F2
Chadleigh Gr BS4 22 D7
Chad's Hill TA5 135 B2
Chadwyck Cl TA24 124 A4
CHAFFCOMBE 194 C5
Chaffcombe La TA20 194 B5
Chaffcombe Rd TA20 223 E6
Chaffeymoor Hill SP8 161 E1
Chaffinch Ave
Frome BA11 120 B6
Keynsham BS31 24 C3
Chaffinch Cl TA1 212 B4
Chaffinch Dr BA3 97 B8
Chaffins The BS21 6 E2
Chain Gate Ct BA6 206 D4
Chains Rd EX16 178 D1
Chalcombe Rocks La TA4 164 E5
Chalcot La BA13 121 F5
Chalcroft Wlk BS13 21 E4
Chalfield Cl BS31 25 A2
Chalfont Rd BS22 49 C8
Chalice Ct BA6 206 E4
Chalice Hill Cl BA6 206 E4
Chalice Mews 11 TA6 208 F5
Chalice Way BA6 206 F3
Chalice Well* BA6 206 F4
Chalk Farm Cl BS39 40 A7
Chalks The BS40 39 B3
CHALKWAY 194 E2
Challenger Way BA22 218 B6
Challick La TA4 166 A6
Challoner Ct BS1 227 A1
Challow Dr BS22 31 B2
Chamberlain Ho TA1 212 D5
Chamberlain Rd BS24 50 C5
Chamberlain St BA5 203 D4
Chamberlin Ave TA6 209 C6
Chambray Rd 11 TA6 154 A5
Champford La TA21 222 D5
Champford Mews 2 TA21 222 D5
Champion Cross TA4 165 E3
Champion Rd BS30 25 E8
Champney Rd BA11 120 A7
Chancel Cl
Bristol BS9 5 D3
Nailsea BS48 8 D1
Chancellor Cl BA16 156 D7
Chancellor Rd BA16 156 D7
Chancellor's Pound BS40 36 D3
Chandag Inf Sch BS31 25 A4
Chandag Jun Sch BS31 25 A4
Chandag Rd BS31 25 A4
Chandler Cl BA1 27 B1
Chandlers DT9 225 E5
Chandlers La TA7 137 C3
Chandos Ct BS23 48 D6
Chandos Rd BS31 24 E7
Chandos St TA6 208 F5
Change La TA4 164 D6
Channel Cl TA5 134 A2
Channel Ct
Burnham-on-S TA8 104 B5
Weston-super-Mare BS22 31 B3
Channel Dash Pl BA22 173 E2
Channel Hts BS24 48 F1
Channells La TA19 183 C1
Channel Rd BS21 6 E5
Channel View Cres BS20 2 B5
Channel View Farm La BS49 35 A7
Channel View Rd BS20 2 B5
Channing Cl TA8 104 B5
Channon Rd 2 TA2 169 B2
CHANTRY 117 F3
Chantry Cl
Nailsea BS48 8 C1
Taunton TA2 213 B7
Chantry Ct
Bristol BS1 226 C2
Somerton TA11 211 C3
Chantry Dr BS22 32 A4
Chantry Dro TA7 155 B1
Chantry Gdns BA14 83 F3
Chantry Ho 2 BA4 205 B6
Chantry La BA22 174 D3
Chantry Mead Rd BA2 44 E3
Chantry The BS26 87 B5
Chantry View BA22 197 D8
CHAPEL ALLERTON 88 D2
Chapel Barton BS48 8 C2
Chapel Cl
Castle Cary BA7 214 C5
Chew Stoke BS40 56 E8
Chilton Polden TA7 137 B2
Farrington Gurney BS39 76 F4
Keinton Mandeville TA11 158 A1
Nailsea BS48 8 E2
North Curry TA3 170 B4
Winford BS40 38 A6
CHAPEL CLEEVE 131 D5
Chapel Cross
North Cadbury BA22 175 D5
Porlock TA24 129 C7
Chapel Ct
Bath BA1 228 B2
Clandown BA3 78 E4
Clevedon BS21 6 D3
Chapelfield BA3 115 A3
Chapel Field
Peasedown St John BA2 79 E8
South Petherton TA13 220 D3
Chapelfield La TA11 158 C3
Chapel Forge Cl TA9 136 B8
Chapel Hill
Ashcott TA7 156 B8
Backwell BS48 19 D7
Chewton Mendip BA3 94 E5
Clevedon BS21 6 D3
Kingsdon TA11 173 D5
Kington Magna SP8 177 E1
Odcombe BA22 186 C2
Ubley BS40 55 C5
Wrington BS40 35 D3
Chapel La
Bishops Lydeard TA4 167 E8
Butleigh BA6 157 E4
Chew Stoke BS40 56 D8
Claverham BS49 34 F8
Cleeve BS49 35 B7
Chapel La *continued*
Dinnington TA17 195 B7
East Huntspill TA9 136 E8
Gurney Slade BA3 114 E7
Holcombe BA3 116 C8
Milborne Port DT9 217 D2
North Cadbury BA22 175 D6
Oxenpill BA6 138 C4
Penselwood BA9 161 E2
South Cadbury BA22 175 F5
Sparkford BA22 175 A6
Winford BS40 38 A6
Wingfield BA14 83 C6
Yenston BA8 189 F7
Yeovil Marsh BA21 187 A5
Zeals BA12 161 F3
Chapel Lawns BA3 78 E4
CHAPEL LEIGH 167 A8
Chapel Leigh La TA4 167 A8
Chapel Pill La BS20 4 E4
Chapel Rd
Bristol, Bishopsworth BS13 22 A6
Clandown BA3 78 E4
Fordgate TA7 154 C3
Isle Abbotts TA3 183 E7
Pawlett TA6 135 F6
Rooks Bridge BS26 87 C5
South Cadbury BA22 175 D4
Chapel Row
Bath BA1 228 B2
Bathford BA1 29 C2
Dunster TA24 201 D2
Norton St Philip BA2 81 F4
Pill BS20 4 C4
Chapel St
Bridgwater TA6 209 A5
Burnham-on-S TA8 104 A7
Dulverton TA22 163 D6
Exford TA24 128 D1
Horningsham BA12 144 D4
Upton Noble BA4 142 F2
Chapel Yd BA7 214 B4
Chaplains Wood BS20 1 E5
Chapman Ct TA1 212 C1
Chapmans Cl
Frome BA11 119 F6
Wookey BA5 139 D8
CHAPMANSLADE 121 C5
Chapmanslade CE VA Prim Sch BA13 121 D4
Chaps Hollow TA11 211 E2
Chapter St BS2 227 B4
Charbury Wlk BS11 4 E5
Charcroft Hill BA10 160 F6
CHARD 223 D4
Chard Bsns Pk TA20 223 D6
Chard Cl BS48 18 F8
Chard Com Hospl TA20 223 E4
Chard Ct BS14 23 B6
CHARD JUNCTION 198 E7
Chard La
Chard TA20 223 B1
Drimpton DT8 199 F8
Ilminster TA19 194 D6
Tatworth EX13, TA20 193 E1
Woolminstone TA18, TA20 195 B2
Chardleigh Gn TA20 193 E5
CHARDLEIGH GREEN 223 A7
Chard Mus* TA20 223 B4
Chard Rd
Axminster EX13 198 B4
Clevedon BS21 6 E1
Crewkerne TA18 224 A6
Drimpton DT8 199 F7
Chard Sch TA20 223 C4
Chard St
Chardstock EX13 198 B7
Thorncombe TA20 199 B6
CHARDSTOCK 198 B7
Chardstock Ave BS9 5 D8
Chardstock La TA20 223 C2
Chardyke Dr BS39 58 E1
Charing Cross DT6 199 E1
Charity La BA11 98 C1
CHARLCOMBE 27 E3
Charlcombe La BA1 27 F3
Charlcombe Pk BS20 1 D3
Charlcombe Rise BA1 27 F2
Charlcombe View Rd BA1 28 A2
Charlcombe Way BA1 27 F2
Charlcome Rise BS20 1 D3
Charlecombe Ct BS9 5 F6
Charlecombe Rd BS9 5 F6
Charlecote BA1 27 F1
Charles Cres TA1 213 D4
Charles Ct 1 BS8 226 A2
Charles Pl BS8 226 A2
Charles Rd
Frome BA11 119 F3
Yeovil BA21 219 D6
Charles St
Bath BA1 228 B2
Bristol BS1 227 A4
Charlestone Rd TA8 104 B8
Charleton Ho 8 BS2 227 C3
Charlock Cl 3 BS22 49 D7
Charlock Rd BS22 49 D7
Charlotte Ct BA20 219 A4
Charlotte St S BS1 226 C2
Charlotte St
Bath BA1 228 B2
Bristol, Brandon Hill BS1 226 C3
CHARLTON
Creech St Michael 169 F5
Radstock 97 E5
Shepton Mallet 205 E5
CHARLTON ADAM 173 F7
Charlton Ave BS23 48 D4
Charlton Cl
Bridgwater TA6 209 C4
Crewkerne TA18 224 D5
Shepton Mallet BA4 205 D5
Yeovil BA21 219 D5
Charlton Crossroads BA4 205 D5
Charlton Dr BS48 9 C7
Charlton Field La DT9 175 D1
Charlton Hill DT9, BA8 176 B3
CHARLTON HORETHORNE 176 B2
Charlton Horethorne CE Prim Sch DT9 176 A1
Charlton La
Creech St Michael TA3 169 E5
Radstock BA3 97 D6
Sparkford DT9 175 F3
CHARLTON MACKRELL 173 E7
Charlton Mackrell CE Prim Sch
Charlton Mackrell TA11 173 E7
Charlton Mackrell TA11 173 E7
CHARLTON MUSGROVE 161 A2
Charlton Park Rd BA3 97 F6
Charlton Pk
Keynsham BS31 24 D5
Midsomer Norton BA3 97 B7
Charlton Rd
Creech St Michael TA3 169 E6
Holcombe BA3 97 D3
Keynsham BS31, BS14 24 C3
Midsomer Norton BA3 97 B8
Shepton Mallet BA4 205 D5
Weston-super-Mare BS23 48 D4
Charlton Road Cotts TA3 169 D6
Charlton Trad Est BA4 205 E5
Charlton View BS20 2 C5
CHARLYNCH 152 F8
Charlynch Hill TA5 152 F8
Charlynch La TA5 153 B8
Charlynch Rd TA5 153 A8
Charmborough Farm Rural Bsns Pk BA3 97 D3
Charmoor Dro TA20 182 F1
Charmoor La TA20 182 F1
Charmouth Rd BA1 44 B7
Charn Hill DT9 176 A2
Charnwood Cl TA6 208 F7
Charnwood Dr BS27 90 B7
Charnwood Rd BS14 23 B4
Charolais Dr 8 TA6 154 A5
Charter Cl TA6 209 A4
Charter Ho BS1 226 B2
CHARTERHOUSE 72 C4
Charterhouse Cl
Cheddar BS27 90 C6
Nailsea BS48 8 F1
Charterhouse Dr BA11 120 C7
Charter Rd BS22 49 B8
Charter Way BA5 203 B4
Charter Wlk
Bristol BS14 23 A6
Taunton TA1 213 C5
Chartley BS9 5 D2
Chase Cl BA6 206 C3
Chasey's Dro BA6 139 C4
Chatham Ave TA6 208 E6
Chatham Ct TA10 171 C4
Chatham Pk BA2 45 C6
Chatham Pl TA10 171 C4
Chatham Row BA1 228 C3
Chatley Furlong BA2 81 F3
Chatsworth Rd BA21 219 D7
Chattenden Ho BS9 5 F3
Chatterton Gn BS14 22 F3
Chatterton Ho 5 BS1 227 B1
Chatterton Sq BS1 227 C1
Chatterton St BS1 227 C1
Chaucer Cl 4 TA6 153 F4
Chaucer Rd
Bath BA2 44 F4
Midsomer Norton BA3 97 B8
Weston-super-Mare BS23 49 A4
Chaundey Gr BS13 22 B5
Cheapside
Bristol BS2 227 C4
Langport TA10 171 F5
Taunton TA1 212 F3
Wiveliscombe TA4 210 C4
Cheap St
Bath BA1 228 C2
Frome BA11 119 F5
Sherborne DT9 225 D4
Cheats Rd TA3 169 C3
Checcombe La DT9 188 B4
Checkridge La EX13 198 D2
CHEDDAR 90 D8
Cheddar Bsns Pk BS27 90 A6
Cheddar Bsns Pk BS27 90 A6
Cheddar Cl
Burnham-on-S TA8 104 C8
Frome BA11 120 C7
Nailsea BS48 18 F8
Cheddarcoombe La BS25 70 E8
Cheddar Ct BS27 90 B7
Cheddar Fields BS27 90 A7
Cheddar Fst Sch BS27 90 B7
Cheddar Gorge* BS27 71 E1
Cheddar Gorge Rural Village* BS27 90 C8
Cheddar Gr BS13 22 A8
Cheddar Grove Prim Sch BS13 22 A8
Cheddar Gr Prim Sch 1 BS13 22 A8

Cheddar Moor Dro BS27 90 C4
Cheddar Moor Rd BS28 89 E3
Cheddar Rd
Axbridge BS26 70 E2
Clewer BS28 89 D2
Wedmore BS28 108 D6
Cheddar Valley Bldgs 2
BA5 203 C3
CHEDDON FITZPAINE 169 A6
Cheddon Fitzpaine CE Prim
Sch TA2 168 F6
Cheddon Lawns TA2 169 A6
Cheddon Mews TA2 212 F7
Cheddon Rd TA2 212 F7
Chedworth Cl BA2 45 F3
CHEDZOY 154 E8
Chedzoy La TA7 209 E7
Cheeks La BA10 215 E6
Cheer La TA7 154 F5
Cheese Factory Rd TA5 135 A1
Cheese Hill BA11 143 D8
Cheese La BS2 227 B2
Chelmer Cl TA1 213 D4
Chelmer Gr BS31 24 F4
Chelmsine La TA21 181 B5
Chelscombe BA1 27 B1
Chelscombe Cl BA1 27 E4
Chelsea Cl BS31 25 A5
Chelsea Rd BA1 44 C7
Chelsfield BS48 19 A7
CHELSTON 180 D8
Chelston Ave BA21 219 B7
Chelston Bsn Pk TA21 180 D8
CHELSTON HEATHFIELD 180 E7
Chelston Rd BS4 22 D7
Chelston Terr TA21 180 D8
Chelswood Ave BS22 49 C8
Chelswood Gdns BS22 49 D8
Cheltenham St BA2 228 A1
CHELVEY 18 D5
Chelvey Batch BS48 18 F3
Chelvey La BS48 18 E4
Chelvey Rd BS48 18 D5
Chelvey Rise BS48 9 A1
Chelvy Cl BS13 22 D3
CHELWOOD 59 A8
Chelwood BS23 48 F8
Chelwood Dr
Bath BA2 44 D1
Taunton TA1 212 E1
Chelwood Rd
Bristol BS11 4 D7
Saltford BS31 25 E4
Chelwood Rdbt BS39 58 E8
CHELYNCH 141 E6
Chelynch Pk BA4 141 E6
Chelynch Rd BA4 141 F7
Chepstow Ave TA6 209 A2
Chepstow Ct BA21 219 D6
Chepstow Ho BA10 215 D6
Chepstow Rd BS4 22 D8
Chepstow Wlk BS31 24 D5
Cher TA24 200 F6
Cherfield TA24 200 F6
Cherington Rd BS48 9 A2
Cheriton St BA8 176 D3
Cherry Ave BS21 6 E2
Cherry Cl
Bridgwater TA6 209 C3
Yatton BS49 34 B8
Cherry Ct 12 BS1 227 A4
Cherry Garden La BA2 100 D7
Cherry Gr
Frome BA11 119 E3
Taunton TA2 212 F6
Yatton BS49 34 B8
Cherry Hay BS21 6 D1
Cherry La
4 Bristol BS1 227 B4
Odcombe BA22 186 C2
Cherry Orch TA3 168 D1
Cherry Orchard Dr BA5 203 C5
Cherry Pie La BA22 175 A5
Cherry Rd
Long Ashton BS41 10 F1
Nailsea BS48 8 D1
Cherry Tree Cl
Keynsham BS31 24 C4
Radstock BA3 78 E1
Cherry Tree Ct
Crewkerne TA18 224 D8
Kingston Seymour BS21 16 C2
1 Wells BA5 203 C3
Wincanton BA9 216 D4
Cherry Tree Dr BA20 218 D2
Cherry Tree La TA1 212 F1
Cherry Tree Rd EX13 198 A1
Cherry Tree Way TA23 202 D6
Cherrywood Cl TA6 208 D3
Cherrywood Rd BS22 31 F2
Cherrywood Rise BS22 31 F2
Chertsey Cl TA7 136 E4
Cherwell Rd BS31 25 A4
Chescombe Rd BS49 34 B7
Chesham Rd N BS22 49 B8
Chesham Rd S BS22 49 B8
Cheshay's Hill TA19 183 D1
Cheshire Ave BS24 50 C5
Chesle Cl BS20 1 E3
Cheslefield BS20 1 E3
Chesle Way BS20 1 E3
Chessell La BA4 140 C4
Chessels Cl BA22 197 B8
Chessels La TA11 173 F7
Chessington Ave BS14 23 B5
CHESTERBLADE 142 A4
Chesterblade Rd
Chesterblade BA4 142 A4
Evercreech BA4 141 F3
Chester Cl BS24 50 A8
Chester Cres BS13 22 B8
Chesterfield TA20 223 D4
Chesterfield Cl BS29 50 F3
Chesterfield Ho BA3 78 B1
Chesterfield Nuffield Health
Bristol Hospl The BS8 226 A2
Chester Pl TA6 209 C8
Chester Terr TA20 223 D4
Chesterton Dr BS48 9 A2
Chesterton Ho 6 BS2 227 B4
Chestertons The BA2 45 F8
Chestnut Ave
Axbridge BS26 70 C2
Chapel Cleeve TA24 131 D5
Crewkerne TA18 224 D7
Weston-super-Mare BS22 32 A1
Chestnut Barn Ind Est
BS24 33 D3
Chestnut Chase BS48 9 A3
Chestnut Cl
Baltonsborough BA6 158 A5
Banwell BS29 51 A3
Bridgwater TA6 209 C4
Bristol BS14 23 F5
1 Carhampton TA24 131 A5
Congresbury BS49 34 D4
Frome BA11 120 C7
Maiden Bradley BA12 144 C2
Paulton BS39 77 E6
Radstock BA3 78 E1
Somerton TA11 211 C3
Wellington TA21 222 E5
Chestnut Ct BS13 22 A7
Chestnut Dr
Claverham BS49 17 F1
Taunton TA1 213 C1
Yeovil BA20 218 C3
Chestnut Gr
Bath BA2 44 C4
Clevedon BS21 6 E4
Westwood BA15 64 F4
Chestnut Ho
Brean TA8 65 F2
Bristol BS13 22 D3
Chestnut La
Ashcott TA7 156 B8
Bleadon BS24 67 B7
Chestnut Par BA4 205 D4
Chestnut Park Prim Sch
BS49 16 F2
Chestnut Rd
Long Ashton BS41 11 B2
11 Martock TA12 185 E6
Chestnuts The
Cheddar BS27 71 A1
Winscombe BS25 70 A7
Chestnut Way TA24 201 A5
Chestnut Wlk
Bristol BS13 22 A6
Saltford BS31 25 E3
Chever's La BA2 81 E5
Cheverton Ho 1 BA21 219 B5
Cheviot Mdw BS20 2 F4
Cheviot St 6 TA6 154 A5
Chew Cotts BS31 24 F5
Chew Court Farm BS40 39 B3
Chew Hill BS40 39 A4
Chew La BS40 38 F1
CHEW MAGNA 39 C4
Chew Magna Prim Sch
BS40 39 B3
Chew Rd BS40 38 C5
Chew St BS40 39 A3
CHEW STOKE 56 D8
Chew Stoke CE Prim Sch
BS40 56 D8
Chewton Cheese Dairy*
BA3 94 E6
Chewton Hill BA3 95 A7
CHEWTON KEYNSHAM 24 E2
CHEWTON MENDIP 94 E7
Chewton Mendip CE VA Prim
Sch BA3 94 F7
Chewton Rd BS31 24 F2
Chew Valley Lake Nature
Trails* BS39 57 B7
Chew Valley Sch BS40 38 F1
Cheyne Rd BS9 5 D6
Chibbet Hill TA24 146 B8
Chibbet Post TA24 146 C8
Chichester Cl TA8 104 B8
Chichester Pl BA3 79 A2
Chichester Rd BA16 207 C4
Chichester Way BS24 50 A8
Chicks La BA3 95 D7
Chick's La TA4 210 C6
Chickwell La BA3 81 A1
Chidgey Cl TA6 208 F5
CHILCOMBE 132 F1
Chilcombe La TA4 132 F1
CHILCOMPTON 96 C4
Chilcompton Rd BA3 96 E7
Chilcote Dro BA5 113 E2
Chilcote La BA5 113 D1
Chilcott Cross TA22 163 A7
Chilcott La TA22 163 A7
Childhay La
Childhay DT8 199 F6
Drimpton DT8 199 F6
Chilkwell La BA3 81 C2
Chilkwell St BA6 206 E4
Chillingham Dro 14
TA7 154 A5
Chillington Down TA19,
TA20 194 F4
Chilliswood Cres TA1 212 B2
Chilliswood La
Staplehay TA3 181 B8
Taunton TA3 168 B1
Chillybridge Rocks TA22 147 E1
Chillyhill La BS40 38 F2
Chilpitts TA7 136 F4
CHILSON 198 C6
CHILSON COMMON 198 D7
Chiltern Cl BS14 23 B4
Chiltern Cross EX16 164 B2
CHILTHORNE DOMER 186 E5
Chilthorne Domer CE Sch
BA22 186 E5
Chilthorne Hill BA22 186 E6
Chilthornehill La BA22 186 D6
CHILTON CANTELO 174 D1
Chilton Cantelo House (Sch)
BA22 174 C1
Chilton Cl TA6 208 F7
Chilton Ct 7 BA1 28 B1
Chilton Dro TA7 137 C6
Chilton Gr BA21 219 A7
Chilton Pk TA6 208 F7
CHILTON POLDEN 137 B2
Chilton Rd
Bath BA1 28 B1
Bridgwater TA5, TA6 208 F8
Bristol BS4 23 A8
Chilton Polden TA7 137 B4
Chilton Right Dro TA7 155 B6
Chilton St TA6 208 F7
CHILTON TRINITY 135 F2
Chilton Trinity Sch TA6 208 F7
Chilworthy La TA19, TA20 193 F7
Chimes The BS48 18 C8
Chinehorn Dro TA5 135 F3
Chinnock Hollow BA22 196 E8
Chinnock Huts La TA18 196 E8
Chinnock Rd BA6 206 F5
Chip La TA1 212 E5
CHIPLEY 166 F2
Chippel La DT10 190 F5
Chippenham Rd
Doynton BS30 12 D6
Marshfield SN14 13 C7
Chipping Cross BS21 16 C8
CHIPSTABLE 165 E6
Chi-Rio Cl BA4 205 E4
CHISELBOROUGH 185 F1
Chiselborough Hill La
TA14 186 A1
Chisland Dr TA24 129 C8
Chistles La TA11 158 A1
Chitcombe Rocks La TA4 149 C1
Chivers St BA2 45 A2
Choke Wlk BS4 23 E8
CHOLWELL 58 D2
Cholwell Cotts BS39 58 D2
Chorwell La TA21 166 E2
Chovel La BA11 142 F6
Chowins Rd TA18 224 C5
Christ Church CE Fst Sch
BA11 119 F2
Christ Church CE Prim Sch
Bristol BS8 226 A3
Victoria Park BS8 226 A3
Weston-super-Mare BS23 48 E8
Christ Church Cl 1 BS48 8 E2
Christ Church Ct 9 TA18 224 C6
Christchurch Hall 2 BA1 228 B3
Christ Church Path S 12
BS23 48 E8
Christchurch Rd BS8 226 A3
Christchurch St E BA11 119 F4
Christchurch St W BA11 119 E4
Christian Cl BS22 32 A3
Christian's Cross BA6 157 E1
Christina Terr BS8 226 A1
Christmas St 6 BS1 227 A3
Christmas Steps 2 BS1 227 A3
CHRISTON 68 D7
Christon Hill BS26 68 B8
Christon Rd
Banwell BS29 51 A1
Loxton BS26 68 C6
Christon Terr BS23 48 F2
Christopher Brain St BS14 22 E5
Christopher Cl BA20 218 E5
Christopher Way BA4 205 A5
Chritchard Parkway TA1 213 B4
Chrysanthemum Cl 3
DT9 225 E4
Chrysanthemum Flats 2
DT9 225 E4
Chrysanthemum Row 4
DT9 225 E4
Chubbards Cross Cvn Site
TA19 183 E5
Chubbs Lawn TA18 224 C5
Chubworthy Cross TA4 165 D5
Church Ave BS9 5 E4
Church Cl
Bathampton BA2 28 F2
Bathford BA1 29 B2
Bourton SP8 161 E1
7 Carhampton TA24 131 A5
Clevedon BS21 6 A2
East Huntspill TA9 136 E8
Evercreech BA4 141 E1
Great Elm BA11 118 F7
Lydeard St Lawrence TA4 151 A3
24 Martock TA12 185 E6
Norton Fitzwarren TA2 168 B4
Portishead BS20 2 D5
Shapwick TA7 137 F1
Church Cl *continued*
South Brewham BA10 160 F6
Stoke St Gregory TA3 170 E6
Stoke St Mary TA3 169 C1
West Chinnock TA18 196 B8
Yatton BS49 34 C7
Church Cnr BS24 67 B1
Church Cotts
Chilton Trinity TA5 135 F2
Monkton Combe BA2 63 E8
Newton St Loe BA2 43 B6
Church Ct
Midsomer Norton BA3 78 A1
Redhill BS40 36 D3
Churchdown Wlk BS11 4 E5
Church Dr
Congresbury BS49 34 D4
West Buckland TA21 180 F7
Church Farm Bsns Pk BA2 43 A7
Church Farm Cl
Marksbury BA2 42 B1
Stawell TA7 137 A1
Church Farm La BA2 82 D7
Church Farm Pl 18 BA8 190 A6
Churchfield La TA3 183 F7
Church Field La TA7 136 C4
Churchfields
Rode BA11 101 F8
Wellington TA21 222 D7
Church Fields
Wellington TA21 222 E6
Wincanton BA9 216 C3
Churchfield Sch TA9 104 D4
Churchfields Dr BA7 214 C6
Churchfields The Village Sch
BA15 46 E7
Church Gdns BA6 206 D5
Church Hayes Cl BS48 18 E8
Church Hayes Dr BS48 18 E8
Church Hill
Beckington BA11 101 E4
Buckhorn Weston SP8 177 D3
Charlton Adam TA11 173 F7
Combwich TA5 135 B5
Dinnington TA17 195 B7
Exford TA24 128 D1
Freshford BA3 64 B5
Kington Magna SP8 177 E2
Pitney TA10 172 C7
Radstock BA3 79 C3
South Cadbury BA22 175 C3
Stalbridge DT10 190 B5
Templecombe BA8 176 E1
Timsbury BA2 60 B2
Church Ho BA4 141 F1
Church House Rd TA8 84 F5
CHURCHILL 52 F5
Churchill Ave
Clevedon BS21 6 C2
Wells BA5 112 E1
Churchill Batch La BA4 140 D6
Churchill Bsns Pk BS23 49 A7
Churchill CE VA Prim Sch
BS40 53 A5
Churchill Cl
Burnham-on-S TA8 104 C5
5 Clevedon BS21 6 C2
Wells BA5 112 E1
Churchill Com Sch BS25 52 D5
Churchill Dr BS9 5 D7
Churchill Gate BS25 52 F4
Churchill Gn BS25 52 C5
CHURCHILL GREEN 52 D5
Churchill La
Axminster EX13 198 A5
Chipstable TA4 165 C5
Churchill Rd
Frome BA11 119 D4
Shepton Mallet BA4 205 A5
Wells BA5 112 E1
Weston-super-Mare BS23 49 A7
Churchill Rd E BA5 112 E1
Churchill Way
Taunton TA1 212 F1
Watchet TA23 202 C6
CHURCHINFORD 192 A7
Church La
Axbridge BS26 70 C2
Backwell BS48 19 C5
Badgworth BS26 88 A6
Baltonsborough BA6 158 A5
Bath BA2 45 C4
Batheaston BA1 28 F4
Bicknoller TA4 132 F2
Bishop Sutton BS39 57 D4
Bitton BS30 25 E7
Blackford BS28 107 D5
Brent Knoll TA9 86 A2
Bristol BS1 227 B2
Bristol, Clifton Wood BS8 226 B2
Bristol, Dundry Hill BS14 23 B3
Carhampton TA24 131 B5
Chew Stoke BS40 56 D8
Chewton Mendip BA3 94 F7
Chilcompton BA3 96 D5
Chilton Polden TA7 137 B2
Churchill BS25 52 D5
Clutton BS39 58 E3
Coleford BA3 116 F7
Compton Bishop BS26 69 B3
Compton Dando BS39 41 D6
Doulting BA4 141 E6
Downside BA3 96 A2
Dulverton TA22 163 D6
East Coker BA22 197 E8
East Harptree BS40 74 E4
East Huntspill TA9 136 E8
East Lambrook TA13 220 C8
Church La *continued*
Evercreech BA4 141 E1
Farmborough BA2 60 A6
Farrington Gurney BS39 77 A4
Flax Bourton BS48 19 F7
Glastonbury BA6 206 D5
Haselbury Plucknett TA18 196 C5
Hatch Beauchamp TA3 182 E8
Horningsham BA12 144 E4
Horton TA19 183 C2
Hutton BS24 49 E2
Ilminster TA19 221 C4
Kingston St Mary TA2 168 E8
Limpley Stoke BA3 64 A5
Long Ashton BS41 11 C2
Long Sutton TA10 172 D2
Loxton BS26 68 D4
Lympsham BS24 67 B1
Lynford-on-F TA11 158 D2
Meare BA6 138 D4
Midsomer Norton BA3 78 A1
Milborne Port DT9 217 D2
Misterton TA18 224 E3
Monkton Combe BA2 45 F1
Nailsea BS21 8 C4
Nailsea BS48 8 C1
North Perrott TA18 196 C4
Norton Sub Hamdon TA14 185 F2
Norton Sub Hamdon,
Chiselborough TA14 185 E1
Paulton BS39 77 E6
Portbury BS20 3 E3
Rimpton BA22 188 B8
Rode BA11 101 F8
Ruishton TA3 169 C4
Ruishton, Thornfalcon TA3 169 E2
Seavington St Mary TA19 184 E1
22 Shepton Mallet BA4 205 B6
Shepton Mallet, Cannards Grave
BA4 205 D2
Sherborne DT9 225 D4
Stratton-on-t F BA3 96 F2
Timsbury BA2 60 B2
Westonzoyland TA7 154 F5
West Pennard BA6 140 B1
Wingfield BA14 83 C6
Winscombe BS25 69 E6
Yatton BS49 34 C7
Churchlands TA9 106 D4
Churchlands Ct TA8 104 A7
Churchland Way BS22 50 B8
Church Lane Cnr TA9 86 A2
Church Lane End BS48 19 F8
Church Leaze BS11 4 D6
Church Mdw TA6 208 E6
Church Mdws BS14 23 C4
Church Mead SP8 161 E1
Churchmoor La BA6 158 A5
Church Pass 4 TA6 208 F5
Church Path
Aller TA10 171 D8
Bridgwater TA6 208 E5
Crewkerne TA18 224 B6
Meare BA6 138 D4
Minehead TA24 200 F8
Queen Camel BA22 174 F3
South Petherton TA13 220 C2
2 Yeovil BA20 219 B5
Church Path Rd BS20 4 C4
Church Pl
Milborne Port DT9 217 D2
Pill BS20 4 C4
Church Rd
Abbots Leigh BS8 11 A8
Bath, Combe Down BA2 45 C1
Bath, Weston Park BA1 27 C1
Bawdrip TA7 136 E2
Bitton BS30 25 E7
Bourton SP8 177 F8
Bradford Abbas DT9 187 E1
Brean TA8 65 F4
Bristol, Bishopsworth BS13 22 A6
Bristol, Sneyd Park BS9 5 D3
Chapel Leigh TA4 167 A7
Churchinford TA3 191 F8
Churchstanton TA3 181 B1
Coxley BA5 139 E6
Dundry BS41 21 D2
East Brent TA9 86 C4
Easton-in-G BS20 4 A4
Edington TA7 137 C2
Fitzhead TA4 166 F7
Fordgate TA7 154 D3
Huntspill TA9 136 A8
Ilton TA19 183 E4
Keenthorne TA5 134 D3
Kilmington BA12 161 F7
Leigh Woods BS8 11 D6
Lympsham BS24 67 B1
Middlezoy TA7 155 B3
Minehead TA24 200 F8
North Curry TA3 170 B4
North Newton TA7 154 A2
Peasedown St John BA2 79 B8
Pensford BS39 40 A7
Redhill BS40 36 D3
Shapwick TA7 137 F1
South Cadbury BA22 175 D4
Sparkford BA22 175 A4
Spaxton TA5 152 E7
Street BA16 207 D7
Sutton Mallet TA7 155 B7
Taunton TA3 168 D1
Wembdon TA6 208 D6
Weston-super-Mare BS22 31 E2
Whitchurch BS14 23 C4
Winford BS40 38 A7
Winscombe BS25 69 E7

Church Rd *continued*
Yatton BS49 34 C7
Church Rd N BS20 2 D5
Church Rd S BS20 2 D4
Church Rise BS40 38 A7
CHURCH ROW 101 F8
Church Row BA3 96 F2
Church Row Cotts TA3 181 E6
Church Sq
Clutton BS39 58 E2
Midsomer Norton BA3 78 A1
8 Taunton TA1 212 F4
Church St
Babcary TA11 174 C7
Banwell BS29 51 B3
Barton St David BA6 157 F2
6 Bath BA1 228 C2
Bathford BA1 29 B2
Bath, Weston park BA1 27 B1
Bath, Widcombe BA2 45 B4
Beckington BA11 101 E4
Bishops Lydeard TA4 167 E8
Blackford BS28 107 D4
Blagdon BS40 54 F2
Bridgwater TA6 209 A5
Bristol BS1 227 B2
5 Cannington TA5 135 B2
Castle Cary BA7 214 B4
Chard TA20 223 C3
Cheddar BS27 90 B7
Coleford BA3 116 F7
Crewkerne TA18 224 C6
Croscombe BA5 204 C7
Dinder BA5 140 D7
Donyatt TA19 183 D1
Drayton TA10 171 E3
Dunster TA24 201 E2
2 Frome BA11 119 F4
Halstock BA22 197 C3
8 Henstridge BA8 190 A6
Highbridge TA9 104 E4
Hinton St George TA17 195 C7
Horningsham BA12 144 D4
Ilchester BA22 173 E1
Isle Abbotts TA3 183 F7
Keinton Mandeville TA11 158 A1
Kilmersdon BA3 98 B5
Kingsbury Episcopi TA12 185 B8
Kington Magna SP8 177 E2
Lopen TA13 185 A1
Maiden Bradley BA12 144 C1
Mark TA9 106 D4
Martock TA12 185 E6
Merriott TA16 195 F7
Milborne Port DT9 217 D2
Minehead TA24 200 F8
Minehead, Alcombe TA24 201 B5
Norton St Philip BA2 81 E4
Nunney BA11 143 B8
Paulton BS39 77 D6
Pensford BS39 40 D4
Podimore BA22 174 A3
Radstock BA3 78 F2
Shepton Beauchamp TA19 184 E4
Southwick BA14 83 F3
Stogursey TA5 134 C5
Stoke St Michael BA3 116 A2
Taunton TA1 213 B3
Timberscombe TA24 130 B5
Tintinhull BA22 186 B6
Upton Noble BA4 142 F2
Wanstrow BA4 142 F4
Wedmore BS28 108 D4
West Coker BA22 197 A8
Wincanton BA9 216 C4
Wiveliscombe TA4 210 C4
Woolavington TA7 136 E4
Woolley BA1 27 F6
Yeovil BA20 219 B5
Yeovilton BA22 174 A1
CHURCHSTANTON 181 B1
Churchstanton Prim Sch TA3 191 E8
Church Steps TA24 200 F8
Church Terr
7 Bampton EX16 164 B1
East Coker BA22 197 C7
Odcombe BA22 186 C2
4 Yeovil BA20 219 B5
Church Tk SP8 161 E1
CHURCH TOWN 19 C5
Church Town BS48 19 C5
Church View
Bourton SP8 161 E1
Chilton Trinity TA5 135 F2
Clatworthy TA4 149 F1
Evercreech BA4 141 E1
North Wootton BA4 140 C4
Porlock TA24 124 A3
Wraxall BS48 9 B2
Church View Cl TA10 171 E8
Churchview Cl BA6 206 D4
Churchward Dr BA11 120 C6
Churchward Rd BS22 32 B3
Churchway
Curry Rivel TA10 171 D4
Faulkland BA3 80 D1
Church Way TA7 137 D2
Churchway Cl TA10 171 D4
Churchways BS14 23 C4
Churchwell Cl DT9 187 E1
Churchwell St DT9 187 E1
Church Wlk
Baltonsborough BA6 158 A5
Bawdrip TA7 136 E2
Bratton Seymour BA9 176 B8
Ilminster TA19 221 C4
Leigh u M BA3 117 A3
Church Wlk *continued*
Long Sutton TA10 172 F4
Marston Magna BA22 174 F1
9 North Petherton TA6 153 E3
Pill BS20 4 C4
Wrington BS40 35 D2
Chur La BA22 197 A8
Churlands Cl BA22 197 A8
Churston Cl BS14 23 A3
Cinder Ash La TA18 195 D4
Cinnamon La BA6 206 F3
CircleBath Hospl BA2 79 E6
Circle The BA2 44 B3
Circular Rd BS9 5 E2
Circus Field Rd BA6 206 D4
Circus Mews BA1 228 B3
Circus Pl BA1 228 B3
Circus The BA1 228 B3
City of Bath Coll BA1 228 B2
City of Bristol Coll BS1 226 C2
City of Bristol Coll (South Bristol Skills Acad) BA11 22 E5
City Rd BS2 227 B4
City The TA9 106 C4
City View BA1 228 C4
Clammer Hill La TA18 224 D6
Clanage Rd BS3 11 E4
Clanders Batch BS40 54 D3
CLANDOWN 78 E4
Clandown Rd BS39 77 F4
Clanfield DT9 225 B2
Clan Ho BA2 45 C7
CLANVILLE 159 C3
Clanville TA24 200 F7
Clanville Cotts BA7 214 A7
Clanville Rd TA24 200 F7
CLAPTON
Crewkerne 195 C1
Midsomer Norton 96 C7
Clapton Court Gdns* TA18 195 D1
Clapton Dro BS20 2 D1
Clapton Gate TA18 195 C2
CLAPTON IN GORDANO 2 E1
Clapton La
Holton BA9 176 B6
Portishead BS20 2 E2
Clapton Rd
Hewish TA18 195 D2
Midsomer Norton BA3 77 D1
CLAPTON WICK 7 E6
Clapton Wlk BS9 5 C5
Clare Gdns BA2 44 D1
Claremont Bldgs BA1 28 A1
Claremont Cres BS23 30 B1
Claremont Ct TA1 212 C1
Claremont Cvn Pk TA8 84 F6
Claremont Dr TA1 212 C1
Claremont Gdns
Clevedon BS21 6 E1
Hallatrow BS39 77 B7
4 Nailsea BS48 8 D1
Claremont Gr TA6 209 D6
Claremont Hall BS21 6 E4
Claremont La TA1 212 C1
Claremont Pl 13 BA1 28 A1
Claremont Rd BA1 28 B1
Claremont Wlk BA1 28 A1
Clarence Ct 1 BA20 219 A5
Clarence Dr 1 TA6 153 F4
Clarence Grove Rd BS23 48 E5
Clarence Pl
Bath BA1 44 B6
Bristol BS2 226 C4
Clarence Rd BS1 227 B1
Clarence Rd E BS23 48 E5
Clarence Rd N BS23 48 D5
Clarence Rd S BS23 48 D5
Clarence St
Bath BA1 228 C4
Taunton TA1 212 E4
Yeovil BA20 219 A5
Clarence Ter TA6 136 B2
Clarence Terr
Bath BA2 45 D5
8 Yeovil BA20 219 B4
Clarendon Rd
Bath BA2 45 B5
Weston-super-Mare BS23 48 F8
Clarendon Villas BA2 45 B5
Clares Rd BA5 203 D3
Clare St
Bridgwater TA6 208 F5
Bristol BS1 227 A2
2 North Petherton TA6 153 F4
Clark Cl
Woolavington TA7 136 E4
Wraxall BS48 9 B2
Clarken Cl BS48 8 E1
Clarken Coombe BS41 11 B3
Clarke's Cl TA20 223 D4
Clarkes Ct BA20 219 A4
Clarke's Row TA20 223 D4
CLARKHAM CROSS 197 E2
Clarkham Cross BA22 197 E2
Clarks Cl BA22 218 A5
Clark's La TA18 224 F3
Clarks Meadow BA4 205 C3
Clarkson Ave BS22 31 C1
Clarkson Ho BA1 228 A2
Clarks Rd TA6 209 C4
Clarks Shopping Village BA16 207 C6
Clarks Way BA2 44 C2
Classeys House Rd TA10 172 A8
Classic Bldgs TA6 208 F4
Clatcombe La DT9 188 D6
CLATWORTHY 149 F1
Clatworthy Dr BS14 23 A7
Clatworthy Resr* TA4 149 D2
Claude Ave BA2 44 C5
Claude Terr BA2 44 C5
Claudius Rd BS31 24 F7
Clavelshay Rd TA6 153 C2
CLAVERHAM 17 E1
Claverham Cl BS49 34 D7
Claverham Dro BS49 17 D5
Claverham Pk BS49 34 F8
Claverham Rd BS49 34 E8
CLAVERTON 46 B5
Claverton Bldgs BA2 228 C1
Claverton Ct BA2 45 E4
CLAVERTON DOWN 45 F3
Claverton Down Rd BA2 45 F3
Claverton Dr BA2 45 F3
Claverton Hill BA2 46 A4
Claverton Lodge BA2 45 C5
Claverton Pumping Sta* BA2 46 C5
Claverton Rd BS31 25 E2
Claverton Rd W BS31 25 D3
Claverton St BA2 228 C1
Clay Castle TA18 196 C5
Clay Castle La TA18 196 C6
Claydon Cl TA23 131 E4
Claydon Gn BS14 22 F3
Clayford La TA22 163 C5
Clayford Rd TA22 163 C5
CLAYHANGER 165 C1
Clayhanger Common TA19 194 A6
Clayhanger Cross
Combe St Nicholas TA20 193 E6
Combe St Nicholas TA20 193 E6
Clayhanger La
Chard TA20 223 A8
Combe St Nicholas TA20 193 E6
CLAYHIDON 180 E2
Clayhidon Crossway EX15 180 E2
Clay La
Barrington TA19 184 B5
Bitton BS30 25 D8
Chewton Mendip BA3 94 C5
Higher Chillington TA19 194 F5
Millmoor EX15 179 A1
Rode BA11 101 F8
Clayland Cnr TA5 134 E5
Claylands Cnr TA5 134 E5
Claypiece Rd BS13 22 A4
Claypit La TA5 134 E8
Claypit Rd BS41 22 B1
CLAYPITS 164 C4
Claysend BA2 43 D5
CLAYS END 43 D6
Clays End La BA2 43 D6
Clayton Cl
Portishead BS20 2 E4
Yeovil BA22 218 A6
Clayton Rd BS8 226 A4
CLEARWOOD 121 F8
Clearwood BA13 121 F8
Clearwood View BA13 121 E4
Cleaveside Cl BA22 174 F3
CLEEVE 35 B8
Cleeve Abbey* TA23 131 E3
Cleevedale Rd BA2 45 A1
Cleeve Dr BS49 35 B8
Cleeve Gn BA2 44 A6
Cleeve Gr BS31 24 D5
Cleeve Hill
Ubley BS40 73 E8
Watchet TA23 202 A7
Cleeve Hill Rd BS40 35 C7
Cleeve Pk TA24 131 D5
Cleeve Pl BS48 9 A1
Cleeve Rd TA2 213 B7
Cleeveways DT9 176 A2
Clemence Rd BA16 207 D4
Clements Cl BA5 203 C3
Clement St BS2 227 C4
Cleve Ct 3 BS8 11 F6
CLEVEDON 6 B3
Clevedon Com Hospl BS21 6 E3
Clevedon Court* BS21 7 A4
Clevedon Craft Ctr* BS21 7 A1
Clevedon La BS21 8 B7
Clevedon Min Rly* BS21 6 B3
Clevedon Pier* BS21 6 C4
Clevedon Rd
Flax Bourton BS48 9 F2
Midsomer Norton BA3 78 A2
Nailsea BS21 8 B4
Portishead BS20 1 E1
Portishead BS20 2 D3
Walton In Gordano BS21 7 C8
Weston-super-Mare BS23 48 E6
Wraxall BS48 9 B4
Wraxall BS48 9 D6
Clevedon Sch BS21 6 F5
Clevedon Terr BS6 227 A4
Clevedon Wlk 2 BS48 8 E2
Cleveland Cotts BA1 228 C4
Cleveland Ct BA2 45 C6
Cleveland Pl BA1 228 C4
Cleveland Pl E BA1 228 C4
Cleveland Pl W BA1 228 C4
Cleveland Reach BA1 228 C4
Cleveland Row BA1 45 B8
Clevelands TA24 200 F8
Cleveland St TA1 212 E4
Cleveland Terr BA1 228 C4
Cleveland Wlk BA2 45 C6
Cleve The BA21 218 C6
CLEWER 89 D3
Clewer La BS28 89 D2
Clewer Rd BS28 89 D3
Clewson Rise BS14 22 F3
Cleyhill Gdns BA13 121 D4
Cliffe Dr BA3 64 A6
Clifford Ave TA2 212 E8
Clifford Cres TA2 212 E8
Clifford Dr BS39 77 D6
Clifford Gdns BS11 4 E6
Clifford Ho BS23 48 D6
Clifford Lodge 3 TA5 135 B2
Clifford Mews TA21 222 E6
Clifford Pk TA5 135 B2
Clifford Terr TA21 222 E6
Cliff Rd
North Petherton TA6 153 E3
Weston-super-Mare BS22 31 A2
Cliffs Rd The BA5 72 A1
Cliff St BS27 90 C8
Cliffs The
Cheddar BA5 72 A1
Cheddar BS27 90 C8
Clift House Rd BS3 11 F4
Clift House Spur BS3 11 F4
CLIFTON 226 A4
Clifton Ave BS23 48 E5
Clifton Cl
1 Bristol BS8 11 F7
Yeovil BA21 219 E6
Clifton Coll BS8 226 A4
Clifton College Prep Sch BS8 5 F1
Clifton Ct 10 BS21 6 C2
Clifton Down BS8 11 F7
Clifton Down Rd BS8 226 A3
Clifton High Gr BS9 5 E5
Clifton High Sch BS8 226 A4
Clifton Hill
Barwick BA22 197 F8
Bristol BS8 226 A2
Clifton Park Rd BS8 11 F8
Clifton Pk BS8 226 A3
Clifton Rd
Bristol BS8 226 A2
Weston-super-Mare BS23 48 E5
Clifton Rocks Railway* BS8 11 F6
Clifton St BS20 2 C2
Clifton Suspension Bridge* BS8 11 E7
Clifton Suspension Bridge Rd BS8 11 F7
Clifton Terr 7 TA2 212 F6
Clifton Vale BS8 226 A2
Clifton Vale Cl BS8 226 A2
Clifton View 9 BA22 197 F8
CLIFTON WOOD 226 A2
Cliftonwood Cres BS8 226 B2
Clifton Wood Ct BS8 226 B2
Clifton Wood Rd BS8 226 B2
Cliftonwood Terr BS8 226 A2
Clift Pl BS1 227 A1
Clifts Bldgs BA11 119 F4
CLINK 120 C6
Clink Farm Ct BA11 120 C6
Clink Rd BA11 120 D6
Clink The TA6 209 A5
Clipper Cl TA6 209 C4
Clipper Ct BA16 207 B5
Clipper Quay TA24 201 B7
Clitsome View TA23 131 D2
Clive Rd BS14 23 C8
Clivey BA13 102 E1
Clock Ho TA5 134 B2
Clock Ho The BA10 160 D4
Clockhouse Mews BS20 2 D6
Clockhouse The TA4 167 E6
Clockhouse View BA16 207 D6
CLOFORD 143 A7
CLOFORD COMMON 143 B6
Cloisters Croft TA8 104 B6
Cloisters The BA5 203 D3
Cloister The DT9 225 D4
Closemead BS21 6 D1
Close The
Glastonbury BA6 206 E5
9 Merriott TA16 195 F7
Minehead TA24 201 B5
North Cadbury BA22 175 D6
Portishead BS20 1 F1
CLOSWORTH 197 F5
Clotfurlong La DT9 188 F1
Clothier Mdw BA7 214 B6
Cloudberry Cl TA20 223 F5
Cloud Hill Ind Est BS39 77 A8
Clovelly Rd BS22 32 A2
Clover Cl
Clevedon BS21 6 F3
Frome BA11 120 B3
Paulton BS39 77 E4
Clover Ct 2 BS22 49 D7
Clover Gd BA4 205 C5
Clover Hill Way
Barrow Gurney BS48 20 F7
Bristol BS48 21 A6
Clover Mead TA1 213 C1
Clover Rd BS22 32 A6
Cloverton Dr TA6 209 D7
Clover Way
Bridgwater TA6 208 E1
Highbridge TA9 104 E4
Clumber Dr BA11 119 F6
Clumber Ho BA11 119 F6
CLUTTON 58 E3
CLUTTON HILL 59 B4
Clutton Hill BS39 59 B4
Clutton Prim Sch BS39 58 E3
Clyce Rd TA9 104 D3
Clyde Ave BS31 24 F4
Clyde Gdns BA2 44 B6
Clydesdale Cl BS14 23 A6
Clynder Gr BS21 6 E6
Clyntonville BS22 31 A4
Coach House Mews BS23 30 D1
Coachmans Yd BA6 206 D5
Coach Rd TA24 124 A3
Coalash La BA11 119 D8
Coal Barton BA3 116 E8
Coalbridge Cl BS22 31 F2
Coaley Rd BS11 4 D5
Coal La BA11 119 C8
Coal Orch TA1 212 F4
Coalpit La
Chilcompton BA3 96 A2
Stoke St Michael BA3 116 B3
Coalpit Rd BA1 29 A4
Coape Rd BS14 23 F5
Coast Cvn Pk BS21 1 B1
Coastguard Cotts TA24 201 A8
Coast Rd TA8 84 F7
COAT 185 D7
Coates Est BS48 8 F3
Coates Gr BS48 9 A2
Coates Wlk BS4 22 D6
Coate Turn TA4 166 A6
Coatmead Dro TA12 185 C8
Coat Rd TA12 185 D7
Cobbetts Rise TA13 220 B5
Cobblers Way BA3 97 C8
Cobblestone Mews BS8 226 A4
Cob Castle TA21 180 D8
Cobhorn Dr BS13 21 F4
Cobley Croft BS21 16 C8
Cobthorn Way BS49 34 E5
Coburg Cl TA21 180 F7
Coburg Villas 11 BA1 28 A1
Cock And Yew Tree Hill BS40 38 A2
Cock-Crowing Stone TA20 193 D4
Cockercombe Rd TA5 151 F7
Cockers Hill BS39 41 C5
Cockhill Elm La BA7 214 B4
Cockhill La BA22 175 D7
COCKLAKE 108 E7
Cocklake La BS28 108 D8
Cockland Hill TA21 166 C1
Cockmill La BA4 140 F1
Cockpit Hill DT6, DT8 199 F4
Cockpit La BA4 142 C2
Cock Rd
Buckland Dinham BA2, BA11 100 B5
Horningsham BA12 144 C4
COCKWOOD 134 E5
Cockwood Rd TA5 134 D5
Cod La BA22 196 D7
Codrington Pl BS8 226 A3
Codsend Rd TA24 129 B2
Cogley Rd BA10 215 F8
Cogsall Rd BS14 23 F6
Coity Pl BS21 6 C4
Coker Hill BA22 196 F8
Coker Hill La BA22 197 A7
Coker Ho BA22 197 C8
Coker Marsh
East Coker BA22 197 D7
East Coker BA22 197 D7
Coker Rd BS22 32 B2
Coker's La BA12 161 F8
Coking La SP8 190 E7
Colbourn Cl BA3 114 E7
Colbourne Rd BA2 44 D1
Colchester Cres BS4 22 D7
COLD ASHTON 12 F6
Cold Harbour
Milborne Port DT9 217 D2
Sherborne DT9 225 E5
Coldharbour Bsns Pk DT9 225 E6
Coldharbour La BS23 48 D3
Cold Harbour La BA22 196 F6
Coldhills La BA8 176 D2
Cold Nose BS28 138 D8
Coldpark Gdns BS13 21 E5
Coldpark Rd BS13 21 E5
Cold Rd TA3 182 D6
Coldrick Cl BS14 22 F3
Cole Cl
Cotford St Luke TA4 167 E6
Nether Stowey TA5 134 A3
Cole Cross BA22 186 C6
COLEFORD 116 F7
Coleford La TA14 185 E2
COLEFORD WATER 150 F4
Cole Hill BA11 144 B7
Colehouse La BS21 16 C8
Cole La 5 TA14 185 F4
Colemead BS13 22 B5
Cole Mead BA10 215 D5
Cole Rd BA10 215 D5
Coleridge Cottage* TA5 134 B2
Coleridge Cres TA1 213 B3
Coleridge Gdns TA8 85 B2
Coleridge Gn TA6 208 E5
Coleridge Rd
Bridgwater TA6 208 E6
Clevedon BS21 6 C3
Nether Stowey TA5 134 A2
Weston-super-Mare BS23 49 A4
Coleridge Sq TA6 208 E6
Coleridge Vale Rd E 1 BS21 6 D2
Coleridge Vale Rd N BS21 6 C2
Coleridge Vale Rd S BS21 6 D2

Coleridge Vale Rd W 2
BS21 . . . . 6 C2
Coles Cotts TA5 . . . . . 135 F2
COLE'S CROSS 199 D5
Coles Cross Cotts DT8 . . . 199 D5
Coles Gdns BA3 . . . . . 98 B5
Coleshill Dr BS13 . . . . . 22 B5
Cole's La
Chewton Mendip BA3 . . . . . 95 A6
South Petherton TA13 . . . . . 220 D3
Colesmore TA4 . . . . . 167 A4
Coles Place TA20 . . . . . 223 C3
Coles's La EX13 . . . . . 198 B1
COLEY 75 C4
Coley Hill BS40 . . . . . 75 D5
Coley La TA19 . . . . . 194 F5
Coley Narrow BS40 . . . . . 75 C3
Coley Rd BS40 . . . . . 75 B4
Colham La TA20 . . . . . 194 E1
Colin Ave TA2 . . . . . 212 F7
Colin Rd TA2 . . . . . 213 A7
Collarway La BA22 . . . . . 196 F8
College BA22 . . . . . 196 E8
College Cl TA10 . . . . . 172 E2
College Ct TA8 . . . . . 104 A7
College Fields BS8 . . . . . 11 F8
College Gn
Bristol BS1 . . . . . 226 C2
Yeovil BA21 . . . . . 219 B6
College Rd
Bath BA1 . . . . . 27 E1
Bristol, Clifton BS8 . . . . . 11 F8
Taunton TA2 . . . . . 212 D6
Wells BA5 . . . . . 203 E5
College Sq BS1 . . . . . 226 C2
College St
Bristol BS1 . . . . . 226 C2
Burnham-on-S TA8 . . . . . 104 A7
College View
18 Bath BA1 . . . . . 28 A1
Taunton TA1 . . . . . 212 C2
College Way
Bridgwater TA6 . . . . . 209 C6
Taunton TA1 . . . . . 212 C1
Colles Cl BA5 . . . . . 203 F5
Colles Rd BA5 . . . . . 203 F5
Collett Ave BA4 . . . . . 205 C5
Collett Cl BS22 . . . . . 32 C4
Collett Rd TA2 . . . . . 212 A7
Collett Way BA11 . . . . . 120 C7
Colley Farm La TA20 . . . . . 192 E8
Colley La TA6 . . . . . 209 B4
Colleylake Cotts TA3 . . . . . 181 C5
Colley Lane Ind Est TA6 . . . 209 B3
Collickshire La TA3 . . . . . 170 E6
Collie Cnr BA11 . . . . . 118 A1
Collier Cl BA2 . . . . . 78 D8
Colliers Gdns BS48 . . . . . 18 F7
Colliers La BA1 . . . . . 27 F4
Collier's La BA11 . . . . . 99 D2
Colliers Rise BA3 . . . . . 79 A3
Colliers Wlk 4 BS48 . . . . . 8 E2
Colliery La BA2 . . . . . 79 D5
Collingwood Cl
Saltford BS31 . . . . . 25 E2
Weston-super-Mare BS22 . . . 31 E4
Collingwood Ct TA6 . . . . . 208 F5
Collingwood Rd BA21 . . . . . 219 F8
Collin's Farm TA19 . . . . . 183 E2
Collins' La TA11 . . . . . 173 F7
Collinson Rd BS13 . . . . . 22 B5
Collins St BS11 . . . . . 4 B8
Colliters Way
Bristol BS13 . . . . . 21 D7
Bristol BS3 . . . . . 11 D1
Collum La BS22 . . . . . 31 E6
Colman Rd TA1 . . . . . 212 B1
Colmer Rd
Bridgwater TA6 . . . . . 208 F7
Yeovil BA21 . . . . . 219 B6
Colne Gn BS31 . . . . . 25 A4
Colombo Cres BS23 . . . . . 48 E3
Colston Ave BS1 . . . . . 227 A2
Colston Cross EX13 . . . . . 198 B4
Colston Fort 2 BS2 . . . . . 227 A4
Colston Par BS1 . . . . . 227 B1
Colston's Almshouses 1
BS1 . . . . . 227 A3
Colston St BS1 . . . . . 227 A3
Colston Yd BS1 . . . . . 227 A3
Colton La TA4 . . . . . 149 F7
Columbus Cl 7 BA21 . . . . . 219 F8
Columbus Ho BA2 . . . . . 45 D8
Colyton 11 BS22 . . . . . 32 A2
Combe Ave BS20 . . . . . 2 C6
Combe Batch BS28 . . . . . 108 D4
Combe Batch Rise BS28 . . 108 D4
Combe Beacon La TA20 . . . 193 C7
Combe Cl
Bicknoller TA4 . . . . . 132 E2
Yeovil BA21 . . . . . 219 A8
Combe Cross
Halse TA4 . . . . . 167 B7
Monksilver TA4 . . . . . 150 C8
Shillingford EX16 . . . . . 164 D4
Combecross Hill TA4 . . . . . 150 B8
Combecross La
Monksilver TA4 . . . . . 150 B8
Stogumber TA4 . . . . . 150 C8
COMBE DOWN 45 B1
Combe Down CE Prim Sch
BA2 . . . . . 45 B1
Combe Down CEVC Prim Sch
Bathwick BA2 . . . . . 45 B1
Combe Down BA2 . . . . . 45 B1
Combe Down La TA4 . . . . . 151 C2
Combe Fields BS20 . . . . . 2 C6
COMBE FLOREY 151 C2
Combe Gn BA5 . . . . . 204 B7
Combe Gr BA1 . . . . . 44 B8
COMBE HAY 62 D4
Combe Hay La BA2 . . . . . 62 B6
COMBE HILL 217 A4
Combe Hill
Barton St David TA11 . . . . . 158 A2
Combe St Nicholas TA20 . . . 193 D5
Hemyock EX15 . . . . . 180 C2
Milborne Port DT9 . . . . . 217 B3
Templecombe BA8 . . . . . 176 E1
Yenston BA8 . . . . . 189 F8
Combe Hill Dro TA20 . . . . . 193 C5
Combe Hill La TA7 . . . . . 156 B7
Combe La
Brompton Ralph TA4 . . . . . 150 B3
Charlton Adam TA11 . . . . . 173 F8
Chilton Polden TA7 . . . . . 137 B3
Churchstanton TA3 . . . . . 181 A2
Combe St Nicholas TA20 . . . 193 B5
Dulverton TA22 . . . . . 163 D6
East Anstey TA22 . . . . . 162 F6
Exford TA24 . . . . . 128 D1
Hallatrow BS39 . . . . . 77 B6
Langport TA10 . . . . . 171 F7
North Curry TA3 . . . . . 170 A4
Parbrook BA4 . . . . . 158 D8
Rodhuish TA24 . . . . . 131 B3
Wedmore BS28 . . . . . 108 D4
Wiveliscombe TA4 . . . . . 210 C8
Woolavington TA7 . . . . . 136 F4
Combeland La TA22 . . . . . 164 A5
Combeland Rd TA24 . . . . . 201 B4
Combe Pk
Bath BA1 . . . . . 44 C8
Yeovil BA21 . . . . . 218 F8
Combe Rd
Bath BA2 . . . . . 45 B1
Portishead BS20 . . . . . 2 D5
Combe Road Cl BA2 . . . . . 45 B1
COMBE ST NICHOLAS 193 D6
Combeshead Hill TA22 . . . 148 A3
Combeshead La
Brompton Regis TA22 . . . . . 148 A4
West Anstey EX36 . . . . . 162 A7
Combeside BA2 . . . . . 45 A3
Combe Side BS48 . . . . . 19 A7
Combe St TA20 . . . . . 223 C4
Combe Street La BA21 . . . . . 219 A8
Combe Street Lane Rdbt
BA21 . . . . . 218 F8
Combe Terr TA9 . . . . . 136 E8
Combe The
Burrington BS40 . . . . . 53 F2
Lydeard St Lawrence TA4 . . . 151 C2
COMBE THROOP 176 F2
COMBWICH 135 B5
Combwich Rd TA5 . . . . . 135 B4
Comer Rd BS27 . . . . . 90 A7
Comer's Cross TA24 . . . . . 146 E6
Comer's Gate TA24 . . . . . 146 E6
COMEYTROWE 212 B1
Comeytrowe Ctr TA1 . . . . . 212 C1
Comeytrowe La TA1, TA4 . . 212 A2
Comeytrowe Orch TA1 . . . 212 A2
Comeytrowe Rd TA1 . . . . . 212 B1
Comeytrowe Rise TA1 . . . . . 212 B2
Comfortable Pl BA1 . . . . . 228 A3
Commerce Pk BA11 . . . . . 120 D8
Commerce Way TA9 . . . . . 104 F2
Commercial Rd
Bristol BS1 . . . . . 227 A1
Shepton Mallet BA4 . . . . . 205 B6
Commercial Row TA20 . . . 223 C4
Commercial Way BS22 . . . . 32 B2
Common La
Charlton Adam TA11 . . . . . 174 A8
Churchill Green BS25 . . . . . 52 B5
Easton-in-G BS20 . . . . . 4 B2
Halstock BA22 . . . . . 197 C2
Hardington Mandeville
BA22 . . . . . 197 A5
Holcombe BA3 . . . . . 116 D7
Huish Champflower TA4 . . . 165 D7
Kington Magna SP8 . . . . . 177 E1
Marnhull DT10 . . . . . 190 E4
North Perrott TA18 . . . . . 196 D4
South Cheriton BA8 . . . . . 176 F4
Templecombe BA8 . . . . . 177 A1
Wincanton BA9 . . . . . 216 D3
Yenston BA8 . . . . . 189 F8
Common Moor Dro BA6 . . 206 E7
Common Rd
Horningsham BA12 . . . . . 144 C3
Wincanton BA9 . . . . . 216 E3
Como Ct BS20 . . . . . 2 C6
Compass Ave TA6 . . . . . 153 F5
Compass Hill TA1 . . . . . 212 E3
Compass Rise TA1 . . . . . 212 E3
Com Prim Sch
Sydenham TA6 . . . . . 209 B5
Weston-super-Mare BS22 . . . 32 A5
Compton Acres DT9 . . . . . 187 E4
COMPTON BISHOP 69 A3
Compton Cl
Glastonbury BA6 . . . . . 206 F7
Shepton Mallet BA4 . . . . . 205 B5
Taunton TA2 . . . . . 213 A6
Yeovil BA21 . . . . . 219 E8
Compton Cnr BA4 . . . . . 205 B5
Compton Ct Mews DT9 . . . 187 F3
COMPTON DANDO 41 D6
Compton Dr
Ansford BA7 . . . . . 214 A6
Bristol BS9 . . . . . 5 C7
Compton Dr *continued*
Weston-super-Mare BS24 . . . 49 E7
COMPTON DUNDON 157 B4
COMPTON DURVILLE 184 F4
Compton Flats BA21 . . . . . 219 C6
Compton Gdns BA11 . . . . . 120 D7
Compton Gn BS31 . . . . . 24 E4
Compton Hill TA13 . . . . . 220 A5
Compton La
Axbridge BS26 . . . . . 70 B1
Shepton Mallet BA4 . . . . . 205 B2
COMPTON MARTIN 74 A7
COMPTON
PAUNCEFOOT 175 E5
Compton Rd
Shepton Mallet BA4 . . . . . 205 B4
South Cadbury BA22 . . . . . 175 D4
South Petherton TA13 . . . . . 220 B5
Yeovil BA21 . . . . . 187 E3
Compton St
Butleigh BA6 . . . . . 157 D4
Compton Dundon TA11 . . . . . 157 B4
Comrade Ave BS25 . . . . . 70 E8
Concorde Dr BS21 . . . . . 6 B1
Condell Cl TA6 . . . . . 208 F7
Condor Cl BS22 . . . . . 49 D8
Conduit Hill BA11 . . . . . 99 B1
Conduit La TA24 . . . . . 201 D2
Conegore BA22 . . . . . 174 D4
Conegore Cnr BA22 . . . . . 174 D4
Coneygree BS13 . . . . . 21 F6
Conference Ave BS20 . . . . . 2 F5
Conference Cl BS20 . . . . . 2 F4
CONGRESBURY 34 E4
Conies The TA2 . . . . . 168 E8
Conifer Cl TA24 . . . . . 128 D1
Conifer Way BS24 . . . . . 49 E5
Coniston Ave BS9 . . . . . 5 E6
Coniston Cres BS23 . . . . . 48 F4
Coniston Gdns BA21 . . . . . 219 A7
CONKWELL 46 C1
Conkwell BA15 . . . . . 46 C2
Connaught Ho TA6 . . . . . 209 C5
Connaught Mans BA2 . . . . 228 C3
Connaught Pl BS23 . . . . . 48 D8
Connaught Rd BS4 . . . . . 22 E8
Connection Rd BA2 . . . . . 44 A6
Connelly Dr BS28 . . . . . 108 C4
Connock Sq BA4 . . . . . 205 C4
Conquest Bsns Pk TA19 . . . 184 A4
Constable Cl
Keynsham BS31 . . . . . 24 F6
Yeovil BA21 . . . . . 219 E8
Constable Dr BS22 . . . . . 31 F3
Constantine Ct BA4 . . . . . 205 E4
Constitution Hill BS8 . . . . . 226 B2
Convocation Ave BA2 . . . . . 45 E5
Conway Cres TA8 . . . . . 85 C1
Conway Gn BS31 . . . . . 25 A3
Conway Rd TA5 . . . . . 135 B2
Conygar Cl BS21 . . . . . 6 F5
Conygar View TA24 . . . . . 201 E3
Conygre Gn BA2 . . . . . 60 B2
Conygre Rise BA2 . . . . . 59 F6
Cook Ave TA20 . . . . . 223 D3
Cooke's La TA10 . . . . . 156 B2
Cookley La TA4 . . . . . 150 F8
Cook Rd BA21 . . . . . 219 F8
Cooks Bridle Path BS48 . . . 36 D8
Cooks Cl TA3 . . . . . 169 D5
Cook's Folly Rd BS9 . . . . . 5 D3
Cooks Gdns BS48 . . . . . 9 A2
Cooks Hill BS39 . . . . . 58 E3
Cooks La DT9 . . . . . 225 D3
Cook's La
Banwell BS29 . . . . . 51 A4
Clevedon BS21 . . . . . 7 B2
Cranmore BA4 . . . . . 142 A6
Milverton TA4 . . . . . 167 B5
Stalbridge DT10 . . . . . 190 B2
Cooksley La TA4 . . . . . 149 A2
Cookson Cl TA8 . . . . . 104 D5
Cook St BS11 . . . . . 4 C8
Cook Way TA2 . . . . . 212 C6
COOMBE
Crewkerne 195 B4
Sampford Peverell 178 A4
Taunton 169 C8
Coombe DT9 . . . . . 225 C5
Coombe Bridge Ave BS9 . . . 5 D6
Coombe Brook BA5 . . . . . 203 A7
Coombe Cl BA7 . . . . . 214 C6
Coombe Cotts BA5 . . . . . 204 C7
Coombe Dale
Backwell BS48 . . . . . 37 A8
Bristol BS9 . . . . . 5 C6
Coombe Dell BA4 . . . . . 205 A6
COOMBE DINGLE 5 C8
Coombe Gdns BS9 . . . . . 5 E6
Coombe Hill
Blagdon Hill TA21 . . . . . 181 A5
Bruton BA10 . . . . . 215 E7
Coombe Hill La TA11 . . . . . 158 A2
Coombe La
Bristol BS9 . . . . . 5 E6
Compton Bishop BS26 . . . . . 69 B4
East Harptree BS40 . . . . . 74 E4
Easton-in-G BS8 . . . . . 4 A2
Kingsbury Episcopi TA12 . . . 185 B8
Shepton Mallet BA4 . . . . . 205 A6
Coomb End BA3 . . . . . 78 F3
Coombend Ho BA3 . . . . . 78 F3
Coombe Rd
Dinnington TA17 . . . . . 195 B7
Nailsea BS48 . . . . . 8 E1
Weston-super-Mare BS23 . . . 30 E1
Coombe's Cider Farm & Mus★
TA9 . . . . . 106 A4
Coombe Side TA9 . . . . . 86 B2
Coombe St
Bruton BA10 . . . . . 215 E7
Penselwood BA9 . . . . . 161 E2
Coombe's Way BS26 . . . . . 87 E8
Coombe Terr
Glastonbury BA6 . . . . . 206 E5
Sherborne DT9 . . . . . 225 C5
Coombe The
Blagdon BS40 . . . . . 54 C3
Compton Martin BS40 . . . . . 74 A6
Coombe View BA4 . . . . . 205 A6
Coombe Water La DT8 . . . 199 E5
Coomb Rocke BS9 . . . . . 5 D6
Cooperage La BS3 . . . . . 226 B1
Cooperage The BA11 . . . . . 119 F3
Cooper Rd BS9 . . . . . 5 F7
Cooper's Ash La BA7,
BA22 . . . . . 214 A2
Coopers Barns BA22 . . . . . 174 F1
Coopers Hts TA4 . . . . . 210 C4
Cooper's La BA11 . . . . . 101 E7
Coopers Mead BA4 . . . . . 205 D4
Coopers Mill TA2 . . . . . 168 B4
Coot Hide EX16 . . . . . 178 D1
Coots The BS14 . . . . . 23 E6
Copeland Dr BS14 . . . . . 23 B5
Copford La BS41 . . . . . 11 B1
Copis La TA11 . . . . . 158 B3
Coplestons TA3 . . . . . 168 D1
Copley Gdns BS22 . . . . . 31 F2
Coppack Ho 6 BS21 . . . . . 6 C2
Copper Beeches TA1 . . . . . 212 A2
Copper Beech Rd TA11 . . . 173 D5
Copper Cl BS27 . . . . . 90 A8
Copperfield Dr BS22 . . . . . 31 F4
Coppern Way DT10 . . . . . 190 B4
Coppice Cl BA20 . . . . . 218 D2
Coppice End Cnr BS24 . . . . . 67 C2
Coppice Mews BS21 . . . . . 6 C4
Coppice The BS13 . . . . . 21 E4
Coppin Cl BA6 . . . . . 206 F3
Coppin Rd TA2 . . . . . 168 B4
Coppits Hill La
Yeovil BA21 . . . . . 218 D8
Yeovil Marsh BA21 . . . . . 187 A5
COPPLEHAM 147 D5
Copplesbury La BA4, BA10 160 D8
Copse Cl
Watchet TA23 . . . . . 202 C5
Weston-super-Mare BS24 . . . 49 A1
Copse Cnr BS24 . . . . . 67 C2
Copse Dro
Baltonsborough BA6 . . . . . 158 C5
Barrington TA19 . . . . . 184 B5
Copse End BS25 . . . . . 51 F2
Copse La
Ashill TA19 . . . . . 183 D4
Barrington TA19 . . . . . 184 D4
Hambridge TA3 . . . . . 184 B7
Ilton TA19 . . . . . 183 F4
Pilton BA4 . . . . . 140 F3
Copseland BA2 . . . . . 45 D5
Copse Rd
Clevedon BS21 . . . . . 6 C4
Keynsham BS31 . . . . . 25 C4
Yeovil BA22 . . . . . 218 B7
Copse Shoot La TA19 . . . . . 184 C5
Copse Stile TA20 . . . . . 193 F1
Copse The
Bridgwater TA6 . . . . . 209 D5
Cossington TA7 . . . . . 136 F3
Frome BA11 . . . . . 120 B6
Weston-super-Mare BS22 . . . 32 D2
Copsewood La BS26 . . . . . 88 B2
Copthorne Cl BS14 . . . . . 23 B5
Copthorn La BS40 . . . . . 53 F6
Coral Ave TA6 . . . . . 209 C8
Coralberry Dr BS22 . . . . . 31 F1
Corams La TA21 . . . . . 222 B6
Cording's Ball TA4 . . . . . 150 A1
Corewell La TA5 . . . . . 133 E3
CORFE 181 F6
Corfe Cl BS48 . . . . . 8 D1
Corfe Cres BS31 . . . . . 24 E4
Corfe Rd BS4 . . . . . 22 D7
Corinthian Ct 9 BS1 . . . . . 227 B1
Cork Pl BA1 . . . . . 44 D7
Corkscrew La
North Cadbury BA22 . . . . . 175 E7
Staplegrove TA2 . . . . . 212 D8
Cork St
Bath BA1 . . . . . 44 D7
Frome BA11 . . . . . 119 F5
Cork Terr BA1 . . . . . 44 D7
Cormorant Cl
Bridgwater TA6 . . . . . 209 C3
Weston-super-Mare BS22 . . . 31 F1
Cornborough Pl TA6 . . . . . 209 B5
Cornbrash BA11 . . . . . 120 D7
Corner Cl TA21 . . . . . 222 D4
Corner Croft BS21 . . . . . 6 D1
Cornfields The BS22 . . . . . 31 F5
Cornflower Cl TA6 . . . . . 208 D1
Cornhill
Bridgwater TA6 . . . . . 208 F5
Shepton Mallet BA4 . . . . . 205 C6
Sherborne DT9 . . . . . 225 C4
5 Wellington TA21 . . . . . 222 D6
Cornhill Dr BS14 . . . . . 23 A7
Cornish Gr BS14 . . . . . 23 E6
Cornishmen's Rd BA1 . . . . . 27 E4
Cornish Rd BS14 . . . . . 23 E6
Cornishway E TA1 . . . . . 212 B3
Cornishway N TA1 . . . . . 212 B3
Cornishway S TA1 . . . . . 212 B2
Cornishway W TA1 . . . . . 212 B3
Cornish Wlk BS14 . . . . . 23 E6
Cornlands EX16 . . . . . 178 D1
Cornleaze BS13 . . . . . 22 A5
Cornmoor Cres TA9 . . . . . 136 E7
Cornmoor La TA9 . . . . . 136 E7
Corn St
Bath BA1 . . . . . 228 B2
Bristol BS1 . . . . . 227 A3
Cornwallis Ave
Bristol BS8 . . . . . 226 A2
Weston-super-Mare BS22 . . . 31 F4
Cornwallis Cres BS8 . . . . . 11 F6
Cornwallis Gr BS8 . . . . . 226 A2
Cornwall Rd BA4 . . . . . 205 A6
Coromandel Hts BA1 . . . . . 228 B4
Coronation Ave
Bath BA2 . . . . . 44 C4
Keynsham BS31 . . . . . 24 D4
Yeovil BA21 . . . . . 218 F7
Coronation Cl
Ruishton TA3 . . . . . 169 C3
Wanstrow BA4 . . . . . 142 F4
Coronation Ct BA3 . . . . . 115 A3
Coronation Est BS23 . . . . . 48 F3
Coronation Ho TA6 . . . . . 209 C6
Coronation Pl BS1 . . . . . 227 A2
Coronation Rd
Banwell BS29 . . . . . 51 A3
Bath BA1 . . . . . 44 D7
Bleadon BS24 . . . . . 67 C6
Bridgwater TA6 . . . . . 208 E5
Bristol BS3 . . . . . 226 B1
Frome BA11 . . . . . 120 B5
Highbridge TA9 . . . . . 104 D4
Wells BA5 . . . . . 203 B4
Weston-super-Mare BS22 . . . 31 E2
Coronation St TA20 . . . . . 223 C3
Coronation Terr
Chilcompton BA3 . . . . . 96 D5
Oakhill BA3 . . . . . 115 A3
Coronation Villas BA8 . . . . . 176 E1
Corondale Rd BS22 . . . . . 49 D8
Corporate Rd BA22 . . . . . 174 A2
Corporation St TA1 . . . . . 212 F3
Corpus Christi RC Prim Sch
BS23 . . . . . 48 D6
Corrick Cl BS27 . . . . . 90 F2
Corridor The 2 BA1 . . . . . 228 C2
Corscombe Rd BA22 . . . . . 197 C2
Corsham Dr TA8 . . . . . 104 C8
CORSLEY 121 D2
CORSLEY HEATH 144 E8
Corsley Heath BA11 . . . . . 144 D8
Corsley Wlk BS4 . . . . . 22 F8
CORSTON 43 B7
Corston BS24 . . . . . 49 A2
Corston Dr BA2 . . . . . 43 B6
Corston La BA2 . . . . . 43 A8
Corston View BA2 . . . . . 44 C2
Corston Wlk BS11 . . . . . 4 D7
Corton Cl BA21 . . . . . 219 E8
CORTON DENHAM 175 D1
Corton Denham Rd DT9 . . 175 D2
Coryate Cl BA22 . . . . . 186 C2
Cory Rd TA2 . . . . . 213 A8
Cosgates Feet or County Gate
EX35 . . . . . 122 D5
Cosmos Dr TA6 . . . . . 208 D1
COSSINGTON 136 F3
Cossington La TA7 . . . . . 136 E3
Cossington Rd BS4 . . . . . 22 F8
Cossins La TA18 . . . . . 224 C6
Costello Hill BA22 . . . . . 173 F2
Costiland Dr BS13 . . . . . 21 F6
Cote Cnr TA9 . . . . . 136 F7
Cote House La BS9 . . . . . 5 F5
Cote La BA12 . . . . . 161 F6
Cote Paddock BS9 . . . . . 5 F4
Cote Pk BS9 . . . . . 5 E6
COTFORD ST LUKE 167 E6
Cotford St Luke Prim Sch
TA4 . . . . . 167 E5
Cotham Hill BS6 . . . . . 226 C4
Cotham Lawn Ho BS6 . . . . . 226 C4
Cotham Lawn Rd BS6 . . . . . 226 C4
Cotham Pl BS6 . . . . . 226 C4
Cotham Rd BS6 . . . . . 226 C4
Cotham Rd S BS6 . . . . . 227 A4
Cotham Sch BS6 . . . . . 226 C4
Cothay Manor Gardens★
TA21 . . . . . 179 C8
COTHELSTONE 152 A2
Cothelstone Cl TA6 . . . . . 208 B4
Cothelstone Rd TA4 . . . . . 151 F1
Cotlake Cl TA1 . . . . . 212 F1
Cotlake Rise TA1 . . . . . 168 E1
Cotleigh Crossing EX14 . . . 191 F1
Cotley La TA20 . . . . . 193 D2
Cotman Wlk 1 BS22 . . . . . 31 F2
Cotswold Cl BS20 . . . . . 2 E4
Cotswold Gdns BA3 . . . . . 97 A6
Cotswold Rd BA2 . . . . . 44 E4
Cotswold View BA2 . . . . . 44 B5
Cotswold Way SN14 . . . . . 13 A6
Cottage Cnr TA19 . . . . . 183 F4
Cottage La TA22 . . . . . 163 D6
Cottage Pl
3 Bath BA1 . . . . . 28 C2
Bristol BS2 . . . . . 227 A4
Cottage Row TA8 . . . . . 104 A6
Cottages The BS40 . . . . . 35 D2
Cotterell Ct BA1 . . . . . 228 B2
Cottiford La TA4 . . . . . 132 D2
Cottiford Rd TA4 . . . . . 132 D2
Cottle Gdns BS14 . . . . . 23 F6
Cottle Rd BS14 . . . . . 23 F6
Cottles La
West Pennard BA6 . . . . . 140 B1
Winsley BA15 . . . . . 64 F6

COTTLE'S OAK 119 C5
Cotton Cnr 13 BA8. . . . . . . .190 A6
Cotton Mead BA2 . . . . 43 B7
Cotton Patch Wlk 6 TA6 .209 A1
Cotton's La TA11. . . . . .158 B2
Cottonwick Cl BS11 . . . . 4 D5
Cotty La BA5. . . . . .139 B8
Coulson Dr BS22 . . . . 32 B3
Coulson's Cl BS14. . . . . 23 A3
Coulson's Rd BS14 . . . . 23 A3
COULTINGS. 134 F4
Council Hos
Babcary TA11. . . . . .174 D7
Bleadon BS24. . . . . 67 B5
Clapton TA18 . . . . .195 C1
Hewish TA18. . . . . .195 D3
Kingston Seymour BS21. . . . . 16 C3
Podimore BA22 . . . . .174 A4
Wick St Lawrence BS22 . . . . . 32 B8
Council Houses BS24. . . . . . 33 C3
Council Houses The
Butcombe BS40 . . . . 55 B8
Hinton Blewett BS39 . . . . 75 E6
Counterslip BS1 . . . . .227 B2
Counterslip Gdns BS14 . . . . 23 C6
Countess Ave TA6. . . . . . . .208 E7
Countess Gytha Prim Sch
BA22. . . . . .174 F3
County Wlk TA1. . . . . .213 A3
Couple Cross TA24 . . . . . . .130 B1
COURSHAY 198 E3
Coursing Batch BA6. . . . . .206 F3
COURSLEY 151 B4
Court Acres 6 BA22. . . . . .197 F8
Court Ash BA20 . . . . .219 B5
Court Ave BS49 . . . . 34 C7
Court Barn La BA6 . . . . . . .158 A8
Court Barton
Crewkerne TA18. . . . . .224 B6
Ilminster TA19 . . . . .221 C4
Court Cl
Portishead BS20 . . . . 2 D4
Weston-super-Mare BS22 . . . 32 C2
Court Cl The BS48. . . . . 19 C5
Court Cotts SP8. . . . . .177 D3
Court-de-Wyck Prim Sch
BS49. 17 F1
Court Dr
Sandford BS25. . . . . 52 B4
Wellington TA21. . . . . .222 D5
Courtenay Cres BS4 . . . . 22 D7
Courtenay Rd BS31. . . . . 25 B2
Courtenay Wlk BS22. . . . . . . 32 A3
Court Farm BA11. . . . . .100 A3
Court Farm Cl TA20 . . . . . .194 E1
Court Farm Country Park★
Banwell BS29. . . . . 50 F5
Weston-super-Mare BS24 . . . 50 F5
Court Farm Rd BS14. . . . . . . 22 F3
Courtfield
Langport TA10 . . . . .172 A5
Milverton TA4. . . . . .166 F4
Court Field La TA20 . . . . . .193 B5
Court Fields Com Sch
TA21 . . . . .222 C5
Court Gdns
Batheaston BA1. . . . . 29 A4
Marston Magna BA22. . . . . .174 F1
Yeovil BA21 . . . . .218 E8
Court Gr TA7. . . . . .136 C4
Court Hay BS20 . . . . 4 A4
Court Hill
Compton Dando BS39. . . . . . . 41 D5
Taunton TA1 . . . . .212 D2
Court Ho BS26 . . . . 70 B2
Court La
7 Barwick BA22 . . . . .197 F8
Bathford BA1. . . . . 29 B2
Clevedon BS21. . . . . 7 A3
Lye's Green BA12. . . . . .121 B1
Milborne Port DT9 . . . . .217 C3
Morebath EX16 . . . . .164 D4
Shipham BS25 . . . . 70 F8
Courtland Rd TA21 . . . . . . .222 D6
Courtlands BS31. . . . . 24 E5
Courtlands Cl TA23. . . . . . .202 C6
Courtlands Farm Ind Est
TA2 .168 B5
Courtlands La BS3 . . . . 11 E4
Courtlands Unit BS4. . . . . . . 22 D8
Courtmead BA2. . . . . 62 F7
Courtmead La TA24 . . . . . .123 F4
Court Mill TA20 . . . . .223 A8
Court Mill La TA20 . . . . . . .223 A8
Court Moors La TA21 . . . . .179 E5
Court Orch TA5 . . . . .135 B2
Court Pl BS22. . . . . 31 F2
Court Place La TA24. . . . . .131 B4
Court Rd
Norton Fitzwarren TA2 . . . . .168 B4
Weston-super-Mare BS22 . . . 31 A5
Court's Barton BA11. . . . . .119 D2
Court St
5 Bridgwater TA6 . . . . .208 F5
Winsham TA20 . . . . .194 E1
Court Terr TA21. . . . . .222 C5
Court The TA24 . . . . .131 A5
COURTWAY. 152 C4
Court Way EX16. . . . . .178 D1
Courtway Ave TA6. . . . . . . .209 C4
Courtyard The
Dunster TA24 . . . . .201 E2
Evercreech BA4 . . . . .141 F2
Minehead TA24. . . . . .200 F7
Shapwick TA7 . . . . .137 F1
3 Taunton TA1 . . . . .212 F4
West Harptree BS40 . . . . 74 E6
Couture Gr BA16 . . . . .207 B6
Coverdale Ct BA21 . . . . . . .218 F6
Cowan Cl TA8. . . . . .104 C7
COWBRIDGE. 130 B5
Cowbridge Cross TA24 . . .200 D1
Cow Bridge Rd BA6 . . . . . .157 C7
Cow Down Rd TA20. . . . . . .194 C1
Cowdray Cl TA24. . . . . .200 E6
Cowdray Rd
Bristol BS4. . . . . 22 D7
Minehead TA24. . . . . .200 E6
Cowen Cl TA18. . . . . .224 C4
Cowleaze Dro TA3 . . . . . . .169 D3
Cowleaze La BS40. . . . . 74 C6
Cowler Wlk BS13. . . . . 21 F4
Cowling Dr BS14 . . . . 23 C5
Cowling Rd BS14. . . . . 23 D5
Cowl St BA4 . . . . .205 B7
Cowpath La DT9 . . . . .176 A1
COWSLIP GREEN 54 B8
Cowslip Green La BS40 . . . . 54 B8
Cowslip La
East Rolstone BS22 . . . . 33 A2
Loxton BS26. . . . . 68 D3
Cowslip Wlk TA6. . . . . .208 E1
Coxbridge Dro BA6. . . . . . .158 A6
Cox Hill DT10 . . . . .190 E4
Coxland's Rock TA4 . . . . . .167 B7
COXLEY. 139 F6
Coxley Cl BA6. . . . . .206 F7
Coxley Dr BA1 . . . . 28 B2
Coxley Prim Sch
Coxley BA5. . . . . .139 E6
Coxley BA5. . . . . .139 E6
COXLEY WICK. 139 E7
Cox Rd TA21 . . . . .222 C4
Coxs Cl BA22. . . . . .175 D6
Cox's Cl
Bruton BA10. . . . . .215 E5
Glastonbury BA6 . . . . .206 E6
Cox's Dr BA6. . . . . .158 A5
Cox's Gn BS40 . . . . 35 E1
COX'S GREEN 35 E1
Cox's La TA4. . . . . .167 C5
Coxton End La BA5 . . . . 92 B3
Coxway BS21 . . . . 6 F2
Coxwithy La BA6 . . . . .139 D1
Coxwynne Cl BA3 . . . . 97 C8
Crabtree Cl BS41. . . . . 21 D1
Crab Tree Dro BA6 . . . . . . .206 F8
Crabtree La
Curry Rivel TA10. . . . . .171 C1
Dundry BS41 . . . . 21 D2
Wyke Champflower BA10. . .215 B7
Crab Tree La BA11 . . . . . . .117 D2
Crackmore DT9 . . . . .217 C1
Craig Lea TA2. . . . . .212 E7
Cranberry Wlk BS9. . . . . 5 C8
Cranbourne Chase BS23. . . 31 A1
Cranbourne Cl TA6. . . . . . . .208 F6
Crancombe La TA7 . . . . . . .136 D3
Crandale Rd 3 BA2 . . . . 44 D5
Crane Cotts BA4 . . . . .142 B6
Crane Hill TA10, TA11 . . . . .173 C4
Crane Rd BA22. . . . . .218 A6
Cranes Cl TA2. . . . . .213 D7
Cranford Cl BS22. . . . . 31 D1
Crangs La BA22 . . . . .175 D4
Cranhill Rd
Bath BA1 . . . . 44 D8
Street BA16 . . . . .207 B6
Cranleigh BA2 . . . . 62 F8
Cranleigh Ct TA13. . . . . . . .220 B4
Cranleigh Gdns
Bridgwater TA6 . . . . .209 A4
Bristol BS9. . . . . 5 E4
Cranleigh Rd BS14 . . . . 23 B5
Cranmer Rd TA1 . . . . .213 A4
Cranmoor La BS49 . . . . 16 D2
CRANMORE. 142 B6
Cranmore BS24 . . . . 49 A2
Cranmore Ave BS31 . . . . 24 E6
Cranmore Ct 3 BA11. . . . . .119 E3
Cranmore Pl BA2 . . . . 62 E8
Cranmore Sta★ BA4. . . . . . .142 A5
Cranmore View BA11. . . . . .119 D2
Cranmore West Sta★
BA4. .142 A5
Cransey La
Washford TA4, TA23 . . . . . . .131 F2
Williton TA4 . . . . .132 A2
Crantock Ave BS13. . . . . 22 B8
Cranway La TA20. . . . . .223 F2
Cranwell Cl TA7. . . . . .154 F5
Cranwell Gr BS14 . . . . 23 A5
Cranwell Rd
Locking BS24 . . . . 50 C5
Locking BS24 . . . . 50 C5
Cranwells Pk BA1 . . . . 44 D8
Crapnell La BA5. . . . . .140 F8
Crawford Cl 1 BS21. . . . . 6 B1
Crawford La BA22 . . . . .175 D7
CRAWLEY 192 F2
Crawlic La TA4. . . . . .151 E1
Crawl La BA3 . . . . 78 C4
Crawter Dr TA24 . . . . .124 A3
Craydon Gr BS14. . . . . 23 D4
Craydon Rd BS14. . . . . 23 D5
Craydon Wlk BS14 . . . . 23 D5
Crease Cl BA5 . . . . .203 B4
Create Ctr★ BS1 . . . . 11 F5
Crediton 5 BS22. . . . . 32 A2
Creechbarrow Rd TA1. . . . .213 C5
Creechberry Orch TA1. . . .213 D5
Creeches La BA16. . . . . .156 D7
CREECH HEATHFIELD 169 E5
Creech Hill La BA10 . . . . . .215 B7
Creech Hill Rd BA10. . . . . . .160 B7
Creech Mill Est TA3. . . . . . .169 C4
Creech Paper Mill TA3 . . . .169 C4
CREECH ST MICHAEL. 169 D4
Creech St Michael CE Prim
Sch TA3 . . . . .169 D4
Creechwood Terr TA3 . . . .169 D5
Creedwell Cl TA4 . . . . .167 A4
Creedwell Orch TA4. . . . . . .167 A4
Creedy Bridge Rd TA13 . . .185 D2
Creighton Cl BA5. . . . . .140 C8
Crescent Gdns BA1. . . . . . .228 A3
Crescent La BA1 . . . . .228 B4
Crescent The
Backwell BS48 . . . . 19 A6
Bristol, Sea Mills BS9. . . . . 5 C6
4 Carhampton TA24 . . . . . .131 A5
Coleford BA3 . . . . .117 A7
Farrington Gurney BS39. . . . . 77 B3
Golsoncott TA23. . . . . .131 D1
Ilminster TA19 . . . . .221 B2
Lympsham BS24. . . . . 67 C5
South Cadbury BA22 . . . . . .175 E4
Stanton Drew BS39 . . . . 39 F1
Taunton TA1 . . . . .212 F3
Weston-super-Mare BS22 . . . 31 B1
Yeovil BA20 . . . . .219 A4
Crescent View BA2. . . . . . .228 B1
Crescent View Ct BS22 . . . . 31 B1
Crescent Way TA1. . . . . . . .212 F3
Creslands Ind Units BS24 . . 49 A3
Cressey The TA19 . . . . .184 E4
Cresswell Ave TA2 . . . . . . .212 D7
Cresswell Cl BS22. . . . . 32 A2
Crestfield Ave TA6 . . . . . . .208 F7
Crest Heights BS20. . . . . 1 E4
Creswicke Rd BS4. . . . . 22 E7
Creswick Way TA8 . . . . . . .104 C8
CREWKERNE. 224 D6
Crewkerne Bsns Pk TA18. .224 D6
Crewkerne Cl BS48. . . . . 9 B1
Crewkerne Com Hospl
TA18 . . . . .224 B5
Crewkerne & District Mus★
TA18 . . . . .224 C6
Crewkerne Rd TA20 . . . . . .223 E4
Crewkerne Sta TA18 . . . . . .224 E4
Crewkerne Turning EX13 . .198 C6
Cribb's La BS40 . . . . 36 D1
Crib Cl TA20 . . . . .223 D6
Crib House La BS28 . . . . 89 C1
Crickback La
Chew Magna BS40. . . . . 39 A2
Chew Magna BS40. . . . . 39 A3
Cricket Cotts TA3 . . . . .170 B3
Cricket Cross
Cricket Malherbie TA19 . . . .194 D6
Ilminster TA19 . . . . .194 C6
Cricket Field Gn BS48 . . . . . . 8 D2
Cricket La TA19, TA20 . . . . .194 C6
CRICKET MALHERBIE 194 D6
CRICKET ST THOMAS 194 E3
Cricket St Thomas Miniature
Rly★ TA20 . . . . .194 E3
Cricket View DT9 . . . . .225 D3
CRICKHAM 108 D8
Crickham La BS28. . . . . . . .108 D8
Cricklade Ct BS48. . . . . 9 A1
Cridlake 7 EX13 . . . . .198 A1
Cridlands Mdw TA6 . . . . . .208 E6
CRIMCHARD 223 B5
Crimchard TA20 . . . . .223 B5
Crimthorne Cotts TA3 . . . .183 A7
Cripple St TA12 . . . . .185 D7
Crispin Ctr BA16 . . . . .207 C6
Crispin Sch BA16. . . . . .207 D7
Cristata Wy TA6. . . . . .208 D1
Critch Hill BA11. . . . . .119 C3
CRITCHILL. 119 C3
Critchill Cl BA11 . . . . .119 D3
Critchill Gr BA11 . . . . .119 D3
Critchill Rd BA11. . . . . .119 D3
Critchill Sch BA11. . . . . . . .119 C4
Crockerne CE Prim Sch
BS20. . . . . 4 C4
Crockerne Dr BS20. . . . . 4 C3
Crockerne Ho BS20 . . . . 4 D4
Crockers Hill TA7 . . . . .136 E4
Crocker's Hill BA9 . . . . . . .175 F8
Crocker Wy BA9 . . . . .216 A3
CROCOMBE. 60 C3
Crocombe BA2. . . . . 60 C3
Crocombe La BA2. . . . . 60 C3
Croford Hill TA4 . . . . .166 E6
Croft Cl BS30 . . . . 25 D8
Croft Cotts
Moorlinch TA7 . . . . .155 E7
Wrantage TA3 . . . . .170 B1
Croft La
Brushford TA22 . . . . .163 C4
Skilgate TA4 . . . . .164 E6
Westbury-sub-Mendip BA5 .110 C6
Croftland La TA10. . . . . . . .171 E2
Croft Mdw TA4. . . . . .202 F1
Crofton Ave BA21 . . . . .219 B6
Crofton Ct BA21. . . . . .219 B5
CROFTON PARK 219 B6
Crofton Pk BA21 . . . . .219 B5
Crofton Rd BA21 . . . . .219 B6
Croft Rd
Bath BA1 . . . . 28 B1
Holcombe BA3 . . . . .116 C8
Crofts Mead BA9. . . . . .216 C2
Croft The
Backwell BS48 . . . . 19 A7
Cheddar BS27 . . . . 90 C8
Clevedon BS21. . . . . 6 F4
Hutton BS24. . . . . 49 E3
Mark TA9 . . . . .106 A4
Monkton Combe BA2 . . . . . . 45 E1
Croft The *continued*
Watchet TA23. . . . . .202 C7
Westwood BA15. . . . . 64 F3
Williton TA4 . . . . .202 D3
Wookey Hole BA5. . . . . .203 A8
Yeovil BA20 . . . . .218 C2
Croft Way TA4 . . . . .210 C4
Croftways TA4 . . . . .202 D4
Cromer Ct BS21. . . . . 6 D5
Cromer Rd BS23 . . . . 48 E5
Cromwell Dr BS22. . . . . 32 A4
Cromwell Rd
Bridgwater TA6 . . . . .209 A2
Taunton TA1 . . . . .213 B5
Yeovil BA21 . . . . .219 D6
Crooked Dro TA3 . . . . .170 E7
Crooked La
Brent Knoll TA9. . . . . 85 E3
Burnham-on-S TA8 . . . . 85 D1
Cucklington SP8. . . . . .177 E6
Rode BA11 . . . . .101 E7
Crooked Lane TA8 . . . . 85 D2
Crookes La BS22 . . . . 31 A4
Cropmead TA18. . . . . .224 D6
Cropmead Trad Est TA18 . .224 D6
Cropways Ct BA21. . . . . . . .218 C8
Crosby Row BS8 . . . . .226 A2
CROSCOMBE. 204 B8
Croscombe CE Prim Sch
BA5. .204 C7
Croscombe Gdns BA11 . . .120 D6
CROSS 69 E2
Crossacre TA6 . . . . .208 D6
Crosscombe Dr BS13 . . . . . . 22 C3
Cross Combe Wlk BS13. . . . 22 B3
Crosscroft Cotts TA4 . . . . .151 A3
Cross Dro TA7 . . . . .154 C1
Crosselm Rd BA4. . . . . .143 A2
Cross Elms Hill
Kilton TA5. . . . . .133 F7
Kilve TA5. . . . . .133 F7
Cross Elms La BS9 . . . . 5 E5
Cross Farm Cl TA24 . . . . . .201 A5
Cross Farm Green BS28. . .108 D4
Cross Farm Rd BS27. . . . . . . 90 F3
Crossfield Cl TA6 . . . . .208 D6
Crossfields DT9. . . . . .187 F4
Crossing Dro BS28 . . . . . . .109 D3
Cross Keys Cl TA2. . . . . . . .212 A7
Cross La
Axbridge BS26 . . . . 70 A2
Brendon EX35 . . . . .122 A4
Long Sutton TA10 . . . . .172 F4
Crossland La EX14 . . . . . . .191 F2
CROSSLANDS 222 C8
Crosslands TA21 . . . . .222 B8
Cross Lanes BS20 . . . . 4 C4
Crossman Wlk BS21. . . . . 6 F2
Crossmead TA7 . . . . .136 E4
Cross Moor Dr BS26. . . . . . . 70 B1
Cross Moor Dro BS26. . . . . . 69 E1
Cross Moor Rd BS26. . . . . . . 70 B1
Crosspost La BA2 . . . . 42 B4
Cross Rd DT9 . . . . .187 E1
Crossroads The BA9. . . . . .216 C3
Cross St
Burnham-on-S TA8 . . . . .104 A7
Keynsham BS31 . . . . 24 F7
3 Weston-super-Mare
BS23 . . . . 48 E7
Cross The
Baltonsborough BA6 . . . . . .158 A5
Bradford Abbas DT9. . . . . . .187 E1
Buckland Dinham BA11 . . . .100 A3
East Harptree BS40 . . . . 74 F4
9 Henstridge BA8. . . . . .190 A6
Ilminster TA19 . . . . .221 C3
Milverton TA4. . . . . .167 A4
Minehead TA24. . . . . .200 F8
Nether Stowey TA5. . . . . . . .134 B2
Street BA16 . . . . .207 D7
Cross View Rise TA6. . . . . .208 D6
Crossway TA1. . . . . .213 C5
Cross Way DT9. . . . . .187 E1
Crossway La BA3. . . . . 96 B7
Crossways
Coleford BA3 . . . . .116 F7
Tatworth TA20 . . . . .198 D8
Crossways Cvn Pk BA2 . . . . 61 F5
Crossways La
Barrow BA4 . . . . .140 C4
Combe Hay BA2 . . . . 62 A5
Crossways Rd TA6. . . . . . . .209 B1
Crosswell Cl 7 TA6 . . . . . .153 E3
Cross Wlk BS14 . . . . 23 A6
Crouds La TA10 . . . . .172 E4
Crow Castle La TA18. . . . . .224 B7
CROWCOMBE. 151 C7
Crowcombe CE VA Prim Sch
TA4 .151 C7
Crowcombe Combe TA4 . .151 C8
Crowcombe Heathfield Sta★
TA4 .151 B5
Crowcombe Rd TA2 . . . . . .212 F8
Crowcombe Wlk TA6 . . . . .208 C4
Crowe Hill BA3. . . . . 64 B5
Crowe La BA3. . . . . 64 B5
Crow La
Ashill TA19 . . . . .183 C4
Bridgwater TA7 . . . . .209 E7
Bristol BS1. . . . . .227 A2
Broadway TA19 . . . . .194 A8
Slape Cross TA7 . . . . .209 E6
Westbury-sub-Mendip BA5 .110 E6
Crown Cl TA2 . . . . .213 C6
Crowne Trad Est BA4 . . . . .205 D5
Crown Gdns BA11 . . . . .119 F3
Crown Glass Pl 5 BS48. . . . . 8 E2
Crown Hill
Bath BA1 . . . . 27 C1
West Buckland TA21. . . . . . .180 F7
Winford BS40. . . . . 38 A5
Crown Ho BS48 . . . . 8 C1
Crown Ind Est TA2 . . . . . . .213 C6
Crown La
Creech St Michael TA3 . . . . .169 D6
South Petherton TA13. . . . . .220 C4
Crown Mews TA21 . . . . . . .180 F7
Crown Rd BA1 . . . . 27 B1
Crown Wlk TA1 . . . . .212 F3
Crowpill Cotts TA6 . . . . . . .208 F6
Crowpill La TA6. . . . . .208 F6
Crow's Hill BA4 . . . . .142 C1
Crowshute Flats TA20 . . . .223 C3
Crowshute Link TA20. . . . .223 C3
Crufts Mdw TA3. . . . . .169 D4
Cruikshank Gr BS24 . . . . . . 50 B5
Crusader Cl TA6 . . . . .208 E6
Crusty La BS20. . . . . 4 C5
Cruwy's Cross TA4 . . . . . . .210 B7
Crypton Tech Bsns Pk
TA6. .209 B8
Cubitt Cl BS24 . . . . 49 C4
Cuck Hill BS25 . . . . 70 E7
CUCKLINGTON 177 D6
Cucklington Rd BA9. . . . . .177 D6
Cuckold's Row TA5. . . . . . .152 E8
Cuckoo Cnr TA1. . . . . .213 B2
Cuckoo Hill
Bruton BA10. . . . . .160 D6
Bruton BA10. . . . . .215 F8
Frome BA11 . . . . .119 E8
Cuckoo La
Frome BA11 . . . . .119 F8
High Littleton BS39 . . . . 59 B3
Thorncombe TA20. . . . . .199 C7
Wraxall BS48. . . . . 9 A6
CUDWORTH 194 E5
Cudworth Hill TA20 . . . . . .194 F4
Cudworth Rd TA19 . . . . . . .194 E6
Cudworth St TA20. . . . . . . .194 E5
Cuff's Common Dro BA16 156 D4
Cuffs Mead TA20. . . . . .223 F1
Cufic La BS27. . . . . 90 C8
CULBONE 123 B5
Culliford Cl BA16. . . . . .207 D7
Cullimore's La BA1. . . . . 26 C4
Culliver's Grave BA22 . . . . .197 C8
Cullivers Grave Rd BA20 . .218 C1
CULM DAVY 180 A2
Culmhead Cl TA1 . . . . .212 D1
Culmstock Prim Sch EX15 179 E1
Culvecliffe Ct TA24. . . . . . .125 C4
Culvercliffe Rd TA23 . . . . .202 D7
Culverhay BS39. . . . . 41 D6
Culverhay Cl TA7. . . . . .136 C4
Culverhay Dr BA21 . . . . . . .218 C8
Culverhayes TA20. . . . . . . .223 C2
Culverhay La TA4 . . . . .210 B4
CULVERHAYS 132 F1
Culverhays La TA4 . . . . . . .132 F1
Culverhill BA11 . . . . .119 F3
Culver Hill TA10. . . . . .172 B7
Culver La
Carhampton TA24. . . . . .131 B4
East Harptree BS40 . . . . 74 F3
Culverlake La EX13. . . . . . .199 A3
Culvers Cl
Keynsham BS31 . . . . 24 E6
Sherborne DT9. . . . . .225 C4
Culvers Rd BS31 . . . . 24 E6
Culver St BS1 . . . . .226 C2
Culver Street La TA5 . . . . .134 A7
Culvert Dro BS27. . . . . .109 B6
Culverwell Cotts BA4. . . . .140 F3
Culverwell Rd BS13 . . . . 22 A4
Culvery La BS39. . . . . 40 D4
Cumberland Basin Rd BS8 . 11 F5
Cumberland Cl BS1 . . . . . .226 A1
Cumberland Ho BA1. . . . . .228 A2
Cumberland Pl 6 BS8. . . . . . 11 F6
Cumberland Rd BS1. . . . . . .226 B1
Cumberland Row BA1 . . . .228 B2
Cumberland St BS2 . . . . . .227 B4
Cumhill Hill BA4 . . . . .140 E3
Cumnock Cres BA7. . . . . . .214 C6
Cumnock Rd BA7 . . . . .214 C6
Cumnock Terr BA7 . . . . . . .214 C6
Cunningham Ave EX13. . . .198 A2
Cunningham Ct TA1. . . . . .213 A5
Cunningham Rd TA8 . . . . . .104 C7
Cunningham Rd BA21 . . . . .219 F8
Curdleigh La TA3 . . . . .181 D5
CURLAND 182 D4
CURLAND COMMON 182 D4
Curland Gr BS14 . . . . 23 B5
Curlew Cl TA24 . . . . .201 C4
Curlew Gdns BS22. . . . . 31 F1
Curlew Pl BS20 . . . . 2 F6
CURLOAD 170 E7
Currells La BS40 . . . . 20 B1
Curriott Hill TA18 . . . . .224 B4
Curriott Hill Rd TA18 . . . . .224 B5
Curry Hole La BA22. . . . . . .197 C2
Curry La TA3. . . . . .169 E6
CURRY MALLET 183 C8
Curry Mallet CE Prim Sch
TA3 .183 D8
Currymead La TA10 . . . . . .171 C2
Currypool La TA5 . . . . .134 E1
CURRY RIVEL 171 C4
Curry Rivel CE Prim Sch
TA10 . . . . .171 D4

Curry Rivel CE VC Prim Sch
TA10 171 C4
Currywoods Way TA10 171 D4
Cursley Path BA5 203 D3
Curtis Units BA11 119 E2
Curvalion House Gdns
TA3 169 D4
Curvalion Rd TA3 169 D4
CUSHUISH 152 B1
Cushuish La TA2 & TA5 152 C2
Cushuish Lane Cotts TA2 152 B1
Cussacombe Gate EX36 145 J1
Cussons St BA2 45 C8
Custom Cl BS14 23 A7
Custom Ho
Bristol BS1 227 A1
Minehead TA24 201 B7
CUTCOMBE 129 F2
Cutcombe CE Fst Sch
Wheddon Cross TA24 129 E1
Wheddon Cross TA24 129 E2
Cutcombe Cross TA24 129 E1
Cutcombe Hill TA24 129 F2
Cuthays La EX13 198 B1
Cuthbert St TA9 104 D3
Cutler Rd BS13 21 F6
CUTLER'S GREEN 94 F4
Cutliff Cl TA1 212 E1
Cuts Rd TA3, TA7 170 E8
Cutter's Wharf TA24 201 B7
CUTTIFORD'S DOOR 223 C7
Cutt Mill La DT10 190 F3
Cut Tongue La TA20 193 C7
Cutty Cotts BA22 175 D6
Cutty La BA22 175 D6
Cygnet Cres BS22 31 F1
Cynthia Rd BA2 44 D5
Cypress Ct
Bristol BS9 5 D3
Somerton TA11 211 E4
Cypress Dr
Puriton TA7 136 C4
Yeovil BA20 218 E2
Cypress Gdns BS8 11 E6
Cypress Terr BA3 78 D1
Cypress Way BA11 120 C7
Cyril St W TA2 212 E6
Cyril St TA2 212 E6

D

Dabinett Cl TA2 168 B5
Dabinett Dr BS25 52 A4
Dadley La BA11 102 A3
Daffodil Pl TA5 208 D1
Dafford's Bldgs BA1 28 C2
Dafford St BA1 28 C2
Dagg's La BS28 138 E8
Dagg's Lane Dro BA5, BS28 138 D7
Daghole BS27 90 C8
Daglands The BA2 78 E8
Dahlia Gdns 9 BA2 45 B7
Dairs Orch TA20 198 C8
Dairy Cl
Horsecastle BS49 17 A2
Sherborne DT9 225 C5
Wells BA5 203 B5
Dairycroft BS2 227 B4
Dairy Ct 3 TA18 224 C5
Dairy Flats DT9 225 E5
Dairy Hill BA2 80 B5
Dairy House La TA3 182 E5
Dairylands TA24 131 D4
Daisey Bank BA2 45 B4
Daisy Cl
Bridgwater TA6 153 F5
Frome BA11 120 B3
Daisyfield BA22 188 A8
Dakota Dr BS14 23 A4
Dale La BA5 92 C3
Daley Cl BS22 32 B3
Dalimores La BA11 143 B8
Dalleston BA3 114 C8
Dallimore La BA4 142 B8
Dallimore Mead BA11 143 B8
Dalton Sq BS2 227 B4
Dalwood 12 BS22 32 A2
Dalwoods DT9 225 D3
Damas Dro TA7 154 F5
Dame Court Cl BS22 31 F4
Dame Withycombe Villas
TA5 135 B5
Dampier Pl BA21 219 C5
Dampier St BA21 219 C5
Dampiet St TA6 208 F4
Damson Cres TA21 222 F7
Damson Orch BA1 29 A4
Damson Rd BS22 49 E7
Damson Row TA21 222 F7
Dancey Mead BS13 21 F6
Dancing Cross BA9 176 B5
Dancing Hill TA6 153 E4
Dancing La BA9 216 A4
Dandelion Rd BA11 120 B2
DandO's La BS28 108 C4
Dandy's Mdw BS20 2 E4
Daneacre Rd BA3 79 A3
Dane Cl BA15 64 E7
Dane Rise BA15 64 E7
Danesboro Rd TA6 208 C4
Danesborough View TA4 202 D3
Danesborough View E
TA4 202 D3
Danesborough View W
TA4 202 D3
Danes Cl EX14 191 F2
Danesfield CE Com Mid Sch
TA4 202 D4
Dane's Lea BS28 108 C4
Dangerfield Ave BS13 21 F6
Daniel Cl BS21 6 F3
Daniel Mews 2 BA2 45 B7
Danielsfield Rd BA20 218 F2
Daniels La BA5 111 A4
Daniel St 3 BA2 45 B7
Dapps Hill BS31 24 F5
Dapwell La BS14, BS31 24 A1
Darby Cl SP8 161 F1
Darby's Knap TA24 147 C5
Darby Way TA4 151 F1
Darcis Row TA20 223 B4
Dare Cl TA2 213 A8
Darkey La BA10 215 F7
Darkfield Way TA7 136 E3
Dark La
Ashbrittle TA21 178 E8
Backwell BS48 19 B5
Banwell BS29 51 C2
Berkley BA11 120 E8
Blagdon BS40 54 E3
Chew Magna BS40 38 F3
Freshford BA3 64 B5
Hockworthy EX16 178 B8
Holcombe BA3 97 C1
Kilmersdon BA11 98 A1
North Wootton BA4 140 C5
Sandford Orcas DT9 188 C7
Seavington St Mary TA19 184 E1
Stoke St Gregory TA3 170 F6
Stoke St Michael BA3 116 C2
Upton Noble BA4 142 F2
Wellington TA21 222 D5
Witham Friary BA11 143 D2
Darlick Cnr EX36 145 G4
Darlington Mews 8 BA2 45 B7
Darlington Pl BA2 45 B6
Darlington Rd BA2 45 B8
Darlington St BA2 45 B7
Darmead BS24 32 B1
DARSHILL 204 F6
Dartmouth Ave BA2 44 C5
Dartmouth Cl BS22 32 A2
Dartmouth Wlk BS31 24 D4
Dart Rd BS21 6 D1
Darvole Road BA22 197 E7
Darwin Cl TA2 212 B6
Darwin Dr BA21 219 F8
Dashwoods La TA4 132 E2
Daubeny Ct BS1 227 A1
Daunton Cl TA9 104 D4
David's La TA19 184 F2
David's Rd BS14 23 C6
David St BS2 227 C3
Davies Cl
Bridgwater TA6 208 F2
Winsham TA20 194 E1
Davies Ct BA5 203 B4
Davin Cres BS20 4 C3
Davis La BS21 16 F8
Davis St BS11 4 B8
Davis Terr 5 BA5 203 C4
Dawbins Dr TA7 136 E4
Dawes Cl BS21 6 D1
Dawes Ct 2 BS8 11 F6
Daws Cl TA6 208 E2
Daws La TA6 153 E3
Daw's La DT9 176 A3
Daws Mead TA1 212 A3
Day Cres BA2 43 F6
Deacon Rd TA6 209 C6
DEACONS 168 C7
Deacons Cl BS22 31 E2
Deacons Ct BS22 31 C1
Deacons La BA21 187 D6
Deacons Mill La DT10 190 B3
Deacon Way TA8 104 B6
Deadlands La TA12, TA13 185 A6
Dead Maids Cross Rd
BA13 121 E5
Deadman's Hill DT9 176 A1
Deadmans La TA20 181 F2
Deadmill La BA1 28 C3
Dead Woman's Cnr BA12 161 F8
Deal Cl TA6 209 D5
DEAN 142 B7
Dean Cl
Frome BA11 120 C6
Weston-super-Mare BS22 32 B3
Deane Cl TA4 150 D8
Deane Dr TA1 212 B2
Deane Gate Ave TA1 213 E5
Deane Ret Pk TA1 213 F5
Deanery Rd BS1 226 C2
Deanery Wlk BA3 64 C6
Deanesly Way BA9 216 D3
Deane Way TA20 198 D8
Deanhill La BA1 27 A2
Dean La
Crewkerne TA18 196 B4
Dunster TA24 201 D3
Milverton TA4 167 A6
Oakhill BA3 115 A3
Dean's Cross
Allerford TA24 124 E3
Lydeard St Lawrence TA4 151 A4
Dean's La
Allerford TA24 124 E3
Brompton Ralph TA4 150 F4
Deansley Way BA9 216 E3
Deans Mead BS11 5 A8
Deans Pl 8 BA5 203 D4
Dean St BS2 227 B4
Deans The BS20 2 B4
Dean Vale Pk TA4 167 C4
Debecca's La BS20 4 B4
De Combe Ho TA18 224 D6
De Corcis Cl TA5 134 A3
Decoy La TA11 157 A2
Deep La BA12 121 E1
Deepleigh La TA4 210 C7
Deerleap
Easton BA5 111 B6
Shipham BS25 70 F8
Deer Mead BS21 6 B1
Deerswood Gdns BA16 207 A6
Deer View TA24 201 C4
Delapre Rd BS23 48 D3
Delhorn La BS24 86 C7
Delius Gr BS4 22 D7
Dellers Ct TA1 212 F5
Deller's Wharf TA1 212 F5
Dellshore Cl TA20 223 D4
Dell The
Bristol, Westbury on T BS9 5 F5
Minehead TA24 200 E6
Nailsea BS48 8 D2
Weston-super-Mare BS22 31 E4
Delmore Rd BA11 119 E3
Delta Cl BA11 119 F5
Delta Ct 1 BA11 119 F5
Delta Rise TA4 151 E1
Demelza Ct BA22 174 D3
De Montalt Pl BA2 45 B1
Dempier Mews BA22 218 B6
Dene Barton Com Hospl
TA4 167 F6
Dene Cl BS31 24 F3
Dene Cross TA4 167 F7
Dene Gdns TA24 201 B4
Dene Rd
Cotford St Luke TA4 167 F6
Whitchurch BS14 23 C4
Dening Cl TA20 223 C6
Denleigh Cl BS14 23 A4
Denman's La
Barrington TA19 184 D5
Cannington TA5 135 B2
Denmark Ave BS1 226 C2
Denmark Rd BA2 44 D6
Denmark St BS1 226 C2
Denmark Terr TA2 212 F7
Dennett Cl BA4 205 E4
Denning Cl TA1 212 B1
Denning Ct BS22 32 B4
Dennington La
Churchinford EX14 192 C6
Dulverton TA22 163 B4
Dennor Pk BS14 23 B7
Denny Cl BS20 2 A5
Denny La BS40 39 B1
Denny View BS20 2 A5
Dennyview Rd BS8 10 F8
Denston Dr BS20 2 E4
Denston Wlk BS13 22 A7
Dentwood Gr BS9 5 B8
Denzil Cl BA22 197 A8
Depley Farm La BA9 177 E7
Derek Mead Way BS29 50 C7
Derham Cl BS49 34 B8
Derham Ct BS49 34 B8
Derham Pk BS49 34 B8
Derham Rd BS13 22 A5
Derricke Rd BS14 23 F6
DERTFORDS 144 D8
Dertfords BA12 144 D8
Derwent Gdns BA21 219 D6
Derwent Gr
Keynsham BS31 25 A5
Taunton TA1 213 E4
Derwent Rd BS23 49 A5
Derwent Way BA21 218 C6
De Salis Pk BS24 50 D8
Desmond Rochford
TA1 212 A3
Devenish La BA9 216 F4
Deveron Gr BS31 25 A4
Devonia Pk TA4 168 A1
Devonshire Bldgs BA2 44 F4
Devonshire Ct BS23 48 E4
Devonshire Dr BS20 1 F5
Devonshire Mews BA2 44 F3
Devonshire Pl BA2 44 F4
Devonshire Rd
Bathampton BA2 28 E1
Weston-super-Mare BS23 48 E4
Devonshire St TA6 209 B5
Devonshire Villas BA2 44 F3
Dewar Cl TA8 104 C7
Dewberry Ave TA6 208 E1
Dew Water La TA11 211 D5
Dexter Wlk 8 TA6 209 A1
Dial Hill Rd BS21 6 D4
Dial La BS40 20 D1
Dial's Gate La BA6, TA11 158 D4
Diamond Batch BS24 32 B1
Dibbens Row BA9 161 A2
Dibbles La BA22 197 A8
Dickenson Rd BS23 48 E6
Dickenson's Gr BS49 34 E3
Dicky's Path TA24 129 A5
Digby Ct DT9 225 D3
Digby Rd DT9 225 D3
Dighton Ct 3 BS2 227 A4
Dighton St BS2 227 A4
Digland La TA24 129 F5
Dilkes La TA11 174 C7
DILLINGTON 221 E5
Dillington Farm Cotts
TA19 221 E5
Dillington House Coll
TA19 221 D6
Dillons Rd TA3 169 D4
DIMMER 159 C3
Dimmer La BA7 159 B2
Dimmock's La TA12 185 D5
DINDER 140 D7
Dinder Cl BS48 18 E8
DINGHURST 52 E4
Dinghurst Rd BS25 52 E4
Dingle Cl BS9 5 C6
Dingle Ct BS13 21 F7
Dingle Rd BS9 5 D7
Dingle The BS9 5 D7
Dingle View BS9 5 C7
Dinglewood Cl BS9 5 D7
Dingley Cl TA6 208 E5
Ding Rd
Broadway TA19 183 A2
Dommett TA20 182 F1
Dinhams TA3 169 C4
Dinhay DT10 190 F6
DINNINGTON 195 B7
Dipford Rd TA3 168 D1
Dipland Gr BS40 54 F2
Disraeli Pl TA1 212 D5
DITCHEAT 159 C7
Ditcheat Hill BA4 159 B7
Ditcheat Prim Sch BA4 159 C7
Ditch Furlong Rd TA7 137 A2
Ditton St TA19 221 C3
Dixon Gdns BA1 27 F1
Dobree Pk TA21 222 A4
Dobunni Cl BS14 23 D3
Dock Gate La BS8 226 A1
Doctor's Hill BA5 111 B1
Dodd Ave BA5 203 F5
Dodd's Cnr BA9 215 E1
Dodge Cross DT9 225 F5
Dodham Cres BA20 218 F4
DODHILL 168 D7
Dodinalls House Rd BA22 175 F7
DODINGTON 133 F3
Dod La BA6 206 E4
Dog Down Cross EX16 178 A8
Doleberrow BS25 52 F3
Dolebury Warren Nature
Reserve★ BS40 53 A3
Dolecroft La BS22 32 E7
Dolemead La BS27 90 E2
DOLEMEADS 45 B5
Dolemoor La
Congresbury BS49 34 A4
Congresbury BS49 34 C3
Dolling Cl TA20 223 D6
Dolling's Rd TA3 181 B4
Dolphin Sq BS23 48 D7
Dominion Rd BA2 44 A6
Dominy Cl TA20 223 D3
DOMMETT 182 D1
Dommett Cl EX13 198 A2
Dommett Rd TA20 182 D1
Dommett's La BA11 119 D4
Domus Dr BA4 205 E4
Donald Rd BS13 21 F7
DONIFORD 202 F6
Doniford Beach Halt TA23 202 E6
Doniford Dr TA4 202 D3
Doniford Mdw TA23 202 F6
Doniford Orch TA23 202 F6
Doniford Rd
Watchet TA23 202 E6
Williton TA4 202 D4
Donne La BA22 186 C2
Donnes Terr BA7 214 B5
Donnington Wlk BS31 24 D4
Donstan Rd TA9 104 E5
DONYATT 183 D1
Donyatt Hill TA19 183 D1
Donyatt Hill Est TA19 183 D1
Doone Way TA24 201 B4
Dorchester Cl 6 BS48 8 D1
Dorchester Rd
Barwick BA22 197 F7
East Coker BA22 197 F5
Taunton TA2 213 A8
Yeovil BA22 219 A1
Dorchester St BA1 228 C1
Dore Cl BA21 218 C7
Dormeads View 6 BS24 49 F7
Dorset Cl
Bath BA2 44 D6
Frome BA11 119 E5
Highbridge TA9 104 E2
Dorset Ho BA2 44 D3
Dorset Rd TA6 209 C3
Dorset St BA2 44 D6
Doster's La TA2 169 C6
Double Gates Dro TA11 158 A3
Double Hill BA2 79 F7
Douglas Ct 3 BS23 48 F5
Douglas Dr BA4 205 B5
Douglas Rd BS23 48 F5
Douglas Yates Ct BA3 116 F7
DOULTING 141 E6
Doulting Ct BA11 120 D7
Doulting Hill BA4 205 F4
Doulton Way BS14 23 B5
Dovai Dr TA6 208 E7
Dove Cots Cl BA16 207 C7
Dove La BS2 227 C4
DOVERHAY 124 B3
Doverhay Rd
Horner TA24 123 A1
Horner TA24 129 A8
Dover Ho BA1 228 C4
Dover Pl
6 Bath BA1 28 A1
Dover Pl *continued*
Bristol BS8 226 B3
Dover Rd TA2 213 A8
Dovers La BA1 29 C2
Dovers Pk BA1 29 C2
Dovery Manor Mus★
TA24 124 A3
Dove St S BS2 227 A4
Dove St BS2 227 A4
Doveswell Gr BS13 22 A4
Dovetail Ct 1 TA1 212 E3
Dovetail Dr BS23 49 A7
Dovetons Cl TA4 202 E3
Dovetons Dr TA4 202 E3
Dowding Rd BA1 28 B1
Dowell Cl TA2 212 C6
Dowland 13 BS22 32 A2
Dowland Gr BS4 22 D6
Dowling La BA6 158 A5
Dowling Rd BS13 22 D3
DOWLISH FORD 221 B1
Dowlish La TA19 194 F5
Dowlish Rd TA17 194 F6
DOWLISH WAKE 194 E7
Downash La EX13 198 E3
Down Ave BA2 45 A1
Down Cl BS20 1 F4
Downclose La TA18 196 C3
Downend Cres TA6 136 B4
Downend Rd TA6 136 B4
Downend Terr TA6 136 B4
Downey Field La TA18 196 D6
Downfield
Bristol BS9 5 C7
Keynsham BS31 24 D5
Downhall Dr TA6 208 D6
DOWNHEAD
Stoke St Michael 142 C8
Yeovilton 174 C4
Downhead La BA22 174 C5
Downhead Rd BA22 174 C4
Down La
Bathampton BA2 28 F1
Buckland Dinham BA11 99 C3
Shepton Montague BA9 160 B2
Sherborne DT9 188 A5
Trent DT9 187 F5
West Pennard BA4, BA6 140 C1
Downland Cl 5 BS48 8 D1
Downlands La EX15, TA3 181 A2
Downleaze
Bristol, Stoke Bishop BS9 5 F3
Portishead BS20 2 A5
Yeovil BA20 218 D2
Downleaze Rd BS9 5 F3
Down Rd BS20 1 F4
Downs Cl BS22 31 F1
Downs Cote Ave BS9 5 F6
Downs Cote Dr BS9 5 F6
DOWNSIDE
Chilcompton 96 C1
Felton 19 D1
Shepton Mallet 205 D8
Downside
Portishead BS20 2 C5
Street BA16 207 D6
Downside Abbey★ BA3 96 E2
Downside Cl
Bathampton BA2 28 F1
Chilcompton BA3 96 D3
Downside Rd
Backwell BS48 36 E8
Weston-super-Mare BS23 48 F4
Downside Sch BA3 96 E2
Downslade La TA10 172 D5
Down's Orch BA6 138 C4
Downs Rd BS41 21 D2
Downs Sch The BS48 9 C8
Downs The BS20 2 B4
Downsway BS39 77 D6
Downton Rd BS13 22 D8
Down View BA3 97 F8
Dowry Pl 3 BS8 11 F5
Dowry Rd BS8 226 A2
Dowry Sq BS8 226 A2
DOWSLANDS 168 F1
Dowsland Way TA1 213 C1
DOYNTON 12 A8
Dozen's Cnr TA17 195 A7
Dragon Cross TA24 131 D3
Dragonfly Chase BA22 173 E2
Dragon Ri TA2 212 A7
Dragons Hill Cl BS31 24 F5
Dragons Hill Ct BS31 24 F5
Dragons Hill Gdns BS31 24 F5
Drake Ave BA2 44 F2
Drake Cl
Saltford BS31 25 D2
Staplegrove TA2 212 B7
Weston-super-Mare BS22 31 F4
Drake Mdws TA3 192 A7
Drake Rd BA5 203 F6
Drakes Cl TA6 208 F5
Drake's Cl TA3 169 C4
Drakes Cres TA20 198 D8
Drake's Dro BA5 139 A6
Drakes Mdw
East Coker BA22 197 C7
Yarcombe EX14 192 D3
Drakes Pk TA21 222 D7
Drakes Pk N TA21 222 D7
Drakes Way BS20 2 B5
Drang The
Coxley BA5 139 E6
Evercreech BA4 141 E1
Porlock TA24 124 A3
Dransfield Way BA2 44 C4
Drapers Way TA24 129 D2

Drappel La BA5 ... 110 E7
Draycot Pl BS1 ... 227 A1
DRAYCOTT
Cheddar ... 90 E2
Yeovil ... 187 B8
Draycott Ave TA2 ... 213 A6
Draycott Ct 1 BA2 ... 228 C3
Draycott Moor Dro BS27 ... 90 D1
Draycott Rd
Cheddar BS27 ... 90 D5
Shepton Mallet BA4 ... 205 B6
Draycott & Rodney Stoke CE Fst Sch BS27 ... 90 F3
Draydon La
Ashwick TA22 ... 147 A1
Hawkridge TA22 ... 146 F2
Draydon Rd BS4 ... 22 D8
Dray Rd BA22 ... 186 C2
DRAYTON
Curry Rival ... 171 E3
Southerton ... 185 D3
Drayton BS24 ... 49 A2
Drayton Cl BS14 ... 23 B8
Drayton Ct TA11 ... 211 B4
Drayton La TA10 ... 171 D3
Drayton Rd BS9 ... 5 C8
Drew's La DT10 ... 190 B5
Drials La BA3 ... 94 F6
Drift Rd TA24 ... 201 D4
Drift The
Chard TA20 ... 194 B3
Chard Junction TA20 ... 198 E8
Drill Hall La BA4 ... 205 C5
DRIMPTON ... 199 F7
Drimpton Cross DT8 ... 199 F7
Dring The BA3 ... 78 E2
Drive The
Bristol BS14 ... 23 C6
Burnham-on-S TA8 ... 85 A2
Churchill BS25 ... 52 E4
Keynsham BS31 ... 24 E6
Shipham BS25 ... 70 E8
Stanton Drew BS39 ... 39 F1
Taunton TA1 ... 212 D1
Weston-super-Mare BS23 ... 48 F8
Woolavington TA7 ... 136 E4
Driveway Dro TA10 ... 173 A3
Dropping La BA10 ... 160 D5
Drove Cl DT10 ... 189 F2
Drove Ct BS48 ... 8 E3
Drove La
East Pennard BA4 ... 158 E8
Shepton Beauchamp TA19 ... 184 E4
Drove Rd
Congresbury BS49 ... 34 D3
Stourton Caundle DT10 ... 189 F2
Weston-super-Mare BS23 ... 48 F5
Drove The
Bridgwater TA6 ... 209 A6
Portbury BS20 ... 3 D6
Droveway TA13 ... 220 B5
Drove Way
Churchinford TA3 ... 191 F8
Sandford BS24, BS25 ... 51 E7
Droveway Cl TA13 ... 220 C5
Droveway La BA21 ... 187 C7
Druid Cl BS9 ... 5 E5
Druid Hill BS9 ... 5 E5
Druid Rd BS9 ... 5 D4
Druids Garth BA2 ... 28 D1
Druid Stoke Ave BS9 ... 5 D5
Druids Wlk TA20 ... 223 C5
Druid Woods BS9 ... 5 C5
Druley Hill BA10 ... 161 D8
Drum Ave BA6 ... 206 C5
Drumhead Way The BS25 ... 70 E8
Dr White's Cl BS1 ... 227 B1
DRY HILL ... 2 C6
Dryleaze BS31 ... 24 E7
Drysdale Cl BS22 ... 31 D1
Duchess Cl 1 TA6 ... 208 E7
Duchy Cl BA3 ... 78 E5
Duchy Rd
Clandown BA3 ... 78 E5
Shepton Mallet BA4 ... 205 A5
Duck La
Chard TA20 ... 223 C3
Churchill BS40 ... 53 A8
Horsington BA8 ... 176 E2
Ilchester BA22 ... 173 F1
Kenn BS21 ... 17 A6
Stalbridge DT10 ... 190 B5
Westbury-sub-Mendip BA5 ... 110 E6
Duck Pool Dro BA6 ... 206 B7
Duckpool La TA18 ... 196 B8
Duck Pool La BA11 ... 102 B6
Ducks' Field Crossing TA18 ... 224 C1
Ducks Hill TA10 ... 172 B5
Ducks La BS22 ... 32 A8
Duck St BS25 ... 52 C5
Ducky La TA5 ... 134 A5
Ducky Path TA24 ... 201 D2
DUDDLESTONE ... 181 F8
Dudley Cl BS31 ... 24 E4
Dudmoor TA12 ... 185 B7
Dudwell La BA3 ... 95 A5
Dugdale St TA24 ... 200 F6
Duke Ave 7 TA5 ... 135 B2
Duke Ho TA19 ... 221 B3
Duke's Cl BA9 ... 216 B3
Dukes Field BA4 ... 205 C5
Duke's La
Horningsham BA12 ... 144 A1
Kilmington BA12 ... 161 F8
Dukes Mead TA6 ... 209 A2
Duke St
Bath BA2 ... 228 C2
Duke St *continued*
Bridgwater TA6 ... 208 E7
Frome BA11 ... 119 E5
Taunton TA1 ... 213 A4
DULCOTE ... 140 C7
Dulcote Hill La BA5 ... 140 C7
Dull Cross TA4 ... 151 D3
DULVERTON ... 163 E6
Dulverton La TA4 ... 165 D7
Dulverton Mid & Com Sch TA22 ... 163 D6
Dumfries Pl BS23 ... 48 E5
Dummis La BA5 ... 111 A1
Dumpers La BS40 ... 39 B2
Dumper's La BA3 ... 94 F7
DUNBALL ... 136 A3
Dunball Drove TA7 ... 136 A4
Dunball Ind Est TA6 ... 136 B4
Dunbar Cl TA9 ... 104 C4
Duncan Gdns BA1 ... 27 A3
Duncart La BA5 ... 204 C7
Duncliffe Cl DT10 ... 190 B4
Duncombe Cl TA6 ... 209 D5
Dundas Row TA4 ... 167 E8
DUNDON ... 156 F3
DUNDON HAYES ... 156 E3
Dundon Hayes Dro TA11 ... 211 B8
DUNDRY ... 21 D2
Dundry CE Prim Sch BS41 ... 21 D2
DUNDRY HILL ... 23 B3
Dundry La
Dundry BS41 ... 21 C3
Winford BS40 ... 38 A7
Dunedin Way BS22 ... 32 C4
Dunford Terr BA6 ... 158 A5
Dungarvon Rd BS24 ... 49 F7
Dungeon BS28 ... 108 D7
Dungeon La BA5 ... 204 C6
Dunkerry Rd BS26 ... 88 C4
DUNKERTON ... 61 E4
Dunkerton Cl BA6 ... 206 F3
Dunkerton Hill BA2 ... 61 E2
Dunkerton La
Combe Hay BA2 ... 62 B4
Dunkerton BA2 ... 61 F3
Dunkerton Rise TA2 ... 168 B5
Dunkery Cl BS48 ... 8 E1
Dunkery Hill Rd TA24 ... 129 C7
Dunkery & Horner Wood National Nature Reserve The* TA24 ... 129 A7
Dunkery Rd
Bridgwater TA6 ... 208 D4
Weston-super-Mare BS23 ... 30 F1
Dunkery Vineyard* TA24 ... 200 A1
Dunkirk Bsns Pk BA14 ... 83 D2
Dunkleys Way TA1 ... 213 C2
Dunlin Dr 1 BS20 ... 2 F6
Dunningham La BS28 ... 107 E7
Dunns Cl BS28 ... 108 C4
Dunn's Hill TA21 ... 179 A6
Dunsford Pl BA2 ... 45 B6
Dunsgreen La EX15 ... 191 A8
Dunsham La TA18 ... 195 C2
Dunsley Hill EX16, EX36 ... 162 D5
Dunstan Dr DT9 ... 225 E5
Dunstan Rd
Burnham-on-S TA8 ... 104 B7
Glastonbury BA6 ... 206 F5
Dunstan Way BS27 ... 90 B6
DUNSTER ... 201 E2
Dunster Beach
Alcombe TA24 ... 125 F2
Ellicombe TA24 ... 201 F5
Dunster Beach Chalets TA24 ... 201 F4
Dunster Castle* TA24 ... 201 E1
Dunster Cl
Minehead TA24 ... 201 B4
Taunton TA2 ... 213 B7
Dunster Cres BS24 ... 49 A2
Dunster Ct BS25 ... 70 A8
Dunster Fst Sch
Dunster TA24 ... 201 D2
Dunster TA24 ... 201 D2
Dunster Gdns 5 BS48 ... 8 E1
Dunster Ho BA2 ... 45 A2
Dunster Rd
Bristol BS4 ... 22 F8
Keynsham BS31 ... 24 E4
Dunsters Rd BS49 ... 17 F1
Dunster Sta* TA24 ... 201 F4
Dunster Steep
Dunster TA24 ... 201 E2
Porlock, Doverhay TA24 ... 124 A3
Dunster Visitor Ctr* TA24 ... 201 E2
Dunster Wood Forest Trails* TA24 ... 130 D5
Dunster Working Water Mill* TA24 ... 201 E1
DUNWEAR ... 209 D1
Dunwear Ho 3 TA6 ... 209 C4
Dunwear La TA6 ... 209 D3
Durban Way BS49 ... 17 B1
Durbin Park Rd BS21 ... 6 D5
Durcott Rd BA2 ... 78 D8
Durham Gr BS31 ... 24 D4
Durham Pl 9 TA2 ... 213 A8
Durhams Cotts TA4 ... 210 C5
Durkheim Dr 2 BA5 ... 203 C4
DURLEIGH ... 208 B3
Durleigh Cl
Bridgwater TA6 ... 208 D3
Bristol BS13 ... 22 A7
Durleigh Hill TA5 ... 208 A2
Durleigh Rd TA6 ... 208 C3
Durley Hill BS31 ... 24 C7
Durley La BS31 ... 24 D7
Durleymoor Cross EX16 ... 178 F4
Durley Pk BA2 ... 44 E4
DURNFIELD ... 186 B7
Durnhill BS40 ... 73 F7
Durrant Cl DT9 ... 225 D3
Dursdon Dro
Priddy BA5 ... 111 C8
Wells BA5 ... 112 B6
Dursley Rd BS11 ... 4 E5
DURSTON ... 169 F6
Durston BS24 ... 49 A2
Durston Cl BA16 ... 207 C5
Durston Ho 3 BA16 ... 207 C5
Durston Way TA1 ... 212 E1
Durville Rd BS13 ... 22 B6
Durweston Wlk BS14 ... 23 C8
Dutch Rd TA9 ... 105 E5
Dutton Cl BS14 ... 23 D6
Dutton Rd BS14 ... 23 D6
Dutton Wlk BS14 ... 23 D6
Dwelly Cl TA20 ... 223 C3
Dyehouse Cnr TA22 ... 164 A6
Dyehouse Cross TA22 ... 163 F5
Dyehouse La
Bury TA22 ... 164 A5
Glastonbury BA6 ... 206 C5
Dye La BA3 ... 115 A3
Dyers Cl
Bristol BS13 ... 22 D4
Curry Rivel TA10 ... 171 D4
West Buckland TA21 ... 180 F7
Dyers' Close La BA11 ... 119 E5
Dyers Gn TA6 ... 153 F3
Dyer's La TA2 ... 213 E7
Dyers Rd TA10 ... 171 D4
Dyke Hill Terr TA20 ... 198 D8
Dyke's Way BA9 ... 216 B3
Dymboro Ave BA3 ... 77 F1
Dymboro Cl BA3 ... 77 F1
Dymboro Gdns BA3 ... 77 F1
Dymboro The BA3 ... 77 F1
Dyrham Cl TA8 ... 104 D7
Dyson Cl BS49 ... 34 B8

E

Eagle Cl
Ilchester BA22 ... 173 E2
Weston-super-Mare BS22 ... 49 D8
Eagle Dr 5 BA3 ... 97 B8
Eagle Gdns BA22 ... 173 E2
Eagle La 1 BA11 ... 119 F4
Eagle Pk BA1 ... 28 F5
Eagle Rd BA1 ... 28 F5
Eagles The BS49 ... 34 B8
Eaker Hill La BA3 ... 93 F6
Eames Orch TA19 ... 221 C2
Earlesfield BS48 ... 8 C1
Earle St BA20 ... 219 C5
Earlham Gr BS23 ... 49 A7
Earls Cl
Bridgwater TA6 ... 208 E7
Sherborne DT9 ... 225 F5
Earl St BS1 ... 227 A4
EAST ANSTEY ... 162 E5
East Anstey Prim Sch EX16 ... 162 E5
East Approach Rd TA7 ... 136 D4
East Ave TA9 ... 104 C4
Eastbourne Ave 15 BA1 ... 28 B1
Eastbourne Ct 13 TA1 ... 213 A4
Eastbourne Gate TA1 ... 213 A4
Eastbourne Rd TA1 ... 213 A4
Eastbourne Terr 12 TA1 ... 213 A4
EAST BOWER ... 209 E6
EAST BRENT ... 86 D5
East Brent CE Fst Sch TA9 ... 86 C4
East Bridgwater Com Sch TA6 ... 209 C5
EASTBROOK ... 168 E1
Eastbrook Terr TA3 ... 168 D1
Eastbury Hill TA24 ... 131 B5
Eastbury Rd TA24 ... 131 B5
EAST CHINNOCK ... 196 E8
East Chinnock Rd
East Chinnock TA18 ... 196 F8
Higher Odcombe TA14 ... 186 C1
East Cl
Bath BA2 ... 44 A5
Haselbury Plucknett TA18 ... 196 B5
EAST CLEVEDON ... 6 F3
East Clevedon Triangle BS21 ... 6 F3
Eastcliff BS20 ... 2 E7
EAST COKER ... 197 D7
East Coker Com Prim Sch BA22 ... 197 C7
East Coker Rd BA20 ... 218 F2
East Coker Sawmills BA22 ... 197 C7
EAST COMBE ... 151 E2
Eastcombe Gdns BS23 ... 30 F1
Eastcombe La BA4 ... 142 E2
Eastcombe Rd BS23 ... 30 F1
EAST COMPTON ... 205 A2
East Compton Rd
Pilton BA4 ... 204 E1
Shepton Mallet BA4 ... 205 B1
East Coombe La TA4 ... 165 D8
Eastcote Pk BS14 ... 23 B5
Eastcott La TA24 ... 148 F5
Eastcourt Rd BS39 ... 76 F8
EAST CRANMORE ... 142 C6
Eastcroft BS40 ... 54 E2
Eastcroft Cl BS40 ... 54 E2
East Ct BS3 ... 11 F3
East Ct BA5 ... 113 A1
Eastdown Rd BA3 ... 78 D5
East Dr TA9 ... 86 E4
EAST DUNDRY ... 22 A1
East Dundry La BS41 ... 22 A1
East Dundry Rd BS13, BS14 ... 22 F2
EAST END
Blagdon ... 54 F2
Chewton Mendip ... 94 E4
Nailsea ... 9 A1
South Cadbury ... 175 D4
Stoke St Michael ... 116 C2
East End BS26 ... 88 D7
East End La
Butleigh BA6 ... 157 F5
Chewton Mendip BA3 ... 94 E4
Easterdown Hill
Dinnington TA17 ... 195 B8
Seavington St Mary TA19 ... 184 E1
Easter La EX35 ... 122 B4
Eastermead La BS29 ... 51 C3
Eastern Ave TA6 ... 209 D4
Eastern Ho BS23 ... 30 E1
EASTERTOWN ... 67 D2
Eastertown BS24 ... 67 D1
Eastfield
Bruton BA10 ... 215 F7
29 Martock TA12 ... 185 E6
Shepton Mallet BA4 ... 205 B6
Yarlington BA9 ... 175 F8
Eastfield Ave BA1 ... 27 B2
Eastfield Cl 30 TA12 ... 185 E6
Eastfield Gdn 12 DT9 ... 225 E4
Eastfield Gdns BS23 ... 30 F1
Eastfield La
Barrington TA19 ... 184 D5
Blackford BS28 ... 107 F6
Ditcheat BA4 ... 159 C7
East Chinnock BA22 ... 196 D8
Hambridge TA3 ... 184 B8
Lydford Fair Place TA11 ... 158 D3
North Perrott TA18 ... 196 C4
Norton Sub Hamdon BA22 ... 185 F1
Eastfield Pk BS23 ... 30 F1
Eastfield Rd
Hutton BS24 ... 49 E2
Wincanton BA9 ... 216 D4
East Gate 11 TA1 ... 213 A4
Eastgate Gdns 10 TA1 ... 213 A4
Easthams Rd TA18 ... 224 D6
EAST HARPTREE ... 74 E4
East Harptree CE VA Prim Sch BS40 ... 74 F4
Easthay La TA20 ... 199 A4
EAST HEWISH ... 33 B6
EASTHILL ... 120 B4
Easthill BA11 ... 120 B4
Easthill La BA7 ... 159 D5
EAST HUNTSPILL ... 136 E7
East Huntspill Sch TA9 ... 136 E8
EAST KNOWSTONE ... 162 B2
East La TA18 ... 196 B7
EAST LAMBROOK ... 220 C8
East Lambrook Manor Gdns* TA13 ... 220 C8
East Lambrook Rd TA13 ... 220 D7
Eastland Rd BA21 ... 219 C5
East Lanes BA21 ... 187 D6
Eastlea BS21 ... 6 B1
East Lea Rd BA1 ... 44 A8
Eastleigh Cl
Burnham-on-S TA8 ... 104 C8
Frome BA11 ... 120 A7
Wiveliscombe TA4 ... 210 C5
Eastleigh Rd TA1 ... 213 B3
EAST LYDFORD ... 158 D2
EAST LYNG ... 170 D8
Eastlyn Rd BS13 ... 22 B8
East Mead BA3 ... 78 B2
Eastmead Ct BS9 ... 5 E4
Eastmead La BS9 ... 5 E4
East Mead La
Street BA16 ... 207 F5
Walton BA16 ... 156 E6
East Mere Cross EX16 ... 178 B2
East Mill Ct 11 DT9 ... 225 E4
East Mill La DT9 ... 225 E4
Eastmoor La TA4 ... 164 E8
East Moor La TA10 ... 172 B3
Eastnor Rd BS14 ... 23 A3
EAST NYNEHEAD ... 167 D2
EASTON ... 111 A4
Easton Ct BA3 ... 76 E1
Easton Farm La BA4 ... 159 B8
Easton Hill BA5 ... 111 B3
Easton Ho 9 BA1 ... 28 C1
EASTON-IN-GORDANO ... 4 A4
Easton La
Pylle BA4 ... 141 C1
Sampford Peverell EX16 ... 178 D1
Easton Moor Dro BA5 ... 110 F3
Easton Rd BS20 ... 4 C4
Easton Town La BA4 ... 158 F4
Easton Trow La BA4 ... 159 B5
Eastop La DT10 ... 190 A3
EASTOVER ... 209 B5
Eastover
Bridgwater TA6 ... 209 A5
Langport TA10 ... 172 A6
Eastover Cl TA10 ... 172 A5
Eastover Com Prim Sch TA6 ... 209 B5
Eastover Gr BA2 ... 44 C1
Eastover Rd BS39 ... 59 D1
East Par BS9 ... 5 C6
EAST PENNARD ... 158 F8
EAST QUANTOXHEAD ... 133 B6
East Quay TA6 ... 209 A6
East Quay Mews TA6 ... 209 A6
East Rd BA16 ... 207 E6
East Reach TA1 ... 213 A4
East Ride TA9 ... 86 B1
East Ridge Dr BS13 ... 21 F5
EAST ROLSTONE ... 33 B1
East Side La TA7 ... 136 F2
East Somerset Railway* BA4 ... 205 F3
East Somerset Way BA5 ... 203 D3
East St
Banwell BS29 ... 51 C3
Bourton SP8 ... 161 F1
Cannington TA5 ... 135 C2
Chard TA20 ... 223 D4
Crewkerne TA18 ... 224 C6
Drayton TA10 ... 171 E3
East Coker BA22 ... 197 B8
Ilminster TA19 ... 221 C4
Martock TA12 ... 185 E6
Milborne Port DT9 ... 217 D2
North Perrott TA18 ... 196 C4
Norton Sub Hamdon TA14 ... 185 F1
Shepton Montague BA9 ... 160 B2
Taunton TA1 ... 212 F3
Templecombe BA8 ... 176 F1
EAST STOKE ... 186 A4
East Stoke TA14 ... 185 F4
EAST STREET ... 139 F1
East Street Dro TA12 ... 185 E6
East Street La BA6 ... 140 A1
East Tapps La EX16 ... 163 B2
EAST TOWN
Lydeard St Lawrence ... 150 E3
Shepton Mallet ... 141 A3
East Town La TA4 ... 150 E3
East Town La (Platterwell La) BA4 ... 141 B3
EAST TWERTON ... 44 D7
Eastville
Bath BA1 ... 28 B1
Yeovil BA21 ... 219 C5
Eastville La BS27 ... 90 F1
EAST WATER ... 92 F2
East Water La BA5 ... 92 F2
Eastway BS48 ... 8 E3
East Way BA2 ... 44 A5
Eastway Cl BS48 ... 8 D2
Eastway Sq BS48 ... 8 E3
Eastwell La BS25 ... 69 E6
Eastwick Ave TA2 ... 212 F7
Eastwick Rd TA2 ... 213 B7
Eastwood
Bath BA2 ... 45 F6
Sherborne BS40 ... 75 B2
Eastwood Cl
Bridgwater TA6 ... 209 C4
Frome BA11 ... 119 C4
High Littleton BS39 ... 59 C1
EAST WOODLANDS ... 144 A7
East Woodlands Rd BA11 ... 144 A7
East Wood Pl BS20 ... 2 E7
Eastwoods BA1 ... 29 B3
Eaton Cl BS14 ... 23 E5
Eaton Cres
Bristol BS8 ... 226 A4
Taunton TA2 ... 213 A6
Ebben La TA20 ... 194 F1
Ebbor Gorge Nature Reserve* BA5 ... 111 D6
Ebbor Gorge Nature Trail* BA5 ... 111 C5
Ebbor La BA5 ... 111 B5
Ebden Lo 15 BS22 ... 32 A2
EBDON ... 32 B6
Ebdon La BS22 ... 32 C5
Ebdon Rd BS22 ... 31 F4
Ebenezer La BS9 ... 5 E5
Eckweek Gdns BA2 ... 79 D8
Eckweek La BA2 ... 79 E8
Eckweek Rd BA2 ... 79 D8
Ecos Ct BA11 ... 119 D4
Edbrooke Rd TA24 ... 147 C5
Edbrook La TA5 ... 134 F3
Eddington Ct BS23 ... 48 D7
Eden Croft BS22 ... 49 E8
Eden Dr BA5 ... 203 C2
Eden Park Cl BA1 ... 29 A4
Eden Park Dr BA1 ... 29 A4
Eden Terr BA1 ... 28 B2
Eden Villas 4 BA1 ... 28 C2
EDFORD ... 116 C7
Edford Hill BA3 ... 116 C6
Edgar Bldgs BA1 ... 228 B3
EDGARLEY ... 139 E1
Edgarley Cl BA6 ... 206 F7
Edgarley Ct BS21 ... 6 C5
Edgarley Field La BA6 ... 157 E8
Edgarley Rd
Glastonbury BA6 ... 139 D1
West Pennard BA6 ... 139 F1
EDGCOTT ... 128 C1
Edgcott Rd TA24 ... 128 C1
Edgebury TA7 ... 136 E4
Edgecombe Ave BS22 ... 31 D2
Edgecombe Mews BA1 ... 27 B1
Edgefield Cl BS14 ... 22 F3
Edgefield Rd BS14 ... 22 F3
Edgehill Rd BS21 ... 6 D6
Edgemoor Rd TA24 ... 201 B4
Edgewood Cl BS14 ... 23 B8
Edgeworth Rd BA2 ... 44 C2
Edinburgh Pl 1 BS23 ... 48 E8
Edinburgh Rd
Bridgwater TA6 ... 208 E2

Edinburgh Rd *continued*
Keynsham BS31 24 E4
EDINGTON 137 C3
Edington Rd TA7 137 D4
Edington Right Dro TA7 155 B7
EDINGWORTH 86 F7
Edingworth Rd BS24 86 F7
Edith Cl TA8 85 A2
EDITHMEAD 104 F7
Edithmead La TA9 105 A6
Edmond's Hill TA11 173 D4
Edmund Hill La BA6 206 F6
Edmund Rd BS14 23 A7
Edmunds Way BS27 90 C7
Edward Cl BA22 218 B6
Edward Ct BS31 24 F4
Edward Rd BS21 6 E5
Edward Rd S BS21 6 E5
Edward Rd W BS21 6 E6
Edward St
Bath, Bathwick BA2 45 B7
Bath, Lower Weston BA1 44 C7
Bridgwater TA6 209 B5
Edwin Short Cl BS30 25 E8
Egerton Rd BA2 44 E4
EGFORD 119 B5
Egford Hill BA11 119 C5
Egford La BA11 119 C5
Egg Moor La EX13 198 A7
Eggwood La TA13, TA16 195 E8
Eglin Croft BS13 22 B4
Eglinton Rd BA16 207 B4
Egremont Ct TA4 202 D2
Egret Dr BS49 16 F2
Egrove Way TA4 202 E4
Eight Acre Dro TA7, TA9 137 A5
Eight Acre La
Wellington TA21 222 E5
Wootton Courtenay TA24 129 F8
Eighteen Arce La BA21 218 C6
Eighth Ave BS14 23 A7
Eileen Cl BA16 207 E5
Eirene Terr BS20 4 D4
Elberton Rd BS9 5 B7
Elborough Ave BS49 34 B8
Elborough Gdns BS24 50 C3
Elborough La BA22 186 F8
Elbridge Ho 3 BS2 227 C3
Elderberry Wlk BS22 31 F1
Elder Cl
Chard TA20 223 C5
Frome BA11 120 B3
Highbridge TA9 104 D5
Eldergrove Cl TA6 209 D7
Elder Ho TA8 65 E2
Elderwood Rd BS14 23 B7
Eldon Pl BA1 28 B2
Eldred Cl BS9 5 D5
Eleanor Cl BA2 44 A5
Eleanor Cotts BA2 44 A6
Electric Ho TA14 185 E3
Eleven Ct TA6 208 E4
Elfrida Terr BA5 203 A5
Elgar Cl
Bristol BS4 22 D6
Clevedon BS21 6 E1
Elgin Cl BA16 207 B5
Eliot Cl BS23 49 A3
Eliotts Dr BA21 218 E7
Elizabeth Cl BS24 49 D3
Elizabeth Ct
Burnham-on-S TA8 104 B6
4 Martock TA12 185 E6
Elizabeth Flats BA21 219 C6
Elizabeth Gdns 16 BA8 190 A6
Elizabeth Way
Bridgwater TA6 209 C5
Chard TA20 223 C5
Ellbridge Cl BS9 5 D5
Ellenborough Cres BS23 48 E6
Ellenborough Ct BS23 48 E6
Ellenborough Ho BS8 226 A2
Ellenborough Park Rd
BS23 48 E6
Ellenborough Pk N BS23 48 D6
Ellenborough Pk S BS23 48 D6
Ellen Cl 8 TA6 153 F4
Ellen Ho BA2 44 A5
Ellersdown La TA22 163 E4
Ellesmere Rd
Bristol BS4 23 D8
Weston-super-Mare BS23 48 D2
Ellfield Cl BS13 21 F6
Ellick Rd BS40 54 D1
ELLICOMBE 201 C4
Ellicombe La TA24 201 C4
Ellicombe Mdw TA24 201 C4
Elliot Cl BA11 119 F6
ELLIOTS GREEN 144 B8
Elliots La BA11 119 B8
Elliott's Hill BA22 196 D7
Ellis Ave BS13 22 A8
Elliscombe Pk BA9 176 B6
Ellis Gr TA2 168 B5
Ellis Pk BS22 32 C4
Ellis's La TA5 152 C6
Elliston Dr BA2 44 B4
Ellsbridge Cl BS31 25 B5
Ellworthy Ct BA11 120 B4
Elm Ave TA8 104 B6
Elmbrook BA1 44 D8
Elm Cl
Banwell BS29 50 E4
Broadway TA19 183 C2
Nailsea BS48 8 C1
Elm Cl *continued*
Star BS25 52 D1
Wells BA5 203 A4
Yatton BS49 34 B7
Elm Ct
Bristol BS14 23 A6
Keynsham BS31 24 C4
Elmdale Rd BS8 226 B3
Elm Dr BA9 216 C3
Elm Farm BS48 9 A2
Elm Gr
Bath, Larkhill BA1 28 C2
Bath, The Oval BA2 44 C4
Locking BS24 49 F4
Minehead TA24 201 A5
Taunton TA1 212 E5
Elmgrove Cl TA6 209 D7
Elmham Way BS24 32 B1
Elm Hayes BS13 21 F6
Elmhurst Ave BA21 219 B7
Elmhurst Est
Batheaston BA1 29 A4
Batheaston BA1 29 A5
Elmhurst Gdns BS41 20 F8
Elmhurst Jun Sch BA16 207 D6
Elmhurst La BA16 207 D6
Elmhurst Rd BS24 49 E2
Elmhyrst Rd BS23 48 F8
Elm La
Great Elm BA11 119 A6
Shalford BA9 216 B7
Woolavington TA7 136 F4
Elmlea Ave BS9 5 F5
Elm Lea Cl TA7 136 C4
Elmlea Jun & Inf Schs BS9 5 F5
Elmleigh BA21 218 C7
Elm Leigh BA11 120 C6
Elmleigh Rd 21 TA12 185 E6
Elm Lodge Rd BS48 9 B2
Elm Pk TA1 212 E5
Elm Pl BA2 44 F4
Elm Rd BS39 77 E5
Elms Cl TA1 212 E5
Elms Est TA2 213 F8
Elmside Cl BA16 207 D5
Elmside Ho TA6 208 F2
Elmside Rd TA6 208 E2
Elms La BA7 214 B7
Elmsleigh Rd BS23 48 E4
Elmsley La BS22 31 C5
Elms Rd TA21 222 F5
Elm St TA20 223 C5
Elms The
Banwell BS29 51 A4
Bath, Lambridge BA1 28 C2
Bath, Weston Park BA1 27 C1
Elmswood BS23 48 F8
Elm Terr BA3 97 C8
Elm Tree Ave
Nailsea BS21 8 A4
Radstock BA3 78 D1
Elmtree Dr BS13 21 F5
Elm Tree Pk BS20 3 D3
Elm Tree Rd
Clevedon BS21 6 D2
Locking BS24 50 A4
Elmvale Dr BS24 49 F3
Elm View
Midsomer Norton BA3 78 B1
Temple Cloud BS39 58 E1
Elm Way BA4 205 A6
Elm Wlk
Portishead BS20 2 C4
Yatton BS49 34 B7
Elmwood Ave TA6 208 F3
Elmwood Sch TA6 208 F3
Elsbert Dr BS13 21 E6
Elscombe La
Timberscombe TA24 130 A4
Wootton Courtenay TA24 129 F4
Elton Ho 2 BS2 227 C3
Elton Rd
Bristol BS8 226 C3
Clevedon BS21 6 C3
Weston-super-Mare BS22 32 A4
Elton St BS2 227 C4
Elvard Cl BS13 22 A4
Elvard Rd BS13 22 A4
Elwell La BS40, BS41 21 A1
ELWORTHY 150 C6
Elworthy Cross TA4 150 C5
Elworthy Dr TA21 222 D4
Elworthy La TA4 150 C5
Ely Gr BS9 5 B7
Embankment The TA10 172 A5
Embden Walk 4 TA6 209 A1
Embercourt Dr BS48 19 A6
Emblett La TA10 156 F3
EMBOROUGH 95 C3
Emborough Pond La BA3 95 D2
Emerald Wy TA7 209 C8
Emery Gate BS29 51 B3
Emlet DT9 187 E1
Emletts Way BA21 218 B8
Emley La BS40 54 B6
Emlyn Cl 6 BS22 32 B4
Emmanuel Ct BS8 226 A4
Emmett Wood BS14 23 B3
Empress Menen Gdns BA1 44 A8
Enderleigh Gdns BS25 52 F4
Enfield Dr BA4 141 E2
Enfield Rd BA4 141 E2
Engine Dro TA7 154 F1
Engine La BS48 18 B8
Englands La BA22 174 F3
England's La TA17 195 D8
Englands Mead BA22 174 F3
Englands Rd TA24 124 A3
Englands Way TA20 223 D6
ENGLISHCOMBE 43 F2
Englishcombe La BA2 44 D3
Englishcombe Rd BS13 22 C3
Englishcombe Rise BA2 44 A3
Englishcombe Tithe Barn* BA2 43 F2
Englishcombe Way BA2 44 E3
ENMORE 153 A6
Enmore BS24 49 A2
Enmore Cl TA8 104 C8
Enmore Rd
Bridgwater TA5 153 B6
Taunton TA2 212 F7
Enmore VC Prim Sch TA5 152 F5
Ennerdale Cl BS23 49 A5
Ensleigh Ave BA1 27 E4
Enterprise Ctr The BS24 49 A3
Enterprise Mews BA20 218 D3
Enterprise Trade Ctr BS4 22 E7
Entry Hill BA2 44 F2
Entry Hill Dr BA2 44 F3
Entry Hill Gdns BA2 44 F3
Entry Hill Pk BA2 44 F2
Entry Rise BA2 44 F1
Erin Wlk BS4 22 D8
Erlon La BA5 110 F4
Ermine St BA21 218 D7
Ermine Way BS11 4 C7
Ernest Ashman Pl TA20 223 D5
Ervine Terr BS2 227 C4
ESCOTT 150 C8
Escott Ct TA6 208 F6
Escott La TA4 132 D1
Esgar Rise BS22 31 E3
Eskdale Cl BS22 49 D8
Eskimo Ct BA16 207 B5
Esmonde Dr BA22 173 E2
Esmond Gr BS21 6 D4
Esplanade
Burnham-on-S TA8 104 A7
Minehead TA24 201 A7
Esplanade La TA23 202 C7
Esplanade Rd BS20 2 C7
Esplanade The TA23 202 C7
Essex Cl TA20 223 C4
Essex Ct TA1 212 C2
Essex Dr TA1 212 C2
Estuary Ho BS20 2 E7
Estuary Pk TA5 135 B5
Estune Wlk BS41 11 A2
Esworthy Cross EX16 162 F1
Ethel St BA5 203 C3
Ethpark Gr 1 TA2 212 F6
Etonhurst BS23 48 D6
Eton La BS29 50 E7
Eton Rd TA8 104 B6
Etsome Cl TA11 211 C4
Etsome Hill TA11 211 C7
Etsome Rd TA11 211 C5
Etsome Terr TA11 211 C4
Ettlingen Way BS21 6 F2
Eugene Flats 7 BS2 227 A4
Eugene St
Bristol, Kingsdown BS2 227 A4
Bristol, St Pauls BS2, BS5 227 C4
Eva Turner Cl BS14 23 C6
Eveleigh Ave BA1 28 D2
Evelyn Rd BA1 44 B8
Evelyn Terr 14 BA1 28 A1
Evenlode Gdns BS11 4 F5
Evenlode Way BS31 25 A3
EVERCREECH 141 E1
Evercreech CE Prim Sch
Evercreech BA4 141 E2
Evercreech BA4 141 E2
Evercreech Rd BS14 23 B4
Evercreech Way TA9 104 F2
Everett Cl BA5 112 E1
Evergreen Cl BS25 51 F1
Evergreen Path TA16 195 F7
Everton Rd BA20 219 A4
Evesham Ave BA21 218 C6
Evesham Dr TA6 209 A1
Ewart Rd BS22 49 C8
Ewell Cl TA19 183 C1
Exbourne 10 BS22 32 A2
Exbury Cl TA8 104 C7
Excelsior St BA2 45 B5
Excelsior Terr BA3 78 B1
Exchange Ave BS1 227 A2
EXEBRIDGE 163 F3
Exebridge Ind Est TA22 163 F3
Exeter Cl
Burnham-on-S TA8 104 C7
Nether Stowey TA5 134 B2
Exeter Rd
Portishead BS20 2 E4
Rockwell Green TA21 222 B5
Weston-super-Mare BS23 48 E5
Exeter Road Cvn Pk TA21 222 A4
EXFORD 128 D1
Exford CE Fst sch TA24 128 D1
Exford Cl BS23 48 F2
Exford Rd TA24 147 C6
Exmoor Cl BA3 97 B6
Exmoor Gdns TA22 163 D6
Exmoor Owl & Hawk Centre* TA24 124 B4
Exmoor Pony Centre The* TA22 147 A1
Exmoor Rd BA2 44 F2
Exmoor Way TA24 200 E6
Exmouth Rd BS4 22 F8
Explore La BS1 226 C2
Express Pk TA6 136 A2
EXTON 147 E4
Exton BS24 49 A2
Exton Cl BS14 23 B5
Exton La TA22 147 E4
Eyer's La BS2 227 C3
Eyers Rd BS24 49 F7
EYEWELL 174 E4

F

Faber Gr BS13 22 C4
Factory Hill SP8 161 F2
Factory La
East Huntspill TA9 136 E8
Tatworth TA20 198 D8
FAILAND 10 C3
Failand Cres BS9 5 C5
Failand La
Easton-in-G BS8 4 A1
Portbury BS20 3 F2
Failand Wlk BS9 5 C6
Fairacre Cl BS24 50 B4
Fairacres Cl BS31 24 F5
Fair Ash BS40 74 D7
Fair Cl BA2 81 E4
Fairclose TA20 193 D6
Fair Cross TA23 131 F2
Faircross La SN14 13 D8
Fairdean Rd TA9 104 E4
Fairend La TA20 193 A8
Fairfax Cl TA6 209 C6
Fairfax Rd TA6 209 C5
Fairfax St BS1 227 B3
Fairfield
Coleford BA3 116 E8
Crewkerne TA18 224 B5
Ilminster TA19 221 A4
7 Martock TA12 185 E6
Rode BA11 82 F1
Sampford Peverell EX16 178 D1
Sherborne DT9 225 D5
Somerton TA11 211 E4
Tunley BA2 61 A3
Yarlington BA9 175 F7
Fairfield Ave BA1 28 A2
Fairfield Cl
Backwell BS48 19 D7
Frome BA11 120 A7
Marshfield SN14 13 F8
Weston-super-Mare BS22 31 B1
Fairfield Dr TA4 202 E3
Fairfield Gdns BA6 206 D4
Fairfield Gn TA3 192 A7
Fairfield Hts DT9 225 D5
Fairfield Mdws BA14 83 F3
Fairfield Mead BS48 19 D7
FAIRFIELD PARK 28 A2
Fairfield Park Rd BA1 28 A2
Fairfield Rd
Bath BA1 28 B1
Taunton TA2 213 B7
Fairfield Sch BS48 19 C6
Fairfield Terr
Bath BA1 28 A1
Fitzhead TA4 166 F5
Peasedown St John BA2 79 C7
Fairfield View BA1 28 A2
Fairfield Way
Backwell BS48 19 C6
Saltford BS31 25 B4
Fairford Cl TA9 104 E4
Fairford Rd
Bristol BS11 4 D7
Highbridge TA9 104 E4
Fair Furlong BS13 22 A4
Fair Furlong Prim Sch
Bishopsworth BS13 22 B4
Bristol BS13 22 B4
Fair Hill BS25 70 F8
Fairhouse Rd BA22 197 F8
Fairlands Mid Sch BS27 90 C7
Fairlands Way BS27 90 C7
Fairmead Rd BA21 219 C8
Fairmead Sch BA21 219 C8
Fairmont Terr 7 DT9 225 E4
Fair Pl TA11 158 D3
Fairseat Workshops BS40 56 E7
Fairview
Mells BA11 118 B7
Weston-super-Mare BS22 31 F4
Fair View BA10 161 A7
Fairview Ho BS9 5 F8
Fairview Terr
Taunton TA3 168 D1
Yeovilton BA22 187 A8
Fairwater Cl TA2 212 D6
Fairway BS4 23 D8
Fairway Cl
Berrow TA8 84 F4
Weston-super-Mare BS22 31 B2
Fairway Rise TA20 223 E5
Fairways
Charlcombe BA1 27 E4
Saltford BS31 25 E2
Wells BA5 203 C4
Fairways Cvn Pk TA7 136 E3
Fairways The TA1 212 F1
Fairway View BA21 219 D6
Fairwood Rd BA13 102 F5
Fairy Hill BS39 41 D6
Fakeham Rd BS24 66 F8
Falcon Cl
Bristol, Westbury on T BS9 5 F8
Portishead BS20 2 D4
1 Radstock BA3 97 B8
Falcon Cres BS22 49 D8
Falcon Ct TA1 212 C4
Falcondale Rd BS9 5 F7
Falconer Rd BA1 27 A3
Falcon Rd BA22 218 A5
Falconsmead Wlk BA21 219 D8
Falkland Ho 7 TA18 224 C6
Falkland Sq 6 TA18 224 C6
Falklands Rise TA24 200 D7
Fallow Dr TA9 104 D2
Fallowfield
Blagdon BS40 54 E2
Weston-super-Mare BS22 31 F3
Falmouth Cl BS48 9 A1
Fannybrooks La DT9 187 F1
Fanshawe Rd BS14 23 A7
Faraday Rd 2 BS8 11 F5
FARLEIGH 19 D7
Farleigh Ct BS48 20 B8
Farleigh Further Ed Coll 3 BA11 119 F5
FARLEIGH HUNGERFORD 82 E8
Farleigh Hungerford Castle* BA2 82 E8
Farleigh La
Hinton Charterhouse BA2 63 F1
Westwood BA2 64 A1
Farleigh Rd
Backwell BS48 19 C6
Clevedon BS21 6 B1
Keynsham BS31 24 D4
Norton St Philip BA2 81 F5
Farleigh Rise
Monkton Farleigh BA15 29 E1
Monkton Farleigh BA15 46 E8
Farleigh View BA15 64 F3
FARLEIGH WICK 46 E4
Farleigh Wlk BS13 22 A8
Farler's End BS48 18 F8
FARLEY 1 B1
Farley Cl BA11 120 C6
Farley Dell BA3 116 E8
FARMBOROUGH 60 B6
Farmborough CE VA Prim Sch BA2 59 F6
Farmborough La BA2 60 E6
Farm Cl
Somerton TA11 211 B3
Westbury-sub-Mendip BA5 110 D6
Weston-super-Mare BS22 32 C4
Farm Ct TA13 220 C5
Farm Dr TA11 211 B3
Farmer Rd BS13 21 E4
Farm Hill TA7 156 B8
Farmhouse Cl 7 BS48 8 E2
Farmhouse Ct 1 BS48 8 E1
Farmhouse Dr BA11 119 F7
Farm La
Buckland St Mary TA20 182 A2
Coultings TA5 134 E4
Stogursey TA5 134 D4
Street BA16 207 C7
Wellow BA2 62 E1
Farm Orch DT9 188 C7
Farm Rd
Bradford Abbas DT9 187 E1
Doulting BA4 141 E5
Hutton BS24 49 E2
Street BA16 207 C6
Weston-super-Mare BS22 31 B1
Farm St
Highbridge TA9 104 D2
Tintinhull BA22 186 C6
Farm View TA2 168 F6
Farmwell Cl BS13 22 B5
Farnaby Cl BS4 22 C7
Farnborough Rd BS24 50 C4
Farncombe La BA9 160 B1
Farndale Rd BS22 49 D8
Farrant Cl
Baltonsborough BA6 158 A5
Bristol BS4 22 D6
Taunton TA1 212 A4
Farrant Rd BA11 119 D5
Farriers Gn TA2 213 F7
Farrier Wy BS14 23 D3
Farringdon Hill La TA5 134 D6
Farringdon La TA5 153 D2
Farrington Fields
BS39 77 C3
Farrington Fields Trad Est
BS39 77 C3
FARRINGTON GURNEY 77 A3
Farrington Gurney By-Pass
BS39 77 A3
Farrington Gurney CE Prim
Sch BS39 77 A4
Farrington La BA4 141 F6
Farrington Rd BS39 77 C5
Farrington Way BS39 77 A3
Farrow Cl TA20 223 D3
Farrs La BA2 45 B2
Farr's La BS1 227 A2
Farr's Orch 6 TA16 195 F7
Farr St BS11 4 B8
Farthing Combe BS26 70 D2
Farthing Down TA21 179 E7
Farthing Rd TA6 208 E1
Farthing Row BA11 82 E1
Farthings Cl TA21 167 C2
Farthings Paddock BA7 159 A3
Farthing's Pitts TA21 222 C4
Fashion Mus* BA1 228 B3
FAULKLAND 80 E2
Faulkland La BA2, BA3 80 C4
Faulkland Rd BA2 44 D5
Faulkland View BA2 79 E7
Faversham Dr BS24 49 A1
Fawcus Pl TA20 223 C4
Fawn Cl BA6 206 C3
Fayre Way BA5 204 B7
Fearnville Est BS21 6 C2

Featherbed La
Chew Stoke BS40 38 A3
Clayhanger EX16 165 C1
Clutton BS39 58 C6
Fedden Village BS21 1 F5
Feeder Rd BS2 227 C1
Fellowsmead DT10 190 F5
Felon's Oak La TA24 131 B2
Felsberg Cl BA11 119 E3
Felsberg Way BS27 90 C7
Feltham Dr BA11 120 A3
Feltham La BA11 144 B8
FELTON 37 C8
Felton Gr BS13 22 A8
Felton La BS40 37 E7
Felton St BS40 37 C7
Fender Cl TA5 135 B5
Feniton 6 BS22 32 A2
Fennel La BS26 70 B2
Fennel Rd BS20 3 A5
Fennel Way BA22 218 A5
Fenners BS22 32 B4
FENNINGTON 168 B8
Fennington La TA2 168 B8
Fenns La BS41 10 E1
FENNY CASTLE 139 D7
Fenshurst Gdns BS41 20 F8
Fenswood Cl BS41 10 F1
Fenswood Ct BS41 10 E1
Fenswood Mead BS41 10 E1
Fenswood Rd BS41 10 E1
Fenton Cl BS31 25 D3
Ferenberge Cl BA2 60 A6
Ferguson Cl TA5 134 A3
Fermoy BA11 120 B6
Fern Cl BA3 78 B1
Ferndale Dr TA1 168 D1
Ferndale Gdns BA21 218 E6
Ferndale Rd
Bath BA1 28 C3
Portishead BS20 2 D6
Ferndown Cl
Bristol BS11 5 A7
Taunton TA1 212 D1
Ferne Animal Sanctuary★
TA20 193 A2
Ferney Leaze La BS39 59 C3
Fern Gr BS48 18 C8
Fern Lea BS24 67 B6
Fernlea Gdns BS20 4 B4
Fernlea Rd BS22 49 C7
Fernleigh Ave TA6 209 A3
Fernleigh Cl BA4 141 E1
Fern Lodge BS23 48 D6
Fernside BS48 19 A7
Fernsteed Rd BS13 21 F6
Ferry Ct BA2 45 B6
Ferry La
Bath BA2 45 B6
Lympsham BS24 67 C3
Ferryman Rd BA6 206 E7
Ferryman's Ct BS2 227 B2
Ferry St BS1 227 B2
Fersfield BA2 45 B3
Festival Units TA6 209 B1
Feversham Ave TA6 208 E6
Feversham Ct BA22 173 E2
Feversham La BA6 206 D5
Feversham Way TA2 213 A8
FIDDINGTON 134 D3
Fiddington Rd TA5 134 D2
Fiddle La BA22 174 F1
Fiddlers Green Rd DT9 175 E1
Fideoak Mill TA4 168 B4
FIELD 205 C5
Field Cl BA3 116 A3
Field End
Axminster EX13 198 A1
Minehead TA24 201 A5
Fielders The BS22 32 B4
Fieldfare Ave BS20 3 A6
Fieldfare Cl BS31 24 C3
Fieldfare Gdns BS49 16 F2
Fieldgardens Rd BS39 58 F1
Field Gate TA3 183 C8
Fieldgate La TA3 183 B8
Field Grove La BS30 25 C8
Fielding Ct BA21 219 C6
Fielding Ho BA2 44 A6
Fielding Path BA6 206 E6
Fielding Rd
Street BA16 207 B7
Yeovil BA21 219 C6
Fielding's Rd BA2 44 C6
Fieldins BA15 64 E7
Field La
Chewton Mendip BA3 94 F8
Kington Magna SP8 177 E1
Penselwood BA9 161 D2
Field Lane TA7 136 D3
Field Marshal Slim Ct 24
BS2 227 C3
Field Rd TA10 156 A1
Fields End TA1 213 C2
Fields The BS22 32 D2
Field View BA4 205 C5
Field View Ct BA4 141 E1
Fieldway BS25 52 B4
Field Way TA9 104 D5
Fifehead Bsns Ctr (Manor
Farm Trad Est) BA8 190 F8
Fifehead Hill BA8 190 F8
FIFEHEAD MAGDALEN 190 F8
Fifth Ave BS14 23 B7
Fig Tree Cres TA6 208 D1
Filer Cl BA2 79 D8
Filers Wy BS24 32 C1
Fillymead DT10 190 F5
Filwood Broadway BS4 22 E8
FILWOOD PARK 22 E8
Finch Cl
Houndstone BA22 218 A6
Shepton Mallet BA4 204 F6
Weston-super-Mare BS22 49 E8
Finches The
4 Portishead BS20 2 F6
Portishead BS20 3 A6
Finches Way TA8 85 B1
Finger Cnr DT10 190 F5
Finger La DT9 225 D3
Finisterre Parade BS20 2 F6
Finmere Gdns BS22 32 A4
Fircliff Pk BS20 2 D7
Fire House Mews BA9 216 C3
FIREPOOL 213 A5
Firepool Cres TA1 213 A5
Firepool Vw TA1 213 A5
Firgrove La BA2 61 B1
Fir La BS40 72 B5
Fir Leaze BS48 8 B1
Firs Ct BS31 24 C4
First Ave
Axminster EX13 198 A2
Bath BA2 44 E4
Bristol BS14 23 A7
Portbury BS20 3 E5
Radstock BA3 97 C8
First Dro TA7 155 D3
Firs The
Bath BA2 45 B1
Langport TA10 172 A5
Limpley Stoke BA3 64 A5
Wheddon Cross TA24 129 E1
First Ho BA16 207 B6
First Sedgemoor Dro
TA10 155 E4
Fir Tor Ave BA5 203 C5
Fir Tree Ave
Paulton BS39 77 F4
Weston-super-Mare BS24 49 E4
Firtree Cl TA5 134 A2
Fir Tree Cl TA6 209 D4
Firway Cross EX16 164 C3
Firwood Rd BA11 119 E4
Fishers Brook BA11 120 A5
Fishers Cl DT9 187 F5
Fisher's Hill
Glastonbury BA6 206 D4
Holywell Lake TA21 179 D7
Fisher's La
Dinnington TA17 195 A7
Mark TA9 106 D5
Fishers Mead TA22 163 D6
Fisherway La TA19 195 A5
FISHPOND BOTTOM 199 A1
Fishpond Bottom Rd DT6 199 A1
Fishwell La BA6 157 D4
Fitzharding Ho 8 BS1 227 A3
Fitzharding Rd BS20 4 E3
FITZHEAD 166 F7
FITZROY 168 A6
Fitzroy Circ BS20 2 F6
Fitzroy Ho 3 BA2 228 C3
Fivash Cl TA1 168 D1
Five Acres 3 BA22 197 F8
Five Arches Cl BA3 78 D2
Five Ashes BA22 186 C2
Five Barrows Cross EX36 145 B7
FIVE BELLS 202 B5
Five Bells TA23 202 B5
Five C Bsns Ctr BS21 6 B1
Five Cross Way TA21 180 F6
Five Cross Ways TA22 162 F7
Five Dials TA19 183 C1
FIVEHEAD 170 F2
Fivehead Dro TA3 170 F3
Five Hos TA21 222 B8
Five Lords TA5 134 B2
Fiveways Cl BS27 90 A7
Fiveways Rdbt BA21 219 A6
Fiveways Sch BA21 219 D6
Five Yards 3 TA4 167 F8
Flagstaff Rd BS26 68 D7
Flamingo Cres BS22 49 E8
Flat The BS39 58 D5
Flatts La BS39 59 C4
Flatwoods Cres BA2 45 F3
Flatwoods Rd BA2 45 F3
FLAX BOURTON 19 F7
Flax Bourton CE Prim Sch
BS48 19 F8
Flax Bourton Rd BS8 10 B3
Flaxfield Dr TA18 224 C5
Flax La DT9 187 F4
Flax Meadow La 12 EX13 198 A1
FLAXPOOL 151 C6
Flaxpool Hill TA4 151 C6
Flax Row TA18 224 C7
Flax Way BA21 218 C6
Fleed Cross TA4 166 A6
Fleet Air Arm Mus★ BA22 174 B3
Fletcher Cl TA2 213 B8
Fletcher's La BS26 87 D6
Fleur De Lys Dr BA14 83 F4
Flingers La BA9 216 D4
Flint Cross TA4 149 C1
Flints Cl BA11 119 D4
Flora's Ride TA24 129 A7
Florence Cl 3 TA6 208 E7
Florence Gr BS22 49 B8
Florida Fields BA7 214 B6
Florida St BA7 214 C5
Florida Terr BA3 78 C2
Flowerdale Rd TA23 202 C6
Flowerdown Bridge BS22 49 D7
Flowerdown Rd BS24 50 D4
Flowerfield BA11 143 B8
Flowers Hill BS4 23 E8
Flowers Ho 1 BA20 219 B4
Flowerstone BA3 114 D7
Flowerwell Rd BS13 22 B5
Flushing Mdw BA21 219 E5
FODDINGTON 174 E8
Foddington Rd TA11 174 F8
Foghamshire La BA11 143 D6
Foldhill Cl 25 TA12 185 E6
Foldhill La
Ash BA22 186 A6
Martock TA12 185 F6
Folke La DT9 189 A1
Folleigh Cl BS41 11 B2
Folleigh Dr BS41 11 B2
Folleigh La BS41 11 B2
Follett Cl TA21 222 C8
Folliott Rd BA6 206 E6
Folly Cl
Cannington TA5 135 B2
Midsomer Norton BA3 96 E7
Folly Dr BA4 159 C7
Folly Dro TA19 183 A5
Folly Farm Nature Reserve★
BS39 58 B5
Folly Fields BA21 219 B7
Folly La
Buckland St Mary TA20 182 E1
Kington Magna SP8 177 F2
Nether Compton DT9 187 F4
North Wootton BA4 140 C4
Shipham BS25 70 E7
South Cadbury BA22 175 D4
Weston-super-Mare BS23 48 E1
Folly Rd TA12 185 B7
FOLLY THE 94 F6
Folly The
Cold Ashton SN14 12 F6
Ditcheat BA4 159 C7
Paulton BS39 77 F6
Saltford BS31 25 F2
Fons George TA1 212 F2
Fons George Cl TA1 212 E2
Fons George Rd TA1 212 F2
Fonthill Rd BA1 27 E2
Font La BA22 197 B7
Fontmell Ct BS14 23 D7
Font Villas BA22 197 B8
Football La BA9 216 B4
Footlands Cl TA1 212 F1
Foots Farm La BS26 87 D6
Forbes Fraser Hospital
BA1 44 B8
Forches Cnr EX15 181 A4
Forche's La TA24 131 D3
FORD
Chewton Mendip 94 E8
Holcombe Rogus 178 F5
Wiveliscombe 210 F6
Forde Abbey & Gardens★
TA20 198 F8
Forde Pk BA21 218 C7
FORDGATE 154 C3
Fordhay BA22 196 E7
Fordhay Terr BA22 196 E7
Ford La
Chewton Mendip BA3 94 D8
Pilton BA4 140 F3
Stawell TA7 137 A1
Yarley BA5 139 B8
Fordmill Cross EX16 164 D1
Ford Orch EX16 178 D1
Ford Rd
Bampton EX16 164 C1
Peasedown St John BA2 79 D8
Wellow BA2 62 F1
Wiveliscombe TA4 210 C4
Ford St TA21 222 F4
FORD STREET 180 D5
Forefield Pl BA2 228 C1
Forefield Rise BA2 45 B4
Forefield Terr BA2 45 A4
Forelands BS23 30 B1
Fore Leaze Dro TA12 184 E7
Fore St
9 Bampton EX16 164 B1
Bridgwater TA6 208 F5
Cannington TA5 135 B2
Castle Cary BA7 214 C5
Chard TA20 223 C4
Dulverton TA22 163 D6
Holcombe Rogus TA21 178 F5
Milverton TA4 167 A4
North Petherton TA6 153 E3
Othery TA7 155 C2
Tatworth TA20 198 D8
Taunton TA1 212 F3
Thorncombe TA20 199 B6
Wellington TA21 222 D6
West Camel BA22 174 D3
Westonzoyland TA7 154 E5
Williton TA4 202 D3
Winsham TA20 194 E1
Forest Dr BS23 31 A1
Forest Dro TA3 182 F5
Forester Ave BA2 45 B8
Forester Cl TA6 208 D5
Forester Ct BA2 228 C4
Forester La BA2 45 B8
Forester Rd
Bath BA2 45 B8
Portishead BS20 2 D4
Foresters Cl TA4 202 E3
Forest Farm Units TA19 183 A3
Forest Hill BA20 218 E2
Forest La TA20 193 E8
Forest Mill La TA19 183 B1
Forest Rd
Frome BA11 120 B7
Horningsham BA11, BA12 144 B4
Forest Wlk BA13 121 C4
Forge Cnr
Somerton TA11 211 C4
Stogursey TA5 134 B6
Forge End BS20 3 E3
Forge La
East Chinnock BA22 196 E8
Zeals SP8, BA12 161 F2
Forsythia Wy TA6 208 D1
Fortescue Rd BA3 78 F2
Fortescue St BA2 81 E4
Fortfield Rd BS14 23 B5
Forth Ave BS20 2 F6
Forth Cl BA16 207 A4
Fortnum Pl TA19 221 D3
FORTON 223 F1
Forton La
Chard TA20 223 F1
Tatworth TA20 194 A1
Forton Rd TA20 223 D2
Forts Orch BA22 186 E6
Forum Bldgs BA1 228 C1
Forum La BA4 205 A7
Forum The BA21 218 C6
Forwards La TA19 183 B3
Forward's La TA3 181 C5
Fosgrove La TA3 181 E7
Fosse Barton BS48 8 D2
Fosse Cl
Nailsea BS48 8 C2
Yeovil BA21 218 D7
Fossedale Ave BS14 23 C6
Fossefield Rd BA3 97 B6
Fosse Gdns BA2 62 D8
Fosse Gn BA3 78 E4
Fosse La
Batheaston BA1 29 A4
Blackford BS28 107 C3
Clandown BA3 78 D3
Nailsea BS48 8 D2
Shepton Mallet BA4 205 D4
Fosse Lane Ind Est BA4 205 E4
Fosse Lane Junc BA4 205 E5
Fosse Lane Trad Est BA4 205 D5
Fosse Park Rd BA20 218 F4
Fosse Rd BA3 115 C3
Fosse The TA3 170 C4
Fosseway
Clandown BA3 78 E4
Clevedon BS21 6 C2
Midsomer Norton BA3 97 A5
Radstock BA3 97 C8
Fosse Way
Nailsea BS48 8 C2
Yeovil BA21 218 D7
Fosseway Cl BA2 79 C7
Fosse Way Cotts BA3 78 D2
Fosseway Ct
Bristol BS8 226 A2
Ilchester BA22 173 E2
Fosse Way Est BA2 44 D1
Fosseway Gdns BA3 78 D1
Fosseway S BA3 97 B7
Fosse Way Sch BA3 97 C8
Fosseway The BS8 226 A3
Fosse Wy TA20 194 C2
Foss La BS22 31 D6
Foss Wy TA12 185 E4
Foster Cl BA5 112 E1
Foster Rd BA11 120 A3
Fosters 10 DT9 225 E4
Foster's Almshouses 3
BS1 227 A3
Fosters Farm La TA9 136 D8
Foster's La BA22 175 A7
Foundry Barton 2 BA11 119 F5
Foundry Cotts BA2 60 B4
Foundry Mews
Chard TA20 223 C4
2 Crewkerne TA18 224 C5
Foundry Rd TA1 212 F4
Foundry Sq 1 TA18 224 C5
Foundry The BA1 228 C3
Fountain Bldgs 7 BA1 228 B3
Fountain Ho 8 BA1 228 B3
Fountain La BS25 70 B7
Fountains Cl BA21 218 C7
Four Acre Mdw TA6 208 E6
Four Acre Mead 1 TA4 167 F8
Four Acres
Bristol BS13 21 E4
Shepton Mallet BA4 205 C5
Fouracres Cl TA1 213 B1
Four Acres Cl
Bristol BS13 21 F4
Nailsea BS48 18 E8
Four Acres Prim Sch BS13 21 E4
Four Elms
Crewkerne TA17 195 D6
Holcombe Rogus TA21 179 A6
FOUR FORKS 152 F8
Four Forks La TA5 152 F7
Four Lanes TA20 193 F6
Fourth Ave
Bristol BS14 23 B7
Radstock BA3 97 D8
Fourways Cl BA7 214 D6
Fourways Pk BA6 139 D3
Fouts Cross TA19 184 F2
Fowen Cl BA16 207 B4
Fowey Cl BS48 19 A8
Fowey Rd BS22 32 A4
Fowler's Mead Dro TA6 209 F1
Fowler St TA2 212 E6
Fownes Rd TA24 201 B5
Foxbury Cl BA11 119 F6
Fox Cl TA21 222 A6
Foxcombe Hill BA22 175 C8
Foxcombe La DT9 176 C1
Foxcombe Rd
Bath BA1 44 B7
Bristol BS14 23 B4
FOXCOTE 79 F4
Foxcote BA20 218 C2
Foxcote Ave BA2 79 E7
Foxcote Gdns BA11 120 C7
Foxdon Hill TA20 223 A7
Foxdon Tip Rd
Chard TA20 193 E4
Crimchard TA20 223 A6
Foxdown Hill TA21 222 C4
Foxdown Ho TA21 222 C4
Foxdown Terr TA21 222 D4
Foxes Field Sch TA24 200 F6
Foxglove Cl BS22 32 A5
Foxglove Rd TA11 211 B3
Foxglove Way
Chard TA20 223 F5
Yeovil BA22 218 A5
Foxglove Wlk TA6 208 E1
Foxhanger La TA22 148 A2
FOX HILL 45 A2
Fox Hill BA2 45 A2
Foxhill Ho BA2 45 A1
FOX HILLS 79 A1
Foxhole La TA3 169 E5
Foxholes La BA2, BA11 100 D5
Fox & Hounds La BS31 24 F5
Fox Mdws TA18 224 D7
Foxmoor Bsns Pk Rd
TA21 180 E7
Fox Rd BA16 207 A5
Fox's Dro BA11 102 C1
Fox Way TA5 134 B2
Foxwell La BA22 196 C7
Foye Ho BS8 11 E6
Frampton Rd
Bridgwater TA6 208 F2
Shepton Mallet BA4 205 D3
Francis Cl TA3 169 D5
Francis Fox Rd 7 BS23 48 E7
Francis Gr BA2 45 A2
Francis Ho BS2 227 A4
Francis Reed Cl TA7 154 F5
Francis Wlk DT9 225 E5
Francombe Ho BS1 227 A1
Frankcom Ho BA2 45 B7
Frank Foley Parkway The
TA8 104 D6
Frankford Mans 7 BS23 30 C1
Frankland Cl BA1 27 B1
Frankley Bldgs BA1 28 B1
Frankley Terr 6 BA1 28 B1
Franklin Cl TA2 212 B7
Franklin Ct BS1 227 B1
Franklin's Way BS49 17 F1
Franklyn Terr BS39 77 A4
Frank Webber Rd TA21 222 A5
Fraser Cl
Burnham-on-S TA8 104 C7
Weston-super-Mare BS22 31 F4
Frederick Ave BA2 79 C7
Frederick Ct BA5 203 C4
Frederick Pl BS8 226 B3
Frederick Rd TA6 209 C6
Fredrick Pl 5 BA20 219 B4
Freedom Ave BA21 218 E6
Free Hill BA5 110 E6
Freeland Pl BS8 11 F6
Freelands BS21 16 C8
Freeling Ho BS1 227 B1
Freemans La BS48 20 B2
Freemantle Ho BS2 227 A4
Free St BA22 173 E1
Freeview Rd BA2 44 A5
Freezinghill La BS30 12 B4
Fremantle Rd TA1 213 B1
Frenchay Rd BS23 48 E4
French Cl
Nailsea BS48 8 F3
Peasedown St John BA2 79 D7
Frenchfield Rd BA2 79 D7
French Weir Ave TA1 212 E5
French Weir Cl TA1 212 E4
FRESHFORD 64 B5
Freshford Church Sch BA3 64 B5
Freshford La BA3 64 A4
Freshford Sta BA3 64 C5
Freshmoor 6 BS21 6 F3
Frethey La TA1, TA4 168 B3
Friar Ave BS22 31 E3
FRIARN 133 F1
Friarn Ave TA6 208 F4
Friarn Lawn TA6 208 F4
Friarn St TA6 208 F4
Friars Ave BA21 218 D6
Friars Cl BA22 173 D1
Friars Way TA8 104 B6
Friary BS1 227 C1
Friary Cl
Clevedon BS21 6 C5
Westwood BA15 64 E4
Witham Friary BA11 143 C3
Friary Rd BS20 2 B5
Friary Wood La
Freshford BA3 64 B2
Winsley BA15 64 F6
Friday St TA24 200 F7
Friendly Row BS20 4 C5
Friendship Gr 2 BS48 8 F2

Friendship Rd BS48 8 F3
FRIEZE HILL 212 D5
Friggle St BA11 120 D1
Frithfield La BA4 205 C6
Frobisher Ave BS20 2 B5
Frobisher Cl
Burnham-on-S TA8 104 D8
Portishead BS20 2 A5
Weston-super-Mare BS22 31 E4
Frobisher Way TA2 212 B6
Frog La
Bristol BS1 226 C2
Combe St Nicholas TA20 193 D6
Creech St Michael TA3 169 F6
Dinnington TA17 195 B8
Enmore TA5 153 A6
Felton BS40 37 C8
Galhampton BA22 175 E8
Haselbury Plucknett TA18 196 C6
Holcombe Rogus TA21 178 F5
Ilminster TA19 221 C4
Isle Brewers TA3 184 A8
Kingsdon TA11 173 D5
Langport TA10 171 F5
North Curry TA3 170 D5
Shepton Mallet BA4 205 E4
Stoke St Michael BA3 116 A4
Ubley BS40 55 D1
Wanstrow BA4 142 F4
West Camel BA22 174 D3
Winford BS40 37 F5
Froglands La BS27 90 C7
Froglands Way BS27 90 C7
Frogmary Gn TA13 220 A1
Frogmary St
South Petherton TA13 185 A3
South Petherton TA13 220 A3
Frogmore St BS1 226 C2
Frogs La TA21 180 F7
Frog St
Bampton EX16 164 B1
East Quantoxhead TA5 133 B6
Lopen TA13 185 A1
Frogwell Cross TA4 164 D6
Frogwell La TA22 164 B6
FROME 119 E4
Frome Bypass
Beckington BA11 101 E2
Tytherington BA11 143 E8
Frome Bypass Feeder Rd W
BA11 120 D6
Frome Com Coll BA11 120 A7
Frome Com Hospl BA11 120 A6
FROMEFIELD 120 A6
Fromefield BA11 120 A6
Fromefield Ho BA11 120 A6
Frome Mus* BA11 119 F5
Frome Old Rd BA3 79 A2
Frome Rd
Bath BA2 44 D1
Beckington BA11 101 D3
Bruton BA10 215 F7
Maiden Bradley BA12 144 B3
Norton St Philip BA2 81 F3
Nunney BA11 143 B8
Radstock BA3 79 B2
Rode BA11 101 F7
Southwick BA14 83 F3
Wingfield BA14 83 C5
Frome Sta BA11 120 A4
Frome View BA12 144 C2
Front St
Chapel Allerton BS26 88 D1
Chedzoy TA7 154 D8
Churchill BS25 52 E4
Monksilver TA4 150 B8
FROST HILL 34 C6
Frost Hill BS49 34 D7
Frost La TA19 183 F4
Fry's Bottom
Breach BS39 58 F7
Chelwood BS39 59 A6
Frys House of Mercy 11
BS1 227 B1
Frys La TA7 154 E8
Fry's La BS40 53 F3
Frys Leaze BA1 28 B2
Frys Mews TA1 213 C2
Fry's Well BA3 96 D3
Fry's Wlk BA4 205 A5
Fryth Ho BS48 9 D3
Fryth Way BS48 8 C2
Fst Sch TA16 195 F7
FULFORD 168 C8
Fulford Ct TA24 200 F7
Fulford Rd BS13 22 C5
Fulford Wlk BS13 22 B5
Fullands Ave TA1 168 F1
Fullands Ct TA1 168 F1
Fullands Rd TA1 213 B1
Fullens Cl BS22 49 D7
Fuller Cl BA4 205 D5
Fuller Rd BA1 28 C2
Fullers La BS25 70 A6
Fullers Way BA2 62 D8
Fullpits La TA7 156 B8
Fullwell Cl BA3 80 D1
Fulmar Rd BS22 31 F1
Fulwell La BA3 80 D1
Fulwood Cl TA1 212 D1
Furge Gr BA8 190 A6
Furge La BA8 190 A6
Furland Rd
Crewkerne TA18 224 C5
Weston-super-Mare BS22 31 C2
Furland Way TA18 224 C5
Furlong Cl BA3 96 F7
Furlong Cotts EX16 179 A4
Furlong Gn TA3 168 D1
Furlong La
Curry Rivel TA10 171 C3
Milborne Port DT9 217 B3
Furlong Pl BS26 70 C1
Furlongs Ave TA6 208 E2
Furlongs La TA10 156 C1
Furlongs The DT9 225 D5
Furnace Way BS49 34 E4
FURNHAM 223 D5
Furnham Cl TA20 223 D5
Furnham Cres TA20 223 D6
Furnham Rd TA20 223 D5
Furnleaze BS39 58 E3
Furpits La TA10 172 B6
Furringdons Cross TA18 195 F6
Furs Cl TA2 213 F8
Furze Cl
Bridgwater TA6 208 D4
Weston-super-Mare BS22 31 B2
Furzeclose La BA4 142 C7
Furzehill TA20 223 D5
Furzehill La TA24 147 C6
Furzeland Rd TA24 124 A4
Furze Rd BS22 31 A3
Furze The BA20 218 C2
Fylton Croft BS14 23 B3
Fyne Court Nat Res & Visitor
Ctr* TA5 152 E3

G

Gables Cl BS29 51 B3
Gables The TA21 222 C6
Gabriel Cl BA11 120 C6
Gadds Dro TA7 154 C2
Gadd's La BS27 90 B8
Gagley La BA5 111 B2
Gainesmarsh La TA10 172 C5
Gainsborough DT9 217 C2
Gainsborough Ct BA1 27 B1
Gainsborough Dr
Sherborne DT9 225 B3
Weston-super-Mare BS22 31 F3
Gainsborough Gdns BA1 44 C8
Gainsborough Hill DT9 225 E2
Gainsborough Rd BS31 24 F5
Gainsborough Way BA21 219 E8
Galahad Cl BA21 218 D7
Gale's Dro BA6 139 D3
GALHAMPTON 175 D8
Galhampton Hill BA7,
BA22 214 C2
Galhampton Rd BA22 175 C7
Galingale Way BS20 2 F5
Gallagher Ret Pk
TA6 209 A6
Weston-super-Mare BS23 49 A5
Galleries The BS1 227 B3
Galley Batch BA3 114 F4
Galley Batch La BA3 114 F4
Galloping Bottom La
TA23 149 E5
GALMINGTON 212 C2
Galmington Cl TA1 212 C3
Galmington Dr TA1 212 C2
Galmington La TA1 212 C2
Galmington Rd TA1 212 C2
Galmington Trad Est TA1 212 B3
Gamblyn Cross TA4 164 F5
Gamlin Cl TA21 222 D8
Gammins Cotts TA24 129 E2
Gander Cl BS13 22 B5
Gandstone Cross TA4 150 D2
Ganesfield BA4 141 E6
Ganges Cl TA3 170 F2
Gange's Hill TA3 170 F2
Gannet Rd BS22 31 F1
Gants Mill & Gdn* BA10 215 C5
Gants Mill La BA10 215 D5
Gaol La BA4 205 C6
Garamond Ct BS1 227 B1
Garden City TA10 172 A6
Garden Cl
Bristol BS9 5 C5
Norton Fitzwarren TA2 168 B4
Weston-super-Mare BS22 31 E2
Garden Ct BS8 226 A4
Gardener Cl BS29 50 D8
Gardeners Cl
Bradford On Tone TA4 167 F1
Cheddar BS27 90 B8
Gardeners Wlk BS41 11 B1
Garden Ground BA4 205 C4
Gardenhurst TA8 85 B1
Garden Hurst Cl TA8 104 B8
Garden Plot Hill TA3 183 E7
Gardens Rd BS21 6 C4
Gardens The
Bath BA1 27 E1
Dulverton TA22 163 D7
East Pennard BA4 158 F8
Sherborne DT9 225 C3
1 Wellington TA21 222 D5
2 Wells BA5 203 D4
Garden Terr TA21 222 B7
Garden Way TA24 200 D7
Garden Wlk TA6 208 E2
Gardiners Bsns Pk TA7 136 F3
Gardiners Orch BS28 108 C4
Gardner Ave BS13 21 F7
Gardner Rd BS20 2 D6
Garfield Terr 1 BA1 28 C2
Garland Ave BS24 50 C5
GARLANDHAYES 180 F2
Garlandhayes La EX15 180 E2
Garland Ho 7 BS21 6 C2
Garner Ct 4 BS22 32 B4
Garonor Way BS20 3 F5
Garre Ho BA2 43 F5
Garrett Rd BA20 218 D3
Garrick Rd BA2 43 F5
Garsdale BA11 120 A4
Garsdale Rd BS22 49 D8
Garston Cotts BS40 54 E3
Garstone La TA16 195 F8
Garston La
Blagdon BS40 54 E3
Frome BA11 120 A4
Marston Magna BA22 174 F1
Garston Lodge 11 BA11 119 F4
Garston Mead BA11 120 A4
Garston Rd BA11 120 A4
Garstons
Bathford BA1 29 D2
7 Clevedon BS21 6 B1
Wrington BS40 35 E1
Garstons Cl
Backwell BS48 18 F6
Wrington BS40 35 E2
Garstons Orch BS40 35 D1
Garston St BA4 205 C6
Garstons The BS20 2 D4
Garth Rd BS13 22 A8
Gartons Mead BA4 141 E1
Gartons Mead Rd BA4 141 E1
Garvins Rd BA6 206 C4
Gashay La EX13 199 B3
Gaskin's La TA3 183 D8
Gas La TA17 195 D7
Gason La BA22 174 F4
GASPER 161 E4
Gasper Lodge Rd BA9 161 E2
Gasper St BA12 161 E3
Gass Cl TA9 104 F4
Gassons BA2 79 D4
Gasson's La TA11 211 C3
Gaston Ave BS31 24 F6
Gaston Cl BA16 207 C4
Gaston's La TA12 185 D5
Gastons The BS11 5 A8
Gaswell La TA7 155 E8
Gasworks La BS1 226 B1
Gatchell Gn TA3 168 D1
Gatchell Mdw TA3 168 D1
Gatchells La TA4 132 F2
Gatchell's La TA3 181 B5
Gatcombe Farm Ind Est
BS40 35 D3
Gatcombe La BS48 20 C8
Gatcombe Mill La BS48 10 C1
Gatcombe Rd BS13 22 B5
Gate Cl EX13 198 E3
Gatehouse Ave BS13 22 A5
Gatehouse Cl BS13 22 A5
Gatehouse Ct BS13 22 B5
Gatehouse Ctr The BS13 22 B5
Gatehouse Way BS13 22 A5
Gate La BA5 203 D2
Gaunton Cl TA1 212 D2
Gaunts Cl BS20 1 F4
Gaunt's La BS1 226 C2
Gaunts Rd TA6 135 E6
Gay Cl TA21 222 E6
Gay Ct BA1 28 E3
Gay Elms Rd BS13 22 A4
Gaylard's La TA20 194 B5
Gay's Hill BA1 228 C4
Gay St
Bath BA1 228 B3
Mells BA11 118 B7
Wellington TA21 222 E6
Gazelle Rd
Weston-super-Mare BS24 49 B3
Yeovil BA20 218 D3
Gefle Cl BS1 226 B1
Geldof Dr BA3 78 A2
Gelosia Cl TA7 154 F6
General Higgins Ho TA9 104 E3
Gennes Gr BA9 216 C4
Gentle St
Frome BA11 119 F4
Horningsham BA12 144 E4
Geoffrey Cl BS13 21 E6
George Cl BS48 19 D7
George & Crown Cotts
TA17 195 C7
George La
Marshfield SN14 13 E8
South Petherton TA13 220 C4
George Maher Ct TA19 221 C3
Georges Bldgs BA1 28 C3
Georges Ground BA11 119 E2
George Sh Ctr The TA18 224 C6
Georges Ho BA2 45 B6
Georges Mews TA1 213 C2
George Smith Way BA22 218 A6
George's Pl BA2 45 B6
George's Rd BA1 28 A1
Georges Sq BS1 227 B2
George St
Bath BA1 228 B3
Bath, Bathwick BA2 45 B6
Bridgwater TA6 208 F5
Burnham-on-S TA8 104 A7
Charlton Adam TA11 173 F7
Glastonbury BA6 206 D5
Portishead BS20 2 C2
Sherborne DT9 225 D4
Taunton TA2 212 F6
Wellington TA21 222 D6
Weston-super-Mare BS23 48 E7
George Sweetman Cl
BA9 216 D4
George William Ct TA6 208 F4
Georgian Ct BA11 119 D3
Georgian Ho BA2 228 C2
Georgian House (Mus)*
BS1 226 C2
Georgian View BA2 44 C2
Gerard Rd BS23 48 F8
Gerbestone La TA21 180 E6
Gerrard Bldgs 5 BA2 45 B7
Gerrard Cl BS4 22 D7
Geys Hill BA12 144 D8
Giant's Grave TA20 193 A7
Giant's Grave Rd TA20 193 A7
Gibbet La BS14 23 D1
Gibbet Rd BA9 176 B6
Gibbsfold Rd BS13 22 C4
Gibbs' La TA19 184 D5
Gibbs Marsh Trad Est
DT10 190 D6
Gibraltar Cotts TA24 123 E4
Giddy La BA3 116 A4
Gielgud Cl TA8 104 D6
Gifford Cl TA20 223 D5
Giffords La TA18 196 C5
Giffords Orch TA12 185 A7
Giffords Pl BS13 22 A7
Gigg La SP8 177 C2
Gilbeck Rd BS48 8 C2
Gilbert Rd BA21 219 F8
Gilberts Cnr BA6 158 A6
Gilbert Scott Ho BA5 113 A1
Gilbert Scott Mews BA5 113 A2
Gilbert Scott Rd BA5 113 A1
Gilberyn Dr BS22 32 A3
Gilda Cl BS14 23 C5
Gilda Cres BS14 23 B6
Gilda Par BS14 23 C5
Gilda Sq W BS14 23 B5
Giles Cl TA10 171 D4
Giles Farm BA5 113 A1
Gillards TA1 212 B4
Gillards Cl TA21 222 B4
Gillards Mead TA3 192 A7
Gill Cres TA1 212 B1
Gillebank Cl BS14 23 D5
Gillingham Ct TA20 223 D5
Gillingham Terr 3 BA1 28 B1
Gill Mews BS22 32 B4
Gillmore Cl BS22 31 D1
Gillmore Rd BS22 31 D1
Gills La BS26 87 B5
Gillson Cl BS24 49 D2
Gimblett Rd BS22 32 B4
Ginger Pl 2 TA2 169 C5
Gipsy Cross TA4 166 A2
Gipsy Dro TA20 193 C4
Gipsy La
Burcott BA5 139 E8
Frome BA11 120 B7
Glastonbury BA6 139 D1
Halse TA4 167 B6
Sampford Arundel TA21 179 D5
Staplegrove TA2 212 D7
Street BA16 207 E4
Taunton TA1 212 C3
Wells BA5 203 A4
GIRT 175 C2
Givele Cl BA21 219 C8
Gladstone Ct BA2 45 C2
Gladstone Pl BA2 45 C2
Gladstone Rd
Bath BA2 45 C2
Bristol BS14 23 B6
Gladstone St
Midsomer Norton BA3 78 B3
Taunton TA2 212 E6
Gladstone Terr
Minehead TA24 201 A5
Wellington TA21 222 E6
Gladstone Villas BA3 115 C5
Glanfield Cl TA4 167 E8
Glanfield Terr BA22 173 F1
Glanvill Ave TA20 223 C5
Glanville Dr BS39 75 E6
Glanville Rd BS28 108 C4
Glanvill Rd BA16 207 C3
Glasses Mead TA1 212 B2
Glass House Hill DT9 225 E3
Glass's Cross TA4 149 E1
Glass's Rocks La TA4 149 D1
GLASTONBURY 206 F6
Glastonbury Abbey* BA6 206 E4
Glastonbury Cl BS48 9 B1
Glastonbury Ct BA21 218 D6
Glastonbury Rd
Meare BA6 138 E4
Wells BA5 203 B2
Glastonbury Tor* BA6 139 D1
Glastonbury Way BS22 32 A2
Glastonbury Western Relief
Rd BA6 206 E7
Glaston Ho BA16 207 D7
Glaston Rd BA16 207 D7
Glebe Ave BS20 2 E4
Glebe Cl BS41 11 C2
Glebe Cotts TA3 169 E2
Glebe Cres TA24 200 E8
Glebe Ho
Bath BA2 45 B5
Portishead BS20 2 E4
Weston-super-Mare BS22 31 F3
Glebeland Cl TA7 156 B8
Glebelands
3 Langaller TA2 169 C5
7 Merriott TA16 195 F7
Minehead TA24 200 E8
Glebelands *continued*
Norton Sub Hamdon TA14 185 F3
Nunney BA11 143 B7
Radstock BA3 78 D1
Glebelands Cl BS27 90 B6
Glebe Paddock BA5 139 E8
Glebe Rd
Bath BA2 44 B4
Clevedon BS21 6 C2
Long Ashton BS41 11 C2
Portishead BS20 2 E4
Weston-super-Mare BS23 48 E8
Glebe The
Fivehead TA3 170 F1
Freshford BA3 64 B4
Hinton Charterhouse BA2 63 D2
Queen Camel BA22 174 F3
Timberscombe TA24 130 B4
Timsbury BA2 60 B3
Wrington BS40 35 D2
Glebe Way BS27 90 C6
Glebe Wlk BS31 24 C4
Glebe Yd TA10 172 E4
Glen Ave BS8 10 F8
Glenavon Pk BS9 5 C4
Glen Brook BS9 5 D4
Glencairn Ct BA2 45 B6
Glen Cl TA2 168 B5
Glencoe Bsns Pk BS23 49 A7
Glencoe Terr TA3 168 D1
Glencot La BA5 203 A7
Glencot Rd BA5 203 A6
Glencroft Way BS22 31 E3
Glendale 16 BS8 11 F6
Glendevon Rd BS14 23 A3
Glen Dr
Bristol BS9 5 D5
Taunton TA2 168 F6
Gleneagles Cl
Nailsea BS48 9 A1
Weston-super-Mare BS22 31 F3
Glenmore Rd TA24 201 A7
Glen The
Saltford BS31 25 F1
Weston-super-Mare BS22 31 B2
Glenthorne Ave BA21 219 B7
Glenthorne Nature Trail
Gate* EX35 122 D5
Glenthorne Rd 9 TA2 212 F6
Glentworth Ct 19 BS23 30 C1
Glentworth Rd BS8 226 B2
Glen View BA3 115 E7
Glenview Ho BA2 79 D8
Glenville Rd BA21 219 D6
Glenwood Gdns TA2 212 F8
Glenwood Mans BS23 30 D1
Glenwood Rise BS20 1 F5
Glen Yeo Terr BS49 34 C4
Glider Ave
Haywood Village BS24 49 B4
Weston-super-Mare BS24 49 B4
Globe Orch TA18 196 C6
Gloucester Ho 11 BS2 227 C3
Gloucester La 18 BS2 227 C3
Gloucester Rd
Bath BA1 28 C3
Bridgwater TA6 208 F2
Burnham-on-S TA8 104 C7
Upper Swainswick BA1 28 A7
Gloucester Row 6 BS8 11 F7
Gloucester St
4 Bath BA1 228 B3
5 Bristol BS2 227 B4
8 Bristol, Clifton BS8 11 F7
Taunton TA1 213 A4
Weston-super-Mare BS23 48 D7
Glovers DT9 225 D5
Glovers Cl
Milborne Port DT9 217 D2
4 Stoke sub Hamdon TA14 185 F4
Glovers Ct BA20 218 F4
Glovers Field BS25 70 F7
Glovers Rd BA8 190 C4
Glovers Wlk 18 BA20 219 B4
Glovers Wlk Sh Ctr BA20 219 B5
Glynsmead TA20 198 C8
Glynswood TA20 223 C5
Gnome Rd BS24 49 C5
GOAR KNAPP 219 D5
GOATHILL 189 B4
Goathill La BA8 176 C3
Goathill Rd DT9 189 B4
GOATHURST 153 B5
Goathurst Hill TA5 153 A4
Godhams La TA4 165 A7
Godminster Ct BA10 215 E6
Godminster La BA10 215 E4
GODNEY 139 A5
Godney Cl BA6 206 F7
Godney Dro BA5 139 B6
Godney Rd BA5, BA6 139 A4
Godwin Cl BA5 203 C2
Godwin Dr BS48 8 C3
Goeffrey Farrant Wlk TA1 213 A5
Goes La BA7 158 F2
Gogs Orch BS28 108 C3
Gold Corner Dro TA9 137 A6
Goldcrest Way BS20 2 F6
Goldcroft BA21 219 B6
Goldcroft Ct BA21 219 B6
Goldenhaye La TA20 194 D3
Golden Hill
Stourton Caundle DT10 189 F1
Wiveliscombe TA4 210 C5
Golden Lion Ct BS1 227 B2
Golden Valley La BS30 25 E8
Golden Valley Prim Sch
BS48 8 F2

Goldfinches La BA6 ... 139 D3
Gold Hill
Batcombe BA4 ... 142 D2
Shepton Mallet BA4 ... 205 B7
Golding Cl BA5 ... 203 C4
Golding's La DT9 ... 217 C1
Goldney Ave BS8 ... 226 A2
Goldney Cl BS39 ... 58 F1
Goldney Rd BS8 ... 226 A2
Goldney Way BS49 ... 58 F1
GOLD'S CROSS ... 57 E6
Goldsmiths La EX13 ... 198 A4
Goldsmoor Cross EX16 ... 178 E3
Gold St DT10 ... 190 B4
Golf Club La BS31 ... 25 E2
Golf Course Rd BA2 ... 45 D6
Golf Links La BA3 ... 114 E3
Golf Links Rd TA8 ... 85 A2
Golledge Cl BA3 ... 96 C4
GOLSONCOTT ... 131 D2
Golsoncott La TA24 ... 131 C2
Gooch Cl
Bridgwater TA6 ... 209 B4
Frome BA11 ... 120 D6
Gooch Way BS22 ... 32 B3
Goodard Dr BS22 ... 32 B4
Goodeaves Cl BA3 ... 117 A7
Goodeaves Cotts BA3 ... 117 A7
Goodeve Pk BS9 ... 5 D3
Goodeve Rd BS9 ... 5 D3
Good Hill BA4 ... 142 E2
Goodlands La TA1 ... 212 F4
Good's La TA5 ... 152 C5
Goodwin Dr BS14 ... 22 F4
Goodymoor Ave BA5 ... 203 B5
Goodymoor La BA5 ... 203 B5
Goold Cl BA2 ... 43 A8
Goosander Cl TA24 ... 201 C4
Goosard La BS39 ... 77 E8
Gooseacre Ct BA22 ... 197 B8
Gooseacre La
East Coker BA22 ... 197 B8
Yeovil BA22 ... 218 A1
Gooseham La BS28 ... 108 F4
Gooseham Mead BS49 ... 34 D4
Goose La
Chilton Polden TA7 ... 137 B3
Horton TA19 ... 183 C2
Gooselade BA16 ... 207 C3
Gooseland Cl BS14 ... 22 F3
Gooseland La DT9 ... 188 B3
GOOSENFORD ... 169 A6
Goose St BA11 ... 101 E5
Goosey La BS22 ... 32 C2
Goosey Path TA24 ... 201 C2
Gordano Bsns Pk BS20 ... 2 E5
Gordano Gdns BS20 ... 4 B4
Gordano Rd BS20 ... 3 D7
Gordano Sch BS20 ... 2 D3
Gordano View BS20 ... 2 C5
Gordano Way BS20 ... 3 F5
Gordon Bldgs BA3 ... 79 A3
Gordon Rd
Bath BA2 ... 45 B5
Bristol BS8 ... 226 B3
Peasedown St John BA2 ... 79 D8
Taunton TA1 ... 213 A3
Weston-super-Mare BS23 ... 48 F2
Yeovil BA21 ... 219 C6
Gordon's Cl TA1 ... 213 B1
Gordon Terr TA6 ... 209 A5
GORE ... 187 F6
Gorefield TA13 ... 220 D2
Gorehedge 14 BA11 ... 119 F4
Gore La
Chapmanslade BA13 ... 121 B4
Pitney TA10 ... 172 C7
Gore Rd TA8 ... 85 A1
Gores Pk BS39 ... 59 B2
Gore Sq TA4 ... 167 E8
Gorlangton Cl BS14 ... 23 A7
Gorlegg TA21 ... 179 E5
Gorpit La TA5 ... 134 F8
Gorse La
Bristol BS8 ... 226 B2
Cold Ashton BS30, SN14 ... 12 D7
Gort Rd TA2 ... 168 B6
Gory La BA6 ... 140 A2
Gosford Mans 6 BS23 ... 30 C1
Goshawk Dr 8 BS20 ... 2 F6
Goslet Rd BS14 ... 23 E5
Goss Barton BS48 ... 8 D1
Goss Cl BS48 ... 8 C1
Goss Dr BA16 ... 207 B3
Goss La BS48 ... 8 C1
Goss View BS48 ... 8 C1
Goswell Cl BA16 ... 207 C5
Goswell Rd BA16 ... 207 C5
GOTHELNEY GREEN ... 153 B8
GOTTON ... 169 B7
Gough Cl 11 TA16 ... 195 F7
Gough Pl BS27 ... 90 A8
Gough's Caves★ BS27 ... 90 D8
Gould Cl
Bristol BS13 ... 22 C5
Street BA16 ... 207 E6
Gouldsbrook Terr TA18 ... 224 B6
Gouldsbrook View TA18 ... 224 C7
GOULD'S GROUND ... 119 E5
Gould's Ground 2 BA11 ... 119 E5
Gould's La 1 BA11 ... 119 E5
Goulston Rd BS13 ... 22 A5
Goulston Wlk BS13 ... 22 A5
Gournay Ct BS39 ... 77 A3
Governors Ho BA2 ... 44 D6
Govier's La TA23 ... 202 C7
Grabbist Top Rd TA24 ... 201 B2
Grace Cl BS49 ... 34 B8
Grace Dr BA3 ... 78 A2
Grace Martin's La BA22 ... 174 F3
Grace Rd BS22 ... 32 B4
Gradwell Cl BS22 ... 32 B3
Grafton Cl TA2 ... 213 A8
Graham Rd BS23 ... 48 E7
Graham Way TA4 ... 167 E6
Grainger Ct BS11 ... 4 F7
Grain Store The 9 BS1 ... 227 A2
Graitney Cl BS49 ... 35 A8
Granaries The BA3 ... 115 A3
Granary Orch DT9 ... 187 F5
Granary The 8 BS1 ... 227 A2
Granary Way TA3 ... 181 D8
Granby Hill BS8 ... 11 F6
Granby Rd BA22 ... 174 A2
Grand Par BA2 ... 228 C2
Grand Pier★ BS23 ... 48 D7
Grand Western Canal (Country Pk)★ EX16 ... 178 F2
Granfield Gdns BS40 ... 53 A5
Grange Ave
Highbridge TA9 ... 104 E3
Street BA16 ... 207 B6
Grange Bsns Pk The BS24 ... 33 A5
Grange Cl
Cannington TA5 ... 135 C2
Wellington TA21 ... 222 E5
Weston-super-Mare BS23 ... 48 E1
Grange Cnr DT8 ... 199 E7
Grange Dr
Bridgwater TA6 ... 208 D4
Taunton TA2 ... 213 A6
Grange End BA3 ... 97 B7
Grange Farm Rd BS49 ... 17 A1
Grangefields BA16 ... 207 D5
Grange Gdns TA2 ... 213 A7
Grange La 6 BS13 ... 21 F4
Grange Paddock TA9 ... 106 E4
Grange Rd
Bristol BS8 ... 226 A3
Bristol, Bishopsworth BS13 ... 22 A5
Frome BA11 ... 120 A7
Huntspill TA9 ... 136 A8
Saltford BS31 ... 25 C3
Street BA16 ... 207 D7
Weston-super-Mare BS23 ... 48 E1
Grange The
Bath BA1 ... 27 C1
Bristol BS9 ... 5 D7
Chilton Polden TA7 ... 137 B2
Flax Bourton BS48 ... 19 F7
Kingston St Mary TA2 ... 168 E8
Langport TA10 ... 171 E5
Grange Way TA6 ... 135 F5
Grange Wlk TA2 ... 213 A6
Granny's Ride TA24 ... 123 B1
Grants Cl BA9 ... 216 B4
Grants Hill DT9 ... 187 F1
Grant's Hill EX16, TA22 ... 163 F2
Grants La BA9 ... 216 D4
Grant's La
Wedmore BS28 ... 108 D4
Wiveliscombe TA4 ... 210 D6
Granville Chapel 5 BS8 ... 11 F5
Granville Rd BA1 ... 27 E4
Granville Way DT9 ... 225 E6
Grasmere TA6 ... 208 C5
Grasmere Dr BS23 ... 48 F4
Grass Meers Dr BS14 ... 23 A4
Grassmere Rd BS49 ... 34 B8
Grass Rd TA8 ... 65 F4
Grass Royal BA21 ... 219 C6
Grass Royal Jun Sch BA21 ... 219 C6
Gratton La EX35 ... 122 A4
Gravelands La TA3 ... 169 D3
Gravel Hill BS40 ... 56 B7
Gravel La TA3, TA19 ... 183 F6
Gravel Pit Cross EX36 ... 145 E6
Gravel Wlk BA1 ... 228 B3
Gravenchon Way BA16 ... 207 A6
Graves Cl 7 TA6 ... 209 B4
Gray Hollow BS40 ... 74 F4
Grayling Ho BS9 ... 5 F7
Gray's Almshouses 17 TA1 ... 213 A4
Grays Ave TA7 ... 154 E6
Grays Hill BA2 ... 80 B5
Gray's Hill EX15 ... 180 D1
Gray's La EX15 ... 180 D1
Grays Rd TA1 ... 213 B4
Grays Terr TA1 ... 213 B4
Great Ann St BS2 ... 227 C3
Great Barton BA4 ... 205 D6
Great Bedford St BA1 ... 228 B4
Great Bow Yd TA10 ... 171 F5
Great Brockeridge BS9 ... 5 F6
Great Cl EX15 ... 179 E1
Great Cnr 5 BA21 ... 218 C6
Great Dunns Cl BA11 ... 101 E4
GREAT ELM ... 118 F7
Great Field La TA14 ... 185 F4
Great Gardens BA4 ... 205 C6
Great George St
Bristol, Brandon Hill BS1 ... 226 C2
Bristol, St Pauls BS2 ... 227 C3
Great Hayles Rd BS14 ... 23 A6
Great Hill BA9 ... 161 D2
Great House Ct BA6 ... 138 D4
Great House St TA24 ... 130 B5
Great La
Knole TA10 ... 173 A4
Shepton Beauchamp TA19 ... 184 E4
Great Mdw TA22 ... 163 D6
Great Mead
Taunton TA1 ... 212 B3
Yeovil BA21 ... 219 F7
Great Orch BA22 ... 173 E2
Great Ostry BA4 ... 205 B6
Great Pit La BA22, DT9 ... 188 B7
Great Pulteney St BA2 ... 228 C3
Great Ringaton La EX36 ... 162 B6
Great St TA14 ... 185 E2
Great Stanhope St BA1 ... 228 A2
Greatstone La BS40 ... 37 F5
Great Western La TA11 ... 211 D3
Great Western Rd
Chard TA20 ... 223 D5
Clevedon BS21 ... 6 D2
Martock TA12 ... 185 E7
Great Western St BA11 ... 120 A4
Great Western Terr BA21 ... 219 D5
Great Western Way TA2 ... 212 A6
Great Western Wy TA2 ... 168 B4
Great Withy Dro BA5 ... 206 C8
Greatwood Cl TA6 ... 209 A2
Great Wood Cl BS13 ... 22 C4
Grebe Cl TA6 ... 209 B4
Grebe Ct TA6 ... 209 B4
Grebe Rd
Bridgwater TA6 ... 209 B4
Taunton TA2 ... 213 B6
Grebe Rd BA21 ... 218 A6
Greenacre
Wembdon TA6 ... 208 D6
Weston-super-Mare BS22 ... 31 B2
Green Acre Rd BS14 ... 23 A3
Greenacres
Bath BA1 ... 27 B3
Bristol BS9 ... 5 E7
Midsomer Norton BA3 ... 77 E1
Puriton TA7 ... 136 B4
Green Acres La DT9 ... 187 D5
Greenacres Pk BA21 ... 187 A5
Greenaleigh Lower Rd TA24 ... 125 C4
Greenaleigh Upper Rd TA24 ... 125 C4
Greenbank Gdns BA1 ... 27 B1
Greenbrook Terr TA1 ... 212 E4
Green Cl
Holford TA5 ... 133 D4
Paulton BS39 ... 77 E6
Sparkford BA22 ... 175 A4
Green Cotts BA2 ... 45 C2
Greendale TA19 ... 221 B3
Greenditch Ave BS13 ... 22 C5
Greenditch Cl BA3 ... 96 C3
Green Ditch La BA3 ... 96 B6
GREEN DOWN ... 94 B8
Greendown Pl BA2 ... 45 A1
Green Dragon Ct 4 TA6 ... 208 F4
Green Dro TA11 ... 158 A4
Green Farm Ind Est BA13 ... 121 C4
Greenfield Cres BS48 ... 8 E3
Greenfield La TA7 ... 136 D2
Greenfield Pk BS20 ... 2 C3
Greenfield Pl BS23 ... 48 C8
Greenfield Prim Sch BS4 ... 22 C7
Greenfield Rd
Keynsham BS31 ... 24 D3
WATCHET TA23 ... 202 D6
Greenfields
Bridgwater TA6 ... 208 F3
Crewkerne TA18 ... 224 C7
Greenfields Ave BS29 ... 51 A3
Greenfields Way BS23 ... 49 B4
Greenfield Terr TA20 ... 198 D8
Greenfield Wlk BA3 ... 78 A3
Greenfylde CE First Sch TA19 ... 221 C3
Greenfylde CE Fst Sch TA19 ... 221 C3
Greengage Cl 6 BS22 ... 49 E8
GREEN GATE ... 178 B2
Green Gate EX16 ... 178 B2
GREENHAM
Drimpton ... 199 E7
Wellington ... 179 B7
Greenham Bsns Pk TA21 ... 179 C5
Greenham La TA18 ... 199 E7
Greenham's Cross TA14 ... 185 F2
Greenham Yd TA18 ... 199 E7
Greenhayes BS27 ... 90 B8
Greenhays Foot EX13 ... 198 B6
GREENHILL ... 78 A3
Greenhill DT9 ... 225 D4
Greenhill Cl
Nailsea BS48 ... 8 D2
Weston-super-Mare BS22 ... 32 A3
Greenhill Croft BS25 ... 52 B4
Greenhill Cross EX36 ... 162 B2
Greenhill La
Alston Sutton BS26 ... 88 E5
Sandford BS25 ... 52 B4
Greenhill Pl BA3 ... 78 A3
Greenhill Rd
Midsomer Norton BA3 ... 78 A3
Sandford BS25 ... 52 B4
Yeovil BA21 ... 219 D7
Greenhoop Dro TA12 ... 185 E8
Greenhouse La
Nempnett Thrubwell BS40 ... 55 C6
Regil BS40 ... 37 D1
Green Knap La TA20 ... 193 C2
Green La
Bristol BS11 ... 4 B8
Brompton Regis TA22 ... 148 B1
Butcombe BS40 ... 55 A7
Castle Cary BA7 ... 214 F4
Chard TA20 ... 193 F1
Chard Junction TA20 ... 198 D7
Chardstock EX13 ... 198 B7
Charlton Horethorne DT9 ... 176 A2
Green La *continued*
Charlton Horethorne, Sigwells DT9 ... 175 F2
Corfe TA3 ... 181 E7
Corsley Heath BA12 ... 144 E7
Cricket St Thomas TA20 ... 194 F3
East Chinnock BA22 ... 196 E8
East Coker BA22 ... 197 B8
Failand BS8 ... 10 C4
Farrington Gurney BS39 ... 76 F6
Felton BS40 ... 37 C3
Fivehead TA3 ... 170 E2
Frome BA11 ... 119 D4
Hinton Charterhouse BA2 ... 63 E1
Ilminster TA19 ... 183 E2
Kingston Magna SP8 ... 177 E2
Leigh u M BA3, BA11 ... 117 B2
Marshfield SN14 ... 13 E8
Misterton TA18 ... 224 E4
Oakhill BA3 ... 114 E4
Pitcombe BA7 ... 215 A1
Priddy BS40 ... 73 B7
Queen Camel BA22 ... 174 F3
Sampford Arundel TA21 ... 179 F4
Shepton Beauchamp TA19 ... 184 E3
Sherborne DT9 ... 188 E1
Southwick BA14 ... 83 D2
Stoke St Michael BA3 ... 116 B5
Stratton-on-t F BA3 ... 96 E1
Street BA16 ... 207 C4
Tatworth TA20 ... 193 D1
West Pennard BA6 ... 140 B1
Greenland La TA24 ... 131 B1
Greenland Rd BS22 ... 31 D1
Greenlands TA1 ... 213 B2
Greenlands Rd BA2 ... 79 C8
Green Lane Ave BA16 ... 207 C4
Green Lane End TA19 ... 184 E3
Green Lane Gate BA9 ... 176 A8
Green Mead BA21 ... 218 C5
Greenmoor La BA21 ... 187 A5
GREEN ORE ... 94 C1
Green Ore Est BA5 ... 94 B1
Green Park La BA11 ... 101 F6
Green Park Mews BA1 ... 228 A2
Green Park Rd BA1 ... 228 B2
Green Parlor Rd BA3 ... 79 D1
GREEN PARLOUR ... 79 D2
Green Pastures Rd BS48 ... 9 B2
Green Patch La BA2 ... 59 E7
Green Pits La BA11 ... 143 B7
Green Pk
Bath BA1 ... 228 B2
Rode BA11 ... 101 E8
Green Quarry BA21 ... 219 A6
Green Ride BA12 ... 161 F7
Greenridge BS39 ... 58 F3
Greenridge Cl BS13 ... 21 E4
GREENSBROOK ... 58 F3
Green's Dro BA6 ... 206 C7
Green's Hill TA4 ... 151 C5
Greenslade Gdns BS48 ... 8 D3
Greens Pl BA5 ... 203 D3
Green St
Bath BA1 ... 228 C2
Hinton St George TA17 ... 195 D7
Shoscombe BA2 ... 79 E5
Ston Easton BA3 ... 95 E8
Greenstalls Pk BA22 ... 173 F2
Green The
Backwell BS48 ... 19 A5
8 Barwick BA22 ... 197 F8
Bath BA2 ... 44 D1
Bridgwater TA6 ... 208 E2
Brushford TA22 ... 163 E4
Easton BA5 ... 111 A4
Faulkland BA3 ... 80 D2
Hinton Charterhouse BA2 ... 63 F1
Ilchester BA22 ... 173 E2
Locking BS24 ... 50 A4
33 Martock TA12 ... 185 E6
Pill BS20 ... 4 D4
Pitminster TA3 ... 181 E6
1 Sherborne DT9 ... 225 D4
Williton TA4 ... 202 D3
Winscombe BS25 ... 70 A7
Green Tree Rd BA3 ... 78 B3
GREENVALE ... 60 B1
Greenvale Cl BA2 ... 60 B1
Greenvale Dr BA2 ... 60 B1
Greenvale Rd BS39 ... 77 D5
GREENWAY ... 167 D8
Greenway
Bishops Lydeard TA4 ... 167 E8
Faulkland BA3 ... 80 C1
Ilminster TA19 ... 221 B1
Minehead TA24 ... 200 D6
Monkton Heathfield TA2 ... 169 B6
North Curry TA3 ... 170 B3
Watchet TA23 ... 202 B7
Greenway Ave TA2 ... 212 E6
Greenway Cl BA9 ... 216 D4
Greenway Cotts TA4 ... 167 E8
Greenway Cres TA2 ... 212 E7
Greenway Ct BA2 ... 44 F4
Greenway La
Barrington TA13 ... 184 E5
Bath BA2 ... 45 A4
Blagdon Hill TA3 ... 181 B5
Cold Ashton SN14 ... 12 D5
Combe St Nicholas TA20 ... 193 E6
Stoke St Mary TA3 ... 169 D2
Wiveliscombe TA4 ... 210 A5
Greenway Pk 3 BS21 ... 6 F3
Greenway Rd
Castle Cary BA7 ... 214 B6
Rockwell Green TA21 ... 222 A5
Taunton TA2 ... 212 E6
Greenways BA3 ... 96 C2
Greenway Terr TA2 ... 168 D8
Greenwell La BS40 ... 53 C7
Greenwood Cl TA9 ... 136 B8
Greenwood Rd
Weston-super-Mare BS22 ... 31 E2
Yeovil BA21 ... 218 D7
Gregory Mead BS49 ... 17 A1
Gregorys Cres TA21 ... 222 D7
Gregorys Gr BA2 ... 62 D8
Gregorys Tyning BS39 ... 77 F6
GREINTON ... 155 F7
Greinton BS24 ... 49 A2
Greinton Rd TA7 ... 155 E7
Grenville Ave BS24 ... 50 A4
Grenville Cl BA6 ... 157 E4
Grenville Ho TA6 ... 208 F2
Grenville Pl 7 BS1 ... 11 F5
Grenville Rd
Burnham-on-S TA8 ... 104 C7
1 Longcroft BA21 ... 219 F8
Grenville View TA4 ... 167 E6
GREYFIELD ... 59 C2
Greyfield Comm BS39 ... 59 C2
Greyfield Rd BS39 ... 59 C2
Greyfield View BS39 ... 58 F1
Greyhound Cl BA9 ... 216 C4
GREYLAKE ... 155 C4
GREYLAKE FOSSE ... 155 E6
Greylake Reserve★ TA7 ... 155 D5
Greylands Rd BS13 ... 21 F7
Grey's Cnr BA9 ... 161 A3
Greys Rd TA16 ... 195 F7
Greystoke Bsns Ctr BS20 ... 2 D4
Grey Stone Dro TA12 ... 185 D7
GRIBB ... 199 B6
Gribb View TA20 ... 199 B6
Grib La BS40 ... 54 F2
Griffen Cl TA6 ... 208 E6
Griffen Rd BS24 ... 49 E7
Griffin Cl
Wells BA5 ... 203 B6
Weston-super-Mare BS22 ... 32 B2
Griffin Ct BA1 ... 228 B2
Griffin La TA3 ... 182 F7
Griffin Rd
Clevedon BS21 ... 6 E3
Hatch Beauchamp TA3 ... 182 F7
Griggfield Wlk BS14 ... 23 A7
Grimsey La SP8 ... 177 F8
Grinfield Ave BS13 ... 22 C4
Grinfield Ct BS13 ... 22 C4
Groats 9 TA4 ... 167 F8
Grooms Orch TA21 ... 222 C5
GROSVENOR ... 28 C1
Grosvenor Bridge Rd BA1 ... 28 C1
Grosvenor Ct BA22 ... 173 E2
Grosvenor Pk BA1 ... 28 C1
Grosvenor Pl BA1 ... 28 C1
Grosvenor Rd
Bristol BS2 ... 227 C4
Stalbridge DT10 ... 190 B4
Grosvenor Terr BA1 ... 28 C2
Grosvenor Villas 9 BA1 ... 28 B1
Grove Alley BA10 ... 215 E6
Grove Ave
Bristol BS1 ... 227 A1
Bristol, Coombe Dingle BS9 ... 5 C7
Yeovil BA20 ... 218 F5
Grove Cl
Penselwood BA9 ... 161 E2
Watchet TA23 ... 202 C6
Grove Ct BS9 ... 5 E5
Grove Dr
Taunton TA2 ... 212 F8
Weston-super-Mare BS22 ... 31 C1
Grove Gate TA2 ... 212 B7
Grove Hill TA7 ... 155 B1
Grove Ho
Bath BA2 ... 45 B6
Burnham-on-S TA8 ... 104 A8
Grove Jun Sch BS48 ... 18 D8
Grove La
Faulkland BA3 ... 80 D2
Frome BA11 ... 119 E3
Knole TA10 ... 173 A4
North Cheriton BA8 ... 176 E5
Stalbridge DT10 ... 190 B4
West Anstey EX36 ... 162 D6
Weston-super-Mare BS23 ... 48 D8
Grove Lane Cl DT10 ... 190 B4
Grove Leaze BS11 ... 4 D6
Grove Mead BA11 ... 119 E2
Grove Orch BS40 ... 54 E2
Grove Park Ct BS23 ... 30 D1
Grove Park Rd BS23 ... 30 D1
Grove Pl TA24 ... 201 B4
Grove Rd
Banwell BS29 ... 50 E4
Blue Anchor TA24 ... 131 B6
Bristol, Coombe Dingle BS9 ... 5 D8
Burnham-on-S TA8 ... 104 A8
Huntspill TA9 ... 136 A8
Weston-super-Mare BS23 ... 48 D8
Weston-super-Mare, Milton BS22 ... 31 C1
Groves La TA24 ... 131 B6
Grove St BA2 ... 228 C3
Groves The BS13 ... 22 D4
Grove Terr 8 TA2 ... 212 F6
Grove The
Bath BA1 ... 27 C1
Bristol BS1 ... 227 A1
Burnham-on-S TA8 ... 85 B1
Frome BA11 ... 119 E2

Grove The *continued*
Hallatrow BS39 77 B7
Ruishton TA3 169 C3
Sherborne DT9 225 D3
Winscombe BS25 51 F1
Wraxall BS48 9 C3
Grove Wood Rd BA3 78 F1
Grughay La TA3 182 E5
Grunter's La BA3 114 F7
Gryphon Sch The DT9 225 E6
Guard Ave BA22 218 B6
Guard House La 9 BA5 203 D4
Guernsey Rd BS25 69 F7
Gug The BS39 59 C2
Guild Ct BS1 227 B2
Guildford Pl TA1 212 F3
Guildhall La BS28 108 C4
Guillemot Rd 9 BS20 2 F6
Guineagore La DT9 188 B4
Guinea La BA1 228 C3
Guinea St BS1 227 A1
Guinevere Cl BA21 218 D7
Gullen BA2 80 A6
Gulliford Cl TA9 104 D4
Gulliford's Bank BS21 6 F2
Gullimores Gdns BS13 22 B4
Gullock Tyning BA3 78 B1
Gullons Cl BS13 22 A6
Gullon Wlk BS13 21 F5
Gulway Mead TA20 198 D8
Gumbrells Ct TA6 209 A4
Gunners La BA22 218 A5
Gunning's La BA4 142 F2
Gunville La
Charlton Horethorne DT9 176 A2
East Coker BA22 197 D8
Gunwyn Cl BA6 206 E6
GUPWORTHY 148 C6
GURNEY SLADE 114 F7
Gurney St TA5 135 C2
Gurnville Cotts BA11 119 F2
Guthrie Rd BS8 226 A4
Gwynne La TA1 213 A3
Gwyther Mead TA1 212 A3
Gyffarde Ct 4 TA1 213 A4
Gyffarde St TA1 213 A4
Gypsy La
Cheddar BS28 89 D6
Keynsham BS31 42 B8
Marshfield SN14 13 F7
Gypsy Moth La BS24 49 C5

H

Haberfield Hill BS8 4 E2
Haberfield Ho 1 BS8 11 F6
Hacketty Way TA24 124 B3
Hack La
Holford TA5 133 F2
Nether Stowey TA5 134 A2
Hack Mead La TA9 105 E1
HACKNESS 136 D8
Hackness Rd TA9 136 E8
Hackney La BA4 142 F2
Haddon Cl TA22 148 B2
Haddon Hill TA4 164 E7
Haddon La
Hartford TA4 164 C7
North Petherton TA6 153 C2
Stalbridge DT10 190 C5
Haddon View TA22 148 B2
Hadley Rd BA2 45 B2
Hadrian Cl
Bristol BS9 5 C4
Keynsham BS31 24 F7
HADSPEN 214 F6
Hadspen Garden* BA7 160 A2
Hadworthy La TA6 153 F4
Hafner Gn BS24 49 C4
Hagget Cl TA6 208 F1
Haggetts La TA9 136 E7
Hagleys Gn TA4 151 B7
Haig Cl BS9 5 B7
Haig Rd TA2 168 B6
HAINES HILL 212 E2
Haines Hill TA1 212 E2
Haines La DT8 199 D5
Haines Pk TA1 212 E1
Hains La DT10 190 F7
Halcombe TA20 223 C2
HALCON 213 D5
Halcon Cnr TA1 213 D4
Halcon Com Prim Sch
TA1 213 D4
HALE 177 D6
Hale La BA9 177 C6
Halesleigh Rd TA6 208 E5
Hales Mdw BA21 187 D6
Hale Way TA2 213 D7
Half Acre TA4 202 D2
Half Acre Cl
Bristol BS14 23 A3
Williton TA4 202 D2
Halfacre La BS14 23 B4
Half Acres DT9 225 C3
Half Moon St 6 DT9 225 D3
Halfpenny Row BA11 82 E1
Halfway BA22 186 F6
Halfyard Ct TA21 222 F4
Half Yd BS40 53 D8
Hallam Ct BS21 6 C4
Hallam Rd BS21 6 C4
Hallards Cl BS11 4 F8
HALLATROW 77 B7
Hallatrow Rd BS39 77 C6
Hallen Dr BS9 5 C7
Hallet Gdns BA20 219 A4
Hallets Orch BA22 186 B6
Hallett Rd BA7 214 B7
Halletts Way
Axminster EX13 198 A1
Portishead BS20 2 D5
Hall Hill EX35 122 B5
Halliwell Rd BS20 1 D4
Hall La BA1 12 B3
Hall Rd TA7 136 B4
Hall Terr TA8 104 A8
HALSE 167 B6
Halse Cnr TA4 167 D5
Halse La TA24 147 B5
Halse Manor TA4 167 B6
HALSTOCK 197 C3
Halston Dr BS2 227 C4
HALSWAY 151 B8
Halsway TA6 209 C5
Halsway Hill TA4 132 F1
Halsway La
Bicknoller TA4 133 A1
Crowcombe TA4 151 A8
Halswell Cl TA6 208 E4
Halswell Gdns BS13 22 B4
Halswell Rd BS21 6 D1
Halt End BS14 23 C3
Halter Path Dro TA7 137 C7
Halves La BA22 197 C7
Halwyn Cl BS9 5 D5
Halyard Dr TA6 208 E7
Halyard Pl TA24 201 B7
Halyard Wy BS20 2 F7
Halyars Way BA21 218 C8
HAM
Creech St Michael 169 E4
Holcombe 116 D6
Paulton 77 F5
Wellington 180 D8
Hamber Lea TA4 167 F8
Hambledon Rd BS22 32 C4
HAMBRIDGE
184 D8
Whitecross TA10 171 D1
Hambridge Com Prim Sch
TA10 184 D8
Ham Cl BS39 58 F1
Hamdon Cl 12 TA14 185 F4
Hamdon Hill Country Pk*
TA14 185 F3
Hamdon View TA14 185 E3
Hamdown Ct TA10 172 B6
Ham Gn
Hambridge TA10 184 D8
Pill BS20 4 D3
Ham Gr BS39 77 E5
HAM GREEN 4 E4
Ham Hill
Coleford BA3 116 D6
Combe St Nicholas TA20 193 D8
High Ham TA10 156 A2
Langford Budville TA21 166 A1
Radstock BA3 78 F3
Ham Hill Ctry Pk* TA14 186 A3
Ham Hill Rd
Odcombe BA22 186 C2
Stoke sub Hamdon TA14 185 F4
Hamilton Ct
11 Bristol BS1 227 A4
Taunton TA1 213 C4
Wells BA5 203 B4
Hamilton Dr TA6 209 C8
Hamilton Ho BA1 27 E3
Hamilton Rd
Bath BA1 27 E2
Taunton TA1 213 C4
8 Weston-super-Mare BS23 30 C1
Hamilton Terr BA2 79 F5
Hamilton Wy BS14 23 D3
Ham La
Bishop Sutton BS39 57 C5
Burnham-on-S TA8 104 B6
Compton Dundon TA11 157 A3
Croscombe BA4, BA5 204 E7
Dundry BS41 21 D3
Farrington Gurney BS39 76 F5
Kingston Seymour BS21 16 B2
Marnhull DT10 190 F6
North End BS49 17 A3
Paulton BS39 77 E5
Pawlett TA6 135 E6
Rodhuish TA23 149 C8
Shepton Mallet BA4 205 A7
Sherborne DT9 188 A5
Trent DT9 187 F5
Wraxall BS48 9 B4
Yatton BS49 17 A3
Ham La E BA4 204 F7
Hamlands La TA21 167 D1
Hamlet The
Nailsea BS48 9 A3
Templecombe BA8 176 E1
Hamley La
Buckland St Mary TA20 193 B8
Combe St Nicholas TA20 182 F1
Ham Link BS40 53 F3
Hamlyn Cl TA1 212 C1
Hamlyn Rd BA6 206 E6
Ham Mdw DT10 190 E6
Hammer La BA2, BA3 100 C8
Hammer St BA10 161 B8
Hammet St
8 North Petherton TA6 153 E3
Taunton TA1 212 F4
Hammets Wharf 1 TA1 212 F4
Hammocks Dro TA10 172 D4
Hammond Gdns BS9 5 E7
HAMP 208 F2
Hamp Ave TA6 208 F3
Hamp Brook Way TA6 208 E2
Hamp Com Jun Sch TA6 208 F3
Hampden Rd BS22 31 E2
Hamp Green Rise TA6 209 A3
Hamp Ind Est TA6 209 A3
Hamp Inf Sch TA6 208 F3
Hamp St TA6 208 F3
Hampton Cl
5 Barwick BA22 197 F8
Bridgwater TA6 209 D7
Hampton Cnr BS11 4 E6
Hampton H BA2 45 D8
Hampton Ho 10 BA1 28 C1
Hampton La BS8 226 B4
Hampton Rd BS6 226 C4
Hampton Row BA2 45 B8
Hampton View BA1 28 B1
Ham Rd
Brean BS24, TA8 66 B3
Burnham-on-S TA9 85 E4
Creech St Michael TA3 169 D4
Wellington TA21 180 D8
Hamrod La TA7 154 E5
Hams La BS26 68 C3
Ham's La TA11 174 D7
Hams Rd BS31 24 F7
Ham St BA6 158 B5
HAM STREET 158 B5
Ham Wall Wetland* BA6 138 C2
Hamway La TA20 193 C8
HAMWOOD 68 C7
Hamwood TA1 212 B4
Ham Wood Cl BS24 49 B2
Hamwood Cotts TA1 212 B4
Hamwood La TA3 181 B8
Hamwood Terr TA1 212 B4
Hanbury Ct BS8 226 A4
Hanbury Rd BS8 226 A4
Handel Rd BS31 24 E5
Handlemaker Rd BA11 119 E2
Handy Cross TA4 151 A2
Hanford Ct BS14 23 D7
Hangerland La TA4 150 E6
Hanger's Way TA24 201 D2
Hanger Wy BS14 22 F5
Hang Hill BA2 80 A6
Hanging Hill La TA13 184 F4
Hanglands La BA8 176 C2
Hanham La BS39 77 F7
Hanham Way BS48 8 B2
Hankridge Way TA1 213 E5
Hanna Cl BA2 44 B6
Hannah Dr BS24 50 C5
Hannah More Cl
Cheddar BS27 90 B7
Wrington BS40 35 E2
Hannah More Inf Sch BS48 18 D8
Hannah More Prim Sch
BS1 227 C2
Hannah More Rd BS48 18 C8
Hannahs La BA5 110 E6
Hannay Rd BS27 71 B1
Hann Cl BA5 203 B2
Hanning Cl TA19 221 F6
Hanning Pk TA19 183 C1
Hanning Rd TA19 183 C1
Hanover Cl
Shepton Mallet BA4 205 A6
Weston-super-Mare BS22 32 A4
Hanover Ct
Bath BA1 28 B2
Castle Cary BA7 214 C5
Dulverton TA22 163 D7
Radstock BA3 79 C2
Hanover Gdns BA11 119 D3
Hanover Ho BS20 2 B5
Hanover Pl
Bath BA1 45 B8
Bristol BS1 226 B1
Hanover St
2 Bath BA1 28 B1
2 Bristol BS1 227 A2
Hanover Terr 5 BA1 28 B1
Hansetown Rd TA4 148 F1
Hansford Cl BA2 44 E1
Hansford Mews BA2 44 F1
Hansford Sq BA2 44 E1
Hanson's Way 4 BS21 6 C2
Hans Price Acad BS23 48 F5
Hans Price Cl 18 BS23 48 E8
Hans Price Ho 13 BS23 48 E8
Hantone Hill BA2 45 F8
Hapil Cl BS25 51 F4
Happerton La BS20 4 D2
Hapsburg Cl BS22 32 A4
HAPSFORD 119 B8
Hapsford Hill BA11 119 C8
Harbour BA21 218 C5
Harbour Cres BS20 2 E5
Harbour Ct TA5 135 B5
Harbourne Cl TA8 104 C8
Harbour Rd
Portishead BS20 2 D6
Sherborne DT9 225 E5
Watchet TA23 202 C7
Harbour Road Trad Est BS20 2 F6
Harbour Terr DT9 225 E5
Harbour View TA5 135 B5
Harbour Wall BS9 5 B4
Harbour Way DT9 225 E5
Harbour Wlk BS1 226 C1
Harbutts BA2 28 F1
Harcourt Cl BS31 25 E2
Harcourt Gdns BA1 27 B2
Harcourt Mews BA11 120 A4
Harcourt St TA2 212 E6
Harden Rd BS14 23 E5
Harding Ct TA11 211 D3
Harding Dr BS29 50 C7
Hardings Cl 8 TA6 153 F3
Hardings Ct TA13 220 C5
Harding's Hill TA10, TA11 172 F5
Harding's House La DT9 225 A6
Hardings La BA2 42 A1
Harding's La BA8 176 D4
HARDINGTON 99 E6
Hardington Dr BS31 25 A2
HARDINGTON MANDEVILLE 197 A6
HARDINGTON MARSH 196 F4
HARDINGTON MOOR 197 A7
Hardington Moor National Nature Reserve* BA22 197 A7
Hard Leaze Dro BA22 186 A8
Hardmead La BS27 90 E2
Hardwarden Terr BA22 175 A5
HARDWAY 161 A5
Hardway BA10 160 F4
Hardwick Rd BS20 4 C5
Hardy Cres DT10 190 B4
Hardy Ct TA18 224 C5
Hardy Mead Dro TA9 136 B7
Hardy Rise BA7 214 A7
Hardys Rd
Langaller TA2 169 C5
Taunton TA2 213 F7
HARE 182 F2
Hareclive Acad BS13 22 C4
Hareclive Rd BS13 22 C4
Hare La TA20 182 E2
Harepark Terr TA24 201 A5
Hare Path TA24 147 F8
Hare Path Cross TA24 129 D1
Harepit La BA12 161 F7
Harepits La BA6 157 E3
Hare Pk TA24 124 C4
Harestone Cross EX13 198 B7
Harewell Wlk BA5 203 B3
Harfield Terr 10 BA20 219 B4
Harford Cl BS9 5 C7
Harford Sq BS40 39 B3
Hargrove La DT10 190 C2
Harington Pl 2 BA1 228 B2
Harlech Cl BS31 24 C4
Harley Ct 3 BS8 11 F7
Harley La BS21 7 C6
Harley Mews 2 BS8 11 F7
Harley Pl 4 BS8 11 F7
Harley St BA1 228 B4
Harmony Dr BS20 1 F4
Harnell Cl TA1 213 C3
Harnhill Cl BS13 22 B4
Harp Chase TA1 213 B1
Harper Rd TA18 224 C5
Harper's La TA23 131 D1
Harpitts La SP8 177 F2
Harp Rd
Brent Knoll TA9 105 E6
South Petherton TA13 220 C3
Harpsichord Way BS31 25 B4
Harptree BS24 49 A2
Harptree Cl BS48 18 D8
Harptree Hill BS40 74 B5
Harptree La BA3 75 C1
Harrier Dr BA22 218 A5
Harrier Path 3 BS22 49 E8
Harriets Yd BS31 24 F5
Harrington Ave BS14 23 E6
Harrington Cl BS30 25 E8
Harrington Gr BS14 23 E6
Harrington Rd BS14 23 E6
Harrington Wlk BS14 23 E6
Harris Cl
Frome BA11 120 B4
Westleigh EX16 179 A4
Harris Gr BS13 22 B3
Harris La
Abbots Leigh BS8 10 F8
Curry Mallet TA3 183 C8
Harrison's La TA19 184 E1
Harris Vale BA3 116 F7
Hart Cl BS20 4 E4
HARTCLIFFE 22 C4
Hartcliffe Rd BS4 22 E8
Hartcliffe Way BS3, BS4, BS13 22 C7
Hartcliffe Wlk BS4 22 F8
Harters Cl BA5 139 E6
Harter's Hill La BA5 139 E6
Hartfield Ave BS6 226 C4
HARTFORD 164 C8
Hartford Rd TA22 164 B8
Hartgill Cl BS13 22 B3
Hartlake Cl
Glastonbury BA6 206 F7
Glastonbury BA6 206 F7
Hartland 14 BS22 32 A2
Hartley BA15 64 E8
Hartley Cotts BA4 204 B1
Hartley Ho BA1 228 B3
Hartley Way TA1 213 D2
HARTMOOR 177 F3
Hartmoor Hill SP8 177 E3
Hartrow Cl TA1 212 E1
Harts Cl TA19 221 A4
Hartsfield TA20 223 D2
Hart's La
Hallatrow BS39 77 B7
Huish Champflower TA4 165 D7
Sherborne DT9 188 A3
Harts Paddock BA3 77 F3
HARTSWELL 210 B3
Hartswell TA4 210 C3
Hart Way EX35 122 F3
Harvesters Dr BA16 207 B4
Harvest La
Charlton Horethorne DT9 176 A2
Weston-super-Mare BS22 50 B8
Harvest Way BS22 32 A5
Harvey Cl BS22 32 A4
Harvey's Rd TA13 220 C4
Harvey Way TA19 183 B4
Harwood Cross TA24 130 A4
Harwood Gn BS22 31 E4
Harwood La
Timberscombe TA24 130 A4
Wootton Courtenay TA24 129 F4
Haselbury Gr BS31 25 E2
HASELBURY PLUCKNETT 196 C6
Haselbury Plucknett CE Fst Sch
Haselbury Plucknett TA18 196 C5
Haselbury Plucknett TA18 196 C5
Haselbury Rd TA16 195 F6
Haseley Ct TA1 212 D2
Hassage Farm La BA3 81 A3
Hassage Hill BA2 80 E7
Hassock's La BA10 160 E8
HASTINGS 183 B3
Hastings Cross TA19 183 B3
HATCH BEAUCHAMP 183 A7
Hatch Beauchamp CE Prim Sch
Hatch Beauchamp TA3 183 A7
Hatch Beauchamp TA3 183 A7
Hatch Court* TA3 183 A8
Hatcher Cl TA8 104 D5
Hatchers Ct TA2 212 F7
Hatches La BS24 66 E3
Hatchet Hill BA3, BA11 98 E4
HATCH GREEN 183 A6
Hatch Green La TA3 182 F6
Hatch Mews Bsns Pk TA3 183 A7
Hatfield Bldgs BA2 45 B5
Hatfield Rd
Bath BA2 44 F3
Weston-super-Mare BS23 49 A8
Hathaway Ho 13 BS2 227 A4
Hathermead Gdns BA21 219 D7
Haugh BA15 46 D2
Haunts TA18 196 C8
Havage Cl TA9 104 E5
Havage Dro BS24 51 D8
Haven Cl TA24 201 F3
Haven View BS20 2 E5
Haversham Cl BS22 31 D1
Haviland Gr BA1 27 B3
Haviland Ho 7 BS2 227 C3
Haviland Pk BA1 27 B2
Havory BA1 28 C1
Havyat Rd BS40 53 E8
Havyat Road Trad Est
BS40 35 E1
HAVYATT 157 F8
HAVYATT GREEN 53 F7
Hawarden Terr BA1 28 B1
Hawcombe View TA24 124 A3
Hawcombe Woods National Nature Reserve* TA24 123 E2
HAWKCHURCH 198 E3
Hawkchurch CE Prim Sch
EX13 198 E3
Hawkchurch Cross EX13 198 E2
Hawkchurch Rd EX13 198 E3
HAWKCOMBE 124 A3
Hawke Rd BS22 31 E4
Hawkers Cl 9 TA5 135 B2
Hawkers La TA10 184 D8
Hawker's La BA5 112 E1
Hawkfield Bsns Pk BS14 22 D5
Hawkfield Cl BS14 22 D5
Hawkfield Rd BS13 22 D5
Hawkfield Way BS14 22 D5
Hawkins Cl
Burnham-on-S TA8 104 C7
Street BA16 207 E6
Hawkin's La TA4 165 E7
Hawkins St BS2 227 C3
Hawkins Way 2 BA21 218 C6
Hawkmoor Hill DT6, EX13 199 B2
Hawk Rd BA22 218 A5
HAWKRIDGE 146 D1
Hawkridge Cross TA22 146 D1
Hawkridge Rd TA6 208 B4
Hawksmoor Cl BS14 23 A6
Hawks Rise BA22 218 B5
Hawk's Worth Cl BA11 120 C7
Hawksworth Dr BS22 32 C4
Hawksworth Rd TA24 201 B6
Hawkwell Cross EX16 162 F4
Hawkwell La TA22 163 A4
Hawley Way TA8 104 C7
Hawthorn Cl
Bridgwater TA6 209 D4
High Ham TA10 156 A2
Portishead BS20 1 F5
Hawthorn Coombe BS22 31 E3
Hawthorn Cres
Shepton Mallet BA4 205 A6
Yatton BS49 17 A2
Hawthorne Cl TA18 224 D7
Hawthorne Rd TA21 222 F5
Hawthorn Gdns BS22 31 D2
Hawthorn Gr BA2 45 A1
Hawthorn Hill
Kingsbury Episcopi TA13 185 B6
Weston-super-Mare BS22 31 E2
Hawthorn Hts BS22 31 D3
Hawthorn La BS22 32 C2
Hawthorn Pk BS22 31 E3

Hawthorn Rd
Frome BA11 120 A6
Ilton TA19 183 F4
Minehead TA24 200 D7
Radstock BA3 79 B2
Street BA16 207 E6
Taunton TA1 213 C1
Yeovil BA21 219 D7
Hawthorns La BS31 24 E5
Hawthorns The
Clevedon BS21 6 C3
Stalbridge DT10 190 C4
Hawthorn Way BS48 9 A2
Haxen La TA17 195 A8
Hayboro Way BS39 77 E4
Haybow BS24 32 E2
HAYBRIDGE 203 A5
Haybridge Hill BA5 203 A4
Haybridge La BA5 111 E1
Haybridge Villas BA5 203 A5
Haycombe BS14 22 F6
Haycombe Dr BA2 44 A4
Haycombe La BA2 44 A3
Hayden Cl BA2 228 A1
HAYDON
Milborne Port 189 B2
Radstock 97 F8
Taunton 213 E2
Wells 113 D5
Haydon Cl TA1 212 B4
Haydon Dro BA5 113 C6
Haydon Gate BA3 97 F8
Haydon Hill BA3 98 A8
Haydon Hollow DT9 189 B3
Haydon Ind Est BA3 97 F8
Haydon La TA1, TA3 213 E2
Haydon Rd TA1 213 A4
Hayesdown Fst Sch BA11 120 B5
Hayes Dr BA5 111 F1
Hayes End TA13 220 D4
Hayes End Manor TA13 220 D4
Hayesfield Girls Sch BA2 228 A1
Hayesfield Pk BA2 228 B1
Hayesfield Sch Tech Coll
BA2 44 D6
Hayes La TA11 156 F2
HAYES PARK 78 A2
Hayes Park Rd BA3 77 F2
Hayes Pl BA2 228 B1
Hayes Rd
Compton Dundon TA11 156 F3
Midsomer Norton BA3 77 F1
Hayes The BS27 90 B8
Hayeswood Farm BA15 46 F5
Hayeswood Rd BA2 59 E3
Hayfield Cl TA24 201 B6
Hayfield Rd TA24 201 B6
Haygarth Ct BA1 228 B4
Haygrove Pk TA3 168 D1
Haygrove Pk Rd TA6 208 D3
Haygrove Rd TA6 208 C3
Haygrove Sch TA6 208 C4
Hay Hill
Bath BA1 228 B3
Croscombe BA5 204 B8
Hay La BS40 37 D6
Hayleigh Ho BS13 22 C4
Hayman Rd TA24 200 F7
Haymarket The BS1 227 A3
Haymarket Wlk 9 BS1 227 A4
Haymoor Dro BA5 139 D7
Haymoor La
Coxley BA5 139 E6
Long Sutton TA10 172 D4
Hayne Cross EX16 164 B4
Hayne La TA5 153 B7
Haynes International Motor
Mus★ BA22 175 A6
Hayne Wlk TA7 137 B2
Hay St BA3 96 A8
Haytor Pk BS9 5 D6
Hayward Ave BS24 50 C8
Hayward Cl BS21 6 C1
Hayward Dr BA6 158 A6
Haywater Ave TA6 208 D3
Haywood Cl BS24 49 A1
Haywood Gdns BS24 49 B1
Haywood Rd TA1 213 D2
HAYWOOD VILLAGE 49 C4
Haywood Village Acad
BS24 49 D5
Hazel Barrow BS40 74 A7
Hazelbury Rd
Bristol BS14 23 C7
Nailsea BS48 8 D1
Hazel Cl TA1 213 C1
Hazel Cote Rd BS14 23 B4
Hazel Ct BA11 120 A3
Hazeldene Rd BS23 49 A8
Hazel Gr
Bath BA2 44 D4
Midsomer Norton BA3 97 B8
Hazell Cl BS21 6 E1
Hazel St BS14 22 E5
Hazel Terr BA3 97 C8
Hazel View TA18 224 D7
Hazel Way BA2 62 D8
Hazelwell La TA19 221 A4
Hazelwood Ct BS9 5 D3
Hazelwood Dr TA6 209 E5
Hazelwood Hill TA20 194 E1
Hazelwood Rd BS9 5 D3
Hazlegrove Prep Sch
BA22 174 F5
Hazleton Gdns BA2 45 F3
Head Croft BS48 20 B8
Head Dro
Athelney TA7 170 E8
Head Dro *continued*
Catcott TA7 137 D3
Othery TA7 155 D3
Headley Ct BS13 22 B6
Headley La BS13 22 B7
HEADLEY PARK 22 B6
Headley Park Ave BS13 22 B7
Headley Park Prim Sch
BS13 22 B6
Headley Park Rd BS13 22 A7
Headley Rd BS13 22 A6
Headley Wlk BS13 22 B7
Headon Cross TA24 129 F8
Head St BA22 186 B6
Headstock Cross TA20 198 E6
Headstock Rd TA20 198 E7
Headwell TA3 183 C8
Headwell Cl TA3 183 C8
Headwell Hill TA3 183 C8
Heal Cl TA8 104 D5
HEALE 142 C7
Heale La TA10 171 C4
Healeys TA24 124 A4
Heal's Field EX13 198 A2
Healys Mdw TA4 167 E6
Hearn La BA22 175 D8
Heart Meers BS14 23 B5
Heath Cl BA12 144 D8
Heathcombe Rd TA6 208 B4
Heath Dr BA11 119 F6
Heather Cl
Bridgwater TA6 209 B3
Minehead TA24 201 C4
Somerton TA11 211 B3
Taunton TA1 169 A1
Heatherdene BS14 22 F7
Heather Dr BA2 62 D8
Heather Rd BA21 219 D7
Heatherton Park Ho TA4 180 E8
Heather Way BA22 218 A5
HEATHFIELD 167 E5
Heathfield TA4 151 E4
Heathfield Cl
Bath BA1 27 A3
Creech St Michael TA3 169 D6
Keynsham BS31 24 C5
5 North Petherton TA6 153 F4
West Bagborough TA4 151 E4
Heathfield Com Sch TA2 213 F8
Heathfield Cres BS14 23 B4
Heathfield Dr TA2 213 F8
Heathfield Rd BS48 8 E3
Heathfield Way BS48 8 E2
Heathgate BS49 34 B8
Heathgates BS23 48 D4
HEATH HOUSE 107 F1
Heath Rd BS48 8 F3
Heath Ridge BS41 11 A2
Heathstock Hill TA4 210 D5
Heathway BA12 144 D8
Heathway La BA6 138 B4
HEAVEN'S DOOR 188 A8
Heavitree Way TA2 213 A6
Hebden Rd BA15 64 F3
Heber's La TA19 195 A5
Heckley La BA3 115 B5
Hector Cl BS24 50 D4
Hector Rd TA7 137 D2
Hectors La TA3 170 D8
Hectors Stones TA7 136 E4
Heddon Oak TA4 151 A8
Heddon Wood La TA4 151 A7
Hedge La BA4 141 B2
Hedgemead Ct BA1 228 C4
Hedges Cl 3 BS21 6 B1
Hedges The BS22 32 C3
Hedgestocks BA4 160 C8
HEDGING 170 A8
Hedging La TA7 170 A8
Heggard Cl BS13 22 A5
Heights The TA19 221 B4
HELE 168 A3
Hele La
Langport TA10 172 C4
South Petherton TA13 220 C4
Hele Manor La TA22 144 D3
Helena Rd BA20 218 D1
Helens Rd BS25 52 B4
Helicopter Mus The★ BS24 49 E5
HELLAND 170 C3
Helland Hill TA3 170 C3
Helland La TA3 170 D4
Helliar's La
Curry Mallet TA3 183 D8
Fivehead TA3 170 D1
Hellier's Cl TA20 223 B4
Hellier's La BS27 89 E6
Helliers Rd TA20 223 B4
Hellier Wlk BS13 22 C3
Helling's Cross TA4 166 A4
Helmstedt Way TA20 223 D6
Helston Rd BS48 9 A1
Helvier's La TA4 167 A7
Helwell Gn TA23 202 D6
Helwell St TA23 202 D7
Helyar Cl BA6 206 D5
Hembridge La
East Pennard BA4 158 E7
East Pennard BA4 158 F8
Hembury La BA5 139 C7
HEMINGTON 99 B7
Hemington Prim Sch BA3 99 B7
Hemming Way BS24 49 E3
Hemp Gdn TA24 200 F8
Hempitts Rd BA16 156 E7
Hemplow Cl BS14 23 D7
Hemstich Hill TA7 138 C1
HEMYOCK 180 B1
Henacre Rd BS11 4 F8
Henbury Hill BS9 5 F8
Henbury Ho BA2 45 E4
Henbury Rd BS9 5 F8
Hencliffe Rd BS14 23 D7
Henderson Cl TA1 212 C2
Henderson Dr TA20 223 D2
Henderson Ho 1 BS2 227 B4
Henderson Pl 5 BA5 203 D4
Hendford BA20 219 A4
Hendford Ct BA20 219 A3
Hendford Gr BA20 219 A4
Hendford Hill BA20 219 A3
Hendon Cl TA9 104 E5
Hendon Cross EX16 178 B8
Hengasson La BS39 57 E6
HENGROVE 23 B6
Hengrove Ave BS14 23 B8
Hengrove La BS14 23 B8
Hengrove Pk L Ctr BS14 22 E5
Hengrove Prom BS14 22 E5
Hengrove Way BS14 22 E6
Henhambridge Way BA2 101 A7
Henhayes La TA18 224 C6
Hen La BS40 37 E3
HENLADE 169 D2
HENLEY 156 B3
Henley Cl EX13 198 B7
Henley Cross
Crewkerne TA18 224 B1
Henley TA18 195 E2
Henley Gr TA1 212 D4
Henley La
Butleigh BA6 157 E4
Wookey BA5 139 E8
Yatton BS49 34 D7
Henley Lodge BS49 34 D7
Henley Pk BS49 34 C7
Henley Rd
High Ham TA10 156 B3
Kingsdon TA11 173 E5
Taunton TA1 212 D3
Henley Rise BA4 205 D4
Henley View
Crewkerne TA18 224 C4
Wellow BA2 62 D1
Henley Way BA11 119 F5
Henmore La BS26 88 E6
Hennessy Cl BS14 22 F3
Henning Way DT9 217 D3
Henrietta Ct BA2 228 C4
Henrietta Gdns BA2 228 C3
Henrietta Mews BA2 228 C3
Henrietta Pl BA2 228 C3
Henrietta Rd BA2 228 C3
Henrietta St
Bath BA2 228 C3
Bristol BS2 227 A4
Henry Butt Ho 11 BS23 48 E8
Henry Rogers Ho 2 TA5 135 B2
Henry St BA1 228 C2
Hensley Gdns BA2 44 E4
Hensley Rd BA2 44 E3
Hensman's Hill BS8 226 A2
Henson Pk TA20 223 E5
Hensons Dr EX16 179 A3
HENSTRIDGE 190 A6
HENSTRIDGE ASH 189 F7
HENSTRIDGE BOWDEN 189 D7
HENSTRIDGE MARSH 190 C7
Henstridge Trad Est BA8 190 C7
HENTON 139 B8
Hepburn Rd BS2 227 B4
Herald Cl BS9 5 D5
Herbert Gdns BA2 59 E5
Herbert Ho TA22 163 D6
Herbert Rd
Bath BA2 44 D5
Burnham-on-S TA8 104 A8
Clevedon BS21 6 D4
Herbert St TA2 212 E6
Herblay Cl BA21 219 E6
Hercules Wy BS31 24 C3
Hereford Dr TA2 213 A8
Heritage Cl BA2 79 D8
Heritage Ct BA6 206 D4
Heritage Ctyd BA5 203 D4
Heritage The BA2 78 E8
Herluin Way BS22, BS23 49 B6
Hermes Cl BS31 25 D2
Hermes Pl BA22 173 E2
Hermitage Cl BS11 4 E7
Hermitage Hill TA10 172 D6
Hermitage Rd
Bath BA1 27 E1
Langport TA10 172 D6
Hermitage St TA18 224 C5
Herne Rise TA19 221 B2
Hern La BS48 20 E5
Heron Cl
Minehead TA24 201 C4
Weston-super-Mare BS22 49 E8
Heron Ct BS21 6 C2
Heron Dr
Houndstone BA22 218 A6
Taunton TA1 212 B4
Heron Gate TA1 213 E6
Heron Gate Office Pk TA1 213 E5
Heron Gdns BS20 2 E4
Heron Ho 2 TA6 209 C4
Heron Pk TA8 84 E8
HERONS GREEN 56 C3
Herons Green La BS40 56 C4
Herons La TA4 167 A4
Heronsmead Wlk BA21 219 D8
Herons Moor Acad BS24 50 A8
Heron Way TA19 221 C2
Herridge Cl BS13 22 B4
Herridge Rd BS13 22 B4
Herschel Museum of
Astronomy★ BA1 228 B2
Hersey Gdns BS13 21 E3
Hertford Rd BA21 219 E8
Hervey Cl BS28 108 C4
Hervey Rd
Chard TA20 223 D3
Wells BA5 112 E1
Hestercombe Cl TA6 208 B4
Hestercombe House Gdns★
TA2 169 A7
Hestercombe Rd
Bristol BS13 22 B6
Taunton TA2 169 A7
Hestia Cl BS31 24 C3
Hetling Ct 7 BA1 228 B2
Hewett Cl TA3 168 D1
HEWISH
Crewkerne 195 D3
Weston-super-Mare 33 C5
Hewish Ct BS23 48 E8
Hewish La
Crewkerne TA18 224 A5
Hewish TA18 195 D3
Hext Ct TA11 211 D3
Hexton Rd BA6 206 E5
Heyron Wlk BS13 22 B4
Heywood Rd BS20 4 C4
Heywood Terr BS20 4 C4
Hibbs Cl SN14 13 F8
HICKS GATE 24 B8
Hicks's La BA22 214 D1
Hidcote Mews BS24 49 E7
Hide Mkt BS2 227 C3
Hidewood La EX15 180 F1
Higgin's Grave La TA13 220 B1
High Acre BS39 77 F4
Highaton Head Cross
EX36 162 C4
High Bank
Porlock TA24 124 A3
Watchet TA23 202 C7
High Bannerdown
Batheaston BA1 29 B4
Shockerwick BA1 29 B5
High Bolham EX16 163 C1
HIGHBRIDGE 104 E3
Highbridge TA4 202 F4
Highbridge & Burnham Sta
TA9 104 E3
Highbridge Rd TA8 104 B5
Highbrooks Rd TA11 173 B5
Highburn Cl TA8 104 C4
HIGHBURY 117 A7
Highbury Cotts
8 Bath BA1 28 A1
Coleford BA3 116 F7
Highbury Ct 15 BS23 30 C1
Highbury Farm Bsns Pk
BS39 77 A8
Highbury Par BS23 30 C1
Highbury Pl BA1 28 A1
Highbury Rd
Hallatrow BS39 77 B7
Weston-super-Mare BS23 30 C1
Highbury St BA3 117 A7
Highbury Terr 10 BA1 28 A1
Highbury Villas
9 Bath BA1 28 A1
Bristol BS2 226 C4
Highcroft
Weston-super-Mare BS23 30 F1
Woolavington TA7 136 E4
Highcroft La BA3 114 E6
High Cross EX16 164 A1
Highdale Ave BS21 6 E3
Highdale Cl BS14 23 B4
Highdale Rd BS21 6 E3
High Down Jun & Inf Schs
BS20 2 A4
Higher Actis BA6 206 E3
HIGHER ALHAM 142 C4
Higher Backway BA10 215 E6
Higher Barton
Martock TA12 185 D4
Trent DT9 187 F5
Higher Beacon TA19 221 B4
Higher Beadon TA16 195 E7
Higher Boyston La DT9 188 E6
Higher Brooks BA16 207 C2
Higher Bullen BA22 197 F8
HIGHER BURROW 184 E7
Higher Burton BA22 197 C8
Higher Cemetery La DT9 188 E7
Higher Cheap St 3 DT9 225 D4
HIGHER CHILLINGTON 194 F5
Higher Comeytrowe Farm La
TA1 212 A1
Higher Coombses TA20 198 D8
Higher Cross EX15 179 C1
HIGHER DURSTON 169 E7
Higher Eastern Hill BA21 218 C8
Higher Easthams La TA18 224 F7
Higher Farm La
Podimore BA22 174 A4
Sparkford BA22 175 B3
Higher Farm Trad Est
BA20 218 C5
Higher Folly Rd
Crewkerne TA18 224 A2
Hewish TA18 195 D2
Higher Gunville DT9 217 D2
HIGHER HADSPEN 214 E4
HIGHER HALSTOCK
LEIGH 197 A2
Higher Heathfield TA4 151 E4
Higher Kingsbury DT9 217 D3
Higher Kingsbury Cl DT9 217 C3
Higher Kingston BA21 219 B5
Higher Kingstonwell
TA20 194 C2
Higher Mead TA19 221 B3
Highermill Farm La TA24 128 B2
Higher Millhayes EX15 180 B1
Higher North Town La
BA22 175 D7
HIGHER NYLAND 177 C1
HIGHER ODCOMBE 186 C2
Higher Orch
Martock TA12 185 D4
Minehead TA24 200 C8
Higher Palmerston Rd
TA2 212 D6
Higher Park La TA24 129 E2
Higher Pk TA24 200 D6
Higher Rd
Chedzoy TA7 154 D8
Horsington BA8 176 D3
Shepton Beauchamp TA19 184 E3
Woolavington TA7 136 E4
Higher Ream BA21 218 C6
Higher Rodhuish Rd TA24 131 B3
HIGHER SANDFORD 188 C7
Higher Shepton Rd
Pitcombe BA9 215 D1
Shepton Montague BA9 160 B2
Higher St
Curry Mallet TA3 183 C8
Martock TA12 185 D4
Merriott TA16 195 F8
Norton Sub Hamdon TA14 185 E2
West Chinnock TA18 196 B8
Higher Street TA5 133 B5
Higher Tolbury BA10 215 E6
HIGHER TOWN 200 E8
Higher Town EX16 178 C1
HIGHER VEXFORD 150 E6
Higher Wambrook TA20 193 C3
Higher Weare La TA20 194 F5
Higher Westbury DT9 187 E1
Higher West Hatch La
TA3 182 D7
Higher Westholme Rd
North Wootton BA4 140 D4
Pilton BA4 204 A1
Higher Woodlands TA3 183 E6
Highfield
Coleford BA3 116 E8
Ilminster TA19 221 B4
Taunton TA1 212 A2
Taunton TA1 212 C3
Wells BA5 140 C7
West Chinnock TA18 196 B8
Highfield Cl
Bath BA2 44 B5
Somerton TA11 211 C4
Taunton TA1 212 A2
Highfield Cres
Chilcompton BA3 96 C4
Taunton TA1 212 A2
Highfield Dr BS20 1 E3
Highfield La
Compton Martin BS40 74 B6
East Harptree BS40 75 A3
Highfield Rd
Keynsham BS31 24 F2
Peasedown St John BA2 79 C8
Street BA16 207 B5
Taunton TA1 168 F4
Weston-super-Mare BS24 49 A1
Yeovil BA21 219 C6
Highfields
Barrington TA19 184 C5
Clandown BA3 78 E4
Midsomer Norton BA3 78 D2
Stanton Drew BS39 39 F1
Highfield Terr TA12 185 D5
Highfield Trad Est BA21 219 C6
Highfield View BA3 116 E8
Highfield Way TA11 211 C4
High Gn BA5 111 A4
High Gr BS9 5 B7
Highgrove TA1 212 E1
Highgrove Cl TA6 209 A2
Highgrove Wlk BS24 50 A8
HIGH HAM 156 A2
High Ham CE Prim Sch
TA10 156 A1
High Kingsdown BS2 226 C4
High La
Barton St David TA11 158 A2
Shapwick TA7 155 F8
Highland Cl BS22 31 B2
Highland Ct BA21 219 C6
Highland Rd BA2 44 B5
Highlands TA1 212 E1
Highlands La BS24 50 A8
Highlands Rd
Long Ashton BS41 11 A2
Portishead BS20 2 B5
Highland Terr BA2 44 D6
High Lea BA21 219 B8
HIGH LITTLETON 59 C1
High Littleton CE VA Prim Sch
BS39 59 C1
High Mdws BA3 77 F1
Highmead Gdns BS13 21 E4
High Mead Gdns BS39 57 D3
Highmore Rd DT9 225 C5
High Path TA21 222 C7
High Pk BS39 77 D6
High Rd BA22 175 D8

HIGHRIDGE
Bristol 21 F7
Dundry 21 D3
Highridge Cres BS13 21 F5
Highridge Gn BS13 21 E6
Highridge Pk BS13 21 F6
Highridge Rd BS13, BS41 21 E4
Highridge Wlk BS13 21 E7
High St
AllerTA10 171 E8
Ashcott TA7 156 B8
Axbridge BS26 70 B2
Bampton EX16 164 B1
Banwell BS29 51 A2
Bath BA1 228 C2
Bathampton BA2 28 F1
Batheaston BA1 28 F3
Bathford BA1 29 D2
Bath, Twerton BA2 44 B6
Bath, Weston BA1 27 B1
Bishops Lydeard TA4 167 E8
Bitton BS30 25 E8
Blackford BS28 107 E4
Blagdon BS40 54 E3
Bourton SP8 161 F2
Bridgwater TA6 208 F5
Bristol BS1 227 A2
Bristol, Shirehampton BS11 4 E6
Bruton BA10 215 E6
Buckland Dinham BA11 100 A3
Burnham-on-S TA8 104 A6
Butleigh BA6 157 E4
Cannington TA5 135 B2
Carhampton TA24 131 A5
Castle Cary BA7 214 C5
Chapmanslade BA13 121 C4
Chard TA20 223 B4
Charlton Adam TA11 173 F7
Chew Magna BS40 39 A3
Chewton Mendip BA3 94 F7
Claverham BS49 17 F1
Coleford BA3 116 F6
Congresbury BS49 34 D4
Dulverton TA22 163 D6
Dunster TA24 201 E2
East Chinnock BA22 196 E8
East Harptree BS40 74 F5
Evercreech BA4 141 E1
Faulkland BA3 80 D1
Freshford BA3 64 B5
Frome BA11 119 E5
Glastonbury BA6 206 E4
Hardington Mandeville BA22 197 A6
Henstridge BA8 190 A6
High Littleton BS39 59 D1
Hinton Charterhouse BA2 63 E1
Hinton St George TA17 195 D7
Ilchester BA22 173 E1
Ilminster TA19 221 B4
Keinton Mandeville TA11 158 A1
Keynsham BS31 24 E6
Kingweston BA6 157 E1
Lynford-on-F TA11 158 C2
Maiden Bradley BA12 144 C2
Marshfield SN14 13 F8
Midsomer Norton BA3 78 B1
Milborne Port DT9 217 D2
Milton Clevedon BA4 160 A8
Milverton TA4 166 F5
Monksilver TA4 150 B8
Nailsea BS48 8 F3
North Cadbury BA22 175 D6
North Petherton TA6 153 E4
North Wootton BA4 140 C4
Norton St Philip BA2 81 E4
Nunney BA11 143 B8
Oakhill BA3 115 A3
Othery TA7 155 C2
Paulton BS39 77 E5
Paulton, Plummer's Hill BS39 77 E6
Pensford BS39 40 E4
Porlock TA24 124 A3
Portbury BS20 3 E3
Portishead BS20 2 D5
Queen Camel BA22 174 F3
Rimpton BA22 188 A8
Rode BA11 101 E8
Saltford BS31 25 F3
Shepton Mallet BA4 205 B5
Sparkford BA22 175 A5
Spaxton TA5 152 E7
Stalbridge DT10 190 B5
Stogumber TA4 150 D8
Stogursey TA5 134 C5
Stoke sub Hamdon TA14 185 F4
Ston Easton BA3 95 E8
Stoney Stratton BA4 141 F2
Stourton BA12 161 F5
Stourton Caundle DT10 189 F2
Street BA16 207 C6
Taunton TA1 212 F3
Templecombe BA8 176 E1
Thorncombe TA20 199 B6
Timsbury BA2 60 B2
Wellington TA21 222 E6
Wellow BA2 62 D1
Wells BA5 203 D4
West Coker BA22 197 A8
Weston-super-Mare BS23 48 D8
Weston-super-Mare, Worle BS22 31 E2
Williton TA4 202 D2
Wincanton BA9 216 C4
Winford BS40 38 A7
High St continued
Winsham TA20 194 E1
Wiveliscombe TA4 210 C4
Wookey BA5 139 D8
Wookey Hole BA5 203 A8
Woolley BA1 27 F6
Wrington BS40 35 D2
Yatton BS49 34 C8
Yenston BA8 189 F8
Yeovil BA20 219 B4
Highview BA2 228 A1
High View BS20 2 A4
High View Dr TA7 156 B8
Highwall La BS14, BS31 23 F1
HIGHWAY 185 E7
Highway Rd TA12 185 D7
Highwoods Cl TA14 185 F2
Higson Cl BA22 186 D3
Hilary Rd TA1 212 D3
Hildesheim Bridge BS23 48 F7
Hildesheim Cl BS23 48 F6
Hildeshiem Ct [9] BS23 48 E7
Hilhouse BS9 5 C6
Hill Ave BA2 44 F1
Hillborne Gdns BA21 218 C5
Hillbrook Ct DT9 225 D4
Hill Brow DT9 225 B2
Hill Cl BA9 216 D4
Hillclose La TA19 221 F2
HILL CORNER 120 E6
Hillcote Est BS24 67 B8
Hillcrest
Crowcombe TA4 151 B7
Peasedown St John BA2 79 C7
Pensford BS39 40 E3
Hillcrest Cl
Bristol BS13 22 B6
Nailsea BS48 8 E1
Yeovil BA21 219 C7
Hillcrest Dr BA2 44 C4
Hillcrest Rd
Nailsea BS48 8 E1
Portishead BS20 1 E4
Templecombe BA8 176 E1
Hill Crest Rd BA21 219 C6
Hillcroft Cl BS22 31 A2
Hill Cross BA22 196 F6
Hill Ct BS39 77 E6
Hilldale Rd BS48 19 B5
Hill Dr BS8 10 C3
Hill Dro TA12 185 A7
Hillend BS22 31 E3
HILL END 196 F6
HILLFARRANCE 167 E3
Hillfield BS27 90 B7
Hill Gay Cl BS20 1 F4
Hill Ground BA11 119 E5
Hillgrove Ave BA20 218 F2
Hillgrove Cl TA6 208 E5
Hillgrove Rd BA5 93 C1
Hillgrove St N BS2 227 A4
Hillgrove St BS2 227 B4
Hillgrove Terr BS23 48 D1
Hill Head BA6 206 D3
Hill Head Cl
Glastonbury BA6 206 D3
Taunton TA1 213 A3
Hillhead Cotts TA2 212 C8
Hillhead Cross TA24 128 D3
Hillhouse EX14 192 D3
Hill House Cl DT9 225 E5
Hill House Farm La
Buckland Dinham BA11 99 D2
Buckland Dinham BA11 99 F3
Hillier's La
Churchill BS25 52 D4
Yarley BA5 139 C8
Hillingdon Ct BA21 218 C6
Hill La
Bicknoller TA4 132 F2
Bicknoller, Culverhays TA4 133 A1
Brent Knoll TA9 86 B3
Carhampton TA24 131 A4
Chipstable TA4 165 C6
Clevedon BS21 7 C4
Draycott BS27 90 C2
Portishead BS20 1 F1
Rodney Stoke BS27 91 B2
Rowberrow BS25 53 A1
Shepton Mallet BA4 205 B6
Waterrow TA4 165 E5
West Quantoxhead TA4 132 F4
Hill Lea Gdns BS27 90 B8
Hillmead
Churchill BS40 53 A5
Shepton Mallet BA4 205 B6
Hillmer Rise BS29 50 F3
Hill Moor BS21 6 E2
Hillpath BS29 51 B2
Hill Pk BS49 34 E5
Hill Rd
Allerford TA24 124 E4
Clevedon BS21 6 D4
Dundry BS41 21 D2
Minehead TA24 125 B4
Sandford BS25 52 A3
Weston-super-Mare BS23 48 F8
Weston-super-Mare, Worle BS22 31 E2
Hill Rd E BS22 31 E2
Hillrick Cres BA21 218 C8
Hillsboro TA7 136 E4
Hillsborough BS8 226 A2
Hillsborough Gdns TA8 85 B1
Hillsborough Ho BS23 49 A4
Hills Cl
Chorley Hill BA10 215 F8
Keynsham BS31 25 A5
Hills Cotts TA4 167 A7
Hillsdon Rd BS9 5 F8
HILLSIDE
Axbridge 70 C2
Midsomer Norton 96 E8
Hillside
Bristol BS6 226 C4
Chard TA20 223 B4
Horrington BA5 113 A2
Portbury BS20 3 D3
Puriton TA7 136 C4
West Pennard BA6 140 B1
Hillside Ave
Frome BA11 119 F2
Midsomer Norton BA3 96 F8
Hillside Cl
Curry Rivel TA10 171 D4
Paulton BS39 77 F6
Hill Side Cl BA5 203 C5
Hillside Cres
Midsomer Norton BA3 96 E8
Puriton TA7 136 C4
Hillside Dr
Frome BA11 120 B4
Puriton TA7 136 C4
Hillside Fst Sch BS22 31 E2
Hillside Gdns
Bishop Sutton BS39 57 C3
Weston-super-Mare BS22 31 B1
Hillside Gr TA1 212 C1
Hillside Ho BA11 119 F3
Hillside Rd
Backwell BS48 19 A4
Bath BA2 44 D4
Bleadon BS24 67 B8
Clevedon BS21 6 D3
Long Ashton BS41 11 B2
Midsomer Norton BA3 96 F8
Portishead BS20 1 D4
Hillside Terr BA21 219 C5
Hillside View
[1] Barwick BA22 197 F8
Midsomer Norton BA3 78 A3
Peasedown St John BA2 79 C8
Yeovil BA22 219 D1
Hillside W BS24 49 F2
Hill's La [10] TA12 185 E6
Hills Orch [9] TA12 185 E6
Hill St
Bristol BS1 226 C2
Stogumber TA4 150 D8
Hill Terr TA1 212 A4
Hill The
Freshford BA3 64 C5
Langport TA10 172 A5
Hill Top BS20 2 A4
Hilltop La TA5 133 D6
Hill Top La BS40 37 B3
Hilltops TA8 65 F6
Hillview
Midsomer Norton BA3 96 E7
Timsbury BA2 60 B1
Hill View
Brean TA8 65 E2
Bristol BS8 226 B2
Brompton Ralph TA4 150 C3
Farrington Gurney BS39 77 B3
Marksbury BA2 42 B1
Mudford BA21 187 D6
Priston BA2 61 A5
Queen Camel BA22 174 F4
Yeovil BA21 219 C5
Hillview Ave BS21 6 D2
Hillview Cl TA24 200 D7
Hill View Cl
Ilton TA19 183 F4
[7] Stoke sub Hamdon TA14 185 F4
West Chinnock TA18 196 B8
Hill View Ct
Evercreech BA4 141 E1
Weston-super-Mare BS22 49 D8
Hill View Cvn Pk BS40 20 B1
Hillview Gdns BS40 37 C8
Hill View Park Homes BS22 49 D8
Hillview Rd
Loxton BS26 68 C4
Minehead TA24 200 D7
Hill View Rd
Bath BA1 28 B2
Bristol BS13 22 A8
Carhampton TA24 131 A5
Weston-super-Mare BS23 49 A7
Hillview Terr TA12 185 D5
Hill View Terr
Ilminster TA19 221 B4
Lyng TA3 170 C7
Hill View Trad Est TA4 151 E4
Hillway TA11 173 E7
Hillworth Ho [26] BA4 205 B6
Hillyfield Rd BS13 22 A6
Hillyfields
Taunton TA1 213 C2
Winscombe BS25 70 B8
Hillyfields Way BS25 70 A8
Hilly Head TA21 222 B5
Hilly Pk TA2 168 B5
Hinam Cross TA22 163 B7
Hinckley Cl BS22 32 C4
Hincombe Hill BA4 142 E2
Hindhayes Inf Sch BA16 207 D5
Hindhayes La BA16 207 D6
Hindon La TA24 123 F3
Hind Pitts BS25 70 F7
Hine Rd TA1 212 B1
Hinham La TA22 163 A7
Hinkley Point Nature Trail★ TA5 134 C8
Hinkley Point Rd TA5 134 E6
Hinkley Point Visitor Ctr★ TA6 208 F4
HINTON 187 D7
Hinton BS24 49 A2
HINTON BLEWETT 75 F6
Hinton Blewett Rd
Hinton Blewett BS39 75 E8
Sutton Wick BS39 57 E1
HINTON CHARTERHOUSE 63 E1
Hinton Cl
Bath BA2 43 F6
Hinton St George TA17 195 D7
Saltford BS31 25 E3
Hinton Cross BA22 187 D7
Hinton Dr TA1 212 E1
Hinton Field La TA12 185 D4
Hinton Hill BA2, BA3 63 A1
Hinton La [12] BS8 11 F6
Hinton Rd TA18 224 B8
HINTON ST GEORGE 195 D7
Hinton St George CE Sch
Dinnington TA17 195 C7
Hinton St George TA17 195 C7
Hinton Villas BA2 63 E1
Hippisley Dr BS26 70 D2
Hippisley Ho BA5 113 A1
Hippys Farm La BA3 116 F6
Hiscocks Dr BA2 44 E4
Hiscocks La BA8 176 E2
Hitchen TA16 195 F7
Hitchen Cl SN14 13 F8
Hitchen Hill BA4 140 F3
Hitchings Dro TA12 185 A8
Hitchings La TA3 170 B7
Hitchin La BA4 205 A5
Hither Acre TA19 221 A4
Hither Bath Bridge BS4 23 C8
Hither Gn BS21 6 F2
Hither Green Ind Est BS21 6 F2
Hither Mead TA4 167 F8
Hittsford La EX36 162 A1
Hoare's La BA11 98 B3
Hobart Rd BS23 48 F3
Hobbiton Rd BS22 32 A4
Hobbs Ct [1] BS48 8 F2
Hobbs La BS48 20 E3
Hobb's La BS1 226 C2
Hobbs Mead [7] TA4 167 F8
Hobbs Rd BA4 205 D3
HOBB'S WALL 59 E5
Hob Cl TA2 169 B2
Hobhouse La BA4 140 B4
Hob La TA2 168 E8
Hobwell La BS41 11 C2
Hoccombe Ford TA4 150 F1
Hocken Cl TA20 223 D6
Hockers Hill BA22 186 B2
HOCKHOLLER 180 E8
HOCKHOLLER GREEN 180 E8
Hockley Ct BA1 27 D1
Hockley La BA22 175 E5
Hockpitt La TA5 134 A2
HOCKWORTHY 178 D6
Hodder's Cl BA11 119 E5
Hodders La BS22 32 D6
Hodges Barton TA11 211 C4
Hodshill BA2 62 F6
Hoecroft BA3 96 D2
Hoecroft Gdns BA3 96 D3
Hogarth Mews BS22 32 A3
Hogarth Wlk BS22 32 A3
HOGGINGTON 83 D4
Hoggington La BA14 83 E3
Hogues Wlk BS13 22 B4
Holbeach Way BS14 23 A2
HOLBEAR 223 D2
Holbear TA20 223 D2
Holbrook Cres BS13 22 D4
Holbrook Pk TA13 220 C5
Holburne Museum & Crafts Study Ctr★ BA2 45 B7
Holburne Pk BA2 45 C8
HOLCOMBE 116 C8
Holcombe BS14 23 A5
Holcombe Cl BA2 28 F1
Holcombe Gn BA1 27 B2
Holcombe Gr BS31 24 D5
Holcombe Hill BA3 116 C7
Holcombe La
Bathampton BA2 28 F1
Doulting BA4 141 E4
HOLCOMBE ROGUS 178 F5
Holcombe Vale BA2 28 F1
Holden's Way
Curry Rivel TA10 171 C3
Curry Rivel TA10 171 D3
Holders Wlk BS41 20 F8
Holdfast La TA14 185 D1
Holditch Court La TA20 198 E5
Holditch La EX13, TA20 198 E5
Holdscroft La DT6 199 B1
Holeground Villas BA5 203 A8
Holemoor Farm Rd TA20 193 D6
Holemore Cross EX14 191 F5
Holes La BA11 118 B6
Holes Sq TA24 130 B5
HOLFORD 133 D4
Holford Cl BS48 8 E1
Holford Ct BS14 23 B5
Holford La TA4 151 C5
Holford Rd
Bridgwater TA6 208 B4
Taunton TA2 212 E8
Hollam Cross TA22 163 E7
Hollam Dr TA22 163 D6
Hollam La TA22 163 D7
Holland Ct BA16 207 D7
Holland Rd
Bath BA1 28 B1
Clevedon BS21 6 B1
HOLLANDS 219 A7
Holland's La TA4 149 E1
Holland St BS23 49 A8
Holland's Wash Dro TA20 193 C5
Holleys Cl TA20 198 D8
Hollies Cl
Martock TA12 185 D5
Middlezoy TA7 155 B3
Shepton Mallet BA4 205 C6
Hollies La BA1 29 A6
Hollies The
Crewkerne TA18 224 C4
Midsomer Norton BA3 78 A1
Yeovil BA21 219 C7
Hollis Ave BS20 2 C3
Hollis Cl
Halstock BA22 197 D3
Long Ashton BS41 21 A8
Hollis Cres BS20 2 C3
Hollister's Dr BS13 22 D4
Hollis Way
Halstock BA22 197 D3
Southwick BA14 83 F3
Holloway
Bath BA2 228 B1
Lopen TA13 185 A1
Minehead TA24 200 F7
Holloway Rd TA7 155 B2
Holloway St TA24 200 F7
Holloway The TA21 179 E7
HOLLOW BROOK 57 C6
Hollowbrook La BS39, BS40 57 D6
Hollowell Hill
Norton Sub Hamdon TA14, TA18 185 E1
West Chinnock TA18 196 B8
Hollow La
Baltonsborough BA6 158 B8
Dinnington TA17 195 B7
Lopen TA13 185 A1
Montacute TA15 186 B3
Wembdon TA5, TA6 208 C7
Weston-super-Mare BS22 31 F3
Hollow Marsh La BA3, BS39 76 B4
Hollowmead BS49 34 E8
Hollowmead Cl BS49 34 F8
Hollow Rd
Shepton Beauchamp TA19 184 D3
Shipham BS25 70 F8
Hollow The
Bath BA2 44 B4
Corsley Heath BA12 144 E8
Dunkerton BA2 61 D4
Westbury-sub-Mendip BA5 110 D7
Hollway Cl BS14 23 E5
Hollway Rd BS14 23 E5
HOLLY BROOK 110 F5
Holly Bush BA12 144 E3
Hollybush Cl BA15 64 E7
Hollybush La
Bristol BS9 5 E5
Bristol BS9 5 F4
Leigh u M BA3 117 A2
Holly Cl
Bridgwater TA6 209 E5
Nailsea BS48 9 A3
[7] North Petherton TA6 153 F3
Taunton TA1 213 C1
Weston-super-Mare BS22 32 A1
Holly Ct
Bristol BS2 226 C4
Frome BA11 120 B7
Holly Dr BA2 62 D8
Holly Gr TA18 224 D7
Holly Hill BA4 142 C1
Hollyhock Cl TA6 208 E1
Holly La
Clevedon BS21 6 F6
Drimpton DT8 199 F8
Shepton Mallet BA4 205 C4
Hollyman Wlk [5] BS21 6 F3
Hollymead La BS9 5 E4
Hollyridge BS14 23 C6
Holly Ridge BS20 2 A5
Holly Terr
Chard TA20 223 C4
Odcombe BA22 186 C2
Holly Tree Wlk BA20 218 E3
Holly Wlk
Keynsham BS31 24 D4
Radstock BA3 78 E1
Holman Cl BA6 206 E6
HOLMAN CLAVEL 181 E3
Holman's BA6 157 E4
Holmbury Cl BA11 120 D6
Holmbush TA24 128 E8
Holm Cl TA8 104 B5
Holmlea
Portishead BS20 2 F5
[1] Wookey BA5 139 D8
Holmoak Rd BS31 24 C4
Holm Oaks BA6 157 E4
Holm Rd BS24 49 E2
Holms Rd BS23 49 A5
Holm Vw TA23 202 D7
Holsom Cl BS14 23 F6
Holsom Rd BS14 23 F6
Holstein Ave BS25 69 F7
Holst Gdns BS4 22 D7
Holt Ball Steep TA24 129 D7
Holten's La BA22 196 E6
Holt Hill DT9 189 C1
Holt La
Halstock BA22 197 F3
South Perrott DT8 196 D1

Holt La *continued*
Stourton Caundle DT9, DT10 **189** E1
West Pennard BA6........**140** D2
HOLTON.................**176** C5
Holton Cross BA9........**176** C6
Holton St BA9............**176** C5
Holt Rd
North Brewham BA11......**161** E8
Witham Friary BA11.......**143** D1
Holtsdown La BA1......... **28** F7
Holvert La TA20..........**194** F1
HOLWAY
Sherborne **188** D7
Taunton **213** C2
Thorncombe.............**199** C6
Holway
North Petherton TA6.......**153** F4
Tatworth TA20 ....**198** D8
Holway Ave TA1..........**213** B3
Holway Deane TA1 ....**213** D2
Holway Gn TA1 ....**213** C2
Holway Hill TA1..........**213** B2
Holway House Pk TA19 ...**183** E2
Holway Park Com Prim Sch
Holway TA1..............**213** C2
Taunton TA1 ....**213** C3
Holway Rd TA1...........**213** B3
HOLWELL **143** B8
Holwell Cl BS39...........**77** E4
Holwell Hill BA11 ....**143** B7
Holwell La BS27........... **89** F8
Holworthy La TA22 ....**148** E2
Holy Moor Cross EX36....**162** C1
Holy Moor La EX36 ....**162** C1
Holyoake St TA21 ....**222** C7
Holyrood Com Sch (Lower)
TA20 ....**223** C4
Holyrood Com Sch (Upper)
TA20 ....**223** C5
Holyrood St TA20 ....**223** C3
Holy Tree Cross TA14.....**185** E3
Holy Trinity CE Prim Sch
Holway TA1..............**213** A2
Taunton TA1 ....**213** A3
Yeovil BA20 ....**218** E2
HOLYWELL **197** C8
HOLYWELL LAKE **179** E7
Holy Well Rd TA7.........**137** C2
Homberg Way TA6 ....**208** E6
Homeavon Ho BS31 .... **24** F5
Homecanton Ho BA9 .....**216** C4
Homecastle Ho [2] TA6....**208** F5
Homechime Ho BA5......**203** D3
Home Cl
Westbury-sub-Mendip
BA5..................**110** E6
West Camel BA22.........**174** D3
Wrington BS40............ **35** E3
Homeclose La EX13, TA20 .**198** A8
Home Cotts TA1..........**212** D5
Home Dr
Wincanton BA9 ....**216** C3
Yeovil BA21 ....**218** E5
Home Farm Cl BA2........ **79** B7
Home Farm La BA22......**188** A8
Home Farm Pk TA19.......**183** E2
Home Farm Rd BS8........ **11** B8
Home Farm Way TA19....**183** E2
Homefield
Bishops Lydeard TA4 ......**167** E8
Congresbury BS49......... **34** E3
Locking BS24 .... **50** A5
Timsbury BA2............. **60** C2
Wellington TA21..........**222** E4
Homefield Cl
Beckington BA11 ....**101** E4
Creech St Michael TA3 .....**169** D4
Locking BS24 .... **50** A5
Saltford BS31............. **25** E3
Winscombe BS25.......... **51** F1
Home Field Cl TA11 ......**157** B4
Homefield Ct BA22........**174** F1
Homefield Ind Est BS24.... **50** A5
Homefield Rd BS31........ **25** F3
Homefields BA5..........**110** E6
Home Fields BA4.........**205** C4
Homeground BS21 .... **6** F2
Home Ground BS11 .... **4** D7
Homelea Pk E BA1 .... **44** A7
Homelea Pk W BA1........ **44** A7
Home Mdw TA24.........**200** D7
Homemead BA2........... **43** A8
Home Mead BS4 .... **22** E7
Home Orch
Chew Stoke BS40.......... **56** D8
Hatch Beauchamp TA3 .....**183** A7
Homer Wk BS31........... **24** C3
Homestead BS20........... **1** E3
Homestead Ave TA9.....**104** D3
Homestead Pk BA5.......**203** A7
Homestead The
Clevedon BS21............. **6** C3
Keynsham BS31 .... **24** F2
Homestead Way BS25 ..... **70** A8
Homeville Ho BA20.......**219** A4
Home Way Cnr BA6 ......**138** B4
Hone Cross EX16.........**164** F5
Hone La TA22 ....**147** F4
Honeycombe Rise DT9 ...**225** B2
Honey Crock La TA7......**155** E8
Honeygar La BA6.........**138** B5
Honey Garston Cl BS13 .... **22** B4
Honey Garston Rd BS13.... **22** B4
HONEY HALL.............. **52** C7
Honeyhall La BS49 .... **52** D7
Honeyhurst La BS27 ......**109** F8
Honeylands
Curry Rivel TA10..........**171** D4
Honeylands *continued*
Portishead BS20 .... **2** C3
Honeymead
Bristol BS14.............. **23** C6
Croscombe BA5 ....**204** B8
Honey Mead La BA6, TA11 .**158** B4
Honeypot La TA11........**158** C1
Honey Pot La BA11 ....**144** A4
Honey Row La TA4 ....**132** E2
Honeysuckle Pl BS24...... **50** A8
Honeywell La BA3......... **94** F4
Honeywick Rd BA7.......**214** E5
Honiton [9] BS22 .... **32** A2
Honiton Rd
Clevedon BS21............. **6** E1
Taunton TA3 ....**168** D1
Hood Cl BA6 ....**206** E3
Hood Rd BA21 ....**219** F8
HOOK
Chard...................**198** B8
Timsbury **60** D2
Hook Dro BA22...........**187** B8
Hookedmead La BS26 ..... **88** A1
Hook Hill BA2............. **60** D2
Hook La
Hinton Blewett BA3, BS39 ... **75** E4
North Cheriton BA9 ....**176** C5
Hooks Batch BS40......... **54** C4
Hookway Hill TA24 ....**123** A3
Hooper Ave BA5 ....**112** E1
Hooper Cl
Burnham-on-S TA8 ....**104** D5
Highbridge TA9...........**104** F4
Hooper Rd
Bristol BS14.............. **23** D5
Street BA16 ....**207** B5
Hoopers Barton [9] BA11..**119** E5
Hooper's Cl TA1 ....**212** B2
Hoopers Cross EX16......**164** D3
Hooper's La
East Coker BA22 ....**197** F7
Fordgate TA7 ....**154** E3
HOOPERS POOL........... **83** D1
Hopcott Cl TA24..........**200** E6
Hopcott Rd TA24.........**200** F5
Hopcott Terr TA24 ....**201** A5
Hopechapel Hill [10] BS8.... **11** F6
Hope Cl BA5 ....**203** C4
Hope Corner Cl TA2 ......**212** E8
Hope Corner La TA2......**212** F8
Hope Cote Lodge BA2 ..... **45** C1
Hope Cotts
Highbridge TA9...........**104** D3
Kingston Seymour BS21..... **16** B2
Hope Cross SP8..........**177** D3
Hope Ct BS1 ....**226** B1
Hope Sq BS8............. **11** F6
Hope Terr BA3............ **78** B1
Hopewell Gdns BS11 .... **4** F7
Hopewell St TA6 ....**208** D5
Hopkins Ct BA9 ....**216** C2
Hopkins Field TA3........**169** D5
Hopkins Ho BA22.........**218** A5
Hopkins St BS23 .... **48** E8
Hopton Ct BA4 ....**141** E1
Hopton Wy BA1 .... **27** E4
Hopwoods Corner BS27 ... **90** B8
Horesham Gr BS13 .... **22** C5
Horfield Rd BS2..........**227** A4
HORN ASH...............**199** D7
Hornbeam Cl
Bridgwater TA6 ....**209** D5
Frome BA11..............**120** C6
Taunton TA1 ....**213** D2
HORNBLOTTON **158** F5
Horne Cl BA3 .... **96** F1
HORNER **129** B8
Horner Nature Trails★
TA24 ....**129** B8
Horner Rd TA2...........**213** B7
HORNINGSHAM **144** C4
Horningsham Prim Sch
BA12....................**144** D4
Horn La TA20 ....**194** B2
HORNSBURY.............**223** E7
Hornsbury Hill TA20......**223** E8
Hornsey La TA20 ....**182** B1
Horns La BA9 ....**160** B2
Horn's La BS26............ **70** B2
Horn St BA11 ....**143** B8
Hornswell DT9...........**189** D4
HORRINGTON............**113** A1
Horrington Prim Sch BA5 **113** B3
HORSECASTLE............ **17** A2
Horsecastle Cl BS49....... **17** A1
Horsecastle Farm Rd BS49 **17** A1
Horsecastle La DT9 ......**225** C3
Horsecastles DT9 ....**225** D3
Horse Cl BA11 ....**101** D5
Horsecombe Brow BA2.... **45** A1
Horsecombe Gr BA2....... **45** A1
Horsecombe La TA24.....**129** A1
Horsecombe Vale BA2..... **45** A1
Horsecroft La TA3........**170** B4
Horsefair The BS1........**227** B3
Horseham La TA5 ....**134** E8
Horsehill La BA4 ....**142** D2
Horse La DT9 ....**176** A2
Horseland La TA24 ....**131** A5
Horseleaze La BS25 .... **52** D1
Horsemans Mews BA6....**206** D5
Horse Mill Cross DT6.....**199** D3
Horse Mill La TA11 ....**211** E4
Horsepark La TA24 ....**130** A4
Horse Pond La TA6.......**208** F4
Horsepool Rd BS13........ **21** E3
Horse Race La BS8 .... **10** A6
Horse Rd TA24 ....**130** F5
Horseshoe Cotts TA12....**185** E7
Horseshoe Dr BS9.......... **5** C4
Horseshoe Rd TA20 ......**199** A6
Horseshoe Wlk BA2 .... **45** B5
HORSEY.................**136** C2
Horsey Dro TA10 ....**172** B1
Horsey La
Horsey TA7..............**136** C2
Langport TA10 ....**172** B4
Yeovil BA20 ....**219** A4
Horsey Rdbt BA20........**219** A3
HORSINGTON **176** D2
Horsington CE Prim Sch
BA8....................**176** D3
Horsington Ho BA8.......**176** E2
Horsington Rd BA8.......**176** D2
Horstmann Cl [2] BA1...... **44** B7
Hortmead La TA19 ....**183** E3
HORTON **183** C1
Horton Cl BA21 ....**218** D6
HORTON CROSS..........**183** D2
Horton Ho BA2...........**228** C4
Horton St
Bristol BS2..............**227** C3
Frome BA11..............**119** D5
Horton Way TA7 ....**136** E4
Horts Rd TA1 ....**212** C1
Horwood Rd BS48.......... **8** F1
Hosegood Dr BS24 .... **49** C4
Hosey Wlk BS13........... **22** A5
Hoskins Cl TA10..........**171** C4
Hospital La
Sherborne DT9...........**225** D4
South Petherton TA13......**220** D5
Hospital Rd BS48.......... **20** F7
Hospital Rdbt BA20.......**219** A5
Host St BS1..............**227** A3
Hot Bath St [6] BA1 ....**228** B2
Hotwell Rd BS8 ....**226** B1
HOTWELLS **226** A1
Hotwells Prim Sch BS8 .... **11** F6
Houlgate Way BS26 .... **70** B1
Houlton St BS2 ....**227** C4
Houndsmill BA8..........**176** E2
HOUNDSMOOR...........**167** A4
Houndsmoor La TA4......**167** A4
Hound St DT9............**225** D4
HOUNDSTONE **218** A6
Houndstone Bsns Pk
BA22...................**218** B6
Houndstone Cl BA21 .....**218** C5
Houndstone Cnr BA22....**218** A5
Houndstone Ct BA22 .....**218** A5
Houndstone Pk BA22.....**218** A5
Houndstone Ret Pk BA22 .**218** B5
Houndwood Cl BA16......**207** A6
Houndwood Dro BA16....**207** A6
HOUNSLEY BATCH......... **38** A3
House Gate Rd BA11......**143** F2
House's La TA20 ....**193** F1
Housman Rd BA16 ....**207** D5
Houston Way BA11.......**119** D5
Hoveland Cres TA1.......**212** D2
Hoveland Ct TA1.........**212** E2
Hoveland Dr TA1.........**212** D1
Hoveland La TA1.........**212** C2
Howard Cl
Burnham-on-S TA8 ....**104** C7
Saltford BS31............. **25** D3
Howard Rd
Wellington TA21..........**222** D7
Yeovil BA21 ....**219** E6
Howards Row TA20.......**223** C4
Howecroft Ct BS9 .... **5** E4
Howecroft Gdns BS9 .... **5** E4
Howell Hill BA22 ....**174** D4
Howell's La TA2, TA6......**153** D1
Howgrove Hill La BS40 .... **37** C2
How Hill BA2 .... **44** A6
Howitt Way [1] BS24 .... **49** F7
Howleigh La TA3.........**181** C5
HOWLEY **192** F4
Hownel La TA22..........**147** F2
Howtown La TA24........**147** D5
Hoyles Cl TA21...........**222** E4
Hoyles Rd TA21 ....**222** E4
Hozzard La BS28 ....**107** E2
Huckeymead La BA4 .....**158** F7
Huddleston Ct [10] BA5 ....**203** D4
Hudson St TA8...........**104** B6
Hudson Way TA2.........**212** C6
Huett Cl TA8............. **65** F3
Hugdole La TA7..........**137** D2
Hughenden Rd BS23....... **49** A8
Hughes Cl [6] TA6 ....**209** B4
Hughes Ct BA11..........**101** E8
Hugh Sexey CE Mid Sch
BS28...................**107** E3
Hugo St TA1.............**213** A4
Huish BA20..............**219** A5
Huish Ball Steep TA24 ....**129** D7
HUISH CHAMPFLOWER....**165** F8
Huish Cl
Highbridge TA9...........**104** D4
Taunton TA1 ....**213** D4
Huish Cleeve TA4 ....**165** E7
Huish Ct BA3 .... **79** B2
Huish Dro TA10 ....**171** F5
HUISH EPISCOPI..........**172** B5
Huish Episcopi Acad
TA10...................**172** A5
Huish Episcopi Prim Sch
TA10...................**172** A5
Huish Gdns [2] BA20 ......**219** A5
Huish La
Alweston DT9............**189** B2
Washford TA23...........**131** E4
Wyke Champflower BA10...**215** C7
Huish Mdw TA23.........**131** E4
Huish Park (Yeovil Town FC)
BA22...................**218** B7
Huish Prim Sch
Crofton Park BA20........**219** A5
Yeovil BA20 ....**219** A5
Huish Rd TA11 ....**173** C7
Huish Row TA24..........**129** A8
Hukeley Head Cross EX16 **164** D3
Hulk Moor Dro BA16,
BA16 ....**207** C8
Hulkshay La TA6 ....**153** E3
Hull La DT9, BA8..........**176** B3
Humber Gr TA1 ....**213** D3
Humberstan Wlk BS11...... **4** E8
Hummer Rd DT9 ....**187** E6
Humphreys Rd TA21......**222** E7
Humphry Davy Way [6] BS8. **11** F5
Humpy La DT9 ....**189** A1
Hundredstone Cl BA21 ...**219** B8
Hundry La TA10..........**184** C8
HUNGERFORD **131** E3
Hungerford Cl BS4........ **23** E8
Hungerford Gdns BS4 ..... **23** E8
Hungerford Rd
Bath BA1 .... **44** C7
Bristol BS4............... **23** E8
Hungerford Terr BA2...... **62** D1
Hung Rd BS11 .... **4** E5
HUNSTRETE **41** D2
Hunstrete La BS39 .... **41** B4
Hunstrete Rd BA2......... **59** F7
Huntash La TA4..........**167** A4
Huntenhull Gn BA13......**121** C3
Huntenhull La BA13 ......**121** D4
Hunter's Hill EX15........**179** E1
Hunters Moon Touring Pk
EX13...................**198** E1
Hunters Rest Miniature Rlwy★
BS39.................... **59** A5
Hunter's Way EX15.......**179** E1
Huntham Cl TA3 ....**170** E6
Huntham La TA3 ....**170** E5
Huntham Rd TA3.........**170** D4
Huntingham Rd BS13...... **21** F4
Huntley Cl EX13..........**198** A2
Huntley Gr BS48 .... **9** A1
Huntley La
Chardstock EX13 ....**198** A8
Tatworth EX13, TA20 ......**193** D1
HUNTSCOTT.............**129** E6
HUNTSHAM..............**178** A7
Hunts La TA5 ....**133** D5
Hunt's La BS49........... **34** E8
Huntsmans Ridge BS27.... **90** C7
Hunts Mead DT9 ....**225** B2
HUNTSPILL..............**136** B8
Huntspill Rd TA9.........**104** D2
Huntspill River National
Nature Reserve★ TA9....**136** D6
HUNTSTILE..............**153** C4
HUNTWORTH **154** B5
Huntworth Bsns Pk TA6...**154** A5
Huntworth La
Fordgate TA7 ....**154** C5
North Petherton TA6.......**153** F4
Hurcot La TA11 ....**173** C8
HURCOTT **173** C8
Hurcott Cross TA19 ......**184** D3
Hurcott La TA19..........**184** D4
Hurdle Way TA1..........**213** A3
Hurd's Bldgs BA11 ....**119** F4
Hurley La TA4............**151** B8
Hurlstone Pk TA24 ....**124** B3
Hurmans Cl TA7..........**156** B8
Hurn Dro BA5............**139** B6
Hurn La
Berrow TA8............... **84** F7
Keynsham BS31 .... **25** A3
Pitcombe BA7............**215** A1
Shepton Montague BA7 ....**160** A2
Hurn Rd BS21 .... **6** F2
Hursley Hill
Bristol BS14.............. **40** D8
Whitchurch BS14 .... **23** D1
Hursley La BS14........... **23** E1
HURST..................**185** D5
Hurst TA12 ....**185** D5
Hurst Dro
Compton Dundon TA11.....**157** A3
Hambridge TA10, TA12 .....**184** E8
Hurst Drove BS28 ....**109** C2
Hurst Mews TA12 ....**185** D5
Hurston Rd BS4........... **22** D7
Hurst Pk TA12 ....**185** D5
Hurst Rd
Bristol BS4............... **22** F8
Weston-super-Mare BS23 ... **49** A6
Hurst Wlk BS4 .... **22** F8
Hussey's DT10 ....**190** F5
Hutchings's La TA4.......**167** D4
Hutchin's La BA10........**160** F8
HUTTON **49** E2
Hutton CE Prim Sch BS24 .. **49** E2
Hutton Cl
Bristol BS9................ **5** E7
Keynsham BS31 .... **25** A2
Hutton Hill BS24 .... **49** F2
Hutton Moor La
BS22, BS24............... **49** C6
Hutton Moor Pk BS24...... **49** C6
Hutton Moor Rd BS22 ..... **49** C7
Hutton Moor Rdbt BS22.... **49** C7
Huxham La BA4..........**158** F7
Hyacinth Terr TA21.......**222** C5
Hyatt Pl BA4 ....**204** F5
Hyatts Wood Rd BS48...... **19** E1
Hyde Ct BA21 ....**218** C6
Hyde La
[9] Creech St Michael TA3...**169** C5
Monkton Heathfield TA2....**169** C5
Taunton TA2 ....**213** F6
Hyde Lane Cotts TA2 .....**169** C5
Hyde Park Ave [4] TA6 ....**153** E3
Hyde Pk [5] TA6 ....**153** E3
Hyde Rd
Minehead TA24...........**200** E6
Montacute TA15..........**186** B4
Hyde's La SN14 .... **13** A6
Hyde The
Clevedon BS21............ **16** C8
Keynsham BS31 .... **24** F6
Hyland Gr BS9 .... **5** F8
Hylton Cl TA2............**212** F8
Hynicombe La TA4 ....**165** D6
Hythe La BS27 .... **89** E5

I

Iberry La TA3 ....**183** E8
ICELTON **32** C8
Idson La TA5.............**134** E7
Idwal Cl BA2.............. **79** C8
Iford Cl BS31............. **25** E3
Iford Fields BA15.......... **64** E2
Iford Hill BA15 .... **64** E2
Iford La BA3, BA15 .... **64** C3
IKB Academy BS31 .... **25** A5
ILCHESTER...............**173** E1
Ilchester Com Prim Sch (Inf)
BA22...................**173** E2
Ilchester Com Prim Sch (Jun)
BA22...................**173** E2
Ilchester Cres BS13 .... **22** B8
Ilchester La TA10.........**172** F4
ILCHESTER MEAD **173** D1
Ilchester Mead BA22 .....**173** D1
Ilchester Mead Dro BA22 .**186** C8
Ilchester Mus★ BA22.....**173** E1
Ilchester Rd
Bristol BS13.............. **22** B8
Charlton Mackrell TA11 ....**173** F6
Chilthorne Domer BA21,
BA22..................**186** F6
Yeovil BA21 ....**218** F8
Ile Ct TA19...............**221** C4
Ilex Ave BS21 .... **6** E2
Ilex Cl
Bristol BS13.............. **21** F6
Huntspill TA9 ....**136** B8
Ilex La BS25.............. **51** F1
ILFORD **184** A4
Ilford Bridges TA19.......**184** A4
Ilford Ct TA1.............**212** C2
Illustrious Cres BA22 .....**173** E2
ILMINSTER **221** C4
Ilminster BS24 .... **49** A2
Ilminster Ave BS4 .... **22** F8
Ilminster Ave E-ACT Acad
Bristol BS4............... **23** A8
Filwood Park BS4.......... **22** F8
Ilminster Cl
Clevedon BS21............. **6** E2
Nailsea BS48 .... **18** D8
Ilminster Rd TA1 ....**213** D4
Ilsyn Gr BS14 .... **23** D7
ILTON...................**183** E4
Ilton Bsns Pk TA19.......**183** F5
Imbercourt Cl BS14 .... **23** B8
Immenstadt Dr TA21 .....**222** D4
Imperial Pk BS13.......... **22** C6
Imperial Rd BS14.......... **23** C8
Imperial Way
Bridgwater TA6 ....**136** B2
Frome BA11..............**120** D7
Improvement Pl [5] TA21..**222** D5
Inchalloch [19] BA1......... **28** A1
Incline The TA19 ....**221** B3
Inclosures The [5] BS22.... **49** F8
INGLESBATCH **61** C8
Ingleton Dr BS22.......... **32** A4
Ingrams Mdw TA23.......**202** C6
Inkerman Ct TA1 ....**213** A3
Inman Ho BA1 ....**228** C4
INMAN'S BATCH........... **38** A5
Inn Cotts BS11 .... **5** A7
Inner Circ TA1 ....**213** D5
Inner Elm Terr BA3........ **78** C1
Inner Gullands TA1.......**212** D3
Innicks Cl BS40 .... **55** D1
Innox Gdns BS13 .... **22** A5
Innox Gr BA2 .... **43** F2
INNOX HILL..............**119** F6
Innox Hill BA11 ....**119** E6
Innox La BA1.............. **28** B5
Innox Rd BA2 .... **44** B5
Inns Court Ave BS4........ **22** D7
Inns Court Dr BS4 .... **22** D6
Inns Court Gn BS4......... **22** D7
Innsmead La TA7.........**137** B1
Instow [7] BS22........... **32** A2
Instow Rd BS4 .... **22** E8
Instow Wlk BS4 .... **22** E8
International Coll Sherborne
Sch DT9................**225** D5
Inverness Rd BA2 .... **44** C6
Inwood Rd TA6...........**208** C5
Irene Cl TA6 ....**209** D7
Ireson Cl BA9 ....**216** D4
Ireson La BA9............**216** D4
Iris Rd BA11 ....**120** B3
Irnham Rd TA24..........**201** A7

Iron Dish La TA13 184 E6
Iron Mill La BA11 101 A1
Ironmould La BS31 24 A8
Iron Post TA22 163 B5
Irons Way BS24 50 C8
Irvine Cl TA2 212 C6
Irving Cl BS21 6 F3
Irving Ho BS1 226 C3
Irving Rd TA11 158 A1
Irwell Gn TA1 213 D4
Isaacs Cl BA16 207 B4
Island The BA3 78 A1
ISLE ABBOTTS 183 F7
Isle Abbotts Rd TA3 183 E8
ISLE BREWERS 184 A8
Isle Brewers La TA3 184 B8
Islemoor Dro TA3 184 A8
Islemoor La
Fivehead TA3 170 F1
South Petherton TA13 220 B6
Islemoor Rd TA3 183 F8
Isleport Bsns Pk TA9 104 F4
Isleport Rd TA9 104 F3
Isles La
East Coker, Lyatts BA22 197 C6
East Coker, Sutton Bingham BA22 197 D6
Ison La TA24 147 C7
Ivel Ct BA21 219 C5
Ivel Gdns BA22 173 E1
Ivel Sq BA20 219 B5
Ivelway TA18 224 C5
Ivo Peters Rd BA2 228 A2
Ivors Way TA6 153 E4
Ivy Ave BA2 44 C4
Ivy Bank Pk BA2 44 F2
Ivybridge 8 BS22 32 A2
Ivy Cl BS48 8 D1
Ivy Cotts TA3 181 E3
Ivy Cross TA21 179 D7
Ivy Ct BS20 1 F5
Ivy Gn TA20 223 C3
Ivy Gr BA2 44 C4
Ivy Grove Cl TA6 209 D7
Ivy Ho
Chard TA20 223 B4
Wellington TA21 222 C6
Ivy House Cotts BS29 50 D7
Ivy House Pk TA3 169 C2
Ivy La BS24 50 A8
Ivyleaf Rd TA11 211 C4
Ivy Pl BA2 44 C4
Ivythorn Cl BA16 207 C4
Ivy Thorn La BA16 207 A1
Ivythorn Rd BA16 207 C4
Ivywell Rd BS9 5 E3
Ivy Wlk
Banwell BS29 50 E4
Midsomer Norton BA3 97 B8
Yeovil BA20 218 E3
IWOOD 35 A3
Iwood La BS40 35 A2

J

Jack Price Cl BS13 22 C3
Jack's Dro BS28 137 F8
Jack's La
Croscombe BA5 204 C7
Frome BA11 119 D7
Jackson's La TA5 134 A2
Jack White's Gibbet BA9 176 B8
Jacobs Cl BA6 206 E5
Jacob's Ct BS1 226 C2
Jacobs Mdw BS20 2 F4
Jacob St
Bristol BS2 227 B3
Bristol BS2 227 C3
Jacob's Wells Rd BS8 226 B2
Jade Cl TA7 209 C8
Jagaar Ct TA7 137 D5
Jaguar Ho 3 BA1 228 B3
Jamaica St BS2 227 B4
James Cl
Holcombe BA3 116 C8
Shepton Mallet BA4 205 C4
James La EX14 192 F2
James Lane Cross EX13 193 A1
James St W BA1 228 B2
James's Hill BA10 161 A8
James St BS5 227 C4
Jane Austin Centre The★ BA1 228 B3
Janes Gr BA2 45 A2
Janson Cl TA6 209 D6
Japonica Cl TA6 209 D5
Jarman Way TA20 223 D6
Jarmany Hill BA6 157 F3
Jarmyns TA1 212 A3
Jarvis Cl DT10 190 B4
Jarvis La TA9 86 D4
Jarvis Way DT10 190 B4
Jasmine Cl
Bridgwater TA6 208 D1
Crewkerne TA18 224 D7
Highbridge TA9 104 D4
Weston-super-Mare BS22 32 A1
Yeovil BA22 218 B5
Jasmine Ct 8 BS23 48 E8
Jasmine La BS49 17 F2
Jasmine Way BS24 32 A1
Jay Cl BA11 120 B6
Jaycroft Rd TA8 104 B6
Jay View BS23 49 A5
Jeffreys' Way TA1 212 A2
Jeffries Cl TA19 183 C4
Jeffs Way 3 EX13 198 A1
Jellalabad Ct TA1 212 F3
Jellicoe Ct BS22 31 E4
Jena Ct BS31 25 D3
Jenson Ave BA11 120 D8
Jesmond Rd
Clevedon BS21 6 C3
Weston-super-Mare BS22 32 C4
Jesse Hughes Ct BA1 28 C2
Jessop Ct BS1 227 B2
Jessop Underpass BS3 11 F4
Jewel Cl TA7 209 C8
Jews La Bath BA2 44 C6
Churchill BS25 52 F4
Wiveliscombe TA4 210 B5
Jill Dando Memorial Garden★ 8 BS23 48 D8
Jill's Cl BA4 142 A6
Jim O'Neil Ho BS11 4 D7
Jocelin Dr BS22 31 F4
Jocelin Rd BA6 206 F5
Jocelyn Dr BA5 203 B3
John Beales Hill BA4 140 F3
John Cabot Ct BS1 226 A1
John Carr's Terr BS8 226 B2
John Cole Cl TA21 222 D8
John Cozens Ho 6 BS2 227 C3
John Grinter Way TA21 222 D4
John Gunn Cl TA20 223 C5
John Hall Cl BS14 23 B7
John St S TA8 104 A7
John Slessor Ct BA1 228 B4
Johnson Cl
East Brent TA9 86 D5
Wells BA5 203 F5
Johnson Flats BA21 219 C7
Johnson's Ctyd DT9 225 D3
John St
Bath BA1 228 B3
Bristol BS1 227 A3
Burnham-on-S TA8 104 A7
Highbridge TA9 104 D3
Johnstone Ct BA16 207 B3
Johnstone St BA2 228 C2
John Wesleys Chapel★ BS1 227 B3
Joles La BA11 120 F1
Jones Cl BS49 17 A1
Joselin Ct DT9 225 D5
Joyden Ct TA20 223 D2
Joy Hill BS8 11 F6
Juan's La SP8 177 E1
Jubilee Cl
Bridgwater TA6 209 C4
Castle Cary BA7 214 C6
Chard TA20 223 C3
Midsomer Norton BA3 97 A8
Jubilee Cotts 10 BA11 119 F4
Jubilee Ct
8 Wellington TA21 222 D5
Weston-super-Mare BS23 48 F8
Jubilee Dr BS8 10 B4
Jubilee Gdns
Milverton TA4 167 A4
South Petherton TA13 220 C4
Jubilee La BS40 53 A6
Jubilee Path BS22 31 C1
Jubilee Pl
Bristol BS1 227 A1
Clevedon BS21 6 D1
Yeovil BA21 218 D5
Jubilee Rd
Axbridge BS26 70 C2
Radstock BA3 78 D1
Street BA16 207 C4
Weston-super-Mare BS23 48 E7
Jubilee St
Bristol BS2 227 C2
Burnham-on-S TA8 104 B6
Taunton TA2 212 E6
Jubilee Terr
Frome BA11 119 E5
Hemington BA3 99 C7
Paulton BS39 77 E6
Jubilee Way BS22 32 C3
Judge's Ride
Luccombe TA24 123 C1
Luccombe TA24 129 C7
Judy's Orch TA7 154 F5
Julian Cl
Bristol BS9 5 E3
Shepton Mallet BA4 205 C4
Julian Ct BS9 5 E3
Julian Rd
Bath BA1 228 B3
Bristol BS9 5 E3
Julian's Acres TA8 84 F4
Julier Ho BA1 228 C4
Julius Pl BS31 24 F8
Jumpers Combe TA23 148 E8
Junction Ave BA2 228 A1
Junction Dro TA3 170 C2
Junction Rd BA2 228 A1
Juniper Cl
Bridgwater TA6 209 E4
Yeovil BA20 218 F3
Juniper Pl BS22 31 F4
Juniper Rd TA1 213 C2
Jurston Ct TA21 222 F4
Jurston La
Wellington TA21 222 E6
Wellington TA21 222 F5
Jury Hill TA22 163 E6
Jury Rd TA22 163 E6
Justice Ave BS31 25 E3
Justice La BA11 119 F5

K

Kale St BA4 142 D2
Kale Street Cotts BA4 142 D2
Karen Cl BS48 19 A4
Karen Dr BS48 19 A5
Kaynton Mead BA1 44 B7
Kearvell Pl DT9 225 C5
Keats Ho 4 BS23 48 F4
Keats Rd
Radstock BA3 97 C8
Taunton TA1 213 C3
Kebby's Farm Cl TA4 202 E3
Kebby's La TA19 221 D1
Keble Ave BS13 21 F5
Keeds La BS41 10 F1
Keedwell Hill BS41 10 F1
Keel Ave BS20 2 F7
Keel's Hill BA2 79 C8
Keene's Way BS21 6 C2
Keens Cl BA16 207 D5
Keen's Elm La BA16 207 E4
Keens La TA7 155 C2
KEENTHORNE 134 D2
Keepers Hill BA2 43 C5
Keeper's La BA2 42 C3
Keep St BA22 174 D3
Keep The BS22 32 A3
Keg Store The BS1 227 B2
KEINTON MANDEVILLE 158 B1
Keinton Mandeville Prim Sch
Keinton Mandeville TA11 158 A1
Keinton Mandeville TA11 158 A1
Kellaway La BA2 45 A2
Kellways BS48 19 A4
Kelson's La BS28 108 B3
Kelso Pl BA1 44 D7
Kelso Villas BA1 44 D7
KELSTON 26 C3
Kelston Cl BS31 25 D4
Kelston Gdns BS22 32 B5
Kelston Hill La BA1 26 B4
Kelston Rd
Bath BA1 26 E1
Keynsham BS31 24 D5
Weston-super-Mare BS22 32 B5
Kelston View BA2 44 A5
Kelting Gr BS21 6 F2
Keltings TA6 208 C6
Kelway Rd TA21 222 E7
Kember's Hill BA22, DT9 175 C3
Kemble Cl BS48 9 A1
Kemble Gdns BS11 4 F5
Kemm Cl BS27 90 B6
Kempe's Cl BS41 11 A2
Kempe Way BS24 49 E7
Kemps La TA24 147 B7
Kemp's La BA11 120 F7
Kemps Way TA22 163 D6
Kempthorne La BA2 44 E1
Ken Cl
Chard TA20 223 D3
Wells BA5 140 C8
Kencot Wlk BS13 22 B3
Kendale Rd TA6 208 E6
Kendall Cl TA3 169 D6
Kendrick Ct 1 BA5 203 D4
Kenelm Cl DT9 225 B3
Kenilworth Cl BS31 24 D4
Kenilworth Ct BA1 45 B8
Kenmare Rd BS4 22 E8
Kenmeade Cl BS25 70 E8
Kenmore Dr BA21 219 B6
KENN 16 F7
Kennard Cl BA6 206 F3
Kennard Moor Dro
Butleigh BA6 157 E7
Glastonbury BA6 206 F1
Kennaway Rd BS21 6 E2
Kenn Bsns Pk BS21 16 E8
Kenn Cl BS23 49 A5
Kenn Court BS4 22 E7
Kennedy Cl TA9 104 E4
Kennel Batch BA5 111 D4
Kennel Field Dr TA1 212 A3
Kennel La
Compton Bishop BS26 68 E3
East Pennard BA4 158 F8
Langport TA10 172 A6
West Bagborough TA4 151 D4
Kennel Lodge Rd BS3 11 E4
Kenn Est BS21 16 E5
Kennet Gr TA1 213 D4
Kennet Ho 10 BA1 228 B2
Kennet Pk BA2 28 E1
Kennet Rd BS31 25 A4
Kennford 6 BS22 31 F2
Kennington Rd BA1 44 B7
Kennion Cl TA20 223 D3
Kennion Rd BA5 203 C5
Kenn Moor Dr BS21 6 E1
KENN MOOR GATE 17 F4
Kennmoor Rd BS21 17 A6
Kenn Moor Rd BS49 17 B1
Kenn Rd BS21 16 F6
Kenn St BS21 16 F7
KENNY 183 B4
Kensington Ct
Bath BA1 28 B2
Bristol BS8 226 A3
Kensington Fields BA14 83 F7
Kensington Gdns
Bath BA1 28 B1
Bridgwater TA6 209 D6
Kensington Gr TA24 200 E6
Kensington Pl
Bath BA1 28 B1
Bristol BS8 226 A3
Kensington Rd BS23 48 F5
Kent Ave
Bridgwater TA6 209 A2
Weston-super-Mare BS24 50 C8
Weston-super-Mare BS24 50 D8
Kentisworth Rd DT10 190 F5
Kent La
Shapwick TA7 137 F1
Shepton Mallet BA4 205 A5
Kent Rd
Congresbury BS49 34 D5
Tatworth TA20 198 D8
Kent's Bglws TA20 198 D8
Kents Cl TA20 198 C8
Kent's Cotts TA20 198 D8
Kentshare La BS40 38 B6
Kents La TA20 198 D8
Kent's Orch TA20 198 D8
Kent St BS27 71 B1
Kent Way BS22 32 B4
Kenwyn Cl TA1 213 D3
Keppel Cl BS31 25 D2
Kerry Croft BA11 143 C3
Kersey Ct BA11 119 C5
Kersham La TA24 130 A1
Kestrel Cl TA6 209 C3
Kestrel Dr BS22 31 E1
KEWARD 203 C2
Keward Ave BA5 203 B3
Keward Cl BA5 203 B3
Keward Mill Trad Est BA5 203 B2
Keward Wlk BA5 203 C3
Kew Rd BS23 30 E1
Kewside BS22 31 B4
KEWSTOKE 31 B4
Kewstoke Prim Sch BS22 31 B3
Kewstoke Rd
Bath BA2 45 A2
Bristol BS9 5 E4
Weston-super-Mare BS22 31 C3
Kew Wlk BS4 23 C8
Keyes Path BS22 31 F4
KEYFORD 119 F3
Keyford BA11 119 F3
Keyford Cotts 15 BA11 119 F4
Keyford Ct BA11 119 F2
KEYFORD FIELD 119 F2
Keyford Field Cotts BA11 119 F2
Keyford Gdns BA11 119 F3
Keyford Pl BA11 119 F4
Keyford Rdbt BA22 197 E8
Keyford Terr BA11 119 F4
Keyhaven Bglws BS22 31 B4
Key Hill BA22 197 E8
KEYNSHAM 24 E3
Keynsham By-Pass BS31 24 E7
Keynsham Rd BS30, BS31 25 A8
Keynsham Sta BS31 24 F6
Keyton Hill BS28 107 E2
Kicks Hill TA7 155 B4
Kicks Hill La TA7 155 B4
Kidder Bank BA5 203 F5
Kiddles BA21 219 C5
Kidd's La BA4 205 D6
Kid Gate Dro TA9, BS28 137 D8
Kidner Cl TA7 136 E4
Kidsbury Rd TA6 208 E5
Kielder Dr BS22 31 F3
Kilbirnie Rd BS14 23 A3
Kilburn Dr TA6 209 D6
Kildare BA2 45 B7
Kildare Gdns TA24 200 F6
Kildare Rd BS13 22 D8
Kilkenny Ave 5 TA2 212 F6
Kilkenny Ct TA2 212 F6
Kilkenny La
Bath BA2 62 B8
Wraxall BA4 159 A6
Kilkenny Pl BS20 2 C6
Killams Ave
Staplehay TA3 181 F8
Taunton TA1 168 F1
Killams Cl TA1 168 F1
Killams Cres TA1 168 F1
Killams Dr TA1 168 F1
Killams Gn TA1 168 F1
Killams La TA1 168 F1
Killarney Ave TA8 104 C6
Killick Way TA4 202 D3
KILLING'S KNAP 97 B4
KILMERSDON 98 B5
Kilmersdon CE Prim Sch BA3 98 A6
Kilmersdon Hill BA3 98 A5
Kilmersdon Rd
Bristol BS13 22 B4
Radstock BA3 97 E8
KILMINGTON 161 F7
KILMINGTON COMMON 161 F6
Kilmington Common BA12 161 E7
Kilminster Rd BS11 4 D7
Kilmorie Cl TA1 212 C2
Kiln Cl TA5 135 B5
Kiln Dr
Evercreech BA4 141 E1
Highbridge TA9 104 D3
Kiln Pk BS23 49 A6
KILTON 133 E6
Kilton Cross TA5 133 E5
KILVE 133 C6
Kilve BS24 49 A2
Kilve Cl TA2 212 F7
Kilve Cres TA2 212 F7
Kilve Ct TA5 133 C5
Kilver St BA4 205 D6
Kilver Street Hill BA4 205 D7
Kimber Cl TA9 104 D3
Kimberley Rd BS21 6 C2
Kimberley Terr TA6 209 B7
Kinber Cl BA1 27 A3
Kinforde TA20 223 C5
King Alfred Cl 3 TA6 153 F4
King Alfred Dr TA20 223 C2
King Alfred Sch The TA9 104 C5
King Alfreds Ctyd 7 BA5 203 D4
King Alfreds Way BS28 108 B4
King Alfred Way BA15 64 D7
King Arthur Dr BA21 218 D7
King Arthur's Com Sch BA9 216 A4
King Athelstan Dr TA20 223 D2
King Ceol Cl TA20 223 D2
King Cerdic Cl TA20 223 D2
Kingcott Mill Farm Cvns BS48 20 B8
King Cuthred Cl TA20 223 C2
King Cuthred Dr TA20 223 C2
Kingdom BA5 113 A4
Kingdom La TA2 168 B4
Kingdon Mead TA3 169 D4
KINGDOWN 37 D5
Kingdown Rd BS40 37 C5
King Edward Cl BS14 23 A6
King Edward Rd
Bath BA2 44 D5
Minehead TA24 201 A6
King Edward's Jun Sch BA2 45 C7
King Edward's Pre-Prep Sch BA1 44 C8
King Edwards Sch BA1 44 C1
King Edward's Sch BA2 45 C7
Kingfisher Cl TA6 209 C3
Kingfisher Cl BA20 218 D3
Kingfisher Ct BA3 64 C6
Kingfisher Dr
Houndstone BA22 218 A6
Midsomer Norton BA3 97 B8
Kingfisher Rd
Portishead BS20 2 F7
Portishead BS20 3 A7
Weston-super-Mare BS22 49 F8
Kingfisher Wy BS21 1 B1
King George Ave TA6 208 F2
King George Cl TA6 209 A2
King George Rd TA24 201 A6
King George's Rd
Bath BA2 44 C6
Bristol BS13 21 F5
Bristol BS13 21 F5
King George St 2 BA20 219 B4
King George V Pl 7 BS1 227 A2
King Ina CE Acad TA11 211 E3
King Ina Rd TA11 211 D4
King Ine Cl N TA20 223 C2
King Ine Cl S TA20 223 C2
King La BS39 58 F4
Kinglake Dr TA1 212 E2
Kinglake Villas TA6 209 A2
King Rd BS49 52 E6
Kingsacre BA7 214 B5
Kings Acre TA4 151 B5
KINGSBRIDGE 148 E8
KINGSBURY EPISCOPI 185 A8
Kingsbury Episcopi Prim Sch TA12 185 A6
KINGSBURY REGIS 217 D3
Kings Castle Bsns Est TA6 209 A6
King's Castle Rd BA5 112 E1
Kings Cl
Shepton Mallet BA4 205 B5
Taunton TA1 213 A2
Kingscliffe Terr TA6 209 A2
King's Cnr TA22 163 D6
King's Coll TA1 213 B2
Kingscombe BA3 114 E6
Kingscourt Cl BS14 23 A4
Kings Cres DT9 225 D5
Kings Croft BS41 10 E1
Kings Ct
Bath BA1 228 B2
Bristol BS1 227 A2
Bristol, St Pauls BS1 227 B4
2 Bristol, Withywood BS13 21 F4
Sherborne DT9 225 D6
Yeovil BA21 219 C6
KINGSDON 173 E4
Kingsdon CE Prim Sch TA11 173 D5
Kingsdon Dro TA11 173 C4
Kingsdon Hill TA11 173 D5
Kingsdon Manor Sch TA11 173 D4
KINGSDOWN
Box 29 F3
Bristol 227 A4
Kingsdown Cl TA6 209 D6
Kingsdown Gr SN13 29 F3
Kingsdown Par BS6 227 A4
Kingsdown View 16 BA1 28 A1
Kings Dr
Bridgwater TA6 209 D8
Westonzoyland TA7 154 E6
Kingsettle Hill BA10 161 B5
Kingsfield BA2 44 C3
Kingsford Gate Cross TA24 145 B7
Kingsford Hill TA24 145 C7
King's Hall Sch TA2 168 E6
Kingshams BA22 173 E1
King's Head La BS13 21 F7

Kingshill BS48 . . . . . 8 C2
Kings Hill BA22 . . . . . 186 E6
King's Hill BA3 . . . . . 94 F7
Kingshill CE Prim Sch BS48 . 8 D3
Kingshill Gdns BS48 . . . . . 8 C1
Kingshill La BS40 . . . . . 56 C4
Kingsholme Ct BS23 . . . . . 30 E1
Kings La TA7 . . . . . 156 B8
King's La
Binegar BA3 . . . . . 95 E1
Clevedon BS21 . . . . . 6 D5
6 Weston-super-Mare BS23 . . . . . 48 E8
Kingsland TA23 . . . . . 202 D7
Kingsland Grange 1 BA21 . . . . . 218 C6
Kingsland La TA24 . . . . . 148 D5
Kingsland Rd BA4 . . . . . 205 B5
Kingsland Trad Est BS2 . . . 227 C3
Kings Lear TA19 . . . . . 183 F4
Kingsley Cl TA1 . . . . . 212 C1
Kingsley Ho BS2 . . . . . 227 C2
Kingsley Rd
Clevedon BS21 . . . . . 6 D2
Radstock BA3 . . . . . 78 C1
Weston-super-Mare BS23 . . . 48 F3
KINGSMEAD 228 A2
Kingsmead BS48 . . . . . 8 C2
Kingsmead Cl
Holcombe BA3 . . . . . 116 C8
Wiveliscombe TA4 . . . . . 210 C3
Kingsmead Com Sch TA4 . 210 C3
Kingsmead Ct 8 BA1 . . . . . 228 B2
Kingsmead N BA1 . . . . . 228 B2
Kingsmead Sq BA1 . . . . . 228 B2
Kingsmead St BA1 . . . . . 228 B2
Kingsmead W BA1 . . . . . 228 B2
Kingsmill BS9 . . . . . 5 D5
King's Mill Rd DT10 . . . . . 190 D3
Kingsmoor Dro TA10 . . . . . 173 A2
Kingsmoor Prim Sch TA7 . 136 E2
Kings Oak Mdw BS39 . . . . . 58 E2
Kings of Wessex Sch The BS27 . . . . . 90 B7
King's Pl TA6 . . . . . 208 F5
King Sq
Bridgwater TA6 . . . . . 208 F5
Bristol BS2 . . . . . 227 A4
King Square Ave BS2 . . . . . 227 A4
Kings Rd
Sherborne DT9 . . . . . 225 D5
Stoke sub Hamdon TA14 . . . . 185 F5
Wells BA5 . . . . . 140 C8
Wrington BS40 . . . . . 35 D1
King's Rd
Bristol BS8 . . . . . 226 A3
Clevedon BS21 . . . . . 6 D5
Doulting BA4 . . . . . 141 E7
Portishead BS20 . . . . . 1 F4
Kings Ride TA20 . . . . . 223 B6
King's Sch BA10 . . . . . 215 E6
Kings Sq BS30 . . . . . 25 D8
King St
Bridgwater TA6 . . . . . 209 A5
Bristol BS1 . . . . . 227 A2
Frome BA11 . . . . . 119 F5
Glastonbury BA6 . . . . . 206 D5
Highbridge TA9 . . . . . 104 D3
Yeovil BA21 . . . . . 219 B6
Kingston BA20 . . . . . 219 A5
Kingston Ave
Clevedon BS21 . . . . . 6 E3
Saltford BS31 . . . . . 25 C3
Kingston Bldgs 5 BA1 . . . 228 C2
Kingston Cl
Street BA16 . . . . . 207 D6
Taunton TA2 . . . . . 212 E7
Kingston Dr BS48 . . . . . 18 C8
KINGSTONE 221 E2
Kingstone Cross TA19 . . . . 221 F2
Kingstone Hill TA19 . . . . . 221 F2
Kingstone Rd TA17 . . . . . 195 B6
Kingston La
Felton BS40 . . . . . 37 F8
Maiden Bradley BA12 . . . . . 144 C1
Kingston Mead BS40 . . . . . 37 F7
Kingston Mews 3 TA2 . . . 212 F6
Kingston Rd
Bath BA1 . . . . . 228 C2
Nailsea BS48 . . . . . 18 C8
Taunton TA2 . . . . . 212 E7
KINGSTON ST MARY 168 E8
Kingston St Mary CE Prim Sch TA2 . . . . . 168 D8
KINGSTON SEYMOUR 16 C2
Kingston View BA21 . . . . . 219 B6
Kingston Way BS48 . . . . . 18 C8
Kingston Well La TA20 . . . 194 C2
KINGSWAY 44 C3
Kingsway
Bath BA2 . . . . . 44 C3
Holcombe BA3 . . . . . 116 C8
Mark BS26, TA9 . . . . . 87 D3
Portishead BS20 . . . . . 1 F4
Taunton TA1 . . . . . 168 F1
Kingsway Ctr BA11 . . . . . 119 F4
Kingsway Rd TA8 . . . . . 104 B7
Kingswear 3 BS22 . . . . . 32 A2
Kings Weston Ave BS11 . . . . 4 E8
Kings Weston La BS11 . . . . . 5 A8
Kings Weston Rd BS9 . . . . . 5 B8
Kingsweston Sch BS11 . . . . . 5 A8
Kings Wlk BS13 . . . . . 21 E7
KINGSWOOD 150 E8
Kingswood Chase BA14 . . . . 83 F6
Kingswood Prep Sch BA1 . . 27 E1
Kingswood Rd TA18 . . . . . 224 C4
Kingswood Sch BA1 . . . . . 27 E2
Kingswood Sch Upper Sports Fields
Bath BA1 . . . . . 27 D4
Charlcombe BA1 . . . . . 27 D4
KINGTON MAGNA 177 E2
Kington View BA8 . . . . . 176 E1
Kingwell View BS39 . . . . . 59 D2
KINGWESTON 157 E2
Kingweston Rd
Butleigh BA6 . . . . . 157 E3
Charlton Mackrell TA11 . . . . 173 E8
King William Ave BS1 . . . . 227 A2
King William Rd TA7 . . . . . 137 D2
Kinsale Rd BS14 . . . . . 23 C7
Kinvara Rd BS4 . . . . . 22 E8
Kinver Terr TA8 . . . . . 104 A7
Kipling Ave BA2 . . . . . 44 F4
Kipling Rd
Radstock BA3 . . . . . 78 C1
Weston-super-Mare BS23 . . . 49 A3
Kippax Ave BA5 . . . . . 203 F5
Kipscombe Cross EX35 . . . 122 A6
Kirk Dr TA7 . . . . . 154 E6
Kirke Gr TA2 . . . . . 213 B8
Kirkham St TA11 . . . . . 211 E4
Kirlegate BA6 . . . . . 138 C4
Kissing Batch BA11 . . . . . 119 C6
Kissmedown La BA22 . . . . . 186 C5
KITBRIDGE 198 A6
Kitch Dro TA7 . . . . . 154 D3
Kitchener Rd TA2 . . . . . 168 A6
Kitchens La TA13 . . . . . 185 A1
Kite La BA4 . . . . . 159 C6
Kite Pl BA22 . . . . . 218 A5
Kites Croft BA5 . . . . . 110 E7
Kite's Nest La SP8 . . . . . 161 F1
Kite Wlk 2 BS22 . . . . . 49 E8
Kithill TA18 . . . . . 224 D4
Kitland La BS40 . . . . . 53 C8
Kitley Hill BA3 . . . . . 78 C4
Kitridge La TA24 . . . . . 146 B7
Kitrow La TA24 . . . . . 131 A6
Kit's La TA4 . . . . . 166 A6
Kitswall La TA24 . . . . . 130 D5
Kitt Hill DT9 . . . . . 225 C4
KITTISFORD 166 B1
Kitton La DT9 . . . . . 188 A4
Kitts TA21 . . . . . 222 D4
Kittwake Dr
6 Portishead BS20 . . . . . 2 F6
Portishead BS20 . . . . . 2 F7
KITTWHISTLE 199 D6
Kittyhawk Cl 4 BA3 . . . . . 97 B8
Knacker's Hole La
Churchinford TA3 . . . . . 192 A6
Thorncombe DT6, TA20 . . . . 199 C4
Knap Hill BA3 . . . . . 117 B2
Knaplock La TA5 . . . . . 134 F4
KNAPP 169 F4
Knapp TA16 . . . . . 195 F7
Knapp Cotts TA4 . . . . . 151 E1
Knapp Hill Cl BA5 . . . . . 113 A2
Knapp La
Bishops Lydeard TA4 . . . . . 151 E1
North Curry TA3 . . . . . 170 B4
Knapp Rd
Creech St Michael TA3 . . . . . 169 F4
North Curry TA3 . . . . . 170 A4
Knapps Cl BS25 . . . . . 69 F8
Knapps Dr BS25 . . . . . 69 F8
Knapps La
Chard TA20 . . . . . 194 C4
Langport TA10 . . . . . 172 B5
Knapp The TA24 . . . . . 130 B4
Knap The BA8 . . . . . 176 E1
Knaptons Hill BA11 . . . . . 118 C6
Kneller Cl BS11 . . . . . 5 A8
Knight Cl
Monkton Heathfield TA2 . . . . 213 F8
Weston-super-Mare BS22 . . . 32 A5
KNIGHTCOTT 50 F3
Knightcott BS29 . . . . . 50 F3
Knightcott Gdns BS29 . . . . . 50 F3
Knightcott Ind Est BS29 . . . . 50 E3
Knightcott Pk BS29 . . . . . 51 A3
Knightcott Rd
Abbots Leigh BS8 . . . . . 10 F8
Banwell BS29 . . . . . 50 F3
Knightlands La TA10 . . . . . 172 F4
KNIGHTON 184 D7
Knighton TA5 . . . . . 134 B7
Knighton Dro TA10 . . . . . 184 D7
Knight Rd BA5 . . . . . 203 C2
Knightsbridge Pk BS13 . . . . 22 E4
Knightsbridge Way TA6 . . 209 D6
Knight's Cross TA21 . . . . . 181 A5
Knight's Ct BA11 . . . . . 119 F4
Knight Shute La TA20 . . . . . 193 D6
Knight's La
Axminster EX13 . . . . . 198 A4
Higher Chillington TA19 . . . . 194 E5
Knights Maltings BA11 . . . 120 A3
Knights Rd TA21 . . . . . 180 D8
Knights Templar CE Meth Com Sch TA23 . . . . . 202 D6
Knightstone TA3 . . . . . 169 D3
Knightstone Cl
Axbridge BS26 . . . . . 70 C1
Kingsbury Episcopi TA12 . . . . 185 B8
Peasedown St John BA2 . . . . . 79 B8
Knightstone Cswy BS23 . . . . 48 C8
Knightstone Ct
Burnham-on-S TA8 . . . . . 104 B6
Clevedon BS21 . . . . . 6 D1
Stalbridge DT10 . . . . . 190 B4
Taunton TA2 . . . . . 213 A6
Weston-super-Mare BS23 . . . 30 D1
Knightstone Gn BS23 . . . . . 48 E6
Knightstone Ho
1 Bristol BS2 . . . . . 227 A4
Weston-super-Mare BS23 . . . 48 D8
Knightstone Hts BA11 . . . . 119 F3
Knightstone Mead TA22 . . 148 A2
Knightstone Pk 4 BS23 . . . 48 E5
Knightstone Pl
Bath BA1 . . . . . 27 B1
7 Weston-super-Mare BS22 . 31 F2
Knightstone Rd BS23 . . . . . 48 C8
Knightstone Sq BS14 . . . . . 23 C5
Knightstone Wlk BS2 . . . . . 226 C4
Knights Yd BA7 . . . . . 214 C5
Knobsbury Hill BA3 . . . . . 98 D6
Knobsbury La BA3 . . . . . 98 C7
KNOLE 173 A4
Knole Cswy
Knole TA10 . . . . . 173 A4
Long Sutton TA10 . . . . . 172 F4
Knole Pit La TA10 . . . . . 173 A4
Knoll Ct BS9 . . . . . 5 D3
Knoll Green La TA5 . . . . . 134 F2
Knoll Hill BS9 . . . . . 5 D3
Knoll Hill View BA11 . . . . . 143 C6
Knoll Ho 5 BA11 . . . . . 119 F4
Knoll La BA4 . . . . . 142 E3
Knoll Pk TA8 . . . . . 65 F2
Knoll The BS20 . . . . . 2 D7
Knoll View
Burnham-on-S TA8 . . . . . 104 C8
4 Frome BA11 . . . . . 119 F4
Knotcroft La TA2 . . . . . 153 D1
Knotts Paddock DT9 . . . . . 225 E4
KNOWLE 136 D2
Knowle Bridge Rd BA9 . . . 160 D2
Knowle Cross DT8 . . . . . 199 F6
Knowle Dro
Middlezoy TA7 . . . . . 155 A4
Westonzoyland TA7 . . . . . 154 F5
Knowle End TA7 . . . . . 136 E3
Knowle Hill BS40 . . . . . 57 C7
Knowle La
Chard TA20 . . . . . 194 B6
Dunster TA24 . . . . . 201 B1
Misterton DT8, TA18 . . . . . 224 E2
Shepton Mallet BA4 . . . . . 204 E5
Wookey BA5 . . . . . 110 E1
Knowle Moor Dro BA5 . . . . 110 C2
Knowle Rd TA6 . . . . . 209 C6
KNOWLE ST GILES 194 B6
Knowles Rd BS21 . . . . . 6 C2
Knowleyards Rd TA7 . . . . . 155 B4
KNOWSTONE 162 A2
Korresia Wlk TA6 . . . . . 208 D1
Kuching Rd BA22 . . . . . 174 A2
Kylross Ave BS14 . . . . . 23 B5
Kyrle Gdns BA1 . . . . . 28 F3
Kyte Rd BA4 . . . . . 205 C5

L

Labbott The BS31 . . . . . 24 E5
Labourham Dro BS27 . . . . . 90 B5
Labourham Way BS27 . . . . . 90 B6
Laburnum Cl
Bridgwater TA6 . . . . . 209 D4
Frome BA11 . . . . . 120 B7
Midsomer Norton BA3 . . . . . 96 F8
Somerton TA11 . . . . . 211 D4
Laburnum Cotts 7 TA21 . . 222 D5
Laburnum Cres TA18 . . . . . 224 D7
Laburnum Ct
7 Taunton TA1 . . . . . 213 A4
Weston-super-Mare BS23 . . . 49 B7
Laburnum Dr TA11 . . . . . 211 D4
Laburnum Gr BA3 . . . . . 96 F8
Laburnum Lodges TA9 . . . . 136 A8
Laburnum Rd
Wellington TA21 . . . . . 222 E5
Weston-super-Mare BS23 . . . 49 B7
Laburnum St TA1 . . . . . 213 A4
Laburnum Terr
Batheaston BA1 . . . . . 28 F3
Creech St Michael TA3 . . . . . 169 D4
Laburnum Way BA20 . . . . . 218 D2
Lacey Rd BS14 . . . . . 23 F6
La Ciotat Ho TA6 . . . . . 209 A4
Ladd Cl TA9 . . . . . 104 D3
Ladies Mile BS8 . . . . . 5 F1
Ladman Gr BS14 . . . . . 23 E6
Ladman Rd BS14 . . . . . 23 E5
Ladycroft 5 BS21 . . . . . 6 B1
Ladye Bay BS21 . . . . . 6 D7
Ladye Wake BS22 . . . . . 31 F4
Lady Harriet Acland's Dr TA22 . . . . . 164 A8
Lady Lawn TA3 . . . . . 168 D1
Ladymead BS20 . . . . . 2 F5
Ladymead Cl TA6 . . . . . 208 B4
Ladymeade
Backwell BS48 . . . . . 19 A7
Ilminster TA19 . . . . . 221 B3
Ladymead Ho BA1 . . . . . 228 C3
Ladymead La BS40 . . . . . 52 F5
Ladymead Rd TA2 . . . . . 168 F6
Lady St TA22 . . . . . 163 D7
Lady Victoria's Dr TA22 . . 163 E6
Ladywell BS40 . . . . . 35 D2
Laggan Gdns BA1 . . . . . 27 E1
Laggan Ho BA1 . . . . . 27 E1
Lagger Hill TA5 . . . . . 133 C5
Lahs Pl BA11 . . . . . 101 E4
Lakefields BA22 . . . . . 197 B8
Lakemead Gdns 3 BS13 . . . 21 F4
Lakemead Gr BS13 . . . . . 21 F6
Lake Mews BA22 . . . . . 219 B1
Lake Rd BS20 . . . . . 2 D7
Lake Shore Dr BS13 . . . . . 22 C6
Lakeside TA9 . . . . . 104 E4
Lakeside Cl BS40 . . . . . 55 D5
Lakeside Ct BS24 . . . . . 32 B1
Lakeside Pk
Bridgwater TA6 . . . . . 209 A3
Vobster BA11 . . . . . 117 E8
Lakeview Cres TA9 . . . . . 104 E3
Lake Wall TA7 . . . . . 154 E4
Lambert Cl DT9 . . . . . 217 C2
Lambert Ct DT9 . . . . . 217 D2
Lambert La TA19 . . . . . 194 F5
Lambert Pl BS4 . . . . . 22 D6
Lambert's Hill BA4 . . . . . 204 F3
Lamberts Marsh BA14 . . . . . 83 E2
Lamb La TA6 . . . . . 208 F4
Lambourne Ct TA18 . . . . . 224 D7
Lambourne Way BS20 . . . . . 2 F5
Lambourn Rd BS31 . . . . . 25 A4
Lambpark Ct TA3 . . . . . 191 F6
LAMBRIDGE 28 C2
Lambridge 6 BA1 . . . . . 28 C1
Lambridge Bldgs 1 BA1 . . 28 C1
Lambridge Grange 6 BA1 . 28 C2
Lambridge Mews 5 BA1 . . 28 C1
Lambridge Pl BA1 . . . . . 28 C1
Lambridge St BA1 . . . . . 28 C1
Lambrok Cl BA14 . . . . . 83 F6
Lambrok Rd BA14 . . . . . 83 F6
Lambrook Cl TA1 . . . . . 213 B4
Lambrook Gate TA13 . . . . . 184 F5
Lambrook Ho BA9 . . . . . 216 C4
Lambrook La BA22 . . . . . 174 E2
Lambrook Rd
Shepton Beauchamp TA19 . . 184 E4
Taunton TA1 . . . . . 213 B4
Lambrook St BA6 . . . . . 206 E4
Lambrook Way TA1 . . . . . 213 C4
Lambs Field DT9 . . . . . 225 E5
Lamb St BS2 . . . . . 227 C3
Lamington Cl BS13 . . . . . 21 F6
Lamont Ho 7 BA1 . . . . . 28 C1
Lampard's Bldgs BA1 . . . . . 228 B4
Lamparts Way TA19 . . . . . 183 C2
Lampeter Rd BS9 . . . . . 5 F7
Lampley Rd BS21 . . . . . 16 D2
Lampreys La TA13 . . . . . 220 C3
Lampton Ave BS13 . . . . . 22 E3
Lampton Gr BS13 . . . . . 22 E3
Lampton Rd BS41 . . . . . 10 F1
LAMYATT 159 F6
Lancaster Cl TA6 . . . . . 136 B2
Lancaster House Sch BS23 . 48 F8
Lancer Ct TA21 . . . . . 222 D6
Lanch La SP8 . . . . . 177 F5
Lancin La TA20 . . . . . 193 B2
Lancock St TA21 . . . . . 222 A5
Lancombe La BA10 . . . . . 215 C3
Landacre La TA24 . . . . . 146 A7
Landemann Cir BS23 . . . . . 30 E1
Landemann Path 2 BS23 . . 48 E8
Landing Lights BS14 . . . . . 22 E5
Landlord's Hill TA21 . . . . . 179 E7
Landmark Ct BS1 . . . . . 226 C1
Landmead BA6 . . . . . 206 D5
Landmoor La TA10 . . . . . 172 D4
Landsdown Mews BA11 . . . 119 D5
Landseer BA8 . . . . . 176 D4
Landseer Cl BS22 . . . . . 31 F3
Landseer Rd BA2 . . . . . 44 B6
Lands End BS28 . . . . . 107 E1
Landshire La
Charlton Horethorne DT9 . . . 176 A1
Chilton Polden TA7 . . . . . 137 A3
Henstridge BA8 . . . . . 190 C6
Odcombe BA22 . . . . . 186 C1
LANE END 144 D8
Lane End
Corsley Heath BA12 . . . . . 144 D8
Upper Littleton BS40 . . . . . 38 C5
Lane Foot TA24 . . . . . 129 D7
Lane Head TA24 . . . . . 123 E4
Lanesborough Rise BS14 . . 23 D7
Lanes End Hill BA11, BA12 . 144 D8
Laneys Dro BS24 . . . . . 49 E5
LANGALLER 169 C6
Langaller Hill TA22 . . . . . 163 D4
Langaller Way TA2 . . . . . 169 C4
Langdon Cl TA20 . . . . . 223 D6
Langdon Rd BA2 . . . . . 44 B4
Langdons DT9 . . . . . 225 E5
Langdons Way TA20 . . . . . 198 C8
Langdown Ct BS14 . . . . . 23 E5
Langer's La TA19 . . . . . 194 E5
LANGFORD 212 A8
LANGFORD BUDVILLE 166 E2
Langford Budville CE Prim Sch TA21 . . . . . 166 F1
Langford Cl
Fivehead TA3 . . . . . 170 F1
Plummer's Hill BS39 . . . . . 77 D6
Langford Ct 14 TA1 . . . . . 213 A4
Langford Ct Cotts BS40 . . . . 53 E5
Langford Gate TA4 . . . . . 166 F2
Langford La
Fivehead TA3 . . . . . 170 F2
Lower Langford BS40 . . . . . 53 E5
Norton Fitzwarren TA2 . . . . . 168 C6
Langford Rd
Bristol BS13 . . . . . 21 F8
Lower Langford BS40 . . . . . 53 C6
Weston-super-Mare BS23 . . . 49 A6
Langfords La BS39 . . . . . 77 C8
Langford's La BS39 . . . . . 59 D1
LANGHAM
Chard 223 C7
Gillingham 177 F4
Langham Dr TA1 . . . . . 212 C1
Langham Gdns TA1 . . . . . 212 C1
Langham La SP8 . . . . . 177 F5
Langham Pl BA11 . . . . . 82 F1
Langhill Ave BS4 . . . . . 22 D7
Langland La TA7 . . . . . 137 D2
Langlands 8 TA14 . . . . . 185 F4
Langlands La TA3 . . . . . 169 F2
Langland's La TA9 . . . . . 104 B1
LANGLEY 210 C6
Langley Cres BS3 . . . . . 11 E1
Langley Cross TA4 . . . . . 210 B6
LANGLEY MARSH 210 A7
Langleys Cotts BA3 . . . . . 96 B8
Langley's La BA3, BS39 . . . . 77 C1
Langmead Dro
Middlezoy TA7 . . . . . 155 A4
Westonzoyland TA7 . . . . . 154 F5
Langmead La TA7 . . . . . 155 A4
Langmead Pl TA18 . . . . . 224 C4
Langmead Rd TA18 . . . . . 224 C4
Langmead Sq TA18 . . . . . 224 C4
Langmoor Dro TA7 . . . . . 154 F6
Langmoor La
Axminster EX13 . . . . . 198 D2
South Perrott DT8 . . . . . 196 B1
LANGPORT 172 B5
Langport Gdns BS48 . . . . . 18 E8
Langport Rd
Langport TA10 . . . . . 172 A4
Long Sutton TA10 . . . . . 172 E5
Middlezoy TA7 . . . . . 155 B4
Somerton TA11 . . . . . 211 B4
Weston-super-Mare BS23 . . . 48 E5
Lang Rd TA18 . . . . . 224 C4
LANGRIDGE 27 E7
Langridge La BA1 . . . . . 27 D8
Lang's Cnr TA19 . . . . . 183 B1
Langton Ho 9 BS2 . . . . . 227 C3
Langworthy Orch TA19 . . . 183 C1
LANSDOWN
Bath 27 E1
Langridge 27 B6
Lansdown Cres
2 Bath BA1 . . . . . 27 F1
Timsbury BA2 . . . . . 60 C2
Lansdown Ct BS23 . . . . . 48 F8
Lansdowne Pl BA9 . . . . . 216 C4
Lansdowne Rd TA2 . . . . . 213 A6
Lansdown Gdns BS22 . . . . . 32 B5
Lansdown Gr BA1 . . . . . 228 B4
Lansdown Grove Ct BA1 . . 228 B4
Lansdown Grove Lodge BA1 . . . . . 228 B4
Lansdown Ho BA1 . . . . . 27 F1
Lansdown Hts BA1 . . . . . 27 F1
Lansdown La
Bath BA1 . . . . . 27 B4
Upton Cheyney BS30 . . . . . 26 D8
Lansdown Mans BA1 . . . . . 228 B4
Lansdown Pk BA1 . . . . . 27 E3
Lansdown Pl
Bristol BS8 . . . . . 226 A3
Frome BA11 . . . . . 119 D5
High Littleton BS39 . . . . . 59 D1
Lansdown Pl E BA1 . . . . . 228 B4
Lansdown Pl W 1 BA1 . . . . 27 F1
Lansdown Rd
Bath BA1 . . . . . 27 E2
Bristol BS8 . . . . . 226 A3
Saltford BS31 . . . . . 25 E3
Lansdown View
Bath BA2 . . . . . 44 C5
Faulkland BA3 . . . . . 80 D1
Timsbury BA2 . . . . . 60 C2
Tunley BA2 . . . . . 61 B4
Lanthony Cl BS24 . . . . . 50 A8
Laps Cott TA20 . . . . . 192 F5
Lapwing Cl
Minehead TA24 . . . . . 201 C5
Portishead BS20 . . . . . 2 F6
Lapwing Gdns BS22 . . . . . 31 F1
Larch Ave TA20 . . . . . 223 B5
Larch Cl
Bridgwater TA6 . . . . . 209 D6
Churchill BS40 . . . . . 53 A5
Nailsea BS48 . . . . . 9 A2
Taunton TA1 . . . . . 213 D2
Larch Ct BA3 . . . . . 97 D8
Larches The BS22 . . . . . 32 A3
Larchfield Cl BA11 . . . . . 120 B7
Larchfield Trad Est TA19 . . 221 B1
Larchgrove Cres BS22 . . . . . 31 F1
Larchgrove Wlk BS22 . . . . . 31 F1
Larchwood Ct BA3 . . . . . 79 A3
Lark Cl BA3 . . . . . 97 B8
LARKHALL 28 C2
Larkhall Pl BA1 . . . . . 28 C2
Larkhall Terr BA1 . . . . . 28 C2
Larkhill Rd
Locking BS24 . . . . . 50 B6
Yeovil BA21 . . . . . 218 D7
Lark Pl BA1 . . . . . 44 D7
Lark Rd BS22 . . . . . 31 F1
Larks Mdw DT10 . . . . . 190 C4
Larkspur Cl TA1 . . . . . 213 C1
Larkspur Cres BA21 . . . . . 218 D7
Larkspur Ct TA2 . . . . . 212 D7
Larspur Rd TA6 . . . . . 208 E1
Larviscombe Cl TA4 . . . . . 202 D4
Larviscombe Rd TA4 . . . . . 202 D4
Lasbury Gr BS13 . . . . . 22 C5
Lascelles Ave BA2 . . . . . 45 C8
Lascot Hill BS28 . . . . . 108 C5
LATCHAM 108 F4
Latcham Dro BS27, BS28 . . 109 A4

Latches La BS27 90 D3
Latchmoor Ho BS13 22 A8
Late Broads BA15 64 D7
LATTIFORD 176 D5
Lauder Ct DT9 217 D2
LAUNCHERLEY 140 B5
Launcherley Cross BA5 140 A6
Launcherley Rd BA4, BA5 140 B5
Launder Cl BA6 206 E4
Laura Pl BA2 228 C3
Laurel Ave TA9 86 A2
Laurel Cl
East Coker BA22 197 B8
Frome BA11 120 B7
Taunton TA1 213 C1
Laurel Dr
Nailsea BS48 8 F2
Paulton BS39 77 E5
Weston-super-Mare BS23 48 E2
Laurel Gdns
Chard TA20 223 B5
Timsbury BA2 60 B1
Yatton BS49 17 B1
Laurel La BA22 174 F3
Laurel St BA6 140 A1
Laurels The
Churchill BS25 52 F4
Crewkerne TA18 224 D7
Wembdon TA6 208 C6
Weston-super-Mare BS23 48 E2
Westwood BA15 64 F3
Laurel Terr BS49 17 B1
Lavender Cl BS22 32 A5
Lavender Ct
Frome BA11 120 B7
Street BA16 207 B4
Lavender Gr TA1 212 C3
Lavender Wlk TA6 208 D1
LAVERLEY 140 C2
Laverley Cotts BA6 140 C2
Laverock Ct TA1 212 E5
Lavers Ct TA12 186 A7
Laver's La TA20 198 F5
Lavers Oak TA12 185 E7
LAVERTON 100 F7
Lavington Cl BS21 6 B1
Lavinia Wy TA6 208 D5
LAWFORD 151 B7
Lawfords Gate BS2 227 C3
Lawfords Gate Ho 17 BS2 227 C3
Lawford St BS2 227 C3
Law La
Drayton TA10 171 F3
Langport TA10 172 A3
Lawn La
Galhampton BA22 175 D8
Shapwick TA7 137 F1
Lawn Mdw TA3 169 C3
Lawnmoor La TA10 184 C6
Lawn Rd TA2 212 C8
Lawnside BS48 19 B5
Lawns The
Bristol BS11 4 E7
Combe St Nicholas TA20 193 D6
Weston-super-Mare BS22 32 B3
Yatton BS49 17 A1
Lawn The 1 TA21 222 D6
Lawpool Ct 12 BA5 203 D4
Lawrence Cl
Burnham-on-S TA8 104 D5
Highbridge TA9 104 F4
Somerton TA11 211 D3
Weston-super-Mare BS22 31 E2
Lawrence Hayes BA9 216 D3
Lawrence Hill BA9 216 A2
Lawrence Hill Bsns Ctr
BA9 216 B3
Lawrence Mews BS22 31 E2
Lawrence Rd
Coleford BA3 116 F7
Weston-super-Mare BS22 31 E2
Wrington BS40 35 E2
Laws Dr BS24 49 F7
Lawson Cl
5 Martock TA12 185 E6
Saltford BS31 25 C2
Lawyer's Hill TA5 152 C7
Lax Ct BA5 203 B4
Laxton Cl TA1 213 D5
Laxton Rd TA1 213 E5
Laxton Way BA2 79 D7
Laycock Hill DT9 217 D7
Layfield La TA3 170 C3
LAYMORE 199 C7
Layne Terr TA18 196 B8
Lays Bsns Ctr BS31 24 C4
Lays Dr BS31 24 C5
Lays La BS40 54 D4
Lays The BA11 101 E5
Leach Cl BS21 6 D1
Leaches Cl BA22 186 B6
Leaches Mead 4 TA2 169 C5
Leach Rd TA20 223 D7
Leach's Field TA2 168 D8
Lea Cl BA21 219 B8
Lea Croft BS13 22 A4
Leading Edge The BS8 226 B2
Leadmine La BS40 72 E4
Leadon Gr TA1 213 D4
Leafield Cl TA2 168 B5
Leafy Way BS24 50 B4
Lea Grove Rd BS21 6 C4
Leaholme Gdns BS14 23 A3
Lear's La BA9 177 C6
Leat The 8 TA4 167 F8
Leawood Ct 3 BS23 30 C1
Leaze Cl BA11 119 D5
Leaze Dro BA5 139 A7
Leaze Ho BA11 119 D5
Leaze House Mews BA11 119 D5
Leaze La
Blagdon BS40 72 E8
West Chinnock TA18 196 B8
Yeovil BA21 219 F4
Leazemoor La TA10 172 B8
Leaze Rd BA11 119 D5
Leaze The
Radstock BA3 97 D8
Rode BA2 82 C1
Leazeway Dro TA7 155 C1
Lecher La DT8, TA18 196 B1
Leda Ave BS14 23 A7
Leedham Rd
Locking BS24 50 C5
Locking BS24 50 C5
LEEFORD 122 B5
Leeford La EX35 122 B5
Leeford Rd TA4 165 B7
Leekbeds La TA9 104 A1
Leekbeds Lane TA9 103 F1
Leeming Way BS11 4 C8
Lee Pk TA21 180 F7
Leeside BS20 2 C5
Leet Ct DT9 225 B2
Leeward Cl TA6 209 C4
Leewood Rd BS23 30 F1
Leffman Ct TA11 211 C4
Leggar The TA6 209 A6
Legion Rd BA21 218 F6
Leg La BS40 54 B3
Leg Of Mutton Rd BA6 206 E6
Leg Sq BA4 205 C6
Leg Square Ct BA4 205 C6
Leigh Cl BA1 28 A2
Leigh Court Bsns Ctr BS8 5 A2
Leigh Furlong Rd BA16 207 B4
Leigh La
Cold Ashton BA1 13 B3
Crowcombe TA4 151 A7
Halstock BA22 197 C3
Winsford TA22 147 C2
Winsham TA20 199 A8
LEIGHLAND CHAPEL 149 C7
Leigh-on-Mendip Fst Sch
BA3 117 A3
Leigh Rd
Bristol BS8 226 B4
Leigh u M BA11 117 C2
Street BA16 207 C5
Taunton TA2 213 B8
Leigh St BA3 116 F3
LEIGHTON 142 E6
Leighton Cl BA4 141 E1
Leighton Cres BS24 67 A8
Leighton Dr 10 TA3 169 C5
Leighton La BA4 141 E1
Leighton Lane Ind Est
BA4 141 E1
Leighton Rd BA1 27 A3
LEIGH UPON MENDIP 116 F3
Leigh View Rd BS20 2 E7
Leighwood Dr BS48 8 B1
LEIGH WOODS 11 D6
Leigh Woods Forest Walks*
BS8 5 C1
Leigh Woods National Nature
Reserve* BS8 11 D8
Leinster Ave BS4 22 D8
Lemon La BS2 227 C4
Lenover Gdns BS13 22 B4
Lenthay Cl DT9 225 C2
Lenthay Ct DT9 225 C3
Lenthay La DT9 225 A2
Lenthay Rd DT9 225 B2
Leonard Houlden Ct 7
TA2 213 A8
Leonard La BS1 227 A3
Leonard's Barton BA11 119 E6
Leonides Ave BS24 49 B4
Leopold Bldgs BA1 228 C4
Lerburne The BS28 108 D4
Lesley La 4 TA2 169 B2
Leslie Ave TA2 212 E6
Leslie Rise BA15 64 F3
Les Rosiers Gdns BA9 216 C4
Lester Dr BS22 32 A3
Lester La DT9 176 A2
Letham Ct TA19 221 B4
Lethbridge Pk TA4 151 D1
Lethbridge Rd BA5 203 C4
Level La DT9 176 A2
Level View TA10 172 C5
Leversedge Rd BA11 120 A7
LEWCOMBE 197 E2
Lewins Mead BS1 227 A3
Lewis Cl BA3 96 C4
Lewis Cres BA11 119 F6
Lewisham Gr BS23 49 A8
Lewis Rd
Bristol BS13 22 A8
Taunton TA2 212 E7
Lewis's Dro BA5 138 E7
Lewmond Ave BA5 203 F5
Leycroft Cl TA1 213 B4
Leycroft Gr TA1 213 B4
Leycroft Rd TA1 213 B4
Leyland Wlk BS13 21 F4
Leys Hill BA11 120 A6
Leys La BA11 119 F7
Leys The BS21 6 B1
Leystone Cl BA11 120 A6
Leyton Dr TA6 209 D6
Lias Rd BA16 207 B4
Liberty Gdns BS1 226 C1
Liberty La BS40 54 E2
Liberty Pl TA6 209 B4
Liberty The BA5 203 E5
Lichen Rd
Frome BA11 120 B2
Frome BA11 120 B3
Liddon Hill TA18 195 C5
Liddymore La
Watchet TA23 202 D5
Williton TA4, TA23 202 E4
Liddymore Rd TA23 202 C6
Lightermans Cl TA24 201 B7
Lightgate TA13 220 D5
Lightgate La TA13 220 D4
Lightgate Rd TA13 220 D4
Lilac Cl TA1 213 C2
Lilac Ct BS31 24 C4
Lilac Terr BA3 78 C2
Lilac Way BS22 32 A5
Lilian Terr BS39 77 E5
Lillebonne Cl TA21 222 F6
Lillebonne Wy TA21 222 D7
Lillesdon Terr TA3 170 A2
Lilliana Wy TA6 208 E1
Lillington Cl BA3 79 B2
Lillington Rd BA3 79 B2
Lillington Way TA20 223 C5
Lilly Batch BA11 119 F7
Lillycombe La TA3, EX15 191 B8
Lillypool Cheese & Cider
Farm* BS25 70 F6
LILSTOCK 133 F7
Lilstock Rd TA5 133 E7
Lily La BA8 176 E1
Lily Rd BA11 120 B2
Limber Rd BA22 218 A6
Limbers La BA5 139 B8
Limbury 2 TA12 185 E6
Limbury Cotts 3 TA12 185 E6
Limebreach Wood BS48 8 D3
Limeburn Hill BS40 38 E5
Lime Cl
Frome BA11 120 B7
Locking BS24 50 B4
Minehead TA24 200 D7
Street BA16 207 C5
Weston-super-Mare BS22 32 A1
Lime Cres TA1 213 C2
Lime Ct BS31 24 C4
Lime Gr
Bath BA2 45 B6
Shepton Mallet BA4 205 A6
Lime Grove Gdns BA2 45 B6
Lime Kiln BA21 218 C5
Limekiln La
Bath BA2 45 F4
Chard, Forton TA20 223 D1
Chard, Lydmarsh TA20 194 C3
Cricket St Thomas TA20 194 E2
Leigh u M BA11 117 C3
Oakhill BA3 114 E5
Stoke St Michael BA3 115 F4
Tatworth TA20 193 F1
Lime Kiln La
Castle Cary BA7 214 E4
Clevedon BS21 6 D3
Henstridge BA8 190 A6
Wookey Hole BA5 203 B7
Lime Kiln Rd BS1 226 B2
Limekilns Cl BS31 24 F5
Limepits La TA10 172 D5
Limerick Cl DT9 217 D2
Limerick La BA11 101 F2
Limes Cl TA4 202 E3
Lime St
Bristol BS14 22 E5
Nether Stowey TA5 134 B2
Stogursey TA5 134 C6
Limestone Hill TA5 135 C1
Limestone Link BS40 73 D6
Lime Terr BA3 78 D1
Lime Tree Ave BA20 218 E2
Lime Tree Cl TA6 209 D4
Lime Tree Gr BS20 4 D3
LIMINGTON 174 A1
Limington Rd BA22 173 E1
Limousin Way TA6 209 A1
Limpetshell La TA4 202 E3
LIMPLEY STOKE 64 A6
Limpley Stoke Rd BA15 64 D6
Linch La BA4 142 D2
Lincoln Hill TA19 184 E4
Lincoln Cl BS31 24 C4
Lincoln La BS23 49 B4
Lincombe Rd BA3 97 D8
Lincott View BA2 79 C8
Linden Ave BS23 49 B8
Linden Cl
Bridgwater TA6 209 C4
Bristol BS14 23 E6
Frome BA11 119 D5
Radstock BA3 97 E8
Linden Ct BS21 6 D4
Linden Gdns BA1 44 D8
Linden Gr TA1 212 E5
Linden Hill TA21 222 A6
Linden Rd
Clevedon BS21 6 D4
Yeovil BA20 218 F5
Lindens The BS22 31 E4
Lindisfarne Cl BA15 64 E6
Lindsey Cl BS20 1 F4
Lindsey Cres 1 TA6 153 F3
Linemere Cl BS48 19 D6
Linen Wlk BA1 28 C2
Lines Way BS14 23 C3
Liney Rd TA7 154 F6
Lingfield Ave BA21 219 D7
Linham Rd TA6 208 F6
Linhay Cl EX15 179 E1
Linkhay TA20 198 D8
Linkhay Cl TA20 198 D8
Link La
Burrington BS40 53 F3
Monkton Farleigh BA15 46 F8
Linkmead BA3 96 F2
Link Rd
Nailsea BS48 8 F2
Portishead BS20 2 C5
Links Ct BS23 48 D4
Links Gdns TA8 84 F3
Linkside BS21 6 E6
Links Rd BS23 48 C2
Link The BS27 90 B8
Linley Cl
Bath BA2 44 A5
Bridgwater TA6 209 D7
Linleys The BA1 44 C7
Linne Ho BA2 44 A5
Linnet Cl
Taunton TA1 212 B4
Weston-super-Mare BS22 31 E1
Linnet Gdns 5 BS20 2 F6
Linnet Way
Frome BA11 120 B6
Keynsham BS31 24 C3
Keynsham BS31 24 C3
Midsomer Norton BA3 97 B8
Linnington La TA20 193 B2
Linseed Dr 15 EX13 198 A1
Linsvale Cl BA11 120 C5
Linsvale Dr BA11 120 C5
Lintern Cl BA4 159 C7
Linton's Wlk BS14 23 A7
Lion Cl BS48 8 D2
Lion D'angers TA4 210 D4
Lion Dr DT9 217 E2
Lion Ho 20 BA4 205 B6
Lion Mews TA11 211 E4
Lipe Hill La TA3, TA4 168 B1
Lipe La TA3 169 C3
Lipgate Pl BS20 2 D3
Lippard La TA9 105 F8
Lippetts Way TA7 137 D1
Lippiat Hill BA3 80 C3
Lippiatt La
Cheddar BS27 90 C7
Shipham BS25 70 F8
Timsbury BA2 60 B3
Lippiatt The BS27 90 C8
LIPYEATE 97 E1
Lipyeate La BA3 97 E2
Lisieux Ct TA1 213 D2
Lisieux Way TA1 213 C3
Lisle Rd BS22 32 B4
Listercombe Cl TA19 221 C2
Lister Gr BA15 64 F3
Lister's Hill TA19 221 C2
LISTOCK 170 C2
Litfield Pl BS8 11 F7
Litfield Rd BS8 11 F8
Litt Hill BA3 75 F2
Little Ann St BS2, BS5 227 C4
Little Batch BA5 92 D2
Little Birch Croft BS14 23 A3
Little Bishop St BS2 227 B4
Littlebrook BS39 77 E6
Little Brooks La BA4 205 C4
Little Burrow Dro TA7 155 A1
Little Caroline Pl 4 BS8 11 F5
Little Cl TA2 212 C8
Littledown Rd TA4 148 F3
Little Dro TA7 154 F4
Little Elm Rd TA7 155 C4
Little England TA7 155 C2
Little Entry BA5 203 F5
Littlefield DT9 225 B3
Littlefield Cl BA16 156 E7
Littlefield Dro TA12 185 F8
Littlefield La TA10 172 E4
Little Field La BA5 110 F7
Littlefields Ave BS29 51 B3
Littlefields La TA19 184 F3
Littlefields Rd BS29 51 B3
Littlefields Rise BS29 51 B3
Little George St
Bristol BS2 227 C4
Weston-super-Mare BS23 48 E7
Little Gn BA5 111 A4
LITTLE GREEN 118 B6
Little Halt BS20 1 E4
Little Ham BS21 16 C8
Littleham Cotts TA3 181 E6
Little Headley Cl BS13 22 B7
LITTLE HILL 192 F8
Little Hill TA20 192 F8
LITTLE KEYFORD 119 E1
Little Keyford La BA11 119 E1
Little King St BS1 227 A2
Little La
Farmborough BA2 60 A6
Kingsbury Episcopi TA12 185 A7
Little La Wick TA9 85 F7
Little Leaze La TA7 137 D2
Little Lester TA19 221 C2
LITTLE LONDON 114 F3
Little Marston Rd BA22 174 F1
Little Mdw
6 Bishops Lydeard TA4 167 F8
Ilchester BA22 173 E2
Little Mead TA14 185 F2
Little Mead Cl BS24 49 E3
Little Meadow End BS48 18 E8
Little Moor Rd TA9 106 F3
Littlemore Dro TA7 154 C3
LITTLE NORTON 186 A2
Little Orch
Cheddar BS27 90 C8
Street BA16 207 D7
Weston-super-Mare BS23 48 D1
Little Orchard 32 TA12 185 E6
Little Paul St BS2 226 C4
Little Pen TA8 84 F5
Little Pennard La BA4 159 A8
Little Plover Cl TA24 201 C5
Little Sammons BA22 186 E5
Little Silver Ct TA23 202 C7
Little Silver La TA21 222 D2
Little Solsbury La BA1 28 F4
Little St TA14 185 E2
Little Stanhope St BA1 228 A2
Little Stoke Rd BS9 5 E4
Little Thatch Cl BS14 23 C6
LITTLETON 38 D4
Littleton Hill TA11 211 E6
Littleton La
Wellow BA2 80 C7
Winford BS40 38 D5
Little Trumps BA22 186 B7
LITTLE WESTON 175 B4
Little Weston Rd BA22 175 C4
Little Withey Mead BS9 5 F5
Little Wiveliscombe La
TA4 165 D6
Littlewood BA11 143 C4
Littlewood Cl BS14 23 B3
Littlewood La BS49 18 C2
Littlewood Way BS27 89 F8
LITTON 75 F2
Litton BS24 49 A2
Litton Rd BA3 76 A1
Liver Moor Dro TA11 156 E2
Livingstone Dr 3 BA21 219 F8
Livingstone Rd BA2 44 D5
Livingstone Terr BA2 228 A1
Livingstone Way TA2 212 B6
Llewellyns Almshouses 6
BA5 203 D4
Llewellyn Way BS22 32 B3
Lloyd Cl TA1 212 B1
Loaders La BA21 187 A5
Load La TA7 154 E5
Load Pool TA7 155 C2
Lobelia Cl TA9 104 D5
Lockemor Rd BS13 22 F4
Lockes Paddock BS22 32 C3
Lockett Dr BA7 214 A7
Locketts Barton TA3 170 D7
Lockey Rd BA4 205 B4
Lock Gdns BS13 21 E7
LOCKING 50 A4
Locking Farm Ind Est BS24 50 A5
Locking Head Dro
Locking BS24 49 F5
Weston-super-Mare BS24 50 A6
Locking Moor Rd
Locking BS24 50 B5
Weston-super-Mare BS22 49 D8
Locking Prim Sch BS24 50 B4
Locking Rd BS22, BS23 49 B7
Lockingwell Rd BS31 24 D5
LOCKSBROOK 44 B6
Locksbrook Ct 8 BA1 44 B6
Locksbrook Rd
Bath BA1 44 C6
Weston-super-Mare BS22 32 B5
Locksbrook Trad Est 7
BA1 44 B6
Lock's Hill BA11 119 F3
Lockside BS20 2 E7
Lockside Sq BS20 2 E7
Lock's La BA9 216 C4
Locks Way TA7 136 F3
Lockswell TA7 136 E4
Lockswell Cotts BA4 141 B1
Lockwood Ct 4 BA21 218 F7
Lockyer Dro TA7 156 A5
Lodes La TA2 168 E8
Lodge Cl
Taunton TA1 212 A2
Wellington TA21 222 D6
Yatton BS49 34 B8
Lodge Cotts TA3 181 D6
Lodge Ct
Bristol BS9 5 E4
Castle Cary BA7 214 B4
Lodge Dr
Long Ashton BS41 11 B2
Weston-super-Mare BS23 31 A1
Lodge Fields BA12 144 D3
Lodge Gdns BA2 44 D1
Lodge Hill
Berkley BA11, BA13 120 F5
Bratton Seymour BA9 176 A7
Somerton TA11 211 F4
Westbury-sub-Mendip BA5 110 D5
Yarlington BA9 175 F7
Lodge Hill Ind Pk BA5 110 D5
Lodge La
Axminster EX13 198 B2
Tudhay EX13 198 C3
Wraxall BS48 9 B2
Lodge Pl BS1 226 C3
Lodge Rd
Horningsham BA12 144 D4
Kingsdon TA11 173 D4
Lodge Rocks TA24 131 D3
Lodge St BS1 226 C3
Lodges The BA3 96 D1
LODWAY 4 B5
Lodway BS20 4 C4
Lodway Cl BS20 4 C5
Lodway Gdns BS20 4 C4

Lodwells Orch TA3 170 B4
Lollover La TA10 156 F3
Lombardy Cl 5 BS22 49 E8
London Cross TA4 151 E4
London Dro BA6, BS28 138 D7
London Ho TA4 210 C4
London Rd
Bath BA1 228 C4
Milborne Port DT9 217 E1
London Rd E BA1 29 A3
London Rd W BA1 28 E2
London Sq
28 Martock TA12 185 E6
Portishead BS20 2 E7
London St BA1 228 C4
Longacre BS21 16 B8
Long Acre BA4 205 C4
Longacre Cl TA2 212 E7
Longacre Dro TA7 154 D7
Long Acre Ho BA1 228 C4
Longacre La TA19 194 F6
Long Acre Rd BS14 23 A3
Long Acres Cl BS9 5 D7
LONGALLER 168 B4
LONG ASHTON 11 A1
Long Ashton Bsns Pk BS41 11 B1
Long Ashton By-Pass
Barrow Gurney BS48 20 D7
Bristol BS41 11 C1
Bristol BS41 21 B8
Long Ashton Rd BS41 11 B2
Long Ave BS21 6 B2
Long Barnaby BA3 78 A2
Longbottom BS25 71 A6
Longbridge 16 BA4 205 B6
Longbrook Trad Est BS3 11 E3
Long Cl
Ilminster TA19 221 C2
Yeovil BA21 218 C5
Longcombe Dr BA12 144 F6
Longcombe La TA24 130 E3
LONGCROFT 219 A8
Longcroft Rd BA21 219 C6
LONG CROSS 37 D7
Long Cross
Bristol BS11 4 F8
Doulting BA4 141 F8
Felton BS40 37 D7
Nether Stowey TA5 134 A3
Long Cross Bottom
Doulting BA3 142 A8
Stoke St Michael BA3 116 A1
Longdown Dr BS22 32 B4
Long Dro
Broadway TA19, TA20 183 A2
Buckland St Mary TA20 182 F2
Glastonbury BA5 139 E4
Westbury-sub-Mendip BS27 110 A4
Long Eaton Dr BS14 23 B7
Longfellow Ave BA2 44 F4
Longfellow Rd BA3 97 C8
Longfield BA11 118 A7
Longfield Cl TA4 202 E2
Longforth Rd TA21 222 D6
Longforward Hill
Dinnington TA17 195 A8
Seavington St Mary TA19 184 D1
Longforward La
Dinnington TA17 195 B8
Seavington St Mary TA19 184 D1
Long Furlong La
East Coker BA22 197 C8
Long Sutton TA10 172 E5
Long Ground BA11 119 F3
Long Hay Cl BA2 44 B5
LONGHEDGE 144 E7
Long Hill
Clewer BS28 89 D2
Shepton Mallet BA4 141 C8
Long Holcombe Cross
EX36 145 E6
Longhorn Dr 7 TA6 209 A1
LONGHOUSE 61 D5
Long La
Backwell BS48 19 C2
Barwick House BA22 219 C1
Bourton SP8 161 D1
Cucklington BA9 177 D5
Dinder BA5 140 D7
Felton BS40 37 B5
Fishpond Bottom DT6 199 B1
Walton BA16 156 D7
Wanstrow BA4 142 F5
West Chinnock TA18 196 B7
Wheddon Cross TA24 129 C2
Wootton Courtenay TA24 129 E8
Wrington BS40 36 B2
Yeovil BA22 187 C1
Long Lakes TA4 202 E4
Longlands La
East Coker BA22 197 C8
Westbury-sub-Mendip BA5 110 E7
Longleat Cl BA11 119 F3
Longleat Ct BA11 119 E4
Longleat Forest Holiday Village★ BA12 144 F5
Longleat House★ BA12 144 D6
Longleat La BA3 116 C8
Longleat Rd BA3 116 B8
Longleat Rly★ BA12 144 C6
Longleat Safari & Adventure Park★ BA12 144 D6
Longleaze Gdns BS24 49 F3
LONG LOAD 172 E2
Long Load Rd TA12 185 E8
Longman's Lea BA4 159 C7
Longmarsh La TA10 172 E6
Longmead TA4 165 E8
Long Mead BA21 218 C5
Longmead Cl
Norton St Philip BA2 81 F4
Taunton TA1 212 D2
Wellington TA21 222 B8
Longmead Cotts TA21 222 B8
Longmead Croft BS13 21 F4
Longmeadow Rd BS31 24 C4
Longmead Way TA1 212 D2
Long Moor Dro TA7, TA9 137 A7
Long Orchard Hill TA19 221 E3
Longreach Gr BS14 23 D6
Long Ride Dro BA6 157 F3
Longridge Way BS24 49 F7
Long Row BS1 227 B2
Long Run BA22 186 C2
Longrun La TA1 212 D4
Longs Field TA3 170 C4
Long St
Croscombe BA5 204 B7
Galhampton BA22 175 E8
High Ham TA10 156 A1
Sherborne DT9 225 E4
Williton TA4 202 E3
Longstone Ave TA6 209 C5
Longstone Cl TA5 134 B2
Longstrings La TA18 224 C8
LONG SUTTON 172 F4
Long Sutton CE Prim Sch
Long Sutton TA10 172 E4
Long Sutton TA10 172 E4
Long-Thorn BS48 18 F6
Longthorne Pl BA2 44 F2
Long Thorn La BS40 55 E7
Longton Grove Rd 3 BS23 48 E8
Longton Ind Est BS23 48 F6
Long Valley Rd BA2 43 F5
Longvernal BA3 77 F1
Longvernal Prim Sch
Midsomer Norton BA3 77 E1
Midsomer Norton BA3 77 F1
Longway Ave BS13, BS14 22 F4
Longwood Ho BS8 10 D4
Longwood La
Burlescombe TA21 179 C4
Long Ashton BS8, BS41 10 F4
Lonsdale Ave BS23 48 F4
Lonsdale Rd TA5 135 C2
Look's La BA6 157 C6
Looseall La TA22 163 D8
LOPEN 185 A1
Lopen Head TA13 220 A1
Lopen La TA13 220 C1
Lopen Rd TA13, TA17 195 D8
Lord Bath's Dro BA16 156 D4
Lordsleaze La TA20 223 D3
Lords Meadow La 5
EX16 164 B1
Lords Way TA6 208 E6
Loretto Gdns 5 EX13 198 A1
Loretto Rd EX13 198 A1
Lorna Doone TA23 202 B7
Lorne Pl BA5 203 E5
Lorne Rd BA2 44 D6
Lotment Hill TA11 173 D5
LOTTISHAM 158 D5
Lottisham La BA4, BA6 158 D6
Lottisham Rd BA6 158 C6
Lotts' Ave BS48 19 B5
Lotus Ct BS22 31 C1
Lotus Dr TA6 208 D1
Louisa Gate TA22 163 F7
Louisa St BS2 227 C2
Louvigne Cl TA8 104 C7
Love La
Burnham-on-S TA8 104 C7
Ilminster TA19 221 C3
Marnhull DT10 190 F6
Shepton Beauchamp TA19 184 E4
Wincanton BA9 216 F5
Lovelands DT2 197 A1
Lovelinch Gdns BS41 10 F1
Lovell Dr BS39 57 C4
Lovell's Dro BA4 140 A4
Lovells Mead DT10 190 F6
Lovells Mill BS39 57 D4
Lovells The BS20 4 B4
Loveridge La TA20 198 D8
Lovers La BA3, BS39 78 A5
Lovers Wlk BA5 203 D5
Lovers' Wlk
4 Cannington TA5 135 B2
Weston-super-Mare BS23 48 D8
Loves Hill BA2 60 A1
Loves La BA14 83 C7
Love's La BA2 59 F6
LOVINGTON 158 F1
Lovington CE Prim Sch
BA7 158 F2
Lovington Rd
Alford BA7 159 A1
Galhampton BA22 175 A8
Lowbourne BS14 22 F6
Lower Acreman St 3
DT9 225 D3
Lower Actis BA6 206 E3
LOWER AISHOLT 152 C6
Lower Ansford BA7 214 B7
Lower Backway BA10 215 E6
Lower Batch BS40 39 B3
Lower Bath Rd TA6 209 B6
Lower Beadon TA16 195 F7
Lower Borough Walls
BA1 228 C2
Lowerbourne Terr TA24 124 A3
Lower Boyston La DT9 188 F5
Lower Bristol Rd
Bath BA2 44 B6
Lower Bristol Rd *continued*
Clutton BS39 58 F4
Lower Burlington Rd BS20 2 E7
LOWER BURROW 184 F7
Lower Camden Pl BA1 228 C4
LOWER CANADA 49 F2
Lower Castle St BS1 227 B3
Lower Chapel Ct BA5 113 A1
Lower Cheriton La BA8 176 D4
LOWER CHILTON CANTELO 187 C8
Lower Church La BS2 227 A3
Lower Church Rd
Carlingcott BA2 61 A1
Weston-super-Mare BS23 48 D8
Lower Clapton Farm La
BA9 176 A6
LOWER CLAVERHAM 17 F2
Lower Claverham BS49 17 F3
Lower Clifton Hill BS8 226 B2
Lower College St BS1 226 C2
Lower Coombses TA20 198 D8
Lower Crannel Dro BA6 139 C4
Lower Cross EX15 179 C1
Lower Down Rd BS20 2 B5
LOWER DOWNSIDE 205 C7
LOWER DURSTON 169 F7
Lower East Coker Rd
BA20 218 F1
Lower East Hayes BA1 45 B8
LOWER FAILAND 10 A8
Lower Fairfield TA4 166 F5
Lower Fairmead Rd BA21 219 D8
Lower Fallow Cl BS14 22 F3
Lower Farm DT9 187 E4
Lower Farm La BA2 43 B7
Lower Field Dro TA12 185 C7
Lowerfield La TA19 184 E1
Lower Foxmoor Rd TA21 222 B5
Lower Gay St BS2 227 A4
LOWER GODNEY 138 F5
Lower Guinea St BS1 227 A1
Lower Gully Dro BS28 89 F3
Lower Gunville DT9 217 D2
LOWER HALSTOCK LEIGH 197 B2
LOWER HARMSWELL 12 C3
Lower Hedgemead Rd
BA1 228 C4
Lower High St BS11 4 D7
Lower Hill TA5 133 D6
LOWER HOLDITCH 198 D5
Lower Holway Cl TA1 213 D2
Lower Hyde Rd TA15 186 B4
Lower Innox BA11 119 E6
Lower Kewstoke Rd BS22 31 E3
LOWER KEYFORD 119 F3
Lower Keyford BA11 119 F3
Lower Kingsbury DT9 217 D3
Lower Kingsdown Rd SN13 29 F3
Lower Knowles Rd BS21 6 C2
Lower La
Shepton Mallet BA4 205 C6
Weston Town BA4 142 E5
Lower Lamb St BS1 226 C2
LOWER LANGFORD 53 C5
LOWER LEIGH 207 C6
Lower Linden Rd BS21 6 D3
Lower Lodfin EX16 164 B2
Lower Marshfield Rd
TA24 201 B6
LOWER MARSTON 143 E7
Lower Maudlin St BS1 227 A3
Lower Mdw TA19 221 A4
Lower Mead 14 EX13 198 A1
Lower Meadow Rd TA24 201 B5
LOWER MERRIDGE 152 C5
Lower Middle St TA1 212 F4
LOWER MILTON 203 B8
Lower New Rd BS27 90 A7
Lower Northend BA1 28 F5
Lower North St BS27 90 B8
Lower North Town La
BA22 175 D7
Lower Norton La
Weston-super-Mare BS22 31 E4
Weston-super-Mare, Norton BS22 31 C4
Lower Notlake Dro BS28 89 E4
LOWER ODCOMBE 186 D2
Lower Odcombe BA22 186 C2
Lower Oldfield Pk BA2 228 A1
Lower Orch TA19 184 C5
Lower Parade Ground Rd
BS24 50 C5
Lower Park La TA24 129 E1
Lower Park Row BS1 227 A3
LOWER PEASEDOWN 79 B8
Lower Pitney Rd TA10 172 C7
Lower Pk TA24 200 E7
Lower Queen's BS21 6 D3
Lower Rd
Hinton Blewett BS39 75 E6
Horsington BA8 176 D3
Kingsdon TA11 173 D5
Stalbridge DT10 190 C4
Woolavington TA7 136 E4
Lower Ream BA21 218 C5
LOWER ROADWATER 131 D1
Lower Rocke's Cotts BA6 157 D4
LOWER RUDGE 102 D4
Lower Severalls Gdn★
TA18 196 A6
Lower Shepton Rd BA9 160 B2
Lower Shockerwick La
BA1 29 D5
Lower Shute BA12 144 F3
Lowerside La BA6 206 D7
Lowerside Rd BA6 206 E6
Lower Silk Mill BA4 204 F6
LOWER SOMERTON 211 E3
Lower Somerton TA11 211 F3
Lower St
Buckland Dinham BA11 100 A2
Carhampton TA24 131 B4
Chewton Mendip BA3 94 F7
Curry Mallet TA3 183 C8
Merriott TA16 195 F7
Pilton BA4 140 F3
Rode BA11 101 E8
Upton Noble BA4 142 F2
West Chinnock TA18 196 B8
Lower Stoke BA2, BA3 64 A8
LOWER STRATTON 220 E1
LOWER STRODE 56 A8
Lower Strode BS40 56 A7
Lower Strode Rd BS21 16 A7
LOWER SWAINSWICK 28 C3
LOWER TIPPACOTT 122 A4
Lower Touches TA20 223 E5
Lower Town
Montacute TA15 186 B4
Sampford Peverell EX16 178 D1
Lower Turners Barn La
BA20 218 F2
LOWER VELLOW 132 D1
Lower Vellow TA4 132 D2
LOWER VEXFORD 150 F6
LOWER WEACOMBE 132 E3
LOWER WEARE 88 D8
Lower Wellesley Rd
Wells BA5 140 A6
Wells BA5 203 F1
LOWER WESTFORD 222 A6
LOWER WESTHOLME 140 C3
Lower Westholme Rd
BA4 140 D3
LOWER WESTON 44 C7
LOWER WHATLEY 118 D3
Lower Whitelands BA3 79 B3
Lower Woodcock St BA7 214 C5
Lower Woodrow Rd DT10 189 D2
LOWER WOOLSTON 175 F6
Lower Woolston Rd BA22 175 F6
Lower Wraxhill Rd BA20 218 F1
LOWER WRITHLINGTON 79 C3
LOW HAM 172 B8
Low Ham Rd TA10 172 B8
Lowlands Terr TA1 212 B4
Lowman Cross EX16 178 B2
Lowmoor Ind Est TA21 222 B8
Low's Hill La DT9 188 B3
Lowsome La DT9 188 A5
Lowther Rd BA21 219 E7
LOWTON 181 B5
Lowtrow Cross TA4 165 A8
Low Veale La BS39 58 A4
LOW WATER 119 E6
Loxhams TA10 156 B2
Loxleigh Ave TA6 209 B4
Loxleigh Gdns TA6 209 B4
Loxley Batch TA7 156 A8
Loxley Gdns BA2 44 C4
Loxley Terr TA6 208 F7
LOXTON 68 C4
Loxton Dr BA2 44 B6
Loxton Rd BS23 48 F2
Loxton Sq BS14 23 A6
Lubborn La BA6 158 B5
Lucas La TA20 193 D6
LUCCOMBE 129 D7
Lucerne Cres TA6 208 D1
Luckes La TA4 132 E3
Luckington Cross BA11 98 B2
Lucklands Rd BA1 27 C1
Luckley Ave BS13 22 C5
LUCKWELL BRIDGE 129 C1
Luckwells La TA24 129 E2
Lucott Cross TA24 128 C6
Ludbourne Rd DT9 225 E3
Ludlow Ave TA2 213 A8
Ludlow Cl
Bridgwater TA6 209 A2
Frome BA11 120 C6
Keynsham BS31 24 D5
LUDNEY 194 F7
Ludney Cross TA19 194 F7
Ludney La
Dinnington TA17 195 A8
Ilminster TA19 194 F7
Ludwells Orch BS39 77 E5
LUFTON 186 D3
Lufton Heights Commerce Pk
BA22 218 A7
Lufton La BA22 186 D3
Lufton Manor Coll BA22 186 D4
Lufton Trad Est BA22 218 A7
Lufton Way BA22 218 A6
Luggard's Cross BS21 8 C4
Lugshorn La TA11 211 C8
Lukes Cl TA21 222 D8
Luke's Cl BA3 78 F3
Lukes Gdn TA24 131 B4
Luke St EX16 164 B1
LULLINGTON 101 A4
Lullington La BA11 101 B3
LULSGATE BOTTOM 37 A8
Lulsgate Rd BS13 22 A8
Lulworth Rd BS31 24 E4
Lundy Dr TA8 104 B5
Luns Hill BA6 157 F1
Lunty Mead BS48 18 F6
Lupin Way BA22 218 B5
LUPPITT 191 B1
Luscombe Rd TA4 167 F6
Lush Path DT9 225 E4
Lusty Gdns BA10 215 E5
Luttrell Cl TA2 213 B8
Luttrell Gdns TA24 200 F6
Luttrell Wy TA24 201 C6
Luvers La BS40 54 D1
LUXBOROUGH 148 E8
Luxborough Rd TA6 208 B4
Lux Furlong BS9 5 B7
Luxhay Cl TA2 213 B8
LUXTON 192 A6
Luxton's La BA3, BA4 116 F1
Luxton Way TA4 210 C5
Lyatt La BA5 140 E8
LYATTS 197 B6
Lyatts Hill BA22 197 B6
Lychgate Pk BS24 50 A4
Lyddieth Ct BA15 64 E7
Lyddon Cl TA21 222 D4
Lyddon Rd BS22 32 B3
Lyddon's Hill TA22 148 A1
Lyddons Mead TA20 223 E4
Lydeard Cross TA5 152 E3
Lydeard Down Hill TA4 151 B4
Lydeard Mead TA4 167 E8
LYDEARD ST LAWRENCE 151 B3
Lydeard St Lawrence Com Prim Sch TA4 151 A3
Lyde Ct BA21 219 E6
Lyde Gn BA2 81 E5
Lyde La BA21 219 F6
Lyde Rd BA21 219 E7
LYDFORD FAIR PLACE 158 C3
LYDMARSH 194 C3
Lydon La TA4 165 D5
LYE CROSS 36 C1
Lye Cross Rd BS40 36 C1
Lyefield Rd BS22 31 E4
LYE HOLE 36 E2
Lye Hole La BS40 36 D2
Lye La BA4 158 F6
Lye Mead BS40 38 A6
LYE'S GREEN 121 B1
Lyes The BS49 34 D3
Lyewater TA18 224 B6
Lyme Gdns BA1 44 B7
Lyme Rd
Axminster EX13 198 A1
Bath BA1 44 B7
Crewkerne TA18 224 B4
Lymore Ave BA2 44 C5
Lymore Cl BA2 44 C5
Lymore Gdns BA2 44 C5
Lymore Terr BA2 44 C4
LYMPSHAM 67 B1
Lympsham CE Fst Sch
BS24 67 B1
Lympsham Gn BA2 62 D8
Lympsham Rd BS24 67 B1
Lynbrook BS41 10 F1
Lynbrook La BA2 44 F3
Lynch Cl BS22 31 F3
Lynchcombe La BA5 110 F6
Lynch Cres BS25 69 F7
Lynch Hill BA3 96 A3
Lynch La
Cheddar BS27 90 C8
Hardington Mandeville BA22 197 A6
Westbury-sub-Mendip BA5 110 D8
Lynchmead BS25 70 A7
Lynch The BS25 69 F7
Lyncombe Hall BA2 45 A4
LYNCOMBE HILL 45 A4
Lyncombe Hill BA2 228 C1
LYNCOMBE VALE 45 A3
Lyncombe Vale BA2 45 B4
Lyncombe Vale Rd BA2 45 A4
Lyndale Ave
Bridgwater TA6 208 E5
Bristol BS9 5 D5
Lynde Cl BS13 22 B4
Lyndhurst Cres TA6 208 C5
Lyndhurst Gr TA12 185 D7
Lyndhurst Rd
Bath BA2 44 C6
Bristol BS9 5 F7
Keynsham BS31 24 F3
Midsomer Norton BA3 97 B8
Weston-super-Mare BS23 48 E4
Lyndhurst Terr BA1 228 C4
Lynfield Pk BA1 27 C1
Lynfield Rd BA11 119 D5
Lynford La TA11 158 C1
LYNFORD-ON-FOSSE 158 C2
LYNG 170 C7
LYNGFORD 213 A7
Lyngford Cres TA2 213 A7
Lyngford La TA2 168 F6
Lyngford Park Prim Sch
Priorswood TA2 213 B8
Taunton TA2 213 B8
Lyngford Pl TA2 213 A7
Lyngford Rd TA2 213 A7
Lyngford Sq TA2 213 A7
Lynmouth Cl BS22 32 A2
Lynor Cl TA1 213 D3
Lynton Cl BS20 2 E4
Lynton Rd
Burnham-on-S TA8 104 B6
Midsomer Norton BA3 97 B8
Lynwood Cl
Frome BA11 119 D4
Midsomer Norton BA3 97 A8
Lynx Cres BS24 49 B2
Lynx Trad Est BA20 218 D3

Lynx West Trad Est BA20 218 C3
Lyons Court Rd BS14 23 D7
Lyons Ct BS23 48 F7
Lype La TA22 147 E4
Lypstone Cl BS24 50 A8
Lypyatt La BA6 206 F4
Lysander Rd BA20 218 E3
Lysander Ret Pk BA20 219 A3
Lysander Road Rdbt BA20 218 C3
Lyster Cl BA22 173 E1
Lyster Gdns BA22 173 E1
Lyte's Cary* TA11 173 F5
Lytes Cary Rd BS31 25 A3
Lytton Gdns BA2 44 B4
Lytton Gr BS31 25 A5
Lyveden Gdns BS13 22 B5
Lyvedon Way BS41 11 B1

M

Mabels La BA5 113 C5
Macaulay Bldgs BA2 45 C4
Macey's Rd BS13 22 D3
Macfarlane Chase BS23 49 A5
Machine Cross TA22 163 F6
Macies The BA1 27 B3
MACKHAM 191 A4
Mackley La BA2 81 E3
Macleod Cl BS21 6 A2
Macquarie Farm Cl BS49 17 A1
Macrae Rd BS20 4 E4
Madam La
  Weston-super-Mare BS22 31 F2
  Weston-super-Mare BS22 32 A3
  Weston-super-Mare BS22 32 A4
Madam's Paddock BS40 39 B3
Madden Cl TA8 104 C7
Maddocks Pk BA9 216 C3
Maddocks Slade TA8 104 A8
Madeira Ct BS23 48 C8
Madeira Rd
  Clevedon BS21 6 D3
  Weston-super-Mare BS23 30 C1
Madey Mills La TA12 185 E6
Madgeon La TA20 192 E8
Madison Ct 5 TA18 224 C6
Maesbury Rd BS31 25 A2
Maesdown Cl BA4 141 E2
Maesdown Cotts BA4 141 E2
Maesdown Hill BA4 141 E3
Maes Down Ho 10 BA4 205 B6
Maesdown Rd
  Doulting BA4 141 E4
  Evercreech BA4 141 E2
Maesknoll La BS14, BS39 40 B8
Magdalana Ct BS1 227 B1
Magdalen Ave BA2 228 B1
Magdalene Cl BA6 206 D4
Magdalene Ct 9 TA1 212 F4
Magdalene La 10 TA1 212 F4
Magdalene Rd BA3 79 C2
Magdalene St
  Glastonbury BA6 206 D4
  Taunton TA1 212 F4
Magdalen La BA14 83 B7
Magdalen Rd BA2 228 B1
Magdalen Way BS22 32 A3
Magellan Cl BS22 31 F4
Maggs Folly BS39 59 D2
Maggs Hill BA2 60 B2
Maggs La
  Castle Cary BA7 214 C7
  Whitchurch BS14 23 C4
Maglands Rd TA23 202 D6
Magna Cl BA21 219 D8
Magnolia Ave BS22 32 A1
Magnolia Cl
  Frome BA11 120 C7
  Weston-super-Mare BS22 49 E7
Magnolia Rd BA3 78 E1
Magnolia Tree Rd TA6 209 E5
Magpie Cl
  Burnham-on-S TA8 85 B1
  Weston-super-Mare BS22 49 E8
Maiden Beech Acad
  TA18 224 B4
MAIDEN BRADLEY 144 C1
Maiden Bradley BA12 144 E3
MAIDENBROOK 213 D7
Maidenbrook La TA2 169 A6
Maiden Croft La BA6 139 D2
MAIDEN HEAD 21 F1
Maidenhead Cross EX16 179 C2
Maidenhead Rd BS13 22 D3
Maiden Way BS11 4 C8
Maidstone Gr BS24 49 A1
Maincombe Cl TA18 224 C4
MAINES BATCH 35 E3
Main Frome Road BA11 143 C8
Main Rd
  Brockley BS49 18 D2
  Burrowbridge TA7 154 F1
  Cannington TA5 135 C1
  Coxley BA5 139 E6
  Flax Bourton BS48 19 F7
  Huntspill TA9 136 B8
  Hutton BS24 49 E2
  Kilve TA5 133 C5
  Lyng TA3, TA7 170 C7
  Middlezoy TA7 155 B3
  Othery TA7 155 B2
  Shapwick TA7 155 F8
  Westhay BA6 138 B5
  Westonzoyland TA7 154 F5
Main St
  Babcary TA11 174 C7
  Barton St David TA11 158 A3
  Chilthorne Domer BA22 186 E6
  Farrington Gurney BS39 77 A4
  Martock TA12 185 F7
  Walton BA16 156 D7
Majestic Rd TA6 209 C8
Malago Wlk BS13 21 E4
Malden Mead BS14 23 A5
Malherbie Ct TA20 194 B6
Malin Par BS20 2 F6
Mallard Pl TA9 104 C4
Mallard Rd TA24 201 C5
Mallard Way TA6 209 B4
Mallard Wlk 7 BS22 49 E8
Mallet Gr BA2 45 A2
Mallory Cl TA2 212 C6
Mallory Rd BA21 219 F8
Mallow Cl BS21 6 E2
Mall The
  Bath BA1 228 C2
  Bristol, Clifton BS8 11 F7
Malmesbury Ct 6 BA21 218 C6
Malmesbury Way BA21 218 C6
MALMSMEAD 122 C4
Mal's Mead La TA20 194 C3
Malta Way BA22 174 A2
Malt Ho The TA4 210 C4
Malthouse Cl BA9 216 C4
Malthouse Ct
  Frome BA11 119 E3
  Taunton TA1 212 A4
Malthouse La DT9 187 F5
Malthouses TA21 167 A1
Maltings Ind Est The BA1 44 B6
Maltings The
  Chard TA20 223 C3
  Frome BA11 119 F4
  Midford BA2 63 C5
  Sherborne DT9 225 E4
  Weston-super-Mare BS22 31 F2
Maltlands BS22 49 D8
Malvern Bldgs BA1 28 A2
Malvern Cl TA6 209 D6
Malvern Ct BA21 218 D6
Malvern Rd BS23 48 E5
Malvern Terr
  4 Bath BA1 28 A1
  Taunton TA2 212 F6
Malvern Villas 3 BA1 28 A1
Mamba Gr BS24 49 B4
Mamsey La TA4 202 C3
Manchester Cotts BS22 31 E3
Mancroft Ave BS11 4 F7
Mandarin Cl TA6 209 B4
Mandy Mdws BA3 77 F1
Mangle Cave Hill TA18 195 C5
Manilla Cres
  21 Weston-super-Mare
  BS23 30 C1
  Weston-super-Mare BS23 30 C1
Manilla Pl BS23 30 C1
Manilla Rd BS8 226 A3
Manleaze Cvn Pk BA4 205 D3
Manleys Cotts TA2 168 C6
Manmoor La BS21 7 A1
Manning Cl BA5 203 F5
Manning Rd
  Bristol BS4 22 F7
  Cotford St Luke TA4 167 E6
Manning's La BA3 94 F3
Manor Barton TA14 185 E2
Manor Bldgs TA18 196 C4
Manor Cl
  Berrow TA8 84 F6
  Bradford Abbas DT9 187 E1
  Chard TA20 223 C2
  Charlton Horethorne DT9 176 A2
  Cossington TA7 136 F3
  Ditcheat BA4 159 C7
  East Brent TA9 86 D5
  Easton-in-G BS20 4 A4
  Farrington Gurney BS39 77 A3
  Glastonbury BA6 206 D5
  Kingsdon TA11 173 D5
  Portishead BS20 2 A5
  Sandford Orcas DT9 188 C7
  South Perrott DT8 196 C1
  Sparkford BA22 175 A4
  Taunton TA1 212 E3
  Templecombe BA8 189 E8
  Wellow BA2 62 D1
Manor Cl The BS8 11 A8
Manor Copse Rd BA3 79 C2
Manor Court Com Prim Sch
  Chard TA20 223 C3
  Chard TA20 223 C3
Manor Ct
  Backwell BS48 19 A5
  Burnham-on-S TA8 104 B7
  Cossington TA7 136 F3
  Easton BA5 111 A4
  Horsington BA8 176 D2
  Locking BS24 50 B4
  Sherborne DT9 225 D5
  Stawell TA7 137 A1
  Weston-super-Mare BS23 49 A8
Manor Dr
  Bathford BA1 29 C2
  Berrow TA8 84 F6
  Chedzoy TA7 154 D8
  East Coker BA22 197 B8
  10 Merriott TA16 195 F7
  Staplegrove TA2 212 C7
  Taunton TA1 212 E3
Manor Farm
  Chard TA20 223 C3
Manor Farm *continued*
  East Coker BA22 197 B8
Manor Farm Barns TA7 169 E8
Manor Farm Cl
  Paulton BS39 77 D6
  Tatworth TA20 198 C8
  Weston-super-Mare BS24 49 B2
Manor Farm Cres BS24 49 B2
Manor Farm La
  Cossington TA7 136 D1
  Milborne Port DT9 217 D3
Manor Farm Rd
  Barrow Hill DT9 217 C6
  Blackford BA22 175 F5
  Charterhouse BS40 72 D4
  Milborne Wick DT9 189 B7
Manor Furlong BA11 119 E2
Manor Gdns
  Farmborough BA2 59 F6
  Farrington Gurney BS39 77 A3
  Ilchester BA22 173 E1
  Locking BS24 50 A4
  Weston-super-Mare BS22 31 B4
Manor Gn EX14 191 F2
Manor Grange BS24 67 B7
Manor Ho BS2 226 C3
Manor House Gdns BA6 206 D5
Manor House La BS14 23 C6
Manor House Rd BA6 206 D5
Manor La
  Abbots Leigh BS8 10 F8
  Wedmore BS28 108 D5
Manor Mews TA2 212 D8
Manor Orch TA1 212 D2
Manor Park Cl BA3 79 C2
Manor Pk
  Bath BA1 44 B8
  Keinton Mandeville TA11 158 B1
  Norton Fitzwarren TA2 168 B4
  Pawlett TA6 135 F6
  Radstock BA3 79 C2
  Weston-super-Mare BS23 48 E1
Manor Pl TA11 158 B1
Manor Rd
  Abbots Leigh BS8 10 F7
  Bath BA1 27 C1
  Bridgwater TA6 209 C6
  Bristol, Bishopsworth BS13 22 A6
  Burnham-on-S TA8 104 B7
  Chedzoy TA7 154 D8
  Cossington TA7 136 F3
  Edington TA7 137 D2
  Frome BA11 119 E2
  Isle Abbotts TA3 183 F7
  Kingsdon TA11 173 D5
  Milborne Port DT9 217 C3
  Minehead TA24 201 B4
  Pawlett TA6 135 F6
  Radstock BA3 79 C2
  Saltford BS31 25 C2
  Staplegrove TA2 212 C8
  Taunton TA1 212 D3
  Weston-super-Mare BS23 49 A8
  Yeovil BA20 219 A4
Manor Ride TA9 86 B2
Manor St BA22 197 A8
Manor Terr BA3 79 C2
Manor Valley BS23 31 A1
Manor View
  Crewkerne TA18 224 C4
  Golsoncott TA23 131 D1
Manor Villas BA1 27 C1
Manor Way
  Berrow TA8 84 F6
  Failand BS8 10 C4
  Frome BA11 119 E2
Manse La TA7 136 C4
Mansel Cl BS31 25 C3
Manser Rd BS24 50 C5
Mansfield Ave BS23 49 B8
Mansfield Rd TA1 213 A3
Manshay La DT6 199 D1
Manship Gn BA4 205 B4
Manston Cl BS14 23 C7
Mantle St TA21 222 C5
Mantle VC Rd BA22 174 A2
Manvers St BA1 228 C1
Manworthy Cross TA4 166 C4
MAPERTON 176 B5
Maperton Rd DT9 176 A2
Maple Cl
  Bristol BS14 23 D5
  Evercreech BA4 141 F1
  North Petherton TA6 153 F3
  Puriton TA7 136 C4
  Street BA16 207 C5
  Taunton TA2 213 A7
  Weston-super-Mare BS23 49 A8
  Wincanton BA9 216 C2
Maple Ct
  Bridgwater TA6 209 D6
  Bristol BS9 5 F8
  Frome BA11 120 A7
  9 Weston-super-Mare BS23 30 C1
Maple Dr
  Bristol BS9 5 C4
  Burnham-on-S TA8 104 B5
  Crewkerne TA18 224 D7
  Radstock BA3 78 E1
  Yeovil BA20 218 F3
Maple Gdns BA2 44 E4
Maple Gr BA2 44 E4
Maple Ho BS2 227 A4
Maple Leaf Ct BS8 226 A3
Maple Rd
  Curry Rivel TA10 171 D4
  Langport TA10 172 A6
Maple Rise BA3 79 B2
Maples The
  Nailsea BS48 8 C1
  Shepton Mallet BA4 205 C6
Maplestone Rd BS14 23 A3
Maple Tree Ct TA7 136 F3
Maple Wlk BS31 24 D4
Mapstone Cl BA6 206 E3
Marchant Holliday Sch The
  BA8 176 C5
Marchant's Hill BA3 95 F2
Marchant's La BA2 63 F4
Marchants Pass BA1 228 C1
Marchfields Way BS23 49 A5
March La BA22 175 D8
Marconi Cl BS23 49 B7
Marconi Dr TA9 104 D5
Marconi Rd BS20 1 F5
Marden Gr TA1 213 D3
Marden Rd BS31 25 A4
Mardi's La TA11 158 C2
Mardons Cl 2 BA3 97 B8
Mardyke Ferry Rd BS1 226 B1
Mare La TA13 220 C5
Mare's Dro TA7 154 F3
Mares La BA5 110 E7
Margaret Cres TA8 104 A5
Margaret Rd 4 BS13 21 F4
Margaret's Bldgs BA1 228 B3
Margaret's Hill BA1 228 C4
Margery Fish Gdns*
  TA13 220 C8
Marguerite Rd BS13 21 F7
Marigold Rd
  Bridgwater TA5 208 D1
  Frome BA11 120 B3
Marina Row TA6 209 B4
Marindin Dr BS22 32 B4
Marine Ct BA21 219 D5
Marine Dr TA8 104 B5
Marine Hill BS21 6 C5
Marine Par
  Clevedon BS21 6 C4
  Pill BS20 4 C5
  Weston-super-Mare BS23 30 B1
  Weston-super-Mare BS23 48 D6
Mariners Cl
  Backwell BS48 19 A6
  Bridgwater TA6 209 A5
  Minehead TA24 201 B7
Mariner's Cl BS22 31 D1
Mariners Ct TA6 209 A5
Mariners Dr
  Backwell BS48 19 A6
  Bristol BS9 5 D4
Mariners Way TA23 202 D6
Mariner's Way BS20 4 C5
Maritime Heritage Ctr*
  BS1 226 B1
Marjoram Way BS20 2 F5
MARK 106 D4
MARK CAUSEWAY 106 A3
Mark Coll TA9 106 E4
Mark Cswy TA9 106 B4
Market Ave BS22 32 C3
Market Cl
  4 Bampton EX16 164 B1
  Brushford TA22 163 E4
Market Ct
  8 Bridgwater TA6 208 F5
  2 Crewkerne TA18 224 C6
Market Ent Ctr The TA24 129 E1
Market Gate BS2 227 C3
Market House La TA24 200 F7
Market House Mus The*
  TA23 202 C7
Market Ind Est BS49 17 B1
Market La BS23 48 D8
Market Pl
  Burlescombe EX16 179 B4
  Castle Cary BA7 214 C5
  Frome BA11 119 F5
  Glastonbury BA6 206 D4
  Ilchester BA22 173 E1
  Radstock BA3 78 F2
  23 Shepton Mallet BA4 205 B6
  Somerton TA11 211 E4
  Wells BA5 203 E4
  Wincanton BA9 216 C4
  Winford BS40 37 F7
  Wiveliscombe TA4 210 C4
Market Pl The BA11 143 B8
Market Sq
  Crewkerne TA18 224 C6
  South Petherton TA13 220 C4
Market St
  Bridgwater TA6 208 F5
  Crewkerne TA18 224 C6
  Highbridge TA9 104 E3
  Watchet TA23 202 C7
  Wells BA5 203 D4
  Yeovil BA20 219 B5
Market Terr TA9 104 E3
Mark La BS1 226 C2
Marklands BS9 5 E3
Mark Rd
  Burtle TA7 137 D6
  Highbridge TA9 105 A2
MARKSBURY 42 B1
Marksbury Bottom BA2 42 A2
Marksbury CE Prim Sch
  BA2 42 B2
Marksbury La
  Farmborough BA2 60 E7
  Priston BA2 61 A6
Marks Cl TA3 169 C4
Marksmead DT8 199 F8
Marksview Bsns Ctr BA21 219 F7
Mark VA CE Fst Sch TA9 106 A4
Marlborough Ave TA6 209 A2
Marlborough Bldgs
  Bath BA1 228 A3
  Langport TA10 171 F5
Marlborough Cl TA6 209 A2
Marlborough Ct TA8 85 B1
Marlborough Dr BS22 32 B2
Marlborough Flats 8
  BS2 227 A4
Marlborough Hill BS2 227 A4
Marlborough Hill Pl BS2 227 A4
Marlborough La BA1 228 A3
Marlborough Rd BA21 219 E6
Marlborough St
  Bath BA1 228 A4
  Bristol BS2 227 A4
Marl Cl BA21 218 E7
Marle Ground TA19 184 E2
Marlepit Gr BS13 21 F6
Marley Cl TA24 201 A5
Marley's Row TA24 124 A3
Marleys Way BA11 119 C5
Marlfield Wlk BS13 21 E7
Marling Ho TA24 201 B7
Marl La DT9 187 E3
Marlowe Ho 3 BS23 48 F4
Marl Pits 1 BS48 19 A6
Marl Pits La BA11 143 C7
Marne Cl BS14 23 D5
MARNHULL 190 F5
Marnhull Cl DT10 190 F6
Marriage La DT10 190 F3
Marron Cl BS26 70 C2
Marsa Wy 11 TA6 209 B4
Marsden Rd BA2 44 B3
MARSH 192 E5
MARSHALL'S ELM 207 D2
Marshall Way BA11 120 D8
Marshall Wlk BS4 22 D7
MARSHALSEA 199 C3
Marshalsea Est DT6 199 C3
Marshbarn Farm La BA8 176 F3
Marshbridge Cross TA22 163 C7
Marshclose Hill TA22 146 E2
Marsh Cross TA24 200 D1
MARSHFIELD 13 E8
Marshfield Rd TA24 201 B5
Marshfield Way BA1 28 A1
Marsh Gdns TA24 201 E4
Marsh Hill TA22 163 C8
Marsh Hollow BA21 187 A5
Marsh La
  Barrington TA19 184 E5
  Barton St David TA11 158 A3
  Bridgwater TA6 209 B1
  Buckhorn Weston BA9 177 C4
  Cannington TA5 135 C2
  Dunster TA24 201 E3
  Easton-in-G BS20 4 A4
  Farrington Gurney BS39 77 A3
  Henstridge BA8 190 B7
  Holcombe BA3 116 C5
  Penselwood BA9 161 D2
  Pitney TA10 172 D7
  Portbury BS20 3 F6
  South Cheriton BA8 176 E4
  Temple Cloud BS39 59 A1
  Tintinhull BA22 186 A5
  Yeovil BA21 218 F8
  Yeovil Marsh BA21 187 A5
Marsh Lane Ind Est BS20 3 F7
Marsh Pottinson Ho 16
  BA20 219 B4
Marsh Rd
  Bristol BS3 11 F3
  Rode BA11 82 F1
  Standerwick BA11 102 D1
  Yatton BS49 34 B8
Marsh St
  Avonmouth BS11 4 C8
  4 Bristol BS1 227 A2
  Dunster TA24 201 E3
MARSH STREET 201 F3
Marshway TA3 170 D1
MARSHWOOD 199 C2
Marshwood CE Prim Sch
  DT6 199 C2
Marshwood Cross DT6 199 E1
Marson Rd BS21 6 D3
MARSTON BIGOT 143 D7
Marston Cl
  Frome BA11 119 D2
  Taunton TA1 212 E1
MARSTON GATE 119 C1
Marston La BA11 119 D2
MARSTON MAGNA 174 F1
Marston Mead BA11 119 D2
Marston Rd
  Frome BA11 119 D1
  Nunney BA11 143 D8
  Sherborne DT9 225 B5
Marston Trad Est BA11 119 E2
Martcombe Rd BS20 4 C2
Martha's Orch BS13 21 E7
Martindale Ct BS22 49 D8
Martindale Rd BS22 49 D8
Martingale Wy BS20 2 E6
Martins TA3 169 C4
Martins Bldgs 4 TA21 222 D5
Martins Cl
  Evercreech BA4 141 E1
  Wellington TA21 222 D5
  Wells BA5 203 B3
Martin's Cl TA8 85 A3
Martins Gr BS22 31 E2
Martins La BA4 205 E5
Martins Paddock BA4 142 A6
Martin St BA6 158 A5

Martins The BS20 3 A6
Martland Cl TA7 136 E3
Martlet Rd TA24 200 F7
MARTOCK 185 D6
Martock BS24 48 F2
Martock Bsns Pk TA12 185 D7
Martock CE Prim Sch TA12 185 D6
Martock La TA12 185 F7
Martock Rd
Keynsham BS31 25 A3
Long Sutton TA10 172 E4
Mart Rd TA24 201 B7
Mart Road Ind Est TA24 201 B6
Mart The 6 BS23 48 E7
Martyn Cl TA5 135 B5
Marwin Cl TA12 185 E7
Marwood Cl TA8 104 C8
Marwood Rd BS4 22 E8
Mary Brown Davis La 6 BA5 139 D8
Marybush La BS2 227 B3
Mary Elton Prim Sch BS21 6 B1
Mary Hart Cl BA16 207 B7
Mary La 10 EX16 164 B1
Mary Rd BA5 203 C5
Mary St
Taunton TA1 212 F3
Yeovil BA21 219 B5
Masefield Ho BS23 49 A4
Mason La TA15 186 B4
Masons Way BA11 119 D1
Mason's Way BS27 90 C7
Mason Way BA4 205 A4
Massingham Pk TA2 213 B6
Materman Rd BS14 23 E5
Matfurlong Cl TA12 185 D5
Matthews Cl BS14 23 F6
Matthews Rd
Taunton TA1 212 B1
Yeovil BA21 219 C5
Mattock's Tree Hill TA3 169 E1
Mattravers Wy TA1 168 F4
Matt's La TA14 185 F4
Mattys Cross EX14 191 D3
MAUDLIN 199 C8
Maudlin Cross TA20 199 C8
Maudlin La TA20 199 C8
Maudslay Field BA22 197 C8
MAUNDOWN 165 F7
Maundown Rd TA4 166 A8
Maunsell Rd BS24 49 E7
Maunsel Rd TA7 153 F1
Maurice Jennings Dr TA21 222 D8
Maximus Gdns BS30 24 F8
Max Mill La BS25 69 C8
Maxwell Rd BA4 205 B4
Maxwell St TA2 212 E6
Maybrick Rd BA2 44 D5
Mayfair Ave BS48 8 F1
Mayfield Ave BS22 31 E1
Mayfield Cl BA22 175 D8
Mayfield Dr TA6 208 B4
Mayfield Rd
Bath BA2 44 D5
Yeovil BA21 219 D6
Mayfields BS31 24 E5
Mayfield Terr TA4 210 C4
Mayflower Cl TA6 209 D5
Mayflower Ct TA9 104 E4
Mayflower Gdns BS48 9 A2
May La BA1 44 B8
Maynard Cl
Bristol BS13 22 C5
4 Clevedon BS21 6 F3
Maynard Rd BS13 22 C5
Maynard Terr BS39 58 F3
Maypole Cl BS39 58 E3
MAY POLE KNAP 211 C4
May Pole Knap TA11 211 C4
Maysfield Cl BS20 2 D3
Maysgreen La BS24 33 B3
May's La BS24 33 C3
Maysmead La BS40 53 C6
May Terr TA23 131 E3
Maytree Ave BS13 22 B7
Maytree Cl
Bristol BS13 22 B7
Frome BA11 120 B7
May Tree Cl BS48 8 C1
May Tree Rd BA3 78 E1
McAdam Way BS1 11 F5
McCrae Rd BS24 50 B5
McCreath Cl 3 TA6 153 F3
Mc Creery Rd DT9 225 D6
McKinley Terr TA23 131 E4
Mdwhayes TA24 124 A3
Mead Ave BA22 218 B6
Mead Cl
Bath BA2 44 E3
Bristol BS11 4 E6
Cheddar BS27 90 B6
East Huntspill TA9 136 E8
Stoke St Michael BA3 116 B2
Mead Com Prim Sch The BA14 83 C6
Meade Cl TA6 153 F3
Meade Ho BA2 44 A5
Meade La TA19 184 E1
MEADGATE EAST 60 E2
MEADGATE WEST 60 D2
Mead La
Blagdon BS40 54 E3
Lydford Fair Place TA11 158 C3
Saltford BS31 25 F4
Sandford BS25 51 E4
Stocklinch TA19 184 C4
Mead La *continued*
Wanstrow BA4 142 F4
West Pennard BA6 140 C2
Meadlands BA2 43 B7
Meadowbank BS22 31 F3
Meadow Cl
Backwell BS48 19 B6
Chilton Trinity TA5 135 F2
Farrington Gurney BS39 77 A3
Henstridge BA8 190 A7
Highbridge TA9 104 D4
Kingston St Mary TA2 168 E8
Langport TA10 172 A6
Nailsea BS48 8 E3
Nether Stowey TA5 134 A2
Stalbridge DT10 190 B4
Street BA16 207 B4
Wincanton BA9 216 D3
Meadow Cotts TA24 131 B4
Meadow Croft BS24 49 B2
Meadowcroft Dr TA8 104 C8
Meadow Ct BA1 44 A7
Meadow Dr
Bath BA2 62 D8
Locking BS24 50 B4
Portishead BS20 1 F1
Meadow Gdns
Bath BA1 27 A1
Stogursey TA5 134 C6
Meadow Gr BS11 4 D7
Meadow La
Bathampton BA2 28 D1
Walton BA16 156 E7
Meadowland BS49 17 A1
Meadowlands BS22 32 C2
Meadowlands Ave TA6 208 E6
Meadow Pk
Bathford BA1 29 B3
Wembdon TA6 208 C5
Meadow Pl BS22 32 D3
Meadow Rd
Clevedon BS21 6 E3
Frome BA11 119 F7
Paulton BS39 77 F4
Yeovil BA21 219 E7
Meadow Rise BA4 205 B4
Meadows Cl BS20 1 F5
Meadows End BS25 52 D4
Meadowside
Carhampton TA24 131 A5
Rockwell Green TA21 222 B5
Meadowside Cl TA1 212 B4
Meadowside Dr BS14 23 A3
Meadows Prim Sch The BS30 25 D8
Meadow St
Axbridge BS26 70 C2
Weston-super-Mare BS23 48 E7
Meadows The
2 Bourton SP8 161 F1
Drayton TA10 171 E3
Porlock TA24 124 A3
Meadow Terr TA24 201 A5
Meadow View
2 Bampton EX16 164 B1
4 Barwick BA22 197 F8
East Coker BA22 197 C8
Glastonbury BA6 206 E3
Long Sutton TA10 172 E1
Radstock BA3 79 A1
Timberscombe TA24 130 B5
Meadow View Cl BA1 44 A8
Meadow Villas 14 BS23 48 E8
Mead Rd BS20 2 C2
Mead Run TA11 157 A3
Meads Ct TA6 208 E3
Meads Droveway TA3 169 D5
Mead St BS3 227 C1
Meads The DT9 217 D2
Mead Terr BS40 54 E2
Mead The
Clutton BS39 58 E3
Dundry BS41 21 D2
East Brent TA9 86 E5
Farmborough BA2 60 A6
Henstridge BA8 190 A6
Holcombe BA3 116 C8
Ilchester BA22 173 D1
Ilminster TA19 221 B3
Keynsham BS31 24 E3
Paulton BS39 77 D5
Rode BA11 101 E8
14 Shepton Mallet BA4 205 B6
Shipham BS25 70 E8
Stoke St Michael BA3 116 B2
Stratton-on-t F BA3 96 F2
Street BA16 207 D7
Timsbury BA2 60 C3
Winsley BA15 64 E7
Mead Vale BS22 49 E8
Mead Vale Prim Sch BS22 31 E1
Meadway
Bristol BS9 5 C6
Farmborough BA2 60 A6
Temple Cloud BS39 58 E1
Woolavington TA7 136 E4
Mead Way TA2 169 B6
Meadway Ave BS48 8 D2
Mearcombe La BS24 67 F6
Meardon Rd BS14 23 E6
MEARE 138 D4
Meare BS24 48 F2
MEARE GREEN
Hatch Beauchamp 169 F1
Stoke St Gregory 170 D5
Meare Rd
Bath BA2 45 A2
Glastonbury BA6 206 B6
Meare Village Prim Sch BA6 138 D4
Meareway BA6 138 C5
MEARNS 59 E2
Mearn's Cross BA3 94 B6
Mede Cl BS1 227 B1
Medical Ave BS2, BS8 226 C3
Medway Cl
Keynsham BS31 25 A3
Taunton TA1 213 D4
Medway Dr BS31 25 A3
Meetinghouse La BS49 18 A1
Melbourne House Mews BA5 203 D4
Melbourne Pl TA6 209 B6
Melbourne Terr 2 BS21 6 D2
Melcombe Ct BA2 44 D4
Melcombe La TA6 153 E3
Melcombe Rd BA2 44 D4
Mellanby Cl BA16 207 D5
Mellent Ave BS13 22 C3
MELLS 118 B7
Mells CE Sch BA11 118 A6
Mells Cl BS31 25 A2
MELLS GREEN 118 A6
Mells La BA3 79 B1
Melrose Ave
Bristol BS8 226 B4
Wells BA5 203 C4
Melrose Ct 3 BA5 203 C4
Melrose Gr BA2 44 B3
Melrose Pl BS8 226 B4
Melrose Rd BA21 219 B6
Melrose Terr BA1 28 A2
Melsbury La BA5 139 E6
Memorial Ave TA18 224 C5
Memorial Rd
Wrington BS40 35 E2
Yeovil BA22 218 B6
Mendip Ave
Shepton Mallet BA4 205 E4
Weston-super-Mare BS22 31 F2
Mendip Bsns Pk BS26 87 A6
Mendip Cl
Axbridge BS26 70 D2
Frome BA11 120 A7
Keynsham BS31 24 D5
3 Nailsea BS48 8 E1
Paulton BS39 77 E4
Yatton BS49 34 B7
Mendip Dr BA11 120 A7
Mendip Edge BS24 66 F8
Mendip Fields BA3 96 C2
Mendip Gdns
Bath BA2 62 D8
Frome BA11 120 B7
Yatton BS49 34 B7
Mendip Gn BA3 97 B6
Mendip Green Fst Sch BS22 31 E2
Mendip Ho TA1 212 F3
Mendip Lea Cl BS27 90 F2
Mendip Lodge BS25 70 A8
Mendip Rd
Bridgwater TA6 209 C4
Locking BS24 50 D4
Portishead BS20 2 B5
Rooks Bridge BS26 87 A6
Stoke St Michael BA3 116 A2
Weston-super-Mare BS23 49 A7
Yatton BS49 34 B7
Mendip Rise BS24 50 B4
Mendip Vale BA3 116 E7
Mendip Vale Sta★ BA4 205 F3
Mendip Vale Trad Est BS27 90 A7
Mendip View
Coleford BA3 116 F7
Street BA16 207 B7
Mendip Villas
Cheddar BS27 71 A1
Compton Martin BS40 73 F7
Emborough BA3 95 E3
Mendip Way
Burnham-on-S TA8 104 B7
Radstock BA3 78 F3
Menlea BS40 54 D3
Mercer Ct BS14 23 B8
Merchants' Acad
Bristol BS13 22 A4
Bristol BS13 22 A5
Merchants Almshouses 6 BS1 227 A2
Merchants Barton BA11 119 F4
Merchants' Barton 3 BA11 119 F4
Merchants Barton Ind Est BA11 119 F4
Merchants Ct BS8 226 A1
Merchant Sq BS20 2 E6
Merchants Quay BS1 227 A1
Merchants Rd
Bristol BS8 226 A3
Bristol, Hotwells BS8 226 A1
Merchants Row BS1 226 C1
Merchant St BS1 227 B3
Meredith Cl
11 Creech St Michael TA3 169 C5
Halstock BA22 197 C3
Meredith Ct BS1 226 A1
Merevale Way BA21 218 C7
Meriden BA1 44 D8
Meridian Pl BS8 226 B3
Meridian Vale BS8 226 B3
Meriet Ave BS13 22 B4
Merino Way 7 TA6 154 A5
Merle Cl TA6 209 B4
Merlin Cl
Bristol BS9 5 F8
Merlin Cl *continued*
1 Weston-super-Mare BS22 49 E8
Merlin Dr BA5 203 B5
Merlin Ind Pk TA2 213 B6
Merlin Pk BS20 2 A4
Merlin Rd BA20 218 D3
Merlin Way 3 BA3 97 B8
Merrick Ct BS1 227 A1
Merrick Rd BA6 206 E7
MERRIDGE 152 D5
Merridge Cl TA6 208 A4
Merridge Hill TA5 152 D6
Merrifields TA4 167 E6
Merriman Gdns BA16 207 C5
Merriman Rd BA16 207 C5
Merrimans Rd BS11 4 D8
MERRIOTT 195 E7
Merriott Fst Sch TA16 195 F7
Merriott Rd
Hinton St George TA17 195 D7
Merriott TA16 195 F6
MERRIOTTSFORD 195 F7
Merry-field BA3 116 E8
Merryfield La
Doulting BA4 141 F5
Ilton TA19 183 E4
Merryfield Lane Halt★ BA4 141 F5
Merryfield Rd BS24 50 B6
Merryfields TA9 106 D5
Merry La TA9 136 F8
Merthyr Guest Cl BA8 176 E1
Merton Dr BS24 50 A8
Mervyn Ball Cl TA20 223 C5
Methwyn Cl BS22 49 C7
Metropole Ct TA24 201 A7
Metropolitan The BS1 227 B1
Mews The
Bath BA1 44 A8
5 Bridgwater TA6 209 B4
East Coker BA22 197 C7
Minehead TA24 201 A7
Wiveliscombe TA4 210 C4
Mewswell Dr BS27 71 B1
Meyer Cl TA21 222 F6
Mezellion Pl 14 BA1 28 B1
Mianda Terr TA19 221 C3
Michaels Mead BA1 27 B2
Midas Ct TA11 211 D3
Middle Ave BS1 227 A2
Middle Brooks BA16 207 C3
MIDDLE BURNHAM 104 D8
MIDDLE CHINNOCK 196 C8
Middle Chinnock Rd TA18 196 C8
Middlecombe Cross TA24 200 C6
Middle Dro
Baltonsborough BA6 158 B4
Compton Dundon TA11 156 F3
Glastonbury BA6 206 B5
Hambridge TA10, TA12 184 F8
Lydford Fair Place TA11 158 C3
Rodney Stoke BS27 109 C6
Street BA6 157 C7
Middlefield La
Barrington TA10 184 D6
Merriott TA16 195 E8
Norton Sub Hamdon TA13, TA16 185 D1
West Chinnock TA16 196 A8
Middle Field La DT9 188 B7
Middlefield Rd TA10 172 C7
Middleford Ho BS13 22 C4
Middle Gate TA10 172 D8
Middlegate Rd TA10 172 C7
MIDDLE GREEN 222 D3
Middle Green Rd TA21 222 E3
Middle La
Bath BA1 28 B1
Kingston Seymour BS21 15 F4
Middle Leaze Dro TA12 185 F7
MIDDLE LEIGH 207 C4
Middle Leigh BA16 207 C5
MIDDLE LUXTON 191 F5
Middlemead BA3 96 F3
Middlemoor Dro TA7 154 A1
Middle Moor Drove TA5 134 D7
Middle Moor La BS27 89 E7
Middlemoor Water Pk★ TA7 136 F5
Middle Path TA18 224 B5
Middlepiece La BA2, BS31 42 B7
Middle Rd TA7 137 A3
Middle Ridge La DT9 175 D1
Middleroom Dro TA3 182 E4
Middle's La BA4 140 C4
Middle St
Ashcott TA7 156 B7
Burnham-on-S TA9 85 E5
East Harptree BS40 74 F4
East Lambrook TA13 220 C8
Galhampton BA22 175 D8
Kingsdon TA11 173 D5
Martock TA12 185 D4
Minehead TA24 200 F8
Misterton TA18 224 F3
Montacute TA15 186 B3
North Perrott TA18 196 C4
Puriton TA7 136 C4
Rimpton BA22 188 A8
Shepton Beauchamp TA19 184 E3
Taunton TA1 212 F4
Yeovil BA20 219 B4
Middle Stoke BA3 64 A6
MIDDLE STOUGHTON 108 A8
Middle Stream Cl TA6 208 D2
Middleton La
Clatworthy TA4 149 C2
Shepton Mallet BA4 205 B4
Middleton Rd BS11 4 F8
Middle Touches TA20 223 E5
Middleway TA1 212 E2
Middle Way TA11 157 B4
Middleway Ct TA1 212 E2
Middleway Rd BA4 158 E8
Middlewood Cl BA2 44 C2
Middle Yeo Gn BS48 8 D3
MIDDLEZOY 155 B3
Middlezoy Prim Sch
Middlezoy TA7 155 B3
Middlezoy TA7 155 B3
Midelney Rd TA10 171 E2
MIDFORD 63 C6
Midford BS24 48 F2
Midford Hill BA2, BA3 63 C5
Midford La BA2, BA3 63 E7
Midford Rd
Southstoke BA2 63 B7
Taunton TA1 213 B4
Midhaven Rise BS22 31 E4
MID LAMBROOK 220 A8
Midland Bridge Rd BA1, BA2 228 A2
Midland Mews BS2 227 C3
Midland Rd
Bath BA1 44 D7
Bristol BS2 227 C3
Midland St BS2 227 C2
Midleaze DT9 225 A3
Midney La BA9 177 D8
Midsomer Ent Pk BA3 78 C2
MIDSOMER NORTON 78 B3
Midsomer Norton Prim Sch BA3 78 B1
Midsomer Norton South★ BA3 97 A8
Midsummer Bldgs BA1 28 B2
MIDWAY 115 E2
MILBORNE PORT 217 E2
Milborne Port Bsns Ctr DT9 217 D2
Milborne Port Prim Sch
Milborne Port DT9 217 D2
Milborne Port DT9 217 D2
MILBORNE WICK 217 B6
Milburn Rd BS23 48 F7
Milbury Gdns BS22 31 C2
Mildenhall Rd DT9 225 B4
Mildmay Dr BA22 174 F3
Mildmay's Rd TA10 155 F1
Mildred Rd BA16 156 E7
Miles Cl BS20 4 E3
Miles's Bldgs BA1 228 B3
Miles St BA2 228 C1
Milestone Cl TA6 153 F4
Milestone Ct BS22 32 D2
Mile Wlk BS14 23 A6
Milford Inf Sch BA21 219 B7
Milford Jun Sch BA21 219 B7
Milford Pk BA21 219 C7
Milford Pl 3 TA1 213 A4
Milford Rd BA21 219 C7
Milking La BS27 90 E2
Milk St
Bath BA1 228 B2
Frome BA11 119 E5
Millands La TA5 133 C6
Millands The TA11 211 E4
Millards Ct BA3 78 B3
Millards Hill BA3 78 B3
Millard's Hill
Batcombe BA4 142 D2
Midsomer Norton BA3 78 C3
Mill Ave BS1 227 A2
Millbatch BA6 138 C4
Mill Batch Farm Ind Est TA9 86 F4
Mill Bay TA6 153 E4
Millbourn Cl BA15 64 D7
Millbourne Rd BS27 90 C7
Millbridge Gdns TA24 200 F7
Millbridge Rd TA24 200 E7
MILLBROOK 198 A1
Millbrook BA20 219 A4
Millbrook Cross 1 EX13 198 A1
Millbrook Ct BA2 228 C1
Millbrook Dale EX13 198 A1
Millbrook Gdns BA7 214 B5
Millbrook Pl BA2 228 C1
Mill Cl
Cannington TA5 135 B2
East Coker BA22 197 C8
Frome BA11 119 F6
Highbridge TA9 104 D2
Nether Stowey TA5 134 A2
Portbury BS20 3 D2
Mill Cotts
Creech St Michael TA3 169 D4
Saltford BS31 25 F2
Millcross BS21 16 C8
Mill Cross
Halstock BA22 197 C3
Kingston St Mary TA2 168 E7
Mill Ct
Midsomer Norton BA3 78 A1
Watchet TA23 202 B7
Millennium Cl BA3 116 A3
Millennium Sq BS1 226 C2
Miller Cl BS23 48 F8
Miller Ho BS8 226 A2
Millers Cl
Bourton SP8 161 F1
Pill BS20 4 C4
Millers Ct BS21 16 E8

Millers Gdns BA5 203 E5
Miller's Hill DT9 217 A5
Millers Orch TA3 170 F1
Millers Pl BA1 28 E3
Millers Rise BS22 32 A4
Millers Way 11 TA4 167 F8
Miller Way DT9 225 E5
Miller Wlk BA2 28 F1
Milletts Cl 2 TA24 131 A5
Mill Farm Hill TA5 134 F1
Millfield
Chard TA20 223 D3
Ilchester BA22 173 E2
Midsomer Norton BA3 96 F8
Millfield Cl TA20 223 D3
Millfield Ind Est TA20 223 E3
Millfield Prep Sch BA6 139 D1
Millfield Sch BA16 207 E5
Millford La BA4 159 C6
Mill Gdns TA24 201 D1
Millgreen Cl TA9 136 B8
Millground Rd BS13 21 F5
Millham La TA22 163 D6
MILLHAYES 180 C1
Mill Hill BA2 62 E1
Mill Ho BS1 227 A2
Mill House Ct BA11 119 F5
Mill House Rd TA2 168 B4
Millier Rd BS49 35 B8
Milliman Cl BS13 22 C5
Milliner Ct BA4 205 B5
Mill La
Alhampton BA4 159 C5
Axminster EX13 198 F3
Batcombe BA4 142 C1
3 Bath BA2 44 B6
Bathampton BA2 28 F2
Beckington BA11 101 D5
Bishops Lydeard TA4 167 F8
Bitton BS30 25 E8
Bourton SP8 161 F1
Bradford Abbas DT9 187 E1
Bruton BA10 215 E6
Butcombe BS40 55 A8
Cannington TA5 135 B2
Chard TA20 223 C3
Chard, Wambrook TA20 193 C2
Charlton Mackrell TA11 173 E7
Chew Stoke BS40 56 D8
Clatworthy TA4 149 E2
Compton Dando BS39 41 A5
Compton Martin BS40 74 A7
Congresbury BS49 34 D4
Corfe TA3 181 F6
Corsley Heath BA11, BA12 144 C8
Creech St Michael TA3 169 D4
Crewkerne, Misterton TA18 196 B3
Dinnington TA17 195 B8
Dowlish Wake TA19 194 E7
Dunster TA24 201 D1
East Coker BA22 197 C7
East Coker, Holywell BA22 197 B8
East Huntspill TA9 136 D8
Exford TA24 128 C2
Halstock BA22 197 C3
Higher Chillington TA19 194 E5
Ilchester BA22 173 F1
Ilminster TA19 221 B7
Kingstone TA19 221 F1
Lopen TA13 185 A1
Lynford-on-F TA11 158 C2
Maiden Bradley BA12 144 B3
Marnhull DT10 190 F6
Milverton TA4 167 A5
Monkton Combe BA2 63 E8
Nether Stowey TA5 134 A2
North Wootton BA4 140 D5
Othery TA7 155 C2
Pitcombe BA10 215 C3
Porlock TA24 124 A3
Portbury BS20 3 E3
Priston BA2 61 A7
Shapwick TA7 155 F8
Shepton Mallet BA4 204 E4
Somerton TA11 211 D2
South Petherton TA13 220 E6
Stoke St Michael BA3 116 B3
Stone Allerton BS26 88 D4
Taunton TA3 168 D1
Thurloxton TA2 153 D1
Timsbury BA2 60 B1
Trent DT9 187 F5
Watchet TA23 202 C7
Wedmore BS28 108 E3
Wells BA5 203 A1
West Monkton TA2 169 D8
Wiveliscombe TA4 210 C4
Wrington BS40 53 F8
Yeovil BA20 219 B4
Mill Lane Cl TA3 168 D1
Mill La Trad Est BA20 219 C4
Mill Leat BA6 157 E5
Mill Leg BS49 34 D4
Millmead Ho BS13 22 C4
Millmead Rd BA2 44 C5
MILLMOOR 179 E1
Millmoot La TA7 136 F3
Mill on the Brue* BA10 215 D5
Millpill Cl BS9 5 D5
Mill Rd
Barton St David TA11 158 A3
Radstock BA3 79 B2
Mill Rise
Bourton SP8 161 F1
Staplegrove TA2 212 B7
Mill Road Ind Est BA3 79 B3
Mills Dr TA21 222 F7
Mill St
Carhampton TA24 131 B4
North Petherton TA6 153 F3
Rimpton BA22 188 A8
Watchet TA23 202 C7
Wells BA5 203 D4
Wincanton BA9 216 C4
Millstream Cl TA24 200 F6
Mill Stream Cl BS26 70 C1
Mill Stream Gdns TA21 222 B7
Mill Street Cl BA9 216 C4
Millthorn Ho 2 BA16 207 C5
Millward Terr BS39 77 E6
Millway
Chard TA20 193 C2
Rodney Stoke BS27 110 B8
Millway Rise Ind Est EX13 198 A2
Millwey Ave EX13 198 A2
MILLWEY RISE 198 A2
Mill Wlk TA7 136 E3
Millwood Cl TA6 208 E2
Milne Cl TA6 208 F2
Milsom Pl TA4 167 F6
Milsom St BA1 228 B3
MILTON
Martock 185 E8
Weston-super-Mare 31 C2
Milton Ave
Bath BA2 44 F4
Weston-super-Mare BS23 49 A8
Milton Brow BS22 31 B2
Milton Cl
Nailsea BS48 8 E3
Taunton TA1 213 C3
Yeovil BA21 218 C6
MILTON CLEVEDON 160 A8
Milton Ct BA4 205 B7
Milton Gn BS22 31 C1
Milton Hill
Monkton Heathfield TA2 213 E7
Weston-super-Mare BS22 31 B2
Milton Ho BA21 187 D6
Milton La
Martock TA12 185 E8
Wells BA5 203 D5
Wookey Hole BA5 203 B8
Milton Leaze TA10 172 E2
Milton Lodge Gdns* BA5 203 D7
Milton Park Prim Sch BS22 31 D1
Milton Park Rd BS22 31 C1
Milton Pl TA6 208 E4
Milton Rd
Radstock BA3 78 C1
Taunton TA1 213 C3
Weston-super-Mare BS22, BS23 49 B8
Milton Rise BS22 31 C1
Miltons Cl BS13 22 D4
Milton Terr BA5 203 A8
MILVERTON 166 F4
Milverton BS24 48 F2
Milverton Com Prim Sch TA4 166 F4
Milverton Rd TA21 222 B8
Milward Rd BS31 24 E6
Minchington's Cl TA14 185 F2
MINEHEAD 201 A8
Minehead Com Hospl TA24 201 B5
Minehead Ent Pk TA24 201 B5
Minehead First Sch TA24 200 F6
Minehead Fst Sch TA24 200 F6
Minehead La TA22 164 A7
Minehead Mid Sch TA24 201 A6
Minehead Rd
Bishops Lydeard TA4 167 E8
Bristol BS4 23 A8
Minehead Sta* TA24 201 B7
Miners Cl BS41 10 F2
Minerva Ct BA2 228 C3
Minerva Gdns BA2 44 C4
Minery Rd BA5 93 B3
Minnows The TA20 223 C3
Minsmere Rd BS31 25 A4
Minster Cl TA1 212 C1
Minster Ct TA1 212 C1
Minster Way BA2 45 C8
Minton Cl BS14 23 B5
Mintons TA20 223 B3
Mintons Orch TA20 223 B3
Mint The BA11 119 E5
Misburg Cl BA4 204 F6
MISTERTON 224 E3
Misterton CE Fst Sch TA18 224 F3
Mistletoe La BA4 205 D3
Mitchell Gdns TA20 223 B3
Mitchell La BS1 227 B2
Mitchell's Pool TA21 222 E6
Mitchell's Row BA22 175 D6
Mitchell St TA21 222 C7
Mitchell Terr BA5 112 E1
Mitchelmore Rd BA21 219 B5
Mitford-Slade Ct BS49 34 C7
Mitre Ct TA1 213 B4
Mizzymead Cl 1 BS48 8 D1
Mizzymead Rd BS48 8 E1
Mizzymead Rise BS48 8 E1
Moccasin Way BA16 207 B6
Moffats Dr BA5 113 A2
Moles Rd BS40 53 B6
Molesworth Cl BS13 22 A4
Molesworth Dr BS13 22 A4
Mollifriend La BA2 60 B8
Molly Cl BS39 76 E8
Monarch Ctr TA2 213 C6
Monarch Rd TA18 224 E4
Monday's Court La TA10 172 E5
Money Pit La EX13 193 A1
Monger Cotts BS39 77 F4
Monger La
Greenhill BA3 78 A3
Midsomer Norton BA3 78 A3
Paulton BS39 78 A4
Monington Rd BA6 206 E6
Monk Barton Cl BA21 218 C7
Monk Cross TA24 128 D1
Monkhouse Farm La TA16 195 F7
Monkley La BA11 83 C1
Monks Cl
Rooks Bridge BS26 87 B5
Taunton TA1 213 B5
Monks Dale BA21 218 D6
Monksdale Rd BA2 44 D4
Monks Dr TA7 137 F1
Monks Ford BA5 139 D8
Monksford La BA5 139 C8
Monks Hill BS22 31 B3
MONKSILVER 150 A8
Monks' Path TA23, TA24 131 E4
Monkstone Dr TA8 84 F5
Monkstone Gdns 6 EX13 198 A1
Monksway TA23 131 E4
Monks Way TA8 104 B6
Monkton Ave BS24 49 A2
MONKTON COMBE 45 F1
MONKTON FARLEIGH 46 F7
MONKTON HEATHFIELD 213 E8
Monkton La TA5 134 D5
Monkton Prep Sch
Bath BA2 45 C1
Monkton Combe BA2 63 E8
Monkton Sen Sch BA2 45 E1
Monmouth Cl
Chard TA20 223 E4
Glastonbury BA6 206 D5
Portishead BS20 1 F4
Westonzoyland TA7 154 F6
Monmouth Ct
Bath BA1 228 A2
Chard TA20 223 E4
Pill BS20 4 C5
Monmouth Dr BA11 120 B6
Monmouth Farm Cl TA6 135 F5
Monmouth Paddock BA2 81 E5
Monmouth Pl BA1 228 B2
Monmouth Rd
Keynsham BS31 24 D5
Pill BS20 4 C5
Shepton Mallet BA4 205 A5
Taunton TA1 213 B5
Westonzoyland TA7 154 F6
Yeovil BA21 219 D7
Monmouth St
Bath BA1 228 B2
Bridgwater TA6 209 A5
MONTACUTE 186 B3
Montacute Cir 4 BS22 49 F8
Montacute House* TA15 186 B4
Montacute Rd
Montacute TA14, TA15 186 B4
Tintinhull BA22 186 B6
Montacute TV, Radio & Toy Mus* TA15 186 C4
Montague Ct 4 BS2 227 A4
Montague Flats 6 BS2 227 A4
Montague Gdns BA7 214 B5
Montague Hill BS2 227 A4
Montague Hill S 5 BS2 227 A4
Montague Ho 8 BA1 28 C1
Montague Pl BS6 227 A4
Montague Rd
Saltford BS31 25 D2
Shoscombe BA2 79 E5
Montague St BS1 227 A4
Montague Way TA20 223 C3
Monteclefe CE Jun Sch TA11 211 E3
Montepelier BS23 48 F8
Montgomery Ct BA11 120 A4
Montpelier E BS23 30 F1
Montrose Cotts BA1 27 C1
Montrose Rd BA21 219 E7
Montrose Villas BS27 90 C7
Montsurs Cl BA3 96 D3
Monument Cl TA21 222 E4
Monument Rd TA21 222 E3
MOOLHAM 221 C1
Moolham La
Ilminster TA19 194 D7
Kingstone TA19 221 D1
Moondown La TA13 220 B2
Moonhayes Cross EX14 191 F4
Moon La TA7 153 E1
Moonraker Cl 8 TA6 209 B4
Moon's Dro TA7 155 A1
Moons Hill BA3 116 B4
Moonshill Cl BA3 116 A3
Moonshill Cotts BA3 116 A3
Moonshill Rd BA3 116 A3
Moon St BS2 227 B4
MOOR 220 C3
Moor Cl
Compton Dundon TA11 156 F2
Langport TA10 172 A6
Wincanton BA9 216 C3
Moorclose Dro TA7 137 C3
Moorclose La BA4 158 E6
Moor Croft Rd BS24 49 E3
Moor Dro
Chedzoy TA7 154 F8
Moorlinch TA7 155 F6
Moorend Gdns BS11 4 F7
Moor End Spout BS48 8 D2
Moore's La TA5, TA6 208 C7
Moores Yd BA14 83 C6
Moorfield Gdn TA24 146 C6
Moorfield Rd BS48 19 A6
Moorfields Cl BA2 44 D3
Moorfields Ct BS48 8 D2
Moorfields Dr BA2 44 D4
Moorfields Ho BS48 8 D2
Moorfields Rd
Bath BA2 44 D4
Nailsea BS48 8 D2
Moor Gate BS20 2 F4
Moor Gn BS26 70 C1
Moor Gr BS11 5 A8
Moorgrove Ho BS9 5 C7
Moorham Rd BS25 52 A1
MOORHAYNE 192 D2
Moorhen Rd
Kingston Seymour BS49 16 F2
Kingston Seymour BS49 16 F2
Moorhouse La TA4 165 A8
Moor House La TA5 133 E4
Moorings The
Bath BA2 45 B6
Pill BS20 4 C4
Moor La
Alhampton BA4 159 C5
Backwell BS48 18 F6
Batcombe BA4 142 D1
Brushford TA22 163 F4
Churchinford TA3 192 A7
Clapton in G BS20 2 E1
Clevedon BS21 6 E2
Clevedon BS21 7 A2
Cucklington SP8 177 E5
Draycott BS27 90 F1
East Coker BA22 197 D7
Hardington Mandeville BA22 197 A7
Higher Chillington TA20 194 F5
Hutton BS24 49 D3
North Curry TA3 170 B4
South Petherton TA13 220 B3
Tickenham BS21 7 F4
Walton in G BS21 7 C6
Westbury-sub-Mendip BA5 110 C5
Weston-super-Mare BS24 49 F7
Wincanton BA9 216 C2
Moorland Cl TA1 213 C5
Moorland Cotts BS26 69 F2
Moorland Pk BS24 33 E5
Moorland Pl TA1 213 C5
Moorland Rd
Bath BA2 44 D5
Bridgwater TA6 209 D4
Street BA16 207 B7
Taunton TA1 213 C5
Weston-super-Mare BS23 48 E4
MOORLANDS 44 D3
Moorlands TA4 167 F8
Moorlands Cl
16 Martock TA12 185 E6
Nailsea BS48 8 D2
Moorlands Ct TA16 195 F7
Moorlands Inf Sch BA2 44 D4
Moorlands Jun Sch BA2 44 D3
Moorlands Pk 18 TA12 185 E6
Moorlands Pk Sh Ctr 19 TA12 185 E6
Moorlands Rd TA16 195 E6
Moorland St BS26 70 C1
Moorlands The BA2 44 D3
Moorland Way TA6 209 D5
Moor Lane Cl TA3 170 B4
Moorlay Cres BS40 37 F8
MOORLEDGE 39 E1
Moorledge La BS39, BS40 57 F7
Moorledge Rd BS40 39 B1
MOORLINCH 155 E7
Moorlinch Right Dro TA7 155 D6
Moor Park Rd TA10 171 F5
Moor Pk
Clevedon BS21 6 E2
Langport TA10 171 F5
Moor Rd
Banwell BS29 51 B5
Middlezoy TA7 155 B4
Minehead TA24 200 E8
Moorlinch TA7 155 D7
Sutton Mallet TA7 155 B8
Yatton BS49 17 B2
Moorsfield BS39 58 F3
Moor Sherd BS28 110 C1
Moorside BS49 17 B1
Moorside Ct BS21 6 E2
Moorside Villas BS21 6 E2
Moortown La TA10 171 B2
Moorview Cl BA6 138 C4
Moor Villas TA13 220 B3
Moorway La DT9 188 C6
Moots La TA6 209 D4
Morangis Way TA20 223 B6
Moravia Cl TA6 208 E6
Morden Wlk BS14 23 D7
MOREBATH 164 B3
Moredon Dro TA3 170 C5
Moreton Cl BS14 23 A4
Moreton La BS40 56 E2
Moreton Mans 5 BS23 30 C1
Morford St BA1 228 B4
Morgan Cl
Saltford BS31 25 D2
Weston-super-Mare BS22 50 B8
Morgan Pl BS48 20 B8
Morgans Bldgs BS20 8 F8
Morgans Hill Cl BS48 18 D8
Morgan's La
East Harptree BS40 74 F2
Morgan's La *continued*
8 Frome BA11 119 E5
Morgans Rise TA1 212 A3
Morgan Sweet Pl BS25 52 A4
Morgan Way BA2 79 E7
Morland Rd
Glastonbury BA6 206 B3
Highbridge TA9 104 D4
Morlands Ent Pk BA6 206 B3
Morlands Ind Pk TA9 104 D4
Morley Rd TA14 185 E3
Morley Terr
Bath BA2 44 D6
Radstock BA3 79 A3
Mornington Pk TA21 222 E5
Morpeth Rd BS4 22 D8
Morrell's Cross EX16 164 B4
Morrell's La EX16 178 B6
Morris Cl TA19 184 C5
Morris La BA1 29 B3
Morston Ct BS22 49 C7
Mortimer Cl
Bath BA1 27 B2
Woolavington TA7 136 E4
Mortimer Rd BS8 226 A3
Morton's La TA10 156 C1
Moseley Gr BS23 48 E2
Mosquito End BS23 49 B4
Moss Cl TA6 209 C6
Moss La TA3 169 C3
Mosterton Down La DT8 196 A1
Mottershead Ave BS24 50 C5
Moulton Cl BA4 205 A4
Mound The BA6 206 C4
Mounsdon Cl BA6 157 E4
Mountain Ash BA1 27 D1
Mountain's La BA2 59 E6
Mountain Wood BA1 29 C2
Mountbatten Cl
Burnham-on-S TA8 85 A1
Weston-super-Mare BS22 31 E4
Mountbatten Ho TA6 209 C5
Mountbatten Rd 5 BA21 219 F8
Mount Beacon BA1 28 A1
Mount Beacon Pl 3 BA1 27 F1
Mount Beacon Row 1 BA1 28 A1
Mounters Cl DT10 190 F5
Mounter's Hill EX13, TA20 193 B2
Mountery Cl BA5 203 D5
Mountery Rd BA5 203 D5
Mountfields Ave TA1 213 B1
Mountfields Pk TA1 213 B1
Mountfields Rd TA1 213 B1
Mount Gr BA2 44 B3
Mount Hey TA11 211 E3
Mount Hindrance Cl TA20 223 D6
Mount Hindrance La TA20 223 D6
Mount Ho TA1 212 F3
Mount La
Charlton Horethorne DT9 176 A1
Golsoncott TA23, TA24 131 C1
Mount Nebo TA1 212 E2
Mount Pleasant
Bath BA2 45 D1
Castle Cary BA7 214 C5
Crewkerne TA18 224 D6
Frome BA11 119 F2
Kilmington BA12 161 F6
Pill BS20 4 D4
Pilton BA4 140 F3
Radstock BA3 79 B2
Yeovil BA21 219 C5
Mount Pleasant Ave BA5 203 B5
MOUNT RADFORD 208 C6
Mount Rd
Bath BA1 228 B4
Bath, Southdown BA2 44 B3
Nether Stowey TA5 134 A2
Mountsfield BA11 120 A2
Mount St
Bishops Lydeard TA4 167 E8
Bridgwater TA6 208 F5
Taunton TA1 212 F3
Mount Terr TA1 213 A3
MOUNT THE 119 F2
Mount The
Frome BA11 119 F2
Taunton TA1 212 F3
Yatton BS49 34 C8
Mount View
Bath, Beacon Hill BA1 28 A1
Bath, Southdown BA2 44 B3
Woolavington TA7 136 E4
Mount View Terr TA6 135 F6
Mountway TA1 213 A3
Mountway Cl TA1 212 C4
Mountway La TA1 212 C4
Mountway Rd TA1 212 C4
Movey La BA22 173 F1
Mow Barton
Bristol BS13 21 F6
8 Martock TA12 185 E6
Mow Barton Rd TA11 173 D5
Mowbray Rd BS14 23 C7
Mowcroft Rd BS13 22 D4
Mowes La DT10 190 F4
Mowground La TA7 137 A3
Mowleaze 11 BA22 197 F8
Mowlems The BA14 83 F3
Mowries Ct TA11 211 D4
Moxham Dr BS13 22 C4
M Shed* BS1 227 A1
MUCHELNEY 172 B3
Muchelney Abbey* TA10 172 A3
MUCHELNEY HAM 172 B2
Muchelney Hill BA6 158 B5
Muchelney Ho TA19 221 B3

Muchelney Pottery & The John Leach Gall★ TA10 172 B2
Muchelney Way BA21 218 C7
Muckleditch La TA19 184 D3
Muddicombe Cross TA24 128 B2
Muddicombe La TA24 128 B2
Muddyford La TA4 151 A3
Muddy La BS22 32 A8
MUDFORD 187 D6
Mudford Hill BA21 187 C5
Mudford Rd BA21 219 B8
MUDFORD SOCK 187 B6
MUDGLEY 138 D8
Mudgley Cross Roads BS28 108 F1
Mudgley Hill BS28 108 E1
Mudgley La BS28 108 F1
Mudgley Rd
Rooks Bridge BS26 87 A4
Wedmore BS28 108 E3
Mud La BS49 17 D2
Mulberry Ave BS20 2 E5
Mulberry Cl
Backwell BS48 19 A6
Portishead BS20 2 F5
Taunton TA1 213 C2
Weston-super-Mare BS22 32 A1
Mulberry Ct BA11 120 B7
Mulberry Farm BA6 140 B1
Mulberry Gdns
4 Crewkerne TA18 224 C5
Sherborne DT9 225 C5
Mulberry La
Bleadon BS24 67 C6
Stoke Sub Hamdon TA14 186 A4
Mulberry Rd BS49 34 E3
Mulberry Tree Cl TA6 209 D5
Mulberry Way BA2 45 A2
Mulberry Wlk BS9 5 C8
Mulholland Way TA9 104 D5
Mullins Cl BA5 203 B3
Mullins Way BA7 214 B6
Mundays Mead BA9 216 D3
Munden's La DT9 189 A1
Muntjac Rd BS40 53 B6
Murder Combe BA11 118 E5
Murford Ave BS13 22 B4
Murford Wlk BS13 22 B4
Murhill BA3 64 C6
Muriel Terr BA5 203 D3
Murray-Smith Dr BA22 218 A6
Murray Way BA9 216 B3
Murtry Hill La BA11 100 C2
Musbury Cl DT10 190 F6
Musbury La DT10 190 F6
Muscovy Dr 1 TA6 154 A5
Museum of Somerset★ TA1 212 F4
Museum of South Somerset★ BA20 219 B4
Musgraves TA22 163 E6
Musgrove Pk Hospl TA1 212 C3
Musgrove Rd TA1 212 C3
Musmoor La BA22 174 F7
Mus of Bath at Work★ BA1 228 B4
Mus of East Asian Art★ BA1 228 B3
Mutton La BS28 108 D4
Mutton St DT6 199 D1
Mux's La TA4 151 B3
Myrtleberry Mead BS22 32 A5
Myrtle Cl TA6 209 D5
Myrtle Dr
Bristol BS11 4 E5
Burnham-on-S TA8 104 A7
Myrtle Farm Rd BS22 31 C4
Myrtle Gdns BS49 34 C8
Myrtle Hill BS20 4 C5
Myrtle La TA21 179 E7
Myrtle Rd
Bristol BS2 226 C4
22 Martock TA12 185 E6
Myrtles The BS24 49 D2
Myrtle Tree Cres BS22 31 A6
Myrtlle Cotts TA3 182 D7

N

Nag's La TA18 195 B1
NAILSBOURNE 168 D7
NAILSEA 8 E3
Nailsea and Backwell Station BS48 18 F7
Nailsea Cl BS13 22 A7
Nailsea Moor La BS48 17 F7
Nailsea Park Cl BS48 8 F2
Nailsea Pk BS48 8 F2
Nailsea Sch BS48 8 E1
Nailsea Wall BS21 17 C8
Nailsea Wall La BS48 17 E7
NAILWELL 61 D6
Naishes Ave BA2 79 D7
Naish Farm BA3 96 D3
Naish Hill BS20 2 F1
Naish Ho BA2 44 A6
Naish La BS48 20 D3
Naisholt Rd BA4 204 F6
Naish Rd TA8 85 A3
Naish's Cross BA3 96 D3
Naish's St BA11 119 E5
Naked Boys La TA23 149 B5
Nalder Cl BA4 205 D4
Nanga-gat Rd BA22 174 A2
Nanny Hurn's La BS39 58 A1
Napier Ct
Bristol BS1 226 B1
Napier Ct *continued*
Sherborne DT9 225 B2
Napier Miles Rd BS11 5 A8
Napier Rd BA1 27 A3
Naples View TA6 208 E7
NARFORD'S 193 C1
Narfords La TA20 193 C1
Narrow Plain BS2 227 B2
Narrow Quay BS1 227 A2
NASH 197 C8
Nash Barton BA22 197 C8
Nash Cl BS31 25 A5
Nash Dr TA21 222 F6
Nash Gn TA2 212 B7
Nash La
Dinnington TA17, TA19 195 A6
East Coker BA22 197 C8
Marshwood DT6 199 B2
Yeovil BA20 218 D1
Nates La BS40 35 F1
Nathan Cl BA20 218 D2
Naunton Way BS22 31 B2
Neale's Way BA4 141 E2
Neathem Rd BA21 219 C7
Neat La BA4 204 D1
Nedge Cnr BA3 94 D4
Nedge Hill
Chewton Mendip BA3 94 D3
East End BA3 94 D3
Nedge La BA3 94 C4
Needhams Patch TA4 167 E6
NEIGHBOURNE 115 C5
Nelson Bldgs BA1 228 C4
Nelson Ct
Bridgwater TA6 208 F5
Weston-super-Mare BS22 31 E4
Nelson Ho
Bath BA1 228 A3
5 Bristol BS1 227 A3
Nelson Pl BA1 228 C4
Nelson Pl E BA1 228 C4
Nelson Pl W BA1 228 A2
Nelson St BS1 227 A3
Nelson Terr BA1 228 C4
Nelson Villas BA1 228 A2
Nelson Ward Dr BA3 79 A1
Nelson Way BA21 219 F8
Nempnett St BS40 55 D5
NEMPNETT THRUBWELL 55 D5
Neroche Prim Sch TA19 183 C2
Neroche View TA3 183 A7
Nerrols Dr TA2 213 C7
Neston Wlk BS4 22 F8
NETHERCLAY 182 B7
Netherclay TA1 212 A4
Netherclay La TA3 182 B7
NETHER COMPTON 187 F4
Nethercoombe La DT9 225 C5
NETHERCOTT 151 C3
Nethercott La TA4 151 C3
Nethercott Way TA4 151 A3
NETHERHAY 199 F8
Netherhay La DT8 199 F8
Nethermoor Rd TA7 155 B3
NETHERSTOKE 197 D3
Netherstoke La BA22 197 C3
NETHER STOWEY 134 B3
Nether Stowey CE Prim Sch
Nether Stowey TA5 134 A2
Nether Stowey TA5 134 A2
Netherton Cross BA22 197 E6
Netherton La
East Coker BA22 197 F6
Marston Magna BA22 175 A1
Netherton Rd BA21 219 D7
Netherton Wood La BS48 18 A6
Netherways BS21 6 B1
Netley BA21 218 D6
NETTLEBRIDGE 115 D6
Nettlebridge Hill BA3 115 D5
NETTLECOMBE 149 F8
Nettlecombe Hill
Castle Cary BA7 214 F6
Pitcombe BA7 215 A2
Nettlecombe Ho BA5 113 A1
Nettlecombe Park Rd
Monksilver TA4 132 A1
Sticklepath TA4 149 F7
Nettle Combe View BA5 113 A2
Nettlefrith La TA8 66 B1
Neva Rd BS23 48 E6
Neville Cl 1 TA11 173 F7
Neville Pk BA6 158 A5
Nevilles Batch BA3 114 D7
Nevys La TA4 150 E8
Newark St BA1 228 C1
Newbarn Park Rd TA1 212 B1
Newberrys Patch TA3 192 A7
Newbery Cl 4 EX13 198 A1
Newbery La TA18 224 F3
New Bldgs
3 Bampton EX16 164 C1
Dunwear TA7 209 D1
Frome BA11 119 F3
Ilminster TA19 221 B1
North Perrott TA18 196 C4
Oake TA4 167 C4
Peasedown St John BA2 79 B8
New Bond St BA1 228 C2
New Bond Street Pl BA1 228 C2
Newbourne Rd BS22 49 C8
NEWBRIDGE 44 B8
Newbridge Ct BA1 44 B7
Newbridge Dro TA9 105 A1
Newbridge Gdns BA1 44 A8
Newbridge Hill BA1 44 B7
Newbridge Ho BS9 5 C4
Newbridge La TA9 104 F1
Newbridge Prim Sch BA1 44 B7
Newbridge Rd BA1, BA2 44 B7
New Bristol Rd BS22 31 E1
New Buildings La BA11 119 F3
New Bungalows TA20 223 C3
NEWBURY
Coleford 98 B1
Horningsham 144 E4
Newbury BA12 144 E4
Newbury Cotts BA3 117 A8
Newbury Hill BA3 117 A7
Newbury Manor Sch BA11 98 B1
Newbury Terr 3 BA21 218 F7
Newchester Cross TA16 195 E7
New Church Rd BS23 48 D2
New Cl
Bourton SP8 161 F1
Haselbury Plucknett TA18 196 B5
Horrington BA5 113 A4
Street BA16 207 B4
Newclose La BS40 56 D1
Newclose Terr TA14 185 E4
Newcombe Cvn Pk TA8 104 B8
Newcombe Dr BS9 5 C4
Newcombe La BS25 70 B7
Newcombe Rd BS9 5 F7
Newcot Cross EX15 191 A5
NEWCOTT 192 C3
New Cotts
Milton Clevedon BA4 160 A8
West Chinnock TA18 196 B8
NEW CROSS 184 F6
New Cross TA11 211 C3
Newcross Cres BA21 218 B8
New Cross Hill
Barrington TA12, TA13 184 F6
Kingsbury Episcopi TA12 185 A6
New Cut BA5 203 D7
New Cut Bow BS21 16 A6
New Cut Dro BA6 157 C7
Newditch La BS40 20 C1
Newdown La BS41 22 B2
New Ear La BS22 32 E5
Newell DT9 225 C4
New Farm La TA10 172 A7
Newfield TA4 166 F4
Newfields BS40 72 C8
New Fosseway Rd BS14 23 B6
New Fosseway Sch BS13 22 E4
Newfoundland Rd BS2 227 C4
Newfoundland St BS2 227 C4
Newfoundland Way
Bristol BS2 227 C4
Portishead BS20 2 E6
New Friary Cotts BA11 143 C3
Newgate BS1 227 B3
Newgate Cross TA22 163 D7
Newgate La TA4 210 C5
Newhaven Pl BS20 1 E4
Newhaven Rd BS20 1 D4
New Hill TA11 211 E4
Newhouse La TA4 165 E6
Newington Cl BA11 119 E3
Newington Terr BA11 119 E4
New Kingsley Rd BS2 227 C2
New King St BA1 228 B2
New La
Bampton EX16 163 F2
Charlton Horethorne DT9 176 A1
Creech St Michael TA3 169 D5
Cricket St Thomas TA20 194 E4
Haselbury Plucknett TA18 196 C6
Tatworth TA20 198 C8
Witham Friary BA11 143 C4
Newland DT9 225 E4
Newland Cross TA24 128 B1
Newland Dr BS13 22 A4
Newland Flats 5 DT9 225 E4
Newland Gdn 8 DT9 225 E4
Newland Gdns BA11 120 A4
Newland Ho BA1 27 F1
Newland La TA24 127 F1
Newland Rd
Bristol BS13 22 A3
Weston-super-Mare BS23 48 F6
Newlands Cl BS20 2 C5
Newlands Cres TA3 169 C3
Newlands Gn BS21 6 E1
Newlands Gr TA3 169 C3
Newlands Hill BS20 2 C4
Newlands Rd
Keynsham BS31 24 D4
Ruishton TA3 169 C3
Newland Wlk BS13 22 A3
Newlyn Ave BS9 5 D5
Newlyn Cres TA7 136 B4
Newman Cl BA6 206 E6
New Manor House Rd TA10 172 A8
Newmans La
East Huntspill TA9 105 C1
Timsbury BA2 60 B2
Newmarket Ave 9 BS1 227 A3
New Mdws BS14 23 A6
Newmead Dro TA10 172 A2
Newnham Cl BS14 23 D7
New Orchard St BA1 228 C2
New Park Ho BS21 6 D5
Newpark Rd BA9 161 D3
New Pit Cotts BA2 60 F1
New Pk EX16 162 E4
NEWPORT 170 B2
Newport Cl
Clevedon BS21 6 C2
Portishead BS20 1 F4
Newport Hill TA3 170 B2
Newport Rd BS20 4 C5
Newquay Rd BS4 22 F8
New Rd
Banwell BS29 50 E4
Barwick BA22 197 F8
Bathford BA1 29 D2
Bawdrip TA7 136 D2
Bridgwater TA6 209 A5
Burrowbridge TA3, TA7 170 E8
Cannington TA5 135 C1
Carhampton TA24 131 A5
Chapel Allerton BS26 88 C2
Chard Junction TA20 198 F8
Churchill BS25 52 F4
Clevedon BS21 6 D2
Combe St Nicholas TA20 193 D6
Crewkerne TA18 195 B4
Draycott BS27 91 C3
East Huntspill TA9 136 D8
Freshford BA3 64 B5
Frome BA11 120 B4
Hambridge TA12 184 E7
Haselbury Plucknett TA18 196 E6
High Littleton BS39 59 C3
Hinton St George TA17 195 C7
Ilminster TA19 221 B4
Kilmersdon BA3 98 E4
Lyng TA3 170 B6
North Wootton BA4 140 A4
Norton Sub Hamdon TA14 185 E3
Norton Sub Hamdon, Chiselborough TA14 185 F1
Oare EX35 122 D4
Odcombe BA22 186 D3
Othery TA7 155 C2
Pensford BS39 40 D3
Pill BS20 4 C4
Porlock TA24 123 E3
Rawridge EX14 191 E1
Redhill BS40 37 A4
Seavington St Mary TA19 184 E1
Sherborne DT9 225 E3
Shipham BS25 52 E1
South Cadbury BA22 175 E4
Stalbridge DT10 190 B4
Staple Fitzpaine TA3 182 D5
Taunton TA3 168 D1
West Bagborough TA4 151 E4
Weston Town BA4 142 D5
Wiveliscombe TA4 166 A6
Yeovil BA22 218 A5
New Road Gate EX35 122 D5
New Rock Ind Est BA3 96 D2
New Rock Rd BA3 96 D2
Newsome Ave BS20 4 C4
New Sq BA5 113 A2
New St
Bath BA1 228 B2
Bristol BS2 227 C3
Long Sutton TA10 172 E4
Marnhull DT10 190 F5
Mells BA11 118 B7
North Perrott TA18 196 C4
Somerton TA11 211 E4
Wells BA5 203 D5
New Street Flats 4 BS2 227 C3
New Thomas St BS2 227 C2
NEWTON
Combe St Nicholas 193 A7
Watchet 132 E1
Newton Cl
Burnham-on-S TA8 85 A2
West Harptree BS40 74 E6
Newton Ct
14 Bampton EX16 164 B1
Corfe TA3 181 F6
Newton Gn BS48 18 C8
Newton La
Bicknoller TA4 132 E1
Corfe TA3 181 F6
Newton Rd
Barwick BA22 197 F8
Bath BA2 43 F6
North Petherton TA6 153 F3
Taunton TA1 213 E4
Weston-super-Mare BS23 48 E6
Yeovil BA20 219 D3
NEWTON ST LOE 43 D6
Newton Sq 8 EX16 164 B1
Newton's Rd
Weston-super-Mare BS22 31 E3
Weston-super-Mare BS22 31 E4
NEWTOWN
Axbridge 69 D2
Bridgwater 208 E6
Newtown TA12 185 E7
NEW TOWN
Bishop Sutton 57 D7
Freshford 81 F8
Hatch Beauchamp 182 E4
Kington Magna 177 E1
Milborne Port 217 B2
Paulton 77 D6
Wedmore 138 E8
Yeovil 219 C6
Newtown La BA6 140 A1
Newtown Pk TA10 172 A6
Newtown Rd
Highbridge TA9 104 D3
Langport TA10 172 A6
New Way TA10 172 B7
Nibley Rd BS11 4 E5
Nicholas Cl TA22 163 E4
Nicholls Cl TA6 208 D4
Nichol Pl TA4 167 F6
Nichol's Rd BS20 1 F5
Nick Reed's La EX15 180 D1
Niddon's La TA13 195 E8
Nidon La TA7 137 D3
Nigel Pk BS11 4 E7
Nightingale Acre TA3 183 A7
Nightingale Ave BA11 120 B6
Nightingale Cl
1 Bridgwater TA6 209 C4
Burnham-on-S TA8 85 B1
Wells BA5 203 B3
Weston-super-Mare BS22 31 E1
Nightingale Ct
16 Taunton TA1 213 A4
Weston-super-Mare BS22 31 E1
Nightingale Gdns BS48 8 D2
Nightingale Gr BA4 205 C5
Nightingale La BA22 174 F6
Nightingale Rise BS20 1 F3
Nightingales TA4 167 E6
Nightingale Way BA3 97 B8
Nile St BA1 228 A2
Nimbus Rd BS24 49 C5
NIMMER 223 C8
Nine Acre Dro TA7 138 B2
Nine Acre La TA3 170 C4
Nine Barrows La BA5 92 E4
Nine Commons Dro TA10 173 A4
Nippors Way BS25 69 F8
Nithsdale Rd BS23 48 E4
Nixon Trad Units BS24 49 A3
No 1 Royal Cres Mus★ BA1 228 B3
Noah's Ark Zoo Farm★ BS48 9 B7
Noah's Hill TA2 169 B7
Noake Rd DT9 225 B3
Noble St TA1 213 B4
Noel Coward Cl TA8 104 C6
Nomis Pk BS49 34 E2
No Place La TA5 152 E5
Norbins Rd BA6 206 D5
Nordens Mdw TA4 210 D4
Nordrach La BS40 73 D5
Nore Gdns BS20 2 C6
Nore Park Dr BS20 1 F5
Nore Rd BS20 2 A6
Norfolk Ave BS2 227 B4
Norfolk Bldgs BA1 228 A2
Norfolk Cl TA6 209 C3
Norfolk Cres BA1 228 A2
Norfolk Gr BS31 24 C4
Norfolk Hts 10 BS2 227 B4
Norfolk Rd
Portishead BS20 2 E4
Weston-super-Mare BS23 48 F5
Norland Rd BS8 11 F8
Norlet Ct BA6 206 D5
Normandy Ave TA23 202 E6
Normandy Dr TA1 213 C3
Normandy Ho BA16 207 B6
Norman La TA7 156 B7
Norman Rd BS31 25 E3
Normans The BA2 28 F1
Normans Way BS20 3 E7
Norrington Way TA20 223 D2
Northam Farm Cvn Pk & Camp Site TA8 65 F4
Northampton Bldgs BA1 228 B4
Northampton Ho BS48 9 D3
Northampton St BA1 228 B4
Northanger Ct 5 BA2 228 C3
North Ave TA9 104 C4
NORTHAY
Combe St Nicholas 193 B6
Hawkchurch 199 A3
Northay Cross EX13 199 B3
Northay La
Axminster EX13 199 A3
Combe St Nicholas TA20 193 B6
North Bank BA5 203 A8
NORTH BARROW 175 A8
North Barrow Rd BA22 175 A6
North Bradon La TA3 184 A7
NORTH BREWHAM 161 A7
Northbrook Dr TA7 137 F1
Northbrook Rd
Cannington TA5 135 C2
Shapwick TA7 138 A1
Yeovil BA21 219 D7
NORTH CADBURY 175 D6
North Cadbury CE Prim Sch BA22 175 D6
NORTH CHERITON 176 C4
North Cheriton Rd BA9 176 B5
North Chew Terr BS40 39 B3
North Chine Dro BA5 138 D8
North Cl BS27 90 F3
NORTH COKER 197 D8
Northcombe La TA22 163 E7
Northcote Cres BA11 120 A7
Northcote Rd BS8 5 F1
North Cres DT9 217 D3
North Croft TA4 202 D3
NORTH CURRY 170 C4
North Curry CE Prim Sch TA3 170 B3
North Curry CE VC Prim Sch TA3 170 B3
North Devon Link Rd EX16 178 C1
North Down Cl BS25 70 F8
North Down La BS25 70 F8
Northdown Rd BA3 78 E5
North Dro BS48 8 A2
North Elm La BS40 39 B4
NORTHEND 28 F5
NORTH END
Clutton 58 E5
Millmoor 179 E3
Taunton 169 D5

NORTH END *continued*
Yatton 16 F3
North End
Charlton Horethorne DT9 176 A2
Creech St Michael TA3 169 D5
Midsomer Norton BA3 78 B2
North End Rd BS49 16 F3
Northern Path BS21 6 F3
Northern Way BS21 6 F3
NORTHFIELD
Bridgwater 208 C4
Radstock 79 B1
Somerton 211 C5
Northfield
Bridgwater TA6 208 E4
Radstock BA3 79 A3
Somerton TA11 211 C4
Timsbury BA2 60 C3
Winsley BA15 64 F7
Northfield Ave TA1 212 E4
Northfield Cl TA5 134 C6
Northfield Gdns TA1 212 E5
Northfield Ho
Bath BA1 27 F1
Glastonbury BA6 206 E4
Northfield La
Dinnington TA17 195 B8
South Petherton TA13 220 C2
Northfield Rd
Minehead TA24 201 A8
Portishead BS20 1 E3
Taunton TA1 212 E4
Northfields
Bath BA1 27 F1
Taunton TA1 212 B3
Northfields Cl BA1 27 F1
Northfield Way TA11 211 C5
NORTHGATE 210 C5
Northgate
Bridgwater TA6 208 F5
Wiveliscombe TA4 210 C5
Northgate Prim Sch 9 TA6 208 F5
Northgate St BA1 228 C2
North Gr
Pill BS20 4 C4
Wells BA5 203 E5
North Green St 11 BS8 11 F6
North Hill Mews BA11 119 F5
North Hill Rd TA24 200 F8
North Hills Cl BS24 49 B2
North Hill Woodland Trail* TA24 125 B4
North La
Bath BA2 45 D5
Berrow TA8 65 F1
Challacombe EX31, TA24 126 B4
East Coker BA22 197 A7
Nailsea BS48 8 B1
Othery TA7 155 C2
Stogursey TA5 134 C7
2 Weston-super-Mare BS23 48 E7
Yeovil BA20 219 B5
Northleach Wlk BS11 4 F5
North Leaze BS41 11 B2
Northleaze CE Prim Sch
Long Ashton BS41 11 B1
Long Ashton BS41 11 B2
Northleaze Ho BA16 207 C6
North Leaze La BA22 175 C7
Northleigh Ave BS22 31 C1
Northleigh Rd TA1 213 B3
Northload Bridge BA6 206 C5
Northload Bridge Rdbt BA6 206 D5
Northload Dro BS28 109 E2
Northload La BS28 109 D1
Northload St BA6 206 D5
Northload Terr BA6 206 D5
North Mdws BA2 79 E8
Northmead Ave BA3 77 F2
Northmead Cl BA3 77 F2
Northmead Dro TA3 170 A1
Northmead Rd BA3 77 F2
North Mills La TA13 220 C5
Northmoor Dro TA7 136 E1
Northmoor Gn Rd TA7 154 D3
Northmoor Hill TA22 163 B7
Northmoor La TA3 170 C7
Northmoor Rd
Dulverton TA22 163 D7
Othery TA10 155 D1
NORTH NEWTON 153 F2
North Newton Com Prim Sch
North Newton TA7 153 F2
North Newton TA7 153 F2
NORTHOVER
Glastonbury 206 B3
Ilchester 173 E2
Northover Bldgs BA6 206 B3
Northover Dr TA20 223 B5
Northover Farmhouse BA6 207 D8
North Par
Bath BA2 228 C2
Frome BA11 119 F5
North Parade Bldgs 8 BA1 228 C2
North Parade Pas 7 BA1 228 C2
North Parade Rd BA2 45 B6
NORTH PERROTT 196 C4
North Perrott Rd TA18 196 C5
NORTH PETHERTON 153 F4
North Petherton Com Prim Sch TA6 153 F3
North Rd
Banwell BS29 51 A3
Bath, Bathwick BA2 45 C6
Bath, Combe Down BA2 45 B2
Charlton Horethorne DT9 176 A2
Eastertown BS24 67 D2
Leigh Woods BS8 11 D7
Midsomer Norton BA3 78 A1
Minehead TA24 201 A7
Sherborne DT9 225 E5
Timsbury BA2 60 C2
Wells BA5 203 E5
Williton TA4 202 D4
Northside
Castle Cary BA7 214 C6
Rockwell Green TA21 222 B5
North Side Rd BS48 36 F8
North Somerset Mus* BS23 48 E8
North St
Babcary TA11 174 C7
Bradford Abbas DT9 187 E1
Bridgwater TA6 208 E4
Bristol BS1 227 B4
Castle Cary BA7 214 C5
Crewkerne TA18 224 C7
Drayton TA10 171 E3
Haselbury Plucknett TA18 196 C6
Ilminster TA19 221 C4
Langport TA10 172 A5
Martock TA12 185 E6
Milborne Port DT9 217 D2
Milverton TA4 167 A4
Nailsea BS48 8 B1
North Petherton TA6 153 E4
Norton St Philip BA2 81 E4
Norton Sub Hamdon TA14 185 E1
Shepton Beauchamp TA19 184 E4
Somerton TA11 211 E4
South Petherton TA13 220 C5
Stoke sub Hamdon TA14 185 F4
Taunton TA1 212 F4
Wellington TA21 222 D6
Weston-super-Mare BS23 48 E8
Williton TA4 202 D3
Wincanton BA9 216 C4
Wiveliscombe TA4 210 B4
NORTH STOKE 26 C6
North Stoke La BS30 26 B8
North Terr BA21 219 C6
NORTH TOWN
North Cadbury 175 C7
North Wootton 140 D5
Taunton 212 E5
North Town TA11 173 D5
North Town Com Prim Sch TA1 212 E4
Northtown La
North Wootton BA4 140 C4
Taunton TA1 212 E4
North Town Mews TA1 212 E5
Northumberland Bldgs 1 BA1 228 B2
Northumberland Pl 1 BA1 228 C2
North View BA3 79 B2
North View Cl BA2 44 B5
North View Dr BS29 51 A2
North Villas TA4 167 F6
North Way
Bath BA2 44 A5
Midsomer Norton BA3 78 A1
NORTH WESTON 2 C2
NORTHWICK 105 F6
NORTH WICK 39 D8
Northwick Gdns BS39 57 D4
Northwick Rd
Chew Magna BS39, BS41 39 D7
Mark TA9 106 B5
NORTH WIDCOMBE 57 B1
Northwood Cl TA2 168 B4
Northwood Dro BA6 158 A6
NORTH WOOTTON
Sherborne 188 F1
Wells 140 C4
NORTON 31 D4
Norton Cl
Chew Magna BS40 39 B3
Shepton Mallet BA4 205 A5
Norton Dro TA12 185 B8
NORTON FITZWARREN 168 B4
Norton Fitzwarren CE Com Prim Sch TA2 168 B5
Norton Grange BA2 81 E5
NORTON HAWKFIELD 39 F6
NORTON HILL 97 B7
Norton Hill Sch BA3 97 B8
Norton Ho 7 BS1 227 B1
Norton La
Chew Magna BS39, BS40 39 D5
Wellow BA2 81 B7
Weston-super-Mare BS22 31 E4
Whitchurch BS14 23 C2
NORTON MALREWARD 40 B7
Norton Rd TA14 185 E3
NORTON ST PHILIP 81 F4
Norton St Philip CE Fst Sch BA2 81 E4
NORTON SUB HAMDON 185 F3
Norton sub Hamdon CE Prim Sch TA14 185 F3
NORTON'S WOOD 7 C5
Nortons Wood La BS21 7 A5
Norville Cl BS27 90 B8
Norville La BS27 90 B8
Norwich Cl TA1 212 C1
Norwich Ct TA1 212 D2
Norwood Ave BA2 45 E5
Norwood Gr BS20 1 F5
Notaro Wy TA7 154 A4
Notgrove Cl BS22 31 B2
Notlake Dro BS27 89 E4
Notting Hill Way BS26 88 D6
Nova Quarter BA16 207 B5
Nova Scotia Pl BS1 226 A1
Novers Cres BS4 22 C8
Novers Hill BS4 22 C8
Novers La BS4 22 D7
NOVERS PARK 22 D8
Novers Park Dr BS4 22 C8
Novers Park Rd BS4 22 D8
Novers Rd BS4 22 C8
Nowers La TA21 222 C3
Nowhere La BS48 9 A1
Number 15 BA21 219 F7
Nunnery La TA19 183 B4
NUNNEY 143 C8
Nunney Barton BA11 119 B2
Nunney Castle* BA11 143 B8
NUNNEY CATCH 143 B7
Nunney Catch Rbt BA11 143 B7
Nunney Cl
Burnham-on-S TA8 85 C1
Keynsham BS31 25 A2
Nunney Fst Sch BA11 143 B8
Nunney Rd BA11 119 D4
Nurcott La TA24 147 C7
Nursery Cl TA5 135 B5
Nursery Gdns TA20 223 E4
Nursery La BA9 216 C4
Nursery Rd BA20 219 A3
Nursery Rise BA3 96 E4
Nursery Terr TA6 208 E5
Nursery Villas TA20 223 E4
Nutgrove La BS40 39 A4
Nutshole La TA20 194 B2
Nut Tree Cl TA9 136 E8
Nut Tree La TA18 224 D7
Nutts La BA11 101 F8
Nutwell Rd BS22 31 E2
Nutwell Sq BS22 31 E2
Nydon The TA7 137 D3
NYE 51 E8
Nye Cl BS27 90 C7
Nye Dro BS24 51 E8
Nye Rd BS25 51 F5
NYLAND 90 C1
Nyland Dro BS27 90 B1
Nyland La BA8 190 C8
Nyland View BS27 90 F3
NYNEHEAD 167 C1
Nynehead Hollow TA21 167 C1
Nynehead Rd
Nynehead TA21 167 C1
Wellington TA21 222 F8
Nythe Rd TA7 156 A5

O

Oak Apple Dr TA6 208 D6
Oak Ave BA2 44 C3
Oak Cl TA24 200 D7
Oak Ct
Bristol BS14 23 A5
Weston-super-Mare BS22 32 C3
Oakdale Gdns BS22 31 F2
Oakdale Rd BS14 23 A8
Oak Dr
Crewkerne TA18 224 D7
Portishead BS20 2 B4
OAKE 167 D4
Oake Acres TA4 167 D4
Oake, Bradford & Nynehead CE Prim Sch TA4 167 D4
Oake Cl TA4 167 D4
Oake Gn TA4 167 D4
Oak End Way TA20 223 C5
Oaken Ground TA21 222 B5
Oakfield Acad BA11 119 D4
Oakfield Cl
Bath BA1 44 D8
Frome BA11 119 D5
Oakfield Gr BS8 226 B4
Oakfield Pk TA21 222 E4
Oakfield Pl BS8 226 B4
Oakfield Rd
Bridgwater TA6 208 C4
Bristol BS8 226 B4
Frome BA11 119 D4
Keynsham BS31 24 F2
Street BA16 207 B4
Oakford Ave BS23 48 F8
Oakford La BA1 29 A8
Oak Gr BS20 4 C5
Oakgrove Way TA6 209 D6
OAKHILL 115 A3
Oakhill BS24 49 A2
Oakhill CE Prim Sch BA3 115 B3
Oakhill Cl BS48 9 B1
Oakhill Ct BA3 116 E3
Oakhill Rd BA2 44 F2
Oak Ho
Brean TA8 65 E2
Bristol BS13 22 D4
Oakhurst Rd BS9 5 F5
Oak La
East Anstey TA22 162 E6
Rodhuish TA24 131 A3
Taunton TA2 212 F6
Oakland Ct TA12 185 E7
Oakland Dr
Hutton BS24 49 E3
Martock TA12 185 E7
Oakland La TA13 185 B1
Oakland Rd TA12 185 E7
Oaklands
Cheddar BS27 90 A8
Clevedon BS21 6 C4
Paulton BS39 77 E4
Temple Cloud BS39 58 E1
Oaklands Ave TA20 223 F4
Oaklands Prim Sch BA20 218 F5
Oaklands Rd BA21 219 D7
Oakleigh BA20 218 D2
Oakleigh Cl BS48 19 B5
Oakley
Bath BA2 45 E5
Clevedon BS21 16 B8
Oakley Cl TA7 154 F5
Oakley La BA22 186 F6
Oak Lodge Cres TA24 200 F7
Oakmear Rd TA6 208 E3
Oak Rd
Nether Stowey TA5 134 B2
Winscombe BS25 70 A8
Oakridge Cl BS25 70 B7
Oakridge La BS25 70 C6
Oakridge Pk BA21 219 A6
Oak's Dro BA5 138 E8
Oaksey Gr BS48 9 A1
Oak St BA2 228 B1
Oaks The
Nailsea BS48 9 A2
Taunton TA1 213 C1
Wembdon TA6 208 C6
Winford BS40 37 F7
Oak Terr BA3 78 D1
Oak Tree Arena (Somerset Speedway)* TA9 105 A5
Oak Tree Cl EX14 191 F2
Oaktree Ct BS11 4 E7
Oaktree Gdns BS13 21 E5
Oak Tree Ho 13 TA14 185 F4
Oaktree Pk BS24 49 E5
Oaktree Pl BS22 32 C3
Oak Tree Pl TA8 85 A3
Oak Tree Way TA5 135 B2
Oak Tree Wlk BS31 24 D3
Oak Vale La BA8 190 A6
Oak Way BA22 218 A7
OARE 122 E4
OAREFORD 122 F3
Oare Post TA24 123 B3
Oasis Acad Brightstowe BS11 4 E7
Oasis Acad Brislington BS4 23 F8
Oasis Acad John Williams BS14 23 B7
Oasis Acad Long Cross BS11 4 F8
Oasis Acad New Oak BS14 23 B7
Oatcroft La DT9 188 B4
Oatfield BS48 19 F1
Oath Dro TA7 171 B5
OATHILL 199 E8
Oathill Cotts BA4 140 F3
Oathill La
Clapton TA18 195 C1
Winsham TA18 199 E8
Oatlands Ave BS14 23 A6
Oatley La TA5 134 F2
Oborne La DT9 188 F5
Oborne Rd DT9 225 F5
OBRIDGE 213 A6
Obridge Cl TA2 213 A6
Obridge Cres TA2 213 A6
Obridge La TA2 213 A6
Obridge Rd TA2 213 A6
Obridge Viaduct TA2 213 B6
Observatory Field BS25 70 B8
Observatory The BS22 31 D3
Ocean Way BA22 174 B3
Octagon The 5 TA1 212 F4
Octavia Cl TA6 208 E2
Octavius Rd BS31 24 F8
ODCOMBE 186 D2
Odcombe Hollow BA22 196 E8
ODD DOWN 44 D2
Odeon Bldgs BS23 48 E7
Odins Rd BA2 44 D1
Oggshole Farm La TA5 153 A1
Olands Rd TA21 222 D6
Old Acre Rd BS14 23 A3
Old Airfield Cvn Pk The TA7 155 A4
Old Ansford Inn BA7 214 C6
Old App BA7 159 A3
Old Banwell Rd BS24 50 B4
Oldbarn La
Bampton EX16 163 E1
Compton Martin BS40 56 D1
Old Barn La
Felton BS40 37 A5
Hatch Beauchamp TA3 182 F6
Old Barn Way BA20 218 E3
Old Barrow Hill BS11 4 D7
Old Basin TA6 209 B2
Oldberry La TA22 163 D6
Old Blackditch Rd TA9 136 B6
Old Bond St 4 BA1 228 B2
Old Bowden Way DT9 217 D4
Old Bread St BS2 227 C2
Old Brewery Ind Est The TA4 210 C4
Old Brewery Rd TA4 210 C4
Old Brewery The
6 Frome BA11 119 F4
Rode BA11 101 E8
Old Brewhouse The BA1 27 B2
Old Bridge Cl BA6 206 D5
Oldbridge Rd BS14 23 C3
Old Bristol Rd
East Brent TA9 86 E4
Oakhill BA3, BA4 114 E1
Old Bristol Rd *continued*
Priddy BA5, BS40 93 A6
Shepton Mallet BA4 141 C8
Wells BA5 112 B5
Weston-super-Mare BS22 32 A2
Oldbroach La TA3 213 F2
Old Bull La BA4 141 F7
Old Burnett La BS31 42 A7
Old Burnham Rd TA9 104 D4
Old Chapel BA1 228 C4
Old Chapel Ct TA10 172 A6
Old Chapel La BS48 17 F7
Old Chapel Rd TA7 155 B3
Old Chelsea La BS8 10 C4
Old Church Rd
Axbridge BS26 70 C1
Clevedon BS21 6 C3
Nailsea BS48 18 D8
Weston-super-Mare BS23 48 D2
OLD CLEEVE 131 E5
Old Cleeve CE Sch TA23 131 E4
Old Coach Rd BS26 69 E2
Old Combe Hill TA3 181 F5
Old Compton La DT9 187 F2
Old Co-op Cotts BA3 117 A7
Old Dairy Ct BS21 6 E3
Old Dairy The BA2 44 D4
OLD DITCH 110 E7
Old Ditch BA5 110 E7
Old Ditch La TA7 155 E7
OLD DOWN 95 F3
Old Down La BA4 142 A6
Old Drill Hall The BS2 227 C3
Old England Way BA2 79 E8
Old Farm DT9 225 C4
Old Farm Cl TA24 200 E6
Old Farm Ct
Blackford BS28 107 E4
Queen Camel BA22 174 F3
Old Farm Pl TA17 195 C7
Old Farm Rd
Minehead TA24 200 E6
Nether Stowey TA5 134 B2
Old Ferry Rd BA2 44 C6
Oldfield BS21 6 E1
Oldfield La BA2 44 E4
OLDFIELD PARK 44 E4
Oldfield Park Inf Sch BA2 44 D6
Oldfield Park Jun Sch BA2 44 C4
Oldfield Park Sta BA2 44 D6
Oldfield Pl BS8 11 F5
Oldfield Rd
Bath BA2 228 A1
Bristol BS8 226 A1
Oldfield Sch BA1 26 F1
OLDFORD 101 B1
Oldford Hill BA11 101 B1
Oldford Residential Pk BA11 101 B1
Old Forge Mews BS49 34 D8
Old Forge The BA2 61 B4
Old Forge Way BA2 79 E8
Old Fosse Rd
Bath BA2 44 C1
Clandown BA3 78 E4
Old Frome Rd
Bath BA2 62 E8
Doulting BA4 141 E8
Horrington BA5 113 D3
Oakhill BA3, BA4 115 B1
Old Glove Factory The BA22 186 B6
Old Gore La BA3 95 E3
Old Green The 2 DT9 225 D4
Old Ham TA5 133 D6
Old Hill
Wincanton BA9 216 C5
Winford BS40 37 D6
Wrington BS40 35 F3
Oldhill Farm La BS40 37 D6
Old Hitchen 5 TA16 195 F7
Old Ho The BA3 64 C5
Old Junction Rd BS23 49 B5
Old King St BA1 228 B3
Old King Street Ct BS1 227 B3
Old La
Farmborough BA2 60 A6
Nailsea BS21 8 C4
Porlock TA24 124 B3
Old Main Rd TA6 135 F5
Old Malt Ho BS2 227 C4
Old Maltings The BA3 115 A3
Old Manor Est BA3 116 C8
Old Market 6 TA12 185 E6
Old Market Ct BA6 206 D5
Old Market Mews DT10 190 B4
Old Market Rd
Shepton Mallet BA4 205 B6
Sydenham TA6 209 B6
Old Market Rdbt BS2 227 C3
Old Market St BS2 227 C3
Oldmead La BS26 87 C5
Oldmead Wlk BS13 21 E7
Old Midford Rd BA2 63 B7
Old Millard's Hill BA3 78 B3
Old Mill Rd
Portishead BS20 2 D5
Woolavington TA7 136 E4
Old Mill Road Ind Est BS20 2 E6
OLD MILLS 77 D3
Old Mills Ind Est BS39 77 E2
Old Mills La BS39 77 D3
Old Mill Way
Wells BA5 203 B2
Weston-super-Mare BS24 50 A8
OLDMIXON 49 B1
Oldmixon Cres BS24 49 A3
Oldmixon Prim Sch BS24 49 A2

Oldmixon Rd BS24 49 B1
Old Mixon Rd BS24 49 C2
Old Newbridge Hill BA1 44 A8
Old Oaks Cl TA6 208 D5
Old Orch TA20 223 F1
Old Orchard BA1 228 C3
Old Orchard Cl TA19 183 F4
Old Orchards TA20 223 E4
Old Orchard St BA1 228 C2
Old Orchard The TA19 223 A5
Old Orch The TA13 220 D4
Old Park Hill BS2 226 C3
Old Park Rd
Bristol BS11 4 D7
Clevedon BS21 6 E4
Old Pawlett Rd TA9 136 A7
Old Pensford La BS31 24 D1
Old Pit Rd BA3 97 C8
Old Pit Terr BA3 78 E4
Old Pk BS2 226 C3
Old Police Station The
BA9 216 C4
Old Post Office Cotts TA7 153 F2
Old Post Office La BS23 48 D8
Old Pound Ct SP8 161 E1
Old Print Works 6 BA11 119 E5
Old Print Works Rd BS39 77 D6
Old Priory Rd BS20 4 B4
Old Quarry BA2 44 D2
Old Quarry Rd BS11 4 E7
Old Quarry Rise BS11 4 E7
Old Rd
North Petherton TA6 153 F4
Odcombe BA22 186 C2
Pensford BS39 40 E3
Radstock BA3 79 C1
South Cadbury BA22 175 E4
Old Rd The BA8 189 D6
Old Rectory The TA9 86 C4
Oldrey La TA24 147 C8
Old Saw Mills The BA3 117 A3
Old Sawmill The BA12 161 F6
Old School Cl
Alweston DT9 189 A1
Ashcott TA7 156 B8
Churchill BS25 52 F4
Yeovil BA21 218 C5
Old School Hill BA2 62 F7
Old School Ho BA21 219 C5
Old School Ho The
Bath BA1 228 B4
Whatley BA11 118 A3
Old School La
Bleadon BS24 67 C6
Catcott TA7 137 D2
Clifton Wood BS8 226 B2
Lynford-on-F TA11 158 C2
Old School Pl BA5 203 E5
Old School The BA11 119 E4
Oldshute La TA22 163 C7
Old Sneed Ave BS9 5 D4
Old Sneed Cotts BS9 5 E4
Old Sneed Pk BS9 5 D4
Old Sneed Rd BS9 5 D4
Old St BS21 6 E3
Old Station Cl
Cheddar BS27 90 A7
Wrington BS40 35 D1
Old Station Ct TA20 223 D5
Old Station Gdns BA8 190 A7
Old Station La BA10 215 C4
Old Station Rd BA20 219 C4
Old Station Way BA20 219 C4
Old Stream Farm TA10 171 E3
Old Street La BA5 204 B7
Old Tannery The 20 BS2 227 C3
Old Tarnwell BS39 40 B2
Old Taunton Rd TA6 209 A4
Old Threshing Mill The
BA4 141 B2
Old Tiverton Rd EX16 164 C1
Old Tk BA2 63 F7
Old Town TA20 223 C3
Old Vicarage Cl TA7 137 B2
Old Vicarage Ct BS14 23 C4
Old Vicarage Gdns TA13 220 C4
Old Vicarage Gn BS31 24 E6
Old Vicarage La TA4 167 E8
Old Vicarage Rd BA9 160 C2
Old Vicarage The TA21 222 E6
Oldville Ave BS21 6 D2
Old Walcot Sch The BA1 228 B3
Old Wall BS24 66 D5
Old Water Gdns The BS40 54 E2
OLD WAY 184 A4
Old Way
Chipstable TA4 165 D6
Stogumber TA4 150 D8
Oldway Ho TA21 222 F4
Oldway La TA3 183 A8
Oldway Pk TA21 222 F4
Oldway Pl TA9 104 D4
Oldway Rd
East Anstey TA22 162 F5
Wellington TA21 222 E4
OLDWAYS END 162 E3
Old Wells Rd
Bath BA2 44 F3
Croscombe BA5 204 D6
Doulting BA4 142 A8
Glastonbury BA6 206 F6
Leigh u M BA3, BA4, BA11 117 B2
Shepton Mallet BA4 205 A5
Old Weston Rd
Congresbury BS49 34 B5
Flax Bourton BS48 20 B8
Old Withy Rd TA9 136 C7
Old Yarn Mills The DT9 225 D2
Oliver Brooks Rd BA3 96 E7
Oliver's La TA19 183 B2
Olivers Rd TA7 155 C4
Olivier Cl TA8 104 C6
One Elm TA10 172 B7
Onega Ctr BA1 228 A3
Onega Terr BA1 228 A3
Oolite Gr BA2 44 D1
Oolite Rd BA2 44 D1
Opal Wlk TA6 209 C8
Orange Gr BA1 228 C2
Orange St BS2 227 C4
Orchard Ave
Bristol BS1 226 C2
Midsomer Norton BA3 77 F1
Portishead BS21 7 E4
Orchard Cl
Banwell BS29 51 B3
Bishop Sutton BS39 57 C3
Bradford On Tone TA4 167 F1
Bristol, Westbury on T BS9 5 F5
Carhampton TA24 131 B5
Castle Cary BA7 214 B7
Cheddar BS27 90 B8
Coleford BA3 117 A7
Congresbury BS49 34 D4
Cossington TA7 137 A3
Coxley BA5 139 E6
Drimpton DT8 199 F8
East Brent TA9 86 E4
East Chinnock BA22 196 E8
East Huntspill TA9 136 E8
Felton BS40 37 C8
Flax Bourton BS48 20 A8
Frome BA11 119 D4
Highbridge TA9 104 E4
Keynsham BS31 24 D6
Long Sutton TA10 172 E4
3 North Petherton TA6 153 E3
Odcombe BA22 186 C2
Portishead BS20 2 D5
Queen Camel BA22 174 F3
Rockwell Green TA21 222 A5
South Petherton TA13 220 C5
Sparkford BA22 175 A5
Taunton TA3 168 D1
West Coker BA22 197 A8
Weston-super-Mare, Kewstoke
BS22 31 B3
Weston-super-Mare, Worle
BS22 31 F2
Westwood BA15 64 F3
Wincanton BA9 216 D3
Wrington BS40 35 E2
Yeovil Marsh BA21 187 A5
Orchard Cl The BS24 49 F4
ORCHARD COMMON 182 A8
Orchard Cotts
Croscombe BA5 204 B7
Timsbury BA2 60 F1
Orchard Cres BS11 4 D7
Orchard Ct
Claverham BS49 17 F1
Highbridge TA9 104 E3
Minehead TA24 201 B4
Street BA16 207 C6
Wellington TA21 222 E6
Orchard Dr
Bristol BS13 22 A6
Sandford BS25 52 A4
Southwick BA14 83 E3
Taunton TA1 212 A3
Orchard End BS40 74 F4
Orchard Gdns
Paulton BS39 77 E6
West Buckland TA21 180 F7
Orchard Gn TA2 212 F8
Orchard Gr TA9 105 C8
Orchard Ho
Weston-super-Mare BS22 31 F2
Yeovil BA21 219 A6
Orchard La
Allerford TA24 124 B4
Bristol BS1 226 C2
Chewton Mendip BA3 94 F6
Crewkerne TA18 224 C6
Evercreech BA4 141 E1
Kingsbury Episcopi TA12 185 B8
Thorncombe TA20 199 B6
Wembdon TA6 208 D5
Orchard Lea
Coxley BA5 139 E7
Pill BS20 4 D4
Wells BA5 203 C5
Orchardleigh BA22 196 E8
Orchardleigh View BA11 119 D6
Orchard Lodge BA2 45 F8
Orchard Mead TA19 183 C1
Orchard Paddock BA5 203 A7
Orchard Pk
Bristol BS14 23 D4
West Camel BA22 174 D3
Orchard Pl
Aller TA10 171 D8
6 Langaller TA2 169 C5
1 Weston-super-Mare BS23 48 E7
Orchard Rd
Axbridge BS26 70 C1
Backwell BS48 19 A6
Carhampton TA24 131 B5
Clevedon BS21 6 D2
Hutton BS24 49 E2
Long Ashton BS41 10 F1
Milborne Port DT9 217 C2
Minehead TA24 200 F8
Nailsea BS48 8 D1
Paulton BS39 77 E6
Somerton TA11 211 B4
Orchard Rd *continued*
Street BA16 207 C6
Orchard Rise
Crewkerne TA18 224 C5
Fivehead TA3 170 F2
Porlock TA24 124 A3
Ruishton TA3 169 C4
Orchards Sh Ctr TA1 212 F3
Orchard St
Bristol BS1 226 C2
Frome BA11 119 E5
Weston-super-Mare BS23 48 E8
Yeovil BA20 219 A4
Orchards The
Bristol, Shirehampton BS11 4 E6
Horrington BA5 113 A2
Stocklinch TA19 184 C4
Orchard Terr
5 Bath BA2 44 B6
Glastonbury BA6 206 D5
Orchard The
Banwell BS29 51 A3
Bath, Combe Down BA2 45 B1
Batheaston BA1 28 F5
Bath, Newbridge BA1 44 A7
Chard TA20 223 D2
Corston BA2 43 B8
Freshford BA3 64 C5
Holywell Lake TA21 179 E7
Locking BS24 50 A5
Meare BA6 138 D4
Pensford BS39 40 E4
Pill BS20 4 C4
Ruishton TA3 169 C2
Upper Stanton Drew BS39 40 A2
Orchard Vale
Ilminster TA19 221 B3
Langport TA10 172 A5
Midsomer Norton BA3 77 F1
Orchard View
Baltonsborough BA6 158 B6
Haselbury Plucknett TA18 196 C6
Orchard Way
Charlton Horethorne DT9 176 A2
Cheddar BS27 90 B8
Keinton Mandeville TA11 158 A1
Misterton TA18 224 F3
Peasedown St John BA2 79 D7
Shapwick TA7 137 F1
Taunton TA1 213 D5
Timberscombe TA24 130 B5
Williton TA4 202 E4
Woolavington TA7 136 E3
Orchard Wlk
Churchill BS25 52 E4
Milborne Port DT9 217 C2
Orchard Wyndham★ TA4 132 B2
Orchid Cl TA1 169 A1
Orchid Dr
Bath BA2 44 C2
Keynsham BS31 24 E3
Orchids The TA8 85 A2
Orchid Wy TA6 208 E1
Oriel Dr BA6 206 D4
Oriel Gdns BA1 28 C2
Oriel Gr BA2 44 B4
Oriel Rd BA16 207 C5
Orme Dr BS21 6 D5
Ormerod Rd BS9 5 E5
Ormrod Gr BS24 50 C5
Orneage Cl BA11 101 E8
Orwell Dr BS31 25 A4
Osborne Ave BS23 48 F7
Osborne Gr TA1 212 E3
Osborne Pl TA16 195 F7
Osborne Rd
Bath BA1 44 B7
Bridgwater TA6 208 F6
Bristol BS3 226 C1
Weston-super-Mare BS23 48 F7
Yeovil BA20 219 A5
Osborne's La BA1 27 A3
Osborne Villas BS2 226 C4
Osborne Wallis Ho BS8 226 A1
Osborne Way TA1 212 E3
Osborne Wlk TA8 104 C6
Osmond Dr BA5 203 B3
Osmond Rd 2 BS24 49 F7
Osprey Ct BS14 22 D5
Osprey Gdns BS22 31 F1
Ostlings La BA1 29 B2
Ostrey Mead BS27 90 B7
Otago Terr 5 BA1 28 C2
OTHERY 155 B2
Othery Village Prim Sch
TA7 155 C2
Othery Village Sch TA7 155 C2
Ottawa Rd BS23 48 F3
OTTERFORD 181 E1
Otterford Cl BS14 23 B5
Otterford Gypsy Pk TA3 181 D2
Otterford Lakes Nature
Reserve★ TA3 192 B8
Otterford Lakes Nature Trail★
TA3 181 E1
Otterham La TA3 183 F8
OTTERHAMPTON 135 A6
Otterhampton Prim Sch
TA5 135 B5
Otter Rd 1 BS21 6 E1
Otter Vale Cl EX14 191 F1
Ottery La DT9 225 C3
Our Lady of Mount Carmel RC
Prim Sch
Wincanton BA9 216 C3
Wincanton BA9 216 C3
Our Lady of the Rosary RC
Prim Sch BS11 5 A8
Outer Circ TA1 213 D5
Outer Gullands TA1 212 D2
Outmoor Dro TA10 172 D3
Outmoor Straight Dro
TA10 172 D3
OVAL THE 44 C4
Oval The BA2 44 C4
Overbrook Bsns Ctr BS28 107 D4
Overcombe BA8 189 E8
OVER COMPTON 187 F4
Overdale
Clandown BA3 78 E5
Peasedown St John BA2 60 F3
Overhill BS20 4 D4
Over Innox BA11 119 F6
Overland La TA3 170 C3
Overlands
North Curry TA3 170 C4
Ruishton TA3 169 C4
OVERLEIGH 207 C3
Overleigh
Street BA16 207 C3
Street BA16 207 C4
Overstables La BS21 6 D3
OVER STOWEY 134 A1
OVER STRATTON 220 D1
OVERTON 169 C7
Overton BA9 216 D4
Owen Dr BS8 10 B4
Owen St TA21 222 C6
Owlaborough La EX36 162 B2
Owl St
South Petherton TA13 220 B8
Stocklinch TA19 184 C3
Owsley Cotts TA19 184 E4
Oxendale BA16 207 B5
Oxen Dr TA6 209 B6
Oxen La TA3 170 B3
OXENPILL 138 C4
Oxenpill BA6 138 C4
Oxen Rd TA18 224 C6
Oxford Pl
Bath BA2 45 C2
19 Bristol, Clifton BS8 11 F6
10 Taunton TA2 213 A8
Weston-super-Mare BS23 48 D7
Oxford Rd BA21 219 E7
Oxford Row BA1 228 B3
Oxford Sq BS24 50 B6
Oxford St
Bristol BS2 227 C2
Bristol, Tyndall's Park BS2 226 C4
Burnham-on-S TA8 104 B6
Evercreech BA4 141 E1
Weston-super-Mare BS23 48 D7
Oxford Terr 4 TA6 209 B4
Oxhayes DT8 199 F8
Oxhouse La
Failand BS8 10 B6
Winford BS40 37 D6
Oxleaze
5 Bishops Lydeard TA4 167 F8
Bristol BS13 22 D4
Oxleaze La BS41 21 E3
Oxleaze Way BS39 77 D6
Oxley Cotts DT9 225 C4
Ozenhay BS39 75 E6

P

Packers' Way TA18 196 B3
Pack Horse La BA2 62 F7
PACKSADDLE 119 F7
Packsaddle Way BA11 119 F7
Pacquet Ho BS20 4 D5
Paddles La BA11 119 D1
Paddock Cl TA3 169 D5
Paddock Dr TA9 104 D4
Paddock Gdn BS14 22 F4
Paddock Park BS22 32 B2
Paddocks Cvn Pk The
BS26 87 A7
Paddocks The
Bath BA2 45 B1
Ilchester BA22 173 E1
Sandford BS25 52 C4
Wellington TA21 222 E5
Weston-super-Mare BS23 48 D2
Paddock The
Banwell BS29 51 A3
Clevedon BS21 6 D2
Corston BA2 43 B7
Dulverton TA22 163 D6
Galhampton BA22 175 D8
Portishead BS20 2 D4
Taunton, Dowsland TA1 168 F1
Taunton, Trull TA3 168 D1
Paddock Wlk DT9 217 C2
Paddock Woods BA2 45 D2
Paddons Farm TA5 134 C6
Padfield Cl BA2 44 B5
Padfield Gn BA4 141 E6
Padleigh Hill BA2 44 B2
Padstow Rd BS4 22 F8
Paganel Cl TA24 200 F6
Paganel Rd TA24 200 F6
Paganel Rise TA24 200 E6
Paganel Way TA24 200 E6
Pagans Hill BS40 38 D2
Pageant Dr DT9 225 D3
Page La BA6 140 A2
Page's Ct BS49 34 C8
Page's Hill BA16 207 C1
Pages Mead BS11 4 C8
PAINTMOOR 194 B4
Paintmoor La TA20 194 B4
Palace Ct BA5 203 D3
Palace Gdns TA4 210 C4
Palace Yard Mews BA1 228 B2
Palfrey's La TA20 193 D3
Palmer Cl TA6 208 F2
Palmer Row 7 BS23 48 E8
Palmers Cl TA8 104 D8
Palmer's Elm BS24 33 B4
Palmer's End La TA12 184 F7
Palmers La BA2 61 B3
Palmers Mead TA21 222 D8
Palmers Rd BA6 206 D4
Palmer St
Frome BA11 119 F4
South Petherton TA13 220 C4
Weston-super-Mare BS23 48 E8
Palmerston Rd TA1 212 D5
Palmer's Way BS24 49 D2
Palm Tree Cl TA6 209 E5
PANBOROUGH 138 F8
Panborough Dro BA5 138 F8
Panoramic The BS1 226 C3
Paper La BS39 77 D6
Paper Mill Gdns BS20 2 F6
Parade Nurseries TA24 200 F7
Parade The
1 Bath BA2 44 B6
Bristol, Bishopsworth BS13 22 A6
Bristol, Shirehampton BS11 4 E6
Chardstock EX13 198 A7
Minehead TA24 200 F7
Paradise Cres BA4 141 E2
Paradise La
Croscombe BA5 204 B7
Glastonbury BA6 139 D2
Langport TA10 172 A7
Tatworth TA20 193 F1
Paradise Rd BA6 206 D5
Paradise Row BS39 41 A6
Paragon Ct 13 BS23 30 C1
Paragon Pl TA6 209 A3
Paragon Rd BS23 30 C1
Paragon Sch The BA2 45 A3
Paragon The
Bath BA1 228 C3
Bristol BS8 11 F6
Paray Dr BA5 203 F5
PARBROOK 158 D7
Parbrook Ct BS14 23 B5
Parbrook La BA6 158 D7
Parcroft Gdns BA20 218 F5
PARDLESTONE 133 C5
Pardlestone La TA5 133 C5
Parfields BA20 218 F5
Parish Brook Rd BS48 8 B2
Parish Hill BA22 175 D5
Parish Land La TA5 152 D5
Parish Mews BA20 218 C5
Parish Quarry Rd TA4 150 B4
PARK 156 D1
Park Ave
Bath BA2 228 B1
Bridgwater TA6 208 D4
Castle Cary BA7 214 B4
Yatton BS49 17 B1
Park Barn La TA19 183 C4
Park Batch BS40 54 F3
Park Bglws EX16 179 B3
Park Cl
Barton St David TA11 158 A3
Cossington TA7 136 F3
Keynsham BS31 24 D5
Paulton BS39 77 D5
Staplehay TA3 181 D8
Street BA16 207 C5
Park Cnr
Hambridge TA3 184 B7
Leigh u M BA11 117 D3
Sharpstone BA2 64 A4
PARK CORNER 64 A4
Park Cotts TA20 223 B5
Park Cres
Chard TA20 223 B5
Cossington TA7 136 F3
Park Ct 5 BS23 48 E5
Park End BS29 50 E4
Park End Rd TA5 152 B4
Parker Cl TA21 222 E6
Parkes Ave BS24 50 D4
Parkes Rd BS24 50 C5
Park Farm BA6 206 C4
Park Farm Rd BA6 206 C4
Parkfield Cl TA6 153 F4
Parkfield Cres TA1 212 D2
Parkfield Dr TA1 212 D3
Parkfield Gdns BS39 57 D3
Parkfield Prim Sch TA1 212 D3
Parkfield Rd
Axbridge BS26 70 D1
Taunton TA1 212 D3
Parkfields Orch BA6 157 E4
Parkfields Residential Home
BA6 157 E4
Park Gate TA2 168 F7
Parkgate La BA11 101 E7
Park Gdns
Bath BA1 44 D8
Yeovil BA20 219 A5
Park Gr DT10 190 B4
Park Hayes BA3 116 F3
Park Hill
Bristol BS11 4 F6
Mells BA11 118 C7
Pilton BA4 140 E3
Park Hill Dr BA11 119 F6
Park Ho BA2 44 E4

Parkhouse La BS31 24 C2
Parkhouse Rd TA24 200 E7
Parkhurst Rd BS23 49 A7
Park La
Barton St David TA11 158 A3
Bath BA1 44 D7
Blagdon BS40 54 F3
Cannington TA5 135 B3
Carhampton TA24 131 A5
Castle Cary BA7 214 D7
Combe St Nicholas TA20 193 C6
Downhead BA4 117 A1
Faulkland BA3 80 B1
Goathurst TA5 153 C4
Henstridge BA8 190 A8
High Ham TA10 156 D1
Ilminster TA19 183 E1
Kingsdon TA11 173 E5
Kingston St Mary TA2 168 C8
Langport TA10 171 E4
Montacute BA22, TA15 186 B3
North Newton TA7 154 A3
North Petherton TA6 153 F4
Seavington St Mary TA19 184 C1
Thorncombe TA20 199 A7
Wellington TA21 222 C1
West Buckland TA21 180 E7
Yenston BA8 189 F8
Park La Cl TA24 131 A5
Parklands BS39 59 D2
Parklands Ave BS22 32 A4
Parklands Educate Together Prim Sch BS24 50 B6
Parklands Rd
Bristol BS3 11 E4
Wellington TA21 222 D7
Parklands Rise TA24 200 D7
Parklands Way TA11 211 B4
Parkland Wlk TA18 224 C4
Park Lodge BA20 219 A5
Parkmead TA2 213 E8
Park Pl
Bath BA1 228 A4
Bristol BS2 226 C3
Bristol BS8 226 B3
Castle Cary BA7 214 C5
Weston-super-Mare BS23 48 D8
Park Rd
Bath BA1 44 B7
Bridgwater TA6 208 D4
Bristol BS3 226 B1
Bristol, Shirehampton BS11 4 F6
Bruton BA10 215 E5
Chard TA20 223 C4
Clevedon BS21 6 D4
Congresbury BS49 34 E3
Frome BA11 119 E4
Henstridge BA8 190 A6
Keynsham BS31 24 E4
Paulton BS39 77 D5
Shepton Mallet BA4 205 B5
Stalbridge DT10 190 B4
Street BA16 207 C5
Yeovil BA20 219 B5
Park Row BS1 226 C3
Park Sch The BA20 219 A5
Parks Cotts TA2 168 D8
Parkside Ct 1 TA6 209 B4
Parks La
Brompton Ralph TA4 150 C3
Minehead TA24 200 F7
Park St
Bath BA1 228 A4
Bristol BS1 226 C3
Castle Cary BA7 214 C5
Dunster TA24 201 D1
Exford TA24 128 D1
Minehead TA24 200 F7
Taunton TA1 212 E3
Yeovil BA20 219 B4
Parks The
Bridgwater TA6 208 D4
Minehead TA24 200 E7
Parkstone Ave TA6 209 A2
Park Street Ave BS1 226 C3
Park Street Mews BA1 228 A4
Parks View TA24 124 A4
Parksway Ct TA24 200 E7
Park Terr
Chard TA20 223 B6
Glastonbury BA6 206 D4
Minehead TA24 200 F7
Park The
Castle Cary BA7 214 B4
Keynsham BS31 24 E6
Portishead BS20 2 F5
Yatton BS49 17 B1
Yeovil BA20 219 A5
Park View
Axminster EX13 198 A3
Bath BA2 44 D6
Cotford St Luke TA4 167 F6
Crewkerne TA18 224 C4
Crewkerne, Misterton TA18 196 B3
Montacute TA15 186 B3
Stogursey TA5 134 C5
Park Villas BS23 48 D8
Park Wall BA10 215 F5
Park Wall Dro TA7 209 F4
Park Water La DT8 199 F5
Parkway
Bridgwater TA6 209 C5
Timsbury BA2 60 E2
Park Way
Bruton BA10 215 E5
Park Way *continued*
Midsomer Norton BA3 97 A8
Ruishton TA3 169 C3
Park Way BS22 32 B1
Parkway La BA2 60 D3
Park Wlk BS20 4 D4
Park Wood Cl BS14 22 F4
Parlour Ho TA1 213 B5
Parmin Cl TA1 213 C3
Parmin Way TA1 213 C3
Parnell Rd BS21 6 D3
Parnell Way TA8 104 B8
Parrett Cl TA10 171 F5
Parrett Mead
South Perrott DT8 196 C1
Taunton TA1 213 D3
Parrett Way TA6 209 B3
Parrett Works Cotts TA12 220 F8
Parricks La EX13 198 D3
Parrocks La TA20 198 C8
Parry Cl BA2 44 B4
Parry's Cl BS9 5 E5
Parrys Gr BS9 5 E5
Parry's La BS9 5 F5
Parsonage Cl
Langport TA10 172 A5
Somerton TA11 211 E3
West Harptree BS40 74 E6
Winford BS40 37 F6
Parsonage Cotts
Kingston St Mary TA2 168 D8
West Camel BA22 174 D3
Parsonage Cres BA7 214 B6
Parsonage Ct
Puriton TA7 136 B4
Taunton TA1 212 A4
Parsonage Hill TA11 211 E3
Parsonage La
Ashill TA19 183 C4
Axbridge BS26 70 E2
Bath BA1 228 B2
Charlton Musgrove BA9 161 B1
Chilcompton BA3 96 C4
Kingston St Mary TA2 168 D8
Milverton TA4 167 A4
Pensford BS39 40 D6
Staple Fitzpaine TA3 182 C4
Winford BS40 37 F6
Parsonage Pl TA10 171 D4
Parsonage Rd
Berrow TA8 84 F5
Long Ashton BS41 11 C2
West Camel BA22 174 D3
Parson's Batch BA4 140 E3
Parsons Cl
Bicknoller TA4 132 F2
Long Sutton TA10 172 F4
Nether Stowey TA5 134 A3
Parson's Dro BS28 138 C7
Parsons Gate BA7 214 B7
Parsons Gn
Clevedon BS21 16 C8
Weston-super-Mare BS22 32 A3
Parson's La
Houndstone BA22 186 D2
Kingsdon TA11 173 D5
Parsons' La TA5 152 A7
Parsons Mead BS48 19 F7
Parsons Paddock BS14 23 A7
Parsons Pen BS27 90 B7
Parsons Rd TA9 104 C4
Parson's St TA24 124 A3
Parsons Way
Wells BA5 203 B4
Winscombe BS25 69 E6
Partis Coll BA1 44 A8
Partis Way BA1 44 A8
Partition St BS1 226 C2
Partman's Hill BA3 116 B3
Partridge Cl
Moorlinch TA7 155 F7
Weston-super-Mare BS22 31 F1
Partway La
Chard Junction TA20 198 F6
East Chinnock BA22 196 F7
Passage Leaze BS11 4 D6
Passage St BS2 227 B2
Pastures Ave BS22 32 C3
Pastures The BA15 64 E3
Patch Croft BS21 16 C8
Patch St BA2 45 A2
Patchwood Rd BS48 20 F7
Pathe Rd TA7 155 B1
Pathfinder Terr 3 TA6 209 B4
Patrick's Way TA3 181 D8
Patrum Cl TA1 212 B1
Patson Hill La DT9 188 B5
Patterson Ho 8 BS1 227 B1
Pattinson Cl BA21 219 D6
Pattons TA3 169 C1
Patwell La BA10 215 E6
Patwell St BA10 215 E6
Paullet EX16 178 C1
Paulls Cl TA10 172 A6
Paull's La TA19 183 B2
Paulman Gdns BS41 20 F8
Paulmont Rise BS39 58 E1
Paul's Cswy BS49 34 D4
Pauls Rd TA11 211 C3
Paul St
Bristol BS2 226 C4
Frome BA11 119 F5
Shepton Mallet BA4 205 B6
Taunton TA1 212 F3
Paulto' Hill BA3, BS39 78 B6
PAULTON 77 F5
Paulton Inf Sch BS39 77 E5
Paulton Jun & Inf Sch BS39 77 E5
Paulton Jun Sch BS39 77 E5
Paulton La BA2, BA3 78 D7
Paulton Memorial Hospl BS39 77 F4
Paulton Rd
Farrington Gurney BS39 77 B4
Hallatrow BS39 77 B7
Midsomer Norton BA3 77 F1
Paulwood Rd BS39 58 E1
Pavement The TA3 170 B4
Pavey Cl BS13 22 C4
Pavey Rd BS13 22 C4
Pavyotts La BA22 197 E8
Pawelski Cl BA4 142 B7
PAWLETT 136 A5
Pawlett BS24 49 A2
Pawlett Mead Dro TA6 136 A5
Pawlett Prim Sch TA6 135 F5
Pawlett Rd
Bristol BS13 22 C3
Walpole TA6 136 B4
West Huntspill TA6, TA9 136 A7
Pawletts Almshouses TA5 134 C5
Pawlett Wlk BS13 22 C3
Paybridge Rd BS13 21 F4
Payne Rd BS24 49 D2
Paynes Ho 17 BS23 48 E8
Paynes La TA7 155 C2
Payne's La TA12 185 E8
PAYTON 179 F7
Payton Rd
Holywell Lake TA21 179 F7
Rockwell Green TA21 222 A5
Paywell La BS40 72 E5
Peace Cl TA6 209 D6
Peacehay La TA21 179 E4
Peach Tree Cl TA6 209 E5
Peacocks Cl TA21 180 F7
Peacocks Hill TA11 158 A2
Peadon La TA5 134 C4
Peak La
Compton Dundon TA11 157 A2
Shepton Beauchamp TA19 184 D3
Peaky Corner Dro TA7 156 A4
PEAR ASH 161 E2
Pear Ash La BA9 161 E2
Pearce Dr TA9 104 D4
Pearl Cl TA6 209 C8
Pearmain Rd
Somerton TA11 211 B4
Street BA16 207 B4
Pearse Cl BS22 32 B5
Pearson Ho BA21 219 A6
Peart Cl BS13 21 E5
Peart Dr BS13 21 E4
Pear Tree Ave BS41 20 E8
Peartree Cl BS13 22 B4
Pear Tree Cl
Bridgwater TA6 209 D4
Westleigh EX16 179 A4
Peartree Field BS20 2 F5
Peartree Gdns BS24 67 C6
Pear Tree Ind Est BS40 53 C4
Pear Tree La TA9 136 A4
Pear Tree Way TA21 222 F7
Peartwater Hill TA5 152 D8
Peartwater Rd TA5 152 D7
PEASEDOWN ST JOHN 79 C8
Peasedown St John Prim Sch BA2 79 C7
PEASMARSH 194 B7
Peats Hill BS39 40 F5
Pebbles Orch TA19 184 E4
PECKING MILL 159 D8
Pecking Mill Rd BA4 141 E1
Pedder Rd BS21 6 D1
Peddles Cl TA10 171 D8
Peddles La TA11 173 E8
Pedlars Gr
Chapmanslade BA13 121 C4
Frome BA11 119 E7
PEDWELL 156 A7
Pedwell Cvn Pk TA7 156 A7
Pedwell Hill TA7 156 A7
Pedwell La TA7 156 A7
Peel Ct TA23 202 C7
Peel St BS5 227 C4
Peerage Ct TA24 201 A6
Pegasus Ct 17 BA20 219 B4
Pegasus Pl BS25 51 F4
Peggy's La TA18 196 C5
Peile Dr TA2 212 E7
Peir Cl BS20 2 E7
Pelham Ct TA6 209 D7
Pelican Cl BS22 49 F8
Pelting Dro BA5 92 D1
Pembroke Ave BS11 4 E6
Pembroke Cl
Burnham-on-S TA8 85 B1
Taunton TA1 212 C1
Yeovil BA21 219 E7
Pembroke Ct BS21 6 C4
Pembroke Gr BS8 226 A3
Pembroke Ho 1 BS23 30 C1
Pembroke Mans BS8 226 A4
Pembroke Pl BS8 226 A1
Pembroke Rd
Bridgwater TA6 209 C3
Bristol BS8 226 A4
Bristol, Shirehampton BS11 4 E6
Portishead BS20 1 E4
Weston-super-Mare BS23 48 F4
Pembroke St BS2 227 B4
Pembroke Vale BS8 226 A4
Pemswell Rd TA24 200 F8
Penarth Dr BS24 49 A1
Penarth Rd TA6 208 D4
Pen Cross BA22 197 B6
Pendle Cl BS25 70 A7
Pendlesham Gdns BS23 31 A1
PENDOMER 197 B5
Pendomer Rd BA22 197 B5
Pendragon Pk BA6 206 D5
Pen Elm Cotts TA2 168 B5
Pen Elm Hill TA2 168 B6
Penel Orlieu TA6 208 F4
Penfield BA21 219 C5
Pen Hill BA9 161 C4
Penlea Ave TA6 208 E2
Penlea Cl TA6 208 E2
Penlea Ct BS11 4 D7
Peneigh Rd
Wells BA5 111 F2
Wells BA5 203 B6
Pen Mill Hill SP8, BA12 161 F2
Pen Mill Inf Sch BA21 219 D6
Pen Mill Trad Est BA21 219 F6
Penmoor Pl TA8 84 F5
Penmoor Rd TA8 84 F5
Penmore Rd BA22, DT9 188 B7
Pennant Pl BS20 2 F7
Pennard BS24 49 A2
Pennard Ct
Bath BA2 44 A6
Bristol BS14 23 B5
Pennard Gn BA2 44 A6
Pennard La BA6 140 A2
Penn Cl
Cheddar BS27 90 C7
Wells BA5 112 E2
Penn Ct BS26 70 C1
Penneys Piece BA11 120 C6
Penn Gdns BA1 44 A8
Penn Hill BA20 219 B4
Penn Hill La BS31 24 A3
Penn Hill Pk BA20 219 B4
Penn Hill Rd BA1 27 A1
Pennine Gdns BS23 31 A1
Penn La BA22 197 A6
Pennlea BS13 22 C7
Penn Lea Ct BA1 44 B8
Penn Lea Rd BA1 44 B8
PENN MILL 219 E6
Pennon Rise BS1 226 C1
Penn Rd BS27 90 C7
Penn St BS1 227 B3
Penns The BS21 6 E2
PENNSYLVANIA 12 F7
Pennsylvania Vw BA1 27 E4
Penn View BA9 216 D4
Penn Way BS26 70 C1
Penny Batch La BA5 139 E8
Penny Cl TA21 222 D7
Pennycress BS22 49 D7
Pennycress Wy TA6 208 E1
Penny Lea TA23 202 C6
Pennypost Dro TA10 173 B2
Pennyquick BA2 43 D6
Pennyquick Hill BA2 43 F4
Pennyquick View BA2 43 F6
Penny's Meade TA19 183 F4
Pennywell Est 3 BS21 6 D2
Pennywell Rd BS2 227 C4
Penpole Ave BS11 4 E6
Penpole Cl BS11 4 D7
Penpole La BS11 4 E7
Penpole Pk BS11 4 E7
Penpole Pl BS11 4 E6
Penrice Cl BS22 31 C2
Penrose BS14 22 F7
Penrose Sch TA6 208 E4
PENSELWOOD 161 C2
PENSFORD 40 E4
Pensford Ct BS14 23 D5
Pensford Hill BS39 40 D5
Pensford La BS39 40 A3
Pensford Old Rd BS39 40 E3
Pensford Prim Sch BS39 40 D4
Pensford Way BA11 120 D7
Pentagon The BS9 5 B5
Pental La BA3 116 C1
Penthouse Hill BA1 28 F3
Pentire Ave BS13 22 A6
Pentridge La DT10 190 E2
Penzoy Ave TA6 209 B4
Penzoy Dro TA7 154 E6
Peploe Wy 10 TA6 209 B4
Pepperall Rd TA9 104 D4
Peppershells La BS39 41 C6
Pepys Cl BS31 25 D2
Pera Pl BA1 228 C4
Pera Rd BA1 228 C4
Perch Hill BA5 110 E6
Percivale Rd BA21 218 D7
Percival Rd BS8 11 F8
Percy Pl 13 BA1 28 B1
Percy Rd BA21 219 D6
Percy Terrace BA2 44 D6
Peregrine Cl BS22 31 F1
Perfect View BA1 28 A1
Peridot Cl TA6 209 C8
PERITON 200 D6
Periton Cross TA24 200 D6
Periton Ct TA24 200 D6
Periton La TA24 200 D7
Periton Mead Sch TA24 200 D6
Periton Rd TA24 200 D6
Periton Rise TA24 200 D6
Periton Way TA24 200 D6
Peritrack La BS23 49 B4
Perkins Ct BA5 203 B4
Perley La
Luxborough TA23 148 D8
Luxborough TA24 130 D1
Perrett Ho 22 BS2 227 C3
Perretts Ct BS1 226 C1
Perrett Way BS20 4 E4
Perridge Hill BA4 140 D4
Perrin Cl BS39 76 E8
Perrings The BS48 18 E8
Perrins Hill BA22 186 B6
Perrott Hill Sch TA18 196 B4
Perrow La BS28 89 C2
Perry Cl BA3 78 D1
Perry Court E-Act Acad BS14 23 A6
Perrycroft Ave BS13 22 A6
Perrycroft Rd BS13 22 A6
PERRY GREEN 208 B8
Perry Green Rd TA5 135 D1
Perry Hill TA11 174 D8
Perry Hill Rd TA11 211 D2
Perry La TA9 106 F5
Perry Lake La BA5 139 B7
Perrymans Cl BS30 12 A8
PERRYMEAD 45 B3
Perrymead
Bath BA2 45 B3
Weston-super-Mare BS22 32 B5
Perrymead Ct BA2 45 B4
Perrymead Pl BA2 45 B4
Perry Mead Rd BS40 75 C5
Perry New Rd TA22 163 F4
Perry Pl BA21 219 C5
Perry Rd
Blackford TA9 107 A6
Bristol BS1 227 A3
Long Ashton BS41 20 F8
Perry's Cider Mills* TA19 194 E7
Perry's Cl BS27 90 A7
Perrys Hill BA20 218 C1
Perry St TA20 198 D8
PERRY STREET 198 E8
Pesley Cl BS13 22 A4
Pesters La TA11 211 E3
Pestlefield La TA3 170 C1
Petercole Dr BS13 22 A6
Peter's Gore DT6 199 B1
Peterside BS39 76 E8
Peterson Ave 2 BS13 22 C4
Peterson Sq BS13 22 C3
Peter St
Shepton Mallet BA4 205 B6
Taunton TA2 212 F6
Yeovil BA20 219 B4
Petherton Gdns BS14 23 B7
Petherton Rd
Bristol BS14 23 B7
North Newton TA7 153 F2
Pethick Ho BS4 22 F8
Peto Garden at Iford Manor The* BA15 64 E3
Peto Gr BA15 64 F3
Petrel Cl TA6 209 D7
Petter's Way BA20 219 B4
Petticoat La BA4 205 B6
Pettitts Cl DT9 187 E1
PETTON 165 A3
Petton Cross EX16 165 A3
Petvin Cl BA16 207 D4
Petvins Ct TA18 196 C5
Pevensey Wlk BS4 22 D7
Pharmacy Flats The DT10 190 F6
Pheasant Row BS49 16 F2
Pheasant The TA19 184 E1
Phelps Cl TA20 223 D6
Philippa Cl BS14 23 A7
Philips Ho 4 BS2 227 B4
Phillip Ho TA6 208 F2
Phillips Cl TA6 208 D4
Phillip's Dro TA3 170 D7
Phillips Rd BS23 49 A6
Phillis Hill BS39 77 F4
Phippen St 1 BS1 227 B1
Phoenix Acad TA6 153 F3
Phoenix Ct
Frome BA11 119 D4
Taunton TA1 212 F3
Phoenix Ho
Bath BA1 228 B4
Frome BA11 119 D4
Phoenix Rd TA6 209 B3
Phoenix Terr TA8 104 B6
Phoenix Way BS20 2 F6
Piazza Ct BA16 207 B5
PIBSBURY 172 C5
Piccadilly Pl BA1 45 B8
Piccadily Ho 18 BA4 205 B6
Pickeridge Cl TA2 213 B7
Picket La DT8 196 C1
Pickett La BA21 219 A7
PICKNEY 168 B8
Pickney La TA2 168 B7
Pickpurse La TA4 150 E8
Pickwick Rd BA1 28 A2
Picts Hill TA10 172 B6
PICT'S HILL 172 B6
Picts Hill Rd TA10 172 B6
Piece TA19 184 E4
Piece La TA19 184 E4
Piece Rd DT9 217 C3
Piece The 2 TA16 195 F7
Pier Rd BS20 2 E7
Pierrepont Pl 9 BA1 228 C2
Pierrepont St BA1 228 C2
Piers Rd BA4 142 A6
Pier St TA8 104 A6
Piffin La TA4 167 E8
Pigeon House Dr BS13 22 D4
Pigeon La BS40 36 E1
Pig Hill BA22 197 A7
Pightley La TA5 152 F6

Pightley Rd TA5 . . . . 152 E7
Pig La TA7 . . . . 154 D8
Pig Market La TA1 . . . . 212 F3
Pigott Ave BS13 . . . . 22 A4
Pigs Hill La TA5 . . . . 134 D1
Pike Cl BA6 . . . . 206 C5
Pike Hill BA4 . . . . 205 A7
Pike La BA4 . . . . 205 B6
Pikes Cres
Dunster TA24 . . . . 201 D2
Taunton TA1 . . . . 212 E1
Pilcorn St BS28 . . . . 108 C4
Pile La
Curry Mallet TA3 . . . . 183 C8
Stourton Caundle DT10 . . . . 189 F3
Piles Mill La
Luccombe TA24 . . . . 129 C8
Selworthy TA24 . . . . 123 C3
Piley La TA21 . . . . 179 D8
Pilgrims Way
Bristol BS11 . . . . 4 C7
Chew Stoke BS40 . . . . 56 D8
Lovington BA7 . . . . 158 E2
Weston-super-Mare BS22 . . . 31 E3
Pilgrim's Way TA6 . . . . 135 F5
PILL 4 C4
Pillar La BA11 . . . . 99 D4
Pill Bridge Dro TA12 . . . . . . 173 B2
Pill Bridge La BA22 . . . . 173 D1
Pill Head La TA18 . . . . 196 C4
Pill Mdw SP8 . . . . 177 E2
Pillmead La BS28 . . . . 108 D5
Pillmoor Dro BA5 . . . . 139 F6
Pillmoor La BA5 . . . . 139 F6
Pillmore La
Highbridge TA9 . . . . 105 A4
Watchfield TA9 . . . . 105 C4
Pill Rd
Abbots Leigh BS8 . . . . 4 F1
Pill BS20 . . . . 4 E2
Rooks Bridge BS26, TA9 . . . . . 87 C2
Pill St BS20 . . . . 4 D4
Pill Way BS21 . . . . 6 B2
Pilots Helm TA6 . . . . 153 E4
PILSDON 199 F2
Pilsdon La DT6 . . . . 199 F3
PILTON 140 F3
Pilton Hill BA4 . . . . 140 C4
Pilton Manor Vineyard★
BA4 . . . . 140 E3
Pimms La BS22 . . . . 31 B3
Pimm's La BS22 . . . . 31 B2
Pimpernel Cl BA16 . . . . 207 B7
Pince's Knap TA20 . . . . 198 F5
Pinchay La BS40 . . . . 38 A4
Pinching Cl BA5 . . . . 203 E3
Pinckney Gn BA15 . . . . 46 E5
Pincombe Dro TA3 . . . . 170 F5
Pincushion Cnr BA22 . . . . . 197 E6
Pine Ave TA20 . . . . 223 C5
Pine Cl
Street BA16 . . . . 207 B3
Taunton TA1 . . . . 213 D2
Weston-super-Mare
BS22 . . . . 31 D2
Pinecroft
Bristol BS14 . . . . 22 F7
Portishead BS20 . . . . 1 F6
Pine Ct
Chew Magna BS40 . . . . 39 B3
Frome BA11 . . . . 120 B7
Keynsham BS31 . . . . 24 C4
Radstock BA3 . . . . 79 A2
Pine Hill BS22 . . . . 31 D2
Pine Lea BS24 . . . . 67 B6
Pine Ridge Cl BS9 . . . . 5 C4
Pines Cl
Chilcompton BA3 . . . . 96 D3
Wincanton BA9 . . . . 216 C3
Pines Dro TA10 . . . . 156 C3
Pines Residential Site The
BA11 . . . . 120 D8
Pines Way
Bath BA2 . . . . 228 A2
Radstock BA3 . . . . 79 A2
Pines Way Ind Est BA2 . . . . 228 A2
Pine Tree Ave BA20 . . . . 218 F3
Pine Tree Cl TA6 . . . . 209 D4
Pinetree Rd BS24 . . . . 50 D4
Pine Wlk BA3 . . . . 78 E1
Pinewood TA11 . . . . 211 D4
Pinewood Ave BA3 . . . . 77 F1
Pinewood Dr TA11 . . . . 211 D4
Pinewood Gr BA3 . . . . 77 F1
Pinewood Rd BA3 . . . . 77 F1
Pinewood Way TA8 . . . . 65 F3
Pinford La DT9 . . . . 188 F3
Pinhay Rd BS13 . . . . 22 B6
Pinkham Hill TA20 . . . . 194 B6
Pinkhams Twist BS14 . . . . . . 23 A5
Pink Knoll Hollow DT9 . . . . 188 C8
Pinksmoor La TA21 . . . . 179 E7
Pinkwood La BA10 . . . . 160 E7
Pinmore BA11 . . . . 119 E2
Pinney Cl TA1 . . . . 212 B1
Pinnockscroft TA8 . . . . 84 F5
Pintail Rd TA24 . . . . 201 C5
Pinter Cl TA8 . . . . 104 C6
Pioneer Ave BA2 . . . . 44 F1
Pipehouse BA2 . . . . 63 E4
Pipehouse La BA2 . . . . 63 F4
Pipe La BS1 . . . . 226 C2
Piper's Alley TA19 . . . . 221 B4
Pipers Cl BS26 . . . . 88 E6
Pipers Pl EX14 . . . . 191 F2
Pippard Cl BA16 . . . . 207 E5
Pippin Cl BA2 . . . . 79 D7
Pippin Rd TA2 . . . . 169 C5
Pippins The
Portishead BS20 . . . . 2 F5
Wembdon TA6 . . . . 208 D6
Pipplepen La DT8, TA18 . . . 196 B2
Pistle's La TA13 . . . . 185 B1
Pitchcombe Gdns BS9 . . . . . . 5 D7
Pitcher's Hill TA2 . . . . 168 F7
Pitching The BA7 . . . . 214 C5
Pitch & Pay La BS9 . . . . 5 E3
Pitch & Pay Pk BS9 . . . . 5 E3
PITCOMBE 215 D3
Pitcombe Hill BA10 . . . . 215 B2
Pitcombe La TA4 . . . . 165 B5
Pitcombe Rock BA10 . . . . . . 215 C3
PITCOT 115 F7
Pitcot La BA3 . . . . 115 F7
Pitfield Cnr BA22 . . . . 188 A7
Pitfour Terr BA2 . . . . 60 B2
Pithay Ct BS1 . . . . 227 A3
Pithay The
Bristol BS1 . . . . 227 A3
Paulton BS39 . . . . 77 E6
Pit Hill TA17 . . . . 195 B7
Pit Hill La TA7 . . . . 155 C7
Pit La
Backwell BS48 . . . . 19 A4
Sticklepath TA23 . . . . 149 D7
Sutton Mallet TA7 . . . . 155 C7
Ubley BS40 . . . . 55 F5
Pitman Ct BA1 . . . . 28 C2
Pitman Ho BA2 . . . . 44 D4
Pitman Rd BS23 . . . . 48 E6
PITMINSTER 181 E6
PITNEY 172 C7
Pitney Hill TA10 . . . . 172 C6
Pitney Moor Dro TA10 . . . . 156 C2
Pit Rd
Dinnington TA17 . . . . 195 C7
Midsomer Norton BA3 . . . . . . 78 B1
PITSFORD HILL 150 E1
Pitsham La TA4 . . . . 164 E6
Pitt Ct TA10 . . . . 171 B3
Pitten St BA3 . . . . 116 E3
Pitt La
Huish Champflower TA4 . . . . 165 E8
Porlock Weir TA24 . . . . 123 C3
Waterrow TA4 . . . . 165 F5
Pitts Cl TA1 . . . . 212 C1
Pitts La TA3 . . . . 183 F7
Pitt's La BS40 . . . . 39 B1
Pitway TA13 . . . . 220 D5
Pitway Cl BS39 . . . . 76 F4
Pitway Hill TA13 . . . . 220 D6
Pitway La BS39 . . . . 76 E4
Pixash Bsns Ctr BS31 . . . . . . 25 B5
Pixash La BS31 . . . . 25 C5
Pixey Hole La BS40 . . . . 55 E3
Pix La TA4 . . . . 167 B4
Pixton Way TA22 . . . . 163 E6
Pizey Ave
Burnham-on-S TA8 . . . . 85 A1
Clevedon BS21 . . . . 6 B2
Pizey Ave Ind Est BS21 . . . . . . 6 C2
Pizey Cl BS21 . . . . 6 B2
Place Dro TA7 . . . . 154 F4
Placket La BA20 . . . . 218 D1
Plain Pond TA4 . . . . 210 C5
PLAINSFIELD 152 B7
Plain The BA2 . . . . 81 E4
Plais St TA2 . . . . 212 F6
Plantaganet Chase BA20 . . 218 D2
Plantagenet Pk BA20 . . . . . . 218 E3
Platterwell La (East Town La)
BA4 . . . . 141 B3
Players La TA8 . . . . 85 A1
Playfield Cl 2 BA8 . . . . 190 A6
Playford Gdns BS11 . . . . 4 E8
Playses Gn TA10 . . . . 184 D8
PLEAMORE CROSS 222 A2
Pleasant Pl BA1 . . . . 29 D2
Pleshey Cl BS22 . . . . 31 D2
Plimsoll Ho 3 BS1 . . . . 227 B1
Plot La DT9 . . . . 187 F5
Plott La BA8 . . . . 190 B7
Plough Cl BA16 . . . . 207 A4
Ploughed Paddock BS48 . . . . 8 D1
Plover Cl
Milborne Port DT9 . . . . 217 C2
Minehead TA24 . . . . 201 C5
Weston-super-Mare BS22 . . . 31 F1
Plover Ct BA21 . . . . 218 D6
Plover Rd DT9 . . . . 217 C2
Plovers Rise BA3 . . . . 79 A3
Plowage La BA22 . . . . 174 D3
Plox BA10 . . . . 215 E6
Plox Gn BA10 . . . . 215 E6
Plucknett Row BA20 . . . . . . 218 D5
Plud Farm La TA5 . . . . 134 A5
Plud St BS28 . . . . 108 B3
Plumber's Barton 9 BA11 119 F4
Plumers Cl 4 BS21 . . . . 6 E1
Plum La TA6 . . . . 209 C2
Plumley Cres BS24 . . . . 50 A4
Plumley Ct BS23 . . . . 48 D4
PLUMMER'S HILL 77 E6
Plummer's La BA5 . . . . 92 D5
Plum Orch DT9 . . . . 187 F4
Plumptre Ave BA5 . . . . 203 F5
Plumptre Cl BS39 . . . . 77 E5
Plumptre Rd BS39 . . . . 77 E5
Plumtree Cl BS25 . . . . 52 A1
Plum Tree Cl TA6 . . . . 209 E5
Plum Tree Rd BS22 . . . . 49 E8
Plunder St BS49 . . . . 35 B7
Plunging Dr BA6 . . . . 206 F1
Plymor Rd TA9 . . . . 136 A8
Poachers End TA24 . . . . 201 C4
Pococks Yd TA10 . . . . 171 F5
Podgers Dr BA1 . . . . 27 B2
Podger's La TA19 . . . . 183 F4
PODIMORE 174 A3
Podimore La BA22 . . . . 174 A3
Podimore Rd BA22 . . . . 174 A3
Podium Sh Ctr The BA2 . . . 228 C2
Poets Cnr BA3 . . . . 97 C8
Polden Bsns Ctr The TA6 . . 136 B2
Polden Cl BS48 . . . . 8 E1
Polden Ct TA6 . . . . 209 B5
Polden Rd
Portishead BS20 . . . . 2 B5
Weston-super-Mare BS23 . . . 48 F8
Polden St TA6 . . . . 209 B5
Polden View BA6 . . . . 206 E3
Polden Wk BA3 . . . . 97 B6
Polden Wlk TA7 . . . . 136 E3
Pole Rue La TA20 . . . . 193 C6
POLESHILL 166 C1
Polestar Way BS24 . . . . 50 A8
Polham La TA11 . . . . 211 D3
Police La BS39 . . . . 40 E3
Polkes Field TA3 . . . . 170 F6
Pollard Rd
Bridgwater TA6 . . . . 209 D6
Weston-super-Mare BS22 . . . 49 F8
Pollards Ct TA24 . . . . 124 A3
Pollard's La TA21 . . . . 180 F7
Pollards Way TA1 . . . . 212 E4
POLSHAM 139 D5
Poltimore La TA20 . . . . 193 D8
Polygon Rd BS8 . . . . 226 A2
Polygon The 15 BS8 . . . . 11 F6
Pomeroy La BA14 . . . . 83 B6
Pomfrett Gdns BS14 . . . . 23 E5
Pond Cl 5 BA8 . . . . 190 A6
Pond Cotts BA3 . . . . 80 D2
Pond Head BS20 . . . . 4 D4
Pondhead Cross TA4 . . . . . . 202 E3
Pond La TA21 . . . . 179 D3
Pond Orch TA4 . . . . 150 B8
Pondpool La TA3 . . . . 170 C3
Pond Wlk DT10 . . . . 190 B4
Ponsford Rd
Bristol BS14 . . . . 23 B8
Minehead TA24 . . . . 201 A6
Pookfield Cl BA11 . . . . 143 B7
Pool Alley TA10 . . . . 172 B8
Poolbridge Rd BS28 . . . . 107 C4
Pool Cl TA7 . . . . 136 C4
POOLE 222 F8
Poole Cl BS13 . . . . 22 C5
Poole Hill TA22 . . . . 163 B5
Poole Ho BA2 . . . . 43 F5
Poole Ind Est TA21 . . . . 222 F8
Poolemead Rd BA2 . . . . 43 F5
Pooles Cl TA5 . . . . 134 A2
Pooles La TA20 . . . . 194 E1
Poole St BS11 . . . . 4 B8
Pooles Wharf BS8 . . . . 226 A1
Pooles Wharf Ct BS8 . . . . . 226 A1
Pool Hill TA21 . . . . 165 E1
Pool La BS40 . . . . 38 A2
Pools Barn Rd TA5 . . . . 133 E7
POOLTOWN 148 E8
Poop Hill TA18 . . . . 196 C8
Poop Hill La TA18 . . . . 196 C8
Poor Hill BA2 . . . . 59 F6
Poorhouse La DT6 . . . . 199 E1
Pope Cl TA1 . . . . 168 D1
Popery La TA24 . . . . 129 E1
Pope's La
Milborne Port DT9 . . . . 217 D2
Rockwell Green TA21 . . . . . . 222 B4
Pope's Wlk BA2 . . . . 45 B3
Popham Cl
Bridgwater TA6 . . . . 209 D5
East Brent TA9 . . . . 86 D5
Popham Flats TA21 . . . . 222 D6
Popham Rd TA21 . . . . 222 F7
Pop La EX13, TA20 . . . . 198 B8
Poplar Ave BS9 . . . . 5 D6
Poplar Cl
Bath BA2 . . . . 44 D4
Frome BA11 . . . . 120 B7
Poplar Dr BA21 . . . . 218 C7
Poplar Dro TA10 . . . . 172 C3
Poplar Est TA9 . . . . 104 D3
Poplar Farm BA5 . . . . 111 A4
Poplar La
Catcott TA7 . . . . 137 D1
Mark TA9 . . . . 105 E3
Poplar Pl 16 BS23 . . . . 48 E8
Poplar Rd
Bath BA2 . . . . 62 D8
Bridgwater TA6 . . . . 209 D7
Bristol, Highridge BS13 . . . . . 21 F7
Burnham-on-S TA8 . . . . 104 A8
Street BA16 . . . . 207 C3
Taunton TA1 . . . . 213 D2
Poplars Cl BA21 . . . . 187 A5
Poplars The
Easton-in-G BS20 . . . . 4 B4
Porlock TA24 . . . . 124 A3
Weston-super-Mare BS22 . . . 32 A1
Poplar Tree La BA14 . . . . 83 C2
Poplar Wlk BS24 . . . . 49 E5
Poples Bow TA9 . . . . 104 E5
Pople's La BA11 . . . . 117 F8
Pople's Well TA18 . . . . 224 B6
Poppy Cl
Weston-super-Mare BS22 . . . 32 A5
Yeovil BA22 . . . . 218 B5
Poppy Rd TA11 . . . . 211 B3
Porch EX13 . . . . 198 A3
Porch Cl BA6 . . . . 206 E3
Porchestall Dro BA6 . . . . . . 206 B4
PORLOCK 124 A4
Porlock Cl
3 Clevedon BS21 . . . . 6 E1
Weston-super-Mare BS23 . . . 48 F2
Porlock Dr TA1 . . . . 212 E1
PORLOCKFORD 123 F4
Porlock Gdns BS48 . . . . 8 E1
Porlock Hill TA24 . . . . 123 F3
Porlock Rd
Bath BA2 . . . . 45 A1
Minehead TA24 . . . . 200 C7
Porlock Visitor Ctr★
TA24 . . . . 124 A3
PORLOCK WEIR 123 D4
Porlock Weir Rd TA24 . . . . 123 F4
Portal Rd BS24 . . . . 50 D4
PORTBURY 3 D3
Portbury Comm BS20 . . . . 2 E4
Portbury Gr BS11 . . . . 4 D6
Portbury Hundreds The
BS20 . . . . 3 C4
Portbury La BS20 . . . . 9 E7
Portbury Way BS20 . . . . 3 E5
Portbury Wlk BS11 . . . . 4 D6
Portcullis Rd TA10 . . . . 172 A6
Porter's Hatch BA6 . . . . 138 D4
PORTFIELD 171 E5
Portfield La TA10 . . . . 171 F5
PORTISHEAD 2 B4
Portishead Bsns Pk BS20 . . . 2 E5
Portishead Lodge BS20 . . . . . 2 D6
Portishead Prim sch BS20 . . 2 E6
Portishead Rd BS22 . . . . 32 B4
Portishead Way BS3 . . . . 11 E3
Port La TA22 . . . . 164 A5
PORTLAND 207 A6
Portland Cl
Cannington TA5 . . . . 135 B2
Nailsea BS48 . . . . 8 D1
Portland Ct BS1 . . . . 226 B1
Portland Dr BS20 . . . . 2 E4
Portland Grange 6 TA1 . . 212 E3
Portland Lofts 8 BS2 . . . . . 227 B4
Portland Mans 9 BS2 . . . . 227 B4
Portland Pl
Bath BA1 . . . . 228 B4
Brent Knoll TA9 . . . . 86 B1
Bridgwater TA6 . . . . 208 D5
Frome BA11 . . . . 119 D5
Portland Rd
Bath BA1 . . . . 228 B4
Frome BA11 . . . . 119 D5
Langport TA10 . . . . 172 B5
Street BA16 . . . . 207 A6
Portland Sq BS2 . . . . 227 B4
Portland St
Bristol, Clifton BS8 . . . . 11 F7
Taunton TA1 . . . . 212 E4
Portland Terr
Bath BA1 . . . . 228 B4
Watchet TA23 . . . . 202 C7
Portman Cres 9 TA6 . . . . . 153 F3
Portman Ct BA22 . . . . 196 E8
Portman Dr TA6 . . . . 153 E3
Portman Rd TA6 . . . . 153 E3
Portmans TA3 . . . . 170 B3
Portman St TA2 . . . . 212 F6
Portmeade Dro BS26 . . . . 70 C1
Portmeirion Cl BS14 . . . . 23 B5
Portnell's La BA12 . . . . 161 F2
Portobello Bldgs TA20 . . . . 223 B4
Portreeve Dr BA21 . . . . 219 B6
Port View BS20 . . . . 4 C5
Portview Rd BS11 . . . . 4 B8
Portview Trad Est BS11 . . . . . 4 B7
Portwall Dro TA7 . . . . 209 F5
Portwall La BS1 . . . . 227 B1
PORTWAY 207 D4
Portway
Bristol, Shirehampton BS11 . . . 4 C6
Bristol, Sneyd Park BS8 . . . . . 5 C3
Frome BA11 . . . . 120 A4
Holford TA5 . . . . 133 D4
Street BA16 . . . . 207 D4
Wells BA5 . . . . 203 C4
Port Way BA2 . . . . 100 D7
Portway Ave BA5 . . . . 203 D4
Portway Gdns BA11 . . . . . . 120 A4
Portway Hill
Batcombe BA4 . . . . 142 C1
Bruton BA4 . . . . 159 F6
Portway La
Binegar BA3 . . . . 95 E1
Holford TA5 . . . . 133 E4
Portway Lodge 1 BA5 . . . . 203 C4
Portway Rd BA22 . . . . 174 E1
Portway Rdbt BS11 . . . . 4 C8
Portway Villas BA11 . . . . . . 120 A4
Positano Ct 2 TA6 . . . . 208 E7
Poskitt Ho TA6 . . . . 208 F6
Post Cl TA21 . . . . 222 E4
Post La
Malmsmead EX35 . . . . 122 C4
Skilgate TA4 . . . . 164 E7
Post Office La
Blagdon BS40 . . . . 54 D3
Flax Bourton BS48 . . . . 19 F7
Minehead TA24 . . . . 200 F7
Tatworth TA20 . . . . 198 C8
Post Office Rd BS24 . . . . 50 C5
Post Office Yd DT8 . . . . 199 F7
Poston Way BA15 . . . . 64 E7
Pot La BA11 . . . . 120 F8
Potter's Cross TA4 . . . . 165 C7
POTTERS HILL 20 B1
Potters Ho 1 BA4 . . . . 205 B6
Potters La TA20 . . . . 193 B6
Potters View BS49 . . . . 34 E2
Potterton Cl TA6 . . . . 208 F1
Pottery Cl BS23 . . . . 49 A6
Pottery Rd TA19 . . . . 183 C1
Pottery View TA19 . . . . 183 C1
Pottle St BA12 . . . . 144 D3
Potts Cl BA1 . . . . 28 F3
Poulett Cotts TA17 . . . . 195 D7
POUND 220 F2
Pound Cl
Glastonbury BA6 . . . . 206 D5
Stalbridge DT10 . . . . 190 B4
Yeovil BA21 . . . . 218 C5
Pound Farm Cl TA6 . . . . 208 D3
Poundfield La TA3 . . . . 169 F6
Poundfield Rd TA24 . . . . . . 200 E6
Pound Fold BA5 . . . . 204 C7
Pound Hill TA21 . . . . 179 A5
Poundisford Cl TA1 . . . . 212 D1
Pound La
Bishops Lydeard TA4 . . . . . . 151 F1
Buckland St Mary TA20 . . . . 193 A8
Downhead BA4 . . . . 117 A1
Easton BA5 . . . . 111 A4
Lydford Fair Place TA11 . . . . 158 C3
Martock TA12 . . . . 185 D6
Nailsea BS48 . . . . 8 D3
Oakhill BA3 . . . . 115 B5
Rawridge EX14 . . . . 191 F1
Stocklinch TA19 . . . . 184 C4
Yarcombe EX14 . . . . 192 E2
Yarlington BA9 . . . . 175 F8
Yeovil BA22 . . . . 218 A2
Pound Mead BS40 . . . . 37 C8
Pound Orch TA4 . . . . 151 C7
Pound Pool TA11 . . . . 211 C4
Pound Rd
Axminster EX13 . . . . 198 F2
Broadway TA19 . . . . 183 B2
Pawlett TA6 . . . . 135 F5
Poundsclose TA22 . . . . 163 E4
Pound Terr 3 TA21 . . . . . . 222 D5
Pound The BS40 . . . . 36 D3
Pound Way TA10 . . . . 172 B3
Pounsell La TA10 . . . . 172 B5
Powell Cl TA3 . . . . 169 D4
Powell Ct BA5 . . . . 203 B4
Powells Acres BS21 . . . . 6 E3
Powis Cl BS22 . . . . 31 C2
Powlett Ct BA2 . . . . 45 B7
Powlett Rd BA2 . . . . 45 B8
Pow's Hill BA3 . . . . 78 D5
Pow's Orch BA3 . . . . 78 A1
Powy's Gn DT9 . . . . 225 C4
Powy's La DT9 . . . . 225 C4
POYNTINGTON 188 E6
Poyntz Rd BS4 . . . . 22 F8
Prankerds Rd DT9 . . . . 217 C2
Preachers Vale BA3 . . . . 116 F7
Preanes Gn BS22 . . . . 32 A2
Precinct The BS20 . . . . 2 D5
Prescot Cl BS22 . . . . 31 B2
PRESCOTT 179 C1
Prescott Rd EX15 . . . . 179 D1
PRESTLEIGH 141 D3
Prestleigh La BA4 . . . . 141 E4
Prestleigh Rd BA4 . . . . 141 E2
PRESTON 150 E6
PRESTON BOWYER 167 B5
Preston CE Prim Sch
BA21 . . . . 218 C7
Preston Cross TA4 . . . . 150 E6
Preston Gr BA20 . . . . 218 F5
Preston La TA4 . . . . 150 E6
PRESTON PLUCKNETT 218 D4
Preston Rd
Yeovil BA20 . . . . 218 E5
Yeovil, Houndstone BA22 . . . 218 B5
Preston Road Rdbt BA21 . . 218 C5
Preston Sch BA21 . . . . 218 D5
Prestor 9 EX13 . . . . 198 A1
Pretwood Cl TA19 . . . . 221 C3
Prewett St BS1 . . . . 227 B1
Prey La TA3 . . . . 182 D7
Preywater Rd BA5 . . . . 139 D8
Prices Ave TA21 . . . . 222 D7
Prices Bldgs TA6 . . . . 209 A4
Priddles La TA20 . . . . 193 C8
PRIDDY 92 D3
Priddy Cl
Bath BA2 . . . . 44 B5
Frome BA11 . . . . 120 C7
Priddy Ct BS14 . . . . 23 B5
Priddy Dr BS14 . . . . 23 B5
Priddy Mill Dro BA5 . . . . 92 A6
Priddy Nine Barrows★ BA5 . 92 F4
Priddy Prim Sch BA5 . . . . . . 92 D3
Priddy Rd BA5 . . . . 112 E8
Priddy Veal La BA5 . . . . 111 A5
Priestlands DT9 . . . . 225 D5
Priestlands La DT9 . . . . 225 D5
Priestley Way TA8 . . . . 104 C5
Priest Row BA5 . . . . 203 D4
Priest's House★ TA10 . . . . 172 A3
Priest St TA4 . . . . 202 C2
Priests Way BS22 . . . . 31 D2
Prigg La TA13 . . . . 220 C4
Primmerfield La BA3 . . . . 94 C8
Primore Rd TA7 . . . . 169 F8
Primrose Alley BA2 . . . . 42 D2
Primrose Cl TA11 . . . . 211 B3
PRIMROSE HILL 27 D1
Primrose Hill
Bath BA1 . . . . 27 D1
Charlton Mackrell TA11 . . . . 173 F7
East Coker BA22 . . . . 197 B7
Nunney BA11 . . . . 143 B8

Primrose Hill Pk Homes
TA11 173 F7
Primrose La
Midsomer Norton BA3 78 B1
Yeovil BA21 187 D5
Primrose Wlk TA6 208 D1
Prim Sch
Langport TA10 172 A5
North Petherton TA6 153 F3
Wincanton BA9 216 C3
Prince Philip Cl TA20 223 B3
Princes Bldgs BA1 228 B3
Prince's Bldgs [17] BS8 11 F6
Prince's Cl [11] TA14 185 F4
Princes' La BS8 11 F6
Princes Rd BA5 203 D4
Prince's Rd
Clevedon BS21 6 D3
Shepton Mallet BA4 205 C6
Street BA16 207 B5
Princess Anne Rd BA11 120 A7
Princess Cl
Keynsham BS31 24 E4
[12] North Petherton TA6 153 F4
Princess Rd TA1 212 D2
Princess Row BS2 227 A4
Princess St TA8 104 B7
Princes St
Bath BA1 228 B2
Taunton TA1 213 B4
Yeovil BA20 219 B5
Prince's St
Bristol BS2 227 C4
Clandown BA3 78 E5
Princess Victoria St BS8 11 F6
Prince St BS1 227 A1
Prince Street Rdbt BS1 227 A2
Printers Ct [32] TA12 185 E6
Printworks Rd BA11 120 A3
Prior Park Bldgs BA2 45 B5
Prior Park Coll BA2 45 C2
Prior Park Cotts BA2 228 C1
Prior Park Gdns BA2 45 B5
Prior Park Landscape Gdn★
BA2 45 C3
Prior Park Rd BA2 45 B4
Priors Hill BA2 60 A2
Prior's Wlk TA1 212 F4
PRIORSWOOD 213 B7
Priorswood Ind Est TA2 213 B6
Priorswood Pl [8] TA2 213 A8
Priorswood Prim Sch
Priorswood TA2 213 A6
Taunton TA2 212 F6
Taunton TA2 212 F6
Priorswood Rd TA2 213 A6
Priory TA21 222 E6
Priory Ave TA1 213 A4
Priory Bridge Rd TA1 213 A5
Priory Cl
Bath BA2 45 B2
Cannington TA5 135 C2
Castle Cary BA7 214 B5
Chilton Polden TA7 137 B2
Ilchester BA22 173 E1
Midsomer Norton BA3 78 A1
Yeovil BA20 218 D1
Priory Com Sch BS22 32 B3
Priory Ct
Bridgwater TA6 208 F4
[9] Stoke sub Hamdon TA14 185 F4
[5] Taunton TA1 213 A4
Wellington TA21 222 E7
Priory Farm Trad Est BS20 3 D3
Priory Fields TA1 213 A5
Priory Fields Ret Pk TA1 213 A5
Priorygate Ct BA7 214 B6
Priory Gdns
Bristol, Shirehampton BS11 4 D7
Burnham-on-S TA8 104 B6
Easton-in-G BS20 4 B4
Wellington TA21 222 E6
Priory Glade BA21 218 C6
Priory Gn TA24 201 E2
Priory Hill TA5 134 C5
Priory Hospl BA5 203 C3
Priory Mead BA10 215 F8
Priory Mews BS23 49 B7
Priory Path BA7 214 C5
Priory Pl BA5 203 D3
Priory Rd
Bristol BS8 226 C4
Bristol, Shirehampton BS11 4 D6
Chilton Polden TA7 137 B2
Easton-in-G BS20 4 B4
Ilchester BA22 173 E1
Keynsham BS31 24 E7
Portbury BS20 3 D3
Wells BA5 203 D3
Weston-super-Mare BS23 49 A7
Priory Sch The TA2 213 B7
Priory View BA7 214 B6
Priory Villas BA9 216 C3
Priory Way TA1 213 B5
Priory Way Ind Est TA1 213 B5
Priory Wlk
Portbury BS20 3 D3
Taunton TA1 213 A5
PRISTON 61 B5
Priston Cl BS22 32 B5
Priston Hill BA2 61 C5
Priston La
Farmborough BA2 60 C7
Farmborough BA2 60 C8
Priston BA2, BA3 61 A5
Priston Rd BA2 61 D6
Pritchard St BS2 227 B4
Private Rd
North Brewham BA11 161 E8
Staplegrove TA2 212 D7
Privet Dr BS13 22 C5
Proctor Dr BS23 49 B4
Proctor Ho BS1 227 B1
Proctor Rd TA21 222 D8
Prophet's La TA14 185 E3
Prospect Cl
East Brent TA9 86 E5
Shepton Mallet BA4 205 A6
Prospect Gdns BA1 28 F5
Prospect Ho BS22 31 E3
Prospect Pl
Bath, Beacon Hill BA1 28 A1
Bathford BA1 29 D2
Bath, Weston BA1 27 C2
[9] Weston-super-Mare BS23 48 E8
Prospect Rd BA2 45 C4
Prospect Row TA18 224 F3
Prospect Villas BA4 159 C7
Protheroes Ho BS1 226 C2
Proud Cross BS40 74 E4
Providence Ct BA11 120 A3
Providence La BS41 10 F2
Providence Pl
Bristol BS2 227 C2
Bruton BA10 215 D6
PROVIDENCE PLACE 77 F1
Providence Rise BS41 10 F2
Providence View BS41 11 A1
Provident Pl TA6 208 E5
Prowle's Cross BA22 197 F5
Prowse's La BS26 70 A1
Prowses Mdw TA2 168 B4
PUBLOW 40 F5
Publow La BS39 40 E5
PUCKINGTON 184 B5
Pud Brook DT9 217 D1
Pudding Pie Cl BS40 53 A5
Pudding Pie La BS40 53 A6
Puddle Town TA18 196 B5
Puddy's La TA9 105 D4
PUDLEIGH 223 B8
Pudleigh La TA20 223 B8
Puffin Cl
Minehead TA24 201 C5
Weston-super-Mare BS22 49 F8
Pullen Ct BA4 205 B4
Pulmans La TA18 224 C5
Pulpitsway Dro TA12 185 A8
Pulteney Ave BA2 45 B6
Pulteney Bridge BA2 228 C2
Pulteney Gdns BA2 45 B6
Pulteney Gr BA2 45 B6
Pulteney Mews [4] BA2 45 B7
Pulteney Rd BA2 45 B6
Pulteney Terr BA2 45 B6
Pump La
Bathford BA1 29 B2
Bristol BS1 227 B1
Redhill BS40 36 D2
Pump Sq BS20 4 D5
Punnet Cl BS27 90 B7
Puppy Cross Ways BA3 94 F5
Puppy La BA3 94 F5
Purcell Wlk BS4 22 D7
Purdue Cl BS22 32 B3
Purewell TA7 136 C4
PURITON 136 C4
Puriton Hill TA7 136 C3
Puriton Manor TA7 136 C4
Puriton Pk TA7 136 C4
Puriton Prim Sch TA7 136 C4
Puriton Rd
Pawlett TA6 136 A5
West Huntspill TA9 136 B7
Purlewent Dr BA1 27 C1
Purley Dr TA6 209 D6
PURN 67 A7
Purnell Wy BS39 77 D6
Purn La BS24 67 A8
Purn Rd BS24 66 F8
Purn Way BS24 67 B7
PURSE CAUNDLE 189 D4
Purse Caundle Manor House★
DT9 189 D4
Pursey Ave BA16 207 E5
PURTINGTON 195 A4
Purving Row BS24 67 C1
Purving Row La BS24 67 C1
Putham La TA24 129 F1
Putsham Hill TA5 133 D5
Putsham Mead TA5 133 D5
Puttingthorpe Dr BS22 49 C7
Putts La DT9 175 D1
Putt's La DT9 188 D8
Puxley Cl BS14 23 E6
PUXTON 33 D3
Puxton La BS24 33 D3
Puxton Moor La BS24 33 E2
Puxton Park (Adventure
Park)★ BS24 33 B3
Puxton Rd BS24 33 C2
Pyde La TA10 184 D6
Pye Cnr
Churchill BS25 52 D4
Merriott TA16 195 F6
Somerton TA11 211 D4
Pye La TA20 198 E8
PYLEIGH 151 B1
Pyleigh La TA4 151 A1
Pyle La BA22 174 A2
Pyles Thorne TA21 222 F4
Pyles Thorne Cl TA21 222 E5
Pyles Thorne Rd TA21 222 E4
Pylewell La BS25 52 D1
Pyle Well La TA11 174 E8
PYLLE 141 B1
Pylle Hill BA4 141 A1
Pylle La BA4 141 B1
Pylle Rd BA4 141 A2
Pyncombe La TA4 210 B3
Pyne Point BS21 6 C3
Pynne Cl BS14 23 F5
Pynne Rd BS14 23 F5
Pyracantha Wlk BS14 23 A6
PYRLAND 213 A8
Pyrland Ave TA2 212 F8
Pyrland Pl TA2 213 A8
Pyrland Wlk TA6 208 B4

Q

Quab La
Alston Sutton BS26 88 F3
Wedmore BS28 108 B5
Quab Lane Cl BS28 108 B4
Quaish La BA4 140 C4
Quaker's La
Hartswell TA4 166 B6
Wiveliscombe TA4 210 C3
Quakinghouse La TA4 166 E5
Quantick Gdns TA24 201 B5
Quantock Ave TA6 208 D4
Quantock Cl
Burnham-on-S TA8 104 B7
Midsomer Norton BA3 97 B6
North Petherton TA6 153 E4
Quantock Ct
Burnham-on-S TA8 104 A5
Ilminster TA19 221 C4
Street BA16 207 B5
Williton TA4 202 D2
Quantock Gr TA4 202 E2
Quantock Ho TA6 153 E4
Quantock Mdw TA6 208 C5
Quantock Par TA6 153 E4
Quantock Rd
Bridgwater TA5, TA6 208 B5
Cannington TA5 135 C1
Portishead BS20 2 B5
Taunton TA2 212 E8
Watchet TA23 202 C6
Wellington TA21 222 D7
Weston-super-Mare BS23 48 E4
Quantock Rise
Kingston St Mary TA2 168 E8
Pawlett TA6 135 F5
Quantocks BA2 45 A1
Quantock Terr TA6 209 A6
Quantock View
Bishops Lydeard TA4 167 F8
Highbridge TA9 104 D3
Kilve TA5 133 C6
Quantock Way
Bridgwater TA6 208 C5
Kingston St Mary TA2 168 D8
Quaperlake St BA10 215 F7
Quarante-Ans BA4 142 B7
Quarme La TA24 147 E7
QUARR 177 E5
Quarr BA4 205 C6
Quarr Cross SP8 177 E4
Quarr Dr DT9 225 D6
Quarr La DT9 225 D6
Quarr Lane Pk DT9 225 D6
Quarry Batch
Street BA16 207 A5
Walton BA16 156 E7
Quarry Cl
Bath BA2 44 F1
Limpley Stoke BA3 64 D6
Minehead TA24 201 B5
Quarry Cotts BA22 197 F8
Quarry Hay BS40 56 D8
Quarry Hill BA22 175 F4
Quarry La
Blagdon Hill TA3 181 D4
Bradford Abbas DT9 187 E1
Butleigh BA6 157 D3
Combe St Nicholas TA20 193 D6
Kingston St Mary TA2 168 F7
Quarrylands La BS26 88 B4
Quarrymans Ct BA2 45 B1
Quarry Rd
Bath BA2 45 D6
Kingsdon TA11 173 D5
Portishead BS20 2 C4
Sandford BS25 52 A2
Street BA16 207 B4
Washford TA23 131 F4
Quarry Rise BS24 66 F8
Quarry Rock Gdns BA2 45 D4
Quarry Vale Cotts BA2 45 B1
Quarry Way BS48 8 D2
Quarthill La TA4 166 C5
Quartley Hill EX16 164 E4
Quartly Dr TA1 212 A3
Quay La TA24 201 A8
Quays Ave BS20 2 E5
Quayside TA6 208 F5
Quay St
Bristol BS1 227 A3
Minehead TA24 201 A8
Quays The BS1 226 C1
Quay W TA24 125 D4
Quebec BA2 44 A6
Quedam Sh Ctr [6] BA21 219 B5
Queen Anne Ct TA24 200 F7
QUEEN CAMEL 174 F3
Queen Charlotte St BS1 227 A2
QUEEN CHARLTON 24 B3
Queen Charlton La BS14 23 E2
Queen Elizabeth Ct
Bridgwater TA6 209 A5
Street BA16 207 C6
Queen Elizabeth's Hospital
Sch BS8 226 B3
Queen Quay BS1 227 A2
Queens Acre La TA3 181 E6
Queen's Ave
Bristol BS8 226 B3
Portishead BS20 2 C5
Queens Cl TA20 223 B2
Queen's Coll TA1 212 D1
Queen's Coll Jun Sch TA1 212 D1
Queenscote BS20 2 F5
Queens Cres TA14 185 F5
Queen's Ct BS8 226 B3
Queen's Down TA3 169 C4
Queens Dr TA1 168 D1
Queen's Dr BA2 45 A2
Queens Gate BS9 5 D5
Queens Gate Terr TA1 213 A3
Queens Gr BA9 161 E2
Queens Par BS1 226 C2
Queen's Par BA1 228 B3
Queen's Parade Pl BA1 228 B3
Queens Pl BA2 45 B5
Queen Sq
Bath BA1 228 B2
Bristol BS1 227 A2
North Curry TA3 170 B4
Saltford BS31 25 F3
Queen Square Ave [10]
BS1 227 A2
Queen Square Pl BA1 228 B3
Queens Rd
Banwell BS29 51 A3
Bradford Abbas DT9 187 E1
Frome BA11 119 D4
Keynsham BS31 24 D4
Minehead TA24 201 A6
Nailsea BS48 8 D1
Portishead BS20 1 E4
Somerton TA11 211 D4
Street BA16 207 B5
Wellington TA21 222 E4
Queen's Rd
Bridgwater TA6 208 F2
Bristol BS8 226 B3
Bristol, Bishopsworth BS13,
BS41 21 F4
Clevedon BS21 6 D3
Evercreech BA4 141 E2
Radstock BA3 79 B2
Shepton Mallet BA4 205 A5
Weston-super-Mare BS23 30 D1
Queens Row BS27 90 C8
Queens Sq TA9 104 C4
Queen St
Bath BA1 228 B2
Bridgwater TA6 208 F5
Bristol BS2 227 B3
Keinton Mandeville TA11 158 A1
North Petherton TA6 153 F4
Taunton TA1 213 B4
Tintinhull BA22 186 B7
[11] Wells BA5 203 D4
Yarlington BA9 175 F8
Queens Terr TA1 213 A3
Queen's Terr
Sherborne DT9 225 D6
Wiveliscombe TA4 210 C4
Queensway
Taunton TA1 212 B1
Yeovil BA20 219 A4
Queens Way BS20 1 E4
Queen's Way BS22 31 F4
Queensway Cl TA9 106 E5
Queensway Ctr BS22 32 B2
Queensway Pl BA20 219 A4
Queenswood Rd TA6 208 C4
Queenwood Ave BA1 28 A1
Quicksilver Rdbt BA20 218 F2
Quickthorn Cl BS14 23 A6
Quiet St BA1 228 B2
Quilter Gr BS4 22 D7
Quirke St TA24 200 F7

R

Raby Mews BA2 45 B7
Raby Pl BA2 45 B7
Raby Villas BA2 45 B7
Rackclose Gdns TA20 223 A4
Rackclose Ho TA20 223 A4
Rackclose Pk TA20 223 B4
Rackfield TA21 222 A5
Rackfield Pl BA2 44 B6
Rackhay BS1 227 A2
Rackhouse La TA5 152 D4
Rackley La
Buckland St Mary TA20 182 B1
Compton Bishop BS26 69 B2
Rackstile TA20 223 A7
Rackvernal Ct BA3 78 B1
Rackvernal Rd BA3 78 B1
RADDINGTON 165 B4
Raddon Cl BA4 205 B6
RADFORD 78 C8
Radford Hill
Camerton BA2, BA3 78 C7
Timsbury BA2 60 C1
Radigan La TA3, TA19 183 C5
RADLET 134 C1
Radlet Cl TA2 213 B7
Radnidge La EX16 162 D4
RADSTOCK 78 E1
Radstock & District Mus★
BA3 78 F2
Radstock Rd BA3 78 C2
Raggal Dro BA6 157 F6
Ragged Dro BA6 158 A7
Rag Hill BA3 79 D5
Rag La
Babcary BA22 174 B6
Ilminster TA19 221 B7
Yarcombe EX14 192 D2
Raglan Cl
Bridgwater TA6 209 D7
Chilcompton BA3 96 C4
Raglan Ct [4] TA2 212 F6
Ragland La BA1 28 A2
Ragland St BA1 28 A2
Raglan La BS40 37 E7
Raglan Pl [20] BS23 30 C1
Raglan's Cross TA4 202 F2
Raglan Terr
Bath BA1 28 A2
Yeovil BA21 218 F7
Raglan Wlk BS31 24 D4
Railford Hill BA11 118 B3
Railway Arches BS2 227 C2
Railway Cotts BA11 143 C3
Railway La BA2 62 D1
Railway Pl BA1 228 C1
Railway St
Bath BA1 228 C1
Taunton TA2 212 F6
Railway Terr BA2 79 E4
Railway View Pl BA3 78 B2
Rainbow La TA3 191 C7
Rainham Ct [2] BS23 30 C1
Rains Batch BS40 72 E6
Rainsbury Hill TA4 164 F8
Raisey La TA20 193 C7
Raleigh Cl
Bridgwater TA6 209 C5
Saltford BS31 25 D2
Raleigh Ct
Sherborne DT9 225 E4
[3] Weston-super-Mare BS23 48 E5
Raleigh Ho TA6 209 C5
Raleigh Rd DT10 190 B4
Raleigh Rise BS20 2 B5
Raliegh Pl DT9 225 D2
Ralph Allen Dr BA2 45 B3
Ralph Allen Sch BA2 45 E2
Ralston Ct BA9 216 C4
Rambler Way TA6 208 E6
Ramon Ave TA23 202 D7
Ramsay Cl BS22 31 E4
Ramsay Way TA8 104 C8
Ramscombe Forest Wlks★
TA5 151 E8
Ramscombe La BA1 28 F6
Ramsey La TA21 179 F8
Ramshorn Cl TA1 212 C2
Ramshorn Gn TA1 212 D2
Ramshorn Pl TA1 212 D3
Ranchways BS20 1 F4
Randall Rd BS8 226 B2
Randolph Ave BS13 22 B5
Randolph Cl BS13 22 B5
Randolph Rd BA11 119 F4
Ranger Rd BA6 206 C3
Rangoon Rd TA23 202 E6
Rankers La BS39 41 C5
Rank The
Coxley BA5 139 F6
Maiden Bradley BA12 144 C2
Vobster BA3 117 D6
Ranscombe Ave BS22 31 D2
Ransford BS21 6 B1
Raphael Ct BS1 227 B1
Rapide Wy
Weston-super-Mare BS24 49 B4
Weston-super-Mare BS24 49 C4
RAPPS 183 D3
Rapps La TA19 183 D4
Raps Cl TA1 213 E5
Raps Gn TA1 213 E5
Rashwood La BA11 118 B6
Ratleigh La DT9 188 A3
Rattigan Cl TA8 104 C6
Rattle Row TA24 131 B4
Raven Cl BS22 31 E1
Raven Ct BS9 5 F8
Ravenhead Dr BS14 23 B8
Ravensmead TA20 223 C5
Ravenswood Sch BS48 8 D3
Ravensworth Terr TA8 104 B7
Rawle's Bldgs TA24 124 A3
Rawlings La BS26 88 E2
Rawlins Ave BS22 32 A5
RAWRIDGE 191 F1
Rawridge Rd EX14 191 F2
Rayens Cl BS41 10 F1
Rayens Cross Rd BS41 10 F1
Rayleigh Rd BS9 5 E7
Raymar Flats TA19 221 A4
Raymond St TA2 212 E6
Raymore Rise BS41 10 F1
Rayneswood BS23 48 F8
Read Mead BA6 206 E3
Reakes Cl BA5 203 C4
Rebels Way BA6 206 D5
Reckleford BA20, BA21 219 B5
Reckleford Inf Sch BA21 219 C5
Rector's Cl TA8 65 F3
Rector's Way BS23 48 F6
Rectory Cl
Farmborough BA2 60 A6
[6] North Petherton TA6 153 E3
Staplegrove TA2 212 C8
Wraxall BS48 9 A2

Rectory Ct TA20 193 D6
Rectory Dr
Burnham-on-S TA8 104 B8
Staplegrove TA2 212 C7
Yatton BS49 34 C7
Rectory Farm Cl BA22 174 F3
Rectory Farm La BA2 43 F2
Rectory Gdns TA20 193 D6
Rectory Hill
Chapel Allerton BS26 88 D2
Pitney TA10 172 C7
South Cadbury BA22 175 C3
Rectory La
Bleadon BS24 67 C6
Compton Martin BS40 74 B6
Hardington Mandeville BA22 197 A6
Horsington BA8 176 E2
Norton Sub Hamdon TA14 185 F2
Shalford BA9 216 E6
Sparkford BA22 175 A3
Timsbury BA2 60 B2
Rectory Lawn TA8 104 B8
Rectory Pl TA8 104 C8
Rectory Rd
Ashbrittle TA21 178 F8
Burnham-on-S TA8 104 B8
Easton-in-G BS20 4 B3
Norton Fitzwarren TA2 168 B5
Shepton Mallet BA4 205 B6
Staplegrove TA2 212 C8
Rectory Way
Lympsham BS24 66 F2
Yatton BS49 34 C7
Recurium Lodge BS26 70 B2
Redacre BS40 36 D3
RED BALL 179 C4
Red Barn La TA20 193 D4
Redcliff Backs BS1 227 B2
REDCLIFFE BAY 1 E4
Redcliffe Cl BS20 1 E3
Redcliffe Par E BS1 227 A1
Redcliffe Par W BS1 227 A1
Redcliffe Sixth Form Ctr The BS1 227 B1
Redcliffe St BS27 90 C7
Redcliffe Way BS1 227 B1
Redcliff Hill BS1 227 B1
Redcliff Mead La BS1 227 B1
Redcliff St BS1 227 B2
Red Cotts
Blagdon BS40 54 D6
Corsley Heath BA12 144 E8
Redcroft BS40 36 D3
Redcross Mews 14 BS2 227 C3
Redcross St BS2 227 C3
Red Deer Gdns TA6 208 D3
Redding Pit La BS40 37 E4
Reddings The BS40 74 B7
Redfield Gr BA3 97 A8
Redfield La TA10 156 A2
Redfield Rd BA3 97 A8
Redford Cres BS13 21 F3
Redford Trad Est BS3 22 C8
Redford Wlk BS13 21 F3
Redgate Pk TA18 224 C8
Redgates Rd TA24 200 E7
Redgate St TA6 209 B4
REDHILL 36 D3
Red Hill
Peasedown St John BA2 60 E1
Redhill BS40 36 D2
West Monkton TA2 169 B7
Redhill La BA3 95 A2
Red Hill La TA7 155 E7
Redhole La DT9 225 D8
Red House La BS9 5 E6
Red House Rd TA9 86 D5
Red La
Churchinford TA3 191 F7
Hemyock EX15 180 E3
Seaborough DT8 195 E1
Staplehay TA3 181 E8
Redlake Dr TA1 213 D3
Redland Ave BS20 3 F6
Redland La TA3 183 C8
Redland Pk BA2 43 F6
Redlands La TA7 137 C2
Redlands Terr BA3 96 F8
Redland Terr BA11 119 F3
REDLANE 191 F7
Red Lion Ct
3 Crewkerne TA18 224 C6
Somerton TA11 211 E4
Wellington TA21 222 E6
Red Lodge Bsns Pk BS24 32 D1
REDLYNCH 160 D4
Redlynch Cross BA10 160 E4
Redlynch La BS31 24 D2
Redlynch Rd
Pitcombe BA10 215 F2
Redlynch BA10 160 D3
Redmans Hill BS28 107 E4
Redpoll Dr BS20 3 A6
RED POST 79 B7
Red Post
Chard TA20 193 D3
Isle Abbotts TA3 183 E7
Porlock TA24 124 B3
Red Post Cross TA11 173 D4
Red Post Ct BA2 79 B7
Red Post Lower Rd TA4 151 C5
Red Rd
Berrow TA8 85 A7
Brean TA8 66 A2
Redshard La BS40 53 B7
Redstart Prim Sch The TA20 223 C5
Redstart Rd TA20 223 C6
Redway TA24 124 A3
Red Way The BA12 144 F6
Redwing Dr BS22 31 F1
Red Wing Rd DT9 217 C2
Redwood Cl
Nailsea BS48 9 A2
Radstock BA3 97 E8
Redwood Dr BS8 10 F4
Redwood Ho BS13 22 D3
Redwood La BS48 20 C7
Redwood Rd BA21 219 E8
Reed Cl
Bridgwater TA6 208 F2
Chard TA20 223 D6
Watchet TA23 202 D6
Reedley Rd BS9 5 F5
Reedmace Rd BA11 120 B2
Reedmoor Gdns TA6 208 E7
Reeds Barn EX13 198 F1
Reeds Dr TA7 136 F4
Reed Way BS22 32 C3
Rees Way BS26 87 E7
Reeves Cl
Draycott BS27 90 F2
5 Langaller TA2 169 C5
Regal Rd BA4 205 B6
Regal Way 24 BA4 205 B6
Regency Cl TA8 85 A2
Regency Ct BA5 203 C4
Regency Wlk BA11 119 E4
Regent Ct BA22 173 E2
Regent Gn TA4 167 F1
Regent Mews TA20 223 C3
Regent St
Bradford On Tone TA4 167 F1
Bristol BS8 226 A2
Burnham-on-S TA8 104 A7
Weston-super-Mare BS23 48 E7
Regents The
Cotford St Luke TA4 167 E6
Keynsham BS31 24 F6
4 Yeovil BA21 218 C6
Regents Way TA24 200 E6
Regent Way TA6 209 A2
REGIL 37 F2
Regil La BS40 38 A6
Regil Rd BS40 37 F3
Regina The BA1 228 B3
Reid Ct BA5 203 B4
Remalard Ct BA7 214 B5
Rendcomb Cl BS22 31 B2
Rendell Rise BA20 218 C1
Rennison Ct BS23 48 E4
Reservoir La BA5 203 C6
Reservoir Rd
Chard TA20 193 E4
Crimchard TA20 223 A5
Retford Ho BA2 45 E5
Retreat Caravan Park The TA8 85 A2
Retreat The
Foxcote BA3 79 E3
Frome BA11 120 B4
Taunton TA2 168 F6
Weston-super-Mare BS23 30 C1
Reubens Ct BS22 31 F3
Rex Rd BA22 186 C2
Rex's La
Barwick BA22 197 F8
Yeovil BA22 219 C1
Rexton La TA4 150 F5
Reynald's Way
Butleigh BA6 157 C4
Street BA16 207 D1
Reynolds TA21 166 F2
Reynolds Cl BS31 25 A5
RHODE 153 D5
Rhode Cl BS31 25 A3
Rhode La TA6 208 E2
Rhodes Cl TA2 212 C7
Rhodyate BS40 54 D2
Rhodyate Hill BS49 34 F6
Rhodyate La BS49 35 A7
Rhodyate The BS29 51 C1
Rhydderch Way TA18 224 C5
Rhyll Gate Cross TA22 162 E7
Rhymes Pl BA1 28 C3
Rhyne Bridge 9 TA6 209 A1
Rhyne Terr BS23 48 D2
Rhyne View BS48 8 B1
Richard Beadon Cl TA4 210 B4
Richard Huish Coll TA1 213 A2
Richards Cl
Wellington TA21 222 C8
Weston-super-Mare BS22 32 B4
Richards Cres TA2 169 B6
Richmond Cl
Bath BA1 27 F1
Bridgwater TA6 208 F7
Keynsham BS31 24 D4
Minehead TA24 200 E6
Portishead BS20 2 E5
Sampford Peverell EX16 178 D1
Sherborne DT9 225 C3
Richmond Ct BA22 173 E2
Richmond Gn
Nailsea BS48 8 F1
Sherborne DT9 225 C4
Taunton TA1 212 D5
Richmond Hill
Bath BA1 27 F1
Bristol BS8 226 B3
Richmond Hill Ave BS8 226 B3
Richmond Ho
Crewkerne TA18 224 C6
9 Shepton Mallet BA4 205 B6
Yeovil BA20 219 A4
Richmond Hts
Bath BA1 27 F2
Bristol BS8 226 B3
Richmond La
Bath BA1 27 F1
Bristol BS8 226 B3
Richmond Mews BS8 226 A3
Richmond Park Rd BS8 226 A3
Richmond Pk TA1 212 C4
Richmond Pl BA1 27 F1
Richmond Rd
Bath BA1 27 F1
2 Frome BA11 119 E3
Sherborne DT9 225 C3
Taunton TA1 212 D5
Yeovil BA20 219 A4
Richmond St
5 Sidbrook TA2 169 B2
Weston-super-Mare BS23 48 D7
Richmond Terr BS8 226 A3
Richmond Villas BA6 206 E4
Richmond Way BA21 218 C6
Rich's Farmhouse Cider Farm* TA9 105 D3
RICH'S HOLFORD 151 C4
Ricketts La BS22 32 A2
RICKFORD 54 B3
Rickford La BS40 54 A3
Rickford Rd BS48 8 F1
Rickford Rise BS40 54 A3
Rickhayes BA9 216 B4
Rickhay Rise TA18 196 B8
Ricklands The BS40 38 A6
Ricksey Cl TA11 211 B3
Ricksey La TA11 211 B3
Ricksmead Dro TA7 155 B2
Rickyard Rd BS40 35 E2
RIDGE 74 C5
Ridge Cl BS20 2 A4
Ridge Cres BS40 74 E6
Ridge Green Cl BA2 62 D8
Ridge Highway TA4 166 A3
Ridge Hill TA4 210 D5
Ridge La
Corton Denham DT9 175 D1
East Chinnock BA22 196 F8
East Coker BA22 197 A7
Pitcombe BA7, BA10 215 A2
Ridge BS40 74 D5
Shepton Mallet BA4 205 B3
Ridgemead BA20 218 D2
Ridgemeade BS14 23 B4
Ridgemount Gdns BS14 23 B5
Ridge Rd
Croscombe BA4, BA5 204 D5
West Anstey TA22 162 D7
Ridge The
Bristol BS11 4 E7
Porlock TA24 124 B3
Poyntington DT9 188 F7
Yatton BS49 34 B8
Ridgeview BS41 11 B2
Ridgeview Ho BS20 2 E3
RIDGEWAY 143 C7
Ridgeway
Ashcott TA7 156 B8
Nailsea BS48 8 C1
Nunney BA11 143 C8
Sherborne DT9 225 B3
Ridgeway Ave BS23 48 E6
Ridgeway Cl BS40 74 E6
Ridgeway Ct BS14 23 C5
Ridgeway Gdns
Bristol BS14 23 C5
Glastonbury BA6 206 F5
Ridgeway La
Bristol BS14 23 B5
Fitzhead TA4 166 F6
Moorlinch TA7 155 F7
North Cadbury BA22 175 D6
Nunney BA11 143 C8
Shillingford EX16 164 D2
Stolford TA5 134 E8
Ridgeway Rd BS41 11 A2
Ridgeway The BS22 31 B2
Ridgewood BS9 5 D3
Ridgewood Cross EX15 191 B8
Ridgewood La EX15 191 A8
Ridgway TA18 196 B8
Ridgway Cross EX36 145 K1
RIDING GATE 177 B8
Ridings The BS13 21 E4
Ridley Cnr TA10 171 C5
Ridley Hill TA10 171 E8
Riec-Sur-Belon Way TA19 221 A4
Rigg La DT9 187 F5
Rigg Lane Cotts DT9 187 F5
Riggles Cross EX14 191 D3
RIMPTON 188 A8
Rimpton Hill BA22 188 A7
Rimpton Rd BA22 174 F1
Ringdown La EX15 180 F2
Ringolds Way BA16 207 B4
Ringspit La
Blackrock BS39 40 E8
Bristol BS14, BS39 40 E8
Ring St DT10 190 B4
Ringstone TA9 136 B8
Ringswell Gdns BA1 28 B1
Ringwell BA2 81 E4
Ringwell Hill TA12 185 D4
Ringwell La BA2 81 E4
Ringwood Gr BS23 31 A1
Ringwood Rd
Bath BA2 44 C5
Bridgwater TA6 209 A2
Riphay Cross TA22 163 E3
Rippleside BS20 2 C5
Rippleside Rd BS21 6 E5
Ripple The BS21 8 D4
Risdale Rd BS3 11 F1
Risdon Rd TA23 202 C6
Risedale Cl TA6 208 C5
Risedale Rd BS25 70 A8
Risemoor Rd TA6 208 E2
Ritchie Rd BA22 218 A5
Rivendell BS22 32 A4
Riverbed Ho TA9 104 D3
River Dro
Dundon TA10 156 E1
Othery TA7 155 E4
River La TA7 209 E1
Riverland Dr BS13 21 F5
Riverleaze
Bristol BS9 5 C5
Portishead BS20 1 F6
River Mead BS21 16 D8
River Paddock Dro BA5 110 B2
River Pl BA2 44 B6
River Rd
East Huntspill TA7 137 B8
Mark TA9 106 D1
Pawlett TA6 135 F5
Portbury BS20 3 F8
Riversgate BS1 227 C2
RIVERSIDE
Midsomer Norton 96 F7
Wellington 222 B6
Riverside
Banwell BS24, BS29 51 B5
Bridgwater TA6 208 F6
Burrowbridge TA7 154 F1
Combwich TA5 135 C5
Dinder BA5 140 D7
Horton TA19 183 C2
Meare BA5 138 F5
Taunton TA1 212 E4
Wellington TA21 222 B7
Riverside Cl
Bridgwater TA6 208 F7
Bristol BS11 4 F5
Clevedon BS21 6 B1
Midsomer Norton BA3 96 F7
Weston-super-Mare BS22 32 C3
Riverside Cotts BA3 79 A2
Riverside Ct BA2 228 B1
Riverside Gdns
Bath BA1 228 B2
Dunster TA24 201 E3
Midsomer Norton BA3 96 F7
Riverside Pl 2 TA1 212 F4
Riverside Rd
Bath BA2 228 B2
Midsomer Norton BA3 96 F7
Riverside Row TA24 124 A3
Riverside Terr BA11 119 F5
Riverside Wlk BA3 96 F7
Rivers Rd
Bath BA1 28 A1
Bath BA1 228 C4
Yeovil BA21 219 D8
Rivers Reach BA11 120 A5
Rivers St BA1 228 B3
Rivers Street Mews BA1 228 B3
River St BS2 227 C3
River Street Pl 5 BA1 228 B3
River Terr BS31 24 F5
Riverton Rd TA7 136 B4
River View
Bridgwater TA6 208 F6
Combwich TA5 135 B5
Exebridge TA22 163 F3
Riverway BS48 8 F3
River Wlk BS22 32 D2
RNAS Yeovilton Road BA22 174 A2
Roachill Cross EX36 162 C1
Road Hill
Alcombe SN13 29 E8
Langford Budville TA4 166 B3
Roads La SP8 190 D8
ROADWATER 131 C1
Roake La TA2 168 B5
Roath Rd BS20 2 D5
Robbins Cl SN14 13 F8
Robert Blake Science Coll TA6 208 F3
Robert Ct BS8 11 D7
Roberts Dr TA6 209 A2
Roberts Rd TA2 168 A6
Robert St TA4 202 D2
Robin Cl
Bristol BS14 23 D6
Midsomer Norton BA3 97 B8
Taunton TA1 212 B4
Weston-super-Mare BS22 49 E8
Robin Dr BS24 49 E2
Robinia Wlk BS14 23 A7
Robin La BS21 6 D5
Robin Pl BS20 3 A6
Robins Ct
Chard TA20 223 C5
Frome BA11 119 D5
Robins Dr
Bridgwater TA6 209 A6
Burtle TA7 137 D6
Robins La
Burtle TA7 137 C6
Frome BA11 119 D5
Shepton Beauchamp TA19 184 E4
Robinson Cl BS48 19 A5
Robinson Hts DT10 190 B4
Robinson Way BS48 19 A5
Rob-Lynne Ct BS25 69 F8
Roche Cl BA21 218 C7
Rochester Cl BS24 49 A1
Rochester Rd TA2 213 A8
Rochfort Ct BA1 45 B8
Rock Ave BS48 8 C2
Rock Cotts BS20 4 E4
Rockeries Dr BS25 69 F8
Rockeries The BS25 69 F8
Rockery Pk BA2 45 C2
Rocketts Cl TA3 169 D4
Rocketts Cotts TA3 169 C4
Rockfield Cotts TA21 179 F7
Rock Hall Cotts BA2 45 B1
Rockhall Ho 10 BS23 30 C1
Rock Hall Ho BA2 45 B1
Rock Hall La BA2 45 B1
Rock Hill TA3 170 C1
Rockhill Est BS31 24 F4
Rockingham Gdns BS11 5 A8
Rockingham Gr BS23 31 A1
Rock La
Bath BA2 45 B1
Exford TA24 128 D1
West Bagborough TA4 151 E5
Rockleaze
Bristol BS9 5 E2
Evercreech BA4 141 E2
Rockleaze Ave BS9 5 E3
Rockleaze Ct BS9 5 E3
Rockleaze Mans 12 BS23 30 C1
Rockleaze Rd BS9 5 E3
Rockliffe Ave BA2 45 B8
Rockliffe Rd BA2 45 B8
Rock Rd
Keynsham BS31 24 E5
Midsomer Norton BA3 78 B2
Yatton BS49 34 C7
Rock's Dro BA16 138 F3
Rocks La BS40 20 E1
Rocks St BA5 204 C7
Rocks The BA4 142 B7
Rock Terr BA3 116 F6
Rockway TA3 170 C1
Rockwell Gate TA21 222 B5
ROCKWELL GREEN 222 B5
Rockwell Green CE Prim Sch TA21 222 B5
Rocky Hill TA11 173 D5
Rocky La TA23 131 E2
Rodber Cl BA9 216 B4
Rodber Gdns BA9 216 B4
Roddenbury Cl BA11 120 B5
Roddenbury View BA12 144 D8
Rodden Rd BA11 120 A5
RODE 101 F8
Rode Hill
Rode BA11 82 E1
Southwick BA11 83 A1
Rode Methodist VA Fst Sch BA11 101 E8
Rodfords Mead BS14 23 A7
RODGROVE 177 C3
RODHUISH 131 B2
Rodhuish Cross TA24 131 B3
Rodhuish Hill La TA24 131 A3
Rod La TA19 183 F4
Rodmead La BA5 110 E4
Rodmead Wlk BS13 22 A4
Rodmoor Rd BS20 2 D6
Rodmore Cres BA4 141 E1
Rodmore Rd BA4 141 E1
Rodney BS24 49 A2
Rodney Ct BA22 218 A5
Rodney Ho BA2 44 A6
Rodney Pl BS8 226 A3
Rodney Rd
Backwell BS48 19 A6
Saltford BS31 25 E2
RODNEY STOKE 91 A1
Rodney Stoke National Nature Reserve* BS27 91 B2
RODWAY 135 B3
Rodway TA5 135 B3
Rodwell La
Barrington TA13 184 E5
Lillesdon TA3 170 A3
Roe Ave BA22 218 A5
Roebuck Cl BS22 32 B4
Roebuck Gate La TA4 151 B6
Roe Cl TA6 209 D4
Roe La BA22 188 B8
Roemead La BA3 114 C5
Roemead Rd
Oakhill BA3 114 C4
Westbury Beacon BA5 91 E6
Rogers Cl
Buckland Dinham BA11 100 A3
Clutton BS39 58 E3
North Petherton TA6 153 F3
Rogers Wlk TA4 167 E6
Roland Cl TA1 212 C2
ROLSTONE 32 F2
Roman Baths The* BA1 228 C2
Roman Ct BA21 219 D6
Roman Farm Rd BS4 22 E7
Roman Ho BA1 228 C4
Roman La TA6 208 C3
Roman Rd
Batheaston BA1 29 C7
Bleadon BS24 67 C8
Sandford BS25 51 F4
Taunton TA1 213 C5
Roman Villas BA4 205 E4
Roman Way
Bristol BS9 5 C4
Coleford BA3 116 F7

Roman Way *continued*
Paulton BS39 77 C6
Peasedown St John BA2 79 E7
Watchet TA23 202 C7
Roman Way The BA6 206 C3
Romney Mead TA1 213 D4
Romney Rd 2 TA6 154 A5
Romsey Rd BA21 219 E8
Romulus Cl BS31 24 F7
Ron Jones Ho 3 BS1 227 B4
Rookery Cl
Puriton TA7 136 C4
Rooks Bridge BS26 87 A6
Weston-super-Mare BS22 31 E3
Rookery La
Croscombe BA5 204 B7
Drimpton DT8 199 F6
Rookery Terr TA21 222 C5
Rookery The BA5 140 D7
Rookery Way BS14 22 F4
ROOKHAM 112 B5
Rook La BA11 119 F4
ROOKS BRIDGE 87 C5
Rooksbridge Rd BS24, BS26 87 B6
Rooksbridge Wlk BA2 44 B5
Rookscastle Rd TA5 153 A3
Rooks La BA11 120 E7
Rook's Meade La TA19 184 E1
ROOK'S NEST 150 C4
Room Hill Rd TA24 146 D7
Roper's La BS40 35 E3
Rope Walk Ho 23 BS2 227 C3
Ropewalk The TA20 223 B5
Rope Wk TA24 201 B7
Rope Wlk
Backwell BS48 19 A5
Bridgwater TA6 209 A5
Coleford BA3 116 E8
Evercreech BA4 141 E1
14 Martock TA12 185 E6
Wellington TA21 222 C4
Rope Wlk The TA23 202 C7
Roping Rd BA21 219 B6
Rosa Pl TA6 208 E1
Rosary Dr TA6 208 B4
Rosa Wy TA6 208 E1
Rosebank Rd TA4 167 A4
Roseberry Cotts BA3 117 A7
Roseberry Pl BA2 44 C6
Roseberry Rd BA2 44 C6
Roseberry Terr TA1 212 D5
Rosebery Ave
Bridgwater TA6 209 B5
Yeovil BA21 219 D6
Rosebery St TA2 212 E7
Rosebery Terr BS8 226 B2
Rose Cotts
Taunton TA1 213 B3
Weston-super-Mare BS22 32 C2
Rose & Crown Cotts BA3 116 F6
Rose Ct
Keinton Mandeville TA11 158 A1
Shepton Mallet BA4 205 B6
Rosedale Ave BS23 49 A7
Rose Dale Wlk BA11 119 F6
Rose Gdns BS22 32 B4
Rose Hill
Bath BA1 28 C3
Portishead BS20 2 C6
Spaxton TA5 152 F2
Rose La
Crewkerne TA18 224 B6
Crewkerne TA20 195 A3
Crewkerne, Misterton TA18 196 B3
Purtington TA20 195 A3
Roseland Cl BA1 28 C3
Roselyn Cres DT9 189 A1
Rosemary Cres BS20 2 F5
Rosemary La
Dulverton TA22 163 D6
Freshford BA3 64 B4
ROSEMARY LANE 180 D1
Rosemarylane Cross
EX15 180 D1
Rosemary St DT9 217 C2
Rosemary Way BA11 120 B3
Rose Meadow Vw BS3 11 E1
Rose Meare Gdns BS13 21 E7
Rose Mills Ind Est TA19 183 E2
Rosemont Terr BS8 226 A2
Rosemount La BA2 45 B4
Rosemount Rd BS48 20 B8
Roseneath Ave TA8 84 F4
Rose Terr
Bath BA2 45 C2
Bristol BS8 226 B3
Rose Tree Paddock TA8 84 F4
Rosette Cotts TA12 185 B7
Rosevean Cl TA6 209 D7
Rose Villas TA5 135 B2
Rosewarn Cl BA2 44 A4
Rosewell Ct BA1 228 B2
Rosewood Ave TA8 104 C6
Rosewood Cl TA8 104 C7
Rosewood Dr TA8 104 C6
Roslyn Ave BS22 31 C1
Rossendale Cl BS22 31 F3
Rosshayne La EX14 192 C2
Rossiter Cl 8 TA2 169 C5
Rossiter Grange 5 BS13 21 F4
Rossiter Rd BA2 228 C1
Rossiter's Hill BA11 119 F3
Rossiter's Rd BA11 119 E3
Rosslyn Cl 1 BA1 44 B7
Rosslyn Rd BA1 44 B7
ROTCOMBE 59 D2
Rotcombe La BS39 59 D2
Rotcombe Vale BS39 59 D2
Rotton Row TA4 210 C4
Roughmoor TA4 202 E4
Roughmoor Cl TA1 212 D5
Roughmoor Cotts TA1 212 D5
Roughmoor Cres TA1 212 D5
Roughmoor Ind Est TA4 202 E4
Roughmoor La BA5 110 C7
ROUNDHAM 195 D4
Round Hill BA12 144 C2
Roundhill Gr BA2 44 B3
Roundhill Pk BA2 44 A4
Roundmoor Cl BS31 25 D3
Roundmoor Gdns BS14 23 D7
Roundoak Gdns TA21 167 C2
Round Oak Gr BS27 90 A8
Round Oak Rd BS27 90 A8
Round Pool La TA4 151 B7
Roundwell Cl BA4 204 F6
Roundwell St TA13 220 C4
Rowacres
Bath BA2 44 B3
Bristol BS14 22 F6
Rowan Cl
Nailsea BS48 9 A2
Puriton TA7 136 C4
Wincanton BA9 216 D2
Rowan Ct
Frome BA11 120 B7
Radstock BA3 78 E1
Rowan Dr
Berrow TA8 84 F5
Taunton TA1 213 D1
Rowan Ho BS13 22 D4
Rowan Pl BS24 32 B1
Rowans Cl TA6 209 C6
Rowan St BS14 22 E5
Rowans The BS20 2 B4
Rowan Way
Churchill BS40 53 A5
Yeovil BA20 218 F3
Rowan Wlk BS31 24 C4
Rowbarrow Hill
Rimpton DT9 188 A7
Trent DT9 187 F6
ROWBARTON 212 E7
Rowbarton Cl TA2 212 F7
ROWBERROW 53 A1
Rowberrow BS14 22 F7
Rowberrow La BS25 70 F8
Rowberrow Way BS48 8 E1
Rowcliffe Cotts TA21 178 F8
Rowdells Orch TA19 184 D1
Rowden Mill La DT10 189 F1
Rowdens Rd BA5 203 D3
Rowditch La TA5 133 D5
Rowe Cl TA21 222 A4
Rowe's Hill BA12 144 E4
ROWFORD 168 F6
Row La
Keinton Mandeville TA11 158 A1
Laverton BA2 100 D8
Rowlands Cl BA1 29 B2
Rowlands Rise TA7 136 C4
Rowley Farm La BA2 62 D5
Rowley Rd BA6 206 E5
Rowls La BA9 177 E6
Rowmarsh La TA10 172 D5
Rownham Cl BS3 11 E4
Rownham Ct BS8 226 A1
Rownham Hill BS8 11 E6
Rownham Mead BS8 226 A1
Row Of Ashes La BS40 36 F4
Rows La EX16 164 A1
Rows The BS22 31 E2
Row The
Hambridge TA10 184 D8
Langport TA10 172 B3
Royal Ave BA1 228 B3
Royal Cl BA21 219 C6
Royal Cres* BA1 228 A3
Royal Cres BS23 48 D8
Royal Ct BS23 48 D4
Royal Dr TA6 136 B2
Royal Fort Rd BS2, BS8 226 C3
Royal High School Bath Jun Sch The BA1 27 D1
Royal High School Bath The BA1 27 F2
Royal Ho 4 BA4 205 B6
Royal National Hospl for Rheumatic Diseases BA1 228 B2
Royal Par
Bristol BS8 226 B3
Weston-super-Mare BS23 48 D8
Royal Park Mews BS8 226 A3
Royal Pk BS8 226 A3
Royal Portbury Dock Rd BS20 3 E5
Royal Prom BS8 226 B3
Royal Sands BS23 48 D4
Royal United Hospl BA1 44 B8
Royal West of England Acad BS8 226 B3
Royal York Cres BS8 11 F6
Royal York Ho 7 BS8 226 A2
Royal York Mews 6 BS8 226 A2
Royal York Villas BS8 226 A2
Royces La TA19 184 C5
Roynon Way BS27 90 B7
Roys Pl TA2 213 F7
Royston Lodge BS23 48 D6
Royston Rd TA3 192 A7
ROYSTON WATER 192 B7
Rozel Ho 14 BS23 30 C1
Rubbery La TA11 158 D1
Rubens Cl BS31 25 A5
Ruborough Rd TA6 209 C4
Ruby Dr TA6 209 C8
Ruckley Ford BA3 80 A2
Ruddock Cl BA22 197 B8
Ruddock Way BA22 197 B8
Ruddymead BS21 6 D2
RUDGE 102 D5
Rudge Hill BA11 102 D5
Rudge La
Beckington BA11 102 B6
Standerwick BA11 102 D3
Rudge Rd BA11 102 B2
Rudgeway Rd BS39 77 E4
Rudgewood Cl BS13 22 D4
Rudgleigh Ave BS20 4 C4
Rudgleigh Rd BS20 4 C4
Rudhall Gn BS22 32 B3
Rudmore Pk BA1 44 A7
Rue La
Alweston DT9 189 C2
Hambridge TA3 184 B7
Ruett La BS39 77 B4
Rugg's Dro
Chedzoy TA7 154 D7
West Huntspill TA9 136 B7
Rugg's Hill TA22 148 E2
Rughill BS28 108 D8
Rugmoor La BS40 55 D3
Rugosa Dr TA8 84 F4
RUISHTON 169 C3
Ruishton CE Prim Sch TA3 169 C3
Ruishton La TA3 169 C3
Ruishton Lane Cotts TA3 169 C3
RUMWELL 168 B2
RUNNINGTON 179 F8
Runnymede Rd BA21 219 D8
Runway The BS24 49 C4
Rupert St
Bristol BS1 227 A3
Taunton TA2 212 E6
Rusham BS13 21 F4
Rush Ash La BA3 116 E8
Rushgrove Gdns BS39 57 C4
RUSH HILL 44 B2
Rush Hill
Bath BA2 44 C2
Farrington Gurney BS39 76 F3
Rush Hill La BS28 107 F3
Rushmoor BS21 6 A1
Rushmoor Gr BS48 19 A5
Rushmoor La BS48 19 A5
Rushway BS40 53 F4
Ruskin Cl TA1 213 C4
Ruskin Rd BA3 78 C1
Ruskway La TA10 184 C6
Rusling La BS40 37 A1
Russell Ave BS24 50 C5
Russell Cl BS40 38 A6
Russell Pl
Bridgwater TA6 208 F6
Milborne Port DT9 217 C3
Russell Pope Ave TA20 223 D2
Russell Rd
Clevedon BS21 6 C3
Locking BS24 50 C6
Russell's TA4 210 C4
Russell's Barton BA11 143 B8
Russell St BA1 228 B3
Russet Cl TA21 222 F7
Russet Rd TA11 211 B4
Russets The BS20 2 F4
Russett Cl BS48 19 B6
Russett Gr BS48 18 C8
Russett Rd
Street BA16 207 C4
Taunton TA1 213 E5
Russet Way
Peasedown St John BA2 79 D7
Yeovil BA20 218 D2
Russ St BS2 227 C2
Rust La BS21 16 E4
Rusty Well BA20 218 F3
Rusty Well Pk BA20 218 F3
Ruthven Rd BS4 22 E8
Rutland Cl BS22 49 C8
Rutter's La TA19 221 B4
Ryalls Ct BA21 219 C5
Ryburn Cl TA1 213 D3
Rydal Ave BS24 50 A4
Rydal Rd BS23 48 F4
RYDON 169 E8
Rydon Cres TA5 135 C2
Rydon La
Lopen TA13 185 A1
South Petherton TA13 220 A5
Taunton TA2 212 F8
Rye TA7 136 C4
Rye Cl BS13 21 E6
Ryecroft Ave BS22 31 E2
Ryecroft Rise BS41 11 B1
Ryefields Cl BA22 197 B8
Rye Gdns BA20 218 D2
Rye La TA7 155 C2
Ryelands Farm Ind Est TA21 222 B3
Ryeleaze BS11 4 E5
Ryepool TA4 167 F8
Ryesland Way TA3 169 D4
Rye Water La DT2 197 A1
Rylands BA11 101 E4
Rylands Cl TA4 202 D2
Rylestone Gr BS9 5 F5
Rysdale Rd BS9 5 F6

S

Sabrina Way BS9 5 C4
Sackmore Gn DT10 190 F6
Sackmore La DT10 190 F5
Saco Ho BS1 227 B2
Sadborow La TA20 199 B4
Sadborow Pound TA20 199 B5
Sadbury Cl BS22 32 B4
Sadler St BA5 203 D4
Sadlier Cl BS11 5 A8
Saffin Dr TA2 213 F8
Saffron Cl TA1 168 F1
Saffron Ct
Bath BA1 228 C4
Sherborne DT9 225 E4
Saffron Ho 10 BS23 48 E8
Saffrons The 7 BS22 32 B4
Sage Cl BS20 1 E4
Sage's La BA3 94 D6
Sainsbury Cl TA24 200 D7
Sainsbury Rd TA24 200 D7
St Agnes Cl BS48 9 A1
St Albans Pl TA2 212 F8
St Aldhelm's CE Prim Sch BA4 141 E6
St Aldhelm's Cl BA11 119 D4
St Aldhelms Ct BA11 119 D4
St Aldhelm's Rd DT9 225 D6
St Algars Yd BA11 144 A4
St Andrew's CE Jun Sch TA8 104 B7
St Andrew's CE Prim Acad EX13 198 A7
St Andrew's CE Prim Sch
Bath BA1 228 B4
Taunton TA2 212 F6
St Andrews Cl
Castle Cary BA7 214 B7
Nailsea BS48 9 A1
Weston-super-Mare BS22 31 F3
St Andrew's Cl
Congresbury BS49 34 C4
Curry Rivel TA10 171 D4
High Ham TA10 156 A2
St Andrews Ct TA24 200 F7
St Andrew's Ct BA5 203 F5
St Andrews Dr EX13 198 A2
St Andrew's Dr BS21 6 A2
St Andrews La TA24 200 F7
St Andrews Mews 4 BA5 203 C3
St Andrew's Par 1 BS23 48 F4
St Andrews Pk BA5 203 D3
St Andrew's Prim Sch BS49 34 C4
St Andrews Rd
Backwell BS48 19 B5
Cheddar BS27 90 C7
Yeovil BA20 218 F5
St Andrew's Rd
Burnham-on-S TA8 104 B7
Stogursey TA5 134 C5
6 Taunton TA2 212 F6
St Andrew St BA5 203 E4
St Andrew's Terr BA1 228 B3
St Andrews View TA2 212 F6
St Andrews Wlk 5 BA5 203 C3
St Anne's Ave BS31 24 D6
St Anne's CE Prim Sch BS24 33 B5
St Anne's Cl BA6 158 A5
St Anne's Ct BS31 24 D6
St Anne's Gdns BA21 218 E6
St Ann's Cl TA2 212 E7
St Ann's Dr TA8 85 A1
St Ann's Pl BA1 228 B2
St Ann's Way BA2 45 C6
St Anthony's Cl BA3 78 A2
St Antonys Sq 1 DT9 225 D3
St Aubyn's Ave BS23 48 D2
St Audries Cl TA5 134 C6
St Audries Ct TA23 202 B7
St Augustine of Canterbury Sch The TA2 213 A7
St Augustines Ct 1 TA1 213 A4
St Augustine's Par BS1 227 A2
St Augustine's Pl 1 BS1 227 A2
St Augustine St TA1 213 A4
St Austell Cl BS48 19 A8
St Austell Rd BS22 49 B8
St Barnabas Cl BA3 78 B3
St Bartholomew's CE Fst Sch TA18 224 D5
St Bartholomew's CE VC Fst Sch TA18 224 D5
St Benedict's CE Jun Sch BA6 206 D4
St Benedict's Cl BA6 206 D4
St Benedict's RC Prim Sch BA3 97 C7
St Bernadette RC Prim Sch BS14 23 B6
St Bernadette RC Sch BS14 23 B6
St Bernard's RC Prim Sch BS11 4 E6
St Bernard's Rd BS11 4 E6
St Brides Cl BA6 206 D5
St Bridges Cl BS22 31 A6
St Bridges Ct BS22 31 A6
St Bridget's Cl TA8 65 F5
St Cadoc Ho BS31 24 F5
ST CATHERINE 13 F1
St Catherine La BA1 13 D2
St Catherine's Cl BA2 45 C6
St Catherine's Cres DT9 225 B3
St Catherine's Ct 10 BA11 119 E5
St Catherines Hill BA10 215 E6
St Catherine's Mead BS20 4 D3
St Catherine's Way DT9 225 B3
St Chad's Ave BA3 78 A1
St Chad's Gn BA3 97 A8
St Charles Cl BA3 78 A2
St Christophers Cl BA2 45 C8
St Christopher's Ct BS21 6 C5
St Christopher's Way TA8 85 A2
ST CLEERS 211 C3
St Cleers TA11 211 C3
St Cleer's Orch TA11 211 C3
St Cleers Way TA11 211 C3
St Clements Ct
Bath BA1 27 C1
Bristol BS2 227 C4
Clevedon BS21 6 C4
Keynsham BS31 24 E4
2 Weston-super-Mare BS22 32 A2
St Clements Rd BS31 24 F4
St Congars Wy BS49 34 E4
St Cuthbert Ave BA5 203 B5
St Cuthbert's CE Inf Sch BA5 203 C3
St Cuthberts CE Jun & Inf Sch BA5 203 C3
St Cuthbert's Lodge 3 BA5 203 D4
St Cuthbert St BA5 203 D4
St Cuthbert's Villas BA5 203 A5
St Cuthbert Way BA5 203 B5
St Davids Cl EX13 198 A2
St David's Cl
Glastonbury BA6 206 E4
Taunton TA2 213 A8
Weston-super-Mare BS22 31 B2
St David's Cres BA21 219 B7
St Davids Ct TA6 209 D3
St David's Ct BS21 16 E8
St David's Dr EX13 198 A2
St David's Gdns TA2 212 F8
St Davids Mews BS1 226 C2
St Davids Pl BA10 215 E7
ST DECUMANS 202 B6
St Decuman's Rd TA23 202 C7
St Dubricius CE First Sch TA24 124 A3
St Dunstans Cl
Glastonbury BA6 206 D5
Keynsham BS31 24 E6
St Dunstan's Com Sch BA6 206 D5
St Dunstan's Pk BA6 158 A5
St Edmund's Rd BA6 206 D5
St Edmunds's Rd BA6 206 E5
St Edmund's Terr BA3 117 C7
St Edward's Cl TA7 137 B2
St Edward's Rd BS8 226 B2
St Edyth's Rd BS9 5 C6
St Elizabeth's Way TA13 220 C4
SS Peter & Paul RC Cath* BS8 226 A4
SS Peter & Paul RC Prim Sch BS8 226 C4
St Francis RC Prim Sch BS48 8 F1
St Francis Rd BS31 24 D6
St George CE Prim Sch BS1 226 B2
ST GEORGES 32 D3
St Georges Ave EX13 198 A2
St George's Ave
Taunton TA2 212 F8
Yeovil BA21 219 B7
St Georges Bldgs BA1 228 A3
St George's CE Sch SP8 161 E1
St George's CE Sch, Bourton SP8 161 E1
St George's Cl TA24 201 D2
St George's Cross BA11 101 E1
St Georges Ct BA6 206 E5
St George's Hill
Bath BA2 45 D8
Easton-in-G BS20 4 A3
St George's Ho BS8 226 B2
St Georges La BS20 4 B4
St Georges Mews TA1 212 F3
St Georges Pl BA1 228 A3
St George's Pl TA1 212 F3
St Georges Prim Sch BS22 32 C3
St George's RC Prim Sch TA1 213 A3
St George's RC Sch TA1 213 A2
St Georges Rd BS1 226 C2
St George's Rd
Keynsham BS31 24 D6
Portbury BS20 3 E7
St Georges Sq TA1 212 F3
St George's St TA24 201 D2
St Georges Way TA1 212 E2
St Gildas TA20 223 D4
St Gilda's Cl TA10 172 A5
St Gildas Ct TA10 172 A5
St Gildas RC Prim Sch BA21 219 B5
St Gilda's Way BA6 206 D4
St Gregory's CE Prim Sch
Marnhull DT10 190 F5
Marnhull DT10 190 F5
St Gregory's RC Sch BA2 62 D8
St Helens BA22 175 D8
St Hilary Cl BS9 5 D5
St Ives Cl BS48 9 A1
St Ives Rd BS23 49 A5
St James' Barton BS1 227 B4
St James Cl TA1 212 F4
St James Ct
Bridgwater TA6 209 D3
4 Taunton TA1 212 F4

St James Mews TA13 . . . . . 220 C4
St James's Cl BA21 . . . . 218 D5
St James's Par BA1 . . . . . . 228 B2
St James's Pk
Bath BA1 . . . . 228 B4
Yeovil BA20 . . . . 218 C5
St James' Sq BA6 . . . . 157 D4
St James's Sq BA1 . . . . 228 A4
St James's St
Bath BA1 . . . . 228 B4
South Petherton TA13 . . . . . . 220 C4
St James St
Taunton TA1 . . . . 212 F4
Weston-super-Mare BS23 . . . 48 D7
St James Terr BA22 . . . . . . 197 A7
St John's BA1 . . . . 44 B8
St John & St Francis CE Prim Sch TA6 . . . . 209 D4
St John's Ave BS21 . . . . 6 D3
St John's Bridge 4 BS1 . . 227 A3
St John's CE Fst Sch BA11 119 F4
St John's CE Inf Sch BA6 . . 206 E5
St John's CE Prim Sch
Keynsham BS31 . . . . 24 E5
Midsomer Norton BA3 . . . . . . 78 A1
Midsomer Norton BA3 . . . . . . 78 A1
Wellington TA21 . . . . 222 E6
Wellington TA21 . . . . 222 E6
St John's CE VA Fst Sch
17 Frome BA11 . . . . 119 F4
17 Frome BA11 . . . . 119 F4
St Johns Cl TA21 . . . . 222 E6
St John's Cl
Peasedown St John BA2 . . . . . 79 B7
Skilgate TA4 . . . . 164 E6
Weston-super-Mare BS23 . . . 30 D1
St John's Cres
Midsomer Norton BA3 . . . . . . 78 A2
Trowbridge BA14 . . . . 83 F6
St Johns Ct
Axbridge BS26 . . . . 70 B2
Bath BA2 . . . . 228 C3
Keynsham BS31 . . . . 24 E6
Wells BA5 . . . . 203 D3
St Johns Ho 3 BA20 . . . . . . 219 B5
St John's Pl BA1 . . . . 228 B2
St John's RC Prim Sch (Annexe) BA2 . . . . 44 D4
St Johns Rd BA2 . . . . 60 B1
St John's Rd
Backwell BS48 . . . . 19 B5
Bath BA2 . . . . 228 C3
Bath, Lower Weston BA1 . . . . 44 C7
Burnham-on-S TA8 . . . . 104 B7
Clevedon BS21 . . . . 6 D3
Frome BA11 . . . . 120 B5
Taunton TA1 . . . . 212 E3
Yeovil BA21 . . . . 219 D7
St Johns Ret Pk TA1 . . . . . . 213 B5
St John's Sq BA6 . . . . 206 D5
St John St
Bridgwater TA6 . . . . 209 B4
Wells BA5 . . . . 203 D4
St John's Terr BA11 . . . . . . 119 E3
St Johns Wlk BA6 . . . . 206 D5
St John the Evangelist CE Prim Sch
3 Clevedon BS21 . . . . 6 C1
Clevedon BS21 . . . . 6 C1
St Joseph & St Teresa RC Prim Sch
Wells BA5 . . . . 203 D4
Wells BA5 . . . . 203 D4
St Josephs Field TA1 . . . . . 213 A3
St Joseph's RC Prim Sch
Bridgwater TA6 . . . . 208 D4
Burnham-on-S TA8 . . . . 104 B6
Burnham-on-Sea TA8 . . . . . . 104 B6
Portishead BS20 . . . . 2 D3
St Joseph's Rd BS23 . . . . 30 E1
St Judes Ho 21 BS2 . . . . 227 C3
St Jude's Terr BS22 . . . . 31 C1
St Julian's CE Prim Sch
BA2 . . . . 62 E1
St Julian's Cl BS39 . . . . 77 E4
St Julian's Rd BA2 . . . . 79 F5
St Juthware Cl BA22 . . . . . . 197 C3
St Katherine's Sch BS20 . . . . 4 E3
St Kenya Ct BS31 . . . . 24 F5
St Keyna Prim Sch BS31 . . . 24 D5
St Keyna Rd BS31 . . . . 24 E5
St Kilda's Rd BA2 . . . . 44 D5
St Ladoc Rd BS31 . . . . 24 D6
St Laud Cl BS9 . . . . 5 D5
St Lawrence Ct BS11 . . . . 4 E8
St Lawrence's CE Prim Sch
BA5 . . . . 110 E6
St Lawrences VC Prim Sch
BA5 . . . . 110 E6
St Leonards Ct BA20 . . . . . . 219 A4
St Loe Cl BS14 . . . . 22 F3
St Louis RC Prim Sch
13 Frome BA11 . . . . 119 E5
Frome BA11 . . . . 119 E5
St Luke's Cl TA8 . . . . 104 B7
St Lukes Mews TA4 . . . . 167 E6
St Lukes Rd BA11 . . . . 101 E5
St Luke's Rd
Bath BA2 . . . . 44 F3
Midsomer Norton BA3 . . . . . . 77 F2
St Margarets Cl BS48 . . . . . . 19 A5
St Margaret's Cl BS31 . . . . . 24 D6
St Margarets Ct TA1 . . . . . . 213 B4
St Margarets La TA20 . . . . . 198 C8
St Margaret's La BS48 . . . . . . 19 A5
St Margaret's Rd BA22 . . . . 186 B6
St Margaret's Sch BA22 . . . 186 C6
St Margaret's Terr BS23 . . . 48 D8
St Marks Cl
Chedzoy TA7 . . . . 154 E8
Keynsham BS31 . . . . 24 E6
St Marks Ct TA6 . . . . 209 D3
St Mark's Ecumenical CE/Methodist Prim Sch
BS22 . . . . 31 F4
St Marks Gdns BA2 . . . . 228 C1
St Mark's Rd
Bath BA2 . . . . 228 C1
Burnham-on-S TA8 . . . . 104 B8
Midsomer Norton BA3 . . . . . . 78 A2
Weston-super-Mare BS22 . . . 32 A3
St Mark's Sch BA1 . . . . 28 B2
St Mark's VA Prim Sch
BS22 . . . . 31 F4
St Martins
Clevedon BS21 . . . . 6 C5
Long Ashton BS41 . . . . 11 A1
St Martin's CE Prim Sch
BS22 . . . . 31 D2
St Martin's Cl
Fivehead TA3 . . . . 170 F1
Zeals BA12 . . . . 161 F3
St Martins Ct BS22 . . . . 31 E3
St Martin's Ct BA2 . . . . 44 E1
St Martin's Garden Prim Sch
BA2 . . . . 44 D1
St Martins Hospl BA2 . . . . . . 44 E1
St Martin's La SN14 . . . . 13 F8
St Martin's Pk SN14 . . . . 13 F8
St Martins Way BA20 . . . . . 218 D2
St Mary CE Prim Sch BA2 . . 45 C8
St Mary Redcliffe & Temple CE Sch BS1 . . . . 227 B1
St Mary & St Peter's CE VC Prim Sch
Barrington TA19 . . . . 184 D5
Ilton TA19 . . . . 183 E4
St Mary's Bldgs BA2 . . . . . . 228 B1
St Mary's CE Prim Sch
Bradford Abbas DT9 . . . . 187 E1
Bridgwater TA6 . . . . 208 C4
Radstock BA3 . . . . 79 C1
Thorncombe TA20 . . . . 199 B6
Timsbury BA2 . . . . 60 C3
St Mary's CE VA Prim Sch
BS20 . . . . 3 E3
St Marys Cl
Hutton BS24 . . . . 49 D2
Seavington St Mary TA19 . . . 184 D1
Wedmore BS28 . . . . 108 C4
St Mary's Cl
10 Axminster EX13 . . . . 198 A1
Bath BA2 . . . . 45 B6
Chard TA20 . . . . 223 C2
Cossington TA7 . . . . 136 F3
Timsbury BA2 . . . . 60 B2
St Mary's Cres
Chard TA20 . . . . 223 C3
13 North Petherton TA6 . . . . 153 F4
Yeovil BA21 . . . . 219 C8
St Marys Ct TA6 . . . . 153 E4
St Mary's Ct
1 Bridgwater TA6 . . . . 208 F4
Weston-super-Mare BS24 . . . 49 A1
St Mary's Gdns BS40 . . . . . . 53 B5
St Mary's Gr BS48 . . . . 18 C8
St Mary's La BA4 . . . . 140 E3
St Mary's Park Rd BS20 . . . . . 2 C4
St Mary's Pk
Langport TA10 . . . . 172 A5
Nailsea BS48 . . . . 18 C8
St Marys Pl BA4 . . . . 142 F4
St Mary's RC Prim Sch
Axminster EX13 . . . . 198 A1
Bath BA1 . . . . 27 B1
St Mary's Rd
Bristol BS11 . . . . 4 D7
Burnham-on-S TA8 . . . . 104 B7
Frome BA11 . . . . 120 B5
Hutton BS24 . . . . 49 D2
Leigh Woods BS8 . . . . 11 D6
Meare BA6 . . . . 138 D4
Oxenpill BA6 . . . . 138 C4
Portishead BS20 . . . . 2 C4
Sherborne DT9 . . . . 225 B3
Westonzoyland TA7 . . . . 154 F5
St Marys Rise BA3 . . . . 79 C2
St Mary's St BS26 . . . . 70 C2
St Mary St
Bridgwater TA6 . . . . 208 F4
Nether Stowey TA5 . . . . 134 B2
St Mary's View BA22 . . . . . . 196 F7
St Mary's Wlk BS11 . . . . 4 D6
St Mathew's Pl BA2 . . . . 45 B5
St Mathias Ho BS2 . . . . 227 C3
St Matthew's Cl BS23 . . . . . . 30 D1
St Matthew's Field TA6 . . . 208 E4
St Matthews Gn TA6 . . . . . . 208 E4
St Matthew's Rd BS6 . . . . . 227 A4
St Matthias Pk BS2 . . . . . . 227 C3
St Medard Rd BS28 . . . . 108 C4
St Michael Cl TA3 . . . . 169 D4
St Michael on the Mount CE Prim Sch BS2 . . . . 226 C3
St Michael Rd TA3 . . . . 169 D4
St Michael's Ave
Clevedon BS21 . . . . 6 D1
Weston-super-Mare BS22 . . . 32 A3
Yeovil BA21 . . . . 219 C7
St Michael's CE First Sch
TA24 . . . . 200 F7
St Michael's CE Jun Sch
BA2 . . . . 44 A6
St Michaels Cl
Nether Compton DT9 . . . . . . 187 F3
Stoke St Michael BA3 . . . . . . 116 B3
St Michael's Cl
Buckland Dinham BA11 . . . . 100 A3
Glastonbury BA6 . . . . 206 E3
Nether Stowey TA5 . . . . 134 A2
St Michael's Cres TA2 . . . . 213 A8
St Michaels Ct
Bawdrip TA7 . . . . 136 E2
Walton BA16 . . . . 156 D7
Yeovil BA21 . . . . 219 C8
St Michael's Ct BA2 . . . . 63 E8
St Michael's Gdns TA13 . . . 220 D5
St Michael's Hill
Bristol BS2 . . . . 226 C4
Milverton TA4 . . . . 167 A4
St Michael's Hospl BS2 . . . 226 C4
St Michael's Pk BS2 . . . . . . 226 C4
St Michael's Pl BA1 . . . . . . 228 B2
St Michaels Rd BA2 . . . . 44 A5
St Michael's Rd
Bath BA1 . . . . 44 D7
Burnham-on-S TA8 . . . . 104 B7
Minehead TA24 . . . . 200 F8
Yeovil BA21 . . . . 219 D6
St Michael's View TA15 . . . 186 B4
St Nicholas Almshouses 5
BS1 . . . . 227 A2
St Nicholas CE Prim Sch
Combe St Nicholas TA20 . . . 193 D6
Henstridge BA8 . . . . 190 A7
Radstock BA3 . . . . 78 F2
St Nicholas' CE Prim Sch
BA3 . . . . 79 A2
St Nicholas Chantry CE Prim Sch BS21 . . . . 6 E3
St Nicholas Chantry CE VC Prim Sch BS21 . . . . 6 E3
St Nicholas Cl
4 Henstridge BA8 . . . . 190 A6
Winsley BA15 . . . . 64 D7
Yeovil BA20 . . . . 219 B4
St Nicholas Ct BA2 . . . . 28 F1
St Nicholas Pk BA20 . . . . . . 219 B4
St Nicholas Rd
Bristol BS2 . . . . 227 C4
Weston-super-Mare BS23 . . . 48 D2
Whitchurch BS14 . . . . 23 C4
St Nicholas St BS1 . . . . 227 A2
St Nicholas Way BS48 . . . . . 18 D2
St Oswald's Ct BS13 . . . . 22 A8
St Patricks Cl 3 TA2 . . . . . . 213 A8
St Patricks Ct BS31 . . . . 24 E5
St Patrick's Ct BA2 . . . . 45 B6
St Patrick's Rd
Taunton TA2 . . . . 213 A8
Yeovil BA21 . . . . 218 D7
ST PAULS 227 C4
St Paul's CE Jun Sch BA4 . 205 B5
St Pauls Cl TA13 . . . . 220 D4
St Paul's Cl DT9 . . . . 225 E6
St Pauls Ct TA6 . . . . 209 D3
St Paul's Flats DT9 . . . . 225 E6
St Paul's Gn DT9 . . . . 225 E6
St Pauls Pl
Bath BA1 . . . . 228 B2
Midsomer Norton BA3 . . . . . . 78 A2
St Paul's Rd
Bristol BS8 . . . . 226 B4
Burnham-on-S TA8 . . . . 104 B7
Weston-super-Mare BS23 . . . 48 E5
St Paul St BS2 . . . . 227 B4
St Paul's Terr BA5 . . . . 111 A4
St Peter's Ave BS23 . . . . 30 D1
St Peter's CE Fst Sch TA4 . 202 D4
St Peters CE Prim Sch BS20 . 2 D4
St Peter's CE Prim Sch
BS13 . . . . 21 F6
St Peters Cl
Ilton TA19 . . . . 183 F4
Staple Fitzpaine TA3 . . . . . . 182 C5
Williton TA4 . . . . 202 D2
St Peter's Cl
Horton TA19 . . . . 183 C1
Taunton TA2 . . . . 213 B7
St Peters Ct TA6 . . . . 209 D3
St Peter's Ho BS8 . . . . 226 B2
St Peters Lodge BS20 . . . . 2 D4
St Peters Rd
Portishead BS20 . . . . 2 D4
Shepton Mallet BA4 . . . . 205 A6
St Peter's Rd
Burnham-on-S TA8 . . . . 104 B7
Radstock BA3 . . . . 97 C8
St Peter's Rise
Bristol BS13 . . . . 22 B7
South Petherton TA13 . . . . . 220 D4
St Peters Terr 21 BA4 . . . . . 205 B6
St Peter's Terr BA2 . . . . 44 D6
St Philip's CE Prim Sch
BA2 . . . . 44 D2
St Philips Rd BS2 . . . . 227 C3
St Pius X RC Prim Sch
BS13 . . . . 22 A5
St Quintin Pk TA2 . . . . 213 E6
St Rayn Hill TA17 . . . . 195 B4
St Saviour's Ave TA6 . . . . . 209 A4
St Saviour's Inf Church Sch
BA1 . . . . 28 B2
St Saviour's Jun Church Sch
BA1 . . . . 28 B2
St Saviour's Rd BA1 . . . . 28 C2
St Saviour's Terr 10 BA1 . . . 28 B1
St Saviours Way 4 BA1 . . . . 28 C1
St Stephen's Ave 3 BS1 . . 227 A2
St Stephen's CE Prim Sch
BA1 . . . . 27 F1
St Stephen's Cl BA1 . . . . 27 F1
St Stephen's Ct BA1 . . . . . . 228 B4
St Stephen's Pl BA1 . . . . . . 228 B4
St Stephen's Rd BA1 . . . . . . 228 B4
St Stephen's St BS1 . . . . . . 227 A2
St Swithins Cl DT9 . . . . 225 E4
St Swithin's Pl BA1 . . . . 228 C4
St Swithin's Rd DT9 . . . . . . 225 E4
St Swithin's Yd BA2 . . . . . . 228 C3
St Thomas Cross BA21 . . . 219 C5
St Thomas Ct TA6 . . . . 209 D3
St Thomas' Ct BA5 . . . . 203 F5
St Thomas Mews BA5 . . . . 203 F5
St Thomas Pl BS1 . . . . 227 B2
St Thomas Rd BA3 . . . . 78 B2
St Thomas St E BS1 . . . . . . 227 B2
St Thomas St
Bristol BS1 . . . . 227 B2
Dunster TA24 . . . . 201 E2
Wells BA5 . . . . 203 E5
St Thomas Terr BA5 . . . . . . 203 F5
St Vigor & St John CE Prim Sch BA3 . . . . 96 E3
St Vincent's Rd BS8 . . . . . . 226 A2
St Whites Cl BS14 . . . . 23 D3
St Whytes Rd BS4 . . . . 22 D8
St Winifreds Dr BA2 . . . . 45 D2
Salcombe Gdns BS22 . . . . . . 32 A2
Salcombe Rd BS4 . . . . 23 A8
Sale Piece Dro TA10 . . . . . . 156 F1
Salerno Cl BA22 . . . . 173 E2
Sales Ho 15 BA4 . . . . 205 B6
Salisbury Rd
Bath BA1 . . . . 28 B2
Burnham-on-S TA8 . . . . 104 C7
Paulton BS39 . . . . 77 F4
Weston-super-Mare BS22 . . . 31 C1
Salisbury St TA2 . . . . 212 E6
Salisbury Terr
Castle Cary BA7 . . . . 214 B5
4 Frome BA11 . . . . 119 E3
Frome BA11 . . . . 119 E3
Gurney Slade BA3 . . . . 114 E8
Weston-super-Mare BS23 . . . 48 D7
Sally Hill BS20 . . . . 2 E7
Sally In The Wood BA1,
BA15 . . . . 46 D6
Sally Lovell's La BA8 . . . . . 189 F8
Sally Lunn's Kitchen Mus*
BA1 . . . . 228 C2
Sallysmead Cl BS13 . . . . 22 B4
Salmon Mead BS14 . . . . 23 D3
Salmon Par TA6 . . . . 209 A4
SALTFORD 25 D2
Saltford CE Prim Sch
BS31 . . . . 25 E2
Saltford Ct BS31 . . . . 25 E3
Salthouse Ct BS21 . . . . 6 B2
Salthouse La BA20 . . . . 219 A4
Salthouse Rd BS21 . . . . 6 B2
Saltings Cl BS21 . . . . 6 B2
Saltlands TA6 . . . . 208 F7
Saltlands Ave TA6 . . . . 208 F7
Saltlands Ho TA6 . . . . 208 F7
Saltlands La TA6 . . . . 209 A7
Saltry La TA24 . . . . 131 A6
Saltwell Ave BS14 . . . . 23 C5
Salway Cl BS40 . . . . 38 E1
Salway Gdns 11 EX13 . . . . . 198 A1
Samarate Way BA20 . . . . . . 218 D4
Sambar Pl TA6 . . . . 208 D3
Sambourne La BS20 . . . . 4 C4
SAMPFORD ARUNDEL 179 E5
Sampford Arundel Com Prim Sch TA21 . . . . 179 E5
SAMPFORD BRETT 202 E1
SAMPFORD MOOR 179 F5
SAMPFORD PEVERELL 178 E1
Sampford Peverell CE Prim Sch EX16 . . . . 178 C1
Sampford Rocks TA4 . . . . . 202 F1
Sampsons Rd BS13 . . . . 22 D4
Samuel Ct BA8 . . . . 176 F1
Samuels Ct TA2 . . . . 212 E6
Samways Cl BA22 . . . . 218 B5
Sanctuary Gdns BS9 . . . . 5 D3
Sanctuary La TA22 . . . . 148 A2
SAND 108 C2
Sandalwood Ride TA6 . . . . 153 F5
Sandbrook La BA22 . . . . . . 175 D7
Sandburrows Rd BS13 . . . . . 21 F6
Sandburrows Wlk BS13 . . . . 21 F6
Sandcroft BS14 . . . . 22 F6
Sandcroft Ave BS23 . . . . 48 D2
Sandene Cl TA2 . . . . 212 C8
Sanderling BS20 . . . . 2 F6
Sanderling Pl 7 BS20 . . . . . . 2 F6
Sand Farm La BS22 . . . . 31 A6
SANDFORD 52 A3
SANDFORD BATCH 51 F2
Sandford Cl 2 BS21 . . . . 6 B1
Sandford Hill TA5, TA6 . . . 208 A6
SANDFORD ORCAS 188 C7
Sandford Orcas Manor Ho*
DT9 . . . . 188 C8
Sandford Orcas Rd DT9 . . . 225 B7
Sandford Pk BA14 . . . . 83 F7
Sandford Prim Sch BS25 . . . 52 B4
Sandford Rd
Bristol BS8 . . . . 226 A1
Weston-super-Mare BS23 . . . 49 A7
Winscombe BS25 . . . . 51 F1
Sandhill La TA24 . . . . 131 C4
Sandhills Dr TA8 . . . . 84 F4
Sandhurst Rd BA20 . . . . 218 F1
Sanding's La
Chapel Leigh TA4 . . . . 167 A8
Fitzhead TA4 . . . . 166 F8
Lydeard St Lawrence TA4 . . . 151 A1
Sandlewood Cl BA21 . . . . . 219 E8
Sandmead Rd BS25 . . . . 52 A4
Sandown Cl
Bridgwater TA6 . . . . 209 A2
3 Yeovil BA20 . . . . 219 A5
Sandpiper Cl
Bridgwater TA6 . . . . 209 A4
Minehead TA24 . . . . 201 C5
Sandpiper Dr BS22 . . . . 31 F1
Sandpiper Rd TA6 . . . . 209 A4
Sandpits Hill TA10 . . . . 171 E4
Sandpits Rd BA6 . . . . 206 F5
Sand Rd
Wedmore BS28 . . . . 108 C3
Weston-super-Mare BS22 . . . 31 B5
Sandringham Cl TA6 . . . . . 209 C7
Sandringham Ct 2 BS23 . . . 48 F5
Sandringham Rd
1 Weston-super-Mare BS23 . . . . 48 F5
Yeovil BA21 . . . . 219 E6
Sandrocks La TA24 . . . . 131 B3
Sandscross La BA11 . . . . . . 100 A3
Sand St TA4 . . . . 166 F4
Sandy Cl TA9 . . . . 104 D4
Sandy Hole TA16 . . . . 195 F7
Sandy La
Beckington BA11 . . . . 101 E4
Cannington TA5 . . . . 135 A3
Cannington TA5 . . . . 135 B3
Chew Magna BS40 . . . . 39 C3
Easton-in-G BS8 . . . . 10 A8
Failand BS8 . . . . 10 C7
Stanton Drew BS39, BS40 . . . 39 E3
Wiveliscombe TA4 . . . . 210 C7
Sandyleaze BS9 . . . . 5 E7
Sandy's Hill La BA11 . . . . . 119 E1
Sandy's La EX14 . . . . 191 F2
Sandys Moor TA4 . . . . 210 D4
Sandy View BA11 . . . . 101 E4
Sandyway Cross EX36 . . . . 145 H4
Sansome's Hill DT9 . . . . . . 217 D2
Sansom's Cross DT6 . . . . . . 199 F1
Sapphire Dr TA6 . . . . 209 C8
Sarabeth Dr BA2 . . . . 61 A4
Saracen St BA1 . . . . 228 C3
Saunder's Piece La
TA18 . . . . 224 A7
Saunters Cl BA9 . . . . 216 B4
Saunton Wlk BS4 . . . . 22 E8
Savannah Dr 3 TA6 . . . . 154 A5
Savernake Rd BS22 . . . . 31 F3
Savery or Cottage Row
TA1 . . . . 213 B3
Saviano Way TA6 . . . . 208 E7
Saville Cres BS22 . . . . 49 C8
Saville Gate Cl BS9 . . . . 5 F4
Saville Mews BS6 . . . . 227 A4
Saville Pl BS8 . . . . 226 A2
Saville Rd
Bristol BS9 . . . . 5 F3
Weston-super-Mare BS22 . . . 49 C8
Saville Row BA1 . . . . 228 B3
Savoy The BS11 . . . . 4 E6
Saw Cl BA1 . . . . 228 B2
Sawmill Cotts BA11 . . . . . . 143 B8
Sawmill Gdns BA3 . . . . 96 D3
Sawpit La BA6 . . . . 140 C2
Sawpits Cl TA4 . . . . 150 D8
Sawyers Cl
Chilcompton BA3 . . . . 96 D3
Wraxall BS48 . . . . 9 A2
Sawyers Ct BS21 . . . . 6 E3
SAWYER'S HILL 180 E7
Sawyers Leigh TA2 . . . . 168 D8
Sawyers Mill EX16 . . . . 164 E2
Saxby Cl
Clevedon BS21 . . . . 6 B1
Weston-super-Mare BS22 . . . 32 B4
Saxon Cl
Oake TA4 . . . . 167 D4
Watchet TA23 . . . . 202 B7
Whitchurch BS14 . . . . 23 D3
Saxon Ct
Ilminster TA19 . . . . 221 B4
Weston-super-Mare BS22 . . . 32 D3
Saxondale Ave TA8 . . . . 85 A3
Saxon Gn TA6 . . . . 209 C4
Saxon Pl BS27 . . . . 90 B7
Saxon Rd
Bridgwater TA6 . . . . 209 C4
Weston-super-Mare BS22 . . . 49 C8
Saxon Ridge TA23 . . . . 202 B7
Saxon St BS40 . . . . 53 D6
Saxonvale BA11 . . . . 119 F4
Saxon Way
Cheddar BS27 . . . . 90 B6
Peasedown St John BA2 . . . . . 79 E8
Wedmore BS28 . . . . 108 C4
Wincanton BA9 . . . . 216 B3
Winsley BA15 . . . . 64 F7
Saxony Pl 3 TA6 . . . . 209 A1
Says La BS40 . . . . 53 B4
Scadden's La BS27 . . . . 91 B1
Scafell Cl
Taunton TA1 . . . . 212 C1
Weston-super-Mare BS23 . . . 31 A1
Scamel Ho 11 BA4 . . . . 205 B6
Scarf Dr BS24 . . . . 50 C5
Scaurs The BS22 . . . . 31 F2
Schofield Cl 1 TA2 . . . . 169 C5
School Cl
Bampton EX16 . . . . 164 B1
Banwell BS29 . . . . 51 B3
Bristol, Whitchurch BS14 . . . . 22 F4
Tintinhull BA22 . . . . 186 C6
Watchet TA23 . . . . 202 C7

School Cotts
13 East Coker BA22 . . . . 197 F8
Enmore TA5 . . . . 153 A5
Taunton TA2 . . . . 168 F6
School Dr DT9 . . . . 225 E5
School Fields
Cannington TA5 . . . . 135 C2
2 North Petherton TA6 . . . . 153 F3
School Hill
Ashcott TA7 . . . . 156 B8
Cucklington BA9 . . . . 177 D6
Misterton TA18 . . . . 224 F3
South Perrott DT8 . . . . 196 C1
Westbury-sub-Mendip BA5 . 110 E6
Wookey Hole BA5 . . . . 203 A8
SCHOOL HOUSE 199 A5
School La
Barrow Gurney BS48 . . . . . . 20 D5
Batheaston BA1 . . . . 28 F4
Blackford BS28 . . . . 107 D4
Burrowbridge TA7 . . . . 154 F1
Chew Stoke BS40 . . . . 56 D8
Combwich TA5 . . . . 135 B5
Compton Dundon TA11 . . . . 157 A3
Doulting BA4 . . . . 141 E6
Draycott BS27 . . . . 90 F3
Drimpton DT8 . . . . 199 E6
Farrington Gurney BS39 . . . . 77 A4
Horrington BA5 . . . . 113 A1
Kilmersdon BA3 . . . . 98 A6
Lopen TA13 . . . . 185 A1
7 North Petherton TA6 . . . . 153 F4
Rowberrow BS25 . . . . 53 A1
Seavington St Michael TA19 . 184 E2
Shapwick TA7 . . . . 137 F1
Somerton TA11 . . . . 211 E3
Tatworth TA20 . . . . 198 C8
Templecombe BA8 . . . . 176 E1
Wick St Lawrence BS22 . . . . 32 B7
Woolavington TA7 . . . . 136 E4
School of Christ the King RC Prim BS4 . . . . 22 E8
School Pl BA2 . . . . 46 B5
School Rd
Kingsdon TA11 . . . . 173 D5
Monkton Heathfield TA2 . . . . 213 F8
Parbrook BA6 . . . . 158 C7
Westonzoyland TA7 . . . . . . 154 E5
Wrington BS40 . . . . 35 E2
School St
Curry Rivel TA10 . . . . 171 D4
Drayton TA10 . . . . 171 E3
School View BS48 . . . . 9 B1
Schooner Pl TA24 . . . . 201 B7
Scimitar Rd BA22 . . . . 218 B6
Scobell Rise BS39 . . . . 59 C2
Score La BS40 . . . . 54 E2
Score The BS40 . . . . 54 E2
Scornfield La BS40 . . . . 56 D7
Scotch Horn Cl BS48 . . . . 8 F2
Scotch Horn Way 5 BS48 . . . 8 F2
Scot Cl TA6 . . . . 135 F5
Scot Elm Dr
Weston-super-Mare BS24 . . . 32 D1
Weston-super-Mare BS29 . . . 50 D8
Scot La BS40 . . . . 38 D1
Scotland La
Axbridge BS26 . . . . 107 D8
Chapel Allerton BS26 . . . . . 107 D8
Rudge BA11 . . . . 102 C4
Stockwood Vale BS4, BS14 . . . 24 A7
Scots Pine Ave 3 BS48 . . . . . 8 F2
Scott Cl TA2 . . . . 212 C6
Scott Rd
Frome BA11 . . . . 119 F5
Highbridge TA9 . . . . 104 D3
Weston-super-Mare BS23 . . . 49 A4
Scott Road BA21 . . . . 219 F8
Scotts Cl BA3 . . . . 116 C8
Scotts Hill TA4 . . . . 148 E1
Scott's Hill
Huish Champflower TA4 . . . . 165 E8
Seavington St Mary TA19 . . . 184 D1
Scotts La TA7 . . . . 137 D1
Scott's La TA21 . . . . 222 E6
Scotts Way TA18 . . . . 196 B8
Scouse Cross EX13 . . . . 198 E2
Scouse La EX13 . . . . 198 E2
Scrapton La TA20 . . . . 193 D5
Screech Witch Hill TA12 . . 185 F8
Screedy La TA4 . . . . 166 D4
Scruibbitts La TA7 . . . . 137 B2
Scud La TA18 . . . . 195 B2
Scumbrum La BS39 . . . . 59 C2
SEABOROUGH 195 E1
Seaborough Rd TA18 . . . . . 195 F2
Seaborough Road DT8 . . . 224 D1
Seaborough View TA18 . . . 224 C4
Seabrook Rd BS22 . . . . 31 D1
Sea King Rd BA20 . . . . 218 D3
Sea King Way BS24 . . . . 49 C5
Sea La
Carhampton TA24 . . . . 131 A7
Dunster TA24 . . . . 201 F4
Kilve TA5 . . . . 133 C6
Watchet TA23 . . . . 132 D5
Sealey Cl BS27 . . . . 90 F3
Sealey Cres BA5 . . . . 112 E1
Sealeys Cl TA9 . . . . 136 A8
SEA MILLS 5 B6
Sea Mills Inf Sch BS9 . . . . 5 C7
Sea Mills La BS9 . . . . 5 C5
Sea Mills Prim Sch BS9 . . . . . 5 B5
Sea Mills Sta BS9 . . . . 5 B4
SeaQuarium ★ BS23 . . . . 48 D6
Searle Cres BS23 . . . . 49 A6
Searle Ct
Clevedon BS21 . . . . 6 E2
Somerton TA11 . . . . 211 D3
Seat La BA4 . . . . 142 D1
Seaton Ct BA20 . . . . 219 A4
Seaton Rd BA20 . . . . 218 F4
Seavale Mews BS21 . . . . 6 C4
Seavale Rd BS21 . . . . 6 C4
Seaview Rd
Portishead, Redcliffe Bay BS20 . . . . 1 F4
Portishead, West Hill BS20 . . . . 1 F6
Sea View Rd TA8 . . . . 104 A8
SEAVINGTON ST MARY 184 D1
SEAVINGTON ST MICHAEL 184 F2
Seawalls BS9 . . . . 5 D2
Seawalls Rd BS9 . . . . 5 D2
Seaward Dr TA6 . . . . 208 F6
Seaward Way TA24 . . . . 201 C6
Second Ave
Axminster EX13 . . . . 198 A2
Bath BA2 . . . . 44 D5
Bristol BS14 . . . . 23 B7
Radstock BA3 . . . . 97 C7
Second Dro TA7 . . . . 155 D3
Secret World Wildlife Rescue ★ TA9 . . . . 136 C8
SECTOR 198 B1
Sector Hill EX13 . . . . 198 B1
Sector La EX13 . . . . 198 A1
Sedge Cl TA6 . . . . 208 F2
Sedge Dro TA7 . . . . 137 C3
Sedge Mead BA11 . . . . 119 F7
Sedgemoor Cl
Nailsea BS48 . . . . 18 E8
Yeovil BA21 . . . . 219 D7
Sedgemoor Dro
Sutton Mallet TA7 . . . . 155 A6
Wrantage TA3 . . . . 170 B2
Sedgemoor Hill Dr TA7 . . . 155 B7
Sedgemoor Manor Com Jun Sch TA6 . . . . 209 C6
Sedgemoor Manor Inf Sch TA6 . . . . 209 D5
Sedgemoor Rd
Bath BA2 . . . . 44 F2
Bridgwater TA6 . . . . 209 C3
Weston-super-Mare BS23 . . . 30 F1
Woolavington TA7 . . . . 136 E3
Sedgemoor Way
Glastonbury BA6 . . . . 206 D5
Woolavington TA7 . . . . 136 E3
Sedgemount Ind Pk TA6 . . 136 A2
Sedgewick Ho BS11 . . . . 4 E7
Seeley Cres BA16 . . . . 207 B3
Sefton Sq BS24 . . . . 50 A8
Selbourne Cl BA1 . . . . 44 A8
Selbourne Pl TA24 . . . . 200 F6
Selbourne Rd BS23 . . . . 48 E4
Selden Rd BS14 . . . . 23 E5
Sellbed Cross TA24 . . . . 146 A8
Selley Wlk BS13 . . . . 22 A5
Sellicks Rd TA2 . . . . 213 E8
Selway Ct BA2 . . . . 45 B2
Selwood TA20 . . . . 223 C5
Selwood Acad BA11 . . . . 120 B6
Selwood Cl BS22 . . . . 49 C7
Selwood Cres BA11 . . . . 120 A7
Selwood Rd
Frome BA11 . . . . 119 E5
Glastonbury BA6 . . . . 206 F6
Selwood St BA11 . . . . 118 B7
SELWORTHY 124 D3
Selworthy Cl
Bridgwater TA6 . . . . 208 F1
Keynsham BS31 . . . . 24 D5
Selworthy Gdns 4 BS48 . . . . 8 E1
Selworthy Ho BA2 . . . . 44 F2
Selworthy Rd
Taunton TA2 . . . . 213 B8
Weston-super-Mare BS23 . . . 49 A4
Selworthy Sch
Priorswood TA2 . . . . 213 A6
12 Pyrland TA2 . . . . 213 A8
Selworthy Specl Sch TA2 . 213 A8
Selworthy Terr BA2 . . . . 44 F2
Semington Cl TA1 . . . . 213 D4
Septimus Bldgs BS14 . . . . 22 D5
Serbert Cl BS20 . . . . 2 E5
Serbert Rd BS20 . . . . 2 E5
Serbert Way BS20 . . . . 2 E5
Sercombe Pk BS21 . . . . 6 E1
Serel Dr BA5 . . . . 203 B3
Serenity Rise BA16 . . . . 207 B5
Serlo Ct BS22 . . . . 32 A4
Serotines The TA10 . . . . 171 D8
Serse Cl BS31 . . . . 24 C2
Sevenacres TA11 . . . . 211 C3
Seven Acres La BA1 . . . . 28 F5
Seven Acres The 3 BS24 . . . 49 F7
SEVEN ASH 151 D4
Seven Dials BA1 . . . . 228 B2
Seventh Ave BS14 . . . . 23 A7
Severalls Park Ave TA18 . . 224 C5
Severn Ave BS23 . . . . 48 E5
Severn Cl TA6 . . . . 209 D7
Severn Dr TA1 . . . . 213 C4
Severn Gr TA8 . . . . 104 B5
Severnleigh Gdns BS9 . . . . . . 5 F3
Severnmeade BS20 . . . . 1 F5
Severn Rd
Bristol BS11 . . . . 4 D6
Pill BS20 . . . . 4 C5
Portishead BS20 . . . . 2 C5
Weston-super-Mare BS23 . . . 48 E5
Severn Terr TA23 . . . . 202 C7
Severn Way BS31 . . . . 25 A5
Severus St BS31 . . . . 24 F8
Sevier Rd BS26 . . . . 68 C3
Seville Ct
Portishead BS20 . . . . 2 E7
Taunton TA1 . . . . 212 D2
Seville Rd BS20 . . . . 2 E7
Sewage Works La TA12 . . 185 D6
Seward Terr BA3 . . . . 79 C2
Sewell Ho BS25 . . . . 70 A8
Sexey's Hospl BA10 . . . . . . 215 E6
Sexey's Hospl (Almshouses) BA10 . . . . 215 E6
Sexey's Rd BS28 . . . . 107 E4
Sexey's Sch BA10 . . . . 215 D5
Seymour Cl
Clevedon BS21 . . . . 6 E3
Wells BA5 . . . . 203 C5
Weston-super-Mare BS22 . . . 31 F4
Seymour Rd
5 Bath BA1 . . . . 28 A1
Bridgwater TA6 . . . . 209 D5
Street BA16 . . . . 207 D4
Seymour St TA21 . . . . 222 C6
Shackel Cross EX15 . . . . . . 191 B8
Shackleton Rd BA21 . . . . . . 219 F8
Shadow Wlk BS24 . . . . 50 C3
Shadwell Ct BA9 . . . . 216 C4
Shadwell La BA9 . . . . 216 C4
Shaftesbury Ave 2 BA1 . . . 44 C7
Shaftesbury Cl BS48 . . . . 18 D8
Shaftesbury La BA9 . . . . . . 216 C4
Shaftesbury Mews 7 BA2 . 44 D5
Shaftesbury Rd
Bath BA2 . . . . 44 D5
Henstridge BA8 . . . . 190 C8
Weston-super-Mare BS23 . . . 49 B8
Shaftesbury Terr BA3 . . . . . 79 A3
Shaftgate Ave BA4 . . . . 205 A6
Shaft Rd BA2 . . . . 45 E1
Shaggs Flood La TA20 . . . . 193 B1
Shakespeare Ave
Bath BA2 . . . . 44 F4
Taunton TA1 . . . . 213 C3
Shakespeare Ct BS23 . . . . . . 48 F2
Shakespeare Rd BA3 . . . . . . 78 C1
Shaking Dro TA9 . . . . 137 B6
SHALFORD 216 D8
Shalford La
Charlton Musgrove BA9 . . . . 161 A2
Shalford BA9 . . . . 216 D8
Shallows The BS31 . . . . 25 F3
Shambles The TA3 . . . . 170 B4
Sham Castle La BA2 . . . . 45 C7
Shannon Wlk BS20 . . . . 2 F6
Shapcott La EX36 . . . . 162 C2
Shapcott Wood Hill EX36 . 162 A2
Shaplands BS9 . . . . 5 F4
Shapway TA19 . . . . 184 F3
Shapway Cross TA19 . . . . . 184 F3
Shapway La BA4 . . . . 141 F2
Shapway Rd BA4 . . . . 141 E2
SHAPWICK 137 F1
Shapwick Heath National Nature Reserve ★ TA7 . . . . 137 F4
Shapwick Hill TA7 . . . . 155 F8
Shapwick Rd BA6 . . . . 138 A4
Shapwick Right Dro TA7 . . 155 C6
Shapwick Sch
Burtle TA7 . . . . 137 D6
Shapwick TA7 . . . . 137 F1
Sharland Cl BS9 . . . . 5 E3
Sharland Gr BS13 . . . . 22 C4
Sharlands TA19 . . . . 184 C5
Sharpenton La TA7 . . . . 155 D6
Sharpham Dro BA16 . . . . . . 138 E1
Sharpham La
Glastonbury BA16 . . . . 138 D1
Stoke St Gregory TA3 . . . . . . 170 E5
Sharpham Rd
Cheddar BS27 . . . . 89 F7
Glastonbury BA6 . . . . 206 F7
SHARPSTONE 64 A4
Shatterwell Cotts BA9 . . . . 216 C4
Shatt La TA5 . . . . 152 F3
Shatwell La
Castle Cary BA9 . . . . 214 F1
Yarlington BA9 . . . . 175 F8
Shaulders The TA2 . . . . 213 C7
Shave Cross DT6 . . . . 199 F1
Shave Hill SP8 . . . . 177 D4
Shave La
Crewkerne TA18 . . . . 224 A3
Donyatt TA19 . . . . 183 D1
Horton TA19 . . . . 183 C1
South Brewham BA10 . . . . . 161 A6
SHAWFORD 101 D7
Shawford La BA11 . . . . 101 D7
Shaw Gdns BS14 . . . . 23 A8
Shaw Path TA8 . . . . 104 C6
Shaws Way BA2 . . . . 43 F5
Sheafhayne Cross EX14 . . . 192 E4
Shearing Cross TA20 . . . . . 199 A5
Shearn La TA8 . . . . 104 B7
Shearwater Cl TA6 . . . . 209 D3
Shedrick Hill TA20 . . . . 199 B8
Sheepfair La SN14 . . . . 13 F8
Sheephouse Cvn Pk BS20 . . . 3 E7
Sheeplands La DT9 . . . . 225 B5
Sheeplands The DT9 . . . . . 225 B5
Sheeps Croft BS13 . . . . 22 A5
Sheepstealing La TA4 . . . . 150 E5
Sheepwash La TA19 . . . . . . 184 E5
SHEEPWAY 3 B5
Sheepway BS20 . . . . 3 B5
Sheep Way TA19 . . . . 184 E3
Sheepway La BS20 . . . . 3 C5
Sheldon Cl BS21 . . . . 6 F2
Sheldon Ct TA1 . . . . 212 E4
Sheldon Dr BA5 . . . . 203 C3
Sheldon Mill 3 BA5 . . . . . . 203 C3
Sheldon's La TA22 . . . . 163 A7
Shelduck Cl TA24 . . . . 201 C5
Shelley Ave BS21 . . . . 6 D2
Shelley Cl
Burnham-on-S TA8 . . . . 85 A2
Yeovil BA21 . . . . 218 D6
Shelley Dr TA8 . . . . 85 B2
Shelley Gr TA1 . . . . 213 B3
Shelley Rd
Bath BA2 . . . . 44 F4
Radstock BA3 . . . . 78 C1
Weston-super-Mare BS23 . . . 49 A4
Shell's La
Chard TA20 . . . . 193 A3
Shepton Beauchamp TA19 . . 184 E4
Shellthorn Gr TA6 . . . . 208 F2
Shelthorn Hill TA5 . . . . 152 F3
Shelway La TA19 . . . . 184 C4
Shepherds Cl TA6 . . . . 208 D6
Shepherd's Cl TA11 . . . . 157 A4
Shepherd's Cnr TA23 . . . . . 131 E4
Shepherds Cross BA8 . . . . 176 C5
Shepherd's Dro TA7 . . . . . . 155 A3
Shepherd's Hay TA1 . . . . . . 212 C2
Shepherd's Hill SP8 . . . . . . 177 E4
Shepherd's La
Chard TA20 . . . . 223 B4
Cucklington BA9 . . . . 177 C5
Frome BA11 . . . . 144 B7
Hemyock EX15 . . . . 180 F1
Shepherds Way
Beckington BA11 . . . . 101 F4
Weston-super-Mare BS22 . . . 32 C2
Shepherd Wlk BA2 . . . . 45 A1
Sheppard's Barton 11 BA11 . . . . 119 E5
Sheppard's Cnr TA5 . . . . . . 153 B5
Sheppards Gdns BA1 . . . . . . 27 B1
Sheppards Wlk BA3 . . . . 96 D3
Sheppy Rd TA3 . . . . 183 D8
Sheppy's Cider Farm Centre ★ TA4 . . . . 167 F1
Sheppy's Mill BS49 . . . . 34 D5
Shepton BS24 . . . . 49 A2
SHEPTON BEAUCHAMP . . . 184 E3
Shepton Beauchamp CE Prim Sch TA19 . . . . 184 E4
Shepton Beauchamp CE VC Prim Sch TA19 . . . . 184 E4
SHEPTON MALLET 205 D6
Shepton Mallet Com Hospl BA4 . . . . 204 F6
Shepton Mallet Inf Sch BA4 . . . . 205 C6
SHEPTON MONTAGUE 160 B2
Shepton Old Rd
Croscombe BA5 . . . . 204 A6
Dinder BA5 . . . . 140 D7
Shepton Rd BA4, BA5 . . . . . 204 D7
SHERBORNE
Litton 75 D3
Milborne Port 225 C6
Sherborne Abbey ★ DT9 . . . 225 D3
Sherborne Abbey CE Prim Sch DT9 . . . . 225 B2
Sherborne Castle ★ DT9 . . . 225 F3
Sherborne Girls Sch DT9 . 225 C4
Sherborne Hill DT9 . . . . 225 E1
Sherborne Mus ★ DT9 . . . . 225 D4
Sherborne Old Castle ★ DT9 . . . . 225 F4
Sherborne Pk DT10 . . . . . . 189 A3
Sherborne Prep Sch
Sherborne DT9 . . . . 225 D3
Sherborne DT9 . . . . 225 D3
Sherborne Prim Sch DT9 . 225 E5
Sherborne Rd
Milborne Port DT9 . . . . 217 C2
Yenston BA8 . . . . 189 E6
Yeovil BA21 . . . . 219 D5
Sherborne Rd Milbourne Down DT9 . . . . 188 F8
Sherborne Sch DT9 . . . . . . 225 D4
Sherborne Sch Int Coll DT9 . . . . 225 D5
Sherdon Bridge EX36 . . . . 145 D5
SHERFORD 212 E1
Sherford Rd TA1 . . . . 212 E1
Sherford Terr TA1 . . . . 212 E1
Sheridan Cl TA6 . . . . 209 D3
Sheridan Gdns BA14 . . . . 83 F6
Sheridan Rd
Bath BA2 . . . . 43 F5
Burnham-on-S TA8 . . . . 104 C6
Sherlands 4 TA16 . . . . 195 F7
Sherlands Gdns 3 TA16 . . 195 F7
Shermoor La BA22 . . . . 186 B7
Sherring Rd BA4 . . . . 205 D4
Sherrin Way BS13 . . . . 21 E3
Sherston Cl BS48 . . . . 9 A1
Shervage Ct TA6 . . . . 209 C5
Sherwell Cl BA21 . . . . 219 D7
Sherwood Cl BS31 . . . . 24 E5
Sherwood Cres BS22 . . . . 31 F3
Sherwood Rd BS31 . . . . 24 E5
Shetland Way BS48 . . . . 9 A1
Shickle Gr BA2 . . . . 44 D1
Shiller's La DT9 . . . . 188 C7
SHILLINGFORD 164 E2
Shiners Elms BS49 . . . . 34 B8
SHIPHAM 70 F7
Shipham CE Fst Sch BS25 . . 70 E8
Shipham Cl
Bristol BS14 . . . . 23 B5
Nailsea BS48 . . . . 18 F8
Shipham Cl *continued*
Weston-super-Mare BS23 . . . 49 A7
Shipham Hill BS25 . . . . 70 F5
Shipham La BS25 . . . . 52 B1
Shipham Rd BS27 . . . . 71 A3
Ship La
Bristol BS1 . . . . 227 B1
Combwich TA5 . . . . 135 B5
SHIPLATE 67 F6
Shiplate Rd BS24 . . . . 67 E6
Shipney La DT10 . . . . 190 C5
Shircombe La TA22 . . . . 147 F2
Shire Gdns BS11 . . . . 4 D8
SHIREHAMPTON 4 E7
Shirehampton Prim Sch BS11 . . . . 4 D6
Shirehampton Rd BS9 . . . . . . 5 C6
Shirehampton Sta BS11 . . . . 4 D5
Shiremoor Hill TA16 . . . . . . 195 F7
Shire St
Bridgwater TA6 . . . . 209 A1
13 Bridgwater TA7 . . . . 154 A5
Shires The TA24 . . . . 201 C5
Shires Yd BA1 . . . . 228 B3
SHOCKERWICK 29 F5
Shockerwick Farm La BA1 . 29 E6
Shockerwick La BA1 . . . . . . 29 D4
Shoe La
Paulton BS39 . . . . 77 D6
Slape Cross TA7 . . . . 209 E7
Shoot Hill TA17 . . . . 195 C8
Shophouse Rd BA2 . . . . 44 B5
Shop La
Pilton BA4 . . . . 140 E3
Wingfield BA14 . . . . 83 C6
Shopland Ho 8 BS21 . . . . 6 C2
SHOPNOLLER 151 E3
SHOREDITCH 169 A1
Shoreditch BS40 . . . . 56 C7
Shoreditch Rd
Stoke St Mary TA3 . . . . 169 A1
Taunton TA1 . . . . 213 B1
Shoredown La DT9, BA8 . . . 217 E6
Short Dro
Dundon TA10 . . . . 156 E1
Mudgley BS28 . . . . 138 C7
Somerton TA11 . . . . 211 A8
Westbury-sub-Mendip BA5, BS27 . . . . 110 B4
Short La
Draycott BS27 . . . . 90 E3
Litton BA3 . . . . 75 F2
Long Ashton BS41 . . . . 11 A2
Stone Allerton BS26 . . . . 88 C2
Shortland La BS28 . . . . 108 C3
Shortlands Dr BA21 . . . . . . 218 C8
Shortmarsh La BA22 . . . . . . 196 F4
SHORT STREET 121 F6
Short Way BS8 . . . . 10 B4
Shortwood La BA3 . . . . 75 F2
Shortwood Rd BS13 . . . . 22 E3
Shortwood Wlk BS13 . . . . . . 22 E3
SHOSCOMBE 79 E6
Shoscombe CE Prim Sch BA2 . . . . 79 F5
Shoscombe Gdns BA11 . . . 120 C7
SHOSCOMBE VALE 79 E5
Shovel La TA6 . . . . 153 E3
Showell Pk TA2 . . . . 212 B7
Showering Cl BS14 . . . . 23 D5
Showering Rd BS14 . . . . 23 D5
Showground Bsns Pk The TA6 . . . . 209 B1
Showground Rd TA6 . . . . . . 209 B1
Shrewsbury Bow BS24 . . . . . 50 A8
Shrewsbury Rd BA22 . . . . . 218 B7
Shrubbery Ave BS23 . . . . 30 D1
Shrubbery Cl TA8 . . . . 84 E8
Shrubbery Rd BS23 . . . . 30 D1
Shrubbery Terr 11 BS23 . . . 30 C1
Shrubbery Wlk BS23 . . . . . . 30 D1
Shrubbery Wlk W BS23 . . . . 30 D1
Shudrick La TA19 . . . . 221 C3
Shums Ct 3 BA1 . . . . 228 C2
Shurtland La TA4 . . . . 150 C3
SHURTON 134 C7
Shurton La TA5 . . . . 134 C6
Shurton Rd TA5 . . . . 134 B7
Shute La
Bruton BA10 . . . . 215 D6
Huish Champflower TA4 . . . . 165 C8
Long Sutton TA10 . . . . 172 E4
Shute Lake La TA18 . . . . . . 224 D5
Shuteleigh TA21 . . . . 222 E5
Shutemead TA1 . . . . 212 A4
Shute Row TA21 . . . . 222 E5
Shuter Rd BS13 . . . . 21 E5
Shute's La SP8 . . . . 177 E4
Shutewater Cl TA1 . . . . 212 A4
Shutewater Hill TA1 . . . . . . 212 A4
Shutewater Orch TA1 . . . . 212 A3
Shutgate Mdw TA4 . . . . 202 D3
Shuttern 2 TA1 . . . . 212 E3
Shuttern Bridge 3 TA1 . . . 212 E3
Shutwell La BA4 . . . . 140 E3
Shyners Terr 8 TA16 . . . . . 195 F7
SIDBROOK 169 B6
SIDCOT 70 C7
Sidcot Dr BS25 . . . . 70 A7
Sidcot La BS25 . . . . 70 A7
Sidcot Sch BS25 . . . . 70 B7
Sideland Cl BS14 . . . . 23 E6
Sidelings The BS40 . . . . 73 D8
Side Wood La EX36 . . . . . . 162 A1
Sidings The DT10 . . . . 190 C4
Sidmouth Cl TA8 . . . . 104 C8
Sidney Hill Cottage Homes BS25 . . . . 52 E4

SIGWELLS 175 E2
Silbury Rd BS3 . . . . 11 E2
Silbury Rise BS31 . . . . 25 A2
Silcox Rd BS13 . . . . 22 C4
Silk Cl BA4 . . . . 205 B7
Silk House Barton DT10 . . . 190 B4
Silklands Gr BS9 . . . . 5 C6
Silk Mills La TA2 . . . . 212 B6
Silk Mills Rd TA1 . . . . 212 B4
Silton Rd 1 SP8 . . . . 161 F1
Silverberry Rd BS22 . . . . 32 A1
Silvercombe 1 BS23 . . . . 48 E5
Silver Ct BS48 . . . . 8 C2
Silverdale Cl
Brushford TA22 . . . . 163 E4
Wembdon TA6 . . . . 208 C5
Silverdown Hill TA4 . . . . 150 C7
Silver La BA11 . . . . 144 B7
Silverlake Cotts DT9 . . . . 188 B2
Silverlow Rd BS48 . . . . 8 D2
Silvermead TA24 . . . . 201 B5
Silver Mead BS49 . . . . 34 D2
Silvermead Ct TA24 . . . . 201 B5
Silver Moor La BS29 . . . . 50 F7
Silver Rd BA16 . . . . 207 C5
Silver Springs TA19 . . . . 184 E3
Silver St
11 Bampton EX16 . . . . 164 B1
Barrington TA19 . . . . 184 D5
Barton St David TA11 . . . . 158 A3
Barwick BA22 . . . . 197 F8
Bridgwater TA6 . . . . 208 F4
Bristol BS1 . . . . 227 A3
Bruton BA10 . . . . 215 E6
Chard TA20 . . . . 223 C3
Cheddar BS27 . . . . 90 B8
Chew Magna BS40 . . . . 39 B3
Congresbury BS49 . . . . 34 D2
Crewkerne TA18 . . . . 196 B3
Curry Mallet TA3 . . . . 183 C8
Ditcheat BA4 . . . . 159 C7
East Lambrook TA13 . . . . 220 C8
Fivehead TA3 . . . . 170 F1
Glastonbury BA6 . . . . 206 E4
Holcombe BA3 . . . . 97 C1
Huntspill TA9 . . . . 136 A8
Ilminster TA19 . . . . 221 B4
Kilmersdon BA3 . . . . 98 B5
Kingsbury Episcopi TA12 . . . . 185 B8
Kingsdon TA11 . . . . 173 D5
Langport TA10 . . . . 172 A3
Midsomer Norton BA3 . . . . 97 A7
Milverton TA4 . . . . 167 A4
Nailsea BS48 . . . . 8 D2
Portishead BS20 . . . . 1 F1
Shepton Beauchamp TA19 . . . 184 E3
South Petherton TA13 . . . . 220 D5
Taunton TA1 . . . . 213 A3
Wells BA5 . . . . 203 E3
West Buckland TA21 . . . . 180 F7
Wincanton BA9 . . . . 216 C4
Wiveliscombe TA4 . . . . 210 C4
Wrington BS40 . . . . 35 E2
Yeovil BA20 . . . . 219 B5
Silverstone Way BS49 . . . . 34 D3
SILVER STREET 180 F8
Simbriss Rd BA3 . . . . 114 F5
Simmental St TA6 . . . . 209 A1
Simmons Cl BA16 . . . . 207 D5
SIMONSBATH 127 B2
SIMONSBURROW 180 C3
Simons Cl BS22 . . . . 32 A2
Simon's Cl BS39 . . . . 77 F5
Simons Mews
Chard TA20 . . . . 223 E4
3 Weston-super-Mare BS23 . . 48 F7
Simons Rd DT9 . . . . 225 D5
Sinclair Ho BS8 . . . . 226 A2
Singapore Rd BS23 . . . . 48 E3
Singer Ct BA11 . . . . 119 F5
Singer's Knoll BA11 . . . . 119 F4
SINGLE HILL 80 A5
Single Hill BA2 . . . . 79 F5
Singleton Ct BA5 . . . . 203 C5
SION HILL 27 E1
Sion Hill
Bath BA1 . . . . 27 E1
Bristol BS8 . . . . 11 F7
Sion Hill Pl BA1 . . . . 27 E1
Sion La BS8 . . . . 11 F7
Sion Pl
Bath BA2 . . . . 45 B6
Bristol BS8 . . . . 11 F7
Sion Rd BA1 . . . . 27 E1
Sir Bevil Grenville's Mon★
BA1 . . . . 12 A1
Sir Gilbert Scott Ct TA4 . . . 202 E3
Sirius Wood BA2 . . . . 44 B2
Siskin Wlk BS22 . . . . 49 F8
Sisters The BA4 . . . . 205 A6
Six Acres Cl TA1 . . . . 213 C5
Sixpence BS39 . . . . 59 D2
Six Streams BA1 . . . . 27 B2
Sixteen Acre La TA20 . . . . 193 D8
Sixth Ave BS14 . . . . 23 A7
Sixty Acres Cl BS8 . . . . 10 B4
Six Ways BS21 . . . . 6 C4
SKILGATE 164 E6
Skillgate La TA14 . . . . 185 E1
Skimmerton La TA5, TA6 . . 208 A5
Skinner's Hill BA2 . . . . 78 F7
Skinners La BS25 . . . . 52 F4
Skinner's La TA14 . . . . 185 F2
Skitmoor Dro BS28 . . . . 109 C2
Sky Coll TA2 . . . . 213 A6
Skylark Ave BS21 . . . . 1 B1
Skylark Dr BS31 . . . . 24 C3
Skylark Gr BS49 . . . . 16 F2
Slab Dro TA7 . . . . 155 A1
Sladacre La BS40 . . . . 54 E2
Sladebrook Ave BA2 . . . . 44 C3
Sladebrook Ct BA2 . . . . 44 C3
Sladebrook Rd BA2 . . . . 44 B4
Slade Cl TA4 . . . . 150 E8
Slade La
Barrow Gurney BS48 . . . . 20 C4
Golsoncott TA23 . . . . 131 E1
Hawkridge TA22 . . . . 146 D1
Lympsham BS24 . . . . 67 B1
Rimpton BA22 . . . . 188 A7
Rooks Bridge BS26 . . . . 87 E4
West Anstey EX36 . . . . 162 B6
Slade Rd BS20 . . . . 2 D5
Slade's Cross TA20 . . . . 193 D7
Slades Ct 2 BS48 . . . . 19 A6
Slades Dro TA7 . . . . 154 C1
Slades Hill BA8 . . . . 176 E1
Slades Orch TA19 . . . . 183 C1
Slade Way TA4 . . . . 202 E4
Slait Hill BA4 . . . . 142 C7
Slait La BA9 . . . . 216 C7
SLAPE CROSS 209 F6
Slapes Cl TA2 . . . . 168 F6
Slate La BS14, BS31 . . . . 41 B7
Sleep La BS14 . . . . 23 D3
Sleight Cl BA21 . . . . 218 C6
Sleight House La DT9 . . . . 175 F2
Sleight La BA5 . . . . 140 E8
Slingsby Gdns BS24 . . . . 49 C4
Slippery Batch TA11 . . . . 211 A6
Sloe Cl BS22 . . . . 49 D8
Slopers La BA9 . . . . 176 D5
SLOUGH GREEN 182 D7
Slough Green Cvn Pk
TA3 . . . . 182 D8
Slough Hill TA3 . . . . 182 D6
Slough La
Cold Ashton SN14 . . . . 12 F5
Crowcombe TA4 . . . . 151 A8
North Wootton BA4 . . . . 140 B3
Stoke St Gregory TA3 . . . . 170 F6
Upottery EX14 . . . . 191 F5
Sloway La TA6, TA9 . . . . 136 A8
Slow Court La BA22 . . . . 174 D3
Slowland La BA5 . . . . 110 D8
Slugg Hill BA16 . . . . 207 C3
Smallacombe Hill EX16,
EX36 . . . . 162 D4
Smallbrook La BS39 . . . . 41 B6
Smallcombe Cl BA3 . . . . 78 E5
Smallcombe Rd BA3 . . . . 78 E4
Small Down End BS25 . . . . 51 F2
Small Down La BA4 . . . . 142 B2
Small La EX16 . . . . 179 B2
Small Mead Dro BA6 . . . . 157 F4
Smallmoor Chase BA16 . . . 156 E7
Smallmoor Dro TA7 . . . . 155 C3
Small Moor La BA16 . . . . 156 E7
Smallridge Rd EX13 . . . . 198 A4
Smalls Mead 2 TA11 . . . . 173 F7
Small St BS1 . . . . 227 A3
Smallway BS49 . . . . 34 D5
SMALL WAY 214 B2
Small Way La BA22 . . . . 214 C1
Smallways La TA7 . . . . 137 B3
Smallwood View BA3 . . . . 96 E7
SMEATHARPE 191 E5
Smeathy La EX15 . . . . 180 F3
Smeaton Rd BS1 . . . . 11 F5
Sminhays Cnr TA23 . . . . 149 B5
SMITHAM HILL 74 D2
Smithams Hill BS40 . . . . 93 C8
Smitham's Hill BS40 . . . . 74 D2
Smithfield Rd BA16 . . . . 207 B4
Smithick's La BA11 . . . . 143 E6
Smithmead BS13 . . . . 22 B5
Smiths Cl BS27 . . . . 91 A1
Smith's Forge Ind Est BS49 16 F3
Smith's Hill TA18 . . . . 196 C8
Smiths La TA3 . . . . 170 F2
Smith's La BA4 . . . . 159 C6
Smith's Row TA15 . . . . 186 B4
Smith's Terr BA21 . . . . 219 C6
Smith Way TA9 . . . . 104 D3
Smithy TA1 . . . . 212 B3
Smithyard La TA4, TA23 . . 202 A3
Smithy La
Bridgehampton BA22 . . . . 174 D2
Frome BA11 . . . . 119 E4
Smokeham La TA4 . . . . 151 D5
Smoky Hole La TA18 . . . . 185 F1
Smurl La TA9 . . . . 104 C1
Smythe Croft BS14 . . . . 23 A3
Smythes Cross EX15 . . . . 191 C7
Snagg La BA4 . . . . 159 D5
Snag La BA9 . . . . 216 E3
Snake La BS28 . . . . 109 C1
Snakelake Hill BA10 . . . . 160 C7
Snap Hill TA11 . . . . 173 D8
Snatch BS40 . . . . 55 E2
Snatch La BS40 . . . . 55 E2
Snathe Lea 4 TA4 . . . . 167 F8
Snedden Gr TA1 . . . . 213 B5
SNEYD PK 5 D3
Snipefield La BS28 . . . . 108 A6
Snowberry Cl
Bridgwater TA6 . . . . 208 E2
Weston-super-Mare BS22 . . . 32 A1
Snowberry Ct TA1 . . . . 213 C2
Snowdon Cottage La
TA20 . . . . 223 B4
Snowdon Hill Loop Rd
TA20 . . . . 223 A4
Snowdon Hts TA20 . . . . 223 B4
Snowdon Vale BS23 . . . . 31 A1
Snowdrop Cl BS22 . . . . 32 A5
Snow Hill
Bath BA1 . . . . 28 A1
Bath BA2 . . . . 228 C4
Snow Hill Ho BA1 . . . . 228 C4
Society Rd BA4 . . . . 205 A6
SOCKETY 196 D1
Sock Hill BA21 . . . . 187 C6
Sock La BA21 . . . . 187 C6
Sockmead Dro BA22 . . . . 187 B6
Sock's La BA10 . . . . 160 F8
Sogg Dro TA7 . . . . 154 F6
SOHO 117 A5
Soho BA2 . . . . 81 E5
Soho Hill
Coleford BA3 . . . . 116 F6
Soho BA3 . . . . 117 A5
Solomon's Hollow TA3 . . . . 169 F2
Solomons La BA7 . . . . 214 D6
Solon Ct BS13 . . . . 21 F5
Solsbury Ct BA1 . . . . 28 F3
Solsbury View 17 BA1 . . . . 28 A1
Solsbury Way BA1 . . . . 28 A2
Somer Ave BA3 . . . . 77 F2
Somer Cl BA3 . . . . 96 F8
Somer Ct BA3 . . . . 78 B1
SOMERDALE 24 E7
Somerdale Ave
Bath BA2 . . . . 44 D2
Bristol BS4 . . . . 22 F8
Weston-super-Mare BS22 . . . 49 C8
Somerdale Cl BS22 . . . . 49 C8
Somerdale Rd BS31 . . . . 24 F7
Somerdale View BA2 . . . . 44 C2
Somer Ho BA3 . . . . 78 A1
Somerhouse Orch BA6 . . . 206 E5
Somer Lea BA3 . . . . 96 D5
Somerleaze Cl BA5 . . . . 203 B3
Somer Rd BA3 . . . . 77 F2
Somer Ridge BA3 . . . . 77 F3
Somerset Ave
Taunton TA1 . . . . 212 B2
Weston-super-Mare BS22,
BS24 . . . . 50 A8
Somerset Brick & Tile Mus★
TA6 . . . . 209 A6
Somerset Bridge Prim Sch
TA6 . . . . 209 A1
Somerset Cl
Martock TA12 . . . . 185 E7
Shepton Mallet BA4 . . . . 205 C5
Somerset Coll of Arts & Tech
TA1 . . . . 212 D4
Somerset Ct BA21 . . . . 219 A6
Somerset Cty Cricket Gd★
TA1 . . . . 212 F4
Somerset Distillery The★
TA12 . . . . 184 F7
Somerset & Dorset Joint Rly★
BA3 . . . . 97 A8
Somerset & Dorset Rlwy Trust
Mus★ TA23 . . . . 131 E4
Somerset Fire HQ TA2 . . . . 169 A7
Somerset Folly BA2 . . . . 60 B2
Somerset Gdns TA6 . . . . 209 C3
Somerset Ho
Bath BA2 . . . . 44 D3
12 Bristol BS2 . . . . 227 C3
Somerset La BA1 . . . . 27 E1
Somerset Levels National
Nature Reserve★ TA7 . . . . 155 C6
Somerset Mews BS23 . . . . 48 F6
Somerset Pl
Bath BA1 . . . . 27 E1
Taunton TA1 . . . . 213 B4
Yeovil BA20 . . . . 219 A3
Somerset Rd
Bridgwater TA6 . . . . 209 C3
Clevedon BS21 . . . . 6 E3
Frome BA11 . . . . 119 E4
Portishead BS20 . . . . 1 F5
Somerset Rural Life Mus★
BA6 . . . . 206 E4
Somerset Shire Horses★
TA7 . . . . 156 C6
Somerset Sq
Bristol BS1 . . . . 227 B1
3 Nailsea BS48 . . . . 8 E2
Somerset St
Bath BA1 . . . . 228 C1
Bristol BS1 . . . . 227 B1
Bristol, Kingsdown BS2 . . . 227 A4
Somerset Way
Highbridge TA9 . . . . 104 E3
Paulton BS39 . . . . 77 E6
Somer's Hill BA11 . . . . 117 D3
SOMERTON 211 D3
Somerton BS24 . . . . 49 A2
Somerton Bsns Pk TA11 . . . 211 B5
Somerton Cl TA6 . . . . 209 D4
Somerton Door Dro
Compton Dundon TA11 . . . . 156 E1
Somerton TA11 . . . . 211 A7
Somerton Dro TA11 . . . . 156 E1
Somertonfield Rd TA11 . . . 172 E7
Somerton Gdns BA11 . . . . 120 C7
Somerton Hill
Langport TA10 . . . . 172 E7
Somerton TA11 . . . . 211 A3
Somerton Inf Sch TA11 . . . 211 C4
SOMERTON RANDLE 173 C7
Somerton Rd
Clevedon BS21 . . . . 6 E1
Langport TA10 . . . . 172 A6
Street BA16 . . . . 207 D4
Somervale Rd BA3 . . . . 78 E2
Somervale Sch
Midsomer Norton BA3 . . . . 78 A1
3 Midsomer Norton BA3 . . . 78 A1
Somerville Cl
2 Longcroft BA21 . . . . 219 F8
Saltford BS31 . . . . 25 E2
Shepton Mallet BA4 . . . . 205 D4
Somerville Cotts BA5 . . . . 204 B8
Somerville Rd
Sandford BS25 . . . . 52 A4
Wells BA5 . . . . 203 C5
Somerville Way TA6 . . . . 209 D3
Sommerville Way BS30 . . . . 25 E8
Soper Gdns BS4 . . . . 22 D7
Sopers Field TA20 . . . . 223 D2
Sophia Gdns BS22 . . . . 32 B4
Sorrel Dr TA6 . . . . 208 E1
Sorrel Gdns BS20 . . . . 2 F5
Southampton Row 5
TA2 . . . . 213 A8
South Ave
Bath BA2 . . . . 44 D5
Highbridge TA9 . . . . 104 C4
Portishead BS20 . . . . 2 D6
Sherborne DT9 . . . . 225 B2
SOUTHAY 185 B6
Southay Cross TA20 . . . . 193 A4
Southay La TA20 . . . . 192 F4
South Bank
Castle Cary BA7 . . . . 214 B3
Wookey Hole BA5 . . . . 203 A8
SOUTH BARROW 175 A6
South Barrow Rd TA11 . . . 174 D7
Southbourne Gdns BA1 . . . 28 B1
Southbourne Ho TA6 . . . . 208 E4
Southbourne Mans BA2 . . 228 C2
South Brent Cl TA9 . . . . 85 F3
SOUTH BREWHAM 161 A6
South Bristol Bsns Pk BS4 . 22 E7
South Bristol Com Hospl
BS14 . . . . 22 F5
South Bristol Trad Pk BS3 . . 11 F3
Southbrook TA5 . . . . 135 C2
Southbrook Cl TA5 . . . . 135 C2
Southbrook Cotts BA9 . . . 216 F4
SOUTH CADBURY 175 C4
South Cary La BA7 . . . . 214 A5
SOUTH CHARD 198 C8
SOUTH CHERITON 176 D3
South Cl
Draycott BS27 . . . . 90 E2
Lympsham BS24 . . . . 86 B8
Walton BA16 . . . . 156 E7
South Combe BS24 . . . . 67 B6
Southcombe Way BA22 . . . 186 B6
SOUTH COMMON 198 A4
South Common La EX13 . . 198 A5
Southcot Pl BA2 . . . . 228 C1
South Croft BS25 . . . . 51 F2
Southcroft Dr BA13 . . . . 121 D4
South Ct DT9 . . . . 225 B3
South Dene BS9 . . . . 5 E6
SOUTHDOWN 44 B4
Southdown
Charlton Horethorne DT9 . . . 176 A1
Weston-super-Mare BS22 . . . 31 F4
SOUTH DOWN 191 F6
Southdown Ave BA2 . . . . 44 B3
Southdown Com Inf Sch
BA2 . . . . 44 B3
Southdown Cross EX16 . . . 179 B2
Southdown Jun Sch BA2 . . . 44 B3
Southdown Rd
Bath BA2 . . . . 44 B4
Bristol BS9 . . . . 5 F8
South Dro
Curry Rivel TA10 . . . . 171 B4
North Curry TA3 . . . . 170 D2
Southend Gdns TA9 . . . . 104 E5
Southend Rd BS23 . . . . 48 E4
Southernhay BS8 . . . . 226 B2
Southernhay Ave BS8 . . . . 226 B2
Southernhay Cres BS8 . . . 226 B2
Southern Lea Rd TA8 . . . . 104 C8
Southern Relief Rd BS27 . . . 90 C6
Southern Ring Path 4 BS21 6 B1
Southern Way BS21 . . . . 6 C1
South Espl TA8 . . . . 104 A5
Southey Farm La TA3 . . . . 184 A7
Southey Rd BS21 . . . . 6 D2
SOUTHFIELD 79 A2
Southfield
Cheddar BS27 . . . . 90 B8
Norton St Philip BA2 . . . . 81 F4
Radstock BA3 . . . . 79 A2
Southwick BA14 . . . . 83 F2
Wiveliscombe TA4 . . . . 210 C3
Southfield Cl
Nailsea BS48 . . . . 8 E3
Taunton TA2 . . . . 168 F6
Weston-super-Mare BS23 . . . 48 D2
Woolavington TA7 . . . . 136 E3
Southfield Dr BA21 . . . . 218 B8
Southfield Farm Cvn Pk &
Camp Site TA8 . . . . 65 F4
Southfield Farm Rd BA11 . 120 B3
Southfield Hill BA3 . . . . 99 A6
Southfield Rd
Nailsea BS48 . . . . 8 F3
Shepton Mallet BA4 . . . . 205 A5
Southfield Rd Trad Est BS48 . 8 F3
Southfields
Frome BA11 . . . . 120 A2
Ilminster TA19 . . . . 183 E2
South Fields BA6 . . . . 206 E3
Southfield Way BA11 . . . . 120 A3
Southgate
Bath BA1 . . . . 228 C2
Frome BA11 . . . . 120 D7
Wiveliscombe TA4 . . . . 210 C3
Southgate Ave TA6 . . . . 209 A3
Southgate Dr BA9 . . . . 216 C3
Southgate Rd BA9 . . . . 216 C3
Southgate Sh Ctr BA1 . . . . 228 C2
South Gr BS20 . . . . 4 C4
South Green St 8 BS8 . . . . 11 F6
South Harp TA13 . . . . 220 E1
South Hele Cross EX16 . . . 165 C1
SOUTH HILL 211 A1
South Hill BS25 . . . . 51 F2
South La
Challacombe EX31 . . . . 126 A3
Nether Stowey TA5 . . . . 134 B2
Southlands
Bath BA1 . . . . 27 B1
Carhampton TA24 . . . . 131 B5
Southlands Dr BA2 . . . . 60 B2
Southlands Way BS49 . . . . 34 E5
South Lawn BS24 . . . . 49 F4
South Lawn Cl BS24 . . . . 49 F4
South Lea Rd BA1 . . . . 44 A8
Southleaze BS25 . . . . 70 A6
Southleaze Orch BA16 . . . 207 C6
Southleaze Rd BA16 . . . . 207 B6
Southleigh BS25 . . . . 69 F8
Southleigh Rd
Bristol BS8 . . . . 226 B4
Taunton TA1 . . . . 213 B3
SOUTHMARSH 161 B1
South Mdw BA5 . . . . 113 A1
South Mdws BS40 . . . . 35 E2
Southmead
West Camel BA22 . . . . 174 D3
Winscombe BS25 . . . . 70 A8
Southmead Cres TA18 . . . 224 C5
Southmead La BA8 . . . . 190 A6
Southmead Rd BS22 . . . . 49 B7
Southmead Terr TA18 . . . . 224 C5
South Molton Rd EX16 . . . 164 B1
South Moors La TA7 . . . . 137 B2
Southover BA5 . . . . 203 D3
Southover Rd BS39 . . . . 59 D1
South Par
Bath BA2 . . . . 228 C2
Chew Magna BS40 . . . . 39 B3
Frome BA11 . . . . 119 E4
Weston-super-Mare BS23 . . . 48 D8
South Parade Cotts BA2 . . . 45 C1
SOUTH PERROTT 196 C1
SOUTH PETHERTON 220 C4
South Petherton Com Hospl
TA13 . . . . 220 D5
South Petherton Inf Sch
TA13 . . . . 220 C4
South Petherton Jun Sch
TA13 . . . . 220 D3
South Pk TA24 . . . . 200 D6
South Rd
Brean TA8 . . . . 65 F3
Lympsham BS24 . . . . 67 B1
Midsomer Norton BA3 . . . . 78 B1
Portishead BS20 . . . . 2 D7
Taunton TA1 . . . . 213 A2
Timsbury BA2 . . . . 60 B2
Watchet TA23 . . . . 202 C6
Weston-super-Mare BS23 . . . 30 C1
Southridge Hts BS24 . . . . 67 A8
South Road Villas BA9 . . . 216 C3
South Rock Ind Est BA3 . . . 96 D1
Southside BS23 . . . . 48 E8
South Side BS49 . . . . 34 E5
Southside Cl BS9 . . . . 5 B8
Southside Cres BS22 . . . . 31 A4
South St
Burnham-on-S TA8 . . . . 104 A6
Castle Cary BA7 . . . . 214 B4
Crewkerne TA18 . . . . 224 D5
Hinton St George TA17 . . . . 195 D7
Holcombe Rogus TA21 . . . . 178 F5
Kington Magna SP8 . . . . 177 E1
Milborne Port DT9 . . . . 217 D2
Montacute TA15 . . . . 186 B3
Sherborne DT9 . . . . 225 E3
South Petherton TA13 . . . . 220 D4
Stratton-on-t F BA3 . . . . 96 F2
Taunton TA1 . . . . 213 A3
Walton BA16 . . . . 156 E7
Wellington TA21 . . . . 222 E5
Wells BA5 . . . . 203 D4
West Camel BA22 . . . . 174 D3
Wincanton BA9 . . . . 216 C3
Wiveliscombe TA4 . . . . 210 C4
Yeovil BA20 . . . . 219 B4
SOUTHSTOKE 62 E7
Southstoke La BA2 . . . . 62 F8
Southstoke Rd BA2 . . . . 44 F1
South Terr
Burnham-on-S TA8 . . . . 104 B6
Weston-super-Mare BS23 . . . 48 D8
SOUTHTOWN 183 C3
Southtown La BA6 . . . . 158 B8
SOUTH TWERTON 44 C5
Southview TA3 . . . . 168 D1
South View
12 Barwick BA22 . . . . 197 F8
Bawdrip TA7 . . . . 136 E2
Bradford Abbas DT9 . . . . 187 E1
Broadway TA19 . . . . 183 C2
Clandown BA3 . . . . 78 E5
Ditcheat BA4 . . . . 159 C6
Horrington BA5 . . . . 113 A1
Lynford-on-F TA11 . . . . 158 C1
Monkton Combe BA2 . . . . 45 E1
Paulton BS39 . . . . 77 E6
Portishead BS20 . . . . 2 D7
Queen Camel BA22 . . . . 174 F3

South View *continued*
Timsbury BA2 . . . . 60 B2
Westleigh EX16 . . . . 179 A3
Southview Cl
Hutton BS24 . . . . 49 E2
Westonzoyland TA7 . . . . 154 F5
South View Pl BA3 . . . . 78 B2
Southview Rd TA7 . . . . 154 F5
South View Rd
Bath BA2 . . . . 44 D6
Milborne Port DT9 . . . . 217 C3
South View Terr
Taunton TA3 . . . . 168 D1
Yatton BS49 . . . . 17 B1
South Villas TA4 . . . . 167 F6
Southville BA21 . . . . 219 C5
Southville Rd BS23 . . . . 48 E4
Southville Terr BA2 . . . . 45 B4
SOUTHWAY 139 D5
Southway Cl BA21 . . . . 218 F6
Southway Cres BA21 . . . . 218 F6
Southway Ct BS21 . . . . 6 D1
Southway Dr BA21 . . . . 218 F6
Southwell TA3 . . . . 168 D1
Southwell Cl TA3 . . . . 168 D1
Southwell Cres TA9 . . . . 104 E3
Southwell Ct TA9 . . . . 104 E3
Southwell St BS2 . . . . 226 C4
South Western Bsns Pk
DT9 . . . . 225 D3
South Western Terr BA20 219 C4
SOUTHWICK
Trowbridge 83 F2
Watchfield 105 E2
Southwick CE Prim Sch
BA14 . . . . 83 F3
Southwick Ctry Pk* BA14 . . 83 F5
Southwick Rd TA9 . . . . 106 C1
SOUTH WIDCOMBE 75 C6
Southwood BA4 . . . . 159 D8
Southwood Ave BS9 . . . . 5 C8
Southwood Dr BS9 . . . . 5 B8
Southwood Dr E BS9 . . . . 5 C8
Southwood Gr TA1 . . . . 212 C2
Southwoods BA20 . . . . 219 A3
Southwood Way TA3 . . . . 181 C5
Sovereign Rd TA6 . . . . 209 D7
Sovereign Sh Ctr BS23 . . . . 48 D8
Sowden Hill TA5 . . . . 134 D4
Spanish Hill TA6 . . . . 153 F2
Spargrove La BA4 . . . . 142 B1
SPARKFORD 175 A5
Sparkford Hill BA22 . . . . 174 F4
Sparkford Hill La BA22 . . . 175 A4
Sparkhayes La TA24 . . . . 124 A3
Sparks Way TA9 . . . . 104 D3
Sparrow Hill Way BS26 . . . . 88 E6
Sparrow La
Portbury Wharf BS20 . . . . 3 A6
Withypool TA24 . . . . 146 C7
Sparrow Rd BA21 . . . . 219 B6
Spartley Dr BS13 . . . . 21 F6
Spartley Wlk BS13 . . . . 21 F6
SPAXTON 152 E8
Spaxton Cl TA8 . . . . 104 C8
Spaxton Rd TA5 . . . . 153 C7
Spaxton VC Prim Sch TA5 . 152 E7
Spearcey Cl TA3 . . . . 181 D8
Spearcey La TA3 . . . . 181 D8
Spearhay La TA20 . . . . 198 F5
Spear Mead DT8 . . . . 199 F7
Spears La TA4 . . . . 166 A4
Specket La DT8 . . . . 199 E5
SPECKINGTON 174 C2
Speckington La BA22 . . . . 174 B2
Specklemead BS39 . . . . 77 D5
Speedwell Ind Est 1 BS21 . . 6 C2
Speke Cl
Ilminster TA19 . . . . 221 B4
Merriott TA16 . . . . 195 F7
Staplegrove TA2 . . . . 212 B6
Speke Ct TA19 . . . . 221 B4
Spencer Ave TA2 . . . . 212 E6
Spencer Cl TA6 . . . . 209 D3
Spencer Dr
Midsomer Norton BA3 . . . . 78 A2
Weston-super-Mare BS22 . . . 32 B3
Spencer Ho 6 BS1 . . . . 227 B1
Spencer Rd BA4 . . . . 205 C3
Spencers Belle Vue BA1 . . 228 B4
Sperring Ct BA3 . . . . 96 F8
Sperry Cross TA4 . . . . 149 B1
Spicer Way TA20 . . . . 223 D2
SPIKE ISLAND 226 B1
Spike Island* BS3 . . . . 226 B1
Spillers Cl TA6 . . . . 208 E2
Spindleberry Gr BS48 . . . . 9 A2
Spiningmill Cotts 3 BA11 119 E5
Spinners End BS22 . . . . 32 B4
Spinners Ho 5 BA4 . . . . 205 B6
Spinney Croft BS13 . . . . 21 F5
Spinneyfield TA4 . . . . 167 F7
Spinney Rd BS24 . . . . 50 D4
Spinney The
Ashcott TA7 . . . . 156 A8
Portishead BS20 . . . . 2 C4
Taunton TA1 . . . . 212 D2
Weston-super-Mare BS24 . . . 48 F1
Yeovil BA20 . . . . 218 D2
Spinnings Dro BS48 . . . . 19 D2
Spire Cross TA24 . . . . 147 A4
SPLATT 152 E8
Splatt La TA5 . . . . 152 E8
Splott BS26 . . . . 88 F6
Splott La BA3 . . . . 95 B6
Spoonbill Rd TA6 . . . . 209 B4
Spratts Bridge BS40 . . . . 39 A3
Sprays Hill TA20 . . . . 194 D5
Sprigg Dr BS20 . . . . 1 F1
Springbok Cl BA16 . . . . 207 D7
Spring Cres BA2 . . . . 228 C2
Springer's Hill BA3 . . . . 116 E6
Springfield
Ilminster TA19 . . . . 221 B2
Norton St Philip BA3 . . . . 81 E4
Peasedown St John BA2 . . . . 79 C7
Street BA16 . . . . 207 B5
Springfield Ave
Bridgwater TA6 . . . . 208 C3
Bristol, Shirehampton BS11 . . . 4 D6
Weston-super-Mare BS22 . . . 31 D1
Springfield Bldgs
Midsomer Norton BS39 . . . . 77 D2
Radstock BA3 . . . . 79 A3
Springfield Cl
Bath BA2 . . . . 44 B5
Cheddar BS27 . . . . 90 A8
Cross BS26 . . . . 69 F2
Springfield Cotts
Upton Cheyney BS30 . . . . 26 A8
Winsford TA24 . . . . 147 A6
Springfield Cres BA3 . . . . 79 A3
Spring Field Cres DT9 . . . . 225 C3
Springfield Ct BA4 . . . . 205 A5
Springfield Dr BS28 . . . . 108 C3
Springfield Flats TA20 . . . . 223 C4
Springfield Gdns BS29 . . . . 51 A3
Springfield Ho
Bristol BS6 . . . . 226 C4
Portishead BS20 . . . . 2 C4
Springfield Hts BA3 . . . . 78 E4
Springfield Lawn BS11 . . . . 4 D6
Springfield Pl
Bath BA1 . . . . 27 F1
Clandown BA3 . . . . 78 E4
Yeovil BA21 . . . . 218 E7
Springfield Rd
Cheddar BS27 . . . . 90 A8
3 Highbridge TA9 . . . . 104 E4
Highbridge TA9 . . . . 104 E4
Milborne Port DT9 . . . . 217 D3
Pill BS20 . . . . 4 C4
Portishead BS20 . . . . 2 B5
Wellington TA21 . . . . 222 C7
Wincanton BA9 . . . . 216 B4
Yeovil BA21 . . . . 218 E7
Springfields
East Chinnock BA22 . . . . 196 E8
Stalbridge DT10 . . . . 190 C4
Springfield Terr
Street BA16 . . . . 207 B5
Tatworth TA20 . . . . 198 D8
SPRING GARDENS 119 D8
Spring Gardens Rd BA2 . . . 228 C2
Spring Gdns
Minehead TA24 . . . . 201 B5
Wiveliscombe TA4 . . . . 210 C5
Spring Ground Rd BS39 . . . . 77 E5
Spring Hill
Bristol BS2 . . . . 227 A4
Weston-super-Mare BS22 . . . 31 D2
Springhill Cl BS39 . . . . 77 C6
Spring Hill Dr BS22 . . . . 31 E1
Spring La
Bath BA1 . . . . 28 B2
Dundry BS41 . . . . 22 A1
Sandford Orcas DT9 . . . . 188 C7
Springley Rd TA6 . . . . 209 D6
Springmead TA20 . . . . 223 B3
Springmead Sch BA11 . . . . 101 E4
Spring Rd BA11 . . . . 119 F6
Spring Rise
Portishead BS20 . . . . 2 C3
Puriton TA7 . . . . 136 C4
Wells BA5 . . . . 203 C3
Spring Terr
Frome BA11 . . . . 119 D2
Weston-super-Mare BS22 . . . 31 C2
Spring Vale BA1 . . . . 28 B2
Spring Valley BS22 . . . . 31 C2
Springway Ind Est TA7 . . . . 155 A5
Spring Wood Gdns BS24 . . . 49 E3
Spruce Way
Bath BA2 . . . . 62 E8
Weston-super-Mare BS22 . . . 49 E8
Spurwells TA19 . . . . 183 F4
Squares Rd TA5 . . . . 135 F2
Square The
Axbridge BS26 . . . . 70 C2
Banwell BS29 . . . . 51 B3
Bath BA2 . . . . 228 B1
Edington TA7 . . . . 137 C2
Maiden Bradley BA12 . . . . 144 C2
Shipham BS25 . . . . 70 E7
Taunton TA1 . . . . 213 C2
Temple Cloud BS39 . . . . 58 E1
Wellow BA2 . . . . 62 D1
Westbury-sub-Mendip BA5 . 110 E6
Winscombe BS25 . . . . 69 E6
Wiveliscombe TA4 . . . . 210 C4
Woolavington TA7 . . . . 136 E4
Squibbers Wy TA6 . . . . 209 B2
Squibbs Cl TA6 . . . . 209 D5
Squibbs Ho TA6 . . . . 208 F5
Squire La BS40 . . . . 55 C1
Squirrel Ct TA21 . . . . 222 D5
Stabbins Cl BS22 . . . . 32 B5
Stables The BA3 . . . . 98 B5
Stable Yd BA2 . . . . 44 D6
Stacey's Ct TA10 . . . . 171 F5
Staddlestones BA3 . . . . 96 F7
Staddonhill Rd TA24 . . . . 146 F8
Stafford Pl BS23 . . . . 48 E8
Stafford Rd
Bridgwater TA6 . . . . 209 C3
Portishead BS20 . . . . 2 E4
Sherborne DT9 . . . . 225 C4
Weston-super-Mare BS23 . . . 48 F7
STAFFORD'S GREEN 188 D8
Stagman La TA7, BA16 . . . . 156 C8
Stag Mill Cross EX16 . . . . 178 B3
Stag Way BA6 . . . . 206 C4
Stainer Cl BS4 . . . . 22 D7
Staker's Cross TA20 . . . . 195 B2
Staker's Cross La TA18,
TA20 . . . . 195 B2
STALBRIDGE 190 C4
Stalbridge Cl DT10 . . . . 190 B4
Stalbridge La
Marnhull DT10 . . . . 190 F2
Sturminster Newton DT10 . . 190 F1
Stalbridge Pk DT10 . . . . 190 A4
Stalbridge Prim Sch DT10 190 B5
Stalbridge Rd
Henstridge BA8 . . . . 190 A6
Stalbridge Weston DT10 . . . 190 A3
Stourton Caundle DT10 . . . . 189 F2
STALBRIDGE WESTON 190 A3
Stalcombe La BA2 . . . . 42 B4
Staling Way BA4 . . . . 205 C4
Stallards TA21 . . . . 222 C3
STALLEN 188 A3
Stallgrove La BA16 . . . . 207 D3
Stall St BA1 . . . . 228 C2
Stalls The BA12 . . . . 144 D7
Stambrook Pk BA1 . . . . 29 A5
Stammery Hill EX13 . . . . 198 C1
Stanchester Acad TA14 . . . 186 A4
Stanchester Way TA10 . . . 171 D4
Stancombe La
Flax Bourton BS48 . . . . 19 E7
Westbury-sub-Mendip BA5 . 110 F8
Standards Rd TA7 . . . . 154 E5
Standards The TA7 . . . . 137 D2
STANDERWICK 102 C2
Standerwick BA13 . . . . 102 E3
Standerwick Cross BA11 . . 102 B2
Standerwick Orch TA19 . . . 183 C2
Standfast Pl TA2 . . . . 213 C8
Standhill Rd TA10 . . . . 155 F2
Standing Cross BA2 . . . . 61 D7
Standish Ct TA1 . . . . 212 F4
Standish St TA6 . . . . 208 F7
Stane Way BS11 . . . . 4 C7
Stanford Pl BS4 . . . . 22 D7
Stanhope Pl BA1 . . . . 228 A2
Stanhope Rd BS23 . . . . 48 E3
Stanier Cl BA11 . . . . 120 D6
Stanier Rd BA2 . . . . 228 A2
Stankley View TA19 . . . . 184 F4
Stanley Cl
Bridgwater TA6 . . . . 208 F2
Staplegrove TA2 . . . . 212 C6
Stanley Ct BA3 . . . . 78 B2
Stanley Gr BS23 . . . . 48 F7
Stanley Rd 2 BS23 . . . . 48 F7
Stanley Rd W BA2 . . . . 44 D5
Stanley Terr BA3 . . . . 79 A3
Stanley Villas 12 BA1 . . . . 28 A1
Stanmoor Rd TA7 . . . . 170 F8
Stansell Rd TA1 . . . . 213 A1
Stanshalls Cl BS40 . . . . 37 C8
Stanshalls Dr BS40 . . . . 37 C8
Stanshalls La BS40 . . . . 37 C8
STANTON DREW 39 F2
Stanton Drew Prim Sch
BS39 . . . . 40 A2
Stanton Drew Stone Circles*
BS39 . . . . 40 A3
Stanton La BS39 . . . . 40 D4
STANTON PRIOR 42 E2
Stanton Rd BS40 . . . . 39 B3
STANTON WICK 58 D8
Stanton Wick La BS39 . . . . 40 B1
Stant Way TA20 . . . . 193 C6
Stanway Cl
Bath BA2 . . . . 44 D1
Taunton TA2 . . . . 212 D7
Staple Cl TA4 . . . . 132 E4
Staplecombe Vineyard*
TA2 . . . . 168 C6
STAPLE FITZPAINE 182 C5
Staplegate EX16 . . . . 178 A3
Staple Gr BS31 . . . . 24 D5
STAPLEGROVE 212 C8
Staplegrove CE Prim Sch
TA2 . . . . 212 C7
Staplegrove Manor TA2 . . 212 D8
Staplegrove Rd
Staplegrove TA2 . . . . 212 C7
Taunton TA1, TA2 . . . . 212 E5
STAPLEHAY 181 D8
Staple Hill TA3 . . . . 182 C5
Staple La TA4 . . . . 132 E4
STAPLE LAWNS 182 B5
Staples Cl BS21 . . . . 6 E1
Staples Gn BS22 . . . . 32 B3
Staples Hill BA3 . . . . 64 C4
Staples Mdw TA20 . . . . 198 D8
STAPLETON 185 E8
Stapleton Cl TA12 . . . . 185 E7
Stapleton Cross TA12 . . . . 185 E7
Stapleton Rd TA12 . . . . 185 E7
STAPLEY 191 D8
Stapley Cross TA3 . . . . 181 B1
Stapling La TA24 . . . . 130 F3
STAR 52 D1
Starcross Rd BS22 . . . . 32 A2
Star La BS20 . . . . 4 D4
Starling Cl BS22 . . . . 49 E8
Starrs Cl BS26 . . . . 70 B2
Stars La BA20 . . . . 219 C4
Statham Cl
Cheddar BS27 . . . . 90 B7
Taunton TA1 . . . . 212 C2
Statham Gr TA1 . . . . 212 C2
STATHE 171 B8
Stathe Cotts TA7 . . . . 171 B7
Stathe Rd TA7 . . . . 171 A8
Station App
Bristol BS1 . . . . 227 C1
Frome BA11 . . . . 120 A4
Ilminster TA19 . . . . 183 E1
Pensford BS39 . . . . 40 D5
Weston-super-Mare BS23 . . . 48 E7
Station Cl
Backwell BS48 . . . . 18 F7
Congresbury BS49 . . . . 34 C4
Station Lodge 8 BS23 . . . . 48 E7
Station Mead BA3 . . . . 96 D3
Station Path TA11 . . . . 211 D3
Station Rd
Ashcott TA7 . . . . 156 B8
Axbridge BS26 . . . . 70 C2
Backwell BS48 . . . . 19 A6
Bampton EX16 . . . . 164 B1
Bath BA1 . . . . 28 F2
Bath BA1 . . . . 44 C7
Binegar BA3 . . . . 114 D7
Bishops Lydeard TA4 . . . . 167 E8
Blagdon BS40 . . . . 54 E3
Bristol, Shirehampton BS11 . . . 4 D5
Bristol, Shirehampton BS11 . . . 4 E5
Bruton BA10 . . . . 215 F6
Burlescombe EX16 . . . . 179 B3
Burnham-on-S TA9 . . . . 85 F3
Burtle TA7 . . . . 137 D6
Castle Cary BA7 . . . . 214 B6
Chard Junction TA20 . . . . 198 D8
Cheddar BS27 . . . . 90 B7
Clevedon BS21 . . . . 6 D3
Clutton BS39 . . . . 58 E3
Congresbury BS49 . . . . 34 C4
Cossington TA7 . . . . 136 F3
Draycott BS27 . . . . 90 E2
Dunster TA24 . . . . 201 E4
Flax Bourton BS48 . . . . 20 A8
Freshford BA3 . . . . 64 C5
Hatch Beauchamp TA3 . . . . 183 A7
Ilminster TA19 . . . . 221 A4
Keynsham BS31 . . . . 24 E6
Meare TA7 . . . . 138 C1
Midsomer Norton BA3 . . . . 78 B2
Milborne Port DT9 . . . . 217 D4
Milverton TA4 . . . . 167 A5
Misterton TA18 . . . . 224 E4
Nailsea BS48 . . . . 8 F2
Norton Fitzwarren TA2 . . . . 168 B4
Pill BS20 . . . . 4 C4
Portbury BS20 . . . . 3 D3
Portishead BS20 . . . . 2 D6
Sandford BS25 . . . . 51 F4
Shapwick TA7 . . . . 137 F2
Shepton Mallet BA4 . . . . 205 B5
Sherborne DT9 . . . . 225 E3
Stalbridge DT10 . . . . 190 B4
Stogumber TA4 . . . . 150 D8
Taunton TA1 . . . . 212 F5
Templecombe BA8 . . . . 176 E1
Walpole TA6 . . . . 136 B3
Wanstrow BA4 . . . . 142 F4
Washford TA23 . . . . 131 E4
Wellington TA21 . . . . 222 C7
Wellow BA2 . . . . 62 D1
Westbury-sub-Mendip BA5 . 110 E5
Weston-super-Mare BS23 . . . 48 E7
Weston-super-Mare, St Georges
BS22 . . . . 32 D2
Weston-super-Mare, Worle
BS22 . . . . 31 F2
Williton TA4 . . . . 202 E3
Wincanton BA9 . . . . 216 C3
Wiveliscombe TA4 . . . . 210 C4
Wrington BS40 . . . . 35 D2
Yatton BS49 . . . . 17 B1
Station Rd (Blackmoor La)
BA8 . . . . 190 A7
Station Rd Ind Est BA10 . . . 215 F6
Station Road Bsns Pk
DT10 . . . . 190 B5
Station Terr TA24 . . . . 201 A7
Station Vw BA3 . . . . 96 F8
Station Way BA4 . . . . 141 E1
Station Wlk TA9 . . . . 104 E3
Staundle La TA3 . . . . 183 B8
Staunton Fields BS14 . . . . 23 C4
Staunton La
Minehead TA24 . . . . 201 A4
Whitchurch BS14 . . . . 23 D3
Staunton Rd TA24 . . . . 201 A5
Staunton Rise TA24 . . . . 201 A5
Staunton Way BS14 . . . . 23 D4
Stavordale Gr BS14 . . . . 23 B6
STAWELL 137 A1
Stawell Rd TA7 . . . . 137 B1
STAWLEY 166 A1
Stawley Cty Prim Sch
TA21 . . . . 179 B8
Steamalong TA3 . . . . 183 E7
Steam Mills BA3 . . . . 96 F8
Steam Packet Terr 2
TA6 . . . . 209 B4
STEANBOW 140 D2
Steanbow Cotts BA4 . . . . 140 D3
STEART
Babcary 174 C6
Combwich 135 D8
Steart Ave TA8 . . . . 104 B6
Steart Cl TA8 . . . . 104 B6
Steart Cotts TA3 . . . . 169 C3
Steart Ct TA8 . . . . 104 A7
Steart Dr TA8 . . . . 104 A6
Steart Dro TA10 . . . . 156 D1
Steart Gdns TA8 . . . . 104 B6
Steart Hill BA22 . . . . 174 D5
Steart La TA24 . . . . 129 F3
Steart Rd
Babcary TA11 . . . . 174 B6
Fenning Island TA5 . . . . 103 B1
Stedhams Cl TA21 . . . . 222 D7
Steeds Terr BA3 . . . . 115 D6
Steel La TA7 . . . . 137 D2
Steel Mills BS31 . . . . 24 F4
Steel's La BA9 . . . . 161 D2
Steel Well La BA8 . . . . 190 A6
Steep La TA22 . . . . 164 C8
Steeple View BA3 . . . . 116 A3
Steep The TA24 . . . . 147 C5
Steers Cl TA6 . . . . 209 B6
Steevens Ho (Almshouses) 13
BS2 . . . . 227 C3
STEMBRIDGE 185 A7
Stembridge Rd TA10 . . . . 156 B1
Stembridge Tower Mill*
TA10 . . . . 156 B1
Stembridge Way TA2 . . . . 168 B4
Stennard Gn BA2 . . . . 45 B2
Stent Hill TA24 . . . . 123 B4
Stephen's Hill TA10 . . . . 172 E4
Stephenson Dr BA11 . . . . 120 D6
Stephenson Rd TA24 . . . . 201 B6
Stephen St TA1 . . . . 213 A4
Stephen Way 6 TA1 . . . . 213 A4
Steppes Cres 13 TA12 . . . . 185 E6
Steppes Mdw TA12 . . . . 185 E6
Steps La BA2 . . . . 100 E7
Stert Dro TA5 . . . . 135 B7
Steven's Cl BA4 . . . . 205 A5
Stevens La
Frome BA11 . . . . 119 F3
Lympsham BS24 . . . . 67 C3
Stewart Ct EX13 . . . . 198 A2
Steway La BA1 . . . . 29 B6
STEWLEY 183 B5
Stibbear La TA19 . . . . 194 A8
Stiby Ct BA21 . . . . 218 F7
Stiby Rd BA21 . . . . 218 E7
Stickland BS21 . . . . 6 C1
Stickleball La BA4, BA6 . . . 140 D1
Stickle Hill TA4 . . . . 151 B7
Sticklepark La BA9 . . . . 176 A8
STICKLEPATH
Combe St Nicholas 193 D7
Monksilver 149 E7
Stickle Path EX16 . . . . 165 C1
STICKLINCH 140 C1
Sticklinch Rd BA6 . . . . 140 C2
Stidham La BS31 . . . . 25 B6
Stilemead La BS40 . . . . 55 D1
Stiles Ct BA5 . . . . 203 B4
STILEWAY 138 E3
Stileway BA6 . . . . 138 E4
Stileway Bsns Pk BS21 . . . . 16 B8
Stiling Cl TA9 . . . . 104 D4
Stillingfleet Rd BS13 . . . . 22 C5
Stillington Cl BA5 . . . . 203 B3
Stillman Cl BS13 . . . . 21 E4
Stirling Way
Frome BA11 . . . . 120 C6
Keynsham BS31 . . . . 24 E4
Stirtingale Ave BA2 . . . . 44 C3
Stirtingale Rd BA2 . . . . 44 C3
Stitching La BS28 . . . . 138 C8
Stitchings La BA2 . . . . 61 D7
Stitchings Shord La BS39 . . 57 C4
Stoate Cl TA23 . . . . 202 C5
Stoberry Ave BA5 . . . . 203 E5
Stoberry Cres BA5 . . . . 203 E5
Stoberry Park Sch BA5 . . . 203 E5
STOCK 53 B8
Stockbridge TA17 . . . . 195 D7
Stockbridge La BA6 . . . . 140 B2
Stockditch Rd TA12 . . . . 185 B7
Stockers Cl TA4 . . . . 210 B4
Stockham Cross TA4 . . . . 151 D5
Stockham Hill TA22 . . . . 163 E8
Stock Hill BA3 . . . . 115 B8
Stockhill Cl BA3 . . . . 96 C3
Stock Hill Ct BA3 . . . . 117 B7
Stockhill Rd BA3 . . . . 96 C2
Stock La
Buckhorn Weston SP8 . . . . 177 F5
Lower Langford BS40 . . . . 53 A7
STOCKLAND BRISTOL 135 A6
Stockland Bristol Rd TA5 . 135 A6
Stockland Hill EX14 . . . . 192 A1
Stockland Manor TA5 . . . . 134 F6
Stockland Rd EX14 . . . . 193 A2
STOCKLINCH 184 B4
Stocklinch La TA19 . . . . 184 B4
STOCKLINCH OTTERSEY . . . 184 C4
Stocklinch Rd
Ilminster TA19 . . . . 221 F7
Stocklinch TA19 . . . . 184 B3
STOCKLINCH ST
MAGDALEN 184 C4
Stockman La TA20 . . . . 198 C7
Stockmead BS40 . . . . 53 B5
Stockmoor Cl TA6 . . . . 209 A2
Stockmoor Dr
10 Bridgwater TA6 . . . . 154 A5
Bridgwater TA6 . . . . 209 A1
Stock Moor Dro TA6 . . . . 209 A1
Stock's La
Hatch Beauchamp TA3,
TA19 . . . . 183 B6
Leigh u M BA3 . . . . 116 E3

Stock's La *continued*
North Wootton BA4 . . . . 140 C4
Stockstyle La EX13 . . . . 198 A8
Stockton Cl BS14 . . . . 22 F4
Stock Way N BS48 . . . . 8 F2
Stock Way S BS48 . . . . 8 E2
Stockwell Rd TA1 . . . . 168 F4
Stockwitch Cross BA22 . . . 174 B3
STOCKWOOD 23 F5
Stockwood Bsns Pk BA4 . . 141 C2
Stockwood Hill BS31 . . . . . . 24 C7
Stockwood La BS14 . . . . 23 E5
STOCKWOOD VALE 24 C6
Stockwood Vale BS31 . . . . . 24 C6
Stodden's La TA8 . . . . 104 E8
Stodden's Rd TA8 . . . . 85 C1
Stodden's Wlk TA8 . . . . 104 B8
Stodelegh Cl BS22 . . . . 32 B3
STOFORD 197 F8
Stoford La
Broadway TA19 . . . . 183 C2
West Buckland TA21 . . . . . . 181 A7
Stoford Pl TA19 . . . . 183 C2
STOGUMBER 150 D8
Stogumber CE Prim Sch
TA4 . . . . 150 D8
Stogumber Rd
Kingswood TA4 . . . . 150 F8
Lawford TA4 . . . . 151 A8
Stogumber Sta★ TA4 . . . . . 150 E8
STOGURSEY 134 C5
Stogursey CE Prim Sch
TA5 . . . . 134 B5
Stogursey La TA5 . . . . 134 A3
STOKE BISHOP 5 E5
Stoke Bishop CE Prim Sch
BS9 . . . . 5 D5
Stoke Cotts BS9 . . . . 5 E4
Stoke Cres BA3 . . . . 116 A2
Stoke Cross 10 TA14 . . . . . . 185 F4
Stoke Gr BS9 . . . . 5 E6
Stoke Hamlet BS9 . . . . 5 F6
Stoke Hill
Bristol BS9 . . . . 5 E3
Chew Stoke BS40 . . . . 56 D7
Stoke St Mary TA3 . . . . 169 D1
Stoke St Michael BA3 . . . . . . 116 A2
Stoney Stoke BA9 . . . . 160 E3
Stoke La
Bristol, Westbury on T BS9 . . . . 5 F6
Stoke St Mary TA3 . . . . 169 A1
Wincanton BA9 . . . . 216 F5
Yarlington BA9 . . . . 175 E7
Stokeleigh Wlk BS9 . . . . 5 C5
Stoke Mead BA2 . . . . 63 F7
Stoke Moor Dro BS27 . . . . . 109 D6
Stoke Paddock Rd BS9 . . . . . 5 D6
Stoke Park Rd BS9 . . . . 5 F4
Stoke Park Rd S BS9 . . . . 5 E3
STOKE PERO 128 F6
Stoke Rd
Bristol BS9 . . . . 5 F3
Martock TA12 . . . . 185 E5
North Curry TA3 . . . . 170 C4
Portishead BS20 . . . . 2 D5
Ruishton TA3 . . . . 169 C2
Stoke St Mary TA3 . . . . 169 B1
Street BA16 . . . . 207 E6
Taunton TA1 . . . . 213 B1
Westbury-sub-Mendip BA5 . 110 D6
STOKE ST GREGORY 170 E6
Stoke St Gregory CE Prim Sch
Stoke St Gregory TA3 . . . . . . 170 E6
Stoke St Gregory TA3 . . . . . . 170 E6
STOKE ST MARY 169 C1
STOKE ST MICHAEL 116 B2
Stoke St Michael Prim Sch
BA3 . . . . 116 A3
Stokes Croft BS1 . . . . 227 B4
Stokes La DT10 . . . . 189 F2
Stoke St BS27 . . . . 110 B8
STOKE SUB HAMDON 185 F5
Stoke sub Hamdon Castle Prim Sch TA14 . . . . 185 F4
Stoke sub Hamdon Priory★
TA14 . . . . 185 F4
STOKE TRISTER 177 B7
Stoke Trister Rd BA9 . . . . . 177 C7
STOLFORD 134 F8
Stonage La TA18 . . . . 196 C5
Stoneable Rd BA3 . . . . 79 A3
Stoneage La BA2 . . . . 61 B1
STONE ALLERTON 88 C3
Stone Allerton Dro BS26 . . . 88 B2
STON EASTON 95 E8
Ston Easton La BA3 . . . . 95 D8
Stonebarrow La EX13 . . . . . 198 F2
Stoneberry Rd BS14 . . . . 23 B3
STONEBRIDGE
Banwell 51 A4
Frome 120 A7
Stonebridge BS21 . . . . 6 D1
Stonebridge Dr BA11 . . . . . 120 B7
Stonebridge Rd BS23 . . . . . . 48 F4
Stonechat Green BS20 . . . . . . 3 A6
Stone Cl TA1 . . . . 168 D1
Stone Cross TA24 . . . . 128 E1
Stonedene DT9 . . . . 225 D6
Stone Down La BA6 . . . . . . 139 D1
STONE-EDGE BATCH 8 D4
Stone End Cottage La
TA9 . . . . 136 C8
Stonegallows TA1 . . . . 212 A3
Stonehenge La BS48 . . . . 8 E4
Stonehill
South Cadbury BA22 . . . . . . 175 C3
Stoke Sub Hamdon TA14 . . . 186 A4
Street BA16 . . . . 207 B5
STONE HILL 207 A4
Stone Hill Ct TA24 . . . . 200 F7
Stone Hill La TA4 . . . . 166 D3
Stonehouse Cl BA2 . . . . 45 B2
Stonehouse La BA2 . . . . 45 B2
Stone La
Durnfield BA22 . . . . 186 B8
East Pennard BA4 . . . . 158 E6
Exford TA24 . . . . 128 E1
Winsford TA24 . . . . 147 E6
Yeovil BA21 . . . . 187 B5
Stoneleigh
Chew Magna BS40 . . . . 39 B3
Wellington TA21 . . . . 222 B8
Stoneleigh Cl
Burnham-on-S TA8 . . . . 104 C8
Staplegrove TA2 . . . . 212 C8
Stoneleigh Ct
Bath BA1 . . . . 27 E3
Taunton TA1 . . . . 212 C1
Stoneleigh Mews BA21 . . . 218 C7
Stoneleigh Rise BA11 . . . . . 120 A6
Stone Mead La TA10 . . . . . . 173 A4
Stone Rd TA8 . . . . 104 D5
Stoneridge La TA4 . . . . 165 D5
Stones Cross BA3 . . . . 78 B2
Stonesfield TA18 . . . . 196 B5
Stones Paddock BA3 . . . . . 116 C7
Stonewall Terr BA11 . . . . . 119 F2
Stonewell Dr BS49 . . . . 34 D3
Stonewell Gr BS49 . . . . 34 D3
Stonewell La BS49 . . . . 34 D3
Stonewell Park Rd BS49 . . . 34 D3
Stoneyard La BA3 . . . . 75 D2
Stoney Cl TA24 . . . . 129 F6
Stoneyfield Cl BS20 . . . . 4 B5
Stoneyfields BS20 . . . . 4 B4
Stoney Furlong TA2 . . . . . . 213 B8
Stoney Head Cvn Pk TA3 . . 169 F1
Stoneyhurst Dr TA10 . . . . . 171 C3
Stoney La
Bishops Lydeard TA4 . . . . . . 167 E8
Curry Rivel TA10 . . . . 171 C3
East Coker BA22 . . . . 197 D6
Stocklinch TA19 . . . . 184 C4
Stoney Lane Cross EX16 . . 178 B3
Stoney Littleton Long
Barrow★ BA2 . . . . 80 C7
Stoney St TA24 . . . . 129 C7
Stoney Steep
Portishead BS20 . . . . 2 C6
Wraxall BS48 . . . . 9 A5
Stoney Stile Way
Wells BA5 . . . . 111 F2
Wells BA5 . . . . 203 B6
STONEY STOKE 160 F3
Stoney Stoke Rd BA9 . . . . . 160 B2
STONEY STRATTON 141 F2
STONY HEAD 169 F1
Stonyhead Hill TA3 . . . . 169 F1
STONY KNAPS 199 D7
Stony La
Axminster EX13 . . . . 198 A1
Hawkridge TA22 . . . . 146 E3
Whatley BA11 . . . . 118 A2
STONY LITTLETON 80 B6
Stony St BA11 . . . . 119 F5
STOODHAM 220 D6
Stoodham TA13 . . . . 220 D5
Stoodly La
North Wootton BA4 . . . . 140 D4
Pilton BA4 . . . . 204 A2
Stooper's Hill TA20 . . . . 193 C6
STOPGATE 192 C4
Stopgate Cross EX14 . . . . . . 192 C4
Stoppard Rd TA8 . . . . 104 C6
Stopper's La BA5 . . . . 139 F6
Stormont Cl BS23 . . . . 48 F3
Stormore BA13 . . . . 121 F8
Storridge La
Axminster EX13 . . . . 198 B6
Brompton Regis TA22 . . . . . 148 A1
Storridge View TA22 . . . . . 148 A2
Stothert Ave
Bath BA2 . . . . 228 A2
East Twerton BA2 . . . . 44 D6
STOUGHTON CROSS 108 B8
Stoughton Rd BS28 . . . . 107 E5
Stourhead Gardens★
BA12 . . . . 161 F5
Stourhead House★ BA12 . . 161 F5
Stour Hill SP8 . . . . 177 E1
Stour Hill Pk SP8 . . . . 177 F1
STOURTON 161 F5
STOURTON CAUNDLE 189 F2
Stourton Cl BA11 . . . . 119 E3
Stourton Gdns 1 BA11 . . . . 119 E3
Stourton La BA12 . . . . 161 F6
Stourton View BA11 . . . . . . 119 E3
Stourton Way BA21 . . . . 218 D6
STOUT 156 B2
Stout Cross EX14 . . . . 192 C5
Stout's Way La
Luxborough TA23 . . . . 148 F8
Rodhuish TA24 . . . . 131 A1
Stowborough Cotts BA2 . . . 79 C7
STOWELL 176 C1
Stowell Hill DT9 . . . . 176 C1
Stowell La TA20 . . . . 198 D8
Stowell Rd
Barrow Hill DT9 . . . . 217 D8
Milborne Wick DT9 . . . . 189 B8
Stowers Row 31 TA12 . . . . 185 E6
STOWEY 57 F4
Stowey Bottom BS39 . . . . . . 57 E5
Stowey Cross Rds BS39 . . . . 57 F5
Stowey La
Curry Mallet TA3 . . . . 183 E8
Stowey La *continued*
Fivehead TA3 . . . . 170 E1
Stowey Pk BS49 . . . . 34 D7
Stowey Rd
Pitney TA10 . . . . 172 D7
Taunton TA2 . . . . 212 E8
Yatton BS49 . . . . 34 C8
Stow Ho BS11 . . . . 4 E5
Stradling Ave BS23 . . . . 48 F5
Stradling Cl TA7 . . . . 137 B2
Stradlings Hill TA5 . . . . 135 B2
Stradling's Hill TA5 . . . . . . 135 B3
Stradlings Yd BS2 . . . . 226 C4
Straight Dro
Burrowbridge TA7 . . . . 155 B1
Bussex TA7 . . . . 154 F6
Chilton Trinity TA5 . . . . 135 F2
West Huntspill TA9 . . . . 136 B7
Woolavington TA9 . . . . 137 A6
Straight La BA11 . . . . 101 D7
Straightmead BA3 . . . . 75 F1
Strap La
Ston Easton BA3 . . . . 95 F7
Upton Noble BA4, BA10 . . . . 143 A1
Stratford Cl BS14 . . . . 22 F3
Stratford Ct BS9 . . . . 5 F8
Stratford La BS40 . . . . 56 E1
Stratford Rd BA21 . . . . 218 D5
Stratheden BS8 . . . . 226 A4
Stratton Cl TA6 . . . . 209 D3
Stratton La BS22 . . . . 31 A4
STRATTON-ON-THE FOSSE 96 F1
Stratton Rd
Holcombe BA3 . . . . 116 B8
Saltford BS31 . . . . 25 E3
Strawberry Bank TA19 . . . . 221 C4
Strawberry Cl BS48 . . . . 8 D1
Strawberry Field BS26 . . . . . 70 D2
Strawberry Gdns BS48 . . . . . 18 D8
Strawberry Hill
Clevedon BS21 . . . . 6 F4
Street BA16 . . . . 207 B7
Strawberry La BS13, BS41 . . 21 E3
Strawberry Line BS49 . . . . . 52 A8
Strawberry Way BA5 . . . . . 203 C4
Strawberry Way Rdbt
BA5 . . . . 203 D3
Streaked La TA3 . . . . 170 C6
STREAM 132 A2
Streamcombe La TA22 . . . . 163 B5
Streamcross BS49 . . . . 17 D1
Streamleaze BS40 . . . . 39 B3
Stream Rd TA4 . . . . 132 A2
Streamside
Chew Magna BS40 . . . . 39 B3
1 Clevedon BS21 . . . . 6 F3
Taunton TA1 . . . . 213 C2
STREET
Chard 194 C2
Glastonbury 207 C7
STREET ASH 193 C8
Street Dro
Street BA16 . . . . 207 E7
Street, Marshall's Elm BA16 207 B1
Walton BA16 . . . . 156 F5
STREET END 54 D3
Street End BS40 . . . . 54 D2
Street End La BS40 . . . . 54 D2
Street Hill BA16 . . . . 207 B2
Street Ho TA19 . . . . 221 B3
Street La
Odcombe BA22 . . . . 186 C2
South Brewham BA10 . . . . . 161 A7
STREET ON THE FOSSE 141 C2
Street Rd
Compton Dundon TA11 . . . . 157 A4
Glastonbury BA6 . . . . 206 D3
Street BA6 . . . . 207 D8
Street Rdbt BA16 . . . . 207 D7
Street Shoe Mus★ BA16 . . 207 C6
Street The
Bishop Sutton BS39 . . . . 57 D4
Chew Stoke BS40 . . . . 56 D8
Chilcompton BA3 . . . . 96 D5
Compton Martin BS40 . . . . . . 74 B7
Draycott BS27 . . . . 90 F2
Farmborough BA2 . . . . 59 F6
Kilmington BA12 . . . . 161 F6
Radstock BA3 . . . . 78 F2
Stowey BS39 . . . . 57 F4
Ubley BS40 . . . . 55 D1
Wanstrow BA4 . . . . 142 F4
West Monkton TA2 . . . . 169 C7
Winford BS40 . . . . 37 F1
Stretcholt La TA6 . . . . 135 F6
Stretford La TA19 . . . . 194 F7
Stringfellow Cres TA20 . . . 223 D5
Stringfellow Mews TA20 . . 223 C3
STRINGSTON 133 F5
STRODE 55 E7
Strode Coll BA16 . . . . 207 D6
Strode Ho 7 BA4 . . . . 205 B6
Strode Rd
Clevedon BS21 . . . . 6 C2
Street BA16 . . . . 207 D6
Strode Way
Clevedon BS21 . . . . 6 B1
Shepton Mallet BA4 . . . . 205 A5
Stroud Rd BS11 . . . . 4 E5
Stroud Way BS24 . . . . 49 E7
Strowland La BS24 . . . . 86 F6
Strowlands BS24, TA9 . . . . . 86 E6
Struthers Cl BA16 . . . . 207 B7
Strutter's Hill BA10 . . . . . . 215 D2
Stuart Ho BS23 . . . . 30 D1
Stuart Pl BA2 . . . . 44 D6
Stuart Rd BS23 . . . . 49 A5
Stuarts Cl BA5 . . . . 203 D3
Stubb's La BA11 . . . . 101 D4
Stubby La TA2 . . . . 213 C8
STUDLEY GREEN 83 F6
Studley La BA4 . . . . 142 F4
Studley Mdws BA4 . . . . 142 F4
Stump Cross
Pitcombe BA7 . . . . 215 A1
Shepton Mallet BA4 . . . . 204 D5
STURFORD 144 F7
Sturford La BA12 . . . . 144 E7
Sturmey Way BS20 . . . . 4 E3
Sturminster Cl BS14 . . . . 23 D6
Sturminster Lodge BS14 . . . 23 D5
Sturminster Rd BS14 . . . . . . 23 D7
Sturt La TA3 . . . . 183 E7
Stutts End TA4 . . . . 167 E6
Style Flats TA4 . . . . 210 C5
Style Rd TA4 . . . . 210 C5
Styles Ave BA11 . . . . 120 C4
Styles Cl BA11 . . . . 120 B4
Styles Hill BA11 . . . . 120 B4
Styles Mdw BA11 . . . . 120 C5
Styles Pk BA11 . . . . 120 B4
Sub Rd BA6 . . . . 157 D4
Suffolk Cl TA6 . . . . 209 C3
Suffolk Cres TA1 . . . . 212 C1
Suffolk Ct TA1 . . . . 212 C1
Suffolk Ho BA1 . . . . 44 C8
Sugg's La TA19 . . . . 183 C2
Sulis Manor Rd BA2 . . . . 62 D8
Sullivan Cl BS4 . . . . 22 D6
Sully Cl TA6 . . . . 209 D6
Sumerleaze Cres TA2 . . . . . 213 C8
Sumerlin Dr BS21 . . . . 6 F3
Summer Ct BS8 . . . . 226 B3
Summerfield BS22 . . . . 32 A3
Summerfield Ave TA21 . . . . 180 D8
Summerfield Cl TA7 . . . . . . 154 F5
Summerfield Ct TA1 . . . . . . 212 E4
Summerfield Rd BA1 . . . . 28 A1
Summerfields BA8 . . . . 190 A7
Summerfields Rd TA20 . . . 223 C3
Summerfield Terr BA1 . . . . . 28 A1
Summerfield Way TA21 . . . 180 D8
Summer Ground Dr BS13 . . 22 A5
Summerhedge Cres TA7 . . 155 C1
Summerhedge Rd TA7 . . . . 155 C1
Summer Hill
Frome BA11 . . . . 119 F3
Hinton St George TA17 . . . . . 195 D7
Summerhill La
Burford BA4 . . . . 140 F5
West Shepton BA4 . . . . 204 D4
Summerhill Rd BA1 . . . . 27 D1
Summerhouse BS21 . . . . 8 D4
Summer House Terr BA20 219 B4
Summerhouse View BA21 219 C6
Summer La
Banwell BS29 . . . . 50 E5
Chard TA20 . . . . 194 C4
Hinton St George TA13,
TA17 . . . . 195 C8
Monkton Combe BA2 . . . . . . 63 D8
Weston-super-Mare BS22,
BS24 . . . . 32 B1
Weston-super-Mare BS29 . . . 50 B8
Weston-super-Mare BS29 . . . 50 D7
Summer La N BS22 . . . . 32 A2
Summerland Ave TA24 . . . 201 A7
Summerland Pl TA24 . . . . . 200 F7
Summerland Rd TA24 . . . . 200 F7
SUMMERLANDS 218 F6
Summerlands
Backwell BS48 . . . . 19 B5
Yeovil BA21 . . . . 218 E6
Summerlands Hospl BA21 218 F6
Summerlands Park Ave
TA19 . . . . 221 B4
Summerlands Park Cl
TA19 . . . . 221 B4
Summerlands Park Dr
TA19 . . . . 221 B4
Summerlands Rd BS23 . . . . 49 B8
Summer Lane Cvn Pk BS29. 50 E3
Summer Lane Park Homes
BS29 . . . . 50 E4
Summerlays Ct BA2 . . . . 45 B6
Summerlays Pl BA2 . . . . 45 B6
Summerlea BA2 . . . . 61 A5
Summerleaze BS31 . . . . 24 E7
Summer Leaze BS39 . . . . 57 D4
Summerleaze Cres TA2 . . . 213 C7
Summerleaze Pk BA20 . . . 218 F5
Summer Shard TA13 . . . . . 220 C4
Summers Hill La BA4 . . . . . 204 C2
Summerville Terr TA8 . . . . 104 B6
Summerway TA24 . . . . 129 E1
Summerway Dro TA7 . . . . . 209 E4
Summerwell La BA16 . . . . . 156 D7
Summerwood Rd BA16 . . . 207 B4
Sun Batch BS27 . . . . 91 A3
Sunderland Pl BS8 . . . . 226 B3
Sunderland St 2 BA2 . . . . 228 C3
Sundew Cl TA1 . . . . 213 C1
Sunfield Rd BS24 . . . . 49 E3
Sunningdale BS8 . . . . 226 B4
Sunningdale Cl BS48 . . . . 9 A1
Sunningdale Rd
Weston-super-Mare BS22 . . . 31 F3
Yeovil BA21 . . . . 219 C6
Sunnybank BA2 . . . . 45 B4
Sunny Bank TA4 . . . . 150 B8
Sunnybank Ct BS24 . . . . 32 B1
Sunnybank Rd TA6 . . . . 208 E2
Sunnybank Way BS24 . . . . . 32 B1
Sunnybrow Cl 10 TA6 . . . . . 153 F4
Sunny Cl TA9 . . . . 136 B8
Sunny Hill
Bristol BS9 . . . . 5 C7
Pitcombe BA10 . . . . 215 C4
Sunnyhill Dr BS11 . . . . 4 E6
Sunnyhill Ho E BS11 . . . . 4 E6
Sunnyhill Ho W BS11 . . . . 4 E6
Sunny La BA10 . . . . 215 C4
Sunnymead
Bridgwater TA6 . . . . 208 E2
Keynsham BS31 . . . . 24 F3
Midsomer Norton BA3 . . . . . . 77 F2
Oakhill BA3 . . . . 114 F3
Stratton-on-t F BA3 . . . . 96 F2
Sunnymeade BA6 . . . . 138 C4
Sunnymead La BS39 . . . . 57 D3
Sunnymede Rd BS48 . . . . 8 D3
Sunnyside
Barrington TA19 . . . . 184 C5
Bristol BS9 . . . . 5 E5
Burlescombe EX16 . . . . 179 C2
Clatworthy TA4 . . . . 149 F1
Clutton BS39 . . . . 59 B4
Farrington Gurney BS39 . . . . 77 B3
Frome BA11 . . . . 119 F3
Sunnyside Cotts TA24 . . . . 129 A8
Sunnyside Cres BS21 . . . . 6 D3
Sunnyside Farm Trad Est
BS20 . . . . 4 C2
Sunnyside Gdns BA2 . . . . . . 60 B2
Sunnyside Pl BA11 . . . . 119 F3
Sunnyside Rd
Clevedon BS21 . . . . 6 D3
Weston-super-Mare BS23 . . . 48 E5
Sunnyside Rd N BS23 . . . . . . 48 E6
Sunnyside Terr 6 DT9 . . . . 225 E4
Sunnyside View BA2 . . . . . . 79 C7
Sunnyvale
Camerton BA2 . . . . 78 E8
Clevedon BS21 . . . . 6 B1
Sunridge Cl BA3 . . . . 96 F8
Sunridge Pk BA3 . . . . 96 F8
Sunset Cl BA2 . . . . 79 C7
Sun St BA11 . . . . 119 E5
Suprema Ave TA7 . . . . 137 C2
Suprema Est TA7 . . . . 137 D2
Surrey St BS2 . . . . 227 B4
Susanna's Cross BA3 . . . . . 116 B2
Susanna's La BA3 . . . . 116 C2
Sussex Ave TA6 . . . . 209 B3
Sussex Cl TA6 . . . . 209 B3
Sussex Lodge TA1 . . . . 212 F5
Sussex Pl BA2 . . . . 228 C1
Sutherland Ave TA8 . . . . . . 104 B6
Sutherland Cl TA1 . . . . 212 C1
Sutherland Ct TA1 . . . . 212 C1
Sutherland Dr BS24 . . . . 49 D2
SUTTON 159 B4
SUTTON BINGHAM 197 D6
Sutton Cl
Frome BA11 . . . . 120 B7
Weston-super-Mare BS22 . . . 49 E8
Sutton Cross TA10 . . . . 172 F4
Sutton Grange BA21 . . . . . . 218 C6
Sutton Hill
East Coker BA22 . . . . 197 D6
Long Sutton TA10 . . . . 172 E3
Sutton Hill Rd BS39 . . . . 57 D4
Sutton La
Redhill BS40 . . . . 36 F1
Walton BA16 . . . . 156 D6
SUTTON MALLET 155 B7
SUTTON MONTIS 175 C3
Sutton Montis Rd
Sparkford BA22 . . . . 175 B4
Sutton Montis BA22 . . . . 175 C3
Sutton Pk BS39 . . . . 57 D4
Sutton Rd TA11 . . . . 211 C2
Sutton St BA2 . . . . 45 B7
Sutton View TA10 . . . . 172 E2
SUTTON WICK 57 B2
Swains TA21 . . . . 222 D4
Swains La TA21 . . . . 222 D4
Swain St TA23 . . . . 202 C7
Swainswick BS14 . . . . 22 F6
Swainswick CE Prim Sch
BA1 . . . . 28 B5
Swainswick Gdns BA1 . . . . . 28 C2
Swainswick La BA1 . . . . 28 D4
Swallow Cl BA3 . . . . 97 B8
Swallowcliffe Ct 5 BA20 . 219 A5
Swallowcliffe Gdns BA20 . 219 A5
Swallow Ct BS14 . . . . 23 F6
Swallow Ct EX16 . . . . 178 F1
Swallow Dr BA11 . . . . 120 B6
Swallow Gdns BS22 . . . . 49 E8
Swallow Hill TA10 . . . . 172 A6
Swallow St BA1 . . . . 228 C2
Swallows The BS22 . . . . 49 D7
Swan Cl BS22 . . . . 49 E8
Swancombe
Blagdon BS40 . . . . 54 E2
Clapton in G BS20 . . . . 8 E8
Swan Down TA20 . . . . 194 E4
Swane Rd BS14 . . . . 23 F6
Swan Hill TA18 . . . . 196 C5
Swan Ho 3 BA4 . . . . 205 B6
Swanmead Com Sch
TA19 . . . . 221 C3
Swan Prec TA19 . . . . 221 C3
Swanshard La BA5 . . . . 139 D6
Swans La BS27 . . . . 90 F2
Swan Yd DT9 . . . . 225 D4
Swedish Hos TA13 . . . . 220 D1
Sweetgrass Rd BS24 . . . . 50 A8
Sweethay Cl TA3 . . . . 181 D8

Sweethay Cross TA3 . . . 181 C8
Sweethay La TA3 . . . 181 C8
Sweeting Cl 12 TA3 . . . 169 C5
Sweetleaze BA3 . . . 116 A2
Sweetleaze La BA3 . . . 115 C8
SWELL . . . 171 A2
Swell Cl TA9 . . . 136 B8
Swell Dro
North Curry TA3 . . . 170 F3
Swell TA3 . . . 171 A1
Swell La TA3 . . . 171 A2
Swiddacombe La EX36 . . . 162 C7
Swift Cl BS22 . . . 31 F1
Swift Lodge BA20 . . . 219 A4
Swifts TA21 . . . 166 F1
Swillbridge Cvn Pk TA23 . . 202 F6
SWINEFORD . . . 26 A7
Swingbridge TA2 . . . 213 E7
Swiss Ct 13 BS23 . . . 48 E7
Swiss Dr BS3 . . . 11 F2
Swiss Rd
Bristol BS3 . . . 11 F1
Weston-super-Mare BS23 . . . 48 F7
Sycamore Cl
Bridgwater TA6 . . . 209 D5
Burnham-on-S TA8 . . . 104 A5
Nailsea BS48 . . . 8 E2
Shipham BS25 . . . 70 E8
Taunton TA1 . . . 213 C2
Weston-super-Mare BS23 . . . 49 A8
Weston-super-Mare, Locking BS24 . . . 49 E5
Westonzoyland TA7 . . . 154 E5
Sycamore Ct TA20 . . . 223 C5
Sycamore Dr
Crewkerne TA18 . . . 224 D7
Frome BA11 . . . 120 B7
Langport TA10 . . . 172 A6
Yeovil BA20 . . . 218 F2
Sycamore Rd
Minehead TA24 . . . 200 D7
Radstock BA3 . . . 79 B2
Sycamores BS23 . . . 30 E1
Sycamore Sq TA20 . . . 223 C5
Sycamore Wlk TA3 . . . 169 D4
SYDENHAM . . . 209 C5
Sydenham Bldgs BA2 . . . 228 A2
Sydenham Cl
Bridgwater TA6 . . . 209 C6
Porlock TA24 . . . 124 B4
Sydenham Rd
Bath BA2 . . . 228 A2
Bridgwater TA6 . . . 209 C6
Sydenham Terr BA2 . . . 45 C1
Sydling Rd BA21 . . . 219 D6
Sydnalls La BA12 . . . 144 E8
Sydney Bldgs BA2 . . . 45 B6
Sydney Ho BA2 . . . 45 B7
Sydney Mews BA2 . . . 45 B7
Sydney Pl BA2 . . . 45 B7
Sydney Rd BA2 . . . 45 B7
Sydney Row BS1 . . . 226 B1
Sydney Wharf BA2 . . . 45 B7
Sylvan Rd TA21 . . . 222 E5
Sylvan Way
Bristol BS9 . . . 5 B7
Monkton Heathfield TA2 . . . 213 E8
Symes Ave BS13 . . . 22 C4
Symes Cl
Chard TA20 . . . 223 C4
North Perrott TA18 . . . 196 C4
Symes Pk BA1 . . . 27 A2
Symons Way
Bridgwater TA6 . . . 209 A6
Cheddar BS27 . . . 90 C7
Syndercombe La TA4, TA23 . . . 149 D2
SYNDERFORD . . . 199 C6

T

Tabbitts Steep TA24 . . . 129 B2
Tabernacle La 4 BA20 . . . 219 B4
TACKER STREET . . . 149 C8
Taddywood La BA4 . . . 159 F6
TADHILL . . . 116 F2
Tadhill La BA3 . . . 116 D2
TADWICK . . . 12 E1
Tadwick La BA1 . . . 28 A6
Tail Mill TA16 . . . 195 F7
Tailor's Ct 7 BS1 . . . 227 A3
Talbot Cl TA9 . . . 104 D3
Tallis Gr BS4 . . . 22 D6
Tallowood BA4 . . . 205 D5
Tamar Ave TA1 . . . 213 B1
Tamar Dr BS31 . . . 25 A4
Tamar Rd BS22 . . . 32 A2
Tamblyn Cl BA3 . . . 79 A3
Tamsin Ct BS31 . . . 24 F5
Tamworth Rd BS31 . . . 24 E4
Tancred St TA1 . . . 213 A4
TANGIER . . . 212 E4
Tangier TA1 . . . 212 E4
Tankard's Cl BS8 . . . 226 C3
Tankey's Cl BA11 . . . 120 A7
Tan La SP8 . . . 161 F1
Tanner Cl BA3 . . . 97 C8
Tanner Rd BS29 . . . 50 C7
Tanner's Hill TA4 . . . 165 E7
Tanners La SN14 . . . 13 F8
Tanners Wlk
Bath BA2 . . . 43 F5
Marshfield SN14 . . . 13 F8
Tannery Cl BA16 . . . 207 C5
Tannery Ct TA18 . . . 224 C7
Tanorth Cl BS14 . . . 23 A3
Tanorth Rd BS14 . . . 22 F3
Tansee Hill TA20 . . . 199 B6
Tansey BA4 . . . 142 A6
Tansey Ct TA6 . . . 208 E1
Tansy La BS20 . . . 2 F5
Tanyard
Broadway TA19 . . . 183 C2
Nether Stowey TA5 . . . 134 B2
Tanyard Cotts TA24 . . . 131 A5
Tanyard La
Langport TA10 . . . 172 A5
North Wootton BA4 . . . 140 C4
North Wootton, Lower Westholme BA4 . . . 140 D3
Tan Yard La TA13 . . . 184 F5
Tanyards BA10 . . . 215 F7
Tanyard The BA16 . . . 207 C5
Tape La BA3 . . . 114 F7
Taphouse La DT6 . . . 199 E1
Tapmoor Rd TA7 . . . 155 C8
Tappers La 2 TA6 . . . 153 E3
Tapps La TA7 . . . 136 E4
Tapstone Rd TA20 . . . 223 D4
Taranto Hill BA22 . . . 173 E2
Taranto Way BA22 . . . 174 A2
Target La TA12 . . . 185 D4
TARNOCK . . . 87 D6
Tarnock Ave BS14 . . . 23 A7
Tarnwell BS39 . . . 40 A2
Tarragon Pl BS20 . . . 2 F5
Tarrant La BA20 . . . 218 F1
Tarratt La
East Coker BA22 . . . 197 E8
Yeovil BA20, BA22 . . . 219 A1
Tarratt Rd BA20 . . . 218 F1
Tarr La
Cushuish TA2 . . . 152 D1
Kingston St Mary TA2 . . . 168 D8
Tarr Post TA22 . . . 146 C1
Tarr Steps* TA22 . . . 146 E3
Tarr Steps National Nature Reserve* TA22 . . . 146 E3
Tarr Water Cotts TA23 . . . 148 E8
Tatham Ct TA1 . . . 212 D4
TATWORTH . . . 198 C8
Tatworth Prim Sch TA20 . . 198 C8
Tatworth Rd TA20 . . . 223 C2
Tatworth St TA20 . . . 198 C8
Tauntfield Cl TA1 . . . 213 A3
TAUNTON . . . 212 D5
Taunton Acad The TA2 . . . 168 E6
Taunton Nuffield Health Hospl TA2 . . . 212 B7
Taunton Rd
Ashcott TA7 . . . 156 B7
Bishops Lydeard TA4 . . . 167 F7
Bridgwater TA6 . . . 209 A3
North Petherton TA6 . . . 153 F4
Thurloxton TA6 . . . 153 E2
Wellington TA21 . . . 222 E7
Weston-super-Mare BS22 . . . 32 B4
Wiveliscombe TA4 . . . 210 D4
Taunton Sch TA2 . . . 212 D6
Taunton Sta TA1 . . . 212 F5
Taunton Third Way TA1 . . . 212 F4
Taunton Trad Est TA2 . . . 212 A7
Taunton Vale Pk TA2 . . . 213 F8
Taunusstein Way 12 BA20 219 B4
Taveners Wlk BS48 . . . 8 F3
Taverner Cl BS4 . . . 22 D7
Taverners Cl 6 BS23 . . . 48 F4
TAVERN SCOTT . . . 38 D1
Tavistock Rd BS22 . . . 32 A2
Tawny Way BS22 . . . 49 F8
Taylor Cl TA2 . . . 168 B5
Taylor Ct
Bridgwater TA6 . . . 209 A5
Weston-super-Mare BS22 . . . 32 B4
Taylor Gdns BS13 . . . 21 F4
Taylor Ho TA19 . . . 221 B3
Taylors Fields BS29 . . . 51 B3
Taylor's Meade TA20 . . . 193 D6
Taylor's Orch TA14 . . . 185 E1
Tayman Ridge BS30 . . . 25 D8
Teagle Cl BA5 . . . 203 F5
Teak Cl TA6 . . . 209 D6
Teal Cl
Bridgwater TA6 . . . 209 A4
Weston-super-Mare BS22 . . . 31 F1
Tealham Moor Dro BS28 . . 137 E8
Teal Rd TA24 . . . 201 C5
Teals Acre 8 TA5 . . . 135 B2
Teal Way BS20 . . . 2 F6
Teapot Lane (Worms Lane) BA6 . . . 158 B6
Teasel Wlk BS22 . . . 49 D7
Technical St TA8 . . . 104 B6
Teck Hill TA6 . . . 153 E2
Teckhill La TA6 . . . 153 E2
Teddington Cl BA2 . . . 44 C4
Teesdale Cl BS22 . . . 49 D8
Teeside BA14 . . . 83 F4
Teeswater Way 9 TA6 . . . 154 A5
Teign Ct BA16 . . . 156 D7
Teignmouth Rd BS21 . . . 6 E3
Telephone Ave BS1 . . . 227 A2
Telford Ho
Bath BA2 . . . 44 D3
Leigh Woods BS8 . . . 11 E7
Tellis Cross BA22 . . . 197 D8
TELLISFORD . . . 82 E4
Tellisford La BA2 . . . 81 F4
Tellisford Rd BA2 . . . 82 E7
Tellis La BA3 . . . 114 D8
Temblett Gn TA6 . . . 208 C5
Templars Barton BA8 . . . 176 E1
Templars Ct
Long Sutton TA10 . . . 172 E1
1 Weston-super-Mare BS22 . . . 49 D7
Templars Pl BA8 . . . 176 E1
Templars Way BS25 . . . 70 E7
TEMPLE . . . 144 E7
Temple Back BS1 . . . 227 B2
Temple Back East BS1 . . . 227 C2
Temple Bridge Bsns Pk BS39 . . . 76 F7
Temple Circus Giratory BS1 . . . 227 C1
TEMPLE CLOUD . . . 58 E1
TEMPLECOMBE . . . 176 E1
Templecombe La SP8 . . . 177 C3
Templecombe Sta BA8 . . . 176 E1
Temple Ct BS31 . . . 24 E5
Temple Field TA23 . . . 202 C6
Temple Gate BS1 . . . 227 B1
Temple Inn La BS39 . . . 58 E1
Temple La BA8 . . . 176 F1
Templeland Rd BS13 . . . 21 F5
Temple of Harmony* TA5 . . . 153 B5
Temple Rose St BS1 . . . 227 B2
Temple St
Bristol BS1 . . . 227 B2
Keynsham BS31 . . . 24 F5
Temple Way BS2 . . . 227 B2
Temple Way Underpass BS2 . . . 227 C3
Ten Acre Dro TA7 . . . 170 E8
Ten Acre La BA2 . . . 61 F6
Tenby Rd BS31 . . . 24 D4
Ten Foot Rhyne BA6 . . . 140 A2
Tengore La TA10 . . . 172 C6
Tennis Corner Dro BA11 . . 102 D2
Tennis Court Ave BS39 . . . 77 D5
Tennis Court Rd BS39 . . . 77 D5
Tennyson Ave BS21 . . . 6 B2
Tennyson Cl BS31 . . . 24 F6
Tennyson Rd
Bath BA1 . . . 44 D7
Weston-super-Mare BS23 . . . 49 A3
Tenterk Cl BS24 . . . 67 B6
Tents Hill BA11 . . . 118 B6
TERHILL . . . 151 F3
Terhill La TA4 . . . 151 F3
Termare Cl BA22 . . . 218 B6
Terrace The
Minehead TA24 . . . 201 A5
Shipham BS25 . . . 70 E7
Terrace View DT9 . . . 225 E5
Terrace Wlk BA1 . . . 228 C2
Terrell La TA5 . . . 134 D2
Terrell St BS2 . . . 227 A4
Terry Hill BA3 . . . 98 D8
Terry Ho BS1 . . . 226 C3
Tetbury Gdns BS48 . . . 9 A1
Tetton Cl TA6 . . . 208 B4
Teviot Rd BS31 . . . 25 A4
Tewkesbury BA21 . . . 218 D6
Tewther Rd BS13 . . . 22 D3
Teyfant Com Sch BS13 . . . 22 E4
Teyfant Rd BS13 . . . 22 E4
Teyfant Wlk BS13 . . . 22 E4
Thackeray Ave BS21 . . . 6 E4
Thackeray Ho BS23 . . . 49 A5
Thackeray Rd BS21 . . . 6 E4
Thames Dr TA1 . . . 213 D4
Thatcham Cl 2 BA21 . . . 218 F7
Thatcham Ct 1 BA21 . . . 218 F7
Thatcham Pk BA21 . . . 218 F7
Thatch Cotts TA20 . . . 194 E1
Thatcher Cl BS20 . . . 2 D4
Thatch The TA11 . . . 211 C4
The Acorns BA11 . . . 119 D4
Theaks Mews TA1 . . . 213 A3
THEALE . . . 109 C1
Theatre Royal BS1 . . . 227 A2
The Barton BS25 . . . 69 B5
The Cliffs BS27 . . . 71 E1
The Close House Rd BS28 108 C4
The Court House La BS26 . . 87 D6
The Cypress House Rd BA22 . . . 187 D8
The Drumway BS31 . . . 25 B4
The Great Rd TA4 . . . 132 F4
Theillay Cl TA5 . . . 134 A3
The Lower La BA2 . . . 62 C4
The Mead BS31 . . . 24 D3
The Mendip Sch BA4 . . . 141 D3
The Old School Pl DT9 . . . 225 D3
The Pynes BS31 . . . 25 B4
There-and-Back-Again La BS1 . . . 226 C3
The Sidings BS23 . . . 49 B4
The Uplands TA9 . . . 106 E4
Theynes Croft BS41 . . . 11 B1
THICKET MEAD . . . 77 F3
Thicket Mead BA3 . . . 78 A2
Thickthorn Cross TA19 . . . 183 C3
Thickthorn La
Chilcompton BA3 . . . 96 A4
Southtown TA19 . . . 183 B3
Thimble La DT9 . . . 217 D2
Third Ave
Bath BA2 . . . 44 D5
Bristol BS14 . . . 23 B7
Radstock BA3 . . . 97 D7
Thirlmere Rd BS23 . . . 49 A4
Thistledoo Vine TA7 . . . 136 F2
Thistle Pk TA6 . . . 209 B1
Thomas Bunn Cl BA11 . . . 120 A7
Thomas Cl BS29 . . . 51 A3
Thomas Ct BS1 . . . 227 B2
Thomas La BS1 . . . 227 B2
Thomas Lane Appartments BS1 . . . 227 B2
Thomas Pl TA21 . . . 222 D7
Thomas St
Bath BA1 . . . 228 C4
Bristol BS2 . . . 227 B4
Taunton TA2 . . . 212 F6
Thomas Way BA6 . . . 206 B4
Thomas Way Ind Est BA6 . . 206 B4
Thompson Cl TA6 . . . 209 D6
Thompson Rd
Bristol BS14 . . . 23 E6
Wells BA5 . . . 203 D3
Thompson Way BS24 . . . 50 C8
Thomson Dr TA18 . . . 224 D5
Thong La TA10 . . . 184 D6
Thornash Cl TA2 . . . 213 F8
Thornbank Ct DT9 . . . 225 E4
Thornbank Pl BA2 . . . 228 A1
Thornbury Dr BS23 . . . 48 D2
Thornbury Rd BS23 . . . 48 C2
Thornbush Cross TA4 . . . 150 F3
Thorn Cl BS22 . . . 32 B2
THORNCOMBE . . . 199 B6
Thorncombe Cres TA6 . . . 209 C5
Thorncombe La TA4 . . . 133 A1
Thorncombe Thorn TA20 . . . 199 B5
Thorndale BS8 . . . 226 A4
Thorndale Cl BS22 . . . 49 D8
Thorndale Mews BS8 . . . 226 A4
Thorndun Park Dr TA20 . . 223 D6
THORNE COFFIN . . . 218 A8
Thorne Cross BA22 . . . 218 B7
Thorne Cross Way TA21 . . 178 D8
Thorne Gdns BA21 . . . 218 C7
Thorne La
Wheddon Cross TA24 . . . 147 C8
Winsford TA24 . . . 147 C8
Yeovil BA21 . . . 218 C8
Thorne Pk TA8 . . . 104 B5
THORNE ST MARGARET . . . 179 D8
THORNEY . . . 172 A1
Thorneymoor La TA10 . . . 172 A3
Thorney Rd TA12 . . . 185 B8
THORNFALCON . . . 169 E2
Thornhill Dro TA12 . . . 173 A1
Thornhill La BA22 . . . 187 A8
Thornhill Rd DT10 . . . 190 B4
Thorn La TA3 . . . 169 D2
Thornton Rd BA21 . . . 218 D7
Thornwell La BA9 . . . 216 D3
Thornwell Way BA9 . . . 216 C3
Thorny La BA21 . . . 187 E8
Thornymarsh La BA7 . . . 175 B8
THOULSTONE . . . 121 F4
THREE ASHES
North Cadbury . . . 175 C7
Oakhill . . . 115 E1
Three Ashes DT8 . . . 199 D7
Three Ashes La TA11 . . . 157 B4
Three Corner Mead BA21 . 218 C5
Three Gates Cross TA22 . . 163 C6
Three Hill View BA6 . . . 206 E5
Three Horse Shoes Hill TA5 . . . 152 C4
Three Oaks Cross TA19 . . . 183 C4
Three Queens' La BS1 . . . 227 B2
Three Ways Sch BA2 . . . 62 E8
Three Wells Rd BS13 . . . 21 F4
Thrift Cl DT10 . . . 190 C4
Throgmorton Rd BS4 . . . 22 F8
Throop Rd BA8 . . . 176 F1
Thrubwell La BS40 . . . 37 B4
Thrupe La BA5 . . . 114 A2
Thrush Cl 4 BS22 . . . 49 E8
Thumb La BA4 . . . 158 E7
THURLBEAR . . . 182 C8
Thurlbear CE Prim Sch TA3 . . . 182 C8
Thurlestone BS14 . . . 23 A6
Thurlocks BA22 . . . 186 B6
THURLOXTON . . . 153 D1
Thyme Cl BS20 . . . 2 F5
Thynne Cl BS27 . . . 90 B6
Tibbott Rd BS14 . . . 23 D5
Tibbott Wlk BS14 . . . 23 D5
Tiberius Rd BS31 . . . 24 F7
Tichborne Rd BS23 . . . 30 E1
TICKENHAM . . . 7 F4
Tickenham CE Prim Sch BS21 . . . 7 F4
Tickenham Hill BS48 . . . 8 E4
Tickenham Rd BS21 . . . 7 A4
Tide Gr BS11 . . . 5 A8
Tides Reach TA24 . . . 125 C4
Tiffany Ct BS1 . . . 227 B1
Tiger Moth Rd BS24 . . . 49 C5
Tigers Wy 8 EX13 . . . 198 A1
Tiledown BS39 . . . 58 E1
Tiledown Cl BS39 . . . 58 F1
Tile Hill BA10 . . . 161 A7
Tile House Rd
East Huntspill TA7 . . . 137 B8
Mark TA9 . . . 106 C1
Tilery EX14 . . . 192 D3
Tilham St BA6 . . . 158 B6
Tilley Cl
Farmborough BA2 . . . 60 A5
Keynsham BS31 . . . 25 A2
Tilley La BA2 . . . 60 A5
Tilleys Dro BA5 . . . 138 F7
TILLWORTH . . . 198 D3
Tilsey La TA4 . . . 150 C5
Tilton Ct 5 DT9 . . . 225 D3
TIMBERSCOMBE . . . 130 C4
Timberscombe CE First Sch TA24 . . . 130 B5
Timberscombe CE Fst Sch TA24 . . . 130 B4
Timberscombe Way TA6 . . 208 B4
Timberscombe Wlk BS14 . . 23 C5
Timbers The BA3 . . . 97 B7
Timberyard TA7 . . . 137 F1
Timewell Hill EX16 . . . 164 C4
TIMSBURY . . . 60 B1
TIMSBURY BOTTOM . . . 60 A1
Timsbury Rd
Farmborough BA2 . . . 60 B5
High Littleton BS39 . . . 59 D1
Timsbury Village Workshops BA2 . . . 59 F3
Tin Bridge Rdbt BA6 . . . 139 D3
Tinkers La BS48 . . . 19 F2
Tinker's La
Compton Martin BS40 . . . 74 B7
Cucklington BA9 . . . 177 D7
Halse TA4 . . . 167 C6
Kilmersdon BA11 . . . 98 B1
Tinneys La DT9 . . . 225 E4
Tintagel Cl BS31 . . . 24 D4
Tintagel Rd BA21 . . . 218 D7
Tintern BA21 . . . 218 C6
TINTINHULL . . . 186 C6
Tintinhull Gdn* BA22 . . . 186 C6
Tintinhull Rd BA21 . . . 186 F5
Tipcote Hill 17 BA4 . . . 205 B6
Tipnoller Hill TA4 . . . 210 F7
Tippacott La EX35 . . . 122 A4
Tiptoft 3 TA14 . . . 185 F4
Tirley Way BS22 . . . 31 B2
Titan Barrow BA1 . . . 29 C2
Tithe Barn Cross EX15 . . . 179 D2
Tithe Ct BA20 . . . 218 D5
Tithe Mdw TA4 . . . 167 A7
Tithill La TA4 . . . 167 F7
Titlands La BA5 . . . 203 A7
Titus Wy BS31 . . . 24 F7
Tiverton Gdns BS22 . . . 32 A2
Tiverton Rd
Bampton EX16 . . . 164 C1
2 Clevedon BS21 . . . 6 E1
TIVINGTON . . . 129 F8
Tivington Cross TA24 . . . 129 F8
Tivoli Ho BS23 . . . 48 E8
Tivoli La BS23 . . . 48 E8
Tog Hill BS30 . . . 12 B6
Toghill La BS30 . . . 12 A8
Tolbury La BA10 . . . 215 D6
Tolbury Mill BA10 . . . 215 E6
TOLLAND . . . 150 E3
Tolland BS24 . . . 49 A2
Tolland Cross TA4 . . . 150 E3
Toll Bridge Rd BA1 . . . 28 E3
Tolley's La TA20 . . . 194 C3
Toll Gate TA4 . . . 210 C4
Toll House Rd 1 TA5 . . . 135 B2
Toll Rd
Porlock TA24 . . . 124 A3
Weston-super-Mare BS23 . . . 66 F8
Toms Cl TA20 . . . 223 B3
Tomtit's La TA11 . . . 211 C3
TONE . . . 222 A8
TONEDALE . . . 222 B7
Tonedale Bsns Pk TA21 . . . 222 B7
Tonedale Ind Est TA21 . . . 222 B8
Tone Dr TA6 . . . 209 B3
Tone Gn TA4 . . . 167 E2
Tone Hill TA21 . . . 222 B8
Tone Rd BS21 . . . 6 D1
Toneway TA2 . . . 213 C6
Toose The BA21 . . . 218 C6
Topaz Dr TA6 . . . 209 C8
Top Hill BA4 . . . 142 F2
Top La
Gasper BA12 . . . 161 E4
Mells BA11 . . . 118 B6
Top Rd
Charlton Adam TA11 . . . 173 F7
Shipham BS25 . . . 70 F7
Westbury-sub-Mendip BA5 . 110 E6
Top St
Kingsdon TA11 . . . 173 D5
Pilton BA4 . . . 140 F3
Top Wood BA3 . . . 116 B7
Torbay Cl BA7 . . . 214 B5
Torbay Rd BA7 . . . 214 A5
Torbay Road Ind Est BA7 . . 214 A5
Torbay Villas BA7 . . . 214 A5
Tor Cl BS22 . . . 32 A2
Torhill La BA5 . . . 203 F4
Tor Hole Rd
Chewton Mendip BA3 . . . 93 F4
Chewton Mendip BA3 . . . 94 B4
Tori Green 2 TA6 . . . 209 A1
Tormynton Rd BS22 . . . 31 E3
Torre Cider Farm* TA23 . . . 131 E3
Torre Rocks TA23 . . . 131 E2
Torres Vedras Dr TA21 . . . 222 F7
Torre The BA21 . . . 218 C6
Torridge Mead TA1 . . . 213 D4
Torridge Rd BS31 . . . 25 A4
Torrington Ave BS4 . . . 22 F8
Torrington Cres BS22 . . . 32 A3
Tor St BA5 . . . 203 E4
Tor View
Cheddar BS27 . . . 90 C7
Woolavington TA7 . . . 136 E4
Tor View Ave BA6 . . . 206 D3
Tor Wood View BA5 . . . 203 E5
T'OTHER SIDE THE HILL . . . 115 B7
Totnes Cl BS22 . . . 32 A2
Totney Dro BS28 . . . 137 E8
Totshill Dr BS13 . . . 22 E4
Totshill Gr BS13 . . . 22 E4
Tottenham Pl BS8 . . . 226 B3

Totterdown La
Pilton BA4 204 B1
Weston-super-Mare BS24 49 A1
Totterdown Rd BS23 48 F4
Tottle's Dro TA7 154 C2
Touches La TA20 223 E5
Touches Mdw TA20 223 E5
Touching End La SN14 13 F8
Touch La TA10 156 C1
Touchstone Cl TA20 223 B4
Touchstone La TA20 223 B4
Touchwood La BS26 87 E3
Toulouse Rd 5 TA6 209 A1
TOULTON 152 A2
Tout Hill BA9 216 C3
Tout La BA22,TA11 174 A6
Tovey Cl BS22 31 E4
Tower Cl
Cheddar BS27 90 B6
Stoke St Michael BA3 116 A3
Tower Farms Ind Units TA4 151 A4
TOWERHEAD 51 D4
Towerhead Rd BS29 51 D3
Tower Hill
Bristol BS2 227 B3
Bruton BA10 215 D6
Holcombe Rogus TA21 178 D5
Horsington BA8 176 E2
Locking BS24 50 D4
Stogursey TA5 134 B5
Stoke St Michael BA3 116 A3
Williton TA4 202 E2
Tower Hill Rd TA18 224 B5
Tower House La BS48 9 A4
Tower La
Bristol BS1 227 A3
Taunton TA1 212 E4
Towerleaze BS9 5 D3
Tower Rd
Kilmington BA12 161 D6
Portishead BS20 2 A4
Stawell TA7 137 B1
Yeovil BA21 219 C8
Tower St
Bristol BS1 227 B2
Taunton TA1 212 E4
Tower The BS1 227 B2
Tower View
Frome BA11 119 F2
South Cheriton BA8 176 D3
Wanstrow BA4 142 E4
Tower Wlk BS23 30 D1
Town Barton BA2 81 F4
Town Cl
North Curry TA3 170 B4
Stogursey TA5 134 B6
Town End BA2 81 F4
Townend Villas TA14 185 F2
Town Farm TA3 170 B4
Townhall Bldgs BA5 203 E4
Town Hill EX36 162 C6
Town La BA4 205 C6
Town Marsh TA22 163 D7
Townrise 15 BA20 219 B4
TOWNSEND 92 D4
Townsend
East Harptree BS40 75 A5
Ilminster TA19 221 D3
Marston Magna BA22 174 F1
Middlezoy TA7 155 C3
Montacute TA15 186 B3
Shepton Mallet BA4 205 B5
Westonzoyland TA7 154 F5
Williton TA4 202 E3
TOWNS END 77 E4
TOWN'S END 116 E3
Townsend Cl
Bristol BS14 23 F5
Bruton BA10 215 F7
Townsend Cotts TA24 147 C5
Townsend Gn 10 BA8 190 A6
Townsend La
Chilton Polden TA7 137 B2
Emborough BA3 95 B2
Theale BS28 109 A2
Townsend Orch
Merriott TA16 195 F8
Street BA16 207 B5
Townsend Pk BA10 215 F7
Townsend Rd
Bristol BS14 23 F5
Minehead TA24 201 A6
Townsend Rise BA10 215 F7
Townsend Sh Pk BA4 205 B5
Townshend Rd BS22 32 B5
Town St BA4 205 B6
Town Tree Farm Nature Trail* TA12 185 C8
Town Tree La TA10, TA12 185 D8
TRACEBRIDGE 179 A8
Tracey Cl TA7 209 E8
Trackfordmoor Cross TA22 163 B3
Tracy Cl BS14 22 F7
Trafalgar Ct 12 BS23 48 E7
Trafalgar Rd BA1 27 B1
Traits La BA22 174 E4
Trajan's Way BA4 205 E5
Trajectus Way BS31 24 F7
Tramshed The BA1 228 C3
Transform Ind Est TA6 209 A6
Transom Ho BS1 227 B2
Transom Pl TA24 201 B7
Travers Cl BS4 22 D6
Trawden Cl BS23 31 A1
Treasure Ct TA8 85 A1
Treasurer's Ho* TA12 185 E6
TREBLE'S HOLFORD 151 C4
TREBOROUGH 149 A7
Treborough Cl TA2 213 B8
Tredwin Cl TA21 222 D8
Treefield Rd BS21 6 D2
Tregarth Rd BS3 11 F1
Tregelles Cl TA9 104 C4
Tregonwell Rd TA24 201 A7
Trelawn Cl BS22 32 D2
Trelissick Gdns 3 BS22 49 F8
Trellech Ct 3 BA21 218 C6
Tremes Cl SN14 13 F8
Tremlett Mews 3 BS22 32 B4
Trenchard Rd
Locking BS24 50 D4
Saltford BS31 25 D3
Trenchard St BS1 226 C3
Trenchard Way TA2 212 E5
Trendle La
Bicknoller TA4 132 F2
Stoney Stoke BA9 160 E3
Trendle Rd TA1 212 B1
Trendle St DT9 225 D3
Trendlewood Way BS48 9 A1
Trenleigh Dr BS22 32 A2
TRENT 187 F5
Trent Cl BA21 219 E8
Trent Ct TA1 213 D4
Trent Gr BS31 25 A4
Trent Mdw TA1 213 E4
Trent Path La DT9 225 A5
Trent Young's CE Prim Sch DT9 187 F5
Tresco Spinney BA21 218 C6
Trescothick Cl BS31 24 E6
Trevanna Rd BS3 11 F1
Trevelyan Rd BS23 48 F7
Trevett Rd TA1 212 C2
Trevithick Cl BA11 120 C6
Trevor Rd TA6 209 C6
Trevor Smith Pl TA1 213 A3
Trewartha Cl BS23 48 F8
Trewartha Pk BS23 48 F8
Trewint Gdns BS4 22 F8
Triangle Ct 2 BA2 44 D5
Triangle Ctr The BS21 6 D3
Triangle E BA2 44 D5
Triangle N BA2 44 D5
Triangle S BS8 226 B3
Triangle The
Castle Cary BA7 214 C5
Clevedon BS21 6 D3
North Curry TA3 170 A4
Paulton BS39 77 E6
Portishead BS20 2 B5
Somerton TA11 211 D4
Wrington BS40 35 D2
Triangle Villas 1 BA2 44 D5
Triangle W
Bath BA2 44 D5
Bristol BS8 226 B3
Tribunal & Lake Village Mus* BA6 206 D4
Trickey Warren La TA3 181 C1
Trim Bridge 3 BA1 228 B2
Trim St BA1 228 B2
Trinder Rd BS20 4 B4
Trindlewell La TA18 196 C4
TRINITY 119 E5
Trinity Bsns Ctr TA1 213 A3
Trinity CE Fst Sch BA11 119 C4
Trinity CE VC Prim Sch BA3 79 A4
Trinity Cl
Bath BA1 228 B2
Blackford BS28 107 D4
Burnham-on-S TA8 85 A1
Wellington TA21 222 C5
Trinity Coll BS9 5 E4
Trinity Ct
Bridgwater TA6 208 F6
Nailsea BS48 8 C1
13 Yeovil BA20 219 B4
Trinity Gate TA1 213 A3
Trinity Mews 15 BS2 227 C3
Trinity Pl
3 Bristol BS8 226 A2
4 Weston-super-Mare BS23 30 C1
Trinity Prim Sch BS20 2 F5
Trinity Rd
Bath BA2 45 B2
Nailsea BS48 8 D1
Taunton TA1 213 B3
Weston-super-Mare BS23 30 C1
Trinity Rise TA8 85 A1
Trinity Row
Frome BA11 119 E5
Wellington TA21 222 C5
Trinity St
Bath BA1 228 B2
Frome BA11 119 E5
Taunton TA1 213 B3
Trinity Way
Bridgwater TA6 208 E6
Minehead TA24 201 B7
Trinity Wlk
Bristol BS2 227 C3
Frome BA11 119 E5
Trin Mills BS1 227 A1
Tripps Cnr BS49 34 D7
Tripps Dro BA5 139 A6
Tripps Row BS41 11 A1
TRISCOMBE 151 D6
Triscombe Ave TA6 208 D4
Triscombe Gate TA24 147 D8
Triscombe Ho TA4 151 D5
Triscombe Rd TA2 212 E8
Tristram Dr TA3 169 D4
Trollope's Hill BA2 46 A1
Tropical Bird Garden* TA8 47 F2
Tropiquaria Zoo* TA23 131 F4
Trossachs Dr BA2 45 D8
Trotts La TA19 183 B2
Trottsway Cross TA24 129 C2
TROWBRIDGE 83 F7
Trowbridge Cl TA9 104 D4
Trowell La TA4 165 E4
Trow La BA12 144 C2
Truckwell La TA4 150 D4
TRUDOXHILL 143 C6
TRULL 168 D1
Trull CE Prim Sch TA3 168 D1
Trull Green Dr TA3 168 D1
Trull Rd TA1 212 E2
Trumps Cross EX16 178 E3
Truro Cl TA8 104 C7
Truro Rd BS48 9 A1
Trym Bank BS9 5 D7
Trym Cross Rd BS9 5 C5
Trymleaze BS9 5 C5
Trym Side BS9 5 C5
Trymwood Par BS9 5 D6
Tucker's Cross DT9 188 A4
Tuckers La BA7 214 B7
Tucker's La
Baltonsborough BA6 157 F6
Ubley BS40 73 E8
Tucker's Moor Cross EX16 162 F3
Tucker St BA5 203 C4
TUCKERTON 169 F8
Tuckerton La TA7 153 F1
Tuckerton Rd TA7 169 F8
TUCKING MILL 63 C8
Tuckingmill La BS39 41 E5
Tuckmarsh La BA11 143 E7
Tuckmill BS21 6 B1
Tudballs TA24 128 D1
Tuddington Gdns BA5 203 B4
TUDHAY 198 C3
Tudor Ct
Chard TA20 223 C6
Yeovil BA20 219 A4
Tudor Pk TA2 213 D7
Tudor Rd
Portishead BS20 2 E4
Weston-super-Mare BS22 32 A4
Tudor Way TA6 209 A1
Tudway Cl BA5 203 C4
Tufton Ave BS11 5 A8
Tugela Rd BS13 21 F7
Tuggy's La BA2 63 E1
Tulip Tree Rd TA6 209 E5
Tulse Hill BA12 161 F2
Tunbridge Cl BS40 39 B2
Tunbridge Rd BS40 39 B2
Tuncombe La TA18 195 D4
Tundra Walk 5 TA6 154 A5
TUNLEY 61 B3
Tunley Hill BA2 60 E2
Tunley Rd BA2, BA3 61 D5
Tunnel La BA3 96 F5
Tunnell La 14 TA14 185 F4
Tunscombe La BA4 142 D8
Tunstall Cl BS9 5 E4
Turin Path 4 TA6 208 E7
Turkey Ct 5 TA1 212 E3
TURLEIGH 64 F6
Turleigh Hill BA15 64 F6
Turmo Rd BS23 49 B4
Turnbury Ave BS48 9 A1
Turnbury Cl BS22 31 F3
Turner Cl
Bridgwater TA6 209 A4
Keynsham BS31 25 A5
Turner Ct
Wells BA5 203 D3
Weston-super-Mare BS22 31 F3
Turner Rd TA2 212 E7
Turner's Barn La BA20 218 F2
Turner's Court La BA3 114 D8
Turner's La DT6 199 B2
Turner's Twr BA3 80 A1
Turner Way BS21 6 B1
Turn Hill TA10 155 F2
Turnhill Rd TA10 156 A2
Turnock Gdns BS24 50 D8
Turnpike
Milverton TA4 167 A4
Sampford Peverell EX16 178 C1
Turnpike Cl TA18 196 B3
Turnpike Cnr BA3 95 B8
Turnpike Cross TA14 185 E2
Turnpike Cvn Pk TA20 193 A4
Turnpike Gn TA18 196 B3
Turnpike La BA4 142 B6
Turnpike Rd
Cross BS26 69 E1
Shipham BS25 70 E8
Turnstone 3 BS20 2 F6
Turstin Rd BA6 206 F6
Turtlegate Ave BS13 21 E4
Turtlegate Wlk BS13 21 E4
Tut Hill DT9 189 C1
Tutton Way BS21 6 D1
Tuttors Hill BS27 71 C1
Tuxwell La TA5 152 C8
Tweed Rd BS21 6 C1
Tweed Rd Ind Est 2 BS21 6 C1
Tweentown BS27 90 B8
Twelve Acre Post TA22 163 A4
Twelve Acres DT9 225 B5
Twelve Acres Cl BS39 77 D6
Twelve O'clock La BA2 43 B3
TWERTON 44 A5
Twerton Farm Cl 2 BA2 44 B6
Twerton Inf Sch BA2 44 A5
Twinell La TA5 152 D7
Twines Cl BA22 175 A5
Twinhoe La BA2 62 E2
Twistgates La EX14 192 A4
Twitchen Ball Cnr EX36 145 G3
Twitchens La BS27 90 F2
Two Acres Cvn Pk BS21 1 B1
Two Acres Rd BS14 23 A7
Two Ash Hill TA20 193 F1
Two Ash La TA20 194 A1
Two Bridges TA3 183 E7
Two Elms BA21 187 E8
Two Tower La BA22 219 B2
Two Trees BS40 72 E8
Twyford Pl TA21 222 D5
Tydeman Rd BS20 2 F5
Tyler Gn 2 BS22 32 B4
Tylers End TA9 104 F3
Tyler's La TA4 167 A7
Tyler Way TA9 104 D3
Tyndall Ave BS8 226 C4
Tyndall Ho 5 BS2 227 C3
TYNDALL'S PARK 226 C4
Tyndalls Park Mews BS2 226 C4
Tyndall's Park Rd BS8 226 C4
Tyne Gr 10 BS20 2 F6
Tyne Pk TA1 213 D3
TYNING
Radstock 79 B3
Timsbury 60 A2
Tyning Cl BS14 23 A7
Tyning Cotts BA3 116 C7
Tyning End BA2 45 B5
Tyning Hill
Hemington BA3 99 C8
Radstock BA3 79 B3
Tyning La BA1 28 B1
Tyning Pl BA2 45 C2
Tyning Rd
Bath BA2 45 C2
Bathampton BA2 28 F2
Peasedown St John BA2 79 D7
Saltford BS31 25 E2
Winsley BA15 64 E7
Tynings BS39 58 D3
Tynings La BA5 203 C8
Tynings Mews BS23 48 E4
Tynings Rd BA16 207 B4
Tynings The
Clevedon BS21 6 A1
Portishead BS20 1 F1
Tynings Way
Clutton BS39 58 E3
Westwood BA15 64 F3
Tyning Terr 15 BA1 28 A1
Tyning The
Bath BA2 45 B5
Freshford BA3 64 B4
Tynte Ave BS13 22 E3
Tynte Rd TA6 209 D6
Tyntesfield House (NT)* BS48 9 F4
Tyntesfield Rd BS13 22 A8
Tyrone Wlk BS4 22 E8
TYTHERINGTON 143 E8
Tytherington La BA11 143 E8
TYTHERLEIGH 198 C6
Tythe St BA6 206 E3
Tythings Com Ctr The BA9 216 C3
Tythings Ct TA24 200 F7
Tything Way BA9 216 D3

U

UBLEY 55 E1
Ubley CE Prim Sch BS40 55 D1
Ubley Dro BS40 73 B7
UBLEY SIDELING 73 D8
UDLEY 35 C4
ULLCOMBE 192 A4
Ullcombe La EX14 191 F4
Ullswater Cl BS23 49 A4
Ullswater Dr BA1 28 A2
Uncombe Cl BS48 19 D7
Underbanks BS20 4 D4
Underdown BA21 219 F5
Underdown Ho BS1 227 A1
Underdown Hollow
Bradford Abbas DT9 187 E2
Yeovil BA21 219 F4
Underdown La DT9 225 F6
Underhayes Ct TA18 196 E8
Underhill
Gurney Slade BA3 114 E7
Hambridge TA10 184 D8
Penselwood BA9 161 D1
Underhill Ave BA3 77 F2
Underhill Cl BA16 207 B5
Underhill Dr BS23 48 D1
Underhill La
Midsomer Norton BA3 77 F2
Staple Fitzpaine TA3 182 B4
Underhill Rd BA16 207 B5
Under Knoll BA2 79 E8
Under La BS40 36 D1
Underleaf Way BA2 79 D7
Undertown BS40 74 A7
Undertown La BS40 74 A7
Under Tree Rd BA2 79 A6
Under Way TA20 193 D6
Underwood Ave BS22 31 B1
Underwood Business Park BA5 203 B6
Underwood End BS25 52 A4
Underwood La TA10 172 C8
Underwood Rd
Glastonbury BA6 206 D6
Kingsdon TA11 173 D5
Portishead BS20 2 C3
Union Dro TA10 172 B6
Union Pas BA1 228 C2
Union Pl BS23 48 D7
Union St
Bath BA1 228 C2
Bridgwater TA6 209 B6
Bristol BS1 227 B3
Cheddar BS27 90 B7
Dulverton TA22 163 D6
Nailsea BS48 8 C1
Wells BA5 203 D4
Weston-super-Mare BS23 48 D7
Yeovil BA20 219 B4
Unite Ho BS1 226 C2
Unity Ct BS31 25 A5
Unity Rd BS31 25 A6
Unity St BS1 226 C2
University Cl BS9 5 F4
University of Bristol Dorothy Hodgkin Bldg BS1 227 A4
University Rd BS8 226 C3
University Wlk BS8 226 C3
Univ of Bath BA2 45 E5
Univ of Bristol BS8 226 C3
Univ of Bristol Dept of Ed BS8 226 C3
Univ of Bristol Langford House Sch of Veterinary Science BS40 53 B6
Univ of Bristol Sch of Veterinary Science BS2 226 C4
Univ of the West of England BS3 11 E4
Upcot Cres TA1 212 B2
UPCOTT 168 B3
Upcott La
Bicknoller TA4 132 F1
Winsford TA24 147 D7
Upcott Rd TA1, TA4 168 B3
UPHILL 48 C2
Uphill Ct BS23 48 D2
Uphill Dr BA1 28 B2
Uphill Farm Cvn Pk BS23 48 E1
Uphill Prim Sch BS23 48 D2
Uphill Rd N BS23 48 D4
Uphill Rd S BS23 48 D2
Uphills BA10 215 E7
Uphill Way BS23 48 D1
Upjohn Cres BS13 22 D3
Uplands BA9 176 B8
Uplands Cl BA2 63 F7
Uplands Dr BS31 25 F2
Uplands La BS31 24 F1
Uplands Rd BS31 25 F2
Uplands Terr BA22 197 B8
Uplands The BS48 18 C8
UPLOWMAN 178 B2
Uplowman CE Prim Sch EX16 178 B2
UP MUDFORD 187 D5
Up Mudford Rd BA22 187 D6
UPOTTERY 191 F2
Upottery Prim Sch EX14 191 F2
Upper Belgrave Rd BS8 5 F1
UPPER BENTER 115 C7
Upper Berkeley Pl BS8 226 B3
Upper Bloomfield Rd BA2 44 D1
Upper Borough Walls BA1 228 C2
Upper Breach BA5 113 A2
Upper Bristol Rd
Bath BA1 44 D7
Clutton BS39 58 D3
Weston-super-Mare BS22 31 B1
Upper Byron Pl BS8 226 B3
Upper Camden Pl BA1 228 C4
UPPER CHEDDON 168 F7
Upper Cheddon Rd TA2 168 F7
Upper Church La BS24 49 D2
Upper Church Rd BS23 30 D1
Upper Church St BA1 228 B3
UPPER COXLEY 139 F6
Upper Crannel Dro BA6 139 C4
Upper Ct BA3 97 C8
Upper Draycott Rd BS27 90 E5
Upper East Hayes BA1 28 B1
Upper Farm Cl BA2 81 F4
Upper Flowerfield BA11 143 B7
Upper Furlong BA2 60 B3
UPPER GODNEY 139 A6
Upper Green La BS40 55 B7
Upper Hedgemead Rd BA1 228 B4
Upper High St
Castle Cary BA7 214 C5
Taunton TA1 212 F3
Upper Holway Rd TA1 213 C2
Upper Kewstoke Rd BS23 30 B1
Upper Lambridge St BA1 28 C2
UPPER LANGFORD 53 C3
UPPER LANGRIDGE 27 B7
Upper Lansdown Mews BA1 27 F1
UPPER LITTLETON 38 B6
Upper Maudlin St BS2 227 A3
Upper Mead 16 EX13 198 A1
Upper Merrifield BA3 116 E8
Upper Merryfield BA3 97 E1
UPPER MILTON 203 D7
Upper Mount Pleasant BA3 64 A4

Upper Myrtle Hill BS20 4 C4
Upper New Rd BS27 90 A8
Upper North St BS27 90 B8
Upper Oldfield Pk BA2 228 A1
Upper Pitching BA3 96 D5
Upper Pitney Rd TA10 172 C7
UPPER RADFORD 78 B8
Upper Radford BS39 78 B7
Upper Rd BS39 75 E6
Upper Stanton BS39 40 A2
UPPER STANTON DREW 40 B2
Upper Strode BS40 55 F7
UPPER SWAINSWICK 28 B5
Upper Town La BS40 37 C8
UPPER VOBSTER 117 D8
Upper Vobster Rd BA3 117 D8
Upper Wellesley La BA5 140 B6
Upper Wellesley Rd
Wells BA5 140 B7
Wells BA5 203 E1
Upper Wells St BS1 226 C2
UPPER WESTHOLME 140 D4
UPPER WESTON 27 A3
UPPER WESTWOOD 64 E4
Upper Whatcombe BA11 119 E6
Upper Wood St TA1 212 E4
Upper York St BS2 227 B4
UPPOTERY 191 F2
UPTON
Langport 172 D5
Skilgate 164 F8
Upton BS24 49 A2
UPTON CHEYNEY 26 B8
Upton Cotts BS41 38 F8
Upton La
Dundry BS41 39 A8
Seavington St Michael TA19 184 E2
UPTON NOBLE 142 F2
Upton Noble CE Prim Sch
BA4 142 F2
Urchinwood La BS49 34 F4
URGASHAY 174 C3
Urgashay Rd BA22 174 C3

V

VAGG 186 F5
Vagg Hill BA22 186 E5
Vagg La BA22 186 F5
Vagg Pk BA22 186 F5
Valda Rd BS22 31 C2
Vale Cl TA18 224 C4
Vale Cres BS22 32 C2
Vale Ct BS8 226 A4
Vale End BS48 8 D1
Vale La BS3 22 C8
Vale Mill Way BS24 49 F8
Valentine Cl BS14 23 B5
Valentines TA22 163 E6
Vale Rd
Stalbridge DT10 190 B4
Yeovil BA21 219 E6
Valerian Cl BS11 4 F6
Vale St BA8 190 A6
Valetta Cl BS23 48 F3
Valetta Pl TA6 208 F5
Vale View
Aller TA10 171 E8
Henstridge BA8 190 A7
Radstock BA3 79 A2
Wincanton BA9 216 F5
Vale View Cotts TA4 151 E4
Vale View Gdns BA9 216 C2
Vale View Pl 16 BA1 28 B1
Vale View Terr BA1 28 F3
Valley Cl
6 Nailsea BS48 8 E2
Wells BA5 203 C4
Yeovil BA21 219 B6
Valley Ct BS20 1 E3
Valley Gdns BS48 8 E2
Valley Line Ind Pk BS27 90 A7
Valley Rd
Bristol, Bedminster Down
BS13 22 A8
Clevedon BS21 6 F5
Crewkerne TA18 224 C4
Leigh Woods BS8 11 C7
Portishead BS20 2 A2
Taunton TA1 213 C5
Valley View
Chilcompton BA3 96 D3
Clutton BS39 58 E3
Frome BA11 119 D6
Millmoor EX15 179 E1
Morebath EX16 164 B3
Valley View Cl BA1 28 B3
Valley View Rd
Bath BA1 28 C3
Paulton BS39 77 E6
Valley Way Rd BS48 8 E3
Valley Wlk BA3 78 B2
Vallis Ct 7 BA11 119 E5
Vallis Fst Sch
Frome BA11 119 E5
12 Frome BA11 119 E5
Vallis Rd BA11 119 D5
Vallis Trad Est BA11 119 D5
Vallis Way BA11 119 E5
Vanbrugh Gdns BS11 4 F8
Van Diemen's La BA1 27 F2
Vandyck Ave BS31 24 F6
Vane St 2 BA2 45 B7
Vanguard Ct BA22 218 A5
Varsity Way BS24 50 B6
Vaughan Ct BA5 203 B4
Veales DT10 189 F2
Veale The BS24 67 C6
Veal La
Horrington BA5 113 B2
Walton BA16 156 E6
Vedal Dro TA10 172 D4
Vee La BS40 37 D8
Vellore La BA2 45 C7
Vellow Rd TA4 150 D8
Vellow Wood La TA4 132 D1
Velvet Bottom BS40 72 E3
Vemplett's Cross TA23 131 E1
Venford Hill
East Anstey TA22 162 E8
Hawkridge TA22 146 D1
Venland Bsns Pk TA24 201 B6
Venland Ind Pk TA24 201 A6
Venley La TA18 195 C4
Venn Cl TA4 167 E6
Venn Cross TA4 165 D3
Venn Hill DT6, TA20 199 C6
Venniford Cross TA24 129 F8
Vennland Way TA24 201 A6
Venns Cl BS27 90 B7
Venns Gate BS27 71 A1
Venture 20 BA20 218 C3
Venture 7 BA20 218 C3
Venture Eleven The TA2 213 B6
Venture Way TA2 213 B6
Venus La BS39 58 E3
Venus St BS49 34 E2
Vera St TA2 212 F7
Verbena Way BS22 32 A1
Verbena Wlk TA6 208 E1
Verdun Terr TA23 131 E4
Vereland Rd BS24 49 E3
Verlands BS49 34 E5
Vernal La BA11 119 D6
Vernalls Rd DT9 225 D5
Vernham Gr BA2 44 C1
Vernhamwood Cl BA2 44 C1
Vernon Cl BS31 25 D3
Vernon La BS26 69 B3
Vernon Pk BA2 44 C6
Vernon Terr BA2 44 C6
Vernslade BA1 27 A2
Verriers 10 TA6 153 E3
VERRINGTON 216 A5
Verrington La BA9 216 B5
Verrington Park Rd BA9 216 B4
Vesey's Hole Hill SP8 177 E4
Vestry Cl BA16 207 C5
Vestry Ct 1 BA16 207 C5
Vestry La BS5 227 C4
Vestry Rd BA16 207 C5
Vian End BS22 31 F4
Via Traversus BS31 24 F7
Vicarage Cl
Chard TA20 223 C3
Coxley BA5 139 E6
Creech St Michael TA3 169 D4
8 Frome BA11 119 F4
Stogursey TA5 134 C6
Weston-super-Mare BS22 32 A3
Westonzoyland TA7 154 F5
Vicarage Ct
Burnham-on-S TA8 104 A7
Timberscombe TA24 130 B5
Vicarage Gdns BA2 79 B7
Vicarage Hill
Combe St Nicholas TA20 193 D6
Dulverton TA22 163 D6
Vicarage La
Barrow Gurney BS48 20 C6
Compton Bishop BS26 69 B3
Compton Dando BS39 41 D6
Creech St Michael TA3 169 D4
Draycott BS27 90 F3
Mark TA9 106 E5
Norton St Philip BA2 81 E4
Pawlett TA6 135 F5
Shapwick TA7 137 F1
7 Wookey BA5 139 D8
Vicarage Lawns TA3 169 D4
Vicarage Rd
Bristol, Bishopsworth
BS13 22 A6
Carhampton TA24 131 B5
Leigh Woods BS8 11 D6
Minehead TA24 200 F8
Stogursey TA5 134 C6
Wookey BA5 139 E8
Woolavington TA7 136 E4
Vicarage St
Burnham-on-S TA8 104 A7
Frome BA11 119 F4
Tintinhull BA22 186 C6
6 Yeovil BA20 219 B4
Vicarage Wlk BA20 219 B5
Vicar's Cl BA5 203 E5
Vicars La TA6 208 D5
Vicar's La TA12 184 F7
Vicars Path BA5 92 D3
Vickery Cl
Bridgwater TA6 208 D3
Curry Rivel TA10 171 D4
Victoria Art Gall The★
BA2 228 C2
Victoria Ave TA20 223 D4
Victoria Bldgs
Bath BA2 44 D6
Glastonbury BA6 206 E4
Victoria Bridge Ct BA1 228 A3
Victoria Bridge Rd
BA1, BA2 228 A2
Victoria Bsns Pk TA20 223 D4
Victoria Cl
Bath BA2 44 C5
Portishead BS20 2 D5
Yeovil BA21 219 D6
Victoria Cotts BA2 62 F7
Victoria Ct
Castle Cary BA7 214 B5
Chard TA20 223 D4
Frome BA11 120 A4
Ilminster TA19 221 C4
Portishead BS20 2 D5
Victoria Gate TA1 213 B4
Victoria Gdns
Batheaston BA1 28 F3
Castle Cary BA7 214 B6
15 Henstridge BA8 190 A6
Victoria Gr BA4 205 D5
Victoria Ho
Bath BA1 44 D8
Keynsham BS31 24 F4
Victoria Jubilee Homes
BS40 53 C6
Victoria La BA4 141 E1
Victoria Lodge BS22 31 E2
Victoria Mews BA7 214 B5
VICTORIA PARK 226 B3
Victoria Park Bsns Ctr BA1 44 D7
Victoria Pk
Castle Cary BA7 214 B5
Weston-super-Mare BS23 30 D1
Victoria Pl
Bath, Combe Down BA2 45 C1
2 Bath, Lambridge BA1 28 C1
Chardstock EX13 198 A7
Highbridge TA9 104 D3
Paulton BS39 77 D5
Weston-super-Mare BS23 48 D8
Victoria Quadrant BS23 48 E8
Victoria Rd
Avonmouth BS11 4 B7
Bath BA2 44 D6
Bridgwater TA6 208 E5
Castle Cary BA7 214 B5
Clevedon BS21 6 C3
Frome BA11 120 A4
Minehead TA24 201 A5
Saltford BS31 25 D3
Yeovil BA21 219 D6
Victoria Sh Mews TA18 224 C6
Victoria Sq
Bristol BS8 226 A3
Crewkerne TA18 224 B6
Evercreech BA4 141 E1
Portishead BS20 2 D5
Weston-super-Mare BS23 48 D7
Victoria St
Bristol BS1 227 B2
Burnham-on-S TA8 104 A7
Taunton TA1 213 B4
Wellington TA21 222 D6
Victoria Terr
Bath BA2 44 D6
14 Bristol, Clifton BS8 11 F6
14 Henstridge BA8 190 A6
Paulton BS39 77 E6
Victoria Way TA5 152 E7
Victory Rd TA2 213 A7
Vienna Way 4 TA6 154 A5
Vigor Rd BS13 22 B5
Viking Cl TA23 202 D7
Vilberie Cl TA2 212 A7
Village Hill
Huish Champflower TA4 165 A7
Upton TA4 164 F7
Village Rd
Hatch Beauchamp TA3 182 F6
Newton St Loe BA2 43 C6
Villa Rosa 16 BS23 30 C1
Villes La TA24 124 A4
Villice La BS40 74 A8
Vincent Cl TA8 104 C7
Vincent Pl BA20 219 B5
Vincents Cl DT9 189 A1
Vincent St 5 BA20 219 B5
Vine Gdns
Frome BA11 119 F6
Weston-super-Mare BS22 32 A2
Vine Gr BA8 176 E1
Vine House Gdns TA20 223 C3
Vinery The BS25 70 A7
Vine St BA8 176 E1
Vineyards BA1 228 C3
Viney Bridge Mills TA18 224 D5
Viney La EX14 191 F1
Viney St TA1 213 B3
Viney's Yd BA10 215 F6
Vining's Hill BA4 142 D1
Vinney La BA11 143 F8
Vinnicombe Straight
TA22 147 F5
Violet La DT9 176 A2
Virginia Cl 1 BA8 190 A6
Virginia Orch TA3 169 C3
Viscount Sq TA6 208 E7
Vivary Ct TA1 212 E3
Vivary Gate TA1 212 F3
Vivary Hts TA1 212 E2
Vivary Rd TA1 212 E3
Vivien Ave BA3 78 A2
Vixen Cl BA22 174 A3
VOBSTER 117 C7
Vobster Cross BA3 117 D7
Vobster Hill BA3 117 D7
VOLE 106 B8
Vole Rd
Brent Knoll TA9 86 D1
Mark TA9 106 B7
Volis Cross TA5 152 F1
Volis Hill TA2 168 F8
Vowell Cl BS13 22 B4
Vowles Cl BS48 9 A3
VOXMOOR 222 F1
Vulcan Ho BA2 228 C3
Vulcan Rd TA24 201 B6
Vynes Cl BS48 9 A1
Vynes Ind Est BS48 9 A3
Vynes Way BS48 9 A1
Vyvyan Rd BS8 226 A3
Vyvyan Terr BS8 226 A3

W

WADBROOK 198 C4
Wadbrook Cross EX13 198 C4
WADBURY 118 D7
WADDICOMBE 162 E6
Wade Cl TA7 154 E6
WADEFORD 193 D5
Wadeford Hill TA20 193 D5
Wade St BS2 227 C3
Wadham Cl
Bridgwater TA6 209 D6
Ilminster TA19 221 A4
Wadham Cross
Knowstone EX36 162 A2
West Anstey EX36 162 A4
Wadham Hill EX36 162 A2
Wadham's Almshouses
TA19 183 E4
Wadham Sch TA18 224 D7
Wadham St BS23 48 D8
WAGG 172 B5
Wagg Dro TA10 172 B5
WAGGS PLOT 198 B4
Waggs Plot EX13 198 B4
Wagon And Horses Hill
BA4 141 E8
Wagtail Cres BS20 3 A6
Wagtail Gdns BS22 49 E8
Wains Cl 3 BS21 6 C2
Wainwright Cl 5 BS22 32 B4
Wainwright Ct BA4 205 B4
Wainwright Dr BA11 120 C7
Waits Cl BS29 50 F3
Wakedean Gdns BS49 17 A1
WALCOMBE 203 E7
Walcombe La BA5 203 E6
Walcot Bldgs
Bath BA1 45 B8
Bath BA1 228 C4
Walcot Ct BA1 228 C4
Walcot Gate BA1 228 C4
Walcot Ho BA1 228 C4
Walcot Par BA1 228 C4
Walcot St BA1 228 C3
Walcot Terr BA1 228 C4
Waldegrave Rd BA1 27 E1
Waldegrave Terr BA3 79 A3
Walden Rd BS31 25 A4
Waldock Barton TA13 220 D4
Waldron's Cross TA21 165 E1
Waldrons La TA5 135 D2
WALES 174 E3
Wales La BA22 174 E3
WALFORD 169 D7
Walford Ave BS22 32 C3
Walford Cross Ind Pk
TA2 169 D6
Walford Cross Roads TA2 169 D7
Waling La BA2 43 D6
Walker Rd BA11 120 A3
Walkers Dr BS24 49 F7
Walkers Gate TA21 222 D5
Walkers Ri TA2 213 E8
Walker St BS2 226 C4
Walk La TA13 184 F1
WALLACE 74 E3
Wallace La BS40 74 E3
Wallace Rd BA1 28 B1
Wallace Wells Rd TA8 104 D5
Wallbridge BA11 120 B4
Wallbridge Ave BA11 120 A4
Wallbridge Gdns BA11 120 A4
Wallbridge Ho BA11 120 A4
Wallbridge Ind Est BA11 120 B4
Wall Ditch La TA16 196 A8
Wallenge Cl BS39 77 F6
Wallenge Dr BS39 77 F6
Waller Gdns BA1 27 E4
Walley La BS40 57 B7
Wall Gn BS26 70 C1
Wallingford Rd BS4 22 D7
Wallington Way BA11 119 D6
Walliscote Grove Rd 11
BS23 48 E7
Walliscote Prim Sch BS23 48 E7
Walliscote Rd BS23 48 D6
Walliscote Rd S BS23 48 D4
WALL MEAD 60 C4
Walls La BS28 108 B8
Walls The TA7 137 C2
Wall The TA9 106 D5
Wally Court Rd BS40 56 E8
Walmsley Terr 4 BA1 28 B1
Walnut Bldgs BA3 79 A3
Walnut Cl
Axbridge BS26 70 B1
Cheddar BS27 90 B7
Easton-in-G BS20 4 A3
Keynsham BS31 24 C4
Nailsea BS48 18 E8
Puriton TA7 136 C4
Rode BA11 101 E8
Taunton TA1 212 B4
Weston-super-Mare BS24 49 B2
Walnut Dr
Bath BA2 44 E4
Bridgwater TA6 209 D3
Somerton TA11 211 D4
Walnut Gr BA4 205 C4
Walnut La TA7 136 F3
Walnut Rd TA10 172 A6
Walnuts The TA7 137 B2
Walnut Tree Cl
Ubley BS40 55 D1
Wells BA5 203 C5
Walnut Tree Cnr TA23 131 F4
Walnut Tree Ct BS49 34 D4
Walnut Tree Dr TA24 131 A5
Walnut Wlk
Bristol BS13 22 A6
Frome BA11 120 B7
Keynsham BS31 24 C4
WALPOLE 136 B4
Walpole Dro TA9 136 A5
Walridge Cross TA4 166 A4
Walrond Ct TA19 221 B3
Walrond's Pk TA3 184 B7
WALROW 105 C2
Walrow TA9 104 E3
Walrow Ind Est TA9 104 F2
Walrow Terr TA9 104 E3
Walscombe Cl 1 TA14 185 F4
Walsh Ave BS14 23 A7
Walsh Cl BS24 49 B2
Waltham End BS24 50 A8
WALTON 156 E7
Walton BS24 49 A2
Walton Bay House Park
Homes BS21 1 B1
Walton CE Prim Sch BA16 156 E7
Walton Cl
Bridgwater TA6 209 D5
Keynsham BS31 24 D4
Walton Cres BS40 37 F8
Walton Cross BS21 7 B7
Walton Ct TA24 201 A7
Walton Dro BA16 156 D5
Walton High Rd BA16 207 A2
WALTON IN GORDANO 7 B7
Walton Rd
Bristol BS11 4 D6
Clevedon BS21 6 F4
WALTON ST MARY 6 E5
Walton St
Portishead BS21 1 A1
Walton in G BS21 7 A8
Walwyn Cl BA2 44 A6
Walwyn Gdns BS13 22 C3
WAMBROOK 193 C3
Wambrook Cl TA1 212 E1
Wambrook Rd
Chard TA20 223 A4
Wambrook TA20 193 D3
Wand Rd BA5 203 C2
Wansbeck Gn TA1 213 D3
Warne Rd BS31 25 A4
Wansbrough Rd BS22 32 B4
Wansdyke Bsns Ctr BA2 44 D4
Wansdyke Ct BS14 23 B5
Wansdyke Prim Sch BS14 22 F4
Wansdyke Rd BA2 44 D1
Wansdyke Way BS14 23 D3
Wansdyke Workshops
Keynsham BS31 25 A6
Peasedown St John BA2 79 D6
WANSTROW 142 F4
Wapping Rd BS1 227 A1
Warbler Cl 6 BA3 97 B8
Warden Rd TA24 200 F6
Ward La TA7 154 E8
Wardleworth Way TA21 222 C7
Wardour Rd BS4 22 D8
Wareham Cl BS48 8 D1
Wareham Cross EX13 198 E1
Wareham Rd EX13 198 E2
Wares La TA6 208 D6
Waring Ho BS1 227 A1
WARLEIGH 46 C6
Warleigh Cl BA11 119 D4
Warleigh Dr BA1 29 A3
Warleigh La BA1 46 C5
Warleys La BS24 32 C1
Warman Cl BS14 23 F6
Warman Rd BS14 23 F6
War Memorial Hospl TA8 104 B7
Warmington Rd BS14 23 C8
Warminster Rd
Beckington BA11 101 E4
Claverton BA2, BA3 46 B5
Frome BA11 120 B4
Warne Pk BS23 49 A6
Warner Cl BS49 35 A7
Warne Rd BS23 49 A6
Warren Cl
Bridgwater TA6 208 F6
Bruton BA10 215 E6
Charlton Horethorne DT9 176 A2
Fenn's Wood BS41 10 E1
Hutton BS24 49 D2
Warren Farm Cvn Pk & Camp
Site TA8 65 F5
Warren Gdns BS14 23 F5
Warren La BS41 20 E8
Warren Rd
Brean TA8 65 F6
Minehead TA24 201 B7
Warren's Cl BS27 71 B1
Warrens Hill BS27 71 B1
Warrens Hill Rd BS27 71 D4
Warren St
Rockwell Green TA21 222 A4
3 Sidbrook TA2 169 B2

Warrens Way BA5 . . . . 113 A1
Warren The BA16 . . . . 207 A5
Warren Way DT9 . . . . 225 C5
Warres Rd TA2 . . . . 213 C8
Warrilow Cl BS22 . . . . 32 B5
Warrior Ave BA22 . . . . 218 B6
Warry Cl BS48 . . . . 9 B2
Warth La BS22 . . . . 32 A8
Warwick Ave TA6 . . . . 209 C3
Warwick Cl BS22 . . . . 49 C8
Warwick Gdns
Burnham-on-S TA8 . . . . 85 B1
Clutton BS39 . . . . 58 D3
Taunton TA1 . . . . 213 C2
Warwick Rd
3 Bath BA1 . . . . 44 B7
Keynsham BS31 . . . . 24 D4
Taunton TA2 . . . . 213 A8
(was BS22 . . . . 31 E1
WASHBROOK 89 A1
Washcross La TA19 . . . . . . 184 E3
WASHFORD 131 F4
Washford Cross TA23 . . . . . 131 F3
Washford Hill TA23 . . . . . . 202 A5
Washford Sta TA23 . . . . . . 131 E4
Washingpool DT9 . . . . 188 E7
Washing Pound La
Bristol BS14 . . . . 23 B4
Nailsea BS48 . . . . 8 B4
Washington Gdns TA6 . . . . 208 E5
Washington Terr TA20 . . . . 223 B5
Wash La TA15 . . . . 186 B4
Washpool La BA2 . . . . 43 F2
Wassail Cl 5 TA24 . . . . 131 A5
Wassail View TA2 . . . . 168 B4
Waste Dro BA5 . . . . 139 A4
WATCHET 202 B6
Watchet Boat Mus* TA23 . 202 C7
Watchet Sta TA23 . . . . 202 C7
WATCHFIELD 105 D2
Watch House Pl BS20 . . . . 2 E7
Watch House Rd BS20 . . . . . . 4 D4
Watchill Ave BS13 . . . . 21 F6
Watchill Cl BS13 . . . . 21 F6
Watchwell Dro BA6 . . . . . . 157 D7
Waterbridge Rd BS13 . . . . . 21 F4
Watercombe Hts BA20 . . . . 218 D2
Watercombe Pk BA20 . . . . 218 D3
Watercress Cl BS48 . . . . 9 B2
Waterfield Cl TA1 . . . . 212 B3
Waterfield Dr TA1 . . . . 212 B3
Waterford Beck BA14 . . . . . 83 F6
Waterford Cl TA6 . . . . 209 A2
Waterford Pk BA3 . . . . 78 E1
Waterfront Ho BA2 . . . . . . 228 B1
WATERGORE 220 B2
Water Hill TA4 . . . . 150 F7
Waterhouse La BA2 . . . . 63 F8
Water La
Bristol BS1 . . . . 227 B2
Butleigh BA6 . . . . 157 E4
Charlton Horethorne DT9 . . . 176 A2
Crowcombe TA4 . . . . 151 A7
Frome BA11 . . . . 119 E3
Horningsham BA12 . . . . 144 D4
Keenthorne TA5 . . . . 134 C1
Lopen TA13 . . . . 185 A1
Nether Stowey TA5 . . . . 134 A1
Paulton BA3, BS39 . . . . 78 A4
Pill BS20 . . . . 4 C4
Somerton TA11 . . . . 211 C3
Stogumber TA4 . . . . 150 F7
Waterlake DT10 . . . . 190 B4
Waterlake Rd TA20 . . . . . . 198 C8
Waterlands La TA18 . . . . . 224 C8
Waterleaze TA2 . . . . 213 D7
WATERLIP 142 A7
Waterlip BA4 . . . . 141 F7
Waterloo
Frome BA11 . . . . 119 F5
Puriton TA7 . . . . 136 C4
Waterloo Bldgs 4 BA2 . . . . 44 B6
Waterloo Cl TA7 . . . . 136 C4
Waterloo Cotts TA1 . . . . . 212 B4
Waterloo Cres DT9 . . . . . . 176 A1
Waterloo Ho BS20 . . . . 4 D5
Waterloo La
Stalbridge DT10 . . . . 190 A1
Yeovil BA20 . . . . 219 A4
Waterloo Pl 19 BS2 . . . . . . 227 C3
Waterloo Rd
Bristol BS2 . . . . 227 C3
Radstock BA3 . . . . 79 A2
Shepton Mallet BA4 . . . . 205 B7
Wellington TA21 . . . . 222 C6
Waterloo St
Bristol BS2 . . . . 227 C3
9 Bristol, Clifton BS8 . . . . . . 11 F7
Weston-super-Mare BS23 . . . 48 E8
Waterloo Terr DT9 . . . . . . 225 F4
Watermans Mdw TA6 . . . . . 208 E6
Watermead TA20 . . . . 198 D8
Watermead Cl 9 BA1 . . . . 228 B2
Water Path TA21 . . . . 222 A5
Waterpits TA5 . . . . 152 C4
WATERROW 165 F4
Waters Edge BS20 . . . . 2 E7
WATERSIDE 78 E1
Waterside Cres BA3 . . . . . . 78 D1
Waterside La BA3 . . . . 98 A6
Waterside Pk BS20 . . . . 1 D4
Waterside Rd
Radstock BA3 . . . . 78 D1
Wincanton BA9 . . . . 216 C4
Waterside Way BA3 . . . . 97 D8
Waters La BS27 . . . . 90 C8
Watersmeet Cl
Golsoncott TA23 . . . . 131 D1

Watersmeet Cl *continued*
Rooks Bridge BS26 . . . . 87 B5
Water St
Barrington TA19 . . . . 184 D5
Curry Rivel TA10 . . . . 171 C4
East Harptree BS40 . . . . 74 F4
East Lambrook TA13 . . . . . . 220 C8
Hambridge TA10 . . . . 171 D1
Lopen TA13 . . . . 185 A1
Martock TA12 . . . . 185 D5
Seavington St Michael TA19 . 184 E1
Watery Combe BA3 . . . . 94 E7
Watery La
Axminster EX13 . . . . 198 A3
Bath BA2 . . . . 44 A6
Broadway TA19 . . . . 194 B8
Charlton Horethorne DT9 . . . 176 C1
Clatworthy TA4 . . . . 149 C2
Coultings TA5 . . . . 134 E3
Doynton BS30 . . . . 12 A8
Halstock BA22 . . . . 197 D3
Hewish TA18 . . . . 195 D3
Langford Budville TA4, TA21 . 166 C2
Marshfield SN14 . . . . 13 F6
Minehead TA24 . . . . 200 F7
Nailsea BS48 . . . . 8 B2
North Petherton TA6 . . . . . . 153 E4
Spaxton TA5 . . . . 152 F4
Stogursey TA5 . . . . 134 C5
Stratton-on-t F BA3 . . . . 97 A3
Winford BS40 . . . . 38 B4
Watling St BA21 . . . . 218 D7
Watling Way BS11 . . . . 4 D7
Watsons La TA6 . . . . 209 A5
Watts Corner BA6 . . . . 206 F7
Watts La TA4 . . . . 151 E1
Watts's Quarry La TA10,
TA11 . . . . 173 A5
Watts's Rd TA7 . . . . 137 D8
Waveney Rd BS31 . . . . 25 A3
Wavering Down Rise BS26 70 A3
Waverley TA11 . . . . 211 C4
Waverley Cl
Frome BA11 . . . . 120 C6
Somerton TA11 . . . . 211 C4
Waverley Rd
Backwell BS48 . . . . 19 A7
Bridgwater TA6 . . . . 208 F6
Bristol, Shirehampton BS11 . . . 4 E6
Weston-super-Mare BS23 . . . 48 F4
Waverly Ct BS49 . . . . 34 D3
Waverney Cl TA1 . . . . 213 D3
Wayacre Dro BS24 . . . . 66 E6
Wayclose La BA9 . . . . 177 D5
Waycroft Acad BS14 . . . . 23 E5
Waydown Cross TA24 . . . . 130 A4
Waydown La TA24 . . . . 130 A4
Wayfarer Cl BS23 . . . . 49 B4
Wayfield Gdns BA1 . . . . 28 F4
WAYFORD 195 B1
Wayford Cl BS31 . . . . 25 A3
Wayford Hill TA18 . . . . 195 C1
Wayland Rd BS22 . . . . 31 E3
Waysdown La TA4 . . . . 149 D1
Wayside
Staplehay TA3 . . . . 181 D8
Weston-super-Mare BS22 . . . 31 D2
Wayside Cl BA11 . . . . 120 C6
Wayside Dr BS21 . . . . 6 E5
WAY WICK 32 E1
WCA Ho BS1 . . . . 227 A2
WEACOMBE 132 F3
Weacombe Rd
Bridgwater TA6 . . . . 209 C5
Taunton TA2 . . . . 212 F7
Weal Terr BA1 . . . . 27 B2
Weal The BA1 . . . . 27 C2
WEARE 88 E6
Weare CE Fst Sch BS26 . . . . 88 D7
Weare Ct BS1 . . . . 226 A1
We are Curious* BS1 . . . . . 226 C1
Weare Rd BS26 . . . . 88 E2
Weares La TA7 . . . . 137 D2
WEARNE 172 A7
Wearne Main Rd TA10 . . . . 172 A7
Weatherley Dr BS20 . . . . 1 F3
Weatherly Ave BA2 . . . . 44 D2
Weavers Cl
Crewkerne TA18 . . . . 224 D5
Shepton Mallet BA4 . . . . 205 D4
Weavers Ct BA11 . . . . 119 E3
Weavers Orch BA2 . . . . 62 D1
Weaver's Reach TA21 . . . . 222 B7
Weavers The BA11 . . . . 101 E4
Webber Rd BA4 . . . . 205 D4
Webbers TA4 . . . . 167 F7
Webbers CE Prim Sch
TA21 . . . . 178 F5
Webbers Cl TA21 . . . . 222 E4
Webbers Way TA7 . . . . 136 B4
WEBBINGTON 68 E4
Webbington Rd BS26 . . . . . . 69 C3
Webb's Cl BA5 . . . . 203 D3
Webb's Hill BA11 . . . . 119 B5
Webbs Mead
Beckington BA11 . . . . 101 E4
Chew Stoke BS40 . . . . 56 D8
Wedgwood Cl BS14 . . . . 23 B5
Wedgwood Rd BA2 . . . . 44 A5
Wedlakes TA23 . . . . 202 C6
Wedlands TA2 . . . . 212 F7
Wedlock Way BS3 . . . . 11 F3
WEDMORE 108 D3
Wedmore Cl
Bath BA2 . . . . 44 A3
Burnham-on-S TA8 . . . . 104 C8
Frome BA11 . . . . 120 C7
Weston-super-Mare BS23 . . . 48 F2

Wedmore Fst Sch BS28 . . . 108 B4
Wedmore Pk BA2 . . . . 44 A3
Wedmore Rd
Cheddar BS27 . . . . 90 A7
Clevedon BS21 . . . . 6 B1
Nailsea BS48 . . . . 18 E8
Saltford BS31 . . . . 25 D4
Weekesley La BA2 . . . . 60 D1
Weekes Mdw TA21 . . . . 179 E6
Week La TA22 . . . . 147 D4
WEEKMOOR 167 B3
Weekmoor La TA4 . . . . 167 B4
Weetwood Rd BS49 . . . . 34 E5
Weind The BS22 . . . . 31 D2
Weir Cl BS39 . . . . 77 D6
Weirfield Gn TA1 . . . . 212 D5
Weirfield Rd TA24 . . . . 201 A8
Weir Head Cotts TA22 . . . . 163 D7
Weir La
Abbots Leigh BS8 . . . . 10 F5
Marshfield SN14 . . . . 13 F8
Pilton BA4 . . . . 140 E3
Yeovilton BA22 . . . . 174 A1
Weir Rd BS49 . . . . 34 E3
Welbeck Rd BA21 . . . . 219 E7
WELHAM 160 A2
Welham TA11 . . . . 173 C7
Welland Cl TA1 . . . . 213 D4
Welland Rd
Keynsham BS31 . . . . 24 F4
Yeovil BA21 . . . . 219 D7
Wellard Cl 1 BS22 . . . . 32 B4
Well Cl
Long Ashton BS41 . . . . 11 B1
Weston-super-Mare BS24 . . . 49 B2
Winscombe BS25 . . . . 70 A8
Wellesley Ct TA1 . . . . 212 C1
Wellesley Gn BA10 . . . . 215 E6
Wellesley Park Prim Sch
TA21 . . . . 222 E4
Wellesley Pk TA21 . . . . 222 D4
Wellesley St TA2 . . . . 212 F6
Wellesley Way TA3 . . . . 192 A7
Wellfield Hill DT6, EX13 . . . 199 B2
Well House Cl BS9 . . . . 5 E3
Wellhouse La BA6 . . . . 206 F4
Wellings Cl TA20 . . . . 198 C8
WELLINGTON 222 D7
Wellington Bldgs BA1 . . . . . 27 B2
Wellington Com Hospl
TA21 . . . . 222 D5
Wellington Ct BS21 . . . . 6 C5
Wellington Flats BA20 . . . . 219 A4
Wellington Hill TA21 . . . . . 222 F2
Wellington Jun Sch TA21 . 222 E5
Wellington Mews BS11 . . . . . 4 D5
Wellington Monument*
TA21 . . . . 180 B4
Wellington Mus TA21 . . . . . 222 D6
Wellington New Rd TA1 . . 212 B3
Wellington Pl
Cheddar BS27 . . . . 90 B7
Weston-super-Mare BS23 . . . 48 D7
Wellington Rd
Bridgwater TA6 . . . . 209 B5
Bristol BS2 . . . . 227 C4
Taunton TA1 . . . . 212 D4
Wellington Sch TA21 . . . . . 222 E5
Wellington Sq TA24 . . . . . . 200 F7
Wellington Terr
18 Bristol BS8 . . . . 11 F6
Clevedon BS21 . . . . 6 D5
Wiveliscombe TA4 . . . . 210 C5
WELLISFORD 179 D8
Well La
Banwell BS29 . . . . 50 E3
Purse Caundle DT9 . . . . 189 D4
Timberscombe TA24 . . . . 130 A5
Yatton BS49 . . . . 34 C8
WELLOW 62 D1
Wellow Brook Ct BA3 . . . . . . 78 B3
Wellow Brook Mdw BA3 . . . 78 B2
Wellow Dr BA11 . . . . 120 C7
Wellow La
Hinton Charterhouse BA2 . . . 63 D1
Norton St Philip BA2 . . . . 81 D5
Peasedown St John BA2 . . . . . 79 C6
Shoscombe BA2 . . . . 79 E6
Wellow Mead BA2 . . . . 79 B7
Wellow Rd BA2 . . . . 80 B8
Wellow Tyning BA2 . . . . 79 D7
Well Pk BS49 . . . . 34 E4
WELLS 203 E4
Wells Cathedral* BA5 . . . . 203 E4
Wells Cathedral Jun Sch
BA5 . . . . 203 E5
Wells Cathedral Sch BA5 . 203 E5
Wells Central CE Jun Sch
BA5 . . . . 203 C3
Wells Cl
Bristol BS14 . . . . 23 C5
Burnham-on-S TA8 . . . . 104 C7
Nailsea BS48 . . . . 9 B1
Taunton TA2 . . . . 213 A8
Wellsea Gr BS23 . . . . 49 B7
Wellshead La TA24 . . . . 128 A3
Wells Hill Bottom BA5 . . . . 113 E7
Wells & Mendip Mus*
BA5 . . . . 203 E4
WELLSPRINGS 212 F8
Wellsprings Prim Sch
TA2 . . . . 212 F8
Wellsprings Rd TA2 . . . . . . 212 F7
Wells Rd
Bath BA2 . . . . 228 B1
Bristol BS14 . . . . 23 C7
Chilcompton BA3 . . . . 96 F4
Clevedon BS21 . . . . 6 D1

Wells Rd *continued*
Corston BA2 . . . . 43 B7
Dundry BS40, BS41 . . . . 38 F7
Glastonbury BA6 . . . . 206 E6
Glastonbury, Southway BA5,
BA6 . . . . 139 D4
Hallatrow BS39 . . . . 77 B7
Norton St Philip BA2, BA3 . . . . 81 C3
Priddy BA5 . . . . 92 E2
Radstock BA3 . . . . 78 E2
Rodney Stoke BS27 . . . . 91 B1
Shepton Mallet BA4 . . . . 204 E6
Theale BS28 . . . . 109 B1
Westbury-sub-Mendip BA5 . 110 E6
Wookey Hole BA5 . . . . 203 A7
Yarley BA5 . . . . 139 C8
Wells Road Trad Est BA6 . . 206 F7
Wells Sq BA3 . . . . 78 D1
Wellsway
Bath BA2 . . . . 44 F3
Keynsham BS31 . . . . 24 F3
Wells Way BS28 . . . . 107 F3
Wellsway Pk BA2 . . . . 62 D8
Wellsway Sch BS31 . . . . 25 A5
Well The TA21 . . . . 222 B5
Welsford Ave BA5 . . . . 203 C5
Welsford Cl BA5 . . . . 203 B5
Welsh Back BS1 . . . . 227 A2
Welsh Ct BA5 . . . . 203 B4
WELSHMILL 119 F6
Welshmill La BA11 . . . . 119 F5
Welshmill Rd BA11 . . . . 119 F5
WELTON 78 B2
Welton Gr BA3 . . . . 78 B3
WELTON HOLLOW 78 D2
Welton Prim Sch BA3 . . . . . . 78 C2
Welton Rd BA3 . . . . 78 E2
Welton Vale BA3 . . . . 78 B2
WEMBDON 208 C6
Wembdon Ct TA6 . . . . 208 E4
Wembdon Hill TA6 . . . . 208 C6
Wembdon Orch TA6 . . . . . . 208 C6
Wembdon Rd TA6 . . . . 208 E4
Wembdon Rise TA6 . . . . 208 D5
Wembdon St George's CE
Prim Sch TA6 . . . . 208 C6
Wemberham Cres BS49 . . . . 17 A1
Wemberham La BS49 . . . . . . 33 E8
Wendick Dro TA10 . . . . 171 E3
Wentwood Dr BS24 . . . . 49 A1
Wentworth Cl BS22 . . . . 32 A3
Wentworth Rd BA21 . . . . . . 219 E7
Werren Cl TA23 . . . . 202 B7
Wesley Ave BA3 . . . . 78 C1
Wesley Cl
Brean TA8 . . . . 65 F3
Frome BA11 . . . . 119 F4
Southwick BA14 . . . . 83 E2
Taunton TA1 . . . . 212 C1
Wanstrow BA4 . . . . 142 F4
Wesley Ct BS23 . . . . 48 F8
Wesley Dr BS22 . . . . 32 A3
Wesley La BA14 . . . . 83 E2
Wesley Mews BS27 . . . . 90 B7
Wesley Rd BA3 . . . . 78 D1
Wesley Slope 13 BA11 . . . . 119 F4
Wesley Villas
Coleford BA3 . . . . 116 F6
12 Frome BA11 . . . . 119 F4
Wessex Bldgs TA11 . . . . 211 B5
Wessex Bsns Ctr BS27 . . . . . 90 A7
Wessex Cl
Bridgwater TA6 . . . . 209 C4
Chard TA20 . . . . 223 C2
Street BA16 . . . . 207 D6
Wessex Ct 4 DT9 . . . . 225 D3
Wessex Dr DT9 . . . . 187 E1
Wessex Fields BA11 . . . . . . 119 D2
Wessex Fields Ret Pk
BA11 . . . . 119 D2
Wessex Ho 10 BS2 . . . . 227 C3
Wessex Pk TA11 . . . . 211 B5
Wessex Rd
Stalbridge DT10 . . . . 190 C4
Taunton TA1 . . . . 168 E1
Weston-super-Mare BS24 . . . 49 B2
Yeovil BA21 . . . . 218 D8
Wessex Rise TA11 . . . . 211 E3
Wessex Way BA9 . . . . 216 B3
Westacre BA16 . . . . 207 A4
Westacre Cl BS27 . . . . 90 B8
Westacre Rd SP8 . . . . 90 B8
WEST ANSTEY 162 C6
West Anstey School Cross
EX36 . . . . 162 C5
West Approach Rd TA7 . . . 136 D4
West Ave
Bath BA2 . . . . 44 C5
Highbridge TA9 . . . . 104 C4
Westaway Cl BS49 . . . . 34 C7
Westaway Pk BS49 . . . . 34 D7
WEST BAGBOROUGH 151 F4
West Bagborough Rd TA4 152 A4
West Bank BA5 . . . . 203 A8
Westbourne Ave
Clevedon BS21 . . . . 6 B2
Keynsham BS31 . . . . 24 E5
Westbourne Cl BA20 . . . . . 218 E5
Westbourne Cres BS21 . . . . . 6 B2
Westbourne Gr BA20 . . . . . 218 E5
Westbourne Ho BA2 . . . . . . 228 C2
Westbourne Pl BS8 . . . . 226 B3
WEST BOURTON 177 E8
West Bourton Rd SP8 . . . . 177 E8
West Bower La TA5 . . . . . . 153 C7
West Bow Ho TA6 . . . . 208 E4
WEST BRADLEY 158 C7
Westbridge Pk DT9 . . . . 225 B2

West Brook BA21 . . . . 218 D6
Westbrook Ct BA4 . . . . 141 E1
Westbrooke Ct BS1 . . . . . . 226 A1
Westbrook Pk BA1 . . . . 27 A2
Westbrook Rd
Bristol BS4 . . . . 23 D8
Evercreech BA4 . . . . 141 E1
Weston-super-Mare BS22 . . . 31 D1
Westbrook Vale BA4 . . . . . 141 E1
WEST BUCKLAND 180 F7
West Buckland Com Prim Sch
TA21 . . . . 180 F7
West Buckland Rd TA21 . . 180 D7
Westbury
Bradford Abbas DT9 . . . . 187 E1
Sherborne DT9 . . . . 225 D3
Westbury Court Rd BS9 . . . . . 5 F7
Westbury Cres BS23 . . . . 48 F2
Westbury Dro
Priddy BA5 . . . . 92 A3
Westbury Beacon BA5 . . . . . . 91 F2
Westbury Gdns BA22 . . . . . 186 C2
Westbury La BS9 . . . . 5 C7
WESTBURY ON TRYM 5 F7
WESTBURY-SUB-
MENDIP 110 D6
Westbury Terr
Dunkerton BA2 . . . . 61 E5
2 Sherborne DT9 . . . . 225 D3
Westbury View BA2 . . . . 79 E8
WEST CAMEL 174 D3
West Camel Farm BA22 . . . 174 E3
West Camel Rd BA22 . . . . . 174 E3
West Charlton TA11 . . . . . . 173 E7
WEST CHINNOCK 196 B8
West Chinnock CE Prim Sch
TA18 . . . . 196 B8
West Cl
Bath BA2 . . . . 44 A5
Dunster TA24 . . . . 201 D2
WEST COKER 197 A8
West Coker CE Prim Sch
BA22 . . . . 197 A8
West Coker Rd BA20 . . . . . 218 E2
WESTCOMBE
Batcombe 142 B2
Somerton 172 E7
Westcombe BA8 . . . . 176 E1
Westcombe Hill BA4 . . . . . 142 C2
Westcombe Rd
Evercreech BA4 . . . . 141 F2
Westcombe BA4 . . . . 142 A2
Westcombes EX13 . . . . 198 B7
Westcombe Stables La
BA4 . . . . 142 B2
Westcombe Trad Est
TA19 . . . . 183 E1
WEST COMPTON 204 C3
West Compton La BA4 . . . . 204 E3
West Coombe
Bristol BS9 . . . . 5 D6
Yeovil BA21 . . . . 218 D6
West Coombe La TA4 . . . . . 165 D8
West Cornmoor Dro TA9 . . 136 D7
Westcott Cl BA11 . . . . 120 C6
Westcott Cross TA23 . . . . . 130 D1
Westcott La TA4 . . . . 148 F2
Westcott Mead TA24 . . . . . 128 E1
West Cotts TA24 . . . . 127 A2
West Cres TA19 . . . . 221 B2
West Croft
Blagdon BS40 . . . . 54 E2
Clevedon BS21 . . . . 6 B2
West Ct
Horrington BA5 . . . . 112 F1
Portishead BS20 . . . . 2 D4
Templecombe BA8 . . . . 176 E1
West Dene BS9 . . . . 5 E6
West Dro TA7 . . . . 137 D4
West Dundry La BS41 . . . . . . 21 E2
WEST END
Blagdon 54 E3
Chewton Mendip 93 F6
Clevedon 6 B2
Frome 119 F5
Nailsea 17 F7
Somerton 211 C3
West End
Bristol BS3 . . . . 226 C1
Bristol, Kingsdown BS2 . . . . 227 A4
Frome BA11 . . . . 119 F5
Lower Weare BS26 . . . . 88 D8
Marston Magna BA22 . . . . . . 174 E1
Somerton TA11 . . . . 211 C4
Street BA16 . . . . 207 B5
Wedmore BS28 . . . . 108 C3
West End Cl
Somerton TA11 . . . . 211 C4
South Petherton TA13 . . . . . . 220 B4
West End Ct
Chedzoy TA7 . . . . 136 D1
South Petherton TA13 . . . . . . 220 B4
West End Farm Cvn Pk
BS24 . . . . 49 E4
West End La BS48 . . . . 18 A8
Westend La N BA11 . . . . . . 143 C6
West End Trad Est BS48 . . . . . 8 B1
West End View
Barrington TA19 . . . . 184 C5
South Petherton TA13 . . . . . . 220 B4
West End Way TA13 . . . . . . 220 B4
Westerkirk Gate TA2 . . . . . 212 C7
Westerleigh Rd
Bath BA2 . . . . 45 B1
Clevedon BS21 . . . . 6 B2

Westerly Ct TA19 221 B4
Western Approaches BA22 174 A2
Western Ave BA21 218 B6
Western Ct
Clevedon BS21 6 D3
Shepton Mallet BA4 205 B6
Western Dr BS14 22 E6
Western Gate TA10 172 C7
Western La
East Quantoxhead TA5 133 A5
Minehead TA24 200 F7
Ridge BS40 74 C3
Western Retreat BA5 203 B5
Western St DT9 187 E4
Western Way
Bridgwater TA6 208 F7
Winsham TA20 194 E1
Westex Ho BS23 49 B5
West Farm La TA20 194 D5
WESTFIELD 97 C8
Westfield
Bruton BA10 215 D5
Clevedon BS21 16 D8
Curry Rivel TA10 171 C3
Shepton Mallet BA4 205 A6
Sherborne DT9 225 B2
Westfield Acad BA21 218 E6
Westfield Ave BA21 218 E6
Westfield Cl
Backwell BS48 19 A6
Bath BA2 44 E3
Bridgwater TA6 208 E4
Burnham-on-S TA8 104 B8
Keynsham BS31 24 C5
Weston-super-Mare BS23 48 D2
West Field Cl TA1 212 A2
Westfield Cres
Banwell BS29 51 A3
Yeovil BA21 218 F6
Westfield Ct TA8 104 B8
Westfield Dr
Backwell BS48 19 A6
Burnham-on-S TA8 104 B8
Westfield Gr BA21 218 F6
Westfield Ho
Bath BA2 44 E3
Bridgwater TA6 208 E4
Westfield Ind & Trad Est BA3 97 C7
Westfield La
Curry Rivel TA10 171 C3
Draycott BS27 90 E3
North Curry TA3 170 C3
Rodney Stoke BS27 110 C8
Street BA6, BA16 207 E2
West Field Lawn TA8 104 B8
Westfield Pk BA1 44 A7
Westfield Pk S BA1 44 A7
Westfield Pl
Bristol BS8 11 F7
Yeovil BA21 218 E6
Westfield Prim Sch BA3 97 C8
Westfield Rd
Backwell BS48 19 A6
Banwell BS29 51 A3
Burnham-on-S TA8 104 B8
Frome BA11 119 D3
Wells BA5 203 C4
Weston-super-Mare BS23 48 D2
Yeovil BA21 218 F6
Westfields TA19 184 C5
Westfield S BA12 161 F2
Westfield Terr BA3 78 D1
WESTFORD 179 F7
Westford Cl TA21 222 A5
Westford Ct TA21 222 A5
Westford Dr TA21 222 A5
West Garston BS29 51 A3
Westgate BS1 226 B1
Westgate Bldgs BA1 228 B2
Westgate St
Bath BA1 228 B2
4 Taunton TA1 212 E3
Westhall Rd BA1 44 D7
WESTHAM 107 C2
WEST HARPTREE 74 E6
West Harptree Rd BS40 74 F5
WEST HATCH 182 E7
West Hatch La TA3 182 F8
Westhaven Cl BS48 19 A6
Westhaven Sch BS23 48 D2
WESTHAY 138 A5
Westhay Broad Dro TA7 137 E6
Westhay Cross EX13 198 F3
Westhay Moor Dro BA5, BA6 138 D6
Westhay Rd BA6 138 C4
West Hay Rd BS40 35 C3
West Hendford BA20 218 F3
West Henley Rd TA10 156 A2
WEST HEWISH 33 A5
WEST HILL
Nailsea 9 A5
Portishead 2 A5
Wincanton 216 B4
West Hill
Milborne Port DT9 217 D2
Nailsea BS48 9 A5
Portishead BS20 2 B5
Wincanton BA9 216 B4
West Hill Ct BS20 2 C6
WEST HILL GARDENS 78 E1
Westhill Gdns BS20 2 C5
West Hill Gdns
Radstock BA3 78 D1
Radstock BA3 78 E1
Westhill La TA9 105 C2
West Hill Rd BA3 78 D1
Westholm Rd TA11 211 B4
WEST HUNTSPILL 136 A7
West Huntspill Com Prim Sch TA9 104 C1
West La
Alhampton BA4 159 C5
Alweston DT9 189 A2
Barrington TA13 184 F5
Croscombe BA5 140 F8
Felton BS40 37 C8
Lynford-on-F TA11 158 D2
Sherborne DT9 188 F1
Westlake Cl TA7 155 C2
WEST LAMBROOK 184 F5
Westland Rd BA20 218 F4
Westlands Distribution Pk BS24 49 B3
West Lea Rd BA1 27 A1
West Leaze BA16 207 B6
WESTLEIGH 179 A4
WEST LEIGH 150 F1
Westleigh Gdns BA4 205 A6
West Leigh Inf Sch BS48 19 A6
Westleigh Pk BS14 23 B8
Westleigh Rd TA1 213 B3
Westley Mews BS24 32 C1
West Links BS23 48 D2
West Links Cl BS22 31 B3
West Littleton Rd SN14 13 F8
West Lodge BA4 205 A5
WEST LUCCOMBE 124 C3
West Luccombe Rd
Luccombe TA24 123 C2
Luccombe TA24 129 C8
WEST LYDFORD 158 C2
WEST LYNG 170 B7
West Lynne BS27 90 B8
West Mall BS8 11 F7
Westmans Est TA8 104 C7
Westmarch Way BS22 32 A4
Westmead BA3 96 D3
Westmead Gdns BA1 27 A2
West Mendip Com Hospl BA6 139 D3
Westmere Cres TA8 104 C8
West Mill La
Marnhull DT10 190 D6
Sherborne DT9 225 C2
Westminster BA21 218 C7
Westminster Bldgs DT10 190 B4
Westminster Cotts DT10 190 B4
Westminster St BA20 219 A4
Westminster Way TA6 136 B2
Westminster Wy TA6 209 C8
WEST MONKTON 169 C7
West Monkton CE Prim Sch TA2 213 F8
Westmoor Dro
Hambridge TA10, TA12 184 E7
Knapp TA3 169 F4
Westmoor La TA10 184 D8
Westmoreland Dr BA2 228 A2
Westmoreland Rd BA2 228 A1
Westmoreland St BA2 228 A2
Westmoreland Station Rd BA2 228 A1
WEST MUDFORD 187 C7
West Mudford Rd BA22 187 C7
WEST NEWTON 169 F8
WESTON 27 B1
Weston All Saints CE Prim Sch BA1 27 A2
WESTON BAMPFYLDE 175 B3
Weston Bampfylde Rd BA22 175 B3
Weston Bsns Pk BS24 49 E5
Weston Cl
Bristol BS9 5 C7
East Chinnock BA22 196 E8
Weston Coll BS48 8 E2
Weston College BS23 48 D8
Weston Coll South West Skills Campus BS22 49 C8
Weston Coll Uni Campus BS23 48 F2
Weston Ct BS24 49 B3
Weston Dro BS20 7 F8
Weston Euro Pk BS24 49 B4
Weston Express Bsns Pk BS22 49 C6
Weston Farm La BA1 27 C2
Weston Gateway Tourist Pk BS24 32 C1
Weston General Hospl BS23 48 E2
Weston Hill SP8 177 D3
Westonia BS22 31 E2
Westonian Ct BS9 5 C4
Weston Ind Est BS24 49 B2
WESTON IN GORDANO 1 F1
Weston La
Bath BA1 44 C8
Christon BS26 68 C7
East Coker BA22 197 E5
Halstock DT2 196 F1
Weston Lock Ret BA2 44 C6
Weston Lodge BS23 48 D8
Weston Milton Sta BS22 49 C7
Weston Miniature Rly* BS23 48 D5
WESTON PARK 27 C1
Weston Park Ct BA1 27 D1
Weston Pk BA1 27 C1
Weston Pk E BA1 27 D1
Weston Pk W BA1 27 C1
Weston Rd
Bath BA1 44 D8
Brean TA8 66 A5
Congresbury BS49 34 B5
East Brent BS24, TA9 86 D6
Failand BS8 10 C3
Long Ashton BS41 20 D8
Weston Ret Pk BS23 49 A6
Weston St
Buckhorn Weston SP8 177 D3
East Chinnock BA22 196 E8
WESTON-SUPER-MARE 48 B7
Weston-super-Mare Sta BS23 48 E7
WESTON TOWN 142 E5
Weston Town BA4 141 E1
Weston Way BS24 49 F2
Weston Wlk BA11 119 C6
Weston Wood Rd BS20 2 C3
WESTONZOYLAND 154 E5
Westonzoyland Prim Sch
Bussex TA6 153 F6
Westonzoyland TA7 154 F5
Westonzoyland Pumping Sta* TA7 154 D3
Westonzoyland Rd TA6, TA7 209 E4
Westover
Frome BA11 119 D4
Nunney BA11 143 B7
Westover Ct BA11 119 D4
Westover Gdns BS9 5 F8
Westover Gn TA6 208 E4
Westover Green Com Sch TA6 208 E4
Westover La
Crewkerne TA18 224 B7
Martock TA12 185 F8
Westover Rd BS9 5 F8
Westover's Cnr BS28 108 B4
Westover Trad Est TA10 171 F5
Westover View TA18 224 C7
WESTOWE 151 A3
Westowe Hill TA4 151 A3
West Par BS9 5 C7
Westpark TA21 180 D7
Westpark TA21 180 D7
Westpark 26 TA21 180 D7
West Park Cl TA24 200 E7
WEST PENNARD 140 B1
West Pennard CE Prim Sch BA6 140 B1
West Pk
Bristol BS8 226 B4
Butleigh BA6 157 E4
Castle Cary BA7 214 B6
Minehead TA24 200 E7
Yeovil BA20 218 F5
WEST PORLOCK 123 F4
WESTPORT 184 C7
Westport La TA3, TA10 184 B7
West Port Lodge Rd TA20 194 D2
WEST QUANTOXHEAD 132 E4
West Quay TA6 208 F5
West Rd
East Brent BS24, TA9 86 B7
Lympsham BS24 67 B1
Midsomer Norton BA3 78 A3
Wiveliscombe TA4 210 B4
Yatton BS49 34 B7
Westridge DT9 225 C3
Westridge Way TA4 167 E7
West Rocke Ave BS9 5 D6
West Rolstone Rd BS24 33 A1
West Sedgemoor Nature Reserve* TA3 170 F3
West Sedgemoor Rd TA3 170 D3
WEST SHEPTON 205 A4
West Shepton BA4 205 A5
West Somerset Com Coll The TA24 201 B5
West Somerset Community College Farm TA24 201 D4
West Somerset Railway* TA4 150 F7
West Somerset Rly* TA4 151 C4
West Somerset Rural Life Mus* TA24 124 C4
West St
Ashcott TA7 156 B8
Axbridge BS26 70 B2
Bampton EX16 164 B1
Banwell BS29 51 A3
Banwell BS29 51 B3
Bishops Lydeard TA4 167 E8
Bridgwater TA6 208 E4
Bristol BS2 227 C3
Carhampton TA24 131 B4
Crewkerne TA18 224 B6
Dunster TA24 201 D1
Hinton St George TA17 195 C7
Ilchester BA22 173 E1
Ilminster TA19 221 B4
Kington Magna SP8 177 E1
Martock TA12 185 E8
Minehead TA24 200 E6
Seavington St Mary TA19 184 D1
Somerton TA11 211 D4
South Petherton TA13 220 B4
Stoke sub Hamdon TA14 185 E3
Templecombe BA8 189 E8
Watchet TA23 202 B7
Wells BA5 203 C3
Weston-super-Mare BS23 48 D8
Wiveliscombe TA4 210 C4
Yarlington BA9 175 F7
West St continued
Yeovil BA20 218 F4
WEST STOKE 185 E4
WEST STOUGHTON 107 E6
West Terr BA2 82 C1
WEST TOWN
Backwell 18 F5
Baltonsborough 157 F6
Ubley 55 B6
West Town Gr BS4 23 D8
West Town La
Baltonsborough BA6 157 F5
Bristol BS4, BS14 23 C8
West Town Pk BS4 23 D8
West Town Rd
Backwell BS48 19 A5
Bristol BS11 4 C7
West Tyning BA2 42 B1
Westview BS39 77 C5
West View
Creech St Michael TA3 169 D5
Long Sutton TA10 172 E4
Milborne Port DT9 217 D3
Queen Camel BA22 174 F4
South Cadbury BA22 175 D4
West Monkton TA2 169 D8
West View Cl TA7 155 B4
Westview Orch BA3 64 B5
West View Rd
Batheaston BA1 29 A3
Keynsham BS31 24 E5
West Villas TA4 167 F6
Westville BA21 219 C5
Westward BS41 11 B2
Westward Cl BS40 35 D2
Westward Dr BS20 4 C4
Westward Gdns BS41 11 B2
Westward Rd BS13 21 F7
Westway
Nailsea BS48 8 E2
Street BA16 207 B6
West Way BS21 6 C3
Westway Ctr BA11 119 F5
Westway La BA4 205 B4
West Ways BA22 196 E8
West Well La BS28 109 C1
WEST WICK 32 C1
West Wick BS24 32 C1
West Wick Rdbt BS22, BS24 50 B8
WESTWOOD 64 E3
Westwood BA2 45 E6
Westwood Ave BS39 59 C2
Westwood Cl 2 BS22 31 F2
Westwood Cotts BA8 176 E1
Westwood Dr BA11 119 C4
Westwood Dro TA11 158 C3
WEST WOODLANDS 143 F6
Westwood Rd
Bridgwater TA6 209 D7
Bristol BS4 23 D8
Westwoods BA1 29 B3
Westwood with Iford Prim Sch BA15 64 F3
West Yeo Rd TA7 154 F1
Wetherell Pl BS8 226 B3
Wet La BS27 90 F2
Wetlands La BS20 2 C3
Wetlands & Willows Visitor Ctr* TA3 170 D5
Wetmoor La
Langport TA10 172 C2
Westbury-sub-Mendip BA5 110 E1
Wexford Rd BS4 22 D8
WEYCROFT 198 B2
Weycroft Ave EX13 198 A2
Weylands BA11 119 E6
Weymont Cl TA7 155 B3
Weymouth Ct BA1 45 B8
Weymouth Rd
Evercreech BA4 141 E1
Frome BA11 119 E4
Weymouth St BA1 45 B8
Whaddon Hill BA10 160 C7
Whaites Dr TA19 221 A5
Wharf Cotts TA21 222 B8
Wharf Ho TA19 221 B4
Wharf La
Ilminster TA19 221 B3
Portbury BS20 3 B5
Wharf Rd BS24 49 B4
Wharfside BS24 66 E3
Wharnecliffe Cl BS14 23 B5
Wharnecliffe Gdns BS14 23 B5
Whatcombe Rd BA11 119 E6
Whatcombe Terr BA11 119 E6
WHATLEY
Frome 118 D4
Winsham 194 C1
Whatley TA10 171 F5
Whatley Cross TA20 194 C1
Whatley La
Buckland St Mary TA20 192 D7
Langport TA10 172 A5
Tatworth TA20 194 C1
Winsham TA20 199 A8
Whatley Mews TA10 171 F5
Whatley Vineyard & Herb Gdn* BA11 118 D4
Wheatear Rd BS49 16 F2
Wheatfield Dr BS22 32 A5
Wheatfield La BA3 95 A6
Wheathill Cl
Keynsham BS31 24 D5
Milborne Port DT9 217 D2
Wheathill La DT9 217 E3
Wheathill Rd TA11 158 E2
Wheathill Way DT9 217 D2
Wheatleigh Cl TA1 212 E2
Wheatley Cres TA1 213 B5
Wheatsheaf La
Burnett BA2 42 C6
Stone Allerton BS26 88 D3
Wheatstones 10 TA4 167 F8
WHEDDON CROSS 129 E1
Wheeler Gr BA5 203 B4
Wheelers Cl BA3 78 D2
Wheelers Dr BA3 78 C2
WHEELER'S HILL 78 C2
Wheelers Rd BA3 78 D2
Wheel House La TA20 199 B7
Wheel La TA12 185 A6
Whellers Mdw TA12 185 E7
Whetham Mill Cross DT8 199 F5
Whetham Mill La DT8 199 F6
Whetstones Almshouses TA19 183 F4
Whimbrel Ave 2 BS20 2 F6
WHIPCOTT 179 B5
Whippington Ct BS1 227 B3
Whirligg La 15 TA14 185 F4
Whirligig La TA1 212 F4
Whirligig Pl 7 TA1 212 F4
Whistley La BS40 74 F6
Whitaker Rd BA2 45 A2
Whitbourne Moor BA12 144 E8
WHITBOURNE SPRINGS 144 F7
Whitbourne Springs BA12 144 F7
Whitchey Dro TA9 137 A5
WHITCHURCH 23 D4
Whitchurch District Ctr BS14 23 A5
Whitchurch La
Bristol, Bishopsworth BS13 22 B5
Bristol, Hartcliffe BS13 22 C5
Bristol, Whitchurch BS14 22 E5
Dundry BS41 22 C1
Henstridge BA8 190 A7
Yenston BA8 189 F8
Whitchurch Prim Sch BS14 23 C4
Whitchurch Rd BS13 22 A6
Whitchurch Trad Est BS14 22 F5
WHITCOMBE 175 D2
Whitcombe Farm La DT9 175 D2
Whitcross 10 BA22 197 F8
White Ash La TA20 193 A5
WHITE BALL 179 D6
Whitebeam Cl TA6 209 D5
Whitebrook La BA2 79 A8
Whitebrook Terr TA21 178 F5
White Cats Cotts BA8 176 E3
Whitechapel La BA11 101 C1
Whitecroft TA4 202 E4
WHITECROSS 171 E3
WHITE CROSS
Bishop Sutton 57 E1
Burnham-on-Sea 105 B8
Hallatrow 76 F6
Zeals 161 F3
White Cross
Brent Knoll TA9 105 C8
Exford TA24 128 B1
White Cross BS39 76 F6
Whitecross Ave BS14 23 C6
White Cross Gate BS39 76 F6
Whitecross La
Banwell BS29 51 A4
Minehead TA24 200 E7
Whitecross Rd
East Harptree BS40 74 F4
Weston-super-Mare BS23 48 E6
Whitecross Way TA24 200 E7
Whitedown Cross EX15 191 B4
WHITEFIELD 210 B8
Whitefield Cl BA1 29 B4
White field Cross EX36 162 D3
Whitefield La TA19 184 D4
Whitefield Rocks TA4 150 B1
WHITE GATE 194 B1
Whitegate Cl
Bleadon BS24 67 B6
Minehead TA24 201 A6
Whitegate Rd TA24 201 A6
Whitegates Gdns TA24 200 F6
WHITEHALL 180 A1
Whitehall
Taunton TA1 212 F5
Watchet TA23 202 B7
Whitehall Cl TA13 220 D4
Whitehall Ct TA18 224 C7
Whitehall Rd TA6 136 B2
White Hart La TA21 222 D6
WHITE HILL 79 F6
White Hill
Langport TA10 172 A7
Shoscombe BA2 79 F6
White Hill Dro TA20 193 C5
Whitehole Hill BA3 116 E4
White Horse Dr BA11 120 C6
White Horse La BS28 138 D8
White Horse Rd BA15 64 E7
Whitehouse Ctr (PRU) BS13 22 C5
Whitehouse La
Litton BA3 75 D3
Wraxall BS48 9 A6
White House La
East Huntspill TA9 136 E7
Loxton BS26 68 A3
Whitehouse Rd BS49 34 F8
White House Rd TA5, TA6 135 D5
WHITELACKINGTON 184 C2
Whiteladies Rd BS8 226 B4
Whitelands Hill BA3 79 B3
Whiteleaze La
Thurloxton TA2 153 C1
West Monkton TA2 169 D8

White Lodge Pk BS20 2 D6
White Mead BA21 218 D6
Whitemill La BA11 119 C3
Whitemoor Hill TA20 194 C4
Whitemoor La TA4 150 F3
Whitemore Ct BA1 29 A4
Whiteoak Way BS48 18 D8
White Oxmead La BA2 61 E1
White Ox Mead La BA2 61 F1
White Post
Midsomer Norton BA3 97 B6
Twitchen EX36 145 K2
Whitepost Gate DT9 188 D6
Whites Cl TA6 208 E2
White's Dro BA5 138 F7
Whitesfield Ct BS48 8 D2
Whitesfield Rd BS48 8 D1
White's La TA4 133 A1
Whitesome's Dro BS27 109 C6
White St
Bristol BS5 227 C4
Creech St Michael TA3 169 E4
Horningsham BA12 144 E4
North Curry TA3 170 C4
WHITESTAUNTON 193 B5
Whitestaunton Cross
TA20 193 B5
Whitestone Rd BA11 120 B6
Whitestown La BS40 73 E3
Whitewall Cnr TA3 181 D2
WHITEWAY 44 A4
Whiteway TA20 193 E6
Whiteway Rd BA2 44 A3
Whitewell Pl BA11 119 E3
Whitewell Rd BA11 119 E3
Whitewells Rd BA1 28 A2
Whitewick La TA5 134 F8
Whitfield Rd TA6 209 D6
Whitford Hill
Corfe TA3 182 A4
Pitminster TA3 181 F5
Whitford La TA3 182 A4
Whithys The BA16 207 C7
Whiting Cl BA4 205 C4
Whiting La 1 TA6 153 E3
Whiting Rd
Bristol BS13 22 A4
Glastonbury BA6 206 F5
Whiting Way BA5 203 D4
Whitland Ave BS13 22 B5
Whitland Rd BS13 22 B5
WHITLEY BATTS 40 F2
Whitley La BA16 156 D7
Whitley Rd TA7, BA16 156 C8
Whitling St BS40 38 A2
Whitmead Gdns BS13 22 C4
Whitmore La TA2 212 D8
Whitmore Rd TA2 212 E8
WHITNAGE 178 C2
Whitnage La EX16 178 C2
WHITNELL 134 D2
Whitnell Cnr BA5 113 F6
Whitnell La
Binegar BA3 114 B8
Keenthorne TA5 134 D2
Whitney Cres BS24 49 C5
Whitney Hill TA19 193 F8
Whitson Ho 1 BS2 227 C3
Whitson St BS1 227 A4
Whitstone BA4 205 C5
Whitstone Cl BA4 205 C6
Whitstone Cnr BA4 205 D1
Whitstone Ct BA4 205 D5
Whitstone Hill BA4 204 C1
Whitstone La BA4 205 E1
Whitstone Rd BA4 205 D4
Whitstone Rise BA4 205 D4
Whitswood Steep TA24 130 D4
Whittakers Ho 6 BA4 205 B6
Whitting Rd BS23 48 E4
Whittington Dr BS22 31 D2
Whittock Rd BS14 23 D6
Whittock Sq BS14 23 D7
Whittox La BA11 119 E5
Whitwell Rd BS14 23 B8
Whitworth Rd
Frome BA11 119 F2
Minehead TA24 200 D7
WICK
Burnham-on-Sea 85 E8
Glastonbury 139 E2
Stogursey 134 D7
Wick TA10 171 E5
Wicketsbeer Rd BA22 197 C6
Wickfield BS21 6 C1
Wickham Ct BS21 6 C3
Wickham Rise BA11 119 F6
Wickham's Cross or Beggar's Grave BA6 157 C3
Wickham Way
East Brent TA9 86 D4
Shepton Mallet BA4 205 A6
Wick Hill
Charlton Horethorne DT9 176 A1
Milborne Port DT9 217 B6
Wickhill Rd TA10 171 D5
Wick Hollow BA6 206 F5
Wick House Cl BS31 25 D3
Wick La
Burnham-on-S TA9 85 E6
Glastonbury BA6 139 E2
Lympsham BS24 66 E1
Norton Fitzwarren TA2 168 A6
Peasedown St John BA2, BA3 60 F1
Pensford BS39 40 D3
Upton Cheyney BS30 26 A8
WICKLANE 61 A1
Wicklow Rd BS4 22 E8
Wickmoor TA3 171 D6
Wick Moor Dro TA5 134 C7
Wick Oath Rd TA10 171 E6
Wick Pound TA5 134 D7
Wick Rd
Bishop Sutton BS39 57 C3
Lympsham BS24 66 D2
Milborne Port DT9 217 C4
Wick St Lawrence BS22 32 B7
WICK ST LAWRENCE 32 B7
WIDCOMBE 45 C4
Widcombe BS14 23 A6
Widcombe CE Jun Sch
BA2 45 B5
Widcombe Cres BA2 45 B5
Widcombe Hill BA2 45 C4
Widcombe Inf Sch BA2 45 B5
Widcombe Par BA2 228 C1
Widcombe Rise BA2 45 B5
Widcombe Terr BA2 45 B5
Wideatts Rd BS27 90 A7
Widmore Gr BS13 22 B5
Widness Dro TA3 170 C2
WIGBOROUGH 220 F1
Wigeon Cl TA24 201 C5
Wight Row BS20 2 F6
Wigmore Gdns BS22 31 D2
Wiindsor Cres TA20 223 B3
Wilbye Gr BS4 22 D7
Wildcountry La BS48 20 E6
Wilde Cl TA8 104 C6
Wilder Ct BS2 227 B4
Wilderness Dro BA16 138 E2
Wilderness The 9 DT9 225 E4
Wilder St BS2 227 B4
Wildmoor La TA21 180 F6
Wild Oak Ho TA3 168 D1
Wild Oak La TA3 168 D1
Wilfred Rd TA1 213 A4
Wilfrid Rd BA16 207 D6
Wilkins Cl TA20 223 E4
Wilkins Rd TA6 209 D5
WILKINTHROOP 176 C2
WILLAND 191 E8
Willan Pl BS24 32 C1
Willcocks Cl 6 TA21 222 D5
Willcox Cl BA6 206 E5
Willet Cl TA9 104 D3
Willet's La BA3 94 D6
WILLETT 150 E4
Willett Hill Cross TA4 150 D5
Willey Rd TA3 170 E6
WILLHAYNE 223 A8
William Daw Cl BS29 50 F3
William Jessop Wy BS14 22 E4
William Reynolds Ho
BA16 207 D7
William St
Bath BA2 228 C3
Taunton TA2 212 F6
Williamstowe BA2 45 C1
William's Yd BS40 38 A7
Willie Gill Ct TA1 212 E4
Willinton Rd BS4 22 F8
Willis Hay DT9 225 D3
Willis Rd BA2 45 B2
Willis's La TA18 196 C4
WILLITON 202 D3
Williton Com Hospl TA4 202 D3
Williton Cres BS23 48 F3
Williton Ind Est TA4 202 E4
Williton Sta TA4 202 F4
Will La TA4 151 A3
Willmott Cl BS14 22 F3
Willmotts Cl TA7 137 B2
Willoughby Cl BS13 22 B7
Willoughby Pl TA20 223 D3
Willoughby Rd TA6 208 C4
Willowbank TA24 130 B4
Willow Cl
Bath BA2 62 E8
Clevedon BS21 6 E3
East Huntspill TA9 136 E7
Frome BA11 119 E3
Langport TA10 172 A6
Long Ashton BS41 10 F1
Portishead BS20 2 C4
Radstock BA3 78 E2
Taunton TA1 213 D1
Weston-super-Mare, St Georges
BS22 32 D2
Weston-super-Mare, Uphill
BS23 48 E2
Westonzoyland TA7 154 E5
Williton TA4 202 E3
Willow Ct TA6 209 D5
Willowdown BS22 31 E4
Willowdown Prim Acad
TA6 209 C8
Willow Dr
Bleadon BS24 67 C6
Hutton BS24 49 E2
Shepton Mallet BA4 205 A6
Weston-super-Mare BS24 49 E5
Willowfalls BA1 28 E3
Willow Gdns BS22 32 D2
Willow Gn
Bath BA2 44 D4
Chedzoy TA7 154 D8
Willow Gr TA23 131 E4
Willow Ho BS13 22 D4
Willow La EX15 180 F2
Willow Rd
Street BA16 207 B3
Yeovil BA21 218 F6
Willows The
Brent Knoll TA9 86 A2
Nailsea BS48 8 F3
Willow The BA3 96 F2
Willow Tree Cl BA22 174 A4
Willow Vale BA11 119 F5
Willow Way TA18 224 D7
Willow Wlk
Bridgwater TA6 209 C4
Keynsham BS31 24 D4
Wills Ind Est TA6 209 A4
Wills Rd TA6 208 F1
Wills Way BS4 22 D6
Willway St BS2 227 C3
WILMINGTON 43 A1
Wilmington Hill
Englishcombe BA2 43 C2
Marksbury BA2 42 E1
Wilmots Way BS20 4 D4
Wilsham Cross EX35 122 A5
Wilsham La EX35 122 A5
Wilson Cl BA5 203 C2
Wilson Gdns BS24 32 C1
Wilson Pl BS2 227 C4
Wilsons Cl TA5 134 B2
Wilson St BS2 227 C4
WILSTOCK VILLAGE TA6 153 F5
WILTON 212 F2
Wilton Cl
Burnham-on-S TA8 104 C8
Street BA16 207 D5
Taunton TA1 212 E3
Wilton Ct BS23 48 D7
Wilton Gdns BS23 48 D7
Wilton Gr TA1 212 E3
Wilton Orch
Street BA16 207 D5
Taunton TA1 212 E2
Wilton Rd BA21 219 E8
Wiltons BS40 35 D2
Wilton St TA1 212 E3
WILTOWN
Curry Rivel 171 C3
Wellington 180 F3
Wiltown TA10 171 D3
Wiltown La EX15 180 F3
Wiltshire Cl TA1 212 C2
Wiltshire Ct TA1 212 C2
Wiltshires Barton 4
BA11 119 E5
Wiltshire Way BA1 28 A2
Wilway La TA22 163 C6
Wimble Stock Way BA21 218 C8
Wimblestone Rd BS25 51 F2
Wimborne Cl TA1 213 D3
Wimborough La BA22 196 F6
Winash Cl BS14 23 D7
WINCANTON 216 A4
Wincanton Bsns Pk BA9 216 B3
Wincanton Cl BS48 9 B1
Wincanton Com Hospl
BA9 216 B4
Wincanton Mus★ BA9 216 C4
Wincanton Prim Sch BA9 216 C3
Wincanton Rd TA10 172 A5
Winchcombe Cl BS48 19 A8
Winchcombe Gr BS11 4 F5
Winchester Cotts TA19 184 E1
Winchester Gdns BA21 219 C7
Winchester Ho 2 TA1 213 A4
Winchester Rd
5 Bath BA2 44 D5
Burnham-on-S TA8 104 C7
Winchester St TA1 213 A4
Windcliff Cres BS11 4 E7
Wind Down Cl TA6 208 C4
Windell St BA2 45 A2
Windermere Ave BS23 48 F4
Windermere Cl BA20 218 F2
Windmill TA3 170 F5
Windmill Bsns Pk BS21 16 E8
Windmill Cl TA9 105 B7
Windmill Cotts TA15 186 C4
Windmill Cres TA7 136 E3
WINDMILL HILL 183 B3
Windmill Hill
Hutton BS24 50 A2
Wrantage TA3 170 A2
Windmill Hill La
Ashill TA19 183 B3
Westbury-sub-Mendip BA5 110 D4
Windmill Hill Rd BA6 206 E5
Windmill La
Langport TA10 172 C5
Montacute TA15 186 C4
West Pennard BA6 140 C1
Windmill Rd
Clevedon BS21 16 E8
High Ham TA10 156 A1
Windmill Rise TA18 224 C7
Windrush Cl BA2 43 F4
Windrush Gn BS31 25 A4
Windrush Rd BS31 25 A4
Windsbatch Hill BA11 101 C1
Windsbatch La BA11 101 B1
Windsor Ave BS31 24 E4
Windsor Bridge Rd BA1,
BA2 44 D7
Windsor Castle BA1 44 D7
Windsor Cl
Burnham-on-S TA8 85 B1
Clevedon BS21 6 D2
Minehead TA24 200 E6
Taunton TA1 212 C1
Windsor Cres BA11 120 A5
Windsor Ct
4 Bath BA1 44 C7
13 Bristol, Clifton BS8 11 F6
Windsor Dr
Bridgwater TA6 209 D7
Nailsea BS48 8 E2
Windsor Hill La BA4 141 B8
Windsor Ho TA6 209 C5
Windsor La TA14 186 A4
Windsor Pl
5 Bath BA1 44 C7
Bristol, Clifton BS8 11 F6
Windsor Rd
Bridgwater TA6 209 D7
Weston-super-Mare BS22 31 C2
Windsor Terr
Bristol, Clifton BS8 11 F6
17 Henstridge BA8 190 A6
Paulton BS39 77 E5
Windsor Villas 3 BA1 44 C7
Windway Hill TA4 164 D6
Windwhistle Circ BS23 48 F4
Windwhistle La
Sticklepath TA4 149 F6
Weston-super-Mare BS23 48 E3
Windwhistle Prim Sch
BS23 48 F3
Windwhistle Rd BS23 48 D3
Windy Ridge TA17 195 D7
Windyridge La TA11 211 B1
Wine St
Bath BA1 228 C2
Bristol BS1 227 A3
Frome BA11 119 E4
Yeovil BA20 219 B4
WINFORD 37 F7
Winford CE Prim Sch BS40 37 F7
Winford Cl BS20 2 E4
Winford Gr BS13 22 A8
Winford La BS41 21 C1
Winford Rd BS40 38 F3
Winford Rural Workshops
BA22 197 A2
Winford Terr
Bridgwater TA6 209 B6
Bristol BS41 21 C5
Wingard Cl BS23 48 D2
Wingard Ct 6 BS23 48 E5
Wingate Ave BA21 219 C7
WINGFIELD 83 C6
Wingfield Rd DT9 225 C3
Winifred Cliff Ct 1 EX16 164 B1
Winifred's La BA1 27 E1
Winkworth Way TA1, TA2 213 A5
Winnibrook La TA24 131 A5
Winnowing End BS25 52 A3
Winpenny La TA2 168 E8
Winsbeer La
Rockwell Green TA21 222 A6
Runnington TA21 179 F8
Winsbury View BA2 42 B1
WINSCOMBE 69 F7
Winscombe Cl BS31 24 D6
Winscombe Ct BA11 120 B5
Winscombe Dro
Shipham BS25 70 D6
Winscombe BS25 70 A5
Winscombe Hill BS25 69 F5
Winscombe Rd BS23 49 A7
Winscombe Woodborough
Prim Sch BS25 70 A8
WINSFORD 147 C5
WINSHAM 194 D1
Winsham Cl BS14 23 B5
Winsham Prim Sch TA20 194 E1
Winslade Cl TA2 213 B7
WINSLEY 64 D7
Winsley Bypass BA15 64 E7
Winsley CE VA Prim Sch
BA15 64 E7
Winsley Hill BA3 64 B6
Winsley Rd BA15 64 F7
Winsmoor Hill TA19 184 B4
Winsors La TA24 131 A5
Winstitchen Cross TA24 127 C2
Winstitchen La TA24 127 C2
Winston Cl TA2 212 E6
Winston Dr BA21 218 F8
Winstone Ct BS2 226 C3
Winstones Rd
Barrow Gurney BS48 20 F6
Bristol BS48 21 A6
Winterfield TA18 196 B5
Winterfield Pk BS39 77 E4
Winterfield Rd BS39 77 E5
WINTERHAY GREEN 221 A5
Winterhay La TA19 221 A5
WINTERHEAD 70 D8
Winter La DT9 188 C8
Winters Cross TA4 165 C8
Winters Field TA1 213 A5
Wintershead Rd TA24 145 F7
Winters Hill La BA4 204 C3
Winters La BS40 36 D6
Winter's La TA4 150 C3
Winters Orch TA3 169 C1
Winterstoke Commercial Ctr
BS23 49 A6
Winterstoke Hundred Acad
Haywood Village BS24 49 D6
Haywood Village BS24 49 D6
Winterstoke Rd
Bristol BS3 11 F3
Weston-super-Mare BS23,
BS24 49 B4
Winterstoke Underpass
BS3 11 F4
WINTER WELL 182 C7
Winterwell La BA4 141 F4
Winter Wlk BS14 23 C6
Wint Hill BS29 51 B2
WINYARD'S GAP 196 E1
Winyards View TA18 224 D4
Wireworks Est The TA6 136 A2
Wirral Park Rd BA6 206 C3
Wirral Park Rdbt BA6 206 C3
Wirral Park Trad Est BA6 206 B3
Wirral Pk Ind Est BA6 206 B4
Wishford Mews BA3 78 C2
Wisley Wlk BS22 49 F7
Wisteria Ave BS24 49 D2
Wiston Cross EX36 162 D2
Witches Wlk TA6 208 E2
Witch Hazel Rd BS13 22 E3
WITCOMBE 185 F8
Witcombe Dro
Ilchester TA12 172 F1
Knole TA12 173 B2
Witcombe La TA12 185 F8
Witham Cl TA1 213 D3
WITHAM FRIARY 143 C3
Witham Rd BS31 25 A3
Withers La 1 BS13 22 C4
Withey Cl E BS9 5 F6
Withey Cl W BS9 5 F5
Witheys The BS14 23 C4
Withial Hill BA4 158 D8
Withial La BA6 158 D7
Withiel Dr TA5 135 B2
WITHIEL FLOREY 148 E4
Withiel Hill TA24 148 F6
Withiel La TA24 148 E5
Withies La BA3 97 A8
Withies Pk BA3 96 F8
Withies Wy BA3 96 F8
Withmoor Dro TA10 172 E4
Withybed La BA9 177 E6
WITHYBROOK 115 E3
Withy Cl BS48 8 F3
WITHYCOMBE 131 B4
Withycombe Cross TA24 131 C4
Withycombe Hill TA5 135 A5
Withycombe Hill Gate
TA24 130 F4
Withycombe La TA24 131 B5
Withy Cotts BA3 115 C5
WITHYDITCH 61 C3
Withyditch La BA2 61 C4
Withy Gr TA9 136 C7
Withy Grove Cl TA6 209 D7
Withy Hays Rd 3 TA11 173 F7
Withy La
Barton St David TA11 158 A3
Clatworthy TA4 149 B2
Hemyock EX15 180 B1
Oakhill BA3 115 C5
Withymead BS49 17 F1
WITHY MILLS 78 A7
WITHYPOOL 146 C6
Withypool Cross
Hawkridge TA22 146 C2
Twitchen EX36 145 J4
Withypool Gdns BS14 23 B5
Withy Rd TA9 136 C7
Withy Road Farm La TA9 136 C7
Withys The BS20 4 D4
Withywine La TA22 164 C5
WITHYWOOD 22 A4
Withywood Gdns 1 BS13 21 F4
Withy Wood La BA4 142 C5
Withywood Rd BS13 21 F4
Witney Cl BS31 25 D3
Witney La
Chard TA20 223 B8
Tatworth TA20 193 F1
Wittey's La TA20 199 B6
WIVELISCOMBE 210 B4
Wiveliscombe Prim Sch
TA4 210 B5
Wivenhoe Ct BA11 120 C6
Woburn Rd BA21 219 E7
Wolfester Terr BA22 174 F4
Wollens Cl BA6 206 C4
Wolmer Cl TA6 208 E2
Wolsey Cl BA5 203 B3
Wolverlands BA22 175 A6
Wolvershill Ind Units BS29 50 C6
Wolvershill Pk BS29 51 A3
Wolvershill Rd
Banwell BS29 50 E6
Weston-super-Mare BS24 50 C8
WONDERSTONE 67 D6
Wonhouse Dro BS28 138 B6
Woodacre BS20 2 E7
Woodadvent La TA23 131 E1
Woodbarton TA4 166 F4
Woodbirds Hill La TA10 172 C8
WOODBOROUGH 70 B8
Woodborough Cres BS25 70 A7
Woodborough Ct BS25 70 A8
Woodborough Dr BS25 70 A8
Woodborough Hill Cotts
BA2 79 C4
Woodborough La BA3 79 A4
Woodborough Mill La
BS39 41 B5
Woodborough Rd
Radstock BA3 79 A3
Winscombe BS25 69 F8
Woodburn Cross EX16 162 F2
Woodburn Hill EX16 162 F2
Woodburn Water Cross
EX16 162 F1
Woodbury Ave BA5 203 F5
Woodbury Cl BA5 203 F5
Woodbury Rd TA6 208 D4
Wood Cl BA5 203 B4
Woodcliff Ave BS22 31 C1
Woodcliff Rd BS22 31 C1

Wood Close La TA17 . . . . . 195 A8
Woodcock St BA7 . . . . 214 C5
Woodcock Way EX13 . . . . . 198 B7
WOODCOMBE 200 C8
Woodcombe Brake TA24 . 200 D7
Woodcombe Cotts TA24 . . 200 C8
Woodcombe La TA24 . . . . . 200 C8
Woodcote BA20 . . . . 218 D2
Woodcroft BS39 . . . . 57 C3
Woodcroft Mdws TA20 . . . 192 E7
Wooddene BS25 . . . . 70 A8
Wood Dro TA10 . . . . 171 E8
Wood End Wlk BS9 . . . . 5 C6
Wood Farm Cotts TA5 . . . . 134 E4
Woodfield Cl TA8 . . . . 104 C5
WOODFORD
Watchet 132 A1
Wells 140 A6
Woodford Cl BS48 . . . . 9 A1
Woodford Cotts TA4 . . . . . 132 A1
Woodford Ct 2 BS23 . . . . . 48 E5
Woodford La
Coxley BA5 . . . . 139 F6
Wells BA5 . . . . 203 B1
Woodford Rd BA5 . . . . 140 A6
Woodfords Gn BA7 . . . . 214 B6
WOODGATE 179 E2
Woodhayes BA8 . . . . 190 A6
Woodhayes Ct 13 BA8 . . . . 190 A6
Woodhayes Ho 12 BA8 . . . . 190 A6
Woodhayes Rd BA11 . . . . . 120 C6
Woodhenge BA22 . . . . 218 B5
WOODHILL
Portishead 2 D7
Stoke St Gregory 170 F6
Woodhill BS49 . . . . 34 E6
Woodhill Ave BS20 . . . . 2 D6
Woodhill Ct BS20 . . . . 2 D6
Wood Hill Pk BS20 . . . . 2 D7
Woodhill Rd BS20 . . . . 2 D6
Woodhill Terr TA3 . . . . 170 F6
Woodhill Views BS48 . . . . 8 F3
Woodhouse Cross SP8 . . . 177 F6
Woodhouse La
Axminster EX13 . . . . 198 D1
Chard TA20 . . . . 194 B6
Marston Magna BA22 . . . . . 175 B1
Montacute TA15 . . . . 186 C3
Woodhouse Rd
Axminster EX13 . . . . 198 D1
Bath BA2 . . . . 44 A6
Woodhurst Rd BS23 . . . . . . 49 A7
Woodington Rd BS21 . . . . 6 C1
Wood Kilns The BS49 . . . . . . 17 A1
Wood La
Axbridge BS26 . . . . 70 D2
Blue Anchor TA24 . . . . 131 C6
Butleigh BA6 . . . . 157 C4
Carhampton TA24 . . . . 131 B4
Chapmanslade BA13 . . . . . . 121 D4
Clapton in G BS20 . . . . 8 E8
Crowcombe TA4 . . . . 151 C7
Drimpton DT8 . . . . 199 E7
High Ham TA10 . . . . 155 E1
Marnhull DT10 . . . . 190 F2
Moorlinch TA7 . . . . 155 E8
North Perrott TA18 . . . . 196 D3
Rodney Stoke BS27 . . . . 91 B1
South Cheriton BA8 . . . . 176 C4
Stalbridge DT10 . . . . 190 B4
Stawell TA7 . . . . 137 A1
Stogumber TA4 . . . . 150 D7
Weston-super-Mare BS23 . . . 30 F1
Woodland Ave TA7 . . . . 154 F5
Woodland Cl
6 Carhampton TA24 . . . . . . 131 A5
Failand BS8 . . . . 10 B4
Woodland Cotts BA3 . . . . . . 64 D6
Woodland Ct BS9 . . . . 5 C3
Woodland Glade BS21 . . . . . . 6 E5
Woodland Gr
Bath, Bushey Norwood BA2 . . 45 E5
Bath, Weston Park BA1 . . . . . 27 C1
Bristol BS9 . . . . 5 D6
Yeovil BA20 . . . . 219 B4
Woodland Pl BA2 . . . . 45 D5
Woodland Rd
Bristol BS8 . . . . 226 C4
Frome BA11 . . . . 119 F4
Nailsea BS48 . . . . 8 E3
Taunton TA2 . . . . 213 A7
Watchet TA23 . . . . 202 C6
Weston-super-Mare BS23 . . . 48 D4
WOODLANDS 183 E6
Woodlands
Axbridge BS26 . . . . 70 D2
Wellington TA21 . . . . 222 F3
Weston-super-Mare BS23 . . . 30 D1
Woodlands Bsns Pk EX16 . 179 C3
Woodlands Court Bsns Pk
TA6 . . . . 136 B2
Woodlands Ct BS11 . . . . 4 E5
Woodlands Dr
Ruishton TA3 . . . . 169 C3
Winsley BA3 . . . . 64 B6
Woodlands La
Holcombe BA3 . . . . 116 B7
Isle Abbotts TA3 . . . . 183 E6
Woodlands Mead DT10 . . . 190 F6
Woodlands Pk BA1 . . . . 28 C2
Woodlands Rd
Baltonsborough BA6 . . . . . . 158 A8
Clevedon BS21 . . . . 6 C4
Woodlands Rd *continued*
Portishead BS20 . . . . 2 D8
Woodlands The
Peasedown St John BA2 . . . . . 60 F3
Shepton Mallet BA4 . . . . 205 D5
Woodland Way
Failand BS8 . . . . 10 B4
Frome BA11 . . . . 120 D7
Woodleaze BS9 . . . . 5 B6
Woodleigh Gdns BS14 . . . . . 23 C6
Woodmarsh Cl BS14 . . . . 23 A4
Woodmead Gdns BS13 . . . . 22 C4
Woodmill BS49 . . . . 17 A1
Woodmill Cl DT10 . . . . 190 B5
Woodpecker Ave BA3 . . . . . 97 B8
Woodpecker Cl BS31 . . . . . . 24 C3
Woodpecker Dr BS22 . . . . . . 49 E8
Woodram La TA3 . . . . 181 E5
Wood Rd
Ashill TA19 . . . . 183 B4
High Ham TA10 . . . . 172 A8
Woodridge Mead TA4 . . . . 167 F8
Wood Rock EX36 . . . . 162 C5
Woodrush Cl TA1 . . . . 213 C1
Woods Batch BA16 . . . . 207 B6
Woods Cnr TA11 . . . . 173 E8
Wood's Cross EX36 . . . . 162 C5
Woods Hill BA3 . . . . 64 A6
Woodside
Bristol BS9 . . . . 5 D3
Midsomer Norton BA3 . . . . . . 77 E1
Woodside Ave BS24 . . . . 49 B2
Woodside Cl TA24 . . . . 200 D7
Woodside Ct BS23 . . . . 49 A8
Woodside Gdns BS20 . . . . 1 E5
Woodside Rd BS21 . . . . 6 E5
Woodspring Ave BS22 . . . . . 31 B3
Woodspring Cres BS22 . . . . 31 A3
Woodspring Mus* BS23 . . . 48 E8
Woodspring Priory* BS22 . 14 C1
Woods Rd BA16 . . . . 207 A6
Wood St
Bath BA1 . . . . 228 B2
Bath, Beechen Cliff BA2 . . . . 228 B1
Milverton TA4 . . . . 166 F5
Taunton TA1 . . . . 212 E4
Woodstock Rd
Taunton TA1 . . . . 212 E5
Weston-super-Mare BS22 . . . 49 B8
Yeovil BA21 . . . . 219 C7
Woodview
Chilcompton BA3 . . . . 96 E5
2 Clevedon BS21 . . . . 6 F3
Paulton BS39 . . . . 77 C5
Wells BA5 . . . . 203 E5
Woodview Cl BS11 . . . . 4 E7
Woodview Dr BS49 . . . . 35 B8
Woodview Rd BS27 . . . . 90 C7
Woodview Terr
Nailsea BS48 . . . . 8 F2
Weston-super-Mare BS23 . . . 49 A6
Wood Way EX35 . . . . 122 D4
Woodwell Rd BS11 . . . . 4 E5
WOOKEY 139 E8
Wookey Cl BS48 . . . . 18 F8
WOOKEY HOLE 203 A7
Wookey Hole Cave* BA5 . . 111 E5
Wookey Hole Papermill &
Mus* BA5 . . . . 203 A8
Wookey Hole Rd BA5 . . . . . 203 B5
Wookey Prim Sch
Wookey BA5 . . . . 139 D8
Yarley BA5 . . . . 139 D8
Wookey Rd BA5 . . . . 139 E8
WOOLAVINGTON 136 F4
Woolavington Hill TA7 . . . 136 E3
Woolavington Rd TA7 . . . . 136 D4
Woolavington Right Dro
TA7 . . . . 154 D6
Woolavington Village Prim
Sch TA7 . . . . 136 E4
Woolcombe Rd
Wells BA5 . . . . 111 F2
Wells BA5 . . . . 203 A6
Woolcott La SP8 . . . . 161 E1
Wooler Rd BS23 . . . . 48 E8
Wooley La TA19, TA20 . . . . 194 C6
Woolhayes La TA20 . . . . . . 223 A8
WOOLLARD 41 A6
Woollard La
Bristol BS14, BS39 . . . . 41 A7
Whitchurch BS14 . . . . 23 E1
Woollen La BA22 . . . . 174 F1
WOOLLEY 27 F5
Woolley La BA1 . . . . 28 A4
Woolley Rd BS14 . . . . 23 E5
Woolmersdon Rd TA5 . . . . 153 E5
WOOLMINSTONE 195 B3
Woolminstone Rd TA18 . . . 195 C3
Woolpit La TA24 . . . . 146 B7
Woolshed Cl TA24 . . . . 129 E1
WOOLSTON
North Cadbury 175 E6
Watchet 132 D2
Woolstone La TA5 . . . . 134 F7
Woolston Rd BA22 . . . . 175 E6
Woolvers Way BS24 . . . . 50 B6
WOOLVERTON 82 C1
Wooton Hill BA6 . . . . 157 C5
WOOTTON COURTENAY . . . 129 F6
Wootton Cross EX13 . . . . . . 198 F1
Wootton Gr DT9 . . . . 225 E5
Wootton Hill DT6 . . . . 199 A1
Wootton St BA6 . . . . 157 C6
Wootton Vineyard* BA4 . . 140 C5
Worberry La BA3 . . . . 95 B7
Worcester Bldgs BA1 . . . . . . 28 B2
Worcester Cl BA2 . . . . 79 D7
Worcester Cres BS8 . . . . . . 226 A4
Worcester Ct BS8 . . . . 226 A4
Worcester Gdns BS48 . . . . . 18 C8
Worcester Pk BA1 . . . . 28 B2
Worcester Pl BA1 . . . . 28 B2
Worcester Rd BS8 . . . . 226 A4
Worcester Terr
Bath BA1 . . . . 28 B2
Bristol BS8 . . . . 226 A4
Wordsworth Ave TA6 . . . . . 208 E6
Wordsworth Cl TA8 . . . . 85 B2
Wordsworth Dr TA1 . . . . . . 213 B3
Wordsworth Rd
Clevedon BS21 . . . . 6 C2
Weston-super-Mare BS23 . . . 49 A3
Worely La TA11 . . . . 211 F8
Workshop La BA2 . . . . 43 C6
World's End La BS31 . . . . . . 25 C5
WORLE 31 F2
WORLEBURY 31 A2
Worlebury Cl BS22 . . . . 31 B3
Worlebury Hill Rd BS22,
BS23 . . . . 31 B2
Worlebury Park Rd BS22 . . . 31 A2
Worlebury St Pauls CE VA Fst
Sch BS22 . . . . 31 B3
Worle Com Sch BS22 . . . . . . 31 E1
Worle Ct BS22 . . . . 31 F3
Worle Ind Est BS22 . . . . 32 B2
Worle Moor Rd BS24 . . . . . . 49 E7
Worle Sta BS22 . . . . 32 B1
Worle Village Prim Sch
BS22 . . . . 31 E2
Wormcliff La SN13 . . . . 29 F3
WORMINSTER 140 C5
Worminster Batch BA4 . . . 140 D5
Worston La TA8 . . . . 104 C5
Worston Orch TA9 . . . . 104 E4
Worston Rd TA9 . . . . 104 E5
WORTH 139 D8
Worthings The BS24 . . . . 67 B1
Worthington Cl BS28 . . . . . 108 D5
Worth La TA22, TA24 . . . . . 146 C4
WORTHY 123 E5
Worthy Cres BS24 . . . . 67 B1
Worthy La
Creech St Michael TA3 . . . . . 169 D5
Pilton BA4 . . . . 140 F3
5 Weston-super-Mare BS23 . 48 E8
West Pennard BA4, BA6 . . . . 140 D1
Worthy Pl 4 BS23 . . . . 48 E8
Worthy Rd TA24 . . . . 123 E5
Worthy Toll Rd TA24 . . . . . . 123 D4
Wouldham Rd TA23 . . . . . . 202 D6
Wrangcombe La TA21 . . . . 180 A4
Wrangcombe Rd TA21 . . . . 180 A4
Wrangle Farm Gn BS21 . . . . . 6 E2
WRANGLE THE 74 A5
Wrangle The 5 BS24 . . . . 49 F7
WRANGWAY 180 A4
Wrangway Rd EX15 . . . . . . 180 A3
WRANTAGE 170 A1
WRAXALL
Ditcheat 159 A7
Nailsea 9 C3
Wraxall CE VA Prim Sch
BS48 . . . . 9 B4
Wraxall Cross Rds BA4 . . . 159 A7
Wraxall Gr BS13 . . . . 22 A8
Wraxall Hill
Ditcheat BA4 . . . . 159 A8
Wraxall BS48 . . . . 9 C5
Wraxall Rd BA4 . . . . 159 B7
Wraxall Vineyard* BA4 . . . 159 A7
Wraxhill Cl BA16 . . . . 207 D5
Wraxhill Rd
Street BA16 . . . . 207 C5
Yeovil BA20 . . . . 218 E1
WREATH 194 C3
Wreath La TA20 . . . . 194 B3
Wren Cl
Frome BA11 . . . . 120 B6
Taunton TA1 . . . . 212 C4
Weston-super-Mare BS22 . . . 49 D8
Wren Gdns BS20 . . . . 3 A7
Wrenmoor Cl TA6 . . . . 209 C3
WRINGTON 35 E1
Wrington CE Prim Sch
BS40 . . . . 35 E2
Wrington Cres BS13 . . . . 22 A7
Wrington Hill BS40 . . . . 35 F5
Wrington La BS49 . . . . 34 E5
Wrington Mead BS49 . . . . . . 34 E5
Wrington Rd BS49 . . . . 34 F4
Wristland Rd TA23 . . . . 202 D7
WRITHLINGTON 79 C2
Writhlington Ct BA3 . . . . . . 79 C2
Writhlington Sch BA3 . . . . . 79 C1
Writh Rd DT9 . . . . 189 B1
Wroughton Dr BS13 . . . . 22 D4
Wroughton Gdns BS13 . . . . 22 D4
Wry La TA4 . . . . 149 F2
Wyatt Ave BS13 . . . . 21 F5
Wyatt Cl BS13 . . . . 21 F5
Wyatt's Cl BS48 . . . . 8 D2
Wyatts Ct TA17 . . . . 195 C7
Wyatts Field TA3 . . . . 168 D1
Wyatts Way TA19 . . . . 183 C4
Wych Ct EX13 . . . . 198 E3
Wych Elm Rd BA11 . . . . 120 C6
Wycotte Hill BA2 . . . . 62 C6
Wydford Cl DT9 . . . . 225 B3
Wydon La TA24 . . . . 124 F3
Wye Ave TA6 . . . . 209 D3
Wyedale Ave BS9 . . . . 5 C7
WYKE CHAMPFLOWER 215 A6
Wyke La
Wyke Champflower BA10 . . . 215 A5
Wyke Champflower BA10 . . . 215 A6
Wyke Rd
Castle Cary BA7, BA10 . . . . . 214 E7
Wyke Champflower BA10 . . . 215 C6
Wylds Rd TA6 . . . . 209 A7
Wylds Road Ind Est TA6 . . . 209 A7
Wyllie Ct BS22 . . . . 32 A5
Wymbush Cres BS13 . . . . . . 22 C5
Wymbush Gdns BS13 . . . . . . 22 C5
Wyndam Ct BS2 . . . . 227 B4
Wyndham Cres BS20 . . . . 4 B4
Wyndham Ct BA21 . . . . 219 C5
Wyndham Rd
Bridgwater TA6 . . . . 209 C6
Taunton TA2 . . . . 212 E7
Watchet TA23 . . . . 202 C6
Wyndham's TA4 . . . . 210 C4
Wyndham St BA20 . . . . 219 C5
Wyndham View BA21 . . . . . 219 D5
Wyndham Way BS20 . . . . 2 E5
Wyndham Way Ret Pk BS20 . 2 D5
Wynford Rd BA11 . . . . 120 B5
Wynnes Cl DT9 . . . . 225 C3
Wynnes Rise DT9 . . . . 225 C3
Wynsome St BA14 . . . . 83 F3
Wynter Cl BS22 . . . . 32 A3
Wyrral Cl BA6 . . . . 206 D3
Wytch Gn EX13 . . . . 198 E3
Wythburn Rd BA11 . . . . 120 C5
Wyvern Cl
Bruton BA10 . . . . 215 F7
Weston-super-Mare BS23 . . . 48 F7
Yeovil BA20 . . . . 218 C1
Wyvern Ct TA18 . . . . 224 C6
Wyvern Mews 5 BS23 . . . . . . 48 F7
Wyvern Rd TA1 . . . . 168 E1
Wyville Rd BA11 . . . . 120 C6

Y

Yadley Cl BS25 . . . . 70 A7
Yadley La BS25 . . . . 70 A6
Yadley Way BS25 . . . . 70 A7
Yallands Hill TA2 . . . . 213 E8
YALWAY 153 A1
Yanel La BS25 . . . . 52 B5
Yanhey Hill EX16 . . . . 162 E4
Yanleigh Cl BS13 . . . . 21 D6
YANLEY 21 C8
Yanley La BS41, BS13 . . . . . . 21 C7
Yarbury Way BS24 . . . . 32 B1
YARCOMBE 192 D3
YARDE 132 A2
Yarde Pl TA1 . . . . 212 F4
Yard La
Marshwood DT6 . . . . 199 F3
Wiveliscombe TA4 . . . . 210 C6
Yardleigh Cross EX13 . . . . . 198 D4
Yard Rd TA14 . . . . 185 E1
Yard The BA11 . . . . 143 C4
Yardwall Rd TA9 . . . . 106 A3
YARFORD 168 C8
Yarford Rd TA2 . . . . 168 C8
YARLEY 139 C8
Yarley Cross BA5 . . . . 139 C8
Yarley Field La BA5 . . . . . . 139 B7
Yarley Hill BA5 . . . . 139 C7
YARLINGTON 175 F8
Yarlington Cl TA2 . . . . 168 B4
Yarnbarton BA8 . . . . 176 E1
Yarn Barton BA20 . . . . 219 A4
Yarn Mews BA20 . . . . 218 C1
YARROW 106 E3
Yarrow Ct BS22 . . . . 32 A5
Yarrow Rd TA9 . . . . 106 D3
YATTON 34 C8
Yatton CE VA Jun & Inf Schs
BS49 . . . . 34 C8
Yatton Cl BS13 . . . . 21 F8
Yatton Station BS49 . . . . 17 A1
YEABRIDGE 220 E2
Yeabsleys Way BA7 . . . . 214 C6
Yealscombe La TA24 . . . . . . 128 B2
Yeamen's Ho BS1 . . . . 227 B1
Yeap's Dro BA5 . . . . 139 A7
Yearmoor La TA5 . . . . 134 F8
Yearnor Mill La
Oare TA24 . . . . 122 F5
Porlock Weir TA24 . . . . 123 B5
Yeates Ct BS21 . . . . 6 E3
Yeatman Cl BS39 . . . . 57 D4
Yeatman Hospl DT9 . . . . 225 D4
Yellingmill La BA4 . . . . 141 C8
Yellowcombe La TA24 . . . . . 147 C5
Yellow Rose Cvn Pk TA20 . 193 D6
Yellow Way Rd
Maiden Bradley BA11,
BA12 . . . . 144 A3
Witham Friary BA11 . . . . 143 F3
Yellow Wood Cross TA4 . . 132 D2
YENSTON 189 F8
Yenston Hill BA8 . . . . 189 F8
Yeo Bank La
Icelton BS22 . . . . 32 D7
Kingston Seymour BS21 . . . . . 15 F1
Yeo Cl
Cheddar BS27 . . . . 90 B6
Weston-super-Mare BS23 . . . 49 A5
Yeo Ct
Clevedon BS21 . . . . 6 C2
Congresbury BS49 . . . . 34 D4
Yeo La
Bridgwater TA6 . . . . 209 B2
Long Ashton BS41 . . . . 10 F1
Yeolands Dr BS21 . . . . 6 B1
Yeo Leisure Pk* BA20 . . . . . 219 C4
Yeomanry Way BA4 . . . . . . 205 D5
Yeomans Cl BS9 . . . . 5 D5
Yeomanside Cl BS14 . . . . 23 C5
Yeomans Lodge BA11 . . . . . 119 C4
Yeomans Orch BS40 . . . . 35 E3
Yeomead BS48 . . . . 8 F3
Yeomeads BS41 . . . . 10 F1
Yeo Mill Cross EX36 . . . . . . 162 C5
Yeo Moor BS21 . . . . 6 E2
Yeo Moor Dro
BS27, BS28 . . . . 109 D3
Yeo Moor Inf Sch BS21 . . . . . 6 E2
Yeo Moor Jun Sch BS21 . . . . . 6 E2
Yeo Moor Prim Sch BS21 . . . 6 E2
Yeo Rd TA6 . . . . 209 B2
Yeo Valley 2 BA22 . . . . 197 F8
Yeo Valley Way BS48 . . . . 9 B2
YEOVIL 218 E4
Yeovil Bsns Ctr BA21 . . . . . 219 F7
Yeovil Coll BA21 . . . . 219 A6
Yeovil District Hospl
BA21 . . . . 219 B5
Yeovil Innovation Centre
BS22 . . . . 218 B7
Yeovil Junction Sta
BA22 . . . . 219 E1
YEOVIL MARSH 187 A6
Yeovil Marsh Pk BA21 . . . . 187 A5
Yeovil Marsh Rd BA21 . . . . 187 A5
Yeovil Pen Mill Sta BA21 . . 219 E5
Yeovil Railway Ctr*
BA22 . . . . 219 D1
Yeovil Rd
Crewkerne TA18 . . . . 224 E7
Halstock BA22 . . . . 197 D3
Montacute TA15 . . . . 186 B3
Sherborne DT9 . . . . 225 C4
Tintinhull BA22 . . . . 186 C6
Yeovil BA22 . . . . 218 F1
Yeovil Small Bsns Ctr
BA22 . . . . 218 B6
YEOVILTON 174 A1
Yeovil Trinity Foyer 7
BA20 . . . . 219 B4
Yeoward Rd BS21 . . . . 6 E1
Yeo Way BS21 . . . . 6 B2
Yet Mead La BS27 . . . . 110 B7
Yeovil Coll BA20 . . . . 219 A6
Yewcroft Cl BS14 . . . . 23 A4
Yewtree Batch BS40 . . . . 37 A1
Yew Tree Cl
Bishop Sutton BS39 . . . . 57 D4
Lower Langford BS40 . . . . 53 E6
Nailsea BS48 . . . . 8 C1
Yeovil BA20 . . . . 218 E2
Yew Tree Cotts BS40 . . . . . . 54 E3
Yew Tree Ct BS14 . . . . 23 B5
Yew Tree Dr BS22 . . . . 50 B8
Yew Tree Gdns
Nailsea BS48 . . . . 8 C1
Pill BS20 . . . . 4 C4
Sandford BS25 . . . . 52 A4
Yew Tree La
Compton Martin BS40 . . . . . . 74 A7
Kingston Seymour BS21 . . . . . 16 B1
Taunton TA2 . . . . 213 E6
Yew Tree Pk BS49 . . . . 34 D3
Yomede Pk BA1 . . . . 44 A7
Yonder Dro TA10 . . . . 184 E8
Yonder Hill Cotts TA20 . . . 198 E7
Yonder Mead TA4 . . . . 167 F7
York Bldgs TA6 . . . . 208 F5
York Cl
Axminster EX13 . . . . 198 A1
Weston-super-Mare BS22 . . . 32 A4
York Ct BS2 . . . . 227 B4
York Gdns BS8 . . . . 11 F6
York Lodge 4 BA20 . . . . 219 A5
York Pl
Bath BA1 . . . . 45 B8
Bristol, Brandon Hill BS1 . . . 226 C2
Bristol, Victoria Park BS8 . . 226 B3
Yeovil BA20 . . . . 219 A5
York Rd
Bridgwater TA6 . . . . 208 F2
Bristol BS2 . . . . 227 C1
Taunton TA1 . . . . 213 C5
York's La BA3 . . . . 94 B6
York St
Bath BA1 . . . . 228 C2
Bristol BS2 . . . . 227 B4
5 Frome BA11 . . . . 119 E5
Weston-super-Mare BS23 . . . 48 D7
Youngwood La BS48 . . . . . . 18 D7
Yoxter Rd
Charterhouse BA5 . . . . 72 F1
Ubley Sideling BS40 . . . . 73 B2
Westbury Beacon BA5 . . . . . . 91 E8

Z

ZEALS 161 F2
Zeals Rise BA12 . . . . 161 F2
Zembard La TA20 . . . . 223 C4
Zeta Cl TA7 . . . . 209 E8
Zig Zag BS21 . . . . 6 D4
Zion Hill
Midsomer Norton BA3 . . . . . . 96 B7
Oakhill BA3 . . . . 115 A3
18 Shepton Mallet BA4 . . . . . 205 B6